An Anatomy of Louisiana Evidence Law

An Anatomy of Louisiana Evidence Law

Code, Commentary, Cases, & Problems

Shenequa L. Grey
Southern University Law Center

Carolina Academic Press
Durham, North Carolina

ISBN 978-1-61163-819-6
LCCN 2015940831

Carolina Academic Press
700 Kent Street
Durham, NC 27701
Telephone (919) 489-7486
Fax (919) 493-5668
www.cap-press.com

Printed in the United States of America

To my parents,
The late Mrs. Minnie L. Grey & Mr. Louis Grey, Jr.

"All that I am or hope to be, I owe to you."
Abraham Lincoln

~Moo

Summary Table of Contents

Contents

Table of Principal Cases

Preface and Acknowledgments

This casebook is the first of its kind in Louisiana, representing a rising trend in law school casebooks across the country. Apart from the traditional compilation of cases and notes from which students are required to extract and deduce the legal principles and to consult outside sources for explanation, commentary, and problems—this book is much more. It is a complete *coursebook* that presents a detailed, thorough, and comprehensive examination of the law of evidence through the use of concise commentary and a number of pedagogical elements that introduces, teaches, and reinforces the legal principles. You will find that this casebook provides the student with everything needed to learn and effectively apply Louisiana evidence law in one place, without the need for outside sources-thus the name, "*An Anatomy of Louisiana Evidence Law: Code, Commentary, Cases, & Problems.*"

An "anatomy" has been defined as "a separating or dividing into parts for detailed examination and analysis." Incorporating thoughtful feedback and comments from both students and reviewing professors on the format, depth, and breadth of coverage, you will find that this casebook indeed anatomizes Louisiana evidence law. At the outset of the book is the entire Louisiana Code of Evidence for easy access and reference by the students throughout the course. With a few exceptions, each article is covered in a different section of the book, with a treatise-like explanation of the legal principles, written in a reader-friendly style. The commentary contains various elements that attempt to appeal to different types of learning styles and for easy reading and comprehension such as illustrated diagrams of complicated concepts, as well as charts, lists, callout boxes, and numerous examples and illustrations.

While the casebook retains the traditional use of carefully selected and rigorously edited Louisiana cases and select U.S. Supreme Court cases directly affecting Louisiana law, each case is also accompanied by discussion questions to help guide the students through the concepts and principles covered in the cases and commentary. Culminating with a summary of the key points covered in each section, students are presented with a straightforward presentation of the law, designed to better equip them to more fully engage in classroom lectures and discussion.

This style of presentation of the law is coupled with numerous opportunities for application of the principles covered. The book contains over 400 original problems that test the exceptions and nuances of the rules. Select problems have full analysis to demonstrate how to apply the law to the facts. Further, to help bridge the ever-so-wide gap between law school theory and real-life application of the rules, are practical application exercises that present the concepts in ways in which they are likely to be encountered in real-life scenarios.

This casebook further sets itself apart from other Louisiana casebooks by drawing comparisons of important distinctions between the Louisiana Code of Evidence and the Federal Rules of Evidence, where applicable. The book is punctuated with a common thread of the discussion of public policy concerns underlying the evidentiary principles to serve as a guide to understanding how the law should be applied and to show how state public policy concerns drive many of the distinctions in the state and federal laws. Throughout the book students are encouraged to think beyond the plain language of the law to the underlying interests and reasons for the rules—an overriding concern in evidence law.

In *An Anatomy of Louisiana Evidence Law,* these and other features come together to create a comprehensive examination of Louisiana Evidence—an *anatomy,* so to speak. Every element of this casebook was thoughtfully incorporated or developed with two primary goals in mind—both theory and application. I hope that you find the casebook to be everything it was intended to be and more, and I look forward to your thoughtful feedback. Please send any corrections, questions, comments, or suggestions to sgrey@greyevidence.com.

Acknowledgments

I extend a warm thank you to Professor Michelle Ghetti for your guidance, feedback and mentorship over the last ten years, as well as your contributions to case selections for this book. I also thank Vice Chancellor Russell Jones for your support on this project. I thank my dedicated research assistants Jasmine Henderson and Amira Makke for your excellent and timely contributions to this book which greatly contributed to its quality and overall status as an authoritative source on evidence law. Additionally, I thank my good friend Shayna Pitre for your willingness to discuss issues, review problems, suggest examples, discussing pedagogy, and contribute to discussion questions and cases. Most of all, I appreciate your support and encouragement. Finally, I thank my evidence class for the fall of 2014 and all of my students for the spring of 2015 for your patience, understanding, support, and motivation over the last year as I was writing this book.

Editorial Note

To save space and to make judicial decisions read more smoothly, most internal citations and footnotes are omitted. These deletions are not noted. Deleted text is indicated by ellipses. Most problems contain names to help make the actors seem like real people; however, with the exception of instances in which problems are based on cases, the actors in the problems are not intended to represent the actions or events concerning an actual person. Any resemblance to any actual events are purely coincidental.

An Anatomy of Louisiana Evidence Law

Chapter 1

Introduction to Evidence and the Adversarial Trial

§ 1.1 Overview of the Study of Evidence Law

Even if you were to tell a 5-year-old child that you have a quarter balled up in your fist, he's going to skeptically say to you, "Let me see it!" He'll want ***proof***. Proof is the heart of persuasion and believability. It cuts across all aspects of life, helping to resolve personal and professional disputes among colleagues, family, and friends. But there's no place where its presence is more important than in the context of the adversarial trial, where the sole purpose is to resolve conflicts between parties whose contentions conflict. While both parties to a trial will usually present a theory of their case to the jury, which, if believed, could cause the jury to reasonably decide in their favor, the party who prevails is the one who can present the most reliable and believable proof to support their contentions—"evidence" of their assertions.

Evidence has been defined as "any species of proof, or probative matter, legally presented at the trial by the act of the parties and through the medium of witnesses, records, documents, exhibits, concrete objects, etc., for the purpose of inducing belief in the minds of the court or jury as to their contention."[1] This definition succinctly defines the broad scope of the various types of evidence that may be presented at a trial by the parties as well as sets out the purpose of evidence in a trial: to convince the trier of fact of the assertions necessary to decide in their party's favor. In short, evidence is proof. The law of evidence encompasses the rules that govern proof in both civil and criminal trials,[2] and other hearings. It governs not only what may be used as evidence, but also how evidence may be used in a trial—for what purposes, its limitations, as well as exclusions to the rules.

As such, evidence is one of the most important courses you will take in law school. It is an integral part of both the study and practice of law. While much time is spent in law school studying and learning the substantive legal principles relative to issues and elements that must be proven for various claims, and how to apply those principles to a set of facts, in this course you will learn the rules that govern how those facts are proven in the actual trial. But it is important for you to know at the outset of the course, and to keep in mind as you study the law of evidence, that evidence is much broader than in the courtroom. The rules are not something that only litigators will need to know *during* a trial.

---

1. Phillip v. Home Ins. Co., 671 So. 2d 943 (La. Ct. App. 5th Cir. 1996) *citing* Black's Law Dictionary; *See also* La. Prac. Civ. Trial § 5:1.

2. *See* La. Code of Evid. art. 101 Official Comment (b) ("[W]hen a rule is designed and intended to apply solely in criminal matters, the use of the work "accused" in the text will signify its limited applicability or the rule will expressly state its limited applicability.").

The need for a keen understanding of the rules of evidence extends far in advance of trial, and is relevant even if a case never goes to trial. Knowledge of the rules can assist an attorney preparing for trial in determining which motions to file, which witnesses to depose and subpoena, which discovery to seek, whether he should settle the case, and so on. An attorney must even be able to recognize, develop and preserve relevant evidence that might be needed in the event a case must be tried. For example, an attorney should recognize when something should be put into writing rather than merely orally communicating information, when a document or item should be kept, or even when photos should be taken of something that might later be needed in a trial. Thus, knowledge of the rules is an essential component of effective client representation from the very outset of a case.

At trial, an attorney must be familiar with the rules to prove his case—to ensure that he can elicit the necessary testimony from the witnesses, to admit the necessary documents and real evidence, to prevent inadmissible evidence from being admitted by opposing counsel, and to be able to make and respond to objections to admissibility of evidence quickly and correctly, with little or no advance notice.

The most efficient way to learn the rules of evidence is through application of the rules to numerous fact patterns. In law school, that will entail working numerous problems. In practice, mastering the rules of evidence requires the advocate to consistently apply the rules in trials and hearings. Over time, making and meeting objections can become second nature. You will find that an in-depth understanding of the evidentiary rules can garner an attorney a great deal of respect in the courtroom—not to mention victories as well. Thus, you are encouraged to master the rules of evidence. This task will begin in this course.

§ 1.2 Reasons for the Rules of Evidence[3]

Applicable Code Articles

Art. 102. Purpose and Construction

These articles shall be construed to secure fairness and efficiency in administration of the law of evidence to the end that the truth may be ascertained and proceedings justly determined.

The Louisiana Code of Evidence (the "Code"), like many other legal principles and bodies of law, is not an arbitrary set of rules with no underlying legal bases, reasoning, and public policy concerns. To the contrary, the Code is based upon important public policy considerations both internal and external to the trial, constitutional protections, and other considerations necessary for the fair and efficient administration of justice. Article 102 specifically provides that the rules of evidence should be construed "to secure fairness and efficiency in administration of the law of evidence to the end that the truth may be ascertained and proceedings justly determined."[4] Thus, **fairness**, **efficiency**, ascertainment of the **truth**, and

---

3. *See* Christopher Mueller & Laird Kirkpatrick, Evidence § 1.1 at 2–3 (4th ed., 1999) (discussing the reasons for the rules of evidence).

4. La. Code of Evid. art. 102.

just outcomes are the primary reasons for and the ultimate goals of the rules, and are the underlying principles upon which the rules of evidence are based.

Accurate Truth-Finding. At the very core of these principles lies the ultimate goal of accurate truth-finding. Many of the rules are specifically designed for this purpose. For example, the requirement that witnesses have first-hand knowledge[5] of the matters about which they will testify rather than relying on hearsay,[6] the out-of-court statements of others, is more likely to garner the truth at the trial. This rule not only helps to protect a person's right to confront witnesses against him, both a state and federal constitutional right,[7] but also ensures a more effective cross-examination of such witnesses, who can be questioned about their *own* perception, memory, sincerity, and other issues that can assist the trier of fact in discerning the truth.[8]

Additionally, the requirement of original documents, photos, and recordings[9] and that evidence be authenticated, i.e., shown to be what it purports to be,[10] and other foundational requirements prior to admitting evidence at trial, helps to ensure that evidence offered at trial is what the proponent claims and further ensures that more reliable and trustworthy evidence is considered in a case. The Code also includes several other provisions that help ensure accurate truth-finding such as the requirement that witnesses take an oath or affirmation prior to testifying,[11] the requirements that provide for testing the credibility of witnesses in a number of ways, including questioning them about any biases, interest in the case, prior inconsistent statements, prior convictions, and rules allowing evidence of a witness's character for truthfulness or untruthfulness.[12]

Public Policy. In addition to accurate truth-finding, a number of public policy considerations underlie many of the rules—both intrinsic and extrinsic to the trial. For example, the spousal testimonial privilege[13] that precludes a person from being compelled to testify against his or her spouse is designed to foster support and respect for harmonious marriages. The spousal communications privilege[14] encourages open communications between spouses and respects the confidentiality of such statements. Other privileges contained in Chapter 5, such as the attorney-client privilege,[15] the healthcare provider-patient privilege,[16] and other privileges, also encourage open communications within the relationships, where such openness is essential to fostering the true nature of the relationship. Chapter 4 of the Code also contains provisions that further other policy considerations extrinsic to the trial, such as the encouragement of pleas and settlement negotiations,[17] offers to pay medical and other expenses,[18] and to take subsequent remedial measures

---

5. *See* LA. CODE EVID. art. 602.
6. *See* LA. CODE EVID. Chapter 8.
7. *See* U.S. Const. amend. VI ; *See also* La. Const. art. 1 Sec. 16 (1974) ("... An accused is entitled to confront and cross-examine the witnesses against him, ...")
8. *See* MCCORMICK ON EVIDENCE § 245 (5th ed., 1999); *See infra* Chapter 5, Part A for a thorough discussion on the dangers of hearsay.
9. *See* LA. CODE EVID. Chapter 10.
10. *See* LA. CODE EVID. Chapter 9.
11. *See* LA. CODE EVID. art. 603.
12. *See* LA. CODE EVID. arts. 404(A)(3), 607–610.
13. *See* LA. CODE EVID. art. 505.
14. *See* LA. CODE EVID. art. 504.
15. *See* LA. CODE EVID. art. 506.
16. *See* LA. CODE EVID. art. 510.
17. *See* LA. CODE EVID. art. 408.
18. *See* LA. CODE EVID. art. 409.

after an accident or incident occurs,[19] by excluding such evidence from being offered against a party at the trial to show negligence.

Policy considerations relating to the trial itself include rules that help to avoid undue delay and waste of time[20] at the trial. For example, the requirement that only relevant evidence be admitted at trial,[21] and rules that allow the judge to limit the scope of certain examinations of witnesses,[22] are all in the interest of judicial economy.

Basic Fairness. Basic fairness also underlies many of the rules. Several rules are designed to protect jurors from what is referred to as "unfairly prejudicial evidence,[23] or in other words, evidence that might lead them to decide a case on an improper basis such as an emotional one, rather than based on the evidence presented. For the same reason evidence of a person's character[24] is also excluded. It is feared that it might lead the jury to convict a person, not on the merits of the case, but on their perception of the *kind* of person they may think stands before them on trial. These rules presume that the lay juror may not always be able to exclude issues that have nothing to do with the case and decide it based only on the *evidence* presented. Thus, there are rules in place to exclude such evidence to help to ensure a trial is fair and just.

Throughout the course, you will be reminded of these underlying principles as various rules are covered. It is important that you keep these concerns in mind as you study the law of evidence as they will assist you in not only understanding the rules of evidence, but will also assist you in the proper construction and application of the rules.

§ 1.3 Development of the Louisiana Code of Evidence[25]

This casebook focuses on the study of the Louisiana Code of Evidence (the "Code"), which is relatively new. The Code was enacted by the Louisiana Legislature in 1988 and became effective on January 1, 1989.[26] Chapter 5 of the Code was enacted in 1991,[27] and the final chapter of the Louisiana Code of Evidence to be adopted, Presumptions and Burdens of Proof,[28] was enacted by the Legislature in 1997.

The development of the Code was not a simple task, but has best been described as a "long and rocky" road by historians and scholars instrumental in its final development in 1989.[29] The first attempt to codify the Louisiana Code of Evidence began more than

19. *See* LA. CODE EVID. art. 407.
20. *See* LA. CODE EVID. art. 403.
21. *See* LA. CODE EVID. arts. 401, 402.
22. *See* LA. CODE EVID. art. 611.
23. *See* LA. CODE EVID. art. 403.
24. *See* LA. CODE EVID. art. 404.
25. For a complete history of the efforts to develop the LOUISIANA CODE OF EVIDENCE see, George W. Pugh, *Federal Rules of Evidence: Foreword*, 36 LA. L. REV. 59 (1975); George Pugh, Robert Force, Gerald Rault, & Kerry Triche, *The Louisiana Code of Evidence—A Retrospective and Prospective View*, 49 LA. L. REV. 689 (1989) [hereinafter Pugh, Force, Rault, & Triche, *A Retrospective and Prospective View*]; Gerald Rault, *An Overview of the New Louisiana Code of Evidence—Its Imperfections and Uncertainties*, 49 LA. L. REV. 697 (1989) [hereinafter Rault, *An Overview of the New Louisiana Code of Evidence*]. These sources are generally relied upon for this section.
26. Enacted by La. Acts 1988, No. 515.
27. Enacted by La. Acts 1992, No. 376.
28. Enacted by La. Acts 1997, No. 577 § 1.
29. *See* Rault, *An Overview of the New Louisiana Code of Evidence*, *supra* note 25, at 697–698 (1989).

160 years ago in 1822 when the Louisiana Legislature appointed Edward Livingston to prepare a penal code for the state, which was to include a code of evidence as part of the project. Livingston produced a code of evidence that applied to both civil and criminal cases, but for reasons that are unclear, the code was never enacted.[30]

For decades after that, Louisiana continued to utilize general common law of evidence in both civil and criminal cases. Several of the rules were set out in various statutes in Title 15 of the Revised Statutes, the Civil Code, the Code of Criminal Procedure and the Code of Civil Procedure; however, courts primarily looked to judicial decisions for guidance and interpretation of the various provisions.

The confusion and inconsistencies in the law led to a second attempt to codify a code of evidence that began in 1956 when the Louisiana Legislature commissioned the Louisiana State Law Institute to develop a code. This effort also proved to be controversial and after more than 10 years, this project was also abandoned as the Federal Rules of Evidence were then on the horizon.[31]

After the Federal Rules of Evidence were enacted in 1975 the Louisiana Legislature again expressed interest in the development of a code based on the Federal Rules, and in 1979 directed the Judicial College to develop a code to present to the Louisiana Law Institute for recommendations. This effort also proved to be fruitless. However, the enactment of the Federal Rules generated a new belief in the idea that a code could be developed for the state.

So just two years later, the Law Institute again decided to undertake the task of developing a code of evidence. The Reporters, charged with the task of developing the code, considered the Federal Rules, Louisiana's existing law, and the model rules, and after much debate, additions, deletions and modifications, the proposed Louisiana Code of Evidence was published and submitted to the legislature in 1986. Failing to have been enacted in the 1986 and 1987 legislative sessions amid controversy from competing factions,[32] the Code of Evidence was finally enacted in 1988 following a special compromise session that led to several last-minute amendments on the evening before it was considered by the Senate Committee.[33] The Louisiana Code of Evidence was enacted and became effective on January 1, 1989.

Federal Rules of Evidence Distinction. The Code is largely modeled after the Federal Rules of Evidence of 1975, but is different in many ways. For instance, while the Federal Rules do not contain a chapter on privileges, Chapter 5 of the Louisiana Code of Evidence contains rules governing spousal privileges, the attorney-client privilege, the healthcare provider-patient privilege, as well as others. Other significant distinctions between the Louisiana Code of Evidence and the Federal Rules of Evidence are highlighted in the applicable sections of the book as they appear. It is also important to note that in

---

30. *See* Pugh, *Federal Rules of Evidence: Foreword*, 36 LA. L. REV. 59 (1975) n 9 (citing Moore, *The Livingston Code*, 19 J. CRIM. L. & CRIMINOLOGY 344, 354 (1928) (noting that there was great opposition surrounding various provisions of Livingston's proposed code in judicial and legal circles, and also citing Livingston's election to the United States House of Representatives in 1822, taking his seat in December 1823, Moore states that Livingston never returned to Louisiana to complete the project)).

31. *See* Pugh, Force, Rault, & Triche, *A Retrospective and Prospective View, supra* note 25, at 690 (noting that in 1965 Chief Justice Earl Warren appointed an advisory committee to begin formulating evidence rules for the federal courts that looked promising that might provide guidance in developing Louisiana rules). Other models, however, were already available, including the Model Code of Evidence (1942) and the Uniform Rules of Evidence (1953).

32. *See id.* at 693 (noting strong opposition in positions taken by the Louisiana District Attorneys Association, Louisiana Trial Lawyers Association, Louisiana Association of Criminal Defense Lawyers).

33. *See Id.*

enacting the Louisiana Code of Evidence, variations from the Federal Rules were primarily based upon certain underlying state public policy interests, such as the greater protection provided to its citizens under the Louisiana State Constitution.[34] The Louisiana legislature made clear and emphasized that the rules should be construed and applied with a view towards furthering those state interests.

The Louisiana Code of Evidence contains eleven chapters as follows:

Chapter 1:	General Provisions
Chapter 2:	Judicial Notice
Chapter 3:	Presumptions and Burden of Proof
Chapter 4:	Relevancy
Chapter 5:	Privileges
Chapter 6:	Witnesses
Chapter 7:	Opinions and Expert Testimony
Chapter 8:	Hearsay
Chapter 9:	Authentication and Identification
Chapter 10:	Contents of Writings, Recordings, Photographs
Chapter 11:	Miscellaneous Rules

The Louisiana Code of Evidence is a comprehensive guide to the admissibility of evidence in Louisiana courts that clarifies and codifies prior Louisiana evidence law.

§ 1.4 Scope and Application of the Rules of Evidence [La. C.E. art. 1101]

Applicable Code Articles

Art. 101. Scope

This code governs proceedings in the courts of Louisiana to the extent and with the exception stated in Article 1101.

Art. 1101. Applicability

A. Proceedings generally; rule of privilege.

(1) Except as otherwise provided by legislation, the provisions of this Code shall be applicable to the determination of questions of fact in all contradictory judicial proceedings and in proceedings to confirm a default judgment. Juvenile adjudication hearings in non-delinquency proceedings shall be governed by the provisions of this Code applicable to civil cases. Juvenile adjudication hearings in delinquency proceedings shall be governed by the provisions of this Code applicable to criminal cases.

34. *See* La. Code Evid. art. 102 Official Comment (b); Compare La. Const. Art. 1 (1974) (Declaration of Rights) with the U.S. Const. amends. 1–10, (Bill of Rights).

(2) Furthermore, except as otherwise provided by legislation, Chapter 5 of this Code with respect to testimonial privileges applies to all stages of all actions, cases, and proceedings where there is power to subpoena witnesses, including administrative, juvenile, legislative, military courts-martial, grand jury, arbitration, medical review panel, and judicial proceedings, and the proceedings enumerated in Paragraphs B and C of this Article.

* * *

Now that we've covered the history and development of the Louisiana Code of Evidence as well as the reasoning and policy underlying the rules, let's focus now on the proceedings and courts to which the rules apply. Article 101 provides that the rules contained in the Louisiana Code of Evidence govern proceedings in the courts of Louisiana to the extent and with the exception stated in Article 1101. Thus Article 101 must be read in conjunction with Article 1101.

Pursuant to this provision, there are certain proceedings in which application of the rules is **mandatory**, others in which the rules serve only as **guides** to admissibility of evidence, and some proceedings in which the rules specifically **do not apply**. Additionally, the Article notes that the courts have **discretion** to apply certain provisions of the code in all judicial proceedings as outlined below.

Mandatory Application. Article 1101 provides that the Code of Evidence ***shall apply*** to the determination of questions of fact in all contradictory judicial proceedings and in proceedings to confirm a default judgment.[35] Juvenile adjudication hearings in *non-delinquency* proceedings shall be governed by the provisions of the Code applicable to *civil* cases.[36] Juvenile adjudication hearings in *delinquency* proceedings shall be governed by the provisions of the Code applicable to *criminal* cases.[37]

Furthermore, Chapter 5 of the Evidence Code with respect to **testimonial privileges** applies to **all stages** of **all actions**, **cases**, and **proceedings** where there is a power to subpoena witnesses, including administrative, juvenile, and legislative proceedings, military courts-martial, grand jury proceedings, arbitrations, medical review panels, and the proceedings enumerated in Paragraphs B and C of this Article. The provisions relative to privileges are applicable in all proceedings due to the confidential nature of the information involved, and the need to protect that privacy regardless of the nature of the proceeding. Thus, they apply to all stages of all actions.

Applicable Code Articles

Art. 1101. Applicability

* * *

B. Limited applicability. Except as otherwise provided by Article 1101(A)(2) and other legislation, in the following proceedings, the principles underlying this Code shall serve as guides to the admissibility of evidence. The specific exclusionary rules and other provisions,

35. LA. CODE EVID. art. 1101(A)(1).
36. LA. CODE EVID. art. 1101(A)(1); *See also* CHILDREN'S CODE art. 105.
37. LA. CODE EVID. art. 1101(A)(1); *See also* CHILDREN'S CODE art. 105.

however, shall be applied only to the extent that they tend to promote the purposes of the proceeding.

(1) Workers' compensation cases.

(2) Child custody cases.

(3) Revocation of probation hearings.

(4) Preliminary examinations in criminal cases, and the court may consider evidence that would otherwise be barred by the hearsay rule.

(5) All proceedings before mayors' courts and justice of the peace courts.

(6) Peace bond hearings.

(7) Extradition hearings.

(8) Hearings on motions and other summary proceedings involving questions of fact not dispositive of or central to the disposition of the case on the merits, or to the dismissal of the case, excluding in criminal cases hearings on motions to suppress evidence and hearings to determine mental capacity to proceed.

* * *

Limited applicability of the Rules of Evidence. The Code also serves as a ***guide*** to the admissibility of evidence in the following proceedings to the extent that they are not in conflict with other legislation: workers' compensation cases; child custody cases; revocation of probation hearings; preliminary examinations in criminal cases and the mayor's courts and justice of the peace courts; peace bond hearings; extradition hearings; and hearings on motions and other summary proceedings involving questions of fact not dispositive of or central to the disposition of the case on the merits, or to the dismissal of the case. This provision does not include hearings on motions to suppress evidence and hearings to determine mental capacity to proceed in criminal cases.[38]

Under this provision, the specific exclusionary rules and other provisions are applied only to the extent that they tend to promote the purposes of the proceedings.[39]

Applicable Code Articles

Art. 1101. Applicability

* * *

C. Rules inapplicable. Except as otherwise provided by Article 1101(A)(2) and other legislation, the provisions of this Code shall not apply to the following:

(1) The determination of questions of fact preliminary to admissibility of evidence when the issue is to be determined by the court under Article 104.

(2) Proceedings with respect to release on bail.

(3) Disposition hearings in juvenile cases.

38. La. Code Evid. art. 1101(B).
39. La. Code Evid. art. 1101(B).

(4) Sentencing hearings except as provided in Code of Criminal Procedure Article 905.2 in capital cases.

(5) Small claims court proceedings except as provided in R.S. 13:5203 and 13:5207.

(6) Proceedings before grand juries except as provided by Code of Criminal Procedure Article 442.

* * *

Instances Where the Louisiana Rules of Evidence Do Not Apply. The provisions of this Code ***shall not apply*** to the following: the determination of questions of fact preliminary to admissibility of evidence when the issue is to be determined by the court under Article 104; proceedings with respect to release on bail; disposition hearings in juvenile cases; sentencing hearings except as provided in Code of Criminal Procedure Article 905.2 in capital cases; small claims court proceedings except as provided in R.S. 13: 5203 and 13: 5207; and proceedings before grand juries except as provided by Code of Criminal Procedure Article 442.

Applicable Code Articles

Art. 1101. Applicability

* * *

D. Discretionary applicability. Notwithstanding the limitations on the applicability of this Code stated in Paragraphs A, B, and C of this Article, in all judicial proceedings a court may rely upon the provisions of this Code with respect to judicial notice, authentication and identification, and proof of contents of writings, recordings, and photographs as a basis for admitting evidence or making a finding of fact.

Discretionary Applicability of the Louisiana Rules of Evidence. A court ***may*** rely upon the provisions of this Code with respect to judicial notice, authentication and identification, and proof of contents of writings, recordings, and photographs as a basis for admitting evidence or making a finding of fact in all judicial proceedings, subject to the limitations stated above.

Federal Rules of Evidence Distinction. The Federal Rules of Evidence do not contain a corresponding provision specifically providing for the discretionary application of certain rules.

§ 1.5 The Participants in the Adversarial Trial

While the rules of evidence apply to a wide range of proceedings as outlined above, the rules have the greatest impact in a civil or criminal trial. As you begin to study the law of evidence, it is important to understand the parties involved in a trial and the scope of their role. While you might already be fairly familiar with the parties involved in a trial, we will briefly cover it here as a refresher.

The Parties—Plaintiff and Defendant. The party who initiates the action is the plaintiff (or the prosecution in a criminal trial), and they have the burden of proving every element of the action they have brought. In a civil case, the plaintiff must prove the elements of the action by a preponderance of the evidence. In a criminal case, the prosecution must prove the essential elements of the offense with which the accused is charged beyond a reasonable doubt.

The party against whom the case or lawsuit is brought is the defendant. The defendant generally has no burden of proof, although they must prove the elements of any affirmative defenses they may assert that would preclude a finding of guilt or liability.

The Advocates. The attorneys for the parties are responsible for the presentation of the cases. They will call and question witnesses, present the evidence, and make arguments to the jury. They develop their own case strategy and must make and respond to objections. The attorneys have an important role in ensuring that they apprise themselves of the applicable law and have a duty to zealously advocate on their client's behalf and to protect their interests. They must do so in an ethically responsible manner, observing the rules of professional conduct and upholding the state and federal constitutions. In most trial settings, this will be your role, or the role of the judge.

The Witnesses. Evidence is primarily presented through the testimony of witnesses. There are several rules of evidence that limit who may testify, to what information they may testify, and what foundational requirements must be met prior to testifying, which is fully discussed in Chapter 4, *infra*. For example, witnesses must take an oath or affirm that they will tell the truth, and they must testify from their own personal knowledge of the facts, rather than from information related to them by others. Additionally, witnesses must be competent, i.e., they must be capable of understanding the difference between the truth and a lie, and must understand their duty to give their testimony in a truthful manner.

The Judge. The primary role of the judge is to maintain order and control over the courtroom and the proceedings. Judges act somewhat as referees. They ensure that matters before them proceed in an "orderly, expeditious, and fair manner."[40] Additionally, judges make determinations of law at the trial, and some determinations of fact on preliminary matters[41] such as the admissibility of evidence as discussed in Chapter 2, *infra*. They control the mode and order of interrogation of witnesses,[42] as outlined in Chapter 4, *infra*, and in some instances may even call and question witnesses.[43] Judges do not, however, decide case strategy, make opening statements, closing arguments, make or respond to objections made by either party, or give their own opinions about witnesses' credibility or the sufficiency of the evidence in a trial in which the judge is not the trier of fact.

The Jury. In a jury trial, the jury is the trier of fact. The jury is typically composed of neutral individuals who must decide a case based solely on the facts and evidence presented at the trial. In deciding the case, the jury will make credibility determinations as they decide which evidence they will accept and reject. The jury must also make factual determinations that are typically not disturbed on appeal. Ultimately, the most important role of the jury is to determine guilt/innocence/liability. The role of the jury is an important one that is enshrined in our history and Constitution—the right to have cases decided

---

40. Robert Force & Gerald Rault, Handbook on Louisiana Evidence, Art. 611A, Author's Note (1) (West Publishing 2014) [hereinafter Force & Rault, Handbook].

41. La. Code Evid. art. 104.

42. La. Code Evid. art. 611(A).

43. La. Code Evid. art. 614.

by a jury of our peers.[44] However, as laymen, jurors may not always be able to detach their prejudices, biases, beliefs, presumptions, or personal experiences from their roles in deciding a case. Thus, as outlined above, and as will be discussed in various places throughout the course, many of the rules of evidence are crafted to protect jurors from information that may impermissibly or unfairly affect their ability to decide the case in a fair manner.

§ 1.6 The Stages of the Adversarial Trial

What will become increasingly important as we move through the rules is understanding the various stages of a trial, and what takes place during each stage. This will assist you in putting the concepts in context as you study the law of evidence. Throughout the course we will refer to matters that may only be brought out in a party's case-in-chief, during cross-examination, on redirect, in rebuttal, and so on. As you tackle these concepts, you must understand where you are spatially within the adversarial trial. A trial in a Louisiana court (and in most courts across the country) generally proceeds in the following order:

Pre-Trial: Prior to trial, attorneys have an opportunity to attempt to come to an amicable resolution of the case without the need for a trial, and to prepare the case for an efficient trial, in the event the case cannot be settled. Two of the most important pre-trial procedures are: 1) obtaining discovery, including taking depositions; and 2) filing pre-trial motions. Discovery is the process by which attorneys obtain information needed to present and defend their cases. They learn what evidence is available, what evidence will be offered against them by the other party, what witnesses are available, and to what each witness will testify. Additionally, attorneys can file motions to get pre-trial rulings on the admissibility of evidence. Having prior knowledge as to what evidence will be admitted at trial, and what will be excluded, helps the attorneys prepare more efficiently for trial, helps the trial move along more efficiently, and avoids undue delay and inconvenience to juries that would occur if the issues were taken up after the trial began.

Voir Dire (Jury Selection). Voir dire, or jury selection, is the stage of a trial in which the attorneys (or judges in some jurisdictions) talk with prospective jurors to obtain information from them that will enable the attorneys to select the jurors who will hear a particular case. During the voir dire (or questioning of the prospective jurors) the parties are trying to determine whether any fact, circumstance, belief, or any other factor exists that will prevent a juror from being fair and impartial in deciding a particular case. Parties will want to ensure that the jurors do not know the parties or witnesses involved, that preferably they have not heard about the case, or in the alternative, that if they have, they have no preconceptions about guilt/innocence/liability. Additionally, jurors may be asked questions as simple as what types of magazines they subscribe to, their hobbies, or to what organizations they belong[45] in an attempt to determine any particular interests or beliefs they may have that could affect their ability to be fair or impartial.

The mere fact that a prospective juror may appear to be biased does not automatically prevent the juror from being able to serve on the jury. The adverse party will have an op-

44. The Sixth Amendment of the U.S. Constitution provides, in pertinent part, "In all criminal prosecutions, the accused shall enjoy the right to ... an impartial jury of the State and district wherein the crime has have been committed...."

45. For example, members of MADD (Mothers Against Drunk Driving) might be perceived to have a particular bias against drunk drivers and will likely be excluded by the defense in a DWI case.

portunity to rehabilitate a juror, in which they can inquire as to whether, despite the circumstances, the juror's belief, etc., he or she can be fair and impartial in deciding the case. A prospective juror who indicates that they can be fair and impartial cannot be challenged on that basis for cause.

Each party is limited in the number of prospective jurors they can cut (challenge), preventing them from being a part of the final jury. In a criminal trial, each party has an unlimited number of challenges for cause. A cause challenge exists when the prospective juror does not meet statutory requirements to serve on a jury, or has indicated that he or she cannot be fair and impartial in a particular case. Each party also has six peremptory challenges in a trial that will be heard by a six-person jury; and twelve peremptory challenges in a trial that will be heard by a twelve-person jury. Peremptory challenges are challenges of a prospective juror that do not require explanation or justification. While peremptory challenges can be for a wide range of reasons, it is impermissible to challenge prospective jurors based solely on race.[46]

Opening Statements. The opening statement is the opportunity for attorneys to give an overview of their case—their case theory, or what they believe the evidence will show. The opening statement provides a roadmap for the jury. They learn what the case is about, they become familiar with the facts that will be proven, what defenses will be raised, which witnesses they may hear from and what they will likely testify to, and ultimately, what remedy is being sought—guilty, not guilty, liable, etc.

In a criminal case, the prosecution is required to give an opening statement in a jury trial so that a defendant will not be unfairly surprised by the evidence that will be offered against him. While the defense is not required to give an opening statement, it is extremely rare that the defense will waive the opportunity to speak to the jury about their version of what they believe the evidence will show and to lay the foundation for their defense. Opening statements are not arguments. Instead, the opening statement is an overview of the case. Argument about what has been proven or disproven, and how the jury should construe the facts to the law, is reserved for closing arguments.

Plaintiff's/Prosecution's Case-In-Chief. The plaintiff or the prosecution presents their case-in-chief first. The plaintiffs have the burden of proof and must prove all elements of their claim or cause of action. They must do this by calling witnesses who will give testimony, and by admitting physical evidence, documents, photographs, expert opinions, or any other evidence they can obtain to help them prove their case.

When a party calls a witness, he conducts a direct examination of the witness.[47] He asks the witness open-ended questions, preferably in the form of who/what/where/when/why/how, to elicit information about the case. A witness should testify from first-hand knowledge—meaning relating what he perceived with his own senses rather than what he may have been told by another person.

After a party conducts a direct examination on a witness he has called, the opposing party has an opportunity to conduct a cross-examination of the witness.[48] During cross-examination, an opposing party may use leading questions in examining the witness to test the witness's memory, perception, credibility, etc. Cross-examination is a very im-

46. *See* Baton v. Kentucky, 476 U.S. 79 (1986) (restricting exercise of peremptory challenge based solely on race).

47. Direct examination of witnesses is covered thoroughly *infra* Chapter 4 § 4.6.

48. Cross-examination is covered *infra* Chapter 4 § 4.6.

portant component of a party's case, so much so that in a criminal trial, the right is protected in the Sixth Amendment of the United States Constitution.[49]

After the plaintiff has presented all of the evidence in support of his claim, he rests. The evidence presented must have been sufficient to support a jury finding in favor of the plaintiff for every proposition for which he bears the burden of proving—this is referred to as a prima facie case. This basically means that the plaintiff has offered enough evidence in his case-in-chief to prove each and every element of the claim he has brought, such that if uncontradicted and unrebutted, the jury could find in his favor. If a plaintiff has failed to make out a prima facie case, then a judge can find in favor of the defense without the defense ever having to present its case.

Motions for Judgment of Acquittal or Directed Verdict. As stated above, in a plaintiff's case-in-chief, he must have established a prima facie case in order for the case to move forward. The judge generally makes a ruling as to whether plaintiffs have established a prima facie case upon a motion from the defense to the court for a directed verdict[50] (in a civil case), or a motion for judgment of acquittal[51] in a criminal bench trial. If the judge grants the motion in favor of the defense, the trial is over and the defense is not required to put on a case. If the motion is denied, then the defense may move forward with the presentation of its case-in-chief.

Defendant's Case-in-Chief. After the plaintiff/prosecution has rested, the defense has an opportunity to present their case-in-chief. In presenting their case, they may also call witnesses who will be subject to cross-examination by the plaintiff/prosecution. The defendant's evidence may be offered to prove facts that may discredit the plaintiff's witnesses, counter evidence offered by the plaintiff, or to prove his affirmative defenses.

Plaintiff's Rebuttal. After the defendant rests, the prosecution may reopen its case and present additional evidence to rebut evidence presented by the defense in its case-in-chief. For example, if the defense calls a character witness to testify to his good character, after the defense rests the prosecution may call a witness to testify to character traits of the defense that rebuts and contradicts the character evidence presented by the defendant.

Defendant's Surrebuttal. In some rare circumstances, a defendant may be able to reopen his case to rebut any new evidence that was brought out by the plaintiff in its rebuttal. However, surrebuttal by the defendant is not a matter of right, but may be allowed at the court's discretion.[52] Particularly in a criminal trial, if the defense claims he has new evidence, the denial of which might deprive him of an opportunity to present a defense, he may be allowed to reopen his case in surrebuttal.[53]

Closing Arguments. After both parties have rested, they each have an opportunity to make closing arguments to the jury. During closing arguments each party has an opportunity to argue to the jury about what they believe the evidence has shown, and what they believe has been proven or disproved. The parties can go through the law and explain what evidence has been offered to prove the elements of the claim. The parties can address

---

49. See U.S. Const. amend. VI; *See also* Chapter 5, Part E (§ 5.25) *infra*, relative to the Confrontation Clause as it relates to hearsay for a more thorough discussion of the effect of the Confrontation Clause at trial.

50. La. C.C.P. Art. 1810.

51. C.Cr.Pr. art. 778 (the motion for judgment of acquittal is not available in Louisiana for a criminal jury trial).

52. *See* Bowden v. Brown, 114 So. 3d 1194 (La. Ct. App. 2d Cir. 2013); *See also* La. Prac. Trial handbook for La. Lawyers § 9:4.

53. See *State v. George*, 661 So. 2d 975 (La. 1995); LSA-C.Cr.P. Art. 765(5).

the credibility of witnesses that have been offered. Ultimately, closing arguments provide an opportunity for both parties to summarize their cases and explain to the jury why they should ultimately find in their favor.

The plaintiffs have an opportunity to make their closing argument first, followed by the defense. The plaintiff/prosecution has an opportunity to speak to the jury again, the rebuttal, after the defense's closing argument to respond to arguments made by the defense.

Jury Instructions. After all the evidence has been presented to the jury and both parties have made their closing arguments, the judge instructs the jury on the law to be used in the case. Prior to finalizing the jury instructions, both parties usually meet with the judge to review the law on which the jury will be instructed. A party can request that the jury be instructed on particular law or that the law should be applied in a particular manner. The judge may or may not grant the request, a ruling which a party may seek to have reviewed on appeal.

Deliberations and Verdict. After the jury is instructed on the applicable law in the case, the jury retires to deliberate in private and come together on a verdict. Depending on the case, jurors may have to be unanimous, or in some cases, only ten out of twelve jurors may have to concur to render a verdict. During deliberation, jurors may have access to the evidence presented at trial to review it more closely. The jurors usually select a foreman who will help guide their deliberations. After the jury has reached a verdict, the foreman will fill out the verdict form, sign it, and give it to the judge. The verdict is then read aloud in the courtroom in the presence of all parties and the jury.

After the verdict has been read aloud, a party may request that the jury be polled to ascertain in open court from each juror individually whether the verdict read is their verdict. A party (other than the government in a criminal trial) may make a motion for a judgment notwithstanding the verdict, or for a new trial. Those motions are rarely granted.

Discussion Questions

1. While you have not begun to learn the rules of evidence, what are some public policy interests that might have resulted in distinctions between the state and federal rules of evidence? Do the state and federal governments have competing interests they might each want to further in a trial court setting? What might some of those competing interests be?

2. In reading about the early efforts to develop a Code of Evidence, you have briefly read about competing interests between organizations aligned with the prosecution in criminal cases and organizations representing the defense that for decades prevented them from agreeing on several provisions of the Code. Discuss these competing interests and the resulting types of rules they might have had difficulty agreeing on.

   Based on your general knowledge of how jury trials work, do you believe a fair balance has been struck in terms of the types of evidence that might be admissible in a criminal trial against the other party?

3. A major reason that certain types of evidence in a trial are excluded is because of the fear that the lay juror may use this evidence to convict on an improper basis. For example, evidence that a defendant has several prior convictions is excluded from being offered against him for fear that the jury would convict him based on the type of person they think he is rather than based on the evidence presented. Considering

these fears, why do you think that juries are entrusted with such an important role, which is protected by the U.S. Constitution?

4. In § 1.2 we discussed several reasons for the rules of evidence. Do you think that the rules actually further many of the listed reasons? Why or why not? Can you think of other reasons why the rules of evidence might be needed?

Chapter 1 References and Additional Authority on the Introduction to Louisiana Evidence and the Adversarial Trial

1. La. C.E. arts. 101, 102, 1104 and Official Comments
2. Force & Rault, Handbook on Louisiana Evidence Law, Arts. 101, 102, 1104 Author's Comments (West Publishing 2014)
3. Harges & Jones, Louisiana Evidence Art. 101, 102, 1104 Author's Comments (West Publishing 2014)
4. **Applicability of Code of Evidence:** 19 La. Civ. L. Treatise, Evidence And Proof § 1.1–1.4 (2nd ed.)
5. **Burden of proof; Order of Trial:** 0..119 La. Civ. L. Treatise, Evidence and Proof § 3.1–3.10, 4.2 (2d ed.); La. Practice Trial Handbook for La. Lawyers Chapters 8–11 (3d Edition)
6. **History of the development of the Louisiana Code of Evidence Commentary**: Pugh, *Federal Rules of Evidence: Foreword*, 36 La. L. Rev. 59 (1975); See also Pugh, Force, Rault, and Triche, *The Louisiana Code of Evidence—A Retrospective and Prospective View*, 49 La. L. Rev. 689 (1989); Rault, *An Overview of the New Louisiana Code of Evidence—Its Imperfections and Uncertainties*, 49 La. L .Rev. 697 (1989); Papale, *Editorial: Reflections on the Proposed Code of Evidence*, 12 Loyola L. Rev. 51 (1956); Sponsler, *Evidence: Louisiana Style*, 21 Loyola L. Rev. 273 (1975)
7. **Reasons for the rules of evidence**: See Christopher B. Mueller & Laird Kirkpatrick, Evidence § 1.1, at 2–3 (4th ed. 2009) (Identifying five functions served by modern rules of evidence: (1) to protect the jury from receiving information it might improperly use at trial; (2) to promote substantive policies, such as the burden of persuasion and standard of proof, at trial; (3) to further extrinsic social policies that are considered to outweigh the importance of some types of relevant evidence at trial; (4) to ensure accurate fact-finding; and (5) to control the scope and duration of trials).

Chapter 2

Rulings on Evidence and Preserving Issues for Appeal

§ 2.1 Preliminary Questions [La. C.E. art. 104]

Applicable Code Articles

Art. 104. Preliminary questions

A. Questions of admissibility generally. Preliminary questions concerning the competency or qualification of a person to be a witness, the existence of a privilege, or the admissibility of evidence shall be determined by the court, subject to the provisions of Paragraph B. In making its determination it is not bound by the rules of evidence except those with respect to privileges.

* * *

In Chapter 1 we briefly discussed the roles of the parties involved in a trial, including the judge's role to act as a gatekeeper and to maintain order in the courtroom. But perhaps the judge's most important role in a trial is to make **preliminary determinations** of the **admissibility of evidence**. Throughout the course of a trial, and even pre-trial, the judge is repeatedly called upon to resolve questions of admissibility that depend upon contested facts between the parties. While in a jury trial, the jury is the finder of fact and the judge determines questions of law, on a number of preliminary matters the judge must make factual determinations to resolve the issues. The authority for such determinations is found in Article 104(A), which provides that the court shall determine "preliminary questions concerning the competency or qualification of a person to be a witness, the existence of a privilege or the admissibility of evidence."[1] This is a very important article to keep in mind as you study evidence, in that most of the rules we will study in this course deal with the admissibility of evidence that the judge must determine under the authority of this rule. Thus, throughout the course we will often refer back to this rule as the standard by which various questions of admissibility will be resolved.

Let's consider an example. In Chapter 5 we will cover hearsay, and you will learn that while such statements are ordinarily excluded from evidence, there are a number of exceptions to this rule. One such exception is referred to as a dying declaration. The exception applies if a person who made an out-of-court statement is unavailable for the trial, the statement was made while the person believed he was dying, and the statement concerns

1. La. Code Evid. art. 104(A).

the cause or circumstances of what he believed to be his impending death.[2] An example would be if, after being shot, the victim stated, "John shot me!" If an attorney seeks to have the statement admitted under this exception, the judge would have to resolve certain factual questions in order to determine if the exception applies. He would have to determine whether the person who made the statement was actually unavailable based on the representations of the proponent of the evidence and whether the person actually believed he was dying when the statement was made.[3] How the judge resolves these and the other issues would determine whether the exception applies, and thus whether the evidence would be admissible or not.

In addition to determining the admissibility of evidence, under this article the judge also determines if a person is competent to testify under Article 601, i.e., whether the person is capable of understanding the difference between the truth and a lie. Similarly, the judge must make preliminary determinations as to whether a privilege exists. For example, one such privilege is the spousal communications privilege that protects confidential communications between spouses.[4] This would not be an issue that attorneys would present to a jury and the jury would then decide whether the information is privileged or not; instead, the judge hears the facts and circumstances surrounding the making of the statement and determines whether the privilege applies under the authority of this rule.

Standard of proof. The trial judge should generally apply the **preponderance of the evidence** standard when making preliminary determinations of admissibility under Article 104(A),[5] unless the law prescribes a particular foundation or sets forth other special prerequisites for the admissibility of evidence.[6] In most situations, however, the preponderance of the evidence standard should apply. Thus, in the scenario above, the court must decide whether based on the evidence presented by the proponent of the hearsay statement "John shot me!" it is **"more likely than not"** that the person who made the statement is in fact unavailable, believed he was dying, etc. If the judge finds that the standard is met, then the judge should rule in the proponent's favor.

There are certain circumstances in which the law requires that the judge use a particularly specified standard to determine the admissibility of evidence. In such a case, the judge should use that standard rather than preponderance of the evidence. For instance, in Chapter 6 you will learn that in certain circumstances the prosecution may offer evidence of an unrelated crime or other bad act of a defendant to prove a relevant issue at trial, such as the defendant's motive for committing the crime with which he is charged.[7] The Louisiana Supreme Court has held that in determining the admissibility of *that* evidence, the prosecution must prove that the defendant committed the prior crime by

---

2. See Chapter 5, Part C (§ 5.16) for a full discussion of La. Code Evid. art. 804(B)(2), "Statements Under the Belief of Impending Death" also commonly referred to as the "Dying Declaration."

3. *See* State v. Ball, 824 So. 2d 1089 (La. 2002).

4. La. Code Evid. art. 505; *See also* Chapter 8, for a full discussion of privileges.

5. See La. Code Evid. art. 104 Official Comment (c); *See also* Ortego v. Roy Motors, Inc., 635 So. 2d 649 (La. Ct. App. 3d Cir. 1994) ("[W]hen factual questions must be decided to determine admissibility of evidence, a question of law, court should follow preponderance of evidence standard unless special rule of law requires different standard.").

6. *See, e.g.* La. Code Evid. art. 602 relative to the standard for establishing personal knowledge; La. Code Evid. art. 901 et seq. relative to the evidence sufficient to authenticate evidence; La. Code Evid. art. 1103 and State v. Prieur, 277 So. 2d 126 (La. 1973), and State v. Davis, 449 So. 2d 466 (La. 1984) (establishing a clear and convincing standard to admit evidence of other criminal acts under La. Code Evid. art. 404(B)).

7. *See* La. Code Evid. art. 404(B).

"clear and convincing"[8] evidence rather than by a preponderance of the evidence standard.[9] However, when no standard is specified, the preponderance of the evidence should apply. We will point out other instances where a different standard is used as we cover them throughout the course.

Not bound by rules of evidence. As the court evaluates the admissibility of evidence under this article, the rules of evidence do not apply. If you recall from Chapter 1, many of the rules of evidence were developed to protect the untrained *juror* from potentially prejudicial and unreliable evidence that may later be determined to be inadmissible.[10] Thus, when preliminary matters are determined by the judge alone, the rules need not be recognized except as to privileges. Because of the confidential nature of privileges, they are generally recognized at all stages of all actors, cases, and proceedings. Thus, in the example above, as the judge determines the unavailability of the person who made the dying declaration, he may consider hearsay evidence or an unauthenticated document, such as an affidavit prepared by someone who claims that the person is deceased.[11]

Applicable Code Articles

Art. 104. Preliminary questions

* * *

C. Hearing of jury. Hearings on matters to be decided by the judge alone shall be conducted out of the hearing of the jury when the interests of justice require. Hearings on the admissibility of confessions or admissions by the accused or evidence allegedly unlawfully obtained shall in all cases be conducted out of the hearing of the jury, but when there has been a ruling prior to trial, it shall not be necessary to conduct another hearing as to admissibility before presentation of the evidence to a jury.

* * *

Out of hearing of the jury. Further, Article 104(C) provides that hearings on matters to be decided by the judge alone shall be conducted out of the hearing of the jury when the interests of justice require. The provision does not require that *all* preliminary issues be determined out of the presence of the jury, but instead gives the judge discretion in deciding which issues are likely to affect the jury's ability to fairly decide the case. The ultimate goal here is to ensure that to the extent possible, the jury is not exposed to potentially prejudicial evidence or evidence that might ultimately be excluded.

However, when the potential for prejudice is minimal, the issue may appropriately be determined in the presence of the jury, as in the case of determining the qualifications of an expert.[12] While the judge determines whether a person possesses the necessary qualifications to testify as an expert witness, the questions posed to the witness regarding his qualifications are usually conducted in the presence of the jury. In such a case, hearing

8. *See* State v. Blank, 955 So. 2d 90, 95 (La. 2007) (upholding the clear and convincing standard that state must meet in proving the other bad act occurred); *See also* Chapter 6, § 6.6 for a full discussion of non-conformity evidence under La. Code Evid. art. 404(B).

9. For additional examples see La. Code Evid. art. 104 Official Comment (c).

10. La. Code Evid. art. 104 Official Comment (d).

11. *See* Tutorship of Price v. Standard Life Ins. Co., 569 So. 2d 261 (La. Ct. App. 2d Cir. 1990) (using inadmissible evidence to determine unavailability).

12. *See* Force & Rault, Handbook, Art. 104, Author's Note (7).

the witness's qualifications and argument as to whether or not the witness should be able to testify as an expert witness does little to impact the jury's ability to fairly decide the issues.

While Article 104(C) does not contain an exhaustive list of matters that must be decided outside of the presence of the jury, it does specifically require that the determination of the admissibility of confessions or admissions of an accused or whether evidence was unlawfully obtained be conducted outside of the presence of the jury in all cases. Whether other issues will be decided outside of the presence of the jury will be up to the court's discretion subject to an "abuse of discretion" standard on appeal.[13]

If the judge makes a pretrial ruling on the admissibility of the evidence, it shall not be necessary to conduct another hearing on its admissibility prior to presenting the evidence to the jury.

Applicable Code Articles

Art. 104. Preliminary questions

* * *

D. Weight and credibility. The preliminary determination by the court that evidence is admissible does not limit the right of a party to introduce evidence relevant to weight or credibility at the trial.

Opposing party may still challenge admitted evidence. Further, even though a judge has made a preliminary determination that evidence is admissible, it does not limit the right of an adverse party to introduce evidence relevant to the weight or credibility that the jury should give to the evidence at the trial. For example, a judge might determine that a witness possesses the necessary qualifications to testify as an expert witness at trial. However, this does not preclude an opponent from offering evidence to argue, for example, that, based on his qualifications, the witness is not as qualified as *their* expert witness, or that his opinions are not as reliable because of the methodologies he utilized in coming to his conclusions.

While this provision allows the judge to determine admissibility of the evidence, ultimately the jury must determine its weight. Thus, evidence may always be offered on this issue.

Applicable Code Articles

Art. 104. Preliminary questions

* * *

B. Relevancy conditioned on fact. Subject to other provisions of this Code, when the relevancy of evidence depends upon the fulfillment of a condition of fact, the court shall admit it upon, or subject to, the introduction of evidence sufficient to support a finding of the fulfillment of the condition.

* * *

13. *Id.* Author's Note (2); See also *State. v. Ball*, 824 So. 2d 1089 (La. 2002).

Conditional Relevancy. Article 104(B) is another important part of the article relative to preliminary questions. In some instances, whether or not evidence is relevant depends upon the determination of a preliminary question. For example, if a letter confessing to a crime was supposedly written by the defendant in a case, the letter is not relevant unless it can be shown that the defendant did in fact write it.[14] Clearly, if the letter was written by someone other than the defendant, it would not be relevant to the case at hand. Thus, its relevancy depends upon the determination of a preliminary question, in this case, whether the defendant wrote the letter.

Article 104(B) provides that when determining the admissibility of such evidence, the court shall admit it upon, or subject to, the introduction of evidence "*sufficient to support a finding*" of the fulfillment of the condition. Thus, as it relates to the letter, it should be admitted if the proponent offers evidence **"sufficient to support a finding"** that the defendant wrote it. Evidence is "sufficient to support a finding" if **"a reasonable juror could find the existence of the fact."** So provided the proponent can offer evidence where a reasonable juror could find that the defendant wrote the letter, the standard is met, and the evidence should be admitted.

This is a different and lower standard than is used in addressing other preliminary questions. Under this provision, the preponderance of the evidence standard is not used. Instead, under Article 104(B) the court need only find "evidence sufficient to support a finding" that the preliminary fact exists, or in other words it should be admitted if "a rational juror could conclude that the condition exists or was fulfilled."[15]

Once this precondition is met, the judge should allow the evidence to be admitted at trial **for consideration by the jury**. Thereafter, it will be left to the jury to make the determination as to whether the defendant actually wrote the letter. Thus, as it pertains to conditional relevancy under this provision, the *jury* makes the preliminary factual determinations, rather than the judge.[16]

Further, the fact that the provision provides that the evidence may be admitted either "upon" or "subject to" evidence sufficient to support a finding of its relevance allows the court to either require that the fulfillment of the condition be offered *prior to* admitting the evidence or it may be admitted upon counsel's assurance that the evidence "connecting it up" may be *forthcoming*. Of course, if such evidence never materializes, then the judge may withdraw the evidence from consideration by the jury and instruct the jury to disregard it if practicable, or if not, declare a mistrial.[17]

The distinction between preliminary questions to be decided by the judge in Article 104(A) and those to be decided by the jury in Article 104(B) is subtle. After we have studied relevance in Chapter 3 more thoroughly, the distinction will become clearer. For now, it is important to know that the key difference between the two provisions is that under Article 104(B) the determination of the preliminary question determines whether the evidence is *relevant*. In such a case, if the judge determines that a rational juror could find that a condition exists or was fulfilled, then the evidence goes to the jury to determine

14. *See also* FED. R. EVID. 104(b) advisory committee notes.

15. LA. CODE EVID. art. 104 Official Comment (f).

16. *See* Force & Rault, HANDBOOK ON LOUISIANA EVIDENCE, Art. 104, Author's Note (2) (West Publishing 2014).

17. *See* Force & Rault, HANDBOOK ON LOUISIANA EVIDENCE, Art. 104, Author's Note (2) (West Publishing 2014).

the fact. However, under Article 104(A), the judge makes the preliminary determinations of fact in deciding the admissibility of the evidence. If admitted, the jury decides the weight and credibility to give to the evidence.

Key Points

The key points to keep in mind regarding preliminary questions.

1. **Judge's ruling on preliminary questions.** Judges make preliminary determinations on: 1) admissibility of evidence; 2) competency of witnesses; and 3) availability of privileges.
2. In making preliminary determinations, the judge is not bound by rules of evidence, except as to privileges.
3. Court decides preliminary questions using preponderance of evidence standard, unless other standard specified in law.
4. Typically decided outside of presence of jury.
    - However, hearings on confessions or whether evidence unlawfully seized, must be out of presence of jury.
5. Reviewed on abuse of discretion standard.
6. If relevancy of evidence depends upon the determination of the preliminary question, the judge admits it upon evidence "sufficient to support a finding" of the fact or condition.
    i. Evidence "sufficient to support a finding" is evidence in which a rational juror could find the existence of the fact or fulfillment of the condition.
    ii. If the standard is met, evidence goes to jury to decide if the fact exists.

Problems on Preliminary Questions

PROBLEM 2-1. Janet is involved in an accident and sues the man who hit her. At the time of the accident two of her friends are in the car, Maria is in the front seat and Tania is in the backseat. Prior to trial, Tania states in her deposition that she was asleep at the time of the accident. Based on this information, the defense seeks to object to her testimony prior to trial claiming lack of first-hand knowledge regarding how the accident occurred. Does the judge have the authority to exclude her testimony? Why or why not?

PROBLEM 2-2. Should the judge decide the following issue or is it one that the jury should decide, and why?

a. Whether the witness is qualified to testify as an expert in a particular field?
b. Whether the witness's testimony conforms to a particular exception to the hearsay rule?
c. Whether a witness is exempt from the rule of sequestration under Article 615?
d. Whether statements made by one spouse to another are protected by the confidential communications privilege under Article 504?

§ 2.2 Preserving Issues for Appeal [La. C.E. art. 103]

> **Applicable Code Articles**
>
> **Art. 103. Rulings on evidence**
>
> **A. Effect of erroneous ruling.** Error may not be predicated upon a ruling which admits or excludes evidence unless a substantial right of the party is affected, and
>
> **(1) Ruling admitting evidence.** When the ruling is one admitting evidence, a timely objection or motion to admonish the jury to limit or disregard appears of record, stating the specific ground of objection; or
>
> **(2) Ruling excluding evidence.** When the ruling is one excluding evidence, the substance of the evidence was made known to the court by counsel.
>
> **B. Record of ruling.** The court may add any other or further statement which shows the character of the evidence, the form in which it was offered, the objection made, and the ruling thereon.
>
> **C. Hearing of jury.** In jury cases, proceedings shall be conducted, to the extent practicable, so as to prevent inadmissible evidence from being suggested to the jury by any means, such as making statements or asking questions in the hearing of the jury.

Most of the preliminary determinations on the admissibility of evidence discussed in § 2.1 above will involve the determination of factual questions on matters that are in dispute between the parties. In making such determinations, the trial judge has broad discretion, and its findings will not be disturbed on appeal absent an abuse of that discretion. However, if a party does not agree with a trial court's ruling against him on these as well as determinations of law, he may seek to have the court's ruling reviewed on appeal. Article 103 sets forth the requirements that must be met for an appellate court to find error on a trial court's ruling. It is extremely important that a trial court attorney comply with the requirements of Article 103 to give his client somewhat of a second bite at the apple by having the trial court's rulings reviewed on appeal. If the attorney does not strictly comply with the requirements to preserve issues for appeal, he forever waives the right to complain and the ruling will be final.

Requirements for finding error on appeal. The procedural requirements for finding error on appeal are found in Article 103, and depend upon whether the ruling is one admitting evidence or a ruling excluding evidence.

If the ruling is one ***admitting*** evidence, the following requirements must be met:

1) a **timely objection** *or* **motion to admonish** the jury to limit or disregard must appear of record;
2) the party must state the **specific grounds** upon which he objects; and
3) a **substantial right** of the party must be **affected.**

If the ruling is one ***excluding*** evidence, the following requirements must be met:

1) the **substance of the evidence** must be **made known to the court** by counsel, i.e., proffered for the record; and
2) a **substantial right** of the party must be **affected.**

The Contemporaneous Objection Rule

Objection, your honor! It is a familiar scene in television courtroom dramas when an attorney rises in disapproval of various matters taking place during courtroom proceedings with a resounding, **"Objection, your honor!"** An objection is universally recognized as the procedural vehicle by which a party to a proceeding formally makes known to the court its disagreement or disapproval of conduct of another party or the court that he deems illegal or improper, and properly places the issue before the court for resolution at that time, or if necessary, for later review on appeal. Article 103(A) preserves the **contemporaneous objection rule** as a requirement for a party to preserve an issue for appeal on a ruling **admitting evidence**, and requires that the party must do two things:

1) he must make a **timely objection** to a court's ruling admitting evidence; and
2) he must **state the grounds** upon which he objects.[18]

Once a party makes a timely objection with specific grounds upon which he claims the impropriety or illegality of the matter to which he is objecting, the opposing party to the objection is then given an opportunity to respond, explaining why his conduct is indeed proper or legal. Thereafter, the court either **sustains the objection**, agreeing with the objecting party and providing for the remedy he seeks, i.e., exclusion of evidence, etc., or he **overrules the objection**, denying the objecting party any remedy.

Objections at the trial level serve many purposes. While it is the judge's responsibility to make rulings on the admissibility of evidence and to make legal determinations, the parties to an action are given an opportunity to assist the judge in identifying potential illegalities by making objections and stating the legal basis. It also "promote[s] judicial efficiency by preventing a defendant from gambling for a favorable verdict and then upon conviction, resorting to appeal on errors which either could have been avoided or corrected at the time."[19] By placing the issues before the court for a ruling at the trial level, not only are juries precluded from potentially being exposed to illegal evidence, but issues are quickly resolved at the trial level rather than having to be appealed and then possibly having to be remanded for a new trial.

A party's failure to make a timely and specific objection typically constitutes a **waiver of the alleged error**, and he may not complain about the issue on appeal.[20]

1. **Timely objection**. The first important requirement that must be met when making an objection is that it must be timely made. An objection is considered timely if made **at or before the time** in which a **witness testifies** to the objectionable testimony, and **at or before the time** in which **physical evidence is offered** into evidence.[21] If the witness testifies to the inadmissible evidence prior to counsel having an opportunity to object, then counsel should object to the inadmissible evidence as soon as practicable and make a **motion to admonish** the jury to **disregard** the excluded evidence.

18. See also CCr.P art. 841 (A) for authority in criminal trials and La. Cod Civ.P. 1635 for authority relative to civil cases on procedures for preserving issues for appeal. La. CCrP art. 841 also provides that, in a criminal case, a contemporaneous objection to a judge's ruling on a written motion is unnecessary.

19. State v. Carter, 75 So. 3d 1 (La. Ct. App. 5th Cir. 2011).

20. *See* State v. Lanieu, 734 So. 2d 89 (La. Ct. App. 1st Cir. 1999).

21. See, e.g. State v. Spears, 350 So. 2d 603 (La. 1977), where objection to photographs of victim, which was not made at time photographs were introduced into evidence, but rather when State attempted to show photographs to jury, was not timely.

2. **Specific grounds**. Additionally, in order to preserve an issue for appeal on a ruling **admitting** evidence, a party must also state the grounds upon which he objects. For example, the objecting party might state, "Objection your honor. The question calls for hearsay!" Following a brief argument from both counsels, the court either sustains or overrules the objection. With respect to just how specific the grounds should be, "[g]iven the underlying purpose of the rule ... whatever term or phrase ... used ought simply be sufficient, in context, **to clearly apprise the trial judge of the grounds** of the objection."[22]

When stating the grounds upon which a party claims he is entitled to a favorable ruling, it is important to keep in mind that a "party may not successfully urge a new and different ground on appeal."[23] Thus, it is imperative that the party make every effort to state the **correct or proper grounds** upon which the party claims he is entitled to the remedy sought because those grounds will be the only grounds upon which the party may appeal.

To assist in this respect, the objecting party should **raise all possible pertinent grounds** to ensure all possible arguments may be made on appeal. Objecting on multiple grounds is permissible. Thus, a party might state, "Objection your honor. The affidavit is hearsay, it is irrelevant, it has not been properly authenticated, and its admission would deprive my client of his Sixth Amendment right to confrontation."

Additionally, in instances in which a judge makes a ruling on an objection prior to counsel having an opportunity to state the grounds, both counsels should insist upon having the objecting party state the grounds upon which he objects. The objecting party has then ensured he may raise the appropriate ground on appeal, and the opposing party can ensure the objecting party is limited to only those grounds raised when the issue is appealed. It is also important that if the judge makes the ruling at a bench conference, which is typically not recorded, counsel should put the objection and ground(s) on the record as soon as practicable.[24]

Finally, pursuant to Article 103(A)(2), there is no requirement to object with specific grounds if the ruling is one excluding evidence. By offering the evidence, the court is already apprised of the fact that its ruling is contrary to the wishes of the litigant.[25]

Federal Rules of Evidence Distinction. The Louisiana requirement of specifically stating the grounds of all objections to proffered evidence is stricter than the requirement in the Federal Rules of Evidence. Under the Federal Rules, an objecting party need only state the specific ground for the objection if it is not apparent from the context.[26] Thus in federal court, if the grounds upon which a party is objecting are apparent from the context, counsel need not state the grounds. However under Louisiana law, even if the grounds are obvious, in order to preserve an issue for appeal on a ruling **admitting** evidence, the specific grounds upon which a party is objecting must be stated.

22. Force & Rault, HANDBOOK, Art. 103, Author's Note (3).

23. Force & Rault, HANDBOOK, Art. 103, Author's Note (1); See also State v. Barnes, 685 So. 2d 1148 (La. Ct. App. 2d Cir. 1996); Tartar v. Hymes, 656 So 2d 656 (La. Ct. App. 5th Cir. 1995).

24. *See* Tingle v. American Home Assurance Co., 40 So. 3d 1169 (La. Ct. App. 3d Cir. 2010).

25. *See* Force & Rault, HANDBOOK, Art. 103, Author's Note (4).

26. *See* FED. R. EVID. 103(b).

Motion to admonish the jury (when objectionable evidence is inadvertently heard by jury). In lieu of a timely objection with grounds, a party may also preserve an issue for appeal by making a timely motion to admonish[27] the jury to limit or disregard inadmissible evidence. A motion to admonish the jury is a **request by counsel** that the court **instruct the jury** to **disregard or limit inadmissible evidence** that may have been inadvertently overheard by the jury. As stated above, in some instances, a witness may testify to inadmissible evidence before a party has an opportunity to object; or in some instances, the question did not call for objectionable testimony, but the witness nonetheless unexpectedly testifies to inadmissible evidence. While the inadmissible evidence has already been heard by the jury, the objecting party may still request that the court instruct the jury not to consider it. Quite often, counsel will not take advantage of this remedy due to the added attention the admonition may bring to the inadmissible evidence. However, if a party chooses to, he may have the jury so instructed and by doing so will properly preserve the issue for later appeal.

Proffer (when evidence is excluded). As stated above, when preserving an issue for appeal on a ruling **excluding** evidence, the party must also **make known to the court the substance** of the **excluded evidence**.[28] This procedure is referred to as a **"proffer"** of the evidence or an **"offer of proof."** This requirement is a matter of practicality in that without a proffer of the evidence, the reviewing court would have no way of knowing the substance of the excluded evidence and would thus be unable to determine if the trial court erred in excluding it. For example, if a party seeks to have a witness testify to what another person said outside of the present trial or hearing, and the evidence is excluded as inadmissible hearsay, the offering party must put into the record what the witness would have testified to had he been allowed to give the testimony. Thus, counsel might state on the record and outside of the presence of the jury, that had the witness been allowed to give the testimony, he *would have* testified that just before the defendant shot the victim, the victim stated to the defendant that she wanted a divorce. Only by making the substance of the excluded evidence known can the appellate court review it and determine if the trial court correctly ruled on it.

A proffer of evidence may take the form of an **informal statement** in which counsel states the nature of the evidence sought to be admitted, or the proffer may be a more **formal hearing** in which counsel fully questions the witness about the nature of the excluded testimony outside of the presence of the jury.[29]

It is important that a judge allow a party whose evidence has been excluded to proffer it to properly preserve the issue for review on appeal. In a criminal case, the failure of a court to do so can result in reversible error for denial of a defendant's right to present a defense.[30]

Substantial Right of the Party Affected. Pursuant to Article 103, once alleged errors are under review on appeal, error may not be found unless "a substantial right of the party is affected." "The proper inquiry for determining whether a party was prejudiced

---

27. *See also* C.Cr.P. Art. 771; In other jurisdictions and the Federal Rules of Evidence the motion is referred to as the Motion to Strike.

28. See LA. CODE OF CIV. P. art. 1635 for the type of procedure contemplated by this requirement.

29. *See* Michelli v. Michelli, 655 So. 2d 1342 (La. Ct. App. 1st Cir. 1995); Whitehead v. The Kansas City Southern Railway Company, et al., 758 So. 2d 211 (La. Ct. App. 3d Cir. 1999); *See also* LA. CODE CIV. P. art 1635, 1636; Harges & Jones, LOUISIANA EVIDENCE Art. 103, Authors Comments (West Publishing 2014) [hereinafter Harges & Jones, Louisiana Evidence].

30. *See* State v. Adams, 537 So. 2d 1262 (La. Ct. App. 4th Cir. 1989); *See also* State v. Brooks, 734 So. 2d 1232, 1241 (La. Ct. App. 1st 1999) (remanding back to the trial court for hearing after trial court restricted defendant's proffer and defendant's right to present a defense was significantly impaired).

by a trial court's alleged erroneous ruling on the admission or denial of evidence is whether the alleged error, when compared to the entire record, had a **substantial effect on the outcome of the case**. If the effect on the outcome of the case is not substantial, reversal is not warranted."[31] The party alleging prejudice by the evidentiary ruling of the trial court bears the burden of so proving.[32] If the error found on appeal is harmless then no substantial right of the party is affected and error will not be found on appeal. Thus, the ultimate inquiry in determining whether reversal is warranted, is whether the party alleging prejudice can prove the error had a substantial impact on the outcome of the case.

Motion in Limine. Quite often, issues are brought to the court's attention via a motion in limine. "Motion in limine" literally means, "*at the threshold*," and simply means that the moving party seeks a pre-trial ruling on the admissibility of evidence. The motion may be to admit or exclude evidence. A motion in limine to exclude evidence may be based on any objectionable grounds. Raising an issue in a motion in limine provides a party with an opportunity for a more in-depth opportunity to argue the substance of the objection or response thereto as well as an opportunity to brief the court on the issues. It also provides the parties with an opportunity to more effectively prepare for trial by knowing in advance if certain evidence will be admissible or not.

Most Louisiana courts have held that a motion in limine (without more) properly preserves an issue for appeal;[33] however, it would be good practice for a party making a motion in limine to object to the court's ruling on the motion to ensure the issue is properly preserved for appeal. However, La. C.Cr.P. art. 841 specifically states that in a criminal proceeding a contemporaneous objection to a judge's ruling on a written motion is not necessary to preserve the issue for appeal.

Hearing of jury. In Louisiana, issues of admissibility are argued outside of the presence or hearing of the jury to protect the jury from inadmissible and potentially prejudicial evidence pursuant to Article 103(c).[34] Thus, during a jury trial, while an objecting party may object in open court, he should ask for a bench conference to argue to the court the basis for admitting or excluding evidence outside of the hearing of the jury. If the judge makes a ruling on the admissibility of evidence during a bench conference, it is paramount that the objecting party ensure that he fully places his objection, grounds, and/or arguments on the record as soon as practical, preferably at the first available recess.[35]

Remedy for finding error on appeal/Authority of Appellate Courts. The remedies for finding error on appeal may include reversal of the trial court's decision, or having a verdict set aside, effectively voiding it. Additionally, the appellate court could set aside a conviction or sentence of a person found guilty at trial, or a party could be granted a new trial.

Record of ruling. Finally, pursuant to Article 103(B), when ruling on evidence, the court may add any other or further statement which shows the character of the evidence, the form in which it was offered, the objection made, and the ruling thereon.

---

31. Wright v. Bennett, 924 So. 2d 178 (La. Ct. App. 1st Cir. 2005).

32. Emery v. Owens-Corporation, 813 So. 2d 441, 449 (La. Ct. App. 1st Cir. 2001).

33. Whitehead v. The Kansas City Southern Railway Company, 758 So. 2d 211 (La. Ct. App. 3d Cir. 1999) ("A party need not make a formal objection at the time a trial court rules on the admissibility of the evidence, but need only make known the action he desires of the court and his grounds therefor"). *See also*, La. Code of Civ.P. art. 1635; C.Cr.Pr Art. 841, a contemporaneous objection on a judge's ruling to a written motion is not necessary.

34. *See also* La. Code Evid. art. 104(C) and La. Code Evid. art. 104 Official Comment (g).

35. *See* Force & Rault, Handbook, Art. 103 Author's Note (5); *See also* Savin v. Allstate Ins. Co. 579 So. 2d 453 (La. Ct. App. 1st Cir. 1991).

Cases on Preserving Issues for Appeal

State v. Lobato
Supreme Court of Louisiana
603 So. 2d 739 (La. 1992)

HALL, Justice.

Defendant, Daniel Lobato, was convicted of conspiracy to possess marijuana with intent to distribute, LSA-R.S. 14:26 and 40:966, and was sentenced to four and one-half years at hard labor with a fine of $1,250 plus court costs, in default of which defendant is to serve six additional months....

[FACTS]
I.

On Sunday, December 14, 1986, defendant was stopped by Louisiana State Police Trooper Mike Epps on an I-20 exit near Monroe, Louisiana, for a routine traffic violation. After Epps discovered defendant was a Texas resident and the vehicle he was driving was registered in Texas in the name of a third party, defendant told Epps, in conversation, that the vehicle belonged to his girlfriend and that he had traveled from Austin, Texas to Biloxi, Mississippi for the weekend. Defendant stated he did not bring any luggage with him although Epps had noticed a suitcase in the backseat of the vehicle. Epps requested and received written consent from defendant to search the vehicle after Louisiana State Police Trooper Jackie Coleman arrived at the scene. Epps noticed an odor of marijuana during his search of defendant's vehicle. A stronger odor of marijuana was noticed in the empty suitcase where marijuana gleanings were discovered. Upon his arrest for simple possession of marijuana, defendant produced approximately $18,000 cash in small bundles from his person and explained that he had picked up the money for a roofing job and that it belonged to a third party.

At Louisiana State Police headquarters in Monroe, Sgt. James Cannon spoke with defendant to investigate the possibility that a marijuana smuggling operation had been uncovered. According to Cannon, defendant admitted transporting fifteen to sixteen pounds of marijuana for Robert Phillips from Austin, Texas to Jackson, Mississippi, delivering the marijuana to Gary Veazey, and receiving $18,000 in cash from Veazey. Defendant agreed to cooperate with the State Police and, in a plan formulated by the State Police, called Robert Phillips, the alleged seller, in Austin, Texas and informed him that he had been robbed of the $18,000 at a truck stop enroute from Jackson to Austin by associates of Gary Veazey, the alleged purchaser. After several telephone conversations between defendant and Phillips and defendant and Veazey, Veazey met defendant in Monroe to deliver the $3,000 balance owed on this marijuana transaction and to check on the robbery. Veazey was arrested after the money was handed to defendant.... Defendant testified he did not tell Cannon that he had transported marijuana for Phillips from Austin to Jackson. Rather, defendant testified the only statement made to the State Police was that made on December 15, 1986, the day after his arrest and cooperation. During his testimony, defendant indicated his employer had told him Phillips needed someone to travel to Mississippi to collect an overdue roofing debt and that he agreed to do so because he needed the money. Defendant stated he did not search the vehicle which had been borrowed by Phillips from a third party before embarking on his trip and did not suspect anything illegal. Defendant also stated he was not suspicious about being instructed to give Veazey the keys to the vehicle because Veazey arrived at the motel in a company vehicle. Defendant testified he became nervous and suspected something illegal was transpiring when Veazey handed him the cash because he expected to receive a check. Defendant stated he never knew he was transporting drugs and told Trooper Epps he had traveled to Biloxi when stopped for the traffic violation because it was the first thing that came to mind....

IV.

We next consider defendant's contention that evidentiary rulings of the trial court prevented him from presenting a defense. In this assignment of error, defendant argues the trial court erroneously excluded testimony on the state's hearsay objections and general objections where the state failed to provide grounds therefor. Furthermore, defendant claims it was unnecessary for defense counsel to object to the trial court's evidentiary rulings as the objections were made by the state when defendant was testifying during direct examination.

The court of appeal noted defense counsel neither made timely objection to the court's ruling, nor made known the substance of the evidence excluded by the trial court as required by LSA-C.E. Art. 103(A)(2). For error to be predicated on a ruling excluding evidence, that article requires that a substantial right of a party be affected and the substance of the evidence be made known to the trial court by counsel. The court of appeal concluded defendant was able to and did present a defense through his testimony and defense counsel's cross-examination and argument. Accordingly, the court of appeal concluded this assignment of error to be meritless.

Defendant argues he was prevented from presenting his defense of no knowledge of or participation in the conspiracy by the trial court's ruling sustaining hearsay objections and other general objections by the state to his testimony regarding conversations he had with his then employer in which defendant learned of the alleged roofing debt collection for Phillips. Defendant claims those conversations would have shown defendant's motivation for his actions.

Defendant argues he was also prevented, by state objection, from testifying as to instructions given him by Phillips and as to his conversation with Veazey at the motel. Defendant contends the trial court erroneously sustained the state's objections because much of what was offered was non-hearsay since such statements were not offered to show the truth of the conversations, but rather the circumstances of defendant's participation in the transaction and how he was innocently misled by Phillips. Defendant claims he was prevented from showing what, if any, inducement was made by Phillips to persuade him to go to Mississippi and what occurred while he was there.

In response, the state contends such alleged error was not preserved for review on appeal because of defense counsel's failure to make a contemporaneous objection to the trial court ruling sustaining the state's objections as well as defense counsel's failure to make an offer of proof of such evidence for review on appeal.

We agree with the court of appeal's conclusion that defendant was able to present his defense of no knowledge of or participation in the conspiracy through his testimony and the introduction of his recorded statement given to the state police, regardless of the trial court ruling. There is no indication that the excluded testimony would have differed from or added to the statement given by defendant the day after his arrest and cooperation and admitted into evidence. We also agree with the appellate court that defense counsel did not preserve this alleged error for review on appeal by his failure to make a contemporaneous objection to the trial court ruling and make known the substance of such evidence for the purpose of consideration by the trial court and review on appeal. LSA-C.E. Art. 103(A)(2). There is no exception to this requirement when such testimony is solicited and objected to on direct examination. Further, any error in excluding the testimony offered by defendant did not materially affect defendant's opportunity to offer a defense and is harmless beyond a reasonable doubt. This assignment of error is without merit.

Discussion Questions

1. What are the procedural requirements for error to be found on appeal on a ruling excluding evidence?
2. After Lobato attempted to testify to statements purporting to prove his defense, and the court sustained the State's hearsay objections excluding the statements, explain procedurally what steps Lobato's attorney should have taken to preserve the issue for appeal. Specifically explain how one should comply with the requirements of Article 103.
3. What argument does Lobato make as to why or how a substantial right was affected? What other types of arguments could be made in this or other cases to satisfy this procedural requirement for finding error? In other words, what does it mean for a "substantial right" to be affected? What has to be shown on appeal? How does the court ultimately determine if this requirement has been met?

State v. Taylor

Supreme Court of Louisiana
669 So. 2d 364
February 28, 1996

VICTORY, Justice

Feltus Taylor was indicted by the grand jury for the first degree murder of Donna Ponsano, in violation of La.R.S. 14:30. After trial, the jury found the defendant guilty as charged, and unanimously recommended a death sentence.... The defendant raises 339 assignments of error for reversal of his conviction and sentence....

FACTS

On the morning of March 27, 1991, the victim, Donna Ponsano, was working as a cook at Cajun's Fabulous Fried Chicken restaurant on Florida Boulevard in Baton Rouge. At approximately 7:00 a.m., Keith Clark, the restaurant's manager, arrived to assist Ponsano in opening for business. After tending to morning chores in the rear of the restaurant, Clark returned to the front and noticed the defendant at the front door knocking. The defendant was a former employee of the restaurant whom Clark had hired approximately six months earlier....

Clark opened the door for the defendant and allowed him to enter the restaurant. At this time, the defendant, who was experiencing financial problems, asked Clark to rehire him. Clark refused, but assisted the defendant in searching for another job by giving him money to buy a newspaper and sitting with him in a restaurant booth to review classified job advertisements.... As Clark was placing money into the cash registers, the defendant decided that robbery was the solution to his financial problems.... [He] grabbed Ponsano, held the gun to her head and demanded that Clark open the restaurant's floor safe which was located in a storeroom towards the rear of the building.... The defendant then handcuffed Clark and Ponsano together. Clark opened the safe, and gave the defendant its contents, approximately $800.00.... The defendant ... instructed Clark not to inform the police about the robbery. After Clark told the defendant that he would not lie to the police, the defendant again asked Clark to rehire him. Ponsano expressed her opposition to rehiring the defendant, and Clark agreed. The defendant then shot Ponsano, hitting her five times in the head and upper forearm. After emptying the gun, he exited the room, reloaded and returned to shoot Clark in the head. He then emptied the cash register of approximately $580.00, exited through the front door, got into his car and drove away.... When the police and emergency medical personnel arrived at the scene they found Ponsano and Clark lying in the storeroom handcuffed together, each with multiple gunshot wounds to the head. Ponsano died two days later, after treatment and surgery in a nearby hospital. Clark survived, but suffers with paralysis and minor brain damage.... At trial, the defendant conceded guilt, and the jury found him guilty. After a four-day penalty phase hearing, the jury recommended a death sentence, finding four aggravating circumstances....

SCOPE OF REVIEW

As in most capital cases, the defendant asserts numerous assignments of error which were not objected to during the trial. In *State v. Smith*, 554 So. 2d 676 (La.1989), this Court enunciated a new and expanded rule regarding consideration of alleged errors that are not contemporaneously objected to in capital cases. La.Code Crim.P. art. 841(A). A narrow majority of the Court held that in death penalty cases it would notice all possible errors occurring during both the guilt and sentencing phases, even if they were not properly raised.

Smith changed the Court's long-standing policy regarding the scope of review in death cases. Prior to *Smith*, only those unobjected to errors occurring during the *sentencing phase* of the trial were reviewed by the Court. This practice was based upon the Court's statutory obligation to review every death sentence for excessiveness by examining the record for passion, prejudice or arbitrary factors which may have contributed to the death penalty recommendation....

One of the Court's primary reasons for expanding the scope of review in capital cases was "efficiency." Specifically, the Court was concerned that failure to review unobjected to errors occurring during the guilt phase would add "to the burgeoning delays of post-conviction proceedings in state and federal courts." While this concern may have been well-placed when *Smith* was decided, it has been minimized by subsequent events.

Since its decision in *Smith*, the Court has adopted La.Sup.Ct.R. XXXI, which established the Louisiana Indigent Defender Board ("LIDB") and which requires, in capital cases, the appointment of at least two attorneys to represent indigent defendants—one trial lead counsel and one trial associate counsel—both of whom must be "certified" in accordance with the rules and standards of the LIDB....

These Standards will apply in many capital cases since numerous capital defendants are indigent. With able counsel at the helm, most significant errors occurring during the guilt phase should be contemporaneously objected to as required by La.Code Crim.P. art. 841(A). Thus, the concern expressed in *Smith*, that failure to consider unobjected to errors occurring during the guilt phase would result in undue delay in the form of ineffective assistance of counsel claims during postconviction relief proceedings, is lessened in most cases.

Additionally, we note that the contemporaneous objection rule contained in La.Code Crim.P. art. 841(A) and La.Code Evid. art. 103, does not frustrate the goal of efficiency. Instead, it is specifically designed to promote judicial efficiency by preventing a defendant from gambling for a favorable verdict and then, upon conviction, resorting to appeal on errors which either could have been avoided or corrected at the time or should have put an immediate halt to the proceedings.

For these reasons, we abandon the expanded scope of review in capital cases established in *Smith* and its progeny, overrule them and return to previously existing law. This Court's scope of review in capital cases will be limited to alleged errors occurring during the guilt phase that are contemporaneously objected to, and alleged errors occurring during the sentencing phase, whether objected to or not.

Discussion Questions

1. Explain the Louisiana Supreme Court's evolution of the rules regarding the review of unobjected-to errors in capital cases: 1) Pre-*Smith* (pre-1989); 2) under *Smith* (1989–1996); and 3) Post-*Smith*, as enunciated here in *Taylor*.
2. At all points, the court has reviewed errors in the sentencing-phase of capital cases whether objected to or not. What policy reasons underlie this rule? Do you believe this rule is warranted?
3. What public policy reasons does the court cite to support its return to prior law reviewing only properly preserved errors during both phases of capital cases, as well as unobjected-to errors during the sentencing phase? Do the reasons seem to support the conclusion?

Key Points

The key points to keep in mind regarding preserving issues for appeal.

1. **Contemporaneous objection rule**. To preserve an issue for appeal on a ruling admitting evidence a party must: 1) make a timely objection to a court's ruling admitting the evidence; and 2) state the specific grounds upon which he objects.
2. **Timely objection**. An objection is timely if made at or before the time a witness testifies to objectionable testimony or at or before the time physical evidence is offered into evidence. If the witness testifies before counsel has an opportunity to object, he must do so as soon as practicable.
3. **Specific grounds**. A party must state the specific grounds upon which he objects. Since a party may not state new and different grounds on appeal, he must object on the *proper* grounds.
4. **Requirements to find error on appeal**:
   a. Ruling *admitting* evidence: 1) a timely objection *or* motion to admonish the jury to limit or disregard must appear of record; 2) the party must state the specific grounds upon which he objects; and 3) a substantial right of the party must be affected.
   b. Ruling *excluding* evidence: 1) the party must make an objection to the court's ruling excluding the evidence; 2) the substance of the evidence must be made known to the court by counsel, i.e., proffered for the record; and 3) a substantial right of the party must be affected.
5. **Motion to admonish.** A request by counsel that the court instruct the jury to disregard or limit inadmissible evidence that might have been inadvertently stated and heard by the jury. This preserves the issue for appeal.
6. **Proffer**. When a judge makes a ruling excluding evidence, counsel must make known in the record the substance of the evidence so that it may be reviewed on appeal. A

proffer of evidence may be an informal statement by counsel or he may call a witness and question them regarding the full nature of the excluded testimony.

7. **Substantial right of party affected.** "Whether the alleged error as compared to the entire record had a substantial effect on the outcome on the case." **Court considers:**
   1. whether erroneously admitted evidence was the primary evidence relied upon;
   2. whether the aggrieved party was nonetheless able to present the substance of its claim;
   3. the existence and usefulness of curative jury instructions;
   4. the extent of jury argument based on tainted evidence;
   5. whether erroneously admitted evidence was merely cumulative; and
   6. whether other evidence was overwhelming.
8. **Motion in limine.** A motion for a pre-trial ruling admitting or excluding evidence. May be based on any grounds. Gives parties an opportunity for a more in-depth opportunity to argue substance of objections. In criminal proceedings, rulings on written motions preserve the issue for appeal.
9. **Argued out of presence of jury.** Motions and objections should be argued out of the presence of jury to protect them from inadmissible evidence. If argued at the bench, counsel must remember to put the substance of objections on the record as soon as practicable.

Problems on Rulings on Evidence

PROBLEM 2-3. The victim in a domestic battery trial was called by the prosecution to testify about the night her live-in boyfriend beat her nearly to death, leading to the charges. On direct examination, the prosecution asked the victim how she and the defendant met. The victim testified, "Well, right after he got out of jail, he needed a place to stay, so he approached me and asked me if he could move in with me." The defense counsel immediately stood up and made a motion to strike the testimony claiming it brought out the inadmissible evidence of other crimes regarding the defendant's prior time in jail that was unfairly prejudicial to him. The judge responded, "They've already heard it. But don't go any further with that line of questioning, prosecutor." Has the defense properly preserved the issue for appeal? Why or why not?

Assume that instead of asking for a motion to strike, the defense counsel made a motion to the judge to admonish the jury about the fact that the jury was not to consider the defendant's prior conviction/time in jail towards his guilt or innocence in the case. Would this request change your answer regarding whether the defense had properly preserved the issue for appeal? Why or why not?

PROBLEM 2-4. James was found guilty of second-degree murder following a six-day jury trial in which the prosecution offered the testimony of Jason (the victim's 27-year-old son) who witnessed James stab his father to death during a carjacking of his father's truck in which he was a passenger at the time of the incident. The son positively identified James in a six-person photographic lineup and at the trial. James's fingerprints were on the truck's door handle, even though they didn't know James. James confessed to the murder, but later filed a motion to suppress the confession claiming it was unconstitutionally obtained because he claims he made it only because he was promised an offer of a lighter sentence, which he did not receive. Following a hearing on the motion, the judge denied James' motion to exclude the statement, and the statement was offered into evidence against James at trial. James was found guilty and now appeals. On appeal, James claims the court erred in allowing the statement into evidence. Has James properly preserved the issue for appeal? Has he satisfied all procedural requirements for a finding of error at the trial court? What factors will be considered? What will be the likely outcome?

PROBLEM 2-5. During a jury trial, after the defense attempted to question the victim regarding the content of letters that she sent to the defendant prompting the attack for which the defendant is on trial, the prosecution objected and asked to approach the bench. During a bench conference, the prosecutor objected that the witness's testimony was not the best evidence of the content of the letters in violation of Article 1002 and that the defense should be required to produce the letters rather than have the witness testify about the content. The judge sustained the objection and excluded the witness's testimony about what was written in the letter. The defendant was convicted. On appeal, the defense claimed the trial court erred in excluding the victim's testimony regarding the content of the letter because the testimony did not violate Article 1002 and also because the exclusion violated the defendant's Sixth Amendment right under the United States Constitution to present a defense. Was either or both issues properly preserved for appeal? Why or why not?

PROBLEM 2-6. During a domestic violence case in which the victim failed to show up to testify at the trial, the prosecution attempted to offer the witness's statement into the record that was given to the police officer on the evening in which she called the police to their residence after being badly beaten by the defendant. The defense rose and stated, "I'm gonna have to object to that, judge." The judge overruled the objection and allowed the prosecution to offer the affidavit into the record. The defendant was convicted. On appeal the defense alleges that the affidavit was hearsay. Was the issue properly preserved for appeal? Why or why not?

Chapter 2 References and Additional Authority on Preliminary Questions [La. C.E. art. 104] and Preserving Issues for Appeal [La. C.E. art. 103]

1. La. C.E. arts. 103, 104 and Official Comments
2. Force & Rault, HANDBOOK ON LOUISIANA EVIDENCE LAW Arts. 103, 104 Author's Comments (West Publishing 2014)
3. Harges & Jones, LOUISIANA EVIDENCE Art. 103, 104 Author's Comments (West Publishing 2014)
4. 19 La. Civ. L. Treatise, Evidence And Proof § 2.10, § 5.12 (2nd ed.)
5. **Motion in Limine:** *Whitehead v. Kansas City Southern Ry. Co.*, 758 So. 2d 211, (La. Ct. App. 3d Cir. 1999) writ denied, 2000-0209 (La.4/7/00), 759 So. 2d 767 (holding that opposing counsel may object to the introduction of evidence prior to trial by filing a motion in limine; a party need not make a formal objection at the time the trial court rules on the admissibility of the evidence, but need only make known the action he desires of the court and his grounds therefor; La. Code Civ. P. art. 1635).
6. **Failure to timely object resulting in not being able to object on appeal**: *Bechtel v. Entringer Bakeries, Inc.*, 422 So. 2d 1299 (La. Ct. App. 5th Cir. 1982) (holding that

because plaintiffs did not timely object to omission of jury charge, nor to form of jury interrogatories given by trial judge, they waived their right to object on appeal to such omission and interrogatories).

7. **Failure to state proper grounds resulting in not being able to complain on appeal:** *State v. Schrader*, 518 So. 2d 1024 (La. 1988) (holding that when counsel voiced only a general hearsay objection to the question, and backed away from even that complaint when the prosecutor asked a question, counsel had no answer for that, and died on his own objection, he thereby failed to state the proper grounds for his objection and now cannot complain of the court's ruling).

8. **Proffer:** *State v. Lavy*, 142 So. 2d 1000 (La. Ct App. 1st Cir. 2014) (Defendant failed to properly preserve for appeal whether he was improperly restricted from cross-examining witness regarding whether her probation for prior forgery conviction had been revoked in prosecution for second-degree murder where the defendant did not proffer evidence that the witness had been revoked nor that she received favorable treatment for her testimony on the issue of her credibility); *Our Lady of the Lake Regional Medical Center v. Helms*, 754 So. 2d 1049 (La. Ct. App. 1st Cir. 1999) (worker's compensation claimant waived right to argue on appeal that trial court erred in allowing portion of surveillance videotape into evidence, where claimant failed to proffer the entire surveillance tape she claims should have been admitted).

9. **Motion to admonish:** *State v. McPherson*, 733 So. 2d 634 (La. Ct. App. 5th Cir. 1999) (holding that trial court was not required to admonish the jury regarding allegedly improperly admitted evidence of other crimes, in second-degree murder case, in the absence of such a request by the defendant).

10. **Substantial right of party affected:** *Board of Sup'rs of La. State University v. Boudreaux's Tire & Auto Repair, L.L.C.*, 133 So. 3d 1262, (La. Ct. App. 4th Cir. 2014) rehearing denied, writ denied 2014-0942 (La. 8/25/14), 2014 WL 4401319 (If the effect of an erroneous evidentiary ruling on the outcome of the proceedings is insubstantial, reversal is not warranted); *State v. Jarreau*, 692 So. 2d 33 (La. Ct. App. 1st Cir. 1997) writ denied, 703 So. 2d 612 (La. 1997) (Motorist was found guilty of driving while intoxicated. Motorist appealed. The trial court's ruling was a clear abuse of discretion that resulted in prejudice to the defendant's fundamental right to present a defense. La. Const. art. I, sec. 16).

11. **Substantial right of party (not) affected:** *Morrison v. Kappa Alpha Psi Fraternity*, 738 So. 2d 1105 (La. Ct. App. 2d Cir. 1999) writ denied, 747 So. 2d 1120 (La. 1999) and writ denied, 749 So. 2d 634 (La. 1999) and writ denied, 749 So. 2d 635 (La. 1999) (holding that in a claim by a university student injured during a fraternity hazing incident and his parents, plaintiffs were not prejudiced by exclusion of evidence of other specific instances of hazing at other chapters of the national fraternity, where jury imposed liability even without that evidence).

12. **Arguing objection within hearing of jury:** *Savin v. Allstate Ins. Co.*, 579 So. 2d 453, (La. Ct. App. 1st Cir. 1991) (held that the trial court erred in allowing jury to hear a psychiatrist's testimony about the out-of-court hypnosis of a witness where the results of the hypnosis were inadmissible hearsay; jury was also allowed to hear impermissible testimony regarding a planned in-court hypnotic experiment).

Chapter 3

Relevance

§ 3.1 Logical Relevance [La. C.E. arts. 401, 402]

Applicable Code Articles

Art. 401. Definition of "relevant evidence"

"Relevant evidence" means evidence having any tendency to make the existence of any fact that is of consequence to the determination of the action more probable or less probable than it would be without the evidence.

Art. 402. Relevant evidence generally admissible; irrelevant evidence inadmissible

All relevant evidence is admissible, except as otherwise provided by the Constitution of the United States, the Constitution of Louisiana, this Code of Evidence, or other legislation. Evidence which is not relevant is not admissible.

One of the most basic principles underlying the admissibility of evidence at trial is that it must be **relevant** under Article 401. Relevant evidence "means evidence having any tendency to make the existence of **any fact** that is **of consequence** to the determination of the action **more probable** or **less probable** than it would be without the evidence."[1] Article 402 sets forth the general rule that **relevant evidence is generally admissible**, subject to limitations provided under the law.[2] However, **irrelevant evidence is *always* inadmissible.**[3]

The requirement that only relevant evidence may be admitted furthers judicial economy because it precludes evidence from being admitted in a case that would have no bearing on the outcome. The rule also promotes fairness because it protects the trier of fact from exposure to evidence that would divert from the true issues and elements in the case. Thus, evidence may only be offered in a trial if it is related to and could somehow affect the **issues** and **elements** in the case, as defined by the **substantive legal principles** involved. This would also include evidence affecting any **defenses**, **weaknesses**, **theories of the case**, the **credibility of witnesses**,[4] and evidence establishing any **background facts** that would be "helpful in enabling the trier of fact to understand the evidence."[5]

Determining relevancy of evidence. Under the definition of relevant evidence contained in Article 401, two basic requirements must be met to satisfy the standard for determining whether proffered evidence is relevant:

1. La. Code Evid. art. 401.
2. See La. Code Evid. art. 402, which must be read in conjunction with La. Code Evid. art. 401.
3. *See* La. Code Evid. art. 402.
4. Force & Rault, Handbook, Art. 401 Author's Note (1).
5. *Id.*

1. it must make a fact more probable or less probable than it would be without the evidence; and
2. the fact must be a consequential fact, i.e., it must tend to prove or disprove an issue, element, or defense in the case, based on substantive law as outlined above.

Consequential facts. What are consequential facts? Answering this question begins with identifying the **substantive legal principles** in the case. The substantive law in a particular action governs what evidence is relevant because the **substantive law defines the issues, elements** and **defenses** that must be proven in a case. For example, evidence offered to show intent would not be relevant in a negligence action because intent is not required in a negligence case. However, evidence that shows intent, e.g., statements by the accused or preparatory acts, would be relevant in a first-degree murder trial, because intent is an element of the crime. Facts that prove or disprove those issues or elements are "consequential facts." Consequential facts, as stated above, also include facts that affect **defenses, weaknesses, credibility of witnesses**, and evidence establishing **background information** helpful in enabling the trier of fact to understand the evidence. To be relevant, the evidence sought to be admitted must make one or more consequential facts more or less probable than it would be without the evidence.

More or less probable. When evidence makes a fact more or less probable, that means the evidence is **"probative" of the fact**, i.e., it affects its *probability*. For example, evidence that shows that a defendant was in a city where a crime occurred would make it ***more probable*** that he committed the crime, thus the evidence would be *probative* of the fact. Similarly, evidence that the defendant was incarcerated at the time a crime occurred would make it ***less probable*** that he committed the crime. Thus, *that* evidence would also be probative. Either piece of evidence would be probative of the fact of whether the defendant committed the crime because the evidence makes it more or less probable that the defendant had the *opportunity* to do so—one piece of evidence tends to prove the defendant committed the crime, and the other tends to disprove it.

Keep in mind that for purposes of relevance, the "facts" that the evidence must tend to prove or disprove are the "consequential facts" we discussed above—those related to the issues, elements, etc., in the case. Further, the evidence sought to be admitted need only *tend to* prove or disprove the legal proposition by making its existence more or less probable than it would be without the evidence. Thus, referring back to our example above, even though the defendant's presence in the town where the crime occurred does not prove he committed the crime, it is relevant because it makes it more probable that he committed it than if he were not in the town where it occurred.

The Relevance Analysis

Based on the points discussed above, the determination of whether evidence is relevant, requires the following analysis:

1. Identify the **evidence** to be offered. **E**
2. What **fact** or legal proposition is the evidence offered to prove? **F**
3. Is the fact or legal proposition **consequential**; i.e., does it relate to an issue, element, or defense in the case based on substantive law, credibility, or background facts? **C**
4. Is the evidence **probative** of the consequential fact, i.e., does the evidence sought to be admitted actually tend to prove or disprove the consequential fact (make it more or less probable)? **P**

E → F → C → P

Application of law: Using the analysis outlined above, consider whether the evidence sought to be admitted is relevant in the following scenario: The defendant is on trial for murdering his wife. The prosecution would like to offer evidence to show that two weeks prior to the murder, the defendant wrote a love letter to another woman in which he professes his love for her and tells her he wants to be with her. The prosecution's theory is that the defendant was having an affair with the woman to whom he wrote the letter and that he killed his wife to be with her. Is the love letter relevant?

1. **E**: The evidence offered is the love letter.
2. **F**: The fact(s) or legal proposition(s) that the love letter is being offered to prove is that there was an affair between the defendant and the woman, which was the motive for killing his wife.
3. **C**: The affair/motive are consequential facts because they relate to and help to establish a reason *why* the defendant may have killed his wife, which makes it more likely that he killed her. This ultimately helps to prove his guilt—an issue or element in the murder trial.
4. **P**: The love letter is probative of the affair because it actually makes it more likely that there was an affair by common sense inference. One could infer that when a man tells a woman he loves her and wants to be with her, it makes an affair more probable than it would be without the letter. One could also infer that if a man loves a woman and wants to be with her, that he'd take action to make that happen, such as by killing his current wife. Thus, the letter is probative of the consequential facts of the affair and motive because it makes them more likely than they would be without the letter.

Based on the analysis above, the evidence of the man's love letter to another woman is relevant in his murder trial for killing his wife. While the love letter does not *prove* the affair or that the man killed his wife, it *tends* to prove it by making the affair more probable than it would be without the letter. Absent any provision excluding the letter on other grounds, such as hearsay, it would be admissible in evidence. Relevancy determinations are within the discretion of the trial court, and will not be disturbed on appeal absent an abuse of that discretion.

Relevance Illustration

Consequential facts go to.... As illustrated below, consequential facts are the link, like a chain, between the evidence sought to be admitted and the issues, elements, defenses, or credibility issue(s) that must ultimately be proven in a particular case, based upon the substantive legal principles involved. To be relevant, the evidence does not necessarily need to prove the ultimate issue in the case (guilt, liability, etc.), but it must help to prove facts that prove or disprove the issues, elements, etc. in the case. Those facts that form the link between the evidence and ultimate issues are referred to as "consequential facts," because as the name suggests, they have consequence on the case.

Thus, when responding to relevancy objections, it is good practice to simply begin your response by saying, "*Your honor, this evidence goes to ...*" (whatever issue, element, defense, or credibility issue in the case it bears upon), such as damages, intent, motive, preparation for the action, or other. As a result, in response to an objection to the love letter, counsel can respond, "*Your honor, the letter helps to prove an affair which ultimately goes to the defendant's motive for killing his wife.*"

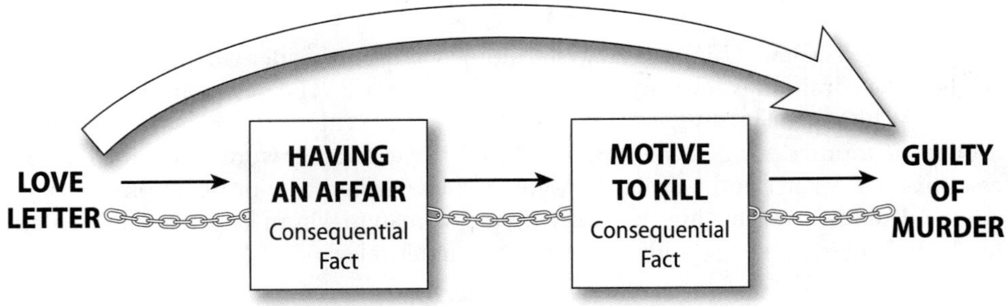

Irrelevant evidence—Not probative of consequential facts. While the proponent of evidence may offer it in support of a consequential fact, in order to be relevant, the evidence must actually help to prove or disprove it. If it is not probative of the consequential fact, it is not relevant. For example, suppose that instead of offering the love letter as evidence to prove the consequential fact that the defendant and the woman were having an affair, the prosecution offers evidence that the defendant and the woman once worked for the same company. While an affair would be a consequential fact, the evidence sought to be admitted, that defendant and woman once worked for the same company, does not make the fact that an affair occurred more or less probable than it would without the evidence. It simply has no bearing on whether they were having an affair and would certainly have no bearing on whether the defendant killed his wife. Thus, the proffered evidence is not probative of the consequential fact, and therefore is not relevant and should be excluded.

A Brick Is Not a Wall[6]—Weight vs. Relevance

It is also important to keep in mind that to be relevant, evidence need not have "any predetermined minimum weight."[7] In other words, as we pointed out in the examples above, to be relevant, the evidence sought to be admitted need only ***help to*** prove or disprove a consequential fact, or ***tend to*** prove or disprove it. Many commentators often refer to this principle by stating that **"a brick is not a wall,"** meaning that to be relevant, evidence need only be a brick in the wall, it need not be the entire wall. For purposes of relevancy, any degree to which the evidence helps to prove or disprove the consequential fact is sufficient. It need not be strong evidence or highly believable in order to be relevant.

It is not uncommon that a young attorney or law student might object to the admissibility of the letter in the example above, claiming that it doesn't "prove" the defendant killed his wife. However, the degree to which it actually proves the offense goes to the **weight of the evidence**, and does not affect the admissibility of it. While a love letter to another woman might only be a brick in the wall, one brick is enough for the evidence to be relevant. A confession by the defendant to killing his wife, on the other hand, which would be closer to an entire wall, would have greater weight, yet both pieces of evidence are relevant.

---

6. *See* McCormick On Evidence § 185 (5th ed., 1999) and Fed. R. Evid. 401 Advisory Committee's Notes.
7. La. Code Evid. art. 402 Official Comment (c).

To be relevant, evidence needs only to be one brick in the wall, not the entire wall. The love letter is a brick in the wall of proving defendant's guilt. While it does not prove guilt by itself, it tends to prove it.

Direct Evidence vs. Circumstantial Evidence

Relevant evidence may be either direct or circumstantial.[8] "Direct evidence is evidence, which if believed, proves a fact. Circumstantial or indirect evidence is evidence, which if believed, proves a fact, and from that fact you may logically and reasonably conclude that another fact exists."[9] For example, if a person testifies that he saw the man stealing the television set, if believed, the testimony proves the fact that the man stole the television. That is direct evidence of the theft and is obviously relevant.

Circumstantial evidence of the crime would be relevant as well. For example, assume that instead of calling the eyewitness to the burglary, the prosecution calls the following three witnesses. Witness #1 testifies that he saw the man's truck in the vicinity of the burglary (circumstantial evidence). Witness #2 testifies that the man's fingerprint was on the case in which the television set was located inside of the residence (circumstantial evidence). Further, witness #3 testifies that the same man pawned the television the same day that it was stolen (also circumstantial evidence). If each witness is believed, his testimony would prove the facts to which he testified, and from those facts one can logically and reasonably conclude that another fact exists—which is that the man stole the television. Circumstantial evidence requires that inferences of guilt be made, while direct evidence does not require such inferences. But circumstantial evidence is nevertheless relevant. As stated above, while evidence that the man's vehicle was in the vicinity of where the burglary occurred does not prove he committed the crime, it *tends* to prove it by making it more probable that he committed the crime than if the evidence were not admitted.[10] Thus, the evidence is relevant.

Cases on Logical Relevancy

In the cases below, we will examine a number of recurring issues of relevance, including guilty mind, motive, its relationship to weight and credibility of evidence, as well as its relationship to circumstantial evidence. We begin with *State v. Mosby*[11] below, where the court examines the relevance of evidence of similar offenses committed by a person other than the accused offered by him in support of his defense theory of mistaken identity to show that he did not commit the instant offense.

---

8. Harges & Jones, LOUISIANA EVIDENCE, Art. 401 Author's Comments.

9. 17 La. Civ. L. Treatise, Criminal Jury Instructions § 3:5 (3d ed.); See Rice v. ABC Ins. Co., 672 So. 2d 1109 (La. Ct. App. 4th Cir. 1996), for a discussion of circumstantial evidence in civil cases.

10. You cannot find a defendant guilty solely on circumstantial evidence unless the facts proven by the evidence exclude every reasonable hypothesis of innocence. 17 La. Civ. L. Treatise, Criminal Jury Instructions § 3:5 (3d ed.); See State v. Chism, 436 So. 2d 464 (La. 1983), for a discussion of the sufficiency of circumstantial evidence to convict.

11. State v. Mosby, 581 So. 2d 1060 (La. Ct. App. 1st Cir. 1991).

State v. Mosby

Court of Appeal of Louisiana, First Circuit
May 16, 1991
581 So. 2d 1060

LANIER, Judge.

The defendant, James Kevin Mosby, was charged by bill of information with simple robbery, in violation of La.R.S. 14:65. He pled not guilty and, after trial by jury, was found guilty as charged ...

FACTS

At approximately 10:00 a.m. on March 9, 1987, the victim, Guy McFarland, drove to the Louisiana National Bank (LNB) located in the Republic Tower Building at 5700 Florida Boulevard in Baton Rouge, East Baton Rouge Parish, Louisiana. As he exited his vehicle, he observed a young, black male (later identified as the defendant) standing outside. McFarland made eye contact with the young, black male, who quickly looked away and walked off. McFarland entered the lobby of the bank, intending to make a deposit from his seafood business ... As he stood in line in the lobby, the same person he had observed outside only a few minutes earlier approached from behind, grabbed the bank bag, and ran to the door ... McFarland immediately gave chase ... McFarland chased the perpetrator until he drove off and obtained a partial license plate number. McFarland then returned to the bank and gave a description of the perpetrator to bank officials and the police.

Baton Rouge Police Detective Greg Phares showed McFarland a photographic lineup a few weeks after the robbery which contained pictures of six black males, including a suspect named Michael Jackson. McFarland identified no one in this lineup. Thereafter, the defendant's former girlfriend, Diane Johnson, informed Det. Phares that defendant had committed a bank robbery. After receiving this information, Det. Phares prepared another photographic lineup containing pictures of six black males, including a picture of the defendant ... McFarland immediately identified the defendant's picture and stated that he was the perpetrator ... [Defendant was subsequently arrested and tried for simple robbery. He was found guilty as charged.]

ADMISSIBILITY OF EVIDENCE OF SIMILAR OFFENSES

The defendant contends that the trial court erred by refusing to allow him to introduce evidence of similar offenses committed by another person to show that he did not commit the instant offense. The defense theory in the case was that someone other than the defendant committed the robbery of McFarland. In support of this theory, the defense attempted to introduce evidence that Michael Jackson, who is also a young, slim-built black male, had been arrested and charged with committing two similar robberies of white males at nearby banks. These robberies involved the taking of bank deposit bags at two banks within a few miles of the Republic Tower Branch of Louisiana National Bank on January 7, 1987, and April 1, 1987.

A defendant in a criminal case has a constitutional right to present a defense; he can testify to or give evidence on any matter relevant to an issue material in the case ... A "material issue" is one which is "of solid or weighty character, of consequence, or importance" to the case.... Relevant evidence is that tending to show the commission of the offense and the intent, or tending to negate the commission of the offense and the intent.... The relevancy of evidence must be determined by the purpose for which it is offered ...

Any evidence, whether direct or circumstantial, is relevant if it tends to prove or disprove the existence of any material fact. *State v. Patch,* 470 So. 2d 585 (La.App. 1st Cir.), *writ denied,*475 So. 2d 358 (La.1985).

An attempt by the defense to introduce evidence of similar offenses or acts often occurs when mistaken identity is alleged as a defense. *State v. Armstrong,* 453 So. 2d 1256 (La.App. 3d Cir.), *writ denied,*457 So. 2d 16 (La.1984). Similar problems arise in cases wherein self-defense is an issue, and the defense wishes to introduce evidence of prior violent acts by the victim or other evidence which might support a finding of self-defense ...

In the instant case, the defendant relied on *State v. Patch* in support of his argument that the evidence of similar offenses was relevant and admissible. In *Patch,* the defendant attempted to introduce evidence of a similar obscenity offense to show that another committed the instant offense. The alleged perpetrator of this similar obscenity offense apparently had a striking resemblance to Patch, and the similar offense occurred in the same area as the offense for which Patch was on trial. This evidence of a similar offense committed by a man resembling the accused, combined with the accused's alibi defense, tended to support the defense theory of mistaken identification. In *Patch,* this Court held that the trial court committed reversible error by excluding relevant evidence of an offense similar to the offense for which the accused was being prosecuted (obscenity).

The trial court herein distinguished *Patch* on the basis that the defendant therein had produced an alibi defense. The trial court ruled that the defense could not introduce evidence that Michael Jackson allegedly committed two similar robberies without also introducing alibi evidence. This ruling was erroneous. Evidence that Michael Jackson allegedly committed two similar robberies was relevant because it tended to support the defense theory of mistaken identification. While *Patch* involved an alibi defense in addition to evidence of the similar obscenity offense, and the alibi clearly supported the argument that the other individual actually committed the offense for which Patch was charged, we did not hold that evidence of an alibi was a prerequisite to the introduction of evidence of a similar offense to support a theory of mistaken identification ...

Although the trial court erred in excluding the evidence of similar offenses herein, we conclude this error was harmless beyond a reasonable doubt ... McFarland identified this picture of the defendant and later identified the defendant in a physical lineup and in court.... Furthermore, the inference (circumstantial evidence) that Michael Jackson committed the instant offense is significantly rebutted by the direct evidence that McFarland did not identify Jackson's picture in the first photographic lineup conducted a few weeks after the offense. Thus, we conclude that the exclusion of the proffered evidence, although error, was harmless beyond a reasonable doubt. *Cf. State v. Bennett,* 517 So. 2d at 1117–1118.

Discussion Questions

1. Is evidence that another person has previously committed a similar offense for which the defendant is charged relevant in his trial to support his defense theory? Knowing what you know about analyzing relevance, what issues or elements does evidence that someone else has committed a similar crime tend to prove or disprove? From *Mosby* you can see how the defense's theory can make evidence relevant that might not otherwise be. How so?
2. Do you believe the evidence is actually probative of the issues for which it was proffered? Why or why not?
3. How far do you believe a defendant should be allowed to go in showing possible "other" suspects that could be responsible for the crime? How closely connected must the cir-

cumstances of the other suspect and crimes be to the instant case to be allowed? What test would you apply or what factors would you consider in limiting such evidence?

Evidence of Motive

In *State v. Wilkinson*,[12] the court addresses the relevance of evidence that tends to show a person's motive to commit a crime. Evidence offered to show motive must truly be the type of evidence that might have compelled a person to commit the crime. *Wilkinson* deals with a showing of the lack of money as motive to commit a robbery.

State v. Wilkinson

Court of Appeal of Louisiana, First Circuit
612 So. 2d 833
Dec. 23, 1992

REMY CHIASSON, Judge Pro Tem.

The defendant, Ellis R. Wilkinson, was charged by bill of information with armed robbery, in violation of La.R.S. 14:64. He pled not guilty and, after trial by jury, was found guilty as charged . . .

FACTS

On the evening of June 4, 1991, the victim, Clara Watson, was working as a cashier at the Ellis Corner Grocery Store . . . At approximately 10:00 p.m., the defendant entered the store. He reached into his pocket and removed a rag and his wallet before producing a gun. The defendant then pointed the gun at the victim and ordered her to open the cash register. When the victim refused, the defendant reached across the counter and began pushing buttons on the register in an unsuccessful attempt to open it. The defendant then took the cash register and began to walk out the door . . .

The victim immediately called the police, who arrived shortly thereafter. They had no trouble identifying the defendant as the perpetrator because he left his wallet at the scene of the robbery. The wallet contained an identification card with the defendant's name and photograph. The police located the defendant the next day at the Salvation Army Lodge on North Boulevard. After his arrest, the defendant confessed to the robbery but denied using a gun . . .

The defendant took the stand and admitted he took the cash register. However, he denied having a gun during the robbery. The defendant also admitted having prior felony convictions for possession of stolen things and forgery, and that he had been released from prison on April 16, 1991, less than two months before he committed the instant offense.

RELEVANCY OF THE PAROLE REPORT
(Assignment of error number 3)

In this assignment of error, the defendant contends that the trial court erred in overruling a defense objection to a question posed by the prosecutor concerning the defendant's parole report.

12. State v. Wilkerson, 612 So. 2d 833 (La. Ct. App. 1st Cir. 1992).

During cross-examination of the defendant, the prosecutor asked the defendant to identify his June 1, 1991, parole report. The prosecutor then asked how often the defendant was required to submit such a report, and he replied that a parole report was due on the first day of each month. At this point, defense counsel objected that this line of questioning was irrelevant and prejudicial. Defense counsel argued that the parole report had no bearing on the only issue presented at the trial, i.e., whether or not the defendant used a gun during the robbery. The prosecutor argued that the line of questioning was relevant to the issue of motive. The trial court overruled the objection and allowed the prosecutor to proceed. The defendant then identified his handwritten statement on the report indicating that he could not pay his $43.00 parole supervision fee on June 1, 1991.

La.Code of Evidence art. 401 provides:

> "Relevant evidence" means evidence having any tendency to make the existence of any fact that is of consequence to the determination of the action more probable or less probable than it would be without the evidence.

La.Code of Evidence art. 403 provides:

> Although relevant, evidence may be excluded if its probative value is substantially outweighed by the danger of unfair prejudice, confusion of the issues, or misleading the jury, or by considerations of undue delay, or waste of time.

In his brief to this court, the defendant contends that his inability to pay the June 1st parole supervision fee was irrelevant to the issue of whether a gun was used during the robbery. He argues that, because of the danger of unfair prejudice and confusion of the issues, his objection should have been sustained and, therefore, the trial court committed reversible error.

This court disagrees because the defendant's inability to pay his parole supervision fee on June 1st, three days before the instant robbery occurred, has relevance to this case. If the defendant had little or no money on June 1st, he could have been desperate enough to use a gun to commit armed robbery. Therefore, this evidence relates to the issues of motive and intent ...

AFFIRMED.

Discussion Questions

1. Do you think that evidence that the defendant did not have the $43.00 to pay his parole supervision fee three days before the crime was committed was relevant to the instant robbery? Why or why not?
2. Does the fact that many people who lack money do not rob others for it make the evidence irrelevant? What effect should such arguments have in a case? Referring to our example above, a similar argument would be that just because a man has an affair doesn't mean he'll kill his wife. Do such arguments make the evidence irrelevant? Why or why not?
3. The defense claims that the only disputed issue was whether the defendant had a gun. Assuming he is correct, does that fact render all other evidence bearing on any of the other issues in the case irrelevant? What effect does the fact that issues are not in dispute have on a case?
4. Motive has always been considered very strong evidence in showing guilt of committing a crime. How about the lack of motive? For example, should a defendant in an armed robbery be able to offer evidence of the large amount of money in his bank account as evidence that he had no need to commit a crime? Why or why not?

Evidence of Flight, Concealment as Consciousness of Guilt

When might evidence of flight or concealment be relevant to consciousness of guilt? As you will learn from reading *State v. Davies*[13] below, quite often the evidence can be probative of this issue. In the next section in *State v. Harris*,[14] you will read a case in which the court concludes that such evidence should be excluded under Article 403.

State v. Davies

Supreme Court of Louisiana
350 So. 2d 586
Sept. 19, 1977

SANDERS, Chief Justice . . .

The defense complains of the court's admitting testimony which revealed a "possible burglary or assault which occurred after the attempted aggravated rape for which (he) was tried, and for which he had been charged under a separate bill of information." He alleges that such testimony was inadmissible as it was irrelevant and evidence of other crimes or misconduct for which the defendant was not on trial.

We adduce the following relevant facts:

The defendant, the victim, and her friends socialized at Sonny's Night Club in the early morning hours of March 13, 1976. There, the defendant asked the victim to have sexual relations with him, but she refused.

About 3:30 a. m., when the victim and her friends left the club, the defendant ran behind them. In order to conceal themselves from the defendant, they ran into an alley. The defendant followed and entered the alley. He grabbed the victim by the neck and pulled her away. As her friends came to her aid, the defendant told them to "back off" or he "would blow (her) head off." When he spoke, he reached into the waistband of his trousers. Believing he was reaching for a gun, everyone ran.

The defendant pinned his victim against a house, and began to choke her. He told her that he had observed her previously and that he was going to "have her" that night . . .

. . . He choked her so strongly that she passed out for a few minutes. As she regained her senses, the police arrived and flashed a light on the defendant. Upon seeing this light, he jumped a fence and ran through a maze of alleyways.

. . . . About 4 a. m., he went to Jerry Ann, a former girl friend's, house. No one let him in. Jerry Ann arose when she heard the door open. She first saw the defendant when he entered her bedroom carrying the board with which she blocked her back door . . .

Jerry Ann and the defendant drank coffee and spoke for a few hours in her kitchen. Charles, a friend of Jerry Ann, stated that the defendant acted abnormal and that he said he had a problem.

As it approached 7 a. m., Charles told the defendant he must leave so Jerry Ann could dress for work. The defendant reacted by trying to shove Charles and Charles' sister, Patricia, into the kitchen. When he did so, Charles asked Patricia for a gun. Upon seeing the gun, the defendant said "Ladies, I wouldn't advise you to do this because I have a .25." As he

13. State v. Davies, 350 So. 2d 586 (La. 1977).
14. State v. Harris, 381 So. 2d 792 (La. 1980).

spoke, he reached into his pants. Jerry Ann and Charles, fearing that he had a gun, hid themselves. Before Charles could retrieve the gun from Patricia, she shot the defendant.

He left Jerry Ann's immediately. The defendant went to another friend, Minnie's, house. Minnie called his mother, who then called the police.

About 7:30 a. m., the police apprehended him.

Evidence of flight, concealment, and attempt to avoid apprehension is relevant. It indicates consciousness of guilt and, therefore, is one of the circumstances from which the jury may infer guilt. This rule applies notwithstanding that the evidence may disclose another crime.... A court may admit a wide range of evidence to prove flight, concealment, and attempt to avoid apprehension. State v. Nelson, supra.

In 22A C.J.S., Criminal Law, s 625A, pp. 460 et seq., the general principles are correctly summarized as follows:

> "While evidence of flight is not substantive evidence of guilt, or of premeditation or deliberation, since it is as consistent with innocence as with guilt, it is universally recognized that testimony as to flight, attempted flight, or concealment after the commission of an offense, or after one is accused of crime, is relevant evidence which may be shown as a criminating circumstance, particularly where such conduct is apparently inconsistent with the idea of innocence ...
>
> "Testimony or evidence as to the conduct and actions of accused during the period of his flight is generally relevant, and criminal conduct by accused during this period may be shown where such conduct was an inseparable part of the flight, as where the criminal activity was to secure funds to finance and accomplish further flight, and to avoid apprehension for the original crime ...
>
> "'Flight,' as evidence of guilt, consists not only in the act of leaving the jurisdiction, but it also comprehends continued concealment to avoid arrest and prosecution, and in criminal law the term is defined as the evading of the course of justice by voluntarily withdrawing oneself in order to avoid arrest or detention, or the institution or continuance of criminal proceedings. The term signifies, in legal parlance, not merely a leaving, but a leaving or concealment under a consciousness of guilt and for the purpose of evading arrest. Such consciousness and purpose is that which gives to the act of leaving its real incriminating character." (Footnotes deleted.)

The record reflects that defendant fled from the scene of the crime. His entry into the house of a third party and his resistance to leaving is evidence of his continued efforts to avoid apprehension. Thus, we hold that the evidence was admissible. This assignment of error is without merit....

Discussion Questions

1. The court states that a wide range of evidence may be offered to prove flight, concealment, and attempt to avoid apprehension. What are your thoughts as to whether the following evidence is relevant: searching flights online after a crime; withdrawing a large sum of money from the bank after a crime; contacting a family friend out of town, such as evidence of a cell phone log showing calls made to a friend that lived in California; bleaching one's hair and buying a fake beard; in a possession of marijuana trial, evidence that prior to being stopped, the defendant attempted to hide it under the seat; in a DWI trial, evidence that prior to being stopped that defendant threw liquid from a cup in his console?

2. Can you think of a scenario when flight or other evasive behavior might not be probative of consciousness of guilt, or in the alternative, might be excluded on other grounds? This issue is revisited in the next section in *State v. Harris*.[15]

Relevancy vs. Weight of Evidence

In the introductory material, we distinguished relevance of evidence from weight of evidence. The two concepts are often confused. Some attorneys argue that evidence is not relevant because of its minimal weight. While evidence with minimal weight might be excluded on other grounds, as you will learn more about in the next section, evidence need not have any predetermined weight to be relevant, as we discussed above. It need only have *some* weight. The distinction between the two concepts is demonstrated in *State v. Lee*[16] below.

State v. Lee
Court of Appeal of Louisiana, Third Circuit
625 So. 2d 645
Oct. 13, 1993

DOUCET, Judge.

In November 1990, the New Iberia Police Department was conducting an undercover narcotics operation aimed at street dealers in the City of New Iberia. Officer Tony Gant from St. Mary Parish was recruited to make narcotic purchases after being introduced to local drug dealers by a confidential informant. Undercover Agent Gant made a purchase of "crack" cocaine from Nathaniel Lee, defendant herein. The defendant was later charged. After his arrest, he admitted selling cocaine. An audiotape recording of the drug sale was admitted into evidence....

AUDIOTAPE EVIDENCE

By his third assignment of error the defendant claims the trial court erred in admitting into evidence an audiotape of the defendant's sale of "crack" cocaine to Agent Gant because this audiotape was unintelligible and therefore unduly prejudiced the defendant. Defendant argues it is inadmissible because it has absolutely no probative value, and any weight it had was far outweighed by its prejudice to defendant. No authority is cited by the defendant in his appellate brief. The State simply argues that if the audiotape was truly unintelligible, then it could have no prejudicial effect, and if the audiotape was intelligible, then its probative value outweighed any prejudice to defendant.

Lt. Kerry LeBlanc testified that, in addition to the background noises, one could hear defendant telling Agent Gant he had some $40 and $25 rocks of "crack" cocaine. Counsel for defendant had previously objected to the introduction of the audiotape and the trial judge recessed trial in order to listen to it and rule on defendant's objection:

> Having listened to the tape, the Court will overrule defense counsel's objection to the tape. It is, as defense counsel points out, very difficult to understand. Many parts of it are in fact unintelligible. However, it is a tape that was made of the transaction. It's been identified by the, by Detective LeBlanc. And the Court

---

15. State v. Harris, 381 So. 2d 792 (La. 1980).
16. State v. Lee, 625 So. 2d 645, (La. Ct. App. 3d Cir. 1993).

> is going to allow the prosecution to play it for whatever weight the jury wants to give it. I believe that if the prosecution wants to offer it, that the jury can assess its weight as effectively as it possibly can.

The audiotape of the alleged transaction is relevant evidence which tends to make the existence of a fact at issue more probable or less probable. La.C.E. art. 401. Relevant evidence is generally admissible. La.C.E. art. 402. Relevant evidence may be excluded if its probative value is substantially outweighed by the danger of unfair prejudice, confusion of the issues, or misleading the jury, or by considerations of undue delay, or waste of time. La.C.E. art. 403.

Counsel for the defendant appears to confuse weight of the evidence with relevancy of the evidence. The comments following La.C.E. art. 402 note that to be admissible under the Code of Evidence, relevant evidence need not have any pre-determined minimum weight. La.C.E. art. 402, comment (c). Article 402 is derived from former La.R.S. 15:441 (repealed), and in *State v. O'Quinn,* 342 So. 2d 202 (La.1977), the court noted that the evidence offered does not need to have strong, full, representative value, or to produce persuasion by its role and intrinsic form, but it is sufficient if it is worth consideration by the jury. Previously, in *State v. LaCoste,* 256 La. 697, 237 So. 2d 871 (1970), a surveillance videotape of a bank robbery was found admissible, and the Supreme Court ruled it was for the jury to decide whether or not it bore upon the guilt or innocence of the accused.

These same principles apply in the present case; the audiotape was found admissible by the trial judge and it was then up to the jury to determine what weight, if any, it would give the recording. The defendant introduced no evidence to support his claim of prejudice. Therefore, the defendant has failed to establish reversible error in the trial court's ruling. La.C.E. art. 103 and La.C.Cr.P. art. 921....

Discussion Questions

1. Explain how and why the evidence in *Lee* was relevant despite its minimal weight.
2. Distinguish the concepts of "probative value" of evidence and "weight" of evidence. How are they different, and how are they the same? How does each concept relate to relevance?
3. What does it mean to say that the jury decides the weight to give to evidence? What does it mean to say that an argument goes to the weight of evidence rather than its admissibility?

Direct vs. Circumstantial Evidence

State v. Badon
Court of Appeal of Louisiana, Fourth Circuit
664 So. 2d 1291
Nov. 16, 1995

WALTZER, Judge.

Officer Byron Adams of the New Orleans Police Department's Homicide Investigations Division testified at the motion [to suppress] hearing. He testified that during his investigation of the death of Gollia McGee, Badon made several statements. In the first, Badon told Adams that at 9:30 a.m., he and Mrs. McGee (Badon's grandmother) were sleeping.

Badon answered a knock on the door, and, upon opening the door, saw two black males in Sewerage and Water Board uniforms. One of the men grabbed Badon around the neck, dragged him to the back room, cut him, punched him in the jaw and rendered him unconscious. Badon awoke to the ringing telephone, kicked it off the hook and asked whoever was on the phone to call the police because he and his grandmother had been stabbed. In response to Badon's initial statement, Adams and other NOPD officers conducted a thorough scene investigation, lasting approximately 45 minutes to one hour which revealed that Badon's story was untrue. The doors were locked from the inside with a deadbolt, and there was very little blood in the room wherein Badon claimed he was stabbed and beaten.... Adams then approached Badon, advised him he was under arrest for first degree murder and advised him of his Miranda rights.... During the interview prior to the formal statement, Badon said a drug dealer to whom he owed a great deal of money sent people to Badon's apartment to collect the debt. Because Badon did not have the money owed, the collection agents beat and cut him and killed his grandmother as an example. Adams questioned Badon about details of his story, and Badon offered a third version, that he brought a man named Charles to his house, where they smoked crack cocaine, became intoxicated, and Charles killed Badon's grandmother, took the hammer and knife used in the murder, wrapped them in a bag and threw them into a sewer drain. Badon and Adams went to the drain and found the evidence. Badon told Adams he did not think Adams believed his story, and admitted that he had killed his grandmother.... Mr. Badon then related the following:

> [Badon] had started drinking Cisco and was talking to his girlfriend on the telephone. Upon completion of the telephone conversation, he had the sudden urge for crack cocaine. He stated that he just clicked and he went in the room and he asked his grandmother to lend him the vehicle. That's when he said upon her refusal, he then clicked. And he went into the kitchen and got a knife and a hammer, went back into the bedroom and then beat the victim about the head and face with the hammer, then continuously stabbed her. He stated that after that, he then went in the room and realized what he had done, at which time he then orchestrated the cover-up and all and had the police notified by his brother who had called him.

Dr. William P. Newman, III, professor of pathology at the Louisiana State University School of Medicine and consultant to the Orleans Parish Coroner's Office, who performed the autopsy on the sixty-three year old victim, testified that he found twenty-five incised wounds, three or four of which would have been fatal, and two blunt trauma wounds. She had a skull fracture and a fracture of the jaw, and both her lungs and her heart were perforated....

FIRST ASSIGNMENT OF ERROR:

Badon contends the [bloodstained blue-jean jacket and the machete] are not relevant because there was no proof offered at trial that the spots on the jacket were actually blood and there was no evidence that the machete was used in the crime. The items are objectionable, he argues, for their prejudicial value....

Relevant evidence is defined by La.C.E. art. 401 as:

> evidence having any tendency to make the existence of any fact that is of consequence to the determination of the action more probable or less probable than it would be without the evidence.

The standard of relevancy is based upon logic and experience. So long as the proffered evidence has a tendency to make a consequential fact more or less probable, the logical relevancy test is satisfied....

Absent a clear abuse of discretion, the trial court's ruling as to relevancy should not be disturbed on appeal. *State v. Whittaker,* 463 So. 2d 1270, 1272 (La.1985).

The blood stains on Badon's jacket were not shown to be his blood or the victim's blood. Because the State has not clearly connected the jacket to the crime or the attempted cover-up, its admission into evidence was error. We find that the defendant was not prejudiced by admission of the evidence. The trial court's error was harmless.

The machete found in a corner of the grandmother's bedroom near the head of her bed is also evidence of Badon's attempted cover-up. It corroborates Adams' testimony that Badon first declared that two men in Sewerage and Water Board uniforms burst into the house and committed the murder and his later story that a drug dealer killed her. The machete was evidence that Badon attempted to cover up his crime by planting the machete, which was not the murder weapon, in order to distract the investigation from its proper object.

. . .

PLOTKIN, J., concurs. PLOTKIN, Judge, concurring.

A foundation was not laid to establish that it was more probable than not that the jacket and machete were connected to the crime.... .Therefore, the trial judge's ruling that the jacket and machete were relevant was incorrect and a clear abuse of discretion. I concur, however, because the error was harmless. The evidence against the appellant is overwhelming and the prejudicial value of those items is slight.

Discussion Question

1. Do you think the evidence (the blood-stained jacket) was relevant absent a showing that it was either the defendant's or victim's blood on it? Why or why not?
2. How closely connected to a crime does circumstantial evidence have to be to be relevant? Isn't the connection part of the inference that the trier of fact must make whenever circumstantial evidence is offered? For example, if the prosecution proves that a defendant's GPS showed that he was in the neighborhood where the crime occurred, must the prosecution also establish that he was actually at the scene of the crime in order for the evidence to be admissible, or is that the inference the jury is being asked to make by offering the circumstantial evidence? How much of a connection should have to be established? What are your thoughts?

Effect of Credibility on Relevance

A witness's credibility may be attacked in a number of ways that we will cover in Chapter 6, infra.[17] You will learn that a witness's credibility may be attacked by showing his bias, interest in the case, prior inconsistent statements, conviction of a crime, and in several other ways. What effect does this have on the relevance of the witness's testimony? Should a witness not be allowed to testify because his testimony has been shown to be untruthful or if he has a motive to lie? Is such testimony irrelevant? As we pointed out above, such issues go to the weight that the trier of fact will give to the witness's testimony, but it does not affect its admissibility. This is the issue presented in *Evans v. Olinde*[18] below.

---

17. See Chapter 6, *infra*. See also La. Code Evid. arts. 607, 608, 609, 609.1, 613.
18. Evan v. Olinde, 609 So. 2d 299 (La. Ct. App. 3d Cir. 1992).

Evans v. Olinde

Court of Appeal of Louisiana, Third Circuit
609 So. 2d 299
Nov. 4, 1992

STOKER, Judge.

Defendant-appellant Steven Otterstatter appeals a judgment holding defendant-appellee Elizabeth Olinde free from fault for an automobile accident. The accident occurred on I-10 west over the Atchafalaya swamp at about 7:10 p.m. on October 21, 1983. The drivers involved in the accident, Otterstatter and Olinde, presented conflicting versions of how the accident occurred.

Otterstatter contends he was driving down the highway with his lights on when Olinde rear-ended his car, pushing it into the guardrail. His car then bounced off of the guardrail, flipped upside down and slid 180 feet. Otterstatter's two young daughters were thrown from the car and seriously injured.

Olinde states that, as she was driving down the highway, Otterstatter's car suddenly loomed before her as a large beige object. Its lights were not on. She braked immediately but was unable to avoid hitting it. According to Olinde, Otterstatter must have already struck the guardrail inadvertently, which knocked the battery out of his car and caused his car lights to go out. Since his car lights were not on, she did not see his car until it was too late to avoid hitting it.

... After a jury trial on the merits of Otterstatter's claim, the jury held that Olinde was free from fault for the accident and, therefore, did not reach the issue of Otterstatter's damages....

Motion in Limine

Otterstatter asserts that the trial judge erred in reversing a prior order granting his motion in limine to exclude expert testimony about the headlights and taillights on Otterstatter's car.

Three days after the accident, on Monday morning, Leo Brassett and Gene Moody investigated Otterstatter's vehicle in the lot where it was impounded. They removed the head and taillights from Otterstatter's car without first filing a discovery request and without any notice to or authorization from Otterstatter or the court. The lights were then sent to Olinde's expert in electrical engineering, Dr. Adams, for testing to discover whether Otterstatter's lights were on or off when Olinde rear-ended his car. After Dr. Adams concluded his tests, Olinde offered to return the lights to Otterstatter.

Otterstatter filed a motion in limine to exclude any evidence concerning Dr. Adams's testing of the lights. The trial judge granted the motion on the grounds that the chain of custody could not be proven sufficiently to identify the lights as those which were on Otterstatter's car and that it was fundamentally unfair to exclude Otterstatter from the testing conducted by Dr. Adams and then offer to return the lights to him afterward.

Olinde subsequently called Dr. Adams as a witness, despite the trial judge's order excluding his testimony. Upon objection by Otterstatter, a bench conference which was not transcribed for the record was conducted before the jury. We assume the trial judge reversed his earlier order and decided to allow Dr. Adams to testify as to the tests on the car lights, since Dr. Adams proceeded to testify after the bench conference was concluded. There are no reasons or ruling by the judge in the record or in the court's minutes.

As we see it, the issue presented is not one of *admissibility* but one of *weight* or *credibility* to be accorded the evidence. However, we will initially note that admissibility is a question of law to be determined by the court. The court should follow the preponderance of evidence standard when factual questions must be decided to determine the admissibility of evidence. LSA-C.E. art. 104 A and D and the comments thereunder and *McLoughlin v. Fireman's Fund Ins. Co.*, 582 So. 2d 203, 207 (La.App. 1st Cir.), writ denied, 586 So. 2d 536 (La.1991).

Cases in the jurisprudence often state it is a fundamental law of evidence that an article or substance which is introduced as demonstrative evidence, or to which a witness is asked to testify, must be sufficiently identified as the one involved in the occurrence in question. The foundation must be laid which connects the specimen with its source, showing that it was properly taken by an authorized person, properly labeled and preserved, properly transported for analysis, and properly tested....

The purpose of the chain of custody rule is to assure the integrity of the evidence, i.e. to prevent the evidence from being tampered with or from being lost.... At least in a civil case, the chain of custody rule does not require a twenty-four hour vigilance of the evidence. It requires that its integrity be preserved, and that it be protected from being tampered with or lost ...

... Otterstatter argues that he has no way of knowing whether the lights tested really came from his car, whether Dr. Adams received the lights in the same condition they were in before Brassett and Moody handled them, or whether they were offered to him, after Dr. Adams's tests, in the same condition they were in before the tests. The lights could have been tampered with, inadvertently damaged en route, or altered by Dr. Adams's tests.

Both Brassett and Moody admitted to removing the lights from Otterstatter's car, an action which the trial judge characterized as a theft since they lacked authority to do so. No testimony was given as to the subsequent handling of the lights, i.e. labeling and transportation to Dr. Adams. Dr. Adams testified that he did not know, of his own knowledge, that the lights came from Otterstatter's car. The lights themselves were not offered into evidence at trial.

We must decide whether the trial court abused its wide discretion in changing its pretrial ruling regarding the admissibility of the evidence in question and allowing the evidence to be introduced at trial. In doing so we bear in mind the distinction between *admissibility* of the evidence to be ruled on by the trial court and the *weight* and *credibility* to be accorded the evidence by the jury as the trier of fact.

This case is a *civil* case. Proof of connexity between Otterstatter's car and the laboratory samples examined by Dr. Adams is sufficient if proven by a preponderance of evidence. These principles and distinctions are clearly enunciated in *McLoughlin v. Fireman's Fund Ins. Co.*, supra, which involved a civil case in which the admissibility of a blood alcohol test of a deceased driver was at issue. In *McLoughlin* the court of appeal observed:

> "Stanley S. Chigoy, a medical technologist, testified that TPL dispatched a courier who during his routine day would pick up specimens (blood samples) at Dr. Maxwell's office, or a place specified by him, and the courier would transport the specimen back to TPL for testing. *The courier in the instant case was not identified and did not testify.* However, this is not necessarily fatal to the admissibility of the evidence. It is gaps in possession of the sample as opposed to lack of evidence pertaining to the taking of the sample and its analysis which result in different language by the courts as to foundation evidence necessary to introduce a sample. Gaps in a chain of custody usually affect the *weight* of the evidence, not its *ad-*

missibility, and an unbroken chain of custody is not essential for the admissibility of the evidence *as long as the foundation evidence as a whole shows it is more probable than not that the evidence tested was that which was originally taken....*"

Leo Brassett testified at trial that he removed two or three bulbs and portions of a red lens from a car and handed them to Gene Moody. It is apparent from Brassett's complete testimony that he believed the questioned items were taken from Otterstatter's car and that Brassett accompanied Moody to view the car because Brassett had identified and located the car.

Gene Moody was qualified as an accident reconstruction expert. Moody testified he and Brassett removed the bulbs, removed the headlights and the taillights, and Moody took those items to Leonard Adams....

In our view, the preponderance of the evidence establishes that the items examined by Adams were the same items removed from Otterstatter's car by Brassett and Moody. We find nothing in the record to seriously question the connexity between the items examined and the items removed and delivered by Moody to Adams.

Further, in our opinion, the cross-examination of Adams goes more to the *weight* of the evidence than to its admissibility. It was the jury's duty of accept or reject Moody's testimony concerning the source of the samples. Also, the failure to produce the questioned items into evidence goes to the weight of Adams's testimony.

... We find the trial judge did not abuse his much discretion, after viewing the demeanors and listening to the testimony of Leo Brassett and Gene Moody, in reversing his prior order and permitting Dr. Adams to testify as to the results of the tests he conducted on Otterstatter's car lights.

Discussion Questions

1. Contrary to the last case, here evidence is offered to connect the evidence to the case at hand. However, the opposing party effectively argues that the evidence offered "is not good enough." Is it ever appropriate to exclude evidence because a witness is shown to be biased, to have an interest in the case, or for other issues bearing on the witness's credibility? Are these issues for the court to decide, or for the trier of fact to decide in determining how much weight to give to the evidence and/or testimony of the witness?
2. What does it mean to say that the witness's credibility "goes to the weight of the evidence, rather than to its admissibility"? How does that concept apply in *Evans v. Olinde*?

Effect of Stipulation on Relevancy

We will visit *Old Chief v. United States*[19] in both this section as well as in § 3.2. In this section we consider whether evidence is logically relevant when certain alternative evidence exists on the same issue—in this case, a stipulation by opposing counsel to the issue. In the next section we will deal with whether such evidence should be excluded on other grounds, namely under Article 403.

---

19. Old Chief v. United States, 519 U.S. 172 (1997).

Old Chief v. United States (I)
Supreme Court of the United States
519 U.S. 172, 117 S.Ct. 644 (1997)

Justice SOUTER delivered the opinion of the Court.

Subject to certain limitations, 18 U.S.C. § 922(g)(1) prohibits possession of a firearm by anyone with a prior felony conviction, which the Government can prove by introducing a record of judgment or similar evidence identifying the previous offense. Fearing prejudice if the jury learns the nature of the earlier crime, defendants sometimes seek to avoid such an informative disclosure by offering to concede the fact of the prior conviction. The issue here is whether a district court abuses its discretion if it spurns such an offer and admits the full record of a prior judgment, when the name or nature of the prior offense raises the risk of a verdict tainted by improper considerations, and when the purpose of the evidence is solely to prove the element of prior conviction. We hold that it does.

I

In 1993, petitioner, Old Chief, was arrested after a fracas involving at least one gunshot. The ensuing federal charges included not only assault with a dangerous weapon and using a firearm in relation to a crime of violence but violation of 18 U.S.C. § 922(g)(1). This statute makes it unlawful for anyone "who has been convicted in any court of, a crime punishable by imprisonment for a term exceeding one year" to "possess in or affecting commerce, any firearm...." "[A] crime punishable by imprisonment for a term exceeding one year" is defined to exclude "any Federal or State offenses pertaining to antitrust violations, unfair trade practices, restraints of trade, or other similar offenses relating to the regulation of business practices" and "any State offense classified by the laws of the State as a misdemeanor and punishable by a term of imprisonment of two years or less." 18 USC § 921(a)(20).

The earlier crime charged in the indictment against Old Chief was assault causing serious bodily injury. Before trial, he moved for an order requiring the Government "to refrain from mentioning—by reading the Indictment, during jury selection, in opening statement, or closing argument—and to refrain from offering into evidence or soliciting any testimony from any witness regarding the prior criminal convictions of the Defendant, *except* to state that the Defendant has been convicted of a crime punishable by imprisonment exceeding one (1) year." He said that revealing the name and nature of his prior assault conviction would unfairly tax the jury's capacity to hold the Government to its burden of proof beyond a reasonable doubt on current charges of assault, possession, and violence with a firearm, and he offered to "solve the problem here by stipulating, agreeing and requesting the Court to instruct the jury that he has been convicted of a crime punishable by imprisonment exceeding one (1) yea[r]." He argued that the offer to stipulate to the fact of the prior conviction rendered evidence of the name and nature of the offense inadmissible under Rule 403 of the Federal Rules of Evidence, the danger being that unfair prejudice from that evidence would substantially outweigh its probative value. He also proposed this jury instruction:

> "The phrase 'crime punishable by imprisonment for a term exceeding one year' generally means a crime which is a felony. The phrase does not include any state offense classified by the laws of that state as a misdemeanor and punishable by a term of imprisonment of two years or less and certain crimes concerning the regulation of business practices. [I] hereby instruct you that Defendant JOHNNY

LYNN OLD CHIEF has been convicted of a crime punishable by imprisonment for a term exceeding one year."

The Assistant United States Attorney refused to join in a stipulation, insisting on his right to prove his case his own way, and the District Court agreed, ruling orally that, "If he doesn't want to stipulate, he doesn't have to." At trial, over renewed objection, the Government introduced the order of judgment and commitment for Old Chief's prior conviction. This document disclosed that on December 18, 1988, he "did knowingly and unlawfully assault Rory Dean Fenner, said assault resulting in serious bodily injury," for which Old Chief was sentenced to five years' imprisonment. The jury found Old Chief guilty on all counts, and he appealed....

As a threshold matter, there is Old Chief's erroneous argument that the name of his prior offense as contained in the record of conviction is irrelevant to the prior—conviction element, and for that reason inadmissible under Rule 402 of the Federal Rules of Evidence. Rule 401 defines relevant evidence as having "any tendency to make the existence of any fact that is of consequence to the determination of the action more probable or less probable than it would be without the evidence." Fed. Rule Evid. 401. To be sure, the fact that Old Chief's prior conviction was for assault resulting in serious bodily injury rather than, say, for theft was not itself an ultimate fact, as if the statute had specifically required proof of injurious assault. But its demonstration was a step on one evidentiary route to the ultimate fact, since it served to place Old Chief within a particular sub-class of offenders for whom firearms possession is outlawed by § 922(g)(1). A documentary record of the conviction for that named offense was thus relevant evidence in making Old Chief's § 922(g)(1) status more probable than it would have been without the evidence.

Nor was its evidentiary relevance under Rule 401 affected by the availability of alternative proofs of the element to which it went, such as an admission by Old Chief that he had been convicted of a crime "punishable by imprisonment for a term exceeding one year" within the meaning of the statute. The 1972 Advisory Committee Notes to Rule 401 make this point directly:

> "The fact to which the evidence is directed need not be in dispute. While situations will arise which call for the exclusion of evidence offered to prove a point conceded by the opponent, the ruling should be made on the basis of such considerations as waste of time and undue prejudice (see Rule 403), rather than under any general requirement that evidence is admissible only if directed to matters in dispute."

If, then, relevant evidence is inadmissible in the presence of other evidence related to it, its exclusion must rest not on the ground that the other evidence has rendered it "irrelevant," but on its character as unfairly prejudicial, cumulative or the like, its relevance notwithstanding.[4]

[The Court continues with a discussion of the Federal Rule of Evidence 403 which is set forth in § 3.2 infra.]

4. Viewing evidence of the name of the prior offense as relevant, there is no reason to dwell on the Government's argument that relevance is to be determined with respect to the entire item offered in evidence (here, the entire record of conviction) and not with reference to distinguishable sub-units of that object (here, the name of the offense and the sentence received). We see no impediment in general to a district court's determination, after objection, that some sections of a document are relevant within the meaning of Rule 401, and others irrelevant and inadmissible under Rule 402. ...

Discussion Question

What effect does the stipulation to the underlying felony have on the relevance of the evidence? Does it make such evidence irrelevant? Why or why not?

Key Points

The key points to keep in mind regarding relevancy.

1. **General rule of relevant evidence.** Relevant evidence is admissible, subject to other legal provisions. Irrelevant evidence is always inadmissible.
2. **Relevance defined.** Relevant evidence makes the existence of consequential facts more or less probable than they would be without it.
3. Evidence **E** → Facts **F** → Consequential facts **C** → Probative of the consequential fact **P**

   (1) Identify evidence; (2) determine what fact or legal proposition the evidence is being offered to prove; (3) is the fact a consequential fact; (4) is the evidence probative of the fact; if so, the evidence is relevant.
4. **Consequential facts** are facts that effect the issues, elements, defenses, weakness, and theories of the case, based on the substantive law, including credibility issues, and background facts.
5. **Probative value.** The evidence sought to be admitted must make one or more consequential facts more or less probable than it would be without the evidence. It need not prove the fact—it need only "tend" to prove or disprove it.
6. **No predetermined weight.** To be relevant the evidence need only be a "brick in the wall," i.e., make the consequential fact more or less probable.
7. **Circumstantial evidence** is also relevant if it meets the standard.
8. Relevancy determinations are within the discretion of the trial court, and will not be disturbed on appeal absent an abuse of that discretion.

Logical Relevancy Problems

PROBLEM 3-1. The Chateau Dijon restaurant was sued after the leg on a customer's chair broke, causing him to fall on the floor and break his hip. The defendant's attorney intends to offer evidence that the restaurant has received three awards from the American Best Foods Society for the quality and taste of their food to show that they are one of the best restaurants in town and take pride in their business. Upon what basis should the plaintiff object? How will the court likely rule and why?

PROBLEM 3-2. Jim is on trial for murder. He is 31 years old. The prosecution would like to have him display an old tattoo that reads "KILLER" which he had placed on his arm when he was 16 years old. His attorney objects that the tattoo is not relevant. How should the court rule and why?

PROBLEM 3-3. Kevin is a delivery truck driver for a major company. One day while out making his deliveries, he was involved in a major accident preventing him from continuing to work. During worker's compensation proceedings, the defendant (employer) would like to offer evidence that at the time of the accident, Kevin had veered off of his route to travel to his daughter's school to drop off her lunch. They would also like to offer evidence that at the time of the accident, Kevin was sending a text message. Kevin objects to the admissibility of both pieces of evidence, claiming they are irrelevant in a worker's compensation proceeding. How should the court rule on each piece of evidence and why?

PROBLEM 3-4. Shortly after an armed robbery of a convenience store was reported, where the cashier stated that she shot the suspect, a 911 call was received where a young man indicated that he'd just been shot. The caller, Ken, was in his apartment, which was about a block from the store that had been robbed. Police arrived at Ken's house and found that he matched the description of the suspect from the robbery. While standing in the doorway, the officer observed a gun stuffed between the pillows of the sofa in the living room next to the front door. Ken stated that the gun belonged to his roommate. Gloves were also found stuffed in the sofa. There were no fingerprints on the gun. The cashier was unable to identify whether the gun was the one used in the robbery and doesn't remember if the robber was wearing gloves. At Ken's trial, the defense objects to the gun and gloves being offered into evidence claiming that the prosecution cannot prove that the items were used in the robbery. How should the court rule on the admissibility of the evidence and why?

PROBLEM 3-5. Mitchell is on trial for second-degree (felony) murder. During a traffic stop, Mitchell pulled off and began fleeing from the officer when the officer went back to his cruiser to check for warrants. During a high-speed chase from the police officer, Mitchell went the wrong way down a one-way street and hit another car head-on, immediately resulting in the driver's death. The prosecution would like to offer evidence that the week before the incident, Mitchell told his landlord that he was wanted in Texas on armed robbery charges, and said that if the police ever got after him, he would make sure that if they take him down, he's going to take somebody else down with him. The prosecution believes the statement goes to Mitchell's state of mind during the chase. Mitchell objects that the statement is not relevant. Should the evidence of Mitchell's statement to his landlord be admitted in a trial for felony murder under the statute below? How should the court rule and why? *[La. R.S. 14:30.1 The killing of a human being when the offender is engaged in the perpetration or attempted perpetration of aggravated escape, even though he has no intent to kill or to inflict great bodily harm.]*

PROBLEM 3-6. Ms. Peirce brought a wrongful death action against her husband's former employer, Bigco, Inc. and its CEO, Emanuel Sims, who she claims negligently shot and killed her husband on a hunting trip. In support of her case, the plaintiff intends to offer evidence of the following: 1) That Emanuel misrepresented the trip as a business trip to the company to get them to pay for it, even though no business was being handled or discussed on the trip; 2) That the gun had been purchased just before 9:00 p.m. the night before they left for the trip and Emanuel had never fired the weapon, even though he was a very experienced marksman and was properly licensed; and 3) That Emanuel also killed a black bear on the trip, a violation of state law. The defense objects to the admissibility of all three pieces of evidence claiming they are irrelevant in the case. What, if any, evidence will likely be admitted at trial? Why or why not?

PROBLEM 3-7. Shayna, a former employee of University USA, has brought a sexual harassment lawsuit against the university claiming the president sexually harassed her. She intends to call Cole to testify that on several occasions he observed the president go into Shayna's office and close and lock the door behind him. Shayna claims that those were instances in which the harassment occurred. The defense would like to offer evidence that Cole had been subsequently fired from the university when it was discovered that he had lied on his job application when he was hired at the university. The plaintiff objects to the admissibility of the evidence, claiming it is not relevant. How should the court rule and why?

PROBLEM 3-8. Melody is suing her employer for employment discrimination because she claims that she was passed over for several promotions even though she was the most qualified person for the job. As a part of her case, she would like to offer evidence of the qualifications, attendance records, and performance evaluations of the last five individuals who were promoted. The defense claims that the qualifications, attendance records, and performance evaluations of other employees are irrelevant in *her* case, since they are not parties to the case. Should the evidence be admitted over the defense's objection? For what purpose(s) might the evidence be relevant? Explain.

PROBLEM 3-9. Dennis had a large aggressive dog. After attacking a little boy named Donovan, Dennis sent his dog to obedience school to make sure he was better trained. After being at obedience school for a month, Dennis went to pick him up and talked with the trainer who told Dennis to be very careful around small children because the dog had a tendency to become aggressive and could possibly attack. Dennis took great care around children with his dog. Shortly after Dennis' dog finished school, Donovan's mother sued Dennis for negligently keeping a vicious dog and for the damages caused by the dog when he bit Donovan. The plaintiff would like to offer evidence that the trainer told Dennis about the dog having a tendency to bite children to help prove that Dennis knew or should have known that his dog posed a danger to others as required under the statute to prove liability. Will the evidence be admissible? Why or why not?

PROBLEM 3-10. Deen was convicted of a felony and placed on probation. During his plea, he was informed that as a convicted felon, he was not to possess any firearms. The very next day, he reported to his probation officer (P.O.) and asked him for a suggestion on how he should get rid of his shotgun that he'd had for many years now that he could not possess weapons. The P.O. told Deen that he should pawn it. He asked the P.O. if it was okay for him to take it to the pawn shop the next day to pawn it, and the P.O. told him that it would be okay. On his way to the pawn shop the next morning, Deen was stopped for speeding and a quick check revealed that he was a convicted felon who was not to be in possession of a firearm. He told the officer that he was on his way to the pawn shop to pawn the shotgun as he was advised to do by his P.O., but the officer told him that was *his* problem and arrested Deen anyway. At the trial, the defense sought to introduce testimony that the P.O. had told Deen that it was okay for him to take the shotgun to the pawn shop the next day to show Deen's good faith. The prosecution objected to the evidence, claiming his good faith was irrelevant to the charged offense. How should the court likely rule and why? [See *State v. Recard*, 704 So. 2d 324 (La. Ct. App. 3d Cir. 1997).]

PROBLEM 3-11. Dug was on trial for the rape of Vicky. In his defense, Dug sought to introduce evidence of a message Vicky left in his voicemail about three weeks before the alleged rape where she stated, "Hey Dug, this is Vicky, just returning your call. Yes, I'm free this weekend. Let's definitely hang out. Looking forward to hearing from you. Talk to you soon. Bye." The prosecution objected to the message being played at the trial claiming that it was irrelevant to the rape. Should the recording be admitted? Why or why not? [See *State v. Probst*, 623 So. 2d 79 (La. Ct. App. 1st Cir. 1993).]

Assume that rather than Dug seeking to admit the voicemail above that Vicky left, that instead Vicky sought to admit a message that she left in his voicemail stating, "Look, I've told you to stop calling me. I am *not* interested in you, so please do not contact me again. I am not going out with you. Goodbye!" Dug objects to this message being played, claiming the voicemail is irrelevant to whether she consented to sleeping with him on the night in question. Should the recording be admitted? Is your answer different than when Dug sought to introduce the message above? Why or why not?

PROBLEM 3-12. One morning, Deidra was driving her boyfriend's car when she was stopped for a traffic violation. During a search of the vehicle, police found marijuana and hydrocodone in the console. Deidra claims she was not aware of the drugs in the car and told officers it was not her vehicle. She was arrested anyway for possession of the controlled dangerous substances. That afternoon, when her mother found out about the arrest, she bonded Deidra out of jail and immediately took her to the hospital to find out if her daughter was doing drugs. A drug test revealed that neither marijuana nor hydrocodone were in Deidra's system. Deidra would like to offer the results of the drug test in her trial for the possession of the controlled dangerous substances. Should the evidence be admitted? Why or why not? Would evidence that hydrocodone *was* located in Deidra's system be relevant? [See *State v. Malone*, 56 So. 3d 336 (La. Ct. App. 2d Cir. 2010).]

§ 3.1 References and Additional Authority on Logical Relevancy [La. C.E. art. 401, 402]

1. La. C.E. arts. 401, 402 and Official Comments
2. Force & Rault, HANDBOOK ON LOUISIANA EVIDENCE LAW Arts. 401, 402 Author's Comments (West Publishing 2014)
3. Harges & Jones, LOUISIANA EVIDENCE Arts. 401, 402 Author's Comments (West Publishing 2014)
4. 19 La. Civ. L. Treatise, Evidence And Proof § 5.1 (2nd ed.)
5. **Evidence relevant to show identity**. *State v. Gilmer*, 604 So. 2d 117 (La. Ct of App. 2d Cir. 1992) (fact that defendant had gold tooth at time of trial was relevant to defendant's identity and defendant was required to display the gold tooth at trial after victim had given the information to the police officer at the time of the initial interview and again stated at the trial that her assailant had a gold tooth).
6. **Evidence irrelevant because it is not probative of stated consequential fact**: *State v. Ramirez*, 30 So. 3d 833 (La. Ct. App. 5th Cir. 2009) (holding that victim's earlier statement about being threatened with a knife, which her son did not believe, was not relevant to show that the victim was senile, making her description of the perpetrator less credible; the fact her son may not have believed her statement about being threatened with a knife prior to the beating does not make it more probable that the victim was senile, it does not make it more probable that the statement was false thereby rendering her statements after the attack less credible, nor does it make it more probable that he should not have believed her later statement describing her assailant while she lay bleeding on the floor. Because the statement in question was not relevant to attack the victim's credibility or faculties, it was correctly excluded.).
7. **Evidence relevant to prove motive**: *State v. Combs*, 600 So. 2d 751 (La. Ct. App. 2d Cir. 1992) writ denied, 604 So. 2d 973 (La. 1992) (holding that defendant's statements related by police officer asserting his membership in the KKK and that he would not let black people take what belonged to him were logically relevant in an arson trial to show his motive for burning property owned by black man); *State v. Weatherspoon*, 948 So. 2d 215 (La. Ct. App. 5th Cir. 2006) (evidence of defendant's gang affiliation was relevant to show defendant's motive in murder trial when the state's theory was

that defendant committed offense in revenge for prior altercation); *State v. Smith*, (La. Ct. App. 1st Cir. 2014) (holding that statements made by state witness about statements made in three rap videos and a "behind the scenes" video by defendant were admissible to show proof of motive, intent, preparation, plan, and knowledge); *State v. Marinello*, 49 So. 3d 488 (La. Ct. App. 3d Cir. 2010) (holding that bad acts evidence regarding defendant's alleged bigamy and filing of false public record was probative of motive and intent, and thus admissible in murder trial when the State's theory was that defendant killed victim due to acrimonious divorce proceedings).

8. **Opening the door:** *O'Neal v. Church's Fried Chicken*, 580 So. 2d 706 (La. Ct. App. 4th Cir. 1991) (A person may open the door to otherwise inadmissible, irrelevant evidence by the content of his testimony. In action to recover damages for loss of love and affection and companionship due to the shooting death of her son while he attempted to rob a Church's chicken, the mother opened the door to 21 prior arrests of her son when she testified that her son was a "good boy," and was a "kind, well-respected individual." Thereafter, evidence showing a lack of love, affection and companionship was relevant and admissible); see also *State v. Jackson*, 734 So. 2d 658, 662 (La. Ct. App. 3d Cir. 1999) (for more on the "opening the door" doctrine).
9. **Irrelevant evidence:** *State v. Hutchinson*, 817 So. 2d 500 (La. Ct. App. 5th Cir. 2002) (holding that defendant's attempt to show jeans irrelevant when he admitted wearing jeans on the night in question); *State v. Joseph*, 854 So. 2d 914 (La. Ct. App. 3d Cir. 2003) (holding that wife's attempt to drop charges against husband in domestic abuse case irrelevant in husband's trial for possession of firearm by convicted felon); *State v. Wix*, 838 So. 2d 41 (La. Ct. App. 4th Cir. 2003) (holding that evidence of an AK-47 clip found in defendant's home was irrelevant in trial where robbery and attempted murder committed with 9mm).

§ 3.2 Excluding Relevant Evidence [La. C.E. art. 403]

Applicable Code Articles

Art. 403. Exclusion of relevant evidence on grounds of prejudice, confusion, or waste of time

Although relevant, evidence may be excluded if its probative value is substantially outweighed by the danger of unfair prejudice, confusion of the issues, or misleading the jury, or by considerations of undue delay, or waste of time.

While evidence must be relevant to be admissible, not all relevant evidence is admissible. As we covered in § 3.1, Article 402 specifically provides that relevant evidence is admissible subject to limitations by the state or federal Constitution, other provisions in the Code of Evidence, or other legislation. As you have learned, the standard of determining whether evidence is relevant is extremely low since it need not have any predetermined weight. As a result, in some instances other interests may outweigh the value of admitting the evidence. For example, if a crime took place in front of a crowd of 50 people, while each person's testimony as to what occurred would be relevant because they are all eyewitnesses to the crime, not all 50 people would need to testify due to the time it would take to call all 50 witnesses to testify to the same thing. The value of some witnesses' testimony, regarding what has already been testified to by 20–30 other people, would be outweighed by the interest in avoiding undue delay or a waste of time.

Other provisions in the Code exclude relevant evidence that is privileged,[20] that furthers certain public policy reasons,[21] or that might lead a juror to convict on an improper basis, such as evidence that might cast the defendant as a bad person because of his prior bad acts, possibly leading the jury to convict him because of the kind of person they believe he is rather than based on the evidence before them.[22] Additionally, while a defendant's confession to a crime would certainly be relevant in a criminal trial regarding his guilt or innocence, the evidence would be excluded if it was obtained in violation of the defendant's Fifth Amendment privilege against self-incrimination. We deem the constitutional right to be free from the compulsion of making statements against oneself more important than allowing the evidence to be used against the defendant in a trial, even though it is relevant.

Article 403 is another important provision in the Code that places limitations on the admissibility of relevant evidence. It provides that relevant evidence may be excluded if its probative value is substantially outweighed by the danger of unfair prejudice, confusion of the issues, misleading the jury, or by considerations of undue delay, or waste of time.

Article 403 Balancing Test. Let's take a closer look at Article 403, which limits the admissibility of relevant evidence. While the general test of relevancy provided for in Article 401 does not depend upon the weight of the evidence, i.e., the degree to which it actually proves the consequential fact or the ultimate issue in the case, Article 403 requires such a consideration. Article 403 requires that some value be placed on the probity of the evidence because under Article 403 the probative value of the evidence is balanced against the danger that the evidence will be unfairly prejudicial, will confuse the issues, mislead the jury, or will result in undue delay, or waste of time. If the dangers of Article 403 substantially outweigh the probative value of the evidence sought to be admitted, then the evidence should be excluded. Because of the balancing required under Article 403, the rule is often referred to as the **"Article 403 balancing test."**

Throughout the course you will learn that this is a very important evidentiary test that the court applies in many different contexts to determine whether evidence should be admitted. For example, whenever prior criminal activity is offered against an accused under Article 404(B) to prove a relevant purpose in the trial, it will only be allowed if the probative value towards proving the relevant purpose in the trial outweighs the prejudicial effect that admitting the evidence would have. This chapter is the first of many instances in which we will refer to the Article 403 balancing test. Below we will take a closer look at both sides of the test.

Probative Value. In § 3.1 we discussed the probative value of evidence and learned that evidence is probative if it makes a fact more or less probable than it would be without the evidence. You learned that to be relevant, the evidence must have a bearing on the issues and elements in the case; however, the evidence need only have "any tendency" to prove or disprove a consequential fact. It need not have any predetermined weight. However, as we stated above, in order to apply a balancing test under Article 403, we must consider the weight of the evidence towards proving the consequential fact.

---

20. See Chapter 5 of the Louisiana Code of Evidence covering Privileges, which are discussed in Chapter 8 of the casebook.

21. *See* La. Code Evid. arts. 407–411, 413–415; Social Policy Exclusions are discussed further in Chapter 9 of the casebook.

22. *See* La. Code Evid. art. 404; Character evidence is covered in Chapter 6 of the casebook.

As you might imagine, not all evidence has the same weight. Let's refer back to our example of the man on trial for murdering his wife. Suppose the prosecution wanted to offer three pieces of evidence against the defendant: 1) evidence that the defendant had written a love letter to his mistress, as we discussed above; 2) evidence that the defendant purchased the murder weapon used in the crime on the morning of the murder; and 3) eyewitness testimony from the couple's 16-year-old son who saw the defendant, his father, shoot his wife.

While all three pieces of evidence are relevant, in that they all make consequential facts more probable than they would be without the evidence, they clearly do not all have the weight. Evidence that the defendant purchased the murder weapon on the morning it was used to kill his wife is much stronger evidence than the love letter and carries more weight than the love letter which requires several inferences towards proving the actual murder. However, an eyewitness is even more probative than having purchased the gun. It is direct evidence of the commission of the crime itself.

Determining probative value of evidence. While it is pretty clear in the example above that the eyewitness testimony has a higher probative value than a love letter, what factors or tests do the courts use to determine probative value, a relatively abstract concept? As you will learn from reading the following cases, among the factors the court considers in assessing probative value is the number of inferences between the offered evidence and the legal proposition it is offered to prove. As discussed in the example above, a love letter has a lower probative value than eyewitness testimony because the love letter requires a chain of inferences between the evidence sought to be admitted and the ultimate issue it is being offered to prove.

For instance, in order for the love letter to tend to prove the defendant murdered his wife, one would have to infer that if the defendant wrote the love letter, he loves the woman; that if he loves her, he might want to be with her; and that if he wants to be with her, he might want to get rid of someone else who stood in his way; and that he'd be willing to get rid of them by killing them.[23] The more inferences involved, the lower the probative value of the evidence. Additionally, the court considers the strength of the inferences and whether some of them can be easily explained away. This concept is explored more in *State v. Ludwig*[24] below.

Additionally, the court considers the availability of alternative evidence to prove the same point, some of which may be less prejudicial than the proffered evidence.[25] For example, if there is only one eyewitness to an incident, then the probative value of that witness's testimony is high. If there are 20 eyewitnesses to an incident, then witness #19's testimony is less probative since several other witnesses have testified to the same thing. When witness #19's testimony is balanced against the danger of the waste of time it may take to call 19 witnesses to testify to the same thing, the Article 403 balancing test may require its exclusion.

As you read the cases below, consider how the court assesses the probative value of the proffered evidence in determining whether it should be excluded under the Article 403 balancing test.

---

23. See State v. Ludwig, 423 So. 2d 1073 (La. 1982), below for an example of how the inferential steps affect probative value of evidence.

24. State v. Ludwig, 423 So. 2d 1073 (La. 1982).

25. See Old Chief v. United States, 519 U.S. 172 (1997), below.

Unfairly Prejudicial. On the other side of the Article 403 balancing test is the prejudicial effect of the evidence. While all evidence offered against a party is said to be prejudicial to them, evidence will only be excluded if it is *unfairly* prejudicial. Evidence is said to be *unfairly* prejudicial if it has **"an undue tendency to suggest decision on an improper basis, commonly, though not necessarily, an emotional one,"**[26] such as based on passion, prejudice, bias, etc. It has also been defined as "evidence that makes conviction more likely because it provokes an emotional response in the jury or otherwise tends to affect adversely the jury's attitude toward the defendant wholly apart from its judgment as to his guilt or innocence of the crime charged."[27]

Evidence of a defendant's character or the fact that he may have committed other crimes is generally excluded because of its tendency to make a jury convict merely because they perceive the defendant as a bad person, rather than based on the evidence before them. Similarly, gruesome photos that depict blood or gruesome details may invoke an emotional response in jurors that could cause them to convict based on passion rather than on the evidence.

While such evidence might have the potential to be unfairly prejudicial, i.e., have the tendency to lead the jury to decide the case based on passion, emotion, etc., the evidence is not automatically excluded. Such evidence is only excluded under Article 403 if its probative value, toward proving/disproving a consequential fact, is substantially outweighed by the danger of unfair prejudice. In such a case, the evidence is said to have failed the Article 403 balancing test. This is an evidentiary determination made by the trial judge and depends upon the facts of each case.

Article 403 also excludes evidence if the probative value is substantially outweighed by confusion of the issues, misleading the jury, or by considerations of undue delay, or waste of time. Those concepts are discussed further below in § 3.2.1–§ 3.2.6.

Cases on Excluding Relevant Evidence under Article 403

State v. Ludwig[28] provides an excellent analysis of assessing the probative value of evidence by considering the inferential steps between the evidence sought to be admitted and the legal proposition the evidence is being offered to prove. Assessing the probative value of evidence is an important component of applying the Article 403 balancing test.

State v. Ludwig

Supreme Court of Louisiana
423 So. 2d 1073
Nov. 29, 1982

DENNIS, Justice.

On December 7, 1979, the body of Stephen Harr was found on a street in Jefferson Parish. He had been shot four times in the head and neck. The investigating police officers found a key to Room 31 of the nearby Holiday Motel in the victim's pocket. One of the

26. *See* Fed. R. Evid. 403 advisory committee notes.

27. U.S. v. Bailleaux, 685 F. 2d 1105 (9th Cir. 1982); *See also* State v. Rose, 949 So. 2d 1236 (2007) (explaining the term "prejudicial effect" of other crimes as it pertains to a criminal case, as a "substantial risk of grave prejudice to the defendant").

28. State v. Ludwig, 423 So. 2d 1073 (La. 1982).

officers, Detective Hidding, proceeded to the manager's office at the motel. The manager informed Hidding of an altercation earlier in the evening at a local lounge between the victim and a man named Ludwig, who lived in Room 11. Hidding went to Room 31, but got no response. In front of Room 11 he saw blood on the porch and in the parking lot. A spent .25 caliber casing lay on the ground nearby. Hidding knocked on the door of Room 11, but received no response, although he could hear the sound of a television inside the room.

The officer had the manager open the door with a pass key. When Hidding and other police officers entered, they observed beer cans, .25 caliber shells and spent casings scattered about the room. There was a spot of blood on one piece of furniture. A cedar chest had been shot several times. After finding that no one was there, the officers left without touching anything, and secured the door.

The manager informed Detective Hidding that the occupant of Room 11 was Alfred Ludwig. A short time later, Hidding observed a man get out of a pickup camper parked in the motel parking lot. The officer approached the man who identified himself as Alfred Ludwig and who confirmed that he was the occupant of Room 11. Detective Hidding then advised Ludwig of his constitutional rights. Although he appeared to have been drinking, Ludwig responded coherently to Hidding's questions. He said he did not know where his car was and that he was not acquainted with Stephen Harr, the victim.

... Just before being transported to the Jefferson Parish Correctional Center, Ludwig informed the officers that his automobile was parked in front of the motel. He handed them the car keys, gave them consent to search the vehicle, and signed another consent to search form. The officers noticed blood on the rear bumper of the automobile. Inside the trunk they discovered a substantial amount of blood.

Under interrogation at the Correctional Center, Ludwig made several incriminating remarks. He stated that he had gotten rid of the weapon where no one would find it. He also stated that the victim's wife had killed Harr in Ludwig's room with Ludwig's gun and then told Ludwig to dispose of the victim's body.

Ludwig's first trial for first degree murder ended in a mistrial. However, he was subsequently indicted for second degree murder and in September, 1980 was found guilty as charged. He was sentenced to life imprisonment without benefit of probation, parole, or suspension of sentence ...

ASSIGNMENT OF ERROR NUMBER TWO

By this assignment of error the defendant contends that the trial court erred in denying him an opportunity to present evidence that the victim's wife had shot the victim in his foot or leg some six months prior to the night of the murder with which the defendant was charged. In his proffer, the defense lawyer did not specify if the evidence would indicate whether the shooting had been intentional or accidental or any other circumstances of the incident.

The defendant attempted to present evidence of the prior shooting several times during the trial. He first sought to elicit the evidence during the cross-examination of Detective Hidding concerning his investigation of Mrs. Harr's possible implication in the charged offense. The trial court sustained the state's objection on the ground that the evidence was not relevant. The defendant next called the victim's wife as a witness, and, outside the jury's presence, requested permission to question her on redirect examination about the prior shooting. After objection by the state, the trial judge ruled that the evidence was irrelevant and constituted impermissible impeachment by the defendant of his own witness. Finally, the defendant attempted to introduce the written police report of the earlier shooting and testimony of the police officer who investigated the prior incident. However, the trial court ruled that this evidence was irrelevant and hearsay.

All evidence which is relevant to a material issue, necessary to be known to explain a relevant fact, or which supports an inference raised by such a fact, is admissible, … except as otherwise provided by the constitution of the United States or this state, by law or by rule of this court.… Relevant evidence is defined by our law as "that tending to show the commission of the offense and the intent, or tending to negative the commission of the offense and the intent." Relevancy of evidence is determined by the purpose for which it is offered …

Applying these precepts to the present case, we conclude that the trial court was in error in finding that the evidence was not relevant. The evidence does have a slight tendency to make the fact that Mrs. Harr fatally shot her husband more probable than it would be without the evidence.

Nevertheless, we think that he properly excluded the evidence because its slight probative value was substantially outweighed by the risk that its admission would consume too much time, unnecessarily confuse the jury concerning the issues to be determined, and tend to excite the emotions of the jury to the undue prejudice of the opponent. See *State v. Moore*, 278 So. 2d 781 (1973).

In this case in which the contested proposition is whether the defendant is the person who killed Stephen Harr, and the evidence proffered is that six months before the homicide, Harr's wife had shot him in the leg or foot, the inferences which the defendant sought to invite from the jury were that (1) because Harr's wife shot him on the previous occasion and was a beneficiary of his life insurance policy, (2) she intended to kill him at that time, (3) she continued in her desire to get rid of him for the next six months, (4) she formulated a plan to kill her husband and blame it on another person, (5) she in fact executed her plan by killing him in defendant's motel room with defendant's gun after a quarrel between the two men, and (6) she persuaded the defendant to use his own car to dispose of the body and the murder weapon. The unarticulated premises conjoined with and supposed to justify the inferential steps are: (1) a woman who shoots her husband in the leg or foot, whether the injury appears to have been intentional or accidental, is more likely to have intended to kill him for his life insurance than a person of whom nothing is known; (2) it is also more likely that she would persist in her intention to kill her husband for six months after the shooting; (3) it is similarly more likely that she would conceive a plan to kill her husband that would place the guilt on the defendant, (4) and the fact that she had either accidentally or intentionally shot her husband six months before makes it more likely that she would execute her plan by shooting her husband to death in the defendant's room after the two men had quarreled and persuade the defendant to use his car to dispose of the body and the weapon. Obviously, the value of the first item of evidence as probative of the fact that Harr's wife, and not the defendant, killed Harr, varies inversely with the number and dubiousness of the intervening inferences. The reasoning is progressively attenuated and is fractionalized at several successive points.

It is generally accepted that the trial judge should exclude circumstantial evidence, even though logically relevant, if its probative value is outweighed by the risk that its admission will consume too much time, unnecessarily confuse the jury concerning the issues to be determined, tend to excite the emotions of the jury to the undue prejudice of the opponent, or unfairly surprise the opponent.… The probative value of evidence of a possibly accidental shooting six months before the charged offense was substantially outweighed by the danger of unfair prejudice, confusion of the issues, misleading the jury, and undue delay or waste of time. Accordingly, the evidence was properly excluded by the trial court despite the fact that it was relevant and of some slight probative value.

Defendant argues that the trial court's exclusion of the evidence violated his federal and state constitutional rights to present a defense and to confront and cross-examine his accusers. These constitutional guarantees do not, however, require a trial court to permit the introduction of evidence that is irrelevant or which has so little probative value that it is substantially outweighed by other legitimate considerations in the administration of justice. For example, in *Chambers v. Mississippi,* 410 U.S. 284, 93 S.Ct. 1038, 35 L.Ed.2d 297 (1973) [leading constitutional case regarding a defendant's right to present a defense], upon which defendant relies primarily, the evidence which the high court held had been unconstitutionally excluded was highly relevant and "critical to Chambers' defense." 410 U.S. at 302, 93 S.Ct. at 1049. The proffered evidence included: (a) The cross-examination of trial witness McDonald concerning his confession to the very crime for which defendant Chambers was on trial and (b) the examination of three other witnesses who would testify to McDonald's confessions to the crime on separate occasions and to corroborating circumstances. The evidence was, of course, extremely relevant, because it related to the crime for which the defendant was on trial and tended to completely exculpate him. The fact that the evidence was highly probative of a very consequential fact was an essential ingredient in the high court's determination that Mississippi deprived Chambers of a fair trial by excluding critical evidence under its voucher and hearsay rules. In the present case, the evidence which the defendant sought to introduce was at most of only slight probative value because it concerned a shooting which occurred six months before the charged offense involving a leg or foot wound which may have been unintentional under the terms of the proffer.

Other states allow the introduction of evidence incriminating a third person only when such third person has been closely linked to the commission of the crime. See Wharton, Criminal Evidence § 195 (1972). One early Louisiana case stated a broad rule which allows evidence incriminating a third person when such evidence would establish a reasonable hypothesis of that person's guilt or a reasonable doubt of the guilt of the defendant. *State v. Jenkins,* 134 La. 185, 63 So. 869 (1913). This early expressed, less vigorous, rule of Louisiana arguably has validity in Louisiana today through the constitutionally guaranteed "right to represent a defense" of Art. I, § 16 of the Louisiana Constitution of 1974. However, even this test is not met in the present case because the mere evidence of the earlier incident between the victim and his wife does not establish a reasonable hypothesis of her guilt nor does it create a reasonable doubt as to the defendant's guilt.

Discussion Questions

1. Was the evidence that the victim's wife shot him in the foot or leg six months prior to the instant offense relevant under Art. 401? Why or why not? Do you agree with the court?
2. The court in *Ludwig* finds that the evidence fails the Article 403 balancing test. Articulate the test applied by the court. How does the court assess the probative value of the proffered evidence? Discuss its prejudicial effect. Do you agree with the court's finding under the Article 403 balancing test?
3. What test do you take from *Ludwig* as to how to assess probative value?
4. The *Ludwig* court also addresses an appropriate test for when evidence that a third person committed the crime may be offered, similar to the issue discussed in *State v.*

Mosby[29] supra. What test is articulated by the court as to when such third party evidence is relevant in a case?

State v. Harris

Supreme Court of Louisiana
381 So. 2d 792
Feb. 15, 1980

DENNIS, Justice

This criminal appeal calls upon us to decide when evidence of an attempted escape by a person in custody may be introduced as an admission of guilt by conduct of the crime for which he was arrested. Since evidence of an attempted escape constitutes other crimes evidence, we conclude that unless the evidence forms part of the res gestae of the charged offense, it may be introduced only if it is probative of defendant's consciousness of guilt of the crime charged and its probative value outweighs its prejudicial effects. In the present case, evidence of defendant Harris' attempted escape, which occurred while he was being transported from jail to a hospital over six weeks after his arrest for the crime charged, was clearly not sufficiently probative of his consciousness of guilt of the crime charged to outweigh its prejudicial effects. Accordingly, the trial court's refusal to grant a mistrial because of the prosecuting attorney's reference to the attempted escape in the presence of the jury was reversible error.

Defendant, Grady E. Harris, was convicted by a jury of armed robbery, La.R.S. 14:64, and sentenced to serve forty years at hard labor ...

Defendant Harris was arrested and charged with the crime of armed robbery. After he had been incarcerated in the Bossier Parish Jail for six weeks, he was taken to a hospital in Shreveport for treatment. En route to the hospital, at an interstate highway exit ramp, Harris jumped from the police car and attempted to flee, but was apprehended quickly by the officers. At the armed robbery trial, when the prosecuting attorney asked Harris, on cross-examination, if he jumped from the car and ran, the trial judge sustained defense counsel's objection and admonished the jury to ignore the remark. However, the defense motion for a mistrial was overruled.

The prosecuting attorney's remark, which referred within the hearing of the jury to another crime committed by the defendant as to which evidence was not admissible, was mandatory ground for a mistrial; an admonition to the jury to disregard the remark was not sufficient. See La.C.Cr.P. art. 770. The defendant's conduct referred to by the prosecutor was "another crime" because an intentional departure of a person in lawful custody of any law enforcement officer constitutes simple escape. La.R.S. 14:110 ...

The prosecution may not introduce evidence of other criminal acts of the accused unless the evidence is substantially relevant for some other purpose than to show a probability that he committed the crime on trial because he is a man of criminal character ...

[E]vidence of an accused's escape or attempted escape may, in compliance with applicable safeguards, be introduced to show his admission of guilt by conduct. By the same token, however, evidence of escape must be excluded if its admission would violate any of the rules protecting a defendant from unfair prejudice.

---

29. State v. Mosby, 581 So. 2d 1060 (La. Ct. App. 1st Cir. 1991).

Applying these rules to the present case, we conclude that the evidence of attempted escape by Harris did not form part of the res gestae, that it had no significant probative value as circumstantial evidence of his guilt, ad that its prejudicial effect clearly outweighed its probative value.

Defendant's flight, a momentary departure from a vehicle transporting him from jail to a hospital for treatment which occurred over six weeks after his arrest for armed robbery, was not significantly probative of his guilt, since it may have been motivated by many other reasons, such as prison or hospital conditions, a simple desire for freedom, or a lack of confidence in his right to a fair and speedy trial. Accordingly, while there was no question of defendant's attempted escape, consciousness of guilt of the crime charged reasonably could not be inferred from his flight, and the prejudicial effect of the evidence clearly outweighed its probative value ...

The conviction and sentence of defendant Grady E. Harris are reversed and a new trial is ordered.

Discussion Questions

1. Applying the Article 403 balancing test to the proffered evidence in *Harris*, is evidence of the escape probative of "consciousness of guilt" at all, i.e., is it relevant? Why or why not? What is the potential prejudicial effect of offering the evidence?
2. Compare this case to *Davies*, *supra*. How do the cases differ? Why would *Davies* pass the Article 403 balancing test and *Harris* does not?

§ 3.2.1 Prejudicial Effect of "Other Crimes" and Effect of Stipulation

One type of evidence that is most often objected to on the grounds that it is unfairly prejudicial is evidence of "other crimes" offered against a defendant in a criminal case. Article 404 specifically excludes evidence of other crimes, wrongs, or acts from being offered against an accused because of its potential to cause the trier of fact to convict the defendant on an improper basis—here, their belief that the accused is a bad person who likely acted in conformity with the bad character in the case at hand. Thus, such evidence is generally excluded. However, the law specifically provides for situations in which evidence of other crimes may be admissible for other purposes that are relevant in the case at hand.[30] Even then, the probative value toward the relevant purpose for which it is offered must outweigh the risk of prejudice to the defendant.

In *Old Chief v. United States*[31] and *State v. Ball* below, the United States and Louisiana Supreme Courts address the prejudicial impact of "other crimes evidence" when it is a relevant element of the crime charged (possession of a firearm by a convicted felon), and also addresses the impact that a stipulation to such other crimes will have on the probative value of the proffered evidence under an Article 403 balancing test. The United States Supreme Court arrives at a different conclusion in *Old Chief* than the Louisiana Supreme Court arrives in *Ball*. As you read the cases, consider the various issues the courts deem relevant in assessing the prejudicial impact of the other crimes evidence, in light of the stipulation, when applying the Article 403 balancing test.

---

30. The full scope of the admissibility of "other crimes, wrongs, or acts" is fully discussed in Chapter 6, *infra*.
31. Old Chief v. United States, 519 U.S. 172 (1997).

Old Chief v. United States [II]
Supreme Court of the United States
519 U.S. 172, 117 S.Ct. 644 (1997)

Justice SOUTER delivered the opinion of the Court.

[For the facts and the ruling as to the evidence's logical relevance, see *Old Chief* I, *supra* § 3.1.]

... If, then, relevant evidence is inadmissible in the presence of other evidence related to it, its exclusion must rest not on the ground that the other evidence has rendered it "irrelevant," but on its character as unfairly prejudicial, cumulative or the like, its relevance notwithstanding ...

B

The principal issue is the scope of a trial judge's discretion under Rule 403, which authorizes exclusion of relevant evidence when its "probative value is substantially outweighed by the danger of unfair prejudice, confusion of the issues, or misleading the jury, or by considerations of undue delay, waste of time, or needless presentation of cumulative evidence." Fed. Rule Evid. 403. Old Chief relies on the danger of unfair prejudice.

1

The term "unfair prejudice," as to a criminal defendant, speaks to the capacity of some concededly relevant evidence to lure the factfinder into declaring guilt on a ground different from proof specific to the offense charged.... So, the Committee Notes to Rule 403 explain, " 'Unfair prejudice' within its context means an undue tendency to suggest decision on an improper basis, commonly, though not necessarily, an emotional one." ...

Such improper grounds certainly include the one that Old Chief points to here: generalizing a defendant's earlier bad act into bad character and taking that as raising the odds that he did the later bad act now charged (or, worse, as calling for preventive conviction even if he should happen to be innocent momentarily). As then-Judge Breyer put it, "Although ... 'propensity evidence' is relevant, the risk that a jury will convict for crimes other than those charged—or that, uncertain of guilt, it will convict anyway because a bad person deserves punishment—creates a prejudicial effect that outweighs ordinary relevance." ... Justice Jackson described how the law has handled this risk:

> "Courts that follow the common-law tradition almost unanimously have come to disallow resort by the prosecution to any kind of evidence of a defendant's evil character to establish a probability of his guilt. Not that the law invests the defendant with a presumption of good character, but it simply closes the whole matter of character, disposition and reputation on the prosecution's case-in-chief. The state may not show defendant's prior trouble with the law, specific criminal acts, or ill name among his neighbors, even though such facts might logically be persuasive that he is by propensity a probable perpetrator of the crime. The inquiry is not rejected because character is irrelevant; on the contrary, it is said to weigh too much with the jury and to so overpersuade them as to prejudge one with a bad general record and deny him a fair opportunity to defend against a particular charge. The overriding policy of excluding such evidence, despite its admitted probative value, is the practical experience that its disallowance tends to prevent confusion of issues, unfair surprise and undue prejudice." *Michel-*

son v. United States, 335 U.S. 469, 475–476, 69 S.Ct. 213, 218-219, 93 L.Ed. 168 (1948) (footnotes omitted).

Rule of Evidence 404(b) reflects this common-law tradition by addressing propensity reasoning directly: "Evidence of other crimes, wrongs, or acts is not admissible to prove the character of a person in order to show action in conformity therewith." Fed. Rule Evid. 404(b). There is, accordingly, no question that propensity would be an "improper basis" for conviction and that evidence of a prior conviction is subject to analysis under Rule 403 for relative probative value and for prejudicial risk of misuse as propensity evidence. Cf. 1 J. Strong, McCormick on Evidence 780 (4th ed.1992) (hereinafter McCormick) (Rule 403 prejudice may occur, for example, when "evidence of convictions for prior, unrelated crimes may lead a juror to think that since the defendant already has a criminal record, an erroneous conviction would not be quite as serious as would otherwise be the case").

As for the analytical method to be used in Rule 403 balancing, two basic possibilities present themselves. (1) An item of evidence might be viewed as an island, with estimates of its own probative value and unfairly prejudicial risk the sole reference points in deciding whether the danger substantially outweighs the value and whether the evidence ought to be excluded.

Or (2) the question of admissibility might be seen as inviting further comparisons to take account of the full evidentiary context of the case as the court understands it when the ruling must be made. This second approach would start out like the first but be ready to go further. On objection, the court would decide whether a particular item of evidence raised a danger of unfair prejudice. If it did, the judge would go on to evaluate the degrees of probative value and unfair prejudice not only for the item in question but for any actually available substitutes as well. If an alternative were found to have substantially the same or greater probative value but a lower danger of unfair prejudice, sound judicial discretion would discount the value of the item first offered and exclude it if its discounted probative value were substantially outweighed by unfairly prejudicial risk.

As we will explain later on, the judge would have to make these calculations with an appreciation of the offering party's need for evidentiary richness and narrative integrity in presenting a case, and the mere fact that two pieces of evidence might go to the same point would not, of course, necessarily mean that only one of them might come in. It would only mean that a judge applying Rule 403 could reasonably apply some discount to the probative value of an item of evidence when faced with less risky alternative proof going to the same point.

Even under this second approach, as we explain below, a defendant's Rule 403 objection offering to concede a point generally cannot prevail over the Government's choice to offer evidence showing guilt and all the circumstances surrounding the offense.[7]

The first understanding of the Rule is open to a very telling objection. That reading would leave the party offering evidence with the option to structure a trial in whatever way would produce the maximum unfair prejudice consistent with relevance. He could choose the available alternative carrying the greatest threat of improper influence, despite the availability of less prejudicial but equally probative evidence. The worst he would have to fear would

7. While our discussion has been general because of the general wording of Rule 403, our holding is limited to cases involving proof of felon status. On appellate review of a Rule 403 decision, a defendant must establish abuse of discretion, a standard that is not satisfied by a mere showing of some alternative means of proof that the prosecution in its broad discretion chose not to rely upon.

be a ruling sustaining a Rule 403 objection, and if that occurred, he could simply fall back to offering substitute evidence. This would be a strange rule. It would be very odd for the law of evidence to recognize the danger of unfair prejudice only to confer such a degree of autonomy on the party subject to temptation, and the Rules of Evidence are not so odd.

Rather, a reading of the companions to Rule 403, and of the commentaries that went with them to Congress, makes it clear that what counts as the Rule 403 "probative value" of an item of evidence, as distinct from its Rule 401 "relevance," may be calculated by comparing evidentiary alternatives. The Committee Notes to Rule 401 explicitly say that a party's concession is pertinent to the court's discretion to exclude evidence on the point conceded. Such a concession, according to the Notes, will sometimes "call for the exclusion of evidence offered to prove [the] point conceded by the opponent...." As already mentioned, the Notes make it clear that such rulings should be made not on the basis of Rule 401 relevance but on "such considerations as waste of time and undue prejudice (see Rule 403)...." *Ibid.* The Notes to Rule 403 then take up the point by stating that when a court considers "whether to exclude on grounds of unfair prejudice," the "availability of other means of proof may ... be an appropriate factor." The point gets a reprise in the Notes to Rule 404(b), dealing with admissibility when a given evidentiary item has the dual nature of legitimate evidence of an element and illegitimate evidence of character: "No mechanical solution is offered. The determination must be made whether the danger of undue prejudice outweighs the probative value of the evidence in view of the availability of other means of proof and other facts appropriate for making decision of this kind under 403." Thus the notes leave no question that when Rule 403 confers discretion by providing that evidence "may" be excluded, the discretionary judgment may be informed not only by assessing an evidentiary item's twin tendencies, but by placing the result of that assessment alongside similar assessments of evidentiary alternatives. See 22 C. Wright & K. Graham, Federal Practice and Procedure § 5250, pp. 546–547 (1978) ("The probative worth of any particular bit of evidence is obviously affected by the scarcity or abundance of other evidence on the same point").

2

In dealing with the specific problem raised by § 922(g)(1) and its prior-conviction element, there can be no question that evidence of the name or nature of the prior offense generally carries a risk of unfair prejudice to the defendant. That risk will vary from case to case, for the reasons already given, but will be substantial whenever the official record offered by the Government would be arresting enough to lure a juror into a sequence of bad character reasoning. Where a prior conviction was for a gun crime or one similar to other charges in a pending case the risk of unfair prejudice would be especially obvious, and Old Chief sensibly worried that the prejudicial effect of his prior assault conviction, significant enough with respect to the current gun charges alone, would take on added weight from the related assault charge against him.[8]

8. It is true that a prior offense may be so far removed in time or nature from the current gun charge and any others brought with it that its potential to prejudice the defendant unfairly will be minimal. Some prior offenses, in fact, may even have some potential to prejudice the Government's case unfairly. Thus an extremely old conviction for a relatively minor felony that nevertheless qualifies under the statute might strike many jurors as a foolish basis for convicting an otherwise upstanding member of the community of otherwise legal gun possession. Since the Government could not, of course, compel the defendant to admit formally the existence of the prior conviction, the Government would have to bear the risk of jury nullification, a fact that might properly drive the Government's charging decision.

The District Court was also presented with alternative, relevant, admissible evidence of the prior conviction by Old Chief's offer to stipulate, evidence necessarily subject to the District Court's consideration on the motion to exclude the record offered by the Government. Although Old Chief's formal offer to stipulate was, strictly, to enter a formal agreement with the Government to be given to the jury, even without the Government's acceptance his proposal amounted to an offer to admit that the prior-conviction element was satisfied, and a defendant's admission is, of course, good evidence.

Old Chief's proffered admission would, in fact, have been not merely relevant but seemingly conclusive evidence of the element. The statutory language in which the prior-conviction requirement is couched shows no congressional concern with the specific name or nature of the prior offense beyond what is necessary to place it within the broad category of qualifying felonies, and Old Chief clearly meant to admit that his felony did qualify, by stipulating "that the Government has proven one of the essential elements of the offense." As a consequence, although the name of the prior offense may have been technically relevant, it addressed no detail in the definition of the prior-conviction element that would not have been covered by the stipulation or admission. Logic, then, seems to side with Old Chief.

3

There is, however, one more question to be considered before deciding whether Old Chief's offer was to supply evidentiary value at least equivalent to what the Government's own evidence carried. In arguing that the stipulation or admission would not have carried equivalent value, the Government invokes the familiar, standard rule that the prosecution is entitled to prove its case by evidence of its own choice, or, more exactly, that a criminal defendant may not stipulate or admit his way out of the full evidentiary force of the case as the Government chooses to present it. The authority usually cited for this rule is *Parr v. United States,* 255 F.2d 86 (CA5), *cert. denied*, 358 U.S. 824, 79 S.Ct. 40, 3 L.Ed.2d 64 (1958), in which the Fifth Circuit explained that the "reason for the rule is to permit a party 'to present to the jury a picture of the events relied upon. To substitute for such a picture a naked admission might have the effect to rob the evidence of much of its fair and legitimate weight.'"

This is unquestionably true as a general matter. The "fair and legitimate weight" of conventional evidence showing individual thoughts and acts amounting to a crime reflects the fact that making a case with testimony and tangible things not only satisfies the formal definition of an offense, but tells a colorful story with descriptive richness. Unlike an abstract premise, whose force depends on going precisely to a particular step in a course of reasoning, a piece of evidence may address any number of separate elements, striking hard just because it shows so much at once; the account of a shooting that establishes capacity and causation may tell just as much about the triggerman's motive and intent. Evidence thus has force beyond any linear scheme of reasoning, and as its pieces come together a narrative gains momentum, with power not only to support conclusions but to sustain the willingness of jurors to draw the inferences, whatever they may be, necessary to reach an honest verdict. This persuasive power of the concrete and particular is often essential to the capacity of jurors to satisfy the obligations that the law places on them. Jury duty is usually unsought and sometimes resisted, and it may be as difficult for one juror suddenly to face the findings that can send another human being to prison, as it is for another to hold out conscientiously for acquittal. When a juror's duty does seem hard, the evidentiary account of what a defendant has thought and done can accomplish what no set of abstract statements ever could, not just to prove a fact but to establish its human significance and so to implicate the law's moral underpinnings and a juror's obligation to sit in judgment. Thus, the prosecution may fairly seek to place its evidence before the jurors, as much to tell a story of guiltiness as to support an inference of guilt, to convince the jurors that a guilty verdict would be morally reasonable as much as to point to the discrete elements of a defendant's legal fault.

But there is something even more to the prosecution's interest in resisting efforts to replace the evidence of its choice with admissions and stipulations, for beyond the power of conventional evidence to support allegations and give life to the moral underpinnings of law's claims, there lies the need for evidence in all its particularity to satisfy the jurors' expectations about what proper proof should be. Some such demands they bring with them to the courthouse, assuming, for example, that a charge of using a firearm to commit an offense will be proven by introducing a gun in evidence. A prosecutor who fails to produce one, or some good reason for his failure, has something to be concerned about. "If [jurors'] expectations are not satisfied, triers of fact may penalize the party who disappoints them by drawing a negative inference against that party." Saltzburg, A Special Aspect of Relevance: Countering Negative Inferences Associated with the Absence of Evidence, 66 Calif. L.Rev. 1011, 1019 (1978) (footnotes omitted).[9]

Expectations may also arise in jurors' minds simply from the experience of a trial itself. The use of witnesses to describe a train of events naturally related can raise the prospect of learning about every ingredient of that natural sequence the same way. If suddenly the prosecution presents some occurrence in the series differently, as by announcing a stipulation or admission, the effect may be like saying, "never mind what's behind the door," and jurors may well wonder what they are being kept from knowing. A party seemingly responsible for cloaking something has reason for apprehension, and the prosecution with its burden of proof may prudently demur at a defense request to interrupt the flow of evidence telling the story in the usual way.

In sum, the accepted rule that the prosecution is entitled to prove its case free from any defendant's option to stipulate the evidence away rests on good sense. A syllogism is not a story, and a naked proposition in a courtroom may be no match for the robust evidence that would be used to prove it. People who hear a story interrupted by gaps of abstraction may be puzzled at the missing chapters, and jurors asked to rest a momentous decision on the story's truth can feel put upon at being asked to take responsibility knowing that more could be said than they have heard. A convincing tale can be told with economy, but when economy becomes a break in the natural sequence of narrative evidence, an assurance that the missing link is really there is never more than second best.

---

9. Cf. Green, "The Whole Truth?": How Rules of Evidence Make Lawyers Deceitful, 25 Loyola (LA) L.Rev. 699, 703 (1992) ("[E]videntiary rules ... predicated in large measure on the law's distrust of juries [can] have the unintended, and perhaps ironic, result of encouraging the jury's distrust of lawyers. The rules do so by fostering the perception that lawyers are deliberately withholding evidence" (footnote omitted)). The fact that juries have expectations as to what evidence ought to be presented by a party, and may well hold the absence of that evidence against the party, is also recognized in the case law of the Fifth Amendment, which explicitly supposes that, despite the venerable history of the privilege against self-incrimination, jurors may not recall that someone accused of crime need not explain the evidence or avow innocence beyond making his plea. The assumption that jurors may have contrary expectations and be moved to draw adverse inferences against the party who disappoints them undergirds the rule that a defendant can demand an instruction forbidding the jury to draw such an inference.

4

This recognition that the prosecution with its burden of persuasion needs evidentiary depth to tell a continuous story has, however, virtually no application when the point at issue is a defendant's legal status, dependent on some judgment rendered wholly independently of the concrete events of later criminal behavior charged against him. As in this case, the choice of evidence for such an element is usually not between eventful narrative and abstract proposition, but between propositions of slightly varying abstraction, either a record saying that conviction for some crime occurred at a certain time or a statement admitting the same thing without naming the particular offense. The issue of substituting one statement for the other normally arises only when the record of conviction would not be admissible for any purpose beyond proving status, so that excluding it would not deprive the prosecution of evidence with multiple utility; if, indeed, there were a justification for receiving evidence of the nature of prior acts on some issue other than status (*i.e.*, to prove "motive, opportunity, intent, preparation, plan, knowledge, identity, or absence of mistake or accident," Rule 404(b) guarantees the opportunity to seek its admission. Nor can it be argued that the events behind the prior conviction are proper nourishment for the jurors' sense of obligation to vindicate the public interest. The issue is not whether concrete details of the prior crime should come to the jurors' attention but whether the name or general character of that crime is to be disclosed. Congress, however, has made it plain that distinctions among generic felonies do not count for this purpose; the fact of the qualifying conviction is alone what matters under the statute. "A defendant falls within the category simply by virtue of past conviction for any [qualifying] crime ranging from possession of short lobsters to the most aggravated murder." The most the jury needs to know is that the conviction admitted by the defendant falls within the class of crimes that Congress thought should bar a convict from possessing a gun, and this point may be made readily in a defendant's admission and underscored in the court's jury instructions.

Finally, the most obvious reason that the general presumption that the prosecution may choose its evidence is so remote from application here is that proof of the defendant's status goes to an element entirely outside the natural sequence of what the defendant is charged with thinking and doing to commit the current offense. Proving status without telling exactly why that status was imposed leaves no gap in the story of a defendant's subsequent criminality, and its demonstration by stipulation or admission neither displaces a chapter from a continuous sequence of conventional evidence nor comes across as an officious substitution, to confuse or offend or provoke reproach.

... In this case, as in any other in which the prior conviction is for an offense likely to support conviction on some improper ground, the only reasonable conclusion was that the risk of unfair prejudice did substantially outweigh the discounted probative value of the record of conviction, and it was an abuse of discretion to admit the record when an admission was available.[10]

The judgment is reversed, and the case is remanded to the Ninth Circuit for further proceedings consistent with this opinion.

---

10. There may be yet other means of proof besides a formal admission on the record that, with a proper objection, will obligate a district court to exclude evidence of the name of the offense. A redacted record of conviction is the one most frequently mentioned.

Justice O'CONNOR, with whom THE CHIEF JUSTICE, Justice SCALIA, and Justice THOMAS join, dissenting.

The Court today announces a rule that misapplies Federal Rule of Evidence 403 and upsets, without explanation, longstanding precedent regarding criminal prosecutions. I do not agree that the Government's introduction of evidence that reveals the name and basic nature of a defendant's prior felony conviction in a prosecution brought under 18 U.S.C. § 922(g)(1) "unfairly" prejudices the defendant within the meaning of Rule 403. Nor do I agree with the Court's newly minted rule that a defendant charged with violating § 922(g)(1) can force the Government to accept his concession to the prior conviction element of that offense, thereby precluding the Government from offering evidence on this point. I therefore dissent. [A lengthy discussion follows].

Discussion Questions

1. How does an offer to stipulate affect the Article 403 balancing test? How does the stipulation factor into the overall probative value of evidence of the actual name and nature of the crime? Does it also affect the prejudicial effect of the evidence? How so?
2. What does the court mean by the "twin tendencies of evidence," and what role does the concept play in assessing the probative value of evidence?
3. What makes offering other crimes against a defendant prejudicial? Will other crimes always be "unfairly" prejudicial? What factors should be considered when making such a determination?
4. What does the court mean by the "evidentiary value" of evidence? How does that concept play into the Article 403 balancing test?
5. What specific factors does the court consider in determining if the probative value of evidence is outweighed by unfair prejudice?

State v. Ball

Supreme Court of Louisiana
756 So. 2d 275
November 30, 1999

VICTORY, Judge.

Ricko C. Ball, convicted of a violation of La. R.S. 14:95.1, possession of a firearm by a convicted felon, claims that because he offered to stipulate at trial he had been convicted of a prior felony offense listed in La. R.S. 14:95.1, it was error for the trial court to allow the state to introduce evidence of the name and nature of the prior offense. After reviewing the record and the applicable law, we affirm the judgment of the lower courts.

FACTS AND PROCEDURAL HISTORY

On the morning of November 4, 1996, Mary Upton discovered that her Plymouth minivan, which had been parked in front of her son's truck in her driveway, was missing. Her son's truck had been pushed out of the way and the side window pushed open. Several items were stolen from the truck, including the keys to the minivan, stereo equipment, a shotgun and a rifle. Three hours later, a Shreveport police officer spotted the minivan, but the driver/defendant refused to stop, leading the police on a high speed chase which ended when the minivan ran into a ditch. The defendant fled on foot but was apprehended by police. In plain view on the floorboard of the minivan between the front bucket seats, police found the rifle and shotgun. The key in the ignition was the key that had been stolen from the son's truck. Fingerprints taken from the window of the truck matched defendant's fingerprints. Upon learning he had pleaded guilty to simple burglary of an inhabited dwelling in Bossier Parish in 1993, the district attorney charged and tried the defendant as a felon in possession of a firearm in violation of La. R.S. 14:95.1.

Before the commencement of the trial, defendant unsuccessfully filed a Motion in Limine offering to stipulate that he had been convicted of a felony that was a predicate offense under La. R.S. 14:95.1 and asked that the state be precluded from introducing evidence of his prior conviction. At trial, the state introduced the bill of information, minutes, and guilty plea transcript from defendant's prior simple burglary of an inhabited dwelling conviction. In addition, his fingerprints were matched to those found on the back of the prior bill of information. After the jury found him guilty as charged, the trial judge sentenced him to 13 years at hard labor without benefit of probation, parole or suspension of sentence, and assessed a $1,000 fine.

The court of appeal affirmed his conviction and sentence. We granted defendant's writ to consider whether the lower courts erred in allowing the state to introduce evidence of the name and nature of the defendant's prior conviction of simple burglary of an inhabited dwelling when the defendant had offered to stipulate that he had been convicted of a prior felony.

DISCUSSION

The law prohibiting certain felons from possessing firearms is codified in La. R.S. 14:95.1 and reads in pertinent part:

> A. It is unlawful for any person who has been convicted of a crime of violence as defined in R.S. 14:2(13)3 which is a felony or simple burglary, burglary of a pharmacy, burglary of an inhabited dwelling, unauthorized entry of an inhabited dwelling, felony illegal use of weapons device, manufacture or possession of a bomb, or any violation of the Uniform Controlled Dangerous Substances Law which is a felony, or any crime defined as an attempt to commit one of the above enumerated offenses under the laws of this state, or who has been convicted under the laws of any other state or of the United States or of any foreign government or country of a crime which, if committed in this state, would be one of the above enumerated crimes, to possess a firearm or carry a concealed weapon.

Possession of a firearm by a convicted felon requires proof of: (1) the possession of a firearm; (2) a previous conviction of an enumerated felony; (3) absence of the 10-year period of limitation; and (4) general intent to commit the offense. La. R.S. 14:95.1; *State v. Husband*, 437 So. 2d 269 (La.1983). We have held that because "[a]n essential element of the crime defined in [La. R.S. 14:95.1] is a defendant's prior conviction for one of the enumerated felonies," the state may introduce evidence of defendant's previous felony convictions as proof of an element of the crime charged and the manner in which the present offense was committed.

Defendant, citing *Old Chief v. United States*, 519 U.S. 172, 117 S.Ct. 644, 136 L.Ed.2d 574 (1997), argues that his trial was tainted by unfair prejudice because the jury was told the name and nature of his previous felony conviction. In *Old Chief*, the defendant, who had previously been convicted of assault causing serious bodily injury, was charged with various federal crimes, including being a felon in possession of a firearm under 18 U.S.C. § 922(g)(1). That statute makes it unlawful for anyone "who has been convicted in any court of a crime punishable by imprisonment for a term exceeding one year" to possess a firearm....

The defendant in *Old Chief* sought a pre-trial ruling to prohibit the government from mentioning or offering any evidence at trial of his prior conviction; in exchange, he offered to stipulate to it. The prosecutor refused to do so, and the district court denied the defendant's motion. Consequently, the government proved the prior conviction to the jury who found Old Chief guilty as charged, and the Court of Appeals affirmed the conviction.

The United States Supreme Court, in a five–four decision, reversed the conviction. The majority accepted Old Chief's argument that evidence of a prior conviction could result in "unfair prejudice," *i.e.*, a tendency to lure the trier of fact into finding guilt on a ground different from proof specific to the offense charged. *Id.* at 180, 117 S.Ct. 644. The Court considered the countervailing principles: (1) the prior offense is unquestionably an essential element of 18 U.S.C. § 922(g)(1); (2) the prosecution traditionally has broad discretion in the manner of presenting evidence; and (3) the prosecution's "burden of persuasion" is normally better served by evidence which "tells a continuous story" rather than a defense stipulation. The Court weighed these probative factors against the risk of unfair prejudice, as required by F.R.E. 403, and concluded that with the "peculiarities of the element of felony-convict status," there is "no cognizable difference between the evidentiary significance of an admission and of the legitimately probative component of the official record the prosecution would prefer to place in evidence." *Id.*, 519 U.S. at 191, 117 S.Ct. 644. The Court concluded that in a felony possession of a firearm case under § 922(g)(1), the federal government may not reject the defendant's offer to stipulate the prior conviction, and evidence of the name and nature of the prior conviction are inadmissible.

We conclude that *Old Chief* is not controlling and decline to follow it for the following reasons. First, the Court's decision was not based on constitutional principles which would be binding on the states, but instead was based on the specific language of 18 U.S.C. § 922. Also, we note that where a state statute is patterned after a federal statute, the United States Supreme Court's interpretation of the federal statute should be a persuasive influence on the interpretation of our own state enactment. *Louisiana Power & Light v. United Gas Pipe Line,* 493 So. 2d 1149, 1158 (La.1986). Although the Louisiana statute was enacted after the federal statute, we have no indication that it was "patterned" after the federal statute and in fact we have held that the Louisiana statute is less restrictive than the federal statute, which applies to all felonies, and does not provide for a prescriptive period. *State v. Williams,* 392 So. 2d 448 (La.1980). In other words, the Louisiana statute does not apply to all felonies, but only to some, and under the Louisiana statute there is a ten year prescriptive period, whereas under the federal statute there is none.

Second, because the Louisiana statute defines the crime by specific enumerated prior offenses, contrary to the broad definition in the federal statute, *Old Chief* is distinguishable. Several courts have declined to adopt *Old Chief* solely because of such a distinction. *See State ex rel. Romley v. Galati, supra; Maibauer v. State,* 968 S.W.2d 502 (Tex.App.Waco 1998); *Sisson v. State,* 232 Ga.App. 61, 499 S.E.2d 422 (1998); *State v. Hamilton,* 327 S.C. 440, 486 S.E.2d 512 (1997), *writ denied, Hamilton v. South Carolina,* 525 U.S. 904, 119 S.Ct. 239, 142 L.Ed.2d 196 (1998). In fact, the language of the majority opinion in *Old Chief* itself makes this distinction:

> Old Chief's proffered admission would, in fact, have been not merely relevant but seemingly conclusive evidence of the element. *The statutory language in which the prior-conviction requirement is couched shows no congressional concern with the specific name or nature of the prior offense beyond what is necessary to place it within the broad category of qualifying felonies,* and Old Chief clearly meant to admit that his felony did qualify, by stipulating "that the Government has proven one of the essential elements of the offense." App. 7. As a consequence, although

> the name of the prior offense may have been technically relevant, *it addressed no detail in the definition of the prior-conviction element that would not have been covered by the stipulation or admission.* Logic, then, seems to side with Old Chief. (Emphasis added).

Old Chief, 519 U.S. at 186, 117 S.Ct. 644. Thus, the majority reasoned that because Congress had made it plain that distinctions among generic felonies were irrelevant for purposes of the crime charged, the most the jury needed to know was that the admitted conviction fell within the class of crimes that Congress felt should bar a convict from possessing a gun. *Id.* at 190–91, 117 S.Ct. 644. To the contrary, under the Louisiana statute, "the statutory language in which the prior conviction requirement is couched" *does* show "concern with the specific name or nature of the prior offense" and the name of the prior offense *does* address a "detail in the definition of the prior conviction element that would not have been covered by the stipulation." Because proof of one of the enumerated felonies is an essential element of the crime under La. R.S. 14:95.1, the probative value of the name and nature of the prior conviction is greater than the "generic" felony required by the federal statute.

Further, we hold that any additional prejudice to defendant by proving to the jury the name of the prior conviction is minimal, that is, it is much less damaging than telling the jury the defendant is a prior felon, which is absolutely essential under our statute and must be covered either by the state's proof or by defendant's stipulation.

We cannot accept the Supreme Court's concerns that the jury will be lured into finding guilt of the instant charge because of the prior conviction. We note that under La. C.E. art. 609.1, evidence of a prior criminal conviction, including its name, is admissible against a testifying criminal defendant upon the issue of his credibility. Yet contrary to the concerns of the five-member majority in *Old Chief,* under these circumstances, the jury's attention is not unduly focused on the prior conviction and the defendant is not unfairly prejudiced because the jury is told why the conviction is admissible and is instructed not to use the evidence of the prior conviction to infer guilt in connection with the present offense. The same principles apply here where a specific prior felony conviction is one element of the present offense under La. R.S. 14:95.1 and the jury is instructed to consider that evidence only with respect to whether that element has been proven and not to infer that defendant is guilty merely because he has a prior felony conviction.[6] In both instances, an admonishment to the jury greatly lessens the danger of unfair prejudice and focuses the jury's attention on the proper issues, not the prior convictions.[7]

---

6. In this case, the jury was given the following limiting instruction:

Mr. Rico Ball is alleged to have possessed a firearm after having been convicted of a felony, namely, simple burglary of an inhabited dwelling. You are instructed that you may consider evidence regarding the simple burglary of an inhabited dwelling conviction only with respect to whether that element of prior convicted of an enumerated felony has been proven for purposes of the charge for which the defendant is now on trial. That is to say, you should not infer or conclude any negative impression solely and only because you may believe that the defendant has a prior felony conviction.

7. In addition, it should be noted that under Louisiana law, other acts or convictions of a defendant are admitted into evidence for purposes other than showing bad character. Specifically, La. C.E. art. 404(B)(1) prevents the introduction of crimes, wrongs, or acts of a defendant to prove his character in order to show he acted in conformity therewith. However, 404(B) does allow the introduction of such evidence for other purposes such as to prove motive, opportunity, intent, preparation, plan, knowledge, identity, and absence of mistake or accident. While such evidence may be prejudicial, it is nevertheless admissible for purposes other than proving the character of the accused and an admonishment to the jury tends to diminish any prejudice in that instance. Even more so, if the prior conviction is an element of the crime, introduction of that crime should be allowed. To argue that it is prejudicial is not enough; there must be unfair prejudice. As Justice O'Connor argued in her dissent,

Further, to fully and fairly implement the defendant's desired result in this case, more would be required than merely accepting the defendant's stipulation and prohibiting the state from mentioning the name of the prior felony conviction. In addition, the trial court would be required to prohibit the reading of the indictment in its entirety, which in this case contained the name and date of the prior conviction as well as the sentence imposed, and the judge would not be allowed to fully instruct the jury as to the law governing the case, both of which are required under general principles of law. First, under La.C.Cr.P. art. 483, "an indictment shall not contain an allegation of a prior conviction of the defendant unless such allegation is necessary to fully charge the offense." The state correctly argues that a convicted felon's specific prior offense is "absolutely necessary to fully charge the offense and, therefore, must be contained in the charging instrument" and that this Court's jurisprudence requires the indictment or information to be read to the jury in its entirety. *State v. Pounds,* 359 So. 2d 150 (La.1978).[9] Second, under Louisiana Code of Criminal Procedure article 802, "[t]he court shall charge the jury: (1) As to the law applicable to the case; ..." Official Revision Comment (c) provides that "[t]he general language of Clause (1) makes all questions of law applicable to a case mandatory charges to be given by the judge to the jury." Thus, the trial judge must fully advise the jury as to the law of La. R.S. 14:95.1, and that includes naming the prior felony convictions that disqualify a defendant from firearm possession.

Lastly, as recognized by the majority in *Old Chief,* the general rule is that "the prosecution is entitled to prove its case by evidence of its own choice, or, more exactly, that a criminal may not stipulate or admit his way out of the full evidentiary force of the case as the government chooses to present it." 519 U.S. at 186–87, 117 S.Ct. 644. We have held that "[t]he State cannot be robbed of the moral force of its case merely because the stipulation is offered." *State v. Watson,* 449 So. 2d 1321, 1326 (La.1984), *cert. denied,* 469 U.S. 1181, 105 S.Ct. 939, 83 L.Ed.2d 952 (1985) (citing *State v. Harvey,* 358 So. 2d 1224 (La.1978) (allowing the admission of autopsy photographs at sentencing phase and rejecting defendant's argument that because he offered to stipulate to the facts of the crime, the photographs were not probative)). To force the state to accept defendant's stipulation would frustrate this general rule as well.

CONCLUSION

Proof of a prior specifically enumerated felony conviction is an essential element under La. R.S. 14:95.1 and evidence of name and nature of the defendant's prior conviction may be presented to the jury by the state. For the reasons previously stated, *Old Chief* is not controlling and we decline to follow it....

AFFIRMED....

---

it is not unfairly prejudicial for the state to establish an essential element of its case against a defendant with direct proof of his prior conviction. *Old Chief,* 519 U.S. at 201, 117 S.Ct. 644 (O'Connor, dissenting). Necessarily, all the evidence introduced by the state will be prejudicial to the defendant. However, a defendant should not be allowed to enter a "partial plea of guilty" in order to avoid having a jury hear all the negative evidence against him. *Id.* at 200, 117 S.Ct. 644.

9. If the jury is not told the name of the defendant's prior conviction, it may assume that the defendant was convicted of much more heinous crime than simple burglary of an inhabited dwelling. On the opposite end of the spectrum, as noted by the majority in *Old Chief,* certain prior offenses may even be unfairly prejudicial to the state, such as an old conviction for a relatively minor felony, which might strike the jury as a foolish basis for convicting an otherwise upstanding member of the community of otherwise legal gun possession. 519 U.S. at 185, n. 8, 117 S.Ct. 644. But the state would not be allowed to force the defendant to stipulate to his "status" as a felon in that case.

Discussion Questions

1. Compare *Ball* to *Old Chief II*. Upon what basis does Louisiana distinguish the cases? How does the Louisiana Supreme Court arrive at a different outcome than the United States Supreme Court? Do you agree with the court's ruling?
2. Specifically, are there public policy reasons that the State of Louisiana might have that the federal government would not that would lead to a different outcome in such a case?

§ 3.2.2 Gruesome Photographs

Aside from evidence of "other crimes," gruesome photos are probably the other type of evidence most often objected to on the grounds that they are unfairly prejudicial. Blood spatter, the depiction of post-mortem murder victims, mortal wounds, and other factors could have the tendency to "overwhelm the jurors' reason and lead them to convict without sufficient other evidence."[32] However, Louisiana courts have held that the mere fact that a photograph is gruesome does not necessarily render it inadmissible.

Generally, photographs are admissible if they "illustrate any fact, shed light upon any fact or issue in the case, or are relevant to describe the person, place, or thing depicted."[33] In other words, the content of the photos must be relevant for some reason other than simply exciting the emotions of the jurors. For example, the photos may be "relevant to show the manner of death and the location, placement, and number of the bullet wounds on the victim's body,"[34] how the crime was committed, or some other relevant issue in the case.

In some instances, courts will attempt to lessen the prejudicial effect of gruesome photos by limiting the number of photos introduced into evidence, by limiting the size of the photos, or by ordering that the photos be presented in black and white rather than in color. However, there is no requirement that photos be in black and white to be admitted. Each situation is considered on a case-by-case basis. In *State v. Harvey*[35] and *State v. Perry*[36] below, the Louisiana Supreme Court in two pre-code cases analyzes the admissibility of gruesome photos.

State v. Harvey
Supreme Court of Louisiana
358 So. 2d 1224
April 10, 1978

DENNIS, Justice.

James Harvey, Rennie Atwell, and Diane Lawrenson were indicted for the first degree murder of one Robert A. Alexander. Lawrenson's indictment was subsequently severed

---

32. Harges & Jones, Louisiana Evidence, Art 403 Author's Comments.

33. State v. Logan, 986 So. 2d 772 (La. Ct. App. 5th Cir. 2008); See also Harges & Jones, Louisiana Evidence Art. 403 Author's Comments.

34. State v. Logan, 986 So. 2d 772 (La. Ct. App. 5th Cir. 2008); See also Harges & Jones, Louisiana Evidence Art. 403 Author's Comments.

35. State v. Harvey, 358 So. 2d 1224 (La. 1978).

36. State v. Perry, 502 So. 2d 543 (La. 1986).

from her co-defendants'. She was granted immunity by the State and testified at the trial of Harvey and Atwell, implicating both in the crime. According to the State's theory of the case, as presented through Lawrenson's testimony, Atwell, Harvey and Lawrenson conspired to rob Alexander; the murder of Alexander occurred during an armed robbery committed by Atwell and Lawrenson pursuant to the conspiracy; and the proceeds of the robbery were later divided among the three co-conspirators.

After a trial by jury, both Harvey and Atwell were found guilty of first degree murder without capital punishment. They were subsequently sentenced to life imprisonment without benefit of parole, probation, or suspension of sentence.

ASSIGNMENTS OF ERROR: HARVEY'S NO. 2 AND ATWELL'S NO. 9

Defendants argue that the trial judge erred in allowing the introduction of State's Exhibits 3, 4, 5, 6, and 7, photographs of the victim taken at the scene of the crime and at the morgue prior to the coroner's autopsy. They contend that, under State v. Gilmore, 332 So. 2d 789 (La.1976), their offers to stipulate as to the victim's identity, the cause of his death, and the fact of his death deprived the photographs of any probative value which they might have had and rendered their admission highly prejudicial. The State, however, asserts that the photographs were probative as tending to corroborate the testimony of its eyewitness, Diane Lawrenson, as to the manner in which the robbery was committed and Alexander killed.

In State v. Gilmore, 332 So. 2d 789 (La.1976), we discussed the effect of a defense offer to stipulate to the content of photographs offered into evidence by the State. We stated:

> "... Particularly where, as here, the fact to be proved is not seriously at issue a judicial admission offers an expeditious means of serving both the State's interest in meeting its burden of proof and the defendant's interest in excluding prejudicial material. To reserve to the State the right to accept or reject the stipulation is to forego an objective balancing of these countervailing interests and to invite the State to exploit the prejudicial impact of the evidence. This was demonstrated in the instant case. When the State asked at trial that the photograph be shown to the jury, the judge remarked, 'I don't see why the jury has to see the picture;' but at the State's insistence, he complied with the request. Implicit in the State's refusal to accept the stipulation is the suggestion that it sought to gain something more from the admission of the photograph than proof of the murder victim's identity. If this 'something more' was merely the inflammatory effect of the photograph, the trial judge should have had the authority to prevent it.
>
> "On the other hand, a defendant may not be permitted to rob the State's evidence of its fair and legitimate weight by means of a unilateral stipulation:
>
> > "'Nevertheless, a colorless admission by the opponent may sometimes have the effect of depriving the party of the legitimate moral force of his evidence; furthermore, a judicial admission may be cleverly made with grudging limitations or evasions or insinuations (especially in criminal cases), so as to be technically but not practically a waiver of proof.' Id. (9 Wigmore on Evidence, s 2591 (3d ed. 1940))
>
> The sensible solution, offered by Wigmore, is to leave the question of admissibility to the trial judge:
>
> > "... Hence, there should be no absolute rule on the subject; and the trial Court's discretion should determine whether a particular admission is so plenary as to render the first party's evidence wholly needless under the circumstances." Id.

> "Therefore, when the case is tried again, it will be for the trial judge to determine whether a stipulation may prevent the admission of the photograph into evidence." 332 So. 2d at 796.

From an examination of the photographs and a survey of the record before us, we are unable to conclude that the trial court abused its discretion in allowing admission of the photographs. Unquestionably, the photographs of the robbery scene and of the victim's body, showing the entry wound made by the bullet, are corroborative of Diane Lawrenson's account of the commission of the crime. Further, the photographs in question are not particularly gruesome, although the use of black and white film is certainly preferable to the color photographs here admitted. Taking into account the fact that the defendants' offer to stipulate diminished considerably the probative value of the evidence, we are nevertheless unable to find that the trial judge abused his wide discretion in determining that the stipulation was not so plenary as to render the State's evidence wholly needless under the circumstances. Consequently, these assignments present a serious question, but not reversible error.

Discussion Questions

1. Why do gruesome photos have the potential to be so highly prejudicial? What is the potential impact they could have on jurors deciding a case?
2. The defense stipulated to the identity of the victim, as well as to the cause and fact of death. For what purposes(s) are the photographs relevant beyond the information stipulated to by the defense? Would photos potentially be highly probative of those issues?
    a. How does the probative value of the photographs toward their relevant reasons, measure against the risk of prejudice of the photos considering the number and size of photos offered here?

State v. Perry

Supreme Court of Louisiana
502 So. 2d 543
Nov. 24, 1986

COLE, Associate Justice pro tempore.

On July 17, 1983 defendant apparently entered the unlocked house on Louisiana Street in the early morning. He walked first to the living room couch where [his cousin] Randy Perry lay asleep. From a short distance of only a few feet, he fired into the left eye of his cousin. The accused then entered the bedroom where [his cousin] Bryan LeBlanc slept, and again fired the gun at the victim's head.

It appears defendant then walked across the yard to his parents' home at 810 Seventh Street and broke into the house. He listened to music for a while, awaiting his parents' arrival home from an out of town trip. His parents, on their return home, stopped to pick up the two-year-old, Anthony Bonin, whom they cared for when his father worked offshore.... [D]efendant indicated his father came through the door first, followed by the child and the mother. According to his statement, he shot his father first, then his mother, and then the child. There appeared to be some struggle with his father, whose body was found crouching behind the television in the living room. Because his first attempt did not kill either of his parents, he shot both of them a second time in the head. Not being sure the child was dead, he shot him a second time also. After dragging his mother's body away from the door so he could close it, he took his father's billfold containing $3,000 cash, and a strongbox belonging to his mother. He left the scene in his father's car.

ASSIGNMENT OF ERROR NO. FIVE

Defendant argues the trial court erred in allowing the State to present to the jurors numerous color photographs of the five homicide victims. He contends the photographs were not necessary for any probative purpose and inflamed the jury, overwhelming their reason.... The photographs were unnecessary, he argues, because the pathologist who performed the autopsies testified to the cause of death, the location and number of gunshot wounds, the type of weapon used and the approximate distance of the victim from the gun when fired. Sheriff's deputies testified in great detail to the location of the victims in the house, the location of gunshot holes in the walls, the splatter of blood, tissue and brains; the deputies used drawings, cut outs and body figures to illustrate their testimony.

The State introduced a total of 170 color photographs in evidence. The photos show the interior and exterior of the two houses, the condition of the house as it was found and photos of the houses after the victims were removed. There are eight photos taken at the pathologist's directions before he began autopsies. The total also includes four portraits of the victims as they appeared in life. The great majority of the photographs are a painstaking photographic tour through the two houses, with officers taking pictures of all conceivably relevant evidence. Of the 158 photos taken at the two murder scenes, 23 show one or more of the victims.

The photographs of the remains of five murdered persons cannot be less than gruesome. The pictures are unpleasant. All the victims were struck in the head with blasts from a shotgun fired at close range, sometimes at point-blank range. Many of the photographs show the destruction of the skulls, particularly the photographs taken prior to autopsy. No amount of testimony or the use of diagrams can depict the murders with such effect as the photographs.

The defendant cannot force the State to use drawings or other evidence instead of photographs. The defendant cannot deprive the State of the moral force of its case by offering to stipulate to what is shown in photographs. The court's admission of allegedly gruesome photographs will be overturned on appeal only if the prejudicial effect of the photographs clearly outweighs their probative value.

The photographs of the murder scenes are clearly relevant, corroborating the testimony of the State's witnesses as to the location of the bodies, the apparent sequence the murders occurred in and the multiple gunshot wounds to at least two of the victims.

This Court will not find the photographic evidence was admitted in error unless the photographs are so gruesome as to overwhelm the jurors' reason and lead them to convict the defendant without sufficient other evidence.

The photographic evidence was admitted during the trial's guilt phase following testimony of the investigating officers and the pathologist on Friday, October 25, and Saturday, October 26, 1985, respectively. The court recessed for the weekend following introduction of the last of the photographs. Trial resumed Monday, October 28, 1985. Guilty verdicts were returned October 31, 1985, and the jury deliberated and decided on the death penalty the same date. The emotional impact of the photographs had time to dissipate before the State concluded its case and the jury reached the deliberative stage. Without doubt, the primary effect of having viewed the photographs was to impress upon the individual juror the seriousness of the task to which he or she was sworn. The State was entitled to no less.

This Court, in *State v. Lowenfield*, 495 So. 2d 1245 (La.1985), considered the admissibility of photographs of five murder victims. Lowenfield was convicted of murdering four adults and one child in his former girlfriend's house. All the victims were shot in the head and all suffered multiple gunshot wounds. The weapons used were a .38 caliber pistol and a .22 caliber rifle. This court found the prejudicial effect of the pictures did not outweigh their probative value. The photographs of murder victims are admissible to prove corpus delicti, to identify the victims, to corroborate the cause of death and to show location, placement and severity of wounds. One photograph of each victim was put into evidence.

We find the photographic evidence was relevant and probative in proving the State's case against Michael Owen Perry. They proved corpus delicti, helped identify the victims, corroborated the cause of death, the types of weapons used and the location and severity of the wounds. We find no merit in this assignment of error.

Discussion Questions

1. In *Perry*, the court stated that the pictures, "proved corpus delicti, helped identify the victims, corroborated the cause of death, the types of weapons used and the location and severity of the wounds," which are all relevant reasons for offering photos. Do you think that the number of photos used in *Perry* was excessive? What specific factors would justify the introduction of 170 photos?
2. How much is too much? How do you determine an appropriate limit on the number of photographs needed in a particular case? What guidance would you offer?

§ 3.2.3 Admissibility of Videos

The admissibility of videos are evaluated under the same standard as gruesome photos. "A video may be admitted into evidence to corroborate other testimony in a case such as the location of the body, the manner of death, the specific intent to kill, the number, location and severity of wounds, and the cause of death."[37] While it is not uncommon for an opposing party to object that a video is cumulative and does nothing more than offer the same evidence that has been testified to by a witness, an actual video of an incident certainly can give additional insight as to the specifics of how an incident occurred that words could not likely explain. Additionally, a video of an incident can corroborate a witness's testimony, significantly increasing the witness's believability.

State v. Davis
Supreme Court of Louisiana
637 So. 2d 1012
May 23, 1994

MARVIN, Justice Ad Hoc.

At about 3 a.m. on June 29, Johnny Hall, an employee of Fat's Exxon, an outlet or convenience store owned by Calvin Moore ... became another victim of Percy Davis. There Davis robbed and shot Johnny Hall. Ballistics showed that the cartridge from which

37. Harges & Jones, Louisiana Evidence Art. 403 Author's Comments; See also State v. Denby, WL 832498 (La. Ct. App 3d Cir. 2011).

the shot was fired came from Davis's pistol. During the penalty phase of the murder trial, Johnny Hall identified Davis as his robber and assailant.

Near midnight on June 30 Davis returned to Fat's Exxon where he committed the armed robbery and murder of Calvin Moore some 20 hours after he had robbed and shot Johnny Hall in the same store. Moore and his wife were working that night because Hall was hospitalized. The video tape of the murder-robbery clearly shows those persons who were at the counter and cash register being served by Calvin Moore and his wife.

Davis was accompanied by an acquaintance, Rodney Hill. When Davis and Hill appear on camera, Hill stands at the counter while Moore places small items in a paper sack ... Davis quickly bends or stoops below the counter and pulls his pistol from his sock. Arising from that position with pistol in hand, Davis, in one quick and continuous motion, without saying anything to Moore, shoots Moore in the chest at point blank range ... Moore obviously does not notice or react to the pistol, but is thrown on his back by the gunshot and is twitching, breathing heavily and immediately on the floor in the throes of death.

Immediately after shooting Moore, Davis shoots at Mrs. Moore ... Fortunately, Davis missed Mrs. Moore. She immediately reacts, falling to the floor and quickly scoots under the counter.

Davis thereafter opens and ransacks the cash register, removing all currency, some of which was in an envelope, and some coins, while observing his wounded victim on the floor in the throes of death. While removing the money from the cash register, Davis keeps the pistol pointed at Moore and threatens to shoot him again if he attempts to get up. Mrs. Moore testified that she heard Davis say to her husband, "Are you trying to get up from there? I'll shoot you again, you m----- f-----!" Lip reading the videotape corroborates what Mrs. Moore said Davis said.

After removing the money Davis departs toward the front door of the store and out of the range of the camera. Shortly after Davis departs, Mrs. Moore rises from under the cabinet and comes to the aid of her husband, telephoning for help. She is soon assisted by a customer who enters the store and by Thomas Adgate, who had been an earlier customer....

In response to the telephone calls, police arrived and learned that the video camera in the store was functioning before, during and after the robbery-murder. Police provided a copy of the videotape to news media, requesting help ... Once Hill was told about the videotape he voluntarily went to the police, attempting to exculpate himself as much as possible, while identifying Davis as the perpetrator of the crimes. Davis's picture was placed in a photographic lineup which was separately presented to Adgate and Hill. Each identified Davis's photograph....

Nos. 9, 24, 26 and 32—The Videotape: Davis contends that the jury should not have seen the video tape of the murder at Fat's Exxon. Davis initially filed a motion in limine to preclude the state from introducing the tape taken by a stationary remote video camera. He argued the prejudicial impact of the video outweighed its probative value and that it unfairly appealed to the jury's emotions. See La.C.E. Art. 403. He claims the introduction of the tape denied him the opportunity to cross-examine his accusers and was presented solely to inflame the jury. Davis argues the videotape is merely cumulative of other testimony and photographs and mentions that he offered to stipulate to the manner of death and the sequence of events. He claims the court should have undertaken to determine if the video camera was tested and in working order and should have required testimony in connection with the tape showing it was preserved and that it was not edited. At least three times at trial Davis objected to the introduction of the tape, especially when the court permitted the jury to take the tape, State's Exhibit # 10, to the jury room during death penalty deliberations, which he argued was the same as having *testimony* repeated during deliberations and requires reversal.

A videotape, which is like a photograph, is neither testimony nor written evidence and is not excluded by La.C.Cr.P. Art. 793. A photograph is a reproduction of a physical object or scene. It is not "written" evidence of "testimony" within the meaning of La.C.Cr.P. Art. 793, which prohibits the use of written material during deliberations. Hence, a jury's request to see a videotape after it retired to deliberate on the penalty phase is not an abuse of the court's statutory discretion.

Concerning the admission of the video during the guilt phase, we see no reason why the law on still photos should not apply equally to this video. See La.C.E. Art. 1001(2). The video is in black and white, without sound, and contains no close-ups. The video is extremely probative considering the State's burden of proving the robbery, specific intent and negating Davis's intoxication defense. The tape portrays Davis's deliberate and unhesitating murder of Calvin Moore, the unnecessary shooting at Norma Moore, and the taking of money from the cash register. Even without audio, the tape reveals the specific threat of Davis to again shoot Mr. Moore, easily determined by lipreading Davis in the light of Mrs. Moore's testimony. Merely because the video may be "cumulative" evidence does not render the tape inadmissible. The video was not wholly cumulative because the testimony did not cover everything shown on the video. Mrs. Moore did not see the initial shooting or realize that Davis had fired at her. Mrs. Moore testified that the video was an accurate recording of the events on the fatal night. She and Detective Ashley testified that the video was taken from Fat's Exxon on the night of the murder. The video was not edited in any way and was highly probative.

... The trial court correctly ruled at the pre-trial motion in limine that the issue was similar to the admissibility of still photographs, holding that the videotape was admissible to corroborate other testimony in this case, such as location of the bodies, manner of death, specific intent to kill, and cause of death.

The tape's probative value, especially regarding Davis's intoxication/lack of specific intent argument, was not outweighed by its possible prejudicial effect.

Discussion Questions

1. The defense objected to the videotape on several grounds. What were the extensive grounds argued by the defense against admitting the video? How was each issue resolved?
2. What additional relevant information does a video provide that is not presented through testimony? Since a video could always potentially add additional detail to how an incident occurred, and be highly probative, should it always be admitted? Why or why not?

§ 3.2.4 Confusing the Issues

Evidence may be excluded as *confusing the issues* if it would tend to distract the jury from the proper issues and lead them to focus on issues that are not before them to decide. If the danger of confusing the issues outweighs the probative value, then such evidence should be excluded. Do you agree with the court in *Laing v. Honda Motor Co., Inc.*[38] below, that the evidence sought to be admitted would have confused the issues before the jury?

38. Laing v. Honda Motor Co., Inc., 628 So. 2d 196 (La. Ct. App. 2d Cir. 1993).

Laing v. Am. Honda Motor Co., Inc.

Court of Appeal of Louisiana, Second Circuit
628 So. 2d 196
Dec. 1, 1993

BROWN, Judge.

A 25-year-old Morehouse Parish farmer, Thomas Laing, purchased a three-wheel all-terrain vehicle (ATV) manufactured by Honda. Four days later, while riding the ATV in the course of his farming operation, Laing was seriously injured.... Plaintiffs alleged that the ATV was unreasonably dangerous for normal farm use.

A jury found for the Laings. The distributor and manufacturer (collectively referred to as "Honda") were held responsible. The action against the retailer was dismissed. Damages of $5,654,794.37 were awarded to Laing. Mrs. Laing was awarded $250,000 for loss of consortium. The jury apportioned to Honda 75% and to Laing 25% of the fault ...

FACTS

... On November 18, 1985, between 4:00 and 5:00 p.m., Laing left riding this newly purchased three wheeler to inspect his fields to determine if they were ready for planting. That evening Laing's wife reported him missing and the following morning at 8:30 a.m. a search party found Laing lying unconscious, face down, in a turn row or tractor path running between cotton fields....

There were no witnesses to the accident and Laing was unable to recall what happened. Reconstruction experts for both parties conducted tests on Laing's and a similar ATV, considered the description of the scene given by members of the search party, viewed photographs of the scene taken on the day Laing was found and personally viewed the scene. Although these experts disagreed on the plaintiff's speed and the specific maneuver causing the accident, they did agree that: 1) Laing was riding the ATV along a rough path between cotton fields when he encountered a dirt clod or mound; 2) Laing and the ATV were found approximately 20 to 30 yards beyond the clod, which was about a foot high and more than a foot in diameter; 3) the ATV was damaged on its left side; 4) the top of the clod appeared to have been knocked off; 5) ATV tracks led up to the clod; 6) the headlights of the ATV were not on; and 7) Laing, an experienced motorcycle and ATV rider, was not wearing a helmet at the time of the accident. According to plaintiffs' experts, Laing was traveling 15 to 25 m.p.h. when he turned to avoid the mound and the ATV flipped over. Defense experts believed Laing drove over the mound at about 35 m.p.h., causing him to go airborne and lose control. In estimating speed, plaintiff's experts emphasized the light damage to the ATV while defense experts stressed the distance traveled by the ATV from the mound to its final location.

Laing suffered a severe traumatic brain injury and was in a coma for approximately two months. Thereafter, he underwent intensive rehabilitation and had to be retaught such basic functions as speaking, reading and bowel and bladder control. Laing, who was discharged from the hospital in June 1986, approximately 7 months after his accident, still requires assistance and cannot feed himself or perform other simple tasks such as writing or cooking.

Laing's two-year-old daughter was sent to St. Louis, Missouri, to live with her mother's parents while Mrs. Laing devoted all of her time to caring for her husband during his comatose and recovery period. The daughter was frightened when she finally saw her father. After doing all she could for her husband, Mrs. Laing moved to St. Louis to care for her daughter and eventually obtained a divorce.

...

EVIDENTIARY RULINGS
COMPARATIVE RISK EVIDENCE

Honda argues that the trial court committed an error of law and thus abused its discretion by excluding its study of comparative risks. The trial court's rulings occurred prior to trial pursuant to a motion in limine filed by plaintiffs. The trial judge excluded Honda's evidence under L.C.E. Articles 401 and 403, stating:

> [T]he testimony that Dr. McCarthy (Honda's expert) would purport to give deals with the notion of comparative risk analysis in which, in this context, the risk of riding an all-terrain vehicle (ATV) must be compared with other encountered recreational activities such as snowmobiling, skate-boarding, parachuting and the like....
>
> This court is inclined to agree..., that the all-terrain vehicle manufactured by Honda must be judged and evaluated on its own merits, not in regard to snowmobiles, or bungee jumping apparatus, go-carts or any other remotely analogous recreational activity.
>
> [T]he Court feels that the introduction of the comparative risk evidence will only serve to confuse the jury, introduce extraneous, arcane and abstruse issues into the trial and needlessly prolong the presentation of evidence in a case which is already promising to be quite tedious and lengthy.

L.C.E. Article 401 defines relevant evidence as evidence having any tendency to make the existence of any fact of consequence more or less probable than it would be without the evidence. The trial court is allowed wide discretion in determining relevant evidence and its ruling will not be disturbed absent a clear abuse of this discretion....

L.C.E. Article 403 provides that though relevant, evidence may be excluded "if its probative value is substantially outweighed by the danger of unfair prejudice, confusion of the issues, or misleading the jury, or by considerations of undue delay or waste of time." A trial judge's assessment of the probative value of evidence is accorded great weight.

Whether the utility of the 1985 Honda ATC 250SX as a farm machine outweighed its risk of danger was an issue for the jury. Honda countered evidence introduced by plaintiffs regarding the risks associated with the ATC with testimony from several experts of the ATC's utility as a recreational vehicle, in addition to its use in farming and industrial situations. Honda's proffered evidence of risks associated with a myriad of different products and recreational activities, such as snowmobiles, go-carts and bungee jumping, though interesting, was not necessary for the jury's determination of this particular product's utility as a farm instrument. As noted by the trial judge, this study had the potential of confusing the issues. We find no error in the trial judge's exclusion of this evidence.

Discussion Question

Do you agree with the court that the evidence would distract the jury from the proper issues and lead them to focus on issues not before them? Why or why not?

§ 3.2.5 Waste of Time/Cumulative Evidence

Evidence may also be excluded if its probative value is substantially outweighed by the danger that the evidence will result in undue delay or waste of time. Undue delay and waste of time "apply where the evidence relates to the event in question but is 'overkill.'"[39] "That rule permits a judge undertaking the article 403 balancing test to exclude the testimony of additional witnesses as cumulative." Although Louisiana's version of article 403 excludes the "cumulative" language, "the result should be the same, because the evidence would be a 'waste of time.'"[40]

Varnell v. Service Merchandise

Court of Appeal of Louisiana, Third Circuit
613 So. 2d 1042
Feb. 3, 1993

DOUCET, Judge.

This case arises out of a trip and fall in a Service Merchandise store.

On October 19, 1985, Sheila Varnell tripped over a display in a Service Merchandise showroom located in Lafayette, La.... After the trial the jury ... found that Service was not negligent....

On appeal Mrs. Varnell contends that the trial judge erred in excluding from evidence OSHA regulations and the defendant's safety manual which incorporates OSHA regulations by reference. In her brief, Mrs. Varnell argues that OSHA regulations were relevant and admissible to establish the standard of care owed by a retail merchant to an invitee.

29 U.S.C.A. § 654, which is part of the legislation known as the Occupational Safety and Health Act of 1970 (OSHA), provides that:

> (a) Each employer—
>
> (1) shall furnish to each of his employees employment and a place of employment which are free from recognized hazards that are causing or are likely to cause death or serious physical harm to his employees;
>
> (2) shall comply with occupational safety and health standards promulgated under this Act.
>
> (b) Each employee shall comply with occupational safety and health standards and all rules, regulations, and orders issued pursuant to this Act which are applicable to his own actions and conduct.

The trial judge excluded evidence of the OSHA regulations on a finding that their prejudicial effect would outweigh their probative value....

[I]n this case the trial court allowed extensive testimony on safety and safety standards from the plaintiff's expert, Wilfred Gallardo. As a result, the effect of admission of the OSHA regulations and the Service safety manual would have been cumulative. The admission of cumulative evidence is within the discretion of the trial court....

Additionally, in light of dicta set out in *Rabon v. Automatic Fasteners, Inc.*, 672 F.2d 1231 (C.A. 5th Cir.1982), we question the relevancy of OSHA regulations to an action by a non-employee since OSHA regulations are designed to protect employees.

Accordingly, we conclude that the trial court acted within its discretion in excluding the OSHA regulations and the Service safety handbook from evidence.

---

39. Frank L. Maraist, Louisiana Civil Law Treatise, Evidence & Proof § 5.1, at 68 (1999).
40. Entergy Gulf States, Inc. v. Louisiana Public Service Commission, 730 So. 2d 890 (La. 1999).

Discussion Questions

1. Do you agree with the finding that the manual should be excluded? Do you think that it is irrelevant altogether (having no probative value toward the standard of care that should've been exercised), or do you think it fails the Article 403 balancing test?
   a. Could offering the manual have taken up a substantial amount of time as the court feared? How much additional time would it have taken to offer the OSHA safety manual?

§ 3.2.6 Misleading the Jury

Misleading the jury refers to the possibility that the jury might attach *undue weight* to the evidence. For example, a government report on safety of tires was excluded under Article 403 because the jury may have been influenced by the official character of the report to afford it greater weight than it was worth. Additionally, polygraph tests are generally excluded because of the weight the jury might give them. When the court finds that the danger that the evidence will mislead the jury substantially outweighs its probative value, the evidence should properly be excluded under Article 403.

Key Points

The key points to keep in mind regarding Article 403 Balancing.

1. Under Article 403 relevant evidence may be excluded if the probative value is substantially outweighed by the danger of unfair prejudice, confusion of the issues, misleading the jury, or by considerations of undue delay, or waste of time.
2. **Article 403 Balancing Test.** Article 403 requires a balancing of the probative value of the evidence against the danger of unfair prejudice, confusion of the issues, misleading the jury, or considerations of undue delay, or waste of time.
3. **The probative value** of evidence is the degree to which it actually proves or disproves a relevant issue in the case, as opposed to the relevancy standard which only requires "any" tendency to prove a consequential fact.
4. **Assessing probative value.** Probative value is assessed by the considerations of various factors including the number and dubiousness of intervening inferences between the proffered evidence and the proposition it is being offered to prove, the strength of the inferences, or whether the inferences can be fractionalized. Additionally, probative value is determined by the availability of evidentiary alternatives, and the existence of less prejudicial evidentiary alternatives.
5. **Unfairly prejudicial evidence** is evidence that has an undue tendency to suggest decision on an improper basis, most commonly an emotional one, such as passion, prejudice, or bias. It is also evidence that adversely affects the jury's attitude towards the defendant on factors unrelated to the case, such as other crimes evidence or evidence of bad character.
6. The most common types of unfairly prejudicial evidence are gruesome photos and evidence of other crimes, wrongs, or bad acts.

7. ***Old Chief/Ball.*** Courts weighed the probative value of offering the actual name and nature of another crime that is an element of a crime or charge, when the issue has been stipulated to, against its risk of unfair prejudice. The U.S. Supreme Court found the actual name/nature of the crime to be unfairly prejudicial in light of the stipulation. The Louisiana Supreme Court, in *Ball*, found the name/nature of an underlying crime not unfairly prejudicial even in light of the stipulation.
8. **Gruesome photos.** Photos are not automatically excluded because they are gruesome. The content of the photos must be relevant for some reason other than simply exciting the emotions of the jurors, e.g., to show the manner and location of death, placement and number of the bullet wounds on the victim's body, how the crime was committed, or some other relevant reason. The probative value of the photo is weighed against the risk of unfair prejudice.
9. **Confusing the issues.** Relevant evidence might be excluded if it would tend to distract the jury from proper issues and lead them to focus on issues not before them to decide.
10. **Waste of time.** Evidence might be excluded if its probative value is substantially outweighed by the danger that the evidence will result in undue delay or waste of time.
11. **Misleading the jury.** Evidence may be excluded if the jury might attach undue weight to it.

Article 403 Balancing Problems

PROBLEM 3-13: Lolita stabbed her husband Mark to death in their bedroom following a heated altercation that occurred after Lolita learned that Mark was having an affair. After killing Mark, Lolita dragged his bloody body from their upstairs bedroom down the stairs though the living room, dining room, and kitchen, and into the garage where she put him in the trunk of the car, then drove to a canyon where she dumped his body. Following a thorough investigation, Lolita was arrested and was subsequently tried for Mark's murder. The prosecution offered 67 color photos that showed the bloody bedroom, traces of blood along the staircase and wall and in various rooms throughout the house, garage, vehicle, and canyon that supported their theory of how Lolita committed the murder then attempted to cover up the crime. Assuming the photos have been properly authenticated by the crime scene investigator who took them, how will the court likely rule on the objection to their admissibility?

Discussion:

When analyzing a photograph under the Article 403 balancing test, you must consider its probative value for some relevant purpose other than just to excite the emotions of the jury, such as demonstrating the cause or manner of death, or the location, placement, and number of wounds. Here, the photos are being offered by the prosecution to demonstrate how Lolita was able to commit the murder alone by approaching Mark from the back when she stabbed him, and was then able to remove the body by dragging it through the house and garage, and into the car where she took it to the canyon to dispose of it. The photos here are needed to support the prosecution's theory that it was Lolita alone who killed Mark and to rebut her theory that it would have been impossible for her to have singlehandedly overcome Mark. Thus, the photos are highly probative.

The probative value is then weighed against the risk of unfair prejudice, i.e., its tendency to lead the jury to convict on improper basis—here, the excitement of seeing the gruesome photos. In this case, the photos indeed have some prejudicial effect in that they depict a bloody crime scene, there are 67 photos that are being offered by the prosecution, and they are all in color. While the prejudicial effect could certainly be reduced by limiting the number of photos offered or requiring the prosecution to offer black and white photos, considering the high probative value in helping to prove the prosecution's theory of the case, the probative value will likely outweigh the prejudicial effect and the photos will likely be admitted into evidence.

PROBLEM 3-14. The defendant is on trial for murder, but he claims self-defense. He would like to offer a computer-animated reenactment of the incident as he claims it occurred. The prosecution objects, claiming the evidence should not be admitted. How will the court likely rule and why?

PROBLEM 3-15. Casey is on trial for murder of his parents to obtain life insurance proceeds. Seven of the prosecution's 14 witnesses are various creditors who will testify that Casey was either late or had defaulted on various accounts, including credit cards, his vehicle, and his home. The evidence is being offered to show Casey's motive for killing his parents, and his irresponsibility and/or obsession with money and finances. On what grounds should the defense object? How will the court likely rule and why?

PROBLEM 3-16. Johnon called 911 and claimed that he'd arrived home from a business trip and found his wife stabbed to death. The first officer to arrive was Ofc. Demery. Shortly thereafter several other officers within the vicinity of the incident arrived on scene including Officer Mitchell. The officers secured the scene and waited for about 15 minutes for the lead detective to arrive who immediately took over the investigation, which led to Johnon's arrest for his wife's murder. About a year later, just before Johnon's trial, his lawyer discovers that Officer Mitchell is no longer employed with the police department. He learns that a few months after Johnon was arrested, the officer was terminated from the police force for profiling vehicles for stops, then falsifying information on speeding tickets he issued. Due to his insignificant role in Johnon's case, the prosecution had no plans to call him as a witness. Johnon's lawyer would like to call him to the stand to question him about the circumstances surrounding his dismissal from the force. The prosecution does not think he should be called as a witness. Upon what basis should they object? How will the court likely rule and why?

PROBLEM 3-17. Sue was killed in a car accident one night while driving home after the brakes on her car gave out, causing her to hit a tree. Sue died on impact. Sue's husband (Husband) sues the manufacturer of the vehicle claiming the brakes on the car were defective. He seeks damages for loss of consortium, including loss of love and affection, society, and companionship. In support of his claim, Husband seeks to introduce a photograph of him and his wife Sue on a camping trip before she died, hugging each other and enjoying each other's company. The plaintiffs plan to offer the photo into evidence during Husband's testimony as he gives further detail about what Sue meant to him. The defense objects that the photograph is unfairly prejudicial. Assuming the photograph has been properly authenticated for admissibility, how should the court rule on the defense's objection and why?

PROBLEM 3-18. John is on trial for possession of a firearm by a convicted felon. One of the elements the prosecution must prove is that John is in fact a convicted felon. John's previous felony conviction is armed robbery, for which he served a 10-year sentence. At the trial, John has agreed to stipulate to his felony status to prevent the prosecution from introducing the exact name of the crime for which he was convicted because he does not want the jury to know that he has committed a crime with a weapon in the past. The State, however, does not wish to agree to the stipulation. Upon what grounds will John argue that he is entitled to the stipulation in a federal court? How should the court rule and why? Would your answer change if the matter was in a Louisiana state court? How and why?

PROBLEM 3-19. Bill, 27, is on trial for the aggravated rape and attempted murder of Pearl, a 71-year-old elderly lady. After raping her, Bill strangled her and left her for dead. She survived, but has been on life support in the ICU since the incident. She has various tubes in her and is connected to a breathing apparatus. Two months after the incident, Pearl remains unconscious in ICU and is unable to testify at the trial. The prosecution would like to show a picture or a video of her in the hospital in her current state, claiming it will show that Bill really did "almost kill" her. How should the judge rule on the jury seeing Pearl in the ICU?

PROBLEM 3-20. The prosecution would like to offer evidence that when Dion called the police to report that his wife had been shot and that he needed an ambulance, he added, "I've been arrested before and I know that the deputies are going to blame me for the shooting." The defense has objected to the deputy (lead investigator) testifying to the statement claiming that the statement is unfairly prejudicial. Should the statement be admitted? Why or why not? [See *State v. Bailey*, 664 So. 2d 665 (La. Ct. App. 3d Cir. 1995).]

PROBLEM 3-21. Carey is on trial for the armed robbery of a convenience store. There were two clerks present at the time of the robbery. Clerk 1 was behind the cash register and will testify to everything she saw and heard as she followed Carey's instructions to empty the cash register into a Ziploc bag that Carey gave to her. Clerk 2 was on break at the time of robbery, but listened to the whole thing from the break room just behind the counter. Clerk 2's statements about what he heard are consistent with Clerk 1's testimony. There was also a black and white video of the entire incident as well. The video had no sound and was a frame by frame of several still pictures. At Carey's trial, the prosecution intends to offer the testimony of both clerks as well as the video. The defendant objects that Clerk 2's testimony is irrelevant because he did not see anything, but only heard stuff through the door. The defendant also objects that the video should be excluded because it is cumulative and unfairly prejudicial. How will the court likely rule on the admissibility of Clerk 2's testimony and the video and why?

PROBLEM 3-22. Jackson is the defendant in a civil case arising out of an accident where he ran a red light. In the damages phase of the trial, he would like to offer evidence that a couple of months after the accident, the victim/plaintiff had been in jail on an unrelated incident. He claimed that any mental anguish that plaintiff may have suffered was a result of his time in jail, rather than from the accident. Should the evidence be admitted? [See *State v. Haley*, 709 So. 2d 992 (La. Ct. App. 3d Cir 1998).]

PROBLEM 3-23. Benjamin is on trial for murder. He is accused of the murder in a hotel room of a male prostitute whom he'd hired for sex. The prosecution would like to offer photos of the deceased male victim dressed in women's lingerie in obscene sexual poses that were found at the crime scene. The defense objects that the photos are unfairly prejudicial. How should the court rule and why? [See *State v. Brasseaux*, 919 So. 2d 738 (La. Ct. App. 5th Cir. 2005).]

PROBLEM 3-24. Phillip is on trial for the sexual abuse of a 10-year-old boy. The prosecution seeks to introduce evidence that Phillip is a homosexual. Should the evidence be admissible? [See *State v. Taylor*, 663 So. 2d 336 (La. Ct. App. 3d Cir. 1995).]

PROBLEM 3-25. Joe is on trial for armed robbery. The defense calls Joe's mother to the stand to testify that on the night of the robbery, Joe was at home watching the game with her. On cross-examination of Joe's mother, the prosecution asks her if she believes robbing someone is okay? Upon what basis would you object to the witness answering this question? How will the court likely rule and why?

PROBLEM 3-26. University president Jimmy White accuses a student, Russell Mason, of slandering him in a speech that Russell made at a rally attended by about 750 students as they gathered to protest hikes in tuition. Russell stated that the students should not be required to buy new cars and houses for the president, who he claims wants the extra money for personal use. At the trial, President White would like to call at least the seniors who attended the rally to testify to what Russell stated at the rally—over 200 of the students. If you were Russell's attorney, upon what grounds would you object to the testimony? How will the court likely rule and why?

PROBLEM 3-27. David is on trial for capital murder. He is accused of shooting an entire family in cold blood during an armed robbery at a gas station. The prosecution would like to offer evidence that the defendant's nickname is "Gunslinger" to show that the defendant is violent and is likely to use a gun to kill. Should the evidence be admissible? Why or why not?

Assume instead that during the trial several eyewitnesses testified that they saw the defendant commit the crime, who they only knew by the name "Gunslinger." The police had asked them to identify the person they knew as Gunslinger in a photo lineup, and they had each identified the defendant. The prosecution would like to offer evidence that the defendant was known as Gunslinger. Should the evidence be admissible? Why or why not? How are the two scenarios different? Does your answer change? Why or why not? [See *State v. Edwards*, 750 So. 2d 893, (La. 1999).]

§ 3.2 References and Additional Authority on Article 403 Balancing

1. La. C.E. art. 403 and Official Comments
2. Force & Rault, HANDBOOK ON LOUISIANA EVIDENCE LAW Art. 403, Author's Comments (West Publishing 2014)
3. Harges & Jones, LOUISIANA EVIDENCE Art. 403 Author's Comments (West Publishing 2014)
4. 19 La. Civ. L. Treatise, Evidence And Proof § 5.1 (2nd ed.)
5. **Unfairly prejudicial evidence**: *Young v. Longue*, 660 So. 2d 32 (La. Ct. App. 4 Cir. 1995) (holding that evidence was properly excluded under balancing test of La.C.E. art. 403, because of the danger that it would unfairly prejudice the jury by revealing that plaintiff had already compromised his claims against a variety of other defendants; such evidence could have "tainted" the jury against plaintiff, and defendant offers no persuasive reason why the evidence should have been admitted or what purpose it would have served had it been admitted); *Malloy v. Vanwinkle*, 662 So. 2d 96 (La. Ct. App. 4th Cir. 1995) (holding that trial court properly excluded medical records of insured which were unrelated to automobile accident and described substance abuse by insured based on finding that probative value of records was outweighed by their risk of prejudice, even though insurer contended that past history of substance abuse was relevant to establish motive to exaggerate injuries in order to obtain prescription drugs); *State v. Washington*, 788 So. 2d 477 (La. Ct. App. 4th Cir. 2001) writ denied,

816 So. 2d 866 (La. 2002) (holding that unfair prejudice substantially outweighed probative value, as impeachment evidence, of newspaper article alleging that the arresting officer and another officer had "jacked people up and stuff like that," in prosecution for possession with intent to distribute heroin).

6. **Gruesome photos:** *State v. Ellis*, 28 So. 2d 282 (La. Ct. App. 2d Cir. 1996), 677 So. 2d 617 writ denied, 96-1991 (La. 2/21/97); 688 So. 2d 521 (holding that photos of the victim at the murder scene are generally admissible to prove the corpus delicti, corroborate other evidence and establish the cause of death, identity, or the number, location and severity of wounds); *State v. Hardeman*, 467 So. 2d 1163 (La. Ct. App. 2d Cir. 1985) (holding that the admission of gruesome photos, such as dead body of victim, autopsy photos, and photos of the angulation of the bullet and entrance wound will not constitute reversible error unless it is clear that the prejudicial effect of the photographs outweighs their probative value).

7. **Gruesome videotapes**: *State v. Denby*, 58 So. 3d 1096 (La. Ct. App. 3d Cir. 2011) (holding that probative value of one-minute video that depicted child victim prior to death in a hospital bed with his head heavily bandaged and making seizure-like movements outweighed prejudicial effect, such that video was admissible in murder prosecution, where video accurately depicted victim's injuries).

8. **Misleading the jury**: *State v. Harris*, 79 So. 3d 1037 (La. App. 1st Cir. 2011) (holding that the probative value of defendant's prior possession of a valid prescription for dextroamphetamine was substantially outweighed by danger of confusing and misleading the jury in his current trial for possession of amphetamine).

9. **Waste of time/Cumulative evidence**: *State v. Volentine*, 565 So. 2d 511 (La. App. 2d Cir. 1990) (holding that a certified public accountant who testified as state expert witness in theft prosecution and traced flow of funds from husband and wife's accounts to defendant corroborated wife's testimony and was not merely cumulative; expert testimony served to enhance and not confuse jury's understanding of events in light of number of checks involved); *State v. Fleming*, 593 So. 2d 1298 (La. Ct. App. 1st Cir. 1991) (holding that a videotape of interior and exterior of laundromat, burglary scene, was not merely cumulative since it corroborated prosecution witness's testimony); *Nguyen v. Pausina*, 607 So. 2d 675 (La. Ct. App. 4th Cir. 1992) (holding that restricting testimony of pathologist to conclusion and explanation as to cause of death was not abuse of discretion when his testimony as to history provided to him by investigator of accident would have been a waste of time because it would be repetitive of testimony already given by emergency room physician); *Askins v. Barbazon, III et al.*, 593 So. 2d 792 (La. Ct. App. 4th Cir. 1992) (holding that "[t]he videotape would have been cumulative and was unnecessary to plaintiff's case since what it was intended to prove was already established").

10. **Confusion of issues:** *State v. Lee*, 569 So. 2d 1038 (La. App. 3d Cir. 1990) (holding that danger of unfair prejudice and confusion of issues outweighed any probative value of evidence of homicide defendant's homosexuality; though it was conceivable that defendant's killing of 13-year-old male victim while on camping trip may have been result of rejected sexual advances, there was no evidence of homosexual activity between victim and defendant); *State v. Gay*, 697 So. 2d 642 (La. Ct. App. 2d Cir. 1997) (In defendant's trial for first degree murder, the court excluded evidence that there had been a prior drug raid at the residence where the murder occurred about 8 1/2 months prior to the incident in which the defendant killed the victim. The victim was at the residence selling clothes from his clothing business out of the trunk of his

car. The defendant sought to introduce the evidence of the prior drug raid to show that he had gone to the residence that day to buy drugs, and not to kill anyone. He claimed the killing was an accident. In excluding the evidence of the prior drug raid, the court held, "Without a showing that the victim had something to do with the drug sales from the Young residence, evidence about those sales tends to confuse the issue of the defendant's intent to kill with his motive for going to the house (to buy drugs). This motive is irrelevant to the murder charge. Therefore, under La. C.E. art. 403 and art. 609.1(C), evidence about the raid on the house tended simply to confuse without proving a fact at issue and was properly excluded.").

11. **Polygraph tests**: *State v. Cosey*, 779 So. 2d 675 (La. 2000) (holding that evidence of polygraph results was inadmissible because of undue weight trier of fact will attach to results; prejudicial effect substantially outweighs any relevance results would have); *Hines v. Arkansas Louisiana Gas Co.*, 613 So. 2d 646 (La. App. 2d Cir. 1993) writ denied, 617 So. 2d 932 (La. 1993) (holding that evidence that employee had offered to submit to lie detector test was not admissible in defamation action arising out of his dismissal for allegedly harassing his female subordinates, as the prejudicial effect of the evidence clearly outweighed whatever relevance it had in demonstrating employee's state of mind).

Chapter 4

Witnesses and Testimonial Evidence

In this chapter we will examine witnesses. As the primary manner through which evidence is introduced at trial, witnesses play a key role in the presentation of a party's case. Thus, a number of evidentiary rules are dedicated to regulating various aspects of a witness's testimony at trial—from who may testify, to the types of information about which a witness may testify, to procedural and foundational requirements that must be met prior to their testimony.

Many of the rules relative to the nature and scope of a witness's testimony are found in Chapter 6 of the Code of Evidence, including the basic rule for **competency** of a witness [Article 601], the requirement of **first-hand knowledge** [Article 602], and the requirement that a witness take an **oath** or make an **affirmation** that they will tell the truth when testifying [Article 603]. Additionally Chapter 6 contains rules for the **examination of witnesses** [Article 611], the **sequestration** of witnesses [Article 615] and rules relating to testing the **credibility** of witnesses [Articles 607–610, 613]. Many of these rules will be discussed in this chapter. This chapter will also cover the rule governing **opinion testimony of lay witnesses**, which is contained in Article 701. The rules regarding the credibility of witnesses are covered in Chapter 6 of the casebook.

§ 4.1 Competency [La. C.E. art. 601]

Applicable Code Article

Art. 601. General rule of competency

Every person of proper understanding is competent to be a witness except as otherwise provided by legislation.

A basic requirement for all witnesses testifying at trial is that they be deemed **competent.** As in the everyday sense of the word, a competent witness is one that is capable and up to the task of testifying at the trial. The general rule for competency in Louisiana is set out in Article 601 and provides that every person of **"proper understanding"** is competent to be a witness in a trial, except as otherwise provided by law. " 'Proper understanding'[1] is the exclusive test for determining the competency of a witness under Louisiana evidence law," and basically refers to the "witness's general ability to appreciate truth and falsity and to understand the proceedings."[2] The competency of a witness is not a matter of the witness's

1. La. Code Evid. art. 601 Official Comment (b).
2. La. Code Evid. art. 601 Official Comment (c).

age, but rather, whether the witness can determine the difference between the truth and a lie, and can understand his duty to be truthful as a witness in a proceeding.

The competency of a witness does not depend upon whether the witness is likely to lie, has a motive to lie, or any other issue bearing on his credibility or the weight that the trier of fact should give to his testimony. Provided the witness can appreciate the difference between the truth and a lie, he is competent to testify.

Thus, the fact that the witness has been convicted of a crime, has an interest in the case, has reason to be biased, or has previously made a statement that is inconsistent with his current testimony at trial does not render him incompetent to testify.[3] Such issues affect the weight and credibility the trier of fact may give to the witness's testimony, but they do not prevent him from testifying, nor do they render his testimony inadmissible.

Challenge of Competency. Generally, the person claiming lack of competency has the burden of proving it. An objection to a witness's competency must be made before the witness is sworn. The judge makes competency determinations under the authority of Article 104, and "great weight is given to a trial judge's competency determinations because of his ability to see and hear the witness. His determination of competency will not be overturned absent manifest error."[4] In making such determinations, evidence rules are not used except as to the rules relative to privileges due to the confidentiality of the privileged information. However, expert opinions may be considered in determining competency.[5]

While there is no specific test used to determine if the witness possesses the necessary proper understanding to find him competent to testify, generally, the court asks general questions of a person whose competency has been challenged to satisfy itself that the witness is competent. The questions could be anything ranging from whether Santa Claus is real to what grades she makes in school.

Competency of Children. An often heavily contested issue at trial is the competency of a young child to testify. Since a person's competency is not determined by his age, a child is not automatically deemed incompetent because he or she is a young child. Article 601 changed prior Louisiana law, wherein the courts were required to use a specific test to determine the competency of a witness under the age of twelve.[6] Under current law, the standard for determining if a child is competent to testify is the same as for any other witness—whether he has proper understanding, i.e., whether he can understand the difference between the truth and a lie and can understand his duty to be truthful as a witness in a proceeding.

When a child's competency is challenged, the court will typically ask the child questions to determine the child's competency. The court considers not only the child's answers to questions, but also the child's overall demeanor, including whether it appears as though the child has been coached. There are no specific questions the court is required to ask, provided the court can satisfy itself of the child's understanding of the difference between telling the truth and telling a lie, and that he understands that he must testify truthfully in the court proceeding. Thus, a judge might determine the competency of a child as follows:

---

3. Madere v. Tranchina, 62 So. 2d 871 (La. Ct. App., Orleans 1953) (holding that a witness was not incompetent to testify due to past arrest); State v. Henry, 197 La. 999, 3 So. 2d 104 (1941) (witness not incompetent due to criminal conviction); Middleton v. Consolidated Underwriters, 185 So. 2d 307 (La. Ct. App. 1st Cir. 1966) (prior conviction does not affect competency, but does affect witness's credibility); *See also* McCormick on Evidence § 62–§ 66 (6th ed. 2006).

4. State v. Bean, 582 So. 2d 947 (La. Ct. App. 2d Cir. 1991).

5. Force & Rault, Handbook, Art. 601 Author's Comment (4); *See also* State v. Troulliet, 643 So. 2d 1267 (La. Ct. App. 5th Cir. 1994).

6. *See* La. R.S. 15:469. Repealed by Acts 1988, No. 515, § 8, eff. Jan. 1, 1989.

Question: Mandy, do you know what a lie is?
Answer: Yes.
Question: What is a lie?
Answer: It's when you make up a story.
Question: Do you ever make up stories?
Answer: Yes.
Question: Do you know you are not supposed to make up stories today?
Answer: Yes.
Question: Can you tell us only true stuff today?
Answer: Yes.
Question: Did anyone tell you what to say today?
Answer: No.
Question: Did anyone tell you not to tell the truth today?
Answer: No. My mother told me to tell the truth and I wouldn't get in trouble.

It is important to note that when a witness testifies to a statement made by a person outside of the present trial or hearing, the person who made the out-of-court statement is not subject to the competency rules outlined in Article 601. They are effectively not a "witness" for purposes of this provision. Thus, a witness could be permitted to testify to a statement made by a child outside of court that conforms to a hearsay exception, even if the child would be incompetent to testify personally at the trial. This issue is discussed further in *State v. Bean*, below.[7]

Mental Disorders/Defects. Additionally, the fact that a person suffers from a mental disorder or defect does not automatically render a person incompetent to testify. The same test of "proper understanding" applies. If the person has the general ability to distinguish between the truth and a lie, and understands his duty to tell the truth, the witness may be found competent to testify at trial.[8] Any issues regarding mental diseases, disorders, or defects could be inquired into on the issue of the witness's capacity or credibility, but would not automatically render the witness incompetent.

Conviction of Crime and Other Credibility Issues. Further, as stated above, issues bearing on a witness's credibility do not affect the witness's competency to testify. The fact that a witness has been convicted of a crime, or the fact that other credibility issues may exist, such as bias, interest, prior inconsistent statements, etc., will not affect the witness's competency to testify. Such issues go to the witness's credibility and may affect the weight the trier of fact gives to the witness's testimony, but they do not preclude the witness from being competent to testify. Arguments that go toward a witness's credibility should be presented to the jury.

7. *See also* La. C.E. art. 601 Official Comment (e).

8. *See* State v. Morris, 429 So. 2d 111, 120 (La. 1983); *See also* State v. Burleson, 516 So. 2d 1159 (La. Ct. App. 4th Cir. 1987) (addressing competency determination for a mentally retarded adult).

Federal Rules of Evidence Distinction. The first part of Federal Rule of Evidence 601 provides that "[e]very person is competent to be a witness unless these rules provide otherwise."[9] Under this provision, "every witness is presumed competent to testify, unless it can be shown that witness does not have personal knowledge of matters about which he is to testify, that he does not have capacity to recall, or that he does not understand duty to testify truthfully."[10] Under the Federal Rules, the prior statutes that once rendered a person incompetent to testify no longer exist, such as conviction of crime, interest in the case, and others. Today, as in Louisiana, such issues are merely credibility issues that do not prevent a witness from testifying altogether. As to young children, the appropriate test of competence "is whether he has requisite intelligence and mental capacity to understand, recall and narrate his impressions of an occurrence."[11] The court typically asks questions of the child prior to his testimony to ensure the child is competent to testify.

The second sentence of Rule 601 is where the rule differs from Louisiana law. It provides that, "in a civil case, state law governs the witness's competency regarding a claim or defense for which state law supplies the rule of decision."[12] This provision means that, "state law governs competency of witnesses where proof is directed at substantive issues governed by state law."[13] Thus, in a diversity case, for example, in which the federal court is required to follow state substantive principles, the court would be required to follow the state law for determining competency.

Cases on Competency

State v. Bean
Court of Appeal of Louisiana, Second Circuit
582 So. 2d 947
June 19, 1991

VICTORY, Judge.

Defendant, convicted of second degree murder by a jury and sentenced to life imprisonment, appeals his conviction, assigning twelve errors. We affirm.

FACTS

On April 17, 1989, defendant, John Wesley Bean, known as "Sugar Boy," telephoned his wife, Elgie Palmo Mack, from whom he was physically separated, to tell her he was coming to her home to get some of his personal items. Ms. Mack and four-year-old Cherdaria (her and defendant's daughter) were living with Jessie Mae Anderson, Ms. Mack's aunt.

Upon arriving at the house, defendant spoke to Cherdaria and her seven-year-old cousin, Barbara Peterson, who were playing in the front yard. Ms. Mack and James Smith,

9. Fed. R. Evid. 601.

10. U.S. v. Lightly, C.A.4 (Va.) 1982, 677 F.2d 1027.

11. U.S. v. Perez, C.A.5 (Tex.) 1976, 526 F.2d 859, rehearing denied 531 F.2d 575, certiorari denied 97 S. Ct. 129, 429 U.S. 846, 50 L. Ed. 2d.

12. Fed. R. Evid. 601.

13. Barton v. American Red Cross, M.D. Ala. 1993, 829 F. Supp. 1290, affirmed 43 F.3d 678, certiorari denied 116 S. Ct. 84, 516 U.S. 822, 133 L. Ed. 2d 41, rehearing denied 116 S. Ct. 550, 516 U.S. 1002, 133 L. Ed. 2d 452, affirmed 43 F.3d 679.

known as "Bay Bay," were inside. Defendant entered and asked Smith whether he intended to marry Ms. Mack. Smith responded that he was already married.

Defendant and Ms. Mack left the house in his father's car with the two children in the back seat, and headed down the street to Ms. Mack's car, located on a parking lot about a block away. Peterson testified that she heard defendant say to Ms. Mack several times on the way to the parking lot that he was going to bury her at the funeral home.

Defendant had a .38 caliber semi-automatic pistol in the car with him. Ms. Mack was shot, the passenger door opened and she fell out backwards onto the street. Peterson and Dorothy Mae Johnson, a bystander, said the gun was fired again after Ms. Mack had fallen out of the car. The two children ran from the car and defendant drove away. Ms. Mack died soon afterwards from the gunshot wounds.

Defendant disposed of the gun and fled for about a week, going as far away as Chicago, Illinois, never checking on the extent of his wife's injuries. On April 24, 1989, he turned himself in to police.

On May 9, 1990, a twelve-member jury found defendant guilty of second degree murder and he was thereafter sentenced by the trial judge to life imprisonment at hard labor without benefit of parole, probation or suspension of sentence.

ADMISSIBILITY OF HEARSAY STATEMENTS

Defendant contends the trial judge erred in allowing two hearsay statements, one from police officer John Clary and another from Dorothy Mae Johnson, both of whom testified about what other people had said to them....

Defendant further contends the trial judge erred in allowing Dorothy Mae Johnson to tell the jury statements made to her by four-year-old Cherdaria. Johnson and a neighbor were standing on the porch of the neighbor's house when they observed the defendant and Ms. Mack in a car at a stop sign, with two children in the back seat. Johnson heard two to three shots, saw Ms. Mack come out of the passenger door, land on her back, and then heard another shot. The two children ran to Johnson. She testified that Cherdaria immediately stated to her "Sugar Boy shot my mama," and then asked "why would my daddy kill my mama?"

The trial judge ruled the testimony was not hearsay because it was part of the res gestae under LSA-C.E. Art. 801 D(4), and that it fell within the excited utterance exception to the hearsay rule.

LSA-C.E. Art. 803(2) defines an excited utterance as:

> A statement relating to a startling event or condition made while the declarant was under the stress of excitement caused by the event or condition.

In *Morgan v. Foretich,* 846 F.2d 941 (4th Cir.1988), defendants argued the statements from a four-year-old child should be excluded because they did not meet the excited utterance exception to the hearsay rule, and also that the child's age made her incompetent to testify. The court disagreed, and held that under the federal excited utterance hearsay exception, which is identical to the Louisiana provision, the declarant must (1) have experienced a startling event or condition and (2) reacted while under the stress or excitement of that event and not from reflection and fabrication. The court held that the test was met, and with respect to the child's incompetency, it stated:

> We agree with the majority of courts that have studied this issue and reached the conclusion that "although a child is incompetent to testify, testimony to his spon-

> taneous declarations or res gestae statements is nevertheless admissible." ... Likewise, the leading commentators have concluded that "an excited utterance is admissible despite the fact that the declarant was a child and would have been incompetent as a witness for that reason." ...

In 6 *Wigmore on Evidence* § 1751 (Chadbourn Rev. 1976), the rhetorical question is posed whether the disqualification of infancy should exclude declarations which are otherwise admissible. The suggested answer is negative because the principle of the exception obviates the usual sources of untrustworthiness in children's testimony.

The general test for determining a witnesses' competency does not include the person who makes an out-of-court declaration which is subsequently admitted into evidence as an exception to the hearsay rule. Competency questions as to such declarants are best determined in their particular contexts....

In *State v. Bennett,* 549 So. 2d 398 (La.App. 4th Cir.1989), writ denied 558 So. 2d 1123 (1990), a pre-code case, the court, without discussing the issue of incompetency, allowed a statement into evidence made by a three-year-old child to an eight-year-old child as part of the res gestae, even though the three year old had been ruled incompetent to testify. The court ruled that her statements were "certainly a product of a shocking episode and not a fabrication." The court further commented that the statements were corroborated to a great extent by a neighbor and therefore any prejudice which may have occurred to the defendant was cured.

In the instant case, the statements fall within the excited utterance exception. First, the shooting was an event of a startling nature that would render a four year old's reflective thought processes inoperative. Second, Cherdaria immediately ran to Johnson and made the statements, with virtually no time allowed for fabrication of the statement. The statements therefore fall within the ambit of the hearsay exception and are not barred by the child's incompetency. Thus the trial judge committed no error in allowing this testimony....

COMPETENCY OF EIGHT-YEAR-OLD WITNESS

Defendant argues the district court erred in finding eight-year-old Barbara Peterson was competent to testify.

Every person of proper understanding is competent to be a witness except as otherwise provided by legislation. LSA-C.E. Art. 601. The question of competency of a person to be a witness is determined by the trial judge. See LSA-C.E. Art. 104 and Comments. The specific rules previously used for determining competency of witnesses under the age of twelve were abandoned with the adoption of the Code of Evidence....

Therefore understanding, rather than age, is the test of competency for any witness, and great weight is given a trial judge's determination of competency because of his opportunity to see and hear the witness. His determination of competency should not be overturned absent manifest error....

At the competency hearing, Peterson first appeared scared and shy, but testified that she understood the difference between the truth and a lie, and seemed to have the intelligence that one of a similar age would possess. After reviewing the lengthy question-answer session posed to the child on the issue of competency, we cannot say the trial judge abused his discretion in ruling that she was competent.

Defendant further contends Peterson was "coached", and was therefore incompetent. At the competency hearing, Peterson's great-grandmother attempted to help her answer some questions. The great-grandmother was removed by the court upon discovery of her actions and was not present in court during the child's testimony before the jury. The great-grandmother's actions had no substantial bearing on whether Peterson was of a proper understanding to be competent as a witness.

Likewise, Peterson's earlier statements to authorities, which appear to contradict some of her statements at trial, have little bearing on her *competency,* but rather go to her *credibility,* which is a jury question. This assignment of error is without merit.

Discussion Questions

1. How did the judge in *Bean* determine whether the child was competent to testify?
2. Why do you presume a statement could be admissible that a person made outside of court even if the person might not be found to be competent to testify at trial, such as the statement of the 4-year-old in *Bean*? What facts or circumstances differ in the courtroom setting that would require a witness to be competent that do not exist for statements made by persons outside of court?
   a. What does the statement cited by the court that "the principle of the exception obviates the usual sources of untrustworthiness in children's testimony" mean to you? Do you agree with the principle? See also *State v. Bennett*, 591 So. 2d 1193 (La. Ct. App. 1st Cir. 1991).
3. The defendant pointed out that the witness was being "coached" by her great-grandmother at the hearing and that she also made prior inconsistent statements. Do such issues have any bearing on a witness's competency? Why or why not? Do they have any effect at all? Explain.

State v. Deutor

Court of Appeal of Louisiana, Fourth Circuit
842 So. 2d 438
March 19, 2003

LEON A. CANNIZZARO, JR., Judge.

On an application for post conviction relief, the trial court granted the defendant, Silvio Deutor, a new appeal. Thus, this matter is before this Court for the second time....

STATEMENT OF FACTS

During the early morning hours of September 27, 1993, Silvio Deutor, the defendant herein, entered the bedroom of his apartment located at 10204 Plainfield Street where his "common law" wife, Anita, and her four year old daughter, Ashley, were sleeping. He woke Anita and asked her to go outside with him. She refused and he began raising his voice. Ashley was awakened by the disturbance.

The two adults then went into the living room and argued. Anita returned to the bedroom, packed a suitcase, and she and Ashley went outside. Anita planned to call a taxicab to take them to her grandmother's house. The defendant came outside and told them to come back into the house. When they went inside, the defendant resumed the argument. Anita, fearing the defendant, took Ashley into the bathroom, locking the door behind them. The defendant, in a rage, kicked the door open and then brandished a gun. He pushed them both onto the bed. He then pointed the gun at Ashley and shot her. Thereafter, the defendant repeatedly shot Anita, striking her six times. He stopped only after emptying his gun of its bullets. Despite this Anita was able to leave the apartment in an effort to find help. She called 911 from a pay phone and then returned to the apartment out of concern for Ashley whom she found lying lifelessly in the bedroom.

After New Orleans Police Officer Harry Parker was dispatched to the scene, he observed the two victims being transported by ambulance. The defendant was standing outside the apartment, which appeared to have been ransacked. The defendant told Officer Parker that someone had burglarized his residence. Officer Parker later learned, as a result of Anita informing medical personnel at the hospital, that the defendant was responsible for the shooting. Officer Parker then arrested the defendant. A search of the apartment's exterior produced a .38 caliber gun. A background check revealed that the defendant had prior convictions for possession of cocaine and for being a convicted felon in possession of a firearm....

The defendant argues in his second assignment of error that the district court erred in finding six-year-old Ashley Annunciation competent to testify.

La. C.E. art. 601 provides: "Every person of proper understanding is competent to be a witness except as otherwise provided by legislation." Understanding, not age, is the test of whether any person shall be sworn as a witness. A key determination to be made is whether the witness is able to understand the difference between truth and falsehoods. *State v. Troulliet, supra.* Determination that a child is competent to testify as a witness is based not only on the child's answers to questions testing his understanding but also in the child's overall demeanor. *State v. Bennett,* 591 So. 2d 1193 (La.App. 1 Cir.1991).

The trial court is vested with wide discretion in determining the competency of child witnesses. Its ruling as to competency is entitled to great weight on appeal, and will not be disturbed absent manifest abuse of discretion. *State v. Foy,* 439 So.2d 433 (La.1983); *State v. Troulliet, supra.*

Before allowing Ashley Annunciation to testify, the trial judge questioned the child out of the jury's presence. Ashley correctly stated her age, date of birth, grade in school, school attended, and her teacher's name. At the judge's request, she correctly spelled and wrote her name. Although she hesitated, and denied knowing the difference between the truth and a lie, she ably remonstrated the judge when he purposely misidentified the color of her dress, telling him that if he said her pink dress was blue, "It would be a lie." A child's sometimes hesitant or unresponsive answers do not necessarily indicate incompetency. Instead, they may be part of an overall demeanor in the unfamiliar courtroom experience, which favorably reflects testimony only as to what is clear to the child. *State v. Foy, supra. See also State v. Sharp,* 338 So.2d 654 (La.1976), in which the defendant asserted that the murder victim's eight-year-old son was not competent to testify. The Supreme Court stated that, reviewing the child's testimony in its entirety, it was clear that the child had sufficient understanding to be a witness. Although the witness had stated that he did not know what an oath was or what would happen if he told a lie, "it was evident that he was simply unfamiliar with the courtroom experience." *Id.* at 661.

In this case, a review of Ashley's testimony, as a whole, demonstrates that she had sufficient understanding to be deemed a competent witness. Although she had difficulty with abstract questions about telling the truth and lying, the victim was able to understand more specific questions applying those concepts. Additionally, the courtroom experience was apparently somewhat stressful for this young child, as reflected by her fear and inability to look at the defendant when requested to do so by the prosecutor. The trial judge, who had the benefit of observing the child's demeanor, did not abuse his discretion by concluding that Ashley Annunciation was a competent witness. This assignment is without merit.

Accordingly, for the above reasons, the defendant's conviction and sentence are affirmed.

AFFIRMED.

Discussion Questions

1. Based on what you have seen in *Bean* and now *Deutor*, how should a court determine whether a child understands the difference between the truth and a lie? Specifically how many and what types of questions would you recommend the court ask?
2. The court often refers to the child's overall demeanor as being a relevant factor in assessing the child's competency to testify. If proper understanding, i.e., knowing the difference between the truth and a lie, is the sole test for competency, what type of demeanor does the court consider in determining the child's competency?

State v. Pierce

80 So. 3d 1267
Court of Appeal of Louisiana, Fifth Circuit
Dec. 29, 2011

MARC E. JOHNSON, Judge.

Defendant, Preston Lee Pierce, appeals his convictions and sentences for two counts of aggravated rape and two counts of sexual battery. For the reasons that follow, we affirm his convictions and sentences.

FACTS

In August 2007, J.G., [initials are used to protect the identity of minor children] at the age of seven, lived with her mother, father, and two older sisters in Kenner, Louisiana. Although her mother and father were married and lived together, they were not emotionally together; J.G.'s mother often dated, and in August 2007, she was dating defendant. On August 25, 2007, J.G.'s mother attended a party with defendant's sister while defendant babysat J.G. While babysitting J.G., defendant took her to his bedroom, applied a lubricant to her vaginal and anal area, and contacted her vagina and anus with his penis.

Defendant was arrested the next day and news of his arrest was published in the newspaper. As a result of the publicity, other women came forward with similar accusations against defendant, including defendant's adult daughter, C.P. C.P. alleged that her father had "messed" with her when she was a child. C.P. testified that starting when she was six or seven years old until she was 15 or 16, defendant made her spread her legs, applied his saliva to her vaginal area, contacted her clitoris with his penis, and ejaculated on her stomach. C.P. also testified that on one occasion defendant achieved full penetration of her vagina with his penis.

J.T. was another victim of defendant. J.T. and her boyfriend were friends with defendant's son, Preston Lee Pierce, Jr. ("Lee"). J.T. testified that in June 2003, she, her boyfriend, and Lee were at Lee's aunt's house for defendant's birthday. Alcohol was consumed and J.T. became intoxicated to the point of vomiting. J.T. then went to bed with her boyfriend, with whom she had consensual sex before going to sleep without putting her pants back on. In the bed, J.T.'s boyfriend slept closest to the wall while J.T. slept on the open side of the bed. J.T. was awakened in the middle of the night by a penis penetrating her vagina. She thought it was her boyfriend at first, but when she opened her eyes, she saw her boyfriend sleeping next to her and discovered it was defendant who was on top of her.

The fourth person to come forward with similar accusations against defendant was M.B. M.B.'s mother testified that she and her two daughters shared an apartment with defendant from about April 1994 until September 1994. M.B., the younger daughter, testified that around this time, on more than one occasion, defendant took her to his bedroom, laid her on his bed, told her she had a rash, and applied Vaseline to her vagina and vaginal area.

LAW & DISCUSSION . . .

ASSIGNMENT OF ERROR NUMBER TWO

In his second assignment of error, defendant argues that the trial court erred in finding J.G. competent to testify. Defendant contends that J.G. was incompetent to testify because she had been diagnosed with two mental disorders (bipolar disorder and post-traumatic stress disorder), she made illogical statements to the examining physician, her mother testified that J.G. often lied, and her testimony appeared coached.

La. C.E. art. 601 provides that every person of proper understanding is competent to be a witness except as otherwise provided by legislation. Understanding, not age, is the test of whether any person shall be sworn as a witness. A key determination to be made is whether the witness is able to understand the difference between truth and falsehoods. The competency of a child to testify as a witness is based not only on the child's answers to questions testing his understanding, but also on the child's overall demeanor. *Id.*

The trial court is vested with wide discretion in determining the competency of child witnesses. Its ruling as to competency is entitled to great weight on appeal, and will not be disturbed absent abuse of discretion. *Id.*

Prior to trial, a hearing was held to determine the competency of J.G. At the hearing, J.G. stated her name, age, birth date, school, grade level, and address. She was asked about the difference between telling the truth and telling a lie. J.G. was given specific statements and asked if they were true or false. She correctly distinguished all examples as truths or lies. J.G. was also asked about her understanding of her surroundings. She knew she was in a courtroom and that the person in the black robe was a judge. J.G. stated that before she could tell her story in a courtroom, she had to "pledge that [she] will tell the truth and only the truth." She explained that "you can get in trouble," maybe go to jail, and probably would not be able to tell your story, if you lie. J.G. promised to tell the truth if the judge allowed her to tell her story. When asked why she should tell the truth, J.G. replied, "Because if someone tries to prank you just for a not good reason and you tell a lie, you don't go to heaven you go underground. So it's best to tell the truth so someone can know how to help you in what way."

On cross-examination, J.G. stated that she had met with the prosecutor prior to the hearing to practice the questions he would ask. She also admitted that she had lied before. At the conclusion of the hearing, the trial judge found J.G. competent to testify.

Cases with similar circumstances have upheld the competency of a child witness. In *Cedrington, supra,* this Court found a seven-year-old boy competent to testify. The boy was able to tell the judge his birth date and year. He explained that to tell the truth meant to "don't story." He stated he would be able to tell the truth. The boy further stated that "God will punish you" if you do something wrong. This Court found the boy's testimony before the jury was coherent, and his answers were responsive to the questions asked.

Also, in *State v. Gaal,* 01–376 (La.App. 5 Cir. 10/17/01), 800 So.2d 938, 940, *writ denied,* 02–2335 (La.10/3/03), 855 So.2d 294, this Court found a six-year-old boy, who was a victim of sexual battery and aggravated oral sexual battery, to be competent. In *Gaal,* the child stated that he attended church, believed in God, and promised to tell the truth. He gave the name of his school and his grade level. When questioned about what "subjects" he took in school, he did not understand. However, he answered correctly when he was provided with specific examples. When asked what it meant to tell a lie, the child responded that it was to "tell a different story." The boy further stated that your mom and dad punish you when you tell a lie. He was given concrete examples and correctly distinguished between truth and falsehood. He admitted telling lies in the past, but stated he would tell the truth when sitting in the witness chair.

In finding the child witness competent, this Court noted that the record revealed the victim knew the difference between the truth and a lie, as demonstrated by his ability to differentiate when confronted with concrete examples. We also noted that despite an incorrect response given by the child regarding the number of days in a month, the child understood and correctly responded to questions presented in a way a six-year-old child could understand. *Id.* at 947.

Finally, in *State v. Linson*, 94–61 (La.App. 1 Cir. 4/7/95), 654 So. 2d 440, 441, *writ denied*, 95–1120 (La.9/22/95), 660 So. 2d 470, the Court found two children, ages seven and eight, competent to testify in a sexual abuse case. The Court focused on the girls' ability to demonstrate through examples that they understood between telling the truth and telling a lie. Both children admitted telling lies in the past, but stated they would tell the truth when asked questions at trial. They both testified they believed in God and they knew God wanted them to tell the truth.

Similar to these cases, J.G. correctly stated her name, age, birth date, school, grade level, and address. She stated she understood the difference between the truth and a lie, which was confirmed by two examples. She testified that she believed in God and that God wanted her to tell the truth. She was aware of her surroundings, acknowledging her presence in a courtroom in front of a judge. She was aware that she would be punished if she did not tell the truth, and she understood the meaning of the oath given to witnesses. J.G. also understood the importance of telling the truth to policemen and doctors. Although she admitted she had told lies in the past, she promised that she would tell the whole truth when asked questions at trial. Lastly, in regard to J.G.'s mental disorders, Dr. Hutton testified that bipolar disorder would not affect J.G.'s ability to know the difference between right and wrong.

Considering the record before us, including the testimony of the child, we find the trial judge did not abuse his discretion when he found the child victim competent to testify. Accordingly, this assignment of error is without merit....

CONVICTIONS AND SENTENCES AFFIRMED ...

Discussion Questions

1. Mental disorders or defects do not automatically preclude a witness from being competent to testify, provided he has proper understanding as defined by the courts. Do you agree with the court's finding that J.G. was competent considering, "she had been diagnosed with two mental disorders (bipolar disorder and post-traumatic stress disorder), she made illogical statements to the examining physician, her mother testified that J.G. often lied, and her testimony appeared coached"? Were her answers sufficient to overcome any concerns about her competency in your view? Why or why not?
2. Do you believe that mental disorders/defects are competency issues or credibility issues, along with bias, interest, convictions of crimes, and other issues bearing on credibility?[13] Explain.

13. See Chapter 6, §6.11 for a complete discussion of credibility and issues bearing on credibility.

Key Points

The key points to keep in mind regarding competency.

1. **The test.** "Proper understanding" is the general test of competency in Louisiana.
2. Proper understanding is the ability to distinguish between the truth and a lie, and to understand the duty to be truthful as a witness in the proceeding.
3. **Challenge of competency.**
   a. Challenges should be made before the witness is sworn.
   b. Trial judges make competency determinations that will not be overturned on appeal absent manifest error.
   c. There is no set method the court must use to determine a witness's competency. The court generally asks questions to determine if the person has the proper understanding to testify.
4. **Children.** No specific test for children. Age is not dispositive. The court considers answers to questions and overall demeanor to determine if they have general ability to distinguish between truth and a lie and to understand their ability to tell the truth in the trial.
5. **Credibility.** The fact that a witness's credibility may be attacked due to bias, interest, prior inconsistent statement, or prior convictions under Articles 609/609.1 does not affect his competency to testify. Those issues go to the witness's credibility and not to whether he may be accepted to testify.
6. **Mental disorders/defects.** Mental diseases or disorders do not automatically render a person incompetent to testify. The same test of "proper understanding" applies. If they understand the difference between the truth and a lie, and understand their ability to tell the truth in the proceedings, they may be found competent.

Problems on Competency of Witnesses

PROBLEM 4-1. Mary is rushing out of her driveway to take her 15-year-old daughter to cheerleading practice. Her 2-year-old son is in the back seat. Mary is attempting to back out of her driveway when her 2-year-old son says, "Man waving mommy." Mary runs over the man standing behind her car who was signaling for her to stop. The deceased man's family has brought a wrongful death action against Mary. During cross-examination of Mary's 15-year-old daughter, the plaintiff asks her to repeat what the 2-year-old said. Mary's attorney objects that the 2-year-old's statement should not be admitted because he is incompetent. Should the daughter's testimony regarding the son's statement be excluded on competency grounds? Why or why not?

PROBLEM 4-2. Mildred's husband is on trial for battering her. She reluctantly agrees to testify against him, but tells the prosecutor that she is not going to say anything that will hurt him. During Mildred's testimony, she repeatedly contradicts her prior statement to police. The prosecution warns her that she can be charged with perjury, but Mildred continues to knowingly lie on the stand. The prosecution has asked the court to find that Mildred is incompetent to testify. The defense objects. How should the court rule and why?

PROBLEM 4-3. Dan is testifying as a witness for the plaintiff in a civil case. Dan took a deposition some time before the trial. During cross-examination, the defense has impeached Dan several times on prior inconsistent statements Dan made in the deposition. After the forth impeachment, the defense attorney objected to Dan's continued testimony and claims that Dan is incompetent to testify due to the number of prior inconsistent statements that Dan has made. How should the judge rule and why?

PROBLEM 4-4. The prosecutor called six-year-old Mandy to the stand to testify about a crime she witnessed. Before she began testifying, the defense attorney objected to her testimony on the ground that she was not competent. After excusing the jury from the courtroom, the trial judge asked the child the following questions after which the judge declared the child was a competent witness. Was the competency of the witness properly determined? Why or why not?

Judge: Do you know the difference between telling the truth and telling a lie?

Mandy: Yes.

Judge: I'm going to ask you a few questions and I want you to tell me if it's the truth or a lie, okay?

Mandy: Okay.

Judge: Your name is Mandy? Is that the truth?

Mandy: Yes.

Judge: You are a little boy ... is that the truth?

Mandy: No, I'm a girl, judge.

Judge: Your mother's name is Jane. Is that the truth or a lie, Mandy?

Mandy: That's a lie too. My mommy's name is Sharon.

Judge: Mandy, do you know that you are only supposed to tell the truth here today?

Mandy: Yes.

Judge: Will you only tell the truth?

Mandy: Yes.

PROBLEM 4-5. Betty is a witness to a murder that occurred while she was living in a half-way house for women. Betty has been diagnosed with bipolar disorder and schizophrenia. Upon being called as a witness to testify in the trial, the defense objected that Betty was incompetent to testify due to her mental disorders. Do Betty's mental disorders automatically preclude her from testifying in the trial? What steps should be taken and what standard should be met in order for her to be able to testify in the trial?

PROBLEM 4-6. Victor has been sued for sexual harassment. In his defense, he plans to call several employees to testify on his behalf. The plaintiffs object that the witnesses are incompetent to testify because they all have an interest in the case since they are employed by the defendant and have a motive to lie to keep their jobs. How should the judge rule on the objection and why?

PROBLEM 4-7. Coleman, an inmate, was called to testify as a witness to a jailhouse confession made to him. The trial court knew that Coleman had been diagnosed as a paranoid schizophrenic with auditory hallucinations. The following are the questions that were asked of Coleman at the hearing:

Mr. Holland: All right. Mr. Coleman, do you know the difference in telling the truth and telling a lie?

Mr. Coleman: Yes.

Mr. Holland: Do you know what perjury is?

Mr. Coleman: Yes.

Mr. Holland: Would you explain to the Court what your understanding of perjury is?

Mr. Coleman: Perjury is lying under oath.

Mr. Holland: All right. The determination the Court would need to make is that you know the difference in telling the truth and telling a lie right now.

Mr. Coleman: Sure.

Following the hearing, the court found that Coleman was competent. The defense objected to the finding. What ruling? See, *State v. Guidry*, 953 So. 2d 943 (La. Ct. App. 2d Cir. 2007).

§ 4.1 References and Additional Authority on Competency of Witnesses [La. C.E. art. 601]

1. La. C.E. art. 601 and Official Comments
2. Force & Rault, Handbook on Louisiana Evidence Law Art. 601, Author's Comments (West Publishing 2014)
3. Harges & Jones, Louisiana Evidence Art. 601 Author's Comments (West Publishing 2014)
4. 19 La. Civ. L. Treatise, Evidence And Proof § 6.1 (2nd ed.)
5. McCormick on Evidence § 61, § 63–§ 66 (6th ed. 2006)
6. **Finding children competent:** *State v. Allen*, 647 So. 2d 428 (La. Ct. App. 2d Cir. 1994) (finding eight-year-old at time of trial competent to testify at trial); *State v. Crandell*, 604 So. 2d 123 (La. Ct. App. 2d Cir. 1992) (finding nine-year-old competent); *State v. Bennett*, 591 So. 2d 1193 (La. Ct. App. 1st Cir. 1991) (five-year-old competent to testify as to circumstances occurring when she was four); *State v. Murphy*, 515 So. 2d 558 (La. Ct. App. 1st Cir. 1987), decision rev'd, on other grounds 542 So. 2d 1373 (La. 1989) (finding that child four years old at time of alleged events had sufficient understanding to testify).
7. **Finding children incompetent**: *State v. Dykes*, 440 So. 2d 88 (La. 1983) (holding the victim, three years and ten months old at the time of the trial, to be incompetent; the victim was vague as to what happened to him and contradicted himself during this testimony; the victim's responses relative to his understanding of the need to tell the truth were also vague, and he also testified that others had told him what to say in court).
8. **Cases concerning competency and mental diseases/defects**: *State v. Leonard*, 543 So. 2d 975 (La. Ct. App. 3d Cir. 1989); *State v. Peters*, 441 So. 2d 403, 408 (La. Ct. App. 4th Cir. 1983) (holding that mentally retarded rape victim who had chronological age of 29 but mental age of six or seven was competent to testify as to what took place at time of crime, where trial judge himself questioned victim and observed her demeanor, and was satisfied that she knew the difference between the truth and a lie and would tell the truth); *State v. Burleson*, 516 So. 2d 1159 (La. App. 4th Cir. 1987) writ denied, 521 So. 2d 1168 (La. 1988) (holding that adult mentally retarded victims, with mental ages between six and ten years, were competent witnesses in sexual battery prosecution, where they indicated that they knew what it meant to tell the truth and the moral and legal consequences of lying on witness stand, and demonstrated an ability to understand

questions and provide answers which were responsive and intelligent); *State v. Atkins*, 713 So. 2d 1168, 1175 (La. Ct. App. 4th Cir. 1998) (evidence that 16-year-old alleged victim of forcible rape knew the difference between right and wrong was sufficient to support finding that she was competent to testify, even though her testimony indicated that she was special education student and had difficulty communicating with counsel).

9. **Illness**: *Davis v. Schwegmann Giant Super Markets*, 631 So. 2d 479 (La. App. 4th Cir. 1994) (holding that a grocery store customer was competent to testify in slip and fall case, despite her testimony that a brain tumor had caused memory loss, difficulty in telling right from left and up from down, and intermittent severe headaches; although customer had made conflicting statements in her deposition and trial testimony, her answers were generally responsive to questions posed).
10. **Competency v. credibility**: *State v. Wilkerson*, App. 448 So. 2d 1355 (La. Ct. App. 2d Cir. 1984) (holding that eyewitness's defects of capacity, sensory or mental, which would have lessened her ability to perceive facts which she purported to have observed were provable to attack her credibility either upon cross-examination or by producing other witnesses to prove the defect; such matters go to credibility of the witness and not to her competency to testify).

§ 4.2 Personal Knowledge Requirement [La. C.E. art. 602]

Applicable Code Articles

Art. 602. Lack of personal knowledge

A witness may not testify to a matter unless evidence is introduced sufficient to support a finding that he has personal knowledge of the matter. Evidence to prove personal knowledge may, but need not, consist of the testimony of the witness himself. This Article is subject to the provisions of Article 703, relating to opinion testimony by expert witnesses.

Another important rule relative to a witness's qualifications to testify at trial is the requirement that a witness have first-hand knowledge of the information about which he will testify. In other words, all witnesses must testify about information acquired "from the use of their own senses"[14] rather than from information obtained from someone else. As we discussed in Chapter 1, one of the most basic principles underlying the rules of evidence is the goal of accurate truth-finding in the trial. The requirement that a witness testify from first-hand knowledge is one such rule with this goal in mind. In such a case, not only is the witness's testimony more likely to be accurate, but he can also be more effectively cross-examined on the information about which he is testifying.

To help ensure compliance with the rule, the article requires that there be evidence "sufficient to support a finding" that the witness is in fact testifying from personal knowledge. In other words, before the witness testifies to a matter, it must first be shown,

14. *See* La. C.E. Art. 602 Official Comment (b); See also Hidalgo v. General Fire & Cas. Co., 254 So. 2d 493 (La. Ct. App. 3d Cir. 1971).

through testimony or otherwise, that the witness has first-hand knowledge of the matter about which he will testify. This portion of the article imposes the requirement that the necessary **foundation** be laid prior to the witness testifying about a particular issue to establish that the witness acquired the knowledge of the matter about which he will testify from the use of his own senses—information that he personally saw, heard, touched, etc. For example, a witness who will testify about the way in which an accident occurred will first be asked questions such as the following:

Question:	*What were you doing on June 4th at around 1:00 p.m.?*
Answer:	*I was traveling to a doctor's appointment.*
Question:	*Where is the doctor's office located that you were traveling to?*
Answer:	*It is located on the corner of Hillcrest and Maple St.*
Question:	*What route were you traveling to get to that location?*
Answer:	*I was traveling south on Main St. towards Hillcrest, and was going to turn right onto Maple, where the office is located.*
Question:	*While traveling down Main Street, did you notice anything unusual?*
Answer:	*Yes.*
Question:	*What did you notice?*
Answer:	*I saw an accident occur.*

From this point on, the witness could be asked questions about the accident, including the vehicles involved, their color, position, location, and exactly how the accident occurred. The foundational questions have established that the witness is testifying from his own personal knowledge of what occurred. The questions are "sufficient to support a finding" that the witness is basing his testimony on information obtained from the use of his own senses, rather than from information obtained from others.

While the evidence to prove personal knowledge may come from the witness himself, as in the case above, the evidence may also come from another witness. For example, a witness may be asked whether anyone else was around when the accident occurred to which the witness will name the eyewitnesses. Those eyewitnesses may then take the stand and testify as to what occurred. The court will likely find that testimony from the third party witness was sufficient to support a finding that the witness has first-hand knowledge.

While the foundational information may come from sources outside of the witness himself, it is most common, and probably most effective, to always ask a witness himself the necessary foundational questions prior to eliciting his testimony, or a combination of both. Doing so will likely add value, credibility, and structure to the witness's testimony. It might also prevent unnecessary objections from opposing counsel that insufficient foundation has been laid to establish that the witness has first-hand knowledge of the information about which he will testify.

Relationship to hearsay rules. Since this provision limits testimony from a witness about information he learned from others, it will often overlap with the rules precluding hearsay testimony *(discussed infra in Chapter 5)*. As a result, the provision should be read in conjunction with hearsay rules (and exceptions), where in some situations a witness may be allowed to testify about certain out-of-court statements made by others if certain requirements for the exception or exemption are met. In such cases, the witness need only have first-hand knowledge of the statement rather than first-hand knowledge of the substance of the statement.[15] This issue will be discussed in greater detail in the next chapter.

Relationship to opinion testimony. Finally, the first-hand knowledge requirement when read in conjunction with the provision governing lay witness opinions places certain limitations on a lay witness's ability to give opinion testimony.[16] Article 701 requires that lay witnesses may only give opinions that are rationally based on their own personal perceptions. Thus, a lay witness's opinions must be based on first-hand knowledge of the information upon which he bases his opinion. For example, before a witness testifies that a substance in a cup was an alcoholic beverage, the witness must first testify that he saw it, smelled it, tasted it, or concluded that the substance was an alcoholic beverage based on first-hand information. As with all other testimony, lay witness opinions must be based on first-hand knowledge.[17]

This requirement is different than when opinions are given by expert witnesses, whose opinions may be based on first-hand knowledge ***or*** information made known to them.[18] Expert witnesses need not have personal knowledge of the underlying facts upon which they base their opinions. As a result, an expert may consider witness statements, medical examinations, accident reports, or other information in coming to his conclusions or opinions. The information upon which experts may base opinions is discussed in greater detail in Chapter 7, infra.

The first-hand knowledge requirement favors a preference that witnesses testify to factual testimony, with conclusions and inferences about such testimony being left to the trier of fact to make. Thus, rather than a lay witness testifying that the driver drove "recklessly," we'd much rather have a witness testify that the driver, "ran stop signs, exceeded the speed limit, and weaved across the dividing line." The trier of fact can then conclude that the driver drove recklessly.

Key Points

The key points to keep in mind regarding first-hand knowledge.

1. All witnesses must testify from first-hand knowledge—information acquired from the use of their own senses.
2. **Foundation required prior to testifying.** Prior to testifying, there must be evidence sufficient to support a finding that the witness is testifying from first-hand knowledge.
3. The first-hand knowledge requirement often intersects with other rules, such as hearsay, when a witness begins to testify to what someone else may have said or told him.

Problem on First-Hand Knowledge Requirement

PROBLEM 4-8. Jim was on trial for armed robbery. His attorney called Jaiden to testify as an alibi witness in Jim's defense. Jaiden will testify that he and Jim were at his house

15. *See* La. C.E. art. 602 Official Comment (c).
16. *See* Force & Rault, Handbook , Art. 602 Author's Comment (4).
17. Lay witness opinions are discussed further in § 4.8 *infra*.
18. *See* La. Code Evid art. 702.

watching a football game at the time of the robbery. On direct examination by the defense counsel, Jaiden was asked the following questions:

Question: State your name for the record, please.

Answer: My name is Jaiden James.

Question: Where was Jim when the robbery occurred?

The prosecution objected that the question lacked foundation. Should the judge sustain or overrule the objection? Explain. Rewrite the questions to improve the examination.

§ 4.2 References and Additional Authority Regarding First-Hand Knowledge [La. C.E. art. 602]

1. La. C.E. art. 602 and Official Comments
2. Force & Rault, Handbook on Louisiana Evidence Law Art. 602, Author's Comments (West Publishing 2014)
3. Harges & Jones, Louisiana Evidence Art. 602 Author's Comments (West Publishing 2014)
4. 19 La. Civ. L. Treatise, Evidence And Proof § 7.1 (2nd ed.)
5. **Sufficient foundation to establish first-hand knowledge**: *State v. Wright*, 931 So. 2d 432 (La. App. 2d Cir. 2006) writ denied, 952 So. 2d 694 (La. 2007) (holding that testimony of officer regarding items removed from defendant's vehicle after vehicle stop was admissible even though the officer was not the one who collected the evidence); *Abbyad v. Mathes Group*, 671 So. 2d 958 (La. Ct. App. 4th Cir. 1996) (holding that a homeowner could testify regarding cost of rebuilding home, in negligence action against architectural firm, where homeowner had seen project through to completion and had paid bills, and thus, the evidence was within his personal knowledge).
6. **Lack of first-hand knowledge**: *Williams v. Lafayette City-Parish Consol. Govt.*, 72 So. 3d 1023 (La. Ct. App. 3d Cir. 2011) writ denied, 79 So. 3d 1027 (La. 2012) (holding that in action for damages against the city-parish based on passenger's fall on bus as a result of bus driver's alleged negligence, statements of witness, another city-parish bus driver, concerning policy for reporting accidents were outside her personal knowledge and, thus, were properly excluded, where witness testified that she "had to radio it in" if someone fell on one of her buses, but that she had no idea whether the driver had done so); *State v. Jackson*, 523 So. 2d 251 (La. Ct. App. 2d Cir. 1988), writ denied 530 So. 2d 565 (holding that defense questions posed to officer on whether officer would make confession without talking to attorney and whether officer had ever known attorney to advise client to confess unless some deal had been worked out called for opinion testimony not within scope of officer's personal knowledge); *State v. Brown*, 6 So. 3d 966 (La. Ct. App. 3d Cir. 2009), writ denied 24 So. 3d 860, 2009-0979 (La. 1/8/10) (holding that the act of the trial court in sustaining the State's objection when the defense asked one of the State's witnesses whether knew how to get to the victim's house did not constitute reversible error in prosecution for second-degree murder; witness testified that he did not know defendant, so he would have had no personal knowledge of what defendant did or did not know); *State v. Jarreau*, 444 So. 2d 340 (La. Ct. App. 1st Cir. 1983) (holding that court's refusal to allow defense counsel to complete a cross-examination of a police officer as to whether anything in photographs he took at scene of alleged burglary looked "abnormal" or "unusual" was not error

since the officer had no knowledge of the condition of the premises prior to the time he took photographs).

7. **Relative to lay witness testimony:** *State v. Beason*, 653 So. 2d 1274 (La. Ct. App. 2d Cir. 1995), rehearing denied, writ denied 661 So. 2d 1359, 1995-1388 (La. 10/27/95) (lay witness's testimony that negligent homicide defendant's vehicle was going at high rate of speed was properly admitted; testimony was based on personal knowledge and was rationally based on witness's perceptions).

§4.3 Oath or Affirmation [La. C.E. art. 603]

Applicable Code Articles

Art. 603. Oath or affirmation

Before testifying, every witness shall be required to declare that he will testify truthfully, by oath or affirmation administered in a form calculated to awaken his conscience and impress his mind with his duty to do so.

Another important prerequisite to a witness giving testimony is that prior to testifying, each witness must declare that he will testify truthfully, by oath or affirmation, administered in a form calculated to awaken his conscience and impress his mind with his duty to do so. This requirement is contained in Article 603 and changes prior Louisiana law, which required that prior to a witness "affirming" that he will testify truthfully, the witness must have first *refused* to take an oath or to swear, and was required to explain why he chose not to do so.[19] Today, in order to avoid any embarrassment to a witness who chooses to affirm rather than swear, the oath is often administered by asking a witness to "solemnly swear or affirm" that he will tell the truth. The provision also requires that the oath or affirmation take place *prior* to the witness testifying. It is not sufficient that a witness be sworn *after* he has testified, and then be asked whether he was in fact previously telling the truth.[20] It has been held reversible error for a court to fail to require such an oath or affirmation prior to accepting testimony from a witness.[21]

In re Custody of Landry

Court of Appeal of Louisiana, First Circuit
662 So. 2d 169
Oct. 6, 1995

GONZALES, Judge.

This case involves a dispute over the custody of three minor children. The mother of the children, Margie Odet Wilson, and the father of the children, Kenneth Craig Landry, were not married, however, they lived together for over ten years.

19. See Force & Rault, HANDBOOK ON LOUISIANA EVIDENCE LAW Art. 603 Author's Comment (1) (West Publishing 2014).

20. *See* Coffman v. Coffman, 926 So. 2d 809 (La. Ct. App. 2d Cir. 2006).

21. *See* In re Custody of Landry, 662 So. 2d 169 (La. Ct. App. 1st Cir. 1995).

Mr. Landry filed a petition for temporary custody on April 11, 1994, alleging that on March 17, 1994, Ms. Wilson abandoned the parties' domicile in Livingston Parish, leaving the minor children with Mr. Landry and refusing to return. By judgment dated April 11, 1994, the trial court awarded Mr. Landry temporary custody of the children.

...

On November 4, 1994, Ms. Wilson filed a rule for sole custody, child support, psychological evaluation of Mr. Landry, and for contempt. A hearing was held on November 15, 1994. After evidence was presented, the trial court stated that it would continue a joint custody plan, changing the domiciliary parent to Ms. Wilson, with Mr. Landry to have liberal visitation. The trial court then set child support at $300 per month. Mr. Landry began to argue with the court about the designation of Ms. Wilson as the custodial parent, and the trial court found Mr. Landry in contempt and sentenced him to a weekend in jail....

At that point in the hearing, Mrs. Desdemona Landry, the children's paternal grandmother, (who was not a party to the proceedings) began to address the court. She stated that she and her husband would like to have custody of the children and could provide a good home for the children. The following discussion took place:

> BY THE COURT: It would be easy for me to say, that that is too late, your offer I am talking about, because I have already ruled. But the law dictates that I make a decision as to what is in the best interest of the children.
>
> BY MRS. LANDRY: That is our concern.
>
> BY THE COURT: I have not considered, because no evidence was put forth as an alternative placement with you. As I have indicated on the record, I had concerns about Ms. Wilson, and if it had not been for Mr. Landry's temper problem, I would not have removed the children from his house.
>
> BY MRS. LANDRY: Your honor—
>
> BY THE COURT: Based upon—is it Mrs. Landry?
>
> BY MRS. LANDRY: Yes.
>
> BY THE COURT: What I am inclined to do is leave the case open at this time for additional—I will vacate my earlier ruling. My findings still apply. I have some questions about Ms. Wilson. I have some questions about Mr. Landry and when I weighed between the two of them I believed and still do, that Mr. Landry's problems with his anger are such that it would not be appropriate for the children to continue to reside with him as the domiciliary parent.

The trial court then vacated its previous ruling and continued the stipulated plan for visitation (with Mr. Landry as the domiciliary parent and Ms. Wilson to have visitation every other weekend) until a hearing set for December 5, 1994.

At the close of the December 5, 1994 hearing, Ms. Wilson made a motion for involuntary dismissal of Mrs. Landry's request for custody, which motion was denied by the trial court. The trial court then awarded provisional custody to Mrs. Landry, with reasonable visitation to Ms. Wilson and Mr. Landry. The judgment was set for review on June 19, 1995.

...

ASSIGNMENT OF ERROR NO. 3 UNSWORN TESTIMONY FROM A NONPARTY

We note that, in several other cases, the courts have approved an award of child custody to a grandparent who was not a party to the suit. *Roller v. Roller,* 213 So. 2d 161 (La.App.

3d Cir.1968); *Schloegel v. Nettle*, 584 So. 2d 344 (La.App. 4th Cir.1991); *Stuckey v. Stuckey*, 276 So. 2d 408 (La.App. 2d Cir.1973).

However, we agree with Ms. Wilson that the trial court erred in allowing unsworn testimony by Mrs. Landry at the November 15, 1994 hearing. Because Mrs. Landry was not sworn in as a witness, but merely carried on a conversation with the trial court at the close of the hearing, this unsworn "testimony" was presented in a non-adversarial manner, with no opportunity for Ms. Wilson to conduct a cross examination.2 This was a clear violation of La.C.E. art. 603. Louisiana Code of Civil Procedure article 603 provides:

> Before testifying, every witness shall be required to declare that he will testify truthfully, by oath or affirmation administered in a form calculated to awaken his conscience and impress his mind with his duty to do so. The judge's failure to sustain Ms. Wilson's objection on this point was clear error, and the only issue is for us to decide whether or not "a substantial right of the party is affected" under La.C.E. art. 103. As stated in *Kaltenbach v. Breaux*, 690 F.Supp. 1551, 1556 (W.D.La.1988):
>
> > The rights to confront and cross-examine witnesses and to call witnesses in one's own behalf have long been recognized as essential to due process. [citations omitted] These rights are among the minimum essentials of a fair trial:
>
> A person's right to reasonable notice of a charge against him, and an opportunity to be heard in his defense—a right to his day in court—are basic in our system of jurisprudence; and these rights include, at a minimum, a right to examine the witnesses against him, to offer testimony, and to be represented by counsel. *In re Oliver*, 333 U.S. 257, 273, 68 S.Ct. 499, 507, 92 L.Ed. 682 (1948).

We find that this error affected a substantial right of Ms. Wilson's under La.C.E. art. 103. This constitutional violation additionally affected the rights of the parties in that the judge predicated his ruling to vacate his earlier judgment upon this constitutionally prohibited "testimony."

This assignment of error has merit.

Therefore, for the foregoing reasons, the trial court judgment awarding custody to Mrs. Desdemona Landry is **REVERSED;** and the case is **REMANDED** to the trial court for an evidentiary hearing to determine child custody. Costs are assessed against Mrs. Desdemona Landry.

Discussion Questions

1. What is the true purpose of the oath? Consider the overriding purpose of the rules of evidence in accurate truth-finding. Does the requirement that a witness be under oath help further these goals, i.e., does it actually impress upon a person's mind their duty to be truthful and make them more likely to tell the truth?
2. In *Landry*, the court considers a person's courtroom outburst in not only overruling itself in a custody determination, but also in determining provisional custody of the children. What was the true extent of the consequences of the court not requiring the witness to take the stand and testify under oath? In addition to possible constitutional issues, what are the practical consequences in such a case regarding the court's ability to determine the best interest of the child, i.e., could the judge have been sure that the witness was the best custodial arrangement for the children? Why or why not?
3. What should the court have done in *Landry* upon having a witness volunteer information the court deemed relevant to its determination of an issue before it?

Key Points

The key points to keep in mind regarding oath or affirmation.

1. Before testifying, all witnesses are required to declare that he will testify truthfully, by oath or affirmation administered in a form calculated to awaken his conscience and impress his mind with his duty to do so.
2. A witness is not required to explain why he chooses to affirm rather than swear.

Problems on Oath or Affirmation

PROBLEM 4-9. Kathy brought an action against her husband for interim spousal support pending their divorce. Prior to taking the stand at the proceeding, the judge asked Kathy several questions about her living situation and living expenses. The questions were asked in open court and on the record. Following the questioning, and upon request by opposing counsel to ask questions of Kathy, the judge ordered that Kathy take the stand for cross-examination, at which time Kathy was placed under oath. Prior to allowing the cross-examination, the judge asked Kathy if her prior answers to his questions were truthful, to which Kathy answered yes. The judge then stated on the record that all of Kathy's prior answers to the court shall be incorporated into the record. The defense attorney was then allowed to cross-examine Kathy. Following the cross-examination, the judge ordered the interim spousal support over defense counsel's objection to the manner in which the court elicited testimony from Kathy upon which the order was based. Kathy's husband has appealed the order. What outcome? [*See Coffman v. Coffman*, 926 So. 2d 809 (La. Ct. App. 2d Cir. 2006).]

PROBLEM 4-10. Bo was called to the stand to testify in a personal injury case. Upon being given the oath, Bo stated that he does not swear. He was then asked if he "affirmed" that he would tell the truth. Bo then responded, "I promise I am going to tell the truth on the stand." Is Bo's statement sufficient to allow Bo to testify? Why or why not?

§ 4.3 References and Additional Authority Concerning Oath/Affirmation [La. C.E. art. 603]

1. La. C.E. art. 603 and Official Comments
2. Force & Rault, HANDBOOK ON LOUISIANA EVIDENCE LAW Art. 603, Author's Comments (West Publishing 2014)
3. Harges & Jones, LOUISIANA EVIDENCE Art. 603 Author's Comments (West Publishing 2014)
4. **Reversed for lack of oath or affirmation**. *Searles v. Searles*, 9 So. 3d 997 (La. Ct. App. 1st Cir. 2009) (reversed and remanded where court decided case based on unsworn informal discussion with the parties); *Vallius v. Vallius*, 53 So. 3d 655 (La. Ct. App. 4th Cir 2010) (holding that appellate court could not consider the unsworn statement of a trial witness).

§4.4 Disqualification of Judge and Juror as Witness [La. C.E. arts. 605, 606]

Applicable Code Article

Art. 605. Disqualification of judge as witness

The judge presiding at the trial may not testify in that trial as a witness. No objection need be made in order to preserve the point.

Art. 606. Disqualification of juror as witness

A. At the trial. A member of the jury may not testify as a witness before that jury in the trial of the case in which he is sitting as a juror. If he is called so to testify, the opposing party shall be afforded an opportunity to object out of the presence of the jury.

B. Inquiry into validity of verdict or indictment. Upon an inquiry into the validity of a verdict or indictment, a juror may not testify as to any matter or statement occurring during the course of the jury's deliberations or to the effect of anything upon his or any other juror's mind or emotions as influencing him to assent to or dissent from the verdict or indictment or concerning his mental processes in connection therewith, except that a juror may testify on the question whether any outside influence was improperly brought to bear upon any juror, and, in criminal cases only, whether extraneous prejudicial information was improperly brought to the jury's attention. Nor may his affidavit or evidence of any statement by him concerning a matter about which he would be precluded from testifying be received for these purposes.

Judge as Witness

Disqualification of Judge as Witness. Pursuant to Article 605, a judge may not testify in a trial over which he is presiding. This exclusion also relates to other hearings in which the defendant's liberty is at stake, such as a hearing on ineffective assistance of counsel.[22] "To violate this rule, it is not necessary that the judge actually be sworn as a witness and formally testify. Statements from the bench of a testimonial nature during the presentation of evidence may violate the prohibition."[23] Additionally, the judge shall not comment upon the facts of the case, either by commenting upon or recapitulating the evidence, repeating the testimony of any witness, or giving an opinion as to what has been proved, not proved, or refuted."[24] Such comments could result in reversible error.[25]

---

22. Harges & Jones, Louisiana Evidence Art. 606, Author's Comments; *See also* State v. Willie, 595 So. 2d 1149, 1153 (La. 1992), where trial court judge was disqualified to testify as witness in subsequent hearing on ineffective assistance of counsel resulting in attorney's trial court performance.

23. Ford v. Wycoff, 757 So. 2d 833, 839 (La. Ct. App. 3d Cir. 2000); *See also* Harges & Jones, Louisiana Evidence Art. 606, Author's Comments.

24. La.C.C.P. art 1791 and La. C.Cr.P. art. 77.

25. In State v. Brooks, 499 So. 2d 741 (La. Ct. App. 3d Cir. 1986), an issue at trial was the loudness of a gun when its trigger was pulled on an empty chamber. During the trial, which the jury was present, the judge took the gun and pulled the trigger several times. The judge's actions were considered an impermissible comment on the evidence and the conviction was reversed. Even a brief good-natured gibe from the bench, which nonetheless casts a shadow on the credibility of a witness, may constitute reversible error.

Further, no objection need be made in order to preserve the issue for appeal. The rule recognizes that a party might not object out of fear that the judge would retaliate against him for making such an objection. Thus, the requirement of contemporaneous objection to preserve the issue for appeal is waived.

If a judge is to take the stand as a witness, regardless of the nature of his testimony, the judge should be recused from presiding over the trial or hearing. If a party anticipates that the judge may be called as a witness in a trial or hearing, he should make a motion to have the judge recused.[26]

Juror as Witness

Disqualification of Juror as Witness. Similarly, a juror may not testify as a witness in a trial in which he will serve as a juror. This issue is a matter that will typically be discovered and cured during voir dire of prospective jurors as they are usually thoroughly questioned on matters that could affect their ability to decide the case, including questions regarding any knowledge of or involvement in the case. In the rare instance in which a juror is to serve as a witness in a case, the opposing party shall be given an opportunity to object outside of the presence of the jury to avoid the possibility of having a juror biased against the party for so objecting. Because counsel may wait until the jury is outside of the courtroom to object, the rule is also an exception to the contemporaneous objection rule.

Jury Shield Law. Additionally, Article 606(B) contains what is commonly referred to as the "Jury Shield Law." This provision precludes a juror from being called to testify as a witness regarding a verdict rendered while sitting as a juror on a case. Specifically the article states that "upon an inquiry into the validity of a verdict or indictment, a juror may not testify as to any matter or statement occurring during the course of the jury's deliberations or to the effect of anything upon his or any other juror's mind or emotions as influencing him to assent to or dissent from the verdict or indictment or concerning his mental processes in connection therewith."[27] This provision recognizes and expects that jurors will influence each other during deliberations, and will encourage each other's votes either way. Thus, **internal influences** are protected under this provision. Jurors may not testify regarding those factors nor may any affidavit or other statement by him concerning a matter about which he would be precluded from testifying be received for such purposes.[28] This provision is designed to further finality of jury verdicts by preventing inquiry into the basis upon which a jury based their decision.

Exception to Jury Shield Law—Outside Influences. The jury shield law found in Article 606(B) does not, however, prohibit a juror from testifying on the question of whether any **outside influence** was improperly inserted into the jury deliberations. Further, in a criminal case, a juror may be allowed to testify not only about outside influences, but also about any **"extraneous prejudicial information"** improperly brought to the jury's attention. This rule is in recognition of a defendant's important constitutional right to a fair trial when his liberty is at stake in a criminal trial.

---

26. This article should be read in conjunction with provision governing recusal of judges. See C.Cr.Pr. arts. 671–674; CCP art. 4861, and 151; *See also* State v. Skipper, 861 So. 2d 796 (La. Ct. App. 3d Cir. 2003).

27. La. Code Evid. art. 605(B).

28. See La. Code Evid. art. 605(B).

***State v. Wallace*, 110 So. 3d 1199, 1202–1204 (La. Ct. App. 5th Cir. 2013).** In upholding the trial court's ruling excluding testimony of a juror regarding improper jury considerations in support of the defendant's motion for post-verdict judgment of acquittal, the Louisiana 5th Circuit Court of Appeal, in *State v. Wallace*,[29] described the scope of the "Jury Shield Law," as follows:

> In defendant's motion to adduce testimony, he alleged that after his trial, one of the jurors, Ms. Lorraine Broderick, contacted defense counsel to express concerns with the verdict and the jury's deliberations. Ms. Broderick informed counsel that the jury returned a verdict of attempted illegal possession of a firearm because the jury believed defendant was a convicted felon and wanted to punish him for being a felon in possession of a firearm. Ms. Broderick also filed into the record a sworn affidavit, in which she states that during a break in the trial, one juror informed the other jurors that because defendant had been charged with illegal possession of a firearm, he was a convicted felon. Her affidavit contends that two other jurors also stated that they recognized defendant from The Times–Picayune crime reports. The affidavit also provides that during deliberations, the jurors all agreed that neither Mr. nor Mrs. Goertz were actually concerned with being shot by defendant, and that the jury returned the conviction based on the belief that defendant was a convicted felon.
>
> In denying the motion, the trial court stated:
>
> I have a real problem with bringing jurors in, because I do not want to hear from one juror without hearing from the others, and I have a real problem with bringing jurors in to question them as to what they did in their deliberations. I feel that that goes beyond what we're asked to do.
>
> I mean, I understand your argument, that this is what your belief is, is that they believed that Mr. Wallace was a convicted felon. The verdict, as I remember it came down, they found him guilty of one count—
>
> ...
>
> And an attempt was a lesser included offense under the charges. I found it to be a valid verdict. It's not that they reached any conclusions that were beyond that which was presented. I just—I think we'd be violating the jury room.
>
> I invite you to take it up on appeal. If they tell me that we need to have the hearing, I'll have the hearing. But, you know, at this time, I'm denying your motion, and I'm denying the motion for post-verdict judgment of acquittal.
>
> Louisiana's jury shield provision, codified in La. C.E. art. 606(B), generally precludes inquiry into the course and conduct of a jury's deliberations. *State v. Ingram,* 10–2274, p. 5 (La.3/25/11), 57 So. 3d 299, 301. This shield is intended to preserve the confidentiality and finality of jury verdicts, and the confidentiality of discussion among jurors. *State v. Videau,* 04–923, p. 11 (La.App. 5 Cir. 3/1/05), 900 So. 2d 855, 863, *writ denied,* 05–0841 (La.1/9/06), 918 So. 2d 1037. It provides:
>
> Upon an inquiry into the validity of a verdict or indictment, a juror may not testify as to any matter or statement occurring during the course of the jury's deliberations or to the effect of anything upon his or any other juror's mind or emotions as influencing him to assent to or dissent from the verdict or in-

29. State v. Wallace, 110 So. 3d 1199, 1202–1204 (La. Ct. App. 5th Cir. 2013).

> dictment or concerning his mental processes in connection therewith, except that a juror may testify on the question whether any outside influence was improperly brought to bear upon any juror, and, in criminal cases only, whether extraneous prejudicial information was improperly brought to the jury's attention. Nor may his affidavit or evidence of any statement by him concerning a matter about which he would be precluded from testifying be received for these purposes.

> The prohibition against juror testimony is not absolute, but must yield to a substantial showing that the defendant was deprived of his constitutional rights. *Videau,* 04–923 at 12, 900 So. 2d at 863 (citations omitted).
>
> The intent behind the jury shield provision was explained by the court in *State v. Currie,* 00–2284 (La.App. 4 Cir. 2/13/02), 812 So. 2d 128, 136–7:
>
> > Historically, the law was intended to preserve the finality of jury verdicts and the confidentiality of discussions among jurors. *State v. Richardson,* 91,2339 (La.App. 1 Cir. 5/20/94), 637 So. 2d 709; *State v. Harris,* 597 So. 2d 163 (La.App. 2 Cir.1992). As the Supreme Court has further stated: "[N]o juror is competent to impeach the verdict of the jury on which he served.... .This firmly-established rule prevents jurors from impeaching their verdict by disclosure of jury deliberations or even by testimony of misconduct within the jury room." *State v. Abney,* 347 So. 2d 498, 502 (La.1977).
> >
> > Although not strictly held in criminal cases where, as explained above, there are additional constitutional considerations, in civil cases "affidavits and other testimony by jurors cannot be used as evidence to impeach a jury's verdict." *Uriegas v. Gainsco,* 94–1400 (La.App. 3 Cir. 9/13/95), 663 So. 2d 162, 170, citing *Pitts v. Bailes,* 551 So. 2d 1363 (La.App. 3 Cir.1989); "One reason for this rule is that if, after being discharged and mingling with the public, jurors are permitted to impeach verdicts which they have rendered, it would invite tampering with the jurors and would place it in the power of a dissatisfied or corrupt juror to destroy a verdict to which he had deliberately given his assent under the sanction of oath." *Parker v. Centenary Heritage Manor,* 28,401 (La.App. 2 Cir. 6/26/96), 677 So. 2d 568, 574.
>
> In this case, it is not alleged that an outside person presented evidence to the jury that was not adduced at trial. Rather defendant contends that comments made by jurors unfairly contributed to the verdict. This is exactly the situation addressed by *Currie,* where a juror is attempting to impeach a verdict that the jury had rendered. We find no error in the trial court's decision to deny defendant's motion to adduce testimony from a juror. This allegation is without merit.

Thus, in most cases it will only be the interjection of outside influences that might allow inquiry into jury deliberations. However, in a criminal case the rule must yield to a substantial showing that the defendant was deprived of his constitutional rights.

Discussion Questions

1. How and from what does this provision "shield" the jury? What is the significance of such protection? Why is it important? What types of issues could you foresee occurring if such a rule did not exist?
2. Do you agree with the court in *Wallace*? Explain why the juror's testimony did or did not fall squarely within the scope of the protections of the jury shield law.

Key Points

The key points to keep in mind regarding disqualification as judge or juror as witness.

Disqualification of Judge as Witness

1. A judge may not testify in a trial over which he or she is presiding.
2. Testimony includes informal statements from the bench that amount to testimony.
3. If a party anticipates that the judge is to testify, he may file a motion to have the judge recused.
4. No objection need be made to preserve the issue for appeal.

Disqualification of Juror as Witness

1. A juror may not testify in a trial in which he serves as a juror—includes affidavits and other statements.
2. **Jury Shield Law** prevents inquiry into influences in jury deliberations.
    a. Does not preclude inquiry into outside influences affecting deliberations. In such situations, the jury may be so questioned.
    b. In criminal cases, the exclusion applies to both "outside influences" as well as "extraneous prejudicial information" improperly brought to the jury's attention.

§ 4.4 References and Additional Authority Concerning Judge and Juror as Witness [La. C.E. arts. 605, 606]

1. La. C.E. arts. 605, 606 and Official Comments
2. Force & Rault, Handbook on Louisiana Evidence Law Arts. 605, 606, Author's Comments (West Publishing 2014)
3. Harges & Jones, Louisiana Evidence Arts. 605, 606 Author's Comments (West Publishing 2014)
4. 19 La. Civ. L. Treatise, Evidence And Proof § 6.2 (2nd ed.)
5. **Judge's informal statements amounting to unsworn testimony from bench:** *State v. Talley*, 572 So. 2d 230 (La. Ct. App. 1st Cir. 1990) (holding that judge's statements amounted to unsworn testimony when, during a contradictory hearing to determine whether defendant validly waived right to trial by jury, judge stated on record without being sworn as a witness that " 'for the record' he distinctly remembered conducting a colloquy with defendant in the presence of defense counsel" and that "although he could not remember the date on which it occurred, he was satisfied that defendant did intelligently waive his right to trial by jury," and further stated that "he had no explanation for why the court reporter did not record the waiver or why it was not in the record, however, 'it was done' ").
6. **Use of juror affidavits in civil case:** *Fabacher v. Labord, McCauley & Wilson, Anesthesiologist*, 563 So. 2d 1305 (La. Ct. app. 3d Cir. 1990) (holding that court properly excluded a juror's affidavit from consideration in a civil case on motion for new trial alleging improper juror deliberations).

7. **Use of juror affidavit in criminal case:** *State v. Currie*, 812 So. 2d 128 (La. Ct. App. 4th Cir. 2002) (a defendant's constitutional rights might compel consideration of juror affidavit that deliberations that ran from 12:15 a.m. to 6:20 a.m. might have seriously compromised a juror's ability to be alert and a fair decision maker).
8. **Juror testimony excluded on jury deliberations:** *Young v. Armadores de Cabotaje, S.A.* 617 So. 2d 517 (La. Ct. App. 4th Cir. 1993); *Lablanc v. Western Heritage Ins. Co.*, 837 So. 2d 81 (La. Ct. App. 5th Cir. 2002).

§ 4.5 Examination of Witnesses [La. C.E. art. 611(A)–(E)]

Now that we have covered the basic qualifications that witnesses must have to testify, in this section we turn to the basic structure and other procedural issues surrounding the examination of witnesses. As we stated in the introduction, evidence is primarily elicited at trial through the examination of witnesses conducted by attorneys for the parties, and with some exceptions, questions from the court as outlined in § 4.6, *infra*. Examinations of witnesses take the form of:

- **Direct examinations,** conducted by the party calling the witness;
- **Cross-examinations,** conducted by the adverse party;
- **Redirect examinations**, conducted by the party calling the witness after he has been cross-examined, if necessary;
- **Recross examinations**, conducted by the party adverse to the party calling the witness after he has been redirected if necessary; and
- Further recross and redirect examination at the discretion of the court.

Most of the rules related to the interrogation of witnesses are contained in Article 611. This article sets forth the role and duties of the attorneys and judge with respect to examining witnesses, as well as the nature and scope of the examinations.

Applicable Code Articles

Art. 611. Mode and order of interrogation and presentation

A. Control by court. Except as provided by this Article and Code of Criminal Procedure Article 773, the parties to a proceeding have the primary responsibility of presenting the evidence and examining the witnesses. The court, however, shall exercise reasonable control over the mode and order of interrogating witnesses and presenting evidence so as to:

(1) Make the interrogation and presentation effective for the ascertainment of the truth;

(2) Avoid needless consumption of time; and

(3) Protect witnesses from harassment or undue embarrassment.

* * *

Judge's role in examination of witnesses. While the basic rule is that the parties to an action have the primary responsibility of examining witnesses, Article 611(A) also sets forth an important role of the judge in the interrogation of witnesses. Since trial judges have a responsibility to ensure that all matters before them proceed in a legally proper, orderly, and expeditious and fair manner, they must also regulate and exercise such control in the interrogation of witnesses. Under this article, judges are to exercise such authority with specific goals in mind. Specifically, judges are to regulate the examination of witness so as to:

1. Make the interrogation and presentation effective for the ascertainment of the truth;
2. Avoid needless consumption of time; and
3. Protect witnesses from harassment or undue embarrassment.[30]

The powers granted to the judge under Article 611(A) and jurisprudence recognizes the "broad discretion of trial judges in evaluating the sufficiency of the foundation laid for the introduction of evidence, and controlling interrogation of witnesses with respect to relevance, proper cross and redirect examination, leading forms of questions, narrative answers, irrelevant answers, irrelevant direct examinations, and the scope of testimony in rebuttal."[31] Additionally, judges are also granted the power to control the manner in which counsel may question or interact with witnesses to protect them from harassment or undue embarrassment.

The broad powers granted to judges under this article are limited only by the provisions of this article, the constitutional rights of the litigants,[32] "other provisions of evidence law,"[33] and the "conventions of practice."[34]

Applicable Code Article

Art. 611. Mode and order of interrogation and presentation

* * *

B. Scope of cross-examination. A witness may be cross-examined on any matter relevant to any issue in the case, including credibility. However, in a civil case, when a party or person identified with a party has been called as a witness by an adverse party to testify only as to particular aspects of the case, the court shall limit the scope of cross-examination to matters testified to on direct examination, unless the interests of justice otherwise require.

C. Leading questions. Generally, leading questions should not be used on the direct examination of a witness except as may be necessary to develop his testimony and in examining an expert witness on his opinions and inferences. However, when a party calls a hostile witness, a witness who is unable or unwilling to respond to proper questioning, an adverse party, or a witness identified with an adverse party, interrogation may be by leading questions. Generally, leading questions should be permitted on cross-examination. However, the court ordinarily shall prohibit counsel for a party from using leading questions when that party or a person identified with him is examined by his counsel, even when the party or a person identified with him has been called as a witness by another party and tendered for cross-examination.

---

30. La. Code Evid. art. 611(A).

31. La. Code Evid. art. 611 Official Comment to Paragraph A; *See also* State v. Peters, 302 So. 2d 888 (La. 1974) .

32. Force & Rault, Handbook, Art. 611 Author's note (1); *See also*, State v. Shannon, 388 So. 2d 731 (La. 1980); State v. Banks, 362 So. 2d 540 (La. 1978).

33. Force & Rault, Handbook, Art. 611 Author's note (1); See also La. R.S. 15:270–15:501; C.C. Arts. 1831, et. seq.; State v. Mullins, 353 So. 2d 243 (La. 1977).

34. Force & Rault, Handbook, Art. 611 Author's note (1); *See also* 3 J. Weinstein & M. Berger, Weinstein's Evidence 611-12 through 611-74 (1981).

D. Scope of redirect examination; recross examination. A witness who has been cross-examined is subject to redirect examination as to matters covered on cross-examination and, in the discretion of the court, as to other matters in the case. When the court has allowed a party to bring out new matter on redirect, the other parties shall be provided an opportunity to recross on such matters.

E. Rebuttal evidence. The plaintiff in a civil case and the state in a criminal prosecution shall have the right to rebut evidence adduced by their opponents.

Direct examination of witnesses. Now let's take a closer look at the examinations themselves. The party who calls a witness conducts a direct examination of the witness. He asks open-ended questions of the witness, usually in the form of who, what, when, where, why, and how to elicit testimony from the witness. During direct examinations, the party allows the witness to testify from his own first-hand knowledge of events about which he is called to testify, without prompting or suggestion from the examining attorney. During direct examination, the examining attorney should ask short, open-ended questions to walk the witness through his testimony eliciting the evidence needed to build his case.

Generally, an attorney is not permitted to ask leading questions on direct examination. A leading question is one that suggests the answer to the witness. While oftentimes, a leading question may require a yes or no answer, the fact that the question calls for a yes or no answer does not automatically render the question leading.[35] For example, the questions below are not leading:

Q: "Ms. Wilson, do you know the defendant?"

A: "Yes."

Q: "How do you know the defendant, Ms. Wilson?"

A: "He is my former student."

Another example:

Q: "Ms. Brown, are you currently employed?"

A: "Yes."

Q: "Where are you currently employed?"

A: "I work at the county zoo."

In each example above, while the questions call for a yes or no answer, the questions are not leading. The difference between direct and leading questions is demonstrated below in the following chart. As you can see, direct examinations (left) allow the witness to tell the story in his own words. The attorney's questions are slightly dimmed in the

35. *See* State v. Clayton, 570 So. 2d 519 (La. Ct. App. 5th Cir. 1990) (noting that a question suggesting a yes or no answer is not necessarily leading unless it suggests to the witness which answer to give).

chart to demonstrate this point. If the witness's answers *alone* are read aloud, you can see that the story is told through the witness's testimony.

Alternatively, during cross-examination (right), the examiner tells the story. His questions suggest the answer and tells the story. If his questions alone are read aloud, his examination makes sense.

Direct Examination

Q: Please state your name for the record.

A: My name is Mary Wilson.

Q: Where are you currently employed?

A: I work at the Tasty Tavern.

Q: How long have you been employed there?

A: I've been there for three years.

Q: In the course of the three years in which you've been employed there, in what capacities have you worked?

A: I have been a cook, a cashier, a waitress, an assistant manager, and I'm currently a manager.

Q: As manager, what do your duties entail?

A: Basically, I manage the employees—I hire and fire, I make work schedules, order supplies, generally supervise the running of the restaurant.

Q: Were you working on September 28, 2006?

A: Yes, I was.

Q: What times did you work that day?

A: I worked from 11:00 a.m. until around 10:00 p.m.

Cross-Examination

Q: Ms. Wilson, you began working at the Tasty Tavern in October of 2012, right?

A: Yes

Q: And you are still employed there today?

A: Yes.

Q: As of today, you've been working at the Tasty Tavern about 3 years and four months?

A: Yes.

Q: Now, since you've been there you've held several different positions, haven't you?

A: Yes.

Q: You began as a cook?

A: Yes.

Q: You've been a waitress?

A: Yes.

Q: You've been an assistant manager?

A: Yes.

Q: And now you're the manager?

A: That's right.

Q: An in that capacity, your duties entail basic managerial duties, right?

A: Yes.

And so on ...

Because leading questions suggest the answer to a witness, an attorney is generally not permitted to examine his own witness by using leading questions. A witness who can testify based on his own personal knowledge (rather than from suggestion by his attorney) is much more credible and his testimony more reliable. Leading questions are, however, permissible on cross-examination, because even though the answers are suggested, an adverse witness is not likely to agree with the answer just because the opposing attorney suggests the answer he desires.

Use of leading questions on direct examination. While leading questions are generally not permissible on direct examination, there are a number of exceptions to this rule set out in Article 611(C) as follows:

1. when necessary to develop his testimony;
2. in examining an expert witness on his opinions and inferences;

3. when a party calls a hostile witness;
4. a witness who is unable or unwilling to respond to proper questioning;
5. is an adverse party; or
6. a witness identified with an adverse party.[36]

In these situations, counsel may use leading questions on direct examination. Thus, if a plaintiff were suing her employer company for sexual harassment and called the president of the company during direct examination, it would be proper for counsel to ask the witness the following questions:

Question: *Mr. President, didn't Ms. Brown report Mr. Wayne's sexual advances toward her on multiple occasions?*

Answer: *Yes.*

Question: *Yet neither you nor anyone else in the company management ever took any action, did you?*

While the questions are leading questions on direct examination, the questions are proper because the witness is an adverse party or identified with an adverse party because he is the president of the company she is suing. If opposing counsel objects to the leading question(s), counsel should respond that an exception to asking leading questions on direct examination applies when examining a witness identified with an adverse party.

Additionally, counsel may lead a witness when asking introductory or basic information, or otherwise undisputed preliminary issues such as the following:

Question: *Ms. Williams, the defendant is your son, right?*

Answer: *Yes, he is.*

Question: *And he was living with you at the time he was arrested for this offense, correct?*

Answer: *Yes, he was.*

Question: *Okay, now let's talk about the events that transpired that evening. About what time did you first become aware that your son had not returned home from the previous night?*

In this scenario counsel asks a couple of undisputed preliminary questions before getting to the substance of his examination, which is generally permissible. However, if opposing counsel were to object, the examining attorney could either respond that he may question the witness as such under the exception to Article 611(C), or he may simply rephrase the questions. The same applies for the other exceptions contained in Article 611(C). Counsel may ask leading questions during direct examination of expert witnesses, a hostile witness, or other witnesses who are unwilling or unable to respond to questioning.

Cross-examination of own party—leading questions precluded. While leading questions are permissible on cross-examination, the court should prohibit counsel from using

---

36. La. Code Evid. art. 611(C).

leading questions when a person (or party) is examined by his own counsel, even when the party was called as a witness by another party and tendered for cross-examination to his own counsel.[37] For example, if the plaintiff in a personal injury action calls the CEO of the company he is suing to testify to a specific point that he must prove in his case-in-chief, such as an employee/employer relationship for the purpose of proving vicarious liability, when the plaintiff tenders the witness for cross-examination, the defense now has his own party (or a party identified with the defense) on cross-examination. Article 611(C) precludes the defense counsel from using leading questions to question the CEO of the company he represents (a party identified with him), even though the defendant's CEO was called by the plaintiffs and has been tendered to the defense for cross-examination. Leading questions should generally not be used when questioning one's own client, even if the client has been tendered to them for cross-examination, unless an exception above exists.

Cross-examination. As outlined above, after a party who calls a witness has completed an examination of the witness, he tenders the witness to the opposing party, who conducts a cross-examination of the witness. Cross-examination may be conducted using leading questions, except as provided above when a party is being cross-examined by his own counsel.

In Louisiana, cross-examination is usually referred to as **"wide open cross"** because the law specifically states that a witness may be cross-examined on "*any matter* relevant to any issue in the case, including credibility."[38] Cross-examination is not limited to only those matters covered during direct examination by the opposing party.

Federal Rules of Evidence Distinction. Federal Rule of Evidence 611(b) specifically limits the scope of cross-examination to "the subject matter of the direct examination and matters affecting credibility of the witness" and, in the court's discretion, "any additional matters as if on direct examination."[39] While the Federal Rule limits the scope of cross-examination to only those matters brought out on direct examination, the scope is broad and should not be taken literally. For example, if the defendant is accused of running into the back of the plaintiff's vehicle, the mere fact that the plaintiff did not question the witness about the fact that he was not wearing his glasses that day does not preclude the issue from being brought up on cross-examination. The courts generally liberally construe scope for purposes of the rule.

Cross-examination of own party—scope limited. While cross-examination is generally open to any relevant matter under Louisiana law, under Article 611(B), in a civil case, when a party or person identified with a party has been called as a witness by an adverse party to testify as to particular aspects of the case, the court shall limit the scope of cross-examination to those matters he testified to on direct examination, unless the interests of justice otherwise require.[40] Let's take the example above, where the CEO of the defendant company was called by the plaintiff only to testify as to the employer-employee relationship. When the witness is tendered back to his own counsel for cross-examination, not only should his counsel be prohibited from questioning him in the form of leading questions, as outlined above, but his counsel should only be allowed to question him regarding the specific issue(s) about which he was called to testify by the adverse party. In this case,

---

37. La. Code Evid. art. 611(C); *See also* Force & Rault, Handbook, Art. 611(C), Author's Note (3).

38. La. Code Evid. art. 611(B).

39. Fed. R. Evid. 611(b).

40. La. Code Evid. art. 611(B).

Overview of Examination of Witnesses

Type of Examination	Type of Questions		Scope of Examination	
	Type of Questions	Exception to Type	Scope of Examination	Exception to Scope
Direct Examination	Open-Ended Questions	**Exceptions when leading questions may be used:** 1. when necessary to develop witness's testimony; 2. in examining an expert witness on his opinions and inferences; 3. when a party calls a hostile witness; 4. if a witness is unable or unwilling to respond to proper questioning; 5. if witness is an adverse party or someone identified with an adverse party.	Any relevant matter	
Cross-Examination	Leading Questions	**Exception when leading question may <u>not</u> be used:** when a person or party is being examined by his own counsel (even when called by another party and tendered for cross-examination)	Wide-Open Cross-Examination Any relevant matter	**Exception to scope of cross**: When cross-examining one's own party, scope of cross-examination limited to those matters he testified to on direct examination, unless the interests of justice otherwise require (Civil Cases only)
Redirect Examination	Open-Ended Questions	Same as above regarding direct examination	Limited to new matters brought out on cross-examination, other matters within court's discretion	
Recross Examination	Leading Questions	Same as above regarding cross-examination	Limited to new matters brought out on cross-examination, if court allows new matters on redirect	

counsel should only be allowed to cross-examine the witness concerning the employee-employer relationship.

Scope of redirect examination. After a witness has been cross-examined, if the party calling him examines him again, it is referred to as redirect examination. Article 611(D) limits the scope of redirect examination to "matters covered on cross-examination and, in the discretion of the court, other matters in the case." Since Louisiana provides for wide-open cross-examination, it is very likely that issues will be brought out during cross-examination that the party who called the witness did not specifically inquire into. On redirect examination the calling party may then examine the witness on those issues, as well as other issues, in the court's discretion[41] considering factors such as time, whether counsel had sufficient opportunity to inquire into the issue on direct examination, whether the matter has been proven by another witness(es), and the defendant's constitutional right to present a defense as well as other factors.

Scope of recross examination. If the court, in its discretion, allows a party to bring out new matters on redirect, the opposing party shall be provided an opportunity to recross the witness on such matters. While cross-examination is not limited, recross examination is in fact limited in scope to only those matters brought out on redirect examination.[42]

Rebuttal. The plaintiff in a civil case and the prosecution in a criminal case has a right to rebut evidence presented by the defense after the defense closes their case.[43] The evidence presented by the plaintiff/prosecution in rebuttal "must truly contradict or counter" the evidence presented by the defense rather than just be a repetition of evidence already presented in the case-in-chief.

Case on Examination of Witnesses

State v. Rodriguez
Court of Appeal of Louisiana, Fifth Circuit
839 So. 2d 106
Jan. 14, 2003

CLARENCE E. McMANUS, Judge.

[A] Grand Jury for the Parish of Jefferson returned a bill of indictment charging the defendant, Luis Rodriguez, with one count of second degree murder and one count of attempted second degree murder, charges to which the defendant pled not guilty at arraignment.... Trial began on September 21, 1999 and lasted until October 1, 1999, when the twelve-person jury found the defendant guilty as charged on both counts.... [T]he trial judge sentenced defendant to life imprisonment on count one and to [seventy-five] years of imprisonment on count two. Both sentences were ordered to be served at hard labor without benefit of probation, parole or suspension of sentence, and to be served concurrently with each other.

41. La. Code Evid. art. 611(D).
42. La. Code Evid. art. 611(D).
43. La. Code Evid. art. 611(E).

FACTS

On the night of August 31, 1997, Danny Heiness, who was eighteen years old, was shot in the head in the parking lot of Don Carter's bowling alley in Kenner. Another boy, Danny Landry, was shot in the hand....

Detective Powell compiled a photographic lineup that contained defendant's photograph along with several others. Detective Ortiz showed the lineup to three of the four witnesses, Daniel Landry, Jeffrey Clark, and Ernie Gardner. The first two positively identified the defendant as the shooter.... [T]he police seized a blue knit "Tommy Hilfiger" cap, a pair of "London & London" denim overalls, a gold cross, and several photographs [depicting defendant with a gold cross around his neck from defendant's residence]....

Daniel Landry, who was twenty-one at the time of trial, testified that ... Heiness and Landry went to the parking lot to obtain some change from Heiness' car for the pool table. While Heiness was getting change, Landry saw a man, whom he later identified as the defendant, walking around the parking lot....

As Heiness and Landry walked toward the bowling alley, the rest of their friends were walking out into the parking lot. Landry said that he saw the defendant walk behind the group.... Shortly thereafter, Robert Craig, who was the last in the group, told them to stop walking. Landry looked behind him and noticed that the defendant was four or five feet away from Craig. According to Landry, the defendant said, "You about handling business?" Craig replied, "We what?" Then Landry saw the defendant pull a gun from his overalls, cocked it, and then fired. Landry said that he and Craig ducked and began running. When they got a short distance away, they noticed Heiness was not there.... Landry was shot in the hand, and he found out later that his friend had been mortally wounded.

Landry said that he saw the shooter's face clearly, and described him as a "black male, skinny," wearing blue jean overalls with the right strap hanging down, a black and blue shirt, with a black "cango" hat. Also, Landry said the shooter was wearing a gold cross, "with a little Jesus in the middle." Landry identified the pendant that was seized from the defendant's home as the one that the shooter wore....

According to Landry, he could not completely see the shooter's hairstyle because of the hat, but stated that the shooter's hair was shaved on the sides. He did not remember seeing a pony tail or pig tail.... Landry stated that he had positively identified the defendant from the photographic lineup that he was shown, and he acknowledged that he had no doubts that the defendant was the shooter. When shown a photograph of Jorge Serrano, Landry said that he did not see that person at the bowling alley that night.

... Twenty-year-old Jeffrey Clark related essentially the same account of the events immediately preceding the shooting.... Clark said that he saw the shooter clearly, since Clark was only ten feet from him. According to Clark, the shooter wore overalls with the right strap hanging down. Clark identified the pendant seized from the defendant's residence as the one worn by the shooter. Additionally, Clark stated that the shooter wore a "blue denim cango hat" that was turned around backwards, and that the shooter had "like a braid going down the back of his neck."

When the prosecutor showed Clark the photograph of defendant taken at the time of his arrest, Clark acknowledged the defendant did not have a braid. However, Clark denied that the fact defendant did not have a braid at the time of his arrest failed to change his mind that the defendant was the shooter. When shown a photograph of Serrano, Clark was not sure if he had seen Serrano that night. But, Clark stated that Serrano did not resemble the defendant. Finally, Clark stated that he was 90 percent certain the defendant was the shooter when he identified him from the photographic lineup, but after seeing the defendant in person at a prior motion hearing, Clark was 100 percent sure of his identification. Clark also identified the defendant in court.

Robert Craig corroborated much of the foregoing testimony leading up to the shooting. Craig added that the defendant asked whether Craig was a Cripp. When Craig answered affirmatively, the person uttered an expletive and fired the gun. Craig said that the shooter wore a maroon long-sleeved shirt, overalls with one of the straps unhooked and a black "cango" hat. Craig identified the pendant seized from the defendant's residence as the one worn by the shooter. According to Craig, the shooter had a "little rat tail" hanging down. However, he said that the fact that the defendant did not have a rat tail in his arrest photograph did not change his identification of the defendant as the shooter. When shown a photograph of Serrano, Craig denied that he had seen Serrano at the bowling alley. Further, Craig said that Serrano did not resemble the defendant....

The State's theory of the case was that the defendant and Jorge Serrano had conspired to have Serrano claim responsibility for the murder because Serrano was already serving a 20-year sentence at hard labor on a rape conviction. To that end, letters written in Spanish from Serrano to the defendant and vice versa, were seized from their respective prison cells. The letters were translated into English.] ... The letters reflect that the defendant considered Serrano his brother, and the defendant expressed his affection for Serrano in the letters. In one of the letters, defendant inquired whether Serrano still wanted to help the defendant, and in another, he asked whether Serrano had the tattoo with the "five points" made. In the same letter, defendant urged Serrano to "have everything memorized when the party begins." In one of Serrano's letters to the defendant, he responds that he is going to have two tattoos made, "the crown and the five points." He says that he is ready to go to court with the defendant and "begin the fight." ...

Through an interpreter, Jorge Serrano testified that he committed the murder, not the defendant.... Serrano stated that a friend, who was not the defendant, drove him from the scene in a black Nissan Altima. An hour later, another friend, whom Serrano also refused to name, drove him to Miami where Serrano stayed with another friend, whom he refused to name. Serrano returned to Louisiana three months later when he was arrested for allegedly raping his former girlfriend. When he was brought to jail, Serrano saw the defendant there. Serrano learned that the defendant had been arrested for the crime he had committed. Serrano denied that he was lying in order to save the defendant from prison.... Finally, Serrano claimed that he sold the gun to "Felix," who was later identified as Felippe Gomez. The defense established that the .45 caliber casing found at the scene was fired from a gun that was later unlawfully discharged in a bar by Felippe Gomez, with whom both the defendant and Serrano were acquainted.

Christy Mora testified that she was at Wendy's near the bowling alley and heard the gunshot. She stated that she noticed a person carrying a weapon enter the passenger's side of a black Nissan Altima....

Defendant [testified and] denied that he committed the crimes for which he was charged. Defendant further claimed that Serrano did not act in self-defense but actually committed the crime to advance his position as a Latin Kings gang member. Defendant denied being a member of a gang, and removed his shirt to demonstrate to the jury the absence of gang tattoos. He denied owning the overalls that had been seized from his home. Defendant stated that the pants were not a man's garment, since there was no zipper in the front. Defendant denied that he and Serrano had confected a scheme by which Serrano would take responsibility for the crime. Finally, defendant claimed that he did not wear his hair in a pony tail. Rather, defendant described his hairstyle as a "poopy doo," which is characterized by more hair on top with the sides and back of the head shaved.

During trial, Aida Fuentes, the defendant's "common-law" wife, testified defendant was not at home earlier on the evening of the shooting, but that he arrived home at approximately 10:15 p.m....

Ms. Fuentes said that the overalls seized from her residence belonged to her sister, Julia Aguilar, who was staying with them at the time. Further, Ms. Fuentes stated that the cross that was seized was actually at the jewelry shop on August 31, 1997. Ms. Fuentes claimed that she picked up the cross on the following day, September 1, 1997. Both Ms. Fuentes and Julia Fuentes Aguilar stated that Serrano wore his hair in a pony tail, but defendant never had.

Ms. Aguilar said that the overalls belonged to her, not the defendant, and that the defendant came home later that evening, but she was not certain of the time. Further, Ms. Aguilar claimed that the defendant had borrowed her light-blue Toyota Tercel that night. Arecio Conde, who lived across the street from Ms. Fuentes' parents, confirmed in his testimony that the defendant wore his hair short in the back....

ASSIGNMENT OF ERROR NUMBER FOUR

The defendant next argues that the court erred in refusing to allow the defense to ask Jorge Serrano, on redirect or as recalled witness, whether he had a pony tail at the time of the crime. The defendant contends that his right to present a defense was abridged.

The record reflects that the court allowed the defense to examine Serrano at length. In fact, direct examination alone encompassed approximately a day and a half, and the entirety of Serrano's testimony spans volumes eight, nine and ten of the appellate record. During the protracted direct examination, the defense did not ask Serrano about his hairstyle at the time of the shooting. It was only on redirect that the subject was addressed. The State objected on the basis that Serrano's hairstyle was beyond the scope of redirect examination, since the subject was not covered in cross-examination. Mr. Regan responded that he had neglected to inquire about Serrano's hairstyle during direct. The court sustained the State's objection, and denied the defendant's motion for a mistrial.

At the conclusion of redirect, the defense moved to recall Serrano for the purpose of inquiring into his hairstyle. The State objected on the basis that recalling Serrano could raise additional issues, which would entitle the State to recross Serrano and would unduly prolong the trial. The trial judge sustained the State's objection and denied defendant's mistrial motion. The defense then proffered Serrano's testimony, in which Serrano stated that he wore his hair in a pony tail at the time of the shooting.

The scope of redirect examination of a witness is governed by LSA-C.E. art. 611D, which states:

> A witness who has been cross-examined is subject to redirect examination as to matters covered on cross-examination and, in the discretion of the court, as to other matters in the case. When the court has allowed a party to bring out new matter on redirect, the other parties shall be provided an opportunity to recross on such matters.

In the present case, the prosecutor did not ask Serrano any questions about his hairstyle on cross-examination. Therefore, the questions about his hairstyle were not technically within the scope of redirect examination.

Defendant alternatively contends that the trial judge abused his discretion in refusing to permit the defense to recall Serrano to inquire about Serrano's hairstyle. Although the trial judge has discretion to allow a party to recall a witness after the witness has been dismissed, the trial court may deny permission to recall a witness if it will cause undue delay and if the facts show that the party had a reasonable opportunity on the witness's first appearance to question the witness about the matter for which recall is sought. *State v. Griffin,* 288 So.2d 636, 638 (La.1974).

The defendant relies on *State v. Davis,* 498 So.2d 723 (La.1986), which held that the trial judge abused his discretion by refusing to permit the defense to recall the victim. In *Davis,* the key issue was identification of the defendant as the perpetrator of a robbery. During cross-examination, the victim denied that she told anyone that she had not seen the robber's face. Other defense witnesses, however, testified to the contrary. When another witness was asked to relate the details of what the victim had said, the trial judge interrupted, though the prosecution had not objected, and stated no foundation had been laid to impeach the victim. The trial judge denied the defendant's motion to recall the victim to lay the proper foundation. *Id.* at 725.

The Louisiana Supreme Court concluded that the trial judge's ruling was an abuse of discretion because the evidence was relevant and recalling the victim would not have consumed a great deal of time. The *Davis* court observed that virtually all of the State's case rested on the strength of the victim's identification, and the evidence would have served to undermine the victim's identification of defendant as the perpetrator. Therefore, the *Davis* court held that the exclusion of this evidence infringed on the defendant's right to present a defense. *State v. Davis,* 498 So.2d at 726.

The facts in this case are distinguishable from *Davis* because the jury was not deprived of the information that the defense sought to elicit from Serrano on redirect or by recalling him. Both defendant and Aida Fuentes testified that Serrano wore his hair in a pony tail, but that defendant never had a pony tail. Rather, defendant described his own hairstyle at the time he was arrested as a "poopy-doo," which is shaved all of the way around the head with more hair on top.

By the time that the defense sought to ask the questions on redirect, the trial was in its seventh day. The defense had the entire sixth day, and one half of the seventh day to ask Serrano this question. The trial judge's comments indicate he was concerned that recalling Serrano or permitting these questions on redirect, would be unduly time consuming.

The trial court is vested with much discretion in controlling the scope of redirect examination, and those rulings are not to be disturbed on appeal absent an abuse of that discretion. *State v. Wright,* 593 So.2d 759, 764 (La.App. 5 Cir.1992). Considering the length of the trial, the length of Serrano's testimony, and the fact that the defense had an ample opportunity to develop the testimony regarding the hairstyle on direct, it appears that the trial judge was within his discretion to refuse the defense requests.

In addition, for an error to be predicated on a ruling excluding evidence, LSA-C.E. art. 103A(2) requires that a substantial right of a party be affected and that counsel inform the trial court of the substance of the excluded evidence.... In this case, the defendant's substantial rights were not affected by the exclusion of this evidence from Serrano, since the jury heard the same testimony from defendant and Ms. Fuentes. Further, when the prosecutor asked Clark and Craig whether it would alter their identification testimony if it turned out the defendant did not have a pony tail, they answered negatively. Most importantly, all four of the eyewitnesses said that Serrano did not resemble the defendant. Accordingly, even if the trial judge's ruling was improper, the error was harmless.

Discussion Questions

1. What factors do you think a court should consider in determining the extent to which it will limit a party's right to examine a witness, particularly in reference to redirect and recross examinations?
2. What are the underlying policy reasons in giving judges discretion to limit the scope of examinations?
3. Specifically what factors did the court consider in *Rodriguez* in determining whether the trial court abused its discretion in refusing to allow the witness to be recalled?
4. What do you think about the court's analysis of whether the defendant was deprived of an opportunity to present a defense? Should a defendant also have an interest in presenting his defense in the manner in which he chooses?

Key Points

The key points to keep in mind regarding examination of witnesses, i.e., direct, cross, and redirect.

1. On direct examination, witnesses should be asked open-ended questions, usually in the form of who, what, when, where, why, and how. Leading questions are generally not permitted on direct examination.
2. Leading questions suggest the answer. Leading questions are permissible on cross-examination.
3. **When leading is okay on direct exam:** 1) when necessary to develop witness's testimony; 2) in examining an expert witness on his opinions and inferences; 3) when a party calls a hostile witness; 4) is a witness who is unable or unwilling to respond to proper questioning; 5) is an adverse party; or 6) is a witness identified with an adverse party.
4. **Wide open cross-examination.** In Louisiana, a witness may be questioned on any relevant matter.
5. **Calling adverse parties.** When adverse party is called on direct exam, when tendered to his own counsel for cross-examination: 1) leading questions are not permissible; and 2) if in a civil case and called only for one issue, the cross –examination (from own counsel) should be limited to questions only on that issue.
6. **Redirect** is limited to new matters brought out on recross and other matters in the court's discretion.
7. **Recross** is limited only to new matters brought out on redirect.
8. **Rebuttal**. The plaintiff or prosecution can rebut evidence presented by the defense upon closing their case that directly *contradicts* evidence presented in their case.
9. The trial court has the discretion to limit the scope of examinations in time and scope and also with respect to how witnesses are examined so as to protect them from harassment and embarrassment.

Problems on Examination of Witnesses

PROBLEM 4-11. Plaintiff brings a personal injury action against the driver (Driver) of a truck and the company that employed the driver. At the time of the accident, the sole owner (Owner) of the company was present in the truck as a passenger. At trial, the plaintiff calls Owner to the stand in its case-in-chief to elicit information about Driver's employment status and other relevant information to its case. During the course of the examination, Plaintiff asks Owner, "The traffic light facing Driver was red at the time he approached the intersection, was it not?" The defendant's attorney jumps up and objects that Plaintiff is using leading questions on direct examination. Is the question leading? Is the question permissible? Why or why not?

PROBLEM 4-12. Will sued André for damages following a car accident that occurred after André failed to stop at a four-way stop sign. During the defense's case-in-chief, André (D) testifies that he hit Will only because Will (P) proceeded through the intersection ahead of him even though he (André) had the right of way. André continued to testify that he was traveling at the appropriate speed limit and that all of the equipment on his vehicle was in proper working order. On cross-examination of André, Will's attorney immediately asked André the following questions:

Question: *Mr. André, you're single, right?*

Answer: *Yes.*

Question: *You've been divorced for about five years now, right?*

Answer: *Yes.*

Question: *And on the day of the accident, you had a date that evening didn't you?*

Answer: *Yes.*

Question: *You were supposed to be meeting a young lady at The Bistro restaurant at 7:00 p.m. that evening weren't you?*

Answer: *Yes.*

Question: *You testified on direct examination that you arrived at the intersection at around 7:15 p.m. right?*

Answer: *Yes.*

Question: *So when you made it to that intersection you were running late for that date, weren't you?*

Answer: *Yes.*

During the cross-examination of André by Will's attorney, André s attorney objects that the line of questioning is irrelevant and beyond the scope of direct examination because he said nothing about his marital status, where he was going or the fact that he had a date that evening. If you were Will's attorney, how would you respond to the objections to your questions? How will the court likely rule and why? Would your answer change if you were in federal court? Why or why not?

PROBLEM 4-13. The same facts as in Problem 4-12 above. Following the conclusion of the cross-examination of André, his attorney asks if he may redirect the witness. He forgot to question André about the fact that the route on which the accident occurred was on the route that André takes to work each day to establish that André is familiar with the intersection. Assuming the information is relevant in the case, will André's attorney be able to question him about this information during redirect examination? How will the court likely rule and why? Discuss all arguments for both allowing the redirect and denying it. [*Assume that André had testified on direct examination most of the morning about his version of what happened that day. He had been cross-examined most of the afternoon. It was around 4 p.m. when his attorney sought to ask a few more questions on this issue.*]

PROBLEM 4-14. The plaintiff in a civil case called a witness to the stand in its case-in-chief who had worked for the defendant company about 2 years prior to the trial and immediately began asking leading questions during his direct examination. The defense objected that the plaintiff could not ask leading questions on direct examination. How should the court rule and why? Are there any steps that should be taken before the court allows the witness to be led on direct examination? Would your answer change if the witness was a current employee of the business as opposed to a former employee of the business? [*See Brown v. Diamond Shamrock, Inc.*, 671 So. 2d 1049, 1060 (La. Ct. App. 3d Cir. 1996).]

PROBLEM 4-15. In a civil trial, plaintiff is suing a company for injuries she suffered in a car accident with one of the company's delivery drivers when the driver fell asleep behind the wheel after driving for 15 consecutive hours without a break. The plaintiff called an executive of the company to testify to the driver's employment status with the company, to help prove vicarious liability. After laying the proper foundation for the testimony, the plaintiff specifically limited her questions to the fact of the driver's employment with the company, the driver's dates of employment, his duties, and the fact that he was in the course and scope of his employment at the time of the accident. The witness was tendered for cross-examination. On cross, the defendant company would like to question the company executive about all matters they believe are relevant in the case. The plaintiff objects to the line of questioning. In response, the defendant states that under Louisiana law's "wide-open" cross-examination, they are entitled to do this. How should the court rule on the plaintiff's objection and why?

PROBLEM 4-16. Marlon Stephens is the plaintiff in a civil lawsuit against his former employer, LacLus Chemical Company. He is suing the company for injuries he sustained after he was severely burned in a fire after he was locked in a control room during a chemical fire at the plant. He claims the company was negligent in failing to follow several safety procedures (for purposes of this problem, please disregard any worker's compensation laws). The company claims that Marlon negligently caused the fire due to his disregard of all safety protocol. The following is an excerpt from Marlon's deposition in the matter. Using the deposition, please prepare the following: 1) a direct examination of Marlon that his attorney will ask him when he takes the stand; and 2) a cross-examination of Marlon that counsel for LacLus will ask Marlon on cross-examination.

> My name is Marlon Stephens and I've been working for LacLus Chemical Co.—a chemical plant in Louisiana—for 8 years. I am currently a chemical control room operator. I've been working in that capacity about six months. Up until then, I loaded chemicals and filled machines. I've been working at LacLus since I graduated from college with a degree in chemical engineering. It was my first job even though I'd interned there for two summers prior to graduating from college. I had no other experience. Although I'd only been operating that specific machine for three months, I was very familiar with

this type of machinery. I'd received the highest level of training and had all the certifications needed for proper operation of the machine. So it was a complete surprise to me on August 11, 2013 when the machine inadvertently caught fire. After it caught on fire, I exercised all the proper protocols to extinguish the fire and call for backup, but the alarms weren't working and I was unable to put the fire out with the extinguisher in the control room. It seemed like forever before anyone came to assist me. I could feel my skin starting to burn and I could smell it also. I thought I was going to die. I had no way out of the control room. The door was locked in accordance with policy. Protocol provides that there are always two people working in the chemical control room—one to monitor temperatures and one to work controls, but we haven't really practiced that in the last few years and no one ever really said anything about it. It seemed okay. I never had a problem doing both. The fire happened around 2:00 in the afternoon. I had returned from lunch and was feeling fine. I had worked a double shift the day before, but I was alert. I had all of my protective gear on. When I began the afternoon shift, all of the equipment seemed to be working fine. I'd ran all the tests that morning. All of a sudden, while I was operating the controls, I noticed the temperature gauge starting to rise very quickly and within a matter of minutes, flames exploded from the rear of the machine. There was no one around. I have never been so afraid for my life. All I could think about was my kids.

PROBLEM 4-17. Roscoe, a prosecutor, called the victim of a domestic battery to the stand. Before taking the stand, the victim advised Roscoe that no matter what, she would not say anything to hurt her boyfriend. She was nonetheless called to the stand. After stating her name and address, the victim failed to answer the next three questions: Do you know the defendant? How do you know him? What is the nature of your relationship? The prosecutor then asked the judge to direct the witness to answer the questions, which she did. The witness then stated, "Yes, I know him so what?" At this point, Roscoe began to ask a series of questions. Roscoe typically had to ask each question two to three times before the witness said anything, and even then, it would be one-word responses. Roscoe feels that he is getting nowhere. Is there any action he can take to assist him in getting testimony from the witness? What action should he take? What steps are involved?

§ 4.5 References and Additional Authority on Examination of Witnesses [La. C.E. art. 611]

1. La. C.E. art. 611 and Official Comments
2. Force & Rault, Handbook on Louisiana Evidence Law Art. 611, Author's Comments (West Publishing 2014)
3. Harges & Jones, Louisiana Evidence Art. 611 Author's Comments (West Publishing 2014)
4. 19 La. Civ. L. Treatise, Evidence And Proof § 7.1 (2nd ed.)
5. **Court's discretion to limit scope of redirect:** *State v. Wiley*, 614 So. 2d 862 (La. Ct. App. 2d Cir. 1993) (holding that in the discretion of the trial judge, however, matters

outside the scope of cross-examination may be covered on redirect); *State v. Bolden*, 852 So. 2d 1050 (La. Ct. App. 5th Cir. 2003) (holding that court properly limited scope of redirect examination of defendant when issues brought out by prosecution during cross-examination were not new issues).

6. **Limiting scope of recross examination:** *Crane v. Diamond Offshore Drilling, Inc.*, 743 So. 2d 780 (La. Ct. App. 5th Cir. 1999) (holding that recross is not allowed where the redirect examination is merely a clarification of prior testimony and does not involve new matters; the trial judge has broad discretion to permit or deny recross examination); *State v. Brooks*, 656 So. 2d 772 (La. Ct. App. 5th Cir. 1995) (holding that defendant was not entitled to recross examination of witness who was asked about hypothetical paths that shooting victim would have taken in light of showing that redirect questions did not involve new matters but only clarification of previous testimony as witness was shown same picture of layout of apartment complex that she had been shown during direct testimony; redirect questions clarified fact that victim could have taken either of two different routes in coming to apartment after shooting); *State v. Seals*, 83 So. 3d 285 (La. Ct. App. 5th Cir. 2011), writ denied, 99 So. 3d 53 (La. 2012) (court properly limited scope of recross after finding that new issues not brought out on redirect).
7. **Prohibiting leading on direct examination:** *Diamond Shamrock, Inc.*, 671 So. 2d 1049, 1060 (La. Ct. App. 3d Cir. 1996) (holding defendant was properly prevented from asking leading questions on direct of a former employee of D because he failed to lay a proper foundation to show continuing loyalty, sympathy or bias, on the part of the witness to establish that witness was a person identified with an adverse party).
8. **Allowing leading on direct of hostile witness:** *State v. Jones*, 132 So. 3d 505 (La Ct. App. 2d Cir. 2014) (holding that defendant's fiancée, who at trial contradicted her statements to police officer responding to 911 call as to how she had been injured, insisting that there had been just a disagreement and a fall that caused such severe injuries, demonstrated that she would not be cooperative to prosecution, and it was within trial court's discretion to treat her as a hostile witness, according prosecution ability to ask leading questions); *State v. Young*, 576 So. 2d 1048 (La. Ct. App. 1st Cir. 1991), writ denied 584 So. 2d 679 (holding that prosecution could properly use leading questions during direct examination of defendant's family members, in that they were hostile or identified with the defense, despite contention that they became identified with the State once they were offered immunity from prosecution in exchange for testifying).
9. **Allowing leading of expert witness:** *State v. Jackso*n, 629 So. 2d 1374, 1385 (La. Ct. App. 2d Cir. 1993) (leading questions are permitted in examining an expert).
10. **Limiting leading on cross-examination of own party:** *State v. Alfaro*, 128 So. 3d 515 (La. Ct. App. 5th Cir. 2013) (holding that since witness was identified with adverse party, court did not err in allowing the prosecution to lead on direct and did not err in not allowing the defense to lead on cross-examination).

§ 4.6 Calling and Questioning of Witnesses by Court [La. C.E. art. 614]

Applicable Code Articles

Art. 614. Calling and questioning of witnesses by court

A. Calling by court. The court, at the request of a party or if otherwise authorized by legislation, may call witnesses, and all parties are entitled to examine witnesses thus called.

B. Questioning by court. The court may question witnesses, whether called by itself or by a party.

C. Objections. Objections to the calling of witnesses by the court or to questioning of witnesses by it may be made at the time or at the next available opportunity when the jury is not present.

D. Exception. In a jury trial, the court may not call or examine a witness, except upon the express consent of all parties, which consent shall not be requested within the hearing of the jury.

Calling and questioning witnesses. In a **bench trial**, the court may also call witnesses upon the request of at least one party. When the court calls a witness, all parties are entitled to examine the witnesses called by the court.[44] Additionally, the court may question witnesses, whether called by itself or by a party.[45] Objections to the calling of witnesses by the court or to questioning of witnesses by it may be made at the time the witness is called or at the next available opportunity when the jury is not present.[46]

In a **jury trial**, the court may only call or examine witnesses, if all parties expressly consent. The court should not request consent to call or question a witness within the hearing of the jury.[47]

§ 4.7 Sequestration of Witnesses [La. C.E. art. 615]

Applicable Code Articles

Art. 615. Exclusion of witnesses

A. As a matter of right. On its own motion the court may, and on request of a party the court shall, order that the witnesses be excluded from the courtroom or from a place where they can see or hear the proceedings, and refrain from discussing the facts of the case with anyone other than counsel in the case. In the interests of justice, the court may exempt any witness from its order of exclusion.

---

44. La. Code Evid. art. 614(A).
45. La. Code Evid. art. 614(B).
46. La. Code Evid. art. 614(C).
47. La. Code Evid. art. 614(D).

B. Exceptions. This Article does not authorize exclusion of any of the following:

(1) A party who is a natural person.

(2) A single officer or single employee of a party which is not a natural person designated as its representative or case agent by its attorney.

(3) A person whose presence is shown by a party to be essential to the presentation of his cause such as an expert.

(4) The victim of the offense or the family of the victim.

C. Violation of exclusion order. A court may impose appropriate sanctions for violations of its exclusion order including contempt, appropriate instructions to the jury, or when such sanctions are insufficient, disqualification of the witness.

Article 615 contains another rule that helps to further the goal of accurate truth-finding at trial and other court proceedings. This article contains a rule that requires that witnesses remain outside of the courtroom during the proceedings in which they will testify to prevent them from being influenced by the testimony of other witnesses. The rule is commonly referred to as the "**rule of sequestration**," and specifically provides that upon request of a party the court *shall*, or on the court's own motion it *may*, order that the witnesses to a proceeding be excluded from the courtroom where they cannot see or hear the proceedings. Further, under the rule, witnesses are instructed to refrain from discussing the facts of the case with anyone other than the attorneys in the case. "The purposes of sequestration are to guard against a witness's testimony being influenced by that of earlier witnesses, and to enhance the utility of cross-examination in developing the facts."[48]

This rule is not to be confused with "sequestering a jury" where a jury is held together during the duration of a trial to prevent exposure to outside influences such as news, media, family, friends, etc. Article 615 specifically deals with witnesses, and requires that during a proceeding they remain in a position where they are unable to view or hear the proceedings until they are called to testify, and further precludes them from discussing the case with anyone except counsel.

Exceptions to the rule of sequestration. Once a party requests that the court place the witnesses under a sequestration order, the court *shall* grant the request. However, the court *may* exempt a witness from the order in the interest of justice, allowing the witness to remain in the courtroom during the proceedings. Additionally, the article specifically excludes certain witnesses from the rule, giving them a *right* to remain in the courtroom throughout the proceedings, even if they will later testify as witnesses themselves. They are:

1. A party who is a natural person;
2. A single officer or single employee of a party which is not a natural person designated as its representative or case agent by its attorney;
3. A person whose presence is shown by a party to be essential to the presentation of his cause such as an expert;
4. The victim of the offense or the family of the victim.[49]

48. Johnson v. E.I. DuPont deNemours & Co., Inc., 7 So. 3d 734 (La. Ct. App. 5th Cir 2009) (citing *State v. Doleman*, 835 So. 2d 850 (La. Ct. App. 4th Cir. 2002)).

49. La. Code Evid. art. 615(B).

Aside from the parties to the case (or a representative of an unnatural party), and the victim and victim's family, other persons must be shown to be "**essential to the presentation of the party's case**" in order to remain in the courtroom during the proceedings. This means that there must be some **demonstrable need** to have them in the courtroom while other witnesses are testifying, as explained below as it pertains to expert witnesses.

Expert witnesses. Expert witnesses are ordinarily exempt from the rule of sequestration and are allowed to remain in the courtroom during the proceedings. They are typically considered to be "essential to the presentation of the case." In situations in which an expert "is not primarily a fact witness and his presence is helpful to a party in the presentation of his case, such as when an expert assists counsel, or will be called to answer hypothetical questions based on facts testified to by other witnesses, the expert witness should not be sequestered."[50]

For example, as you will learn in Chapter 7 infra, an expert witness may base his opinions and conclusions on information made known to him at or before the proceeding. He may review depositions, police reports, or other information before arriving at the hearing, as well as consider information testified to by the witnesses *at* the hearing. Thus, an accident reconstructionist could be allowed to listen to testimony from a witness about the speed in which he claims to have been driving, the position of the cars, how he maneuvered his vehicle and other information, to use in coming to a conclusion about how the accident occurred. He could then be asked in a hypothetical form, " ... taking that information as true, what would your opinion be about ..." If the expert's purpose at trial is to give such opinion testimony, it could be shown that his presence in the courtroom during the testimony of the other witnesses is essential to the presentation of his party's case, and he will likely be excluded from the sequestration order. Keep in mind though that if the expert witness is primarily a fact witness, then it is proper that he also be placed under the sequestration order.

Victim or victim's family. The victim of a crime and her family are also exempt from a sequestration order and may remain in the courtroom even though they will testify in the proceeding. While the defendant in a criminal case also has a right to remain in the courtroom throughout the proceedings as a party to the action, his family has no right to remain inside of the courtroom during the trial if they will be called as witnesses. As a caveat to the defendant's right to remain in the courtroom during the proceedings, he could be deprived of this right for reasons such as outbursts in the courtroom or other behavioral problems.

Representatives of party who is not a natural person. Typically only one person is designated as a representative of a non-natural party to be exempt from a sequestration order. For example, the CEO of a company may be the only person allowed in the courtroom as a representative of the non-natural party being sued. The entire board of directors, for example, would have no right to remain in the courtroom during the proceedings, unless of course they are not testifying in the trial. However, in some instances more than one person may be designated to represent the non-natural party if counsel can demonstrate the article's requirement that their continued presence in the courtroom throughout the proceedings is essential to the presentation of the party's case. Specifically, counsel must demonstrate a "need to have the witness in the courtroom while other witnesses are testifying."[51]

Allegation of violation/burden of proof. Typically, once there has been an allegation that a sequestration order has been violated, the court will hold a hearing and question

50. La. Code Evid. art. 615 Official Comment (e).
51. La. Code Evid. art. 615 Official Comment (e).

witnesses regarding their conduct as well as call other witnesses to the alleged violation. At the hearing, the party alleging the harm has the burden of proving the following by a preponderance of the evidence through witnesses and/or argument:

1. that a violation has occurred; and
2. that the violation substantially prejudiced his case in being able to cross-examine witnesses, or in developing facts.[52]

The burden is not on the party whose witnesses have been accused of violating the sequestration order to prove that the order was not violated. Only after a ***violation <u>and</u> prejudice*** has been shown is the party entitled to a remedy. Such a violation is considered harmless where there is no evidence that the violation of the sequestration order actually altered or influenced that witness's testimony.[53]

Violation of exclusion order/sanctions. If the court determines that a violation has occurred under the standard above, various sanctions may be imposed including: holding the witness in contempt, instructions to the jury, limiting testimony of witnesses, or in extreme situations, when all other sanctions are insufficient, disqualification of the witness.[54] Exclusion of witnesses should always be a last resort. In a case in which the party has no knowledge of the violation and did not acquiesce in or procure the violation, excluding his witnesses significantly impairs his ability to present a case. In a criminal trial such an exclusion may violate a defendant's constitutional rights to call witnesses on his behalf.[55] In fact, Louisiana courts have held that, "[e]xcluding the witness's testimony, in the absence of a sequestration violation with the consent or knowledge of the defendant or his counsel, is not a constitutionally permissible means [of] insuring reliable testimony."[56] As a result, in a criminal case, witnesses should not be excluded when the rule has been violated unless the party in some way consented to, knew about, procured or acquiesced in the violation. Otherwise, the court should attempt to exercise other less extreme measures such as sanctions, limiting instructions to the jury, or holding the person or party in contempt.

Preserving sequestration rulings for appeal. In order to preserve for appeal a trial court's ruling excluding a witness's testimony from trial for violating a sequestration order, counsel should object to the court's ruling and proffer into the record the substance of the testimony to which the witness would have testified. The substance of a witness's testimony must be known in order for the appellate court to determine whether a substantial right of the party was affected by the court's ruling excluding the evidence to which the excluded witness would have testified.[57] Further, a party who claims that his case was prejudiced by witnesses remaining in the courtroom and not being placed under the rule of sequestration must have requested that the witness(es) be placed under the rule of sequestration in order to complain about the issue on appeal.

---

52. *See* State v. Lucas below.
53. *See* Cory v. Cory, 989 So. 2d 855 (La. Ct. App. 2d Cir. 2008).
54. See La. Code Evid. art. 615(C).
55. See La. Code Evid. art. 615 Official Comment (f); *See also* State v. Warren, 437 So. 2d 836, 839–40 (La. 1983).
56. State v. Jones, 354 So. 2d 530, 532 (La. 1978); *See also* Briscoe v. Brisco, 641 So. 2d 999 (La. Ct. App. 2d Cir. 1994), for an example of a flagrant violation of the rule with knowledge and participation of the calling party, warranting exclusion of the witnesses; *See also* State v. Trahan, 576 So. 2d 1, 12 (La. 1990).
57. La. Code Evid. art. 103(A)(2).

Case on the Rule of Sequestration

In *State v. Lucas* below, the Louisiana Second Circuit Court of Appeal presents an excellent illustration of the standard that must be met in determining whether a violation of a sequestration order has occurred and the factors to consider in determining the appropriate sanctions that should be imposed.

State v. Lucas

Court of Appeal, Second Circuit
896 So. 2d 331
March 9, 2005

STEWART, Judge.

This matter was tried before a jury on February 11 and 12, 2004. Prior to the taking of testimony, the trial court placed all of the witnesses under the "Rule Of Sequestration," advising the witnesses that they would not be allowed in the courtroom to hear the other witnesses' testimony, that they could not "discuss the testimony of another witness with anyone," and that if they discussed their own testimony with either one of the attorneys, they had to do it outside the presence of the other witnesses. The first day, the defendant had four witnesses: Ron Lucas, Sr., Paula Lucas, April Hider, and Sonny Clary placed under sequestration.

At the trial of this case, Shannon Mack ... testified that around 3:30 p.m. on May 10, 2003, she was traveling west on the right lane of U.S. Highway 80, where it intersected with La. Highway 157, in the Haughton area.... [A] dark blue truck ... accelerated and pulled up alongside Mack's vehicle. Mack slowed down to let the truck pass. As she slowed down, so did the truck to where it remained alongside of her vehicle.... Mack saw the driver of the truck had straightened his body out to "where his chin was pushed all the way into his chest ... the top of his pelvic [*sic*] was even or a little above his window. He had his right hand on his exposed penis. And he was moving it up and down and looking at me and smiling ..." ...

After the Macks had testified, the state asked for a hearing outside the presence of the jury, regarding an allegation of a violation of the sequestration order by the defendant's witnesses. Monica Hudson, the Victim Assistance Coordinator for the Bossier Parish District Attorney's Office, testified that earlier that morning she saw the defendant's witnesses in the hallway. She described what she saw by saying, "I got a demonstration and laughing going on about ... the driving." When asked what demonstration did the witnesses give, Hudson testified, "Well, I think it [sic] was trying to duplicate what they said the defendant was doing because it [sic] had—he was pushed up."

When asked whether she heard the witnesses talk about the case, Hudson testified, "[t]hey were laughing. And I don't know what verbally was being said, but they were talking among themselves." ...

After Hudson testified, the trial court told the defendant's counsel, "Mr. Johnson, evidently you didn't listen to the Court's instructions when the Court instructed all the witnesses not to discuss the case with anyone.... Demonstrating and talking about how somebody performed something in a truck is discussing the case, Mr. Johnson."

Thereafter, Ron Lucas, the defendant's father, testified that he did not discuss the details of the case with the other witnesses during the course of the trial. Ron Lucas also testified that one witness, Sonny Clary, did not even know he was going to be called to testify until sometime around lunchtime. On cross, Ron Lucas testified he was sitting next to Clary. When asked if Clary was demonstrating something while beside him, Ron Lucas testified, "[h]e may have been. I don't know what he was demonstrating really.... I think he was trying to relate to an incident that happened sometime back to him or someone that he knew or something to that nature."

Cullen David "Sonny" Clary testified that ... he had not discussed the details of the case or his testimony with anyone out in the hallway, and did not recall giving some sort of demonstration of someone raising his pelvis up, while sitting with the other witnesses. On cross, Clary acknowledged that at some point, the bailiff came over and told the witnesses not to talk about the case. Clary testified they were not talking about the case, but were talking about a football half-time show....

April Rider testified that she had been with the defendant's other witnesses all day, and that she had not talked about the details of her testimony with any other witness. Rider denied seeing any "demonstration" by any of the other witnesses. On cross, Rider testified that she did not see Clary make any "certain bodily displays" or "particular bodily positions" in relation to the case. She did testify that Clary may have made some form of "body contortions" regarding either a football game or a halftime show. She stated she didn't know much of what was said because she was "pacing the floor."

The next witness was Paula Lucas, the wife of Ron Lucas. She testified that she did not discuss the details of the case with any other witness. As to her conversation with Clary, Paula Lucas testified that she hadn't seen him for some years and they were just catching up on children and past history. She testified Clary talked about his son. Clary also talked about the Super Bowl halftime show incident with Janet Jackson, and he was making some sort of demonstration about football when the "gentleman" came out and made a motion for them to quit. "We were laughing at that point and he said don't be talking about the case. I said we're not." Paula Lucas further testified that they were laughing about the Janet Jackson halftime show incident....

The trial court found that the witnesses had violated the court's rule of sequestration. The trial court further found, "I have no idea to what extent because nobody would be truthful." The trial court ruled, "I'm going to order that they not be allowed to testify for violation of the Rule of Sequestration. That would be the order of this Court." The trial court further ruled that since the witnesses violated the rule of sequestration, "the only thing the Court can do is limit their testimony based upon what they're going to testify to." ...

The jury found the defendant guilty of obscenity....

Disqualification of Witnesses

Lucas argues the trial court's order excluding all of his witnesses from testifying was based on insufficient evidence and deprived him of a fair trial.

The state argues the trial court's action was not an abuse of discretion, and if it was, the appropriate action would be to remand the case for an evidentiary hearing to determine the materiality of the testimony to the defendant's case.

We find that the trial court violated defendant's constitutional right to compel the attendance of witnesses and to present his defense by disqualifying all of his witnesses for a perceived violation of a sequestration order....

The record shows that pursuant to La. C.E. art. 615, all of the witnesses, including the defendant's four witnesses, were placed under the "rule of sequestration." ...

There is no evidence that the defendant was aware of the witnesses' actions. There is also no evidence that any of the witnesses ever heard or watched the testimony in the courtroom.

At the hearing on the matter, all of the defendant's witnesses denied discussing their testimony with any of the other witnesses, each giving a varying account of what did or did not happen in the hallway. A couple of the witnesses attributed the "demonstration" to Sonny Clary, a character witness for the defendant who had only arrived at the court an hour or so earlier. These witnesses testified the conversation was either about football or the halftime show involving Janet Jackson's wardrobe malfunction. The trial court found none of the witnesses to be truthful, and further ruled that when the witnesses violated the rule of sequestration, "the only thing the Court can do is limit their testimony based upon what they're going to testify to." The trial court barred all of the witnesses from testifying at trial.

The trial court's ruling was based on clear errors of law. First, disqualification of the witnesses was not the only option available to the trial court....

Even if the evidence presented to the trial court was sufficient to find the witnesses had discussed the case, excluding all of the defendant's witnesses was not the only option available. It is the last option available. This is particularly true in cases where the evidence shows that the defendant neither consented to, nor had any prior knowledge of the infraction by his witnesses. To automatically exclude all of a party's witnesses without any review of other possible appropriate sanctions, "... is not a constitutionally permissible means of insuring reliable testimony." *State v. Jones, supra,* at 532.

The second error by the trial court was to shift the burden of proof in the hearing to the defendant by ruling that it would automatically exclude the witnesses unless the defendant could produce evidence to support a reason not to exclude the witnesses.

The purpose of sequestration is to assure that a witness testifies as to his own knowledge, to prevent witnesses from being influenced by the testimony of others, and to strengthen the role of cross-examination in developing facts. The mere fact that a witness speaks to other witnesses does not establish a violation of the order of sequestration and does not show possible prejudice. Exclusion of witnesses would not be an appropriate sanction without a showing of how the infraction prejudiced the opposing side's right to cross-examine the witnesses and develop needed facts in the case.

In the present case, the state asserted the motion. Accordingly, the state, as the injured party, should have had the burden of proving not just that a sequestration violation occurred, but also how the violation prejudiced its case before being entitled to having witnesses excluded. The state provided the trial court with no evidence or argument as to how the witnesses' testimony was tainted by the violation or how its ability to cross-examine these witnesses was in any way hampered or prejudiced by the violation. Without any showing, by a preponderance of the evidence, that a sequestration violation occurred and that the violation substantially prejudiced his case, a complaining party is not entitled to having his opponent's witnesses excluded from the trial.

... In *State v. Jones, supra,* the state chose not to use a subpoenaed witness, who was not sequestered and allowed to remain in the courtroom. After the trial had progressed, the defendant attempted to call the witness, but the trial court excluded the witness from testifying. The court remanded the matter for an evidentiary hearing on the materiality of the witness's testimony, since the record was silent as to what he would have testified about.

In the present case, *all* of the defendant's witnesses were excluded, thereby virtually eliminating the defendant's constitutional right to compel witnesses to testify on his behalf.

Unlike in *State v. Jones, supra,* the present record shows the defendant was prejudiced by the exclusion of all of his witnesses. For example, the defendant repeatedly attempted to introduce photographs of his truck into evidence to contradict the victim's version of the story. But, the defendant could not lay the foundation for the introduction of the photographs, since the photographs had been taken by excluded witnesses. The defendant testified he was home by the time that the victim first called 911. He also testified about a large wooden pallet being in the back of the truck at the time of the alleged incident, which was not seen by the victim. But, his girlfriend, who was home when the defendant returned, was excluded from testifying....

Consequently, we reverse the defendant's conviction and sentence and remand this matter for a new trial.

Discussion Questions

1. What are your thoughts about how the *Lucas* court handled the following: 1) placing the burden on the defense to prove that no violation of the rule occurred; 2) its determination that there had been a violation of the rule of sequestration on the evidence presented (all witnesses denying having discussed the case, and neutral witnesses not hearing anything about the case being discussed); 3) not requiring a showing of prejudice; and 4) its imposition of the maximum sanction?
2. Describe the appropriate steps the court should have taken once the allegation of the violation of the rule was made. Procedurally, what should have happened? Who had the burden? What should have been shown? What remedy? Based on the cursory view of the witness's testimony outlined in the case above, did it appear to be reasonable that the court found that a violation had occurred?
3. If the State had been able to show that their case had been substantially prejudiced by a violation of the rule of sequestration and that the defendant was not aware of nor procured the violation, what sanction should be imposed considering the defendant's right to present a defense? What are the two competing interests in such a situation? Which of the two interests should outweigh the other and why?

Key Points

The key points to keep in mind regarding the rule of sequestration.

1. The rule requires witnesses to remain outside of the courtroom, and not discuss the case with other witnesses.
2. **Should be requested.** Counsel should request that the witnesses be placed under the rule of sequestration in order to be able to later complain on appeal. If requested, the court *shall* order that the witnesses be placed under the rule. If not requested, the court *may* order witnesses be placed under the rule.
3. **Exempted from rule.** The statute specifically exempts certain persons from the rule: parties to the action, including a representative of non-natural parties; victims and victim's family; and others who are essential to the presentation of the case.
4. **Other exempted persons.** Other persons may only be exempted from the rule if they are deemed *"essential to the presentation of the case,"* meaning that there must be a

demonstrable need to have them in the courtroom while other witnesses are testifying, such as an expert witness who will rely on their testimony to answer hypothetical questions, or perhaps the parent of a young child.

5. **Proving violation.** Once there has been a reported violation of the rule, the party alleging the harm has the burden of proving: 1) that a violation has occurred; and 2) that the party was prejudiced as a result of the violation (in cross-examining witnesses, or developing their facts).
6. Only a party who can prove that a violation occurred, and that they were prejudiced, has a right to a remedy.
7. **Sanctions for violation.** If the court determines that a violation has occurred, possible sanctions include: holding witnesses in contempt, limiting instructions to jury, limiting testimony, and in extreme cases, excluding the witness. Exclusion of witnesses should be a **last** resort, especially when the defendant had no knowledge of the violation, and did not consent to or procure it.
8. **Defendant's right to present defense.** In a criminal case, exclusion of witnesses violates a defendant's right to present a defense when he had no knowledge of the violation and did not procure or acquiesce in the violation.
9. **Preserving issue for appeal.** If a party's witnesses are excluded for violating the rule, particularly if the party had no knowledge of the violation, the party should object and proffer the substance of the excluded witnesses' testimony to properly preserve the court's ruling for appeal.

Sequestration Problems

PROBLEM 4-18. Nancy attacked Patricia at the PTA meeting. During the altercation, Nancy stabbed Patricia. Nancy is now on trial for aggravated battery of Patricia and claims self-defense. Patricia says Nancy attacked her simply because she disagreed with her at the meeting. There were several witnesses to the altercation, and both the prosecution and Nancy's lawyer plan to call several witnesses that will each testify that the other started the altercation. The prosecution does not want any of the witnesses in the courtroom during the trial because he doesn't want them to change their stories to go along with anyone else's testimony. However, he would like for Patricia to remain in the courtroom. What should he do? Does he have a right to have the witnesses excluded? Can either Nancy or Patricia (or both) remain in the courtroom? Why or why not? Fully explain your answer.

PROBLEM 4-19. Johnon had several witnesses who he planned to call as witnesses in his trial for armed robbery. At Johnon's request, the witnesses were placed under the rule of sequestration. After the first witness testified, the bailiff observed him chatting with the other witnesses outside the courtroom. If the prosecution objects that the witnesses have violated the sequestration order, what action should the court take? Explain why the court should or should not take each of the following actions:

A. Order a new trial.

B. Exclude the witnesses from testifying at the trial.

C. Inquire as to whether the rule has been violated, and if so, the court may exercise its discretion in ordering one of various remedies.

D. Overrule the objection because there's been no proof of violation of the rule.

E. Allow the defense to respond and if their response satisfies the court that the rule has not been violated, then overrule the objection and proceed with the trial.

PROBLEM 4-20. Morris is on trial for armed robbery. He plans to call two witnesses in his defense, both his brother and mother, who are both alibi witnesses. Both will testify that Morris was at home with them watching television at the time of the robbery. Following Brother's testimony in Morris' case-in-chief, he went outside and told Mother what the prosecution was going to imply during the cross-examination. The bailiff overheard it and reported it to the court. During the hearing the prosecution established that the witnesses had discussed the case, and the court excluded Mother from testifying at the trial. What must Morris do to preserve the issue for appeal? What outcome on appeal? Did the court err in excluding the testimony? Do you believe Morris was deprived of an opportunity to present a defense by having his mother's testimony excluded from trial? Why or why not?

PROBLEM 4-21. Dr. Milton is the Parish Coroner who will testify to the fact and cause of death of the victim in a first-degree murder trial. The defense has requested that all witnesses be placed under the rule of sequestration. Should he be required to take a place outside of the courtroom or may he be exempt from the rule? What must be shown in order for the expert witness to be allowed to remain in the courtroom during the proceedings?

PROBLEM 4-22. The defendant is 16 years old and is being tried as an adult for second-degree murder for killing a high school classmate at school. At the trial, the parties request that the witnesses be placed under the rule of sequestration. The State has requested that the parents of the victim and their attorney in the civil case against the school be allowed to remain in the courtroom, even though they are all scheduled to be witnesses in the case. The defense has also requested that the parents of the defendant be allowed in the courtroom due to his young age, for moral support. They are also scheduled to testify. How should the court rule on whether each party (victim's parents, parents' attorney, and defendant's parents) should be allowed to remain in the courtroom and why?

PROBLEM 4-23. Gorge is on trial for raping his 16-year-old stepdaughter. All of the prosecution's witnesses are inside of the courtroom when the victim gives compelling testimony. After the victim testifies, the defense requests that the prosecution's remaining 11 witnesses be placed under the rule of sequestration. The defendant had no witnesses that he planned to call. The court granted the motion and placed the witnesses outside of the courtroom for the remainder of the trial. During each witness's testimony it appeared as though their stories had slightly changed from the statements they'd given to the police. On appeal, Gorge claims that he was prejudiced by having the witnesses inside of the courtroom during the victim's testimony. How should the issue be handled and why?

§ 4.7 References and Additional Authority Concerning Sequestration of Witnesses [La. C.E. art. 615]

1. La. C.E. art. 615 and Official Comments
2. Force & Rault, Handbook on Louisiana Evidence Law Art. 615, Author's Comments (West Publishing 2014)
3. Harges & Jones, Louisiana Evidence Art. 615 Author's Comments (West Publishing 2014)

4. 19 La. Civ. L. Treatise, Evidence And Proof § 7.1 (2nd ed.); La. Prac. Civ. Trial § 6:15.
5. **Witnesses improperly excluded from testifying, depriving defendant of right to present a defense:** *State v. Trahan,* 576 So. 2d 1, 12 (La. 1990) (holding that excluding witnesses for violation "without consent, connivance, procurement or knowledge of the defendant or counsel is not a constitutionally permissible means of insuring reliable testimony"); *State v. Joubert,* 534 So. 2d 91, 93 (La. Ct. App. 3d Cir. 1988) (finding exclusion of witnesses improper and reversible error).
6. **Exclusion generally disfavored without procurement by party or counsel:** *State v. Watson,* 844 So. 2d 198 (La. Ct. App. 5th Cir. 2003) (holding that exclusion was a disfavored sanction absent showing that the violation occurred with the consent, connivance, procurement or knowledge of the party or his counsel for whom the witness was to testify).
7. **Victim's family properly allowed in Courtroom:** *State v. Johnson,* 833 So. 2d 508 (La. Ct. App. 4th Cir. 2002) (witness was victim in case and properly allowed to remain in courtroom); *State v. Lyles,* 858 So. 2d 35 (La. Ct. App. 5th Cir. 2003) (because witnesses were victims in case, they were properly allowed to remain in courtroom).
8. **Witness essential to presentation of case**: *Ortego v. Pratt-Farnsworth, Inc.*, 423 So. 2d 780 (La. Ct. App. 4th Cir. 1982) (finding that an "insured," although not a party, may be essential to the presentation of the insurer's defense); *Hopkins v. Department of Highways,* 350 So. 2d 1271 (La. Ct. App. 3d Cir. 1977) (holding that if experts are primarily fact witnesses, exclusion may be proper); *Basic Home Care Services, Inc. v. Dore,* 945 So. 2d 861 (La. Ct. App. 3d Cir. 2006) (Mrs. Dore was the individual to whom the services were provided by Basic Home Care. As such, it was she who would have knowledge of the facts and the truthfulness of the witnesses' testimony necessary to assist defense counsel. Therefore, we find no abuse of the trial court's broad discretion in his refusal to order the sequestration of Mrs. Dore. Nevertheless, this issue is rendered moot since this court affirms the trial court's grant of directed.); *Rhone v. Boh Bros.*, 804 So. 2d 764 (La. Ct. App. 4th Cir 2001) (employer's medical expert allowed to remain in courtroom in worker's compensation hearing).
9. **Representative properly allowed to remain in courtroom:** *Spears v. Ryan's Steakhouse,* 965 So. 2d 435, (La. Ct. App. 1st Cir. 2007), writ denied 964 So. 2d 364, 2007-1348 (La. 9/28/07) (holding that employer's general manager was a company representative not subject to the sequestration order, and thus, he could testify in workers' compensation action, even though he remained in court in spite of sequestration order); *Prater v. Town of Elton,* 2008 WL 4801712 (La. Ct. App. 3d Cir. 2008) (town mayor not sequestered when the town is a party to suit).
10. **Violation requires showing of prejudice, i.e., that violation "tainted" testimony**: *Cory v. Cory,* 989 So. 2d 855 (La. Ct. App. 2d Cir. 2008) (sanctions appropriate only with showing of actual prejudice—witness's testimony tainted, altered, or influenced by violation); *State v. Firmin,* 637 So. 2d 1143 (La. Ct. App. 4th Cir. 1994); *State v. Babin,* 637 So. 2d 814 (La. Ct. App. 1st Cir. 1994).
11. **Media exposure**: *State v. Clarkson,* 86 So. 3d 804 (La. Ct. App. 3d Cir. 2012) (where reporter did real-time blog of court proceedings).
12. **Not a party:** *Duhon v. Duhon,* 801 So. 2d 1263 (La. Ct. App. 3d Cir. 2001) (holding that husband's new wife was not a party to child custody litigation and was subject to the rule of sequestration, even though wife had named new wife as a defendant to the action; new wife was a witness, rather than a party in child custody dispute between the biological parents).

§ 4.8 Lay Opinion Testimony [La. C.E. art. 701]

Applicable Code Articles

Art. 701. Opinion testimony by lay witnesses

If the witness is not testifying as an expert, his testimony in the form of opinions or inferences is limited to those opinions or inferences which are:

(1) Rationally based on the perception of the witness; and

(2) Helpful to a clear understanding of his testimony or the determination of a fact in issue.

The final topic we will cover in this chapter pertains to the extent to which a lay witness may testify in the form of opinions and conclusions.[58] While the preference is that a lay witness's testimony be factual and to allow the *jury* to draw conclusions based on those facts, the law provides authority for opinion testimony from witnesses if specific criteria are met. Chapter 7 of the Louisiana Code of Evidence governs the admissibility of opinion testimony of witnesses. The rules depend upon whether the person has been qualified as an expert witness or if the witness is testifying as a lay witness. If a witness is not qualified to testify as an expert in a particular field based on specialized knowledge, then the witness is testifying as a lay witness. Lay witnesses are generally prohibited from giving opinion testimony; however, Article 701 provides for limited circumstances in which lay witness opinions may be offered.

While certain opinions, such as testimony regarding a person's cause of death, obviously require specialized expertise, there are some opinions that any reasonable person can give. For example, any reasonable person might be able to testify that another person appeared to be happy, sad, or anxious; that a beverage was water, milk, or coffee; or that a substance smelled like smoke, gasoline, or bleach. All of these examples are opinions or conclusions that could be drawn by any reasonable person based on common experiences. Article 701 provides authority for rendering such opinions by witnesses, even if the witness has no specialized skills or training, if he can base his opinion testimony on information that he personally perceived, and the opinion would be helpful to the jury in some way.

Thus, if a witness has not been qualified as an expert witness to give expert opinions pursuant to Articles 702–706, he may only give testimony in the form of opinions or inferences if two requirements are met. The opinions or inferences must be:

1. **rationally based** on the witness's own **personal perceptions**; and
2. **helpful** to a clear understanding of the witness's testimony or the determination of a fact in issue.

Based on the requirements set out in Article 701 and accompanying case law, there are five major issues we will examine in this section relative to a lay witness's testimony in the form of opinions and conclusions:

1. the opinion testimony must be **reasonable** common sense **inferences**;

58. Expert witnesses are covered in Chapter 7 of the casebook.

2. the opinions/inferences must be **rationally based** on facts ***perceived*** by the witness;
3. the underlying facts/perceptions must be ***personal*** **perceptions**, of which the witness has first-hand knowledge;
4. the opinions must be **helpful** to a clear understanding of testimony or determination of a fact in issue; and
5. sufficient **foundation** must be laid to establish the underlying facts upon which the opinion is based, i.e., the witness must state the facts.

Rationally based opinions or inferences. The limitation on lay witness opinions to only those opinions that are "**rationally based**" on perceptions, is for the most part another way of stating that the opinions of lay witnesses can be no more than "reasonable inferences" that could be drawn by any reasonable person, and not requiring any specialized knowledge, skill, training, or expertise.

In Louisiana, lay witnesses have been permitted to testify to their opinions and reasonable inferences in various situations, including: a person's emotional state or appearance, a person's handwriting, voice, intoxication, the speed of vehicles, that various fluids appeared to be blood, semen, or urine, smells, tastes, and a person's age, height, or weight.[59] In all of these situations, any reasonable person could have drawn the reasonable inferences or conclusions that were the substance of the witness's opinion testimony after perceiving the underlying facts upon which the inferences were based.

Based on personal perceptions. Additionally, the opinions and inferences of lay witnesses must be based on **personal perceptions**. This requirement contains two significant aspects: 1) the witness must have personal first-hand knowledge of the underlying facts upon which his opinion is based, and not based on information relayed to him by someone else; and 2) the opinion or inferences of the lay witness must be based on facts *perceived* by the witness, i.e., what he personally saw, heard, touched, smelled, etc.

As we discussed in § 4.2, testimony must be based on first-hand knowledge. If a witness is to give an opinion, he must have first-hand knowledge of the facts upon which his opinion is based. Such knowledge must have been obtained through his own personal perceptions—that which he personally saw, touched, smelled, or even heard, upon which he could rationally base an inference or opinion. For instance, if a witness will testify that gasoline was poured on his vehicle, he must have personally **seen** or **smelled** it. There must have been something about the liquid that appealed to his senses that led to his conclusion that it was in fact gasoline being poured on his car. A witness might be able to testify that the beverage was coffee because he **tasted** it or **smelled** it. He might know that a baby was in the room because he **heard** it crying; or he might be able to testify to a person's mood or emotion because he personally **saw** their demeanor (smile, tears, laughing, etc.).

A lay witness should not be allowed to give an opinion based on information relayed to him by someone else. For example, a witness should not be allowed to testify that, "*I think my daughter's husband was drunk last night. She told me that when he got home he was stumbling, had slurred speech and bloodshot eyes.*" Such testimony amounts to mere speculation and conjecture and is unreliable. While the daughter could testify that her

59. Harges & Jones, Louisiana Evidence, Art. 701 Author's comments.

husband appeared to be drunk, based on her personal observations, i.e., speech, eyes, stumbling, etc., the mother, who was told the information by the daughter, could not.

Foundation to show first-hand knowledge. An important prerequisite to a lay witness testifying to his opinion or inferences is that a sufficient **foundation** must be laid to establish the underlying facts upon which the opinion is based. As with all testimony, prior to the witness giving an opinion, there must be evidence "sufficient to support a finding" that the witness has first-hand knowledge of that to which he testifies. Consequently, a witness must not only base his opinion on information that he personally perceived, but he must also **state those facts** prior to giving the testimony.[60] For example, the witness might testify that he saw a white substance in a cup that he concluded was milk, or that he heard a loud sound and in his opinion a gun had been fired.

If a witness is to testify that a person appeared to be happy and excited about something, a proper foundation will include the facts upon which he based that conclusion—that the person was smiling and laughing and jumping up and down. He will then testify that based on what he saw (or otherwise heard, smelled, touched, tasted, etc.), he concluded that the person was happy and excited. If counsel has not laid sufficient foundation to establish that the witness personally perceived the facts upon which the lay witness based his opinion, the opposing party should object to insufficient foundation for a lay witness opinion, and the opinion testimony should be excluded.

Helpfulness. Another important requirement that must be met for a lay witness to give an opinion is that the opinion testimony must be **helpful to the finder of fact** to either: 1) understanding the witness's testimony; or 2) determining a fact in issue. If the court does not find that the opinion testimony is helpful, the testimony should be excluded. In some instances the courts have found the opinion testimony not to be helpful if it is not based on personal observations because it merely constituted speculation.[61] Testimony might also not be helpful if it embraces the ultimate issue to be determined by the trier of fact.

Additionally, the courts construe whether the "helpfulness" requirement is met with respect to whether the opinion is relevant to any issue that must ultimately be determined at the trial. The helpfulness requirement is further discussed below in *State v. Butler*.[62]

Lay witnesses with expertise in a particular field. As you have learned, if a witness has not been qualified as an expert witness in a particular field based on his specialized knowledge, education, or training, then his testimony should be confined to the scope of a lay witness's opinion as we've discussed in this section. In Chapter 7 we will study the procedures for qualifying a witness as an expert in detail, but for now you should know that prior to a witness testifying as an expert, he usually testifies to whatever training, skills, experience, education, etc. qualifies him to give expert testimony. He is then tendered as an expert in a particular field based on those qualifications. The court usually then declares that the witness has or has not been accepted as tendered prior to the witness giving such expert testimony. If this procedure is not followed, recognizing the witness as an ex-

60. *See* State v. Decay, 798 So. 2d 1057 (La. Ct. App. 5 Cir. 2001) ("Where subject of testimony is such that any person of experience may make a natural inference from observed facts, a lay witness may testify as to such inferences, provided he also states the observed facts"); *See also* La. Code Evid. art. 602 (requiring first-hand knowledge, and evidence sufficient to prove witness has first-hand knowledge).

61. *See* Shaw v. Fidelity & Cas. Ins. Co., 582 So. 2d 919, 924 (La. Ct. App. 2d Cir. 1991).

62. State v. Butler, 563 So. 2d 976 (La. Ct. App. 1st Cir. 1990).

pert, then he is considered a lay witness, even if he might otherwise have the necessary qualifications to be recognized as an expert.

This is important here because some Louisiana courts have allowed witnesses to testify to opinions that required specialized knowledge that the witness actually possessed, even though the witnesses had not been qualified as an expert in the field based on the procedures outlined in Articles 702–706. These witnesses are sometimes referred to as "quasi-experts." For example, say a psychologist takes the stand and is not qualified as an expert in any particular field, but proceeds to testify to a person's mental or psychological diagnosis. The testimony would ordinarily only be testimony to which an expert clinical psychologist could testify. However, some courts allow witnesses to testify to such opinion testimony even though the witness has not been qualified as an expert in the field, if the witness *could have been* qualified as an expert in the field because they actually possess the necessary training, education, etc. The fact is, however, if a witness is not qualified as an expert, he should only be allowed to testify within the scope of giving lay witness opinions—those opinions or inferences that are rationally based on personal perceptions.

Federal Rules of Evidence Distinction. The Federal Rules have specifically addressed the issue of these quasi-experts in Federal Rule of Evidence 701, by requiring all three of the following be present in order to allow lay witness opinion testimony. The testimony must be: 1) rationally based on the perception of the witness; 2) helpful to a clear understanding of his testimony or the determination of a fact in issue; and 3) ***not* based on scientific, technical, or other specialized knowledge.**[63] Federal Rule of Evidence 701(3) specifically excludes from the realm of lay witness opinion testimony any opinion that should ordinarily only be elicited from an expert qualified in a particular field, even if the witness possesses the necessary expertise to give the opinion in question. Federal Rule, if the testimony is based on scientific, technical or specialized knowledge, then it does not meet the requirements for a lay witness opinion.

While Louisiana has not specifically enacted this provision, many courts construe the statute to have this intent, and will not allow a witness to testify to areas requiring specialized knowledge if the witness has not been qualified as an expert, even if the witness could have easily been qualified as an expert in the field. In some instances, these "quasi-experts" have been allowed to testify as lay witnesses to opinions requiring expertise in a field in which he is testifying. While some Louisiana courts have allowed such testimony, a better approach is to qualify the witness as an expert prior to having him testify as to areas requiring specific expertise.

Opinions specifically excluded. One final point to keep in mind as it relates to opinion testimony is that in certain areas of Louisiana law, opinion testimony has been specifically excluded. Article 608(A) sets forth the manner in which the credibility of a witness may be proven and provides that a "character witness shall not express his personal opinion as to the character of the witness whose credibility is in issue." For example, a witness may not testify that in his opinion a witness is truthful or has a truthful character.[64] Additionally, Article 412 excludes opinion evidence of the past sexual behavior of the victim in cases in which the accused is charged with a crime involving sexual assaultive behavior. Under Article 412, evidence such as, "I think the woman is easy," would be excluded.

---

63. As amended in 2000.

64. *See* Morrison v. Johnston, 571 So. 2d 788 (La. Ct. App. 2d Cir. 1990) (noting that an expert witness should not give an opinion directly concerning the particular victim's credibility).

Cases on Lay Witness Opinions

Mitchell v. Roy

Court of Appeal of Louisiana, Third Circuit
51 So. 3d 153
Nov. 3, 2010

CHATELAIN, Judge.

Darion, who was ten years of age at the time, was injured on March 14, 2008, when he rode his bicycle into the path of a 1999 Chevrolet Venture minivan that Roy was driving. The accident occurred on 8th Avenue between 9th and 10th Streets in Lake Charles, Louisiana, at approximately 4:30 p.m. Upon impact, Darion, who was not wearing a safety helmet, struck his head on the windshield when he was thrown onto the minivan's hood.

Acadian Ambulance transported Darion from the scene of the accident to Christus St. Patrick's Hospital. He underwent CT scans of the head and cervical spine and X rays of his right shoulder, chest, pelvis, and abdomen. The CT scan of Darion's head revealed some mild soft tissue swelling; otherwise, the test results were within normal limits and no fractures were noted. He was diagnosed with a head injury and scalp lacerations, and he received sutures and staples to those areas before being discharged from the hospital later that same evening.

On September 23, 2008, the plaintiff filed a petition for damages against Roy and his automobile liability insurer, Imperial. She alleged that Roy had negligently caused the accident by traveling in excess of the posted speed limit, by failing to keep a proper lookout, and by failing to do what he should have done to avoid the collision. The defendants answered the petition, asserting that the plaintiff's damages were caused when Darion recklessly operated his bicycle.

The matter proceeded to a bench trial on January 5, 2010, following which the trial court stated from the bench that Roy's negligence was the sole cause of the accident....

The defendants now appeal, asserting that the trial court erred in the following respects: (1) in allowing Angela Dodd (Dodd), a witness, to offer a lay opinion concerning the speed the Roy vehicle was traveling prior to the accident; ...

DISCUSSION

In the present case, the trial court ruled as follows:

> The Court finds in favor of the plaintiffs specifically finding that the accident was caused by the sole fault and negligence of Mr. Roy, the defendant. And that's based primarily on the third party independent witness, Ms. Dodd, who has some rather compelling testimony regarding the speed of the Roy vehicle. And even though she gave an estimate of the speed, I think looking at her testimony as a whole, it's clear that she was able to determine that his vehicle was traveling greater than 25 miles an hour. How much greater, we don't really know. It kicked up dust. It immediately brought itself to her attention because of that. And she made a contemporaneous comment to her niece about the speed of that vehicle. That is very compelling, persuasive testimony that is more persuasive, much more persuasive than the testimony of Mr. Roy and/or Mr. Fernandez....
>
> So Mr. Roy was going too fast. He did not take into account that there were children in the area. He ignored his friend's warning until it was too late....

So the fault is a hundred percent against the defendant.

Admissibility of Opinion Testimony Regarding Roy's Speed

The defendants contend that Dodd's testimony regarding the speed the Roy vehicle was traveling based on the movement of dust on the street "was not rationally based on perception." Dodd explained that she had in the past operated her own vehicle at various speeds ranging from twenty to forty miles per hour and that the environment appeared different at those varying rates of speed. Based upon those prior observations, she estimated that the Roy vehicle was traveling between thirty-five and forty miles per hour just before the accident. The defendants submit that Dodd should not have been allowed to present testimony as to the speed of the Roy vehicle because her observations were made when she was sitting stationary in her front yard, thus giving her the impression that the Roy vehicle was moving faster than the speed at which it was actually traveling. Finally, the defendants point out that the testimony of Officer Andrea LeLeaux contradicted some of Dodd's testimony. Specifically, Dodd stated that Roy had slammed on his brakes and skidded, but Officer LeLeaux testified that she had looked for skid marks in her investigation of the accident and had found none. The defendants argue that this contradiction "further undercut[s] the reliability of Dodd's testimony" regarding the speed of the Roy vehicle. The plaintiff counters that Dodd's testimony met the requirements of La.Code Evid. art. 701, and, thus, the trial court acted within its discretion when allowing her to testify.

Louisiana Code of Evidence Article 701 guides us in our assessment of the admissibility of a lay witness's opinion testimony. It provides as follows:

> If the witness is not testifying as an expert, his testimony in the form of opinions or inferences is limited to those opinions or inferences which are:
>
> (1) Rationally based on the perception of the witness; and
>
> (2) Helpful to a clear understanding of his testimony or the determination of a fact in issue.

"The general rule is that a lay witness is permitted to draw reasonable inferences from his or her personal observations." *State v. LeBlanc,* 05–885, p. 7 La.App. 1 Cir. 2/10/06), 928 So.2d 599, 603. "If the testimony constitutes a natural inference from what was observed, no prohibition against it as the opinion of a non-expert exists as long as the lay witness states the observed facts as well." *Id.* The *LeBlanc* court discussed the appellate standard of review regarding testimony admitted pursuant to La.Code Evid. art. 701:

> A reviewing court must ask two pertinent questions to determine whether the trial court properly allowed lay opinion testimony: (1) was the testimony speculative opinion evidence or simply a recitation of or inferences from fact based upon the witness's observations; and (2) if erroneously admitted, was the testimony so prejudicial to the defense as to constitute reversible error.

LeBlanc, 928 So.2d at 603....

In overruling the defendants' evidentiary objections to Dodd's lay opinion testimony about the speed of the Roy vehicle, the trial court stated that it would "take into consideration that [Dodd] is not an expert on speed" and that it would consider her opinion "in the context of just a lay impression." We are satisfied that the trial court properly allowed Dodd to testify as to the inferences she drew based upon her personal observations, that the trial court gave the proper weight to Dodd's opinion testimony, and that Dodd's testimony aided the trial court in determining a fact in issue. Moreover, we are convinced that even if the testimony was erroneously admitted, it was not so prejudicial to the defendants as to constitute reversible error, especially because this matter was a bench trial....

AMENDED IN PART, REVERSED IN PART, AND AFFIRMED AS AMENDED.

Discussion Questions

1. *LeBlanc* requires that a lay witness state the observed facts upon which he bases his opinions, which establishes the foundation upon which the lay opinion is based. Upon what foundation did Dodd base her opinion (prior experience and observations)? Has Dodd established sufficient foundation to support her opinion of the speed the Roy vehicle was traveling? Is there anything more or less that you would require?
2. Can anyone observing a traveling vehicle give an opinion of its speed regardless of prior experience or vantage point, for example, someone who has never driven, or someone looking down from a 15-story building? What minimum foundation would you require to give such an opinion?
3. Should the defendant's arguments that Dodd was only stationary in her yard, and that her testimony was contradicted by the officer, go to the admissibility of Dodd's opinion or to the weight and credibility of her opinion? In other words, should the fact that a person's reasonable inferences may not be correct prevent them from being able to testify to those inferences with the proper foundation? For example, should a person be able to testify that, based on his observations, someone appeared to be drunk when the opposing party plans to offer testimony that at the time in question the person was actually suffering from a diabetic episode and was in need of something sweet?

State v. Butler

Court of Appeal of Louisiana, First Circuit
563 So. 2d 976
May 30, 1990

COVINGTON, Chief Judge.

The victim of the instant offense was defendant's former girlfriend. Defendant met Ms. Poche at Southern University, and they were both students at the time of the incident. The couple frequently quarreled during their lengthy relationship. Defendant testified that, on at least three occasions, he moved into her residence; and each time he moved out, believing she was involved with other men. At the time of the victim's death, they had been separated for several months. According to his testimony, defendant had resolved to move away from the area and attend school elsewhere.

Poche was shot at close range as she was seated in her car, apparently attempting to flee from defendant. She died as the result of massive blood loss caused by five gunshot wounds.

The shooting occurred in the parking lot of her apartment complex. Defendant confronted the victim and her escort, Anthony Druilhet, as they walked to the door of her apartment. Druilhet testified that he recognized defendant from a photograph that the victim had shown him. When defendant approached the couple, Poche said, "What are you doing here, Herbert? I don't want any trouble." Defendant ran to the nearby shrubbery and pulled out a rifle hidden there. Druilhet related that he immediately fled on foot and that he believed the victim was with him. From across the street, he heard a car ignition start, followed by several gun shots. When he returned to the parking lot of the victim's apartment, he saw that her car had moved a few feet and that she was slumped over in the front seat. Butler was no longer in the vicinity.

Druilhet went to a neighboring apartment to summon help. When the police arrived, he named defendant as the victim's assailant. Several hours later, he identified Butler from a physical lineup.

Defendant testified on his own behalf. He claimed that he had gone to the victim's apartment to tell her that he was leaving town. He testified that he saw Druilhet reach into his car; and, therefore, he went to his car and retrieved his gun. He claimed that he did not know that he hit anyone, but he shot the gun in self-defense.

EXCLUSION OF TESTIMONY

By assignments of error five and seven, defendant complains of the trial court's rulings restricting his examination of two witnesses. In assignment of error number five, he submits that the trial court erred by sustaining the state's objection to a question concerning his state of mind shortly after the shooting. In assignment of error number seven, defendant argues that the court erred by refusing to permit him to ask a witness his opinion of the relationship between defendant and the victim.

Assignment of error number five is concerned with the testimony of Namon Harris, a witness for the state, who had worked with the defendant for approximately two years. Harris testified that defendant came to his apartment in the early morning hours of the day after the shooting and told him, "I got in trouble with a gun." Harris claimed that Butler initially did not tell him many of the details of his difficulty; rather, he asked a number of questions concerning possible future actions. Unable to provide the information defendant sought, Harris and Butler called another co-worker, Kevin Guillory. When Guillory and Harris attempted to determine the seriousness of the incident, defendant repeatedly told them that he did not know. However, he admitted that he went to the victim's apartment and saw her with another man; that he saw the man reach into the car to retrieve an object, so he returned to his car and got his gun; and that he shot the gun, but he did not know whether or not he hit anyone.

On cross-examination, Harris repeated that defendant was aware that he had fired the gun but did not know whether or not he hit anyone. Defense counsel then asked him, "Is it safe to say that he was basically in a trance?" The state objected on the grounds that the witness had no way of determining whether or not defendant was in a trance, and the court sustained the state's objection. Thereafter, through specific questions, defense counsel elicited Harris's opinion that defendant was thought by his fellow workers to be a fun, easy-going person who enjoyed joking with the persons with whom he worked; however, on the night of the shooting, he acted quite differently. The following exchange then occurred:

> Q. Now, when you gave a statement to the police that night, didn't you tell them that you thought Herb was in a trance?
>
> A. When I—I thought—when I looked at Herb I could tell he wasn't the same guy that he used to be when he—he wasn't the same guy that when I would see him that time in the morning—when I would see Herb in the mornings it was always a laughing and a joking and nicknaming me or saying something to me that made me laugh or something to get the day through or at break we would all go up to the upstairs to, it's like a candy machine or something, and Herb always had something funny to say to make the—to make the time pass, so I could relate to that incident and the time that he walked into my bedroom that it was two different Herb Butlers.

Defendant contends that the court erred by sustaining the state's objection because the testimony was admissible pursuant to LSA-C.E. art. 701, authorizing the introduction of opinion testimony by lay witnesses. He contends the evidence was relevant to his defense of insanity, and the court's ruling prevented him from introducing evidence critical to that defense.

LSA-C.E. art. 701 provides for the admission of opinion testimony by lay witnesses, as follows:

> If the witness is not testifying as an expert, his testimony in the form of opinions or inferences is limited to those opinions or inferences which are:
>
> (1) Rationally based on the perception of the witness; and
>
> (2) Helpful to a clear understanding of his testimony or the determination of a fact in issue.

LSA-C.E. art. 103 further provides, in pertinent part, as follows:

> **A. Effect of erroneous ruling.** Error may not be predicated upon a ruling which admits or excludes evidence unless a substantial right of the party is affected, and
>
> * * *
>
> (2) When the ruling is one excluding evidence, the substance of the evidence was made known to the court by counsel.

Initially, we note that, at the time of the objection, defense counsel did not make the substance of the excluded testimony, that is, Harris's opinion, known to the court. Thus, we are unable to determine whether or not the witness actually would have testified as defendant claimed.

However, even if we were to assume Harris would have testified that he believed defendant was in a trance after the shooting, we doubt that his opinion would have been helpful to the determination of the issue of defendant's sanity in this case, as necessary for admission under Article 701. Harris previously testified that defendant drove to his apartment and walked and talked clearly. He asked questions concerning the repercussions of his actions, and he even drank beer with his co-workers while he discussed the incident. He was able to relate the events which led up to the shooting. Therefore, even if he would have testified that defendant acted as though he were in a trance, that opinion would not have prompted a clear understanding of defendant's sanity in light of his specific testimony relating non-abstract behavior which did not support that conclusion.

...

In assignment of error number seven, defendant submits that the trial court erred by sustaining the state's objection to the question through which he sought to obtain a witness's opinion as to whether or not the defendant's relationship to the victim was unusual. Defendant called Joe Collier, a bail bondsman, to testify on his behalf. Collier testified that the victim called him several times after defendant was arrested December 23, 1987, for the burglary of the victim's apartment and that she furnished money for his bond. On cross-examination by the state, Collier indicated that it was not unusual for a girlfriend to post bond for her boyfriend. Thereafter, on redirect examination, defendant asked, "Would you consider this case compared to the other cases you've seen unusual?" The state objected because defendant had failed to define "unusual," and the court agreed that the foundation was insufficient.

Defendant claims Collier's opinion testimony was important to establish the unusual nature of the relationship between defendant and the victim, which was important to support his defense of insanity. He contends the information was admissible under LSA-C.E. arts. 701 and 704 as the opinion of a lay witness.

As previously noted, article 701 permits the introduction of opinion testimony by a lay witness only if such opinion is rationally based on the perception of the witness and is helpful to a clear understanding of his testimony or to the determination of a fact in issue. A defendant is presumed to be sane at the time of the offense. La.R.S. 15:432. In order to establish that he should be exempt from criminal responsibility, the defendant must show that, because of a mental disease or defect, he was incapable of distinguishing between right and wrong with reference to the conduct in question. LSA-R.S. 14:14. Louisiana does not recognize the doctrine of diminished responsibility. [Citations omitted]

Although defendant contends the information was relevant to his defense of insanity, we find no manner in which the witness's personal opinion of defendant's relationship with the victim as it existed several months prior to the commission of the offense could have assisted the trier of fact in its determination of defendant's ability to distinguish between right and wrong at the time in question. Accordingly, we find no error in the court's ruling....

AFFIRMED.

Discussion Question

What does it mean that lay opinion testimony must be helpful? Helpful in what way? Is it the same standard as relevant? Is it more or less?

Yellott v. Underwriters Ins. Co.
Court of Appeal of Louisiana, Third Circuit
915 So. 2d 917
Aug. 31, 2005

THIBODEAUX, Chief Judge.

I. ISSUES

This appeal presents multiple issues. First, both sides of this dispute have asked this court to determine whether the trial court's admission of certain lay opinion testimony from multiple fact witnesses constituted error that necessitates a new trial....

II. FACTS

On August 21, 2000, a car accident occurred between Yellott, who was driving a Pontiac Grand Am, and David Bunch ("Bunch"), the employee/driver of a Sabine Pools GMC 3500 extended cab, heavy duty pickup truck. The events leading up to and during the accident are disputed, as well as the extent of Yellott's resulting injuries.

...

Yellott, who was traveling westward in the right lane of Highway 379 in her Pontiac Grand Am, approaching Independence Road, was being followed by her friend, Rebecca Hoffpauir ("Hoffpauir"), who was driving a Ford Mustang. They both testified to seeing the Sabine Pools truck turn left onto Highway 379 off of Independence Road as they approached ... Both denied seeing a turn signal or any other indication from the driver that he was intending to make a turn.

Yellott testified that after driving behind the truck for a short distance, she decided to pass it. Hoffpauir testified that she continued to drive in the right lane of the highway behind the Sabine Pools truck while Yellott began to pass. Yellott contends that after determining there was no oncoming traffic, she drove across the centerline into the left lane of the highway and increased her speed to attempt to pass the Sabine Pools truck. While in the process of overtaking the truck, she asserts its driver, without warning or signaling in any manner, began a left turn, crossing over the centerline, directly into her lane of travel. Because of her position virtually parallel to the truck, she applied her brakes, but claims to have been unable to avoid the collision....

Sabine Pools' theory of how the accident occurred is based primarily on the testimony offered by Bunch and a co-worker, Michael LeLeux ("LeLeux"), who was riding as a passenger in the Sabine Pools truck at the time of the accident. Bunch claims that Yellott was solely responsible for the accident because she crashed into the truck as he was in the process of a lawful, left turn.... Bunch went on to testify that he saw Yellott speeding at approximately 90 miles per hour when he checked his mirrors. He opined that this, in addition to her inattention to his turn signal, resulted in her crashing into the truck as he made his turn.

Moreover, Bunch and LeLeux identified and measured skid marks on the day *after* the accident, which began in the right lane of the highway and extended into the left lane, concluding that they were those left by Yellott's vehicle. Relying on these witnesses' identification of this set of skid marks as those having been made by Yellott's vehicle, although other skid marks were also noted at the scene, Sabine Pools argues that this establishes that Yellott initiated an unsafe passing maneuver after Bunch had already turned left and was driving into the driveway....

The investigating state trooper at the scene, Ronald Mann ("Trooper Mann"), reached different conclusions. He testified that during his investigation at the scene, he observed multiple sets of skid marks and was able to ultimately determine that those skids made by Yellott's vehicle were located wholly in the left lane of the highway. He determined that there was no yaw or other evasive action apparently made by Yellott's vehicle immediately prior to the accident. In addition, he concluded that Yellott had not been traveling at a rate of 90 miles per hour at the time of the impact, but opined, based upon calculations made from measurements of skid marks taken at the scene *on the day* of the accident, that she had been traveling at a rate of about 70 miles per hour while overtaking the Sabine Pools truck. As a result of his findings, he testified that Yellott's car was already completely in the left lane of the highway when Bunch initiated his left turn, contrary to Bunch's assertions, and that Bunch crossed the centerline into the left lane of the highway, striking Yellott's vehicle, apparently unaware of her location....

III. LAW AND DISCUSSION

Objection to Lay Testimony

Both sides to this case contend that the trial court committed error by allowing inadmissible and prejudicial lay opinion testimony from various witnesses over their respective motions *in limine* and objections made during trial. Yellott contends that Bunch and LeLeux were able to voice opinions as to which skid marks located at the scene were made by Yellott's vehicle and, based on these unskilled observations, were further allowed to testify as to Yellott's allegedly negligent actions immediately prior to the accident. Likewise, Sabine Pools argues that the trial court improperly allowed the investigating state trooper, Trooper Mann, to testify that Bunch was issued a citation at the scene of the accident and also to improperly offer his opinion regarding Bunch's fault in causing the accident.

Testimony by a witness who is not testifying as an expert can be offered in the form of opinions and inferences, if such opinions and inferences are limited to those which are (1) "[r]ationally based on the perception of the witness;" and are (2) "[h]elpful to a clear understanding of his testimony or the determination of a fact in issue." La.Code Evid. art. 701.

Testimony by Sabine Pools Employees

Yellott contends that no proper foundation was laid for the introduction of the opinion testimony offered by LeLeux and Bunch about the skid marks, numerous markings, or about how the accident occurred.... We agree with Yellott's argument that the trial court erred in allowing this testimony from Bunch and LeLeux.

While a lay witness may identify the *existence* of markings near an accident scene, that witness does not possess the requisite level of skill and expertise to assign skid markings to a particular vehicle nor can a lay witness reconstruct an accident based on their subjective assignment of skid marks to a vehicle. Such testimony goes beyond mere identification of markings and skid marks and crosses the line into accident reconstruction. That is what occurred in this case. The opinions and inferences of Bunch and LeLeux were not rationally based on their perceptions. La.Code Evid. art. 701. Thus, it was legally impermissible to allow their testimony on this issue. We conclude that this error tainted the fact-finding process and prejudiced Ms. Yellott's case. See La.Code Evid. art. 103(A).

Testimony by Trooper Mann

Sabine Pools argues that Trooper Mann "rendered highly prejudicial and inadmissible opinion testimony, testifying that he issued a citation to Mr. Bunch after he concluded where the vehicles were when the accident events began." ...

The question prompting the response at issue was as follows: "Why were skid marks a focus of your investigation at the scene of this crash on Houston River Road on August 21, 2000?" Following this question, the trial court advised Trooper Mann, "Sir, in the presence of the jury, I want to instruct you that you are not permitted to give opinions." The trial court further advised the Trooper to "restrict [his] answer to non-opinion answers." Trooper Mann responded as follows:

> In order to issue the citation of 32:79, improper lane usage [the] investigating officer must determine where each vehicle was at the time of the crash. To do that, you need to determine if the vehicle in possession of each lane was in that lane or in possession properly.
>
> Mr. Bunch was westbound on 379, he was in possession of the westbound lane of LA 379, or Houston River Road. Ms. Yellott, to determine where Ms. Yellott was at for the citation issued, I had to determine exactly where she was at when Mr. Bunch began her [sic] turn and caused Ms. Yellott to apply her brakes and start the skid marks....

We recognize that, in some instances, our appellate courts have affirmed the admission of opinion testimony by police officers who are not experts, based on their training, investigation, perception of the scene, and observation of physical evidence. *See Eldridge*, 888 So.2d 365 (citing *Cooper v. State Dep't of Transp. & Dev.*, 03–1847 (La.App. 1 Cir. 6/25/04), 885 So.2d 1211, *writ denied*, 04–1913 (La.11/8/04), 885 So.2d 1142); *Bozeman v. State Dep't of Transp. & Dev.*, 34,430 (La.App. 2 Cir. 4/4/01), 787 So.2d 357, *writ denied*, 01–1341 (La.6/29/01), 794 So.2d 813. Trooper Mann was not tendered as an expert in accident reconstruction at trial. He possessed experience in accident investigation, as most troopers do. However, this experience did not talismanically allow Trooper Mann to determine the location of the parties' vehicles and the resulting *cause* of the accident. The admission of this testimony was legal error.

Allocation of Fault

... The objective evidence, we find, dilutes the power of the self-serving testimony of the Sabine Pools employees and dominates substantially in favor of the plaintiff. The photographs of the vehicles in the accident provide a clear picture of where the vehicles collided—at the passenger side front quarter panel of Yellott's vehicle and at the truck's driver side mirror and tire....

To begin with, Trooper Mann testified that he identified skid marks belonging to Yellott's vehicle located wholly within the left lane of the highway, leaving him to rationally conclude that she was already in the left lane and in the process of passing, prior to the collision occurring. He was also able to determine from skid marks, that he found consistent with this scenario, that there was no yaw or other such evasive action made by Yellott's vehicle prior to impact....

Additionally, Bunch's testimony regarding the speed of Yellott's vehicle before the collision is not reasonably supported by the evidence in the record. For one, Trooper Mann was able to estimate an approximate speed of Yellott and Hoffpauir's vehicles as 70 miles per hour. The speed was based on measurements taken from the skid marks that Trooper Mann believed had been made by Hoffpauir's vehicle.... It cannot be ignored also that the impact of a vehicle traveling at 90 miles per hour, as Bunch proposes, would have resulted in considerably more damage than that which was suffered by the vehicles in this accident.

.. As a result, we find that based on the facts presented, the left-turning motorist, Bunch, breached his high duty of care and should be assessed with 90% of the fault in causing this accident. We find Yellott 10% at fault in causing the accident....

AFFIRMED IN PART; REVERSED IN PART; AND RENDERED....

Discussion Questions

1. Do you think that a lay witness with absolutely no experience in accident investigation and reconstruction should ever be allowed to give an opinion about the cause of an accident based on observation and measurement of skid marks? Was the testimony of LeLeux and Bunch reasonable common sense inferences, rationally based on perceptions or much more? Explain.
2. This case is further complicated by the fact that the witnesses were also allowed to offer an opinion regarding which set of skid marks were made by the plaintiff's vehicle the day after the accident occurred. Are there inferences a lay witness might be able to draw from the appearance of skid marks? Are there any circumstances, other than actually viewing an accident, under which a lay witness might be able to conclude the cause of the accident?
3. Trooper Mann also did not testify as an expert witness. Are your thoughts different regarding whether or not an officer with his experience and training should be able to testify to the cause of the accident and the location and approximate speed of the vehicles prior to the accident based on the skid marks? This case crosses into a grey area in which courts sometimes allow witnesses to testify beyond the scope of a lay witness based on their experience in the field, without allowing the witness to testify as an expert. These "quasi-experts," quite often police officers, are allowed to give rationally based inferences based on perception, in light of their own personal experiences. Is this appropriate or should all lay witnesses' testimony fall within the same objective standard?
    - While the *Yellott* court points out that many courts have affirmed such opinions, many courts have also expressed disapproval of this type of testimony. (See e.g. *Carter v. Travelers Ins. Co.*, 535 So. 2d 1001 (La. Ct. App. 2d Cir. 1988) (finding

that a trooper could not give an opinion as to the manner in which a vehicle spun after impact); *Fontenot v. Cooper*, 599 So. 2d 883 (La. Ct. App. 3d Cir. 1992) (finding that the trial court erred in permitting a state trooper who did not see the accident and was not qualified as an accident reconstruction expert, to express an opinion as to the point of impact of the accident).)

4. Do you find it unusual that although the court found that Trooper Mann should not have been able to give opinions regarding the "location of the vehicles" and the "resulting cause of the accident," they ultimately relied on his opinions in determining that the trial court erred in its allocation of fault? Specifically the court relied on Trooper Mann's opinion that based on the skid marks he identified he was able to "rationally conclude that she [Bunch] was already in the left lane and in the process of passing, prior to the collision occurring," and based on his measurements of the skid marks that he was "able to estimate an approximate speed of Yellott and Hoffpauir's vehicles as 70 miles per hour." How do you reconcile the courts conclusion's regarding Trooper Mann's opinions and its subsequent reliance on them?

Key Points

The key points to keep in mind regarding lay witness opinion testimony.

1. Lay witness opinion testimony must be reasonable common sense inferences.
2. The opinions/inferences must be rationally based on facts *perceived* by the witness.
3. The underlying facts/perceptions must be *personal* perceptions, of which the witness has first-hand knowledge.
4. Foundation must be laid as to the underlying facts upon which the witness bases his opinions.
5. The opinions must be helpful to a clear understanding of testimony or determination of a fact in issue.

Lay Witness Opinion Testimony Problems

PROBLEM 4-24. Marilyn's husband is on trial for assaulting her and you represent the defendant husband. During direct examination of Marilyn, the prosecutor asked her whether there was anything unusual that she noticed about him that night. Marilyn responded, "*Yes, he was drunk when he got home.*" Upon what basis will you object to her answer to the prosecutor's question? How will the court likely rule and why?

PROBLEM 4-25. Joe is on trial for rape, and took the stand in his own defense. During the direct examination Joe testified that the victim "wanted it." On what grounds should the prosecution object? How should the court rule and why? Is there anything that Joe's attorney might be able to do to allow such testimony? What steps should be taken?

PROBLEM 4-26. Jack and Jill were getting a divorce and were fighting over custody of their daughter Kendyl. Jill does not want Kendyl to spend time at Jack's house with his new wife Janet because she believes he beats his wife at night and doesn't want Kendyl around the violence. Jill's lawyer plans to call Jill to the stand to testify to the beatings at the custody hearing. She will testify that she has come to this conclusion because her daughter told her that at night she often hears her father screaming very loudly at Janet, followed by loud thumps, and then Janet screams and cries. Jill will testify that based on that information she believes Jack is beating Janet at night. Will her conclusion about Jack's conduct be admissible? Why or why not?

PROBLEM 4-27. University of USA has been sued for discriminating against female professors in granting tenure. The attorney for the University calls the dean to the stand who is accused of denying tenure to the plaintiff because she was female. The very first question the attorney for the University asks the dean on direct examination is, "Dean Williams, did you discriminate against the plaintiff?" Upon what basis would you object to this question? How will the court likely rule and why?

PROBLEM 4-28. The victim's mother took the stand to testify in a second degree battery case in which her son was the victim. The prosecution asked her what happened the night of the incident. She stated that her son arrived home around midnight and had been "beaten up by some thugs." The defense objects that the witness cannot testify to what occurred because she was not there. Can she testify that her son had been beaten up? Why or why not?

PROBLEM 4-29. Can Carletta testify that while sitting on the train, she noticed the lady sitting next to her was having a seizure? Can she testify that the lady had epilepsy? Why or why not?

PROBLEM 4-30. In a trial for damages resulting from his dog biting a child in the neighborhood, the defendant testified that he didn't keep his dog on a leash when he walked him through the neighborhood because "none of the kids were afraid of him." Are there any circumstances under which the defendant could make such a statement? Explain.

PROBLEM 4-31. The police officer who reported to the scene of the accident testified that after speaking with everyone at the scene, he concluded that the man driving the green car was at fault. Will his finding be admissible in court? Why or why not?

PROBLEM 4-32. Sheila has brought an action against her employer for wrongful termination. She calls Dr. Kimberly Bach to the stand, a licensed clinical psychologist, who has not been qualified as an expert in any field. Sheila would like for Dr. Bach to testify that she (plaintiff) was clinically depressed over the last six months, and that it was her condition that caused her poor performance at work. Dr. Bach will further testify that rather than being terminated, Shelia should have been offered treatment and that with proper treatment she could have performed her duties. Should Dr. Bach be allowed to testify to those conclusions? Are there any circumstances in which she can testify as to Sheila's condition?

PROBLEM 4-33. The school board was found liable in the death of a young boy who was killed after he was negligently let off a school bus in the middle of the highway and struck by a car. In the damages phase of the trial, the school board would like to offer testimony from a teacher that she taught the little boy in the second grade and that he was a "poor" student and would not have likely gone to and graduated from college. Should she be allowed to testify to this on the issue of the little boy's future earning capacity? Why or why not?

PROBLEM 4-34. Assume the following testimony was given with the proper foundation. To which of the following would a lay witness be able to testify and why?

A. Donna testifies that the man was very strong.

B. Donna testified that the waitress seemed tired the night of the robbery.

C. Donna testified that it was about 50 degrees outside the night of the robbery.

D. Donna testified that the handwriting in the letter appeared to be that of her husband.

E. Donna testified that the defendant seemed very nervous.

PROBLEM 4-35. Ms. Sadie is on trial for illegal discharge of a dangerous weapon within the city limits for firing her shotgun at five youths she saw standing in a huddle downstairs in the open area of her apartment complex. She fired the shots from her fourth floor apartment. At trial, Ms. Sadie testified that she was sitting in her living room and heard commotion outside. She says she got up, looked outside and saw some boys smoking marijuana. She says that she got her shotgun and shot in the air to scare them away. The prosecution objects to the witness testifying that the boys were smoking marijuana. How should the court rule on the objection?

§ 4.8 References and Additional Authority on Lay Witness Opinions [La. C.E. art. 701]

1. La. C.E. art. 701 and Official Comments
2. Force & Rault, Handbook on Louisiana Evidence Law La. C.E. art. 701 Author's Comments (West Publishing 2014)
3. Harges & Jones, Louisiana Evidence Art. 701 Author's Comments (West Publishing 2014)
4. 19 La. Civ. L. Treatise, Evidence And Proof § 11.2 (2nd ed.)
5. **Emotional State (fear, nervousness, upset, excitement, etc.):** *State v. Adams*, Sup.1981, 394 So. 2d 1204 (Lay witness was allowed to testify that child victim of rape was "scared" of defendant based upon witness's observations that child desired to stay close to witness and did not want to go near defendant.); *State v. Walder*, 504 So. 2d 991 (La. Ct. App. 1st Cir. 1987), writ denied 506 So. 2d 1223 (lay witness was allowed to testify that rape victim was nervous based on witness's observations); *State v. Matthews*, Sup.1907, 119 La. 665, 44 So. 336 (witness was allowed to testify that accused in murder trial seemed excited, walked very fast, and was panting when talking, after testifying that he had seen the accused after the shot); *State v. Anthony*, Sup.1928, 166 La. 793, 117 So. 921 (witness was allowed to testify that defendants were nervous, and one of them had "ghastly" look on face in murder prosecution); *State v. Hattaway*, 674 So. 2d 380 (La. Ct. App. 2d Cir. 1996), rehearing denied, writ denied 685 So. 2d 141, 1996-1900 (La. 1/10/97) (deputy was allowed to testify that wife of murder victim was "visibly upset" after being shown clothing husband was wearing at time of murder).
6. **Helpfulness:** *State v. Robertson*, 723 So. 2d 500 (La. Ct. App. 3d Cir. 1998) (holding that testimony of witness's opinion regarding whether or not defendant intended to inflict serious bodily injury not helpful because witness could not have known defendant's state of mind unless he expressed it; defendant's conduct speaks for itself); *State v. McSweeney*, 619 So. 2d 861 (La. Ct. App. 3d Cir. 1993) (holding that mother and brother-in-law's opinion regarding whether defendant's voice was on tape recording made by undercover officer during drug transaction was not helpful to jury's determination of whether one of the voice was defendant's where voice identification was not essential to either defendant's arrest or his conviction).
7. **Intoxication:** *State v. Kestle*, 996 So. 2d 275 (La. 2008) (trooper was permitted to give lay opinion testimony that defendant was under the influence of narcotics based upon his observations of defendant during the field sobriety tests); *State v. Davis*, 722 So.

2d 1049, (La. Ct. App. 1st Cir. 1998), writ denied 764 So. 2d 960 (deputy permitted to give lay witness opinion testimony that he wrote "unable to perform" on standardized field sobriety test form because of defendant's "impaired state, from the alcohol from drinking").

8. **Speed:** *Rideau v. State Farm Mut. Auto. Ins. Co.*, 970 So. 2d 564 (La. Ct. App. 1st Cir. 2007) (lay witness was allowed to testify that vehicle was not going any, "faster than the speed limit" based on observations); *Gianfala v. State Farm Mut. Auto. Ins. Co.*, 615 So. 2d 558 (La. Ct. App. 3d Cir. 1993) (witness permitted to testify that "plaintiff was traveling at a fast rate of speed ...").

9. **Bodily fluids (blood, urine, semen):** *State v. Poche*, 924 So. 2d 1225 (La. Ct. App. 3d Cir. 2006) (lay witnesses were allowed to testify that a substance thrown at them was urine); *State v. Strother*, 990 So. 2d 130 (La. Ct. App. 2d Cir. 2008) (teenage rape victim was allowed to testify that substance on her shirt was semen after she testified that she was familiar with its appearance).

10. **Value:** *Abbyad v. Mathes Group*, 671 So. 2d 958 (La. Ct. App. 4th Cir. 1996) (homeowner was permitted to testify to cost of rebuilding his home); *State v. Bolton*, 739 So. 2d 364 (La. Ct. App. 5th Cir. 1999) (store security officer was allowed to give lay witness testimony as to value of stolen merchandise given fact that he had direct contact with the merchandise on the night of the crime).

11. **Lay witnesses with experience who should have been qualified as experts:** *Eldridge v. Carrier*, 888 So. 2d 365 (La. Ct. App. 3d Cir. 2004) (officer permitted to testify as to location of cars at time of impact, based upon skid marks without being qualified as expert); *Cooper v. Louisiana State Dept. of Transp. and Development*, 885 So. 2d 1211 (La. Ct. App. 1st Cir. 2004) (state trooper permitted to give his opinion as to what caused the accident, even though he was not qualified as an expert in accident reconstruction); *Whetstone v. Dixon*, 616 So. 2d 764, 768 (La. Ct. App. 1st Cir. 1993) (state trooper permitted to give opinion concerning the point of impact based on his perception of the accident scene and the physical evidence he observed without being qualified as expert); *Figeroha v. State Farm Mut. Auto. Ins. Co.*, WL 1564686 (La. Ct. App. 1st Cir. 2012) (police officer not qualified as expert was permitted to testify regarding how far the plaintiff traveled from the impact of the collision to his final resting place); *Precht v. Case Corp.*, 756 So. 2d 488 (La. Ct. App. 3d Cir. 2000) (mechanical engineer/safety consultant/accident reconstructionist not qualified as expert was permitted to testify in products liability action about origin of tractor fire).

Chapter 5

Hearsay Rule and Exceptions

Part A
Definition of Hearsay and Hearsay Rule

Introduction to Hearsay

In Chapter 5 Parts A–E we will cover the hearsay rule and exceptions. The law governing hearsay is contained in Chapter 8 of the La. Code of Evid. arts. 801–806. It is the largest body of law covered in the Code and will be the most often encountered objection that occurs in a courtroom. The rule is implicated every time a document of any kind is presented in court, e.g., letters, reports, medical records, etc., and potentially every time a witness testifies to what someone else might have said.

What makes the rule so intimidating for many students to learn, and for many practitioners to apply, is that while there is a general rule excluding hearsay from being admitted at trial, hearsay can sometimes be difficult to identify, and the rule excluding it has a lot of exceptions. The hearsay ban is largely policy-based, with an eye toward accurate truth-finding in the adversarial process. It is designed to increase the reliability and accuracy of testimony by helping to ensure that a witness's testimony is based on first-hand knowledge, and is presented personally in court where he is under oath and subject to cross-examination on the subject matter about which he has testified.[1] It is important to keep these concerns in the back of your mind as you study hearsay, as the rule and many of the exceptions are based on whether, under the circumstances in which these statements are made, these interests are protected and/or furthered.

§ 5.1 Definition of Hearsay and the Hearsay Rule [La. C.E. arts. 801(A)–(C), 802]

Applicable Code Articles

Art. 801. Definitions

The following definitions apply under this Chapter:

A. Statement. A "statement" is:

(1) An oral or written assertion; or

1. *See generally*, McCormick on Evidence § 245 (5th ed., 1999); *See also* Force & Rault, Handbook, Art. 801 Author's Comment (1).

(2) Nonverbal conduct of a person, if it is intended by him as an assertion.

B. Declarant. A "declarant" is a person who makes a statement.

C. Hearsay. "Hearsay" is a statement, other than one made by the declarant while testifying at the present trial or hearing, offered in evidence to prove the truth of the matter asserted.

* * *

Art. 802. Hearsay rule

Hearsay is not admissible except as otherwise provided by this Code or other legislation.

Pursuant to Article 801(C), "hearsay" is defined as "a statement, other than one made by the declarant while testifying at the present trial or hearing, offered in evidence to prove the truth of the matter asserted." Another way of saying this is that hearsay is a statement made by a person outside of the present trial or hearing, that is being offered in evidence to prove what the statement "asserts," and in doing so, the trier of fact is required to believe that the assertion is in fact true.

For instance, say Bob is on trial for killing his wife. In order to prove that Bob stabbed his wife to death, the prosecution calls the neighbor to the stand who testifies: "*Yes, Bob did it. I was standing outside of the house and the maid ran outside and said, 'Bob is in there stabbing his wife.'*" On cross-examination of the neighbor by the defense, the neighbor is asked the following questions: "Are you sure that it was Bob who was stabbing her? Where was Bob standing? Where was she? Did Bob appear to be angry? Did Bob's wife have a weapon? Did he approach her from behind or from the front? From where did Bob retrieve the knife? Are you sure she didn't stab herself?"

Clearly, the neighbor cannot answer any of these questions. His testimony is hearsay. Only the maid can answer questions relative to what actually occurred, because she personally witnessed the events. Thus, the maid's testimony is essential to getting to the truth. Not to mention that as a criminal defendant, Bob has a constitutional right to confront and cross-examine witnesses against him.[2] Because of these and other concerns, hearsay statements are generally inadmissible in a trial.[3]

Reasons for the hearsay ban. There are several dangers associated with allowing statements from witnesses who are not present in court to be offered to prove the truth of the matters asserted within those statements. It is widely recognized that the value of testimony depends upon the **perception**, **memory**, **narration**, and **sincerity** of the witness.[4] When a witness testifies, it is imperative to be able to determine whether the witness was able to perceive what he testified to (perception); whether the witness remembers accurately (memory); what the witness means by what he is saying (narration); and whether the witness is being sincere in his testimony (sincerity).[5] The danger of admitting hearsay statements into evidence

2. See the Confrontation Clause of the Sixth Amendment of the United States Constitution, which provides that "In all criminal prosecutions, the accused shall enjoy the right ... to be confronted with the witnesses against him; to have compulsory process for obtaining witnesses in his favor, and to have the Assistance of Counsel for his defense." The Confrontation Clause as it relates to hearsay is covered in Chapter 5 Part E, § 5.25.

3. La. Code Evid. art. 802.

4. McCormick on Evidence § 245 (5th ed., 1999).

5. *Id.*

is that these four factors cannot be tested when the witness is not present in court, making the statements unreliable and untrustworthy.

When a witness testifies personally at a trial, there are mechanisms in place that help to minimize these dangers. First, a witness is under oath.[6] As discussed in Chapter 4, supra, the oath or affirmation is required of all witnesses to impress upon him his duty to tell the truth. A person who makes an out-of-court statement is generally not under oath when his or her statements are made. Second, if present in court, a witness's demeanor is capable of being observed by the jury who can determine the weight and credibility to assign to the witness's testimony[7]—was he fidgeting? Did he appear confident or unsure? Finally, and most importantly, a witness who is present in court is capable of being cross-examined about the substance of his testimony.[8] During cross-examination, any defects in a witness's memory, sincerity, perception, and narration can be tested and exposed. Thus, the hearsay ban and the preference for in-court testimony ultimately assists the trier of fact in getting to the truth.

Throughout this chapter we will often refer back to these concerns. Many of the exceptions to the hearsay rule are based on the fact that the potential dangers of admitting hearsay statements are minimized due to circumstances under which the statements were made, increasing the reliability of the statement. As we cover the exceptions to the hearsay rule later in the chapter, we will continue to point out which dangers of admitting the statement are minimized under the circumstances of each exception, and what factors help to increase the reliability and trustworthiness of the statement despite its hearsay status.

Identifying Hearsay

Identifying hearsay begins with understanding the components of the rule. As stated above, hearsay is defined as "a statement, other than one made by the declarant while testifying at the present trial or hearing, offered in evidence to prove the truth of the matter asserted." Based on this definition, a hearsay statement requires the following: 1) that there be a statement (within the meaning of the rule); 2) that the statement was made outside of the present trial or hearing; 3) the declarant must be a person; 4) the statement must assert something; and 5) the statement is being offered to prove what the statement asserts. Each aspect is examined more closely below.

Statements. First, hearsay only applies to "statements" as defined by the Code. Article 801(A) defines a statement as: (1) An oral or written assertion; or (2) Nonverbal conduct of a person, if it is intended by him as an assertion. So not only is a statement one that may be written or orally made, it may also include the "conduct" of a person, but only if that conduct is intended to assert something, or to otherwise convey a message of some sort.[9] For example, if a person points to something or someone to convey the message, "that is him, her, or it," such as in making an identification,[10] the person's nonverbal conduct is a statement for purposes of the hearsay rule.

Keep in mind that even if the statement is oral or written, to be a statement for purposes of hearsay, it must assert a fact or convey a message. For instance, "*The sky is blue,*" asserts

6. *Id.*
7. *Id.*
8. *Id.*
9. *See* LA. CODE EVID. art. 801(A)(c) Official Comments.
10. *See* State v. Jones, 642 So. 2d 151 (La. 1994).

that the sky is blue. "*He ran a red light*" asserts that the person ran a red light. Information is being conveyed in the statements. If no message is conveyed, such as in the case of a command ("*Put your hands up!*") or most questions ("*Can I have your French fries?*"), then hearsay is not implicated, although some rare exceptions exist.

Whether the statement is oral or written, or is nonverbal assertive conduct, it is hearsay only if it is being offered to prove the truth of the matter asserted by the statement. But first, you must determine that you have a statement as defined by the rule.

Outside of present trial/hearing. Hearsay refers to statements that were made outside of the *present* trial or hearing at a time prior to the trial or hearing at which the witness is currently testifying. Even if the prior statement was made at some *other* trial or hearing, or was made under oath at a deposition or in an affidavit, it can be hearsay if the other components of the rule are met.

Declarant. The person who made the statement in question is referred to as the declarant.[11] Thus, if Neighbor testifies at trial, "*The maid said Bob is stabbing his wife,*" then the *maid* is the declarant. She made the out-of-court statement in question. While the declarant is usually a third person who made a statement to which the witness is now testifying, the declarant may also be the witness himself if he is currently testifying about a statement he or she previously made outside of the present trial.[12] For example, the witness is asked the following at the trial:

Q: "*Mr. Witness, what did you tell the police when they arrived on scene?*"

A: "*I told them that John shot Henry in the shoulder.*"

In this instance, the witness is testifying to his own statement that was made outside of the present trial or hearing. In this instance the witness himself is the declarant.

Further, the rule specifically refers to a declarant as a "person"[13] who makes a statement. So an animal such as a drug-sniffing dog would not be subject to the hearsay rule as to any assertions it might make. Similarly, computer-generated information, such as a phone bill with a log of the numbers dialed, cannot be hearsay.[14] Assertions made by animals and computers do not present the dangers of hearsay—memory, perception, narration, or sincerity. Thus, the rule is not designed to address such statements. However, as will be discussed further in *State v. Carter*[15] below, if the information is a printout of human input or is human-stored information, then it is subject to the hearsay rule. So while a log of the numbers dialed on a phone bill (computer-generated) is not hearsay, if a person printed out his list of contacts from his phone (human-stored information), it would be subject to the hearsay rule.

Truth of the matter asserted. Finally, and perhaps the most difficult aspect of the rule, is the fact that the statement in question is now being offered in evidence to prove what the statement is asserting, which requires the trier of fact to believe that what the statement asserted is true. As stated above, to be a statement for purposes of the hearsay rule, it must assert something, or convey a message. The statement "*The light was red when John*

---

11. La. Code Evid. art. 801(B).

12. See Force & Rault, Handbook Art. 801 Author's Comment (1); In State v. Martin, 356 So. 2d 1370 (La. 1978), the Louisiana Supreme Court upheld trial court's ruling excluding a letter written by the testifying defendant to his attorney relating events preceding his arrest as inadmissible hearsay.

13. La. Code Evid. art. 801(B); *See also* Force & Rault, Handbook, Art. 801 Author's Comment (1).

14. *See* State v. Carter, 762 So. 2d 662 (La. Ct. App. 4th Cir. 2000).

15. *Id.*

went through it" asserts a message that when John proceeded through the light, it was red. "*Bob was stabbing Henry*" conveys the message that Bob was, in fact, stabbing Henry. To determine if a statement is hearsay, you must first determine what the statement is asserting.

For a statement to be hearsay, it is not enough that a statement assert *something*. A statement is hearsay only if the statement is being *offered to prove what it is asserting*, which will require the trier of fact to believe that what the statement asserts is true. This raises questions of sincerity and puts the out-of-court declarant's credibility at issue. If the statement is being offered in evidence to prove something other than what it asserts, and it is irrelevant as to whether the statement is true, the statement is not hearsay.

Let's take the example above again, where Neighbor testifies that the maid said that Bob was stabbing his wife. In this case, the statement asserts **that Bob was stabbing his wife.** The assertion is very literal—that Bob stabbed his wife. Bob is on trial for murder, so the prosecution is offering the maid's testimony through Neighbor for the purpose of trying to prove **that Bob stabbed his wife.** Thus, the statement is being offered to prove what it is asserting, and is therefore hearsay. As a result, the maid's credibility is at issue because the jury must believe that what she said is true without her being present to testify under oath and subject to cross-examination about what she claims she saw.

If the statement were being offered to prove something other than what it is asserting, then it would not be hearsay. For example, if Bob's wife had lived and sued the maid for failing to take action to assist her, Neighbor might testify at the trial that the maid ran outside to notify someone of what Bob was doing to his wife. In this case, the jury does not have to believe the statement was true, only that the maid made the statement. Here, the statement is not being offered to prove that Bob was actually stabbing his wife, but instead, only to prove that the maid called for help. Thus, in this situation the statement would not be hearsay.

Hearsay requirements. Therefore, the requirements for a statement to be hearsay are: 1) that there be a **statement**; 2) that the statement was made **other than at the present trial** or **hearing**; 3) the declarant must be a **person**; 4) the statement must **assert something**; and 5) the statement is being **offered to prove what it asserts** and that the assertion is true. Therefore, determining whether a statement is hearsay requires the following steps:

1. Identify the statement.
   - *i. Which may be an oral or written assertion, or assertive conduct;*
   - *ii. Was made by a person; and*
   - *iii. Was made outside of the present trial or hearing.*
2. Determine what is being asserted in the statement.
3. Determine what the statement is being offered into evidence to prove.

If "Step 2" and "Step 3" are the same, i.e., "Step 2" = "Step 3," then the statement is hearsay—it's being offered to prove the same thing that it asserts.

If "Step 2" and "Step 3" are not the same, i.e., "Step 2" ≠ "Step 3," then the statement is *not* hearsay—it's not being offered to prove the same as it asserts. It is being offered for some other reason.

Discussion and Application of the Hearsay Rule

In learning to identify hearsay, consider the two following scenarios. In which of the scenarios is the statement in question hearsay, i.e., is being offered to prove what it is asserting; and which one is not hearsay, but is only going to the declarant's state of mind? Follow the steps outlined above to determine which statement is hearsay and which statement is not.

Scenario A: Megan is on trial for murdering her son's teacher. In order to prove Megan's motive, the prosecution calls Joann to the stand. Joann testifies that the day before the teacher was killed, she attended a PTA meeting with Megan, and while Megan's son's teacher was speaking about how the "slower" kids stopped progress in the classroom (which included Megan's son), Megan said to her, "*I'm so furious right now!*" Megan objects that the statement is hearsay. How will the court likely rule and why?

Scenario B: Megan is on trial for murdering her son's teacher. In order to prove Megan's motive, the prosecution calls Megan's friend Joann to the stand to testify that on the day of the murder she was visiting Megan when Megan's son came home from school and said to her, "*My teacher pinched me really hard until I started crying. She then made me stand in the corner until I stopped.*" Megan's friend testified that, at that point, Megan left her house with a gun and shot the teacher. Upon what grounds will the defense likely object? How will the court likely rule and why?

Explanation of the problem:

As outlined above, hearsay is a statement, other than one made by the declarant while testifying at the present trial or hearing, offered in evidence to prove the truth of the matter asserted. Identifying hearsay requires the following three steps:

1. Identify the statement (*i. oral/written/assertive conduct; ii. by a person; iii. outside of present hearing*).
2. Determine what is being asserted in the statement.
3. Determine what the statement is being offered into evidence to prove.

If "Step 2" and "Step 3" are the same, then the statement is hearsay, i.e., **if Step 2 = Step 3 = hearsay.** The statement is being offered to prove what it is asserting.

If "Step 2" and "Step 3" are not the same, then the statement is not hearsay, **i.e., Step 2 ≠ Step 3 ≠ hearsay.** The statement is not being offered to prove what it is asserting.

Scenario A:

1. The statement: "I'm so furious right now."
2. What is being asserted in the statement?
   a. That Megan killed the teacher. (no)
   b. That Megan had the motive to kill the teacher. (no)
   c. **That Megan was furious at the time she made the statement.** (yes)
3. What is it being offered to prove?
   a. That Megan killed the teacher. (no)
   b. That Megan had the motive to kill the teacher. (no)
   c. **That Megan was furious at the time she made the statement (which will ultimately prove her motive for killing the teacher).** (yes)

Here Step 2 = Step 3, therefore it is hearsay. Here, the statement is being offered to prove ("Step 3") the same thing that it is asserting ("Step 2"). As a result, the trier of fact is required to believe that the assertion in the statement (that Megan was furious) is true. Thus, the trier of fact is required to rely on the credibility of a person who is not on the stand to be cross-examined on the substance of his statement. (Example: Were you *really* furious? Aren't you always furious? What did you mean by furious? etc.) When the credibility of a person is at issue who is not present to testify to his out-of-court statements, and to be cross-examined on them, his statements are generally excluded under the hearsay rule, subject to exceptions discussed later. Since the statement is being offered to prove the truth of the matter asserted, it is hearsay by definition.

Keep in mind that when trying to determine what the statement is being offered to prove, do not be confused by what the statement will *ultimately* help to prove in the case, such as motive or guilt/innocence above. Instead, ask whether you must prove what is asserted within the statement, here that Meagan was furious, in order to prove the ultimate fact, her guilt.

Here you must prove that Megan was in fact **furious** to establish Megan's motive to kill the teacher. So this statement is being offered to prove the truth of what it asserts.

Scenario B:

1. The statement: "My teacher pinched me really hard until I started crying. She then made me stand in the corner until I stopped."
2. What is being asserted in the statement?
    a. **That the teacher pinched son really hard; and the teacher made son stand in the corner until he stopped crying.** (yes)
    b. That Megan killed teacher. (no)
    c. That Megan had the motive to kill teacher. (no)
3. What is the statement being offered to prove?
    a. That the teacher pinched son really hard; and the teacher made son stand in the corner until he stopped crying. (no)
    b. That Megan killed teacher. (no)
    c. **Why Megan killed the teacher (her motive) because she believed her son (even if not true)** (yes)

Here Step 2 ≠ Step 3, therefore it is not hearsay. Here, the statement is **<u>not</u>** being offered to prove ("Step 3") what it is asserting ("Step 2"), therefore it is not hearsay. Here, son's statement is not being offered to prove that the teacher pinched son. Thus, the trier of fact does not have to believe that the statement is true. The statement is relevant even if it is not true because it is being offered to show the effect it had on Megan in giving her the motive to kill her son's teacher, because it was made. All that matters in this case is that Megan heard it and *she* believed it. Thus, the credibility of the person who made the statement (the son), is not at issue at the trial, and it is not necessary that he take the stand to be cross-examined about what he said to Megan.

While the statement is being offered to ultimately prove Megan's motive, and to help prove that she in fact killed the teacher, the trier of fact is not required to first believe that what the statement asserts is true, which is that the teacher pinched the son. While in Scenario A, you must first believe that what the statement asserts is true, here one need only believe that the statement was made. Thus, it is **<u>not</u>** hearsay by definition.

Case on the Definition of Hearsay and the Hearsay Rule

State v. Carter
Court of Appeal, Fourth Circuit
762 So. 2d 662
May 10, 2000

McKAY, Judge.

The defendant Yvette Scott was charged by grand jury indictment on January 27, 1994 with the second degree murder of Roger Scott, in violation of La. R.S. 14:30.1. The defendant pleaded not guilty and not guilty by reasons of insanity at her February 2, 1994 arraignment. Following trial by a twelve-person jury, the defendant was found guilty of manslaughter. After waiving all delays, the defendant was sentenced to serve twenty-one years at hard labor, with sixteen years suspended, and five years active probation.

FACTS

... New Orleans Police Officer Christopher Joseph Smith Sr. testified that he was working a uniformed paid detail at the Bottom Line Lounge on the morning of November 21, 1993. He said he saw the victim sitting alone on the second floor of the bar sometime before midnight. He later observed the defendant enter the bar and go upstairs. Officer Smith testified that as the couple came downstairs to leave, the defendant was walking behind the victim "fussing" at him, apparently engaged in a "one-sided" argument with the victim. He said the victim did not hit the defendant nor lay his hands on her at any time. Prior to the couple leaving, the officer had not been informed of any disturbance involving the two of them. Approximately one hour after that, ... people came running through the front door saying that the defendant had shot the victim. Officer Smith went outside and found the victim lying in a pool of blood, with a gun approximately five feet from his body. He said the defendant was upset and crying, and pacing back and forth near the body. Officer Smith said the defendant told him a young man had attempted to rob her and the victim. He observed that the window of the Explorer had been shot out and that there was blood inside the vehicle. He said that he did not notice any injuries to the victim.

New Orleans Police Officer Gregory Clay ... went outside and saw the victim lying on the ground in pool of blood, and mumbling something to the effect that, "She shot me." ...

The defendant, who was thirty-three years old at the time of trial, testified.... On the night of the killing, defendant said she went ... to the Bottom Line Lounge to meet the victim. She claimed that the victim began berating her, asking why she took so long to get there. She said he loudly cursed her, and that he was talking like he was going to "stomp" her. They walked outside, where he allegedly called her a "hoe" and said he was going to start stomping her. He then hit her on the side of her face with some keys. She pleaded with him to stop, but he kept on hitting her. She said he was "steady beating me and beating me." She said she hit him back and that he then became furious and started punching her. The victim then allegedly threatened to kill defendant, and asked for the gun she had in her purse. When she refused to give it to him, he said he would get another one he had, and went to his truck.... After the victim went to his truck, defendant said she got the gun out of her purse and aimed it at him. When she saw him reach for something, she shot him.... She then telephoned her sister to inform her that she had just shot the victim, and told her that he might "need some blood or something." ...

Georgette Lemon, the defendant's sister, testified ... that after the defendant telephoned her at 3:00 or 4:00 a.m. on the morning of the shooting, she went to Charity Hospital to donate blood for the victim, but discovered upon her arrival that he had died.... Ms. Lemon said that when the defendant telephoned her on the night of the shooting to ask her to go and donate blood for the victim, she did not say how the victim had gotten shot....

ASSIGNMENT OF ERROR NO. 4

By this assignment of error, the defendant claims the trial court erred in admitting telephone records into evidence.

The defendant testified on direct examination that after she shot her husband she telephoned her sister, Georgette Lemon, so she could go to the hospital and donate blood for the victim.

In rebuttal, the State called Mark Pitre, a Bell South Mobility loss prevention specialist, who identified records for a cellular telephone account in the name of Roger Scott [the victim]. The records had been faxed from Bell South's Atlanta office, where the information was stored. He testified from the telephone records that one telephone call was placed on November 21, 1993 at 3:58 a.m. to 504-948-7143, that the call prior to that one had been placed at 3:19 a.m., and that there had been no calls placed after that during the billing cycle, through November 28, 1993.

Kathleen Causey, a security department specialist for BellSouth, testified that records for telephone number 504-948-7143 reflected that the subscriber and person responsible for that account was Shwanda Matthews [not the sister].

The defendant argues on appeal that the records introduced by Mr. Pitre constitute hearsay evidence, and that a proper foundation was not laid to introduce them pursuant to the business records exception of La. C.E. art. 803(6)....

Hearsay is a statement, other than one made by the declarant while testifying at the present trial or hearing, offered in evidence to prove the truth of the matter asserted. Hearsay is not admissible except as otherwise provided by the Code of Evidence or other legislation. Evidence is only considered hearsay if it is a "statement." A statement is an oral or written assertion, or nonverbal conduct of a person, if it is intended by him as an assertion.

In *Armstead*, the State linked the defendant to a number of obscene telephone calls by introducing telephone company computer printouts showing that several of the calls had been traced to a number assigned to the defendant's mother. The defendant objected to the introduction of those computer printouts on the same basis as defendant in the instant case—that the State failed to lay the proper foundation for the printouts to be admissible under the business records exception to the hearsay rule. In rejecting the defendant's argument, and finding that the computer printouts did not even constitute hearsay statements, the court stated:

> There is no doubt that computer printouts which reflect computer stored human statements are hearsay when introduced for the truth of the matter asserted in the statements. The output represents only the by-product of a machine operation which uses for its input "statements" entered into the machine by out-of-court declarants.
>
> From our understanding of the record, however, we are not dealing with computer stored human statements or assertions which have been retrieved from the computer and introduced into evidence in printout form. The invention of electronic switching systems in telecommunications has eliminated the need for manual involvement in a telephone trace. Since the computer is actually responsible

for making the telephone connection, the computer can be programmed to record the source of any incoming call. Thus, the printout of a telephone trace in this type of system does not represent evidence of computer stored declarations. The computer generated data by recording the source of various telephone connections as it was making them. Therefore, the evidence in this case was generated solely by the electrical and mechanical operations of the computer and telephone equipment, and was not dependent upon the observations and reporting of a human declarant.

We therefore view the printout offered as evidence in this case differently from printouts of human statements fed into the computer. Since the computer was programmed to record its activities when it made the telephone connections, the printout simply represents a self-generated record of its operations, much like a seismograph can produce a record of geophysical occurrences, a flight recorder can produce a record of physical conditions onboard an aircraft, and an electron microscope can produce a micrograph, which is a photograph of things too small to be viewed by the human eye.

We pretermit consideration of the defendant's contention that the printout in this case was not properly qualified as a business record, since we find that such a foundation was not required. The printout of the results of the computer's internal operations is not hearsay evidence. It does not represent the output of statements placed into the computer by out-of-court declarants. Nor can we say that this printout itself is a "statement" constituting hearsay evidence. The underlying rationale of the hearsay rule is that such statements are made without an oath and their truth cannot be tested by cross-examination. Of concern is the possibility that a witness may consciously or unconsciously misrepresent what the declarant told him or that the declarant may consciously or unconsciously misrepresent a fact or occurrence. With a machine, however, there is no possibility of a conscious misrepresentation, and the possibility of inaccurate or misleading data only materializes if the machine is not functioning properly. For this reason, apparently, most definitions of hearsay are limited to out-of-court statements by a person made out of court and thus not under oath, and not the subject of cross-examination or confrontation. We therefore view the computer generated data in this case as demonstrative evidence of a scientific test or experiment. The defendant's argument that the person who made the record should have been called is without merit since the computer itself made the record, not a person who could have been called to the stand.

One last note is in order. The defendant, in his objection to the introduction of the printout, only argued that Mr. Henry Arceneaux, security manager for South Central Bell, was not the proper person to introduce the evidence. He did not argue that a proper foundation had not been laid in terms of the accuracy and reliability of the computer trace. While we are certain that such a predicate would be required, we need not decide in this case the appropriate standard to be utilized in evaluating the sufficiency of evidence elicited in such a predicate since no contemporaneous objection on this ground was made. (Footnotes omitted).

... Mr. Pitre did not testify as to how the information contained in these records was compiled, or how the physical records themselves were generated. However, it can only be concluded that, as in *Armstead,* the telephone records were not compiled by human beings entering information into a computer. Taking judicial notice of the advances in technology since *Armstead,* decided in 1983, it would defy logic to even suggest that the information contained in the cellular telephone records of Roger Scott be considered as statements, i.e., oral or written assertions by a person or persons. Rather, the records are obviously computer-generated printouts of the computer-recorded numbers of telephone calls placed by a person or persons using a cellular telephone under an account in the name of Roger Scott. As in *Armstead*, the records are not hearsay evidence....

Discussion Questions

1. Why are the dangers associated with admitting hearsay into evidence not present when a computer compiles and generates the information? Why is the same true with respect to animals?
2. Can you think of other types of computer-compiled and -generated information that would be offered to prove the truth of the matter asserted, but would not be subject to the hearsay rule?
3. Why was the issue of the foundation for the business record exception pretermitted by finding that the phone records were not hearsay? When are the hearsay exceptions applicable?

Key Points

The key points to keep in mind regarding defining hearsay and the hearsay rule.

1. **Hearsay** is an out-of-court statement offered to prove the truth of the matter asserted. Hearsay is generally inadmissible, subject to other legislation.
2. The **dangers of hearsay are**: 1) memory; 2) perception; 3) narration; 4) insincerity. The **protections at trial** against the dangers of hearsay are: 1) oath; 2) cross-examination; and 3) being personally present to be observed by the jury.
3. **The components of hearsay rule**: 1) that there be a statement; 2) that the statement was made other than at the present trial or hearing; 3) the declarant must be a person; 4) the statement must assert something; and 5) the statement is being offered to prove what it asserts and that the assertion is true.
   a. Statement — oral or written assertion, or non-verbal conduct intended as an assertion.
   b. Outside of present trial — made outside of present trial or hearing, even if made in another trial.
   c. Declarant must be a person — the person who made the out-of-court statement must be a person, and does not include computer-generated information or animal assertions.
   d. Offered in evidence to prove what the statement asserts — if statement offered to prove what it asserts, it is hearsay. If it is not offered to prove what it asserts, it is not hearsay.
4. **Identifying hearsay:**
   a. Identify the statement;
   b. Determine what the statement is being offered to prove; and
   c. Determine what the statement is asserting (that trier of fact must accept as true).

If what statement is being offered to prove = what the statement asserts = hearsay.

Problems on Identifying Hearsay

For each problem you should determine whether or not the statement in question is hearsay pursuant to the definition contained in Article 801. Some of the statements that are hearsay, might fall into an exception to the hearsay rule, but in this section you are not required to discuss any exceptions to the hearsay rule that might apply.

PROBLEM 5-1. Flip was at the annual office Christmas party with his friend Jake and other coworkers. Shortly after Jake left the party, Flip and the others heard that Jake had been involved in a serious car accident killing two people. When Flip heard the news he commented to his boss, "*Jake had been drinking all night long prior to leaving the party in his red Lamborghini.*" The family of the victims want the boss to testify at the trial to what Flip told him to help prove Jake's negligence in driving his vehicle after drinking at the party. Jake objects that the statement is hearsay. What ruling?

PROBLEM 5-2. During an argument over finances, Tiffany stabbed her husband to death and immediately called 911. She told the operator, "*I stabbed my husband and he's dead.*" At Tiffany's trial, the prosecutor played the 911 call and Tiffany's attorney objected that the statement is hearsay. What ruling? Would your answer change if Tiffany testified to what she told the operator when the call was made rather than merely playing the call to the jury? Why or why not?

PROBLEM 5-3. David is on trial for attempting to kidnap a teenager as she walked home from school. During the trial, the prosecutor asked the teenager what David said to her when he pulled up beside her in his truck. Terry testified that he said, "*Get in the car now or I'll blow your head off!*" The defense objects that the statement is hearsay. 1) What ruling? 2) Would your answer change if instead he'd said, "*Do you need a ride home, Sweetheart?*" Why or why not?

PROBLEM 5-4. Jane is on trial for conspiracy to commit murder because she paid a hit man to kill her husband's mistress. At the trial, to help prove the conspiracy, the prosecution offers into evidence Jane's telephone records that show 31 calls between Jane and the hit man on the day of the murder and more than 100 calls in the couple of weeks leading up to the murder. When the records are offered, Jane's attorney objects that the records are hearsay. What ruling?

PROBLEM 5-5. As the police officer began to testify at the murder trial about which photo the victim selected as her assailant, the defense objected that the testimony was hearsay. Is the officer's testimony about which person the victim picked from the lineup to prove the identity of the offender hearsay? Why or why not?

PROBLEM 5-6. Freddie Mack was on trial for illegal discharge of a dangerous weapon. The prosecution has called several witnesses to help prove that it was Freddie Mack who discharged the weapon. Among the witnesses was the mother of one of the neighborhood kids who testified that within a matter of seconds after she heard gunshots, her son ran into the house and said, "*Ma, Freddie Mack has a gun and he's out there shooting at us. He almost hit me and several others.*" She stated that she then called the police. At the trial the prosecution calls the mother to the stand to testify to what her son told her to help prove that Freddie Mack fired the shots. Freddie Mack objects that the statement is hearsay. How should the court decide the admissibility of the statement?

PROBLEM 5-7. Ryan is accused of an armed robbery that took place around noon in Lafayette on June 1. One of his college professors in a nearby city about 75 miles away testified that Ryan was in his class at the time of the murder. The class is at noon. The defense attorney asked him how he could be sure that Ryan was in class. He stated that after class Ryan said to him, "*I won't be in class on Friday because I have an interview in Dallas.*" The professor was intrigued because he used to live in Dallas. As the professor testifies about what Ryan told him, the prosecution objects that the testimony is hearsay. How should the court rule and why?

PROBLEM 5-8. Adrian is suing the Dew Drop Inn because he fell down a steep flight of stairs that were poorly lit and did not have a handrail. After she fell, a manager ran to her rescue and said, "*I've told him to fix this stairwell. People keep falling down these stairs.*" At the trial, Adrian wants to testify to what the manager said to her to prove that the owner had been given notice of the condition, yet still failed to make the repairs. The owner of the Dew Drop objected that the statement is hearsay. What ruling and why?

PROBLEM 5-9. Diamond and Dee Dee are sisters and began fighting over their late mother's pearls. During the encounter, Diamond grabbed a bat and hit Dee Dee with it. Dee Dee grabbed a vase and hit Diamond back. The neighbor observed the whole thing and called the police. When the police officer arrived he went to the neighbor's house, and she told him, "*I saw the two sisters that live in that house fighting over their mother's pearls and it looks like the oldest sister, Diamond, started the whole thing. They were screaming and yelling and Diamond was chasing Dee Dee around the yard with a bat. Eventually Dee Dee armed herself with a vase and defended herself.*" The officer went over and arrested Diamond for attacking her sister. At Diamond's trial, the police officer was called to the stand to testify about what led to Diamond's arrest. He stated he was dispatched to the house of a neighbor who called and reported an incident next door. He was asked what the neighbor told him when he arrived. The defense objected that the testimony would be hearsay. The prosecution responded that they were not trying to prove the truth of the matter within the statement, but only to explain why the officer went next door and subsequently arrested Diamond. How should the court rule and why?

PROBLEM 5-10. Tim's son was thought to be involved in some gang-related violence and looting that took place around midnight Saturday night. During the investigation, when police asked Tim if his son was home, he told them that his son was at home all evening and couldn't have been involved. Later on that day, Tim told his neighbor, "*My son did not arrive home last night until well after 2 a.m.*" The neighbor called the police, and Tim's son was arrested. At Tim's son's trial, the prosecution called the neighbor to testify to what Tim told him to help prove Tim's son was not home at the time of the incident. The son's attorney objects that the statement is hearsay. How should the court rule and why?

PROBLEM 5-11. Gunner was having lunch with his fiancée at a small café on the corner when he observed an accident over his date's shoulder. When the cars crashed, she looked around to see what happened and Gunner immediately told her, "*The blue car went through the intersection on a red light and hit that little brown truck.*" Gunner did not want to be involved, but his fiancée was called to the stand by the victims of the accident to testify to what Gunner told her after the accident. The defense objects that the statement is hearsay. How should the court rule and why?

PROBLEM 5-12. Shepherd was sitting at the bar when he observed a couple across from him. The man got up and walked towards the restroom. When he returned, the bartender told him, "*That lady put something in your drink when you went to the restroom.*" The couple began to argue, and she denied the allegation. Convinced the drink was okay, the man drank it. It was later determined that the lady was a prostitute and had taken the man to a hotel room and had robbed him after he fell asleep. During her trial, Shepherd was called to the stand by the prosecution to testify to what he had heard the bartender tell the man after he returned from the restroom to help prove that the prostitute drugged the guy by putting something in his drink. The defense objected that the question called for hearsay. What ruling?

PROBLEM 5-13. Chucky was on trial for possession of marijuana. An element of the crime is that the substance he possessed must have actually been marijuana. To prove this, the prosecution offered into evidence a crime lab report where the substance that was found in his possession had been tested. The report stated, "*The tested substance was determined to be 100% pure marijuana.*" Chucky objected that the report was hearsay. How should the court rule and why?

PROBLEM 5-14. Roxanne was a witness to an accident. She was called to the stand to testify for the plaintiff and was asked to tell the court what she told the police officer at the scene when he asked her what happened. Roxanne testified, "I told him, '*That lady was sending a text message when the accident happened.*'" The plaintiff wishes to prove what the defendant was doing when the accident occurred to show that she was at fault. The defendant objected that the testimony is hearsay. The plaintiff's attorney responds that the statement is not hearsay because Roxanne is present and can be cross-examined about what she told the officer. How should the court rule and why?

§ 5.2 Non-Hearsay — Statements Not Being Offered to Prove the Truth of the Matter Asserted

Since statements are subject to the hearsay rule only if they are offered in evidence to prove the truth of the matter asserted, a statement is not hearsay, and not subject to exclusion, if it is being offered for some *other* reason. These statements are commonly referred to as **non-hearsay** statements. As a result, a first line of defense whenever an opponent of a statement objects that a statement is hearsay is to examine whether the statement is in fact being offered to prove the truth of the matter asserted, as outlined above. If it is determined that the statement is not being offered to prove the truth of the matter asserted, then the statement will not be excluded by the hearsay rule. However, in such a case, it typically must be shown that the statement is relevant for a reason other than its assertive value. In other words, why *is* the statement being offered?

There are several categories of non-hearsay that have been identified by the courts as alternative reasons why a statement might be relevant other than for the truth of the matter asserted. Typically, if a proponent of a statement argues that the statement is not being offered to prove the truth of the matter asserted, he should be able to articulate a non-hearsay purpose for which the statement is relevant. Common categories of non-hearsay include:

1. verbal acts;
2. verbal parts of acts;
3. non-assertive conduct;
4. state of mind of hearer/receiver;
5. state of mind of the declarant;
6. notice or knowledge of the hearer/receiver;
7. notice or knowledge of the declarant; and
8. prior inconsistent and prior consistent statements.

§ 5.2.1 Verbal Acts

A "verbal act" is a statement, the making of which has **substantive legal significance** apart from its truth or **gives rise to legal consequences**. This type of statement is also referred to as an "**operative fact**."[16] A prime example of this type of statement is a defamatory statement. In a defamation case, a statement referring to one's boss as a thief has independent legal significance simply because the statement was made.[17] The statement itself gives rise to legal consequences because it *is* the defamatory statement at issue. In this type of case, the statement is not being offered to prove that the boss is actually a thief, in which case it would be hearsay, but instead is being offered to prove that the employee made the statement and defamed his boss.

Other examples include the statements constituting the offer and the acceptance in a contract case. The statements themselves give rise to legal consequences—being bound by a contract. Additionally, a statement granting permission ("*Yes, you may.*") as in *Buckbee* below, or a statement requesting services in a solicitation of a prostitute case ("*Looking for a date tonight, Hun?*"), are verbal acts. In each of these instances, the statements themselves have legal significance aside from their truth, to which the law attaches "duties and liabilities."[18] Just as a punch is the "act" that would form the battery in a battery case, a statement threatening someone ("*I will kill you!*") would be the "verbal" act that forms the threat in a stalking case. The fact that the statement was uttered is what is relevant. As a result, these statements are not hearsay and are not subject to the hearsay exclusion.

Cases on Verbal Act

Buckbee v. United Gas Pipe Line Company
Supreme Court of Louisiana
561 So. 2d 76
April 30, 1990

CALOGERO, Chief Justice.

Buckbee was employed as the maintenance foreman for LCR. He was assigned the job of reassembling and installing a second-hand box heater previously owned by United Gas Pipe Line Company Inc. ("United Gas").[19] In the process of readying the heater for service, Buckbee and a co-employee, Roosevelt Vincent, attempted to remove a tapered metal

---

16. *See* Force & Rault, Handbook, Art. 801 Author's Comment (1); *See also* 19 La. Civ. L. Treatise, Evidence And Proof § 10.1(2d ed).

17. *See* Meloncon v. Hyatt, below.

18. Buckbee v. United Gas Pipe Line Co., 561 So. 2d 76 (La. 1990).

19. The box heater consisted of a steel frame full of firebrick and six-inch steel tubes welded into coils. It weighed approximately 200 tons, and measured forty feet long, fifteen feet wide, and thirty feet high. It was originally used by United Gas at its plant in Carthage, Texas. When United Gas closed its Carthage plant, it sold its equipment, including several box heaters, to the Jerry R. Watt Co., a used equipment dealer. The Watt Co. sold the heaters to LCR. The heaters were dismantled and transported from Carthage to the LCR refinery near Lake Charles, Louisiana. LCR had to reassemble the heaters before placing them in service....

plug protruding from a mule-ear header on the exterior of the heater. After two hours of work with wrenches and sledge hammers, they found themselves unable to remove the plug. Buckbee then left the scaffold where he and Vincent were working, went into the plant office, remained there for about ten minutes, returned, and remounted the scaffold. At that point, Buckbee and Vincent used an acetylene torch in an effort to loosen the plug. Although the heater had been out of service for several years, and although it had been "cleaned," dismantled, and transported from Texas to Louisiana, the tube behind the plug apparently contained some volatile flammable matter. Application of the acetylene torch to the plug and surrounding heater surface caused a fire to erupt, coincident with expulsion of the plug. The fire burned both Buckbee and Vincent severely. Vincent recovered; Buckbee died three weeks later from his injuries.

Buckbee's surviving wife and child sued United Gas, among others, alleging that United Gas negligently failed to inspect, test, and clean the heater before selling it to the Jerry R. Watt Co., and failed to warn LCR of the dangerous condition of the heater. Upon motion by United Gas, the trial court consolidated the Buckbee plaintiffs' suit with a suit filed by Roosevelt Vincent.

At trial, the jury heard evidence that United Gas had used in the heater a kerosene-like substance called "absorbing oil" and that a sample of a kerosene-like liquid was taken from the tube shortly after the explosion. Apparently it was the absorbing oil which fueled the explosion and fire. The jury also heard evidence that the contract between United Gas and the first purchaser, the Jerry R. Watt Co., required United Gas to provide an inspector to "assist in monitoring" the dismantling of the heaters at United Gas's site. The jury concluded that United Gas's negligence was a proximate cause of the accident.

The jury also heard testimony from Buckbee's superiors, plant co-owner Joseph Chamberlin and plant superintendent Blane Sheley, that the accepted safe practice was to remove the first plug from this type of heater "cold," that is, through use of chisels, hammers, and wrenches, just as Buckbee and Vincent first tried. The jury heard evidence that Buckbee, who had worked in refineries for at least ten years, was aware of this safety procedure. Over plaintiffs' hearsay objection, the trial court permitted Chamberlin to testify that he instructed Buckbee "probably a month before and probably a day before" the accident that the first plug should always be removed cold. The trial court permitted Sheley to testify that on the evening before the accident he and Buckbee discussed the procedure for removing the first plug cold with a third employee, a trainee who was not later involved in the accident.

Contrariwise, the jury was not permitted to hear plaintiffs' evidence which indicated that on the morning of the accident Buckbee had sought and secured his superiors' permission to use heat just before he applied heat to the plug. The trial court refused to permit Roosevelt Vincent to testify about two oral statements which Buckbee allegedly made just before the accident, statements which indicated that Buckbee had (1) sought permission to apply heat to the plug and (2) secured such permission.

The court permitted Vincent to testify that prior to applying heat Buckbee descended the scaffold on which they were working, entered the plant office, remained there for approximately ten minutes, returned and remounted the scaffold. The court also permitted Vincent to testify that after receiving instructions from Buckbee he and Buckbee then, in turn, applied heat to the plug with an acetylene torch. However, the court did not permit Vincent to testify about what Buckbee told him just before descending and just after reascending the scaffold. Plaintiffs proffered Vincent's testimony in the form of a stipulation of the parties:

> [I]f Mr. Vincent were called as a witness and asked what was his understanding of why Mr. Buckbee left to go to the office, it would be to obtain permission to apply heat to the plug to remove it. Secondly, that if he were asked to testify as to what Mr. Buckbee said before he went to the office, he would say that he was going to get permission to apply heat, and that when he came back he said that he had obtained permission and they could go ahead and apply the heat.

The jury found that Buckbee's negligence was a proximate cause of the accident, precluding any recovery by Buckbee's surviving spouse and child. By contrast, the jury found no negligence on the part of Vincent and awarded him $750,880.00 in damages. Buckbee's widow and child appealed, arguing that the trial court erred in excluding Vincent's testimony and that such exclusion constituted reversible error....

In each instance, the issue before this Court is whether the testimony is hearsay under the definition of hearsay adopted by this Court, and therefore inadmissible; whether the testimony is, by definition, nonhearsay and therefore admissible; or whether the testimony, even though hearsay, is admissible under an exception to the hearsay rule.

In proceeding to answer these inquiries, we look first to the definition of hearsay ... :

Hearsay evidence is testimony in court, or written evidence, of a statement made out of court, the statement being offered as an assertion to show the truth of matters asserted therein, and thus resting for its value upon the credibility of the out-of-court asserter.[20]

In its broadest sweep, the hearsay rule excludes all testimony regarding statements made out-of-court by declarants who at the time of making the statements were not under oath, not in the presence of the trier of fact, and thus not subject to cross-examination. By excluding testimony which fails these three requirements, the hearsay rule increases the reliability of in-court testimony, and seeks to admit only that testimony which the factfinder can evaluate for the witness's perception, memory, narration and sincerity.

The hearsay rule, however, does not bar testimony not properly defined as hearsay, needless to say. When testimony concerning an out-of-court statement is not "offered as an assertion to show the truth of the matters asserted therein," such testimony is, by definition, not hearsay. Such testimony may therefore be admissible if it otherwise meets the requirements of relevancy and materiality, and overcomes the risk of undue prejudice.

An out-of-court statement may be admissible as nonhearsay in the following instances, among others: (1) to prove that the out-of-court statement was made, rather than to prove the truth of the fact or facts asserted in the statement; (2) to illustrate the impact and consequent effect that the out-of-court statement had upon the state of mind of the

---

20. This case commenced prior to the effective date of the Louisiana Code of Evidence with the filing of plaintiff's petition on January 12, 1981. ...The case is thus governed by pre-Codal statutes and jurisprudence on the admissibility of hearsay testimony. The L.C.E. adopts a definition of hearsay which comports substantially with the definition previously adopted by this Court. The Code defines hearsay as "a statement, other than one made by the declarant while testifying at the present trial or hearing, offered in evidence to prove the truth of the matter asserted." L.C.E. art. 801(C).

listener or to illustrate the state of mind of the speaker;[21] and (3) to prove the occurrence of a "verbal act" to which the law attaches duties and liabilities.[22]

Chamberlin's and Sheley's testimony to out-of-court statements made by them was, by definition, not hearsay. This testimony was not offered to prove the truth of the matters asserted in the out-of-court statements, that it was only safe to remove the first plug cold. Rather, Chamberlin's and Sheley's testimony to their out-of-court statements was offered as evidence that Buckbee had received cautionary advice instructing him in the safe procedure for removing this plug. Their testimony was offered as evidence of Buckbee's mental state, i.e., that he had notice, knowledge, and information concerning the industry's accepted safe method for removing a first plug from this type of equipment, and that he was advised by experienced individuals to follow that procedure. Chamberlin's and Sheley's testimony was offered for this nonhearsay purpose and, for this reason, was properly admitted by the lower courts. This testimony was relevant to the central legal issue in the case: whether Buckbee acted negligently when he applied heat to the plug.

Plaintiffs urge that Vincent's testimony concerning Buckbee's second statement, that he had received permission to apply heat, is also admissible as nonhearsay evidence of Buckbee's state of mind, that is, as evidence that Buckbee might reasonably have concluded that it was safe to heat the plug. We do not find that Buckbee's second statement is admissible for the nonhearsay purpose suggested by plaintiffs, for these reasons. To admit Vincent's testimony to Buckbee's second statement as evidence that (1) Buckbee reasonably concluded that it was safe to heat the plug, and that (2) Buckbee acted reasonably and not negligently when he applied heat to the plug, one must first assume the truth of the underlying hypothesis, i.e., that Buckbee did in fact receive a favorable response from his superiors to his request for permission to apply heat. Unless that underlying assertion is true, that Buckbee received the sought-after permission, Buckbee's second statement has no credible relevance to the issue of whether Buckbee was reasonable in concluding that it was safe to heat the plug.

Plaintiffs cannot be permitted to rely on the nonhearsay use of this statement to prove the effect upon Buckbee, the listener, of an expression of permission which is contested and not otherwise proven. Whether Buckbee acted reasonably in concluding that it was safe to apply heat depends, at least in part, upon whether he reached this conclusion in consequence of receiving his superiors' permission. And the only proof of whether Buckbee received permission is Buckbee's own statement to that effect, presented through the tes-

---

21. Weinstein gives the following examples of the nonhearsay use of statements to show state of mind:

> [S]tatements of complaint may be admitted to show that the recipient was on notice that his customers were generally dissatisfied; continued operation despite this knowledge may then be indicative of a scheme to defraud. An accused may proffer statements consistent with good faith on his part to rebut the inference of criminal intent which might otherwise be drawn from his actions. Statements may likewise be proffered in civil cases to show the presence or absence of intent in actions in which intent is in issue.
>
> Statements may also be admitted to show other states of mind such as knowledge, motive, fear, or reasonableness in taking particular action or in reaching a particular conclusion.

4 J. Weinstein & M. Berger, Weinstein's Evidence § 801(c)(01) at 801–78 to 801–80 (1988).

22. For example, in a suit for defamation, the defaming statement is the "operative fact which gives rise to legal consequences." See also *McCormick on Evidence* § 249 n.4 for citations to cases which hold that specific verbal acts, such as a command, a fraudulent representation, and an agent's testimony to a principal's statement granting him agency authority, are not hearsay.

timony of Vincent. Since Buckbee's statement was made out of court, not under oath, and not subject to cross-examination, Vincent's testimony to that statement is hearsay when offered to prove that Buckbee in fact received permission to apply heat[23] and would not be admitted in this instance solely for a nonhearsay purpose. The lower courts properly excluded this testimony.

Plaintiffs also urge that, even if Vincent's testimony to Buckbee's second statement is hearsay, it should be admitted under a jurisprudential exception to the hearsay rule. This Court, in the search for truth, recognizes exceptions to the hearsay rule when there exist both sufficient guarantees of trustworthiness and a necessity for the evidence. Plaintiffs urge the Court to rule that Vincent's testimony to Buckbee's second statement is admissible under a broad residual exception to the hearsay rule equivalent to that permitted by L.C.E. art. 804(B)(6) and Fed.R.Evid. 804(b)(5). Both the federal rule and the Louisiana code article reflect concerns articulated by this Court in *State v. Smith, supra,* that the hearsay possess circumstantial guarantees of trustworthiness and that a necessity exist for its introduction in a particular case.

Although the instant case is not governed by the L.C.E., we find that L.C.E. art. 806(B)(6) provides the appropriate standard—trustworthiness and necessity—by which to judge the admissibility of the hearsay evidence at issue here. In this case, Vincent's testimony to Buckbee's statement, that he had received permission to apply heat, is the only available evidence (except for Vincent's testimony to Buckbee's first statement) which supports plaintiffs' version of events in this case. Plaintiffs have been unable to adduce any other evidence countering Chamberlin's and Sheley's testimony that Buckbee disobeyed instructions and acted hastily and incautiously in his effort to remove the plug, but rather that he in fact got permission. Vincent's testimony therefore meets the necessity requirement of the residual hearsay exception.

However, Vincent's testimony regarding Buckbee's second "permission" statement lacks circumstantial guarantees of trustworthiness which would overcome the hearsay bar posed by Buckbee's unavailability to testify in court under oath and subject to cross-examination. Admittedly, there is one item of evidence which could be interpreted as circumstantial support for Buckbee's declaration that he had received permission: the fact that he descended the scaffold, entered the plant office, and remained there for ten minutes. This fact alone, however, is insufficient to offset the other equally plausible explanation for Buckbee's statement, i.e., the possibility that Buckbee was unable to procure assent to his request for permission to apply heat, or that his request was denied and he chose in either event to proceed with what he perceived as the thing to do while conveniently misleading Vincent by telling him that he had obtained permission to proceed with heat. The court cannot test, and the jury cannot evaluate, the trustworthiness of this statement by placing

23. Had Buckbee survived, he would have been permitted to testify about his superiors' statements permitting him to apply heat as a nonhearsay "verbal act" (a giving of permission by a superior with authority to do so) with concomitant legal consequences. Had Vincent personally heard Buckbee's superiors giving Buckbee permission to apply heat, he too would have been permitted to testify to that statement. However, since Vincent did not personally hear the statement being made, he is not permitted to testify to Buckbee's out-of-court assertion that such a statement occurred. *See Knorr v. Pearson,* 671 F.2d 1368, 1372–73 (C.C.P.A.1982) (third party's testimony to what he heard first inventor say to second inventor held admissible nonhearsay as proof of a verbal act with legal consequences between the two inventors, but third party forbidden to testify to what the first inventor told him the second inventor said); *General Tire of Miami Beach, Inc. v. N.L.R.B.,* 332 F.2d 58, 60–61 (5th Cir.1964) ("The verbal act, as any other act, may be proved by one who heard it, saw it, or felt it.").

Buckbee on the witness stand under oath and subject to cross-examination. In his absence, the statement is inadmissible for the reason that the circumstantial guarantees of the statement's reliability are insufficient. On the admittedly limited evidence presented, the trustworthiness of Buckbee's "permission" statement is not preponderantly shown.

Our conclusion here is of course different from *State v. Gremillion,* 542 So.2d 1074 (La.1989), where, guided by the residual hearsay exception standard in L.C.E. art. 804(B)(6), we found that a decedent's statement, although hearsay, was admissible. In *Gremillion,* we found that the statement was corroborated by other evidence which rendered it reliable and trustworthy. The defendant in *Gremillion* was accused of beating a man who later died of internal injuries. After being admitted to a hospital, the victim stated to an investigating officer that he had been attacked by three white males. In a separate statement, made part of the hospital record and admitted at trial, the victim told the admitting physician that he was kicked and beaten by "several others." The victim was otherwise unable to identify his attackers. The Court found that several factors rendered the victim's statement to the investigating officer reliable and trustworthy: first, it was made to an officer investigating the crime; second, an equivalent statement was made to the admitting physician; and third, the decedent failed to identify the defendant as his attacker although he had known the defendant for approximately eleven years.[24]

Unlike the hearsay statement in *Gremillion,* Buckbee's second statement lacks similarly persuasive other corroborative evidence and is therefore not admissible under the residual hearsay exception urged by plaintiffs.

Plaintiffs have also suggested that Buckbee's second statement to Vincent may be admissible as part of the *res gestae* of the incident or under the "present sense impression" exception to the hearsay rule. We reject both of these analyses for the following reasons.

In Louisiana, *res gestae* was formerly defined and rendered admissible by statute. La.R.S. 15:447–448.[25] Although Louisiana's statutory definition of *res gestae* was narrowly drawn, the exception often received expansive treatment in the courts. Nevertheless, the *res gestae*

---

24. In *Robinson v. Shapiro,* 646 F.2d 734 (2d Cir.1981), the court found adequate physical evidence to corroborate and render trustworthy a worker's statement made shortly before his death in a fatal work-related accident to a co-employee. The decedent told the co-worker that the building superintendent at the job site had instructed that, to prevent the superintendent's dog from escaping its rooftop kennel, the work crew was forbidden to open a large iron gate in order to reach the garage rooftop work area. Decedent also stated that the superintendent forbade the crew to reach the roof by passing through his apartment because that would soil the carpets. Throughout the day, the workcrew climbed over the gate to reach the work area. At the end of the day, when the decedent was climbing over the gate for the last time, the gate came loose, the decedent fell down the stairs leading to the roof, and the gate fell on top of him. He died three days later from injuries.

The trial court admitted the co-worker's testimony about the decedent's statement and the court of appeals affirmed, holding that the testimony met the requirements of the residual hearsay exception in Fed.R.Evid. 804(b)(5). The statement was corroborated by other physical evidence, giving it "equivalent circumstantial guarantees of trustworthiness": First, there was evidence that a dog was kept on the roof; and second, the weather on the day of the accident was wet and snowy. Moreover, the evidence was material; it was "more probative on the point for which it (was) offered than any other" reasonably available evidence; and its admission served the best interest of justice. *Robinson,* 646 F.2d at 742.

25. Res gestae was formerly defined by La.R.S. 15:447 as follows:

> Res gestae are events speaking for themselves under the immediate pressure of the occurrence, through the instructive, impulsive and spontaneous words and acts of the participants, and not the words of the participants when narrating the events. What forms any part of the res gestae is always admissible in evidence.

exception was more properly limited to "spontaneous words or acts of the participants at the time of the occurrence" rather than a participant's narration of events. As the *Williams* Court explained, "(t)he res gestae exception permits admission of events speaking through participants, but not the testimony of participants speaking about events." *Williams,* 331 So.2d at 470.[26]

In the instant case, Buckbee's statement was made narratively, upon his return from the plant office. He recounted an event which had purportedly transpired. It is not rendered admissible under the *res gestae* exception by the mere fact that it was made during what, in retrospect, appears a continuing sequence of events leading up to the fatal accident.

Nor is this statement admissible under the exception for a "present sense impression," an exception now codified at L.C.E. art. 803(1). As McCormick explains, a present sense impression is "confined to 'describing or explaining' " an event or condition perceived by the speaker. The critical factor is whether the statement was made while the individual was "perceiving" the event or "immediately thereafter." The statement may follow "immediately" after perceiving an event, allowing only for "the time needed for translating observation into speech."

In this case, Buckbee's statement did not "immediately" follow his "perception" of an event. Rather, Buckbee's statement was sufficiently distant from events which may have taken place in the plant office to rule out admitting it as Buckbee's present sense impression of those purported events. Consequently, Buckbee's second statement to Vincent fails to meet the requirements of the present sense exception to the hearsay rule and was properly excluded by the lower courts. We turn now to the admissibility of Buckbee's first statement, which Buckbee made to Vincent before descending the scaffold, that he intended to seek permission to heat the plug.

One well-recognized exception to the hearsay rule admits testimony concerning a speaker's out-of-court declaration of intent. Although such a statement is hearsay when offered to prove the truth of the matter asserted therein, i.e., that the declarant actually intended to take, and did subsequently take, certain action, such a statement is nonetheless excepted from the bar of the hearsay rule. This exception is now codified at L.C.E. art. 803(3), which provides, in pertinent part, that a "statement of the declarant's then existing state of mind, emotion, sensation, or physical condition (such as intent, plan, motive, design, mental feeling, pain, and bodily health)," is admissible as an exception to the hearsay rule when that statement is "offered to prove the declarant's then existing condition or his future action."[27]

---

26. The *res gestae* exception predates many recent developments in the theory of hearsay; it served historically to admit words spoken contemporaneously with or directly after the event that formed the subject of the legal action. Statements formerly admitted under the *res gestae* exception are now described and rendered admissible by separate specific hearsay exceptions and exemptions in both the L.C.E. and the Federal Rules of Evidence, including an excited utterance; a present sense impression; a statement of then existing mental, emotional, or physical condition; statements made for purposes of receiving medical treatment; and statements offered as nonhearsay proof of something other than the truth of the matter asserted. These specific exceptions reflect the rationale underlying the original *res gestae* exception: that statements made contemporaneously with an event, without opportunity for reflective thought, possess sufficient guarantees of reliability to overcome the hearsay bar.

27. Testimony about a *declarant's* out-of-court statement of intent is hearsay when offered to prove the truth of the matter asserted, that the declarant did in fact intend to take certain action, and did subsequently take such action. It is nonetheless admissible under this statutory exception to the hearsay rule.

Testimony concerning an out-of-court statement is nonhearsay, and therefore not barred, when used to prove the effect of an out-of court statement on the *listener's* state of mind. Testimony con-

In this case, Vincent's testimony to Buckbee's first statement, that he intended to seek permission to apply heat to the plug, a statement which Buckbee made just before descending the scaffold and going into the plant office, falls squarely under this exception to the hearsay rule. It is hearsay *and* it is nevertheless admissible to show the declarant Buckbee's state of mind, i.e., his intent to seek permission.

This testimony is not only evidence that Buckbee formulated the intention to seek his superiors' permission to apply heat. It could also be offered as some evidence that Buckbee did indeed act in accordance with his expressed intention, that he did approach his superiors in the moments before the accident and that he did request of them permission to apply heat.[28] Coupled with Vincent's testimony that Buckbee thereupon descended the scaffold, and Vincent's testimony that he watched Buckbee walk to, enter, and remain in the plant office for about ten minutes, the testimony regarding what Buckbee said just before descending the scaffold is powerful circumstantial proof that Buckbee in fact sought his superiors' permission to apply heat.

Vincent's testimony concerning this statement was admissible as an exception to the hearsay rule and the lower courts erred in excluding this statement. Moreover, because this testimony is relevant to the issue of Buckbee's negligence, its exclusion was not harmless error but was decidedly prejudicial to plaintiffs' case. It probably explains why the jury found Buckbee contributorily negligent and without the right to recover damages while allowing Vincent, Buckbee's co-employee, to recover.

...

In summary, the lower courts correctly admitted Chamberlin's and Sheley's testimony concerning the advice they gave Buckbee. The courts correctly excluded Vincent's testimony concerning Buckbee's second statement, that he had obtained permission to apply heat. However, the courts erred in excluding Vincent's testimony concerning Buckbee's first statement, that he was going to seek permission to heat the plug. Moreover, because this error may have affected the jury's conclusion on the central issue of Buckbee's contributory negligence, the court of appeal erred in concluding that the exclusion of this evidence constituted harmless error. We therefore reverse the lower courts' decision and remand....

Discussion Questions

1. The *Buckbee* court defines a "verbal act" many times in the case and in many ways. What are some of the ways in which a "verbal act" is defined? Put this concept in your own words. What does it mean to you?
2. The court acknowledges that a statement of permission is a verbal act. What types of legal consequences would the statement of permission have had in *Buckbee*, had the statement been admitted?

---

cerning an out-of-court statement may be admissible as nonhearsay to demonstrate a *declarant's* state of mind when the testimony is not offered to prove the truth of the matter asserted in the statement. For example, a declarant's statement "I am the king" may be admissible nonhearsay when offered to prove the speaker's mental condition; the statement would be inadmissible hearsay if offered to prove the truth of the assertion, that the speaker is in fact the king.

28. In *State v. Doze*, we determined that "(d)eclarations of state of mind are usually admissible for the purpose of proving that the intention of the declarant was actually carried out." This dual evidentiary function of the statement of intent is carried over in L.C.E. art. 803(3), which provides that such a statement may be offered "to prove the declarant's then existing condition *or his future action*." (Emphasis added).

3. The court gives several examples of statements that constitute verbal acts. What are some of these examples? Explain the legal significance of the statements. What legal consequences do the given statements implicate?
4. Why is it that if Vincent had heard the statement from the supervisors, it would've been admissible, but it was not permissible for Vincent to testify to it in the instant case? We will revisit this issue again in § 5.3 *infra*.
5. Another verbal act addressed in the case was the supervisors' comments to Buckbee that it was only safe to remove the first plug cold, as "cautionary advice." Explain how and why those comments were verbal acts. The court stated that these statements went to the central issue in the case. How so?
6. After the court determines that Buckbee's statement to Vincent was hearsay, the court attempts to analyze whether the statement fit into exceptions to the hearsay rule, including the residual catchall exception found in Article 804(6), which considers the trustworthiness of the statement. While we have not covered the exceptions at this time, what are your thoughts on the reliability of any statement that Buckbee may have made? What factors seem to increase or reduce the trustworthiness of the statement?

Melancon v. The Hyatt Corporation

Court of Appeal of Louisiana, Fourth Circuit
589 So. 2d 1186
Nov. 14, 1991

KLEES, Judge.

Defendant, the Hyatt Corporation, appeals the trial court's judgment awarding damages to plaintiffs, Mack Melancon and his wife Jacqueline, for defamation and loss of consortium, respectively....

From November of 1983 until February 7, 1987, Mack Melancon was employed as a shift engineer at the Hyatt Regency hotel in New Orleans. Melancon's job was to operate and maintain the boilers, refrigeration units, heating and air conditioning systems in the hotel. He sometimes had to go into the hotel laundry room, which was kept unlocked, to get rags.

Sometime in November of 1986, the hotel laundry manager, Mr. Dorsky, discovered during a routine inventory that there were some new Regency Club towels missing from the laundry room. He reported this fact to Mr. Conrad, the hotel director of security, who told him to put out more towels and keep a daily count. Mr. Conrad then had a hidden video camera installed in the laundry room. There were towels missing again in December, but the pictures taken by the video camera were inconclusive because the lights had been turned off. Mr. Conrad then had the laundry room lights wired to remain on at all times.

On January 7th, more towels were reported missing. Mr. Conrad checked hotel records and determined that Mack Melancon and Joseph Celestine had been on duty in the Engineering Department from midnight until 8:00 a.m. on January 7th. Mr. Conrad then viewed the videotape, which showed someone enter the laundry room at about 3:46 a.m., climb up on a cart, reach into a box of Regency Club towels on a high shelf, and then walk out. From the tape, Mr. Conrad determined that the person who did this was Mack Melancon.

Mr. Conrad then showed the tape to Mr. Dorsky and Mr. Besmehn, the employee representative in the Personnel Department, without telling them who he believed was on the tape. Mr. Dorsky and Mr. Besmehn each independently recognized Mack Melancon. Finally, the tape was shown to Mr. Gros, a security supervisor, who could not identify the person and said it did not look like Mack Melancon.

Mr. Besmehn discussed the problem with other supervisors in the Personnel Department and with the director of the Engineering Department. The general reaction was one of surprise because Mr. Melancon had always been a good employee.

On February 6, 1987, Mr. Besmehn called Mack Melancon and told him that he was suspected of misappropriating towels based on the videotape. Mr. Melancon denied any involvement in the incident and denied that he was the person shown on the tape. Mr. Melancon was asked to resign; he refused, and was sent home for the day and told not to say anything to anyone. The next day when Melancon came into work, a fellow employee named Charlotte Guidry told him that she had heard "what happened to him." He then went to Personnel, and was fired for stealing towels. He asked to see the videotape, but was denied permission.

Mr. Melancon testified that when he went to clean out his locker, his fellow employees didn't speak to him, and he felt that they all knew the reason he was discharged. Larry Washington, a former employee in the Maintenance Department of the Hyatt, testified at trial that he was told by Betty Mullens, a cafeteria employee, that Mack Melancon was fired for stealing towels. Richard Johnson, another former Hyatt employee, stated that he was told the same thing by fellow employees Vic Sperling, West Young, Victor Artist, and "a lot of guys" sitting at the table during a break time at the Hyatt....

On June 4, 1987, Mack Melancon filed suit against the Hyatt Corporation and its employees Greg Besmehn and Elwood Conrad, alleging defamation and wrongful discharge from his employment....

On June 18, 1990 the jury rendered its verdict that the Hyatt had defamed Mack Melancon, awarding $176,000 in damages to Mr. Melancon plus $25,000 to Mrs. Melancon for loss of consortium.

Defendant's third assignment of error is that the trial judge failed to exclude the testimony of Larry Washington and Richard Johnson as hearsay. Mr. Johnson and Mr. Washington are former employees of the Hyatt who testified that certain other employees communicated to them that Mack Melancon had been fired for stealing towels.

This assignment of error has no merit. Hearsay is testimony in court of a statement made out of court, which statement is being offered to show the truth of the matters asserted therein. *Buckbee v. United Gas Pipeline Company,* 561 So.2d 76 (La.1990). In the instant case, the testimony of Washington and Johnson was not offered to prove the truth of the statement made to them; i.e., that Melancon had stolen towels, but rather was offered to prove publication of that statement. If an out-of-court statement is offered merely to prove that the statement *was made,* it is not hearsay. See *Buckbee, supra.* Therefore, the testimony complained of was not hearsay, and the trial judge's ruling was correct.

Discussion Questions

1. What was the statement in *Melancon* that was the subject of dispute? What duties or liabilities are attached to the statement based solely on whether or not it was made, even if not true?
2. In the case of defamation, the statement also has legal significance if it is deemed to be true as well, doesn't it? What would be the significance of proving the statement was true? Does that in any way affect whether or not it is hearsay? Why or why not?

Problems on Non-Hearsay Verbal Acts

In the following problems, you should determine whether or not the statement in question is hearsay pursuant to the definition contained in Article 801 or if it is a verbal act. Some of the statements that are hearsay might fall into an exception to the hearsay rule, but in this section you are not required to discuss any exceptions to the hearsay rule that might apply.

PROBLEM 5-15. Skip is suing his opponent in the governor's race for slander. Skip claims that during a fundraiser the opponent (Opponent) stated that Skip had had an illicit affair with his secretary. Skip adamantly denies it. Several guests from the fundraiser will testify to what Opponent stated. Opponent claims that testimony to what he said at the fundraiser would be hearsay and is inadmissible. How should the court rule and why?

PROBLEM 5-16. Gray is on trial for stalking and harassing Vera (V). V plans to testify that Gray came to her home and stated, "*I will kill you! You will be mine or dead! I will have who and what I want!*" As V is testifying to what Gray said to her, Gray objects that the statements are hearsay. What ruling?

PROBLEM 5-17. Kane is on trial for solicitation of a prostitute. The undercover police officer will testify that Kane approached her on the corner and stated, "*What can I get for $20?*" Kane objects that the statement is hearsay. How should the court rule and why?

PROBLEM 5-18. Billup is on trial for bribery of a law enforcement officer. After being pulled over for a speeding ticket, Billup said to the officer, "*Wouldn't you rather have this $100 for yourself to forget about this whole thing than to give it to the city?*" As the officer testified to what Billup said to him, Billup's attorney objected that the statement was hearsay. Ruling?

PROBLEM 5-19. Blade and Jagger are on trial for conspiracy to commit a murder for making plans to kill their parents to receive their inheritance. One day while going over the details in their basement apartment, the homeowner who lived upstairs in the residence overheard the conversation and contacted the police. A search of their apartment yielded very large knives, rope, tape, black ski masks, and written plans as to how the murder would be carried out. At the trial, as the homeowner began to testify to the conversation that she overheard between Blade and Jagger discussing the murder of their parents, their attorney objected that the conversation was hearsay. How should the court rule and why?

§ 5.2.1 References and Additional Authority on Verbal Acts

1. Force & Rault, Handbook on Louisiana Evidence Law Arts. 801, 802 Author's Comments (West Publishing 2014)
2. Harges & Jones, Louisiana Evidence Arts. 801, 802 Author's Comments (West Publishing 2014)
3. 19 La. Civ. L. Treatise, Evidence And Proof § 10.1 (2d ed.)
4. **Defaming statement is an operative fact giving rise to legal consequence:** *N.D. v. Ochsner Clinic, L.L.C.*, (La. App. 5th Cir. 05/27/08) WL 8872547 (In an action against Ochsner Clinic, L.L.C. for wrongful disclosure of medical records to those outside of the medical facility by an Ochsner employee, Deanna Dawson, the court held that the

witness's testimony that Dawson came into their workplace and told "all employees in the office" about plaintiff's test results which she obtained through the Ochsner computer system was not hearsay because the witness personally witnessed the alleged publication and testified to the operative facts giving rise to the violation of the privacy claim.).

5. **Threats as verbal acts**: *State of Louisiana in the interest of RT*, 781 So. 2d 1239 (La. 2001) (characterizing bomb threat as verbal act).
6. **Offer/Acceptance in contract:** *Cloverland-Green Spring Dairies, Inc. v. Pennsylvania Milk Marketing Bd.*, 298 F.3d 201 (3d Cir. 2002) (holding that offer to sell a product at a particular price is verbal act and is not hearsay, because the statement has legal effect); *Preferred Properties, Inc. v. Indian River Estates, Inc.*, 276 F.3d 790 (6th Cir. 2002) (holding that words constituting offer and acceptance create a contract and are not inadmissible hearsay).
7. **Trade Secret:** *Harvey Barnett, Inc. v. Shidler*, 338 F.3d 1125 (10th Cir. 2003) (holding that information downloaded from the Internet is not hearsay if offered to prove that the material was there, where contention was that certain information was a trade secret).
8. **Other non-hearsay:** *Spears v. Grambling State University*, 111 So. 3d 392 (La. Ct. App. 1st Cir. 2012) (holding that newspaper articles about head football coach did not constitute inadmissible hearsay evidence in coach's breach of employment contract action against the university when the newspaper articles were not offered into evidence to prove the truth of the matter, but, rather, to show evidence of the adverse impact of coach's actions on university's reputation); *State v. Lutcher*, 700 So. 2d 961 (La. Ct. App. 1st Cir. 1997) (holding that order of justice of the peace informing defendant that his wife did not want him on her property following domestic dispute was offered to establish existence and nature of order, not to prove utterances contained therein, and was thus not hearsay and was admissible in prosecution of defendant for subsequent murder of wife); *Cenval Leasing Corp. v. Nunnery*, 577 So. 2d 1042 (La. Ct App. 4th Cir. 1991) (holding that three written bids which were obtained on vehicle prior to its sale pursuant to lease agreement were properly admitted in action brought by lessor under lease contract for balance due under defaulted lease despite claim that evidence constituted inadmissible hearsay; bids were not introduced into evidence to prove value of vehicle at time of sale, but rather were introduced to prove that bids were received as required by lease and to demonstrate amount of highest offer).

§ 5.2.2 Verbal Part of an Act

A "verbal part of an act"[29] is a statement made that accompanies an act that **characterizes and gives meaning to the act**. For example, if a person hands another individual $5.00, along with the statement, "*Here's the $5.00 I owe you,*" it will be allowed into evidence to explain the act of giving the money. Since giving money could have several meanings (repayment of a loan, payment of a bribe, offering of a gift, payment of a bet, etc.),[30] the words are needed to explain the action and to give color to the otherwise ambiguous conduct. The explanatory words that accompany and give character to the act are not hearsay when, under the substantive law, only a person's outward manifestations, rather than the

29. *See* McCormick on Evidence, § 249 (5th ed., 1999).
30. *Id.*

person's subjective intent, is at issue.[31] Such words that accompany the act are considered to be the verbal part of the act. In such a case, the statement is not being offered to prove the truth of the matter asserted and, therefore, will not be excluded by the hearsay rule.

Case on Verbal Part of an Act

State v. Gonzales
Supreme Court of Louisiana
245 So. 2d 372
Feb. 24, 1971

SANDERS, Justice

The background facts are these: On the night of November 20, 1969, New Orleans Policeman Tim Freel entered the Golden Slipper Club in plain clothes for a routine vice check in cooperation with the vice squad. He ordered a drink. Ernest B. Gonzales, the defendant, was in the establishment. Gonzales motioned to Freel and called to the barmaid, Ruth Cray. She approached the officer and asked him to buy her a drink. After the officer had purchased her a drink, she offered to engage in prostitution. Ultimately, he gave her three twenty dollar bills, the numbers of which had been recorded.

The woman placed the money in the cash register and accompanied the officer to an apartment owned by Gonzales. After she had disrobed, the officer placed her under arrest. He then summoned two other officers, and they returned to the Golden Slipper. There, they arrested Gonzales, advised him of his rights, and asked him to empty his pockets. He produced a large roll of bills in which the officers found the three twenty dollar bills received by the barmaid.

BILLS OF EXCEPTIONS NOS. 1 and 2: Admission of Hearsay Evidence.

Defendant reserved these Bills of Exceptions to the following testimony of Officer Freel:

> 'I sat at the bar and ordered a drink and the subject before the bar there motioned to me and called to the barmaid. The barmaid approached me and asked if I would buy her a drink. * * *
>
> 'She asked me to buy her a drink which I did. She asked me if I would like to go to a party. At this time I said how much and where and when. She told me it would be $50.00 and S10.00 for a room. I told her that would be all right. She said, 'Do you have a way to get there?' I said, 'No, I don't.' She said she would call a cab at which time I handed her $60.00, three twenties.'

The defendant asserts that this out-of-court statement of the barmaid was inadmissible hearsay; that the barmaid was available as a witness; and that the admission of the officer's testimony prejudiced the substantial rights of the defendant.

The State asserts that the statement was uttered during the commission of a crime and was admissible under the doctrine of Res gestae, a frequently used exception to the hearsay rule embodied in our statutory law as LSA-R.S. 15:447, 448.

These Bills of Exceptions lack merit. Hearsay evidence is generally inadmissible in criminal prosecutions. LSA-R.S. 15:434. This rule, however, excludes only those out-of-court statements offered to prove the truth of the matter contained in them....

---

31. *Id.*

To sustain the charge in the present case, the State was required to prove that the barmaid from whom defendant received the money engaged in prostitution. In such proof, her solicitation of men to engage in sexual relations is pertinent. The evidentiary question is whether the words of solicitation were spoken. Without the words, the transfer of money to the barmaid is at best ambiguous. Under these circumstances, her conversation with the officer is usable, not to prove the truth of its content, but that the utterance occurred. The utterance gives color to the non-verbal conduct. The officer, of course, is able to testify as to her statement from his own perception. Such evidence is non-hearsay. Because of its relevance, it is admissible in the present case.

... For the reasons assigned, the conviction and sentence are affirmed.

Discussion Questions

1. Why are the words of solicitation in *Gonzales* not being offered for the truth of the matter asserted?
2. How or why are the words at issue here a "verbal part of an act"?
3. Could words of solicitation also qualify as a "verbal act"? Why or why not? Do words of solicitation have independent legal significance in a solicitation case?

Problems on Non-Hearsay Verbal Part of an Act

In the following problems, you should determine whether the statement in question is hearsay pursuant to the definition contained in Article 801 or if the statement is a verbal part of an act. Some of the statements that are hearsay might fall into an exception to the hearsay rule, but in this section you are not required to discuss any exceptions to the hearsay rule that might apply.

PROBLEM 5-20. The teacher claims a student attempted to bribe her with cash in exchange for a grade. She claims the student offered her the money right before class one day. The student will offer the testimony of Laura, who came to class early that day, and as Laura walked into the classroom behind him and the teacher, Laura just happened to overhear him say to the teacher as he handed her the money, "*Here's the rest of the money for the flashcards. Thanks for selling me your old copy.*" Is the statement hearsay? Would your answer change if the student was in fact offering the money for the grade? Why or why not?

PROBLEM 5-21. Joe claims his best friend Jake owes him $500 for the motorcycle that Joe sold to Jake. Jake claims that he doesn't owe any money for the bike because Joe gave it to him. Joe sues Jake for the remainder of the money. In order to prove that the bike was not a gift, Joe calls Jake's neighbor who was present when Joe delivered the bike, who will testify that, after Joe took the bike off of the truck, he said to Jake, "*And they say don't do business with friends. I really trust that you'll pay me on time.*" Jake objects that the statement is hearsay. How should the court likely rule and why?

§ 5.2.2 References and Additional Authority on Verbal Part of an Act

1. Force & Rault, HANDBOOK ON LOUISIANA EVIDENCE LAW Arts. 801, 802 Author's Comments (West Publishing 2014)
2. Harges & Jones, LOUISIANA EVIDENCE Arts. 801, 802 Author's Comments (West Publishing 2014)

3. 19 La. Civ. L. Treatise, Evidence and Proof § 10.1 (2d ed.)
4. McCormick on Evidence § 249 (5th ed., 1999)
5. *State v. Jones*, 769 So. 2d 28 (La. Ct. App. 4th Cir. 2000) (Defendant was in possession of three slabs of crack cocaine. Defendant attempted to sell one of the three slabs to an officer one hour before he was arrested. The officer testified that he saw the defendant break off a piece of cocaine and give it to another person who then gave it to the officer.); *Simon v. Trahan*, 235 So. 2d 610 (La. Ct. App. 3d Cir. 1970) (in an action by the son-in-law against his mother-in-law, the court was left to decide whether medical bills paid by son-in-law for mother-in-law's hospital stay was a gift or a loan); *See also Sanders v. Worthington*, 382 S.W.2d 910, 916 (Tex. 1964).

§ 5.2.3 Non-Assertive Conduct

As outlined above, nonverbal conduct *may* be hearsay if the conduct is intended by the declarant to assert a matter or to convey a message, *and* the conduct is being offered to prove the truth of the matter that it asserts. Thus, non-assertive conduct, conduct that does not convey a message, is not hearsay, and therefore is not excluded by the hearsay rule. A common example of assertive conduct is when a person makes an identification.[32] For example, if the victim of a robbery points out an individual in a lineup, he is asserting that the person he has pointed out is the person who robbed him. By pointing (the conduct), he intends to assert a fact (that's the person who robbed me). If his assertive conduct is offered to prove what he asserted, that the person he pointed out actually robbed him, such as in that person's criminal trial for the robbery, then his nonverbal conduct is hearsay.

It follows then that non-assertive conduct is *not* hearsay.[33] If a person does not intend to assert a message by his conduct, then his conduct is non-assertive conduct, and is not hearsay. Keep in mind that the test is whether the person *intends* to assert a message from the conduct, not whether another person inadvertently *received* a message from the conduct. For example, if you observe a colleague leave the office for lunch, then come back into the office to retrieve his umbrella, you might conclude that it must be raining outside. However, the colleague was not *intending* to convey the message that it was raining. Thus, his conduct is non-assertive and is not hearsay.

If, however, the colleague left the office with his umbrella, then peeped back into the office at you while you were on the telephone, and waved his umbrella to you pointing at it, he may be trying to convey the message that it was raining outside and to tell you not to forget your umbrella. In this instance, he is *intending* to assert a message—that it's raining outside. If that conduct is offered to prove that it was in fact raining outside, then the assertive conduct is hearsay. While assertive conduct may be hearsay, depending upon the purpose for which it is offered, non-assertive conduct is another category of non-hearsay.

---

32. *See* State v. Jones, 642 So. 2d 151 (La. 1994), for a post-code case holding identification to be assertive conduct, and hearsay. However, Article 801(D)(1)(c) contains an exemption to the hearsay rule for identifications made after perceiving a person if the declarant testifies at trial and is subject to cross-examination on their identification.

33. *See* 19 La. Civ. L. Treatise, Evidence And Proof § 10.1(2d ed).

Case on Non-Assertive Conduct

State v. Arbuthnot
Supreme Court of Louisiana
367 So. 2d 296
Jan. 29, 1979

TATE, Justice

The defendants Arbuthnot and Williams were convicted of armed robbery, La.R.S. 14:64, and sentenced to 65 years and 99 years respectively at hard labor....

Context Facts

The defendants were jointly charged with the armed robbery of Larry Tedley. From the truncated record before us, it appears that one robber (allegedly Williams) went into the store wearing a ski mask, which he took off when he demanded the money. The other robber (Arbuthnot) was shot during the getaway.

From the truncated record, it appears that only two persons were able to observe the identity of the robber (allegedly Williams) who went into the store: Tedley, who testified at the trial; and a Mrs. Silver, who did not testify. The improper elicitation of hearsay testimony as to Mrs. Silver's identification of Williams as the robber who went into the store is the basis of our reversal of his conviction.

The excerpts of testimony in the record indicate that Arbuthnot, the co-defendant, was apparently identified by a bystander as he left the scene. He was arrested at the hospital to which he was taken after he was shot during or following the robbery.

...

The Defendant Williams

The defendant Williams' Assignment 4 complains of the admission of prejudicial hearsay identification evidence. It requires reversal of his conviction.

As noted, the defendants are charged with the armed robbery of Tedley, who identified Williams as one of the robbers. There was one other witness to Williams' participation in the robbery, a Mrs. Silver. The state did not call her to testify.

Nevertheless, over objection, the state introduced testimony of a police officer that she also had identified Williams as one of the robbers. This hearsay evidence, in effect doubling the eyewitness identification of Williams, was clearly inadmissible, and clearly reversible....

In Louisiana criminal trials, hearsay evidence is inadmissible except under certain recognized exceptions. Hearsay evidence is testimony in court, or written evidence, of an out-of-court statement offered to show the truth of the matter asserted therein and resting for its value upon the credibility of the out-of-court assertor.

The traditional exclusion of hearsay evidence is based upon considerations of unreliability and of potential unfairness to the accused to permit the introduction of out-of-court statements which cannot be tested by cross-examination of the out-of-court declarant. Moreover, there is a chance that the witness will consciously or unconsciously misrepresent what the declarant told him.

It is suggested that the officer did not testify to any out-of-court statement, merely that the (absent and unsworn) witness had identified Williams' photograph as that of the robber.

In State v. Ford, 336 So.2d 817 (La.1976), we expressly rejected this argument that a non-oral communication of picking out a photograph is not subject to exclusion as hearsay. We there pointed out, 336 So.2d 821: "The assertive action of Summerville (the victim) was a communication to the officers that the photograph before him was one of his robber. It was introduced for the purpose of proving the truth of the matter so asserted, i.e., that the defendant Ford was his robber. It was therefore hearsay, as an assertive communication introduced for the truth of the assertion thereby made."

... Here, however, the identifying witness did not herself testify at the trial. As we noted, in reversing a conviction in State v. Jacobs, 344 So.2d 659, 662 (La.1976), "the state may not bolster its case with an inadmissible extrajudicial identification when the identifier has not testified that she made such a pre-trial identification."

By use of the hearsay description of the identification by Mrs. Silver, the state was improperly permitted to introduce an out-of-court assertion by an unsworn and un-cross-examined witness to bolster (double) its identification testimony and thereby to strengthen improperly the testimony of what, at least under the truncated record before us, is its only identification witness.

The improper use of hearsay evidence on a material contested issue of its case is reversible error. This is especially so here: The uncross-examined hearsay identification testimony, which deprived the defendant Williams of his cross-examination rights, was used to corroborate substantially the sole eyewitness who testified to identify him as the robber, whose testimony standing alone may not have been as readily believed by the trial jury.

Accordingly, defendant Williams' conviction must be reversed....

Discussion Questions

1. Why does hearsay only encompass conduct *intended* as an assertion, and does not include conduct from which a message was otherwise received, even if there was no intent to assert a message?
2. Are there situations in which non-assertive conduct should be excluded because it poses the same risks as admitting hearsay? Consider this example: John is struck in the crosswalk by a speeding vehicle driven by Speedy. Speedy claims the light was green and that John walked out in front of his car. John wishes to call two bystanders to testify that prior to the time he stepped into the crosswalk, another car traveling in the same direction as Speedy had come to a stop when he approached the light as Speedy continued through the light. John wishes to offer the evidence that the other driver had come to a stop to prove that the light was red when Speedy went through it. Speedy objects claiming the evidence is hearsay. He claims he is unable to cross-examine the other driver about why and if he stopped. Are any of the dangers associated with admitting hearsay present in such a case (memory, narration, perception, sincerity)? Make arguments both for and against excluding the evidence under the rationale of why hearsay statements are excluded.

Problems on Non-Assertive Conduct

In the following problems, you should determine whether the statement in question is hearsay pursuant to the definition contained in Article 801, or if the statement is non-assertive conduct. Some of the statements that are hearsay might fall into an exception to the hearsay rule, but in this section you are not required to discuss any exceptions to the hearsay rule that might apply.

PROBLEM 5-22. As Jillian was leaving school for the day, she remembered she left her house keys at home, so she ran back upstairs to the classroom where her roommate was in class to get her roommate's house key. When she looked into the classroom, she saw that everyone was looking down very focused and writing vigorously, and the professor was in front of the class looking at his watch. Realizing they were taking an exam, she decided not to disturb them, so she ran back downstairs and decided she would simply break into the apartment through the window. At the trial brought by the landlord to recover the cost of the window and other damage the roommates left when they moved out, Jillian sought to testify to what she saw when she looked into her roommate's classroom—that roommate was taking an exam. The landlord objected that what Jillian saw in the classroom was hearsay and that the roommate would need to come into the courtroom herself to testify as to what was going on in the classroom that day. How should the judge rule on the objection and why?

PROBLEM 5-23. Jim walked outside and saw his neighbor and neighbor's brother standing outside in the driveway. Neighbor asked Jim if he wanted to buy some tickets from him to the football game that Sunday. Jim asked how much they were and the neighbor said, "*$200 for great seats.*" He continued, "*If you buy them, I can get the tickets to you in a couple days.*" As Jim spoke to Neighbor, Neighbor's brother stood behind Neighbor shaking his head in a "no" manner and holding his hands up circling his eyes as if he were holding binoculars. Thinking that the tickets were too far away, based on what he saw the brother doing, Jim declined to buy the tickets. In a subsequent trial, would it be hearsay for Jim to testify to what Neighbor's brother did behind Neighbor's back to show either of the following: a) that Neighbor had a tendency to engage in shady business practices; b) Neighbor's brother's thoughts about Neighbor; c) that Neighbor's seats were far away from the field, i.e., "nosebleed"; or d) that the size of the stadium in question was very large? Address each scenario.

PROBLEM 5-24. In a medical malpractice trial, Evelyn wants to prove that emergency personnel in the ER made no efforts to revive her dying husband. The doctor claims numerous efforts were made that Evelyn did not see because she was crying in the bathroom. Evelyn seeks to testify that, as she observed through the window, she saw no medical procedures performed before she observed the doctor pull a sheet over her husband's face and body. She states that it wasn't until after she saw that, that she knew her husband was dead, and that it was then that she ran into the bathroom to cry. Evelyn wants to offer the moment at which time the sheet was pulled over her husband's face as the moment at which he was pronounced dead, so that the jury will only consider the doctor's conduct before that time in determining whether the doctor was negligent. The defense objects that the testimony would be hearsay. Explain the argument the defense is attempting to make. How should the court rule?

PROBLEM 5-25: Christopher is five years old and came to school one day with bruises on his body. Christopher lives with his dad. When his teacher asked him what happened, he refused to say anything. Later that day, the teacher told him to draw a picture of him and his daddy that shows life at home, and Christopher drew a picture that depicted a tall stick man labeled "Dad" with his hand around the neck of the small stick man, which was labeled "me." The small figure had tears coming down his face. The father was arrested for abuse of Christopher. At father's trial, the prosecution calls the teacher to the stand to admit the drawing as evidence of father's abuse of Christopher. The defense objects to the admissibility of the drawing claiming that it is hearsay. How should the court rule on the hearsay objection?

PROBLEM 5-26. Homeowner has sued Plummet Roofing Company, LLC for installing a faulty roof. The roof leaked less than a month after it was replaced by Plummet, and when Homeowner went onto the roof to check things out, well you know what happened. Mr. Plummet would like to offer the testimony of Homeowner's neighbor who will testify that on the day the roof was completed, he looked out of his front window and saw Mr. Plummet stomping around on the roof to prove that the roof was sound when it was finished. Homeowner objected that Neighbor's testimony would be hearsay. How should the court rule and why?

PROBLEM 5-27. Miller crashed into a vehicle one late Friday night after he ran a red light. Following the accident, Miller jumped out of his car and ran home, so he was not found and arrested until the next day. The driver (Driver) of the vehicle has filed suit against Miller for her injuries. As evidence that Miller might have been intoxicated when the accident occurred, the plaintiff calls Condi from Miller's job who will testify that earlier that Friday evening Miller passed her office heading toward the exit while talking on his phone. Condi will testify that she stopped Miller and asked him to stay at work with her to help her finish up some paperwork. In response, Miller shook his head from left to right, pointed at his phone then made a motion of a person drinking from a glass as he threw his head back. Miller then waved goodbye and left. Condi assumed Miller couldn't stay because he had a drinking date with a friend for the evening. At trial, Driver (P) calls Condi to the stand. When Condi begins to testify as to what Miller did after she asked him to stay and help her, Miller objected that the testimony was hearsay. Should the testimony of Miller's conduct be admitted at trial? Why or why not?

§ 5.2.3 References and Additional Authority on Non-Assertive Conduct

1. Force & Rault, Handbook on Louisiana Evidence Law Arts. 801, 802 Author's Comments (West Publishing 2014)
2. Harges & Jones, Louisiana Evidence Arts. 801, 802 Author's Comments (West Publishing 2014)
3. 19 La. Civ. L. Treatise, Evidence And Proof § 10.1 (2d ed.)
4. McCormick on Evidence § 250 (5th ed., 1999)
5. **Non-Assertive Conduct**: *State v. Ratliff*, 796 So. 2d 101 (La. Ct. App. 2d Cir. 2001) (holding that conduct was non-assertive and therefore could not be excluded as hearsay when person flees from a scene even though their conduct may imply that they are guilty); *State v. Feazell*, 486 So. 2d 327 (La. Ct. App. 3 Cir.1986) (holding that testimony of crisis intervention unit employee that defendant's son played with cylindrical vibrator and put it on female doll's genitalia and breast was not assertive in nature and was offered to prove circumstantially son's state of mind and, therefore, was not hearsay); *State v. Ellison*, 572 So. 2d 262 (La. Ct. App. 1st Cir. 1990) (holding that codefendant's actions in connection with drug sale, as described by narcotics agent at trial, did not constitute "statement," within meaning of this article defining that term for hearsay purposes); *State v. Price*, 636 So. 2d 933 (La. Ct App. 1st Cir. 1994) (During the trial of an armed robbery, the victim's son testified that he found his father after the robbery. Within the conversation, the son testified that his father stated that "the girl's boyfriend" beat him up. Additionally, the father asked about the money underneath the seat where he was sitting. The son testified that he looked under the seat but did not find the bag with money in it. The defendants objected to the testimony as hearsay, but the court ruled that the testimony was not hearsay because it was offered non-assertively to prove the conversation had taken place.).

§ 5.2.4 State of Mind of Hearer/Receiver

Another purpose for which a statement may be offered other than to prove the truth of the matter asserted is to prove the state of mind of the hearer or receiver of the statement, or to show the effect that the statement had on the receiver/hearer.[34] For example, if a man tells another man, "I'm having an affair with your wife," the statement may be offered into evidence in a murder trial to show the effect that the statement had on the hearer (the defendant), which led to his killing the man with whom his wife was having the affair. Here, the statement is being offered to prove the hearer's motive for the killing. It is irrelevant as to whether the statement was actually true. All that matters is that the defendant heard it, and since *he* believed it to be true, he killed the declarant. Other examples of states of mind that a statement may be offered to prove are **good/bad faith**, **fear**, **bias**, the **reasonableness/unreasonableness of a person's conduct**, or **why a person took the action that he took.**[35] For example, a person may testify that the reason he left town so abruptly was because he was told a terrible storm was coming. In such a case, the statement would be offered only to show the effect it had on the person who heard it. It would be irrelevant as to whether the statement were true.

State of mind must be relevant in case. It is important to note that in order for a statement to be offered into evidence on the issue of the hearer's state of mind, the hearer's state of mind must be relevant in the case. For example, if a person is charged with fraud for selling counterfeit paintings, evidence that he was told by the gallery from which he purchased the paintings that they were authentic could be offered to prove his good faith. It would show that he believed the paintings to be authentic based on what he was told. The purchaser would be allowed to testify to the statements made to him to show the effect that they had on him (the hearer/receiver), or his state of mind. Clearly in this instance, his state of mind is at issue. On the issue of his good faith, it is irrelevant as to whether the statements made to him were actually true. Here, the statements are only relevant because he was told the information and *he* believed it to be true, and it would be relevant to prove that he did not intend to defraud anyone by selling the paintings.

Hearsay state of mind vs. non-hearsay state of mind. This category of non-hearsay state of mind is not to be confused with the state of mind *exception* to the hearsay rule in Article 803(3) and discussed in Part B—§ 5.7. While this category of statements is not hearsay because they are not being offered to prove the truth of the matter asserted within the statement, there are some statements that *are* hearsay, but may fall into the state of mind exception to the hearsay rule. For example, if a person states that he is very upset, and the statement is being offered into evidence to prove that he was, in fact, very upset at that particular time, the statement is hearsay, but may fall into the state of mind exception to the hearsay rule in Article 803(3). However, the statement above ("I'm having an affair with your wife") is not being offered to prove the truth of the matter asserted, that the declarant was having an affair with the wife, so *that* statement is non-hearsay and is admissible to show the state of mind of the person who heard it. The distinction is discussed further in the section covering Article 803(3).

---

34. *Id.*

35. *See* State v. Bruno, 526 So. 2d 1287 (La. Ct. App. 3d Cir. 1988); *See also* State v. Wille, 559 So. 2d 1321 (La. 1990) below.

Cases on State of Mind of Hearer

State v. Wille
Supreme Court of Louisiana
559 So. 2d 1321
March 12, 1990

LEMMON, Justice.

This is an appeal from a conviction of first degree murder and a sentence of death....

FACTS

These proceedings arose out of the June 2, 1985 abduction, rape and murder of eight-year old Nichole Lopatta. This tragic episode began when defendant, accompanied by his girlfriend, Judith Walters, and Walters' fourteen-year-old daughter, Sheila, drove from their residence in Milton, Florida to Louisiana, where defendant had lived most of his life. After they entered Louisiana, defendant stopped to pick up an acquaintance, Billy Phillips, who was hitchhiking on the highway. Defendant had been drinking alcohol during the trip, and he continued drinking with Phillips as they drove into New Orleans.

The following excerpts from defendant's tape-recorded confession, given on August 27, 1985 while he was in custody in Florida on unrelated charges, vividly relate the events surrounding the murder:

...

[Graphic excerpts from defendant's tape-recorded confession of the kidnapping and repeated rape of the 8-year-old victim by both the defendant and Phillips, her murder, the murder of Phillips, and subsequent dumping of the bodies follow.]

Hearsay Testimony

Defendant urges that the trial court erred in allowing FBI Special Agent Victor Harvey to testify as to the substance of assertions made by Judith and Sheila Walters in interviews conducted by Harvey. Even though Judith and Shelia Walters did not appear as witnesses in this case, Agent Harvey was allowed to testify as follows:

> A. We had, once again, the usual investigative steps, but no real suspects. This continued for approximately two months, from the 6th [of June] to the, about August the 10th, when one of the agents assigned to the task force advised that perhaps we should go to Milton, Florida. Specifically to interview one Judy Walters of Norco that may have some, some information concerning the Lopatta killing. Myself and another agent traveled to, to Milton, Florida. And on the 10th of August interviewed Miss Walters for an extensive period. *Based upon the information supplied, and the investigative conclusions that we were able to draw, we were able to force or focus our entire investigative attention on Judy Walters and her alleged boyfriend, John Wille. John Wille, based upon not only the interview of the 10th but all of the interviews with Miss Wille, I mean Miss Walters, immediately became a prime suspect in this matter. Through Walters' information we were able to determine that her daughter might have information, Sheila Walters. We interviewed her on two difference [sic] occasions and became certain that John Wille was, was our prime suspect....* ..
>
> Q. So what did you do at that time?
>
> A. All right. Like I said, one of, we interviewed Miss Walters on numerous occasions. *Each time she would tell us more about the crime, more specific facts, things*

> *that were, were possible to cooberate [sic].* One of the first things we did, of course, was show her a picture of the child to make sure that we were dealing with, with the same abduction. There are abductions going on all over the country. Miss Walters had—(Interrupted by objection).... .
>
> A. Yes, sir. *Based upon the series of interviews with Miss Walters our investigative conclusion became very strengthened that John Wille was responsible for these, these crimes. These crimes being both the murders we've discussed. Further cooberation [sic] was, as to this conclusion, was, was, furnished by the two interviews of her daughter.... ..*
>
> Q. After that what was done?
>
> A. *Based upon the peculiarity of the story as it was related to me personally I asked prior to the formal interview of Mr. Wille that Miss Walters be brought back to this area and her story physically retraced as to times, dates, movements. This was also done in my presence and recorded by me. I have a log of that. Once again, this meshed chronologically and totally with her, with her, with her evidence that she had supplied to me concerning Mr. Wille.* I have that available. On the 27th I asked that Special Agent Terry Scott and Lieutenant Boy Hay of this Sheriff's Office formerly interview Mr. Wille. They did. Mr. Wille furnished them with a taped statement as to his involvement in both murders.... ..
>
> Q. After, what did you do after this was done?
>
> A. *Based upon, based upon the statements given, the fact that the information and the statements matched the, matched the peculiarity of the offense, and the other information I mentioned, the State, I prepared and submitted a report, and the State charged Mr. Wille with the crimes he's on trial here for.*
>
> Q. *Was Sheila Walters ever interviewed?*
>
> A. *Yes, sir. I personally interviewed Sheila Walters, the fourteen year old daughter of Judy Walters, on two occasions and she completely cooberated [sic]*—(interrupted by objection). (emphasis added).

Although defense counsel entered several hearsay objections about identification of the victim and corroboration of the eyewitnesses' statements, Agent Harvey was permitted to testify that assertions by the eyewitnesses to the murder had led him to conclude defendant was the prime suspect and to become "certain" defendant was responsible for the two killings. Defendant argues that the jury could only conclude from Harvey's testimony that Judith and Sheila Walters had told him defendant was the murderer while admitting to their own involvement in the events.

Hearsay evidence is testimony in court, or written evidence, of a statement made out of court, when the statement is being offered as an assertion to show the truth of matters asserted therein and thus rests for its value upon the credibility of the out-of-court asserter. One of the primary justifications for the exclusion of hearsay is that the adversary has no opportunity to cross-examine the absent declarant to test the accuracy and completeness of the testimony. The declarant is also not under oath at the time of the statement. Moreover, the confrontation clause of the United States Constitution provides that "[i]n all criminal prosecutions, the accused shall enjoy the right ... to be confronted with the witnesses against him". U.S. Const amend. VI. There is no opportunity for confrontation when an assertion by one party is presented through the testimony of another party....

In the present case the prosecutor, citing *State v. Calloway,* 324 So.2d 801 (La.1976), *State v. Monk,* 315 So.2d 727 (La.1975), and *State v. Smith,* 400 So.2d 587 (La.1980), argues that testimony by a police officer, as to his action taken in response to a person's out-of-court statement, is admissible, not to prove the truth of the out-of-court statement, but to explain the sequence of events leading to the arrest of the defendant from the viewpoint of the investigating officer. However, those cases are distinguishable from the present case. The substance of Officer Harvey's testimony in the present case was that two eyewitnesses named defendant as the perpetrator of the crime, while the substance of the out-of-court assertions in the cited cases did not significantly connect the defendant with the crime.[36]

Admission of information received by a police officer in the investigation of a crime, on the basis that such information explains the officer's presence and conduct and therefore does not constitute hearsay evidence, is an area of widespread abuse.[37] Such information frequently has an impermissible hearsay aspect as well as a permissible nonhearsay aspect, and the court in determining admissibility should balance the need of the evidence for the proper purpose against the danger of improper use of the evidence by the jury. The fact that an officer acted on information received in an out-of-court assertion may be relevant to explain his conduct, but this fact should not become a passkey to bring before the jury the substance of the out-of-court information that would otherwise be barred by the hearsay rule.[38]

---

36. In the *Smith* case an officer was allowed to testify that he was advised of the shooting incident. Because this testimony was offered to show why the officer began an investigation of the incident and not to prove the truth of the assertion, this court concluded that the testimony was not hearsay. Significantly, the report of the shooting did not connect the defendant with the crime.

In the *Calloway* case an arresting officer was allowed to testify that he had received a radio communication that the two suspects in a store robbery were travelling in a black Cadillac. This court held that the admission of the testimony was not hearsay since it was admitted merely to explain events preceding the arrest of the defendants in a black Cadillac. Significantly, there was other proper evidence that a black Cadillac was parked in front of the store at the time of the robbery, and the officer's testimony was merely cumulative as to this fact.

Finally, the *Monk* case held it was not hearsay when a deputy testified that he had received a radio message that a robbery had been committed at a bank by two men who fled on a motorcycle. The robbers were apprehended on a motorcycle shortly after the robbery four miles from the bank. Significantly, numerous other witnesses testified that the two robbers wearing motorcycle helmets and ski masks were seen leaving the bank on a motorcycle, and the deputy's testimony as to the motorcycle was merely cumulative as to this fact.

37. The treatise identified the area of widespread abuse as follows:

> In criminal cases, an arresting or investigating officer should not be put in the false position of seeming just to have happened upon the scene; he should be allowed some explanation of his presence and conduct. His testimony that he acted "upon information received", or words to that effect, should be sufficient. Nevertheless, cases abound in which the officer is allowed to relate historical aspects of the case, replete with hearsay statements in the form of complaints and reports, on the ground that he was entitled to give the information upon which he acted. The need for the evidence is slight, the likelihood of misuse great.

38. This court has previously restricted the admission of this kind of evidence. In *State v. Thompson*, 331 So.2d 848 (La.1976), the trial court permitted an officer, under the guise of explaining his subsequent conduct, to testify that an anonymous informant had specifically identified the defendant as one of two men involved in an armed robbery. In reversing the conviction, this court stated that the officer could testify as to his receipt of information from the informer and his subsequent conduct, but not as to "the content of the statement of this anonymous witness, not sworn o[r] subject to cross-examination at the trial, to the effect that this defendant had committed the crime for which he was on trial". *Id.* at 849. The court noted that the content of the out-of-court statement (which was used before the judge to obtain a search warrant) was not admissible at trial for any *relevant* issue before the jury.

When an out-of-court statement, such as information received by a police officer during an investigation of a crime, has both an impermissible hearsay aspect and a permissible nonhearsay aspect, the issue of relevancy becomes significantly interrelated with the hearsay issue. If the nonhearsay content of the statement has little or no relevance, then the statement should generally be excluded on both relevance and hearsay grounds. Marginally relevant nonhearsay evidence should not be used as a vehicle to permit the introduction of highly relevant and highly prejudicial hearsay evidence which consists of the substance of an out-of-court assertion that was not made under oath and is not subject to cross-examination at trial.

There was no true issue in the present case as to the propriety of any action taken by Agent Harvey during his investigation of the Lopatta murder. Indeed, an investigating officer's testimony at trial (as opposed to testimony at a motion to suppress), explaining his conduct after an investigation, almost always has only marginal relevance at best.[39] The real purpose of Harvey's testimony in the present case about the information received from Judith and Sheila Walters was to place before the jury the fact that their statements had named defendant as the killer of Nichole Lopatta.[40] The value of the statements rested upon the credibility of the out-of-court assertions. Because Judith and Sheila Walters did not testify, evidence of the fact that their statements named defendant as the killer was otherwise barred by the hearsay rule. Clearly, the extremely marginal relevance of Agent Harvey's testimony for the purpose of explaining his conduct in the investigation was greatly outweighed by the danger that the jury would use this testimony as substantive evidence that Judith and Sheila Walters had named defendant as the killer.[41] The only truly relevant information conveyed by Agent Harvey to the jury was his conclusion, after interviewing two eyewitnesses to the crime for which defendant was on trial, that defendant was the perpetrator and that the eyewitnesses' version of the events was completely corroborated by physical and other evidence uncovered by the investigation. Because the assertions related by Judith and Sheila Walters to Agent Harvey, the substance of which was conveyed to the jury, were presented almost solely for their relevance and assertive value in establishing defendant's guilt and were not given under oath or ever subjected to cross-examination, and because such assertions by accomplices are inherently suspect, the testimony should have been excluded as hearsay and irrelevant evidence.

Nevertheless, the erroneous admission of the hearsay and irrelevant evidence does not require a reversal of defendant's conviction because the error was harmless beyond a reasonable doubt. Reversal is mandated only when there is a reasonable possibility that the evidence might have contributed to the verdict....

---

39. In *Teague v. State*, 252 Ga. 534, 314 S.E.2d 910 (1984), the court observed:

> It will be seen that only in rare instances will the "conduct" of an investigating officer need to be "explained", as in practically every case, the motive, intent, or state of mind of such an officer will not be "matters concerning which the truth must be found." At heart, a criminal prosecution is designed to find the truth of what a defendant did, and, on occasion, of why he did it. It is most unusual that a prosecution will properly concern itself with *why* an investigating officer did something. (emphasis in original).

40. Harvey, an experienced investigator, carefully avoided saying that the Walters told him defendant killed the child. However, his testimony that statements by the Walters caused him to conclude defendant was the prime suspect and to become convinced that defendant was responsible for the crimes clearly conveyed to the jury the substance of the Walters' out-of-court assertions, as well as his belief in the reliability of the statements.

41. The relevancy issue is at the core of the problem. The statements by the Walters may have been relevant to the issue of probable cause for arresting defendant, but that issue was one for the judge and not for the jury.

Identification by Deborah Davis

Defendant contends that the trial court erred in allowing Deborah Davis, who was not called upon to identify defendant in court, to testify as to her out-of-court identification of defendant as the person who asked for a bag at Popeye's on the night of the murder. Relying on *State v. Jacobs,* 344 So.2d 659 (La.1977), defendant argues that a positive identification by Davis of defendant in court was a prerequisite to her testimony that she had previously identified a picture of defendant as the man she saw at Popeye's on June 2, 1985.

In the *Jacobs* case the victim testified that the defendant "looked very much like" the perpetrator of the crime. The state then called several police officers who testified that the victim had made a positive identification of the defendant prior to trial at a photographic lineup. The court, distinguishing *State v. Ford,* 336 So.2d 817 (La.1976), noted that an officer's testimony concerning a pretrial identification by a witness may be allowed to corroborate the testimony of the witness, but is inadmissible, because of its hearsay nature, when the witness does not testify about the pretrial identification, especially when the witness could not make a definite identification at trial.

This court held earlier in *Ford* that the admission of hearsay identification testimony is not reversible error if the person who made the pretrial identification also testifies at trial as to the identification. The case at bar is factually more closely aligned with *Ford* than with *Jacobs,* where the positive pretrial identification was used to bolster a tentative identification at trial. In the present case Davis specifically testified, without objection, as to her pretrial identification of defendant's picture in a photographic lineup as the person who entered the restaurant on June 2, 1985 and asked for a specific size bag. Since there was no suggestion that Davis could not identify defendant in court, the fact that she was not specifically asked to make an identification in court relates only to the weight of her testimony regarding the photographic lineup. Moreover, Davis did answer affirmatively a question by defense counsel asking if Photograph No. 3 was "Mr. Wille's photograph". The record as a whole establishes that Davis' out-of-court identification, repeated by her at trial, referred to the accused who was in court at the trial.

Finally, in *United States v. Owens,* 484 U.S. 554, 108 S.Ct. 838, 98 L.Ed.2d 951 (1988), the Court allowed evidence that the witness had previously identified the defendant as his assailant, even though the witness could not remember at trial (because of injuries inflicted in the attack) enough details of the attack to positively identify the defendant in court. The Court concluded that the use of the witness' prior identification as substantive evidence did not violate the confrontation clause which insures only the opportunity to cross-examine a witness, and not necessarily cross-examination which is beneficial to the defendant.

In the case at bar, even if Davis did not make (or could not make) a positive identification of defendant in court, her prior out-of-court identification would not necessarily be excluded because she was available for cross-examination.

Discussion Questions

1. The court notes that using hearsay statements for the purpose of "explaining an officer's actions" is an "area of widespread abuse"[42] by prosecutors. The statements often have both a non-hearsay purpose and a hearsay purpose. What test does the court suggest be used to determine the admissibility of an out-of-court statement that has both a

42. State v. Wille, 559 So. 2d 1321, 1331 (La. 1990).

permissible non-hearsay purpose and an impermissible hearsay purpose? In making this determination, how does "relevancy become[ ] significantly interrelated with the hearsay issue"?[43]

2. Some argue that prosecutors are in a difficult situation at times because they no doubt have to explain how a particular house or car came to be searched, or a particular person came to be arrested or chased. Otherwise a police officer might be testifying, "Well, so I was walking through this abandoned house two blocks from where the robbery occurred, and saw the suspect hiding behind an old refrigerator." To add context to the officer's testimony, prosecutors usually attempt to ask the witness why were they looking for that particular person in that particular place. Quite often, the reason is because of information they were told. Someone said, "He went that way," or "He's wearing a black hoodie," as in *Wille*. How would you suggest a prosecutor get around the issue of testifying to hearsay statements that led to the officer's actions? The court gives guidance in footnote 37 in *Wille*.[44] This approach is referred to as the "explanatory exception."[45] Does the suggested approach give the needed context?

3. In another important Louisiana Supreme Court case, *State v. Hearold*, 603 So. 2d 731, 738–39 (La. 1992), in reversing the defendant's conviction and sentence after inadmissible hearsay was admitted by the trial court that purportedly "explained" the officer's conduct, the court held that:

   > Generally, an explanation of the officer's actions should never be an acceptable basis upon which to admit an out-of-court declaration when the so-called "explanation" involves a direct assertion of criminal activity against the accused.... Absent some unique circumstances in which the explanation of purpose is probative evidence of a contested fact, such hearsay evidence should not be admitted under an "explanation" exception. The probative value of the mere fact that an out-of-court declaration was made is generally outweighed greatly by the likelihood that the jury will consider the statement for the truth of the matter asserted.[46]

   Can you think of a unique situation or circumstance in which an explanation of the officer's conduct is probative of a contested fact, such that hearsay statements directly asserting criminal activity of the accused might be permissible?

Patrick v. Iberia Bank

Court of Appeal of Louisiana, Fifth Circuit
926 So. 2d 632
March 14, 2006

FREDERICKA HOMBERG WICKER, Judge.

Plaintiff appeals from the granting of defendant's Motion for Summary Judgment. For the following reasons, we affirm the judgment of the trial court.

---

43. *Id.*

44. *See also* McCormick on Evidence § 249 (5th ed).

45. For an excellent discussion of the history and full application of the "Explanatory Exception," see Joshua P. Clayton, *The Louisiana "Explanatory Exception": Faithfulness to Louisiana's Hearsay Framework or Mere Storytime with the Prosecution*, 71 La. L. Rev. 1259 (2011).

46. State v. Hearold, 603 So. 2d 731, 738–39 (La. 1992).

Plaintiff filed a Petition for Damages against defendant, alleging that on January 9, 2002 defendant was "willfully negligent and malicious in misinforming the Jefferson Parish Sheriff's Office" that plaintiff was attempting to fraudulently remove funds from her mother, Rosemary Patrick's (Mrs. Patrick), account, causing plaintiff to be transported from the premises and charged with attempted theft.

After filing an Answer and Defenses, defendant filed a Motion for Summary Judgment, asserting that plaintiff's claims against it should be dismissed because the undisputed facts surrounding her arrest support a conclusion that defendant had a reasonable and honest belief that she presented a check that was not properly payable, and that, therefore, she was attempting to illicitly remove funds from Mrs. Patrick's account.

In its judgment granting defendant's Motion for Summary Judgment, the trial court stated:

> After reviewing the memoranda of the parties and hearing the argument of counsel, the Court found that the undisputed facts surrounding plaintiff's arrest supported a finding of probable cause for plaintiff's arrest. Therefore, no genuine issue of material fact exists as to the liability of Iberia Bank, and defendant is entitled to Summary Judgment as a matter of law.

It is from this judgment that plaintiff appeals. Plaintiff argues that the trial court erred, because 1) it misapplied the standard of proof pursuant to La.C.C.P. art. 966; 2) it considered an affidavit which did not meet the legal standards of La.C.C.P. art. 967; and 3) it granted defendant's summary judgment solely on the grounds of "probable cause" when intent was a consideration....

The essential elements of malicious prosecution are: (1) the commencement or continuance of an original criminal proceeding; (2) its legal causation by the present defendant against plaintiff who was defendant in the original proceeding; (3) its bona fide termination in favor of the present plaintiff; (4) the absence of probable cause for such proceeding; (5) the presence of malice therein; (6) damage conforming to legal standards resulting to plaintiff.

In the instant case, the trial court determined that plaintiff could not establish the fourth essential element, the absence of probable cause for such proceeding.

In support of its motion, defendant submitted a memorandum and attached plaintiff's deposition, an affidavit by Kathey Simmons (IberiaBank Teller), and a copy of Mrs. Patrick's Certificate of Death listing January 8, 2002 as her date of death. Attached to plaintiff's deposition is a copy of an IberiaBank signature card indicating that Mrs. Patrick opened an account (hereinafter "the checking account") on September 8, 2001. Plaintiff is not listed on the signature card; only Mrs. Patrick is listed as an authorized individual. Also attached to the deposition is a copy of a check for $1,885.00, drawn on the account, dated January 9, 2002, made payable to defendant, and signed "Rosemary Patrick" (hereinafter "the check").

In opposition to the motion, plaintiff submitted a memorandum with attachments—signature cards from the checking and savings account showing "Rosemary Patrick" as the only authorized individual on both accounts; a statement from the savings account, and an affidavit by plaintiff.

In plaintiff's deposition she testified that she accompanied her mother to IberiaBank on September 8, 2001 to open Mrs. Patrick's checking and savings accounts. Plaintiff further testified that, although only her mother's name is listed and signed twice on the account signature card, in actuality plaintiff signed one of the "Rosemary Patrick" signatures.

According to plaintiff, she and her mother signed "Rosemary Patrick" on the card at the same time in front of an IberiaBank representative. Plaintiff further stated that she believed that this signature was her authorization to sign on the account.

Plaintiff testified that she received a telephone call on January 9, 2002 from an IberiaBank representative asking to speak to Mrs. Patrick; plaintiff told the representative that Mrs. Patrick was deceased. Plaintiff further testified that later that day she drove to IberiaBank to cash a check for $1,885.00 drawn on Mrs. Patrick's checking account. According to plaintiff, Mrs. Patrick had signed the check on January 6, 2002 and filled in everything but the date, which plaintiff filled in. Plaintiff stated that she walked into the bank, waited in line for a period of time, and then presented the check to the teller, without speaking. The teller asked for and received plaintiff's ID1, then told plaintiff to wait a few minutes "because the computer was down." She had no further conversations with anybody from the bank that day. Plaintiff stated that after waiting five to ten minutes, a Jefferson Parish Sheriff's Deputy arrived and questioned her for approximately three minutes in the bank's conference room. She told him that her mother was deceased and:

> "... basically he asked me what was I doing in the bank. I told him that I came to cash a check. He asked me who the check was for. I told him that it was for me, but it was under my mom's name. He said, okay. He started reading me my rights."

Plaintiff further testified that the charges against her were eventually dropped.

As stated above, defendant submitted Kathey Simmons' affidavit in support of its motion. Three exhibits are attached to the affidavit, one identified as an IberiaBank account application, and the other two are statements for Mrs. Patrick's checking and savings accounts at IberiaBank.

Simmons states that she is a teller at IberiaBank in Marrero, Louisiana, and that in connection with her work as a teller, she has access to all official bank records. She attests that the account application attached to the affidavit is the account application completed by Mrs. Patrick to open the checking account. Further, the only individual authorized to sign checks drawn on the checking account was Mrs. Patrick.

Simmons states that there were multiple requests for telephone transfers of money from Mrs. Patrick's savings account to her checking account in January 2002. Mrs. Patrick's checking and savings account statements attached to the affidavit indicate these telephone transfers—January 2, 2002 for $500 and January 8, 2002 for $900. After a third telephone request was made on January 9, 2002, a bank employee spoke to Simmons "regarding the fact that the individual making the request sounded younger than a 63 year old woman." After speaking to bank employees, Simmons telephoned West Jefferson Hospital and spoke to a representative in the medical records department who verified that Mrs. Patrick died on January 8, 2002. Thereafter an "alert" was placed on Mrs. Patrick's account. Simmons further stated that she was present during plaintiff's arrest.

Plaintiff contends that the trial court erred by considering the affidavit of Kathey Simmons because it did not meet the legal standard of La.C.C.P. art. 967. La.C.C.P. art. 967(A) provides, in pertinent part:

> Supporting and opposing affidavits shall be made on personal knowledge, shall set forth such facts as would be admissible in evidence, and shall show affirmatively that the affiant is competent to testify to the matters stated therein ...

Plaintiff argues that certain assertions by Simmons in her affidavit do not comply with La.C.C.P. art. 967(A) because they are hearsay and are not made on her personal knowledge but rather on information provided to her by an unknown third person. The assertions pertain to conversations Simmons had on January 9, 2002, and are as follows:

> 11. After the January 9, 2002 request, a bank employee spoke to her regarding the fact that the individual making the request sounded younger than a 63 year old woman;
>
> 12. After speaking to the bank employees, she called West Jefferson Hospital and spoke to a representative in the medical records department who verified that Rosemary Patrick died on January 8, 2002;

La.C.C.P. art. 967(A) provides that "affidavits shall be made on personal knowledge." Simmons would clearly have personal knowledge of conversations that she asserts she participated in. Further, La.C.E. art. 801(C) defines hearsay as "a statement, other than one made by the declarant while testifying at the present trial or hearing, offered in evidence to prove the truth of the matter asserted." The statements which Simmons refers to above are not being offered in evidence to prove the truth of the matter asserted, i.e., that the person who made the third telephone transfer request was in fact younger than sixty-three years of age and that Mrs. Patrick died on January 8, 2002. Rather, they are being offered into evidence to show what information the bank had at the time of plaintiff's arrest. And even if the above statements were omitted as hearsay, the record includes Mrs. Patrick's certificate of death indicating a January 8, 2002 date of death and plaintiff's testimony that a representative of IberiaBank telephoned on January 9, 2002 asking to speak to Mrs. Patrick and that she informed the representative that Mrs. Patrick was deceased.

Finally, plaintiff argues that the trial court erred because it granted defendant's summary judgment solely on the grounds of "probable cause" when intent was a consideration.

In the present case, the defendant, as the party bringing the summary judgment motion, bears the burden of proof. However, because defendant will not bear the burden of proof at trial, its burden on the motion for summary judgment does not require it to negate all essential elements of plaintiff's claim, but rather to point out to the court that there is an absence of factual support for one or more elements essential to plaintiff's claim. As stated above, one of the five essential elements in a malicious prosecution case is that plaintiff must prove that there was no probable cause.

Probable cause does not depend upon the actual state of the case in point of fact, but on the honest and reasonable belief of the party prosecuting. *JCM Const. Co., Inc. v. Orleans Parish School Bd., supra* at 1123. In support of its motion for summary judgment, defendant submitted a deposition, affidavit, and exhibits pointing out that defendant's records indicated that Mrs. Patrick was the only authorized signatory on her checking account; that Mrs. Patrick died on January 8, 2002; that the bank learned of Mrs. Patrick's death on January 9, 2002; and that after Mrs. Patrick's death, plaintiff entered a bank branch and without explanation attempted to cash a check drawn on the deceased Mrs. Patrick's checking account, dated January 9, 2002, and made payable to plaintiff for $1,885.00. Plaintiff does not dispute any of these facts. Once defendant pointed out the absence of factual support for an element essential to plaintiff's claim, the burden then shifted to plaintiff to produce factual support sufficient to show that she will be able to meet her evidentiary burden of proof at trial. La.C.C.P. art. 966(C)(2). Because plaintiff failed to produce factual support sufficient to establish that she will be able to satisfy her evidentiary burden of proof as to this element at trial, the trial court properly granted summary judgment in favor of defendant.

Therefore, we affirm the judgment of the trial court granting defendant's motion for summary judgment.

AFFIRMED.

Discussion Question

In *Patrick*, the out-of-court statements are being offered to prove the effect on the hearer, her good faith in the actions she took, and/or the reasonableness of her conduct based on statements made to her. What are the statements at issue? How do the statements in *Patrick* show the teller's good faith? Why is her good faith at issue here?

Problems on Non-Hearsay State of Mind of Hearer/Receiver

In the following problems, you should determine whether the statement in question is hearsay pursuant to the definition contained in Article 801 or if the statement is non-hearsay state of mind of the hearer/receiver. If you determine that a statement falls within the category of non-hearsay state of mind of the hearer/receiver, please indicate which relevant state of mind is at issue. Some of the statements that are hearsay may fall into an exception to the hearsay rule, but in this section you are not required to discuss any exceptions to the hearsay rule that might apply.

PROBLEM 5-28. Randal is on trial for the murder of his sister's husband. At the murder trial, his sister's maid testified that on the day of the murder, Randal's sister called him over to her house, and once he arrived she heard her tell Randal, "*My husband has been molesting our five-year-old daughter.*" In a rage, Randal immediately went over to the husband's (his brother-in-law) office where he was working and shot him one time in the head. At the murder trial, when the maid began testifying about what Randal's sister told him about her 5-year-old daughter (Randal's niece), the prosecution objected that the sister's statement to Randal was hearsay and that only the sister could testify to what she told Randal. How should the court rule and why?

PROBLEM 5-29. Rudy and Mitch were members of two rival gangs. Rudy is on trial for murdering Mitch, but claims self-defense. Rudy will offer the testimony of Ciara who will testify that she was in a nightclub and overheard Mitch say, "*If I ever catch that rat Rudy out in his gang colors, I'm gonna bust a cap in him.*" She immediately sent a text message to Rudy that said, "*Mitch said he's gonna put a cap in you.*" The prosecution objects that the text message is hearsay. How should the court rule?

PROBLEM 5-30. There was a serial killer/rapist on the loose in the small town of Bossville. One evening while canvassing the neighborhood and looking for witnesses, the police knocked on Macy's apartment door and told her, "*One of your neighbors in your apartment complex has been raped and killed, so be careful out here.*" Macy hadn't seen or heard anything strange, but the next day she packed her bags and moved back home with her parents. In an action by her landlord for payment of the remaining month's rent, Macy sought to testify as to what the officer told her to show that the apartment was not safe (a grounds for breaking leases in the lease agreement). The landlord objected that the testimony was hearsay. How should the court rule and why? Would your answer change if the officer's statement was being offered to prove that her move was reasonable? Why or why not?

PROBLEM 5-31. Kelly was injured on the job when he used a blow torch to remove steel hinges from a stove that blew up and seriously injured him. Kelly sued his boss for damages. They claimed that Kelly negligently used the blow torch on a gas stove, and should have used an iron pipe to remove the hinges. They claim he acted unreasonably. In response, Kelly offered evidence that his boss told him that it was okay for him to use the blow torch to remove the steel hinges on the stove when he asked if it was okay. The boss objected that the statement would be hearsay. Is it? What if Kelly came back and told his coworker that the boss told him it was okay? Could the coworker testify that Kelly told him that the boss had given him permission to use the torch? Why or why not?

PROBLEM 5-32. Coty was attempting to sell a lamp he'd purchased from an auction that had supposedly been passed down from the British Royal Stroganoff family. Someone had anonymously reported that the lamp could not have been authentic because the last member of the family had died before electricity was invented. In Coty's trial for attempted fraud, he offered the Certificate of Authenticity he'd received from the auction house when he purchased the lamp. The certificate had a stamp and seal on it and appeared to be authentic. The prosecution objected that the certificate was hearsay and additionally that they had learned that the certificate had been fraudulently created by the auction house, who also faced fraud charges. Should the court allow the certificate over the prosecution's objection to show that Coty believed the lamp was authentic? Explain.

PROBLEM 5-33. Cynthia called the police and reported that she was being beaten by her boyfriend. When the police arrived she recanted and told them that it was a prank call. Cynthia was arrested for intentionally making a false police report. At her trial she claimed she was telling the truth when she called, but claims her boyfriend had stated, "*If you have me arrested, I will kill you*," just before police arrived. Cynthia seeks to offer the statement made to her by her boyfriend before police arrived at her house to help explain her actions. The prosecution objects that the statement is hearsay. How should the court rule and why?

§ 5.2.4 References and Additional Authority on State of Mind of the Hearer/Receiver

1. Force & Rault, Handbook on Louisiana Evidence Law Arts. 801, 802 Author's Comments (West Publishing 2014)
2. Harges & Jones, Louisiana Evidence Arts. 801, 802 Author's Comments (West Publishing 2014)
3. 19 La. Civ. L. Treatise, Evidence And Proof § 10.1 (2d ed.)
4. **Commentary**: Joshua P. Clayton, *The Louisiana "Explanatory Exception": Faithfulness to Louisiana's Hearsay Framework or Mere Storytime with the Prosecution*, 71 La. L. Rev. 1259 (2011).
5. **To show why hearer took action taken (non-law enforcement):** *Ashworth v. Ashworth*, 86 So. 3d 134 (La. Ct. App. 3d Cir. 2012) (holding that Katherine's statement about her brother and niece telling her that her husband was committing adultery was admissible and not hearsay because it was offered to prove why she took the action of leaving her home); *State v. Rios*, 44-132 La. App. 2 Cir. 4/8/09, 2009 WL 929380 (La. Ct. App. 2d Cir. 2009) (holding that statement made by one employee of auto dealership to another employee stating, "That Mexican dude that was just in the showroom jumped in a truck and took off" was not hearsay because not offered for truth of the matter asserted, but to explain why second employee called the police and initiated the use of OnStar communications system to locate stolen vehicle); *State v. Taylor*, 550 So. 2d 712 (La. Ct. App. 2d Cir. 1989) (holding that testimony of attorney as to statement made by representative of District Attorney's office when representative came to attorney's office to recover gun taken by attorney from defendant's house, was propounded to explain impetus for attorney's action, not for truth of statements; thus, statements were not hearsay).

6. **To show reasonableness of hearer's conduct:** *State v. Stewart,* 656 So. 2d 677 (La. Ct. App. 2d Cir. 1995) (holding that statement relevant to state of mind of listener in determining the reasonableness of listener's belief); *State v. Stewart,* 656 So. 2d 677 (La. Ct. App. 2d Cir. 1995) (holding that statements made by hotel manager to searching officer that officer had authority to begin search were not hearsay as significant suppression issues turned on reasonableness of officer's belief that he had obtained consent to search of hotel room).
7. **To show bias of hearer:** *State v. Bruno*, 526 So. 2d 1287 (La. Ct. App. 3d Cir.1988) (holding that defense counsel's question to witness regarding whether witness had heard from anyone that defendant had told others that witness was receiving compensation benefits to which he may not have been entitled, was not offered to show truth of statements, but rather to show witness's state of mind, namely that witness was biased against defendant, and hence, trial court erred in sustaining prosecutor's hearsay objection to question).
8. **Interpretation of "Explanatory Exception":** *State v. Legendre*, 942 So. 2d 45 (La. Ct. App. 4th Cir. 2006) (holding that detective's testimony that the unidentified witness provided him with the first name of Marvin was inadmissible hearsay and did not fit within the limits of the explanatory exception); see also 19 La. Civ. L. Treatise, Evidence and Proof § 10.28 (2d ed.) for good explanation of explanatory exception.
9. **Explanation of police officer conduct (permissible):** *State v. Hawkins*, 688 So. 2d 473 (La. 1997) (The detective's statement that the caller stated that there were several individuals in a car was relevant and not hearsay because the detective was explaining the course of police investigation and the steps that lead to the defendant's arrest.).

§ 5.2.5 State of Mind of Declarant

Just as evidence may be offered to show the state of mind of a person who *heard* a statement, a statement may also be offered to show the state of mind of the person who *made* the statement (the declarant).[47] For example, evidence that a person claimed that she could fly could be offered to show that the person had psychological problems. This type of statement is not hearsay because it is not being offered to prove the truth of the matter asserted within the statement, that the patient can actually fly, but is being offered to show the state of mind of the person who made the statement. As stated above, this category of non-hearsay is not to be confused with the state of mind exception to the hearsay rule found in Article 803(3), where the statement itself is hearsay, but may be admitted under the exception.

A way to distinguish the two situations is that in the case of the hearsay state of mind, the declarant is actually stating what his state of mind is at the time (I am sad, angry, upset, crazy, etc.), whereas with the non-hearsay state of mind, the hearer is required to *infer* the state of mind of the declarant. So when a woman states that she can fly, one can infer that she has psychological problems. In such a case, since the statement is not being offered to prove the truth of the matter asserted within the statement, that the declarant can fly, it is not hearsay and will not be excluded by the hearsay rule.

A person's statement may be used to show his **fear**, **intent**, **bias**, **good/bad faith**, **knowledge**, among other states of mind. In *Raymond* below, the court infers the declarant's state of mind from his statement.

---

47. *See* 19 La. Civ. L. Treatise, Evidence And Proof § 10.1(2d ed).

Case on State of Mind of Declarant

State v. Raymond
Supreme Court of Louisiana
245 So. 2d 335
Feb. 24, 1971

SANDERS, Justice.

This is a criminal prosecution. The charred body of a person identified as James Quinn was found in a burned building near Northwestern State College at Natchitoches. Medical experts reported that death resulted from a gunshot wound, rather than from fire. On November 15, 1967, the investigating officers arrested James Raymond for the homicide. The Grand Jury of Natchitoches Parish later indicted him for murder. After hearing the evidence, the jury found him guilty of manslaughter, and the trial judge sentenced him to a term of seven years in the Louisiana State Penitentiary.

The defendant Raymond has appealed, relying upon nineteen bills of exceptions reserved in the trial court. The main legal questions presented relate to the denial of defendant's right to a speedy trial, the sequestration of the witnesses at the trial, and the admission in evidence of an oral statement of the victim made before his death.

...

BILLS OF EXCEPTIONS 15 and 15A: Admission in Evidence of Victim's Statement.

The State called John Luther Jackson as a witness. He testified that on November 12, 1967, about 7:00 p.m., (several hours before the alleged homicide) the victim, James Quinn, was at Chip's Place. As the defendant approached in his automobile and inquired as to the victim's whereabouts, the victim moved behind a tree.

Over defense objection, the State elicited the following additional testimony:

'Q. Why did he say he was hiding?

'A. Because that punk (referring to defendant) would want him * * * (to have abnormal sexual relations with him) tonight, and he hid behind the tree.

'Q. It was after he made the statement that he went and hid behind the tree?

'A. That's right. He said that and then he hid behind the tree.

'Q. And who was coming at that time?

'A. Mr. Raymond.'

We construe the testimony in this sequence: As the defendant approached, the victim declared, that punk will want me to have sexual relations with him tonight, and then moved behind a tree.

The defense strongly contends that the victim's utterance was inadmissible, because it was hearsay and connected the defendant with another crime, that is, sodomy.

The trial judge admitted the utterance as evidence of the victim's state of mind. He instructed the jury that the utterance was not to be considered as evidence of the truth of the facts recited.

Subject to several exceptions, hearsay evidence is inadmissible in a criminal prosecution. LSA-R.S. 15:434. The hearsay rule generally excludes out-of-court statements offered to prove the truth of the matter contained in them. The reason underlying this rule is that such statements are made without an oath and their truth cannot be tested by cross-examination in the presence of the trier of fact.

In the present case, one factual issue is whether the defendant was with the victim at the time of the alleged homicide, several hours after the present incident. The state of mind of the defendant is important insofar as it either increases or decreases the likelihood that contact between the victim and defendant occurred. Hence, evidence of the victim's fear of defendant or his emotional reaction to the presence of defendant is relevant.

The victim's state of mind, of course, can be proved by circumstantial evidence, that is, by utterances from which the jury may infer the existence of fear or revulsion. When an out-of-court statement is offered to prove circumstantially the declarant's state of mind, it is non-hearsay. It is admitted in evidence, not to prove the truth of the facts recited, but to prove that the utterance occurred as a basis for inference. McCormick On Evidence, s 228, p. 465 (1954); 6 Wigmore On Evidence (3d ed.) s 1715, p. 60; 29 Am.Jur.2d, Evidence, s 355, p. 404.

The victim's utterance immediately preceded his act in moving behind the tree. As phrased, the utterance does not appear to be a direct statement that the victim was afraid of the defendant. From it, however, the jury might well infer fear or revulsion. The utterance gives color to the victim's conduct in moving behind the tree. The utterance, as well as the non-verbal conduct, is circumstantial evidence of the victim's state of mind, or emotional attitude toward defendant. The testimony is non-hearsay and, because of its relevance, was admissible in evidence. See State v. Dunn, 161 La. 532, 109 So. 56; State v. Thomas, 159 La. 1076, 106 So. 570; State v. Morgan, 142 La. 755, 77 So. 588; Comment, Hearsay and Non-Hearsay as Reflected in Louisiana, Criminal Cases, 14 La.L.Rev. 611, 614.

Assuming arguendo, however, that the contested statement is hearsay, it would nonetheless be admissible in evidence under either of two exceptions to the hearsay rule. As a spontaneous declaration of apparent sincerity, it would be admissible under the 'Declaration of Mental State' exception to the hearsay rule. See McCormick On Evidence, s 268, p. 567 (1954); 6 Wigmore On Evidence (3d ed.), s 1730, p. 93. It would likewise be admissible under the broad Res gestae exception as applied in Louisiana. See State v. Reese, 250 La. 151, 194 So.2d 729.

The need for this type of evidence in a homicide case is apparent. The victim is dead. In many instances, the jury must determine the facts from a mosaic of circumstantial evidence. This is true in the present case. We conclude that the statement was properly admitted in evidence.

...

For the reasons assigned, the conviction and sentence are affirmed.

...

Discussion Question

As we pointed out above, the non-hearsay purpose for which a statement is offered must be relevant in a case. Why was the declarant's state of mind relevant in *Raymond*? What state of mind were you able to infer from his statement?

Problems on Non-Hearsay State of Mind of Declarant

In the following problems, you should determine whether the statement in question is hearsay pursuant to the definition contained in Article 801, or whether it is non-hearsay state of mind of the declarant. Relevant states of mind of the declarant or hearer may include **knowledge**, **motive**, **bias**, **fear**, **intent**, or even **reasonableness of the declarant's conduct**. If you determine that a statement falls within the category of non-hearsay state of mind of the declarant, please indicate which relevant state of mind is at issue. Some of statements that are hearsay, may fall into an exception to the hearsay rule, but in this section you are not required to discuss any exceptions to the hearsay rule that might apply.

PROBLEM 5-34. Ms. Beth brought an action for false imprisonment against the hospital where she was held for three months in a psychiatric ward against her will, claiming that she was wrongly held there. Dr. Davit seeks to testify that prior to admitting Ms. Beth to the psychiatric ward at the hospital, she told him in an examination, "*Each night I am abducted by aliens who take me onto their spaceship, take over my body and roam the earth until just before dawn, at which time they bring me back. I must find the aliens and kill them. I've already purchased a gun.*" Based on her statement, she was admitted to the hospital against her will because Dr. Davit believed she was a danger to society. Her attorney objected on the grounds that Ms. Beth's statement to the doctor was hearsay. How should the court rule?

PROBLEM 5-35. Didly Poe has died and left his entire estate to his youngest son, Youngster, and nothing to the oldest son, Oldest. Oldest is contesting the will claiming that there *must* be fraud because their father loved him and would never have excluded him from the will. Youngster disputes that assessment. He will have Didly's lifelong friend testify that on numerous occasions Didly repeatedly said to him, "*My oldest son is so lazy. I have no respect for a lazy man.*" Oldest objects that their father's friend's testimony about what Didly said is hearsay. How should the court rule and why?

PROBLEM 5-36. Charisma is suing her apartment complex for wrongful eviction. She was evicted for "causing a disturbance in the apartment complex" which led to several police cars coming to the apartment complex in the middle of the night to conduct a criminal investigation. All of the lights and noise had tenants outside looking on at the disturbance. The apartment complex has this provision for eviction in the lease agreement because they believe such disturbances will deter potential tenants. However, the lease contains an exception if the disturbance is caused "due to no fault of the tenant." Charisma seeks to have the 911 call played to the jury that she frantically made on the night in question reporting the incident. In the call she stated that an intruder was in her apartment, and that she believed that he was going to rape and kill her. She then ran out of the apartment and began yelling and screaming and knocking on doors until police arrived. It was later determined that it was her brother who had unexpectedly dropped by to spend the night because he was intoxicated and did not want to drive all the way back across town. Charisma had given him a key years earlier but had forgotten. When the 911 call is played, the apartment complex objects that what she told the 911 operator is hearsay. Is it? How should the court rule and why?

PROBLEM 5-37. Randall is on trial for murdering his brother-in-law after his sister told him that her husband was molesting their daughter. During Randall's defense, he claimed that he only went to his brother-in-law's office to scare the husband with his gun and that he did not intend to shoot him. He claims he only shot him after the brother-in-law attacked *him* during the confrontation. To counter Randall's argument, the husband's secretary will testify that when Randall walked into the office, he immediately pushed her out of the way and said, "*Your boss is going to hell today!*" Randall objects that the statement is hearsay. Is it? Why or why not?

PROBLEM 5-38. Big Bubba was a judge in the cooking contest at the Culinary Institute of the USA (CIUSA). Just before judging started, he commented to another judge that one of the contestants looked like his niece, but he wasn't sure. After judging, the contestant who Big Bubba thought was his niece won, largely due the very high score Big Bubba had given her. The first runner up sued to get her money back for her travel and food expenses claiming the contest was rigged. At trial, the CIUSA argued and proved that the lady was in fact determined *not* to be Bubba's niece. They further argued that as long as there was no actual relation to a contestant, the judging was fair. The first runner up sought to introduce the statement that Bubba made to the other judge about *thinking* it was his niece. The CIUSA argues the statement is hearsay. How should the court rule and why?

§ 5.2.5 References and Additional Authority on State of Mind of the Declarant

1. Force & Rault, Handbook on Louisiana Evidence Law Arts. 801, 802 Author's Comments (West Publishing 2014)
2. Harges & Jones, Louisiana Evidence Arts. 801, 802 Author's Comments (West Publishing 2014)
3. 19 La. Civ. L. Treatise, Evidence And Proof § 10.1 (2d ed.)
4. McCormick on Evidence § 249 (6th ed.)
5. **Commentary**: McLain, Lynn, "*I'm Going to Dinner with Frank*": *Admissibility of Nontestimonial Statements of Intent to Prove the Actions of Someone Other Than the Speaker—and the Role of the Due Process Clause*, 32 Cardozo L. Rev. 373 (2010).
6. **To show declarant's fear:** *State v. Parks*, 2 So. 3d 470 (La. Ct. App. 5th Cir. 2008) writ denied, 09-0142 (La. 10/02/09), 18 So. 3d 101 (Ms. White, a sixty-one-year-old woman, was invited to spend New Year's Eve with her niece, Ms. Johnson, and her boyfriend, the defendant. At the trial, Ms. Johnson stated that her aunt called her crying on the phone stating that the defendant brought a woman to her house and said "if there is any sh*t in the house tonight that he had a gun." Ms. Johnson testified that her aunt was scared and had never heard her aunt sound so upset. Here, the court found that the victim's statement was admissible to prove the state of mind of the declarant because it established the victim's fear of defendant and her request for help.); *State v. Coleman*, 647 So. 2d 1355, 1360 (La. Ct. App. 4th Cir. 1994) (victim's statement was offered to show that victim feared defendant).
7. **To show declarant's actions were retaliatory:** *Bergene v. Salt River Project Agr. Imp. and Power Dist.*, 272 F.3d 1136 (9th Cir. 2001) (holding that in retaliation claim, the fact that supervisor said plaintiff would not be promoted if she held out for too much money in settlement negotiations of her pregnancy discrimination claim was relevant to show that subsequent denial of promotion was retaliatory, and thus was not hearsay).
8. **To show declarant's intent**: *State v. Huff*, 660 So. 2d 529 (La. Ct. App. 2 Cir.1995) (holding that defendant's statement to witness concerning codefendant's call for a cab was admissible to show defendant's state of mind at the time he talked to witness, shortly before he was seen entering the cab; defendant's belief that codefendant had called cab, making it possible to rob driver, went to defendant's intent to commit robbery).
9. **To show motive of declarant:** *State v. Smith*, 710 So. 2d 1187 (La. Ct. App. 5th Cir. 1998) (holding that witness's testimony that defendant said he was tired of waiting for his money from the victim, which was introduced by state against defendant, was offered to show defendant's motive for killing victim, and therefore, statements did not constitute hearsay in second-degree murder prosecution).

§ 5.2.6 Notice/Knowledge of Receiver/Hearer

Another category of non-hearsay includes statements that are being offered to show that the receiver/hearer had notice or knowledge of some relevant information contained in the statement. These statements are typically relevant in cases where a person claims he was unaware of something that he should have known, and the statement is being offered to show that he did, in fact, have notice or knowledge of the information contained in the statement because the statement was made to him. One such situation is if a person claims to have no knowledge of a dangerous condition of something in his custody, the fact that someone had complained about the condition would be admissible to show that he had knowledge of the condition. For instance, if a person falls in a puddle of water in a grocery store, evidence that prior to the fall someone had told a clerk that there was water on the floor on aisle three would be admissible to show that the store had knowledge of the dangerous condition and should have corrected it. In this situation, the statement is not being offered to prove that there was water on the floor; that point might even be conceded. But the statement would be offered for the non-hearsay purpose of showing the hearer's knowledge that the water was on the floor—a relevant issue in the case.

For purposes of this category of non-hearsay, the notice might come from an oral statement, or it might even be a sign posted stating, **"Danger! Do Not Enter!"** showing that a person was on notice of a dangerous condition.

Cases on Notice/Knowledge of Receiver/Hearer

Bordelon v. Henderson
Supreme Court of Louisiana
604 So. 2d 950
July 31, 1992

PER CURIAM.

The plaintiffs seek damages for the death of their husband and father allegedly caused by the malpractice of the defendant physician in failing to perform proper diagnostic tests and to diagnose the decedent's cancer. Plaintiffs intend to offer evidence, composed in part of decedent's perpetuation deposition, that the physician failed to perform certain x-rays required by the appropriate standard of care.

The defendant physician intends to testify that he advised the decedent to undergo the x-rays but that the decedent declined or refused. Plaintiffs' in limine motion sought to exclude the doctor's testimony of decedent's refusal to take the x-rays as hearsay. The trial court ruled the testimony inadmissible, finding it to be hearsay and unfairly prejudicial. The court of appeal reversed, finding the testimony admissible as non-hearsay under LSA-C.E. Art. 803(4). On original consideration of plaintiffs' writ application, this court reversed the court of appeal and reinstated the trial court judgment, 601 So.2d 665, finding that even if the testimony is otherwise admissible under one of the hearsay exceptions, there is no reason to disturb the trial court's conclusion that the evidence was inadmissible.

Upon defendants' application for rehearing, we conclude our original decision was erroneous and the result reached by the court of appeal was correct. The proposed testimony, the physician's account of decedent's statement of refusal of the x-ray, is not hearsay. The declarant's statement is not offered to prove the truth of the matter asserted. LSA-C.E. Art. 801(C). It is offered to prove the statement was made for the purpose of its legal effects or consequences. The legal effect of the statement becomes operative regardless of the credibility of the declarant or the truthfulness of the statement. Further, a party's own statement offered against the party is not hearsay. LSA-C.E. Art. 801(D)(2)(a). Decedent was an original party plaintiff in this action. Under relational and privity concepts, a statement is not hearsay if the statement is offered against a party and the statement is "[a] statement by a declarant offered against the party in an action for damages arising from the death of that declarant; ..." LSA-C.E. Art. 801(D)(3)(e).

Plaintiffs' contentions that the physician's testimony is unreliable because contemporaneous notation of the decedent's refusal to take the x-ray was not made in the medical records and because decedent was not cross-examined about the refusal during his perpetuation deposition, goes to the credibility and weight of the evidence which should be determined by the jury, not the court. While the proposed testimony may be detrimental to plaintiffs' case, it is highly relevant to the central issue in the case which plaintiffs intend to support by use of the decedent's perpetuation deposition, and it cannot be said to be "unfairly" prejudicial so as to justify exclusion under LSA-C.E. Art. 403.

Discussion Questions

1. In *Bordelon*, the physician's statement is one of notice to the receiver. Why is notice relevant here?
2. Does the patient's refusal of treatment also fall into another category of non-hearsay we have studied thus far? Which one? Explain.

Problems on Notice/Knowledge of Receiver/Hearer

In the following problems, you should determine whether the statement in question is hearsay pursuant to the definition contained in Article 801, or whether it is non-hearsay notice/knowledge of receiver/hearer. Some of the statements that are hearsay might fall into an exception to the hearsay rule, but in this section you are not required to discuss any exceptions to the hearsay rule that might apply.

PROBLEM 5-39. Several tenants are suing their apartment complex for damages resulting from exposure to mold in the apartment. The apartment claims that they were not aware of the state of the apartment and would have made the repairs if they had known. The tenants sought to introduce letters they'd written to the apartment manager complaining of various conditions that they believed posed a danger to their health including leaking water under the floorboards, and wet walls and floors for extended periods of time. The apartment objects that the letters are hearsay. How should the court rule on the objection and why?

PROBLEM 5-40. After Dennis' dog turned 6 months old, Dennis put him in obedience school to make sure he was well trained. After being at obedience school for a month, Dennis went to pick him up and talked with the trainer who told Dennis to be very careful around small children because the dog had a tendency to become aggressive and could possibly attack. A month later, Dennis' dog attacked Donovan while off of his leash in the park. Donovan's mother sued Dennis for negligently keeping a vicious dog and for the damages caused by the dog when he bit Donovan. Donovan would like to offer evidence that the trainer told Dennis about the dog having a tendency to bite children to help prove

Dennis knew his dog was vicious, yet let him off the leash. Dennis objected that the evidence was hearsay. What ruling?

§ 5.2.6 References and Additional Authority on Notice/Knowledge of the Receiver/Hearer

1. Force & Rault, HANDBOOK ON LOUISIANA EVIDENCE LAW Arts. 801, 802 Author's Comments (West Publishing 2014)
2. Harges & Jones, LOUISIANA EVIDENCE Arts. 801, 802 Author's Comments (West Publishing 2014)
3. 19 La. Civ. L. Treatise, Evidence And Proof § 10.1 (2d ed.)
4. MCCORMICK ON EVIDENCE § 249 (5th, ed. 1999)
5. **Notice to or knowledge of hearer/receiver:** *Jackson v. Tyson*, 526 So. 2d 398 (La. Ct. App. 4th Cir. 1988) (Jackson filed suit against Tyson when she fell at the duplex which she rented from defendant. Jackson testified that she complained to the landlord about the stairs. The testimony about the complaint to landlord was admissible to show landlord had notice of the condition of stairs, and was not hearsay.); *Green v. Administrators of Tulane Educational Fund*, 284 F.3d 642 (5th Cir. 2002) (holding that evidence of three prior sexual harassment complaints against physician not hearsay when offered to show that university was on notice that physician may have been sexually harassing women); *Guillot v. Doughty*, 142 So. 3d 1034 (La. Ct. App. 1st Cir. 2014) (holding that inspection report completed prior to sale of home went to home purchasers' knowledge of its existence and notice of its conclusion that the home they purchased contained mold, rather than to the truth of its conclusions, and thus was not hearsay in purchasers' action against vendor for injuries sustained due to presence of toxic mold in the home).

§ 5.2.7 Notice/Knowledge of Declarant

In some instances a statement made by a person that shows his knowledge of something that is relevant is non-hearsay. A statement from a person that he should have his dog trained, or that his dog doesn't like kids, would show that he had knowledge of the dog's vicious nature and what the dog might do to kids. Like the other categories of non-hearsay, since the statement is not being offered to prove what it asserts, and only what the declarant might have known, it is not hearsay.

Problems on Notice/Knowledge of Declarant

In the following problems, you should determine whether or not the statement in question is hearsay pursuant to the definition contained in Article 801 or non-hearsay notice/knowledge of the declarant. Some of the statements that are hearsay might fall into an exception to the hearsay rule, but in this section you are not required to discuss any exceptions to the hearsay rule that might apply.

PROBLEM 5-41. Robin is suing the State Fair Co. claiming that one of their vendors sold her what he said was a magic wand, but she has learned that it doesn't do any magic. The State Fair will offer the testimony of the cab driver who took Robin home from the fair, who will testify that when Robin got into the cab, she said to him, "*This is a pretty nice wand to be a toy.*" Robin objects that the statement to the cab driver is hearsay. How should the court rule and why?

§ 5.2.7 References and Additional Authority on Notice/Knowledge of the Declarant

1. Force & Rault, HANDBOOK ON LOUISIANA EVIDENCE LAW Arts. 801, 802 Author's Comments (West Publishing 2014)
2. Harges & Jones, LOUISIANA EVIDENCE Arts. 801, 802 Author's Comments (West Publishing 2014)
3. 19 La. Civ. L. Treatise, Evidence And Proof § 10.1 (2d ed.)
4. **Notice or knowledge of declarant:** *Hill v. Travelers Ins. Co.*, 128 So. 2d 277 (La. Ct. App. 1st Cir. 1961) (holding that tenant's continuous complaints to landlord over a period of 5–6 months showed that tenant was aware of rotten condition of outside stairway on house, and was contributorily negligent in using stairway, and could not recover for injuries suffered when stairway collapsed while being used by tenant, notwithstanding landlord's negligence in maintaining stairway).

§ 5.2.8 Prior Inconsistent/Consistent Statements

Another type of statement that is not hearsay is a prior inconsistent statement. A prior inconsistent statement is a prior statement of a witness that is inconsistent with his current testimony offered to impeach the witness, i.e., to attack the witness's credibility or truthfulness. For example, if the witness testifies that the light was *green* when he went through it, evidence may be offered to show that at the time of the incident in question, he stated that the light was *red* when he went through it. In such a case, the prior statement is not being offered to show that the light was actually red as the witness previously stated, but instead is being offered only to show that the witness has stated two different versions of the facts, and thus should not be believed.

Prior inconsistent statements used to attack credibility are discussed more thoroughly in Chapter 6, § 6.11 *supra*, where we cover ways of attacking the credibility of witnesses. We will also discuss prior inconsistent statements in Chapter 5, Part D (§ 5.22.1),[48] where in certain circumstances if specific conditions are met the prior statement may be offered for its substantive value, i.e., to prove that what was asserted in the prior statement was in fact true. But for now, it is important to keep in mind that if the prior statement is offered only to show that the witness is not worthy of believing because he has stated two different versions of the facts, then the prior statement is not hearsay.

Also note here that in some instances, if a witness is accused of recently fabricating his current testimony or lying due to some improper motive or influence, a prior statement of a witness that is *consistent* with his current testimony that was made prior to the charge of recent fabrication or undue influence may be offered to rehabilitate the witness's credibility.[49] For example, say a child witness in a custody battle testifies that she was molested

---

48. *See* LA. CODE EVID. art. 801(D)(1)(a) which defines prior inconsistent statements as statements which are not hearsay.

49. *See* LA. CODE EVID. art. 801(D)(1)(b) which defines prior consistent statements as statements

at her father's house. If, during cross-examination, the child is accused of fabricating the story only because she wants to live with her mother, evidence that the child made the same statement before the custody battle began may be offered to rebut the accusation that the child is lying only because of the custody issue.

In this type of situation, the prior consistent statement is similarly not offered for the truth of the matter asserted within the prior statement, but is being offered only to rehabilitate a witness whose credibility has been attacked. Thus, such statements are not hearsay. The use of prior consistent statements for this purpose is thoroughly discussed in Chapter 5, Part D § 5.22.2 *infra*.

Problems on Prior Inconsistent/Consistent Statements

In the following problems, you should determine whether or not the statement in question is hearsay pursuant to the definition contained in Article 801 or whether it is either a prior inconsistent statement to impeach a witness or a prior consistent statement to rehabilitate a witness whose credibility has been attacked. Some of the statements that are hearsay might fall into an exception to the hearsay rule, but in this section you are not required to discuss any exceptions to the hearsay rule that might apply.

PROBLEM 5-42. Jenny was injured leaving her office building when she tripped and fell down the stairs. Immediately after the accident, Jenny wrote up an accident report for the building manager where she stated that the light in the stairwell was on, but while she was distracted on the phone, she missed a step and fell down the stairs. Jenny subsequently brings a lawsuit against the building owners for negligently maintaining the stairs in the building and for inadequate lighting. At the trial, Jenny testifies that there was no light on in the stairwell and that she was not on the phone and was paying close attention. The defense seeks to cross-examine Jenny regarding the statement she made immediately after the accident where she states she was on the phone. Jenny's attorney objects that the statement/accident report is hearsay. How should the court rule and why?

PROBLEM 5-43. Kelsey is the plaintiff in a personal injury trial. At the trial, she testifies that she was sure that she was traveling the speed limit at the time of the accident when she was struck by the defendant. During cross-examination, the defense accuses her of lying because she has since gotten a new job driving delivery trucks, and that she is only testifying to driving the speed limit because it could affect her job. In response, the plaintiff offers a statement that Kelsey made at the time of the accident, long before she got the new job, where she indicated that she was driving the speed limit. The defense objected that the prior statement is hearsay. How should the judge rule on the objection and why?

§ 5.2.8 References and Additional Authority on Prior Inconsistent/Consistent Statements

1. Force & Rault, HANDBOOK ON LOUISIANA EVIDENCE LAW Arts. 801, 802 Author's Comments (West Publishing 2014)

---

which are not hearsay "when offered to rebut an express or implied charge against him of recent fabrication or improper influence or motive." *See also* MCCORMICK ON EVIDENCE § 249 (5th ed., 1999).

2. Harges & Jones, LOUISIANA EVIDENCE Arts. 801, 802 Author's Comments (West Publishing 2014)
3. 19 La. Civ. L. Treatise, Evidence And Proof § 10.1 (2d ed.)
4. MCCORMICK ON EVIDENCE § 249 (5th ed., 1999)
5. See Chapter 6 § 6.11 and Chapter 5 § 5.22.1 and 5 § 5.22.2 infra.
6. **Prior Inconsistent Statements:** *State v. S.L.D.*, 997 So. 2d 759 (La. Ct. App. 3d Cir. 2008) (The victim of a sexual assault testified that she attempted to perform oral sex on the defendant several times during a camping trip. When the State asked whether the oral sex was voluntary, she stated it was. She went on to state that after the third time, the defendant walked out and threatened to tell the victim's parents. The defendant told the detective the same story. There was also a witness that testified that she saw the victim perform oral sex at the defendant's home. The court held that since the victim "testified at the trial, was cross-examined by the defense, offered testimony inconsistent with a prior statement, and then specifically refuted the veracity of her prior statement," the statements to the detective were non-hearsay.); *State v. Bairnsfather*, 591 So. 2d 686 (La. 1991) (At the trial, defense counsel attempted to bring to light prior inconsistent statements made by witness. Witness previously told her neighbor that the defendant never molested her, but she denied ever making the statement. During the trial, defense counsel called the neighbor to the stand and wanted to introduce the prior inconsistent statement but was barred by the court. The Supreme Court held that the inconsistent statements should have been admitted to allow the jury to determine the witness's credibility.).
7. **Prior Consistent Statements:** *State v. Turner*, 82 So. 3d 1245 (La. Ct. App. 4th Cir. 2012) (Defendant was convicted of second-degree battery. Two witnesses identified defendant as the attacker. Patterson, one of the witnesses, initially told officers that she thought the victim had been robbed. Defense counsel attempted to imply that Patterson initially lied to the police. The trial court held that Patterson's prior statements were admissible to rebut claim of recent fabrication.).

Key Points

The key points to keep in mind regarding non-hearsay.

1. Statements are non-hearsay if they are offered to prove something other than the truth of the matter asserted.
2. The non-hearsay purpose for which a statement is offered must be relevant in the case.
   a. If a statement has both a non-hearsay purpose and a hearsay purpose, the court weighs the significance of both purposes to determine if the non-hearsay purpose is at issue. If not, the statement cannot be used as a ruse to admit prejudicial hearsay, such as when the reason that a police officer took the action that he took is not at issue.
3. **Categories of non-hearsay include the following:**
   a. **Verbal acts** — an operative fact that gives rise to legal consequences; a statement to which the law attaches duties and liabilities.

b. **Verbal parts of acts**—words that accompany an ambiguous physical act that gives color to the act.

c. **Non-assertive conduct**—conduct not intended as an assertion.

d. **State of mind of hearer/listener/reader**—a statement offered to show the state of mind of the hearer/receiver, such as that he had notice or knowledge, had a certain emotion, good/bad faith, or behaved reasonably, is not hearsay.

e. **State of mind of the declarant**—a statement offered to show the state of mind of the person making the statement such as knowledge, motive, fear, good/bad faith, or reasonableness in taking particular action or in reaching a particular conclusion, is not hearsay.

f. **Notice or knowledge of receiver/hearer**—a statement offered only to show that the hearer had notice or knowledge of something of which she heard/read is not hearsay.

g. **Notice or knowledge of declarant**—a statement offered only to show that the declarant had certain notice or knowledge of something of which he spoke is not hearsay.

h. **Prior inconsistent statement**—a prior statement of a witness that is inconsistent with his present testimony offered to impeach the witness's credibility is not hearsay.

i. **Prior consistent statement**—a prior statement of a witness that is consistent with his current testimony offered to rebut a charge of recent fabrication or undue influence or motive is not hearsay.

Problems on Categories of Non-Hearsay

In the following problems, you should determine whether or not the statement in question is hearsay pursuant to the definition contained in Article 801. If the statement is not hearsay, please indicate which category of non-hearsay applies. If the statement goes to the state of mind of the declarant or hearer, please indicate which relevant state of mind is at issue. Some of statements that are hearsay might fall into an exception to the hearsay rule, but in this section you are not required to discuss any exceptions to the hearsay rule that might apply.

PROBLEM 5-44. Bill was in a small antique shop in Mississippi when he came across a baseball signed, "Handy Joe Smooth"—a famous pitcher from the major leagues. He asked the owner of the antique shop if he knew if the baseball was authentic and the owner told him that he knew for a fact it was Handy's signature because "*Handy signed the ball in the store,*" he claimed. Little did the owner know, but Bill was Handy's former agent who immediately contacted Handy on his cell phone and asked him if he'd ever been to the small antique shop in Mississippi and signed a ball there. Handy assured him he'd never been there and had not signed the ball. The agent called the police, and the shop owner was arrested for fraud. At the trial, the owner claimed he really believed the signature was Handy's and therefore had no intent to defraud anyone. The state will counter his assertions by offering Bill's testimony that the owner specifically told him that Handy signed the ball in the store. The owner objects that the statement is hearsay. How should the court rule and why?

PROBLEM 5-45. Greta sued the hotel for injures she sustained while swimming in the hotel's pool when she caught a cramp and could no longer swim, but no lifeguard was on duty to help her. The hotel offered six signs posted all around the pool that stated,

"*No Lifeguard on Duty. Swim at Own Risk,*" in their case to show that Greta knew that no lifeguard was on duty, but chose to swim anyway. Greta objects that the signs are hearsay. How should the court rule?

Assume instead that no signs were posted around the pool. After Greta went outside and did not see a lifeguard, she returned inside and told the front desk attendant that there was no lifeguard outside at the pool and asked if one would be on duty at the pool at a later time. The front desk attendant told Greta, "*He's around. He comes and goes. Just yell if there's a problem.*" Believing the lifeguard was in close proximity to the pool, Greta went outside to swim. When she caught a cramp, she cried out, but no one came. Greta was injured. At the trial against the hotel, they would like to offer Greta's statement to the attendant that "no lifeguard was outside" to show that she knew the pool was unattended, yet unreasonably swam in it. Greta would like to offer the attendant's statement to her to show why she swam in the pool even though she didn't see the lifeguard. Both parties object that the other party's statement is hearsay. Will either statement be admitted at trial? Why or why not?

PROBLEM 5-46. Wasted is on trial for DWI. At his trial, the prosecution would like to offer the roadside video after it is properly authenticated, in which Wasted is observed swerving and falling down as he attempts to perform Standardized Field Sobriety Tests. Wasted objects that the video is hearsay and should be excluded. How should the court rule and why?

PROBLEM 5-47. A battered woman called the police and stated that her husband was beating her. When the police arrived the husband had left the scene, but the woman was asked to make a sworn statement about the incident. She completed a sworn affidavit that stated, "*My husband beat me today. He put a gun to my head and a knife to my neck and threatened to kill me. Then he ran away.*" The husband was eventually arrested for domestic battery. At the trial, the woman refused to testify against her husband and invoked her spousal privilege. The prosecution would like to use her sworn affidavit to prove what the defendant did to the wife on the day of the incident. The defense objects that the affidavit is hearsay. How should the court rule and why?

PROBLEM 5-48. Bye was suing Sel to have Sel turnover the Cadillac he'd purchased from him. Bye claims that one day while he was admiring Sel's new Cadillac, Sel said to him, "*You can have her for $15.*" Bye immediately said, "*Deal!*" and handed over the $15. At the trial, Sel denies saying that to Bye, so Bye calls the parking meter attendant who was standing nearby and heard the whole conversation who will testify that he in fact heard Sel tell Bye that he "could have her for $15," and that Bye said, "Deal!" and handed over the money. Sel objects that the statements are hearsay. How should the court rule and why?

§ 5.3 Multiple Hearsay [La. C.E. art. 805]

Applicable Code Articles

Art. 805. Hearsay within hearsay

Hearsay included within hearsay is not excluded under the hearsay rule if each part of the combined statements conforms with an exception to the hearsay rule provided by legislation.

In some instances, the out-of-court statement to which a witness testifies in court also contains another statement, and depending upon the reasons for which each statement is offered (for the truth of the matter asserted or for some other reason), the witness's testimony may constitute hearsay within hearsay. A common situation where this occurs is in written documents that are being offered in court that contain statements made by others. Since documents are out-of-court statements, if offered to prove the truth of the matter asserted, they will always be hearsay. If the document contains a statement made by someone else that is also being offered to prove the truth of the matter asserted, it would constitute double hearsay. Thus, a medical report (out-of-court statement #1) that contains a statement made by a patient that her stomach was hurting (out-of-court statement #2), would be double hearsay. Article 805 provides that in order to be admissible, each statement must conform to an exception (or exemption[50]) to the hearsay rule.

Each statement must conform to exception. To be admissible, a proponent of multiple hearsay must be able to articulate an exception that applies to each statement. Taking the example above, the medical record would conform to the "business records" exception found in Article 803(6), and the patient's statement that her stomach was hurting would conform to the "then existing physical condition" exception to the hearsay rule found in Article 803(3). Since both statements conform to an exception to the hearsay rule, both the medical report and the patient's statement contained in it would be admissible. If the court finds that the statement contained within the record does not conform to an exception, the record would be admissible but the statement contained within it would be excluded. The statement could be excised out of the record.

Similarly, if the medical report *(out-of-court statement #1)* contains a statement from mother (statement #2) that her son, who is now unconscious, had been complaining of certain symptoms prior to collapsing (statement #3), then this scenario would constitute triple hearsay. Essentially, the report is saying, that the mother said, that the son said something. In order to be admissible, each part would have to conform to an exception or exemption to the hearsay rule. The same would be true if a police officer's report (out-of-court statement #1) was offered into evidence that included a statement of an eyewitness to an accident (statement #2).

While any *written* document (letter, record, report, deposition, email, text message, etc.) that contains statements made by others would constitute double hearsay if both are being offered for the truth of the matter asserted within them, double hearsay is also often presented when a person *testifies* about an out-of-court statement that contains other statements. An example would be if a mother testifies, "My son came home and told me (out-of-court statement #1) that his teacher told him (out-of-court statement #2) that if he missed any more days from school he'd be expelled." In order for the mother to testify to what her son told her that the teacher said, both the son's statement and the teacher's statement must conform to an exception to the hearsay rule.

The concept of multiple hearsay can be illustrated as in Figure 5.3.1, on the next page, in the form of each statement being contained within a bubble. Each statement must conform to an exception or exemption, or be non-hearsay, in order to come out of the bubble,

50. La. Code Evid. art. 801(D)(1)–(4) exempts certain statements from being excluded by the hearsay rule. They are titled, "Statements which are not Hearsay." In this textbook they are referred to as "Statutory Non-Hearsay" and are covered in Chapter 5 Part D.

Figure 5.3.1. A medical record contains the following three statements notated by the doctor: A) patient states that she had severe pain in lower left portion of abdomen; B) she states that her husband beat her and stomped her in the stomach last night; and C) she states that her husband said he would kill her if she called the police.

Statement A

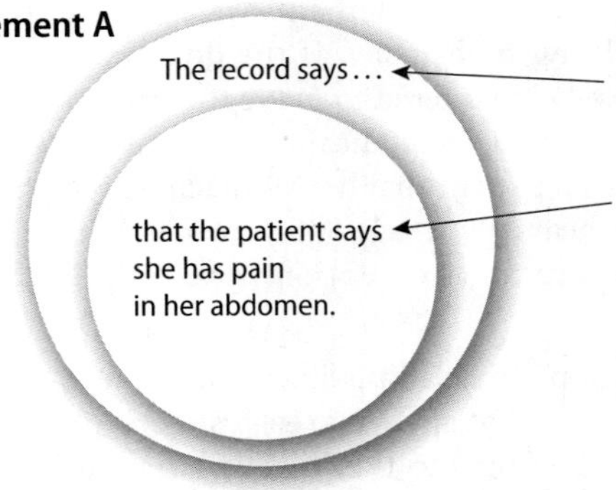

Business Record Exception or
Hospital Record Rule
Article 803(6)

Then-Existing Physical Condition Exception
Article 803(3)

Here, both statements conform to an exception to the hearsay rule, so the report and the statement contained in it are **admissible**.

Statement B

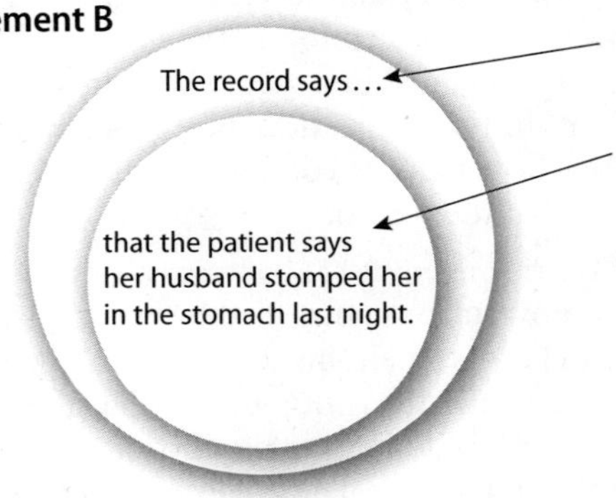

Business Record Exception or
Hospital Record Rule
Article 803(6)

No exception or exemption

Here, although the medical records conform to an exception to the hearsay rule, the patient's statements about her husband stomping her are not admissible. The statement is hearsay because it is being offered to prove that the husband caused the injuries. Since no exception exists, this statement made by the victim would be **inadmissible**. The victim would have to take the stand to testify about what her husband did to her.

Statement C

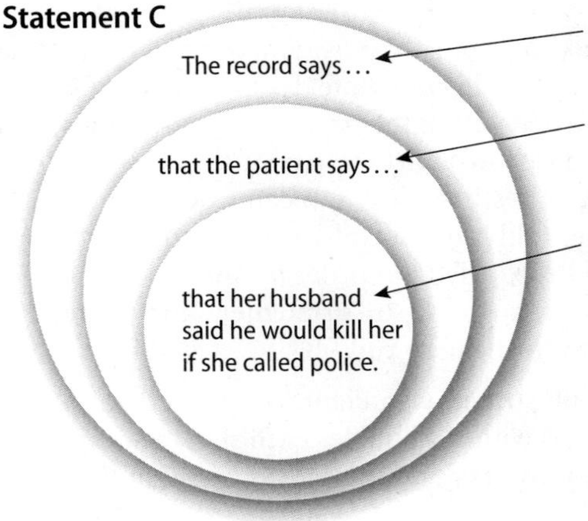

Business Record Exception or
Hospital Record Rule
Article 803(6)

No exception or exemption

This is likely non-hearsay, but depends on why it's being offered. If only to show the assault in assault case (verbal act), or why victim hadn't reported incident (effect on hearer), or to show his intent (state of mind of declarant), then it's non-hearsay.

This is a triple hearsay statement. Although the medical record conforms to an exception, the patient's statement about what her husband said to her is not admissible because no exception exists. Even if husband's statement is non-hearsay or an exception exists, because it is still contained within the bubble of her inadmissible statement to the doctor, it is still inadmissible. Here, the victim would have to take the stand to testify about her husband's threat to her.

allowing the statement to be admissible. While an outer statement may be admitted that excludes an inner statement if no exception applies, if the outer statement is not admissible, then none of the inner statements may be admissible. Also consider whether your answer to the illustrated scenario would change if instead the victim had been immediately rushed to the hospital and the statement had been made to the doctor.

Revisit *Buckbee, supra.* In *Buckbee*, the decedent's coworker, Vincent, testified that the decedent told him that his supervisor gave him permission to use heat—a typical case of double hearsay, both requiring an exception to be admissible. Like the illustration in Figure 5.3.1, Figure 5.3.2 below illustrates that, while the statement to Buckbee was a non-hearsay verbal act (statement giving permission), the statement made to the coworker by Buckbee did not conform to an exception to the hearsay rule, and was therefore inadmissible. As the court pointed out:

> [T]he only proof of whether Buckbee received permission is Buckbee's own statement to that effect, presented through the testimony of Vincent. Since Buckbee's statement was made out of court, not under oath, and not subject to cross-examination, Vincent's testimony to that statement is hearsay when offered to prove that Buckbee in fact received permission to apply heat[FN 8] and would not be admitted in this instance solely for a nonhearsay purpose. The lower courts properly excluded this testimony.
>
> FN 8. Had Buckbee survived, he would have been permitted to testify about his superiors' statements permitting him to apply heat as a nonhearsay "verbal act" (a giving of permission by a superior with authority to do so) with concomitant legal consequences. Had Vincent personally heard Buckbee's superiors giving Buckbee permission to apply heat, he too would have been permitted to testify to that statement. However, since Vincent did not personally hear the statement being made, he is not permitted to testify to Buckbee's out-of-court assertion that such a statement occurred. *See Knorr v. Pearson*, 671 F.2d 1368, 1372–73 (C.C.P.A.1982) (third party's testimony to what he heard first inventor say to second inventor held admissible nonhearsay as proof of a verbal act with legal consequences between the two inventors, but third party forbidden to testify to what the first inventor told him the second inventor said); *General Tire of Miami Beach, Inc. v. N.L.R.B.*, 332 F.2d 58, 60–61 (5th Cir.1964) ("The verbal act, as any other act, may be proved by one who heard it, saw it, or felt it.").

Figure 5.3.2. Illustration of Vincent testifying that Buckbee stated he was given permission by supervisor.

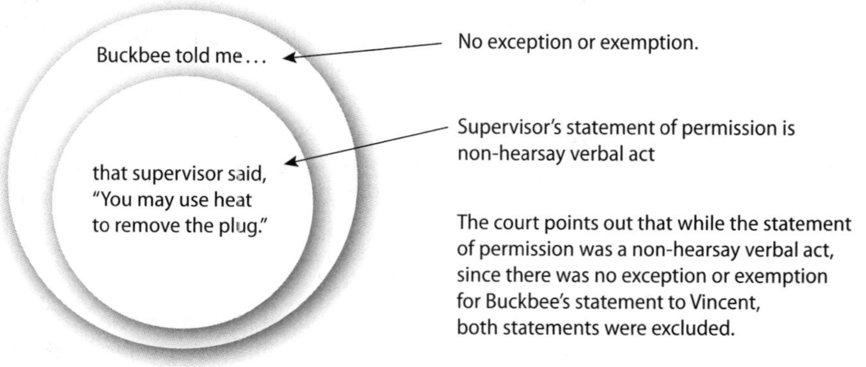

Cases on Multiple Hearsay

State v. Griffin
Supreme Court of Louisiana
783 So. 2d 1241
March 7, 2001

Johnson, Judge.

The State charged defendant with shooting and mortally wounding Patrick Parker and Tiche Carter. After being shot, Carter ran to the apartment of William Thomas and purportedly told him just before dying that Dennis shot him. Subsequently, Thomas related Carter's statement to the police investigator who included the statement in the police report. Five days prior to defendant's trial, Thomas died. After a mistrial was declared in the first trial of defendant, a motion was filed by him seeking to have Thomas declared unavailable and requesting that Thomas's statement to the police be admissible as a dying declaration under La. Code Evid. art. 804(B)(2).[51] The trial court granted defendant's motion The court of appeal, Fourth Circuit, denied the State's writ application. *State v. Griffin,* 01-0350 (La.App. 4 Cir. 3/1/01). The State sought expedited attention in this Court, contending that Carter's statement to Thomas as recorded in the police report constituted inadmissible double hearsay. *State v. Griffin,* 01-KK-0579 (La.3/2/01).

The State contends that the lower courts have improperly sanctioned the use of double hearsay, i.e., Carter's purported statement to Thomas as recorded in Thomas's statement to the police investigators. It contends that there is no indicia of reliability and the jury will not be able to judge his credibility as would normally occur after the State would have an opportunity for cross-examination of this witness. We agree.

In *Buckbee v. United Gas Pipe Line Co., Inc.,* 561 So.2d 76 (La.1990), we reasoned:

> In its broadest sweep, the hearsay rule excludes all testimony regarding statements made out-of-court by declarants who at the time of making the statements were not under oath, not in the presence of the trier of fact, and thus not subject to cross-examination. By excluding testimony which fails these three requirements, the hearsay rule increases the reliability of in-court testimony, and seeks to admit only that testimony which the fact-finder can evaluate for the witness's perception, memory, narration, and sincerity. 4 J. Weinstein & M. Berger, Weinstein's Evidence 800-1 to 800-5 (1988). *Buckbee,* 561 So. 2d at 80.

Although Carter's statement to Thomas may have been a dying declaration, Thomas's testimony is unavailable for evaluation by the fact-finder as to his perception, memory, narration, and sincerity. Thus, the reliability needed to justify an exception to the hearsay rule is fatally lacking. There is no indicia of reliability.

Accordingly, the judgments of the lower courts are reversed and set aside. It is hereby ordered, adjudged, and decreed that defendant's motion requesting that Thomas's statement to the police be admissible as a dying declaration is denied. Our stay order issued on March 5, 2001, in this matter is recalled and this matter is remanded to the trial court for further proceedings.

---

51. The following are not excluded by the hearsay rule if the declarant is unavailable as a witness: "... (2) A statement made by a declarant while believing that his death was imminent, concerning the cause or circumstances of what he believed to be his impending death." La. Code Evid. art. 804(B)(2).

Discussion Questions

1. If the report is admitted, this case presents a situation of triple hearsay. How so? Would the result change if the police officer personally testified? If so, how?
2. Whose credibility is at issue here? How might the opponent of the statement benefit from cross-examining him? Are the potential dangers for admitting hearsay compounded in such a situation? How or why?

State v. Hurst
Court of Appeal of Louisiana, Fourth Circuit
828 So. 2d 1165
Sept. 25, 2002

MICHAEL E. KIRBY, Judge.

On July 29, 1999, the defendant was charged by grand jury indictment with second degree murder. La. R.S. 14:30.1. He was arraigned and pled not guilty August 8, 1999. A twelve member jury found him guilty as charged June 27, 2000.... He was sentenced to life imprisonment at hard labor without benefit of parole, probation, or suspension of sentence....

FACTS

Allen Delatte, nineteen, was killed outside the New Orleans Superdome following an event known as the Super Fair on June 7, 1999. He was shot from the back from some distance in a manner that indicated he may have been running when he was wounded.

Officer Bradley Tollefson said that when he arrived at the scene, there was a large crowd leaving the fair, and that several of the victim's friends and family were present. These people said they were with the victim, heard the shots, and were running with him when he was hit. No witness could identify the perpetrator. Tollefson learned from Detective Davillier, who was also on the scene, that two black men, who had later left the scene, reported to them that two perpetrators had driven by in a red 1993 Oldsmobile with primer paint on the right door.

Detective Archie Kaufman, Homicide, took over the case. He learned from Detective Norman McCord that the suspect's nickname was "Chevy" or "Duvan". He spoke with Detectives Jerry Kuhn, Jerry Farve and Walter Powers of the Second District. He learned that "Duvan–Chevy" was Duvander Hurst....

The defendant turned himself in. In a statement, he said that on the night of the crime he had gotten a ride to the Superdome with Albert Luckettee and Corey Madison, who owned a red four door Buick Skylark in which they were driving. After the fair, the three went to Rally's on Carrollton Avenue and then went home. He said he was not present during the shooting....

The defendant's mother, Ethel Hurst, said she learned about the shooting on television the next day. She did not remember a reporter coming to her house prior to the defendant's arrest. After she watched a tape of the broadcast played to the court room, she said that in fact she had been interviewed. She said the defendant had in fact told her that he had been at the Superdome and had heard the shots, but that he had not been involved in the crime. She said he could not have been in his red car the night of the crime because it was in the shop. She did not actually see the car in the shop, but she had a "paper" to show that it was indeed in the shop. She did not know Louis Silva. She had never seen the defendant with a gun, although he had been arrested for armed robbery. She said she remembered that he had been arrested for marijuana possession, but she did not remember he had been arrested for cocaine.

...

ASSIGNMENT OF ERROR ONE:

The defendant filed a motion in limine to prevent a playing of a videotape which contained a compilation of various news stories surrounding the crime. The stories had appeared on various of the major news stations in the metropolitan region. The trial, after ascertaining that the State had a witness to establish the chain of custody, and limiting the jury's viewing solely to an interview with Ethel Hurst, viewed the tape. After learning that the State would call Ethel Hurst, the trial court allowed the evidence.

On appeal, the judge defendant complains about the jury having viewed the excerpt of the tape which involved a report from WWL–TV, the New Orleans CBS affiliate. The excerpt showed a black woman using her house door to shield her from the cameras such that only a hand was visible. The woman said on the tape that she was the defendant's mother, that he had told her that he had been at the fair, and that he had said that he had nothing to do with the crime.

The defendant complains that allowing the jury to view the tape was an introduction of impermissible hearsay within hearsay. Specifically, the defendant argues that the reporter should have been called to the stand, that the defendant did not testify, and that the only way the State laid a proper foundation was to call Gail Guidry, custodian of records for WWL.

The defendant cites absolutely no law to support this assignment except a cursory reference to La. C.E. arts. 802[52] and 805.[53]

The first level of the "hearsay within hearsay" of which the defendant complains involves the statements of the defendant to his mother. The second level involves the statements by the mother to the reporter. Addressing the latter first, hearsay is defined as "a statement, other than one made by the declarant while testifying at the present trial or hearing, offered in evidence to prove the truth of the matter asserted." La. C.E. art. 801. Here, the statement was made by the declarant, Ethel Hurst, who testified at trial and admitted she had made the statement. As such, the statement does not fall under the definition of hearsay.

As to the hearsay argument concerning the defendant's statement to his mother that he was at the scene of the crime, that statement was a statement against his interest. La. C.E. art. 804(B)(3) specifically sets an exception for statements against interest. The evidence was properly admitted. This assignment is without merit.

...

52. La. C.E. art. 802 provides: "Hearsay is not admissible except as otherwise provided by this Code or other legislation."

53. La. C.E. art. 805 provides: "Hearsay included within hearsay is not excluded under the hearsay rule if each part of the combined statements conforms with an exception to the hearsay rule provided by legislation."

Discussion Question

Do you agree with the court's analysis? How would you have analyzed the admissibility of the video in *Hurst*? Would your answer change if the reporter had testified about what the mother said, instead of offering the video? Why or why not?

Problems on Multiple/Double Hearsay

We will revisit multiple hearsay later on throughout the chapter after we have covered some of the exceptions and exemptions so that you can determine whether the statements would ultimately be admissible. For now, we will practice identifying multiple hearsay.

PROBLEM 5-49. For each statement, please indicate whether the statement is hearsay, double hearsay, or triple hearsay. For purposes of this exercise, we will refer to each level of statements as "hearsay" even it if it might fit into an exemption or a category of non-hearsay. Draw them out if it will assist you in identifying multiple hearsay.

A. The witness testified, "*My husband came home and told me that some guy hit his car driving a big red truck, then ran away.*"

B. The witness testified, "*My husband came home and told me that some guy hit his car driving a big red truck, and that the guy got out of the truck and told him that he was going to drive to the police station, then he got into the car and ran away.*"

C. The plaintiff offered her medical records into evidence that included the statement, "*Patient stated that guy walked up to him and accused him of killing his brother, then shot him in the stomach.*"

D. The plaintiff offers a video into evidence in which a deceased woman talks about why she is going to commit suicide where she states, "*The final straw was when Rick (husband) came home and told me that his boss had informed him that he couldn't afford to keep him on the job and that the last day of the month would be his last day.*"

E. The plaintiff was injured on the job. The former employer testified that when the plaintiff came back to work on the first day, he had a talk with him, and the plaintiff said that he wasn't sure he wanted to come back to work because his lawyer told him that *if he goes back to work he'll get about $25,000, but if he doesn't go back to work, he'll get over $200,000.*

§ 5.3 References and Additional Authority on Multiple Hearsay [La. C.E. art. 805]

1. La. C.E. art. 805 and Official Comments.
2. Force & Rault, HANDBOOK ON LOUISIANA EVIDENCE LAW Art. 805 Author's Comments (West Publishing 2014).
3. Harges & Jones, LOUISIANA EVIDENCE Art. 805 Author's Comments (West Publishing 2014).
4. 19 La. Civ. L. Treatise, Evidence And Proof § 10.29 (2d ed.).

5. **La. C.E. art. 805—Multiple Hearsay:** *Maddox v. Anderson Trucking Services*, 801 So. 2d 593 (La. Ct. App. 3d Cir. 2001) (An affidavit was presented to the court by Stunek but did not state that he was the person who communicated with the plaintiff from which facts were obtained. Affiant only stated that he had personal knowledge of "certain facts." The court held that unless Stunek (the affiant) was the person communicating to the plaintiff, the facts in the affidavit presented to the court would be double hearsay.).

Part B
Introduction to Exceptions to Hearsay Rule
Availability of Declarant Immaterial
[La. C.E. art. 803]

§ 5.4 Hearsay Exceptions Generally [La. C.E. arts. 803, 804]

While the general rule under Article 802 is that hearsay statements are inadmissible, there are numerous exceptions to the rule. As stated in the introduction to Chapter 5, many of the exceptions have been developed recognizing that under certain circumstances, many of the dangers inherent in admitting hearsay statements (insincerity, ambiguity, faulty perception, and flawed memory), are not present, therefore rendering the statements **presumptively trustworthy**.[54] For example, if a person makes a statement describing something that he is observing while he is contemporaneously observing it, a "present sense impression," not only is faulty memory not an issue, but it is also unlikely that the person would've had an opportunity to reflect and fabricate his observations.

Similarly, if a person is dying and knows it, and spontaneously makes a statement about what caused his death, of which he has first-hand knowledge, it is unlikely that the person would be fabricating the statement when he has nothing to lose, nothing to gain, and would not likely want his dying words to be a known lie. Additionally, since the incident leading to his death most likely just occurred, memory wouldn't be an issue either. Similarly, certain records, such as business or public records, because of the manner in which they are stored and kept, are likely to be trustworthy and reliable documents.

As in these situations, other statements have similarly been excluded from the hearsay ban because they fall within certain "**categories of circumstantial reliability**."[55] Because of the reliability of these statements, and in some situations when the statements are also a necessity because the declarant is unavailable to testify personally, the statements may be admissible at trial. Thus, while hearsay statements are generally inadmissible, there are several exceptions to this rule that are covered in Articles 803 and 804 of the Louisiana Code of Evidence.

Keep in mind however, that even though statements falling into these categories are "presumptively trustworthy,"[56] in "circumstances that indicate that [the statement] is grossly and patently unreliable,"[57] the statement should nonetheless still be excluded.

Exceptions apply to hearsay statements only. It is important to remember that the exceptions to the hearsay rule apply to *hearsay* statements only. In other words, it is only after you determine that a statement is in fact hearsay, i.e., that it is being offered to prove the truth of the matter asserted, that the exceptions become applicable. So the first step in analyzing any hearsay issue, whether on an examination or in court, is to analyze whether the statement in question is in fact hearsay. Only if you find that the statement in question is hearsay, do you move on to determining whether the statement fits into an exception to the hearsay rule.

---

54. La. Code Evid., Introductory Note to Chapter 8.
55. *Id.*
56. *Id.*
57. *Id.*

Categories of hearsay exceptions. There are two main categories of hearsay exceptions. One category includes exceptions listed in **Article 803**, which are exceptions that apply whether or not the declarant is available to testify at the trial. For these exceptions, there is no requirement that the declarant be dead or otherwise unable to testify to the statement himself. The circumstances surrounding the making of the statements in Article 803 are deemed sufficiently trustworthy to warrant admitting the statement even if the declarant might be available to testify to the statement himself.

The other main category of exceptions is found in **Article 804**. These exceptions to the hearsay rule *require* that the person who made the statement be *unavailable* to testify prior to admitting his statements. In other words, Article 804 exceptions apply only if the person who made the statement cannot or will not appear in court, such as if he or she is dead, ill, or for some other reason is prevented from testifying in court, not caused by the proponent of the statement. These exceptions are not considered to be as trustworthy as Article 803 exceptions, but because of the necessity for them, since the witness is unavailable, the statement may be admissible.

La. C.E. art. 803 exceptions are covered in Chapter 5 (Part B, §5.5–§5.13). La. C.E. art. 804 exceptions will be covered in Chapter 5 (Part C, §5.14–§5.21).

Hearsay exemptions — Statutory Non-Hearsay. A different but closely related rule to those governing the exceptions is **Article 801(D)(1)–(4)**, which *exempts* certain statements from the hearsay rule titled, **"Statements which are not hearsay."** Some of these statements would technically be hearsay under the definition because they are being offered to prove the truth of what they are asserting. An example is when a declarant makes an identification, which is technically hearsay because it is an out-of-court statement being offered to prove the truth of the matter asserted. However, these statements are exempt from the hearsay ban in Article 801(D)(1)(c).

For purposes of this casebook, the statements referenced in Article 801(D)(1)–(4) will be referred to as **hearsay "exemptions"** or **"statutory non-hearsay,"** since they are *defined* under statute as not being hearsay. The exemptions, discussed at length in Chapter 5 (Part D, §5.22–§5.24), *infra*, work very much like the exceptions. If you find that the requirements of the exemptions are met, the statement will not be excluded under the hearsay rule.

Exceptions do not make statements admissible. Also keep in mind that "[t]he exceptions [to the hearsay rule] are phrased in terms of nonapplication of the hearsay rule, rather than in positive terms of admissibility, in order to repel any implication that other possible grounds for exclusion are eliminated from consideration."[58] In other words, the fact that a statement is not *excluded* under the hearsay rule, because it may fit into an exception, does not mean the statement will automatically be *admitted* into evidence. The statement could still be excluded on other grounds, such as privilege, lack of authentication, the Article 403 balancing test, relevancy, or because admitting the statement would violate a defendant's Sixth Amendment rights to confront and cross-examine witnesses against him.[59]

Hearsay vis-à-vis the Sixth Amendment Confrontation Clause. One final and important consideration to keep in mind as you study the admissibility of hearsay statements is to consider whether offering such statements would violate an accused's rights under the Sixth Amendment Confrontation Clause. The Sixth Amendment of the United States

58. *Id.*, *quoting* Fed. R. of Evid. 803, advisory committee's note.

59. *See* La. Code Evid., Introductory Note to Chapter 8.

Even though a statement conforms with a hearsay exception, it comports with the requirements of the Confrontation Clause only if:

1. the declarant is currently unavailable;
2. the statement is testimonial; and
3. there was a prior opportunity for cross-examination.

Constitution provides that "[i]n all criminal prosecutions, the accused shall enjoy the right ... to be confronted with the witnesses against him."[60] Despite this constitutional right to confront and cross-examine witnesses, prior to *Crawford v. Washington*,[61] once a court determined that a statement was not precluded by the hearsay rule (i.e., fit into a hearsay exception or exemption), the statement was deemed to have complied with any requirements of the Confrontation Clause and was allowed into evidence.

In *Crawford*, the U.S. Supreme Court recognized that despite a statement overcoming the hearsay rule, a statement should still be excluded if it violated the defendant's Sixth Amendment rights under the Confrontation Clause, and thus precluded unconfronted testimony from being used against the accused. *Crawford* clarified, however, that not all statements offered against an accused must be subject to confrontation. The Court concluded that only those statements that constitute *testimony* should be excluded under the Sixth Amendment if the witness is currently *unavailable* and there was *no prior opportunity to cross-examine* the witness.

Thus, even though a statement conforms with a hearsay exception, it will comport with the requirements of the Confrontation Clause only if: 1) the declarant is currently unavailable; 2) the statement is testimonial; and 3) there was a prior opportunity for cross-examination on the statement.[62]

Each of these components of the Confrontation Clause is thoroughly discussed in Part E of this chapter. For now it is important to keep in mind as you study hearsay that even if a statement conforms to the requirements of a hearsay exception, it will also have to overcome confrontation issues in order to be admissible in the same manner in which it must overcome other provisions of the Code of Evidence such as relevance, privilege, etc. As we cover the exceptions, we will note which statements are more likely to implicate the Sixth Amendment Confrontation Clause.

Hearsay Exceptions that Apply Whether or Not the Declarant Is Available [La. C.E. art. 803]

The Louisiana Code of Evidence Article 803 contains twenty-four exceptions to the hearsay rule that apply whether or not the declarant is available and capable of testifying at the trial as a witness himself. "Article 803 hearsay exceptions are generally based upon the policy that when the qualifying circumstances are met, there is *ordinarily* a sufficient basis for crediting the trustworthiness and reliability of the out-of-court statement to justify making an exception to the hearsay rule even though the declarant is available, but

60. U.S. Const. amend. VI; La. Const. Art. 1, Sec. 16 (1974).
61. Crawford v. Washington, 541 U.S. 36 (2004).
62. Crawford v. Washington, 541 U.S. 36 (2004).

not called to testify, at trial."[63] In other words, for the exceptions found in this article, the circumstances surrounding the making of the statements are of sufficient trustworthiness to warrant admitting the statement into evidence even though the witness might be available to testify.

Keep in mind, however, that while these statements are *ordinarily* trustworthy, if the circumstances suggest that a statement is not reliable, it should nonetheless be excluded.[64]

§ 5.5 Present Sense Impressions [La. C.E. art. 803(1)]

Applicable Code Articles

The following are not excluded by the hearsay rule, even though the declarant is available as a witness:

(1) **Present sense impression.** A statement describing or explaining an event or condition made while the declarant was perceiving the event or condition, or immediately thereafter.

* * *

Pursuant to Article 803(1), a statement will not be excluded as hearsay if it is one ***describing*** or ***explaining*** an event or condition while the declarant is ***perceiving*** it, or if the statement is made ***immediately after*** perceiving the event or condition it describes. These statements are deemed trustworthy based on the fact that since the statement is being made contemporaneously with observing what the statement describes, it is unlikely that the declarant would have the opportunity to fabricate his observations. Also, memory is unlikely to be an issue since the event is occurring while the statement is being made.

The rule has two basic requirements: 1) the statement **describes** or **explains** (an event or condition); and 2) is made **while perceiving** (or immediately after) perceiving the event or condition.

For example, a person looking out of a window might exclaim, "*Oh my God, that guy is out in the parking lot breaking car windows and rummaging through cars!*" The statement is one describing what the declarant is perceiving at the moment. Thus, a person who was present and overheard the statement when it was made by the declarant would be able to testify to what he heard the declarant say.

***Perceiving* event or condition.** The declarant must actually perceive the event he is describing or explaining. The statement cannot be concerning an event he merely heard about or was later told about. The exception only applies if the declarant perceives the event he describes or explains.

Substantial contemporaneity requirement. The critical element to this exception is that the statement must be made substantially contemporaneous with perceiving the event

63. Cole Oil & Tire Co. v. Davis, 567 So. 2d 122 (La. 1990).

64. *See* Peters v. Atlanta Intern. Ins. Co., 469 So. 2d 421 (La. Ct. App. 3d Cir. 1985); La. Code Evid., Introductory Note to Chapter 8.

Present Sense Impression Requirements:

1. The statement describes or explains an event or condition;
2. made while (or immediately after) perceiving the event or condition.

it describes.[65] The passage of time allowed between perception and the spoken words is about the amount of "time needed for **translating observations into speech**"[66]—almost instantly, as in a matter of seconds. Thus, in the example above, the person looking out of the window would be able to turn around and make the statement to someone in the room, but the exception would not apply if the declarant had to first run downstairs to tell someone about what he saw or waited for police to arrive to tell them about what he saw. The statement itself must be made contemporaneously with the observations.

Describing or explaining. Further, the statement must be one that "describes or explains" what the declarant is perceiving at that moment, not a statement that merely "relates to" what the declarant perceived, as in the case of an excited utterance.[67] So in the example above, if the person looking out of the window instead stated, "*I hope that guy doesn't break into my car*," the statement would not fit into this exception because it is not *describing* or *explaining* what the declarant is perceiving at that moment.

No excitement necessary. While oftentimes it will be an exciting event that might cause a person to describe or explain an event while he is perceiving it, there is no requirement that the event be an exciting or startling event for the exception to apply. Thus, the exception would apply if a lady were on the phone with her mother and commented, "*Oh we're not doing much tonight. John is sitting here reading the paper. The kids are on the floor playing with their toys*." Here, the declarant is describing what she is observing, while she is observing it, and thus the requirements for the exception are satisfied.

Cases on Present Sense Impression

State v. Heggar
Court of Appeal of Louisiana, Second Circuit
908 So. 2d 1245
Aug. 17, 2005

GASKINS, J.

The victim, Lydell Dabney, had recently begun a relationship with Shadonna Hunter. Ms. Hunter was formerly the paramour of the defendant; Ms. Hunter and the defendant have a five-year-old daughter. On November 3, 2003, after a series of confrontations with Ms. Hunter and Mr. Dabney, Mr. Heggar moved out of the home he shared with Ms. Hunter. On the afternoon of November 8, 2003, Mr. Dabney was at his home in Ruston, Louisiana, with one of his roommates, Mr. Kenyotta Duncan, and Mr. Duncan's child.

---

65. Force & Rault, Handbook, Art. 803(1) Author's comment (3); *See also* State v. Jones, 729 So. 2d 95, 98 (La. App. 5 Cir. 1999).

66. Buckbee v. United Gas Pipe Line Co. Inc., 561 So. 2d 76 (La. 1990).

67. See McCormick On Evidence § 271 (4th ed. 1992); *See also* State v. Price, 952 So. 2d 112 (La. Ct. App. 1st Cir. 2006).

Cellular telephone records show that at 1:51 p.m., Mr. Dabney used his cell phone to call Ms. Hunter on her cell phone. Mr. Dabney went outside and sat on the porch while he was talking to Ms. Hunter; Mr. Duncan remained inside and could not hear the conversation. During the conversation, Mr. Duncan looked out a window at the driveway and saw a black male drive up in a green Honda Accord. Mr. Heggar was known to drive a green Honda Accord, but Mr. Duncan did not know Mr. Heggar and could not identify him as the driver. The driver and Mr. Dabney began talking.

Cell phone records show that the call between Mr. Dabney and Ms. Hunter ended at 2:01 p.m. Ms. Hunter called Mr. Dabney back at 2:16 p.m. and the two talked briefly.

The admissibility of the conversations between Ms. Hunter and Mr. Dabney forms the basis of this appeal. According to Ms. Hunter, Mr. Dabney told her during their first conversation that Mr. Heggar was driving into the driveway. During the second conversation, Mr. Dabney reportedly told Ms. Hunter that he and Mr. Heggar were talking and that there was no problem. Ms. Hunter told Mr. Dabney to call her back when Mr. Heggar left. Over the objection of the defendant, the court allowed Ms. Hunter to testify to these facts.

Shortly after Mr. Dabney's second conversation with Ms. Hunter, the assailant shot Mr. Dabney eight times, killing him....

On March 12, 2004, the state filed a motion *in limine* asking the court for permission to allow Ms. Hunter to testify about the substance of her telephone conversations with Mr. Dabney just prior to his murder. The court held a hearing on the motion, and subsequently ruled that the jury could hear Ms. Hunter testify about the conversations. The defendant objected to the court's ruling. The jury convicted the defendant as charged on March 26, 2004.

... The defendant now appeals.

HEARSAY AND RIGHT OF CONFRONTATION

The defendant's single assignment of error challenges the trial court's ruling on the motion *in limine* that allowed the state to present Ms. Hunter's testimony regarding the content of her conversations with Mr. Dabney immediately prior to his murder. The defendant urges that this testimony denied his right to confront the witnesses against him.

At the hearing on the motion *in limine*, the trial court found that Ms. Hunter's testimony regarding the conversations she had with the victim immediately prior to his death was admissible as present sense impressions and was not inadmissible hearsay. La. C.E. art. 801(C) provides:

> **Hearsay.** "Hearsay" is a statement, other than one made by the declarant while testifying at the present trial or hearing, offered in evidence to prove the truth of the matter asserted.

La. C.E. art. 803(1) provides:

> The following are not excluded by the hearsay rule, even though the declarant is available as a witness:
>
> **(1) Present sense impression.** A statement describing or explaining an event or condition made while the declarant was perceiving the event or condition, or immediately thereafter.

Under a narrow, literal reading of La. C.E. art. 803(1), only a statement describing or explaining an event or condition made while perceiving the event or condition or immediately thereafter will be admissible as a present sense impression. *State v. Brown*, 618 So.2d 629

(La.App. 2d Cir.1993) Ms. Hunter's testimony is hearsay under La. C.E. art. 801 because the statement presented through her testimony is that of Mr. Dabney and because the statement was offered to prove that the person in the green Honda Accord was Mr. Heggar and not some other person. However, Ms. Hunter's testimony qualifies under a "narrow and literal reading of" La. C.E. art. 803(1) as an exception to the general rule against the admissibility of hearsay. Mr. Dabney's statement to Ms. Hunter described the arrival of Mr. Heggar as it happened. Likewise, Mr. Dabney's later statement to Ms. Hunter immediately prior to the shooting that he and Heggar were talking is a description of the event as it happened and the statements also qualify under the present sense exception to the hearsay rule.

[Court continues with Sixth Amendment Confrontation Clause issue.]

AFFIRMED.

Discussion Question

Describe what the declarant perceives as he is speaking in *Heggar*. Explain how his statement describes or explains his perception.

State v. Francois
Court of Appeal of Louisiana, Fifth Circuit
134 So. 3d 42
Jan. 31, 2014

ROBERT M. MURPHY, Judge.

On the ... night of April 28, 2011, Lorraine Harris, ... mother [of the victim], was on the phone at her home with her friend Carolyn Geary. While speaking with Ms. Harris, Ms. Geary heard loud knocking through the phone. Ms. Harris told Ms. Geary: "Somebody is knocking at the door." Ms. Harris asked Ms. Geary to remain on the phone and she relayed to Ms. Geary what was occurring and what was being said. When Ms. Harris opened the door, she recognized the visitor, whom she had seen "many times" before, as Derrick Francois, Defendant. He asked her if "Smurf" was sleeping. After checking on her son and determining that he was awake, Ms. Harris invited Defendant in. He entered, prompting Ms. Harris to say, "You have my condolences for Delast." Defendant thanked her and proceeded into Harris' bedroom where he spoke with him.

Ms. Geary testified that she could hear what Ms. Harris was saying, and could hear the other person's voice, but could not discern what the other person was saying. Ms. Harris told Ms. Geary that the visitor asked to speak to "Smurf." Ms. Geary asked who the visitor was and Ms. Harris explained that it was the brother of the boy who had been killed the day before. Ms. Harris sat on the sofa from where she could see Defendant standing in her son's room talking to her son as he was lying on his bed.

Ms. Harris observed Defendant talking calmly, asking what Harris knew about his brother's death. Then, suddenly, in a raised voice, Defendant asked Harris: "Where that n* * * *r at?" Harris replied: "I don't know, I don't know where he is." Defendant asked: "Is he in Mississippi?" As soon as Harris answered "I don't know," Ms. Harris heard a shot. Ms. Geary testified that she heard two shots—"pop pop"—over the phone and that Ms. Harris exclaimed, "He killed Smurf."

Defendant then walked out of the bedroom, put the gun to Ms. Harris' head and said, "B* * *h, shut the f* *k up." Ms. Harris dropped the phone and pleaded for her life, at which point, Defendant put the gun down and quietly walked out of the house. Ms. Harris called 911 and told the operator, "Delast's brother came here and shot [my son]." She told the operator she thought the perpetrator's name was Darius.

...

ASSIGNMENTS OF ERROR NUMBERS TWO AND THREE

In Defendant's second assignment of error, he argues that the trial court erred in denying his January 7, 2013 motion in limine, which sought to exclude as inadmissible hearsay the testimony of Ms. Geary regarding her telephone conversation with Ms. Harris on the night of Harris' murder. Defendant contends that this testimony should have been excluded because it does not fall under the present sense impression exception in La. C.E. art. 803(1), nor does it qualify as non-hearsay under La. C.E. art. 801(D)(1)(c). He further contends, in his third assignment of error, that the trial court erred in denying his motion for new trial, which also asserted that the trial court improperly admitted the hearsay testimony of Ms. Geary on the same basis. The State contends that this testimony is admissible as a present sense impression under La. C.E. art. 803(1), as well as non-hearsay under La. C.E. art. 801(D)(1)(c), and that the trial court did not err in denying both Defendant's motion in limine and his motion for new trial.

...

Hearsay is "a statement, other than one made by the declarant while testifying at the present trial or hearing, offered in evidence to prove the truth of the matter asserted." La. C.E. art. 801(C). Hearsay evidence is inadmissible except as specified in the Louisiana Code of Evidence or other legislation. La. C.E. art. 802.

Pursuant to La. C.E. art. 803(1), a statement describing or explaining an event or condition made while the declarant was perceiving the event or condition, or immediately thereafter, is not excluded as hearsay, even though the declarant is available as a witness. In determining whether a statement qualifies as a present sense impression exception to the hearsay rule, the critical factor is whether the statement was made while the declarant was perceiving the event or immediately thereafter. *State v. Jones,* 98–1055 (La.App. 5 Cir. 2/23/99), 729 So.2d 95, 98.

...

In the instant case, the evidence established that Ms. Harris told Ms. Geary that Delast Francois' brother was at her door just as Defendant was standing at Ms. Harris' door. Ms. Harris' statement was made immediately after she permitted Defendant to enter her home, and as such, we find that the statement falls within the present sense impression exception to the general rule of hearsay under La. C.E. art. 803(1). Because our review of the record shows that the trial court admitted Ms. Geary's testimony on the basis of La. C.E. art. 803(1), and not on the basis of La. C.E. art. 801(D)(1)(c), Defendant's argument that Ms. Geary's testimony is not admissible under La. C.E. art. 801(D)(1)(c) is moot....

Discussion Question

The critical factor for a present sense impression is whether the statement is made substantially contemporaneous with what the declarant is perceiving. The court notes that some of the statements in *Francois* are being made after the declarant perceives them. How much time may pass for a statement to still be considered substantially contemporaneous with the perception? How much time passed in *Francois*?

§ 5.5 References and Additional Authority on Present Sense Impression [La. C.E. art. 803(1)]

1. La. C.E. art. 803(1) and Official Comments
2. Force & Rault, Handbook on Louisiana Evidence Law, Art. 803(1) Author's Comments (West Publishing 2014)
3. Harges & Jones, Louisiana Evidence, Art. 803(1) Author's Comments (West Publishing 2014)
4. 19 La. Civ. L. Treatise, Evidence And Proof § 10.13 (2nd ed.)
5. **Admitted as Present Sense Impression**: *State v. Smith*, 285 So. 2d 240 (La. 1973) (In a case involving an armed robbery of a dairy truck, the driver was locked in the freezing compartment for about thirty seconds. Upon exiting the freezer compartment, a woman handed him a piece of paper with a license number. The woman did not testify, but the paper was introduced into evidence. The court held that "the fact that the statement is made contemporaneously with the act or immediately thereafter implies reliability since the declarant is unlikely to have had an opportunity to form a purpose to mistake his observations."); *State v. Carvin*, 308 So. 2d 757 (La. 1975) (holding that deputy's statement that motor was too cool for the automobile to have been used in the shooting should have been admitted as present sense impression); *State v. Dillard*, 55 So. 3d 56 (La. Ct. App. 2d Cir. 2010) (holding that declarant's statement giving description of suspect and his location was present sense impression when made it to police on the telephone while declarant pursued suspect in car while he was escaping on his bicycle from robbery).
6. **Not made "while perceiving or immediately thereafter"**: *State v. Everett*, 96 So. 3d 605 (La. App. 4th Cir. 2012) (holding that statements made at a hospital fifteen minutes after a shooting were not within the time needed to translate "observation into speech"; since the statement was not made while perceiving the shooting or immediately after, the present sense impression exception is not applicable); *Carbon v. Allstate Ins. Co.*, 701 So. 2d 462 (La. Ct. App. 1st Cir. 1997) (statements by bystanders were not contemporaneous with event described, and were thus not a present sense impression).

§ 5.6 Excited Utterance [La. C.E. art. 803(2)]

Applicable Code Articles

The following are not excluded by the hearsay rule, even though the declarant is available as a witness:

* * *

(2) Excited utterance. A statement relating to a startling event or condition made while the declarant was under the stress of excitement caused by the event or condition.

* * *

In some instances, a person who has just experienced a startling event might hysterically make a statement related to the event, such as, "*Oh my God! I just got robbed!*" Such statements are typically deemed to be trustworthy and are thus excluded from the hearsay rule

Excited Utterance Exception Requirements:

1. Startling event or condition;
2. Statement "relating to" startling event or condition; and
3. Made while still under stress of startling event.

under the excited utterance exception. The excited utterance exception to the hearsay rule is contained in Article 803(2) and excludes a statement from the hearsay ban relating to a startling event or condition made while the declarant was under the stress of excitement caused by the event or condition. The exception is premised on the fact that a person who is under the stress of a startling event lacks the capacity for reflection and fabrication. Like the present sense impression, since he has just experienced the event, he does not likely have memory issues either. The key to this exception is the spontaneity of the statement in the face of the startling event.[68]

This exception has three primary requirements: 1) **startling event** or condition; 2) statement **"relating to"** a startling event or condition; and 3) made while **"still under stress"** of a startling event or condition.

Startling requirement. This exception requires a "startling" event that triggers the statement. There's no specific type of event required, provided it is one that is sufficiently startling to render the declarant's "normal reflective thought process inoperative."[69] In other words, the circumstances should be such that the declarant would not likely have had the capacity and calmness to reflect and fabricate his words before speaking. Ordinarily, events such as observing a car accident, seeing a crime in progress or an unexpected or tragic event like seeing a child drowning would be the types of events that might be sufficient. While the determination of whether the event was sufficiently startling is a preliminary question to be determined by the trial judge,[70] essentially the event would be sufficient if it would make the average person exclaim, "*Oh my God!*"

While under stress of event. Additionally, the statement must be made while the declarant is still under the stress of excitement caused by the startling event. The court looks to all the surrounding circumstances to determine whether the person is still under the stress of the startling event when the statement was made, including: the person themselves, the time lapsed, whether the statement was made in response to questioning, whether it was self-serving, whether it was an expansion beyond a description of the event and into past or future facts, and whether, between the event and the statement, the declarant performed tasks that required a reflective thought process.[71]

The most important factor is the **time span between the startling event and the statement**. The court will consider whether the time span was of sufficient duration for restora-

---

68. Force & Rault, HANDBOOK, Art. 803(2) Author's comment (1); *See also* State v. Mays, 612 So. 2d 1040 (La. Ct. App. 2d Cir. 1993).

69. State v. Reaves, 569 So. 2d 650 (La. Ct. App. 2d Cir.1990).

70. Force & Rault, HANDBOOK, Art. 803(2) Author's comment (1); *See also* LA. CODE EVID. art. 104(A).

71. *See* State v. Griffin, 30 So. 2d 1039 (La. Ct. App. 2d Cir. 2010), *quoting*, State v. Henderson, 362 So. 2d 1358 (La.1978); State v. Jasper, 28,187 (La.App. 2d Cir.6/26/96), 677 So. 2d 553, 563, *writ denied*, 96–1897 (La.2/21/97), 688 So. 2d 521.

tion of the thought process.[72] However, as noted in *State v. Brown*[73] below, in some instances the time might be suspended such as if the person is unconscious or disoriented. When the person comes to, although more time than usual might have passed, the person would be deemed to still be under the stress of the startling event since he would not have had an opportunity for reflection and fabrication before making the statement. Thus, if immediately after coming out of a coma a person exclaimed, "*Bo did this to me,*" the statement would likely be deemed to conform to the exception.

If the court finds that the declarant is no longer under the stress of the event when the statement is made, then the exception will not apply, since the declarant would have had an opportunity to reflect on the situation and possibly fabricate his statement.

Relating to requirement. The final requirement for this exception is that the statement "relate to" the startling event or condition that triggered it. This is much broader than in the case of the present sense impression, which must be a statement "describing or explaining" the event the declarant perceives. Here, the declarant's statement can be anything *related to* the event, provided the statement is a "spontaneous reaction to the occurrence or event and not a statement that is a result of reflective thought."[74]

For example, if the startling event was a building that was on fire, the declarant might exclaim, "*We've been telling them to fix the faulty wiring in this old building! Let's get out of here!*" While the statement isn't describing anything, it is "related to" the event that caused the excitement, made while the declarant is still under the stress of the event, thus the exception applies.

Case on Excited Utterance

State v. Brown
Supreme Court of Louisiana
395 So. 2d 1301
March 2, 1981

COLE, Associate Justice Ad Hoc.

At trial, the state adduced the following evidence. The victim, Carolee Crowder, was separated from her husband and she was living with Randy Brown, the brother of the defendant Robert Brown. Though there appeared to have been no problems between the Browns (Randy, Robert, and Robert's wife) and Carolee, there is some suggestion that Carolee's estranged husband was an irritation and Robert felt he might cause a problem for his brother. On April 23, 1979, Randy and Carolee quarreled and he left the house. Shortly thereafter, Carolee left in her own car, stopped and bought beer, then encountered the defendant, Robert, and his wife. Robert and Carolee argued, agreed to discuss the situation later, and then went their separate ways. After another brief stop, Carolee made her way to the farm where the Browns lived; it was approximately 4:30 p.m. When Carolee drove up to the Brown's house, Randy came out and the two talked. Randy returned inside and Carolee, still outside, could hear Robert arguing with Randy, trying to turn him against

---

72. State v. Jasper, 28,187 (La. App. 2d Cir.6/26/96), 677 So. 2d 553, 563, *writ denied,* 96–1897 (La.2/21/97), 688 So. 2d 521.

73. State v. Brown, 395 So. 2d 1301 (La. 1981).

74. State v. Henderson, 362 So. 2d 1358 (La. 1978).

Carolee. When Carolee threw a beer bottle at one of the brother's cars, Randy came out of the house and began slapping her. Robert followed, exclaiming that Randy was not hitting her hard enough. Randy punched Carolee as she tried to get back into her car. Randy stopped her and continued to wrestle with and beat her while Robert stood only a few feet away, yelling. Suddenly Randy shouted, "He's got that damn gun," and the victim heard three shots. She then heard Robert's wife shout, "Robert Lee, bring that gun back in this house," and heard two more shots. The next thing the victim could remember was being helped into the hospital emergency room at 8:45 p.m. She did not see the shots fired. Until told by the hospital personnel, the victim did not realize there was a puncture wound to her forehead which had been caused by a bullet that pierced into her skull and entered her brain.

Nurse Lois Taylor was on duty in the emergency room and testified the victim was stable and responsive, considering her injury, and Carolee told her "Randy beat her" and "Robert shot her." The victim also made similar statements to others, including police officers. Based on Carolee's statements, Randy, who had driven her to the hospital, was arrested, as was Robert, who was taken into custody later that night at his residence.

... Though no handgun was found at the Brown residence, Mrs. Brown later gave the police a .22 caliber pistol. Since the bullet could not be retrieved from the victim's brain, and in any event was shattered, no tests were run to determine if the .22 was in fact the weapon used in the shooting.

When admitted to the hospital the victim was said to be suffering numerous bruises and contusions about her face but the main injury was said to have been a close gunshot wound to the right frontal region of the forehead. The gunshot left powder burns on the victim's forehead indicating that it was fired from only inches away. She survived but due to her injury she required lengthy hospitalization and continues to suffer from partial paralysis....

ASSIGNMENT OF ERROR NO. 2

By this assignment defendant contends the trial court erred in admitting hearsay testimony.

The testimony to which defendant objects was introduced into evidence during the examination of Ms. Lois Taylor, a nurse who had attended the victim at the hospital emergency room after the shooting. After questioning the witness about her treatment of the victim and the taking of the victim's medical history, the following occurred:

"Q. All right. Did you ask her anything else after that?

A. I said, 'Can you tell me what happened to you?'

Q. Repeat again, if you will, what's the last question that you asked her?

A. 'Can you tell me what happened to you?'

Q. And what was her response to that?

A. She said, 'Randy beat me and Randy's brother, Robert, shot me.'"

Before this testimony was elicited, the trial judge, after argument of counsel and with the jury removed, had declared it admissible as part of the res gestae exception to the hearsay rule.

The testimony of Ms. Taylor was evidence of an out-of-court statement by the victim and was offered as an assertion to show the truth of matters asserted therein, i. e. that Robert had shot her, resting for its value upon the credibility of the out-of-court asserter. The testimony thus constitutes hearsay. Hearsay is generally inadmissible except as provided by statute or one of the well-recognized hearsay exceptions....

The statement is also admissible as an "excited utterance." Under this hearsay exception, statements made under the influence of a startling event are deemed admissible, provided there was an occurrence or event sufficiently startling to render normal reflective thought processes of an observer inoperative and the statement was a spontaneous reaction to the occurrence or the event and not the result of reflective thought. In *State v. Henderson*, supra, at 1362, this Court examined the excited utterance as follows:

> "Many factors enter into determining whether in fact the second requirement has been fulfilled and whether a declarant was at the time of an offered statement under the influence of an exciting event. Probably the most important of these is the time factor. In this connection, the trial court must determine whether the interval between the event and the statement was long enough to permit a subsidence of emotional upset and a restoration of a reflective thought process. Several additional factors which may indicate that the statement was the result of reflective thought, but which do not automatically justify exclusion, are as follows: Evidence that the statement was self-serving or made in response to an inquiry; Expansion of the excited utterance beyond a description of the exciting event into past facts or the future; Proof that the declarant performed tasks requiring reflective thought processes between the event and the statement....

Here, as noted above, there was an appreciable lapse of time, but the victim testified she had been beaten and shot, and upon her arrival at the hospital, she was still disoriented, had been unconscious, and was obviously suffering from the trauma of the attack. Given her apparent mental and physical condition, especially the fact that, until told by hospital personnel, she did not know she had a bullet wound to the forehead, we find the time lapse was not long enough for her emotional state to diminish, or long enough to allow her to reflect on the events of the battery. Though the statement was in response to an inquiry from Ms. Taylor, the question was merely part of the patient's examination and not leading and is thus admissible as an excited utterance. The fact the statement is made in response to an inquiry does not automatically defeat this exception to the hearsay rule. This assignment is without merit....

Discussion Question

If a person is unconscious, how much time do you think the court might allow and still find him under the stress of the startling event or condition? A few hours? Days? Months? What underlying policy supports this rationale? Do such statements retain their reliability?

Key Points

The key points to keep in mind regarding Excited Utterance and Present Sense Impression.

1. **Exited Utterance**—a statement relating to a startling event or condition made while the declarant is still under the stress of excitement caused by the event or condition.
   a. **Requirements:**
      i. the statement describes or explains (an event or condition); and
      ii. made while (or immediately after) perceiving the event or condition.

2. **Present Sense Impression** — a statement describing or explaining an event or condition made while perceiving it or immediately thereafter.
   a. **Requirements**:
      i. startling event or condition;
      ii. statement "relating to" startling event or condition; and
      iii. made while still under stress of startling event.

Problems on Excited Utterance and Present Sense Impression

PROBLEM 5-50. Dale and Ronnie are on trial for robbing The Corner Store. In order to prove identity and exactly what occurred during the robbery, the prosecution puts their mother on the stand who testifies that she was on the phone with her daughter who had just inadvertently driven up to The Corner Store and said to her, "*Mama, Dale and Ronnie are robbing The Corner Store. Dale is holding a gun to the cashier's head and Ronnie is loading cigarettes into a garbage bag.*" The defense objects that the statement is hearsay. How should the court rule and why?

PROBLEM 5-51. As the professor was standing in front of class and happened to glance out of the window, she commented, "*There's a guy out there looking into car windows and breaking into the cars. Someone call the police.*" The police arrived and arrested Patrick during the commission of the crime. The teacher is not available to testify at Patrick's trial, so one of the students is called to testify to what the teacher said in order to prove that Patrick committed the burglary. The defense objects that the statement is hearsay. How should the court rule on the objection and why?

PROBLEM 5-52. Tim was involved in a fight on the bus. His sister watched the whole thing before the bus driver stopped the bus and broke it up. A few stops later, when Tim and his sister were let off the bus at their home, his sister immediately ran into the house and told their mother, "*Mom, I saw the whole thing. He kept pushing and teasing Tim, and then he hit him in the back of the head. Tim finally got up and charged him, and punched him back. He really defended himself. You should have seen him.*" During Tim's juvenile proceedings, could the mother testify to what Tim's sister told her about what happened to help prove that Tim was fighting in self-defense? How should the court rule and why?

PROBLEM 5-53. Howard was taking a constitutional law examination and observed someone on the row in front of him cheating when the teacher stepped out of the classroom. When the teacher returned, Howard asked her to step outside and told her, "*That student in the front row was cheating when you left the classroom. He looked at a piece of balled up paper with answers on it and put the paper back in his wallet before you returned.*" She immediately removed the student from the classroom, and the student was eventually expelled. In an action against the school by the cheating student, can the teacher testify to what Howard told her to prove the student was cheating? Why or why not?

PROBLEM 5-54. Sissy was in the truck with her boyfriend Hank who had become upset with her for dancing with another man at the nightclub. Sissy called 911 while they were in the truck heading home from the club and stated, "*He's driving like a maniac. He's driving the wrong way on one-ways and swerving through traffic. Help me!*" Hank subsequently crashes the truck. He lives, but Sissy dies. Can the prosecution play Sissy's 911 call to help prove that Hank was driving recklessly at the time of the crash to help prove negligent homicide? Why or why not?

PROBLEM 5-55. Sid was in the crowd at a concert when she heard someone say, "*Hey, this security guard is back here filling up water balloons and throwing them on stage.*" Immediately after that, someone threw several large water balloons on stage striking the drummer and a fight erupted at the concert. The security guard was arrested for throwing the balloons. At the trial, the prosecution wants Sid to testify to what she heard to help prove the security guard threw the water balloons on stage. The defendant objects that the statement is hearsay. How should the court rule and why?

PROBLEM 5-56. Gunner was having lunch with his fiancée at a small café on the corner when he observed an accident over his date's shoulder. When the cars crashed, she looked around to see what happened, and he immediately told her, "*That truck went through the intersection on a red light and hit that little car.*" Gunner did not want to be involved, but his fiancée was called to the stand by the victims of the accident to testify to what Gunner told her after the accident. The defense objects that the statement is hearsay. How should the court rule and why?

PROBLEM 5-57. Bo was on trial for violating several deer hunting regulations arising out of a deer hunting trip that he took with his two young children. He denies going on the trip, hunting, or shooting any deer. During a search of his phone, LDWF located a video where Bo recorded his 7-year-old daughter on the phone with Bo's wife (the little girl's mother) on a camping trip. The little girl states, "*Mommy, mommy, daddy just shot a deer! It was awesome! The deer just came out, daddy aimed, and wham! The deer was down!*" Bo objects that the video is hearsay and inadmissible. Should the court allow the video? Why or why not?

PROBLEM 5-58. Phillip saw a young boy push an old lady down, grab her purse and run towards the subway. Phillip exclaimed, "*Somebody stop that man. He has the lady's purse!*" and began chasing him as another person called the police. Phillip never caught up to the thief, but stopped to rest on a bench about a mile from where the incident occurred. About a half hour later, the police officer finally found Phillip looking rather disappointed about not catching the thief and asked him to recount what he'd seen. Phillip stated, "*This young skinny boy walked up behind this old lady wearing a brown overcoat, pushed her down, took her purse and ran back this way. He was young, like late teens, really skinny, and had a limp.*" In a trial against the robber, the police officer attempts to testify to what Phillip told him to help prove who committed the robbery. The defense objects that the statement is hearsay. How should the court rule? Can someone testify that they overheard Phillips first statement that he made before chasing after the robber?

PROBLEM 5-59. Mona was in the truck with her boyfriend Thumper who was upset with Mona for dancing with another man at the nightclub, so he began driving erratically the wrong way down one-way streets and swerving through cars. Mona screams at him to stop and says, "*Lord, this boy is gonna kill me. Lord, please forgive me for my sins. I'm so sorry for stealing that computer from work, and for fudging my timesheets.*" They all make it home fine and, in revenge, Thumper calls Mona's boss and tells him what Mona said. Will Mona's statements be admissible as an excited utterance in proceedings against Mona for defrauding her employees? Why or why not?

PROBLEM 5-60. Keira was raped and badly beaten by a man who broke into her home and left her for dead. Keira's co-worker discovered her the next morning when she swung by to pick her up for work. Keira was unconscious, but breathing and had a pulse. Keira was taken to the hospital and remained in a coma and clinging to life for about two months. When she awakened from the coma, she immediately stated while crying in the presence of her nurse, "*The maintenance man. Jim, the maintenance man, came into my* *apartment and raped me.*" Can the nurse testify to what Keira said when she first came out of the coma? Why or why not?

PROBLEM 5-61. In the case of *State of Florida v. George Zimmerman*, Zimmerman is accused of murdering 16-year-old Trayvon Martin. Zimmerman claims the murder was in self-defense. The prosecution seeks to prove that the murder was not in self-defense, and that instead, prior to killing Martin, Zimmerman profiled him, chased him down with a weapon, and after Martin attempted to protect himself from the would-be attacker, he was shot and killed. Immediately prior to the shooting, the victim Martin was on the phone with a friend of his named Rachel. In order to prove its case, the prosecution calls Rachel to the stand to testify to the conversation that she was having with Martin immediately prior to and leading up to the shooting to prove that Martin was in fact chased and gunned down by Zimmerman. Below is an excerpt of the direct examination of Rachel. Please state what your responses would be to an objection that the following line numbers in the transcript are **hearsay: 2a; 4a; 6a; 8a; 9a; 10a; 11a; 12a; 14a; 18a; and 20a.** How will the court likely rule and why?

1. **At some point did Trayvon Martin describe going back to the neighborhood where he was staying at (after leaving store)?**

   a. *Yes.*

2. **Did he describe what was happening?**

   a. *Yes. He said a man was watching him.*

3. **When he told you that a man was watching him, did you say anything to him?**

   a. *I asked him what the man looked like.*

4. **After you asked him that, did he say anything else to you or did you say anything back to him?**

   a. *He said he looked like a "creepy a** creep."*

5. **What did he say to you after that?**

   a. *He told me the man was looking at him.*

6. **What else did he say?**

   a. *He said he was going to try to lose him.*

7. **Mr. Martin said he was gonna try to lose him?**

   a. *Yes.*

8. **How did he say he was gonna lose him?**

   a. *He said he was gonna leave the mailing area.*

9. **What did you take that to mean?**

   a. *He was going home.*

10. **Did you say anything else to him?**

    a. *I told him he could be a rapist.*

11. **And what did he say?**

    a. *He said don't play with me like that.*

12. **Then what happened?**

    a. *I told him to run.*

13. **When you told him to run, what did Mr. Martin say?**

a. He said, no, I'm almost by my father's fiancée's house.

14. Then what did he say?

a. He said he was about to run from the back.

15. What did you do next?

a. The phone just shut off, then I called back.

16. When you called him back, did you get him?

a. Yes.

17. What did either of you say when you called back?

a. I asked him where he was, he said at the back of his daddy's fiancée's house.

18. What happened next?

*a. A couple seconds later, Trayvon said, "Oh, sh*t! The 'n-word' is behind me."*

19. Then what?

a. I heard him say, "Why you following me?"

20. Did you hear anything else?

a. Yes, then I heard a deep voice say, "What you doing around here?"

§ 5.6 References and Additional Authority on Excited Utterances [La. C.E. art. 803(2)]

1. La. C.E. art. 803(2) and Official Comments
2. Force & Rault, Handbook on Louisiana Evidence Law Art. 803(2) Author's Comments (West Publishing 2014)
3. Harges & Jones, Louisiana Evidence Art. 803(2) Author's Comments (West Publishing 2014)
4. 19 La. Civ. L. Treatise, Evidence And Proof § 10.14 (2nd ed.)
5. **Admitted statements as Excited Utterance**: *State v. Dalton*, 759 So. 2d 180 (La. App. 4th Cir. 2000) (While suspect was being handcuffed, a glass pipe was dropped. At that time, the defendant's husband shouted, "She on that sh*t. She on that sh*t. She's always smoking crack. That's the problem." The court found that when the defendant dropped the crack pipe to the floor, her husband's response was a spontaneous and reflexive response.); *State v. Falkins*, 146 So. 3d 838 (La. App. 4th Cir. 2014) (holding that statements admissible as excited utterances when made by declarant during 911 call while the defendant was kicking in her front door; declarant began crying and begging for the police, then stated that the intruder was "dragging her sister up the street"); *State v. Etienne*, 649 So. 2d 1230 (La. Ct. App. 3d Cir. 1995) (holding that statements of three people who appeared hysterical and approached officers within five to ten minutes of shooting were properly admitted as excited utterances); *State v. King*, 604 So. 2d 661, 667 (La. Ct. App. 1st Cir. 1992) (holding that an edited version of an audio tape of an emergency 911 call reporting multiple shootings was admissible under the excited utterance exception because the declarants were severely traumatized from being shot).
6. **Still under stress:** *Hacs v. Romero*, 977 So. 2d 196 (La. Ct. App. 3d Cir. 2008) (statement to police officer twenty minutes after car accident admitted as an excited utterance

when declarant was suffering from multiple injuries, unconsciousness, and an elevated alcohol level sufficiently limited time for reflective thought); *State v. Crawford*, 672 So. 2d 197 (La. Ct. App. 3d Cir. 1996) (holding that rape victim's statement made 45 minutes after victim had been raped at knife point was admissible excited utterance); *State v. Richardson*, 71 So. 3d 492 (La. Ct. App. 2d Cir. 2011) (Victim was asleep in her bedroom when defendants allegedly broke into her house robbed and raped her. Victim was unconscious for unknown period of time before she stumbled outside to get help and told her neighbor that she had been attacked. Court held that considering her age, the perceived length of the event, her state of mind and demeanor when she reported the events to her neighbor, she was likely still under the stress of excitement caused by the startling events.); *State v. Blanche*, 92 So. 3d 508 (La. Ct. App. 2d Cir. 2012) (holding that victim's statement to police 40 minutes after being shot in the neck identifying the defendant as shooter admitted as an excited utterance because during the 40 minutes victim lost consciousness a few times, ran into a ditch multiple times trying to drive, and was found lying in a carport bleeding, and thus had not regained reflective thought).

7. **What constitutes startling event:** *State v. Odoms*, 815 So. 2d 224 (La. Ct. App. 5th Cir. 2002) (holding that statement made by declarant in the midst of a forced entry by police into her home was an excited utterance); *State v. Bagneris*, 830 So. 2d 1047 (La. Ct. App. 4th Cir. 2002) (holding that an inmate's attack on deputy was a sufficient startling event).
8. **Declarant no longer under stress of event or condition/too much time passed:** *State v. Reaves*, 569 So. 2d 650 (La. Ct. App. 2d Cir. 1990) (finding that trial court erred in finding statements excited utterances because several hours had passed by the time statements made and the time in which the victim was attacked at knifepoint and raped); *State v. Winn*, 705 So. 2d 1271 (La. Ct. App. 4th Cir. 1998) (holding that statement of paralyzed, formerly comatose shooting victim not admissible as an excited utterance because it was the product of years of reflective thought).
9. **Admitted excited utterances even though delayed due to incapacity or inability to communicate**: *State v. Griffin*, 30 So. 3d 1039. (La. Ct. App. 2d Cir. 2010) (Defendant beat an 85-year-old man at his home and took his money. When the man's daughter and police arrived, he told his daughter, "He's inside. He's inside." The court found the man's statements to his daughter were excited utterances even though he could not talk immediately upon arrival since the statements were made immediately upon his ability to talk.).

§ 5.7 Then Existing Mental Condition (State of Mind) [La. C.E. art. 803(3)]

Applicable Code Articles

The following are not excluded by the hearsay rule, even though the declarant is available as a witness:

* * *

(3) Then existing mental, emotional, ... condition. A statement of the declarant's then existing state of mind, emotion, ... (such as intent, plan, motive, design, mental feeling, ...), offered to prove the declarant's then existing condition or his future action. A statement of memory or belief, however, is not admissible to prove the fact remembered or believed unless it relates to the execution, revocation, identification, or terms of declarant's testament.

* * *

Article 803(3) contains an exception for statements of the declarant's "then existing mental, emotional, or physical condition." This exception is also referred to as the **"state of mind"** exception to the hearsay rule. While this exception refers to both ***mental*** and ***physical*** conditions, for purposes of this casebook, the different aspects of the rule will be handled separately. This section addresses mental conditions. Statements regarding physical conditions are addressed in § 5.8. The **"then existing mental condition"** exception excludes statements from the hearsay ban that are expressions of the declarant's state of mind at the moment in which the statement is made.

The rule is broad, including a wide range of expressions of the declarant's emotions, sensations, or other mental feelings, such as his **intentions, plans, desires, likes, dislikes,** etc. For example, the rule would include statements such as, "*I am going to . . .*," "*I want . . .*," "*I love . . .*," "*I hate . . .*," "*I admire . . .*," "*I'm happy*," "*I'm sad*," "*I'm lonely*." All of these statements are expressions of a declarant's mental condition at the moment in which the statement is being made. They do not include past mental states, such as "*I didn't love you when I married you.*" The statement must be the declarant's *then* existing mental condition to conform to the exception.

Underlying policy. This exception is premised upon the fact that as opposed to other types of evidence of a person's state of mind, a person's own statement regarding his feelings at a particular time is the best available evidence and the only *direct* evidence of the person's state of mind. Further, because of the requirement that only statements concerning a person's *then* existing mental state are included in the rule, the statements do not rely on memory.

The requirements of the rule are: 1) must be a statement of a person's then existing mental condition; 2) offered to prove the declarant's then existing mental condition or his own future action. The rule excludes statement of memory or belief from being offered to prove the thing remembered or believed except as it relates to testaments.

Must be then existing mental condition (not past mental state). A key component of the rule is that the statement must be one that expresses the declarant's *then* existing mental state—his mental state at the exact moment the statement is being made. As stated above, the rule encompasses statements such as, "*I plan to go to Texas*" or "*I'm about to head home*," because they are the declarant's current plans and intentions. Statements concerning a mental state from some time in the past such as, "*I was very upset yesterday*" or "*I didn't mean to kill him*," are not statements of the declarant's then existing mental condition. Statements concerning a person's past mental feelings are referred to as statements of "memory" in this article, since the declarant is required to recall how he felt at some time in the past. Statements of memory are not included under this rule.

Statements of memory and belief excluded. As discussed above, statements of memory are not included in the exception and may not be offered to prove the thing remembered.

State of Mind Exception Requirements:

1. A statement of a person's then existing mental condition; and
2. Offered to prove the declarant's then existing mental condition or his own future action.

Such statements are not as reliable as statements of present mental conditions, since the declarant is required to remember how he felt at that time. Thus, if a person stated, "*I didn't love my husband when I married him,*" a statement recalling her mental state at that time, it could not be offered under this exception to prove the thing remembered—that at that time the person didn't love her husband.

Similarly, the rule excludes statements of *belief* from being offered to prove the thing believed. Like statements of memory, statements of belief are not reliable. While a statement of belief is in fact a person's mental state, i.e., "*I think my kids are conspiring to kill me,*" the statement is not trustworthy to prove the thing believed since the person has no first-hand knowledge of the assertion—he only *believes* it. Thus, the statement could not be offered under this exception to prove the thing believed, i.e., that the kids were in fact conspiring to kill their mother. There are two points to keep in mind here, though, as it relates to statements of memory or belief.

1. **Statement of memory or belief admissible for other purposes/non-hearsay.** While a statement of memory or belief cannot be offered to prove the "thing remembered or believed" (that kids were conspiring to kill mother), it may be offered for other purposes, such as to explain why mother moved away from home. In such a case, this would be an example of non-hearsay state of mind, since in that case the statement would be offered only to show the state of mind of the declarant, not to prove the truth of the matter asserted.
2. **May be admissible as it relates to testaments.**[75] An exception in the rule, where a statement of memory or belief may be offered to prove the thing remembered or believed, is when the statement relates to the execution, revocation, identification, or terms of declarant's testaments, or wills. Thus, in an action to challenge a will brought by the decedent's adult children who were all excluded, evidence could be offered that shortly before he passed away he stated that he never wanted to have children to prove that he in fact, never wanted kids. While the statement is one of memory, how the decedent felt at some time in the past, it can be offered to prove the thing remembered since it relates to a testament.

May be offered to prove declarant's future action. Further, under this article, a statement may be offered, not only to prove that the declarant actually had the mental condition expressed by him at the time he expressed it; but his statement may also be offered to prove the declarant's future action, i.e., that he acted in conformity with his intentions. For example, if a person says, "*I think I'm going to Texas tomorrow,*" his statement may be offered to prove that he not only planned to go to Texas, but that he actually went to Texas. Thus, if the man went missing, his statement could be offered to prove that he likely went to Texas, since that was his intention. Keep in mind however, that the statement

75. Shephard v. U.S., 290 U.S. 96, 54 S. Ct. 22 (1933).

may only be offered to prove the *future* action of the declarant, not past conduct.[76] The exception is said to be forward-looking.

Federal Rules of Evidence Distinction — May not be offered to prove future action of third party. While this exception may be offered to prove the future action of the declarant, the statement may not be offered to prove the future action of a third party.[77] For example, if the declarant stated, "*Frank and I are going to Texas tomorrow,*" the statement may not be offered to prove that Frank went to Texas. It may only be offered to prove the future action of the declarant. These statements are not as reliable as it pertains to the future actions of third parties who did not make the statements, thus, under Louisiana law they are excluded for that purpose. However, this is a major difference from Federal Rule of Evidence 803(3), where a declarant's words may be offered to prove both the future action of the declarant as well as of a third party.[78]

State of mind must be at issue. Just as we pointed out with respect to non-hearsay state of mind, to be admissible, the declarant's state of mind must be at issue, or otherwise relevant in the case. However, the declarant's state of mind need not be an ultimate issue in the case to be admissible.[79]

Hearsay State of Mind vs. Non-Hearsay State of Mind. This exception is often confused with non-hearsay state of mind discussed in § 5.2.4 and § 5.2.5, *supra*. In some instances a person makes a statement that expresses his actual state of mind at that moment, for example, "*I'm afraid of my husband*" — a statement expressing fear of husband. If the statement is offered to prove *that* then existing state of mind, by definition it is hearsay and would fall into this exception.

In other instances, a person can make a statement that is *not* an actual expression of his present state of mind, but his state of mind can be *inferred* from his statement or from a statement made to him. For example, if a man is told, "*I'm having an affair with your wife,*" it may be inferred that his motive for killing the speaker was that he believed the declarant was having an affair with his wife. In this case, the statement is not being offered to prove the matter asserted, that the speaker is having an affair with the man's wife, so the statement is not hearsay. But since it is helping to prove the hearer's state of mind, it is referred to as non-hearsay state of mind.[80]

A statement that is an actual expression of one's state of mind, offered to prove the declarant's state of mind, is hearsay and falls under this exception. A statement that asserts a fact other than a person's state of mind, from which their state of mind may be *inferred*, is not hearsay and is referred to as non-hearsay state of mind. This concept is illustrated below.

---

76. *See* Force & Rault, HANDBOOK , Art. 803(3) Author's Note (8); *See also* State v. Holland, 544 So. 2d 461 (La. Ct. App. 2d Cir. 1989).

77. LA. CODE EVID. art. 803(3) Official Comment (b); *See also* State v. Weedon, 342 So. 2d 642 (La. 1977).

78. *See, e.g.* United State v. Pheaster, 544 F.2d 353, 374–80 (9th Cir. 1976), Cert. denied, 429 U.S. 1099, 97 S.Ct. 1118 (1977). *See also* Goode & Wellborn, COURTROOM EVIDENCE HANDBOOK, FED. R. EVID 803(3) Author's Comment (8) (West Publishing 2010–2011).

79. LA. CODE EVID. art. 803(3) Official Comment (c); *See also* State v. Doze, 384 So. 2d 351 (La. 1980).

80. *See* Force & Rault, HANDBOOK, Art. 803(3) Author's Note (3).

Hearsay State of Mind
A direct expression of the declarant's state of mind

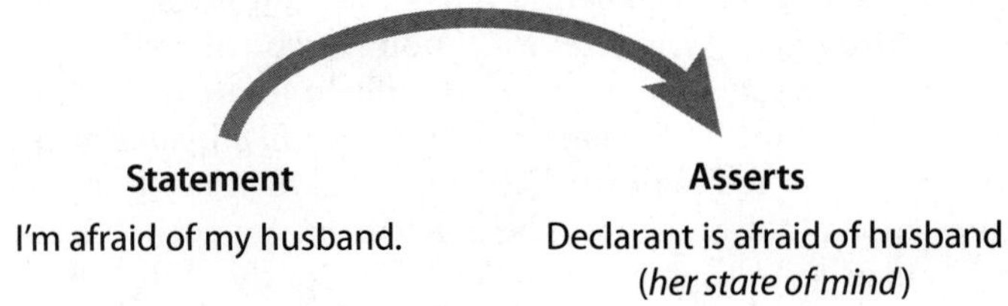

Non-Hearsay State of Mind
Reqires an *inference* of the declarant's state of mind

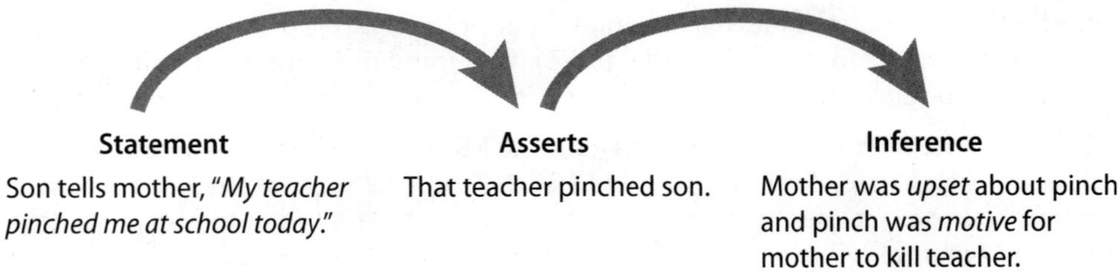

PROBLEM 5-62. Distinguish Hearsay State of Mind vs. Non-Hearsay State of Mind. In each of the following statements, identify whether the statement is an example of non-hearsay state of mind or an example of hearsay state of mind. Explain.

a. Jim is on trial for killing his fiancée Kelly. He claims she ran off with another man while she was living in Paris with him. Kelly's mother will testify for the prosecution that before Kelly left with Jim to move to France, she said, "*I love him more than life itself, mama.*" The prosecution wants to show that Kelly loved Jim way too much to have run off with another man.

b. No one has seen Becky since the Monday before Thanksgiving. Her boyfriend has been accused of kidnapping her. He would like Becky's mother to testify that the week before she went missing Becky told her, "*I'm going to Dallas this weekend for the football game,*" to show that Becky went to Dallas and may still be there.

c. Luke was missing. His friend will testify that on their way home from school last week, Luke stated, "*If my parents see these grades, they will kill me.*"

d. In his defense of murdering his wife, George would like for his wife's best friend to testify that only days before she was found shot in the head, she told her, "*I'm sad and depressed.*" George would like to offer the statement to prove that his wife was so depressed that she killed herself.

e. Neighbor will testify that two days before Jill went missing, Jill told her, "*I'm afraid of my daughter.*" Will the statement be admissible against Jill's daughter in her trial for killing her mother?

f. The hotel concierge will testify that as soon as J.R. brought Candy into the hotel for the weekend, she stated, "*Wow! I like this place.*" J.R. would like to offer the statement in his trial for kidnapping Candy to show that Candy was enjoying her stay and was not being held against her will.

g. After selecting Amanda as the new Strawberry Festival Queen, one of the judges testified that she overhead Amanda's mother telling another judge, "*I will have something for you that you'll really like if my daughter wins tonight.*"

h. Bo's roommate testified that two days before Kip was killed, he overheard Bo say, "*I'm going to get myself a gun and teach him a lesson.*" Will the statement be admissible to prove that Bo subsequently bought a gun and shot and killed Kip?

Cases on Then Existing Mental Condition

§ 5.7.1 Non-Hearsay State of Mind and Hearsay State of Mind

In *Stroud v. Golson*[81] below, the court admits the statements under the Article 803(3) state of mind exception. Consider whether you believe the statements made by the declarant are hearsay state of mind or non-hearsay state of mind, or a combination of both. Isolate the statements of the declarant. Are they being offered to prove the truth of the matter asserted, i.e., a direct assertion of the declarant's state of mind, or are you required to infer the declarant's state of mind?

Stroud v. Golson
Court of Appeal Louisiana, Second Circuit
741 So. 2d 182
June 16, 1999

BROWN, J.

In this medical malpractice action for the failure to diagnose lung cancer, defendant, the Louisiana Patients' Compensation Fund ("PCF"), appeals a $1.5 million jury verdict which was reduced by the trial court's judgment to $400,000 to comply with the PCF's maximum exposure under Louisiana's medical malpractice scheme. We affirm.

FACTS

On March 29, 1994, Gloria Stroud was examined by Lauren J. Mikey, M.D. After viewing x-rays, Dr. Mikey told Mrs. Stroud that she may have lung cancer and referred her to Thomas J. Gullatt, M.D. On March 30, 1994, Dr. Gullatt examined Mrs. Stroud and referred her to St. Francis Medical Center in Monroe for a CT scan. That same day, a CT scan was performed and its findings interpreted by Bruce Golson, M.D. Dr. Golson opined that, according to the CT scan, Mrs. Stroud did not have lung cancer.

Approximately one year later, on April 10, 1995, Mrs. Stroud was hospitalized at St. Francis for a cerebral hemorrhage caused by an unrelated condition known as arteriovenous malformation ("AVM").[82] During this treatment, x-rays and CT scans revealed inoperative [sic] cancer in Mrs. Stroud's left lung.

On May 31, 1995, Mrs. Stroud was discharged from St. Francis. On August 15, 1995, Mrs. Stroud died as a result of the cancer. She was survived by her husband of 33 years, Clarence Stroud, and her two major sons, Jason and Randy Stroud.

---

81. State v. Golson, 741 So. 2d 182 (La. Ct. App. 2d Cir. 1999).

82. AVM is a life-threatening condition that can cause a person's brain to hemorrhage, resulting in "significant morbidity and mortality."

Plaintiffs, decedent's husband and sons, filed the instant suit seeking damages arising from Dr. Golson's failure to properly interpret Mrs. Stroud's CT scan. Before trial, plaintiffs settled with Dr. Golson and his insurer, St. Paul Fire and Marine Insurance Company, for $80,000, while reserving their rights to seek excess damages from the PCF. [83]

On February 23, 1998, a trial by jury was commenced against the PCF that admitted medical negligence but claimed that Mrs. Stroud would have died from the fast-acting cancer even if it had been diagnosed in 1994. On February 25, 1998, the jury returned a verdict finding that Mrs. Stroud lost a less than even chance of survival because of Dr. Golson's negligence and awarded plaintiffs $1.5 million in damages. On March 18, 1998, the trial court entered judgment in favor of plaintiffs consistent with the statutory cap, reducing the award to $400,000, together with legal interest and costs.

Thereafter, the PCF filed JNOV and new trial motions, both of which were denied. The PCF now appeals, citing three assignments of error. Plaintiffs have answered the appeal....

DISCUSSION

... *Hearsay Objection*

Defendant lastly argues that the trial judge erred when he overruled the hearsay objection regarding Mr. Stroud's testimony concerning what Mrs. Stroud's reasons were for declining treatment after her cancer was diagnosed. The testimony at issue is as follows:

> Mr. Thomas: Now, did your wife discuss—You—You and your wife discuss whether or not she should have treatment for her cancer?
>
> Mr. Stroud: Yes, we did.
>
> Mr. Thomas: And were you a part in making a decision with her with why she did not agree to have treatment?
>
> Mr. Stroud: Yes.
>
> Mr. Thomas: Share with the jury what she said about that?
>
> Mr. Stroud: She, ah,—
>
> Mr. Anzelmo: Your Honor, I object to hearsay.
>
> The Court: I understand. But, I think it—It is hearsay but it's reliable. I'll allow it.
>
> Mr. Thomas: Go ahead.
>
> Mr. Stroud: Ah, I had a—My sister passed away in November '94 with lung cancer, and she found out in July of '94 that she had lung cancer. So, she went and took the radium treatments and she weighed a hundred and twenty-five pounds and was eating and doing all right until she started taking the radium treatments, and by the end of the radium treatments she could hardly get about, and actually she just laid down and starved herself to death. She weighed sixty-five pounds when she passed away, and was bed ridden all that time. And the wife felt that it was too far gone in her for any treatments to do any good, plus what few days she had left she didn't want to be like my sister.

83. According to La. R.S. 40:1299.42, Dr. Golson and his personal liability insurer were only liable for the first $100,000 in damages. The PCF was liable for the remaining damages up to a $500,000 cap.

The PCF argues that Mr. Stroud's testimony did not fit any of the hearsay exceptions and the court's statement that the evidence was "reliable" compounded error citing *Cole Oil and Tire Company, Inc. v. Davis,* 567 So.2d 122 (La.App. 2d Cir.1990).

Mr. Stroud's testimony regarding statements his wife made were statements of her then-existing state of mind. La.C.E. art. 803(3). The testimony showed the motive behind Mrs. Stroud's decision not to receive treatment, namely, her belief that the treatments would not be effective, as well as her desire to avoid the severe pain and discomfort that can accompany chemotherapy. This assignment of error is without merit.

Discussion Questions

1. Would the statements in this case be better analyzed as non-hearsay state of mind, or is this actually a mixture of both hearsay state of mind and non-hearsay state of mind? Why or why not?
2. As you know, state of mind must be relevant to a case to be admissible. The court notes that the declarant's statements were relevant to show her reasoning and motive for refusing treatment. For what purpose is her reasoning relevant in the case for defendant's malpractice?

§ 5.7.2 Must Be *Then* Existing Mental Condition, Not Statement of Memory

As we noted above, to conform to the rule, statements of a person's mental condition must be the person's "then" existing mental condition, not statements of past mental states. In *State v. Emerson*,[84] the declarant attempts to offer a statement of memory to prove the thing remembered, which is rejected by the court.

State v. Emerson
Court of Appeal of Louisiana, Second Circuit
722 So. 2d 373
Dec. 9, 1998

WILLIAMS, Judge.

The defendant, Terry Emerson, was indicted by a Ouachita Parish grand jury for the offense of second degree murder, a violation of LSA-R.S. 14.30.1. After a jury trial, the defendant was found guilty of manslaughter, a violation of LSA-R.S. 14.31. The trial court sentenced the defendant to serve thirty-six years imprisonment at hard labor.

FACTS

On December 9, 1994, at approximately 2:00 a.m., the defendant, Terry Emerson a/k/a "T-Love" and Brandon Flintroy began arguing in the parking lot of Nelson's Drive-In, located in Monroe, Louisiana. During this argument, Jerome Hudson approached the defendant and struck him without warning. Hudson and the defendant began fighting. An acquaintance of both men, Charles Owens, testified that he intervened and brought a temporary halt to the fight, but Owens said that the fight resumed when Hudson threw his pager at the defendant, hitting him on the head. The defendant then forced Hudson

84. State v. Emerson, 722 So. 2d 373 (La. Ct. App. 2d Cir. 1998).

to the ground and appeared to have won the fight. Several witnesses testified that defendant then went inside the building, followed by Hudson a short time later.

Joe Bass, the son of Betty Nelson, the owner of the drive-in, testified that he helped to break up the fight and led Hudson into the building. Bass stated that he and Hudson walked into the rear of the building, which Nelson used as a residence. Other witnesses did not see Bass take Hudson inside. Bass testified that when he and Hudson reached the residence kitchen, he tried to calm Hudson while waiting for the police, and that he did not know defendant's whereabouts at the time. Bass stated that as he walked back through the hallway from the residential kitchen, he met the defendant coming the other way. Bass testified that the defendant pushed him aside, approached Hudson and with an "overhand" motion, stabbed the victim in the chest with a large kitchen knife. Bass said that Hudson appeared to have been unarmed.

Myland Cherry, a cook at Nelson's, testified that he saw the defendant in the restaurant's kitchen and told him to leave. Cherry stated that defendant left the kitchen just as Hudson came through the hall. However, Cherry did not see Bass until after the stabbing. Cherry testified that he observed the defendant stab the victim on "the spur of the moment" and that he heard the defendant say, "I'll kill you" just before the stabbing. Cherry stated that as the defendant approached with the knife, Hudson stopped, backed up towards the storage area and said "No, T-Love" just before he was stabbed. Cherry did not notice whether Hudson held anything in his hands.

Hudson, bleeding and holding his chest, stumbled outside and collapsed in the parking lot. Betty Nelson testified that after learning of the disturbance she entered her residence kitchen. Nelson found the defendant standing near a corner and noticed that a picture, which had fallen from the wall onto the floor, was stained with blood. Nelson then walked outside and discovered the victim on the ground. Paramedics transported Hudson to the hospital, where he died....

The defendant fled from the scene. Local police obtained an arrest warrant but were unable to find the defendant. In July 1995, the defendant was finally apprehended in Seattle, Washington, where he was apparently using the name Yatterius Dorsey....

DISCUSSION

... Defendant contends the trial court erred in refusing to allow Rachelle Price to testify about her telephone conversation with the defendant shortly after the stabbing. The defendant argues that the content of this conversation was admissible under LSA-C.E. art. 801(D)(4), which provides:

> A statement is not hearsay if:
>
> The statements are events speaking for themselves under the immediate pressure of the occurrence, through the instructive, impulsive and spontaneous words and acts of the participants, and not the words of the participants when narrating the events, and which are necessary incidents of the criminal act, or immediate concomitants of it, or form in conjunction with it one continuous transaction.

In *Buckbee v. United Gas Pipe Line Co. Inc.*, 561 So.2d 76 (La.1990), the supreme court stated that the *res gestae* rule is properly limited to spontaneous words or acts of the participants at the time of the occurrence, rather than a participant's narration of events. The *res gestae* exception permits admission of events speaking through participants, but not the testimony of participants speaking about events. *State v. Williams,* 331 So.2d 467 (La.1976).

Here, Price testified that defendant telephoned her approximately one hour after the stabbing. When the defense counsel asked about the content of that conversation, the prosecutor objected on the grounds that the evidence was hearsay. The trial court sustained the objection. In accordance with LSA-C.E. art. 103A(2), the defendant proffered Price's testimony. Price testified that during the telephone conversation, defendant stated that "they" were "trying to crowd me" and that he wasn't trying to hurt the victim. "He was just trying to defend himself."

Despite the defendant's contention that his statements were admissible because they were made shortly after the incident, a narrative account of an event, made either by a witness or by a party, is hearsay and thus inadmissible under the ambit of LSA-C.E. art. 801(D)(4), regardless of its proximity in time to the event itself. Pursuant to Article 801D(4), it is not the proximity to the event which removes the statement from hearsay exclusion. Rather, it is the statement's integral connection to the event that permits its admission.

The testimony sought to be introduced falls squarely within the prohibited category of "testimony of participants speaking about events." *Buckbee, supra.* Had the defendant said "Stop crowding me!" during the event, evidence of that statement would not be hearsay. However, the proffered evidence was clearly inadmissible because the defendant's statement was made narratively, recounting an event which had purportedly happened. The argument lacks merit.

The defendant also contends that the evidence is admissible under LSA-C.E. art. 803(3), which Provides an exception to the hearsay rule for statements of the declarant's then existing mental, emotional or physical condition. This contention also fails. Such "state of mind" evidence is not admissible to prove a speaker's past conduct.... Evidence of intent is similarly inadmissible to prove past action. Article 803(3) allows such evidence to prove only the declarant's "then existing condition or his future action." The proffered testimony concerning defendant's later claim not to have intended to hurt the victim does not meet this standard. Because the evidence sought to be introduced was hearsay not admissible under any exception to the rule, we cannot say the trial court erred in excluding the testimony. The assignment of error lacks merit.

Discussion Questions

1. In *Emerson*, the court reasons that the declarant's statements are of his past mental condition. What are the statements? At what point in time did the declarant possess the mental state at issue?
2. Why are statements of a person's past mental condition deemed unreliable, and are thus inadmissible under this exception? Are there both practical and policy reasons for excluding such statements? Explain.

§ 5.7.3 May Be Offered to Prove Declarant's Future Action

Under the rule, a person's statement of his then existing mental condition may be offered to prove that he possessed that mental condition at that moment, as well as to prove his future action. In *Mutual Life Ins. Co. v. Hillmon*,[85] the U.S. Supreme Court presents an excellent example of the use of a person's statements regarding his intentions

85. Mutual Life v. Hillmon, 145 U.S. 285 (1892). For more information on additional background in the *Hillmon* case, including photos of both Hillmon and Walters, visit www.thehillmoncase.com/wesson.html.

and plans to prove his future actions in conformity with those intentions. Additionally, the court discusses relevant background and policy underlying the rule.

Mutual Life Ins. Co. of New York v. Hillmon
Supreme Court of the United States
145 U.S. 285, 12 S.Ct. 909
May 16, 1892

STATEMENT BY MR. JUSTICE GRAY.

On July 13, 1880, Sallie E. Hillmon, a citizen of Kansas, brought an action against the Mutual Life Insurance Company, a corporation of New York, on a policy of insurance, dated December 10, 1878, on the life of her husband, John W. Hillmon, in the sum of $10,000, payable to her within 60 days after notice and proof of his death. On the same day the plaintiff brought two other actions,—the one against the New York Life Insurance Company, a corporation of New York, on two similar policies of life insurance, dated, respectively, November 30, 1878, and December 10, 1878, for the sum of $5,000 each; and the other against the Connecticut Mutual Life Insurance Company, a corporation of Connecticut, on a similar policy, dated March 4, 1879, for the sum of $5,000.

In each case the declaration alleged that Hillmon died on March 17, 1879, during the continuance of the policy, but that the defendant, though duly notified of the fact, had refused to pay the amount of the policy, or any part thereof; and the answer denied the death of Hillmon, and alleged that he, together with John H. Brown and divers other persons, on or before November 30, 1878, conspiring to defraud the defendant, procured the issue of all the policies, and afterwards, in March and April, 1879, falsely pretended and represented that Hillmon was dead, and that a dead body which they had procured was his, whereas in reality he was alive and in hiding.

...

At the trial plaintiff introduced evidence tending to show that on or about March 5, 1879, Hillmon and Brown left Wichita, in the state of Kansas, and traveled together through southern Kansas in search of a site for a cattle ranch; that on the night of March 18th, while they were in camp at a place called 'Crooked Creek,' Hillmon was killed by the accidental discharge of a gun; that Brown at once notified persons living in the neighborhood, and that the body was thereupon taken to a neighboring town, where, after an inquest, it was buried. The defendants introduced evidence tending to show that the body found in the camp at Crooked Creek on the night of March 18th was not the body of Hillmon, but was the body of one Frederick Adolph Walters. Upon the question whose body this was there was much conflicting evidence, including photographs and descriptions of the corpse, and of the marks and scars upon it, and testimony to its likeness to Hillmon and to Walters.

The defendants introduced testimony that Walters left his home at Ft. Madison, in the state of Iowa, in March, 1878, and was afterwards in Kansas in 1878, and in January and February, 1879; that during that time his family frequently received letters from him, the last of which was written from Wichita; and that he had not been heard from since March, 1879. The defendants also offered the following evidence:

Elizabeth Rieffenach testified that she was a sister of Frederick Adolph Walters, and lived at Ft. Madison: ...

'Witness further testified that she had received a letter written from Wichita, Kansas, about the 4th or 5th day of March, 1879, by her brother Frederick Adolph; that the letter was dated at Wichita, and was in the handwriting of her brother; that she had searched for the letter, but could not find the same, it being lost; that she remembered and could state the contents of the letter.

'Thereupon the defendants' counsel asked the question, 'State the contents of that letter;" to which the plaintiff objected, on the ground that the same is incompetent, irrelevant, and hearsay. The objection was sustained, and the defendants duly excepted. The following is the letter as stated by witness:

> Wichita, Kansas, March 4th or 5th or 3d or 4th,—I don't know,—1879. Dear Sister and All: I now in my usual style drop you a few lines to let you know that I expect to leave Wichita on or about March the 5th with a certain Mr. Hillmon, a sheep trader, for Colorado, or parts unknown to me. I expect to see the country now. News are of no interest to you, as you are not acquainted here. I will close with compliments to all inquiring friends. Love to all. I am truly your brother, FRED. ADOLPH WALTERS.'

Alvina D. Kasten testified that she was 21 years of age, and resided in Ft. Madison; that she was engaged to be married to Frederick Adolph Walters; that she last saw him on March 24, 1878, at Ft. Madison; that he left there at that time, and had not returned; that she corresponded regularly with him, and received a letter about every two weeks until March 3, 1879, which was the last time she received a letter from him; that this letter was dated at Wichita, March 1, 1879, and was addressed to her at Ft. Madison, and the envelope was postmarked 'Wichita, Kansas, March 2, 1879;' and that she had never heard from or seen him since that time.

The defendants put in evidence the envelope with the postmark and address, and thereupon offered to read the letter in evidence. The plaintiff objected to the reading of the letter. The court sustained the objection, and the defendants excepted.

This letter was dated 'Wichita, March 1, 1879,' was signed by Walters, and began as follows:

> 'Dearest Alvina: Your kind and ever welcome letter was received yesterday afternoon about an hour before I left Emporia. I will stay here until the fore part of next week, and then will leave here to see a part of the country that I never expected to see when I left home, as I am going with a man by the name of Hillmon, who intends, to start a sheep ranch, and, as he promised me more wages than I could make at anything else, I concluded to take it, for a while at least, until I strike something better. There is so many folks in this country that have got the Leadville fever, and if I could not of got the situation that I have now I would have went there myself; but as it is at present I get to see the best portion of Kansas, Indian Territory, Colorado, and Mexico. The route that we intend to take would cost a man to travel from $150 to $200, but it will not cost me a cent; besides, I get good wages. I will drop you a letter occasionally until I get settled down. Then I want you to answer it.'

... The court, after recapitulating some of the testimony introduced, instructed the jury as follows: 'You have perceived from the very beginning of the trial that the conclusion to be reached must practically turn upon one question of fact, and all the large volume of evidence, with its graphic and varied details, has no actual significance, save as the facts established thereby may throw light upon and aid you in answering the question, whose body was it that on the evening of March 18, 1879, lay dead by the camp fire on Crooked creek? The decision of that question decides the verdict you should render.'

The jury, being instructed by the court to return a separate verdict in each case, returned verdicts for the plaintiff against the three defendants respectively for the amounts of their policies and interest, upon which separate judgments were rendered. The defendants sued out four writs of error, one jointly in the three cases as consolidated, and one in each case separately....

Mr. Justice GRAY, after stating the case as above, delivered the opinion of the court....

This question is of the admissibility of the letters written by Walters on the first days of March, 1879, which were offered in evidence by the defendants, and excluded by the court....

The matter chiefly contested at the trial was the death of John W. Hillmon, the insured; and that depended upon the question whether the body found at Crooked creek on the night of March 18, 1879, was his body or the body of one Walters.

Much conflicting evidence had been introduced as to the identity of the body. The plaintiff had also introduced evidence that Hillmon and one Brown left Wichita, in Kansas, on or about March 5, 1879, and traveled together through southern Kansas in search of a site for a cattle ranch; and that on the night of March 18th, while they were in camp at Crooked creek, Hillmon was accidentally killed, and that his body was taken thence and buried.

The defendants had introduced evidence, without objection, that Walters left his home and his betrothed in Iowa in March, 1878, and was afterwards in Kansas until March, 1879; that during that time he corresponded regularly with his family and Lis betrothed; that the last letters received from him were one received by his betrothed on March 3d, and postmarked at 'Wichita, March 2,' and one received by his sister about March 4th or 5th, and dated at Wichita a day or two before; and that he had not been heard from since.

The evidence that Walters was at Wichita on or before March 5th, and had not been heard from since, together with the evidence to identify as his the body found at Crooked Creek on March 18th, tended to show that he went from Wichita to Crooked Creek between those dates. Evidence that just before March 5th he had the intention of leaving Wichita with Hillmon would tend to corroborate the evidence already admitted, and to show that he went from Wichita to Crooked Creek with Hillmon. Letters from him to his family and his betrothed were the natural, if not the only attainable, evidence of his intention....

But upon another ground suggested they should have been admitted. A man's state of mind or feeling can only be manifested to others by countenance, attitude, or gesture, or by sounds or words, spoken or written. The nature of the fact to be proved is the same, and evidence of its proper tokens is equally competent to prove it, whether expressed by aspect or conduct, by voice or pen. When the intention to be proved is important only as qualifying an act, its connection with that act must be shown, in order to warrant the admission of declarations of the intention. But whenever the intention is of itself a distinct and material fact in a chain of circumstances, it may be proved by contemporaneous oral or written declarations of the party.

The existence of a particular intention in a certain person at a certain time being a material fact to be proved, evidence that he expressed that intention at that time is as direct evidence of the fact as his own testimony that he then had that intention would be. After his death these can hardly be any other way of proving it, and while he is still alive his own memory of his state of mind at a former time is no more likely to be clear and true than a bystander's recollection of what he then said, and is less trustworthy than letters written by him at the very time and under circumstances precluding a suspicion of misrepresentation.

The letters in question were competent not as narratives of facts communicated to the writer by others, nor yet as proof that he actually went away from Wichita, but as evidence that, shortly before the time when other evidence tended to show that he went away, he had the intention of going, and of going with Hillmon, which made it more probable both that he did go and that he went with Hillmon than if there had been no proof of such intention. In view of the mass of conflicting testimony introduced upon the question whether it was the body of Walters that was found in Hillmon's camp, this evidence might properly influence the jury in determining that question.

The rule applicable to this case has been thus stated by this court: 'Wherever the bodily or mental feelings of an individual are material to be proved, the usual expressions of such feelings are original and competent evidence. Those expressions are the natural reflexes of what it might be impossible to show by other testimony. If there be such other testimony, this may be necessary to set the facts thus developed in their true light, and to give them their proper effect. As independent, explanatory, or corroborative evidence it is often indispensable to the due administration of justice. Such declarations are regarded as verbal acts, and are as competent as any other testimony, when relevant to the issue. Their truth or falsity is an inquiry for the jury.'...

In accordance with this rule, a bankrupt's declarations, oral or by letter, at or before the time of leaving or staying away from home, as to his reason for going abroad, have always been held by the English courts to be competent, in an action by his assignees against a creditor, as evidence that his departure was with intent to defraud his creditors, and therefore an act of bankruptcy....

The highest courts of New Hampshire and Massachusetts have held declarations of a servant, at the time of leaving his master's service, to be competent evidence, in actions between third persons, of his reasons for doing so.... And the supreme court of Ohio has held that, for the purpose of proving that a person was at a railroad station intending to take passage on a train, previous declarations made by him at the time of leaving his hotel were admissible....

In actions for criminal conversation, letters by the wife to her husband or to third persons are competent to show her affection towards her husband, and her reasons for living apart from him, if written before any misconduct on her part, and if there is no ground to suspect collusion.... So letters from a husband to a third person, showing his state of feeling, affection, and sympathy for his wife, have been held by this court to be competent evidence, bearing on the validity of the marriage, when the legitimacy of their children is in issue....

Upon an indictment of one Hunter for the murder of one Armstrong at Camden, the court of errors and appeals of New Jersey unanimously held that Armstrong's oral declarations to his son at Philadelphia, on the afternoon before the night of the murder, as well as a letter written by him at the same time and place to his wife, each stating that he was going with Hunter to Camden on business, were rightly admitted in evidence. Chief Justice BEASLEY said: 'In the ordinary course of things, it was the usual information that a man about leaving home would communicate, for the convenience of his family, the information of his friends, or the regulation of his business. At the time it was given, such declarations could, in the nature of things, mean harm to no one. He who uttered them was bent on no expedition of mischief or wrong, and the attitude of affairs at the time entirely explodes the idea that such utterances were intended to serve any purpose but that for which they were obviously designed. If it be said that such notice of an intention of leaving home could have been given without introducing in it the name of Mr. Hunter, the obvious answer to the suggestion, I think, is that a reference to the companion who is to accompany the person leaving is as natural a part of the transaction as is any other incident or quality of it. If it is legitimate to show by a man's own declarations that he left his home to be gone a week, or for a certain destination, which seems incontestable, why may it not be proved in the same way that a designated person was to bear him company? At the time the words were uttered or written they imported no wrongdoing to any one, and the reference to the companion who was to go with him was nothing more, as matters then stood, than an indication of an additional circumstance of his going. If it was in the ordinary train of events for this man to leave word or to state where he was going, it seems to me it was equally so for him to say with whom he was going'....

Upon principle and authority, therefore, we are of opinion that the two letters were competent evidence of the intention of Walters at the time of writing them, which was a material fact bearing upon the question in controversy; and that for the exclusion of these letters, as well as for the undue restriction of the defendants' challenges, the verdicts must be set aside, and a new trial had.

Discussion Questions

1. For what reason was the declarant's then existing mental condition relevant in *Hillmon*?
2. What policy reasons do the Court point out to support admitting statements of a person's intentions, plans, etc. to prove his future action? Do you agree with this reasoning? Is such evidence reliable?

Statements Made in Jest

Consider the application of this rule to statements that could arguably have been made in jest. In *State v. Taylor*,[86] the defendant was found guilty of first-degree murder and sentenced to death by lethal injection on October 10, 2000. Following the penalty phase of the prosecution, the jury returned a death recommendation based on the sole aggravating circumstance urged by the state—that defendant was engaged in the perpetration or attempted perpetration of an armed robbery at the time of the murder.

In rebutting the defendant's claim that he had been "acting under the dominion and control of [co-defendant] Timothy Taylor who was the real mastermind behind the instant offense and the subsequent bank robbery," the prosecution offered evidence of the defendant's state of mind under Article 803(3) to show his intent. Specifically, the prosecution was allowed to introduce evidence that defendant told his friends *he wanted to "kill somebody" before he died*; that he *wanted to go out in a "blaze of glory"*; and that once while watching his favorite movie, *Natural Born Killers*, he critiqued the bank robbery featured in the film and stated that he would have conducted the bank robbery by "*pop[ping] a cap in the [guard's] ass.*"

Although the defense adamantly argued that the statements were made in jest, the court allowed the evidence finding that it constituted direct assertions of defendant's state of mind, was relevant to prove his motive and intent, and was admissible to prove defendant's future acts.

While evidence of a person's then existing mental condition may be used to prove future action, do you think there are circumstances in which a person's statement as to his desires, plans, or future actions should be excluded because of unreliability? Were the statements in *Taylor* reliable? Why or why not?

---

86. State v. Taylor, 838 So. 2d 729 (La. 2003).

§ 5.7.4 May *Not* Be Offered to Prove Future Action of Third Party[87]

As stated above, the rule may only be offered to prove one's own future action, not the future action of a third party. Let's revisit *Buckbee, supra,* where the Louisiana Supreme Court correctly applied this aspect of the exception. If you recall, while the court correctly found that Buckbee's statement of his intent to obtain permission from his supervisors to use heat on the plug could be admitted on the issue of whether Buckbee, in fact, sought permission from his supervisors, it could not be used to prove that Buckbee actually received the permission sought. In that case, his statement of intent would have been used to prove the action of a third party, and not his own, which is prohibited under Louisiana law. Outlining how the rule should be applied, the court in *Buckbee* stated:

> We turn now to the admissibility of Buckbee's first statement, which Buckbee made to Vincent before descending the scaffold, that he intended to seek permission to heat the plug.
>
> One well-recognized exception to the hearsay rule admits testimony concerning a speaker's out-of-court declaration of intent. Although such a statement is hearsay when offered to prove the truth of the matter asserted therein, i.e., that the declarant actually intended to take, and did subsequently take, certain action, such a statement is nonetheless excepted from the bar of the hearsay rule. This exception is now codified at L.C.E. art. 803(3), which provides, in pertinent part, that a "statement of the declarant's then existing state of mind, emotion, sensation, or physical condition (such as intent, plan, motive, design, mental feeling, pain, and bodily health)," is admissible as an exception to the hearsay rule when that statement is "offered to prove the declarant's then existing condition or his future action."[88]
>
> In this case, Vincent's testimony to Buckbee's first statement, that he intended to seek permission to apply heat to the plug, a statement which Buckbee made just before descending the scaffold and going into the plant office, falls squarely under this exception to the hearsay rule. It is hearsay *and* it is nevertheless admissible to show the declarant Buckbee's state of mind, i.e., his intent to seek permission.
>
> This testimony is not only evidence that Buckbee formulated the intention to seek his superiors' permission to apply heat. It could also be offered as some evidence that Buckbee did indeed act in accordance with his expressed intention,

---

87. State v. Weedon, 342 So.2d 642, 646 (La.1977) (An out-of-court declaration by one person is inadmissible to show what another person did.).

88. Testimony about a *declarant's* out-of-court statement of intent is hearsay when offered to prove the truth of the matter asserted, that the declarant did in fact intend to take certain action, and did subsequently take such action. It is nonetheless admissible under this statutory exception to the hearsay rule.

Testimony concerning an out-of-court statement is non-hearsay, and therefore not barred, when used to prove the effect of an out-of-court statement on the *listener's* state of mind. Testimony concerning an out-of-court statement may be admissible as non-hearsay to demonstrate a *declarant's* state of mind when the testimony is not offered to prove the truth of the matter asserted in the statement. For example, a declarant's statement "I am the king" may be admissible non-hearsay when offered to prove the speaker's mental condition; the statement would be inadmissible hearsay if offered to prove the truth of the assertion, that the speaker is in fact the king.

that he did approach his superiors in the moments before the accident and that he did request of them permission to apply heat.[89] Coupled with Vincent's testimony that Buckbee thereupon descended the scaffold, and Vincent's testimony that he watched Buckbee walk to, enter, and remain in the plant office for about ten minutes, the testimony regarding what Buckbee said just before descending the scaffold is powerful circumstantial proof that Buckbee in fact sought his superiors' permission to apply heat.

Vincent's testimony concerning this statement was admissible as an exception to the hearsay rule and the lower courts erred in excluding this statement. Thus, while the *Buckbee* court acknowledged that the statement could be admissible under the exception as evidence to prove that Buckbee actually *sought* permission (his own future action), it stopped short of allowing the statement to be used to prove he was actually *given* permission (future action of a third party).

In ***Garza v. Delta Tau Delta Fraternity***[90] below, the Louisiana Supreme Court rejects the admissibility of a suicide note under the then existing mental condition exception to the hearsay rule, on the issue of whether the defendant's actions led the victim to commit suicide. The Court reasons that the note exceeds several limitations of the rule including those regarding: 1) past states of mind; 2) proving conduct of third parties; and 3) statements of memory/belief offered to prove the thing remembered or believed. As you read the case, reflect on your understanding of the application of this rule. We will revisit the court's reasoning after you have read the case.

Garza v. Delta Tau Delta Fraternity (I)[91]

Supreme Court of Louisiana
948 So. 2d 84
July 10, 2006

WEIMER, Justice.

Certiorari was granted in this matter to determine whether the lower courts erred in ruling on motions in limine that a suicide note would be admissible at trial as an exception to the hearsay rule. In light of the facts of this case and for the reasons assigned, we hold that the suicide note in question does not qualify as a "[s]tatement under belief of impending death" pursuant to LSA-C.E. art. 804(B)(2), or, as plaintiffs argue alternatively, as an exception to the hearsay rule pursuant to LSA-C.E. art. 803(3) for the purpose of proving the "[t]hen existing mental, emotional, or physical condition" of the decedent....

Accordingly, we reverse the holdings of the lower courts finding the suicide note admissible into evidence as a statement under belief of impending death, we vacate the judgment on the motions in limine, and remand this matter to the district court.

---

89. In State v. Doze, we determined that "(d)eclarations of state of mind are usually admissible for the purpose of proving that the intention of the declarant was actually carried out." This dual evidentiary function of the statement of intent is carried over in L.C.E. art. 803(3), which provides that such a statement may be offered "to prove the declarant's then existing condition *or his future action.*" (Emphasis added).

90. Garza v. Delta Tau Delta Fraternity, 948 So. 2d 84 (La. 2006).

91. This case is revisited in § 5.16, *supra*, on the issue of its admissibility under the dying declaration exception.

FACTS AND PROCEDURAL BACKGROUND

This matter arises from a tragic death by suicide. Thomas Garza, Sr., and Sandra Garza, along with their son, Thomas Garza, Jr., the parents and brother of the decedent, filed suit against various defendants for the wrongful death of Courtney Garza, on April 9, 2001. On that date, Courtney, a 21-year-old college student at Southeastern Louisiana University (SLU) in Hammond, Louisiana, took her own life by hanging at her parents' home in Baton Rouge. Prior to the suicide, Courtney authored a handwritten letter.

In their original petition, plaintiffs sued Delta Tau Delta International Fraternity, Epsilon Phi Chapter (DTD Local); Delta Tau Delta, National (DTD National), the fraternal organization headquartered in Carmel, Indiana; Paul Upshaw; and the State of Louisiana, through the Board of Supervisors for the University of Louisiana System and Southeastern Louisiana University.[92] Petitioners aver that Courtney's death was "proximately caused by the concomitant negligence of the defendants," which they particularize as: sexual assault and rape of the decedent; continuous and ongoing harassment of the decedent; failure to properly supervise activities of fraternal organizations on the SLU campus; and failure to prevent the tortious activities described in the petition.

The defendants answered the petition, denying the allegations.

... The note is handwritten on letter-sized, lined paper—three pages, front and back, plus seven lines. It can be broken down into three parts. 1) At the beginning of the note Courtney states she had been thinking about suicide for months, having been constantly depressed; she also talks about seeking counseling and deciding not to seek further counseling. 2) Then, Courtney writes, "I guess I'll begin & explain what happened to me this semester." She relates her account of drinking at a local lounge until closing time, 2:00 a.m. According to the note, she and a sorority sister accepted a ride with a DTD member, and they willingly went to an off-campus house occupied by several fraternity members, where Courtney ended up in the bedroom of Paul Upshaw. She writes, "I was raped." This portion of the note ends with "[a]ll I wanted was to forget about what happened & all it brought me was debt." 3) The final portion of the note consists of goodbyes to family, instructions for getting in touch with friends, and instructions for her funeral.

In a judgment signed on June 15, 2004, the motions were denied in part as to the suicide note up to and including the word "debt" on page three. Thus, the portion of the note preceding the word "debt" was deemed admissible hearsay pursuant to La. C.E. art. 804(B)(2). The motions in limine were granted as to the remainder of the suicide note and pursuant to La. C.E. art. 403 deemed inadmissible. Although the parties argued admissibility of the note pursuant to La. C.E. art. 803(3), this article was not addressed by the trial court.

The excluded portion of Courtney's note begins with "I'm sorry Mom" and ends with "This is goodbye." The plaintiffs did not seek a writ as to the portion of the district court's judgment granting the motion in limine. Thus, the portion of the suicide note after the

---

92. The petition also included allegations against SLU for negligence in providing inadequate and unsupervised "counseling" when, subsequent to a February 6, 2001 incident, Courtney presented herself to the SLU Comprehensive Counseling Center in "acute emotional distress as an 'emergency walk-in'" and was seen by an SLU practicum student counselor. While SLU's writ application was pending in this court, this portion of plaintiffs' claim against SLU was disposed of in a "Partial Judgment of Dismissal" dated September 29, 2005, by the district court based on a consent judgment between the plaintiffs and SLU. The judgment further dismisses the medical review panel for lack of evidence of a breach of the standard of care by the SLU Comprehensive Counseling Center....

word "debt" on page three is not before us. The note was dated April 8, 2001, at 12:30, and Courtney died April 9, 2001.[93]

The sole issue presented for our determination is whether the suicide note in question is admissible in evidence as an exception to the hearsay rule as codified in the Louisiana Code of Evidence enacted in 1988.

DISCUSSION

The task of determining the intent of the legislature begins with the words of the applicable statute or statutes, as words are the means used by the legislature to express its intent.... However, the exceptions to the hearsay rule provided in the Louisiana Code of Evidence are, to a large extent, a systematization and codification of hearsay exceptions previously recognized in Louisiana.... Although we are confined by the statutory language, interpretation of the articles of the Code of Evidence would be superficial if performed in a vacuum rather than in the context of history and jurisprudence where the words are susceptible to different meanings....

Further, Chapter 8 of the Code of Evidence is entitled "Hearsay" and consists of Articles 801 through 806, which are modeled on Federal Rules of Evidence with the same numbers, adding common law history and federal jurisprudence to the instructive arsenal available for our use in interpretation of the Louisiana Code of Evidence....

...

Then existing mental, emotional, or physical condition:

The statutory provision involved with plaintiffs' alternative argument is La. C.E. art. 803(3)....

The exception for then existing mental, emotional of physical condition, like the dying declaration exception, is of long standing. The United States Supreme Court considered—and rejected as inapplicable under the facts of that case—both exceptions in *Shepard, supra.*

The Official Comments to this exception point out that it clarifies prior Louisiana law and generally follows the federal rules. However, the legislature borrowed from the approach taken in Alaska by adding the phrase "offered to prove the declarant's then existing condition or his future action." This insertion establishes the limited scope of the exception as stated by this court in *State v. Weedon,* 342 So.2d 642, 646 (La.1977) (An out-of-court declaration by one person is inadmissible to show what another person did.). Considered in the context of the instant case, the suicide note might be admissible to prove Courtney's state of mind, for example, depressed or despondent or suicidal, at the time of the statement and to prove Courtney's future action of taking her own life, but it is not admissible to prove the actions of Paul Upshaw, other fraternity members, the fraternity itself, and/or SLU.

If the prohibition of the first sentence of the statute for use of the declaration to prove another's action were not sufficient, the legislature sealed the inquiry by its next statement that: "[a] statement of memory or belief ... is not admissible to prove the fact remembered or believed." Courtney's statements in her suicide note not only concerned the defendants' alleged acts, but, in plaintiffs' words, "the connection between her state of mind immediately prior to her death, and what she believed to be the causes of her death."[94] The limitation

93. There is nothing in the record to establish the time of death or whether the 12:30 reference is to A.M. or P.M. As such, based on the record, it is impossible to determine the time frame between the writing of the note and death.

94. Further, in brief to this court urging the suicide note is admissible pursuant to the hearsay exception for then existing mental condition, the plaintiffs state that they "have consistently alleged and

of La. C.E. art. 803(3) could not be clearer: the fact remembered or believed by the declarant cannot be proved by the out-of-court statement, even if the statement otherwise relates to the declarant's then existing mental or emotional condition or to her future action.

The limitation of the exception was eloquently explained in *Shepard*, 290 U.S. at 105–106, 54 S.Ct. at 26:

> Declarations of intention, casting light upon the future, have been sharply distinguished from declarations of memory, pointing backwards to the past. There would be an end, or nearly that, to the rule against hearsay if the distinction were ignored. The testimony now questioned faced backward and not forward. This at least it did in its most obvious implications. What is even more important, it spoke to a past act, and, more than that, to an act by someone not the speaker. Other tendency, if it had any, was a filament too fine to be disentangled by a jury. (The declaration at issue in *Shepard* was, once again, a wife's claim that her husband poisoned her, which could lead to jury confusion over admission of the declaration for the extremely limited purpose of proving present state of mind.)

As we explained previously, the suicide note consisted of three parts, with the final part already excluded by the trial court. Thus, we consider the plaintiffs' argument for admission as referring only to the first two parts of the note.

In the first part of the note, Courtney states she had been thinking about suicide for months, having been constantly depressed. This part, although dealing with state of mind, does not deal directly with her present state of mind. The statement may provide background for her present state of mind, but it is clearly not admissible under this exception since the references were to depression in the past. Further, her state of mind in the past as stated in this first part would not be relevant to the issue in the case, *i.e.*, whether the defendants' acts led her to commit suicide, because she made no accusations against any individuals or entities in this part of the note; she merely described her depression and uncertainty about the suicide.

The second (middle) part of the suicide note is the portion that includes accusations against various members of the fraternity, especially Upshaw. As previously stated, this portion cannot be admitted pursuant to this particular exception to the hearsay rule because Article 803(3) codified the Louisiana rule that a statement of present state of mind cannot be used to prove the acts of a third party....

Although plaintiffs' alternative argument was not ruled on by the lower courts, because of their determination that the suicide note was a dying declaration, we hold that, as a matter of law, this particular suicide note cannot be admitted pursuant to La. C.E. art. 803(3). The note does not fall under this exception to the hearsay rule for three reasons: 1) for the most part, the declarant does not speak of present state of mind, but speaks of past state of mind;[95] 2) the declarant accuses others of wrongdoing, which accusations exceed the statutory limit that the declaration be offered to prove the declarant's future

---

discovered that Ms. Garza committed suicide over the tortuous acts and conduct of the various defendants as well as the omissions to act in response to her allegations."

95. There are some brief references in the note to Courtney's state of mind at the time she penned the note. However, at this point in the litigation, defendants concede that Courtney was depressed and suicidal at the time she penned the note. Thus, her present state of mind is not now at issue. If, at a later date in the proceedings, her present state of mind becomes a disputed issue, the trial court will be able to make an analysis of the contents of the note in light of our pronouncements to determine if a redacted version of the note may be admissible pursuant to La. C.E. art. 803(3) after applying the balancing test of La. C.E. art. 403.

action;[96] and 3) the declarant relates memories and beliefs which are not admissible to prove the facts remembered or believed.

DECREE

Because the portions of the suicide note presently in question do not qualify as an exception to the hearsay rule pursuant to La. C.E. art. 804(B)(2) or art. 803(3), the suicide note is inadmissible hearsay, requiring the reversal of the lower courts' rulings.

JUDGMENT REVERSED; MATTER REMANDED.

JOHNSON, J., & TRAYLOR, J., dissents and assigns reasons; KIMBALL, J., dissents for reasons assigned by TRAYLOR, J.

Discussion Questions

1. Unlike many of the statements you have analyzed thus far, a preliminary issue in *Garza* is the fact that the suicide note, which is more than eight pages long, includes several different statements of various types. Some of the statements point to past and current feelings of the declarant, past actions of the declarant and others, as well as intentions and future actions of the declarant. Despite this, a preliminary issue in analyzing the note (as with all statements) under the hearsay rule is to determine whether the statement is in fact hearsay. What is the suicide note (or portions of it) asserting? What is the note being offered to prove (as stated by the court in this civil action)? Is this note hearsay?
2. Would your analysis of the admissibility of the suicide note change in any way if the note were being offered in a criminal case against Paul Upshaw (the alleged rapist) on the issue of identity or culpability? Why or why not?
3. Apparently finding the note to be hearsay, i.e., being offered to prove the truth of the matter asserted in the suicide note, the Court concludes that the note does not conform to the Article 803(3) exception for three reasons:
   1. the declarant does not speak of present state of mind, but speaks of past state of mind;
   2. that the note is being offered to prove the actions of third parties (*Upshaw, the fraternities, and the university*); and
   3. the declarant relates beliefs which are not admissible to prove the facts believed.

   Explain the Court's reasoning under each aspect of the rule. Do you agree with the court's reasoning? Why or why not?
4. In § 5.2.5 we covered non-hearsay "state of mind of the declarant." Can you make a reasonable argument as to how the suicide note might fit into this category of non-hearsay. Recall the court's rationale in *State v. Raymond, supra*. How would that rationale apply to *Garza*? What result?

96. This limitation is based on the perceived unreliability of the use of the declarant's state of mind to establish the acts of another person.

Key Points

The key points to keep in mind regarding then existing mental condition.

1. The then existing mental condition exception provides that statements of a declarant's then existing mental condition may be offered to prove the declarant's then existing mental condition or future action.

   Requirements:

   a) a statement of the declarant's then existing mental condition; and

   b) offered to prove his then existing mental condition or his future action.
2. Includes statements of present state of mind, emotions, sensations (such as intent, plan, motive, design, mental feelings, desires, likes, dislikes, etc.).
3. State of mind should be a direct statement of a person's mental state—no inference necessary. Non-hearsay state of mind requires an inference of mental state.
4. Must be "then" existing mental condition, not a statement of memory (i.e., a past mental state) or belief.
5. May be offered to prove declarant's "future" action, not past action.
6. May not be offered to prove future action of third party.
7. Statement of belief/memory is ***not*** admissible to prove thing believed.
8. Statement of memory/belief may be offered to prove things other than memory/belief (non-hearsay).
9. A statement of memory/belief can be offered to prove the thing remembered or believed as it pertains to testaments.

Problems on Then Existing Mental Condition

In problems 5-63 to 5-76, please keep in mind these five major sub-issues as they relate to the "then existing mental condition" exception to hearsay.

1. Must be "then" existing mental condition, not statement of memory (a past mental state)
2. May be offered to prove declarant's "future" action, not past action
3. May not be offered to prove future action of a third party
4. Statement of belief/memory is not admissible to prove thing remembered/believed
5. A statement of memory/belief can be offered to prove thing remembered or believed as it pertains to testaments

PROBLEM 5-63. A lady walked into her house and saw her son holding a gun, standing over a dead body. He immediately exclaimed, "*I didn't mean to kill him.*" At trial the lady is called to the stand to testify to her son's statement to prove that her son in fact shot the man. Does the statement conform to the "then existing mental condition" exception to the hearsay rule?

PROBLEM 5-64. While consoling his neighbor, Henry said to him, "*When my mother passed, I actually felt a bit of relief. She was old.*" Does the statement conform to the "then existing mental condition" exception to the hearsay rule? Why or why not?

PROBLEM 5-65. In her trial for the theft of her neighbor's lawnmower, Yolanda's daughter testified that when she went with her mother to return the lawnmower to neighbor, her mother stated, "*I'm sorry I took your lawnmower. I thought it was mine.*" Does the statement conform to the "then existing mental condition" exception to the hearsay rule? Explain.

PROBLEM 5-66. Son is on trial for murder of mother. At the trial, the sister plans to testify that while she was on the phone with mother about a week before the murder, mother told her, "*I plan to change my will.*" Can sister testify to what mother told her to help establish brother's motive for killing mother? Why or why not?

PROBLEM 5-67. Ulga's neighbor accused her of stealing her best china and called the police. When the police questioned Ulga, she immediately stated, "*I don't even like china.*" Can Ulga offer her statement to the police to prove that she didn't likely steal her neighbor's china? Why or why not?

PROBLEM 5-68. Jim is on trial for killing his fiancée Kelly. He claims she ran off with another man while he and Kelly were in Paris together. Jim would like for his brother to testify that after Kelly went missing, he returned home from Paris and told him, "*I love Kelly more than life itself, bro.*" He would like to offer the statement to prove that he loved Kelly too much to have killed her. Does the statement conform to the "then existing mental condition" exception to the hearsay rule?

PROBLEM 5-69. Part I: About a week before spring break, Lamar called his father and told him, "*Taylor and I are going to Mexico for spring break.*" Taylor's parents haven't heard from her since days before spring break. She never returned to school. Can the prosecution offer Lamar's statement to his father to prove that Taylor likely went to Mexico with Lamar under the "then existing mental condition" exception to the hearsay rule? Explain.

Part II: Assume Taylor's body is found several months later in Mexico. There is no other evidence that Lamar went to Mexico other than his statements to his parents that he was going there for spring break. The prosecution would like to call his parents to testify to what Lamar told them in his murder trial fo killing Taylor. The defense objects that the statement is hearsay. Does the statement conform to the "then existing mental condition" exception? Explain.

PROBLEM 5-70. William was riding along with his sister Mary and called up his long time friend Engle, and told her, "*I'm going to drop off the $300 I owe you on Friday.*" No one has heard from Engle since Friday evening. The prosecution would like for Mary to testify to what she overheard William say to Engle to prove that he went there on Friday to help prove that he saw her on the day of her disappearance. Admissible?

PROBLEM 5-71. Zack was a finalist for an important job, but he learned that he was not hired because he showed up late for the interview. Zack claimed he was late because no one ever called him to tell him the exact location, and he got lost on the way. They will offer the testimony of Mable who will testify that she was present when they called Zack to tell him about the interview and during the call she heard Zack say, "*Okay, I'll call you next week to get the exact location for the interview.*" They want Mable to testify to Zack's statement to the company to prove that Zack called and got the location and knew exactly where to go for the interview. Should the statement be admitted?

PROBLEM 5-72. Anna's husband is on trial for killing her. He claims he came home and found her dead in the house after a fishing trip. In the prosecution's case against him, they would like to call Anna's best friend to the stand who will testify that two weeks before Anna was found dead, Anna said to her, "*I think my husband is trying to kill me. I think that accident we had six months ago was staged. And about two months ago, I slept 16 hours* *straight. I think he put something in the tea he brought me before bedtime.*" Can any of Anna's statements be offered to prove that Anna's husband did those things to her to help prove he killed her? Why or why not?

Assume instead that it was Anna on trial for killing her husband. Anna claims self-defense and claims that she killed her husband when he violently attacked her. She claims that it has occurred on numerous occasions, and she was afraid for her life. In Anna's defense, she would like to call her best friend to the stand to testify that about two weeks before the incident Anna made the statements above in Problem 5-72. The prosecution objects that the statements are hearsay. Would your answer now change regarding the admissibility of Anna's statement to her friend? Why or why not?

PROBLEM 5-73. Mother is suing the school because she claims they failed to protect her son from being injured while playing football. The son wants to continue playing, so he denied being hurt to his mother. Finally, one night mother came into the bedroom with father, and said, "*Baby, he must be hurting. I think that was alcohol he was rubbing all over his body.*" Father finally confronted son and he confessed to his injuries and pain. During father's testimony, he testifies to what his wife told him. Can the statement be offered to prove either: 1) why father finally confronted his son about being hurt more than 4 weeks since the purported injury; or 2) that the son was rubbing alcohol on himself that night and was still hurting from an injury that occurred more than 4 weeks prior to that night? Why or why not? Explain.

PROBLEM 5-74. Eric was on trial for the murder of his son. In a heated argument that led to a physical altercation, Eric choked his son to death. When police arrived, the only eyewitness, Eric's girlfriend, told the police officer, "*Based on the way it happened, I don't think he was trying to kill him when he choked him.*" While on the stand during cross-examination by Eric's attorney, the police officer was asked what Eric's girlfriend told him to prove that there was no intent to kill. Should the statement be admitted? Why or why not?

PROBLEM 5-75. Bo Diddly had five daughters. In his will, he left everything to four of his daughters and excluded one of them, Dee Dee, who is now a stripper in New York. (She has changed her name to Deelicious.) In an action she brought to dispute the validity of the will claiming undue influence, the defense calls Bo Diddly's lifelong friend who will testify that Bo Diddly made the following statements to him over the two years before he died. Deelicious objects that the statements are hearsay. How should the court rule on each statement and why?

a. "She was my favorite daughter growing up until she betrayed me up on that pole in New York."

b. "I think Dee Dee is extremely irresponsible."

c. "I think her boyfriend is too controlling and takes every penny she gets her hands on."

d. "Dee Dee doesn't love me."

e. "Dee Dee is better off if I just leave her alone."

PROBLEM 5-76. Dwayne is charged with the kidnapping and murder of his wife, Victoria. The prosecution offers the testimony of a friend of the wife who will testify that Victoria came to her crying and complaining that she was not happy in her marriage to Dwayne and was afraid of him. After discussing the marriage for a while, Victoria said she was going to call Dwayne to tell him how she felt. She picked up her cell phone and called Dwayne and told him that she wanted a divorce. Victoria then hung up the phone, started crying, and said, "He's gonna kill me, I know it. I don't wanna go home." Victoria left her friend's house and was never seen again. The prosecution has called the friend to the stand to testify and seeks to introduce the following evidence of her conversation with Victoria. Which of the following is most likely to be **excluded** from trial and why?

A. That Victoria told her that she was not happy and was afraid of her husband.

B. That Victoria said she was about to call her husband, Dwayne.

C. That Victoria told Dwayne, "I want a divorce."

D. That Victoria said, "He's gonna kill me. I know it."

E. That Victoria said, "I don't wanna go home."

§ 5.7 References and Additional Authority on Then Existing Mental Condition [La. C.E. art. 803(3)]

1. La. C.E. art. 803(3) and Official Comments
2. Force & Rault, HANDBOOK ON LOUISIANA EVIDENCE LAW Art. 803(3) Author's Comments (West Publishing 2014)
3. Harges & Jones, LOUISIANA EVIDENCE Art. 803(3) Author's Comments (West Publishing 2014)
4. 19 La. Civ. L. Treatise, Evidence And Proof § 10.15 (2nd ed.)
5. **Commentary**: Devall, Joseph, "*Whether Federal Rules of Evidence 803(3) Should Be Amended to Exclude Statements Offered to Prove the Subsequent Conduct of a Nondeclarant: Guidance from Louisiana*," 78 Tul. L. Rev. 911 (2004).
6. **Then Existing Mental Condition**: *State v. Adams*, 897 So. 2d 629 (La. Ct. App. 1st Cir. 2004) (showing declarant's intent to remove son from will).
7. **Must be "then" existing mental condition, not statement of memory (a past mental state), or belief**: *State v. Robinson*, 634 So. 2d 1274 (La. Ct. App. 3d Cir. 1994) (holding that when the defendant alleged the shooting was an accident but stated "I told you I was going to do it," statement was admissible to disprove the shooting was accidental).
8. **Offered to prove declarant's "future" action, not past action**: *State v. Ulfers* (La. 1st Cir. 02/08), WL 441488 (holding that victim's statements regarding being choked by defendants on two prior occasions were admissible to prove the victim's state of mind of fear for her life and to prove she was preparing to divorce the defendant); *State v. Lee*, 559 So. 2d 1310 (La. 1990) (holding that in trial for rape and murder, defendant's statements made to his sister eight months prior to crime, that he was "in love" with that woman and planned to marry her, and that when the woman subsequently ended the relationship he was "devastated" and "very unhappy," should have been admissible as his then existing mental condition to prove his future action).
9. **Not admissible to prove future action of third party**: *State v. Magee*, 103 So.3d 285 (La. 2012) (holding that sections of letter from defendant's wife, the victim, to defendant in which wife recalled the abuse, both physical and mental, she ostensibly suffered at the defendant's hands over the previous years of their relationship were not admissible under the state of mind exception to the hearsay rule in murder prosecution; exception precluded admission of a present state of mind to prove the acts of a third party or to prove a fact remembered).
10. **Statement of memory/belief is not admissible to prove thing remembered/believed:** *Lowery v. Herbert*, 909 So. 2d 648 (La. Ct. App. 3d Cir. 2005) (William Lowery wanted

to use statements of his deceased uncle, George Lowery, regarding where he believed the boundary line was and that he possessed the disputed property as the owner. The court found that the statements were not offered to prove the decedent's then existing mental condition or the future action but were statements of memory or belief which were not admissible to "prove fact remembered or believed.").

§ 5.8 Then Existing Physical Condition [La. C.E. art. 803(3)]

Applicable Code Articles

The following are not excluded by the hearsay rule, even though the declarant is available as a witness:

* * *

(3) Then existing..., physical condition. A statement of the declarant's then existing ... sensation, or physical condition (such as..., pain and bodily health), offered to prove the declarant's then existing condition or his future action. A statement of memory or belief, however, is not admissible to prove the fact remembered or believed unless it relates to the execution, revocation, identification, or terms of declarant's testament.

* * *

As stated above, Article 803(3) covers both mental and physical conditions. This section deals with *physical* conditions. Like mental conditions, when a person expresses his present physical condition, his statement may be offered to prove that he was in fact experiencing that physical condition at that time. Also like the mental condition, the exception is premised upon the fact that a person's own statement about his physical condition is the most reliable evidence of his physical condition. Further, there are no issues regarding memory since the exception only applies to a physical condition a person is experiencing at the moment in which the statement is made. This exception does not apply to expressions of memory about *past* physical conditions.

An example of a "then" existing physical condition is "*My stomach hurts*" or "*I feel nauseous*"—both statements express how the declarant feels at the moment the statements were made. A statement such as, "*My back has been hurting me all week,*" or "*That headache kept me up all night,*" would not conform to the exception because both statements speak to *past* physical conditions, or statements of memory about the declarant's physical condition at some prior time.

Additionally, unlike "statements made for purposes of medical treatment and diagnosis in connection with treatment," discussed in the next section, these statements need not be made for purposes of medical treatment, nor must they be made to a medical provider. Like then existing mental conditions, these statements may be made at any time, to anyone, for any purpose, provided they express the declarant's then existing physical condition.

Statements of belief not offered to prove thing believed. Finally, as with then existing mental conditions, a statement of a person's belief about his physical conditions or about what may have caused his physical condition may not be offered to prove the thing believed.

Thus a person who states, "*I think my back is broken*," may not be offered to prove the fact that the person's back is broken. However, the statement could possibly be relevant for non-hearsay purposes. For example, if the statement were offered for the state of mind of the declarant only to show that he was in severe pain, it might be admissible. But it could not be offered as evidence that the declarant's back was actually broken.

Similarly, if a person states, "*I have a sharp pain in my abdomen. I think I have appendicitis,*" while the statement about the sharp pain conforms to the exception, the person's belief about the cause of the pain (appendicitis) does not.

Case on "Then Existing Physical Condition"

Gilchrist v. Ozone Spring Water Company

Court of Appeal of Louisiana, Fourth Circuit
639 So. 2d 489
June 30, 1994

WALTZER, Judge.

STATEMENT OF THE CASE

Lloyd Gilchrist, Sr. (Gilchrist) sued Ozone Spring Water Company (Ozone) for injuries allegedly arising out of a slip and fall injury Gilchrist sustained when he fell on the bottom three to five steps of a staircase located on Ozone's premises. Access to the stairwell was controlled by a combination-controlled locking mechanism on a steel door, the combination of which was available to Ozone employees. Gilchrist claimed his injuries were caused solely by the defective design and/or condition of the steps, or by the presence of a slippery substance thereon. Gilchrist contended that Ozone failed properly to inspect and maintain the stairwell, and failed to warn plaintiff of the alleged defects.

Ozone answered, denying Gilchrist's claims, pleading comparative fault and contending that Gilchrist's injury occurred while he was on Ozone's premises without proper authorization in a limited access area.

Trial was held before the district court judge [Bernette Johnson—now on the Louisiana Supreme Court] on 14–16 June 1994. At the close of Gilchrist's testimony, the court noted that the record of Gilchrist's medical condition prior to the alleged accident was incomplete, and held the case open for reception of evidence including hospital records of two prior surgeries and a 1980 back strain, records of three treating physicians, and Social Security records pertaining to Gilchrist's pre-existing disability arising from accidents occurring seventeen and ten years ago....

The case was argued to the trial court on 10 September 1993, and judgment was rendered on 13 September 1993 in favor of Gilchrist in the amount of $193,703.40, together with legal interest from judicial demand until paid. The trial court set Gilchrist's comparative fault at 40% and Ozone's fault at 60%. The trial judge awarded $118,339.00 for past medical expenses, $29,500.00 for future medical expenses and $175,000 for general damages, reduced by 40% to reflect Gilchrist's comparative fault....

Finding no manifest error in the trial court's judgment, we affirm.

TRIAL COURT'S REASONS FOR JUDGMENT

The trial judge found that on the day of the accident, Gilchrist accompanied his son, Lloyd Gilchrist, Jr. (Junior), to the Ozone plant. The judge did not resolve the issue of whether Junior, a former Ozone employee who had been terminated for cause six days before the alleged accident, and Gilchrist were on the premises for any legitimate purpose, but found that Junior used his employee 4-digit combination code to gain entry for himself and for his father to the stairwell wherein Gilchrist was injured. Gilchrist and Junior went up the employee stairs to Joseph Pierce's office. Following some heated discussion, they descended the stairs. When Gilchrist was approximately three to five steps from the bottom, he fell, suffering an injury.

The trial judge, relying on the testimony of Gilchrist's architect Lawrence Dwyer, found that the stairs were defective because of numerous code violations....

The evidence of record demonstrates that prior to the accident, Gilchrist was 100% disabled, could sit only about one hour without pain, could walk only one or two blocks without back pain, used a cane at all times, was in bed 22 hours a day, experienced shortness of breath, was nervous and had trouble concentrating.

The court awarded documented past medical expenses of $118,339; future medical expenses of $29,500; and general damages arising out of his carpal tunnel and disc surgeries of $175,000.

We find that the record amply supports the trial court's findings....

PLAINTIFF'S SECOND ASSIGNMENT OF ERROR

Gilchrist contends the trial court erred in holding the case open for submission of Gilchrist's medical records and Social Security Administration records. Gilchrist contends these records are inadmissible hearsay evidence and may not be received after the close of the trial.

...

At the close of testimony, in open court, the trial judge told counsel for the parties:

THE COURT:

"The record is not complete and this is what I need to supplement this record. I need the entire hospital records from the 1971 surgery, apparently at Methodist Hospital; the hospital records from the 1978 or '79 surgery, whatever hospital; I need Dr. McLachlan's reports and notes; I need the records from Lafayette General Hospital with reference to this back strain in the 1980's; I need the complete records from Social Security; I need Dr. Provenza's reports and notes; I need Dr. Bourgeois' notes and reports. My preference would be to get all of these records over the summer and *continue this hearing to September.* It's not clear to me, why did Dr. Louis Provenza not testify in person, he's not available?" (Emphasis added.)

[PLAINTIFF'S COUNSEL]:

"Judge, I thought it was convenient for the Court, he's extremely expensive to get to court and hard to get to court, and in a judge trial—"

THE COURT:

"The deposition isn't sufficient. Let me do this, let me look at his reports and records and all of these other medical records. There are questions I need answered in terms of his prior medical history and his percentage of disability prior to this accident so I can come to some kind of conclusion about what percentage of his disability relates to this injury, it's just not there."

...

The medical reports and records sought by the trial court, and provided by both defendant and plaintiff, are relevant both to the issue of causation and to the credibility of the trial testimony of Gilchrist and his wife.

As to causation, the Louisiana Supreme Court held:

> "[a] claimant's disability is presumed to have resulted from an accident, if before the accident the injured person was in good health, but commencing with the accident the symptoms of the disabling condition appear and continuously manifest themselves afterwards, providing that the medical evidence shows there to be a reasonable possibility of causal connection between the accident and the disabling condition." ...

Thus, Gilchrist's pre-accident condition is at issue in this case.

Furthermore, the trial court's requested evidence is relevant to the credibility of Gilchrist's own trial testimony and to that of his wife. At trial, Gilchrist said his prior injuries and surgeries had not altered his ability to function well in his daily life, and that he could do "everything a normal person could do" except, perhaps "playing football or basketball." He alleged that after the injury in the Ozone plant, his mental, physical, and emotional condition so deteriorated that he was required to spend 23 hours of each day in his bed. His statements as reflected in the medical and social security records are admissible as inconsistencies, contradictions, and explanations of his trial testimony.

LSA-C.E. art. 803(3) provides:

> "The following are not excluded by the hearsay rule, even though the declarant is available as a witness:
>
> (3) ... A statement of the declarant's then existing state of mind, emotion, sensation, or physical condition..., offered to prove the declarant's then existing condition or his future action."

In his final decision, issued 27 April 1983 (*five years before the Ozone accident*), [Social Security] Administrative Law Judge Carl W. Sarett reports:

> "Claimant [Lloyd Gilchrist, Sr.] *testified* that he has constant burning in the left leg. He has severe, constant low back pain which is like a 'knuckle pushing hard into his back.' The back pain has gotten worse since the 1978 operation. In addition, his neck hurts all the time. Claimant stated *after sitting one hour the pain is worse.* He can *walk one or two blocks* ... then the back pain is worse and his heart beats fast. He *uses a cane at all times.* He has *shortness of breath and chest pains three or four times a week.* He stated *he was in bed twenty-two hours a day.* He is very nervous and has trouble concentrating. When he sits it feels as if the bones are going into each other." (Emphasis added.)

These findings are clearly within the "statement of physical condition" exception to the hearsay rule and were properly considered by the trial judge.

At trial, Gilchrist's wife testified at length about her husband's condition before and after the Ozone plant accident. It was her testimony that after Gilchrist's 1971 surgery, but before the Ozone plant accident, he had some pain at times, but led an active life, mowing grass, doing housework, shopping, cooking, and caring for her epilepsy and esophagitis. The trial judge reviewed the following statement from Judge Sarett's decision:

> "Claimant's wife [Mrs. Gilchrist, Sr.] testified that claimant is constantly complaining of pain. He *hardly gets out of bed.* In the last year he has been worse. He

> cannot concentrate as he used to. He is *unable to bend or walk more than one block* without his leg giving out." (Emphasis added).

These findings are likewise within the foregoing exception to the hearsay rule.

...

The Social Security Administration proceedings, which concluded with a finding of total disability on 27 April 1983, are admissible under the public records and reports exception to the hearsay rule. LSA-C.E. 803(8) provides:

> "The following are not excluded by the hearsay rule, even though the declarant is available as a witness: ...
>
> (8)(a) Records, reports, statements, or data compilations, in any form, of a public office or agency setting forth: ...
>
> (iii) Factual findings resulting from an investigation made pursuant to authority granted by law. Factual findings are conclusions of fact reached by a governmental agency and may be based upon information furnished to it by persons other than agents and employees of that agency."

On 27 April 1983, [Social Security] Administrative Law Judge Carl W. Sarett found as to Gilchrist:

> "Claimant [Lloyd Gilchrist, Sr.] has a history of surgery of the back, including a fusion from L4 to S1 which was not successful. Claimant continues to have severe impairment in the lower lumbar spine including chronic arachnoiditis, spondylolisthesis, and stenosis. Claimant also has some impairment of the cervical spine, possibly a herniated disc, of a moderately severe nature. He suffers from hypertension, not severe and without organ damage.... As a result of the foregoing claimant continues to suffer with severe pain and severe limitation of normal bodily functions.... Claimant continues to be incapable of performing any sustained substantial gainful activity.... Since April 1982 claimant has been disabled within the meaning of the law.... claimant ... continues to be disabled and entitled to disability insurance benefits. Claimant also is disabled for purposes of supplemental security income...."

The trial judge considered both the contemporaneous trial testimony of the plaintiff, his wife, and physicians, and the records of the Social Security Administration and treating and examining physicians in making her determination of the actual loss sustained by Gilchrist as a result of the Ozone plant accident. We find no error in this consideration, nor do we find the trial court's conclusions to be manifestly erroneous. The plaintiff's second assignment of error is without merit.

...

In the case at bar, the trial judge said in her reasons for judgment that it was her intent to make the plaintiff whole—that is, to compensate him as nearly as possible in a monetary way for the difference between his condition just prior to the Ozone accident and his condition following the accident. She determined that an award of general damages in the amount of $175,000 would compensate Gilchrist for that loss. The trial judge found that prior to the accident, Gilchrist was totally disabled, in constant pain, spending about 22 hours per day in bed, walking breathlessly with a cane. We cannot say that the trial judge was manifestly erroneous in failing to attribute all of the plaintiff's present ills to the Ozone accident. Indeed, were she to have ruled otherwise, the trial judge would have had to have concluded that although Gilchrist was bed-ridden and in constant pain in April of 1982, somehow a miracle occurred between April, 1982 and October, 1988 by which he became functionally whole, and capable of every normal activity except football and basketball, until the Ozone accident returned him to his 1982 disabled condition.[97]

Likewise, the trial judge's apparent conclusion that the services performed by his family members were not increased as a result of the Ozone accident is not manifestly erroneous. Furthermore, the trial judge was acting within her vast discretion as trier of fact in determining that the future medical treatment and comprehensive plan of life care as to which testimony was adduced were not the result of the Ozone injury.

Discussion Questions

1. *Gilchrist* presents an issue of double and triple hearsay. The ALJ Report (statement #1) contains the claimant's statements (statement #2), both requiring an exception or exemption to the hearsay rule to be admissible. Which exceptions were used for each statement here?
2. Does the portion of the report that refers to Mrs. Gilchrist's statement present triple hearsay? The report states (statement #1) that Ms. Gilchrist states (statement #2) that her husband complains (statement #3) of ... Is there an exception for Mrs. Gilchrist's statement? Should that statement have been admitted without reference to an additional exception?
3. Taking a closer look at the statements that were admitted under the "then existing physical condition" exception—does the entire statement refer to the claimant's "then existing physical condition"? Do portions refer to statements of memory being offered to prove the thing remembered? Which portions of the statement would it have been possible to excise?

§ 5.8 References and Additional Authority on Then Existing Physical Condition [La. C.E. art. 803(3)]

1. La. C.E. art. 803(3) and Official Comments
2. Force & Rault, Handbook on Louisiana Evidence Law Art. 803(3) Author's Comments (West Publishing 2014)
3. Harges & Jones, Louisiana Evidence Art. 803(3) Author's Comments (West Publishing 2014)
4. 19 La. Civ. L. Treatise, Evidence And Proof § 10.15 (2nd ed.)
5. **Then existing physical condition**: *Trascher v. Territo*, 89 So. 3d 357 (La. 2012) (Plaintiffs filed suit against several defendants for wrongful death and survival action regarding the illness and death of Mr. Trascher caused by workplace exposure to asbestos. Mr. Trascher's video deposition was taken; however, defendants were not present to

97. The Social Security finding of total disability, and Gilchrist's medical status, cause all of his future medical treatments to be covered either by Social Security, Medicaid and/or Medicare. The payment records show these treatments to have been paid for by Medicare and Medicaid, and the supporting documentation notes that the treatments were not necessitated by an accident or injury.

cross-examine the deponent. The video shows the physical condition of Mr. Trascher when he was hooked to oxygen, in very poor health and in a hospital bed struggling to breathe. Mr. Trascher was asked, "And today how do you feel?" The response by the deponent was objected to but the court stated the answer as admissible under the exception of Mr. Trascher's then existing state of mind and physical condition to prove the existing condition since he was in poor health, had trouble breathing, and was suffering from depression due to his confinement to the hospital bed.).

§ 5.9 Statements Made for Purposes of Medical Treatment and Diagnosis in Connection with Treatment [La. C.E. art. 803(4)]

Applicable Code Articles

The following are not excluded by the hearsay rule, even though the declarant is available as a witness:

* * *

(4) Statements for purposes of medical treatment and medical diagnosis in connection with treatment. Statements made for purposes of medical treatment and medical diagnosis in connection with treatment and describing medical history, or past or present symptoms, pain, or sensations, or the inception or general character of the cause or external source thereof insofar as reasonably pertinent to treatment or diagnosis in connection with treatment.

* * *

Article 803(4) provides that certain statements made to healthcare providers for the purpose of obtaining medical treatment and medical diagnosis in connection with treatment are excluded from the hearsay ban. This exception would include statements a person might make to a nurse upon arriving in an emergency room, such as, "*I'm weak, I have chills, and I've been throwing up all week. I had gallbladder surgery two months ago.*" These statements are deemed reliable because a person is unlikely to fabricate information to a healthcare provider when the person knows that the healthcare provider is relying on the information he provides for the purpose of treating him.

As in the example above, the exception includes statements that describe a person's medical history, past or present symptoms, pain, and sensations. The statements may also include statements relating to the cause or external source of the condition, if the information is reasonably pertinent to the treatment or diagnosis in connection with treatment of the condition.

The basic requirements for the rule are that the statements must be:

1) describing a person's medial history, past or present symptoms, pain, or sensations and/or statements regarding the cause and circumstances of injury (if reasonably pertinent to treatment/diagnosis in connection with treatment);
2) made to a healthcare provider; and
3) made for purposes of medical diagnosis and treatment in connection with treatment.

Medical Treatment Exception Requirements:

1. describing a person's **medical history**, past or present **symptoms, pain, or sensations** and/or statements regarding the **cause and circumstances** of injury (if reasonably pertinent to treatment/diagnosis in connection with treatment);
2. made to a **healthcare provider**; and
3. made for purposes of medical **diagnosis** and **treatment** in connection with treatment.

Types of statements included. Not all statements that a person makes to a physician or medical provider will be permissible under this rule. As noted above, this exception only includes statements describing a person's medical history, past or present **symptoms, pain, sensations** and/or statements regarding the **cause and circumstances** of injury, if **reasonably pertinent to treatment/diagnosis** in connection with treatment. The exception is limited to only those statements that are usually relied upon by physicians in their diagnosis and treatment of patients.[98] There are two important points to keep in mind regarding these statements.

1. Must be in connection with treatment. This exception ultimately envisions actual ***treatment*** by the healthcare provider. As a result, its trustworthiness lies in the fact that a person will be unlikely to fabricate information to a healthcare provider when he knows he will be treated based on the information he provides. As a result, if the statements are being made to a healthcare provider for some other purpose, such as in anticipation of litigation, to only *diagnose* a disorder for which the patient will not be treated, the exception will not apply.[99] In such a case, a person could go on and on about pain and symptoms he claims to have for the purposes of increasing his recovery. Thus, such statements are not reliable and are not included in the rule.

Federal Rules of Evidence Distinction. This is a major difference from Federal Rule of Evidence 803(4), which does not require that the statement actually be in connection with treatment, only diagnosis.[100] Thus, under federal law, a person's statements about his injuries to a chiropractor, for example, who will prepare a report that will be used at trial to show the injury he sustained in an accident, will be allowed under this rule, even if the doctor does not actually treat him for the injury he diagnoses. Such statements would not be admissible under Louisiana law, however, which requires that the statements be made in connection with actual treatment to be trustworthy.

2. Cause or source of pain, symptoms, or injury. In addition to statements about a person's actual symptoms or pain that will assist the healthcare provider in diagnosing and treating him, this exception also allows certain statements about the cause or source of the injuries, if that information is **"reasonably pertinent to the treatment and diagnosis."**[101] This generally includes "statements that are usually relied upon by physicians

98. La. Code Evid. art. 803(4) Official Comment to Exception (4)(b).
99. La. Code Evid. art. 803(4) Official Comment to Exception (4)(a).
100. See Fed. R. Evid. 804(4); La. Code Evid. art. 803(4) Official Comments to Exception (4)(a).
101. La. Code Evid. art. 803(4).

in their diagnosis and treatment."[102] For example, a person who arrives at the hospital with a broken leg might state that he fell down the stairs, or that he fell off of his motorcycle. This information might be deemed reasonably pertinent to assisting the doctor in diagnosing or treating a patient. However, if the person states, "*My employee pushed me down the stairs after I fired him,*" the court will likely find the statement inadmissible. Who pushed the patient down the stairs and why he was pushed are not pertinent to diagnosis and treatment.

Statement to healthcare provider. This exception only applies to statements made to healthcare providers, but they need not be a physician, per se.[103] A healthcare provider might include the nurse, emergency medical technicians, lab technicians, and other healthcare providers working under the direction of a physician.

Others with relationship can make the statements, including doctor to doctor. In addition to the patient's own statements, a third party's statements to the healthcare provider may be included under this exception, including a parent or spouse, provided the third party has a relationship with the patient such that his or her statements are likely to be trustworthy. The exception also includes statements from one doctor to another doctor made for the purpose of medical treatment and diagnosis in connection with treatment of a patient. The declarant must, however, have personal knowledge of whatever information he relates to the healthcare provider for purposes of treatment or diagnosis.[104]

This exception does not include statements made by the doctor to the patient during such interactions.

Distinguished from "then existing physical condition." Although in many instances "statements made for purposes of medical treatment and diagnosis in connection with treatment" will include statements of a person's "then existing physical condition," there are distinct differences between the two exceptions as follows:

1. A statement made for purposes of medical treatment/diagnosis in connection with treatment, must actually be made in connection with *treatment*, while statements of a person's then existing physical condition need not be made for purposes of medical treatment. They may be made for any purpose.
2. Statements made for purposes of medical treatment/diagnosis in connection with treatment must be made to a healthcare provider, while statements of a person's then existing medical condition may be made to anyone at any time.
3. In addition to present symptoms, statements for purposes of medical treatment and diagnosis may also include statements describing medical history, past symptoms, and even statements regarding the cause and circumstances of the injury if pertinent to treatment and diagnosis. Statements of a person's then existing physical condition include only the person's physical condition when the statement is made.
4. Statements for purposes of medical treatment or diagnosis may also be made by someone other than the declarant if the relationship exists such that the other person's statements are deemed trustworthy. Statements of a then existing physical condition must be a statement of a person's own physical condition. They may not be made by another person.

102. LA. CODE EVID. art. 803(4) Official Comment to Exception (4).
103. LA. CODE EVID. art. 803(4) Official Comment to Exception (4)(e).
104. LA. CODE EVID. art. 803(4) Official comment to Exception (4)(d).

Cases on Statements Made for Purposes of Medical Treatment/ Diagnosis in Connection with Treatment

Dardeau v. Ardoin

Court of Appeal of Louisiana, Third Circuit
703 So. 2d 695
Nov. 5, 1997

DECUIR, Judge.

Plaintiff alleges that when she was 28 years old, she came under the care of Dr. James Ardoin for routine female examinations. She contends that after her first visit with Dr. Ardoin, he recommended and performed radical surgery consisting of a bladder suspension, cystocele repair, rectocele repair, complete hysterectomy and removal of her ovaries. According to the plaintiff, Dr. Ardoin injured her obturator nerve during the cystocele surgery and that as a result, she has sustained permanent paralysis in her right leg.

... According to defendant, plaintiff's complaints persisted and Dr. Ardoin ... suggested surgery.... After a discussion of the procedures, plaintiff executed three consent forms, which were introduced into the record. A second opinion was obtained from Dr. Francisco Cantu who agreed with Dr. Ardoin's findings and recommendation for surgery.

... The jury concluded that Dr. Ardoin obtained Ms. Dardeau's informed consent prior to surgery; that a reasonable person would have accepted the risk of an obturator nerve injury based upon the medical condition of the plaintiff at the time of the surgery; that Dr. Ardoin was not guilty of substandard conduct constituting malpractice; and that plaintiff's injury was not caused by any substandard conduct on the part of Dr. Ardoin. For the following reasons, we affirm.

HEARSAY

Dr. Ardoin passed away prior to trial. Plaintiff complains in brief that the introduction of progress notes or office chart by Dr. Ardoin constitute hearsay....

... Dr. Ardoin's office chart is admissible under several articles of the Louisiana Code of Evidence. Specifically, Dr. Ardoin's office chart created during the course of his treatment of the plaintiff constitutes a record maintained in the course of a regularly conducted business activity under La.Code Evid. art. 803(6). Dr. Ardoin's receptionist, Norma Fontenot, testified at trial that the office chart was created in connection with Dr. Ardoin's business, that the entries in the chart were made at the time of treatment, and that the entries were made by Dr. Ardoin who had personal knowledge of the information in the chart. Ms. Fontenot testified that she has never seen any chart being altered or falsified by Dr. Ardoin, nor did Dr. Ardoin request that she alter any office chart. Finally, no evidence was presented by plaintiff to indicate that Dr. Ardoin's records were untrustworthy.

Dr. Ardoin's office chart is likewise admissible under La.Code Evid. art. 803(4) relating to statements made for the purpose of medical treatment and diagnosis in connection with treatment. Dr. Ardoin's records which were made contemporaneously with the history and complaints related by plaintiff constitute statements made for the purpose of medical treatment and diagnosis, and thus the office chart falls under the art. 803(4) exception to the hearsay rule....

Having found no error on the part of the trial court, we affirm the jury verdict and the judgment of the trial court. Costs of appeal are assessed to plaintiff-appellant.

THIBODEAUX, Judge, dissenting.

The trial court incorrectly allowed the records of Dr. James Ardoin into evidence. In my view, those records were clearly hearsay. This hearsay evidence was not supported by the necessary qualifying circumstances which would ensure the trustworthiness of those documents. That evidence was simply lacking. Since this legal error tainted the fact finding process, I would reverse the judgment below and conduct a *de novo* review of the entire proceeding without a consideration of the inadmissible hearsay evidence.

Discussion Question

Would the entire office chart be admissible under this exception, or would only the plaintiff's statements to the doctor be permissible under the exception? Would you need to know exactly what the charts stated to decide? Why or why not?

Weeks v. Byrd[105] below demonstrates the portion of the rule that excludes statements regarding the cause and circumstances of an injury that are not reasonably pertinent to diagnosis and treatment in connection with treatment.

Weeks v. Byrd Medical Clinic, Inc.

Ct of Appeal of Louisiana, Third Circuit
927 So. 2d 594
April 5, 2006

EZELL, Judge.

Ms. Weeks' mother, Goldia Neystel, was transferred from Many Hospital to the senior care unit at Byrd Hospital on February 25, 1997, due to psychotic and schizophrenia problems. On intake, it was noted that she was a high risk for falls. This risk was increased by the fact that the great toe on her left foot had been amputated. Ms. Neystel was listed as a patient requiring specialist precautions II. This type of patient required that the nursing staff observe and make contact with the patient at least every fifteen minutes.

In the early morning hours of March 18, 1997, Ms. Neystel fell while attempting to get out of bed to use her bedside commode. As a result of the fall, she fractured her right hip. The next day, she was transferred to a hospital in Baton Rouge at the request of her daughter. Ms. Neystel died on March 21, 1997.

Ms. Weeks filed suit against Byrd Hospital and other parties. She alleged that Byrd Hospital was negligent in its care of Ms. Neystel and that it breached the appropriate standard of care owed to her.

On March 25, 2004, Byrd Hospital filed a motion for summary judgment that was heard on July 12, 2004. Judgment was signed on February 9, 2005, granting summary judgment in favor of Byrd Hospital and dismissing Ms. Weeks' claim against it. Ms. Weeks appeals.

SUMMARY JUDGMENT

Ms. Weeks appeals the summary judgment dismissal of Byrd Hospital, arguing that there is evidence in the record that indicates that the employees were negligent in their

105. Weeks v. Byrd, 927 So. 2d (La. Ct. App. 3d Cir 2006).

care of Ms. Neystel by failing to follow policies and procedures. She relies on the deposition testimony of Dr. Frank Covington, Ms. Neystel's treating psychiatrist....

In written reasons for judgment the trial court ruled that "[p]laintiff ... presented no evidence that the procedures and policies developed by Byrd Hospital did not meet the required standard of care." The court further stated that:

> The only evidence of a deviation from the standard of care was the hearsay statement of Goldia Neystel that nurses failed to respond timely to her signal for assistance. The hospital records do not corroborate this statement. No evidence was presented which would indicate the statement would be admitted under an exception to the hearsay rules.

Byrd Hospital claims that the record establishes that it complied with the orders of Dr. Covington that Ms. Neystel be checked every fifteen minutes. It argues that Ms. Weeks has not produced any medical evidence that it deviated from the standard of care and that a deviation caused the injuries or death of Ms. Neystel.

On the other hand, Ms. Weeks argues that she does not need any expert testimony to establish the standard of care required of Byrd Hospital, as recognized by the trial court. She claims that Dr. Covington's deposition, taken on July 23, 2003, over six years after Ms. Neystel's fall, establishes a breach of the standard of care required of Byrd Hospital. *Ms. Weeks relies on Dr.* Covington's deposition testimony that Ms. Neystel told him, on the morning after her fall, that she had attempted to call the staff on several occasions to help her. She could not wait, so she got up and fell at the bedside. Ms. Weeks also relies on his statement that a nurse had told him that a nurse from the unit had been pulled to another floor during the night. Dr. Covington did not identify any specific nurse that made this statement and was not sure of the number of nurses that would work the night shift.

...

Byrd Hospital argues that this testimony relied on by Ms. Weeks to establish a breach of the standard of care is inadmissible hearsay testimony that would not be admissible at trial. It claims that this does not create a genuine issue of material fact. We agree.

It is clear that both statements of Dr. Covington relied upon by Ms. Weeks are hearsay testimony pursuant to La.Code Evid. art. 801. Ms. Weeks argues that the statement made by her mother to Dr. Covington is admissible as a statement for the purpose of medical treatment and diagnosis pursuant to La.Code Evid. art. 803(4). Comments to Exception(4)(b) provide that this subsection "has been interpreted to limit the scope of this exception to the kind of statements that are usually relied upon by physicians in their diagnosis and treatment of patients." It further provides that "statements as to the cause of a condition not reasonably pertinent to diagnosis or treatment of it are not within the ambit of this exception." Ms. Neystel's statements to Dr. Covington as to how she fell have nothing to do with the diagnosis or treatment of her condition and are therefore inadmissible.

We have thoroughly reviewed the record and evidence in the case and agree with the trial court that there is no evidence that Byrd Hospital breached any standard of care owed to Ms. Neystel. Records indicate that she was checked on every fifteen minutes.

Discussion Questions

1. While the fact that Ms. Neystel fell might be pertinent to her treatment, do you think the facts and circumstances which led to her attempting to walk in the first place are relevant to treating her? Why or why not?

2. Why are these types of statements excluded from the exception? Do you think the statements are trustworthy? Explain.

Key Points

The key points to keep in mind regarding then existing physical condition and statements made for purposes of medical treatment and diagnosis in connection with treatment.

Then Existing Physical Condition

1. **Then Existing Physical Condition**—Allows statements of a person's then existing physical condition.
   a. **Requirements:** 1) a statement of the person's own then existing physical condition, and not a statement of memory or belief; 2) offered to prove the person's then existing physical condition.
2. **Statements of belief** not admissible to prove the thing believed.
3. **Statements of memory** excluded.
4. Statements may be made to anyone at any time. Need not be made to a healthcare provider.

Statements for Purposes of Medical Treatment and Diagnosis in Connection with Treatment

1. **Statements for purposes of medical treatment and diagnosis in connection with treatment**—permits statements made for purposes of medical diagnosis and treatment in connection with treatment.
2. **Requirements:**
   a. statements describing a person's medical history, past or present symptoms, pain, or sensations and/or statements regarding the cause and circumstances of injury (if reasonably pertinent to treatment/diagnosis in connection with treatment);
   b. made to a healthcare provider; and
   c. made for purposes of medical diagnosis and treatment in connection with treatment.
3. Statements **must be made to healthcare provider** (e.g., nurse, EMT, anyone working under direction of physician).
4. Statements **may be made by a third party,** provided the third party has first-hand knowledge and trustworthy relationship exists.
5. Statements must be **made in connection with treatment**, not merely for diagnosis.
6. **Statements include**: medical history, past or present symptoms, pain, or sensations, etc. Statements need not be present conditions provided they are reasonably pertinent to treatment or diagnosis.
7. May include statements regarding the **cause and circumstances** of injury, provided the statement is *reasonably pertinent to treatment/diagnosis in connection with treatment.*

Problems on Then Existing Physical Condition and Statements Made for Medical Treatment/Diagnosis in Connection with Treatment

PROBLEM 5-77. Which of the following are statements of a person's "then existing physical condition"?

a. *"I'm hungry."*

b. *"I'm exhausted."*

c. *"I killed him."*

d. *"My leg got hurt in a car accident."*

e. *"I'm constipated."*

f. *"My mother embarrasses me every time I introduce her to a new beau."*

g. *"I think I have a brain aneurysm."*

h. *"I have a sharp pain in my chest. I think I'm having a heart attack."*

PROBLEM 5-78. Dillon described his symptoms to his doctor hoping he could help him determine the cause of his problems. "*Every now and then I wake up at night with an excruciating headache. My eyes begin to dim. There is numbness right between my eyes, and my eyes are very sensitive to light. I think it's migraines.*" Would the doctor be able to testify to what Dillon told him about his symptoms? If so, under which exception? Would any portion be excluded? Explain.

PROBLEM 5-79. Part I: Kelly stated to her husband, "*I am nauseated and tired all the time. I think I'm pregnant.*" Kelly was later killed by her husband who didn't want kids. Can Kelly's statement be offered to show her husband's motive for killing her?

Part II: Assume instead that killing a woman when there is reason to believe she is pregnant is first-degree murder. Can Kelly's statement be offered by the prosecution to prove that Kelly was pregnant when she was killed in order to elevate the charges to first-degree murder? Why or why not? (For this part, disregard the allegation that Husband didn't want kids as a motive for killing.)

PROBLEM 5-80. Jim stated to his neighbor, "*Ya know I was in an accident last week. My back was hurting me so bad last night, I didn't sleep a wink.*" Can his neighbor subsequently testify to what Jim told him in Jim's personal injury trial, to help prove how badly Jim was hurt?

PROBLEM 5-81. Only hours before Dena was found dead in her apartment, she said to her mother, "*The pain is so unbearable, I can't live like this.*" Can this statement be offered to prove Dena might have committed suicide? Why or why not?

PROBLEM 5-82. Tim's dad ran into an ER holding Tim in his arms and said to the nurses, "*My son had an accident on his four wheeler. He was speeding and ran into the side of a car.*" The driver of the car sued Tim and his insurance company for damages. At trial, they want to offer the statement Dad made to the nurses to help prove Tim's negligence. How should the court rule and why?

What if, instead of seeking to have a nurse testify to the statement, the plaintiffs discover the statement in Tim's medical records during discovery. At trial the medical records are offered into evidence. Tim objects that the statement should be excised because it is hearsay. Are there any circumstances under which the statement can be admitted? Explain.

PROBLEM 5-83. Sally was transported by ambulance from her church to the emergency room after she had a seizure and fainted during Sunday morning service. Her pastor rode to the hospital in the ambulance with her. Upon arrival at the hospital, the Pastor told the ER doctor that earlier that morning in church Sally looked dizzy, then began sweating and trembling uncontrollably before she fell onto the floor and fainted. The doctor put the pastor's statement in Sally's medical records. Sally subsequently sued her family doctor who gave her the medication that made her sick for medical malpractice. Sally's Pastor has since passed away, so Sally offers the medical records, which include the Pastor's statement, as evidence of the effect that the medication had on her before being taken to the hospital. At trial, her family doctor objects that the medical report is double hearsay. Should the portion of the report containing Pastor's statement be admitted into evidence over Family Doctor's objection?

PROBLEM 5-84. Bob was hit while crossing the intersection. When he got into the ambulance, he immediately said, "*The man my wife is cheating with just ran over me.*" Does this statement conform to the "statement made for purposes of medical treatment/diagnosis in connection with treatment" exception?

PROBLEM 5-85. Billy's parents were suing the school system for Intentional Infliction of Emotional Distress for distress Billy suffered from being bullied at school after the school failed to intervene. In preparation for the trial, Billy saw a therapist who will testify that Billy said to her, "*I don't usually sleep at night. I have no appetite. I'm very nervous now all the time. I've become an introvert and I have trust issues.*" Will the statements be admissible to prove Billy's suffering?

PROBLEM 5-86. Mindy (5) and Harrison (8) were taken from their mother's home by the Office of Community Services over allegations of abuse made by their teachers. In furtherance of their investigation, the OCS had the children examined by Dr. Curtis to determine if they had been sexually abused. Following the examination, the doctor determined that both children had been abused. In a hearing to involuntarily terminate parental rights of the mother, the doctor testified to various statements made by the children concerning the nature of the sexual abuse—when and how it occurred, by whom, etc. Are the children's statements to the doctor hearsay? [*See State in Interest of D.S.*, 694 So. 2d 327 (La. Ct. App. 1st Cir. 1996).]

PROBLEM 5-87. Crystal is trying out for the school soccer team and has to get a medical examination. During the examination, the doctor asks Crystal a series of questions in order to determine if she is healthy enough to play on the team. Crystal informed the doctor that she sometimes has chest pains, but not often, and they're not very severe. The doctor cleared Crystal to play, and Crystal made the team. During the championship game near the end of the season, Crystal suffered a heart attack and died. Crystal's parents sued the school claiming that they negligently allowed Crystal to play on the team despite her heart condition. The school claims that Crystal was thoroughly examined and did not have the heart condition when she made the team, and must have developed it sometime during the season. The parents would like to offer the testimony of the doctor as to what Crystal told him about her chest pains to prove that Crystal had the heart condition at the time she was allowed to play on the team. The school objects that the statement is hearsay. Will the doctor's testimony be admissible? How will the court rule and why?

PROBLEM 5-88. Cane has to get a physical to get a health insurance policy. Cane informed the doctor about the occasional pain in his lower abdomen. The doctor finds no health problems and clears Cane for the health insurance policy. It later turns out that Cane has pancreatic cancer. The insurance company refuses to pay the medical bills claiming the condition was pre-existing—that Cane already had the cancer before he was covered. Cane sues the insurance company to pay his medical bills. The insurance company seeks to admit the statement that Cane made to the doctor about his stomach pains as proof that Cane was having symptoms of the pancreatic cancer when he was examined to help prove that he had the condition before he was covered. Cane objects that the statement is hearsay. How will the court rule and why?

§ 5.9 References and Additional Authority on Statements Made for Purposes of Treatment [La. C.E. art. 803(4)]

1. La. C.E. art. 803(4) and Official Comments
2. Force & Rault, Handbook on Louisiana Evidence Law Art. 803(4) Author's Comments (West Publishing 2014)
3. Harges & Jones, Louisiana Evidence Art. 803(4) Author's Comments (West Publishing 2014)
4. 19 La. Civ. L. Treatise, Evidence And Proof § 10.16 (2nd ed.)
5. **Admitted as Statements Made for Purposes of Medical Treatment and Diagnosis in Connection with Treatment**: *State In Interest of D.S.*, 694 So. 2d 327 (La. Ct. App. 1st Cir. 1996), writ denied 684 So. 2d 930, 1996-2395 (La. 12/6/96) (holding that testimony of emergency room physician in termination of parental rights proceeding regarding results of her examination of child to determine whether she had been sexually abused fell within exception to hearsay for statements made for purposes of medical treatment and medical diagnosis in connection with treatment, though physician did not treat child, where examination provided critical information for physician to recommend various types of treatment for child); *G.N.S. v. S.B.S*, 796 So. 2d 739 (La. Ct. App. 2d Cir. 2001) (holding that, in custody modification case, out-of-court statements made by child to child abuse expert, psychiatrist, and social worker concerning allegations of abuse perpetrated on child by mother were admissible under hearsay exception permitting admission of statements made for purposes of medical treatment and diagnosis); *State v. Thom*, 615 So. 2d 355 (La. Ct. App. 5th Cir. 1993) (holding that the victim of a rape explaining to the nurse how her rape occurred was admissible for the purpose of medical diagnosis and treatment to determine the amount of trauma the victim sustained).
6. **Must be made for purposes of medical treatment**: *State v. Johnson*, 706 So. 2d 468 (La. Ct App. 4th Cir 1997), writ denied 98-0617 (La. 1998), 724 So. 2d 203 (holding that a statement by a rape victim to the examining physician that she was forced into an alley at gunpoint was not admissible because it was not stated for the purposes of medical treatment and diagnosis); *State v. Harris*, 781 So. 2d 73 (La. Ct. App. 4th Cir. 2001) (holding that statements by seven-year-old minor victim to expert witness while witness took a culture from victim to determine presence of sexually transmitted diseases four weeks after last incident of alleged sexual abuse, that defendant went "inside" of her and it "hurt," were not admissible in aggravated rape prosecution under medical treatment exception to hearsay rule; principal purpose of examination was forensic).
7. **Must be made to healthcare provider**: *State v. Ste. Marie*, 801 So. 2d 424 (La. Ct. App. 3d Cir. 2001) (holding that social worker's testimony as to what juveniles told

her regarding sexual abuse was inadmissible under hearsay exception for statement made for purpose of medical treatment and diagnosis, where there was no evidence that social worker was working under physician's direction).

8. **May be made by a third party**: *In re P.H.*, 635 So. 2d 1302 (La. Ct. App. 4th Cir. 1994) (Statements made by relatives of patient).
9. **Made in connection with treatment, not merely for diagnosis**: *State v. Morgan*, 34 So. 3d 1127 (La. Ct. App. 2d Cir. 2010) (holding that statement by the hospital physician that a victim of a rape reported the sexual assault was an exception to the hearsay rule because it was made for the purpose of medical treatment).
10. **Cause/circumstances not reasonably pertinent to diagnosis**: *State v. Bennett*, 591 So. 2d 783 (La. Ct. App. 4th Cir. 1991) (holding that rape victim's statement to physician about being forced to drive to a particular place where the rape occurred was inadmissible because the statement and information was not reasonably pertinent to the treatment and/or diagnosis of the victim); *State v. Merritt*, App. 875 So. 2d 80, (La. Ct. App. 3d Cir 2004) reversed in part on rehearing 884 So. 2d 1283, 2003-946 (La.App. 3 Cir. 10/13/04), writ granted 896 So. 2d 987, 2004-2827 (La. 3/18/05) (holding that child victim's statements to doctor regarding defendant's abuse were not statements necessary for the purpose of medical treatment and diagnosis in connection with any treatment, and thus doctor's testimony regarding statements was not admissible in prosecution for cruelty to juveniles when doctor admitted she was retained to determine whether injuries were a result of child abuse, doctor did not treat injuries, and identity of person who caused injuries was not pertinent to treatment).

§ 5.10 Recorded Recollections and Writings Used to Refresh Memory [La. C.E. arts. 803(5), 612]

Applicable Code Articles

The following are not excluded by the hearsay rule, even though the declarant is available as a witness:

* * *

(5) Recorded recollection. A memorandum or record concerning a matter about which a witness once had knowledge but now has insufficient recollection to enable him to testify fully and accurately, shown to have been made or adopted by the witness when the matter was fresh in his memory and to reflect that knowledge correctly. If admitted, the memorandum or record may be read into evidence and received as an exhibit but may not itself be taken into the jury room. This exception is subject to the provisions of Article 612.

* * *

Art. 612. Writing used to refresh memory

A. Civil cases. In a civil case, any writing, recording, or object may be used by a witness to refresh his memory while testifying. If a witness asserts that his memory is refreshed he must then testify from memory independent of the writing, recording, or object. If, before or during testimony, a witness has used or uses a writing, recording, or object to refresh his memory for the purpose of testifying in court, an adverse party is entitled, subject to Paragraph C, to have the writing, recording, or object produced, if practicable, at the hearing, to inspect it, to examine the witness thereon, and to introduce in evidence those portions which relate to the testimony of the witness. If production of the writing, recording, or object at the hearing is impracticable, the court may make any appropriate order, including one for inspection.

B. Criminal cases. In a criminal case, any writing, recording, or object may be used by a witness to refresh his memory while testifying. If a witness asserts that his memory is refreshed he must then testify from memory independent of the writing, recording, or object. If while testifying a witness uses a writing, recording, or object to refresh his memory an adverse party is entitled, subject to Paragraph C, to inspect it, to examine the witness thereon, and to introduce in evidence those portions which relate to the testimony of the witness.

C. Claim of irrelevance. If it is claimed that a writing or recording contains matters not related to the subject matter of the testimony the court shall examine it in camera, excise any portions not so related, and order delivery of the remainder to the party entitled thereto. Any portion withheld over objections shall be preserved and made available to the appellate court in the event of an appeal.

D. Failure to produce. If a writing, recording, or object is not produced or delivered pursuant to an order under this Article, the court shall make any order justice requires, except that in criminal cases when the prosecution elects not to comply, the order shall only be one excluding the testimony or, if the court in its discretion determines that the interests of justice so require, declaring a mistrial.

In some instances, a witness who once had first-hand knowledge of a matter may be unable to testify from memory about the matter when called upon to testify at trial—perhaps because of the amount of time that has passed, the details involved, the volume of cases handled, or for some other reason. Article 612 provides that in such a case, a witness may use any writing, recording or other object (e.g., deposition, recorded statement, etc.) to attempt to refresh his memory of the matter. If the item refreshes his memory of the matter, he must then testify from his own memory, independent of the writing, recording, or object he used to refresh it. If, however, the witness asserts that even after attempting to refresh his memory of the matter, he still cannot testify from his own independent recollection, the writing, recording, or object may be admitted into evidence and be read or heard by the jury, provided certain foundational requirements are met.

Article 803(5) addresses those instances when the writing or recording that the witness has used to attempt to refresh his memory has failed to do so, and the proponent of the testimony wishes to admit the writing itself into evidence in lieu of the testimony. In such a case, the proponent is attempting to offer the out-of-court statement (the writing or recording) to prove the truth of the matter asserted within it, which as a result, would be hearsay. The recorded recollection exception to the hearsay rule excludes such a writing or recording from the hearsay ban.

The recorded recollection exception found in Article 803(5) specifically requires that prior to introducing an item into evidence under the exception, the proponent must first comply with the requirements of Article 612 and attempt to refresh the witness's independent recollection of the matter. It is only when the witness has asserted that even after attempting to refresh his memory of the matter and he still cannot testify from memory, that the item may be introduced into evidence under Article 803(5). Once the writing is introduced into evidence after establishing the additional foundational requirements of Article 803(5), the writing or recording may be read or heard by the jury, but may not be taken into the jury deliberation room. Thus, for purposes of covering the recorded recollection exception to the hearsay rule in this section, we will first examine the requirements of Article 612.

Refreshing Memory under Article 612—Prerequisite to Article 803(5)

As specifically stated in Article 803(5), a prerequisite to evidence being introduced as a recorded recollection is to first comply with the requirements of Article 612. Article 612, titled, "Writing Used to Refresh Memory," sets out the requirements for refreshing a witness's memory who has indicated upon being asked a question while testifying at trial, that he cannot remember. For instance, if the attorney asks the witness, "*Mr. Witness, what color was the car that you saw run the red light?*" and the witness responds, "*I really don't remember what color the car was,*" then the attorney may attempt to refresh the witness's memory of the matter using a writing, recording, or other object, by following the procedures below:

1. Establish that the witness once had personal knowledge of the incident.
2. Ask the witness if anything would refresh his memory of the incident—can be a writing, recording, or other object.
3. Counsel should approach the witness and hand him the writing, recording, or other object, and ask the witness to review it *silently* to himself.[106]
4. After the witness has reviewed the writing or recording, the attorney should ask the witness if his memory has been sufficiently refreshed to testify from his own independent memory.
5. If the witness asserts that his memory has been refreshed, then the attorney should take the writing/recording/object away from the witness and the witness should then testify from his own independent recollection.
6. If the witness asserts that his independent memory has *not* been refreshed, and he still cannot testify independently, counsel can seek to admit the document as a recorded recollection (*procedures discussed below*), or move on to another topic.

It is important to remember, that for purposes of refreshing a witness's memory, the witness reads the writing ***silently*** to himself. The witness does not read it aloud, nor does the attorney read it aloud to the witness, as in the case of impeachment. The writing is also not admitted into evidence under this provision. The writing is *not* evidence—it is merely being used to jog the witness's independent memory of the incident. Also, if the witness is relying upon a recording to refresh his memory, such as a recorded deposition, he should review it outside of the presence of the jury.[107] Additionally, prior to testifying, the witness must assert that his memory has been refreshed and that he is testifying from his own independent memory of the incident, not merely reciting what he just read.

---

106. If the witness relies upon a recording to refresh his memory, the recording should be heard outside of the presence of the jury.

107. *See* State v. Woods, 619 So. 2d 803 (La. Ct. App. 1st Cir. 1993).

Procedures for Refreshing Memory:

1. Ask the witness if anything would refresh his memory of the incident.
2. Counsel hands witness writing, recording, or other object, and asks the witness to review it *silently* to himself.
3. After the witness has reviewed the item, the attorney should ask the witness if his memory has been sufficiently refreshed to testify from his own memory.
4. If the witness asserts that his memory has been refreshed, then the attorney should take the item away, and the witness should then testify from his own memory.
5. If the witness asserts that his independent memory has *not* been refreshed, and he still cannot testify independently, counsel can seek to admit the document as a recorded recollection or move on to another topic.

Any writing, recording or object may be used. Article 612 specifically provides that ***any*** writing, recording, or object may be used by the witness to refresh his memory. The item need not be a "formal" document. The range of items that may be used should be given their broadest meaning and may include sound recordings, pictures,[108] depositions, unsworn statements, diaries, newspaper articles, police reports, calendars,[109] notes, letters, etc., regardless of who prepared them.[110] It is immaterial who prepared the item used to refresh a witness's memory because when the witness asserts that his memory is refreshed and proceeds to testify from his own memory, his *testimony* is the evidence, not the writing itself.[111]

Adverse party rights. It is also important for an attorney to keep in mind that an adverse party will have certain rights to any writing, document, or recording used by a witness to refresh his memory,[112] so he should be cautious about which documents the witness is allowed to use. In a **criminal trial**, if a witness uses a writing, recording, or object to refresh his memory ***at trial***, the adverse party has a right to: 1) inspect it; 2) examine the witness thereon; and 3) introduce in evidence those portions which relate to the testimony of the witness, subject to certain irrelevant portions being excised pursuant to Article 612(d).[113] In a **civil trial**, the adverse party has a right to items used by the witness both ***before*** and ***during*** his testimony to: 1) inspect it; 2) examine the witness thereon; and 3) introduce relevant portions into the record related to the witness's testimony.

It is not unusual for an attorney to inquire of a witness on the stand as to whether he reviewed anything in preparation for his testimony to determine whether there may be documents to which he is entitled. For example, if the witness states that she used her diary to prepare for trial, or if it is used at trial to refresh her memory, the opposing

---

108. La. Code Evid. art. 612 Official Comments (c).

109. *See, e.g.*, State v. Ester, 490 So. 2d 579 (La. Ct. App. 2d Cir. 1986) (allowing a 13-year-old boy to refresh his memory by referring to a calendar where he had placed checkmarks and other notations on days he was sexually assaulted by mother).

110. La. Code Evid. art. 612 Official Comment (a).

111. *See* State v. Runnels, 101 So. 3d 1046 (La. Ct. App. 3d Cir. 2012) (allowing police officer to used note prepared by another police officer to refresh his memory on the stand).

112. La. Code Evid. art. 612 Official Comment (b).

113. *See* State v. Taylor, 688 So. 2d 1262 (La. 3d Cir. 1997), for an excellent analysis of the circumstances under which an adverse party would be entitled to a document used by a witness to refresh his memory.

counsel may be entitled to inspect it, which might reveal information favorable to that side. If relevant, counsel could seek to have the material offered into evidence. Thus, an attorney should ensure that whatever a witness uses to prepare for trial, or that he uses to refresh a witness's memory, is something he would be comfortable sharing with opposing counsel.

An attorney ordered to turn over an item pursuant to this article, and fails to do so could be held in contempt. However, if the prosecution fails to comply with an order to deliver such item in a criminal trial, the court may only either exclude the testimony or order a mistrial.[114]

Recorded Recollection [Article 803(5)]

The recorded recollection exception to the hearsay rule only comes into play after counsel has attempted to refresh a witness's independent memory of a matter and the witness asserts that he still cannot testify "fully and accurately" from his own independent memory. In such a case, the attorney can then seek to admit the item into evidence as a recorded recollection under Article 803(5) and have the witness read the item aloud in the presence of the jury. Pursuant to the article, the foundation for admitting the item is as follows:

1. Establish that the witness once had personal knowledge of the matter.
2. Establish that, despite an attempt to refresh the witness's memory, the witness still has insufficient recollection to enable him to testify fully and accurately.
3. Establish that the record was made/adopted/verified by the witness.
4. Establish that the record was made/adopted/verified when the matter was fresh in the witness's memory.
5. Establish that the record correctly reflects the witness's knowledge of the matter.

Once the foundational requirements of Article 803(5) are met, the item may not be excluded on hearsay grounds, but must still overcome any other objections that any other document would have to overcome, such as to authentication, relevance, best evidence, etc. If the document is admitted into evidence, it may *then* be read aloud in the presence of the jury. It may not, however, be taken into the jury room. This limitation is imposed to ensure that the jury does not give the item too much weight.

Like the business records exception, the foundational requirements prior to admissibility help to ensure the reliability of the document.

Foundation for admitting recorded recollection. As listed above, there are five primary foundational requirements that must be met to introduce a document into evidence as a recorded recollection. First, counsel must establish that the witness once had personal knowledge of the matter. He may do this through ordinary foundational questions that would be asked prior to any other testimony.

Next, counsel must establish that despite an attempt to refresh the witness's memory, the witness still has **insufficient recollection** to enable him to testify **fully and accurately**. Counsel does this by complying with Article 612 as outlined above. Note that the article only provides that the witness cannot testify "fully and accurately," not that the witness cannot testify at all. In other words, the witness need not have a complete loss of memory

114. La. Code Evid. art. 612(D).

Foundation for Recorded Recollection

1. The witness once had personal knowledge of the matter;
2. Despite an attempt to refresh the witness's memory, the witness still has insufficient recollection to enable him to testify fully and accurately (shown under Article 612);
3. The record was made/adopted/verified by the witness;
4. The record was made/adopted/verified when the matter was fresh in the witness's memory; and
5. The record correctly reflects the witness's knowledge of the matter.

to comply. Counsel need only establish that the witness cannot testify fully and accurately without the item.

Additionally, counsel must establish that the record was **made, adopted, or verified** by the witness. The article clearly provides that the witness need not have made the item, provided the witness has adopted or verified it. Adoption or verification of a document often occurs, for example, when a doctor or other party dictates information to another party, such as his secretary or assistant, who prepares the document, then the person later signs the document adopting its contents. A witness verifies and adopts his statement made in a deposition when he reviews and signs it. Sometimes a police officer writes out a witness's statement and allows the witness to review and sign it. The article does not require any type of "formal" adoption or verification. An officer might simply show a person his statement and the witness can verify it by simply responding, "*Yep, that's what I saw.*"

The attorney must also establish that the verification or adoption occurred **while the matter was fresh in the witness's memory**. Thus, no significant time should have passed between the incident and adoption or verification of the record. Preferably it would occur at the time of the incident, or perhaps within a couple of days. The requirement is simply that it be done while the matter is still fresh in the witness's memory.

The final foundational requirement is that the witness must testify that the record **correctly reflects the witness's knowledge of the matter**. Since the witness made, verified, or adopted the matter while it was fresh in his memory, the witness should be able to testify that the item correctly reflects his knowledge of the matter.

Once all of the foundational requirements are met, the writing is offered into evidence. If admitted, subject to other objections, the witness can then read the item aloud in the presence of the jury.

Police Reports. For public policy reasons, many of which are outlined in § 5.12, *infra*, relative to the public records exception found in Article 803(8), law enforcement reports are usually not admitted under this exception. While an officer will be able to refresh his recollection using his report as needed under Article 612, the entire report will not be admitted. Not only is the document hearsay, but a defendant's Sixth Amendments rights under the Confrontation Clause are also implicated. Under *Crawford v. Washington*,[115] the statement would most likely be excluded since the witness is not currently unavailable, even if there was a prior opportunity for cross-examination, say at a preliminary examination. This issue is further discussed in Part E, *infra*.

---

115. Discussed at length in Chapter 5 Part E, § 5.25.

Federal Rules of Evidence Distinction. The rule on recorded recollection is substantially the same as the federal rules with a couple of minor exceptions. Under Federal Rule of Evidence 803(5), once the foundation is laid, the item may be "read into evidence but may not itself be received as an exhibit unless offered by an adverse party."[116] Thus, unlike the Louisiana Code of Evidence, which allows the item to be admitted into evidence but not taken into the jury room, under the Federal Rule the memorandum or record may not be admitted into evidence *at all* by the proponent, but may be read aloud. The reasoning is the same as to why Louisiana does not allow the jury to take the evidence into the deliberation room, which is so that the jury will not give it too much weight.[117] Under the Federal Rule, while the proponent may not offer the record into evidence, the opposing party may offer the record into evidence if he chooses to do so.[118]

The Litany for Refreshing a Witness's Recollection at Trial

Below are the series of questions counsel should ask his witness to refresh the witness's recollection, and, if needed, to admit an item into evidence as a recorded recollection.

Refreshing Recollection (*Use with your own witness on direct who says "I don't remember."*)

- What color was the vehicle that you saw run the red light? *I don't really remember the color of the car.*
- Is there something that could refresh your memory? *Yes.*
- What is that? *My deposition could refresh my memory.*
- Your honor may I approach the witness?
- I'm handing you your deposition taken in this matter.
- Is that your deposition? *Yes.*
- Is this your signature? *Yes, it is.*
- Take a look at page ___, line ___, and read it *silently* to yourself, and look up when you have finished.
- Do you now remember the color of the vehicle? *Yes.*
- (Take the item back from the witness and restate the question.) What color was the car that you saw run the red light? *It was silver.*

116. Fed. R. Evid. 803(5); *See also* Research Systems Corp. v. IPSOS Publicite, 276 F.3d 914, 923 (7th Cir. 2002) Cir. denied, 537 U.S. 878, (2002) (excluding exhibit when offered into evidence rather than read).

117. *See* U.S. v. Judon, 567 F.2d 1289, 1294 (5th Cir. 1978) ("[In] order to prevent the trier of fact from being overly impressed by the writing").

118. Fed. R. Evid. 803(5).

Recorded Recollection (*If witness still doesn't remember, lay additional foundation to admit as recorded recollection.*)

- At the time the deposition was taken, was this matter fresh in your memory?

If something other than deposition (notes, book, newspaper, diary, etc.), ask:

- Did you make/adopt/verify this item (notes, book, diary, report, etc.)?
- When did you make/adopt/verify the item?
- At the time you made/adopted/verified the item, was it fresh in your memory?
- And does this deposition (or other item) correctly reflect your memory of ____?
- At this time, I offer plaintiff's exhibit P-1 into evidence.
- Could you please **read** (the item) **aloud** for the jury?

Cases on Refreshing Memory and Recorded Recollection

Maricle v. Liberty Mutual Ins. Co.

Court of Appeal of Louisiana, Third Circuit
898 So. 2d 565
March 2, 2005

PETERS, Judge.

The accident giving rise to this litigation occurred on U.S. Highway 165 (Hwy 165) a short distance north of Oakdale, Louisiana....

... Ms. Maricle [the plaintiff] was driving north on Hwy 165 in a 1983 Dodge sedan, which was also occupied by Ms. McDaniel and Ms. Maricle's three small children. At the same time, Mr. Dyer was driving Transwood Trucking's tractor-trailer rig (eighteen-wheeler) north on Hwy 165 and was immediately behind two vehicles, with the lead vehicle of the two being Ms. Maricle's vehicle.

... [T]he impact between the two vehicles occurred as Mr. Dyer attempted to pass Ms. Maricle's vehicle at a time when Ms. Maricle was attempting to make a left turn from Hwy 165 onto Meyers Road. Ms. Maricle's vehicle was struck between the driver's door and the front bumper by the right outside tire of the front axle of the rear tandem of the eighteen-wheeler. The point of impact between the two vehicles was one to two feet across the centerline of Hwy 165 in the southbound lane.... Mr. Dyer parked his eighteen-wheeler on the shoulder of the northbound lane of Hwy 165 beyond the accident scene.

...

Trooper Mire arrived on the scene over one hour after the accident. He interviewed Mr. Dyer at the scene and Ms. Maricle in an Oakdale hospital. According to Trooper Mire, Ms. Maricle told him that she was attempting to turn onto Meyers Road and that she did not see the eighteen-wheeler, while Mr. Dyer told him that as he passed two slow-moving vehicles, Ms. Maricle turned into his path. Trooper Mire examined the accident scene and concluded that the impact occurred inside the southbound lane and that Ms. Maricle's vehicle traveled thirteen feet after impact. After completing his investigation, he issued a traffic citation to Ms. Maricle, charging her with making an unsafe turn in violation of La.R.S. 32:104.

...

OPINION

All four of the plaintiffs' assignments of error relate to evidentiary rulings by the trial court. The first three pertain to rulings admitting evidence unfavorable to Ms. Maricle, and the fourth pertains to a ruling excluding evidence arguably favorable to her....

Assignment of Error Number Three

At the previously mentioned hearing on the evidentiary motions, the trial court also rejected the plaintiffs' motion to exclude Trooper Mire's accident report from being introduced into evidence. At trial, the trial court allowed the accident report to be admitted into evidence pursuant to La.Code Evid. art. 803(5), but declined to allow it to be published to the jury because certain portions contained "inadmissible hearsay." While the trial court did not allow the jury to examine the report, it did allow Trooper Mire to be questioned extensively concerning the contents of the report, and it did allow him to read directly from it. In their third assignment of error, the plaintiffs assert that this was error on the part of the trial court. We agree.

The contents of Trooper Mire's accident report clearly contain hearsay as defined by La.Code Evid. art. 801(C). The report is therefore inadmissible unless it fits within one of the exceptions found in La.Code Evid. art. 803. While public records and reports are generally considered as an exception to the hearsay exclusionary rule pursuant to La.Code Evid. art. 803(8), that same provision specifically excludes "[i]nvestigative reports by police and other law enforcement personnel" from that exception. La.Code Evid. art. 803(8)(b)(i).

The trial court found that the accident report was admissible pursuant to the exception to the hearsay exclusionary rule found in La.Code Evid. art. 803(5), which provides:

> A memorandum or record concerning a matter about which a witness once had knowledge but now has insufficient recollection to enable him to testify fully and accurately, shown to have been made or adopted by the witness when the matter was fresh in his memory and to reflect that knowledge correctly. If admitted, the memorandum or record may be read into evidence and received as an exhibit but may not itself be taken into the jury room. This exception is subject to the provisions of Article 612.

Louisiana Code of Evidence Article 612(A) relates to the use of writings to refresh the memory of a witness and provides in pertinent part:

> In a civil case, any writing, recording, or object may be used by a witness to refresh his memory while testifying. If a witness asserts that his memory is refreshed he must then testify from memory independent of the writing, recording, or object. If, before or during testimony, a witness has used a writing, recording, or object to refresh his memory for the purpose of testifying in court, an adverse party is entitled, subject to Paragraph C, to have the writing, recording, or object produced, if practicable, at the hearing, to inspect it, to examine the witness thereon, and to introduce in evidence those portions which relate to the testimony of the witness.

Louisiana Code of Evidence Article 612(C) provides:

> If it is claimed that a writing or recording contains matters not related to the subject matter of the testimony the court shall examine it in camera, excise any portions not so related, and order delivery of the remainder to the party entitled thereto. Any portion withheld over objections shall be preserved and made available to the appellate court in the event of an appeal.

In the matter before us, Trooper Mire was asked whether he needed his report in order to testify, and he responded: "I'm gonna need the report to be accurate." Significantly, he was never asked whether his review of the report refreshed his memory or whether he had insufficient recollection to testify and was relying solely on the content of the report. Because there is no evidence of insufficient recollection, the trial court erred in admitting the accident report and, at the same time, in allowing the trooper to testify concerning its contents, as if he had independent recollection. Additionally, as pointed out in *Talamo v. Shad*, 619 So. 2d 699, 701–02 (La.App. 4 Cir.), *writ denied*, 625 So.2d 175 (La.1993), for a document to be admissible under La.Code Evid. art. 803(5), "it must be shown, among other things, that the witness had firsthand knowledge of the matter described in the memorandum." While Trooper Mire had firsthand knowledge of matters he observed in his investigation, his conclusions with regard to the accident itself [that Ms. Maricle made an unsafe turn] were acquired from his investigative analysis, and not from firsthand knowledge. Therefore, the trial court erred in allowing introduction of the accident report and in allowing Trooper Mire to read from that report.

Discussion Questions

1. Explain the difference between refreshing memory (Article 612) and recorded recollection (Article 803(5)). What are the key distinctions? What policy reasons justify the differences in the requirements for each? For example, when refreshing a witness's memory, why is it immaterial who prepared the document, while when offering a recorded recollection into evidence, the witness must have made, adopted, or verified the item?
2. In *Maricle*, once the officer asserted that he would "need the report to be accurate," the officer's report was offered into evidence and he was allowed to read from it extensively in testifying. The court noted that he was never asked: 1) whether his review of the report refreshed his memory (Article 612); or 2) whether he had insufficient recollection to testify. Had the witness testified that his review of the report refreshed his memory, what steps should have been taken at that point?

   If the witness had responded that he still had insufficient recollection to testify, what steps should have been taken at that point to elicit testimony from the officer?
3. Do you think that testimony elicited after a witness has "refreshed" his memory under Article 612 is reliable? What potential dangers exist? What are the advantages in support of the viability of this provision?
4. Why do you suppose Article 612 is a prerequisite to Article 803(5)? What potential dangers would exist if documents could be immediately admitted into evidence whenever a witness claims not to remember?
5. If counsel had properly complied with the requirements of Article 803(5) and Article 612, would the officer's report have been admitted into evidence under the recorded recollection exception? Why or why not?
6. Trooper Mire arrived at the scene over an hour after the accident occurred, and concluded that Ms. Maricle made an illegal turn. Trooper Mire was not qualified as an expert in accident reconstruction. Was he competent to draw such a conclusion in this case? Why or why not?

State v. Woods

Court of Appeal of Louisiana, First Circuit
619 So. 2d 803
May 28, 1993

GONZALES, Judge.

Leroy Woods was indicted for second degree murder. He pled not guilty and, after trial by jury, was convicted of the responsive offense of manslaughter, a violation of La.R.S. 14:31.... [T]he court adjudicated him to be a second felony offender and sentenced him to serve a term of twenty years at hard labor, with credit for time served.

FACTS

On February 2, 1991, defendant shot Milton Brown over what apparently was a gambling dispute. Brown had picked up his girlfriend, Gwendolyn Stewart, from her job at about 10:15 p.m. He then drove to the corner of Gus Young Avenue and 48th Street in Baton Rouge. He got out of the car and told Stewart he would return in a few minutes. Then Brown went into a nearby house. After about fifteen or twenty minutes, Brown came out of the house alone. He told Stewart he would be ready to leave soon and walked across the street to where some men were shooting dice.

Later, Stewart observed a man come from the direction of the house where Brown had been; she saw him go across the street in the same direction as Brown. Stewart identified defendant in court as being this man. After defendant went across the street, Stewart heard Brown begging not to be shot and heard three gunshots. Because the men were behind a garbage bin, Stewart could not see either Brown or the person who fired the shots; but immediately afterward she saw defendant with a gun in his hand.

Brown sustained multiple gunshot wounds to various parts of his body and became partially paralyzed. While conscious at the scene, he told the first officer who arrived that Leroy Woods was the person who had shot him. Before surgery, he explained to the surgeon that during a dice game he and another man had argued over which number had rolled. The man left and returned with a gun to shoot Brown. Despite surgery, Brown died a few days later as a result of his injuries.

INTRODUCTION OF WITNESS' TAPED STATEMENT

In the first assignment of error, defendant asserts the court erred when it overruled defendant's objection to the introduction of a taped statement given by Gwendolyn Stewart to the police. Defendant argues, and the state concedes, that the tape was inadmissible under La.C.E. art. 612(B), which allows a witness to review any writing, recording, or object in order to refresh his memory while testifying. Defendant further argues the tape recording was inadmissible hearsay and did not meet the requirements of the recorded recollection exception to the hearsay rule (La.C.E. art. 803(5)) because Stewart did not have a lapse of memory as required by that exception.

When called as a witness, Stewart testified generally about defendant picking her up from work and driving to the location where the offense occurred. After stating that she observed defendant walk across the street before the offense, she indicated she did not see defendant after the offense because she slid down in the car to hide. The prosecutor pursued the line of questioning and referred Stewart to previous statements made by her. Then the prosecutor again asked her "when" she saw defendant at the scene. This time

Stewart replied that she could not remember. When questioned further, she responded as before that she did not see defendant again. Stewart then admitted that she was afraid to testify. After a bench conference, the state asked Stewart if it would assist in her recollection of the events to hear the taped statement she gave to the investigating detective after the offense. When Stewart replied that it would, defendant objected to the playing of the tape, arguing that the recollection of the witness was the best evidence. In response, the state argued the recording was admissible to refresh the witness's recollection. The court overruled the objection, and the recording (State Exhibit 19) was played before the jury. In her taped statement, Stewart told the detective that she saw defendant with a gun in his hand after she heard the gunshots. She also observed defendant walk back into the house after the offense.

After hearing the tape, Stewart testified that she remembered making the statement. She maintained that she was telling the truth when she gave the statement to the police and that the tape is how she remembers the facts of the offense. When questioned further about the offense, Stewart identified clothing viewed in court as being the clothes worn by defendant on the night of the offense. She also testified that she saw a gun in defendant's hand after the shooting.

Hearsay is defined as an oral or written assertion (or a nonverbal assertion if intended as an assertion), other than one made by the declarant while testifying at the present trial or hearing, offered in evidence to prove the truth of the matter asserted. La.C.E. art. 801. Hearsay is not admissible except as provided by the Code of Evidence or other legislation. La.C.Cr.P. art. 802.

On appeal, the state argues the taped statement was admissible as a recorded recollection, an exception to the hearsay rule of exclusion....

Under this provision, the following foundation must be established: (1) the witness should have had firsthand knowledge of the matter described in the memorandum or record; (2) the memorandum or record should have been made or verified by the witness at a time when the matter reported was fresh in his memory; and (3) the memorandum should accurately reflect the witness' earlier knowledge of the matter recorded; and (4) while testifying, the witness should have insufficient recollection.... [119]

In this case, the tape recording consisted of Stewart's statement to the police concerning events she personally witnessed. She made the statement shortly after the offense and testified the crime was "fresh" in her memory when she spoke to the detective. She also testified that she told the truth when she gave the statement. However, the record does not support the state's position that Stewart's memory was impaired. Although Stewart testified inconsistently before the tape was played (alternatively stating that she did not see defendant after the offense and that she could not remember whether or not she saw defendant), upon hearing the tape recording, her memory was refreshed and she specifically testified that the information in her taped statement was how she remembered the events of the night of the offense.

Absent the required memory loss, article 803(5) does not authorize a witness to read the memorandum or listen to the recording before the jury. To do so under these circumstances violates the hearsay rule.... If the witness' memory is refreshed upon consulting the memorandum or recording, then the memorandum or recording may not be presented

119. The memorandum need not be in written form. As a comment to article 803(5) indicates, a tape recording suffices. La.C.E. art. 803(5), comment (b).

before the jury and the provisions of La.C.E. art. 612 apply.... Once the witness' memory is refreshed, he must testify from his memory independent of the writing or recording which was used to refresh his memory. La.C.E. art. 612(B).[120]

Accordingly, the court erred by overruling defendant's objection to the playing of the taped recording before the jury. However, erroneous admission of hearsay evidence requires reversal only when there is a reasonable possibility that the evidence might have contributed to the verdict. The inquiry is whether or not the reviewing court, assuming that the damaging potential of the cross-examination of the declarant were fully realized, is nonetheless convinced the error was harmless beyond a reasonable doubt....

In the instant case, admission of the recording clearly was harmless error. The most damaging evidence emitted from the recording was Stewart's claim that she saw defendant after the offense with a gun in his hand and that people at the scene referred to defendant by name ("Leroy"). However, Stewart later testified in court from her own memory that she saw defendant with the gun. Additionally, Robert Matthews, a defense witness who testified concerning statements made to him by Stewart, testified on cross-examination that Stewart told him she saw defendant after the shooting come from behind the garbage bin with a pistol in his hand. Moreover, while conscious at the scene, the victim identified his shooter by name. Thus, we conclude the trial court's error was harmless beyond a reasonable doubt....

Discussion Questions

1. Was sufficient foundation laid to refresh Ms. Stewart's memory? Compare the foundation that should be laid to refresh a witness's memory under Article 612, to what occurred with Ms. Stewart.
2. To be admitted into evidence under Article 803(5), all of the foundational requirements of the article must be met. The court notes that certain requirements were met and some were not. Which requirements for admissibility were met under Article 803(5) and which were not?
3. The witness in *Woods* stated that she was afraid to testify. How would you suggest an attorney handle such a situation at trial to attempt to elicit testimony from the witness?

Key Points

The key points to keep in mind regarding recorded recollection and refreshing memory.

1. **Recorded recollection exception.** Allows a writing to be offered into evidence if the following requirements are met:
   a. the witness once had personal knowledge of the matter;
   b. despite an attempt to refresh the witness's memory, the witness still has insufficient recollection to enable him to testify fully and accurately (shown under Article 612);
   c. the record was made/adopted/verified by the witness;

120. To avoid the problem peculiar to audio recordings which occurred in this case, the witness initially should be allowed to listen to the recording outside the jury's presence.

d. the record was made/adopted/verified when the matter was fresh in the witness's memory; and

e. the record correctly reflects the witness's knowledge of the matter.

2. Refreshing memory requirements under Article 612.

a. Establish that the witness once had personal knowledge of the incident.

b. Ask the witness if anything would refresh his memory of the incident—can be a writing, recording, or other object.

c. Counsel should approach the witness and hand him the writing, recording, or other object and ask the witness to review it *silently* to himself.

d. After the witness has reviewed the writing or recording, the attorney should ask the witness if his memory has been sufficiently refreshed to testify from his own independent recollection.

e. If the witness asserts that his memory has been refreshed, then the attorney should take the writing/recording/object away from the witness, and the witness should then testify from his own independent recollection.

f. If the witness asserts that his independent memory has *not* been refreshed, and he still cannot testify independently, counsel can seek to admit the document as a recorded recollection (*procedures discussed below*) or move on to another topic.

3. When <u>refreshing memory</u>, keep the following in mind.

- Matter is not admitted into evidence, it is read silently, and if it is a recording, it should be heard outside of the presence of the jury.
- Any writing, recording or object may be used (broadest meaning), and it is immaterial who prepared it—the testimony is evidence, not the object.
- **Adverse party rights.**
- In a **criminal case**, adverse party has right to inspect, question witness from, and admit relevant portions into evidence of item that witness uses to refresh memory *at trial.*
- In a **civil case**, adverse party has a right to inspect, question witness from, and admit relevant portions into evidence, of an item that witness uses to refresh memory either *before* or *during* trial.
- An attorney who fails to comply with order to produce item used may be held in contempt, or if it's the prosecution in a criminal trial, testimony may be excluded or mistrial ordered.

4. If matter is admitted as <u>recorded recollection</u>, keep the following in mind.

- The item is offered into evidence.
- May be read *aloud* or heard by jury, since it is now admitted into evidence.
- Jury may not take it into the jury room.
- While witness need not have made the item, it must have been verified or adopted by the witness while the matter was still fresh in the witness's mind.

Problems on Refreshing Memory and Recorded Recollection

PROBLEM 5-89. Beverly's portable heater caught fire in her office one day. Angie and Rose, two of her coworkers, ran from across the hall to see what all the commotion was about and discovered the fire. While attempting to help put the fire out, Rose was burned and was taken to the hospital for her injuries. Later on that evening when she returned home from the hospital, she jotted down notes about what happed. Rose subsequently sued Beverly and their employer for her damages. By the time the case gets to trial, Angie is called as a witness for Rose, but can't remember what happened. Can Rose attempt to refresh Angie's memory with her notes even though Angie never saw the notes close to the time of the event? Why or why not? If so, what procedure must she use?

Assuming Rose's notes do not refresh Angie's memory of the event, can the notes be offered into evidence as a recorded recollection? Why or why not?

PROBLEM 5-90. Keith worked at a tire repair shop. After repairing Rick's pickup truck, he forgot to tighten the lugs on one of the tires, and the tire came off while Rick was on the highway, causing an accident in which Rick was severely injured. After the accident was reported to the tire shop the next day, the supervisor on duty at the time the truck was serviced, but who had no knowledge of any services rendered on the truck, requested that all five employees who were on duty the day the truck was serviced make a report of the vehicles they serviced and the procedures they followed. After reviewing the statements, the supervisor then signed off on all five of them. At the trial, the supervisor testifies, but cannot remember (or does not know) much of the information contained in the reports even after the plaintiff attempts to refresh his memory with them. Is it possible to have any of the reports admitted into evidence as a recorded recollection since he signed off on them? Why or why not?

PROBLEM 5-91. Paul sues Drake for injuries he sustained when Drake rear-ended Paul. About a year later, Paul and Drake took video depositions in the case. At the trial, when Drake begins to testify, he cannot remember some details of the accident. Can his memory be refreshed from the video? If so, what procedure must be followed for refreshing the witness's memory with a video?

Assume the video does not refresh Drake's memory. Can the relevant portion of the video be offered into evidence as a recorded recollection? Why or why not?

PROBLEM 5-92. The responding police officer to an accident is unable to recall all of the names of the witnesses he interviewed and all of their statements. The prosecution attempts to refresh the officer's recollection with his report, but he still can't remember all of the names. Are there any circumstances under which the report might be admitted into evidence, or in the alternative, the officer might be allowed to read from his report?

PROBLEM 5-93. Samantha is the plaintiff in a civil case. During her testimony, she can't remember some of the details, so her attorney asks her if there is anything that can refresh her memory, and she states that she wrote about the incident in an extensive letter that she'd written to her mother detailing the events the same night it occurred. As Samantha's attorney hands her the letter, the defendant's attorney objects that he is entitled to the letter. Must they give him the letter? Why or why not? Would your answer change if it were a criminal case? Why or why not?

PROBLEM 5-94. Wayne is representing Bill in a products liability action against the manufacturer of an ATV that Bill was riding when the brakes locked up causing Bill to be ejected from the ATV. The ATV landed on Bill, and he was seriously injured. At trial during direct examination, Wayne asks Bill how many times he had the ATV serviced during the six months that he owned it before the accident, and Bill responded, "Six times." Wayne then asked Bill to tell the jury the dates of each time he had the ATV serviced, along with the place, the diagnosis, and any repairs that were made. Bill then stated that he could not remember, but states that if he could take a look at his social media page he could remember because he says that each time he had to get the ATV serviced he wrote about it the same day as he complained about how far he had to drive to have it serviced and all the problems he had to have repaired. Should Bill be allowed to take a look at his social media page to refresh his memory of the information?

§ 5.10 References and Additional Authority on Recorded Recollections [La. C.E. art. 803(5)] and Writings Used to Refresh Memory [La. C.E. art. 612]

1. La. C.E. arts. 803(5), 612 and Official Comments
2. Force & Rault, Handbook on Louisiana Evidence Law Arts. 803(5), 612 Author's Comments (West Publishing 2014)
3. Harges & Jones, Louisiana Evidence Arts. 803(5), 612 Author's Comments (West Publishing 2014)
4. 19 La. Civ. L. Treatise, Evidence And Proof § 10.17 (2nd ed.)
5. **Admitted as Recorded Recollection**: *State v. Sullivan*, 688 So. 2d 1245 (La. Ct. App. 4th Cir. 1997) (declarant recalled certain portions of the incident, but could not recall many of the details); *State v. Dupree*, 950 So. 2d 140 (La. Ct App. 2d Cir. 2007) (Allowing the police officer who took the initial report of a rape to testify from his report which was not admitted into evidence, was admissible under recorded recollection exception.).
6. **Cases allowing use to refresh memory (Article 612)**: *State v. Gremillion*, 428 So. 2d 940 (La. Ct. App. 1st Cir. 1983) (The report served to refresh the witness's present memory and, after a brief review of the report, witness was able to testify independently from the report.).
7. **Distinguishing recollection refreshed and recollection**: *State v. Tharp*, 284 So. 2d 536 (La. 1973) (distinguishing the difference between past recollection recorded and present recollection refreshed. The witness used a report to refresh his mind during examination under oath. The court found that the report was admissible, and the ability to use the report to refresh his memory was admissible.).

§ 5.11 Business Records and Absence of Entry in Business Records [La. C.E. arts. 803(6), (7)]

Applicable Code Articles

The following are not excluded by the hearsay rule, even though the declarant is available as a witness:

* * *

(6) Records of regularly conducted business activity. A memorandum, report, record, or data compilation, in any form, including but not limited to that which is stored by the use of an optical disk imaging system, of acts, events, conditions, opinions, or diagnoses, made at or near the time by, or from information transmitted by, a person with knowledge, if made and kept in the course of a regularly conducted business activity, and if it was the regular practice of that business activity to make and to keep the memorandum, report, record, or data compilation, all as shown by the testimony of the custodian or other qualified witness, unless the source of information or the method or circumstances of preparation indicate lack of trustworthiness. This exception is inapplicable unless the recorded information was furnished to the business either by a person who was routinely acting for the business in reporting the information or in circumstances under which the statement would not be excluded by the hearsay rule. The term "business" as used in this Paragraph includes business, institution, association, profession, occupation, and calling of every kind, whether or not conducted for profit. Public records and reports which are specifically excluded from the public records exception by Article 803(8)(b) shall not qualify as an exception to the hearsay rule under this Paragraph.

(7) Absence of entry in records of regularly conducted business activity. Evidence that a matter is not included in the memoranda, reports, records, or data compilations, in any form, kept in accordance with the provisions of Paragraph (6), to prove the nonoccurrence or nonexistence of the matter, if the matter was of a kind of which a memorandum, report, record, or data compilation was regularly made and preserved unless the sources of information or other circumstances indicate lack of trustworthiness.

* * *

In this section we will cover the **business records exception** to the hearsay rule found in Article 803(6) and the **absence of entry in business records exception** found in Article 803(7). Under the business records exception, certain records made and kept in the course of the regularly conducted business activity may be excluded from the hearsay ban. The business records exception is one of the most commonly used exceptions to the hearsay rule in civil cases,[121] although the rule applies to both civil and criminal cases.[122] In a trial, business records can be valuable and persuasive evidence because they are something in "writing," as it were, that help a party prove his case. But since the records are out-of-court statements being offered to prove the truth of what is asserted within those records,

121. Force & Rault, Handbook, Art. 803(6) Author's Comment (2).

122. This article was made applicable to criminal cases by Section I of Act. 1300 of 1995. Prior to that time, the exception pertaining to criminal cases was contained in La. Code Evid. art. 804(5); *See also* Force & Rault, Handbook, Art. 803(6) Author's Comment (1).

the information is hearsay. This exception addresses the admissibility of the contents of those records, and sets forth specific requirements that must be met to conform with the exception.

Underlying Policy. Business records are deemed reliable if certain requirements are met establishing how the records were made and kept because it is presumed that a business is likely to keep and maintain accurate and reliable records for the success and maintenance of the business. Provided the proponent of the record is able to demonstrate at trial the procedures as to how the records are made and kept through a competent witness with first-hand knowledge of those procedures, the records will be deemed reliable and trustworthy and will not be excluded under the hearsay rule.

Requirements for business records exception. Pursuant to the statute, all of the following requirements must be met to conform to the business records exception.[123]

1. **Must be a business:** any business, institution, association, profession, occupation, calling, including those that are not for profit
2. **Records must be in the form of**: memorandum, report, record, data compilation in any form
3. **Record must concern:** acts, events, conditions, opinions, diagnosis
4. **Foundational requirements through a competent witness:**
   i. that the record was made at or near the time of the event it records;
   ii. that the record was made by: a) a person with personal knowledge; or b) based on information transmitted to him by a person with personal knowledge;
   iii. that the recorded information was furnished to the business by either: a) a person routinely acting for the business in reporting the information; or b) in circumstances in which the statement would not be excluded by the hearsay rule;
   iv. that the record was made and kept in the course of a regularly conducted business activity; and
   v. that it was the regular practice of that business activity to make and to keep the record.
5. The source of information or the method or circumstances of preparation must not indicate lack of trustworthiness.
6. Does not include public records and reports which are specifically excluded from the public records exception by Article 803(8)(b)

Applicability of the exception. For purposes of this exception, a ***business*** includes an institution, association, profession, occupation, or calling, including those that are not for profit. The definition is broad, thus most entities and organizations will qualify as a business for purposes of the exception. ***Records*** are also broadly defined in the article as including memorandums, reports, records, data compilations in any form, not limited to that which is stored by the use of an optical disk imaging system. Thus, records may include records digitally maintained, including portable document formats (pdf)[124] and

123. *See also* Force & Rault, Handbook, Appendix D Checklist 6, for the foundational requirements for offering business records into evidence.

124. Ford Motor Credit Co. v. Jackson, 47 So. 3d 558 (La. Ct. App. 2d Cir. 2010); *See also* Harges & Jones, Louisiana Evidence Art. 803(6) Author's Comments.

Foundation for business records through a competent witness:

1. that the record was made at or near the time of the event it records;
2. that the record was made by: a) a person with personal knowledge; or b) based on information transmitted to him by a person with personal knowledge;
3. that the recorded information was furnished to the business by either: a) a person routinely acting for the business in reporting the information; or b) in circumstances in which the statement would not be excluded by the hearsay rule;
4. that the record was made and kept in the course of a regularly conducted business activity; and
5. that it was the regular practice of that business activity to make and to keep the record.

even voice recordings, as in a recorded meeting,[125] if the other requirements of the exception are met.

The exception does require, however, that the record be actually "kept," meaning that it must be written or otherwise "tangibly recoverable rather than merely oral."[126] The ***contents*** of a business record for purposes of this exception are also broad and must generally record acts, events, conditions, opinions, or diagnosis.

Foundational requirements. The key components to this exception are the foundational requirements that show the reliability and trustworthiness of the record. As stated above, there are five primary foundational requirements that the proponent of the record must establish at trial through a competent witness who has first-hand knowledge of the information to which he will testify. First, it must be shown that the record was made **at or near the time** of the event it records. This would help to minimize memory problems.

Secondly, it must be shown that the record was **made by** either a person with **personal knowledge** or was **transmitted to that person by a person with personal knowledge**. Thus, a doctor dictating information to a nurse who is writing the information into the record would qualify. While the nurse might not have personal knowledge of the information contained in the record, the information was transmitted to her by a person with personal knowledge, the doctor.

Next, the recorded **information** must be **furnished to the business** by either a person who is **routinely acting for the business** in reporting the information or in circumstances in which the statement would **not be excluded by the hearsay rule.**[127] Thus, the information contained in an emergency room hospital record that is provided by the emergency room doctor and nurses, who are routinely acting for the business, would be included under the exception, and admissible. However, if the record contains information provided by the mother of the unconscious victim, a person not routinely acting for the hospital, her statement is considered to be hearsay within hearsay.

---

125. *See. e.g.*, Grady Crawford Const., Inc. v. City of Baton Rouge, 76 So. 3d 513 (La. Ct. App. 1st Cir. 2011), where the court admitted an audio recording of a meeting of the Licensing Board under this exception to show the time the board met and approved a contractor's application for certification to submit public bids.

126. La. Code Evid. art. 803(6) Official Comments to Exception (6).

127. *See* La. Code Evid. art. 803(6) Official Comments to Exception (6); *See also* Suluki v. Veterans Life Ins. Co., 681 So. 2d 52 (La. Ct. App. 2d Cir. 1996).

So while the record may be admitted under the exception, the mother's statement can only be admitted if it "would not be excluded by the hearsay rule," i.e., if it fits within another exception to the hearsay rule, is non-hearsay, or is exempt from the hearsay rule under Article 801(D).[128] Otherwise, her statement would have to be excised from the record.

Finally, the record must be one that is **made and kept** in the course of a **regularly conducted business activity**, and it must be the **regular practice** of that business **to make and to keep that type of record.** Reliability does not attach to everything that is written down on a piece of paper at a business.[129] The exception only encompasses those documents that are routinely made in the course of regularly conducted business activity and those records that the business routinely makes. It is from this routine, day-to-day activity of making and keeping the type of record that the reliability and trustworthiness of the exception lies.

Competent witness must testify.[130] In order to lay the proper foundation to admit a business record, a competent witness must be present to testify. That witness must be one that has first-hand knowledge of the foregoing foundational requirements as set forth in Article 602. In other words, the witness through whom the record will be admitted must be one that can testify from first-hand knowledge as to the practices and procedures of the business for keeping and maintaining its records.

With such knowledge, the witness would be able to testify as to whether the record complies with the foundational requirements that establish its trustworthiness, i.e., that the record was in fact made at or near the time of the event it records, that the record was made and kept as a part of the routine practice of the business, and so on. The witness might be a custodian of the records or other qualified person, such as a company employee or supervisor who would actually have such knowledge, which would be established through foundational questions.

"The witness laying the foundation for admissibility of business records need not have been the preparer of the records,"[131] nor have first-hand knowledge of the contents of the record, provided a foundation can be laid that the witness has **first-hand knowledge** of the **business's practices** and **procedures for making and keeping records** to establish that the foundational requirements for admission of the records have been met.

This person would also be able to **authenticate** the record and testify that the record sought to be introduced is in fact what it purports to be and that it accurately reflects the information contained therein. While it is of utmost importance that a document complies with all of the foundational requirements to be admitted, having a competent witness who can testify that the foundational requirements have been met is equally important. Without it, the record will not be admitted under this exception.

It is important to keep in mind that in situations in which a record is not hearsay, as in the case of computer-generated information like the log of numbers dialed listed on a cell phone bill,[132] while the foundational requirements for the business records exception

---

128. *See* LA. CODE EVID. arts. 803(6)(b) and (d) Official Comments.

129. *See* Goode & Wellborn III, COURTROOM EVIDENCE HANDBOOK 2015–2016 Student Edition (West Publishing) Rule 803 (6),(7) Author's Comments (4).

130. *See* Cole Oil & Tire Co., Inc. v. Davis, 567 So. 2d 122 (La. Ct App. 2d Cir. 1990) below, for an excellent analysis of the need for a competent witness through whom the foundation for admissibility of business record is established.

131. Cole Oil & Tire Co., Inc. v. Davis, 567 So. 2d 122 (La. Ct App. 2d Cir. 1990).

132. *See* State v. Carter, 762 So. 2d 662 (La. Ct. App. 4th Cir. 2000) discussed in Section 5.1 relative to defining hearsay.

need not be established, the record must still be authenticated through a competent witness pursuant to Article 901 et seq. to be admissible.

Must not indicate lack of trustworthiness. As with the other exceptions, a record may not be admitted under this exception if the source of the information or methods or circumstances of preparation indicate lack of trustworthiness, such as if the record appears to have been altered or if portions of it are missing. A record might also be deemed to lack trustworthiness if the source of an entry cannot be determined,[133] if the preparer had an interest in the outcome of the litigation or had a motive to falsify the record, or if the record was prepared in anticipation of litigation.[134]

Certain public records excluded. The last sentence of this article specifically excludes from admissibility, as a business record, any public record that is excluded from admissibility under the public records exception in Article 803(8)(b).[135] Specifically, the public records exception, which provides that certain public records may be excluded from the hearsay ban, lists four types of public records that are specifically excluded from that exception. Those exclusions are listed below. The business records exception provides that these records similarly may not be admitted under the business records exception. The applicable provision of the public records exception states as follows:

> (b) Except as specifically provided otherwise by legislation, the following are excluded from this exception to the hearsay rule:
>
> (i) Investigative reports by police and other law enforcement personnel.
>
> (ii) Investigative reports prepared by or for any government, public office, or public agency when offered by that or any other government, public office, or public agency in a case in which it is a party.
>
> (iii) Factual findings offered by the prosecution in a criminal case.
>
> (iv) Factual findings resulting from investigation of a particular complaint, case, or incident, including an investigation into the facts and circumstances on which the present proceeding is based or an investigation into a similar occurrence or occurrences.

Thus, these four records similarly are not admissible under the business records exception. One of the most common types of public records excluded under the public records exception is "investigative reports by police and other law enforcement personnel," which is found in Article 803(8)(b)(i). As a result, police reports are also excluded from being admitted into evidence under the business records exception.

Keep in mind though, that if a public record or report is not specifically excluded by Article 803(8)(b), there may be circumstances when the record may be introduced under this exception if all the requirements are met, such as when a government agency operates a hospital. In such a case, even though it is a public agency, if the requirements for the business records exception are met, the records may be admitted under this exception.[136] This exclusion is discussed further in § 5.12, *infra*, in *McRay v. Booker T. Washington Nursing Home.*[137]

Hospital Records. While hospital records may be admitted into evidence under this exception, if the requirements are met, hospital records may also be admitted under La.

---

133. *See* State v. Juniors, 915 So. 2d 291 (La. 2005).
134. Harges & Jones, Louisiana Evidence Art. 803(6) Author's Comments.
135. *See* La. Code Evid. art. 803 Official Comments to Exception (6).
136. *See* La. Code Evid. art. 803 Official Comments to Exception (6).
137. McRay v. Booker T. Washington Nursing Home, 711 So. 2d 772 (La. Ct. App. 2d Cir. 1998).

R.S. 13:3714. That statute provides that "a copy of a hospital record certified by the administrator or medical records librarian 'shall be received in evidence ... as prima facie proof of its contents ...' "[138] Like other exceptions allowing for the admissibility of documents, statements contained within the record may constitute hearsay within hearsay and a separate exception must apply to admit those statements. The court in *State v. Juniors*,[139] *infra*, thoroughly analyzes the scope of La. R.S. 13:3714 regarding statements and other information contained within the record.

Earlier cases allowed the entire record to be admitted into evidence under this statute,[140] even though portions may have been double hearsay or untrustworthy. However, in *Juniors* below, the court properly excludes portions of the records not properly falling within the exception.

Federal Rules of Evidence Distinction. Federal Rule of Evidence 803(6) does not specifically contain language providing that if the information furnished to the business is not by a person routinely acting for the business then, it must be "in circumstances under which the statement would not be excluded by the hearsay rule."[141] As outlined above, this phrase in the Louisiana Code basically means that information provided by third parties not routinely acting for the business must fall into a hearsay exception or it will be excluded as double hearsay. While the Federal Rule does not include that language, it has been recognized that the rule has the same effect. Thus, statements by third parties contained in business records under the federal rules are also regarded as double hearsay and must fit into an exception to be admissible.[142]

Further, following amendments to the Federal Rules of Evidence 803(6), (7), and (8), that went into effect on December 1, 2014, the rules now make clear that it is the *opponent* of the record who has the burden of proving that the record "lacks trustworthiness" in order for it to be excluded from admissibility under the business and public records exceptions. Louisiana's article also provides that to be admissible, the record must not indicate lack of trustworthiness, but it does not specify who has the burden of proving such lack of trustworthiness.

Absences of entry. Article 803(7) contains an additional exception to the hearsay rule that deals with business records. This exception provides that evidence may be offered showing that a matter is *not* included in a business record to prove the **nonoccurrence** or **nonexistence** of the matter, if the matter was of a kind of which would have been included in the business record had it occurred. For example, if a business record lists all payments a debtor makes on his accounts, evidence that there was no notation of a payment on a particular occasion may be offered as evidence to prove that no payment was made on that occasion. If hospital records show each time a person was admitted into the hospital, the lack of such records could be offered to show that the person was not admitted on a particular occasion.

While this type of evidence is arguably not a statement under Article 801, the exception likely exists to prevent the exclusion of such evidence, since the entries along with evidence of the non-entries theoretically asserts the non-existence of a fact.

---

138. 19 La. Civ. L. Treatise, Evidence And Proof § 10.18 (2d ed).

139. State v. Juniors, 915 So. 2d 291 (La. 2005). *Cf.* Judd v. State Depart of Transportation and Development, 663 So. 2d 690 (La. 1995).

140. Judd v. State Depart of Transportation and Development, 663 So. 2d 690 (La. 1995).

141. La. Code Evid. art. 803(6); *See also* Fed. R. Evid. 803(6).

142. *See* U.S. v. Snyder, 787 F.2d 1429, 1434 (10th Cir. 1986), *cert. denied*, 479 U.S. 836 (1986); United States v. Bortnovsky, 879 F.2d 30, 34 (2d Cir. 1989).

Like the business records exception, the exception allowing evidence of non-entry of a matter as evidence of non-existence, similarly does not apply if the sources of information or other circumstances indicate lack of trustworthiness. This might include errors, omissions, or erasures in the records, or the inability of the proponent of the record to lay a sufficient foundation to establish that the recordkeeping process is reliable and trustworthy.[143]

Cases on the Business Records Exception

Cole Oil & Tire Co. v. Davis

Court of Appeal of Louisiana, Second Circuit
567 So. 2d 122
Aug. 22, 1990

MARVIN, Judge.

In October 1986, plaintiff Cole Oil purchased the assets, including accounts receivable, of Boss Oil. One of the accounts was Davis's account, which showed a balance due of $8,021.85.

Cole thereafter sold merchandise and fuel to Davis through 1988, at first on credit and later, at Davis's suggestion, for cash. Davis paid Cole for what he purchased from Cole and, according to Cole, paid a total of $5,000 on the Boss Oil balance.

When Cole's efforts to collect the $3,021.85 did not succeed, Cole demanded that amount in writing from Davis. Cole's letter demand was returned "unclaimed."

On December 29, 1988, Cole sued Davis and his wife on open account, alleging that Cole sold to them goods, merchandise and services "on the dates and for the prices" shown on an allegedly "attached" itemized statement of account, subject only to "payments" shown on the itemized statement. The itemized statement, however, was *not* attached to Cole's petition. Cole Oil's bookkeeper, Kim Jones, executed an affidavit generally swearing that $3,021.85 was past due on the account. This affidavit was the only attachment to the petition.

The defendants answered, specifically denying only the correctness of the amount demanded. Defendants did not deny that Boss Oil had delivered merchandise and services to them and did not plead an affirmative defense. Davis did not allege or attempt to show at trial that he made specific payments to Cole which were not properly credited.

Cole, plaintiff's president, the only witness to testify at the September 14, 1989, trial, testified about the 1986 purchase of Boss Oil, his continued business dealings and discussions with Davis thereafter about payment of the Boss Oil balance and about Davis's payments "toward" the Boss account to Cole.

Cole sought to introduce its "Exhibit P-1 in globo," to which Davis promptly objected. Exhibit P-1 is Cole's "monthly" statement, an adding machine tape, and 14 Boss Oil sales invoices to defendant, allegedly for purchases defendant made from Boss Oil between July 3 and September 10, 1986. Overruling Davis' prompt and repeated objections of hearsay and Cole's incompetence and lack of knowledge about the Boss Oil records, the trial court admitted P-1 and allowed the testimony from Cole....

143. *See* State v. Romero, 574 So. 2d 330 (La. 1990) (finding that errors and omission in medical records suggested their unreliability).

EXHIBIT P-1 and OTHER EVIDENCE

As stated, Exhibit P-1 is Cole Oil's printed "MONTHLY STATEMENT" showing a balance due of $3,021.85, to which is stapled an adding machine tape that totals $3,182.31 and 14 Boss Oil printed invoices. Six of the invoices show that "Jerry" signed as "Received Payment." One shows that "Bobby Stuart" signed as "Received Payment." Six of the invoices are unsigned. With the Cole Oil "MONTHLY STATEMENT" and the adding machine tape, we reproduce the remaining invoice which is the only one that bears, beneath the printed name "JERRY," a signature, somewhat illegible, under "Goods Received" (see second column).

As Davis argues, the invoices have facial discrepancies unexplained by Cole. Cole, the only witness, did not identify or relate to Davis any name that was printed or signed on any Boss Oil invoice. The total shown, and the six amounts listed, on the adding machine tape do not correspond to the amount Cole says is owed on the Boss Oil account by Davis.

Before Exhibit P-1 was offered into evidence, Cole identified the Cole Oil monthly statement and explained its content without objection. Contrary to the monthly statement showing "PAYMENT 5000.00," Cole testified that Davis had made several payments that totaled $5,000.

Cole then attempted to identify, authenticate, and verify the 14 Boss Oil sales invoices. Davis promptly objected on the grounds that Cole lacked personal knowledge to identify the invoices, to verify "the amounts were actually delivered and received" by Davis, and to testify about the "prior owner['s]" business records.

Attempting to lay the proper foundation, Cole then explained that when he acquired the Cole Oil accounts receivable the sale documents showed that Davis then owed Boss Oil $8,021.85. The Boss Oil to Cole sale documents were *not* introduced into evidence.

Apparently assuming that the Boss Oil invoices were "records" of Cole Oil, the trial court overruled Davis's initial objections and allowed Cole's testimony. Cole testified, over objection, that the Boss Oil invoices reflected the amount Davis owed in 1986 and offered P-1, including the invoices, as evidence of the account. Davis's objections on the same grounds were again overruled and Exhibit P-1 was admitted.

On cross-examination, Cole stated he had not previously worked for and had no connection with Boss Oil, which was his competitor before he purchased the business and accounts receivables. He had no personal knowledge of and was unfamiliar with either Boss Oil's business records and sales invoices or Davis's alleged purchases from, and payments to, Boss Oil. Cole could not identify or testify regarding the individual's signature indicating "payment received" on the invoices. His only "personal knowledge" concerning Davis's account with Boss Oil was gained from the invoices and sale documents and verbal representations from Boss Oil.

Cole stated Cole Oil's payment records accurately reflected the total of amounts Davis paid on the Boss Oil account. Cole said Davis never questioned or disputed the Boss Oil balance during their discussions about the balance when Davis continued to do business with Cole Oil.

The Boss Oil-Cole "sale documents" and Cole Oil's "payment records" were not offered into evidence in the trial court.

HEARSAY AND THE BUSINESS RECORDS EXCEPTION

Before enactment of the Code of Evidence, hearsay was defined as an "out-of-court, unsworn, oral or written statement by a third party, which was offered for the truth of its content." ... Then, as now, hearsay was deemed unreliable and inadmissible....

The Code of Evidence defines hearsay as "a statement, other than one made by the declarant while testifying at the present trial or hearing, offered in evidence to prove the truth of the matter asserted." Unless specifically excepted or otherwise provided by the Code of Evidence or other legislation, hearsay is inadmissible.

Various exceptions to the hearsay rule are recognized in the Code of Evidence. Article 803 hearsay exceptions are generally based upon the policy that when the qualifying circumstances are met, there is *ordinarily* a sufficient basis for crediting the trustworthiness and reliability of the out-of-court statement to justify making an exception to the hearsay rule even though the declarant is available, but not called to testify, at trial. If the requirements for witness competency, authentication, and exception are met, the hearsay "exclusionary rule" does not bar admission of some "business records."

Relevant here is C.E. Art. 803(6), the "business records" exception, which reads in pertinent part:

> The following are *not excluded* by the hearsay rule, *even though the declarant is available* as a witness: * * *
>
> (6) Records of a regularly conducted business activity. In a *civil* case, *a memorandum, report, record, or other data compilation,* in *any form,* of acts, events, conditions, ... made at or near the time by, or from information transmitted by, a person with knowledge, if made and kept in the course of a regularly conducted business activity, and if it was the regular practice of that business activity to make and to keep the memorandum, report, record, or data compilation, *all as shown by the testimony of the custodian or other qualified witness, unless the source of information or the method or circumstances of preparation indicate a lack of trustworthiness.* This exception is inapplicable unless the recorded information was furnished to the business either by a person who was routinely acting for the business in reporting the information or in circumstances under which the statement would not be excluded by the hearsay rule.... C.E. Art. 803(6) (1989). (Emphasis added.)

The "business records" exception to the hearsay rule in Louisiana is not new. Under prior statutes, the business records admissibility requirements in both civil and criminal cases were more restrictive, however. Often perceiving the business records exception as too strict and inappropriate for modern business practices, some trial courts often ignored the statutory provision and applied common law business records rules....

The C.E. exception is substantially derived from its federal counterpart, with some minor differences. Unlike the federal rule, the Louisiana rule applies only to *civil* cases. Additionally, our rule, incorporating a second sentence not found in the federal rules, *expressly* requires, as a prerequisite to admissibility, that the initial entry information, as well as all subsequent transmitting and recording of it, to have been performed in the course of a regularly conducted business activity by persons owing a duty to that business. Louisiana further requires that the records be "made *and kept*" not only in the course of a regularly conducted business activity but also as a *regular practice* of that business activity. See generally and compare the Introductory Note preceding the Louisiana Code of Evidence, and Arts. 801 and 803(6) and related Comments with Fed.R.Evid., Rules 801 and 803(6), 28 U.S.C.

Like its federal counterpart, our code provides that business records "in any form" escape the hearsay ban if (and only if) the requirements of the law are met. Authenticity and firsthand knowledge of the record or records must be shown before the record is admissible. See C.E. Arts. 602 and 901, et seq.

A verbal statement by an absent declarant is admissible under Art. 803 only when the circumstances sufficiently indicate that the out-of-court declarant had firsthand, personal knowledge of that which he spoke.

To exclude business records from the hearsay rule and render them admissible, Article 803(6) requires the court to determine from testimony of either the "records custodian or other *qualified* witness" that:

1. The record of an event must have been made at or near the time of the event;

2. The record of an event must have been made either by, or from information transmitted by, a person with knowledge;

3. It must be made *and kept* in the course of a regularly conducted business activity;

4. It was the regular practice of that business activity to make *and keep* such records;

5. The recorded information must have been furnished to the business either (a) by a person who was routinely acting for the business in reporting the information; or (b) in circumstances under which the statement would not be excluded by the hearsay rule; and

6. Neither sources of information nor the method or circumstances of preparation must indicate a lack of trustworthiness.

Each of these requirements pose threshold questions for the trial judge. See also C.E. Art. 104(A).

The witness laying the foundation for admissibility of business records need not have been the preparer of the records. The person who keeps the books and records and makes the entries need not testify if a person who is in a position to attest to the authenticity of the records is present to testify.... Nothing in the Code of Evidence specifically requires either that the foundation witness be able to personally attest to the accuracy of the information contained in the documents, or that he personally prepared the documents. Indeed, Article 803 specifically eliminates these requirements....

A party offering business records evidence is no longer generally required to prove the declarant's unavailability or that production of such persons would be a "needless burden." Moreover, the business records sought to be introduced at trial no longer must be the "first collected records available." The former requirements no longer constrain the required "records custodian or other qualified witness" who testifies to the foundation requirements....

The party who seeks to introduce written evidence must in some way, nonetheless, authenticate it by a *qualified* witness. Under Art. 803(6), it is essential that a custodian or other qualified witness testimonially explain the record-keeping procedures of the business and thus lay the foundation for the admissibility of the records.... That witness must, however, be familiar with and able to testify from personal knowledge about the bookkeeping and accounting procedures of the entity whose business records are sought to be introduced.

If the foundation witness cannot vouch that the requirements of the Code of Evidence have been met, the evidence or proffered entry must be excluded....

Nevertheless, the erroneous admission of documentary exhibits does not warrant a reversal unless it is shown that substantial rights of the objecting party were prejudiced or affected. C.E. Art. 103(A). The burden of demonstrating prejudice rests upon the party asserting error....

DISCUSSION

On this record we must conclude that the trial court was clearly wrong in admitting P-1. Boss Oil's invoices, Cole's testimony regarding them, and portions of the Cole Oil statement clearly were hearsay or were founded on hearsay. Cole simply was not the qualified witness that is necessary to establish the C.E. 803(6) business records exclusion in these respects:

Boss Oil invoices.

The 14 Boss Oil invoices were obviously prepared by one or more third parties in connection with and for use by Boss Oil. Third party invoices, prepared by an out-of-court declarant, constitute hearsay. Cole's testimony, which was based entirely on third party oral and written statements, is "double hearsay."

"Double hearsay" does not preclude admissibility if the statutory requirements are met.... The statutory requirements are not met in this record.

Cole had no firsthand or personal knowledge about Boss Oil, its business records and accounting procedures or the "facts" contained in its invoices. He was never employed by or otherwise affiliated with Boss Oil when the invoices were prepared. He played no role in their creation or compilation. He knew nothing about the source or content, the method or circumstances of preparation or accuracy, trustworthiness or authenticity of the invoices.

Cole's only "knowledge" about the amount Davis allegedly owed came, he said, from sale documents, the invoices, and hearsay representations made to him by someone from Boss Oil. Cole testified that Boss Oil represented to him, in writing and verbally, at the time of the 1986 sale that Davis owed Boss Oil $8,021.85 on the accounts receivable Cole purchased. Cole's purchase of Boss Oil's assets does not make Cole "qualified" to verify or authenticate Boss Oil's record-keeping practices or the invoices in question. Though Cole Oil became the "owner" of Boss Oil's accounts receivable in 1986, and although Davis may have owed Boss Oil $8,021.85 at that time, Cole simply has not shown he had the necessary personal knowledge of and connexity with the Boss Oil transactions and business records to qualify him to provide the statutory foundation for admissibility of the records. C.E. Arts. 601, 602, and 901, et seq.

Cole did not know who prepared the documents. He could not identify the persons whose signatures appeared on the invoices or explain the facial discrepancies mentioned. Cole did not have personal knowledge of Boss Oil's record keeping practices or which invoices had or had not been paid by Davis and is in no position to attest to the reliability or trustworthiness of the invoices. Cole was not, then, a "qualified witness." C.E. Arts. 803(6) and 901.

Moreover, other "business records" exception requirements were not met. The record does not show that the invoices were prepared "at or near the time" of the alleged purchases, or by or from a person having knowledge of the information being transmitted, or that the records were made and kept in the course of a regularly conducted business activity, or whether it was Boss's regular practice to make and to keep such records. Art. 803(6).

Cases under the former law have consistently held that third party invoices are not admissible as business records to establish damages unless their reliability is supported by the testimony of the third party....

On this record, we must also find that substantial rights of Davis were prejudiced or affected. Davis's answer specifically denies the accuracy of the account sued on. No itemized statement of Davis' account reflecting credits and debits was attached to Cole's petition or introduced into evidence. Although the evidence of payments by Davis was properly admitted, no knowledgeable person testified and was subject to cross-examination about the accuracy of the account. The hearsay rule addresses the danger of prejudice inherent in such circumstances.

The 14 Boss Oil sales invoices constituted inadmissible hearsay. C.E. Art. 803(6). Cole's testimony about the 14 invoices is likewise inadmissible hearsay.

Cole Oil's "MONTHLY STATEMENT".

Cole's testimony about Cole Oil's monthly statement, which was not specifically objected to, is a "summary statement" under the code. Cole testified that his bookkeeper, Jones, was responsible for Cole Oil's books and business computer and was familiar with Davis's account.

Cole generally testified about Cole Oil's accounting procedures. Cole stated he received Davis' payments, gave them to Jones, who entered these payments on the computer, generated payment receipts and that he was familiar with Davis's account. Cole implied that the original *payment* records, prepared by Jones and supporting a "computer trail" which was not introduced at trial, were made by Jones at or near the time of payment from information Cole supplied to Jones.

That portion of the monthly statement which shows the alleged Boss Oil balance constitutes "hearsay within hearsay" based on another's written and oral declarations even though entered on Cole Oil's business records. See Art. 805 and related Comment. "Hearsay within hearsay" is admissible only if each part of the combined statement conforms with the business records exception. C.E. Art. 805.... Because Cole Oil failed to meet the statutory requirements for admitting the Boss Oil invoices, the portion of Cole Oil's monthly statement, which indicates Davis's September 30, 1986, "Balance Forward," constitutes hearsay.

Neither an itemized statement reflecting total debits and credits nor the actual payment receipts were introduced into evidence. Cole Oil's "monthly statement" reflects only the date of September 30, 1986. Cole testified, however, that Davis made several cash payments from 1986 through the latter part of 1988. The statement shows only the *total* amount of the payments. Thus, Cole Oil offers only a *summary* statement, which does not meet the statutory requirements.

There is no testimony indicating this summary statement was "made and kept" in the course of Cole Oil's regularly conducted business or that the summary form was a routine record-keeping practice of Cole Oil. Davis's objections were to Cole's competency to testify regarding and the admissibility of the *third party business record* and its content. Cole testified, without objection, about Cole Oil's monthly statement and its content. See Art. 103(A)(1). Even should we assume the monthly statement was generally admissible in these circumstances as a Cole business record, it was not admissible to prove the beginning balance owed by Davis on the Boss Oil account because Davis objected to any hearsay evidence to prove the balance owed on the account at any given time....

Having determined that the Boss Oil sale invoices, Cole's testimony regarding their contents, and the portion of Cole Oil's monthly statement reflecting Davis' Boss Oil balance were improperly admitted into evidence, we ignore that evidence as inadmissible, and conclude that Cole Oil did not meet its burden of proof.

The evidence shows only that Davis paid to Cole Oil several payments over a two-year period that totaled $5,000. There is simply no competent evidence to prove a balance of the Boss Oil account either before or after credit is given for payments to Cole by Davis. Cole's assertions that Davis did not dispute the Boss Oil account balance which was $3,021.85 is not sufficient to establish a prima facie case.

At plaintiff's cost, we reverse and render judgment in Davis's favor rejecting Cole's demands.

Discussion Questions

1. Upon what policy interests is the business records exception based? Why are business records deemed reliable and trustworthy?
2. What standards must be met in order for a witness to be competent to lay the foundation to introduce business records into evidence? What questions should be asked to establish that a witness is competent to testify? Is there a particular job or role in the business the witness must hold?
3. What foundation must be asked of a competent witness when introducing business records to ensure the reliability and trustworthiness of the record? How does each of these foundational issues help to ensure the trustworthiness of the evidence?
4. Who was needed in *Cole Oil* to lay the foundation for admission of the records? Why?

State v. Juniors

Supreme Court of Louisiana
915 So. 2d 291
June 29, 2005

WEIMER, Judge.

On November 17, 1997, shortly before 5:00 p.m., Robinson and John C. "Jack" Jackson, Jr., were each shot once inside the offices of Jack Jackson, Inc. and Fleet Boats, Inc., in Convent, Louisiana, in an apparent robbery attempt. The assailant absconded with Robinson's wallet and a knife, and with Jackson's wallet and some cash. Jackson, who was shot in the back, managed to call 911 and a nearby business, Elmwood Marine Services. Jack Haskell, an employee of Elmwood Marine Services and a friend of both Jackson and Robinson, ran to the office and attempted to render aid. Emergency personnel arrived shortly after Haskell, and began providing care to both victims. Robinson, who was shot in the head just above the left eye, was flown by helicopter to Thibodaux Regional Medical Center where he underwent emergency surgery. He died the next day. Jackson was transported by ambulance to Our Lady of the Lake Hospital in Baton Rouge, where he was treated and released two days later.

At trial, Jackson recounted the events of that November 17, 1997. He testified that at approximately 3:00 p.m., he was approached by a well-dressed, African-American male in the parking lot of the Fleet Boats office. The man asked him for a job application. Jackson led the man into the office, handed him the requested paperwork, and accompanied him back to the parking lot where they parted ways. Jackson then left to attend to various work-related tasks, both on and off the premises. He returned to the office at approximately 4:30 p.m. only to find the same individual who had approached him earlier standing outside the door of the office. This time the man asked if the welding job had been filled, and requested a second application. Jackson asked the man if he was Glynn Juniors, a person whom former employee Ronald Williams was going to send. The man responded negatively. Jackson then led the man into the office and handed him another application. The man asked Jackson if "the captain" was in and asked if he could speak with him. Jackson replied that Robinson was in the back office. The man proceeded to the back. Jackson, who remained behind to straighten the desk from which he had pulled the application, heard the man say "Butch." As he walked toward Robinson's office, Jackson could see Robinson standing at his desk holding one hand in the air. He heard a pop. Jackson entered the office only to discover Robinson with a gunshot wound above his eye. The assailant turned to Jackson, instructing him to empty his pockets and lie down on the floor. Jackson attempted to comply, but he was shot in the back before he could finish emptying his pockets. As Jackson lay prostrate on the floor, the man ransacked the office, ripping telephones from their jacks and throwing a computer monitor on top of Robinson. As he exited the room, the assailant kicked Jackson in the head.

...

On February 10, 1998, a St. James Parish grand jury returned indictments charging both defendant and Williams with the first degree murder of Albert "Butch" Robinson....

On April 19, 1999, Williams pled guilty to first degree murder. Pursuant to the plea agreement, the court sentenced Williams to life imprisonment at hard labor without benefit of parole, probation, or suspension of sentence. As part of the plea agreement, Williams agreed to testify against defendant.

Jury selection in defendant's case began on August 12, 1999, with the trial commencing four days later. At trial, Williams testified that on the afternoon of November 17, 1997, he and defendant drove from LaPlace to Convent in a gray Chevrolet Celebrity with the idea of robbing his former employer, whom he knew to carry a large amount of cash. Upon arriving in Convent, Williams dropped defendant off in the vicinity of the Fleet Boats office. The plan was for defendant to walk up to the office and ask for a job application so that he might "scope out" the premises. Williams circled back in his vehicle and retrieved defendant a short time later. The two men then drove around for a while, returning to the same location later in the day. According to Williams, the second time they approached the Fleet Boats office, he parked his car behind the nearby post office, got out, and walked to the front of the building. Defendant walked across a field to the Fleet Boats office. Williams returned to his car, popped the hood, and waited. After a few minutes, Williams heard two shots being fired, and the sound of items being thrown around. The defendant appeared across the field, walking from the direction of the Fleet Boats office. The men got in Williams' car and drove off. Later, defendant gave Williams a knife and approximately $285 to $295 in cash. Williams testified that defendant told him he shot each of the men in the head.

...

On August 17, 1999, following deliberations, the jury found defendant guilty as charged. After waiting the requisite twelve hours, the court began the penalty phase of the trial. The State introduced victim impact testimony, as well as evidence of the BRS Seafood and In & Out Food Store robberies. Defendant introduced testimony from family members.

At the conclusion of the penalty phase, the jury recommended that defendant be sentenced to death by lethal injection. Jurors found two aggravating circumstances: that defendant had knowingly created a risk of death or great bodily harm to more than one person; and that the victim had died during the commission of an armed robbery or attempted armed robbery. The trial court denied defendant's motions for new trial and for post-verdict judgment of acquittal. On June 22, 2000, the trial court sentenced defendant in accordance with the jury's recommendation. Defendant then filed a direct appeal in this court, asserting thirty-four assignments of error....

LAW AND ANALYSIS

... *Exclusion of Evidence*

In assignments of error Numbers 2, 3, 4, and 5, defendant maintains the trial court denied him the right to present a defense when it ruled three crucial items of evidence were inadmissible on hearsay grounds: a letter allegedly written by co-defendant Williams which purports to exonerate defendant; business records maintained by Fleet Boats, Inc. that indicate Williams had tested positive for marijuana while employed there; and, hospital records suggesting Robinson had been shot by a "disgruntled employee." We will address the admissibility of each of the excluded items of evidence in reverse order.

Hospital Records

At the close of his case, defendant attempted to introduce into evidence a Thibodaux Regional Medical Center "History and Physical" form prepared in connection with Robinson's emergency room admission on November 17, 1997. The form is signed by Donald Judice, M.D., and under the heading "History of Present Illness" notes: "The patient is a forty-six year old male who was shot by a disgruntled employee earlier." Defendant sought to introduce the medical report to bolster his claim that it was Williams, a former employee of Fleet Boats, Inc., who was the actual perpetrator of the crime.

The State objected to the introduction of the medical record, arguing that the statement could not have come from the victim because Robinson never regained consciousness. Thus, according to the State, the notation amounts to, at best, double hearsay. In addition, the State asserted the doctor who signed the form had since died and was, therefore, unavailable to testify.

Defendant countered that the report is admissible as an exception to the hearsay rule under LSA-R.S. 13:3714 and LSA-C.E. art. 803(4). Alternatively, defendant postulated the statement is non-hearsay and was being offered, not to prove the truth of the matter asserted, but to prove "that there are many statements made as to how this happened and what happened."

The trial court ruled the medical records admissible, but ordered that the phrase "by a disgruntled employee" be excised from the report as hearsay. Defendant contends the trial court erred in ruling the statement inadmissible.

Hearsay is defined in the Louisiana Code of Evidence as "a statement, other than one made by the declarant while testifying at the present trial or hearing, offered in evidence to prove the truth of the matter asserted." (LSA-C.E. art. 801 C). Hearsay is generally inadmissible unless it falls within one of the exceptions established by law.

As an initial matter, we reject defendant's argument that the statement excised from the medical report is not hearsay because it was being offered to demonstrate the inadequacies of the police investigation and to suggest that someone other than defendant committed the murder, and not for the truth of the matter asserted.[144] The statement is clearly hearsay. It was made out of court by a declarant who was unavailable to testify, and it was being offered for the truth of its content, that is, to prove that someone other than defendant committed the murder. As hearsay, it is not admissible unless it falls within one of the recognized hearsay exceptions.

Louisiana Revised Statutes 13:3714 establishes an exception to the hearsay rule for certified copies of hospital records. It provides:

> Whenever a certified copy of the chart or record of any hospital, signed by the administrator or the medical records librarian of the hospital in question, or a copy of a bill for services rendered, medical narrative, chart, or record of any other state health care provider, as defined by R.S. 40:1299.39(A)(1) and any

---

144. While the adequacy of a police investigation is a legitimate ground of inquiry, it is nevertheless an inquiry subject to hearsay rules.

> other health care provider as defined in R.S. 40:1299.41(A)(1), certified or attested to by the state health care provider or the health care provider, is offered in evidence in any court of competent jurisdiction, it shall be received in evidence by such court as prima facie proof of its contents, provided that the party against whom the bills, medical narrative, chart, or record is sought to be used may summon and examine those making the original of the bills, medical narrative, chart, or record as witnesses under cross-examination.

The purpose of the statute is to save a litigant the difficulty and expense of producing as a witness each person who assisted in the treatment of the patient. *Judd v. State, Dept. of Transportation and Development,* 95-1052, p. 3 (La.11/27/95), 663 So.2d 690, 693. It provides that the opposing party may defend against the record by calling those who made the record as witnesses under cross-examination. *Id.*

Since *State v. Kelly,* 237 La. 956, 112 So.2d 674 (1959), this court has applied LSA-R.S. 13:3714 in criminal as well as civil cases. However, we have also recognized that because the medical records rule is an exception to the hearsay rule created by statute, it must be strictly construed, and all formalities prescribed in the law must be followed. *State v. Trahan,* 332 So.2d 218, 220 (La.1976).

In the instant case, when Robinson's medical records were initially offered in evidence, the State objected on grounds that the doctor who prepared the report had died, and, thus, was unavailable for cross-examination. Defense counsel did not attempt to refute this assertion, stating he would accept counsel's word as to the doctor's demise. However, because the physician who prepared the statement could not be summoned by the State for cross-examination, an essential prerequisite for admissibility of the medical report could not be established. On this basis alone, the records did not qualify for introduction under the hospital records exception to the hearsay rule.

Further, even assuming the records could have been admitted into evidence, we have recognized that LSA-R.S. 13:3714 provides an exception to the hearsay rule with respect to those who made the medical record, *i.e.,* physicians, nurses, and technicians. *Judd,* 95-1052 at 3, 663 So.2d at 693. In this case, the statement sought to be admitted is not the statement of a person who made the record, but the statement of an unknown declarant to the record maker.[145] It is double hearsay. As such, the statement falls outside the ambit of the intended scope of the medical records exception (which must be strictly construed) and was properly excised by the trial court....

In a similar vein, we find the excised statement was not admissible under the alternative exception to the hearsay rule urged by defendant: LSA-C.E. art. 803(4). Article 803(4) provides a hearsay exception for "[s]tatements made for purposes of medical treatment and medical diagnosis in connection with treatment and describing medical history ... insofar as reasonably pertinent to treatment or diagnosis in connection with treatment." Under this exception, the use of hearsay history of a case as told to a physician by a patient is admissible if received, not to show the truth of the facts stated, but only the basis of the physician's opinion. All of the hearsay evidence not necessary to the diagnosis is inadmissible.

---

145. The report itself does not identify the source of the statement. However, it appears from the record that it is most unlikely the statement came from Robinson. The "Physical Examination" section of the medical report states that "[t]he patient is unconscious." Sections of the report entitled "Past History," "Review of Symptoms" and "Family History" all report: "I am not able to obtain." These notes suggest the State was correct when it argued that the statement did not come from Robinson.

Applying this exception in *State v. Bennett,* 591 So.2d 783, 785–86 (La.App. 4 Cir.1991), the court ruled that a rape victim's statements to her examining physician describing the sexual contact were reasonably pertinent and admissible under LSA-C.E. art. 803(4) because the statements were not used to show the truth of the facts stated. However, the court also ruled the victim's added comment that the defendant had forced her to drive to a secluded place was not reasonably related to diagnosis or treatment, and should not have been admitted, although the error was harmless under the facts of that particular case. *See also, State v. Johnson,* 96-0950 (La.App. 4 Cir. 8/20/97), 706 So.2d 468 (Rape victim's statement to physician that he was robbed and forced into an alley at gunpoint did not fall within LSA-C.E. art. 803(4) exception and should not have been admitted at trial.).

Here, the statement defendant sought to introduce—that Robinson was shot "by a disgruntled employee"—was not reasonably related to diagnosis and treatment and, thus, was not admissible as an exception to the hearsay rule pursuant to LSA-C.E. art. 803(4).

Finally, defendant contends that even if the excluded statement constitutes hearsay not fitting within one of the recognized exceptions to the hearsay rule, it was nevertheless admissible because it was critical to the defense and was made under circumstances providing considerable assurances of its reliability.

As a general matter, this court has recognized that under compelling circumstances a defendant's right to present a defense may require admission of statements which do not fall under any statutorily recognized exception to the hearsay rule. *State v. Van Winkle,* 94-0947 (La.6/30/95), 658 So.2d 198; *State v. Gremillion,* 542 So.2d 1074 (La.1989). *See also, Chambers v. Mississippi,* 410 U.S. 284, 93 S.Ct. 1038, 35 L.Ed.2d 297 (1973). Normally inadmissible hearsay may be admitted if it is reliable, trustworthy, and relevant, and if to exclude it would compromise the defendant's right to present a defense. *Van Winkle,* 94-0947 at 6, 658 So.2d at 202.

In the instant case, the statement sought to be admitted by defendant has no indicia of reliability or trustworthiness that would justify its admissibility in evidence as an exception to the well-settled rules of evidence. While the examining physician in this case had no reason to do anything other than report accurately the information that was relayed to him, there is absolutely no indication in the record as to the source of the physician's information. It is highly unlikely the statement that Robinson was shot by a "disgruntled employee" came from the victim; the medical report itself shows Robinson was unconscious during his examination, and the physician was unable to obtain any pertinent medical history, which he would undeniably have been able to do had he been able to speak with Robinson. It is equally unlikely the information came from co-victim, Jackson, as the record reveals the two men were transported from the scene to different hospitals in different cities. The physician, who is deceased, was unavailable to testify as to how he obtained the information. Thus, the circumstances surrounding the making of the statement are simply too speculative and too unreliable to merit their admission. The trial court did not err in refusing to allow defendant to introduce into evidence the hospital records containing the notation that the victim had been shot "by a disgruntled employee."

Business Records

Through the testimony of Debbie Wilson, a secretary at Fleet Boats, Inc., the defendant attempted to introduce into evidence a Corning Clinical Laboratories Forensic Drug Testing Custody and Control Form prepared in connection with Williams' pre-employment drug test. At the bottom of the form is a handwritten notation: "Positive marijuana 11/3/97." Defendant sought to introduce the document as circumstantial proof that

Williams lost his job at Fleet Boats due to alleged drug use, and, thus, had a motive for killing Robinson. The trial court ruled the document inadmissible.

Defendant contends the trial court erred in excluding the document, arguing it was admissible under the business records exception to the hearsay rule, LSA-C.E. art. 803(6). That article provides, in pertinent part:

> The following are not excluded by the hearsay rule, even though the declarant is available as a witness:.... .
>
> (6) Records of regularly conducted business activity. A memorandum, report, record, or data compilation, in any form, ... of acts, events, conditions, opinions, or diagnoses, made at or near the time by, or from information transmitted by, a person with knowledge, if made and kept in the course of a regularly conducted business activity, and if it was the regular practice of that business activity to make and to keep the memorandum, report, record, or data compilation, all as shown by the testimony of the custodian or other qualified witness, unless the source of information or the method or circumstances of preparation indicate lack of trustworthiness. This exception is inapplicable unless the recorded information was furnished to the business either by a person who was routinely acting for the business in reporting the information or in circumstances under which the statement would not be excluded by the hearsay rule. [Emphasis supplied.]

To exclude business records from the hearsay rule and render them admissible, LSA-C.E. art. 803(6) requires the court to determine from testimony of either the "custodian or other qualified witness" that:

> 1. The record was made at or near the time of the event;
>
> 2. The record was made either by, or from information transmitted by, a person with knowledge;
>
> 3. The record was made and kept in the course of a regularly conducted business activity;
>
> 4. It was the regular practice of that business activity to make and keep such records;
>
> 5. The recorded information was furnished to the business either (a) by a person who was routinely acting for the business in reporting the information; or (b) in circumstances under which the statement would not be excluded by the hearsay rule; and
>
> 6. Neither sources of information nor the method or circumstances of preparation indicate a lack of trustworthiness.

The witness laying the foundation for the admissibility of business records need not have been the preparer of the records; however, the witness must be familiar with and able to testify from personal knowledge about the bookkeeping and accounting procedures of the entity whose business records are sought to be introduced. *Cole Oil & Tire Co., Inc. v. Davis,* 567 So.2d 122, 129 (La.App. 2 Cir.1990). "Under Art[icle] 803(6), it is essential that a custodian or other qualified witness testimonially explain the record-keeping procedures of the business and thus lay the foundation for the admissibility of the records." *Id.* If the foundation witness cannot vouch that the requirements of the Code of Evidence have been met, the evidence must be excluded. *Id.*

In this case, Wilson, the secretary of Fleet Boats, Inc. who testified that she handled the accounting and most of the paperwork for the company, provided the necessary predicate for introduction of certain business records of the company. She identified Williams' W-4 form, completed job application, and pink slip as Fleet Boats records that were generated and kept as part of the personnel file. However, when the drug test form from the independent laboratory was presented to the witness for identification, she acknowledged that report was generated by the independent laboratory, and not by Fleet Boats. Further, she was unable to explain how the notation "Positive marijuana" came to be handwritten on the bottom of the form or by whom.[146] Under such circumstances, it is clear the necessary predicate was not established for admissibility of the Corning Laboratories form under the business records exception to the hearsay rule.

The Corning Laboratories test was obviously conducted by a third party for use by Fleet Boats. The form was not generated or made in the course of a regularly conducted business activity of Fleet Boats. Wilson had no personal knowledge as to the procedures and processes of the laboratory; nor could she identify how the handwritten notation came to be placed at the bottom of the form. She was unable to verify that the entry was made by persons who had personal knowledge of the test or of the test results. In short, she was in no position to testify as to the reliability or trustworthiness of the report. As a result, the report was properly excluded by the trial court.... *See and compare, State v. Borne, supra,* (Results of defendant's pre-employment drug test not admissible under business records exception to hearsay rules absent testimony as to who had custody of the result, who conducted the drug testing, and whether the results were kept as records in the regular course of business.); *Ruddock v. Jefferson Parish Fire Civil Service Bd.*, 96-831 (La.App. 5 Cir. 1/28/97), 688 So.2d 112, (Results of drug test properly admitted under business records exception to hearsay rule where associate director of biomedical laboratory performing the test testified he was responsible for the day-to-day operations of the laboratory, that he was familiar with the procedures and processes conducted at the laboratory upon receipt of a specimen for testing, and provided a detailed explanation of the test results.)....

Because the trial court did not err in excluding the Corning Laboratories form indicating that Williams had tested positive for marijuana while employed at Fleet Boats or the hospital records suggesting that Robinson was shot by a "disgruntled employee," ... the defendant was not deprived of the opportunity to present a defense. The trial court's evidentiary rulings do not undermine the reliability of the jury's verdict in this case. Defendant's assignments of error Numbers 2, 3, 4, and 5 lack merit.

Discussion Questions

1. The defense suggests that the statement that the victim was "shot by a disgruntled employee" was being offered for the non-hearsay purpose of showing "shoddy police work." Even so, the statement also had a hearsay purpose of showing that the victim was in fact shot by a "disgruntled employee," who of course would be someone other than the defendant. Recall back to Section 5.2.4 where the court in *State v. Wille* set out a rule for dealing with statements that have both a hearsay and non-hearsay purpose. Under what circumstances, if any, should such a statement be admitted?
2. Why is the statement, "the patient is a forty-six-year-old male who was shot by a disgruntled employee earlier," hearsay within hearsay?

146. Indeed, she could not verify the purpose of the test or when it was conducted. She speculated the test was a random drug screen, but the form itself indicates the test was part of the pre-employment physical.

3. Analyze the admissibility of the statement under the "statements made for medical treatment and diagnosis in connection with treatment" exception. What element(s) of that exception are missing?
4. Because of a defendant's constitutional right to present a defense, in some instances he may be able to offer a hearsay statement into evidence under the "residual catchall" exception (discussed later in the chapter), which might allow a statement to be admitted into evidence if it has "indicia of reliability." The court reasons that this statement had no indicia of reliability. What are your thoughts? Under the circumstances, does it appear that the statement could be reliable and trustworthy?
5. Why was the Fleet Boat employee incompetent to lay the foundation for the lab report? What was needed that she was unable to do?
6. Do you think it's possible that the notation on the lab report could have been non-hearsay? What effect would it have on the hearer/reader? Was the notation "Positive marijuana 11/3/97" being offered to prove that Williams actually tested positive for marijuana, or only to show a motive for why he may have been fired, even if the statement was not true? Is the credibility of the unknown person who made the statement at issue, or do we only care that Fleetwood read it?

§5.11.1 Out-of-State Business Records (Foreign Records of Regularly Conducted Business) [La. C.E. art. 803.1]

Applicable Code Articles

Art. 803.1. Hearsay exceptions; foreign records of regularly conducted activity

A. (1) Except as otherwise provided by this Code, in a criminal proceeding, a foreign record of regularly conducted activity, or a copy of such record, shall not be excluded as evidence by the hearsay rule if a foreign certification attests to the following:

(a) Such record was made, at or near the time of the occurrence of the matters set forth, by or from information transmitted by, a person with knowledge of those matters; and

(b) Such record was kept in the course of a regularly conducted business activity; and

(c) The business activity made such a record as a regular practice; and

(d) If such record is not the original, such record is a duplicate of the original, unless the source of information or the method or circumstances of preparation indicate lack of trustworthiness.

(2) A party intending to offer in evidence pursuant to this Article a foreign record of regularly conducted activity shall provide written notice of that intention to each other party not less than ten days prior to trial. A motion opposing admission in evidence of such record shall be made by the opposing party and determined by the court before trial. Failure by a party to file such motion before trial shall constitute a waiver of objection to such record or duplicate, but the court for cause shown may grant relief from the waiver.

B. As used in this Article:

(1) "Foreign record of regularly conducted activity" means a memorandum, report, record, or data compilation, in any form, of acts, events, conditions, opinions, or diagnoses,

> maintained by a business domiciled in a jurisdiction outside the territorial limits of the state of Louisiana.
>
> (2) "Foreign certification" means a written declaration made and signed in a jurisdiction outside the territorial limits of the state of Louisiana by the custodian of a business record of regularly conducted activity or another qualified person that, if falsely made, would subject the maker to criminal penalty under the laws of the state of Louisiana.
>
> (3) "Business" includes a business, institution, association, profession, occupation, and calling of every kind, whether or not conducted for profit.

Article 803.1 excludes business records from the hearsay rule from businesses domiciled in a state outside of the state of Louisiana in criminal trials. This provision is a relatively new exception to the Louisiana Code of Evidence that became law in 2008.[147] For purposes of this article, a business includes all of the same entities as for the business records exception found in Article 803(6)—a business, institution, association, profession, occupation, and calling of every kind, whether or not conducted for profit.

Records under this exception are similarly broad and include a memorandum, report, record, or data compilation, in any form, of acts, events, conditions, opinions, or diagnoses, maintained by a business domiciled in a jurisdiction outside the territorial limits of the state of Louisiana.

Certification from the state attesting to the following. To be excluded from the hearsay rule, the custodian of the foreign business record of a regularly conducted business activity or another qualified person must attest, i.e., make a written declaration that, if false, such a statement would subject him to criminal penalty, that the following exists:

a. Such record was made, at or near the time of the occurrence of the matters set forth by, or from information transmitted by, a person with knowledge of those matters;
b. Such record was kept in the course of a regularly conducted business activity;
c. The business activity made such a record as a regular practice; and
d. If such record is not the original, such record is a duplicate of the original, unless the source of information or the method or circumstances of preparation indicate lack of trustworthiness.

The foundational requirements for establishing the reliability are substantially the same as under the business records exception, except that rather than having a competent witness to testify personally to the foundational requirements, here, a competent witness *certifies* that the foundational requirements are met.

This exception obviously exists for practical purposes of not having to produce out-of-state witnesses for the sole purpose of having them authenticate records of an out-of-state business, which could be costly and in some cases impractical. However, due to the foundational requirements of the rule, the documents thus produced are likely to be reliable and trustworthy.

Procedures to offer foreign business record. A party intending to offer into evidence a foreign record of regularly conducted business activity pursuant to this Article shall pro-

147. La. Acts 2008, No. 178 § 1.

vide written notice of that intention to the other party not less than ten days prior to trial. A motion opposing admission in evidence of such record shall be made by the opposing party and determined by the court before trial. Failure by a party to file such motion before trial shall constitute a waiver of objection to such record or duplicate, but the court for cause shown may grant relief from the waiver.[148]

Key Points

The key points to keep in mind regarding the business records exception.

1. The business records exception provides that certain business records kept by a business in the course of its routine business practice may be excluded from the hearsay ban.
2. **Requirements:**
   1. **Must be business:** any business, institution, association, profession, occupation, calling, including those that are not for profit;
   2. **Records must be in the form of:** memorandum, report, record, data compilation in any form;
   3. **Record must concern:** acts, events, conditions, opinions, diagnosis;
   4. **Foundational requirements through a competent witness:**
      - i. that the record was made at or near the time of the event it records;
      - ii. that the record was made by: a) a person with personal knowledge; or b) based on information transmitted to him by a person with personal knowledge;
      - iii. that the recorded information was furnished to the business by either: a) a person routinely acting for the business in reporting the information; or b) in circumstances in which the statement would not be excluded by the hearsay rule;
      - iv. that the record was made and kept in the course of a regularly conducted business activity; and
      - v. that it was the regular practice of that business activity to make and to keep the record.
   5. The source of information or the method or circumstances of preparation must not indicate lack of trustworthiness; and
   6. Does not include public records and reports which are specifically excluded from the public records exception by Article 803(8)(b).
3. **Absence of entry in business record.** Under Article 803(7), evidence that a matter is *not* included in a business record may be offered to prove the nonoccurrence or nonexistence of the matter, if the matter was of a kind of which would have been included in the business record had it occurred, unless circumstances indicate lack of trustworthiness.

Foreign Business Record [La. C.E. art. 803.1]

1. A foreign record of regularly conducted activity, or a copy of such record, shall not be excluded as evidence by the hearsay rule if a foreign certification attests to the following:

148. La. Code Evid. art. 803.1(A)(2).

(a) Such record was made at or near the time of the occurrence of the matters set forth, by, or from information transmitted by, a person with knowledge of those matters;

(b) Such record was kept in the course of a regularly conducted business activity;

(c) The business activity made such a record as a regular practice; and

(d) If such record is not the original, such record is a duplicate of the original, unless the source of information or the method or circumstances of preparation indicate lack of trustworthiness.

2. To offer foreign business records, a party must provide notice to opposing party not less than 10 days prior to trial. Opposing party shall file motion to oppose offering the foreign business record and court makes ruling on issue before trial. If opposing party fails to oppose offering the foreign business record before trial, the party is deemed to have waived the right to oppose.

Problems on Business Records and Absence of Entry in Business Records

PROBLEM 5-95. Randall, who'd worked as a CPA all of his life for a major accounting firm, inherited his grandfather's furniture store when his grandfather passed away. Randall immediately quit his lucrative job to run his grandfather's company. Once Randall began going over the books, he noticed that the company accountant was taking money from the company, right under his grandfather's nose, over the last five years his grandfather was alive. Randall fired her and had her arrested. During the criminal trial on direct examination of Randall, the prosecution seeks to admit records from the company's accounting documents over the last five years to prove what was stolen. As the attorney begins to question Randall about the recordkeeping process for accounts receivables, profits, losses, and payments during that time, the defense objects that Randall is not competent to testify to those matters. Can the foundation for the records be laid through Randall? Why or why not?

PROBLEM 5-96. Blackburn Trucking, LLC is suing Minnie for outstanding payments she owes for services they rendered to Minnie. Minnie claims she owes no outstanding balance and claims that she paid every month, on time. At the trial, Blackburn calls their CFO to the stand and through him seeks to introduce their records of each payment Minnie made on her account, when, and for how much. They also plan to argue that where there are no entries in their records, Minnie made no payments. Minnie's attorney reviews the records and notices that all entries on the document are written in pencil and it has several erasures on it. Some of the entries of payments have no dates beside them, and at least one payment that they all agree was actually made, one that Minnie dropped off at the company president's house one Sunday when she was heading out of the country the next day, was not on the record at all. Minnie's attorney objects that the records do not satisfy the requirements for a business record exception. He also argues that even if the record is accepted, it should not be used to prove that Minnie didn't make additional payments that may not have been entered. How would you rule on the objection and why?

PROBLEM 5-97. Dr. Philip's right hand nurse is Jane. During Dr. Philip's examination of Tiffany, Dr. Philip states his findings out loud, as Jane writes down what he says into the official medical record. When Jane finishes, she hands them back to Dr. Philip, who reviews them and signs off on them. At Tiffany's trial, her attorney sought to introduce her medical records through Dr. Philip. The defense objects that the records were made by Jane who had no firsthand knowledge of the contents of the records, and they should be excluded because the foundation for a business record has not been met. How should the court rule on the objection and why?

PROBLEM 5-98. Jeremy's attorney seeks to admit his hospital records into evidence to prove the injuries he suffered in the automobile accident that led to the lawsuit. The records are from the day of the incident just hours after the accident occurred. At the trial, the hospital calls the custodian of records who lays the appropriate foundation for admission of Jeremy's records for the dates/times in question. While the defense does not object to the records in their entirety, they object to the following statements contained in the records. How should the court rule on each of the following statements contained in Jeremy's hospital records?

a. The patient complains of "*severe headache, nausea, states that he regurgitated in route to hospital. Says eyes are dim and can't see out of right eye at all.*"

b. Patient states, "*My ex-boyfriend Roger hit me because he doesn't like me anymore.*"

c. Patient stated upon entering ER, "*I think I have a concussion.*"

d. Patient's mother arrived and stated, "*I think this is intentional because he's been having an issue with the young man driving that other car.*"

e. Patient's mother reported that "*patient is allergic to penicillin and aspirin.*"

f. Doctor writes: "*Diagnosis: Concussion and severe head trauma due to impact with front window after vehicle struck by another vehicle traveling at high rate of speed.*"

PROBLEM 5-99. Twin brothers Tim and Tam determined that they've been together way too long, so they decide to dissolve their partnership, the restaurant they've run together the last 2 years—Tim and Tam's Tavern. They plan to finally go their separate ways to make a life for themselves. After they've sold all of the remaining stock, they dissolve the business. Finally, they sell off the last of the furniture (tables, chairs, counters, refrigerators, etc.) at an auction that took placed about 6 weeks after the two had closed shop. Tim handles this because Tam has already moved out of town. But before Tam left, he and Tim made a list of all the merchandise they had that they intended to sell at the auction. They listed every single table, chair, the refrigerator, freezer, silverware, and everything down to the two commercial ovens. Tim got $8,500 at auction, but writes a letter to Tam and tells him that he received only $2,500 for the merchandise and encloses $1,250 that he claims is the half due to Tam. Tam sues Tim for the rest of the money he claims he is due. At the trial he wishes to offer the list of merchandise they compiled together as evidence of all the items sold by Tim from which he claims he is due a portion of the proceeds. Tim claims the list is hearsay. Tam claims it is a business record. How should the court rule and why?

PROBLEM 5-100. Jonathan slipped and fell in a stairwell at his place of employment seriously injuring his back. The next day he immediately informed his supervisor and filed an accident report. In the report, Jonathan states that he injured himself when he fell on a poorly lit stairwell that also did not have a handrail. Jonathan has sued his employer for damages. In his suit, Jonathan alleges that his company failed to properly maintain the stairwell with inadequate lighting and railing. His employer contends that Jonathan injured his back while sleeping on the roof while at work. Jonathan wants to introduce the accident report at trial. His employer objects. How will the court likely rule?

PROBLEM 5-101. Luke purchased a car in Alabama and then moved to Louisiana where he subsequently put a stolen license plate on the vehicle to rob a bank. The prosecution would like to offer the sales invoice from the Alabama car dealership into evidence to prove that Luke actually purchased the car used in the robbery. The defense objects that the record is hearsay and does not fall with the business records exception because it is a foreign business. They further claim that if such a record could be used, there are several procedural requirements with which they must comply to admit it. How would you respond to the objection?

PROBLEM 5-102. The defendant is charged with credit card fraud. He wants to call someone from the bank to offer records that show that a week prior to the time the charges were made he called and reported his card stolen. The record from the call is introduced through the custodian of records at the bank and contains the defendant's statement. Should the portion of the record that contains his statement be admissible?

PROBLEM 5-103. Monique is suing her realtor Heather for damages she suffered when she was unable to close on a real estate transaction that Heather was handling. At the time of the deal, Monique made several calls to Heather but was unable to reach her. Each time she called, the receptionist put a note on Heather's desk telling her to call Monique, but Heather never returned Monique's call. Each note stated, "Monique called." Monique would like to offer the notes into evidence to prove how often she called Heather. Heather objects that the notes are hearsay. Can the notes be admitted under the business records exception?

PROBLEM 5-104. Kenya worked part-time at a local jewelry store. One of her duties was to count the valuable diamond rings each night before closing the store. A log was kept of the number of diamonds with which they both started and ended the day. One night while in a hurry to get out of the store to finish studying for finals, Kenya does not count the diamonds. She leaves the store. The next morning the manager came in and noticed that the diamonds were not counted from the night before. He then counts them and logs in the number of diamonds from the night before and then puts the same number down for the morning count. It is later discovered that a diamond was in fact missing and Kenya is arrested for theft. She wishes to call the manager to testify to what was noted in the log for the night that she was there. Will the entry in the log be admissible under the business records exception? Are all requirements met?

§ 5.11 References and Additional Authority on Business Records and Absence of Entry in Business Records [La. C.E. art. 803(6), (7)]

1. La. C.E. arts. 803(6),(7) and Official Comments
2. Force & Rault, Handbook on Louisiana Evidence Law Arts. 803(6),(7) Author's Comments (West Publishing 2014)
3. Harges & Jones, Louisiana Evidence Art. 803(6), (7) Author's Comments (West Publishing 2014)
4. 19 La. Civ. L. Treatise, Evidence And Proof § 10.18 (2nd ed.)
5. **Made within course of business activity:** *Brooks v. Reimonenq*, 44 So. 3d 824 (La. Ct. App. 4th Cir. 2010) (Ms. Keys, an adjuster for an insurance company, testified and her claim file was introduced as business record. The court reasoned that Ms. Keys was a litigation adjuster and since she testified that she reviewed the file that was pre-

pared for the investigation of the claim, the document was made within the regularly conducted business activity.).

6. **Qualified witness to lay foundation with first-hand knowledge:** *Cole v. Celotex Corp.*, 599 So. 2d 1058, 1083 (La. 1992) (holding that written deposition questions propounded to physician's custodian of records, indicating that records were made by physician in regular course of business as provider of medical services, established proper foundation for admission of medical records under business records exception to hearsay rule); *State ex rel. Guste v. Green*, 657 So. 2d 610 (La. Ct. App. 1st Cir. 1995) (holding that court-appointed deputy conservator was competent to give testimony as a "custodian or other witness").

7. **Finding not a business record**: *State v. Rainey*, 150 So. 3d 370 (La. Ct. App. 4th Cir. 2014) (Defendant was charged with one count of possession of oxycodone. Defendant claimed to have a valid prescription for the medication and introduced a copy of a prescription and pharmacy's computer printout. The prescription and patient history report were signed with "no name corresponding to the signature and no certification of authenticity" and were not admissible under hearsay exception for records of regularly conducted business activity because it could not be shown as to be authenticated by the custodian or other qualified witness.).

8. **Lacking foundation:** *Vining v. State Farm Life Ins. Co.*, 409 So. 2d 1306 (La. Ct. App. 2d Cir. 1982) (A business record was being offered as a joint exhibit but there was no establishment of the accuracy of the machine, that the record was made in the regular course of business or near the time of the happening and there was a lack of foundation by anyone who would have supervised the computerized records being prepared to show truthfulness and to justify the admission as evidence.); *Newspaper Production Co. v. Perry*, 404 So. 2d 1331 (La. Ct. App. 2d Cir. 1981) (Plaintiff offered defendant's ledger card to prove a balance was remaining and owed by defendant. The witness was the custodian of the ledger card but had not posted all of the entries pertaining to the ledger and did not supervise the other postings. The other person which posted to the ledger was neither called nor identified as a witness. The ledger was not admissible because the plaintiff was not the party who posted the entries to the card nor did she supervise the posting of the data.); *Westberry v. Nguyen*, 650 So. 2d 1218 (La. Ct. App. 4th Cir. 1995) (where witness could not say that documents came from his files, the records introduced were not properly authenticated and were not admissible as business records).

9. **Record made by a person with personal knowledge** or **based on information transmitted to him by a person with personal knowledge**: *Hamby v. Crescent Ford Truck Sales, Inc.*, 839 So. 2d 138 (La. Ct. App. 5th Cir. 2003) (holding that accident report inadmissible because employee could not prove that someone with knowledge made the report).

10. **Recorded information was furnished to the business by either a person who routinely acting for the business in reporting the information**; or **in circumstances in which the statement would not be excluded by the hearsay rule:** *LaSalle Pump & Supply Co., Inc. v. Louisiana Midland R. Co., Inc.*, 433 So. 2d 745 (La. Ct. App. 3d Cir. 1982) (Those preparing the record for the absence of inventory were not the individuals that normally estimated inventory and could not explain the method and procedure used to calculate inventory.); *Phillips v. Joseph Management Services, Inc.*, 861 So. 2d 625 (La. Ct. App. 5th Cir. 2003) (holding that contract accountant was not routinely acting for the business).

11. **Record was made and kept in the course of a regularly conducted business activity:** *State v. Roche*, 341 So. 2d 348 (La. 1976) (The controller of a facility brought records showing the defendant was in debt at the casino and testified that the records presented were kept in the normal course of the business and that anyone in his position at the facility would have access and be familiar with the records.).

12. **La. C.E. art. 803(7) Absence of Entry of Business Records:** *State v. Romero*, 574 So. 2d 330 (La. 1990) (The State was attempting to prove a doctor was committing Medicaid fraud by submitting claims for medical services which he never provided. The documents consisted of patient charts, nurses' notes, progress notes, physician order sheets and doctor order sheets. The custodian of records testified that all pertinent information regarding a patient was in the said documents, thus an absence of an entry would conclude the service did not exist. The custodian stated that she routinely removed charts to her office and took them home to be "thinned." The removed documents were placed in a separate file which the State did not have possession of. Since they were untrustworthy and incomplete, they were not admissible.).

§ 5.12 Public Records and Absence of Entry in Public Records [La. C.E. art. 803(8), (10)]

Applicable Code Articles

The following are not excluded by the hearsay rule, even though the declarant is available as a witness:

* * *

(8) Public records and reports

(a) Records, reports, statements, or data compilations, in any form, of a public office or agency setting forth:

(i) Its regularly conducted and regularly recorded activities;

(ii) Matters observed pursuant to duty imposed by law and as to which there was a duty to report; or

(iii) Factual findings resulting from an investigation made pursuant to authority granted by law. Factual findings are conclusions of fact reached by a governmental agency and may be based upon information furnished to it by persons other than agents and employees of that agency.

(b) Except as specifically provided otherwise by legislation, the following are excluded from this exception to the hearsay rule:

(i) Investigative reports by police and other law enforcement personnel.

(ii) Investigative reports prepared by or for any government, public office, or public agency when offered by that or any other government, public office, or public agency in a case in which it is a party.

(iii) Factual findings offered by the prosecution in a criminal case.

> (iv) Factual findings resulting from investigation of a particular complaint, case, or incident, including an investigation into the facts and circumstances on which the present proceeding is based or an investigation into a similar occurrence or occurrences.
>
> * * *
>
> **(10) Absence of public record or entry.** To prove the absence of a record, report, statement, or data compilation, in any form, or the nonoccurrence or nonexistence of a matter of which a record, report, statement, or data compilation, in any form, was regularly made and preserved by a public office or agency, evidence in the form of a certification in accordance with Article 902, or testimony, that diligent search failed to disclose the record, report, statement, or data compilation, or entry.
>
> * * *

Article 803(8) contains the public records exception, which provides that certain records, reports, or data compilations of state or federal public offices or agencies will not be subject to the hearsay rule. Like other documentary evidence, the records are out-of-court statements being offered to prove the truth of the matter asserted within the record, making them hearsay. However, if all of the requirements for admissibility of the exception are met, the records will not be excluded by the hearsay rule.

Policy for admitting evidence. The basis for excluding public records from the hearsay rule is an "assumption that these records are trustworthy because public officials will perform their duties properly, that they have no motive and thus are not likely to falsify the records, and that open records statutes requiring disclosure of public records will foster accuracy."[149] Additionally with public records, "there is a need for admission of such records because it is unlikely that public officials will remember details of all events or occurrences they encounter in their positions."[150]

Requirements for the public records exception:

1. Must be a record, report, or data compilation;
2. Of a state or federal public agency or public office; and
3. Must set forth: i) its regularly conducted and regularly recorded *activities*; ii) matters *observed* pursuant to duty imposed by law and as to which there was a duty to report; or iii) *factual findings* resulting from an investigation made pursuant to authority granted by law.
4. Not excluded under Article 803(8)(b)(i)–(iv).

Types of Records Included

The public records exception is a narrow exception, and by far does not include a broad range of government records. Article 803(a)(i)–(iii) sets forth only three categories of records that may be admitted under this exception. They include those records setting forth:

i. its regularly conducted and regularly recorded *activities*;[151]

149. La. Prac. Civ. Trial § 8:73.
150. La. Prac. Civ. Trial § 8:73.
151. La. Code Evid. art. 803(a)(i).

Requirements for Public Records Exception:

1. Must be a record, report, or data compilation;
2. Of a state or federal public agency or public office; and
3. Must set forth:
   i. its regularly conducted and regularly recorded *activities;*
   ii. matters *observed* pursuant to duty imposed by law and as to which there was a duty to report; or
   iii. *factual findings* resulting from an investigation made pursuant to authority granted by law.
4. Not excluded under Article 803(8)(b)(i)–(iv).

ii. matters *observed* pursuant to duty imposed by law and as to which there was a duty to report;[152] or

iii. *factual findings* resulting from an investigation made pursuant to authority granted by law.[153]

Regularly conducted and regularly recorded activities. The first two categories of records include matters of which the agency official has **first-hand knowledge**, or is information **supplied to the record maker by** an **agency official who had first-hand knowledge**. "Records made by one official that include information provided by another official who is acting in the course of his duties are covered by the article. Internal hearsay within the government agency will not affect admissibility under the exception."[154]

This provision includes records pertaining to the core activities of the agency—such as certificates of title, registry, death, and birth, records of licensing agencies, serving papers, erecting signs and monuments, hiring and firing people, buying, selling, or maintaining equipment, etc.[155]

Matters observed pursuant to duty imposed by law with duty to report. Like the first category, this category requires **first-hand knowledge of someone from the agency**, or supplied **by someone from the agency**. It may be used to prove things like "temperature and weather conditions, building code violations, geographical features, and prices of commodities studied or regulated by the government."[156]

Factual finding from investigations. The final category of records that may be introduced under this exception sets forth "factual findings resulting from an investigation" made pursuant to authority granted by law. Unlike the first two categories, this category of records sets forth **"conclusions and inferences drawn from the facts."**[157] The conclusions may be drawn from **personal observations** of an **agency official** or from **information supplied** to the agency **by others with first-hand knowledge** who are not affiliated with

---

152. La. Code Evid. art. 803(a)(ii).

153. La. Code Evid. art. 803(a)(iii).

154. Harges & Jones, Louisiana Evidence, Author's Comments; *See also* La. Code Evid. art. 803 (8) Official Comment (d).

155. Christopher Mueller & Laird Kirkpatrick, Evidence, 217 (3d ed. West Publishing) [hereinafter Mueller & Kirkpatrick, Evidence]; *See also* Glen Weissenberge & James J. Duane, Federal Rules of Evidence: Rules, Legislative History, Commentary and Authority § 803.42 (6th ed. 2009).

156. Mueller & Kirkpatrick, Evidence, at 217.

157. La. Code Evid. art. 803(8) Official Comment (c).

the agency.[158] In these circumstances, the court should ensure that the basis for the conclusions is trustworthy.

Records in this category include results of studies conducted in a wide range of subjects such as "reports on the nature, causes, and spread of diseases, on product safety, on discrimination in housing or workplace, on incidence of crime, on educational attainments, and so forth."[159]

In some instances factual findings will include evaluative statements such as expert opinions. In such cases, the record should only be allowed if the person expressing the opinion has the proper qualifications.[160] The trial court should require such a foundation in allowing the report.

While the provision permits factual conclusions, it does not permit legal conclusions. "Thus, a statement made by a qualified official, after investigation, that an airplane involved in an accident had been traveling at approximately 500 miles per hour at impact would be a 'factual finding,' while a statement that the pilot of the plane was 'negligent' would not."[161]

Excluded Public Records under Exception

Excluded public records. The article specifically excludes four categories of public records from the exception in Article 803(8)(b)(i)–(iv). They include:

i. Investigative reports by police and other law enforcement personnel;
ii. Investigative reports prepared by or for any government, public office, or public agency when offered by that or any other government, public office, or public agency in a case in which it is a party;
iii. Factual findings offered by the prosecution in a criminal case; and
iv. Factual findings resulting from investigation of a particular complaint, case, or incident, including an investigation into the facts and circumstances on which the present proceeding is based or an investigation into a similar occurrence or occurrences.

The list of exclusions further narrows the types of public records that may be offered under the exception. The exclusions are "designed to exclude untrustworthy evidence, to avoid encroaching upon an accused's right to confrontation and to preserve the function of the jury as the ultimate finder of fact.[162]

Article 803(8)(b)(i) excludes police reports and other law enforcement investigative reports. For this part, the key is the type of agency that carried out the investigation that determines whether the report is excluded[163]—here, law enforcement. The exclusion applies to police reports in either a civil or criminal case, and regardless to who is offering it, defendant or the government. This exclusion is primarily designed to respect an accused's Sixth Amendment right to confrontation and cross-examination in a criminal case. Thus, the prosecution would never be able to simply offer a police

158. La. Code Evid. art. 803(8) Official Comment (c).
159. Mueller & Kirkpatrick, Evidence, at 217.
160. La. Code Evid. art. 803(8) Official Comment (d).
161. La. Code Evid. art. 803(8) Official Comment (c).
162. La. Code Evid. art. 803(8) Official Comment (e).
163. La. Code Evid. art. 803(8) Official Comment (h).

report as evidence against the accused in lieu of having the officer or individual witnesses involved present to testify.[164]

Article 803(8)(b)(ii) excludes investigative reports of government agencies other than law enforcement from being offered by the agency when the government is a party to the action. Under this provision, it is the **nature of the party** that proffers the report that is crucial to admissibility.[165] This exclusion applies to reports offered ***by an agency*** when they ***are a party*** to the action. Under this provision, the report may be offered against the government agency, such as by an accused in a criminal case, if it fits one of the three categories in Subparagraph (a).

Article 803(8)(b)(iii) excludes factual findings from being offered by the prosecution in a criminal case. This exclusion is in further respect for a defendant's constitutional rights to confrontation and cross-examination. Thus, while certain factual findings may be permissible under Subparagraph (a) as outlined above, this section excludes factual findings offered by the prosecution in a criminal case. The exception does not, however, preclude a criminal defendant from offering such reports.[166] Thus, while Part (i) excludes law enforcement reports whether offered by state or defense, Parts (ii) and (iii) only exclude reports offered by a government agency. The defendant may offer them.

Article 803(8)(b)(iv) excludes reports of factual findings "resulting from an investigation of a particular complaint" including the facts and circumstances on which the present proceeding is based. An example of a particular complaint would be an investigation into the cause of death of a particular person—such as whether a particular person's death was caused by asbestos.

A general investigation would be a study of the relationship between asbestos and deaths. While a person could offer the factual findings of the general investigation, the factual findings in the particular complaint could not be introduced under the exception in any case, whether it is one arising out of the facts of the specific case or another unrelated case.

Neither party may offer reports of factual findings into a particular case or complaint. This exclusion is further elaborated on in *McRay v. Booker T. Washington Nursing Home*,[167] below.

Exclusions may not be offered as business records. It is important to note that a record excluded from admissibility under this exception cannot, in the alternative, be admitted as a business record. The business records exception specifically states that "Public records and reports which are specifically excluded from the public records exception by Article 803(8)(b) shall not qualify as an exception to the hearsay rule under this Paragraph." As a result, the four categories of public records excluded above cannot be admitted as public records *or* business records.

Untrustworthy records excluded. Even when not specifically excluded within the list of exclusions, a public record should be excluded if it is untrustworthy.[168]

---

164. See further discussion of the defendant's Sixth Amendment rights to confrontation and cross-examination as it relates to hearsay in Chapter 5 Part E, *infra*.

165. La. Code Evid. art. 803(8) Official Comment (h).

166. La. Code Evid. art. 803(8) Official Comment (g).

167. McRay v. Booker T. Washington Nursing Home , 711 So. 2d 772 (La. Ct. App. 2d Cir. 1998).

168. La. Code Evid. art. 803(8) Official Comment (e); *See, e.g.*, State v. Nicholas, 359 So. 2d 965 (La. 1978).

Other public records. Keep in mind that while this provision specifically relates to three categories of public records included within the exception, and specifically excludes certain public records, it does not affect the admissibility of public records specifically allowed under special statutes.[169] Among those are these listed below:

R.S. 15:529.1 (F) (prison and clerk of court certificates admissible under the habitual offender law)

R.S. 15:585 (admissibility of records of Louisiana Bureau of Criminal Identification)

R.S. 15:499–500 (admissibility of results of laboratory examinations)

R.S. 32:1473 (admissibility of records of convictions of motor vehicle offenses)

R.S. 13:3714 (admissibility of hospital records)

Absence of entry in public records. Like the business records exception, there is also an exception to the hearsay rule for the absence of entry of public records. Pursuant to Article 803(10), if a public record is one that is regularly made and preserved by a public office or agency, evidence of:

1. the absence of a public record; or
2. the absence of entry in a public record,

is admissible to prove:

1. the absence of the record; or
2. the nonexistence or nonoccurrence of the matter.

To prove such absence of entry or the nonexistence or nonoccurrence of the matter, evidence may be offered in the form of either:

1. a certification in accordance with Article 902 (which would be self-authenticating); or
2. testimony, that diligent search failed to disclose the record, report, statement, or data compilation, or entry.

While the absence of entry in the public record could arguably be said not be a statement, the article is included to prevent the absence of such a record or entry from being excluded in evidence.[170] "The same rationale justifying the admission of the absence of business records justifies this rule. That is, the duty of public officers to make and keep these records is a guarantee of their trustworthiness, even where it is the absence rather than the presence of a particular entry or record that is relevant."[171]

Federal Rules of Evidence Distinction. There are distinctions in the Louisiana and federal public records exceptions. The substantive differences provide for a narrower public records exception under the Louisiana Code of Evidence and require caution in relying on federal cases decided under the federal rule.[172] Specifically, the Federal Rule of Evidence 803(8) states as follows:

> **(8) Public Records.** A record or statement of a public office if:
>
> (A) it sets out:
>
> (i) the office's activities;

---

169. La. Code Evid. art. 803(8) Official Comment (a).
170. *See* Force & Rault, Handbook, Art. 803(10) Author's Comment (2).
171. *See* La. Prac. Civ. Trial § 8:77.
172. Force & Rault, Handbook, Art. 803(8) Author's Comment (2).

(ii) a matter observed while under a legal duty to report, but not including, in a criminal case, a matter observed by law-enforcement personnel; or

(iii) in a civil case or against the government in a criminal case, factual findings from a legally authorized investigation; and

(B) the opponent does not show that the source of information or other circumstances indicate a lack of trustworthiness.[173]

Like the Louisiana article, the federal rule only relates to three types of public records. However, the federal rule does not require that the *activities* of the public agency recorded in the record be the "regularly conducted and regularly recorded" activities, as is required under the Louisiana article. However, like the Louisiana article, the federal rule also includes records that set out certain "matters observed," that the agency official is under a legal duty to report, as well as records of "factual findings" from a legally authorized investigation.

While the federal rule does not have a separate section specifically listing exclusions, the rule does exclude from the exception matters **observed by law enforcement in a criminal case** in Federal Rule of Evidence 803(8)(ii), and excludes **factual findings** from a legally authorized investigation from being offered **by the government in a criminal case** under Federal Rule of Evidence 803(iii). Under this section, however, such records could be introduced by the accused.

While Louisiana's rule is narrower than the federal rule in containing more specific and broader exclusions, the federal rule also shows respect for the Sixth Amendment confrontation and cross-examination rights of the accused by excluding the categories of records in "(ii)" and "(iii)" from being offered against the accused in criminal cases.[174]

Additionally, the federal rule in part (B) specifically provides that such records may not lack trustworthiness. While Louisiana's article does not specifically state this requirement, it has been recognized that a public record should not be permitted if the records lack trustworthiness.[175]

Case on Public Records Exception

McRay v. Booker T. Washington Nursing Home

Ct. of Appeal of Louisiana, Second Circuit
711 So. 2d 772
April 8, 1998

MARVIN, Chief Judge.

In this malpractice action, the defendant nursing home appeals a default judgment and the denial of its motion for new trial. Finding that plaintiffs failed to present evidence sufficient to establish a prima facie case, we vacate the default judgment and remand.

FACTS

Golden McRay, Jr. was rendered a paraplegic after being shot in early 1990. After being hospitalized in LSU Medical Center in Shreveport, McRay was placed in Guest Care Nursing Home. Shortly thereafter, McRay was moved to the defendant nursing home,

173. Fed. R. Evid. 803(8).

174. *See* Goode & Wellborn, Courtroom Evidence Handbook, Student Edition Rule 803(8)–(10) Author's Comments (6) and (7) (West Publishing).

175. Official Comment (e); *See, e.g.*, State v. Nicholas, 359 So. 2d 965 (La. 1978).

BTW, in May 1990. McRay remained there until he was moved to a third nursing home on August 20, 1990, where his condition was quickly recognized as critical and he was again hospitalized in the LSU Medical Center, where he died on November 23, 1990 at the age of 38.

Plaintiffs, McRay's surviving spouse, Virginia McRay, their four minor children, and his one major child, Anthony Jackson, brought their action against BTW on November 22, 1991. They alleged that they made complaints to the Louisiana Department of Health and Hospitals (DHH) regarding neglect of McRay by the BTW staff; that after an investigation by DHH found the complaints to be valid, DHH ordered McRay's transfer from BTW; that McRay was moved to Arcadia Nursing Home, where it was discovered that because of BTW's neglect, severe bed sores had developed, leading to gangrene and requiring hospitalization; that McRay subsequently died from the gangrene and resulting infection; and that McRay's death was the direct result of BTW's failure to provide the standard of care required for a paraplegic.

On November 27, 1991, service was made on Gloria Harrison, BTW's registered agent for service of process. BTW did not file an answer or otherwise plead. No further court action was taken in this matter until October 3, 1996, when plaintiffs filed notice to substitute Frank Ferrell for James Dawson as counsel of record. Ferrell entered a preliminary default on November 6, 1996. On November 18, 1996, the trial court conducted a hearing to confirm the preliminary default. At the conclusion of this hearing, the court rendered a default judgment awarding $30,000 to McRay's estate for his pain and suffering, $15,000 to Virginia McRay for loss of consortium, love and affection, and $5,000 to each of the four minor children. The court rejected the claims of Anthony Jackson.

DISCUSSION

To confirm the default judgment, plaintiffs were required to present to the trial court "proof of the demand sufficient to establish a prima facie case" against BTW. La. C.C.P. art. 1702. We have explained the burden of establishing a prima facie case:

A "prima facie case" is established when the plaintiff proves the essential allegations of the petition, with competent evidence, to the same extent as if the allegations had been specifically denied. In other words, the plaintiff must present competent evidence that convinces the court that it is probable that he would prevail at a trial on the merits. Hearsay evidence does not sustain the burden of proving the prima facie case necessary for confirmation of default....

At the hearing to confirm the preliminary default, Virginia McRay testified that her husband's condition prevented him from walking or using his arms and hands, but he was able to speak; that McRay was at BTW from May 1990 to August 1990, and she would visit him from five to six times per week; that McRay was at the LSU Medical Center when he died on November 23, 1990; that McRay developed bed sores while at BTW, and she complained about this to the BTW staff, but she did not speak to a doctor about her husband's condition; that if McRay had the sores before he came to BTW, she did not know about it; that she did not see the BTW staff take any measures to treat the bed sores; that an investigation of this incident by the state resulted in McRay's removal from BTW; that McRay was transferred to a nursing home in Arcadia, where the staff considered his condition to be so bad that they transferred him to the LSU Medical Center; and that McRay's doctor told her that he died because of a bad infection from the bed sores. No other witnesses testified.

Plaintiff introduced as "P-1" a cover letter to attorney Dawson from the Department of Health and Hospitals (DHH) and copies of two interoffice communications from the regional office of DHH. The first communication, dated July 27, 1990, contains a list of allegations made by a clinic nurse against BTW regarding McRay's treatment. The second interoffice communication, dated August 13, 1990, details the results of the investigation into the July 27, 1990 complaints. Attorney Ferrell acknowledged to the court that these documents were not certified. BTW of course argues that these three documents were hearsay and did not meet the requirements for admissibility of business records under La. C.E. art. 803(6). Plaintiffs counter that the documents were admissible as factual findings under La. C.E. art. 803(8).

Art. 803(8)(a)(iii) provides that a report by a public agency is an exception to the hearsay rule:

> Factual findings resulting from an investigation made pursuant to authority granted by law. Factual findings are conclusions of fact reached by a governmental agency and may be based upon information furnished to it by persons other than agents and employees of that agency.

This exception is limited by Art. 803(8)(b)(iv), which states that except as specifically provided otherwise by legislation, this exception does not apply to:

> Factual findings resulting from investigation of a particular complaint, case, or incident, including an investigation into the facts and circumstances on which the present proceeding is based or an investigation into a similar occurrence or occurrences.

While factual findings from a *general* investigation may be admissible, factual findings from a *specific or particular* investigation are inadmissible under the public records exception. Moreover, if a public report is excluded under Art. 803(8)(b), it is not admissible under the business records exception to the hearsay rule. La. C.E. art. 803(6).

The comments to exception (8) of Art. 803 distinguish a special investigation of a particular complaint from a general investigation. A special investigation is an investigation into the circumstances that give rise to the proceeding in question. An example of a report from a general investigation is a report establishing a link between cigarette smoking and lung cancer. An example of a report from a special investigation is a finding by a government investigator that the cause of an accident which is the subject of the proceeding is a defective tire. See *Green v. Connor,* 94-2120 (La.10/7/94), 644 So.2d 618. There the plaintiff sought social security disability benefits after being injured in an auto accident, while simultaneously filing a claim against his uninsured motorist insurer alleging arbitrary and capricious handling of his claim for UM benefits. In a per curiam opinion, the court ruled that because the social security proceedings involved the same incident as the suit against the insurer, the factual findings made by the social security administration were inadmissible under Art. 803(8)(a). See also *Zatarain v. WDSU-Television, Inc.,* 95-2600 (La.App. 4th Cir. 4/24/96), 673 So.2d 1181 [Letter of Determination from EEOC concluding that television station likely discriminated against news anchor was not admissible under Art. 803(8)(b)(iv) in the anchor's employment discrimination suit against station].

The first interoffice communication contains the allegations that McRay had massive *decubiti* [pressure sores] that were not being cared for and were getting worse, that his penis was draining pus and there was a lesion behind the foreskin, and that McRay had not had a bath in over a week. The second interoffice communication, dated August 13, 1990, contains the results of the investigation into these allegations, with the investigators finding the first two allegations to be valid. The investigators further concluded that because McRay required "SNF" level care, his placement at BTW was inappropriate since BTW is an "ICF" facility, and transfer to a "SNF" facility was therefore ordered. Obviously, the second interoffice communication contains factual findings regarding the same incident

[BTW's treatment of McRay] that is the subject matter of this litigation. Under Art. 803(8)(b)(iv), this communication is not within the public records exception to hearsay and should not have been admitted.

The letter to Dawson and the first interoffice communication likewise constitute inadmissible hearsay. While plaintiffs contend both are exceptions under Art. 803(8)(iii), neither contains "factual findings resulting from an investigation made pursuant to authority granted by law." The cover letter to Dawson simply informs him that the two interoffice communications are attached. The first interoffice communication only lists allegations, not conclusions. Moreover, even if the letter and the first interoffice communication could have been admitted under the business records exception to hearsay found in Art. 803(6), that exception requires the testimony of the custodian or other qualified witness regarding the agency's record-keeping procedures. Plaintiffs did not provide this in this record.

Even if we assume that each of the three documents in P-1 came under an exception to the hearsay rule, we note the lack of authentication. La. C.C.P. art. 1702(B)(2) provides that when the demand is based upon a delictual obligation, a plaintiff's testimony can be corroborated by affidavits and exhibits annexed thereto which shall be self-authenticating. The three documents in P-1 were not accompanied by any affidavit.

La. C.E. art. 902(2)(b) allows for originals of documents from a state agency to be admitted without extrinsic evidence of authenticity when certified as being the original. Copies of documents from a public agency are self-authenticated when certified as being true or correct by the custodian or other person authorized to make that certification. La. C.E. art. 904. Attorney Ferrell correctly responded to the trial court's question that the documents were not certified. P-1 should not have been admitted without certification or extrinsic evidence as to its authenticity.

As noted, hearsay evidence does not sustain a plaintiff's burden of proof to establish a prima facie case necessary to confirm a default. *Carroll, supra.* The three P-1 documents, hearsay and not authenticated, are not competent evidence. We are then left only with the testimony of Virginia McRay, to determine whether it alone is sufficient to confirm the default. The testimony of a plaintiff alone may be sufficient to confirm a default. *Carroll, supra.* We find, however, the testimony of Mrs. McRay does not establish a prima facie case of BTW's negligence. The standard of care imposed on a nursing home is that of reasonable care, considering the patient's mental and physical condition. *McCartney v. Columbia Heights Nursing Home, Inc.*, 25,710 (La.App.2d Cir. 3/30/94), 634 So.2d 927.

Mrs. McRay did not offer testimony regarding the standard of care that BTW owed to her husband. Furthermore, we have no evidence establishing that BTW's alleged failure to provide reasonable care caused the bed sores. Virginia McRay simply said that her husband developed bad bed sores at BTW, without showing what alleged omission by BTW caused the bed sores. Nor do we have evidence to support plaintiffs' *allegation* that the bed sores caused McRay's death within the three months after he left BTW's care. Virginia McRay's testimony that a doctor told her that McRay died because of an infection from the bed sores again is simply hearsay testimony. Her testimony that an investigation of this incident by the state led to her husband's removal from BTW is also hearsay. Because plaintiffs presented essentially hearsay evidence to establish a prima facie case, we must find that the default judgment was improperly granted.

Discussion Questions

1. In *McRay*, the court excludes the communications finding that the records involved factual findings related to an investigation into the facts and circumstances on which

the present proceeding is based. Such reports are specifically excluded under the article. What particular case were the communications in reference to? How are they the same as the facts on which the present proceeding is based?

2. The court gives a good discussion of the difference between an investigation of a specific complaint and a general investigation. Explain the difference between the two. Why do you think the distinction in the rule exists, allowing factual findings of general investigations and not specific ones? Are general investigations more reliable and trustworthy than investigations into specific complaints?
3. What might be an example of factual findings related to a "general investigation" that might have been admissible under the exception in *McRay*? Would a report from DHH showing a pattern of abuse at BTW have been admissible? What about a report from DHH showing a link between deaths and nursing homes? Explain.
4. As it relates to "particular" complaints, the exclusion in Article 803(8)(b)(iv) applies to: 1) factual findings resulting from an investigation of a particular complaint, case, or incident; 2) factual findings from an investigation into the facts and circumstances on which the present proceeding is based; and 3) factual findings from an investigation into a similar occurrence or occurrences. Distinguish these types of particular complaints. Give an example of each.
5. *McRay* also demonstrates the relationship between the exclusion and business records. What is that relationship? May a document be offered as a business record in the event it is excluded under this exception? What is the rationale behind this rule?
6. *McRay* further demonstrates the relationship between the business records exception and the authentication requirement. How did the court address this issue? Had the document been excluded from the hearsay ban, would it have been admissible?
7. The official legislative comments note that one of the purposes of the exclusions is "to preserve the function of the jury as the ultimate finder of facts." How does the exclusion of findings of fact into a particular case help to preserve the function of the jury as ultimate fact finder? What potential dangers exist in allowing such evidence?
8. Perhaps the most important exclusion pertains to an accused's rights to confront and cross-examine witnesses against him. How does this rule show respect for this important constitutional right?

Key Points

The key points to keep in mind regarding the public records exception.

1. The public records exception provides that certain records of state or federal government offices or agencies will not be subject to the hearsay rule.
2. **There are three categories of records included within this exception.** They include those setting forth:
   1) its regularly conducted and regularly recorded activities;
   2) matters observed pursuant to duty imposed by law and as to which there was a duty to report; or
   3) factual findings resulting from an investigation made pursuant to authority granted by law.

3. The records of "activities" and reported "observations" are based on knowledge of which the record maker had first-hand knowledge or information supplied to him by personnel with first-hand knowledge.
4. **Factual findings**. Includes conclusions and inferences based on facts supplied to the agency including persons who are not agency personnel (if trustworthy) and expert opinions (if qualified to express such opinions).
5. **Excluded from the public records exception**:
   i. Investigative reports by police and other law enforcement personnel.
   ii. Investigative reports prepared by or for any government, public office, or public agency when offered by that or any other government, public office, or public agency in a case in which it is a party.
   iii. Factual findings offered by the prosecution in a criminal case.
   iv. Factual findings resulting from investigation of a particular complaint, case, or incident, including an investigation into the facts and circumstances on which the present proceeding is based or an investigation into a similar occurrence or occurrences.
6. The purpose of the exclusions is to avoid encroaching upon an accused right to confrontation and to preserve the function of the jury as the ultimate finder of facts.
7. **Police reports** are excluded from the exception in recognition of an accused's right to confrontation and cross-examination, regardless of who offers it. Further, records of **factual findings** may not be offered against an accused in a criminal case, but may be offered by him. **Investigative reports** from other government agencies (other than law enforcement) may not be offered by the government when the government is a party, but may be offered against the government. Additionally, factual findings resulting from an investigation of a particular complaint are also excluded.
8. A record excluded under the public records exception may not be offered as a business record. However, if the record is not excluded under the exception, if it fits within the business records exception, it may be admitted.
9. Even if not specifically excluded under the article, untrustworthy records should be excluded.
10. This article does not affect the admissibility of public records authorized by specific statute, such as those pertaining to admissibility of hospital records, records of convictions of motor vehicle offenses, results of laboratory examinations.
11. **Absence of entry in public record — Article 803(10).** The fact that information is not included in a public record, that *would* be included if it existed, cannot be excluded as hearsay.

Problems on Public Records and Absence of Entry in Public Records

PROBLEM 5-105. The victim in an attempted first-degree murder case testified on cross-examination that at the time the defendant set her on fire she was not suffering from any physical or mental disability that would impair her recollection. In order to attack her credibility, the defense sought to introduce extracts from the witness's social security file that showed that, six years prior to the incident, she became entitled to SSI benefits for the disability established as "Schizophrenic, Paranoid & Other Functional Psychosis." The prosecution objects that the document is hearsay. Does the record conform to the public records exception to the hearsay rule?

PROBLEM 5-106. In a civil case for personal injury, Mr. Johnson offered a transcript from his prior social security proceedings to show the extent of his preexisting health conditions, to prove that his current injuries had been caused by the accident for which he was at trial. The defendant objected that the social security proceedings were inadmissible hearsay. What ruling?

PROBLEM 5-107. Plaintiff, a teacher, sued the parish school system claiming discrimination. As evidence, she offered a letter from the EEOC which had concluded that the defendant discriminated against her. The defendant objected that the letter was inadmissible hearsay. Does the statement conform to the public records exception? Why or why not?

PROBLEM 5-108. The prosecution in a criminal case cannot locate a police detective who investigated a case and has since left the police force. The prosecution seeks to admit his police report into evidence which details how the defendant came to be arrested and other incriminating information. The defense objects that the report is hearsay. The prosecution claims it is a public record or a business record. Does the report satisfy the admissibility requirements for either exception?

PROBLEM 5-109. A social worker for the Dept. of Family Services investigated a complaint of sexual abuse filed by the mother of a young child against the father. The report concluded that the allegations were unfounded and not credible. Following the investigation, the father sued the agency for reinstatement of all of his rights and privileges that were taken away during the investigation. As evidence, he offered the report from the investigation. DCFS claimed the report was excluded under 803(8)(b). a) How should the court rule? b) If the record cannot be admitted as a public record, can it likely come in under the business record exception? c) Would father be able to use the report in his defense in a criminal case against him for sexual abuse of his child to prove that the agency found the allegations unfounded and not credible? Why or why not?

PROBLEM 5-110. Bron is on trial for murder and pleads not guilty and not guilty by reason of insanity. At trial, since he has been a patient at a state mental institution, Bron seeks to offer medical records of his treatment into evidence. Can the records be admitted under the public records exception? Why or why not?

PROBLEM 5-111. In order to prove that Kelvin Riley was not born in the state of Louisiana, the plaintiffs offer a certification from the custodian of official birth records at the hearing which reads: "*I have examined the birth records under my custody, and find no entry for last name 'Riley' and first name 'Kelvin'.*" Admissible?

PROBLEM 5-112. Wayne is suing his employer for damages caused by inhaling second-hand smoke all day from his co-workers who were allowed to smoke in the small closed-off room in which they worked. Wayne has been diagnosed with lung cancer and COPD. Wayne would like to offer the report from the Department of Health and Hospitals (DHH) which conducted a study of more than 2,000 cases of COPD and found that over 47% of diagnosed cases in the State of Louisiana came from second-hand smoke. Further he wishes to offer the results of the investigation conducted by the DHH in his particular case in which they determined that there was a 97% likelihood that his COPD was caused due to exposure to second-hand smoke. Wayne's employer objects that both reports are inadmissible hearsay. How should the court rule?

§ 5.12 References and Additional Authority on Public Records and Absence of Entry in Public Records [La. C.E. arts. 803(8), (10)]

1. La. C.E. arts. 803(8), (10) and Official Comments
2. Force & Rault, HANDBOOK ON LOUISIANA EVIDENCE LAW Arts. 803(8), (10) Author's Comments (West Publishing 2014)
3. Harges & Jones, LOUISIANA EVIDENCE Arts. 803(8),(10) Author's Comments (West Publishing 2014)
4. 19 La. Civ. L. Treatise, Evidence And Proof § 10.19 (2nd ed.)
5. **Excluded from exception under exclusions**: *Zatarain v. WDSU-Television, Inc.*, 673 So. 2d 1181 (La. Ct. App. 4th Cir. 1996) (holding that an EEOC Letter of Determination which was based on the same facts as those of the present case was inadmissible hearsay under La. Code Evid. Art. 803(8)(b)(iv)); *Green v. Connor*, 644 So. 2d 618 (La. 1994) (holding that actual transcript and judgments from the social security proceedings on which the present proceeding is based are inadmissible).
6. **Inadmissible police reports**: *State v. Black*, 864 So. 2d 836 (La. Ct. App. 5th Cir. 2003) (holding that police report is inadmissible hearsay); *State v. Robinson*, 846 So. 2d 76 (La. Ct. App. 5th Cir. 2003) (holding that police report is not admissible under public records exception to hearsay rule).
7. *Schexnayder v. Gish*, 948 So. 2d 1259 (La. Ct. App. 2d Cir. 2007) (holding that letter from Director of the Investigative Division of the Louisiana Real Estate Commission stating that a party is not a licensed realtor in a real estate transaction case is inadmissible hearsay).

§ 5.13 Other Hearsay Exceptions that Apply Whether or Not the Declarant Is Available [La. C.E. arts. 803(9), (11–24)]

Applicable Code Articles

The following are not excluded by the hearsay rule, even though the declarant is available as a witness:

* * *

(9) Records of vital statistics. Records or data compilations, in any form, of birth, filiation, adoption, or death, including fetal death, still birth, and abortion, or of marital status, including divorce and annulment, if the report thereof was made to a public office pursuant to requirements of law, and any record included within the Louisiana Vital Statistics Laws.

* * *

(11) Records of religious organizations. Statements of births, marriages, divorces, deaths, filiation, ancestry, relationship by blood or marriage, or other similar facts of personal or family history, contained in a regularly kept record of a religious organization.

(12) Marriage, baptismal, and similar certificates. Statements of fact contained in a certificate that the maker performed a marriage or other ceremony or administered a sacrament, made by a clergyman, public official, or other person authorized by the rules or practices of a religious organization or by law to perform the act certified, and purporting to have been issued at the time of the act or within a reasonable time thereafter.

(13) Family records. Statements of fact concerning personal or family history contained in family Bibles, genealogies, charts, engravings on rings, inscriptions on family portraits, engravings on urns, crypts, or tombstones, or the like.

(14) Records of documents affecting an interest in property. Records of documents purporting to establish or affect an interest in property to the extent that their admission is authorized by other legislation.

(15) Statements in documents affecting an interest in property. A statement contained in a document purporting to establish or affect an interest in property if the matter stated was relevant to the purpose of the document, unless dealings with the property since the document was made have been inconsistent with the truth of the statement or the purport of the document.

(16) Statements in ancient documents. Statements in a document in existence thirty years or more the authenticity of which is established, or statements in a recorded document as provided by other legislation.

(17) Market reports, commercial publications. Market quotations, tabulations, lists, directories, or other published compilations, generally used and relied upon by the public or by persons in particular occupations.

(18) Learned treatises. To the extent called to the attention of an expert witness upon cross-examination or, in a civil case, relied upon by him in direct examination, statements contained in published treatises, periodicals, or pamphlets on a subject of history, medicine, or other science or art, established as a reliable authority by the testimony or admission of the witness or by other expert testimony or by judicial notice. If admitted, such a statement may be read into evidence and received as an exhibit but may not be taken into the jury room.

(19) Reputation concerning personal or family history. Reputation, arising before the controversy, among members of his family by blood, adoption, or marriage, or among his associates, or in the community, concerning a person's birth, adoption, marriage, divorce, death, filiation, relationship by blood, adoption, or marriage, ancestry, or other similar fact of his personal or family history.

(20) Reputation concerning boundaries or general history. Reputation in a community, arising before the controversy, as to boundaries of or customs affecting lands in the community, and reputation as to events of general history important to the community or state or nation in which located

(21) Reputation as to character. Reputation of a person's character among his associates or in the community.

(22) Judgment of previous conviction. Evidence of a final judgment, entered after a trial or upon a plea of guilty (but not upon a plea of nolo contendere), adjudging a person guilty of a crime punishable by death or imprisonment in excess of six months, to prove any fact essential to sustain the judgment. This exception does not permit the prosecutor in a criminal prosecution to offer as evidence the judgment of conviction of a person other than the accused, except for the purpose of attacking the credibility of a witness. The pendency of an appeal may be shown but does not affect admissibility.

(23) Judgment as to personal, family, or general history, or boundaries. Judgments as proof of matters of personal, family, or general history, or boundaries, essential to the judgment, if the same would be provable by evidence of reputation.

(24) Testimony as to age. A witness's testimony as to his own age.

The following are additional exceptions to the hearsay rule listed in Article 803 that apply whether or not the declarant is available to testify as a witness. This provision only provides that the evidence will not be excluded under the hearsay rule. All evidence must comply with other requirements for admissibility.

Records of vital statistics. Article 803(9) contains an exception for records of vital statistics. The exception includes records or data compilations, in any form, of birth, filiation, adoption, or death, including fetal death, still birth, and abortion, or of marital status, including divorce and annulment. The exception requires that the report be made to a public office pursuant to requirements of law, and any record included within the Louisiana Vital Statistics Laws.[176]

Louisiana's comprehensive laws governing vital statistics is contained in La. R.S. 40:32 et seq. This provision merely removes the hearsay bar from vital statistics records.[177]

Records of religious organizations. Article 803(11) contains an exception for records of religious organizations. This exception includes statements of births, marriages, divorces, deaths, filiation, ancestry, relationship by blood or marriage, or other similar facts of personal or family history, contained in a regularly kept record of a religious organization.[178]

Marriage, baptismal, and similar certificates. Article 803(12) contains a hearsay exception for marriage, baptismal and similar certificates. The exception includes statements of fact contained in a certificate that the maker performed a marriage or other ceremony or administered a sacrament, made by a clergyman, public official, or other person authorized by the rules or practices of a religious organization or by law to perform the act certified, and purporting to have been issued at the time of the act or within a reasonable time thereafter.[179]

There is overlap between this provision and the public records and vital statistics exceptions; however, this article is broader.[180] This exception "extends the certification procedure to clergymen and the like who perform marriages and other ceremonies or administer sacraments."[181] Further, this exception also "allows a person to offer into

176. La. Code Evid. art. 803(9).
177. *See* La. Code Evid. art. 803(9) Official Comments.
178. La. Code Evid. art. 803(11).
179. La. Code Evid. art. 803(12).
180. *See* La. Code Evid. art. 803(9) Official Comment (a).
181. *See* La. Code Evid. art. 803(9) Official Comment (a) *citing* the Fed. R. Evid. 803(12), advisory committee note.

evidence the certificate given him by the presiding official instead of obtaining a copy of the corresponding vital statistics record."[182]

Family records. Article 803(13) contains a hearsay exception for family records. This exception includes statements of fact concerning personal or family history contained in family Bibles, genealogies, charts, engravings on rings, inscriptions on family portraits, engravings on urns, crypts, or tombstones, or the like.[183] This provision deals with records, i.e., written statements regarding family history that are in family bibles, engravings, charts, urns, and other similar types of places. A similar provision contained in Article 804(B)(4) deals with *statements* of a person's *own* family history that requires the declarant to be unavailable that specifically deal with birth, adoption, marriage, divorce, filiation, and other relationships.

Records of documents affecting an interest in property. Article 803(14) contains an exception for records of documents affecting an interest in property to the extent that their admission is authorized by other legislation.[184] It pertains to both movable as well as immovable property[185] and escapes the hearsay bar only if there is specific statutory authority providing for the admissibility of the evidence.[186]

Statements in documents affecting an interest in property. Article 803(15) contains an exception for statements in documents affecting an interest in property. The exception includes statements contained in a document purporting to establish or affect an interest in property if the matter stated was relevant to the purpose of the document, unless dealings with the property since the document was made have been inconsistent with the truth of the statement or the purport of the document.[187]

While there appears to be little evidence on the issue, in *Succession of Anderson*,[188] a girl was allowed to prove that she was the daughter of the decedent by offering a notarial act of sale executed by the decedent in which he stated that he had been married to the plaintiff's mother until her death.

Statements in ancient documents. Article 803(16) contains an exception for statements contained in ancient documents. It applies to statements in a document in existence thirty years or more, the authenticity of which is established. The exception also applies to statements in a recorded document as provided by other legislation.[189] To be admissible under this provision, the document must be properly authenticated under Article 902(B)(8) to prove its genuineness which also goes to its trustworthiness.[190] Additionally, as with other documents, it must not be excluded under any other provision of the Code. This provision merely overcomes the hearsay bar.

Federal Rules of Evidence Distinction. This exception is different from the Federal Rules of Evidence exception, which only requires that the document have been existence for 20 years rather than for 30 years.[191]

---

182. *See* La. Code Evid. art. 803(9) Official Comment (a).
183. La. Code Evid. art. 803(13).
184. La. Code Evid. art. 803(14).
185. *See* La. Code Evid. art. 803(14) Official Comment (b).
186. Force & Rault, Handbook, La. Code Evid. art. 803(14) Author's Comment (1).
187. La. Code Evid. art. 803(15).
188. Succession of Anderson, 176 La. 66, 145 So. 270 (1932); *see also* Force & Rault, Handbook, Art. 803(15) Author's Comment (1).
189. La. Code Evid. art. 803(16).
190. See La. Code Evid. art. 803(16) Official Comment (c).
191. See Fed. R. Evid. 803(16).

Market reports, commercial publications. Article 803(17) contains an exception to the hearsay rule for market reports and commercial publications. It includes market quotations, tabulations, lists, directories, or other published compilations, generally used and relied upon by the public or by persons in particular occupations.[192] Generally, to fit into this exception the list must be in print, circulated for use by others, relied on by either the general public or by person's in a particular field, and perhaps most importantly, it must pertain to relatively straightforward objective facts.[193]

Learned treatises. To the extent called to the attention of an expert witness upon cross-examination or, in a civil case, relied upon by him in direct examination, Article 803(18) contains an exception for statements contained in published treatises, periodicals, or pamphlets on a subject of history, medicine, or other science or art, established as a reliable authority by the testimony or admission of the witness or by other expert testimony or by judicial notice. If admitted, such a statement may be read into evidence and received as an exhibit but may not be taken into the jury room.[194]

Learned treatises are deemed to be trustworthy for two reasons, "[f]irst, authors of treatises have no bias in any particular case. Second, they are acutely aware that their material will be read and evaluated by others in their field, and accordingly feel a strong pressure to be accurate."[195] Thus, such publications will not be excluded by the hearsay rule.

Reputation concerning personal or family history. Article 803(19) contains an exception regarding reputation concerning personal or family history. The exception includes reputation arising before the controversy, among members of his family by blood, adoption, or marriage, or among his associates, or in the community, concerning a person's birth, adoption, marriage, divorce, death, filiation, relationship by blood, adoption, or marriage, ancestry, or other similar fact of his personal or family history.[196]

Contrary to *records* of family history discussed above contained in Bibles and the like, this provision deals with *reputation* of family history prior to the controversy regarding birth, adoption, marriage, divorce, and other facts regarding a person's family history within the family or community. It does not include rumor or gossip, but instead requires a foundation that the witness is familiar with the reputation at issue.[197] This provision is also different than the provision in Article 804(4) that covers *statements* that a person makes regarding his own family history when the declarant is unavailable.[198]

Reputation concerning boundaries or general history. Article 803(20) contains an exception for reputation concerning boundaries or general history. This exception includes reputation in a community, arising before the controversy, as to boundaries of or customs affecting lands in the community, and reputation as to events of general history important to the community or state or nation in which located.[199]

Reputation as to character. Article 803(21) contains an exception to the hearsay rule for evidence of a person's reputation as to character among his associates or in the com-

---

192. La. Code Evid. art. 803(17).
193. *See* McCormick on Evidence § 321 (5th ed., 1999).
194. La. Code Evid. art. 803(18).
195. McCormick on Evidence § 321 (5th ed., 1999).
196. La. Code Evid. art. 803(19).
197. *See* La. Code Evid. art. 803(19) Official Comments (b) and (c); *See also* La. Code Evid. art. 405.
198. *See* La. Code Evid. art. 804(4).
199. La. Code Evid. art. 803(20).

munity.[200] In Chapter 6 we will study the limited use of character evidence that, pursuant to Article 405, is generally proven by a person's general reputation in the community among his associates. In such cases, the evidence is hearsay because the witness testifies as to what others have said about the person's reputation that is offered to prove that the person does in fact have the reputation testified to, which is hearsay. This provision allows such evidence to escape the hearsay ban.

Adding to the reliability of this exception, in situations in which character evidence is admissible, the appropriate foundation must be laid in which the proponent must establish that the witness is familiar with the person's reputation. There are also measures put in place to test the witness's knowledge of the person's reputation through cross-examination about specific conduct that might contradict the reputation to which the witness has testified.[201]

Judgment of previous conviction. Article 803(22) contains an exception for judgments of previous conviction. The exception includes evidence of a final judgment, entered after a trial or upon a plea of guilty (but not upon a plea of nolo contendere), adjudging a person guilty of a crime punishable by death or imprisonment in excess of six months, to prove any fact essential to sustain the judgment. This exception does not permit the prosecutor in a criminal prosecution to offer as evidence the judgment of conviction of a person other than the accused, except for the purpose of attacking the credibility of a witness under Article 609.1. The pendency of an appeal may be shown but does not affect admissibility.[202]

Judgment as to personal, family, or general history, or boundaries. Article 803(23) contains an exception for judgments as to personal, family, or general history, or boundaries. It provides that such judgments may be offered as proof of matters of personal, family, or general history, or boundaries, essential to the judgment, if the same would be provable by evidence of reputation.[203]

Federal Rules of Evidence Distinction — Testimony as to age. Article 803(24) contains an exception to the hearsay ban for a person's testimony as to his own age.[204] Technically, such testimony is no doubt what the witness has been told. But in most instances, it can reasonably be said to be reliable. The federal rules do not contain a comparable provision.

Problems on Other Exceptions Where the Declarant's Availability Immaterial

PROBLEM 5-113. Henry is involved in a legal battle over his brother's will. Henry is an illegitimate child and his siblings do not believe he is their brother. In order to prove that he is the brother of the testator, Henry offers a deed executed by his brother that was properly recorded and authenticated by the custodian of Parish Records. The deed contains the statement, "*I hereby transfer to my brother, Henry, my property located at 117 Blackburn St.*" Is the statement admissible? Explain.

---

200. La. Code Evid. art. 803(21).

201. See Chapter 6 for a thorough discussion of the admissibility of reputation evidence to prove character.

202. La. Code Evid. art. 803(22).

203. La. Code Evid. art. 803(23).

204. La. Code Evid. art. 803(24).

PROBLEM 5-114. Carrie Wallace died two weeks ago. In her safe deposit box that hadn't been opened since some time in the '80s, her family found a document entitled, "My Will" and dated December 10, 1985, leaving everything to her maid, Kendyl. There is no other evidence surrounding the making of the will. When the will is offered into evidence, the opponent objects that it is hearsay. How would you respond? What ruling and why?

PROBLEM 5-115. In order to prove that Randy did not kill himself so that she (wife) could recover the insurance proceeds (which excludes suicides), his wife offers his death certificate, which was filled out and signed by his doctor listing the cause of death as a "brain tumor." Admissible? Why or why not?

PROBLEM 5-116. In a succession, the plaintiff claimed that the decedent only had a one-half interest in a certain piece of property listed in the succession, and that her deceased mother owned the other one-half interest of the property because the property was purchased while the decedent was married to her mother and is therefore community property. The decedent's other heirs, who are children by a different woman, claim that the property is the decedent's separate property. They claim he was never married to the plaintiff's mother, and therefore the property cannot be community property. In plaintiff's case, she would like to offer into evidence a notarial act of sale, executed by decedent on an unrelated piece of property, where he stated that "*he had been married to the plaintiff's mother until her death.*" Should that document be admitted into evidence in the dispute of the relative interests in property in the succession over a hearsay objection?

PROBLEM 5-117. The Hansen family owns over 250 acres of land in St. Francisville, Louisiana, that was purchased by their ancestor Simon Hansen around 1880. The property is currently owned by over 150 heirs, Hansen's great-great-grandchildren. In order to partition the property, the attorney will have to prove the dates of death and birth of various heirs along the way to determine each person's interest in the Hansen property. The attorney is unable to obtain death certificates of all the heirs, so she must prove when they died in various ways. Can the attorney use a) an urn where an heir's ashes are kept, which is engraved with his date of birth and date of death; b) a picture of a tombstone with date of death and birth on it; c) a page from a family bible that lists the dates of death of one heir's close family members; d) records from the family church in St. Francisville, Louisiana, where the pastor from 1905–1945 kept a record of every eulogy he gave? Are the items hearsay? Do any exceptions apply? Explain.

PROBLEM 5-118. Jamie has brought an action for conversion against her ex-boyfriend for burning up her two-year-old vehicle in a jealous rage. At the trial, she would like to offer the listing in the Yellowbook Vehicle Valuation Guide of the value of her car to prove the value of her car and the damages to which she claims she is entitled. The defendant objects that the listing is hearsay. What ruling?

PROBLEM 5-119. Ivan is on trial for first-degree murder. In his defense, he would like to call two character witnesses pursuant to Article 405 (A), who will testify as to his reputation in the community for being a kind, gentle man. The prosecution objects that the testimony is hearsay. How should the court rule and why?

PROBLEM 5-120. Blade is on trial for possession of a firearm by a convicted felon. To prove that the defendant has in fact been convicted of the underlying felony, the prosecution offers a certified copy of a judgment of conviction for the underlying felony. The defense objects that the judgment is hearsay. What ruling?

PROBLEM 5-121. In a rape trial the prosecution calls the victim to the stand, and after asking her to state and spell her name, the prosecution then asks the witness what is her age. The defense stands up and objects that the question calls for hearsay because the witness does not remember being born and cannot testify from first-hand knowledge as to her age. How should the court rule and why?

PROBLEM 5-122. Brandon is qualified as an expert at trial in civil engineering with a specialization in structural engineering which includes the construction and maintenance of bridges. In a lawsuit against the City after a bridge gave way during a storm killing hundreds of commuters traversing the bridge and injuring thousands more, Brandon testifies for the plaintiffs that the bridge was not properly constructed to handle the estimated capacity the bridge would have to support on the major thoroughfare it covered. During cross-examination, Brandon is asked if he is familiar with the *Treatise on Structural Engineering Technology*. He states that every engineer worth a grain of salt is familiar with the publication because it is the most noted authority in the field. The attorney then cross-examines him from the publication, asking him to explain various statements made in the publication for the jury. He reads what the publication states, then asks Brandon if it is a true statement, and to reconcile his testimony with the treatise. Opposing counsel objects that the statements in the book are hearsay. What ruling and why?

§ 5.13 References and Additional Authority on Other Hearsay Exceptions Where Availability Is Immaterial [La. C.E. arts. 803(9), (11)–(24)]

1. La. C.E. arts. 803(9), (11)–(24) and Official Comments
2. Force & Rault, Handbook on Louisiana Evidence Law Arts. 803(9), (11)–(24) Author's Comments (West Publishing 2014)
3. Harges & Jones, Louisiana Evidence Arts. 803(9), (11)–(24) Author's Comments (West Publishing 2014)
4. 19 La. Civ. L. Treatise, Evidence And Proof § 10.20–26 (2nd ed.)
5. **Article 803(9) Vital statistic exception cases:** *In re Succession of Byrd*, 142 So. 3d 1058 (La. Ct. App. 2d Cir. 06/11/14) (holding that the death certificate, records or compilations of data of a death or any other record included within Louisiana Vital Statistics Laws are not excluded by the hearsay rule and serve as prima facie evidence of the facts stated therein); *State v. Dozier*, 713 So. 2d 729 (La. Ct. App. 3d Cir. 1998) (death certificate); *Morris v. Reve, Inc.*, 662 So. 2d 525 (La. Ct. App. 5th Cir. 1995) (death certificate); *State v. Parham*, 636 So. 2d 991 (La. Ct. App. 5th Cir. 1994) (birth certificate).
6. **Article 804(13) Family records case(s):** *Succession of Rodgers*, 499 So. 2d 492 (1986) (La. Ct. App. 2d Cir. 1986) (Plaintiffs attempted to admit a book from the funeral home that contained a copy of Marvin's obituary, which also appeared in the newspaper. The article not only listed his death, but also his heirs. The trial court held that the article lacked proper foundation because the author was not shown and was therefore inadmissible. Court of appeal held the newspaper article should have been admitted.).
7. **Article 804(16) Statements in ancient documents case(s) — Statutory presumption of genuineness of ancient documents is not conclusive, but rather rebuttable:** *Bailey v. Descendants of Fowler*, 746 So. 2d 130 (La. Ct. App. 3d Cir. 1999); *Cole v. Celotex Corp.*, 588 So. 2d 376, App. 3 Cir. 1991 (holding in negligence trial arising out of asbestos exposure of employees that report published in 1937 documenting relative haz-

ards of asbestos dust and duration of exposure that might result in harm to workers was admissible under ancient document exception to hearsay rule).

8. **Article 804(17) Market reports, commercial publications case(s):** *Dottie v. Safeway Ins. Co. of Louisiana*, 87 So. 3d 942. (La. Ct. App. 2d Cir. 2012) (holding that using the Kelley Blue Book valuation to determine the value of a vehicle in a particular condition and the damages which have been sustained was admissible); *Neloms v. Empire Fire & Marine Ins. Co.*, 859 So. 2d 225 (La. Ct. App. 2d Cir. 2003) (Kelley Blue Book used to establish price of car).
9. **Article 804(18) Learned treatise case(s):** *Regan v. Gore*, 670 So. 2d 268 (La. Ct. App. 3d Cir. 1996) (holding that statements used by an expert and referred to as authoritative and any references to the material are not hearsay; here, the expert did not consider the material as authoritative and the court did not admit the material into evidence).
10. **Article 804(19) Reputation concerning personal or family history case(s):** *State v. Stringer*, 567 So. 2d 758 (La. App. 2d Cir. 1990) (Defendant wanted to rely on the reputation about his ancestry to determine his race but did not present testimony by others to prove the reputation as true. The court accepted the findings of the doctor which relied on the defendant's belief as to his own race.).
11. **Article 804(22) Judgment of previous conviction case(s):** *Brasseaux v. Town of Mamou*, 713 So. 2d 742 (La. Ct. App. 3d Cir. 1998) (The owner of a lounge was injured in an altercation outside of the lounge when he was trying to protect his patrons from further injury. The owner filed suit against the patron. In lounge owner's claim against patron and others arising out of altercation in which owner was injured, plea transcript and sentencing transcript of owner for charges arising out of altercation were not relevant, as owner pled nolo contendere to criminal charges against him.).
12. **Article 804(23) Judgment as to personal, family, or general history, or boundaries case(s):** *State v. Scott*, 823 So. 2d 960 (La. Ct. App. 2d Cir. 2002) (In a case of aggravated incest, the defendant argued that the admissibility of the judgment of paternity was wrongly admitted because it was not final. The judgment of paternity was rendered July 10, 2000, and the defendant received the judgment on July 11, 2000. The court ruled that the judgment of paternity was admissible because it was relevant and probative since the defendant's status as the victim's father went to reputation and that it fell within the exception of the hearsay rule.).
13. **Article 804(24) Age case(s):** *State v. Fickes*, 497 So. 2d 392 (La. Ct. App. 3d Cir. 1986) (holding that victim's statement that she was eight years old at time of offense was not excludable as hearsay, and was sufficient to establish her age, for purposes of charge of aggravated crime against nature).

Part C
Hearsay Exceptions That Apply When the Declarant Is Unavailable

In this part we will move to Article 804, which contains exceptions to the hearsay rule that apply only when the declarant is unavailable to testify at the trial or hearing. Although these exceptions are not considered to be as trustworthy as the exceptions contained in Article 803, they are admissible for two primary reasons: 1) since the declarant is unavailable, and there would be no other way of introducing the statement, they are allowed out of a matter of necessity; and 2) indicia of trustworthiness surrounding the making of the statements.

§ 5.14 Unavailability [La. C.E. art. 804(A)]

Applicable Code Articles

A. Definition of unavailability. Except as otherwise provided by this Code, a declarant is "unavailable as a witness" when the declarant cannot or will not appear in court and testify to the substance of his statement made outside of court. This includes situations in which the declarant:

(1) Is exempted by ruling of the court on the ground of privilege from testifying concerning the subject matter of his statement;

(2) Persists in refusing to testify concerning the subject matter of his statement despite an order of the court to do so;

(3) Testifies to a lack of memory of the subject matter of his statement;

(4) Is unable to be present or to testify at the hearing because of death or then existing physical or mental illness, infirmity, or other sufficient cause;

(5) Is absent from the hearing and the proponent of his statement has been unable to procure his attendance by process or other reasonable means. A declarant is not unavailable as a witness if his exemption, refusal, claim of lack of memory, inability, or absence is due to the procurement or wrong-doing of the proponent of his statement for the purpose of preventing the witness from attending or testifying.

* * *

A preliminary requirement that must be met prior to admitting any statement under an exception listed in Article 804(B) is that the proponent of the statement must prove that the declarant is unavailable to testify to the statement him or herself as provided in Article 804(A). The unavailability of a declarant is a legal determination that the judge makes,[205] and includes not only a witness who is unavailable in the literal sense in that he is physically absent from the court or dead; but also includes situations in which a witness

205. *See* La. Code Evid. art. 804(A)(c) Official Comments; *See also* La. Code Evid. art. 104(A).

may be present, but is unwilling or unable to testify due to a physical or mental illness or infirmity, loss of memory, asserting a privilege, or for some other reason.

The list of situations contained in Article 804(A) is only illustrative and may include a number of other situations in which a court finds that the witness is functionally unable to serve as a witness in the trial. Most often, a witness is deemed unavailable if he cannot be located or is deceased. A witness is also unavailable if he asserts his Fifth Amendment privilege against self-incrimination or other privilege, such as when a spouse asserts his or her spousal testimonial privilege. Additionally, a witness is unavailable if he testifies to lack of memory or refuses to testify even under threat of being held in contempt of court.

Burden of Proof. The proponent of the statement under this exception has the burden of proving that the declarant is unavailable,[206] and must show a "diligent and good faith effort to obtain [the witness's] presence at trial."[207] "The lengths to which the State must go [in a criminal case] to try to procure a witness is a question of reasonableness,"[208] but will require more than a mere statement to the court that the witness is unavailable or that counsel does not know where the witness is located. The proponent must exercise *due diligence* in trying to procure a witness before claiming the witness is unavailable.

Procurement or Wrongdoing. Additionally, pursuant to Article 804(A)(5), the proponent of a statement cannot claim a witness is unavailable for purposes of using an out-of-court statement under this exception, if the witness's absence, refusal, claim of lack of memory, or inability, is due to the procurement or wrong-doing of the proponent of his statement for the *purpose* of preventing the witness from attending or testifying. In other words, if the proponent kills, threatens, or otherwise does anything to the witness for the purpose of preventing the witness from testifying, he cannot then claim the witness is unavailable.

This does not include situations in which a defendant may be on trial for the murder of a person who happened to have made a statement the defense would like to offer under the exception. In such a case, the witness was not killed *for the purpose* of preventing him from testifying. This exclusion also doesn't apply if the procurement was merely negligent.[209] In order for this provision to apply, the proponent of the statement must have killed or otherwise procured the unavailability of the witness for the specific purpose of preventing him from testifying in court.

Confrontation Clause Concerns. The fact that a statement satisfies the requirement of an Article 804 exception to the hearsay rule does not alleviate the defendant's right to confront and cross-examine adverse witnesses, as guaranteed by the Sixth Amendment of the United States Constitution, and Art. I, § 16 of the Louisiana Constitution. In order for the State to admit testimonial statements against a defendant from a witness who is not available for cross-examination, the State must also overcome Confrontation Clause issues under *Crawford*, which requires that the accused must have had a prior opportunity to cross-examine the declarant on the statement. If the State is unable to comply with the requirements of the Sixth Amendment Confrontation Clause as set out in *Crawford*, the statement will nonetheless be excluded. This issue is further discussed, *infra*, § 5.25.

Unavailable Declarant is Not an Exception. Finally, you should also keep in mind that the unavailability of a declarant is *not* in and of itself an exception to the hearsay

---

206. *See, e.g.*, Finch v. ATC/Vancom Management Services Lt. Partnership, 33 So. 2d 215 (La. Ct. App. 5th Cir. 2010).

207. State v. Nicolas, 548 So. 2d 1278, 1280 (4th Cir. 1989).

208. State v. Williams, 833 So. 2d 497, 505 (La. Ct. App. 5th Cir. 2012).

209. *See* La. Code Evid. art. 804(A)(f) Official Comments.

rule. A statement is *not* automatically admissible just because the declarant is unavailable. Article 804 (B) contains specific exceptions that require as a prerequisite to applicability, that the declarant be unavailable. Even if the declarant is unavailable, if the other requirements of the exception are not met, then the statement will be excluded under the hearsay rule.

Exceptions requiring unavailable declarant. Part C of Chapter 5 will cover seven exceptions to the hearsay rule that require the declarant to be unavailable. The exceptions are:

1. §5.15 Former Testimony [La. C.E. art. 804(B)(1)];
2. §5.16 Statement Under Belief of Impending Death [La. C.E. art. 804(B)(2)];
3. §5.17 Statement Against Interest [La. C.E. art. 804(B)(3)];
4. §5.18 Family History [La. C.E. art. 804(B)(4)];
5. §5.19 Complaint of Sexually Assaultive Behavior [La. C.E. art. 804(B)(5)];
6. §5.20 Residual Catchall [La. C.E. art. 804(B)(6)]; and
7. §5.21 Forfeiture by Wrongdoing [La. C.E. art. 804(B)(7)].

Key Points

The key points to keep in mind regarding unavailability of the declarant.

1. **Unavailable requirement.** Article 804 exceptions require a preliminary showing that the declarant is unavailable to admit statements under these exceptions. The seven exceptions are:

   1) Former Testimony; 2) Statement Under Belief of Impending Death; 3) Statement Against Interest; 4) Family History; 5) Complaint of Sexually Assaultive Behavior; 6) Residual Catchall; and 7) Forfeiture by Wrongdoing.

2. **Unavailable includes:** death, lack of memory, privilege, refusing to testify, physical or mental illness, infirmity, unable to be located, or other sufficient cause. The list is illustrative.
3. **Proving unavailability.** The proponent of the statement has the burden of proving the witness is unavailable. He must show "due diligence" to secure the witness's presence. The judge makes the determination of unavailability.
4. **Procurement or wrongdoing.** The proponent of a statement cannot claim a witness is unavailable for purposes of using an out-of-court statement under this exception, if the witness's absence, refusal, claim of lack of memory, or inability, is due to the procurement or wrong-doing of the proponent of his statement for the ***purpose*** of preventing the witness from attending or testifying.
5. **Confrontation clause issue.** If statement is testimonial and witness is unavailable, to avoid violating the accused's Confrontation Clause rights, must comply with requirements of *Crawford*.

Unavailability Problems

PROBLEM 5-123. Part I: Todd Lee is charged with the brutal rape and murder of 17 women—decapitating them after the murder, then scattering their body parts throughout the parish. Only one of his would-be victims, Candice, was able to get away. Her description is what led to Lee's capture. Candice is terrified that if she testifies at Lee's trial, he will certainly have his goonies kill her. Is Candice legally unavailable to the State? To the defense? Explain.

Part II: Assume Candice actually died as well. But before she died, she managed to called 911 and gave a description of the man who raped her indicating that it was a different race and sex than the defendant. The defense would like to use the dying declaration exception, which requires that the declarant be unavailable. The defense claims Candice is unavailable because she is dead. The prosecution objects and claims that the defense cannot claim Candice is unavailable because the defendant is the one who killed her. Is Candice unavailable to the defendant? How should the court rule and why?

PROBLEM 5-124. The prosecution's key witness is eight months pregnant. After having some complications, her doctor has put her on bed rest and she has been instructed not to stand upright, walk, nor endure any mentally stressful situations until after she gives birth. The judge has refused to postpone the trial any longer and forces the prosecution to proceed. Is the woman legally unavailable? Explain.

PROBLEM 5-125. The psychiatrist testifies that forcing the child to relive the traumatic repressed events could be detrimental to his mental stability. Should a court find that he is unavailable under Article 804(A)?

PROBLEM 5-126. The defendant is on trial for aggravated kidnapping and multiple counts of aggravated rape of a 14-year-old girl that he abducted as she walked home from school. After holding her captive for nine months, she managed to escape and returned home. The family moved from their current residence after the girl returned home for privacy reasons—so she wouldn't have to return to the same school and so that the offender would not know where she was. In preparation for trial, the prosecution sent a subpoena to the address the family had when the girl was abducted, but it was returned unsigned because they were no longer living at the residence. On the day of the trial, the prosecution asserts that the victim is unavailable because they do not know where the family moved to. The defense objects. Should the court find the victim is unavailable? Why or why not?

PROBLEM 5-127. The primary witness in a major case was killed in an unrelated car accident a month before the trial against the defendant for armed robbery was set to begin. The witness was the clerk at the convenience store that the defendant was accused of robbing. Before the trial began, the prosecution presented to the court the witness's death certificate showing that the witness was in fact deceased, along with a newspaper article about the tragic accident. The court found that the witness was in fact unavailable. The prosecution then requests that any and all statements that the unavailable witness made to anyone concerning the incident that are relevant to the case be admitted since the witness is unavailable. How should the court rule and why?

§ 5.14 References and Additional Authority on Unavailability [La. C.E. art. 804(A)]

1. La. C.E. art. 804(A) and Official Comments
2. Force & Rault, Handbook on Louisiana Evidence Law Art. 804(A) Author's Comments (West Publishing 2014)

3. Harges & Jones, LOUISIANA EVIDENCE Art. 804(A) Author's Comments (West Publishing 2014)
4. 19 La. Civ. L. Treatise, Evidence And Proof § 10.6 (2nd ed.)
5. MCCORMICK ON EVIDENCE § 253 (5th ed., 1999)
6. **Finding that witness is unavailable Article 804(A):** *Sunlake Apartments Residents v. Tonti Dev. Corp.*, 602 So. 2d 22 (La. Ct. App. 5th Cir. 1992) (finding expert witness unavailable who resided out of the state was not under the subpoena powers of the State and it would have cost the prosecution more than $2500.00 to get the expert to the trial; thus the expert witness was unavailable and the deposition was admissible); *State v. Adams*, 609 So. 2d 894 (La. Ct. App. 4th Cir. 1992) (Although the witness was threatened with contempt of court, the witness refused to testify and the court held that the witness was unavailable.); *Walley v. Vargas*, 104 So. 3d 93 (La. Ct. App. 1st Cir. 2012) (holding that trial court erred in refusing to find witness unavailable due to lack of memory); *State v. Sullivan*, 688 So. 2d 1245 (La. Ct. App. 4th Cir. 1997) (stipulation to unavailability of witnesses); *State v. Myers*, 584 So. 2d 242 (La. Ct. App. 5th Cir. 1991) (co-defendant unavailable due to invocation of Fifth Amendment privilege against self-incrimination).
7. **Efforts to procure witness's presence:** *Finch v. ATC/Vancom Management Services Ltd. Partnership*, 33 So. 3d 215 (La. Ct. App. 5th Cir. 2010) (The party who plans to offer a hearsay statement must first make a diligent and good faith effort in finding the declarant. If a lack of diligence and good faith is found, then the witness will not be found unavailable and the statement will be inadmissible. In this case, the appellant made no attempt in procuring either of the declarants. Therefore, the statement was inadmissible.).

§ 5.15 Former Testimony [La. C.E. art. 804(B)(1)]

Applicable Code Articles

* * *

B. Hearsay exceptions. The following are not excluded by the hearsay rule if the declarant is unavailable as a witness:

(1) Former testimony. Testimony given as a witness at another hearing of the same or a different proceeding, if the party against whom the testimony is now offered, or, in a civil action or proceeding, a party with a similar interest, had an opportunity and similar motive to develop the testimony by direct, cross, or redirect examination. Testimony given in another proceeding by an expert witness in the form of opinions or inferences, however, is not admissible under this exception.

* * *

In some limited circumstances, a witness's testimony that was given at a prior proceeding may be excluded from the hearsay rule under the former testimony exception pursuant to Article 804(B)(1). For example, if the prosecution's key witness in a criminal case has died and is now unavailable to testify at the trial, the prosecution may seek to offer the witness's testimony that was given in the preliminary examination earlier in the proceedings to prove the facts that the witness would have testified to if he were present. Since the witness's prior statement given in the preliminary examination is a statement that was made outside of the present trial or hearing, and would be offered to prove the truth of what it asserts, it would be hearsay, and generally inadmissible. However, in such a situation, the former testimony exception may apply if certain circumstances are met.

Requirements for exception. First, the exception requires that the witness be currently unavailable to testify at the present proceeding pursuant to Article 804(A). Once the proponent of the prior statement has established that the witness is in fact unavailable, the requirements to use the prior testimony depend upon whether the proponent intends to offer the prior testimony in a criminal trial or a civil trial.

A. Criminal trial: If the proponent seeks to offer testimony given by a witness in a prior proceeding in a criminal case, then the party against whom the testimony is now offered (*in the example above, the criminal defendant*), must have had an *opportunity* and similar *motive* to *develop the prior testimony* through direct, cross-examination, or redirect examination.

B. Civil Trial: If the subsequent proceeding is a civil case at which a party seeks to admit testimony given by a witness at a prior proceeding, then either the party themselves, or another party with similar interest must have had an opportunity and similar motive to develop the prior testimony through direct, cross, or redirect examination.

The Former Testimony. First, let's talk about what constitutes former testimony. Under this exception, a witness who is now unavailable in either a civil or criminal trial might have previously given testimony at either a civil or criminal proceeding that was either a part of the same or a different proceeding. For example, say a truck driver was involved in an accident while negligently driving his truck while intoxicated, and criminal charges are brought against him after the accident. The plaintiff also sues the truck driver for her injuries resulting from the accident. The defendant is now involved in both a civil action and a criminal action. Assume the civil case goes to trial first and the defendant has an opportunity to cross-examine the plaintiff, and is found liable. The plaintiff dies before the criminal trial that takes place six months later. In this situation, the prosecution may be able to use the testimony that the plaintiff gave in the prior civil trial against the defendant if the other requirements are met even though the former testimony was given in a different proceeding and in a civil case.

Similarly, if the criminal trial had taken place first, a person may seek to offer a statement in a subsequent civil trial. While this scenario involves different proceedings arising out of the same incident, the former testimony might have been given in an earlier hearing in the same proceeding. For instance, the victim of a crime might testify in a preliminary examination in a criminal case, but is unavailable at the time of the trial.

In either case, under this exception the prior testimony sought to be used could have been given at the same or different proceedings, in either a civil or criminal trial. The admissibility requirements for the prior testimony, as stated above, depend upon whether the *instant case* at which the proponent now seeks to admit the prior statement is a criminal case or a civil case.

Criminal Cases

If a party (usually the prosecution) seeks to admit a witness's statement in a criminal case that was given at a prior hearing (criminal trial, preliminary exam, civil case, etc.), then **the defendant himself** must have had an opportunity and similar motive to develop the witness's prior testimony through the applicable examination—direct, cross, or redirect.

Requirements for Former Testimony Exception: *Criminal Case*

1. declarant is unavailable;
2. the party against whom testimony is now offered must have (himself) had a prior *opportunity* and *similar motive* to develop testimony through direct, cross, or redirect examination; **and**
3. at time of prior testimony:
   1. accused must have had counsel;
   2. witness under oath;
   3. witness was cross-examined or defendant validly waived;
   4. witness is currently unavailable; and
   5. state made a good faith effort to locate the witness.

While the prior hearing might have been a part of the same proceeding in an earlier hearing, such as a motion hearing or preliminary exam, or even a prior criminal or civil trial, it must have been the defendant himself (through counsel) who had the opportunity and similar motive to develop the prior testimony. This rule helps ensure the defendant's confrontation rights are not violated. While he might not have the opportunity to confront and cross-examine the declarant at the current hearing, the rule ensures that he has had an opportunity to confront and cross-examine the witness on a prior occasion on the issue.

1. Similar Motive to Develop Testimony. What does it mean to have had a "similar motive" to develop the testimony? Similar motive would exist if, for example, the examining party in the prior proceeding would have been trying to bring out, test, or address similar types of issues, elements, defenses, etc.[210] For example, if a rape victim is unavailable to testify at the defendant's trial for rape, but she testified at the preliminary examination, the defendant would likely have had a similar motive for developing the victim's testimony at the preliminary examination as he would at trial. If his defense is consent, he would have been questioning her regarding the things she said and did that would show consent, attacking her credibility, memory, and other issues. Since the accused had an opportunity at the prior hearing to bring out the same issues he would if the witness were present at the trial, he would not likely be able to claim that he was highly prejudiced by not being able to examine the witness at the present trial. Thus, this requirement would be met.

2. Additional Protections for Use in Criminal Trials. In further protection of the defendant's rights to confrontation and cross-examination in a criminal trial, the following requirements must have also been met at the prior hearing where the former testimony was given, whether it was a prior civil or criminal proceeding:

1. accused must have had counsel;
2. witness under oath;[211]
3. witness was cross-examined or defendant validly waived;
4. witness is currently unavailable; and

210. *See* R. Ray Orrill, Jr. et al. v. Ram Rod Trucking, et al. below.
211. La. Code Evid. art. 804(B)(1) Official Comment (c).

5. State made a good faith effort to locate the witness.[212]

3. Confrontation Issues. Since the prior statement will always be testimonial, the State must ensure that offering the statement does not infringe upon the accused's right to confront and cross-examine adverse witnesses as guaranteed by the Sixth Amendment of the United States Constitution and Art. I, § 16 of the Louisiana Constitution. Thus, the State must comply with the requirements under *Crawford*, which provide that if the witness is currently unavailable, the accused must have had a prior opportunity to cross-examine the witness. While the requirements of the article generally conform with the requirements of *Crawford*, the additional jurisprudential criteria listed above help to ensure that the accused's rights are protected.

4. Opportunity to Develop Testimony. Further, the statute requires that the examining party (the defendant himself in a criminal case) need only have had a prior *opportunity* to develop the prior testimony; there is no requirement that the examination of the witness in fact took place in the prior proceeding.[213] Thus, if the defendant validly waived the right to cross-examination (not under duress, threats, etc.), then this requirement is met. It is irrelevant as to whether the prior examination was cross-examination, direct examination, or redirect examination.

Civil Cases

If a party seeks to admit a witness's statement in a civil case that was given at a prior hearing (criminal trial, preliminary exam, civil case, etc.), ***any party*** with a similar interest must have had an opportunity and similar motive to develop the witness's prior testimony through the applicable examination—by direct, cross, or redirect. There is no requirement that the party himself have had a prior opportunity and motive to examine the witness.

Party with similar interest. Who is a party with a similar interest? For example, the plaintiff (P1) and her best friend (P2) are injured in an accident when the defendant driver negligently operated his truck and hit the vehicle P1 was driving. P1 sues the truck driver's employer. At the trial the truck driver testifies for the defense, his employer, and is cross-examined by P1. In her cross-examination, P1 attempts to show that the truck driver was driving erratically, speeding, and was not paying close attention when he struck her vehicle. She also shows that she was cautiously operating her vehicle at the time of the accident. The employer is found liable.

Sometime after that, plaintiff's friend P2 brings a suit against the employer for her injuries. By the time her case goes to trial, the truck driver is no longer working for the defendant company and cannot be located. The employer would like to use the truck driver's direct examination he gave in the first trial against P1 in the trial brought by P2. In order to do this, he must show that although P2 will not be able to cross-examine the truck driver, a party with a similar interest as P2 had an opportunity and similar motive to develop the truck driver's testimony at the prior hearing through direct, cross, or redirect examination.

It is likely that the court will find that P1 and P2 have a similar interest in examining the driver. Like P1, P2 would also want to show that the truck driver was negligent and not P1. To show this, P2 will likely want to elicit the same type of information from the

---

212. State v. Ball, 824 So. 2d 1089 (La. 2002); State v. Francois, 926 So. 2d 744 (La. App. 3d Cir. 2006).

213. *See* State v Randall, 830 So. 2d 1062 (La. Ct. App. 4th Cir. 2002); *See also* State v. Jones, 642 So. 2d 151 (La. 1994).

Requirements for Former Testimony Exception: *Civil Case*

1. declarant is unavailable; and
2. the party against whom testimony is now offered (*or a party with a similar interest*) must have had a prior ***opportunity*** and *similar* **motive** to develop testimony through direct, cross, or redirect examination.

driver that P1 did. She would want to show that the driver was driving erratically and speeding when the accident occurred and that P1 was driving cautiously and properly at the time of the accident.

Thus, since a party with a similar interest as P2 had an opportunity and motive to develop the truck driver's testimony in the prior proceeding through cross-examination, the defendant may use the prior testimony given by the truck driver in the second civil trial brought by P2. The fact that the different trial attorneys cross-examining the witness might have had different trial strategies and the like is irrelevant for the exception to apply.[214]

Keep in mind that while it is sufficient in a civil trial for *any party* with a similar interest to have had a prior opportunity and motive to develop the former testimony at the prior hearing, in a criminal trial, the accused himself must have had the prior opportunity and motive to develop the witness's former testimony.

Expert witnesses excluded from exception. The statute specifically excludes from admissibility, under the exception, testimony given in another proceeding by an expert witness in the form of opinions or inferences. Unlike other witnesses who may be the only person who can testify to the substance of his testimony, with expert witnesses there are usually other experts who can testify on a given point.[215]

Depositions. Depositions do not fall into this exception, although there could be some extenuating circumstances in which a deposition might be admissible under this exception.[216] The admissibility of deposition testimony is generally covered in the Louisiana Code of Civil Procedure under La. C.C.P. art. 1450 et seq.[217] The admissibility of depositions in criminal trials as it relates to incarcerated material witnesses can be found in La. R.S. 15:258–259.[218]

Federal Rules of Evidence Distinction. The corresponding provision under the Federal Rules of Evidence does not contain the exclusion of expert testimony from the exception as found under the Louisiana Article.[219] Additionally, while in Louisiana *any party* with a similar interest must have had a prior opportunity and motive to develop the former testimony at the prior hearing in a civil case, Federal Rule of Evidence 804(b)(1) provides for a "predecessor in interest" to have developed the prior testimony in a civil trial.

---

214. *See, e.g.*, U.S. v. Mann, 161 F.3d 840, 861 (5th Cir. 1998).

215. La. Code Evid. art. 804(B)(1); *See also* La. Code Evid. art. 804(B)(1) Official Comment (h).

216. La. Code Evid. art. 804(B)(1) Official Comment (d).

217. La. Code Evid. art. 804(B)(1) Official Comment (d).

218. *See also* La. Code Evid. art. 804(B)(1) Official Comment (d).

219. *See* Fed. R. Evid. 804(B)(1); *See also* La. Code Evid. art. 804(B)(1) Official Comment (h).

Cases on Former Testimony

Orrill v. Ram Rod Trucking

Court of Appeal of Louisiana, Fourth Circuit
557 So. 2d 384
Jan. 30, 1990

WILLIAMS, Judge.

On August 14, 1984, R. Ray Orrill, Jr. was injured when the vehicle he was driving was struck in the rear by a truck owned by Ram Rod Trucking & Storage, Inc. and operated by its employee, Richard E. Harton. The accident occurred on Interstate 10 in the area of Morrison Road in New Orleans East. Orrill and his wife filed suit against Harton and Ram Rod for injuries allegedly sustained as a result of the accident and surrounding events.

At trial, Orrill testified that, after colliding, the drivers parked their vehicles on the side of the Interstate. Harton then went to the cab of his truck, withdrew a nickel-plated handgun and threatened Orrill. Harton denied this allegation throughout his testimony and further testified that, in fact, Orrill threatened him with a brick and appeared to be intoxicated. Police officers found a nickel-plated handgun in the cab of Harton's truck when they arrived on the scene of the accident.

The trial court rejected Harton's testimony as lacking credibility and found that the accident was a result of Harton's inattention, carelessness and failure to properly observe the traffic in front of him and to properly keep his vehicle under control at all times. The court further found that there was no negligence attributable to plaintiff. The court found Ram Rod Trucking and Richard E. Harton liable jointly, severally and in solido in the total amount of $47,417.84....

Assignments of Error by Ram Rod Trucking, Inc. and Harton

Ram Rod and Harton complain that the trial court erred in the following respects: in admitting into evidence the transcript of the criminal trial of Harton for the alleged assault; in concluding that the plaintiff had sustained his burden of proof; in concluding that all medical treatment of Orrill presented at trial was a result of the automobile accident of August 14, 1984, and; in awarding an excessive amount of damages for pain and suffering to Orrill....

Introduction of Transcript

Defendants argue that introduction of the transcript of Harton's criminal trial (in connection with the alleged assault) should not have been allowed primarily because it was not certified. Furthermore, the transcript should not have been introduced because a district court cannot take judicial notice of proceedings in a case from another jurisdiction....

Defendants also complain that, by allowing the transcript to be introduced, the trial judge allowed introduction of testimony of two witnesses, a police officer and a tow truck driver, who were not present and therefore not subject to cross-examination. Furthermore, the testimony of these two witnesses is inadmissible hearsay offered for the truth of the matter asserted.

The trial judge allowed the transcript to be admitted into evidence under: L.C.E. art. 804B(1), which provides:

> B. Hearsay exception. The following are not excluded by the hearsay rule if the declarant is unavailable as a witness:

(1) Former testimony. Testimony given as a witness at another hearing of the same or a different proceeding, if the party against whom the testimony is now offered, or, in a civil action or proceeding, a party with a similar interest, had an opportunity and similar motive to develop the testimony by direct, cross, or redirect examination. Testimony given in another proceeding by an expert witness in the form of opinions or inferences, however, is not admissible under this exception.

... The trial judge noted that the witness could not be found and plaintiff testified at trial that neither he nor defendants were able to locate the tow-truck driver who had appeared at the scene of the accident. The defendant Harton had the opportunity to cross-examine the witness at his criminal trial, and the defendant employer's interest and motive are similar to those of Harton's so that the employer's interests were protected by Harton's ability to cross-examine.

This court finds that the trial court did not commit manifest error in admitting the prior testimony. Furthermore, if the admission of the record had constituted error, we find that any such error would be harmless in light of the remaining evidence.

Discussion Questions

1. Explain how and why the employer's interest and motive in the civil case are similar to that of Harton's in the criminal case for assault. In Harton's criminal trial for assault, what types of issues and elements might he have been cross-examining the witness about? What motive does he have? What is it that both Harton and his employer would have been attempting to show in the civil trial? Did Harton protect both his and his employer's interests in the criminal trial?
2. Based on the evidence presented in the opinion, would you have found that the proponent of the statement met his burden of proving that the declarant was unavailable? Beyond a mere statement, what efforts would you require a proponent of a statement show to secure the declarant's presence at trial?

State v. Crandell

Ct. of Appeal of Louisiana, Second Circuit
987 So. 2d 375
June 18, 2008

STEWART, Judge.

The defendant, James Carl Crandell, was found guilty of second degree murder and sentenced to life imprisonment at hard labor without the possibility of parole. He now appeals his conviction based on the introduction at trial of testimony given in a prior proceeding. Finding no reversible error, we affirm the defendant's conviction and sentence.

FACTS

On the morning of August 21, 1989, two maids at the Beacon Manor, a motel in Bossier City, Louisiana, discovered the body of Charles Parr in a closet in Room 15. Parr had been beaten to death. The motel owner, Margie Theodos called the police. The investigation focused on the most recent occupants of Room 15, namely, James Carl Crandell and his girlfriend, Gail Willars. The couple was traveling with Willars' 8-year-old son, Zachary. From the motel's phone records, the police learned that the missing occupants had placed calls to a residence in Chicago, Illinois. Crandell and Willars were arrested by Chicago police at the residence identified from the phone records and, after waiving formal extradition, they returned to Louisiana.

Crandell and Willars were indicted for first-degree murder and tried together in February 1991. A jury found Crandell guilty of first degree murder and Willars guilty of second degree murder. Because the jury could not reach a unanimous verdict in Crandell's penalty phase, Crandell and Willars both received life sentences. Their convictions were affirmed on appeal. However, Crandell obtained federal *habeas corpus* relief in August 2004, and his conviction and sentence were vacated....

Thereafter, a Bossier Parish grand jury again indicted Crandell for first degree murder, but the state ultimately amended the indictment to a second degree murder charge. On September 21, 2007, the state filed a motion notifying the defendant that it intended to introduce as evidence the transcribed testimony of Margie Theodos, Gail Willars, and Zachary Willars from the 1991 trial. The state asserted that all three were unavailable as witnesses; Ms. Theodos was deceased, Gail Willars had opted not to testify on Fifth Amendment grounds, and Zachary could not be located. The defendant objected to the introduction of the testimony on the grounds that the previous trial had been vacated as an absolute nullity, that Gail Willars had not persistently refused to testify, and that the state had not made adequate efforts to locate Zachary.

In support of its motion, the state introduced a copy of a newspaper obituary for Margie Theodos stating that she died on February 23, 2007, and informed the court that Ms. Theodos' husband and son were also deceased. The trial court overruled the defendant's objection that the obituary did not prove that the decedent was the same Margie Theodos who had testified at the first trial and allowed the obituary to be introduced. The trial court also found that Crandell's right to confront and cross-examine witnesses was not impacted by use of the prior testimony by the three unavailable witnesses and rejected the argument that the testimony could not be used because his prior conviction had been vacated.

Trial commenced on September 25, 2007. During a recess and outside of the jury's presence, the trial court again took up the matter of the unavailability of Theodos, Willars, and Zachary. With regard to Zachary Willars, the state called Amy Noonan, felony supervisor for the Bossier Parish District Attorney's ("BPDA") office, to testify about efforts to locate Zachary. Noonan testified that the BPDA tried to locate Zachary, who was now an adult, about a year and a half prior to trial based on information that he had been in several psychiatric hospitals in Houston, Texas. However, he was not located at any of those facilities. In June 2007, BPDA obtained a material witness warrant for Zachary's last known address at a hospital in Houston and at four other addresses, two in Houston and two in Chicago. But upon learning that he was probably in California, no effort was made to serve the Houston or Chicago addresses.

Noonan testified that she conducted computer searches for Zachary for "months." On September 20, 2007, she searched Accurint.com, Whitepages.com, Nlets.org, and the National Crime Information Center for information on his whereabouts. Noonan found various tenants at the addresses the BPDA had for Zachary, and she discovered the names of an aunt and uncle who lived in Texas. Noonan contacted these relatives, who told her that Zachary had been in a mental institution in California approximately one and a half years ago; however, they did not know where Zachary could be found. Noonan attempted to have Zachary served at an address in Coarsegold, California, without success. Likewise, a summons mailed to another possible address in Camarillo, California, was returned undeliverable. Finally, Bossier Parish District Attorney Schuyler Marvin testified that he had recently spoken with Zachary's mother Gail, who told him that she did not know where he could be found.

With regard to Ms. Theodos, Noonan testified that an Accurint search for her name returned a result with a "D," indicating that she was deceased. Although Noonan was not able to obtain a death certificate or other proof of death through the coroner's office, a cousin of Ms. Theodos confirmed that she had died and a copy of the obituary from the local newspaper was obtained. A former neighbor also confirmed Ms. Theodos' death.

Finally, the trial court addressed Gail Willars' unavailability. Willars, who was continuing to contest her conviction through a petition for *certiorari* to the United States Supreme Court, informed the trial court that she was relying on her Fifth Amendment right not to testify in Crandell's case. Her petition had been returned to her with instructions to provide additional information and refile it before "the end of October." She provided a copy of her petition to the BPDA.

Regarding her son Zachary's whereabouts, Willars told the court:

> I believe he's somewhere in Los Angeles. [Willars said she did not know his address.] He may possibly testify, but I don't believe you would get any results from him because he is extremely mentally ill. He is, to my knowledge, living somewhere on the street. He's been in a forensic facility where he has just been released from recently and he's doing drugs and he's in pretty bad shape. He's been in and out of mental institutions for the last few years.

The court then asked Willars whether she would invoke the privilege against self-incrimination if she were questioned by the state or the defense about the events of August 21, 1989, and she replied, "Yes, sir."

The trial court ruled that all three witnesses were unavailable and that the state could use the transcripts of their prior testimony as evidence against the defendant by allowing them to be read to the jury by members of the court's staff. The defendant objected to the ruling.

Trial resumed on September 26, 2007, with the presentation of Ms. Theodos' testimony from the first trial. The court informed the jury that the testimony was "from a prior proceeding." Ms. Theodos testified that Crandell and Willars began renting a room at the motel in mid-July 1989. On August 21, 1989, they were due to be evicted for non-payment of rent. Although Theodos said that the Beacon Manor rented rooms for as little as an hour at a time, supplied free condoms to its customers, and had free adult movies, she denied problems with prostitution. At the end of Theodos' testimony, the defense objected to references in the transcript to Crandell and Willars being "in court" and to one reference to the word "trial." The objection was overruled.

After additional testimony, the transcript of Gail Willars' testimony was read. Willars met Crandell in 1987, while living in Fayetteville, Arkansas, and married to Jerry Wayne Willars. After her husband was killed in a tractor accident during a hayride in November 1987, Willars received $150,000 in death benefits and monthly payments of $2,500 from her husband's former company. She became close friends with Crandell, and they began traveling together. During a trip to Georgia to scatter her husband's ashes, Crandell introduced Willars to cocaine. Thereafter, she supplied Crandell with money to buy drugs; she claimed the drugs took away her pain and grief. They traveled throughout Texas, Arkansas, and Louisiana, living in motels and using about a pound of cocaine per week. They were arrested for possession in Cass County, Texas, in March 1988, and Willars was arrested again on a drug charge in Houston. They were separated for a time while Crandell was put in the custody of the Texas Department of Corrections, and while she was on probation. Upon Crandell's release, they began traveling again, this time with her son, Zachary.

By the summer of 1989, Willars was out of money except for the monthly payments, which were sent to her father's address in Houston. Because Crandell was "in violation of his parole," the pair did not want to drive back to Houston for the checks, so Willars' father cashed the checks and wired the money to her wherever she happened to be. In July 1989, their location was Bossier City. Willars testified that they had spent all the money for the month, so they sold their car for $250 to pay for a place to stay. When they ran out of money again by the middle of August, Crandell suggested that she prostitute herself to obtain money for rent. Willars noted that they were using little, if any, cocaine at this point due to lack of funds.

On the morning of August 20, the day they were to be evicted from the motel, Willars tried unsuccessfully to call her father for money. While she was at the pay phone, Parr drove up to her and asked if she needed a ride and whether she was a working girl. Willars initially declined his advance, but she eventually agreed to perform oral sex for $30. Willars and Parr entered the motel room and began to disrobe. Willars claimed that Parr called her a whore, cursed and demanded additional sexual favors, so she told Parr that she had AIDS. He became enraged and picked her up. Willars testified that Crandell appeared and hit Parr on the head with a small stick, which shattered. The two men fought until Crandell brandished a knife. Willars described Crandell as "screaming and wild-eyed and crazy looking, acting like a lunatic." She said that Crandell bound Parr's hands with duct tape and, later, with bungee cords, then forced Parr into a closet. While she and Crandell argued, Parr managed to untie himself and burst out of the closet. Parr grabbed a frying pan, and the two men fighting over it. Willars said that as she tried to separate them she heard crying and saw Zachary in the bathroom. She told the men to stop because of the child in the room. She testified that Parr stopped fighting but that Crandell grabbed the frying pan and began hitting Parr on the head. Crandell then choked Parr into submission until he fell to the floor. While Crandell put Parr's body back in the closet, she cleaned the room a little. She recalled that many items were spattered with blood. She and Crandell loaded the contents of their room into Parr's vehicle and left with Zachary. They drove to a McDonald's where they bought food with money found in Parr's car, and then they began driving to the home of Crandell's friend in Chicago.

When asked about statements she made to the Chicago police about the locations of weapons used in the encounter with Parr, she professed to a poor recollection of those statements. She also testified about letters that Crandell wrote to her while they were jailed in Louisiana. In the letters, which were introduced as the states' exhibits 52, 53, and 54, Crandell wrote about a possible insanity defense, his desire not to go to a mental institution, and his claim that what happened to Parr was the result of either self-defense or an accident. Crandell wrote:

> [N]o, I don't want to spend years or the rest of my life in a mental hospital. No, I don't want my brain probed and picked apart by people and made a spectacle. And as you know, I don't want to be executed or spend the rest of my life in prison.... What happened in that room was an accident and nothing but an accident. I just hope these people believe that.... Gail, he was alive when I put him in the closet and we left that motel. I told you he was dead because I thought you'd want to call an ambulance and have him taken to the hospital and I was in one hell of a state of panic. And all I wanted to do was get the hell away from there. I didn't think he was going to die. I thought the worse that might happen was that they would put a warrant on us for robbery. I didn't think I hit him that hard. After I told him to leave you alone and asked him to leave and when he refused and when we started to fighting, I kind of lost it there for a minute. That man was strong and all I could think of was that if he beat and hurt me what would he do to you.

Next, the 1991 testimony of then 9-year-old Zachary Willars was read to the jury. Zachary testified that he and Crandell, who had a knife in his hand, were in the bathroom when his mother and Parr entered the motel room and began undressing. The bathroom door was open, and he could see the rest of the room through a mirror. He testified that Crandell jumped out of the bathroom wielding the knife. His mother picked up a stick and started hitting Parr on the head, while Crandell put down the knife and watched. Zachary said that Crandell then taped Parr's mouth and hands and put him in the closet. Because Parr continued to make noise, Crandell took him out of the closet and "started hitting [Parr] on the head" with a frying pan that Gail had handed him. At that point, Gail told him to stop when she noticed Zachary, and she shut the bathroom door. Zachary testified that he then heard a sound like "dragging [Parr] to the closet." When Zachary came out of the bathroom a few minutes later, Crandell opened the closet door, pointed to Parr's body, and laughed. Zachary said that Crandell took Parr's wallet. The three then packed up and drove Parr's car to Chicago. Zachary also testified that Parr never hit his mother or Crandell.

After the state rested, the defense objected to the introduction of other crimes evidence, namely Crandell's use of cocaine as well as his drug conviction and parole violation, mentioned in the transcript of Gail Willars' testimony. The defense also objected to the repeated references to the jury trial in Willars' testimony, such as questions beginning, "Tell the jury...." Similar objections were made with regard to Zachary's testimony, particularly a reference to the fact that the previous trial was a first-degree murder trial. The trial court overruled these objections.

Crandell did not testify, and the defense rested. The jury returned a unanimous verdict of guilty as charged of second degree murder. Motions for post-verdict judgment of acquittal and a new trial were filed and denied. Crandell was sentenced to life imprisonment at hard labor without the benefit of parole....

DISCUSSION

... *Unavailability of Witnesses*

Appellant counsel's second, third, fourth, and fifth assignments of error all pertain to whether there was a sufficient showing that Willars and Zachary were unavailable and whether allowing their transcribed testimony to be read deprived the jury of the opportunity to assess their credibility. There is also the complaint that Gail Willars' unavailability allowed the state to introduce otherwise inadmissible evidence that the state would not have been able to elicit on direct examination without a proper foundation being laid.

Determining the unavailability of a witness is a preliminary question for the trial court. La. C.E. art. 104(A). Such determinations are subject to manifest error review and will not be overturned absent an abuse of discretion by the trial court....

The defendant asserts that the state's efforts to locate Zachary were perfunctory. To the contrary, the testimony of Amy Noonan established that BPDA made a good faith and diligent effort to locate Zachary, who from all indications had become a transient. It became apparent during the investigation that Zachary had been hospitalized in mental institutions during his adult life and that he had no fixed or permanent address or employment. His mother explained that he might be living somewhere on the street in Los Angeles and that he had been using drugs. Even with powerful cross-referenced databases, the BPDA was unable to determine his whereabouts. The state's two efforts to issue subpoenas for Zachary are not indicia of a lack of effort; rather, the state's investigation simply revealed no likely locations to which a subpoena could or should be sent. The trial court did not err in finding Zachary to be unavailable.

Next, the defendant argues that Gail Willars should not have been found unavailable to testify and her 1991 testimony should not have been admissible in the 2007 trial. At the time of the 2007 trial, Willars had pending a petition for *certiorari* before the U.S. Supreme Court to challenge her 1991 conviction. Because both Crandell and Willars had been indicted by the same grand jury and Crandell's conviction had been reversed due to racial discrimination in the selection of the grand jury foreman, it is reasonable to assume that Willars' efforts to have her conviction overturned were not hopeless or futile. Rather, Willars' petition was pending, and its success depended on whether she timely asserted her rights, a question which had not been conclusively answered. The trial judge accepted that Willars was in the process of refiling her federal petition and that finding is not manifestly erroneous on this record that contains a copy of Willars' petition to the U.S. Supreme Court. Under these peculiar circumstances, the trial court did not err in finding Willars to be unavailable.

Referring to La. C.E. art. 804(B)(1), the defendant argues that Gail Willars' 1991 testimony should not have been introduced. He reasons that in the 1991 trial he did not have a "similar motive to develop the testimony by direct, cross, or redirect examination." He argues that because Willars was also on trial in 1991, she had every interest in shifting the blame for the crime to Crandell rather than onto herself. Finally, he complains that use of Willars' prior testimony allowed the state to introduce evidence, such as Willars' statement to the Chicago police, which would not otherwise have been admissible.

Article 804(B)(1) is a firmly-rooted exception to the hearsay rule. Former testimony given by a declarant who is unavailable as a witness is admissible if the party against whom it is offered "had an opportunity and similar motive to develop the testimony by direct, cross, or redirect examination." La. C.E. art. 804(B)(1). In *State v. Ball,* the Court addressed the requirements for the admissibility of prior testimony:

> This Court has held that use of the prior testimony must not impinge on the defendant's constitutional right to confront and cross-examine adverse witnesses, as guaranteed by the Sixth Amendment of the United States Constitution, Art. I, § 16 of the Louisiana Constitution, and La.Rev.Stat. § 15:273. To protect these constitutional rights, certain conditions must be met before the prior testimony may be introduced: (1) the defendant must have been represented by counsel at the earlier hearing; (2) the witness must have testified under oath; (3) the witness must have been cross-examined (or there must have been a valid waiver of the right to cross-examination); (4) at the time of trial, the witness must be "unavailable" to testify; and (5) the State must have made a good faith effort to locate the unavailable witness. These jurisprudential criteria are subsumed in La.Code Evid. art. 804(B)(1), permitting the use of prior recorded testimony of an unavailable declarant as an exception to the hearsay rule. (Citations omitted.)

The record shows that the conditions set forth in *Ball* are met in this instance for the admissibility of Willars' prior testimony. As discussed, Willars was "unavailable" to testify in the 2007 trial due to the pending review of her conviction. Crandell was represented by counsel in the 1991 trial. Willars testified in that proceeding under oath. In 1991, Crandell was able to fully question Willars. The original transcript of Willars' testimony is 181 legal-sized pages long, the first 67 of which consists of Willars' testimony on direct examination by Crandell's attorney. Crandell's counsel also questioned her on redirect. From our review of Willars' transcript, we have no difficulty in concluding that Crandall had every full and fair opportunity and a similar motive to thoroughly question Willars and develop her testimony at the original trial....

Discussion Questions

1. Upon what basis did the trial court find that Margie Theodos, Gail Willars, and Zachary Willars were unavailable? Do you agree with the court that the prosecution met its burden of establishing that each witness was unavailable?
2. Did Crandell have a similar motive for developing Willars' testimony at the original trial as he would in this subsequent one, considering she was not a co-defendant in the second trial?
3. A final requirement that must be met to use prior testimony in a criminal trial to ensure that the prior testimony does not infringe on the defendant's constitutional right to confront and cross-examine adverse witnesses, as guaranteed by the Sixth Amendment of the United States Constitution, and Art. I, § 16 of the Louisiana Constitution, are five jurisprudential criteria set out in *State v. Ball*. What are these criteria? How do they help to protect a defendant's confrontation rights? Are they met in this case?

Key Points

The key points to keep in mind regarding former testimony.

1. **Requirements in a Criminal Case**
   a. declarant is unavailable;
   b. the party against whom testimony is now offered must (*himself*) have had a ***prior opportunity and similar motive*** to develop testimony through direct, cross, or redirect examination; **and**
   c. ***if offered against an accused, at time of prior testimony:***
      1. accused must have had counsel;
      2. witness under oath;
      3. witness was cross-examined or defendant validly waived;
      4. witness is currently unavailable; and
      5. state made a good faith effort to locate the witness.
2. **Requirements in a Civil Case**
   a. declarant is unavailable; and
   b. the party against whom testimony is now offered (*or a party with a similar interest*) must have had a ***prior opportunity*** **and** ***similar motive*** to develop testimony through direct, cross, or redirect examination.
3. Whether in a civil or criminal case, there is no requirement that the person against whom the testimony is now offered actually examined the witness, only that they had the prior opportunity to do so. The prior examination may be either direct, cross, or redirect examination.
4. Prior testimony could have been given at another hearing of the same or a different proceeding in either a civil or criminal trial.

5. Prior testimony of expert witnesses are not admissible under this exception.
6. The exception does not apply to depositions.

Problems on Former Testimony

PROBLEM 5-128. An eyewitness at a suppression hearing gave extremely damaging testimony against the defendant in a suppression hearing identifying the defendant as the murderer in a drug transaction. At that time, he was thoroughly cross-examined by the defense counsel. Two months before the trial he moved from the address that was originally given in the police reports. At the trial, the prosecution seeks to introduce the testimony given at the motion to suppress hearing. They have informed the court and opposing counsel on the record that the witness has moved. Should the witness's former testimony be admitted at the trial? Why or why not?

PROBLEM 5-129. In a criminal trial in which the defendant pled not guilty and not guilty by reason of insanity, an expert forensic psychologist testified that the defendant was not insane at the time of the commission of the offense and that he was capable of distinguishing between right and wrong at the time the offense was committed. The defendant was found guilty as charged and appealed. On appeal, the appellate court reversed the conviction on technical grounds and ordered a new trial. Prior to the new trial, the expert forensic psychologist who testified at the original trial died, and the prosecution seeks to admit the testimony that he gave at the initial trial under the former testimony exception. The defense objects. How should the court rule and why?

PROBLEM 5-130. Carson is believed to have burned down his house to get the insurance proceeds. Following an investigation, Carson was charged with arson, and the insurance company refused to pay. A witness who saw Carson while he was supposedly away from his home when the fire started testifies that he saw Carson filling up a gas can at a nearby gas station. He says that when he attempted to inquire as to whether everything was okay, Carson hurriedly ended the conversation and drove off. While Carson awaited the criminal trial, he brought an action against the insurance company to collect the proceeds to help pay his legal bills.

a. Assume the civil case proceeds to trial first, and the witness testifies for the insurance company but dies before the criminal trial. In the criminal trial, the prosecution would like to use the witness's statement that he gave in the civil case. Admissible?

b. Would your answer change if the criminal trial proceeded first, and the witness died before the civil case? Should the insurance company be allowed to offer the testimony that the witness gave in the criminal trial in the civil case they are defending against Carson? Why or why not?

PROBLEM 5-131. Dexter murdered his girlfriend and is very wealthy. Criminal charges are brought against him. His girlfriend's estate also brings a civil action. The civil case goes to trial first. In the civil trial, Dexter calls a pimp to the stand who testifies that the girlfriend had worked for him and had only recently stopped working the streets after she met Dexter. He further testifies about several former clients who she had stolen from or owed favors who may have had an opportunity and motive to kill her. Dexter is found not to be liable for her death in the civil case. The criminal case moves forward, but before the trial, the pimp dies and is unavailable to testify. Dexter offers the transcript from the civil case, and the prosecution objects that the testimony is hearsay. Should the court allow the testimony in light of Dexter's constitutional rights to present a defense?

PROBLEM 5-132. Biff is arrested for murder. At the preliminary examination on the charges, Cane is called to testify for the prosecution that following the murder, Biff came to his residence and confessed to the murder wearing bloody clothes and with wounds on his hands. After discussing it over with Biff, Biff's lawyer decides not to cross-examine Cane. Some time after the preliminary examination, but before the trial, Cane dies. In which of the following proceedings arising out of the incident will Cane's testimony from Biff's preliminary examination likely be permissible under the former testimony exception? Explain.

Proceeding A: The prosecution seeks to use Cane's testimony from the preliminary examination against Biff in Biff's murder trial.

Proceeding B: It is later discovered (after Biff's criminal trial has ended) that Bandit was Biff's accomplice in the murder. Bandit is now also being tried for the same murder as Biff. The prosecution would like to use Cane's testimony that he gave at Biff's preliminary examination against Bandit in his murder trial.

Proceeding C: Following both murder trials, the victims' families bring a civil suit against Biff and Bandit. The plaintiffs would like to use Cane's statement that he gave in Biff's preliminary examination against both Biff and Bandit in the civil trial.

PROBLEM 5-133. Buck drove trucks for Panola Co. and was involved in an accident where he injured two teenagers (T1 and T2) when he ran a red light and struck their small vehicle. The teenagers sued Buck, wherein both of them testified and were cross-examined by Buck's attorney. Unable to recover anything from Buck, T2 then sued Johnny Panola, the owner of the company, for her injuries. T1 did not sue Johnny because following the accident she flunked out of school and was forced to move back home to Chicago. T2 was unable to locate T1 for the trial, so she would like to offer T1's testimony that T1 gave at the trial against Buck. Johnny Panola objects that the testimony is hearsay. How will the court likely rule?

PROBLEM 5-134. Raymond's ex-wife (Ex-Wife) accused him of molesting their daughter during her weekend visits with him. As a result, criminal charges are subsequently brought against Raymond. At the criminal trial against Raymond for child molestation, Raymond's attorney cross-examined the Child Protection Services (CPS) worker, whose testimony ultimately revealed that the molestation charges were unwarranted and unsubstantiated. Raymond was found not guilty. Raymond subsequently sued Ex-Wife for slander for spreading the false allegations about molesting their daughter that ruined his reputation and resulted in him losing his job and several clients. By the time the civil case goes to trial, the CPS worker has moved to the UK with her military husband and cannot be located. Raymond wishes to use the testimony that she gave at the criminal trial to support his case that the accusations were false. Ex-Wife objects that the CPS worker's testimony from the criminal trial is hearsay. What ruling and why?

PROBLEM 5-135. Gretchen testified at a grand jury hearing for the prosection after which first-degree murder charges were brought against the defendant. By the time the case goes to trial, the witness has died from AIDS. What must be shown in order for the prosecution to use the grand jury testimony? Will the testimony likely be admissible in the defendant's trial? Why or why not?

§ 5.15 References and Additional Authority on Former Testimony [La. C.E. art. 804(B)(1)]

1. La. C.E. art. 804(B)(1) and Official Comments
2. Force & Rault, HANDBOOK ON LOUISIANA EVIDENCE LAW Art. 804(B)(1) Author's Comments (West Publishing 2014)
3. Harges & Jones, LOUISIANA EVIDENCE Art. 804(B)(1) Author's Comments (West Publishing 2014)
4. 19 La. Civ. L. Treatise, Evidence And Proof § 10.7 (2nd ed.)
5. MCCORMICK ON EVIDENCE § 301 (5th ed., 1999)
6. **Former testimony used in civil case:** *Warren v. Bergeron*, 599 So. 2d 369 (La. Ct. App. 3d Cir. 1992) (holding that testimony of codefendant, who pleaded guilty to second-degree murder of homeowner, as presented in defendant's prior criminal trial was admissible in wrongful death and survival action where codefendant refused to testify and was unavailable, and facts and circumstances of previous criminal trial were very similar to facts and circumstances of wrongful death and survival action, and defendant had full opportunity to cross-examine codefendant in criminal trial).
7. **Former testimony used in criminal cases:** *State v. Seals*, 83 So. 3d 285 (La. Ct. App. 5th Cir. 2011) (allowing prior testimony of the witness after finding that all prerequisites were met; the defendant had proper representation, the witness testified under oath, the witness was cross-examined or validly waived the right to cross-examination, the witness was currently unavailable, and the state made a diligent effort in procuring the witness); *State v. Vincent*, 806 So. 2d 992 (La. Ct. App. 4th Cir. 2002), rehearing denied (In defendant's first-degree murder trial, State was allowed to present at retrial the prior testimony of now-deceased witness given in defendant's first trial, where defense counsel had opportunity to confront and cross-examine witness in first trial.).
8. **Expert witness:** *Southern Message Service, Inc. v. Commercial Union Ins. Co.*, 647 So. 2d 398 (La. Ct. App. 2d Cir. 1994), writ denied 650 So. 2d 1180, 1995-0059 (La. 3/10/95) (holding that former testimony of unavailable expert witness is not admissible as exception to hearsay rule).

§ 5.16 Statement Under Belief of Impending Death (Dying Declaration) [La. C.E. art. 804(B)(2)]

Applicable Code Articles

* * *

B. Hearsay exceptions. The following are not excluded by the hearsay rule if the declarant is unavailable as a witness:

* * *

(2) Statement under belief of impending death. A statement made by a declarant while believing that his death was imminent, concerning the cause or circumstances of what he believed to be his impending death.

* * *

In this section we move to Article 804(B)(2) which contains an exception that excludes statements from the hearsay rule if made by a declarant while believing that his death was imminent, when the statements are concerning the cause or circumstances of what he believed to be his impending death. This exception is commonly referred to as the "dying declaration" exception, and its reliability was historically premised upon the religious belief that a person would not want to meet his maker with a lie on his lips.[220] Other historical underpinnings of the rule reasoned that it would be unfair to allow killers to escape justice because of (or by causing) the unavailability of victims, the only witnesses of the murder.[221] Further, a person who is dying has little motive to lie since he can suffer no consequences from his words.[222] Thus, if a person has just been shot in the heart, and while clutching his chest and lying in a pool of blood proclaims, "*Deen just shot me,*" the statement will likely conform to this exception.

Statute expands and clarifies Louisiana Law. Article 804(B)(2) expands prior Louisiana law in important respects. Under prior law, the exception applied only in criminal homicide prosecutions. Additionally, the declarant must have actually died, and his death must have been the subject of the criminal prosecution in which the statement was used.[223] Under the current Article 804(B)(2), the exception also applies in civil trials as well as in any type of criminal trial, not only homicide prosecutions arising out of the declarant's death. Further, the declarant need not have actually died at the time the statement was made, although he must be otherwise unavailable at the time of the trial for the exception to apply.

Basically, under the current law, the exception may apply in any type of civil or criminal trial if:

---

220. *See* Garza v. Delta Tau Delta Fraternity National, 948 So. 2d 84, 91 n.13 (La. 2006), ("Eighteenth-century rationale was that the impending judgment of God imposed an obligation of honesty upon the dying, so as to justify an exception to the exclusionary hearsay rule.").

221. *See* Garza v. Delta Tau Delta Fraternity National, 948 So. 2d 84, 91 (La. 2006), Harges and Jones, 402.

222. Garza v. Delta Tau Delta Fraternity National, 948 So. 2d 84, 91 (La. 2006) ("when every motive to falsehood is silenced, and the mind is induced by the most powerful considerations to speak the truth").

223. La. Code Evid. art. 804(B)(2) Official Comment (b).

Requirements for Dying Declaration Exception

1. declarant is unavailable;
2. the declarant believes his death is imminent (*whether or not he actually dies*); and
3. the statement concerns the cause or circumstances of what he believed to be his impending death.

1) the declarant is unavailable;

2) the declarant believes his death is imminent when the statement is made, whether or not he actually dies; and

3) the statement concerns the cause or circumstances of what he believed to be his impending death.

Unavailability requirement. As with all Article 804(B) exceptions, the dying declaration exception requires that the declarant be unavailable to testify at the trial. While the unavailability need not be due to the declarant dying as a result of the circumstances which lead to the making of the statement (as outlined above), he must be either dead or otherwise unavailable at the time of the trial as defined in Article 804(A) for the exception to apply.

Must believe death is imminent. An important element of this exception is that the statement must have been made while the declarant believed his death was imminent. This is a **subjective requirement** that is essential to the reliability and trustworthiness of the statement. It is only when the declarant truly believes his death is imminent that he is most likely to be compelled to tell the truth.[224] It is not sufficient that he believe he will die *soon* or *someday* as in the case of a person suffering from a terminal disease who has been told he has six months to live.[225] The declarant must effectively believe that he is in the process of dying *then*, as he makes the statement.

The question of whether the declarant believed his death was imminent is a question for the trial judge to determine.[226] In making the determination, the judge may consider all facts and circumstances surrounding the making of the statement, including: the declarant's own words, the nature of wounds, others present, the time between the wound and injury,[227] the opinion of a physician,[228] or any other factors that suggest that the declarant "has abandoned all hope or expectation of recovery."[229]

Thus, a person who has just been shot, lying in blood, in severe pain, coupled with comments such as, "*I don't think I'm gonna make it*," "*tell my family I love them*," or simply, "*I think I'm dying*," will likely lead to a finding that the person believed his death was imminent. However, making a statement such as, "*Looks like we're gonna have to postpone our camping trip a couple of weeks*," would likely show a person did not believe his death was imminent.

---

224. 4 Weinstein's Evidence, ¶ 804(b)(2)[01] at 804-124 to 804-125 (1993).

225. *See* Trascher v. Territo, 89 So. 3d 357 (La. 2012) (court excluded a deposition made by a declarant that was scheduled to perpetuate witness's testimony who had been told he had six months to live).

226. La. Code Evid. art. 104.

227. State v. Winn, 705 So. 2d 1271 (La. Ct. App. 4th Cir. 1998).

228. State v. Martin, 562 So. 2d 468 (La. Ct. App. 5th Cir. 1990).

229. State v. Unger, 362 So. 2d 1095, 1098 (La. 1978).

Concerning cause or circumstances of death. The second requirement of the exception deals with the "content" of the statement. The exception only includes statements concerning the cause or circumstances about what the declarant believed to be his impending death. Generally, if a person is dying, information regarding "the **person**, **motive**, or **mechanism** which made up the '**cause or circumstances**' "[230] of the impending death is what generally satisfies the "content requirement"[231] of the rule. Thus, the statement, "*John shot me for the insurance money*," which includes the name (*John*), the motive (*for the insurance money*) and the mechanism (*gunshot*), would generally satisfy the requirement.

However, if a person who has been shot makes statements regarding how to deal with his affairs ("*Cremate my body*"), his feelings about loved ones ("*Tell my wife I love her*"), or all of his regrets in life ("*I wish I'd finished college*"), those statements will not conform to the content requirement of the exception. While such statements would assist the judge in determining that the person believed his death was imminent, such statements do not relate to the cause and circumstances of what he believed to be his impending death and would therefore not conform to the rule.

In relating the information, any adequate form of communication is generally sufficient, whether it be words, signals, or handwritten notes. The declarant could even nod his head in response to leading questions.

First-hand knowledge required. The declarant's statement must concern facts about which he has first-hand knowledge, facts that he either saw or heard himself.[232] While he may give an opinion, mere expressions of conjecture or suspicion will be excluded.

Suicide notes. Suicide notes generally are not held to be dying declarations because at the time the note is written the declarant's death is not imminent in that the mortal wound has not been inflicted. Additionally, the time and reflection of writing the note removes the spontaneity and consequent reliability and trustworthiness of a statement made *after* the mortal wound has been unexpectedly inflicted. It is the spontaneity and lack of time for reflection and fabrication, upon which many of the exceptions are based, that are simply not present with suicide notes. The Louisiana Supreme Court thoroughly addressed the admissibility of suicide notes under this exception in *Garza v. Delta Tau Delta*.[233]

Case on Dying Declarations

In section 5.7.4 we examined the Louisiana Supreme Court's analysis of the admissibility of a suicide note in *Garza v. Delta Tau Delta (I)* under the "then existing mental condition" exception to the hearsay rule in Article 803(3). *Garza II* below continues the court's analysis of the suicide note under the dying declaration exception to the hearsay rule. As you read the case, consider the court's discussion of the historical underpinnings of the rule. Do you think the reasoning and rationale exist in the context of a suicide note? Be prepared to explain why you believe suicide notes either should or should not be admitted under the dying declaration exception.

230. Garza v. Delta Tau Delta Fraternity National, 948 So. 2d 84 (La. 2006).
231. *Id.*
232. *See* LA. CODE EVID. art. 804(B) Official Comment to Introductory Clause.
233. Garza v. Delta Tau Delta Fraternity National, 948 So. 2d 84 (La. 2006).

Garza v. Delta Tau Delta Fraternity National (II)

Supreme Court of Louisiana
948 So. 2d 84
July 10, 2006

WEIMER, Justice.

This matter arises from a tragic death by suicide. Thomas Garza, Sr., and Sandra Garza, along with their son, Thomas Garza, Jr., the parents and brother of the decedent, filed suit against various defendants for the wrongful death4 of Courtney Garza, on April 9, 2001. On that date, Courtney, a 21-year-old college student at Southeastern Louisiana University (SLU) in Hammond, Louisiana, took her own life by hanging at her parents' home in Baton Rouge. Prior to the suicide, Courtney authored a handwritten letter.

. . .

The sole issue presented for our determination is whether the suicide note in question is admissible in evidence as an exception to the hearsay rule as codified in the Louisiana Code of Evidence enacted in 1988.

. . .

Dying declaration:

. . .

[The] admissibility of a dying declaration depends upon the physical circumstances in which the dying declaration was made and whether the statement was made under the sense of impending or imminent death.

The exception at issue, commonly called the "dying declaration exception," is provided in La. C.E. art. 804(B):

> (2) Statement under belief of impending death. A statement made by a declarant while believing that his death was imminent, concerning the cause or circumstances of what he believed to be his impending death.

The provision requires that the person seeking to have the declarant's statement introduced into evidence satisfy the court of two factors, sometimes referred to as the timing requirement and the content requirement15: 1) that the declarant believed his death was imminent/impending16; and 2) that the declarant's statement concerned the cause or circumstances of the impending death. A declaration, whether oral or written, that fails to meet either the timing or the content requirement of a dying declaration is inadmissible. *Angleton*, 269 F.Supp.2d at 886.

A court's decision regarding the first factor, timing, rests on an evaluation of the declarant's subjective experience, *i.e.,* what the declarant believed and not necessarily what others knew about his medical condition. In contrast, a court's decision regarding the second factor, content, rests on an evaluation of the objective facts related in the statement concerning the empirical cause and circumstances of the declarant's death. The declarant's *subjective* belief in the impending nature of his death is what is considered to assure the truth of his statement of the *objective* facts about the person, motive, or mechanism which made up the "cause or circumstances" of the impending death. "The pivotal question should be the declarant's belief as to his physical condition, not what it actually was." McNamara, 22 La.L.Rev. at 655. "The actual physical condition of the declarant at the time the statement was made is material and relevant insofar as it casts light on the state of mind of the declarant.... [T]he wider the disparity between the declarant's apparent belief of his approaching doom and his actual physical condition, the less probable it is that he actually believed the end was near." *Id., citing State v. Augustus,* 129 La. 617, 56 So. 551 (1911) (Declarant's belief in the reality of his impending death was a "mere mental operation"; his statement—"I have been shot to death by Isidore for nothing"—was a recitation of observable facts concerning the person (Isidore), motive (nothing), and mechanism (shooting) of his impending death.)

Our research has not shown a departure from this court's holding in *Augustus* that belief in impending death be corroborated by evidence of empirical circumstances, such as a serious wound or illness, at the time the declaration was made.17 Code of Evidence provisions are consistent with this court's pronouncements in *Augustus.* "The amount of time that elapses between the injury and the victim's statement and the victim's circumstances during that interval are important factors in determining whether a court may infer that a witness made the statement under the belief of impending death."18 HANDBOOK 2006, 2006 Authors' Notes (6) at 612. Explicit in this statement is that the injury precedes the declaration and not vice versa, as is the case where a suicide note is penned some time prior to a hanging. In the instant case, there was no "amount of time" between the injury and the declaration during which Courtney's "circumstances" could significantly produce a sufficient motive to tell the truth, because the declaration preceded the fatal injury, hanging.

Historically in Louisiana, a theological belief in a future state of rewards and punishment was not a prerequisite to the admissibility of a dying declaration. Also, secular motives such as hatred or revenge on the part of the declarant did not prevent admission of the dying declaration. McNamara, 22 La.L.Rev. at 662. The rule for admitting a dying declaration was and is intended to allow a declaration by a person who is faced with an unexpected, mortal injury and cast by circumstances into a premature realization of certain death. The rule is in conflict when the declarant takes her own life. When the wrongful death sued upon is inflicted by the declarant herself, her statement that death is imminent is merely self-serving and lacking in any recognized motivation to tell the truth. Citing *Augustus, supra,* this court has established a test for determining whether a declarant's statement was made with a sense of impending death: "[T]he more serious the injury and impairment of the declarant's physical condition, the more probable is his belief that the end is near." *State v. Verrett,* 419 So.2d 455, 457 (La.1982).

The very nature of death by hanging prevents the application of this test in determining the admissibility of a suicide note, as there is no physical injury or impairment at the time the declaration is made. Thus, a caveat from over a century ago is particularly pertinent: a dying declaration "must be received with the utmost caution, and if the circumstances do not satisfactorily disclose that the awful and solemn situation in which [declarant] is placed is realized" by the declarant, the evidence ought to be rejected. *Mattox,* 146 U.S. at 152, 13 S.Ct. at 54.

Although a declarant is seriously ill for a time prior to her eventual death, not all communications made while ill or depressed are admissible under the dying declaration exception. *See Shepard v. United States,* 290 U.S. 96, 54 S.Ct. 22, 78 L.Ed. 196 (1933). The mere fact that death follows a statement does not render it admissible. Death must be imminent when the statement is made.[234] When, as in the instant case, the deadly trauma

234. The lack of impending death at the time an alleged dying declaration was made resulted in a reversal of a conviction for murder in *Shepard.* The defendant was charged with murdering his wife by poison. The wife first collapsed on May 20, 1929, and rallied two days later at which time she told her nurse that her husband had poisoned her. A week after her statement, the victim relapsed and ul-

(hanging) was inflicted subsequent to the declaration, the mortality of an injury could not have been understood or realized by the decedent. The realization of immediate death must be present when the statement is made. The likelihood of death, the awareness of eventual death, or the intention to eventually inflict death on one's self is not enough to place the declarant in the elevated sense of solemnity envisioned by the jurisprudence or the relevant codal provision. In *Shepard*, 290 U.S. at 99, 54 S.Ct. at 23, Justice Cardozo specified an "indispensable condition" of admission of a dying declaration was that "the declarant must have spoken without hope of recovery and in the shadow of impending death." The court noted that nothing in the condition of the declarant on the date of the statement gave "fair support to the conclusion that hope had then been lost. She may have thought she was going to die and have said so to her nurse, but this was consistent with hope, which could not have been put aside without more to quench it." *Id.*, 290 U.S. at 99, 54 S.Ct. at 24.

> Fear or even belief that illness will end in death will not avail of itself to make a dying declaration. There must be a settled hopeless expectation that death is near at hand, and what is said must have been spoken in the hush of its impending presence.... What is decisive is the state of mind ... [which] must be exhibited in the evidence, and not left to conjecture. The [declarant] must have spoken with the consciousness of a swift and certain doom. [Citations and internal quotation marks omitted.]

Shepard, 290 U.S. at 100, 54 S.Ct. at 24.

The control a declarant has over her fate distinguishes a suicide note from the true dying declaration, which the courts have elevated to the level of sworn testimony in the eyes of the law. Because a suicide note is a planned statement made in anticipation of a controlled act, it is not analogous to a dying declaration made under the belief of impending death by a person with a total lack of control over the timing and causation of death. *See* dissent in *State v. Satterfield*, 193 W.Va. 503, 457 S.E.2d 440, 455–456 (1995). A person intent on committing suicide retains the ability to draft a statement to her liking, defeating the assumed truthfulness the law attributes to true dying declarations when all cause for untruthfulness is presumed to have been eliminated by impending death. The motivation of one penning a suicide note differs from the motivation of someone unexpectedly facing imminent death. "The writer of a suicide note might have a motive to implicate another other than the truth.... A declarant who has decided to commit suicide would have no fear, perhaps other than religious convictions ... of punishment for ... the falsity of the note." *State v. Hodge*, 655 S.W.2d 738, 743 (Mo.App.1983).

The desire for revenge or self-exoneration may continue until the moment of death. 5 Jack B. Weinstein & Margaret A. Berger, Weinstein's Federal Evidence, § 804.05[1] at 804–49 (Joseph M. McLaughlin ed., 2d 2006). In her suicide note, Courtney stated she had not told her parents about the events recounted in the note for fear they would blame her. Thus, her accusations of others contained in the note are tainted with possible motives of self-exoneration. *See Angleton*, 269 F.Supp.2d at 883. The suggestion has been made that the dying declaration exception should not apply to suicide notes because of delusional feelings of appeasement related to suicide and characteristic feelings of aggression and guilt associated with the act. Note, *The Judicial Interpretation of Suicide*,

---

timately died on June 15, 1929. The lower courts allowed the wife's declaration to her nurse to be admitted into evidence at the husband's trial. The United States Supreme Court reversed the conviction on the ground that the facts and circumstances surrounding the wife's declaration did not support the conclusion that she made the statement while experiencing a sense of impending death.

105 U.Pa.L.Rev. 391, 405–406 (1957). When the declaration precedes the mortal wound, the decedent's motivation is at best questionable, a condition that robs the statement of the reliability derived from belief in an impending death. Further, the aspect of control involved in an intended death lessens the spontaneity that is important in a dying declaration exception. *Angleton*, 269 F.Supp.2d at 885; *see also, Garza*, 04–1484 at 1, 916 So.2d at 190 (McDonald, J., dissenting).

Our research of jurisprudence nationwide has revealed only one reported case, *Satterfield*, 193 W.Va. 503, 457 S.E.2d 440, that allowed admission of a suicide note as a dying declaration exception to the hearsay rule, and the majority opinion drew a vigorous dissent. Further, the facts and circumstances of *Satterfield* make it substantially distinguishable from this case.

In *Satterfield*, the court admitted a suicide note under West Virginia's dying declaration rule that mirrored the federal rule. The author of the note had been a witness in a murder trial who was "aggressively questioned" at trial in a way that implied his participation in the murder. Prior to the reopening of court the following day, the witness committed suicide. He left a note proclaiming his innocence and stating that he could not take the pressure of going through a trial. The court found the double requirements of the dying declaration exception were satisfied: the decedent wrote the note believing his death was imminent because the suicide occurred soon after the note was written, and the note explained the suicide.

Although the majority opinion in *Satterfield* discussed the dying declaration exception to the hearsay rule, the purpose for which the suicide note was admitted in that homicide case was not to prove the fact of the homicide or who committed the homicide, but to respond to the defendant's allegations implicating the declarant as the person who had actually committed the homicide. The *Satterfield* suicide note itself differs significantly from Courtney's letter, because the *Satterfield* note did not point a finger at anyone; it merely attempted to exonerate the declarant, who was not on trial. Further, the note was not used as proof of the facts contained therein, but as a response to the questioning in court of the declarant.

The final distinction, that the declarant had already been subjected to cross-examination under oath in court in the same case in which the note was admitted into evidence, is the most significant. That opportunity—to cross examine the witness and to have the witness available for the jury's scrutiny—would not be available if Courtney's note is admitted into evidence in the instant case.

All of the cases that discuss the dying declaration exception require evidence of the declarant's perception of imminent death at the time the statement was made. The declarant's belief in impending death may be inferred from the types of wounds inflicted and the nature of the decedent's injuries. *Mattox*, 146 U.S. at 152, 13 S.Ct. at 54. Statements such as this imply that the mortal wound must precede the declaration and not vice versa, when a suicide note is written prior to the act of hanging one's self.

The vigorous dissent in *Satterfield* stated some poignant concerns. The declarant was in complete control of the timing and circumstances of his death. Thus, there is a significant difference between a suicide note and a statement made by a person facing inevitable death due to circumstances beyond his control. The dissent stated a suicide note is a "perfect opportunity to rewrite one's own history in a way calculated to impress one's final audience." *Satterfield*, 193 W.Va. at 519, 457 S.E.2d at 456.

In the instant case, Judge McDonald's analysis is consistent with the dissent in *Satterfield* and consistent with Louisiana jurisprudence that has considered the admissibility of hearsay because a statement qualifies as a dying declaration. In comparison to the instant case, the facts and circumstances of *Satterfield* are so substantially different that the case cannot be considered as support for the decisions of the lower courts in this matter.

In summation, we find that the suicide note does not meet the qualifications of a statement under belief of impending death pursuant to La. C.E. art. 804(B)(2). The article provides that the statement be made at a time when the declarant was "believing that [her] death was imminent"; that is, believing in an "impending death." The use of the words "imminent" and "impending" militate against allowing the use of a suicide note which was written before the mortal wound was inflicted. "Impending" and "imminent" are words which require that a mortal wound or injury be inflicted at the time of the statement. The very act of writing the note militates against spontaneity. Courts have consistently assessed the physical condition of the declarant at the time the declaration was made, and the declarant's belief that she will not survive the injury. The decisions previously cited almost uniformly involved the factual situation in which the mortal injury had been inflicted prior to the statement.

After reviewing the words of the statute in light of the long line of jurisprudence addressing the dying declaration, we conclude it is the declarant's actual physical condition which must be evaluated to determine if it was possible for her to believe death was imminent. In this matter, at the time the note was written, the declarant was not dying; the mortal wound had not been inflicted. As such, death was not imminent or impending as those words are used in the article. Absent a mortal wound at the time of the statement, the statement lacked the "circumstantial probability of trustworthiness" required for admission as a dying declaration. McNamara, 22 La.L.Rev. at 654.

Additionally, it is undisputed that Courtney's death occurred some months after the alleged rape. The temporal element of her declaration relates to a determination of whether Courtney penned the letter at a time when she believed death was imminent/impending. Traditionally, a dying declaration was limited to the facts and circumstances constituting the *res gestae* of the decedent's fatal injury. *Lucas v. Commonwealth,* 153 Ky. 424, 155 S.W. 721, 722–723 (1913); *see also,* discussion of this requirement at 2 MCCORMICK ON EVIDENCE § 311 at 330 (John W. Strong ed., 4th ed. 1992) ("[D]eclarations [were] admissible only insofar as they relate[d] to the circumstances of the killing and to the events more or less nearly preceding it in time and leading up to it.").

Having found that the plaintiffs failed to carry their burden of proving the timing requirement of the statute, it is unnecessary for us to address whether they proved the content requirement. *See* text at footnote 14. However, we do note that the wording of La. C.E. art. 804(B)(2) that restricts the content of the dying declaration to the "cause or circumstances" of the impending death has been evaluated as "generally sound because the connection between these circumstances and the statement helps to enhance its trustworthiness by reducing the dangers of poor memory and insincerity." 2 MCCORMICK ON EVIDENCE § 315 at 334. A declaration that does not meet one of the two requirements of the exception for a statement under belief of impending death is inadmissible pursuant to the hearsay rule. *Angleton,* 269 F.Supp.2d at 886.

The suicide note in the instant case is hearsay. Admitting it into evidence would result in a statement made by someone who was not sworn to tell the truth, who faced no responsibility for falsification, who could not be observed by the fact finder, and who was not subject to cross-examination. *See Donnelly,* 228 U.S. at 273, 33 S.Ct. at 459.

In our analysis of Article 804(B)(2), we have interpreted the language used by the legislature while keeping in mind the admonishment of the legislature barring judicial creation of exceptions to the hearsay rule. *See* La. C.E. art. 802. Thus, we hold the lower courts erred in classifying the suicide note in this case as a dying declaration.

...

DECREE

Because the portions of the suicide note presently in question do not qualify as an exception to the hearsay rule pursuant to La. C.E. art. 804(B)(2) or art. 803(3), the suicide note is inadmissible hearsay, requiring the reversal of the lower courts' rulings.

JUDGMENT REVERSED; MATTER REMANDED.

Discussion Questions

1. The court gives several reasons as to why the mortal wound must be inflicted prior to the statement for it to be deemed reliable—the spontaneity of a statement made after a wound is unexpectedly inflicted, lack of control, and lack of time for reflection and fabrication, among other reasons. Do you think it matters as to when the mortal wound is inflicted in evaluating the reliability of a statement? Why?
2. Consider some of the issues surrounding suicide notes that tend to make them less trustworthy: lacks spontaneity, not unexpected, planned statement, planned controlled act, and time for reflection and fabrication. Do these or any other reasons tend to make suicide notes inherently unreliable?
3. The fact that a person has "no motivation to lie" is often referred to as a basis of reliability for this exception. However, the Louisiana Supreme Court notes that there are in fact reasons a person might lie in a suicide note, observing that such notes are a "perfect opportunity to rewrite one's own history in a way calculated to impress one's final audience" and that it has the potential to be "self-serving" as in Courtney wanting to "shift blame" to someone else for her actions. Do you believe a person has a motive to lie when dying? In other words, would the desire to leave a great name and legacy behind be a compelling reason to lie in a suicide note?
4. The court points out that the "test for determining whether a declarant's statement was made with a sense of impending death" is: "[T]he more serious the injury and impairment of the declarant's physical condition, the more probable is his belief that the end is near." Citing *State v. Verrett*, 419 So. 2d 455, 457 (La.1982). Is it possible to apply this test when, at the time of writing a suicide note, there is no physical injury or impairment?
5. What effect does the fact that the note is not directly related to the cause and circumstances of Courtney's death have on the admissibility of the note? Here, the cause of Courtney's death was hanging, however, the note mostly related to factors that may have motivated her to commit such an act but were not the direct cause of her death. How far does such a connection reach between the direct cause of death and the facts and circumstances possibly leading to such an act? Do you find this element is met?

Key Points

The key points to keep in mind regarding the dying declaration exception.

1. Statements under belief of impending death exclude statements from the hearsay rule if made by a declarant while believing that his death was imminent, when the statements are concerning the cause or circumstances of what he believed to be his impending death.

2. **Requirements**:
    a. declarant is unavailable;
    b. the declarant believes his death is imminent (whether or not he actually dies); and
    c. the statement concerns the cause or circumstances of what he believed to be his impending death.
3. Declarant must believe death is imminent.
    a. **Factors to determine if person believed death was imminent**: the declarant's own words, the nature of his wounds, whether others present, the time between the wound and injury, the opinion of a physician, or any other factors that suggest that the declarant "has abandoned all hope or expectation of recovery."
4. Statement must relate to cause and circumstances surrounding what he believed to be his impending death. Cause and circumstances must generally relate to the ***person, mode, or mechanism.***
5. Statements may be in words, hand signals, writing, or nodding in response to questions.
6. **First-hand knowledge** about which the person speaks. Cannot be mere speculation, conjecture, or speculation.
7. **Suicide notes**—generally not included in this exception because ***death not imminent*** since at the time of statement, the mortal wound has not been inflicted; writing the note removes the spontaneity and consequent reliability and trustworthiness of a statement made *after* the mortal wound has been unexpectedly inflicted; there is time for reflection and fabrication.

Problems on Dying Declaration

PROBLEM 5-136. Shortly after being shot in the chest by his pregnant wife, Dan managed to crawl through a pool of blood clutching his chest to his cell phone and called 911. When the ambulance arrives, Dan says to one of EMTs, "*Make sure my son knows that I already loved him.*" Dan dies in the hospital. Does the statement conform to the dying declaration exception?

Would your answer change if instead Dan had said to his wife in the presence of the EMT, "*Baby, once our son is born, we can't handle our disputes with violence. You can't just threaten me with a gun and shoot.*" Dan dies an hour later. Admissible?

PROBLEM 5-137. Sam's wife is on trial for murdering him. An autopsy revealed that he died from ingesting small doses of antifreeze over time, which eventually killed him. Sam commonly consumed food from various sources daily—his secretary often made his coffee, he had a mistress at whose house he usually ate a couple times per week, and of course he often ate at home. One evening his wife comes home and finds Sam dead in their bed. It was later discovered that before Sam died, he called his mistress and stated, "*My stomach has never hurt me so bad in my life. My wife must have poisoned me. She must be having an affair.*" The prosecution offers the statement against Sam's wife at her trial. Wife objects that the statement is hearsay. Will any portion of Sam's statement be admissible under the dying declaration exception?

PROBLEM 5-138. David arrived at the hospital unresponsive and covered in blood as a result of a gunshot wound through his lower chest. He was considered to be in critical condition. Although he had a pulse, he was not breathing well on his own. After he was resuscitated, his condition improved significantly, and he was taken to surgery about an hour and a half later. Prior to surgery, the victim was questioned by officers concerning his knowledge of who had shot him. Speaking through an oxygen mask and struggling as he spoke, the victim identified the defendant as the perpetrator and the color of his car. The victim was aware that he was going to surgery. During surgery, the victim's heart stopped beating. Victim died during surgery. At defendant's trial, the State sought to admit the statement through the police officer as a dying declaration. The defense objects that there was no showing that at the time the statement was made that the victim believed his death was imminent. How would you respond? *State v. Lucas*, 99-1524 (La. App. 1 Cir. 5/12/00), 762 So. 2d 717.

PROBLEM 5-139. Trevor was riding his motorcycle on the highway one late night when he was struck by a drunk driver and tossed 30 feet into the air before landing on the ground on his head, immediately breaking his neck. The driver of the vehicle kept going. Another driver stopped to assist Trevor. He ran over to him and while calling 911, Trevor stated, "*It was a black Tahoe. Tinted windows. He never tried to stop.*" Trevor then closed his eyes and died. When the state police arrived about 20 minutes later to investigate the accident, the driver told them what Trevor said about the black Tahoe. Meanwhile, an intoxicated man driving a black Tahoe with a large dent in the fender was stopped about five miles away from the accident. He was arrested. At his trial for vehicular homicide, the prosecution sought to introduce the statement made by Trevor through the state police officer as they were unable to locate the good Samaritan who stopped to help Trevor. The defense objects. What ruling and why? Would your answer change if the good Samaritan had been located and testified to what Trevor said? Why or why not?

PROBLEM 5-140. Wes was a key prosecution witness in a double homicide. After being called as a witness in the trial, he was aggressively questioned under cross-examination for more than nine hours in a way that suggested his participation in the murder. At the end of the day, the court recessed for the day, and Wes was scheduled to continue his testimony the next day. That night Wes committed suicide. In a suicide note, Wes stated that he could not go through more of the trial and cross-examination. He proclaimed his innocence and reiterated, "*Everything I said on the stand is true! He did it! He killed those two poor innocent girls! I had nothing to do with it!*" The defense objects to the admissibility of the suicide note. How should the court rule and why? (*See State v. Satterfield*, 193 W. Va. 503, 457 S.E. 2d 440.)

PROBLEM 5-141. Bubba brutally raped Victoria, then slit her neck and dumped her naked body on side of the road. Unbeknownst to Bubba, Victoria was not dead but lied limp to avoid more torture and abuse. After lying there for hours, a truck driver in an 18-wheeler came along and saw Victoria on side of the road. He called 911 without getting out of the truck, "*Looks like a dead naked woman out here on I65N near the 115 mile marker.*" The driver never stopped. His identity was never discovered. When the EMTs arrived, they asked Victoria who attacked her. She was unable to speak, so they asked her a series of questions at the scene, in the ambulance, and at the hospital before she was taken into surgery. "*Do you know your attacker? Was he a man? Was he white? Was he black? Was he short? Was he tall?*" etc. Victoria shook her head either yes or no to each question, and the information led to Bubba's arrest. Miraculously, Victoria recovered and is doing fine. During the trial, as Victoria sat in the back of the courtroom watching (being the victim), the lead investigator testified to Victoria's answers to the questions to help prove that it was in fact the defendant who committed the crime. The defense objects that the exchange is hearsay and inadmissible.

A) Should Victoria's responses to the investigator's questions be admissible as dying declarations? Explain.

B) Assume that the next morning the investigator also brought a photo line-up to the hospital to show to Victoria and she selected Bubba. Should the officer be able to testify to whom Victoria identified as a dying declaration?

C) Would your answer change if instead of fully recovering, Victoria was permanently unable to speak due to the injury to her throat? Why or why not?

D) Should the truck driver's statement be admissible under *any* exception to the hearsay rule?

PROBLEM 5-142. Collette was originally misdiagnosed by her doctor for more than six months while she repeatedly complained of chest pains, coughing, and bloody mucus. Additional testing showed that Collette had stage four lung cancer and she was told that she had only 4 months to live. Collette told her husband, "*I repeatedly told him to check for lung cancer because my dad died from lung cancer, but he would not do it. I told him I was coughing up blood, but he did nothing.*" Collette died two months later. Her husband sued the doctor. At the trial the husband sought to testify about what Collette told her doctor about her symptoms and requests to check for cancer to help prove his negligence in misdiagnosing Collette. The defense objected that the statements were hearsay. Does the statement conform to the dying declaration exception?

§ 5.16 References and Additional Authority on Dying Declaration [La. C.E. art. 804(B)(2)]

1. La. C.E. art. 804(B)(2) and Official Comments
2. Force & Rault, HANDBOOK ON LOUISIANA EVIDENCE LAW Art. 804(B)(2) Author's Comments (West Publishing 2014)
3. Harges & Jones, LOUISIANA EVIDENCE Art. 804(B)(2) Author's Comments (West Publishing 2014)
4. 19 La. Civ. L. Treatise, Evidence And Proof § 10.9 (2nd ed.)
5. MCCORMICK ON EVIDENCE § 309 (5th ed., 1999)
6. **Commentary**: Rose, Stephen, "*Can a Suicide Victim Be Taken At Her Word: The Louisiana Supreme Court Declares a Suicide Note Inadmissible Hearsay in Garza v. Delta Tau Delta Fraternity National*," 81 Tul. L. Rev. 1715 (2007).
7. **Statements admitted as dying declarations Article 804(B)(2):** *State v. Ramirez*, 30 So. 3d 833 (La. Ct. App. 5th Cir. 2009) (holding that statement of a 94-year-old victim telling the first responding police officer that a white female attacked her was admissible as a dying declaration given the victim's age and physical condition, as well as the fact that the victim's son saw the victim on her knees praying, even though victim died more than three weeks after incident); *State v. Bell*, 721 So. 2d 38 (La. Ct. App. 5th Cir. 1998) (holding that victim's statement was a dying declaration when facts showed that the victim was in fact aware of his condition because when the paramedic arrived, the victim was stating, "help me, help me" while rocking back and forth; the paramedic also stated that the victim's heart rate and blood pressure were low).
8. **No belief of impending death:** *Trascher v. Territo*, 89 So. 3d 357 (La. 2012) (holding that Mr. Trascher's deposition could not be admitted as a statement under belief of im-

pending death because at the time of the deposition, while Mr. Trascher had been told that he had six months to live, his death was not imminent or immediate; in this case, the declarant believed that his deposition would be continued at a later time); *State v. Winn*, 705 So. 2d 1271 (La. Ct. App. 4th Cir. 1998) (holding that because the prosecution made no attempt to show that the victim believed that her death was imminent, the victim's statement was inadmissible as a dying declaration).

9. **Not related to cause/circumstances:** *State v. Garner*, 47 So. 3d 584 (La. Ct. App. 2d Cir. 2010) (holding that the statement made by the victim saying the name Eric to the paramedic while on the way to the hospital was inadmissible under the dying declaration exception because there was no evidence that the statement related to the victim's cause of death).

§ 5.17 Statement Against Interest [La. C.E. art. 804(B)(3)]

Applicable Code Articles

* * *

B. Hearsay exceptions. The following are not excluded by the hearsay rule if the declarant is unavailable as a witness:

* * *

(3) Statement against interest. A statement which was at the time of its making so far contrary to the declarant's pecuniary or proprietary interest, or so far tended to subject him to civil or criminal liability, or to render invalid a claim by him against another, that a reasonable man in his position would not have made the statement unless he believed it to be true. A statement tending to expose the declarant to criminal liability and offered to exculpate the accused is not admissible unless corroborating circumstances clearly indicate the trustworthiness of the statement.

* * *

In this section we will cover the exception to the hearsay rule for statements against the declarant's interest, which is contained in Article 804(B)(3). The statement against interest exception excludes from the hearsay rule statements that are so far contrary to the declarant's pecuniary, proprietary, or other interests, or that might subject him to civil or criminal liability, that it is unlikely that the person would have made the statement unless it were true. The exception is deemed reliable because of the presumption that a reasonable person would not ordinarily lie to his own disadvantage.[235] So statements like, "*I'm sorry, you gave me too much change back*," or "*The accident was my fault. I was sending a text message*," are deemed trustworthy—and because there's also an element of necessity for the statement since the declarant is unavailable, such statements are excluded from the hearsay rule.

Keep in mind, though, that should the court find that the declarant likely had a motive to lie, or that the statement is nonetheless unreliable, the statement should still be excluded.[236]

235. Force & Rault, Handbook, Art. 804(B)(3) Author's Comment (3).

236. *See* State v. Adams, 550 So. 2d 595 (La. 1989); State v. Dabney, 633 So. 2d 1360 (La. Ct. App. 4th Cir. 1994).

Requirements for a Statement Against Interest

1. declarant is unavailable; and
2. against the declarant's interest *(when made)*; ***and sometimes***
3. corroborating circumstances of trustworthiness **if** it is an incriminating statement that exculpates a third party.

Requirements for statements against interest. The exception has two basic requirements: 1) unavailable declarant; and 2) against the declarant's interest (when made).

In some instances there is a third requirement. If a declarant makes an incriminating statement, that exculpates a third party, the article requires that there must be corroborating circumstances that indicate the statement is trustworthy.

Scope and applicability. This exception applies in both civil and criminal trials, and like all Article 804 exceptions, requires a preliminary finding by the court that the declarant is unavailable to testify at the trial. Additionally, other requirements for admissibility must also be present. The declarant must have first-hand knowledge[237] of the information of which he spoke, the statement must be relevant, and it must not be unfairly prejudicial under the Article 403 balancing test.[238]

Types of Statements Against Interest

The key element for this exception is that the statement must be against the declarant's interest at the time the statement is made. The determination of whether a statement qualifies as a statement against interest is a question for the trial court to determine considering all of the facts and circumstances surrounding the making of the statement. The types of disserving ("against interest") statements covered by the rule are broad, and generally includes the following types of statements:

1. ***A statement against the declarant's pecuniary (financial) interests.*** A statement against a declarant's pecuniary interest would affect his financial interest. For example, the statements, "*No I didn't drop that $10 bill*," or "*I think my trade-in is worth less than book value*," would both be against the declarant's financial or pecuniary interest because they are against a financial gain that he might otherwise receive. Another example would be, "*I forgot to pay you. I still owe you the $40 for the work that you did.*"

2. ***A statement against his proprietary (property) interests.*** A statement against the declarant's proprietary interest would affect his interest in property. For example, the statement, "*Our home is community property*," affects the declarant's proprietary interests because the declarant is claiming that half of the property is owned by his spouse, rather than the entire piece of property being owned by him alone.

3. ***A statement that might subject the declarant to civil liability.*** A statement is also against a declarant's interest if it could subject him to civil liability. For example, the statements, "*I was texting when I ran into the back of your car*" or "*I may have had a few too many drinks tonight*," made after an accident would subject the declarant to civil liability because the statements could be used against him in a civil case to prove that he was neg-

237. La. Code Evid. art. 804(B)(3) Official Comment .
238. Force & Rault, Handbook, Art. 804(B)(3) Author's Comment (5).

ligent in operating his vehicle. Additionally, a statement would be against a declarant business owner's interest, if after a patron tripped over a broken step and fractured her hip while coming into the business, he stated, "*I knew I should have replaced that broken step after the last lady fell.*" The statement would show that the declarant had knowledge of a dangerous condition, yet failed to repair it, subjecting himself to civil liability.

4. *A statement that might subject the declarant to criminal liability.* A statement that could subject a declarant to criminal liability is also included in the exception. The statements commonly include confessions of a declarant of participation in criminal conduct such as, "*Yes, I killed my neighbor.*" To be included in the exception, a statement need not be a full confession. An admission to an element, such as "*I held the gun*," or "*I drove the getaway car*," could also subject the declarant to criminal liability.

5. *A statement that could render a claim that the declarant has against another person invalid.* If a person has a claim against her boss for sexual harassment, the statement "*My boss did not sexually harass me*," would render the claim invalid. Thus, such a statement is against the declarant's interest.

Statement must be against interest when made and with knowledge. To conform to the exception, the declarant's statement must be against the declarant's interest **at the time the statement is made.**[239] It is not sufficient that the statement *later* becomes against a declarant's interest. For example, if a guy at a bar tells the bartender that he's done drinking for the night because he's had a few too many to drink, the statement is not against his interest because simply being intoxicated is not a crime, nor does it subject the declarant to civil liability or is it otherwise against his interest. If the declarant is later stopped that night by a police officer for driving while intoxicated, and tells the police officer that he's had a few too many, then the statement is against his interest because it would subject him to criminal liability because driving while intoxicated is a crime. If the statement is not against the declarant's interest *when made*, then the reliability is not present.

Similarly, the declarant must be aware that his statement is against his interest when he makes it. For example, suppose the declarant states to his co-workers, "I went for a drive last night and found myself over in Bob's neighborhood." After making the statement they inform the declarant that Bob was found dead that morning to his surprise. Since the declarant did not know that Bob had been found dead when he placed himself near the scene of the crime, the statement was not against his interest. The rule presumes a person would not *knowingly* lie to his disadvantage. But if the person does not know that the statement is to his disadvantage, then the reliability of the rule is not present.

Additionally, these statements may be made to anyone—cellmate, friend, family member, or stranger. There is no requirement that the statement be made to law enforcement.

Special Circumstances in Determining "Against Interest"

In some instances, it can be difficult to determine if a statement is truly against the declarant's interest because some statements may have both self-serving as well as disserving aspects.[240] Additionally, some statements may do more to shift blame to another than to incriminate oneself, yet in other situations, a statement may incriminate oneself while completely exculpating another for clearly improper motives.

239. *See* State v. Gilmore, 332 So. 2d 789 (La. 1976); *See also* Force & Rault, Handbook, Art. 804(B)(3) Author's Comment (4).
240. *See* Force & Rault, Handbook, Art. 804(B)(6) Author's Comment (4).

For purposes of this exception, let's consider these four scenarios of different types of statements that might be made by a declarant regarding the commission of a crime:

1. *"I did it."*
2. *"I did this part, but I did not do that part."*
3. *"I did it, and he helped me do it."*
4. *"I did it, and he didn't do anything."*

"I did it." In the first scenario, "*I did it,*" the entire statement is clearly inculpatory and can easily be deemed a statement against the declarant's interest, as outlined above.

"I did this part, but I did not do that part." In the second scenario, "*I did this part, but I did not do that part,*" the statement contains both a self-serving (exculpatory) component and a disserving (inculpatory) component. In determining whether the statement is in fact against the declarant's interest, the court will try to determine which motivation predominated,[241] and the statement is deemed against the declarant's interest only if the **disserving aspect predominates**. For example, the court has held that the statement, "*I didn't hit her intentionally,*" was designed to protect the declarant's pecuniary and proprietary interest and was therefore not against the declarant's interest.[242] This statement was clearly more exculpatory than incriminating since although the declarant admits to committing the offense, he denies the key element required for liability—"intent." Thus a statement that contains both self-serving and disserving components, "*I supplied the weapon, but I didn't shoot the gun,*" will only conform to the exception if the disserving aspect predominates.

***"I did it, and he helped me do it"*—Interlocking Statements.** The third scenario, "*I did it, and he helped me do it,*" contains an inculpatory statement, but also implicates a third party. This is referred to as an "interlocking statement." In this situation, the U.S. Supreme Court in *Williamson v. United States*,[243] discussed below, has held that in such a situation, only the part of the statement against the declarant's own interest should be admissible, and not the portion implicating the third party. The Court reasons that the fact that the portion implicating the declarant is in close proximity to a statement implicating a third party, does not make the third party implications any more reliable. In fact, the Court notes, "[o]ne of the most effective ways to lie is to mix falsehood with truth."[244] The Louisiana Supreme Court has also adopted this reasoning in *State v. Smith*[245] and has held that when a statement implicates the declarant as well as a third party, the portion implicating the third party is not reliable and should not be included under this exception.

It is also important to briefly note here, that in situations in which the declarant and the third-party codefendant he implicates are being jointly tried, use of the statement against the declarant would violate the third party's confrontation rights if the declarant chooses not to testify. The jury would no doubt consider the statement against both defendants, yet the third-party codefendant would be unable to cross-examine the declarant implicating him. In such a case, the U.S. Supreme Court has held that the portions of

241. *Id.*
242. *See* Holt v. Phipps, 733 So.2d 693, (La. Ct. App. 3d Cir. 1999).
243. Williamson v. United States, 512 U.S. 594, 114 S.Ct. 2431 (1994) .
244. Williamson v. United States, 512 U.S. 594, 114 S.Ct. 2431, 2435 (1994).
245. State v. Smith, 643 So. 2d 1221 (La. 1994); State v. Lucky, 755 So. 2d 845 (La. 1999); State v. Coates, 661 So. 2d 571 (La. Ct. App. 2d Cir. 1995); State v. Anthony, 695 So. 2d 1142 (La. Ct. App. 3d Cir. 1997); See also the discussion in Force & Rault, HANDBOOK, Art. 804(B)(3) Author's Comment (7).

the statement implicating the third-party defendant would have to be redacted if possible, or the parties would have to be severed for separate trials.[246] A limiting instruction to the jury that the statement only be considered against the declarant is insufficient.

***"I did it, and he didn't do anything"* (Incriminating statements offered to exculpate a third party accused).** In the forth scenario, *"I did it, and he didn't do anything,"* the declarant not only incriminates himself, but also seeks to fully exculpate a third party. It is not uncommon for a declarant who has nothing to lose, for example, who is already serving a life sentence or who may be dying, to take full responsibility for a crime to exculpate a third party family member, friend, or other associate. Because of the inherent unreliability of this type of scenario, Article 804(B)(3) requires an additional element to admit the statement. In such a case, there must be **corroborating circumstances that clearly indicate the trustworthiness of the statement**. Absent trustworthy corroborating evidence that it was in fact the declarant who is responsible for the crime for which he implicates himself and exculpates the third party, the declarant's statement will not be admitted in a criminal case to exculpate an accused.[247] The factors the court will consider in determining the reliability of the statement include:

1. Motive to misrepresent
2. Whether statement made spontaneously
3. Timing of declaration
4. Relationship between parties
5. Relationship between witness and accused
6. General character of the witness
7. Whether other people heard the out-of-court statement
8. Whether made voluntarily after *Miranda*
9. Whether made to curry favor with authorities[248]

Confrontation Clause. Because statements against interest are so often utilized in criminal trials, they can raise serious issues regarding a defendant's Sixth Amendment rights under the Confrontation Clause. As a result, many of these statements may be excluded under the Confrontation Clause even though they may conform to the exception because they are often testimonial. It is important to keep in mind the Sixth Amendment requirements under *Crawford* when analyzing such statements which require that a testimonial statement from an unavailable declarant may only be offered against an accused (who is not the declarant) if he has had a prior opportunity to cross-examine the declarant on the out-of-court statement.

Similarity to Admissions found in Article 801(D)(1). In Part D, § 5.22–§ 5.24 infra, we will study exemptions to the hearsay rule contained in Article 801(D)(2) and (3), which are statements that are *defined* as not being hearsay, also referred herein as "Statutory Non-Hearsay."[249] One type of statement exempted from the hearsay rule is "admissions." Admissions are briefly discussed here because they are often confused with statements against interest and in some instances this exception is mistakenly referred to as an "ad-

246. *See* Bruton v. United States, 391 U.S. 123, 88 S.Ct. 1620 (1968).

247. *See* State v. Watts, 835 So. 2d 441 (La. 2003).

248. *See* United States v. Jackson, 540 F.3d 578, 589 (7th Cir. 2008); *See also* United States v. One Star, 979 F.2d 1319, 1322 (8th Cir. 1992).

249. *See* Chapter 5, Part D, *infra.*

mission against interest." To avoid confusion, such a designation is strongly discouraged.[250] However, in some cases, the two articles do in fact overlap. For example, if the prosecution offers a defendant's confession against him in a criminal trial, the statement likely conforms to the requirements of both an admission and a statement against interest. The statement is against a declarant's interest because it subjects him to criminal liability. It is also an admission. An admission is a statement offered against a party and is a party's own statement in his personal or representative capacity. Since the defendant is a party to the action and the statement is offered against him, it will also qualify as an admission.

However, there are four distinct differences in the two types of statements: 1) statements against interest do not require that the declarant be a party in the action, as in the case of admissions; 2) a statement against interest need not be offered *against* the declarant, as in the case of admissions; 3) an admission need not be a statement against the declarant's interest, but instead can be "any" statement made by a party that is being offered against him; and 4) a statement against interest requires that the declarant be unavailable for admissibility, whereas availability is immaterial with respect to an admission.

We will discuss the differences in greater detail after we have covered admissions in § 5.23, *infra*, but for now it is important that you understand that there are distinct differences between the two articles.

Cases on Statement Against Interest

As stated above, quite often a statement that contains inculpatory components may also contain exculpatory components, and may even implicate third parties, often shifting the majority of the blame to the other person. This does not pose a significant problem when the declarant's own statement is offered against *him*. Such statements are admissions and are generally admissible in their entirety absent being excluded on other grounds.[251] However, when a statement against the declarant's interest is offered against a third party accused, a potential problem exists. The courts must ensure that the statement is in fact against the declarant's interest, and does not do more to implicate the third party accused than to implicate himself, if the statement is to be deemed to have any indicators of trustworthiness. *Williamson* is an important case because the United States Supreme Court gives guidance on how to determine whether a statement is against a declarant's interest in such a scenario and how to handle the admissibility of such statements offered against a third party implicated in the statement.

Williamson v. United States

Supreme Court of the United States
114 S.Ct. 2431
June 27, 1994

Justice O'CONNOR delivered the opinion of the Court ...

In this case we clarify the scope of the hearsay exception for statements against penal interest. Fed. Rule Evid. 804(b)(3).

---

250. *See also* discussion in Force & Rault, Handbook, Art. 804(B)(3) Author's Comment (4).

251. Statements offered against a party that are his own statements in his personal or representative capacity are exempt from the hearsay ban in Articles 801(D)(2) and (3), which are covered in Sec. 5.23, *infra*. In a criminal case, a statement may be excluded from being offered against a defendant if obtained in violation of his Fifth Amendment Privilege Against Self-Incrimination.

I

A deputy sheriff stopped the rental car driven by Reginald Harris for weaving on the highway. Harris consented to a search of the car, which revealed 19 kilograms of cocaine in two suitcases in the trunk. Harris was promptly arrested.

Shortly after Harris' arrest, Special Agent Donald Walton of the Drug Enforcement Administration (DEA) interviewed him by telephone. During that conversation, Harris said that he got the cocaine from an unidentified Cuban in Fort Lauderdale; that the cocaine belonged to petitioner Williamson; and that it was to be delivered that night to a particular dumpster. Williamson was also connected to Harris by physical evidence: The luggage bore the initials of Williamson's sister, Williamson was listed as an additional driver on the car rental agreement, and an envelope addressed to Williamson and a receipt with Williamson's girlfriend's address were found in the glove compartment.

Several hours later, Agent Walton spoke to Harris in person. During that interview, Harris said he had rented the car a few days earlier and had driven it to Fort Lauderdale to meet Williamson. According to Harris, he had gotten the cocaine from a Cuban who was Williamson's acquaintance, and the Cuban had put the cocaine in the car with a note telling Harris how to deliver the drugs. Harris repeated that he had been instructed to leave the drugs in a certain dumpster, to return to his car, and to leave without waiting for anyone to pick up the drugs.

Agent Walton then took steps to arrange a controlled delivery of the cocaine. But as Walton was preparing to leave the interview room, Harris "got out of [his] chair ... and ... took a half step toward [Walton] ... and ... said, ... 'I can't let you do that,' threw his hands up and said 'that's not true, I can't let you go up there for no reason.'" App. 40. Harris told Walton he had lied about the Cuban, the note, and the dumpster. The real story, Harris said, was that he was transporting the cocaine to Atlanta for Williamson, and that Williamson was traveling in front of him in another rental car. Harris added that after his car was stopped, Williamson turned around and drove past the location of the stop, where he could see Harris' car with its trunk open. *Ibid.* Because Williamson had apparently seen the police searching the car, Harris explained that it would be impossible to make a controlled delivery. *Id.*, at 41.

Harris told Walton that he had lied about the source of the drugs because he was afraid of Williamson. *Id.*, at 61, 68; see also *id.*, at 30–31. Though Harris freely implicated himself, he did not want his story to be recorded, and he refused to sign a written version of the statement. *Id.*, at 24–25. Walton testified that he had promised to report any co-operation by Harris to the Assistant United States Attorney. Walton said Harris was not promised any reward or other benefit for cooperating. *Id.*, at 25–26.

Williamson was eventually convicted of possessing cocaine with intent to distribute, conspiring to possess cocaine with intent to distribute, and traveling interstate to promote the distribution of cocaine, 21 U.S.C. §§ 841(a)(1), 846; 18 U.S.C. § 1952. When called to testify at Williamson's trial, Harris refused, even though the prosecution gave him use immunity and the court ordered him to testify and eventually held him in contempt. The District Court then ruled that, under Rule 804(b)(3), Agent Walton could relate what Harris had said to him:

> "The ruling of the Court is that the statements ... are admissible under [Rule 804(b)(3)], which deals with statements against interest.
>
> "First, defendant Harris' statements clearly implicated himself, and therefore, are against his penal interest.

"Second, defendant Harris, the declarant, is unavailable.

"And third, as I found yesterday, there are sufficient corroborating circumstances in this case to ensure the trustworthiness of his testimony. Therefore, under [*United States v. Harrell,* 788 F.2d 1524 (CA11 1986)], these statements by defendant Harris implicating [Williamson] are admissible." App. 51–52.

Williamson appealed his conviction, claiming that the admission of Harris' statements violated Rule 804(b)(3) and the Confrontation Clause of the Sixth Amendment....

II A

The hearsay rule, Fed. Rule Evid. 802, is premised on the theory that out-of-court statements are subject to particular hazards. The declarant might be lying; he might have misperceived the events that he relates; he might have faulty memory; his words might be misunderstood or taken out of context by the listener. And the ways in which these dangers are minimized for in-court statements—the oath, the witness' awareness of the gravity of the proceedings, the jury's ability to observe the witness' demeanor, and, most importantly, the right of the opponent to cross-examine—are generally absent for things said out of court.

Nonetheless, the Federal Rules of Evidence also recognize that some kinds of out-of-court statements are less subject to these hearsay dangers, and therefore except them from the general rule that hearsay is inadmissible. One such category covers statements that are against the declarant's interest:

> "statement[s] which ... at the time of [their] making ... so far tended to subject the declarant to ... criminal liability ... that a reasonable person in the declarant's position would not have made the statement[s] unless believing [them] to be true." Fed. Rule Evid. 804(b)(3).

To decide whether Harris' confession is made admissible by Rule 804(b)(3), we must first determine what the Rule means by "statement," which Federal Rule of Evidence 801(a)(1) defines as "an oral or written assertion." One possible meaning, "a report or narrative," Webster's Third New International Dictionary 2229, defn. 2(a) (1961), connotes an extended declaration. Under this reading, Harris' entire confession—even if it contains both self-inculpatory and non-self-inculpatory parts—would be admissible so long as in the aggregate the confession sufficiently inculpates him. Another meaning of "statement," "a single declaration or remark," *ibid.,* defn. 2(b), would make Rule 804(b)(3) cover only those declarations or remarks within the confession that are individually self-inculpatory. See also *id.,* at 131 (defining "assertion" as a "declaration"); *id.,* at 586 (defining "declaration" as a "statement").

Although the text of the Rule does not directly resolve the matter, the principle behind the Rule, so far as it is discernible from the text, points clearly to the narrower reading. Rule 804(b)(3) is founded on the commonsense notion that reasonable people, even reasonable people who are not especially honest, tend not to make self-inculpatory statements unless they believe them to be true. This notion simply does not extend to the broader definition of "statement." The fact that a person is making a broadly self-inculpatory confession does not make more credible the confession's non-self-inculpatory parts. One of the most effective ways to lie is to mix falsehood with truth, especially truth that seems particularly persuasive because of its self-inculpatory nature.

In this respect, it is telling that the non-self-inculpatory things Harris said in his first statement actually proved to be false, as Harris himself admitted during the second interrogation. And when part of the confession is actually self-exculpatory, the generalization on which Rule 804(b)(3) is founded becomes even less applicable. Self-exculpatory statements are exactly the ones which people are most likely to make even when they are false; and mere proximity to other, self-inculpatory, statements does not increase the plausibility of the self-exculpatory statements....

Congress certainly could, subject to the constraints of the Confrontation Clause, make statements admissible based on their proximity to self-inculpatory statements. But we will not lightly assume that the ambiguous language means anything so inconsistent with the Rule's underlying theory.... In our view, the most faithful reading of Rule 804(b)(3) is that it does not allow admission of non-self-inculpatory statements, even if they are made within a broader narrative that is generally self-inculpatory. The district court may not just assume for purposes of Rule 804(b)(3) that a statement is self-inculpatory because it is part of a fuller confession, and this is especially true when the statement implicates someone else. "[T]he arrest statements of a codefendant have traditionally been viewed with special suspicion. Due to his strong motivation to implicate the defendant and to exonerate himself, a codefendant's statements about what the defendant said or did are less credible than ordinary hearsay evidence." ...

"... [A]dmit[ting] the disserving parts of the declaration, and exclud[ing] the self-serving parts ... seems the most realistic method of adjusting admissibility to trustworthiness, where the serving and disserving parts can be severed." See C. McCormick, Law of Evidence §256, pp. 552–553 (1954) (footnotes omitted)....

[W]e conclude that the policy expressed in the Rule's text points clearly enough in one direction that it outweighs whatever force the Notes may have. And though Justice KENNEDY believes that the text can fairly be read as expressing a policy of admitting collateral statements, *post,* at 2442, for the reasons given above we disagree.

B

We also do not share Justice KENNEDY's fears that our reading of the Rule "eviscerate[s] the against penal interest exception," *post,* at 2443 (internal quotation marks omitted), or makes it lack "meaningful effect," *ibid.* There are many circumstances in which Rule 804(b)(3) does allow the admission of statements that inculpate a criminal defendant. Even the confessions of arrested accomplices may be admissible if they are truly self-inculpatory, rather than merely attempts to shift blame or curry favor.

For instance, a declarant's squarely self-inculpatory confession—"yes, I killed X"—will likely be admissible under Rule 804(b)(3) against accomplices of his who are being tried under a co-conspirator liability theory.... Likewise, by showing that the declarant knew something, a self-inculpatory statement can in some situations help the jury infer that his confederates knew it as well. And when seen with other evidence, an accomplice's self-inculpatory statement can inculpate the defendant directly: "I was robbing the bank on Friday morning," coupled with someone's testimony that the declarant and the defendant drove off together Friday morning, is evidence that the defendant also participated in the robbery.

Moreover, whether a statement is self-inculpatory or not can only be determined by viewing it in context. Even statements that are on their face neutral may actually be against the declarant's interest. "I hid the gun in Joe's apartment" may not be a confession of a crime; but if it is likely to help the police find the murder weapon, then it is certainly self-inculpatory. "Sam and I went to Joe's house" might be against the declarant's interest if a reasonable person in the declarant's shoes would realize that being linked to Joe and Sam would implicate the declarant in Joe and Sam's conspiracy. And other statements that give the police significant details about the crime may also, depending on the situation, be against the declarant's interest. The question under Rule 804(b)(3) is always whether the statement was sufficiently against the declarant's penal interest "that a reasonable person in the declarant's position would not have made the statement unless believing it to be true," and this question can only be answered in light of all the surrounding circumstances.[252]

C

In this case, however, we cannot conclude that all that Harris said was properly admitted. Some of Harris' confession would clearly have been admissible under Rule 804(b)(3); for instance, when he said he knew there was cocaine in the suitcase, he essentially forfeited his only possible defense to a charge of cocaine possession, lack of knowledge. But other parts of his confession, especially the parts that implicated Williamson, did little to subject Harris himself to criminal liability. A reasonable person in Harris' position might even think that implicating someone else would decrease his practical exposure to criminal liability, at least so far as sentencing goes. Small fish in a big conspiracy often get shorter sentences than people who are running the whole show, ... especially if the small fish are willing to help the authorities catch the big ones....

Nothing in the record shows that the District Court or the Court of Appeals inquired whether each of the statements in Harris' confession was truly self-inculpatory. As we explained above, this can be a fact-intensive inquiry, which would require careful examination of all the circumstances surrounding the criminal activity involved; we therefore remand to the Court of Appeals to conduct this inquiry in the first instance.

... The judgment of the Court of Appeals is vacated, and the case is remanded for further proceedings. *So ordered.*

Justice SCALIA, concurring.

Justice GINSBURG, with whom Justice BLACKMUN, Justice STEVENS, and Justice SOUTER join, concurring in part and concurring in the judgment.

Justice KENNEDY, with whom THE CHIEF JUSTICE and Justice THOMAS join, concurring in the judgment.

Discussion Questions

1. The Court gives a test for determining whether a statement is sufficiently against a declarant's penal interest—"whether a reasonable person in the declarant's position would not have made the statement unless believing it to be true." The court concluded that Harris' statement ultimately failed in this respect. Taken as a whole, does Harris' statement do more to inculpate him or to reduce his potential criminal liability? Explain. Keep in mind that Harris was caught red-handed.
2. Taking this test a step further, what, if any, additional factors should a court consider in determining whether a reasonable person would have made the statement unless it were true? What guidance would you offer?
3. Do you agree with the court that portions of a statement that are exculpatory should be excluded, even when made in connection with inculpatory statements? What reasoning does the court give for this conclusion? What additional reasoning or rationale do you believe supports this decision?
4. How significant is the context in which a statement is made? Even statements that are on their face neutral may actually be against the declarant's interest when considered

252. Of course, an accomplice's statements may also be admissible under other provisions of Rules 801–804. For instance, statements made in furtherance of the conspiracy may be admissible under Rule 801(d)(2)(E), and other statements that bear circumstantial guarantees of trustworthiness may be admissible under Rule 804(b)(5), the catchall hearsay exception.

in their context. The court gives examples of such statements. What are some of the examples? Can you think of additional examples?

In *State v. Smith* below, the Louisiana Supreme Court indicated that Louisiana courts should follow the United States Supreme Court reasoning in *Williamson* in interpreting Article 803(B)(3).

State v. Smith

Supreme Court of Louisiana
643 So. 2d 1221
Oct. 7, 1994

PER CURIAM.

The district court's decision to admit only a redacted version of Lavalais's videotaped confession to the police in 1992 at trial, omitting direct inculpation of relator, is reinstated. The statement did not advance the objectives of the alleged 1985 conspiracy to murder relator's wife but brought the illegal agreement to the attention of the authorities. The statement is therefore not admissible against relator under the co-conspirator exception to the hearsay rule. La.C.E. art. 801(D)(3)(b). Moreover, to the extent that it directly implicates relator in the death of his wife, the statement is presumptively unreliable in the absence of extraordinary circumstances not revealed by the present record.... The court ruled properly that Lavalais's self-inculpatory admissions in the videotaped confession constituted statements against *his* interest for purposes of La.C.E. art. 804(B)(3). *See Williamson v. United States*, 512 U.S. 594, 114 S.Ct. 2431, 129 L.Ed.2d 476 (1994). Provided that they are properly redacted to omit direct mention of relator, those statements are admissible against relator at a trial based on a co-conspirator theory of liability, as tending to prove that Lavalais accomplished the objective of the conspiracy. *Id.*, at ___, 114 S.Ct. at 2436.

The district court's ruling admitting in their entirety Lavalais's statements to his uncle shortly after commission of the offense is reversed. As with Lavalais's subsequent videotaped confession, these statements did not advance the objectives of the alleged conspiracy and are therefore not admissible under the co-conspirator exception to the hearsay rule in La.C.E. art. 801(D)(3)(b). The district court should reconsider the admissibility of the statements, either in their entirety or redacted to omit direct mention of relator, in light of La.C.E. art. 804(B)(3) and *Williamson v. United States.*

The district court's decision to admit the entirety of the letter written by relator to Lavalais but never delivered to him is reversed. The contents of the letter represent the admissions of a party opponent under La.C.E. art. 801(D)(2)(a), but the court should excise references to other crimes as to which evidence is not admissible. La.C.E. art. 1103; La.C.Cr.P. art. 770(2).

In all other respects, the applications are denied.

Discussion Questions

1. What suggestions does the Louisiana Supreme Court give to the lower court as to how to handle statements made against Lavalais' interest that implicate the relator? They specifically suggest that the court revisit the admissibility of the statement in light of *Williamson*. As such, how should the issue be handled?
2. What is the significance of the court noting that the statements do not advance a conspiracy? If the court were to find that the statements did in fact advance a conspiracy

between Lavalais and the relator, what effect would that finding have on the admissibility of the statement?

Key Points

The key points to keep in mind regarding statements against interest.

1. Excludes from the hearsay ban statements that are so contrary to the person's ***pecuniary*** interests, ***propriety*** interests, or that might ***subject him to civil or criminal liability***, or ***render a claim*** he has against another ***invalid***, that a reasonable person would not have made the statement unless the statement were true.
2. **Two basic requirements:**
   1) unavailable declarant; and
   2) against the declarant's interest (when made); ***and in some instances***
   3) declarant makes an incriminating statement, that exculpates a third party, there must be corroborating circumstances that indicate the statement is trustworthy
3. Applies both in civil and criminal trials.
4. **First-hand knowledge** of information of which the declarant spoke.
5. Must be against interest ***when made*** and declarant must know that statement is against interest when he makes it.
6. May be made to anyone, at any time. Need not be made to law enforcement.
7. **Inculpates Declarant/Exculpates Declarant.** When a statement contains both an inculpatory (disserving) aspect and an exculpatory (self-serving) aspect, the court must determine **which aspect predominates**. The statement is against interest only if the disserving aspect predominates.
8. **Inculpates Declarant/Inculpates 3rd Party (Interlocking Statements).** If statement implicates the declarant as well as a third party, only the part implicating the declarant is trustworthy and admissible.
   a. If defendants are on trial together, *Burton* requires that the cases be severed to use the statement against the declarant. A limiting instruction is insufficient.
9. **Inculpates Declarant/Exculpates 3rd Party.** When a statement is offered that implicates the declarant and is offered to exculpate a third party (the accused), the statement must have corroborating circumstances of trustworthiness.

   Factors to consider trustworthiness: motive to misrepresent; whether statement made spontaneously; time of declaration; relationship between the parties; relationship between the witness and accused; general character of the witness; whether other people heard the out-of-court statement; whether made voluntary after Miranda; whether made to curry favor with authorities.
10. **Confrontation Clause Issues**: Since such statements are usually testimonial, admitting it against an accused (other than the declarant) could violate accused's Confrontation Clause rights under Sixth Amendment unless the accused had a prior opportunity to cross-examination the declarant on the statement under *Crawford*.

Problems on Statement Against Interest

PROBLEM 5-143. Dixie ran into the back of Pippa's car. At the time of the accident, Peppa (Pippa's sister) was a passenger in Pippa's car. Pippa sued Dixie for negligently causing the car accident by running into her rear end. To defend herself, Dixie will call the police officer who will testify that while questioning Peppa alone following the accident, Peppa stated that she and Pippa were taking selfies at the time the accident occurred. Dixie called Peppa to the stand, but she refused to testify to what she said to the police even after being threatened to be held in contempt of court. Dixie then calls the police officer who will testify to what Peppa told him. Pippa objects that Peppa's statement is hearsay and should not be admitted. How should the court rule and why?

PROBLEM 5-144. Phyllis is suing her law school for wrongful expulsion after being accused of cheating with Ruby on her final examination. Phyllis and Ruby both had the exact same answers on their final exam, and were brought before the honor code committee to determine who had cheated and how they would be punished. Both were expelled. After being expelled, Ruby moved to West Africa to help out with the AIDS epidemic. At trial, Phyllis would like to call Shelia to testify that following the exam, Ruby left the classroom and stated to Shelia, "*I'm glad I was sitting next to Phyllis. I copied off of her paper during the exam. I'm just not getting this stuff.*" The school objected that Ruby's statement to Shelia was hearsay and should be excluded. Should the statement be admitted? Why or why not?

PROBLEM 5-145. Dillon is on trial for aggravated battery and claims self-defense. He claims he shot the victim after the victim shot him in the leg first because he believed he'd be shot again. Once the police were able to speak with the victim at the hospital after he came out of surgery, he stated "*I really didn't know the gun was gonna go off. I was just playing around with it and pretending to shoot Dillon to scare him with it and the gun went off and hit him in the leg. I was pointing it at him, but I didn't know it had bullets in it.*" By the time Dillon's case goes to trial, the victim has left the country and cannot be located. The prosecution would like to offer the victim's statement he made to the police to show Dillon's motive for shooting the victim. They claim that although Dillon was shot, he used excessive force in defending himself. The defense objects that the statement is hearsay. Does the statement comply with the requirements of the statement against interest exception to the hearsay rule? Why or why not?

PROBLEM 5-146. Big-T was charged with first-degree murder for killing a rival gang member. Big-T would like to offer the testimony of this mother who will testify that the morning after the murder, her baby Big-T told her what he'd done the night before stating, "*I had to shoot a dude last night when he tried to jack me.*" Should the statement be admitted under the "statement against interest" exception? Why or why not?

PROBLEM 5-147. Omarion and Kendall were arrested for the aggravated kidnapping of a 12-year-old girl, who they sexually assaulted several times while she was in their custody. Omarion stated that Kendall came to pick him up and told him that he wanted to abduct a girl. He says he rode with Kendall past a middle school and watched Kendall offer the victim a ride home. He says Kendall drove him and the victim to an old house in the county where they repeatedly raped her for three days before she escaped. Omarion stated that he never felt very comfortable about the situation and wanted to let her go long before she escaped. Kendall did not make a statement at all. In Kendall's trial, Omarion refused to testify asserting his Fifth Amendment privilege against self-incrimination, so the prosecution would like to offer Omarion's statement against Kendall. Can any portion of Omarion's statement be offered against Kendall in his trial? Which part? Why? Explain.

PROBLEM 5-148. Shane was serving two consecutive life sentences for killing his entire family. Shortly after he was arrested, his brother was also arrested for raping a young girl in their neighborhood. Shane wrote a letter to the prosecutor handling his brother's case and told her that he was the one who'd raped the little girl and that his brother had nothing to do with it. At brother's trial, he sought to admit the letter that Shane had written to the prosecutor to prove that it was his brother and not him who had committed the rape. The prosecution objected that the letter was hearsay. How should the court rule on the objection and why?

PROBLEM 5-149. Graham was shot and killed at work by a disgruntled coworker. David and Edward were the only two people present at the time of the shooting. Both were charged with a conspiracy to kill Graham and murder. They were tried separately. In David's trial, he seeks to offer a statement made by Edward a week before the murder where Edward tells him that he has purchased a new 9mm handgun. The bullet that was recovered from the victim was ammunition for a 9mm handgun. Edward refuses to testify, asserting his Fifth Amendment privilege against self-incrimination. The prosecution objects that the statement is hearsay. What ruling and why?

PROBLEM 5-150. Peter is a driver for Knight Time Trucking. He is involved in an accident where he hit Pedestrian in the crosswalk. Pedestrian sues Knight Time Trucking. Knight will call Emily to testify that immediately after the accident Peter tells her that now he'll never get Worker's Compensation because of instead of finishing his deliveries for the day, he was rushing to spend the afternoon with his mistress when he hit Pedestrian. Knight wants to prove that Peter was not engaged in the course of employment when the accident occurred. Afraid he could face personal liability, Peter leaves town and can't be found. Pedestrian objects that Peter's statement is hearsay. What ruling?

PROBLEM 5-151. After being diagnosed with terminal cancer, Lamar decided he wanted to go out with a bang in the few short months he had left to live. He solicited his son Lawrence and both went on a bank robbery spree across the state and went on the run with the money. One night, while son Lawrence was out getting beer, police burst into the motel room where the guys were staying and arrested Lamar. Lamar immediately confessed, taking full responsibility for the crime, and stated that his son didn't know anything about the robberies and was never with him when any of the robberies were committed. When Lawrence arrived back from the store, he was also arrested, but said nothing. Lamar was tried first, and was swiftly found guilty as charged of 11 counts of armed robbery. By the time Lawrence's case goes to trial, Lamar has already succumbed to the cancer. Lawrence seeks to use the statement that his father Lamar made to the police officers when he was arrested in his defense to help prove his innocence. The prosecution objected that the statement was hearsay. What ruling?

§ 5.17 References and Additional Authority on Statement Against Interest [La. C.E. art. 804(B)(3)]

1. La. C.E. art. 804(B)(3) and Official Comments
2. Force & Rault, Handbook on Louisiana Evidence Law Art. 804(B)(3) Author's Comments (West Publishing 2014)
3. Harges & Jones, Louisiana Evidence Art. 804(B)(3) Author's Comments (West Publishing 2014)

4. 19 La. Civ. L. Treatise, Evidence And Proof § 10.8 (2nd ed.)

5. **Statement Against Interest Article 804(B)(3):** *State v. Aulph*, 114 So. 3d 610 (La. Ct. App. 2d Cir. 2013) (holding that a statement by defendant to his mother that he had gotten into some trouble was admissible as a statement against his interest); *State v. Moore*, 57 So. 3d 1033 (La. Ct. App. 4th Cir. 2010) (allowing the taped statement of the defendant's former codefendant into evidence as a statement against interest after the codefendant refused to testify and was declared unavailable).

6. **Statements not admitted as statement against interest:** *State v. Jackson*, 726 So. 2d 1061 (La. Ct. App. 2d Cir. 1999) (holding that the accomplice's statements regarding the robbery, although they were against his proprietary interest, were not admissible under statements against interest to the hearsay rule because the accomplice was not unavailable at the time of the trial).

7. **Interlocking:** *State v. Smith*, 643 So. 2d 1221 (La. 1994) (holding that although the statement made by the coconspirator was inadmissible under the coconspirator exception to the hearsay rule, the court should allow the statement under the statement against interest exception to the hearsay rule); *State v. Lucky*, 755 So. 2d 845 (La. 1999) (The defendant argued that a statement that his accomplice made to the police should be inadmissible hearsay. As stated in *Williamson*, the only part of an accomplice's statement that should be admitted is the inculpatory part. The court ruled that the statement was inadmissible under this exception or any other exception because the was insufficient inculpatory evidence.); *State v. Coates*, 661 So. 2d 571 (La. Ct. App. 2d Cir. 1995) (The defendant argued that the lower court improperly admitted statements against him made by the co-defendant and violated his right to confront the co-defendant under the Sixth Amendment Confrontation Clause. The court ruled that this case was analogous to *Williamson* and that only the part inculpating the co-defendant should have been admitted.); *State v. Anthony*, 695 So. 2d 1142 (La. Ct. App. 3d Cir. 1997) (holding that the lower court improperly allowed Lewis's confession into evidence because some portions of Lewis's confession inculpated the defendant; the court reiterated that only the portions of the confession that implicated Lewis were admissible).

8. **Corroborating circumstances to prove trustworthiness:** *State v. Kyles*, 705 So. 2d 740 (La. 1998) (holding that the defense has the burden of proving the corroborating circumstances to the matter asserted); *State v. Bailey*, 875 So. 2d 949 (La. Ct. App. 5th Cir. 2004) (Declarant stated that the drugs in question belonged to her and not the defendant. The court ruled that the statement was inadmissible because there were no corroborating circumstances.); *State v. Watts*, 835 So. 2d 441 (La. 2003) (About a year after the defendant's trial, the declarant admitted to killing the victim. The corroborating circumstances were that the declarant had more knowledge of how the victim ended up on her knees, physical evidence, as well as another witness's testimony. Therefore, the statement was admissible under the statement against interest exception to the hearsay rule.).

9. **Not truly disserving:** *State v. Fogelman*, 98 So. 3d 964 (La. Ct. App. 3d Cir. 2012) (Defendant attempted to offer a statement two months after he no longer had criminal troubles as a statement against interest. The court ruled that at the time the defendant made the statement, it was not contrary to the defendant's penal interest. Therefore, the statement was inadmissible as a statement against interest because it was not truly disserving.).

§ 5.18 Family History [La. C.E. art. 804(B)(4)]

Applicable Code Articles

* * *

B. Hearsay exceptions. The following are not excluded by the hearsay rule if the declarant is unavailable as a witness:

* * *

(4) Statement of personal or family history. (a) A statement, made before the controversy, concerning the declarant's own birth, adoption, marriage, divorce, filiation, relationship by blood, adoption, or marriage, ancestry, or other similar fact of personal or family history, even though declarant had no means of acquiring personal knowledge of the matter stated; or

(b) A statement, made before the controversy, concerning the foregoing matters, and death also, of another person, if the declarant was related to the other by blood, adoption, or marriage or was so intimately associated with the other's family as to be likely to have accurate information concerning the matter declared.

* * *

Article 804(B)(4) contains an exception to the hearsay rule for statements of a person's family history, e.g., statements regarding births, adoption, marriage, divorce, relationship by blood, marriage, or adoption, ancestry, or other similar fact of personal or family history. The exception applies to statements of a person's *own* family history (*"I was adopted"*) to statements by a declarant regarding the family history (and death) of a person *related to* the declarant (*"My little sister was adopted"*), as well as to statements regarding family history made by a person *so intimately associated with the family* that the information declared is likely to be accurate. For example, the family physician might state, *"They had four little girls, then finally adopted a son."*

The family history exception includes the following requirements:

1. declarant unavailable; ***and***
2. statement made *before* the controversy began; ***and***
3. ***either***
    a. regarding the declarant's own personal or family history; ***or***
    b. regarding the personal or family history (*including death*) of another person, related to the declarant; ***or***
    c. regarding the personal or family history (including death) of another person who was close enough to family to have accurate information.

No first-hand knowledge requirement. There is no requirement that the declarant have first-hand knowledge of the information about which he speaks for this exception to apply.[253] Even when a person testifies to his own birth date or the fact that he was adopted at birth, he has no first-hand knowledge of the information since he obviously

253. Force & Rault, HANDBOOK, Art. 804(B)(4) Author's Comment (3).

Requirements for Family History Exception

1. declarant unavailable; ***and***
2. statement made *before* the controversy began; ***and***
3) ***either:***
   a. regarding the *declarant's own* personal or family history—ancestry, or other personal or family history; ***or***
   b. regarding the personal or family history (*including death*) of *another person*, related to the declarant; ***or***
   c. regarding the personal or family history (including death) of another person who was *close enough to family* to have accurate information.

cannot remember. But because such information is the type of information that is usually reported accurately, it is thus deemed reliable even without first-hand knowledge. Additionally, there is usually a necessity for the information, since the declarant is unavailable and there would be no other way of obtaining the information.[254]

Statement made prior to the controversy. Contrary to the federal rules, the statement in question must have been made prior to the controversy in question.[255]

Must lay foundation to establish relationship. To admit a statement from a declarant about the family history of another based solely on his close relationship to the family (rather than relationship by blood, adoptions, etc.), the proponent must lay sufficient foundation to establish the close familial type of relationship between the declarant and the person or family he speaks of.[256] Individuals that might have accurate information about the family history of another might include the family physician, attorney, a long-time neighbor, or family friend.[257]

Distinguish from reputation of family history Article 803(19) and family records Article 803(13). This exception should not be confused with Article 803(19), which allows a witness to testify to the general *reputation* in the community of a person's family history arising *before* the controversy. There, it is immaterial whether the person(s) who may have communicated the reputation information to the witness (the declarant) is available or not to testify. The exception in this article, Article 804(B)(4), includes statements by a declarant about his own, a relative's, or close family friend's family history, when the declarant is no longer available to testify to the statement himself.

Another closely related exception that we covered in § 5.13 is Article 803(13), which excludes *records* of family history that are contained in Bibles, inscriptions, engravings, charts, genealogies, family portraits, urns, crypts, or tombstones, or the like from the hearsay ban. The records of family history exception also does not require that the declarant be unavailable to testify personally nor does it require that the "record have been *made ante litem motam* (before the controversy arose)."[258]

---

254. La. Code Evid. art. 804(B)(4) Official Comment.
255. La. Code Evid. art. 804(B)(4) Official Comment.
256. Force & Rault, Handbook, Art. 804(B)(4) Author's Comment (2).
257. *See* Harges & Jones, Art. 804(B)(4), Author's Comments.
258. Force & Rault, Handbook, Art. 803(13) Author's Comment (b).

Thus, Article 803(13) pertains to *records* of family history, Article 803(19) pertains to *reputation* of family history, and this provision, Article 804(B)(9), pertains to *statements* of a person's family history.

Key Points

The key points to keep in mind regarding the family history.

1. Excludes statements of personal family history from the hearsay rule.
2. The exception includes the following requirements:
   a. declarant unavailable; ***and***
   b. statement made *before* the controversy began; ***and***
   c. ***either***
      1. regarding the declarant's own personal or family history-ancestry, or other personal or family history; ***or***
      2. regarding the personal or family history *(including death)* of another person, related to the declarant; ***or***
      3. regarding the personal or family history (including death) of another person who was close enough to family to have accurate information.
3. No first-hand knowledge requirement.
4. Must establish proper foundation to show how third party witness has the relationship necessary to testify to the family history at issue.

Problems on Family History

PROBLEM 5-152. Phyllis and Minnie's mother Carrie passed away without a will and a dispute arose over who her heirs were. Minnie is now senile. Shay, Minnie's daughter, testified that from the time she was a little girl her mother Minnie had always told her that although she (Minnie) and Phyllis had been raised as sisters by Carrie, Phyllis was actually adopted, but she had not ever been legally adopted by Carrie, making Phyllis the only legal heir to Carrie's estate. Should Shay be able to testify to what her mother Minnie told her about their family history at trial? Why or why not?

PROBLEM 5-153. The Thompson and Hewitt families lived next door to one another in the outskirts of town for over 40 years. They both had small farms. The two young couples were very close and over the years had been there for the births of all of the other's children, eight kids in the Thompson family, and seven kids in the Hewitt family. While the kids were growing up, Mrs. Thompson introduced little 3-year-old Timothy to Mrs. Hewitt one day and explained that he had come to live with them because his mother, a distant cousin, was killed in an automobile accident. Timothy never knew that the other Thompson kids were not his sisters and brothers. Some forty years later, after the Thompsons had passed away, the kids called Mrs. Hewitt to testify in a dispute over their assets as to how Timothy came to live with them and that he was not their sibling. Timothy objects that Mrs. Hewitt's statement is hearsay. Should the statement be admissible? What, if anything, will have to be done to allow Mrs. Hewitt to testify?

PROBLEM 5-154. Patty and her brother Dell must prove their grandmother's age at the time of her death. They attempt to prove her age by calling their grandmother's longtime friend of more than 40 years to testify that grandmother had always told her that she was only 16 years old when she got married. They will also offer an engraving on her wedding ring to establish what year she got married and thus prove her age at death. The wedding ring says she was married on February 14, 1945. They conclude that if she got married 69 years before she died, and she was 16 years old when she got married, that would make her 85 when she died in 2014. The insurance company objects to the admissibility of testimony about how old she was when she got married and the date in the ring as both being inadmissible hearsay. Ruling?

§ 5.18 References and Additional Authority on Statement of Personal or Family History [La. C.E. art. 804(B)(4)]

1. La. C.E. art. 804(B)(4) and Official Comments
2. Force & Rault, Handbook on Louisiana Evidence Law Art. 804(B)(4) Author's Comments (West Publishing 2014)
3. Harges & Jones, Louisiana Evidence Art. 804(B)(4) Author's Comments (West Publishing 2014)
4. 19 La. Civ. L. Treatise, Evidence And Proof § 10.10 (2nd ed.)
5. McCormick on Evidence § 322 (5th ed., 1999)
6. **Statement of personal or family history Article 804(B)(4):** *In re Gray's Succession*, 9 So. 2d 481 (La. 1942) (Defendants argued that the plaintiffs' witness could not testify to what he had heard "old folks" say in the community because it was inadmissible hearsay. The court ruled that there was an exception to the hearsay rule when the case involved pedigree; therefore, the statements were admissible.).

§ 5.19 Complaint of Sexually Assaultive Behavior [La. C.E. art. 804(B)(5)]

Applicable Code Articles

* * *

B. Hearsay exceptions. The following are not excluded by the hearsay rule if the declarant is unavailable as a witness:

* * *

(5) Complaint of sexually assaultive behavior. A statement made by a person under the age of twelve years and the statement is one of initial or otherwise trustworthy complaint of sexually assaultive behavior.

* * *

Requirements for Complaint of Sexually Assaultive Behavior Exception

1. the declarant is unavailable; and
2. the statement must be either: one of initial complaint of sexually assaultive behavior ***or*** an otherwise trustworthy complaint of sexually assaultive behavior; ***and***
3. the declarant must be a person under the age of twelve.

Article 804(B)(5) excludes from the hearsay rule statements made by a person under the age of twelve years that are statements of initial or otherwise trustworthy complaint of sexually assaultive behavior. For this exception to apply, **three requirements must be met:**

1. the declarant must be unavailable; and
2. the statement must be either: one of initial complaint of sexually assaultive behavior or a trustworthy complaint of sexually assaultive behavior; and
3. the declarant must be a person under the age of twelve.

This exception applies to not only initial complaints of sexually assaultive behavior, but also subsequent complaints of sexually assaultive behavior if they are found to be trustworthy.[259] For example, if a 6-year-old girl first tells her teacher about being sexually assaulted by a family member, the teacher might then contact the principal or other authority and report the matter to them. At some point the child may subsequently recount her story to her parent, social worker and police. At trial, if the 6-year-old declarant is unavailable, her initial complaint of sexually assaultive behavior to the teacher might be admissible, or in the alternative, her subsequent complaint to the social worker might be admissible if the statement is deemed trustworthy.

Federal Rules of Evidence Distinction. There is no corresponding provision under the Federal Rules of Evidence.

Unavailable requirement. As in all cases of Article 804(B) exceptions, the declarant must be unavailable. A child victim of sexual abuse might be unavailable for a number of reasons including the fact that the child is unwilling or unable to testify due to lack of memory[260] or other reason. In some instances, courts have found that child victim should not be made to testify due to the psychological impact that testifying at trial could have on the child.[261]

Distinction from Prior Statement of Initial Complaint of Sexually Assault Behavior [Article 801(D)(1)(d)]. Article 801(D)(1)(d) also contains a provision pertaining to complaints of sexual assaults. Under that provision, a prior statement of an initial complaint of sexual assault is exempt from the hearsay rule if: 1) the declarant is *available* at trial; 2) capable of being cross-examined on the prior statement; 3) the statement is consistent with a declarant's statement at trial; and 4) is one of initial complaint of sexually assaultive behavior.

---

259. State v. Free, 643 So. 2d 767 (La. Ct. App. 2d Cir. 1994) (subsequent complaints deemed trustworthy).

260. *See* State v. Davis, 26 So. 3d 802 (La. Ct. App. 2d Cir. 2009) (child witness found unavailable due to lack of memory).

261. *See* Folse v. Folse, 738 So. 2d 1040, 1049–50 (La. 1999) (finding that child victim was unavailable due to the fact that testifying could set the child back from progress she had made).

While both rules relate to statements regarding complaints of sexually assaultive behavior, the requirements for each rule are quite different in that under this rule the declarant must be unavailable, under the age of twelve, and includes not only initial complaints of sexually assaultive behavior, but also complaints that are otherwise trustworthy. The rule found in Article 801(D)(1)(d) is discussed further in § 5.23.4, *infra*, and contains a chart comparing the two concepts.

Problems on Complaint of Sexually Assaultive Behavior

PROBLEM 5-155. Seven-year-old Marissa told her teacher that her grandfather touches her inappropriately at night when he comes to tuck her in to bed. The teacher called the social worker and police and told them what Marissa said. The report led to the arrest of Marissa's grandfather for child molestation. By the time the case goes to trial two years later, Marissa is nine years old. a) Can the teacher testify to what Marissa first told her about what her grandfather does to her at night to prove the molestation charges? b) Can the teacher testify to what Marissa first told her about what her grandfather does to her at night to prove the molestation charges if Marissa can't remember what she told the teacher? Why or why not? c) Assume the teacher testifies to what Marissa told her. Can the police officer then take the stand and testify to what the teacher told him that Marissa said to help prove the molestation charges? Why or why not?

PROBLEM 5-156. Five-year-old Kirsten told her teacher that her cousin comes into her bedroom every night and gets on top of her. Her teacher immediately called the principal and told him what Kirsten said. He then asked Kirsten about what happens to her at night with her cousin. Kirsten told him. The principal called her mother and the CPS worker. Both of them questioned Kirsten, and the social worker questioned Kirsten about it alone. After confirming the story, the police were called, resulting in the cousin's arrest and prosecution. At the trial, Kirsten's psychologist informs the judge that she doesn't think Kirsten can endure a trial because she's had difficulty coping, and the trial could set her back. The prosecution agrees and wants to call the CPS worker to testify to the statement Kirsten made to her and her mother that led to the cousin's arrest. The defense objects that the statement is hearsay. How will the court likely rule and why?

§ 5.19 References and Additional Authority on Complaint of Sexually Assaultive Behavior [La. C.E. art. 804(B)(5)]

1. La. C.E. art. 804(B)(5) and Official Comments
2. Force & Rault, HANDBOOK ON LOUISIANA EVIDENCE LAW Art. 804(B)(5) Author's Comments (West Publishing 2014)
3. Harges & Jones, LOUISIANA EVIDENCE Art. 804(B)(5) Author's Comments (West Publishing 2014)
4. 19 La. Civ. L. Treatise, Evidence And Proof § 10.11 (2nd ed.)
5. **Inadmissible as complaint of sexually assaultive behavior:** *State v. Hilton*, 764 So. 2d 1027 (La. Ct. App. 1st Cir. 2000) (The court stated that the declarant of the complaint of sexually assaultive behavior must be the person that is unavailable at the trial.

Because it was the doctor that was unavailable as a witness to testify at the trial and not the children who were the declarants of the statements, the statements were not admissible as complaints of sexually assaultive behavior.).

6. **Complaint of sexually assaultive behavior under Article 804(B)(5) versus complaint of sexual assault under Article 801 D(1)(d):** *State v. Harris*, 781 So. 2d 73 (La. Ct. App. 4th Cir. 2001) (holding that the declarant was not found to be unavailable for purposes of the complaint of sexually assaultive behavior exception to the hearsay rule because the declarant was present at the trial. However, the court ruled that the statement was admissible under 801 D(1)(d) Sexual Assault Complaint because the statement is not hearsay because the declarant is available to testify and is subject to cross-examination.).

§ 5.20 Other Exceptions [La. C.E. art. 804(B)(6)]

Applicable Code Articles

* * *

B. Hearsay exceptions. The following are not excluded by the hearsay rule if the declarant is unavailable as a witness:

* * *

(6) Other exceptions. In a civil case, a statement not specifically covered by any of the foregoing exceptions if the court determines that considering all pertinent circumstances in the particular case the statement is trustworthy, and the proponent of the evidence has adduced or made a reasonable effort to adduce all other admissible evidence to establish the fact to which the proffered statement relates and the proponent of the statement makes known in writing to the adverse party and to the court his intention to offer the statement and the particulars of it, including the name and address of the declarant, sufficiently in advance of the trial or hearing to provide the adverse party with a fair opportunity to prepare to meet it. If, under the circumstances of a particular case, giving of this notice was not practicable or failure to give notice is found by the court to have been excusable, the court may authorize a delayed notice to be given, and in that event the opposing party is entitled to a recess, continuance, or other appropriate relief sufficient to enable him to prepare to meet the evidence.

* * *

In very rare and extraordinary circumstances,[262] a statement that does not fit into any other hearsay exception may be excluded from the hearsay rule on an ad hoc case-by-case basis if compelling circumstances justify it.[263] Article 804(B)(6) contains an exception to the hearsay ban for a statement that is shown to be supported by circumstantial guarantees

262. La. Code Evid. art. 804(B)(6) Official Comment (c), noting that the exception is to be available only in truly extraordinary circumstances.

263. La. Code Evid. art. 804(B)(6) Official Comment (d).

Requirements for Other Exceptions:

1. declarant is unavailable;
2. trustworthiness of the statement;
3. showing that the proponent has done all she can do to get admissible evidence on the issue; and
4. written notice to the opponent/court.

of trustworthiness[264] and where an element of necessity exists[265] to justify allowing the statement into evidence because the declarant is unavailable and the proponent has unsuccessfully made all reasonable efforts to adduce other admissible evidence to establish the fact to which the proffered statement relates. The proponent of such a statement must also comply with certain notice requirements to provide the opposing party an opportunity to meet the statement.

Requirements. Because the exception is a narrow one, intended only to apply in truly extraordinary circumstances, there are specific requirements with which the proponent must comply to offer a statement under this exception. The four key requirements to admissibility of a statement under this exception are:

1. unavailability of the declarant;
2. trustworthiness of the statement;
3. showing that the proponent has done all she can do to get admissible evidence on the issue; and
4. written notice to the opponent/court (of intent to offer statement; particulars of statement; and name and address of declarant).

Trustworthiness of the statement. The true key to admissibility of a statement under this exception is sufficient circumstantial guarantees of trustworthiness of the information contained in the statement. "[T]rustworthiness is determined by 'considering all pertinent circumstances in the particular case,' including circumstances tending to corroborate the truthfulness of the out of court statement."[266] Further, the proponent of the statement could also demonstrate that the potential dangers of admitting the hearsay statements—poor perception, flawed memory, insincerity, and misleading narration, or ambiguity—are minimal under the circumstances. The applicability of this exception is determined on a case-by-case basis.

Notice requirement. The exception requires that the proponent of the statement must give written notice to the adverse party and to the court of: 1) his intention to offer the statement; 2) the particulars of the statement; and 3) the name and address of the declarant. The notice must be provided sufficiently in advance of the trial or hearing to provide the

---

264. Force & Rault, HANDBOOK, Art. 804(B)(6) Author's Comment (3).

265. *See* Buckbee v. United Gas Pipe Line Co. Inc., 561 So. 2d 76 (La. 1990); *See also* Ratcliff v. Normand, 819 So. 2d 434 (La. Ct. App. 3d Cir. 2002) (finding that exception was not applicable because there was no showing that evidence was necessary); While necessity is not a specific requirement under the exception, the exception does require a showing that the declarant be unavailable and that the proponent of the statement has made a reasonable effort to adduce all other admissible evidence on the point before it may be admitted under the exception.

266. Force & Rault, HANDBOOK, Art. 804(B)(6) Author's Comment (3).

adverse party with a fair opportunity to prepare to meet it. In some circumstances, the court may authorize a delayed notice to be given if, under the circumstances, the court finds that giving of the notice was not practicable or the failure to give notice is otherwise excusable. In such a case, the opposing party is entitled to a recess, continuance, or other appropriate relief sufficient to enable him to prepare to meet the evidence.

Application in criminal cases. Despite the fact that Article 804(B)(6) specifically states that the exception applies in civil cases, the Louisiana Supreme Court has held that the exception may also apply in a criminal case if "its exclusion would interfere with the defendant's constitutional right to present a defense."[267] Additionally, the Official Comment (e) to Article 804(B)(6) notes that the provision may also be mandated when an accused in a criminal case offers reliable, trustworthy evidence because of his constitutional right of compulsory process. In *State v. Gremillion*[268] (below), the Louisiana Supreme Court applies this exception in a criminal case.

Cases on Other Exceptions

Revisit *Buckbee*. If you recall, as we discussed supra § 5.2.1 in *Buckbee*,[269] the Louisiana Supreme Court considered the applicability of this exception to Buckbee's statement to his coworker that he had been given permission to use heat to remove the plug. In setting forth the appropriate standard to be used under the exception, the court noted that "in the search for truth, [it] recognizes exceptions to the hearsay rule when there exist both sufficient guarantees of trustworthiness and a necessity for the evidence."[270]

In *Buckbee*, the court easily found that the necessity requirement had been met, concluding that "Vincent's testimony to Buckbee's statement, that he had received permission to apply heat, is the only available evidence"[271] on the issue, "except for Vincent's testimony to Buckbee's first statement"[272] that he was going to seek permission to use heat from his supervisors—a statement the court found admissible under the then existing mental condition exception.

The *Buckbee* court, however, was unable to find the second requirement—sufficient circumstantial guarantees of trustworthiness—noting that "there [was only] one item of evidence which could be interpreted as circumstantial support for Buckbee's declaration that he had received permission: the fact that he descended the scaffold, entered the plant office, and remained there for ten minutes."[273] However, the court reasoned, "other equally plausible explanations for Buckbee's statement, i.e., the possibility that Buckbee was unable to procure assent to his request for permission to apply heat, or that his request was denied and he chose in either event to proceed with what he perceived as the thing to do while conveniently misleading Vincent by telling him that he had obtained permission to proceed with heat," did not support the reliability of Buckbee's statement to Vincent that permission

---

267. State v. Gremillion, 542 So. 2d 1074 (La. 1989); *See also* Article 804(B)(6) Official Comment (d).
268. State v. Gremillion, 542 So. 2d 1074 (La. 1989).
269. Buckbee v. United Gas Pipe Line Co. Inc., 561 So. 2d 76 (La. 1990).
270. *Id.*
271. *Id.*
272. *Id.*
273. *Id.*

had been received. Thus, the court held the plaintiffs had not preponderantly shown the trustworthiness of Buckbee's statement to Vincent.

Distinguish the reasoning in *Buckbee* from *Gremillion* below, in which the court found that a hearsay statement had circumstantial guarantees of trustworthiness.

State v. Gremillion
Supreme Court of Louisiana
542 So. 2d 1074
May 1, 1989

DIXON, Chief Justice.

Douglas R. Gremillion was convicted by a jury of manslaughter and sentenced to serve eighteen years at hard labor. On appeal, the conviction and sentence were affirmed.... We granted writs, and now reverse the defendant's conviction.

During the early morning hours of February 7, 1987, the defendant was drinking at the Chalet Lounge in Alexandria with the victim's ex-wife, Susan Dupuy. The victim, Robert Dupuy, was also present in the bar. Earlier in the evening, Dupuy and Susan were involved in an argument which led to threats by Dupuy, and he knocked a drink out of her hand. In addition Dupuy had threatened William Swain, who was dancing with Susan earlier in the evening, and warned him to stay away from her. As Dupuy was leaving the bar, he turned around and had words with the defendant and Susan, threatening defendant's life. As Dupuy stepped back (defendant claims that he reached into his coat pocket as if to pull out a gun), the defendant punched him in the face, sending him crashing between some tables. As Dupuy lay unconscious on the ground, the defendant stomped him several times in the chest and abdomen. There was also evidence that Susan kicked him several times. The defendant was restrained by several patrons of the bar who grabbed him, and he was eventually escorted out of the bar. Once outside, the defendant waited to continue the fight, but was persuaded by some friends to go home.

When Dupuy regained consciousness, he left the bar and drove a friend home. Several hours later he checked into the Alexandria Veteran's Hospital complaining of severe abdominal pains. He gave a statement to an attending physician and later to a police officer explaining the events of the evening, apparently being unable to identify his attackers. Dupuy and the defendant had been close friends having known each other for approximately eleven years. Dupuy was diagnosed as having traumatic pancreatitis; despite two surgical procedures he died on February 25, 1987....

In these assignments of error the defendant contends that the trial court erred in refusing to allow into evidence a statement made by Dupuy to Deputy Bowden, the police officer who investigated the crime and interviewed Dupuy at the hospital the day he was admitted. When asked by Bowden to describe his attackers, Dupuy could not say who they were, or what they were wearing, but merely described them as "three white males." Bowden was called as a witness for the defense. The defense tried several times to elicit this statement from Bowden, but was met with hearsay objections from the state, which were sustained by the trial court. While one of the objections by the state came too late, allowing Bowden to give the description, the objection was sustained and the jury was later admonished to disregard the statement.

Earlier in the trial, while the state was presenting its case, it called Dr. Balthazar, Dupuy's treating physician, as a witness. Balthazar testified about the events surrounding Dupuy's admittance and stay at the hospital. In conjunction with this testimony, the state introduced the medical records of Dupuy. Included in these records was a statement by Dupuy to the admitting physician in which he stated that he was beaten and kicked by "several others." Reading from the records, Balthazar recited this statement to the jury. Despite the hearsay nature of this statement, it was allowed into evidence by the trial court. While the two statements are not identical, they are similar in nature since in neither one did Dupuy specifically identify the defendant.

The defense attempted to introduce the statement of Deputy Bowden in an effort to present a defense theory in which William Swain, and not the defendant, inflicted the injuries upon Dupuy that eventually led to his death. To corroborate this theory, the defense called Swain as a witness to attempt to show that he had a motive for attacking Dupuy. Swain testified that he had purchased a car from Dupuy for $800, but was forced to return the car when Dupuy was unable to produce a valid title due to a community property dispute between him and Susan. The $800 had not been returned to Swain. Swain also testified that Dupuy had earlier knocked a drink out of Susan's hand while he was present and threatened him, warning him to stay away from her. It was also revealed that two of Swain's friends were with him in the bar. The defense argument was that Dupuy was beaten by Swain and two of his friends, which would have been bolstered by the statement Dupuy made to Deputy Bowden.

The trial court ruled that the statement made by Dupuy to Deputy Bowden was hearsay, and refused to allow the defense to question Bowden about it. Hearsay is an out of court, unsworn, oral or written statement by a third person, which is offered for the truth of its content.... Hearsay statements are inadmissible unless they fit into one of the recognized exceptions. The defense argues that the statement should have been admitted under either the res gestae, excited utterance, business record or dying declaration exception. The defendant contends that the exclusion of the statement impaired his due process right to present a defense.

The statement Dupuy made to Deputy Bowden is hearsay and does not fit into any of the recognized exceptions to the hearsay rule. The statement was made out of court, by a declarant who was unavailable to testify. The statement was unsworn, and the defense attempted to introduce it for the truth of its content, that is, to prove that Dupuy was attacked by "three white males" and not the defendant. Defendant's claim that the statement is part of the res gestae is without merit. R.S. 15:447 provides:

> Res gestae are events speaking for themselves under the immediate pressure of the occurrence, through the instructive, impulsive and spontaneous words and acts of the participants, and not the words of the participants when narrating the events. What forms any part of the res gestae is always admissible in evidence.

The record reveals that the statement by Dupuy was made at 9:00 p.m. on the evening following the incident at the Chalet Lounge, probably nineteen hours later. The statement was too far removed to be considered spontaneous and was more narrative than impulsive. Further, the statement is also not admissible as an excited utterance since it was made after Dupuy had time to contemplate the event, and not while he was still under the influence of a startling event....

Defendant also claims that the statement should be admissible as a dying declaration. Dying declarations are admissible if made when the declarant is fully conscious of his condition and under a sense of impending death, after having abandoned all hope or expectancy of recovery.... While there are indications that Dupuy was enduring great pain at the time he made the statement, it does not appear that he was aware of his impending death. It was not until two surgeries and seventeen days later that Dupuy died. The statement was not a dying declaration and this argument lacks merit.

Defendant also argues that the statement should be admitted under the business records exception, since the statement was recorded by Deputy Bowden in the course of his employment as a police officer. The contents of the report are based on hearsay, and are not admissible as a business record.... This argument lacks merit.

While the statement does not fit into any of the recognized exceptions to the hearsay rule, it should have, nevertheless, been admitted into evidence due to its reliability and trustworthy nature. The statement to Deputy Bowden, while not identical to the one given to the admitting physician who took Dupuy's history, was corroborated by that statement, in which Dupuy stated that he was attacked by "several others." The defendant and Dupuy were close friends, yet in two separate statements Dupuy failed to identify the defendant as his attacker. The statement indicating that Dupuy was attacked by "three white males" was given to a police officer investigating the crime, and there is no circumstance to suggest that the statement was untrustworthy. The state suggests that Dupuy may have been motivated by his friendship with the defendant when he failed to identify him as his attacker. There is no particular support for it in the record. Dupuy left the bar around 2:00 a.m., and there is no indication of his whereabouts from that time until 10:00 a.m. the next day, when he checked into the hospital. The possibility exists that Dupuy was attacked during this time, and the credibility of this defense should have been presented to the jury to assess.

While hearsay should generally be excluded, if it is reliable and trustworthy and its exclusion would interfere with the defendant's constitutional right to present a defense, it should be admitted. Louisiana Code of Evidence, art. 804(B)(6) provides:

> "In a civil case, a statement not specifically covered by any of the foregoing exceptions if the court determines that considering all pertinent circumstances in the particular case the statement is trustworthy, and the proponent of the evidence has adduced or made a reasonable effort to adduce all other admissible evidence to establish the fact to which the proffered statement relates and the proponent of the statement makes known in writing to the adverse party and to the court his intention to offer the statement and the particulars of it, including the name and address of the declarant, sufficiently in advance of the trial or hearing to provide the adverse party with a fair opportunity to prepare to meet it. If, under the circumstances of a particular case, giving of this notice was not practicable or failure to give notice is found by the court to have been excusable, the court may authorize a delayed notice to be given, and in that event the opposing party is entitled to a recess, continuance, or other appropriate relief sufficient to enable him to prepare to meet the evidence."

While this article specifically limits its application to civil cases, comment (d) states:

> "Although the exception set forth in this Subparagraph is limited to civil cases, under certain circumstances results similar to those authorized by this exception may be mandated by the right of compulsory process when an accused in a criminal case offers reliable trustworthy evidence not fitting within the contours of a legislatively recognized exception to the hearsay rule." See *Chambers v. Mississippi,* 410 U.S. 284 [93 S.Ct. 1038, 35 L.Ed.2d 297] (1973)....

Defendant's primary defense was that the injuries causing Dupuy's death were not inflicted by him. Defendant has a constitutional right to present a defense. La. Const. art 1, § 16. The credibility of this statement and the defense's theory should have been placed before the jury, who could have been cautioned by proper instructions as to the weight to be given to the statement. By not allowing the defendant to place this statement before the jury, the trial court impermissibly impaired his right to present a defense to the crime with which he was charged.

For these reasons, the conviction and sentence of the defendant are reversed and the case is remanded to the district court for a new trial in accordance with this opinion.

Discussion Questions

1. Discuss and explain the circumstantial guarantees of trustworthiness in the statement in *Gremillion*. Do you agree that the statement is trustworthy? See *United Investor's Life Insurance Co. v. Alexander*, 662 So. 2d 831 (La. Ct. App. 2d Cir. 1995) (for an excellent application of the trustworthiness component).
2. Explain the policy and constitutional rationale for allowing the exception to apply in criminal cases.
3. Why do you suppose this article has not been *amended* to specifically provide that it may apply in criminal cases when necessary to protect an accused's rights to confrontation and cross-examination?

Key Points

The key points to keep in mind regarding the other hearsay exception.

1. In extraordinary and rare circumstances a statement that does not fit into any other hearsay exception may be excluded from the hearsay ban on an ad hoc case-by-case basis if compelling circumstances justify it.
2. The four key requirements under this exception are:
   1. unavailability of the declarant;
   2. trustworthiness of the statement;
   3. showing that the proponent has done all she can do to get admissible evidence on the issue; and
   4. written notice to the opponent/court (of intent to offer statement; particulars of statement; and name and address of declarant).
3. **Procedural requirements**: 1) give notice of intention to offer the statement; 2) state the particulars of the statement; and 3) state the name and address of the declarant.

   Time of notice: sufficiently in advance of the trial or hearing to give adverse party a fair opportunity to prepare to meet the statement. Time may be extended if giving notice not practical or otherwise excusable. In such cases, the adverse party may be entitled to continue case.
4. May also apply in criminal cases if necessary to protect an accused's rights to confrontation and cross-examination under the Sixth Amendment of U.S. Constitution and Article 1 Section 16 of Louisiana Constitution.

Problems on Other Hearsay Exception

PROBLEM 5-157. Shady J was accused of beating an old childhood friend who later died of internal injuries. There were no witnesses to the alleged beating. After being admitted to a hospital, the victim stated to an investigating officer that he had been attacked by some guy he'd never seen before. The victim was otherwise unable to identify his attacker. In a separate statement made later that afternoon, the victim told the admitting physician that he was kicked and beaten by some tall dude that he thinks is from "out of town." He says he didn't know him. That statement was made part of the hospital record. At the trial, the defendant sought to introduce evidence of the victim's statements through the police officer and the hospital record that he had been beaten by a "guy he'd never seen before" rather than by him—a longtime childhood friend. The prosecution objected that the statement was hearsay. The defendant argued that the statement should be admitted under the residual catchall exception to the hearsay rule. Should the statement be admitted under the exception? Why or why not? Fully analyze whether the requirements for the exception are met. [*See State v. Gremillion*, 542 So. 2d 1074 (La.1989).]

PROBLEM 5-158. Louis was fatally injured in a work-related accident while he and the rest of his crew made rooftop repairs to a commercial apartment building. Shortly after arriving at the jobsite, Louis spoke to the building superintendent privately then told his co-workers that the building superintendent at the jobsite had instructed him that, to prevent the superintendent's dog from escaping its rooftop kennel, the work crew was forbidden to open a large iron gate in order to reach the rooftop work area in which they were working. The gate was a large iron makeshift gate attached by rickety hinges on each side that had been placed at the top of the stairs leading to the roof. The superintendent had installed the gate himself to prevent his dog from escaping the roof. Louis also stated that the superintendent forbade the crew to reach the roof by passing through his apartment because that would soil the carpets. Throughout the day, the work crew climbed over the gate to reach the work area. At the end of the day, when the decedent was climbing over the gate for the last time, the gate came loose from the hinges, the decedent fell down the stairs leading to the roof, and the gate fell on top of him. He died three days later from injuries. Louis was the only member of the crew who had spoken to the building superintendent that morning and received the instructions that he passed on to the remainder of the crew who all complied with the instructions that Louis stated he'd been given by the superintendent. Photos of the scene of the accident as well as testimony from the crew showed that a dog was in fact on the rooftop that could have escaped if the gate were opened. The decedent's family brought a lawsuit against the building and its superintendent. Members of the work crew had also seen Louis speaking to the superintendent that morning. Also, the superintendent had observed the crew entering and leaving the jobsite by climbing over the fence all day and had entered the roof in that manner himself several times during the day.

At the trial, when members of the crew began testifying to what Louis told them about the instructions from the superintendent, the defendants objected that the statements were double hearsay. Does Louis' statement conform to the requirements for the residual catchall exception? Why or why not? [*See Robinson v. Shapiro*, 646 F.2d 734 (2d Cir.1981).]

§ 5.20 References and Additional Authority on Other Exceptions [La. C.E. art. 804(B)(6)]

1. La. C.E. art. 804(B)(6) and Official Comments
2. Force & Rault, Handbook on Louisiana Evidence Law Art. 804(B)(6) Author's Comments (West Publishing 2014)
3. Harges & Jones, Louisiana Evidence Art. 804(B)(6) Author's Comments (West Publishing 2014)
4. 19 La. Civ. L. Treatise, Evidence And Proof § 10.12; 10.27 (2nd ed.)
5. **Commentary**: Losch, Jill, "*State v. Gremillion: The Constitutional and Evidentiary Elasticity of the Louisiana Residual Hearsay Exception in Criminal Cases,*" 50 La. L. Rev. 845 (March 1990).
6. **Other Hearsay Exceptions Article 804(B)(6):** *Morgan City v. City of New Orleans*, 647 So. 2d 1308 (La. Ct. App. 4th Cir. 1994) (Appellant argued that the lower court erred in refusing to allow a statement made by the deceased janitor concerning the condition of the sidewalk in order to prove notice under the residual catchall exception to the hearsay rule. The court affirmed the decision of the lower court and ruled the statement inadmissible because there was no circumstantial evidence to prove trustworthiness of the statement.); *State v. McCullough*, 774 So. 2d 1105 (La. Ct. App. 3d Cir. 2000) (Statements of co-defendants were not admissible under any exception to the hearsay rule because they were not found to be reliable or trustworthy. The only evidence that the prosecution attempted to present was that the statements made by the declarant were made to police officers prior to the arrest of the defendant.); *State v. Green*, 735 So. 2d 723 (La. Ct. App. 3d Cir. 1999) (After co-defendant invoked his 5th Amendment right not to incriminate himself, the defendant wanted to admit the co-defendant's typed statement. The court ruled that the typed statement was inadmissible because the requirements of *Gremillion* were not met and was therefore unreliable or untrustworthy.); *State v. Fernandez*, 50 So. 3d 219 (La. Ct. App. 4th Cir. 2010) (The court ruled that the statement that the defendant wanted to be present was not of much significance to his defense that would warrant reversal of his conviction. Good discussion of reliability requirement.).

§ 5.21 Forfeiture by Wrongdoing [La. C.E. art. 804(B)(7)]

Applicable Code Articles

* * *

B. Hearsay exceptions. The following are not excluded by the hearsay rule if the declarant is unavailable as a witness:

* * *

(7) (a) Forfeiture by wrongdoing. A statement offered against a party that has engaged or acquiesced in wrongdoing that was intended to, and did, procure the unavailability of the declarant as a witness.

(b) A party seeking to introduce statements under the forfeiture by wrongdoing hearsay exception shall establish, by a preponderance of the evidence, that the party against whom the statement is now offered, engaged or acquiesced in the wrongdoing.

Article 804(B)(7) contains an exception to the hearsay rule that allows a statement to be offered into evidence against a person who intentionally caused the unavailability of a witness (declarant) for the specific purpose of preventing the witness from testifying against him at trial. This might include situations in which a defendant kills or threatens a key witness, or causes a witness to become so afraid to testify that the witness cannot or refuses to testify against the defendant. In such a situation, the person who procured the unavailability of the witness to prevent him from testifying against him is said to have "forfeited" his right to confront the witness against him or to object that the witness's statement is hearsay—thus the name, "forfeiture by wrongdoing."

Requirements for exception. The exception does not apply in *every* instance in which the defendant has killed or otherwise caused the declarant to be unavailable. Instead, for the exception to apply, it must be shown that the witness was made unavailable for the specific purpose, i.e., "with the design to prevent the witness from testifying against him."[274]

As a result, a party seeking to introduce statements under the forfeiture by wrongdoing exception must establish two requirements:

1. declarant is unavailable; and
2. proponent must prove by a preponderance of the evidence, that the party against whom the statement is now offered, procured the unavailability of witness for the *purpose of* preventing the witness from testifying.

Illustration. A witness to a murder gives a statement to the police where he details the defendant's involvement in a crime that results in the defendant being arrested and charged with murder. Prior to the trial, the defendant threatens the witness and tells him that if he testifies at the trial he will see to it that the witness is killed. As a result, the witness moves away and cannot be located by the prosecution. At the trial, the prosecution seeks to offer the statement the witness gave to the police where he implicated the defendant and identified him as the killer. The defendant objects claiming that the statement is hearsay. Under this exception, the statement would be excluded from the hearsay rule since the witness is: 1) unavailable; and 2) the party against whom the statement is being offered (the defendant), procured the unavailability of the witness with the specific purpose of preventing the witness from testifying against him.

Assume instead that the defendant is on trial for killing a longtime friend who had not repaid a loan. Prior to killing the victim, the victim had gone to the police to report that he was being harassed by the defendant for the money. If the defendant subsequently kills the victim in an altercation over the money, the statement the victim gave to the police prior to being killed by the defendant may not be offered under this exception. While the defendant's wrongdoing is the reason the witness is unavailable at trial, the victim was not made unavailable for the *purpose* of preventing him from testifying at trial.

274. Giles v. California, 128 S.Ct. 2678 (2008).

Requirements for Forfeiture by Wrongdoing Exception

1. declarant is unavailable;
2. proponent proves by preponderance of evidence that party against whom evidence is offered procured the unavailability of witness for purpose of preventing witness from testifying.

This exception only applies if it is shown by a **preponderance of the evidence** that the party against whom the evidence is offered procured the unavailability of the witness for the purpose of preventing the witness from testifying against him at trial.

The Doctrine of "Forfeiture by Wrongdoing" of the Confrontation Clause

Keep in mind that "forfeiture by wrongdoing" applies to two different contexts—a hearsay exception and the Confrontation Clause. As we have covered from the outset, the hearsay exceptions are separate and apart from the requirements of the right of confrontation under the U.S. Constitution and Article I § 16 of the Louisiana Constitution, in that the fact that a statement conforms to an exception to the hearsay rule does not necessarily overcome an accused's constitutional rights. A testimonial statement must still comply with the requirements of *Crawford v. Washington*[275] to avoid violating an accused's constitutional right to confrontation. *Crawford* requires that if a declarant is currently unavailable and the statement is testimonial as defined by *Crawford* and *Davis v. Washington*,[276] then the accused must have had a prior opportunity to cross-examine the declarant regarding the prior statement.

While the constitutional right to confrontation is an important one, the Courts have long recognized[277] "certain limited exceptions to the right of confrontation"[278] provided under the Sixth Amendment of the United States Constitution. One such exception to the Confrontation Clause is also referred to as the doctrine of "forfeiture by wrongdoing"—the same name as the hearsay exception. Just as in the hearsay exception, under the doctrine of "forfeiture by wrongdoing" as it relates to the Confrontation Clause, if an accused procured the absence of a witness from trial for the *purpose* of preventing his testimony, then he is said to have "forfeited" his right to confront the witness at trial.

In *Giles* below, the United States Supreme Court considered whether the doctrine should only apply to situations in which the accused procured the absence of a witness for the specific purpose of preventing his testimony at trial or if the exception should apply in all situations in which the defendant's wrongdoing resulted in the witness's un-

275. Crawford v. Washington, 541 U.S. 36, 124 S.Ct. 1354 (2004).

276. Davis v. Washington, 547 U.S. 813, 822, 125 S.Ct. 2266 (2006).

277. *See* Giles v. California, 128 S.Ct. 2678, 2683 (2008) (Noting that "[t]he doctrine has roots in the 1666 decision in Lord Morley's Case, at which judges concluded that a witness's having been "detained by the means or procurement of the prisoner," provided a basis to read testimony previously given at a coroner's inquest").

278. Warner *quoting* Crawford v. Washington, 541 U.S. 36, 124 S.Ct. 1354 (2004).

availability.[279] The *Giles* court held that "unconfronted testimony would *not* be admitted without a showing that the defendant intended to prevent a witness from testifying."[280]

Relationship to the Hearsay Exception. In *Giles*, the United States Supreme Court noted that "the Sixth Amendment's Confrontation Clause and the evidentiary hearsay rule stem from the same roots"[281] in that the hearsay rule exists in large part *because* such statements are unconfronted.[282] Having found that the admission of such statements did not violate an accused's confrontation rights under the U.S. Constitution, in 1997 Congress enacted the "forfeiture by wrongdoing" exception to the hearsay rule found in Federal Rule of Evidence 804(b)(6).[283] The exception "codifies the forfeiture doctrine,"[284] and also excludes such statements from the hearsay ban. In 2009 the Louisiana Legislature followed suit and enacted Article 804(B)(7),[285] which similarly excludes a statement from the hearsay rule when it is shown that the person against whom a statement is offered procured the unavailability of a witness for the purpose of preventing him from testifying.

Thus, following *Giles* below, and the enactment of state and federal hearsay exceptions, the admission of a statement against an accused who procured the absence of a witness/declarant for the purpose of preventing his testimony at trial does not violate an accused's constitutional rights to confrontation and cross-examination, nor does it violate the hearsay rule.

Cases on Forfeiture by Wrongdoing

Giles v. California

Supreme Court of the United States
128 S.Ct. 2678
June 25, 2008

SCALIA, J., delivered the opinion of the Court, except as to Part II-D-2.

We consider whether a defendant forfeits his Sixth Amendment right to confront a witness against him when a judge determines that a wrongful act by the defendant made the witness unavailable to testify at trial.

I

On September 29, 2002, petitioner Dwayne Giles shot his ex-girlfriend, Brenda Avie, outside the garage of his grandmother's house. No witness saw the shooting, but Giles' niece heard what transpired from inside the house. She heard Giles and Avie speaking in conversational tones. Avie then yelled "Granny" several times and a series of gunshots sounded. Giles' niece and grandmother ran outside and saw Giles standing near Avie with a gun in his hand. Avie, who had not been carrying a weapon, had been shot six times.

---

279. Giles v. California, 128 S.Ct. 2678, 2681 (2008).

280. *Id.*

281. *Id. quoting*, Dutton v. Evans, 400 U.S. 74, 86, 91 S.Ct. 210 (1970).

282. *Id.*

283. FED. R. EVID. 806(b)(6).

284. Giles v. California, 128 S.Ct. 2678, 2687 (2008) *quoting* Davis v. Washington, 547 U.S. 813, 833, 126 S. Ct. 2266 (2006).

285. LA. CODE EVID. art. 804(B)(7) was enacted by Acts 2009, No. 7. Subparagraph (b) was added by Acts. 2010, No. 543.

One wound was consistent with Avie's holding her hand up at the time she was shot, another was consistent with her having turned to her side, and a third was consistent with her having been shot while lying on the ground. Giles fled the scene after the shooting. He was apprehended by police about two weeks later and charged with murder.

At trial, Giles testified that he had acted in self-defense.... He said that on the day of the shooting, Avie came to his grandmother's house and threatened to kill him and his new girlfriend, who had been at the house earlier.... Giles testified that after Avie threatened him at the house, he went into the garage and retrieved a gun, took the safety off, and started walking toward the back door of the house. He said that Avie charged at him, and that he was afraid she had something in her hand. According to Giles, he closed his eyes and fired several shots, but did not intend to kill Avie.

Prosecutors sought to introduce statements that Avie had made to a police officer responding to a domestic-violence report about three weeks before the shooting. Avie, who was crying when she spoke, told the officer that Giles had accused her of having an affair, and that after the two began to argue, Giles grabbed her by the shirt, lifted her off the floor, and began to choke her. According to Avie, when she broke free and fell to the floor, Giles punched her in the face and head, and after she broke free again, he opened a folding knife, held it about three feet away from her, and threatened to kill her if he found her cheating on him. Over Giles' objection, the trial court admitted these statements into evidence under a provision of California law that permits admission of out-of-court statements describing the infliction or threat of physical injury on a declarant when the declarant is unavailable to testify at trial and the prior statements are deemed trustworthy.

A jury convicted Giles of first-degree murder. He appealed. While his appeal was pending, this Court decided in *Crawford v. Washington,* 541 U.S. 36, 53–54, 124 S.Ct. 1354, (2004), that the Confrontation Clause requires that a defendant have the opportunity to confront the witnesses who give testimony against him, except in cases where an exception to the confrontation right was recognized at the time of the founding. The California Court of Appeal held that the admission of Avie's unconfronted statements at Giles' trial did not violate the Confrontation Clause as construed by *Crawford* because *Crawford* recognized a doctrine of forfeiture by wrongdoing. It concluded that Giles had forfeited his right to confront Avie because he had committed the murder for which he was on trial, and because his intentional criminal act made Avie unavailable to testify. The California Supreme Court affirmed on the same ground.

II

The Sixth Amendment provides that "[i]n all criminal prosecutions, the accused shall enjoy the right ... to be confronted with the witnesses against him." The Amendment contemplates that a witness who makes testimonial statements admitted against a defendant will ordinarily be present at trial for cross-examination, and that if the witness is unavailable, his prior testimony will be introduced only if the defendant had a prior opportunity to cross-examine him. The State does not dispute here, and we accept without deciding, that Avie's statements accusing Giles of assault were testimonial. But it maintains (as did the California Supreme Court) that the Sixth Amendment did not prohibit prosecutors from introducing the statements because an exception to the confrontation guarantee permits the use of a witness's unconfronted testimony if a judge finds, as the judge did in this case, that the defendant committed a wrongful act that rendered the witness unavailable to testify at trial. We held in *Crawford* that the Confrontation Clause is "most naturally read as a reference to the right of confrontation at common law, admitting only those exceptions established at the time of the founding." We therefore ask whether the theory of forfeiture by wrongdoing accepted by the California Supreme Court is a founding-era exception to the confrontation right.

A

... A second common-law doctrine, which we will refer to as forfeiture by wrongdoing, permitted the introduction of statements of a witness who was "detained" or "kept away" by the "means or procurement" of the defendant. The doctrine has roots in the 1666 decision in *Lord Morley's Case*, at which judges concluded that a witness's having been "detained by the means or procurement of the prisoner," provided a basis to read testimony previously given at a coroner's inquest. Courts and commentators also concluded that wrongful procurement of a witness's absence was among the grounds for admission of statements made at bail and committal hearings conducted under the Marian statutes, which directed justices of the peace to take the statements of felony suspects and the persons bringing the suspects before the magistrate, and to certify those statements to the court. This class of confronted statements was also admissible if the witness who made them was dead or unable to travel.

The terms used to define the scope of the forfeiture rule suggest that the exception applied only when the defendant engaged in conduct *designed* to prevent the witness from testifying. The rule required the witness to have been "kept back" or "detained" by "means or procurement" of the defendant. Although there are definitions of "procure" and "procurement" that would merely require that a defendant have caused the witness's absence, other definitions would limit the causality to one that was *designed* to bring about the result "procured." Similarly, while the term "means" could sweep in all cases in which a defendant caused a witness to fail to appear, it can also connote that a defendant forfeits confrontation rights when he uses an intermediary for the purpose of making a witness absent....

B

The manner in which the rule was applied makes plain that unconfronted testimony would *not* be admitted without a showing that the defendant intended to prevent a witness from testifying. In cases where the evidence suggested that the defendant had caused a person to be absent, but had not done so to prevent the person from testifying—as in the typical murder case involving accusatorial statements by the victim—the testimony was excluded unless it was confronted or fell within the dying-declaration exception. Prosecutors do not appear to have even *argued* that the judge could admit the unconfronted statements because the defendant committed the murder for which he was on trial.

Consider *King v. Woodcock*. William Woodcock was accused of killing his wife, Silvia, who had been beaten and left near death. A Magistrate took Silvia Woodcock's account of the crime, under oath, and she died about 48 hours later. The judge stated that "[g]reat as a crime of this nature must always appear to be, yet the inquiry into it must proceed upon the rules of evidence." Aside from testimony given at trial in the presence of the prisoner, the judge said, there were "two other species which are admitted by law: The one is the dying declaration of a person who has received a fatal blow; the other is the examination of a prisoner, and the depositions of the witnesses who may be produced against him" taken under the Marian bail and committal statutes. Silvia Woodcock's statement could not be admitted pursuant to the Marian statutes because it was unconfronted—the defendant had not been brought before the examining Magistrate and "the prisoner therefore had no opportunity of contradicting the facts it contains." Thus, the statements were admissible only if the witness "apprehended that she was in such a state of mortality as would inevitably oblige her soon to answer before her Maker for the truth or falsehood of her assertions." Depending on the account one credits, the court either instructed the jury to consider the statements only if Woodcock was "in fact under the apprehension of death," or determined for itself that Woodcock was "quietly resigned and submitting to her fate" and admitted her statements into evidence.

King v. Dingler, 2 Leach 561, 168 Eng. Rep. 383 (1791), applied the same test to exclude unconfronted statements by a murder victim. George Dingler was charged with killing his wife Jane, who suffered multiple stab wounds that left her in the hospital for 12 days before she died. The day after the stabbing, a Magistrate took Jane Dingler's deposition—as in *Woodcock,* under oath—"of the facts and circumstances which had attended the outrage committed upon her." George Dingler's attorney argued that the statements did not qualify as dying declarations and were not admissible Marian examinations because they were not taken in the presence of the prisoner, with the result that the defendant did not "have, as he is entitled to have, the benefit of cross-examination." The prosecutor agreed, but argued the deposition should still be admitted because "it was the best evidence that the nature of the case would afford." Relying on *Woodcock,* the court "refused to receive the examination into evidence."

. . .

The State offers another explanation for the above cases. It argues that when a defendant committed some act of wrongdoing that rendered a witness unavailable, he forfeited his right to object to the witness's testimony on confrontation grounds, but not on hearsay grounds. No case or treatise that we have found, however, suggested that a defendant who committed wrongdoing forfeited his confrontation rights but not his hearsay rights. And the distinction would have been a surprising one, because courts prior to the founding excluded hearsay evidence in large part *because* it was unconfronted. As the plurality said in *Dutton v. Evans,* 400 U.S. 74, 86, 91 S.Ct. 210, (1970), "[i]t seems apparent that the Sixth Amendment's Confrontation Clause and the evidentiary hearsay rule stem from the same roots."

The State and the dissent note that common-law authorities justified the wrongful-procurement rule by invoking the maxim that a defendant should not be permitted to benefit from his own wrong. But as the evidence amply shows, the "wrong" and the "evil Practices" to which these statements referred was conduct *designed* to prevent a witness from testifying. The absence of a forfeiture rule covering this sort of conduct would create an intolerable incentive for defendants to bribe, intimidate, or even kill witnesses against them. There is nothing mysterious about courts' refusal to carry the rationale further. The notion that judges may strip the defendant of a right that the Constitution deems essential to a fair trial, on the basis of a prior *judicial* assessment that the defendant is guilty as charged, does not sit well with the right to trial by jury. It is akin, one might say, to "dispensing with jury trial because a defendant is obviously guilty."

C

Not only was the State's proposed exception to the right of confrontation plainly not an "exceptio[n] established at the time of the founding," it is not established in American jurisprudence *since* the founding. American courts never—prior to 1985—invoked forfeiture outside the context of deliberate witness tampering.

This Court first addressed forfeiture in *Reynolds v. United States,* 98 U.S. 145, (1879), where, after hearing testimony that suggested the defendant had kept his wife away from home so that she could not be subpoenaed to testify, the trial court permitted the government to introduce testimony of the defendant's wife from the defendant's prior trial. On appeal, the Court held that admission of the statements did not violate the right of the defendant to confront witnesses at trial, because when a witness is absent by the defendant's "wrongful procurement," the defendant "is in no condition to assert that his constitutional rights have been violated" if "their evidence is supplied in some lawful way." *Reynolds* invoked broad forfeiture principles to explain its holding. The decision stated, for example, that "[t]he Constitution does not guarantee an accused person against the legitimate consequences of his own wrongful acts," and that the wrongful-procurement rule "has its foundation" in the principle that no one should be permitted to take advantage of his wrong, and is "the outgrowth of a maxim based on the principles of common honesty."

Reynolds relied on these maxims (as the common-law authorities had done) to be sure. But it relied on them (as the common-law authorities had done) to admit prior testimony in a case where the defendant had engaged in wrongful conduct designed to prevent a witness's testimony. The Court's opinion indicated that it was adopting the common-law rule. It cited leading common-law cases—*Lord Morley's Case, Harrison's Case,* and *Scaife*—described itself as "content with" the "long-established usage" of the forfeiture principle, and admitted prior confronted statements under circumstances where admissibility was open to no doubt under *Lord Morley's Case.*

If the State's rule had an historical pedigree in the common law or even in the 1879 decision in *Reynolds,* one would have expected it to be routinely invoked in murder prosecutions like the one here, in which the victim's prior statements inculpated the defendant. It was never invoked in this way. The earliest case identified by the litigants and *amici curiae* which admitted unconfronted statements on a forfeiture theory without evidence that the defendant had acted with the purpose of preventing the witness from testifying was decided in 1985.

In 1997, this Court approved a Federal Rule of Evidence, entitled "Forfeiture by wrongdoing," which applies only when the defendant "engaged or acquiesced in wrongdoing that was intended to, and did, procure the unavailability of the declarant as a witness." Fed. Rule of Evid. 804(b)(6). We have described this as a rule "which codifies the forfeiture doctrine." Every commentator we are aware of has concluded the requirement of intent "means that the exception applies only if the defendant has in mind the particular purpose of making the witness unavailable."[286] The commentators come out this way because the dissent's claim that knowledge is sufficient to show intent is emphatically *not* the modern view.

---

286. Only a single state evidentiary code appears to contain a forfeiture rule broader than our holding in this case (and in *Crawford*) allow. Seven of the 12 States that recognize wrongdoing as grounds for forfeiting objection to out-of-court statements duplicate the language of the federal forfeiture provision that requires purpose, see Del. Rule Evid. 804(b)(6) (2001); Ky. Rule Evid. 804(b)(5) (2004); N.D. Rule Evid. 804(b)(6) (2007); Pa. Rule Evid. 804(b)(6) (2005); Vt. Rule Evid. 804(b)(6) (2004); see also Tenn. Rule Evid. 804(b)(6) (2003) (identical except that it excludes mention of acquiescence); Mich. Rule Evid. 804(b)(6) (2008) (substitutes "engaged in or encouraged" for "engaged or acquiesced in"). Two others require "purpose" by their terms. Ohio Rule Evid. 804(B)(6) (2008); Cal. Evid.Code Ann. § 1350 (West Supp. 2008). Two of the three remaining forfeiture provisions require the defendant to have "procured" the unavailability of a witness, Haw. Rule 804(b)(7) (2007); Md. Cts. & Jud. Proc. Code Ann. § 10-901 (Lexis 2006)—which, as we have discussed, is a term traditionally used in the forfeiture context to require intent. Maryland's rule has thus been described as "requir[ing] that the judge must find that [the] wrongdoing or misconduct was undertaken with the intent of making the witness unavailable to testify." 6A L. McLain, Maryland Evidence, State and Federal § 804(6):1, p. 230 (West Supp.2007–2008). These rules cast more than a little doubt on the dissent's assertion that the historic forfeiture rule creates intolerable problems of proof. The lone forfeiture exception whose text reaches more broadly than the rule we adopt is an Oregon rule adopted in 2005. See 2005 Ore. Laws p. 1232, Ch. 458 (S.B. 287).

In sum, our interpretation of the common-law forfeiture rule is supported by (1) the most natural reading of the language used at common law; (2) the absence of common-law cases *admitting* prior statements on a forfeiture theory when the defendant had not engaged in conduct designed to prevent a witness from testifying; (3) the common law's uniform exclusion of unconfronted inculpatory testimony by murder victims (except testimony given with awareness of impending death) in the innumerable cases in which the defendant was on trial for killing the victim, but was not shown to have done so for the purpose of preventing testimony; (4) a subsequent history in which the dissent's broad forfeiture theory has not been applied. The first two and the last are highly persuasive; the third is in our view conclusive....

We decline to approve an exception to the Confrontation Clause unheard of at the time of the founding or for 200 years thereafter. The judgment of the California Supreme Court is vacated, and the case is remanded for further proceedings not inconsistent with this opinion. *It is so ordered.*

Justice THOMAS, concurring.

I write separately to note that I adhere to my view that statements like those made by the victim in this case do not implicate the Confrontation Clause. The contested evidence is indistinguishable from the statements made during police questioning in response to the report of domestic violence in *Hammon v. Indiana,* decided with *Davis v. Washington,* 547 U.S. 813, (2006). There, as here, the police questioning was not "a formalized dialogue"; it was not "sufficiently formal to resemble the Marian examinations" because "the statements were neither Mirandized nor custodial, nor accompanied by any similar indicia of formality"; and "there is no suggestion that the prosecution attempted to offer [Ms. Avie's] hearsay evidence at trial in order to evade confrontation." See *id.,* at 840, 126 S.Ct. 2266 (THOMAS, J., concurring in judgment in part and dissenting in part).

Nonetheless, in this case respondent does not argue that the contested evidence is nontestimonial; the court below noted "no dispute" on the issue; and it is outside the scope of the question presented. Because the Court's opinion accurately reflects our Confrontation Clause jurisprudence where the applicability of that Clause is not at issue, I join the Court in vacating the decision below.

Justice ALITO, concurring.

I join the Court's opinion, but I write separately to make clear that, like Justice THOMAS, I am not convinced that the out-of-court statement at issue here fell within the Confrontation Clause in the first place. The dissent's displeasure with the result in this case is understandable, but I suggest that the real problem concerns the scope of the confrontation right. The Confrontation Clause does not apply to out-of-court statements unless it can be said that they are the equivalent of statements made at trial by "witnesses." It is not at all clear that Ms. Avie's statement falls within that category. But the question whether Ms. Avie's statement falls within the scope of the Clause is not before us, and assuming for the sake of argument that the statement falls within the Clause, I agree with the Court's analysis of the doctrine of forfeiture by wrongdoing.

Discussion Questions

1. Explain the rationale that underlies an accused "forfeiting" his rights to confront and cross-examine a witness whose absence he procures for the purpose of preventing him from testifying at trial.
2. Why is this rule not properly extended to situations in which an accused has made the witness unavailable, but not for the purpose of preventing his testimony from trial?

3. Citing *Dutton v. Evans*,[287] the *Giles* Court notes that "[i]t seems apparent that the Sixth Amendment's Confrontation Clause and the evidentiary hearsay rule stem from the same roots." Explain this concept. How are the two concepts interrelated?
4. As we have discussed throughout Chapter 5, most of the hearsay exceptions are rooted in reliability, in that many of the dangers of admitting the statements are not present under the circumstances of each exception, as well as the necessity for the statement in some instances, since there might be no other way to obtain the evidence. Would you say that the "forfeiture by wrongdoing" exception is based on those underlying policy reasons or others? If not, what policy supports this exception?
5. Should a statement be allowed under this hearsay exception and over any objections to violations to the Confrontation Clause even if the statement is not trustworthy? Can it be said that an accused also forfeits any right to only have "trustworthy" out-of-court testimony offered against him? Why or why not?

In a case of first impression the Louisiana Fourth Circuit Court of Appeal, in *State v. Warner*,[288] considers whether a statement was properly admitted against an accused under Louisiana's "forfeiture by wrongdoing" exception to the hearsay rule, and whether the admissibility of such statement violates an accused's rights under the Sixth Amendment to the United States Constitution and Article I, § 16 of the Louisiana Constitution. Relying on *Giles* and *Crawford*, the court held that the statements did not violate the hearsay rule or the accused's constitutional rights, noting that there were certain "limited exceptions to the right of confrontation, i.e. those 'exceptions that existed at the time of our founding'"[289] with one being "known as 'forfeiture by wrongdoing.'"[290]

State v. Warner
Court of Appeal of Louisiana, Fourth Circuit
116 So. 3d 811
May 1, 2013

MADELEINE M. LANDRIEU, Judge.

Appellant, Jimmie Warner, was indicted for the second degree murder of Mr. Walter Jovel in violation of Louisiana Revised Statute 14:30.1. Following a jury trial, Mr. Warner was found guilty of the lesser included offense of negligent homicide and sentenced to serve a five-year sentence. He has filed the instant appeal of his conviction, alleging two assignments of error.

In his first assignment of error, Mr. Warner argues that the trial court erred when it allowed the State to introduce into evidence an out-of-court statement given by a witness who was called to testify but refused to answer questions asked of her....

FACTS AND PROCEEDINGS BELOW

In the early morning hours of July 20, 2008, Mr. Walter Jovel was shot and killed at the corner of N. Derbigny and Spain Streets. He was first found by military police officers who happened to be in the area on the evening of the shooting. They observed the victim to be unresponsive, apparently from multiple gunshot wounds. The military police con-

---

287. Dutton v. Evans, 400 U.S. 74, 86, 91 S.Ct. 210 (1970).
288. State v. Warner, 116 So. 3d 811 (La. Ct. App. 4th Cir. 1013)
289. *Id. quoting* Crawford v. Washington, 541 U.S. 36, 124 S.Ct. 1354 (2004).
290. *Id.*

tacted New Orleans police officers who investigated the shooting as a homicide. The investigation led to the arrest of the defendant, Mr. Jimmie Warner.

According to testimony elicited during Mr. Warner's trial, the victim was found in the driver's seat of a black truck, lying across the console in a large pool of blood. The car was still running when first responders arrived on the scene, and the car had apparently backed into a street sign. An autopsy later determined Mr. Jovel had been shot three times in the left side of his lower abdomen and buttocks and died of massive internal bleeding. The trajectory of the bullets were consistent with Mr. Jovel having been shot through an open door or window of the car, while in the driver's seat leaning across the front seat toward the passenger side of the vehicle.

In addition to those involved in the investigation, such as police, investigators and the coroner, two witnesses whose testimony is at issue in this appeal were called to the stand: Ms. Nadia Stark and Ms. Laverne King....

MS. STARK

On the evening of the shooting, Detective Nicholas Gernon canvassed the area looking for anyone who might have had information that would assist police in their investigation. He testified during the trial that he knocked on the door of 1703 Spain Street, a double on the corner of the intersection where the shooting occurred. Ms. Nadia Stark came to the door in response to his knock but told Det. Gernon she had been sleeping in the back room of the residence at the time of the shooting and had not heard or seen anything. Detective Gernon did not believe Ms. Stark as she was dressed in regular clothing and she did not appear to have been sleeping. However, he did not question her further at that point because it was shortly after the shooting, approximately 3:00 a.m., and he did not have authority to enter her residence. Det. Gernon gave Ms. Stark's name to Det. Regina Williams, the officer in charge of the investigation.

Based upon the information received from Det. Gernon, Det. Williams went to 1703 Spain Street and spoke with Ms. Stark. Det. Williams later took a recorded statement from Ms. Stark and showed her a photographic lineup, from which Ms. Stark identified the defendant, Mr. Jimmie Warner, as the shooter. Following Ms. Stark's statement and identification of Mr. Warner, Det. Williams booked Mr. Warner with the murder of Walter Jovel.

On the day before she was called to testify at trial, the court questioned Ms. Stark in the presence of counsel for the state and defense, but outside the presence of the jury. Ms. Stark informed the court that she would not answer any questions at trial, but would invoke her Fifth Amendment privilege. The court then suspended all questioning of Ms. Stark until such time as Ms. Stark's lawyer could be present. Once Ms. Stark's lawyer was present, the court allowed the parties to question Ms. Stark about her intentions with respect to giving testimony. The transcript of the proceedings reflects a three-fold purpose for this questioning: to ensure that in the presence of the jury no one discussed another alleged murder in which Ms. Stark's boyfriend, Seymour Quinn, and the defendant in this alleged murder, Jimmie Warner, were suspects; to determine whether Ms. Stark had the right to invoke her right against self-incrimination; and to determine the admissibility of Ms. Stark's recorded statement.

During this questioning, Ms. Stark testified that she was in custody for a probation violation in connection with a charge of theft of goods valued over $500 and that she knew Mr. Warner. She then, in response to a question posed by the State, testified that she would invoke her rights under the Fifth Amendment if she were called to testify in Jimmie Warner's case. The State asked if she was invoking her right because she was concerned that she would be prosecuted for perjury. She responded that she was pleading "the Fifth." The State asked if she would testify to the truth if the State called her to testify, and she asked to speak with her lawyer. After she conferred with counsel, Ms. Stark responded: "I have not [sic] intention of testifying at all and I plan to plead the Fifth." She then identified Mr. Warner. The State asked Ms. Stark if she would identify him in court and if she would testify as to the truth of what happened on the night of the shooting. Ms. Stark again conferred with her attorney and then stated: "I don't plan to testify. I just plan to state my name and my voice on the tape."

At this point, the court noted that Ms. Stark could not invoke her Fifth Amendment right in front of the jury and ordered the State to question her more fully. The State then asked her: if she saw Mr. Warner kill a Hispanic man in a black truck on July 20, 2008; if she killed the man; if she was at 1703 Spain Street on that night; if she was drinking or taking drugs that night; if she saw the Hispanic man arrive in the black truck; if she saw where the man came from; if she gave a statement to Det. Williams; if the statement was true; if she knew Mr. Quinn and if he lived at 1703 Spain; for a description of that address; what happened when the Hispanic male pulled up to the scene; who else was on the scene; what she saw when Mr. Warner walked up to the victim's truck; and if she saw Mr. Warner with a gun, get into the truck, and then get out of the truck. In response to all of these questions, with the exception of two, Ms. Stark responded that she pled "the Fifth." Ms. Stark only affirmatively testified that she gave a statement to the police and that she did not kill the man in the black truck.

At this juncture, the State filed a motion to compel Ms. Stark's testimony pursuant to article 439.1 of the Louisiana Code of Criminal Procedure which provides that under certain circumstances a witness who intends to invoke the privilege against self-incrimination may be compelled to give testimony and that any such testimony may not be used against the witness in any criminal case "except a prosecution for perjury, giving a false statement or otherwise failing to comply with the order." The court did not immediately rule on this motion but warned Ms. Stark that it would hold her in contempt each time she invoked the Fifth Amendment if there was no legal basis for doing so. The court then asked Ms. Stark whether she had any pending charges against her; whether she had been offered anything from the State or Mr. Warner for her testimony; and whether anyone had offered her any money or any promise or benefit for her testimony. To each of these questions, Mr. Stark responded "No." The court then asked Ms. Stark if anyone had told her that "something you may say or any testimony you may give could cause you harm" and whether she had been threatened if she were to give her testimony. As to these questions, Ms. Stark's lawyer asked for the opportunity to visit with Ms. Stark before she answered.

The court took a brief recess to allow counsel to consult with his client and Ms. Stark soon returned to the witness stand. Still outside the presence of the jury, Ms. Stark testified that she was receiving threats and had informed victim advocates about these threats. According to Ms. Stark, people came to her and told her to "stay out of it because of my son's sake and I got a one year old son." Ms. Stark testified that she was afraid to testify because of threats she had received—not threats of prosecution but threats of physical danger. The court then held that Ms. Stark she had no privilege against self-incrimination and ordered her to answer the questions asked of her.

In response to questions from the State, Ms. Stark testified that she gave a statement to Det. Williams and that she would be able to recognize her voice on the statement if she heard it. The State then played a portion of Ms. Stark's recorded statement and Ms. Stark identified her voice. The court asked her if she was scared, and she admitted that she was. The court then declared Ms. Stark a hostile witness which allowed the State to ask leading questions of her. La. C.E. art. 611(C). For reasons unrelated to this appeal, counsel for Ms. Stark was unable to continue to represent her at this point so the court suspended the questioning to allow time to procure another lawyer for Ms. Stark.

The next day, just before Ms. Stark was to be called to the stand in front of the jury, the court again recessed the jury to consider Ms. Stark's testimony. At this time, counsel for Ms. Stark informed the court that there had been possible contact between Ms. Stark and Mr. Warner while they were being transported to the court from jail that day. The court then reminded Ms. Stark that she could not raise her Fifth Amendment privilege in front of the jury and that she could be held in contempt of court is she failed to answer questions asked of her. The State then called Ms. Stark to the witness stand in the presence of the jury.

Here, Ms. Stark refused to answer any questions asked of her. When asked her name, whether she gave a statement to police and whether she could identify her voice on the recording, Ms. Stark simply refused to respond. When asked by the State whether the defendant, Jimmie Warner, had tried to contact her the night before, she again refused to respond. The State then asked her a series of leading questions regarding the shooting and she, again, had no response. On cross-examination, defense counsel only asked Ms. Stark if she was in court because she was serving a sentence for a felony theft conviction. Ms. Stark refused to respond. Defense counsel then noted that Ms. Stark was "not going to answer the questions" and did not ask her any more questions.

After Ms. Stark left the courtroom, the judge recessed the jury and, outside of their presence, declared Ms. Stark "unavailable" pursuant to Louisiana Code of Evidence article 804 A(2) because she persisted in refusing to testify despite an order from the court do so. The court then ruled that the statement Ms. Stark gave to police was admissible pursuant to Louisiana Code of Evidence article 804(B)(7) stating that the "defendant forfeited his constitutional right of confrontation" because the defendant "engaged or acquiesced in wrong doing" that was intended to "and did procure the unavailability" of the declarant (Ms. Stark) and "specifically intended the unavailability to prevent the witness from testifying." The State then called Det. Williams before the jury to authenticate the recording of Ms. Stark's statement and played the statement for the jury.

The recording indicated that the statement was taken on December 8, 2008. Ms. Stark stated that she, Seymour [Quinn], Jimmie [Warner] and someone named James were at her apartment at 1703 Spain Street just prior to the murder. Ms. Stark mentioned something about the woman next door, Erica, being outside on her own porch selling cocaine. She said that Jimmie went outside, and she saw him approach a truck that had stopped. She stated that she supposed that Jimmie asked the driver if he wanted anything, and after the two men spoke, Jimmie got into the passenger side of the truck. She stated that she heard shots, and then Jimmie got out of the truck and ran away, hiding the gun. She stated that she kept looking out the window at the truck to see if the driver was alive or dead, and she saw the truck moving after the shooting. She stated that she saw Jimmie with a gun before he got inside the truck. When questioned further, Ms. Stark stated that Jimmie was first standing on the driver's side of the truck, and then he got in the passenger door, and while he was inside she saw the driver struggling with Jimmie, trying to get the gun. She then changed her account, telling the detectives that Jimmie spoke with the driver, and then got inside the truck. She stated that Jimmie then got back out of the truck, went to the driver's side, and at that point, it appeared that the driver was trying to get the gun out of Jimmie's hand. She then heard shots, and Jimmie fled. The truck then backed up onto the curb. She stated that Jimmie hid the gun next to Ms. Keisha's house, which was across the street from her apartment. Ms. Stark stated that she did not see Jimmie after the shooting.

Ms. Stark said that after Jimmie left, she kept looking at the truck, but she never saw anyone leave it. At some point, she left the window and lay down, and then she got up and saw that the police had arrived. She then went back to bed, and soon officers knocked at her door. She admitted that she told them that she did not see or hear anything because she did not want to get involved. Ms. Stark stated that one or two weeks after the shooting she called Crimestoppers and told the person who took her tip that someone whom she thought was named Jimmie shot the man at the corner of Spain and N. Derbigny. She stated that she described the shooter as tall with big dreadlocks and a cross in the middle of his face.

Ms. Stark admitted in her statement that she went to the police station on the day she gave her statement in connection with a different shooting at the same intersection for which her boyfriend, Seymour Quinn, was in jail. She admitted that while discussing that shooting, she told the officers about the present shooting. She denied giving the officers the information about the present shooting because her boyfriend was in jail and she insisted that her statement accurately set forth what she witnessed. She denied that her statement was the product of any promises or force, and she agreed that its contents were true to the best of her knowledge. She denied that she was under the influence of any drugs, medication, or alcohol while giving the statement.

Mr. Warner contends that Ms. Stark's statement should have been excluded because it was testimonial in nature and her refusal to answer questions denied him his constitutional right to "confront the witnesses against him." This argument forms the basis of Mr. Warner's first assignment of error.

...

ASSIGNMENTS OF ERROR

ISSUES PRESENTED

I. Whether admitting the recorded statement of Nadia Stark under the circumstances of this case denied Mr. Warner his constitutional right of confrontation and his constitutional right to a fair trial.

...

DISCUSSION

I. Introduction of Ms. Stark's statement

Mr. Warner contends that the hearsay exception embodied in Louisiana Code of Evidence article 804(B)(7) is inapplicable here as the State did not establish by a preponderance of the evidence the he was the person who threatened Ms. Stark. Mr. Warner further contends that Ms. Stark's refusal to testify denied him his right of confrontation and thereby denied him his right to a fair trial.

It is undisputed that Ms. Stark's statement was hearsay as it was a statement made by her out of court and offered in court to prove the truth of the matter asserted. LSA—C.E. art. 801(C). Hearsay evidence is not admissible except as otherwise specified in the Louisiana Code of Evidence or other legislation. LSA—C.E. art. 802. The only exception relevant here is found in Article 804 B(7), which provides:

> **12 **B. Hearsay exceptions.** The following are not excluded by the hearsay rule if the declarant is unavailable as a witness:
>
> * * *

(7)(a) **Forfeiture by wrongdoing.** A statement offered against a party that has engaged or acquiesced in wrongdoing that was intended to, and did, procure the unavailability of the declarant as a witness.

b) A party seeking to introduce statements under the forfeiture by wrongdoing hearsay exception shall establish, by a preponderance of the evidence, that the party against whom the statement is offered, engaged or acquiesced in the wrongdoing.

Subpart B(7) of this rule was added in 2009 and amended in 2010, and there are no published Louisiana cases that have addressed it. However, here, it is clear that the plain reading of the exception applies to the facts before us. The trial court held the statement admissible because the defendant engaged or acquiesced in wrongdoing. In so finding, the court specifically found that Mr. Warner intended to and did procure Ms. Stark's absence. Thus, the court found Ms. Stark's statement admissible under Louisiana Code of Evidence article 804(B)(7).

Mr. Warner asserts that the State did not establish by a preponderance of the evidence, as required by the article, that he was the person who threatened Ms. Stark. He contends that when Ms. Stark testified during the second day of trial, outside of the jury's presence, that she had received threats of harm if she testified, she did not indicate that Mr. Warner was the person who threatened her.

Article 804(B)(7) does not require that the person who will benefit must be the person who actually threatens a witness. The language of article 804(B)(7) only requires that the person against whom the hearsay is offered "engaged or acquiesced in the wrongdoing." Notably, once the court informed Ms. Stark that she had no basis to assert her Fifth Amendment right and that the court would hold her in contempt if she failed to answer questions when she was called before the jury, Ms. Stark answered various questions. Specifically, Ms. Stark, outside the presence of the jury, identified herself and Mr. Warner. She testified that she would, if called before the jury, identify herself, and her voice on the tape. She also testified that she had been threatened and was scared. Then, according to Ms. Stark's lawyer, as Mr. Warner and Ms. Stark were passing in the jail on the way to court on the day she was to testify in front of the jury, there was "some possible contact between the defendant and Ms. Stark." It was after this contact that Ms. Stark took the witness stand in front of the jury and refused to answer any questions asked of her. She refused to identify herself; refused to identify Mr. Warner; refused to admit that she gave a statement to the police; and refused to admit that she could recognize her voice on the tape. After the State played a portion of the tape, Ms. Stark refused to identify her voice on the tape.

Considering the totality of the facts below, we cannot say that the trial court erred in finding that the State proved, by a preponderance of the evidence that Mr. Warner "engaged or acquiesced in wrongdoing that was intended to, and did, procure the unavailability of the witness."

Our finding that this hearsay exception was properly applied does not end our inquiry. Mr. Warner asserts that his right of confrontation guaranteed by the Sixth Amendment of the United States Constitution was violated when the court allowed Ms. Stark's statement to be admitted into evidence without being subject to cross-examination.

The Sixth Amendment to the United States Constitution and Article I, § 16 of the Louisiana Constitution guarantee an accused in a criminal prosecution the right to confront the witnesses against him. *State v. Jackson,* 880 So.2d 841, 852.

In *Crawford v. Washington,* 541 U.S. 36, (2004), the United States Supreme Court altered the legal landscape of Confrontation Clause analysis involving hearsay by reexamining its holding in *Ohio v. Roberts,* 448 U.S. 56, 66 (1980). Under *Roberts,* the Confrontation Clause did not bar admission of an unavailable declarant's statement if the statement fell under a "firmly rooted hearsay exception" or bore "particularized guarantees of trustworthiness." In *Crawford,* the Supreme Court revisited this issue and held that where "testimonial" statements are at issue, there is no "guarantee of trustworthiness" that can substitute for cross-examination.

In *Crawford,* the defendant was tried in the State of Washington for assault and attempted murder of a man who allegedly raped his wife. The defendant's wife was a witness to the incident between the victim and her husband, and after being questioned by police, provided them with a recorded statement. At trial, the wife was unavailable to testify because of the spousal privilege. The State sought to introduce the wife's statement as a statement against interest. The defendant argued that, notwithstanding state law that allowed the exception, the admission would violate his federal constitutional right of confrontation.

The trial court admitted that statement into evidence, and Mr. Crawford was convicted. The Washington Court of Appeals reversed. It applied a nine-factor test to determine whether Sylvia Crawford's statement "bore particularized guarantees of trustworthiness and noted several reasons why it did not." 541 U.S. at 41, 124 S.Ct. 1354. The Washington Supreme Court reinstated the conviction, unanimously concluding that, "although Sylvia's statement did not fall under a firmly rooted hearsay exception, it bore guarantees of trustworthiness." *Id.* The United States Supreme Court granted certiorari "to determine whether the State's use of Sylvia's statement violated the Confrontation Clause."

In analyzing the concepts of hearsay and the Confrontation Clause, the *Crawford* court distinguished between "nontestimonial" and "testimonial" hearsay. The Court explained that it would be consistent with the Framer's intent to permit the States flexibility in the development of hearsay law. 124 S.Ct. at 1374. However, with testimonial hearsay evidence, the Court concluded that the Confrontation Clause demands that the declarant be unavailable and that there be a prior opportunity for cross-examination. The Supreme Court rejected its prior analysis in *Ohio v. Roberts,* which had held that the test for admissibility under the Confrontation Clause was whether the hearsay falls under a "firmly rooted hearsay exception" or bears "particularized guarantees of trustworthiness. "The *Crawford* court held that this test departed from the historical principles of the Confrontation Clause and held the standard to be too malleable. Justice Scalia, writing for the majority, noted: "Dispensing with confrontation because testimony is obviously reliable is akin to dispensing with jury trial because the defendant is obviously guilty." 124 S.Ct. at 1371.

In reaching its decision that admitting Sylvia's statement violated Mr. Crawford's right of confrontation, the Crawford court drew a distinction between testimonial hearsay and nontestimonial hearsay and held: "Where testimonial statements are at issue, the only indicium of reliability sufficient to satisfy constitutional demands is the one the Constitution actually prescribes: confrontation." 124 S.Ct. at 1374. However, the *Crawford* court recognized certain limited exceptions to the right of confrontation, i.e. those "exceptions that existed at the time of our founding." One exception particularly noted by the *Crawford* court was known as "forfeiture by wrongdoing," first recognized by the Supreme Court in *Reynolds.*

Thus, the first issue is whether Ms. Stark's statement is "testimonial." While the Supreme Court in *Crawford* specifically declined to fully define "testimonial," it recognized that the Confrontation Clause applies to "witnesses' against the accused—in other words, those who bear testimony... An accuser who makes a formal statement to government officers bears testimony in a sense that a person who makes a casual remark to an acquaintance does not." 541 U.S. at 51, 124 S.Ct. 1354. *Internal citations omitted.* Thus, the majority concluded that "statements taken by police officers in the course of interrogations" (custodial examinations) are testimonial under a narrow definition of the term.2

It is undisputed that Ms. Stark's statement at issue here was testimonial, and therefore the trial court was correct to consider its admissibility in light of *Crawford.* A *Crawford* analysis requires two considerations when testimonial hearsay statements are admitted against an accused: (1) Did the accused have the right to cross-examine the statement? (2) If not, was the statement otherwise admissible pursuant to an exception to the confrontation right that "existed at the time of the founding?" *Id.* The *Crawford* court specifically acknowledged that one of the exceptions that existed when our nation was founded was the doctrine of "forfeiture by wrongdoing." Rooted in common law, this doctrine was premised on the principal that a defendant should not be permitted to benefit from his own wrongdoing.

Forfeiture by wrongdoing was first addressed by the United States Supreme Court in *Reynolds v. United States,* 98 U.S. 145, (1878 Term), a case involving the prosecution for the crime of bigamy. In *Reynolds,* the trial court allowed the prosecution to introduce testimony from the defendant's wife from a prior trial because the defendant had procured her absence at his retrial. The *Reynolds* Court found that the introduction of the wife's testimony did not violate the defendant's confrontation right, given the fact that he procured her absence: 98 U.S. at 158:

> The Constitution gives the accused the right to a trial at which he should be confronted with the witnesses against him; but if a witness is absent by his own wrongful procurement, he cannot complain if competent evidence is admitted to supply the place of that which he has kept away. The Constitution does not guarantee an accused person against the legitimate consequences of his own wrongful acts. It grants him the privilege of being confronted with the witnesses against him; but if he voluntarily keeps the witnesses away, he cannot insist on his privilege. If, therefore, when absent by his procurement, their evidence is supplied in some lawful way, he is in no condition to assert that his constitutional rights have been violated.

This doctrine was more recently discussed in *Giles v. California,* 554 U.S. 353, 128 S.Ct. 2678, 171 L.Ed.2d 488 (2008)....

In *Giles,* the Supreme Court refused to extend the forfeiture by wrongdoing exception to the hearsay rule to the *Giles* facts. In reversing the conviction, the Court held that in order to admit testimonial hearsay evidence that would fit within the forfeiture by wrongdoing exception, the prosecution must show that the defendant *intended* to prevent a witness from testifying. [citations omitted]

... The Court noted that it previously described this evidentiary provision as a rule "which codifies the forfeiture doctrine." [Citations omitted]

Louisiana's forfeiture by wrongdoing exception to hearsay was modeled after the Federal Rule. Unlike California's rule discussed in *Giles,* our rule is one firmly rooted in a hearsay exception that existed at the time of our founding. It requires a finding that the defendant " 'had in mind the particular purpose of making the witness unavailable.' " *Id.* at 367, 128 S.Ct. at 2687. Here, the trial court so found.

This assignment of error is without merit.

...

AFFIRMED

Discussion Questions

1. While the witness in *Warner* is clearly unavailable, are you satisfied that the State showed by a preponderance of the evidence that the accused engaged in wrongdoing for the purpose of procuring the unavailability of the witness? What evidence was presented? What, if any, more would you have required be shown?
2. What conduct should be considered as "wrongdoing"? Clearly, killing a witness or threatening a witness is sufficient. But what if a witness writes a letter asking the witness not to testify, or sends a family member or friend to the witness to ask them not to testify? What if they try very hard to persuade the witness and the witness agrees? What type of conduct should be included?
3. Explain Justice Scalia's analogy in *Crawford* that "[d]ispensing with confrontation because testimony is obviously reliable is akin to dispensing with jury trial because the defendant is obviously guilty." What do you think he means by this statement?
4. How does the court determine whether the statement violated the defendant's rights under the United States Constitution and Art. I § 16 of the Louisiana Constitution? What were the three steps applied from *Crawford*? What was the court's analysis of each?
5. Do you believe it is fair for the judge to be permitted to take away constitutional rights upon its own determination that the defendant engaged in wrongdoing? As to the underlying wrongdoing, isn't the judge acting as judge and jury? Is this fair? Why or why not?
6. Should the jury be made aware of the defendant's conduct in procuring the unavailability of the witness? For what purpose(s) might such evidence of any threats, attempt to contact the witness, etc., be relevant in the trial? See *State v. Lewis*, 125 So. 3d 1252 (La. Ct. App. 4th Cir. 2013) (finding that evidence was relevant to proving "consciousness of guilt" and his "desire to evade prosecution" and conviction). Can you think of other reasons?

Key Points

The key points to keep in mind regarding the forfeiture by wrongdoing.

1. Allows a statement of an unavailable declarant to be offered against a party if that person is shown to be responsible for procuring the unavailability of the witness for the specific purpose of preventing the witness from testifying against him.
2. **Two requirements for the exception:**
   a. declarant is unavailable; and
   b. proponent must prove, by a preponderance of the evidence, that the party against whom the statement is now offered, procured the unavailability of witness for *purpose of* preventing the witness from testifying.
3. The proponent must establish by a preponderance of the evidence that the accused actually engaged in wrongdoing for the purpose of preventing the witness from testifying.
4. An accused who procures the absence of a witness for the purpose of preventing the witness from testifying also forfeits his rights under the Confrontation Clause of the United States Constitution and Article I § 16 of the Louisiana Constitution.

Problems on Forfeiture by Wrongdoing

PROBLEM 5-159. Drell's second wife is missing and his first wife is dead. The state brought charges against Drell for his first wife's murder and would like to use statements his second wife made to her attorney about Drell. She claims he told her he killed his first wife. The defense objects that the statement is hearsay. The prosecution claims that the statement should be admissible under the "forfeiture by wrongdoing" exception, but the defense claims that Drell is not responsible for his second wife being missing. What must be shown in order for the prosecution to be able to use the second wife's statement against Drell? What outcome?

PROBLEM 5-160. Richard is under a grand jury investigation for lying on an application to adopt children where he stated that he had no prior convictions and that he had never lived under a different name. The truth is that Richard had been found not guilty of child molestation charges several years before adopting the kids. Thereafter, he changed his name to Richard and adopted the two kids, lying on the application about his past. One of Richard's neighbors tipped the police off about the prior charges when the neighbor became suspicious that he kept receiving mail at his residence for Richard addressed to Graylord. He did some research and determined that Richard may have lived under that name and may have been hiding something, so he called the police. The investigation led to the grand jury investigation in which the neighbor was called to testify. The same day that the neighbor testified at the grand jury hearing, and it looked as though Richard would be indicted, the neighbor was found dead in his home. Richard was also found in his home with a gunshot wound to the head. Richard admitted that he tried to kill himself to avoid being disgraced, but he lived and was forced to stand trial for all of the charges. He denied involvement in the neighbor's murder. At the trial, when the police officer testified as to what neighbor had told him, Richard objected that the statements are hearsay. Can the statements be admitted into evidence over Richard's objection? Why or why not? What, if anything, would have to be shown first?

§ 5.21 References and Additional Authority on Forfeiture by Wrongdoing [La. C.E. art. 804(B)(7)]

1. La. C.E. art. 804(B)(7) and Official Comments
2. Force & Rault, Handbook on Louisiana Evidence Law Art. 804(B)(7) Author's Comments (West Publishing 2014)
3. Harges & Jones, Louisiana Evidence Art. 804(B)(7) Author's Comments (West Publishing 2014)
4. **Forfeiture by wrongdoing Article 804(B)(7):** *State v. Johnson*, 151 So. 3d 683 (La. Ct. App. 4th Cir. 2014) (holding that the State proved by the preponderance of the evidence that the defendant forfeited his right to cross-examine the eyewitness by procuring the unavailability of the witness; defendant had the witness murdered on the same day that he found out the identity of the "unknown witness").

PART D
STATUTORY NON-HEARSAY/EXEMPTIONS TO THE HEARSAY RULE [LA. C.E. ART. 801(D)]

We now move to Article 801(D), which contains a list of several types of statements that are classed as "**not hearsay**" rather than as "exceptions" to the hearsay rule. The statements contained in this article are *exempt* from the hearsay rule even though the statements would technically be hearsay under the definition. Thus this category of statements is usually referred to as "**hearsay exemptions**" or "**statutory non-hearsay.**" For example, identifications are hearsay because the assertive conduct of pointing out someone who did something is offered to prove the truth of the matter asserted within the statement. However, Article 801(D)(1)(c) specifically exempts a statement from the hearsay ban if the declarant testifies at the trial or hearing and is subject to cross-examination concerning the statement, and the statement is "one of identification of a person made after perceiving the person."[291] Even though technically hearsay, the legislature has exempted these and other statements from being excluded by the hearsay rule.

For all practical purposes, the hearsay exemptions are treated the same as the exceptions in that if a statement conforms to the requirements of the hearsay exemption, it may be offered for the truth of the matter asserted. Thus, a proponent of a statement should determine whether a statement conforms to the requirements of any of the provisions of Article 801(D) as another way of avoiding exclusion of the statement by the hearsay rule.

There are three main categories of statements contained in Article 801(D) creating six different types of statements that are exempt from the hearsay rule that we will study in this part. These statements are:

1. Prior statements in Article 801(D)(1)(a)–(d), discussed in § 5.22;
   a. Prior inconsistent statements [Article 801(D)(1)(a)]
   b. Prior consistent statements [Article 801(D)(1)(b)]
   c. Identifications [Article 801(D)(1)(c)]
   d. Prior complaint of sexually assaultive behavior [Article 801(D)(1)(d)]
2. Admissions in Article 801(D)(2) and (3) discussed in § 5.23; and
3. Things said and done contained in Article 801(D)(4) discussed in § 5.24.

§ 5.22 Prior Statements [La. C.E. art. 801(D)(1)(a)–(d)]

The first category of statutory non-hearsay we will cover is contained in Article 801(D)(1). This article exempts four types of statements that a witness made ***prior to*** testifying at the current trial from the hearsay rule. The four types of prior statements contained in Article 801(D)(1) are: 1) prior inconsistent statements; 2) prior consistent statements; 3) identifications; and 4) complaints of sexual assault.

In all four situations, the person who made the prior statement must be present and testifying in court, and is subject to being cross-examined concerning his prior statement.

291. LA. CODE EVID. art. 801(D)(1)(c).

Prerequisites for all Prior Statements:

1. the declarant testifies at the trial or hearing; and
2. the declarant is subject to cross-examination concerning the prior statement.

If the additional requirements for each exemption are met, the witness's prior statement may be offered to prove the truth of the matter asserted.

Thus, there are two prerequisites for admissibility that apply to all prior statements which are: 1) the declarant must testify at the trial or hearing; and 2) be subject to cross-examination concerning the prior statement. These are covered in § 5.22.1–§ 5.22.4.

§ 5.22.1 Prior Inconsistent Statements [La. C.E. art. 801(D)(1)(a)]

Applicable Code Articles

* * *

D. Statements which are not hearsay. A statement is not hearsay if:

(1) Prior statement by witness. The declarant testifies at the trial or hearing and is subject to cross-examination concerning the statement, and the statement is:

(a) In a criminal case, inconsistent with his testimony, provided that the proponent has first fairly directed the witness' attention to the statement and the witness has been given the opportunity to admit the fact and where there exists any additional evidence to corroborate the matter asserted by the prior inconsistent statement;

* * *

Article 801(D)(1)(a) exempts certain prior *inconsistent* statements from the hearsay rule. A prior inconsistent statement is a statement that a witness made prior to currently testifying at the trial that is inconsistent with his current testimony. For example, if a witness testifies at trial that the light was green when he went through it, but told a police officer on the day of the accident that the light was red when he went through it, the statement to the police officer is a prior statement that is inconsistent with his current testimony.

Requirements for Prior Inconsistent Statements for Substantive Value

1. the declarant testifies;
2. the declarant is subject to cross-examination about the prior statement;
3. applies to criminal cases;
4. the prior statement is inconsistent with his current testimony;
5. witness first given opportunity to admit the fact of the prior statement; and
6. additional evidence corroborates the prior statement.

The prior inconsistent statement need not have been made at a prior trial or hearing or under oath. The exemption includes statements given in a variety of circumstances including a statement made to a police officer, to a friend, in a deposition, a written letter, a recording or otherwise, whether formal or informal.

Offered for substantive purposes. The significance of this provision is that in a criminal trial a declarant's prior inconsistent statement may be used/offered for its *substantive value*, i.e., to prove the truth of the matter asserted within it, rather than just for impeachment purposes as provided in Article 607. Under that article, which we will study in Chapter 6, the use of the prior inconsistent statement may be used to attack the witness's credibility only, i.e., to suggest that the witness may be lying since he is testifying differently at trial than in his prior statement.

For example, taking the scenario above regarding the red light, if the witness told the police officer at the scene that the light was red when he went through it, but testifies at the trial that the light was green, under Article 607, the prior inconsistent statement may only be offered to show that the witness may be lying because he previously made a statement inconsistent with his current testimony. The attorney offering the prior statement could not offer the prior statement to prove nor could he argue that the light was actually red, as the witness previously stated. In such a case, the statement is not being offered for its substantive value, but instead is only being offered to attack the witness's credibility.

However, under this provision, in a *criminal trial*, the attorney offering the prior inconsistent statement could use the prior statement to argue that the light was actually red, as the witness previously stated, i.e., he could offer the prior inconsistent statement for its **substantive value**. Technically, this use would be hearsay because the statement is being offered to prove the truth of the matter asserted, but this provision exempts such prior inconsistent statements from the hearsay ban.

This change in Louisiana law was enacted in 2004[292] primarily to address domestic violence situations in which victims commonly recant and change their stories.[293] This provision allows prosecutors to use the victim's prior statements as substantive evidence to prove the truth of the matter asserted within the statements if the requirements of the rule are met including corroborating evidence of the substance of the prior statement.

Requirements to use for substantive value. Should the proponent of the prior inconsistent statement seek to offer evidence of the prior statement for its substantive value under this provision, the following requirements must be met:

1. the declarant testifies at trial;
2. the declarant is subject to cross-examination about the prior statement;
3. applies to criminal cases;
4. the prior statement is inconsistent with his current testimony;
5. witness first given opportunity to admit the fact of the prior statement; and
6. additional evidence corroborates the prior statement.

---

292. Acts 2004 Number 694 of the Louisiana Legislature.
293. *See* State v. Rankin, 965 So. 2d 946 (La. Ct. App. 2d Cir. 2007).

Declarant testifies at hearing/Subject to cross-examination. As with all four types of prior statements contained in Article 801(D)(1), the declarant must testify at the current trial and be subject to cross-examination about the prior statement. If the witness is unavailable, this exemption does not apply.

Opportunity to admit the fact. Additionally, prior to introducing the prior statement, the proponent must first direct the witness's attention to the statement and give the witness an opportunity to admit the fact. If the witness fails to admit the fact, the proponent may offer extrinsic evidence of the prior statement through another witness who heard the prior inconsistent statement made by the witness. The requirements are substantially similar to the foundational requirements contained in Article 613 for admitting evidence of a prior inconsistent statement under Article 607. If the witness admits the prior statement, "*Yes, I said that, but I'm telling the truth now,*" then counsel cannot offer extrinsic evidence of the prior statement under this rule.

Additional evidence corroborates. In order for the prior inconsistent statement to be admitted into evidence for substantive purposes, the prior statement must be corroborated by other evidence. The corroborating evidence may be any other witness's statements, or physical evidence to help establish that the prior statement was in fact true. For example, a witness testifying at trial in a domestic violence case against her husband accused of battering her might testify at trial that her husband did not attack her. However, in the witness's prior statement given to police at the scene, she might have given a detailed account of how her husband physically attacked and beat her.

Evidence corroborating the witness's prior statement, that she was attacked and beaten, might include injuries and bruises consistent with the victim's description of the attack, torn clothes, or a room in disarray. The witness might have described a weapon used, such as a pipe, which was located and recovered by the investigating officer. Additionally, the suspect might be seen leaving the scene upon police arrival. The witness, through whom the prior statement is offered, such as the police officer, could testify to the corroborating circumstances that support the prior statement. The requirement of corroborating circumstances helps to ensure the reliability of the prior statement since it is being offered to prove the truth of the matter asserted within the statement.

Federal Rules of Evidence Distinction. Federal Rule of Evidence 801(d)(1)(a) has several distinctions from the Louisiana rule. Under the Federal Rule the statement must have been made by the declarant at "a trial, hearing, or other proceeding, or in a deposition."[294] Further, the Federal Rule applies in both civil and criminal cases, whereas the Louisiana article only applies in criminal cases, and under Louisiana law the prior statement need not have been made at any type of formal hearing or deposition.

Case on Prior Inconsistent Statement

State v. Updite presents a good example of the application of Article 801(D)(1)(a) in a common scenario—the use of prior inconsistent statements to assist the prosecution to obtain convictions in domestic violence cases —cases in which witnesses/victims often recant and change their stories.

---

294. Fed. R. Evid. 801(d)(1)(a).

State v. Updite
Court of Appeal of Louisiana, Second Circuit
87 So. 3d 257
Feb. 29, 2012

GASKINS, Judge.

The defendant, a Shreveport police officer, married the victim, Joney Pillows–Updite, in January 2010. On the evening of Thursday, March 4, 2010, and into the early morning of Friday, March 5, 2010, there was an altercation between the couple that was both verbal and physical. The victim's nine-year-old daughter was present in the apartment during this event.

On Saturday, March 6, 2010, the victim called the police and reported the incident. In the early morning hours of Sunday, March 7, 2010, she and her daughter gave recorded statements to the police. According to the victim's statement, the defendant came home on Thursday after attending a class at the police academy; he called her lazy and began yelling at her. At this point, they "tussled" but no blows were struck. According to the victim, the defendant shoved her at this time. The defendant then left the apartment to go to a movie. After he returned, their dispute resumed. She was in bed and wanted to go to sleep. The defendant yelled at her, calling her names. He shoved her first. He then began to hit her with a closed fist on the left side of her face, her left arm and chest. In addition to "punching" her, the victim said the defendant also choked her.

...

The police then spoke to the defendant and informed him that he was under investigation for domestic abuse battery. He initially declined to give a statement. He then changed his mind and agreed to talk to the officers in the presence of his mother, who is a pastor. He stated that on Thursday evening, he made a remark to his wife about her being lazy. She hit him in the face four times; he grabbed her shoulder and pushed her against the wall to stop her. He said they were in the bathroom and his stepdaughter was in another room. He denied hitting the victim and said she threatened to call the police, knowing that he could not afford to get in trouble.

...

On March 11, 2010, the victim signed a notarized "withdrawal of complaint" in which she stated that she wanted to withdraw her complaint of March 6, 2010. She asserted that it was not her husband's intent to hurt her and that they both "misinterpreted" and "overreacted" during the incident. She claimed that she just wanted to make a "home report" but did not want charges filed against him. She further accused the police officers involved of "intimidating" and "misleading" her and forcing her to give a statement while she was "groggy" and "foggy" from medication.

The defendant was charged with domestic abuse battery, in violation of La. R.S. 14:35.3, by bill of information filed on May 5, 2010.

On May 28, 2010, the victim filed a petition for protection from abuse in which she alleged that the defendant had slapped, punched, choked, shoved and threatened her with bodily harm.... She signed an affidavit verifying the petition. An order of protection was signed on May 28, 2010.

On June 29, 2010, the victim filed a petition for divorce in which she alleged that she and the defendant had separated on May 17, 2010, without reconciliation....

On February 24, 2011, and April 21, 2011, the instant criminal matter was tried....

The victim took the stand and recanted her allegations of abuse. She admitted signing the divorce petition verification but said she didn't read the petition "line by line" beforehand. She said the protective order petition was written by a woman at the YWCA from the police reports and that she did not read it before signing it. However, she admitted supplying the dates that were filled in. She asserted that she wrote a typed four-page statement dated March 18, 2011, in which she accused the police of "manipulat[ing]" and "deceiv[ing]" her and the DA of defaming her when it requested a material witness warrant for her. When asked if she had told someone that the typed statement was actually written by her mother-in-law, she admitted that she might have said that "just being angry." When her recorded statement was played without objection, she said she remembered "some" of it. She accused the police officers of misleading her and asserted that she "wasn't in my right mind" when the statement was taken because it was late and she was on "medication." She claimed that she did not want her husband arrested; instead she wanted marital counseling and for his supervisor to "talk" to him.

In her trial testimony, the victim insisted that her husband did not intend to hurt her. She said she told the officers that it was dark and she could not see if the defendant punched or pushed her to cause the bruises on her chest. She said that instead of punching her, he could have "just fell on the bed." She additionally insisted he restrained her because she threw something at him and he might have thought she was going to hit him. She admitted that she was physically sore from their "quarrel." In fact, she testified that the next day she was in so much pain, she could not roll over in any direction.

Sergeant Jody Jones, one of the two officers who interviewed the victim and her daughter, testified. He stated that the victim was able to give a clear statement about what happened. She had bruises on her left upper arm, left chest, left upper back and right upper arm. She stated that she got these bruises from being struck by the defendant and that he also twisted her arm. Additionally, she told him that the defendant choked her but she had no visible bruises indicating that. Although she said she had taken some Aleve, the victim appeared lucid and aware. Neither he nor the other detective prompted her to say where the bruises came from. She never said it was too dark to see whether the defendant hit her. Nor did she say she threw anything at him or hit him first.

The defendant testified in his own defense. He insisted that he only restrained his wife when she was physically violent toward him....

At the conclusion of the evidence, the trial court found the defendant guilty as charged, concluding that the testimony indicated that there was a battery initiated by the defendant. The court sentenced him to six months in the parish jail, suspended, and seven months of supervised probation. The defendant was also ordered to complete a domestic violence counseling program.

The defendant sought review of his conviction.

SUFFICIENCY OF EVIDENCE

Law

When issues are raised on appeal both as to the sufficiency of the evidence and as to one or more trial errors, the reviewing court should first determine the sufficiency of the evidence. The reason for reviewing sufficiency first is that the accused may be entitled to an acquittal under *Hudson v. Louisiana,* 450 U.S. 40, 101 S.Ct. 970, 67 L.Ed.2d 30 (1981), if a rational trier of fact, viewing the evidence in accord with *Jackson v. Virginia,* 443 U.S. 307, 99 S.Ct. 2781, (1979), in the light most favorable to the prosecution, could not reasonably conclude that all of the elements of the offense have been proved beyond a reasonable doubt. *State v. Hearold,* 603 So.2d 731 (La.1992).

...

Domestic abuse battery is the intentional use of force or violence committed by one household member upon the person of another household member. La. R.S. 14:35.3(A).

Discussion

The evidence presented at trial demonstrated the following events. The defendant and the victim engaged in an argument after he called her lazy. Subsequently, they argued again and the situation escalated to the defendant choking, punching and hitting the victim. The victim received bruises which she photographed. She gave a recorded statement to the police detailing the abuse. Although she later attempted to justify and excuse her husband's actions, the victim testified that the defendant's confrontation with her became physical. The detective who interviewed the victim testified that she had visible bruising and that the victim had not mentioned any of her later excuses for the defendant's actions in her statement to the police. While the victim's daughter did not see the fight, she heard noises and statements that indicated that the defendant struck the victim. All of the testimony accepted by the trial court as credible indicated that there was a battery initiated by the defendant.

We find that the evidence at trial presented by the state and accepted by the trial judge proves every element of the crime of domestic abuse battery beyond a reasonable doubt and that the *Jackson* standard has been met. Accordingly, this assignment of error lacks merit.

VICTIM'S INCONSISTENT STATEMENTS

In two assignments of error, the defendant complains that the trial court improperly relied upon evidence that was used to impeach the victim as substantive evidence.

Law

While prior inconsistent statements are admissible to attack credibility under La. C.E. art. 607(D)(2), such nonhearsay statements may also be admissible for their assertive value. See *State v. Rankin,* 42,412 (La.App.2d Cir.9/19/07), 965 So.2d 946.

In relevant part, La. C.E. art. 801 now provides:

> D. Statements which are not hearsay. A statement is not hearsay if:
>
> (1) Prior statement by witness. The declarant testifies at the trial or hearing and is subject to cross-examination concerning the statement, and the statement is:
>
> (a) In a criminal case, inconsistent with his testimony, provided that the proponent has first fairly directed the witness' attention to the statement and the witness has been given the opportunity to admit the fact and where there exists any additional evidence to corroborate the matter asserted by the prior inconsistent statement; ... [295]

In *State v. Rankin, supra,* a domestic abuse victim who suffered facial injuries and a broken finger recanted at trial. However, she had previously given two statements to the police identifying the defendant as the person who inflicted her injuries. Following a

---

295. This article was amended to its present wording in 2004, apparently in part to "address cases of domestic violence ... which are among the most fertile grounds for noncooperative nonparty witnesses." *State v. Rankin, supra.*

bench trial, the trial court convicted the defendant of second degree battery. We affirmed the defendant's conviction. The prior inconsistent statements were corroborated as required by La. C.E. art. 801(D)(1)(a), and were thus nonhearsay. We noted that since the defendant failed to object to the use of the prior inconsistent statements at trial, it was impossible to determine whether they were used for strictly impeachment purposes or for their assertive value as well. Therefore, it could only be assumed that they were admitted for both purposes. We found no abuse in the trial court's discretion in deeming the statements admissible under La. C.E. art. 801(D)(1)(a).

In the instant case, the prior inconsistent statements of the victim were corroborated by other evidence. The victim, her daughter and the defendant all testified as to an argument between the victim and the defendant that turned violent. The victim sustained visible bruises that were consistent with her police statement and were observed by the officer who took her statement. Shortly after the incident, the victim contacted the police to report her injuries. The recorded statement she gave to the officers was internally consistent.2 The officer who took the victim's statement testified that she never mentioned it being too dark to see, throwing anything at the defendant or otherwise provoking him into "restraining" her for his own protection.

We find no abuse of the trial court's discretion in admitting the statements under La. C.E. art. 801(D)(1)(a). This assignment of error is meritless.

...

AFFIRMED

Discussion Questions

1. This case illustrates one of the primary purposes for which Article 801(D)(1)(a) was amended in 2004, providing that prior inconsistent statements could be used for substantive value—to "address cases of domestic violence ... which are among the most fertile grounds for noncooperative nonparty witnesses."[296] As amended, if the requirements are met, the witness's prior statement may be used substantively rather than just for impeachment purposes. Without this change to Louisiana law, would the outcome of this case have been different? Based on the facts, does there appear to have been sufficient evidence to have convicted the defendant without the prior statement?
2. Under the statute, several requirements must be met in order to consider the prior inconsistent statement substantively (as well as for impeachment). What are the requirements? How was each requirement met here?
3. Another important requirement for this rule is that there must be corroborating circumstances of what the statement asserts. What corroborating circumstances support the victim's prior statement in *Updite*?
4. One area of debate is whether the requirement of cross-examination on the prior statement should be a "meaningful" cross-examination or whether it is sufficient that the witness be present and available for cross-examination. The victim in *Updite* denied remembering most of the prior statement and claimed to have been groggy and the like. Under these circumstances was the defense capable of effectively cross-examining the witness on the prior statement? Should more be required to allow the prior statement to be used substantively to protect an accused's rights to confrontation or is having the witness present alone sufficient to protect an accused's rights to confrontation?

---

296. State v. Rankin, 965 So. 2d 946, 951 (La. Ct. App. 2d Cir. 2007).

Key Points

The key points to keep in mind regarding the prior inconsistent statements.

A prior statement that is inconsistent with the declarant's testimony at trial may be offered for substantive value as well as for impeachment purposes if the following requirements are met:

1. the declarant testifies at trial;
2. is subject to cross-examination about the prior statement;
3. applies to criminal cases;
4. the prior statement is inconsistent with his current testimony;
5. witness first given opportunity to admit the fact of the prior statement; and
6. additional evidence corroborates the prior statement.

Problems on Prior Inconsistent Statements

PROBLEM 5-161. Bill Billings is accused of attempted murder for firing a shot at Lefty Simpson, star quarterback for the home team, from a secret passageway at the top of the Louisiana Grand Stadium during a game. At the trial, Bill testifies during direct examination, "*I've never been to the Grand Stadium*," and denies having said anything different. The prosecution calls the police officer who arrested Bill who testifies that when Bill was arrested he told police, "*Of course I've been there. I know the Grand Stadium inside and out.*" During closing argument, the prosecution argues that Bill should be found guilty because he had the knowledge and because there is evidence that shows that he knows the Grand Stadium inside and out and has been there. The defense objects that the prior statement Bill made to the police should only be used for impeachment purposes on Bill's credibility and that the prior statement can't be used to prove the truth of the matter asserted in it. How should the court rule and why? Would your answer change if it were a civil trial? Why or why not? If the statement may be considered substantively, what additional evidence, if any, must also be offered at trial?

PROBLEM 5-162. Sam sues Mr. and Mrs. Butler for injuries he received when Cora, a teenager who had just gotten drunk at a party they threw for their teenage son and his friends, ran over him while he was crossing the street. When the police arrived at the accident scene, Cora was charged with DWI and stated that she'd just left the Butler residence where she'd gotten wasted. In fact, she stated that Mrs. Butler had to help her to her car. In the civil suit against the Butlers, Sam claims that they let Cora drink even though she was underage. The Butlers call Cora as a witness, who on direct testimony, says she didn't drink anything at the party that night. On cross-examination, after Cora testifies that she hadn't had anything to drink, Sam would like to introduce Cora's statement she made to police at the scene claiming she got wasted at the Butlers house. The Butlers object that the statement is hearsay. Could the statement be admitted under [801(D)(1)(A)]? Why or why not? Can it be admitted in a criminal trial against Cora? If so, for what purpose?

PROBLEM 5-163. Chance is on trial for holding up a liquor store. When police arrived at Chance's house with the arrest warrant, his friend James was there. After Chance was taken to the patrol car in handcuffs, James immediately told the police that Chance had told him that he'd robbed the liquor store and showed him the stash of liquor in the basement. The officers found the liquor in the basement and confirmed other details of James' statement. Chance also matched the description given by the clerk at the store. At the trial, James changed his story. James testified that Chance had not told him anything and that he had not seen or consumed any liquor. The prosecution asked James about the statement he made to police, but James adamantly denied making a statement to police. The police officer was called to the stand who detailed James' statement that he'd made when Chance was arrested. The defense objects that the statement should be excluded because it is hearsay. How should the court rule and why?

PROBLEM 5-164. Kaleb is on trial for armed robbery for robbing an old man. At the time of Kaleb's arrest, Tristan was a passenger in Kaleb's vehicle. Tristan was also taken to the station for questioning and stated to the police that Kaleb told him that he had in fact robbed the old man and that Kaleb had showed him the ring that the old man had on his pinky finger when he was robbed. He also identified Kaleb in a photo lineup as the person who had made the statements. The police subsequently got a warrant for Kaleb's house and car and found the pinky ring in the car. Kaleb also matched the description given by the victim. At the trial, two years later, Tristan recanted and changed his whole story. Tristan said that Kaleb had not told him anything and that he had not seen a ring. The prosecution confronted Tristan about the statement he made to police. He adamantly denied it. The police officer was called to the stand who detailed the statement and the identification by Tristan. The defense objects that the statement and identification are hearsay. How should the prosecution respond? Will the statement and identification be admitted? If they are admitted, for what purposes can the prosecution use the statement?

Would your answer change if instead Tristan testified that although he made the prior statement, he was lying then, but is now telling the truth? Why or why not?

Assume instead that prior to trial, Tristan is also charged with the robbery and asserts his Fifth Amendment privilege against self-incrimination at trial and refuses to testify. Would this affect the admissibility of his prior statement to the police? Why or why not?

§ 5.22.1 References and Additional Authority on Prior Inconsistent Statements [La. C.E. art. 801(D)(1)(a)]

1. La. C.E. art. 801(D)(1)(a) and Official Comments
2. Force & Rault, Handbook on Louisiana Evidence Law Art. 801(D)(1)(a) Author's Comments (West Publishing 2014)
3. Harges & Jones, Louisiana Evidence Art. 801(D)(1)(a) Author's Comments (West Publishing 2014)
4. 19 La. Civ. L. Treatise, Evidence And Proof § 10.2 (2nd ed.)
5. **Prior Inconsistent Statement [801(D)(1)(a)]:** *State v. Rankin*, 965 So. 2d 946 (La. Ct. App. 2d Cir. 2007) (The victim of domestic violence stated to police officers on the day of the incident that her boyfriend had pistol whipped her and broke her finger. When called to testify, the victim stated that the defendant only slapped her and that she fell off of the porch and caused her own injuries. The court allowed the State to present the victim's prior inconsistent statement for substantive as well as impeachment purposes.); *State v. Robert*, 956 So. 2d 750 (La. Ct. App. 2d Cir. 2007) (Prior to the trial for aggravated assault, an eyewitness stated that the defendant pointed a rifle at

him and put a knife to his throat. However, at the trial, the eyewitness claimed that he did not remember what happened on that night because he was so drunk. The court allowed the state to admit the eyewitness's prior inconsistent statement.); *State v. Harper*, 970 So. 2d 592 (La. Ct. App. 1st Cir. 2007) (The court allowed prior inconsistent statements of minor witnesses for substantive purposes as well as impeachment purposes where the minors admitted to signing the written statements, even though the statements were written by someone other than the minor witnesses.); *State v. Duncan*, 91 So. 3d 504 (La. Ct. App. 4th Cir. 2012) (Defendant was on trial for murder and there were three witnesses who were set to testify against him. At trial, witnesses changed story and prior inconsistent statements were admissible for substantive value.).

§ 5.22.2 Prior Consistent Statements [La. C.E. art. 801(D)(1)(b)]

Applicable Code Articles

* * *

D. Statements which are not hearsay. A statement is not hearsay if:

(1) Prior statement by witness. The declarant testifies at the trial or hearing and is subject to cross-examination concerning the statement, and the statement is:

* * *

(b) Consistent with his testimony and is offered to rebut an express or implied charge against him of recent fabrication or improper influence or motive;

* * *

Article 801(D)(1)(b) also exempts certain prior *consistent* statements from the hearsay rule. A prior consistent statement is one that is consistent with the witness's testimony at the present trial and is offered to rebut an express or implied charge against the witness of recent fabrication or improper influence or motive. In other words, if a witness is accused, either expressly or implicitly, of testifying to a particular matter only because of some improper influence or motive to lie, evidence that the witness made a statement consistent with his current testimony prior to any motive to lie may be offered to rebut the accusation.

For example, a witness testifies for the prosecution that the defendant, an acquaintance and colleague of hers, admitted to her that he committed the crime for which he is on trial and told her how he did it. During cross-examination, the defense questions her about criminal charges she also has pending with the District Attorney's Office for forging her employer's name on a check. The defense implies that the witness is lying to curry favor with the prosecution to have her charges reduced or dismissed. In such a case, the prosecution could offer evidence that the witness came forward and told them about the defendant's statement to her six months before she forged the check and more than three months before she was arrested—long before she had a motive to lie about what the defendant told her.

Under Article 801(D)(1)(b), the witness's prior statement to the police that is consistent with her current testimony at trial may be offered to rebut the charge of recent fabrication or improper motive or influence to lie. A statement that conforms to the requirement of this article may be offered for both its rehabilitative value on the issue of the witness's credibility as well as for its substantive value to prove the truth of the matter asserted.[297]

The requirements for admissibility of a prior consistent statement are:

1. the declarant testifies at the trial or hearing;
2. the declarant is subject to cross-examination concerning the prior statement;
3. the statement is consistent with his current testimony;
4. and is offered to rebut an express or implied charge against him of recent fabrication or improper influence or motive; and
5. the statement was made prior to the motive or influence to lie.

Prior statement must precede motive to lie. The significance of the prior consistent statement is that it must have been made ***prior to*** any motive the witness may have to lie at the trial. The statement must predate the motive to lie. If the motive to lie already existed when the prior statement was made, then the exception does not apply.[298]

For example, if the witness in the scenario above already had forgery charges pending when she went to the District Attorney's Office with information about the defendant having admitted to committing the crime, then this exception would not apply. It would do nothing to rebut the fact that she is lying to have her charges reduced since the motive to have her charges reduced existed when she gave the first statement as well. For the prior statement to be relevant in rebutting the charge that the witness has a motive to lie at trial, the prior statement must have been made prior to the motive to lie.

Only offered *after* opponent attacks witness with motive or influence to lie. Keep in mind that a witness's credibility cannot be supported with a prior consistent statement until after his credibility has been attacked by the opponent with an express or implied charge that he is lying due to the improper influence or motive to lie.[299] A proponent of a prior consistent statement cannot offer evidence of the prior statement merely to bolster the testimony of a witness whose credibility has not been attacked. For example, in the example above, the prosecution could not have the witness testify to what the defendant told her, then follow that question up with, "*Now this is not your first time saying this about the defendant, is it?*" Then ask the question, "*When did you first come forward with this information?*" in an effort to bolster the witness's testimony before the defense has an opportunity to question her about the motive to lie.

This article only allows evidence of the witness's prior statement *after* the opponent has suggested a motive to lie through cross-examination or otherwise. For example, if on cross-examination the opponent asks the witness if she is lying to have her charges reduced, or implies it, then he has now opened to door to evidence that the witness made a statement before the check was forged and before she was arrested for it. The prosecution may now

---

297. *See* Force & Rault, HANDBOOK, Art. 801(D)(1)(b)Author's Comment (3); *See also* Tome v. U.S., 513 U.S. 150, 157, 115 S. Ct. 696 (1995) (in construing the FED. R. EVID. 801(d)(1)(d) the U.S. Supreme Court noted that the "[a]dvisory Committee decided to treat those consistent statements, ... as nonhearsay and admissible as substantive evidence, not just to rebut an attack on the witness's credibility").

298. *See* State v. Milto, 751 So. 2d 271 (La. Ct. App. 1st Cir. 1999).

299. *See* LA. CODE EVID. art. 607(B) ("the credibility of a witness may not be supported unless it has been attacked").

Requirements for a Prior Consistent Statement

1. The declarant testifies at the trial or hearing;
2. the declarant is subject to cross-examination concerning the prior statement;
3. the statement is consistent with his current testimony;
4. is offered to rebut an express or implied charge against him of recent fabrication or improper influence or motive; and
5. the statement was made prior to the motive or influence to lie.

ask the witness about the prior statement on redirect examination and/or offer evidence of the prior statement through another witness, such as the police officer to whom she made the statement.

You should also keep in mind that the charge of recent fabrication or improper influence or motive by opposing counsel need not be expressly made, but could've been implied through the line of questioning, voir dire, or from the defense strategy or case theory.[300] Thus, it would be possible for the prosecution, for example, to offer evidence of a prior consistent statement in its case-in-chief because the accusation that a key witness is lying might occur during opening statement or through cross-examination of another witness as demonstrated above.

The only requirement is that evidence of the prior consistent statement may only be offered *after* the opponent makes the charge of recent fabrication or improper influence. Once this is done, evidence of the witness's prior consistent statement may be offered to rehabilitate the witness's credibility as well as for its substantive value.

In *State v. Milto*,[301] the Louisiana Fourth Circuit Court of Appeal addresses whether a prior consistent statement offered under Article 801(D)(1)(b) must be made prior to the improper influence or motive to lie. In finding that it does, the Court also addresses the reasoning for such a requirement.

Federal Rules of Evidence Distinction. In 2014, Federal Rule of Evidence 801(d)(1)(B) was amended. The amendment exempts prior consistent statements from the hearsay rule that are offered not only to rebut an express or implied charge that the declarant recently fabricated or acted with an improper influence or motive in so testifying, but also those statements that are offered "to rehabilitate the declarant's credibility as a witness when attacked on another ground."[302]

As originally adopted, the Rule only provided for *substantive* admissibility of statements offered to rebut charges of recent fabrication or improper influence or motive, as provided in Louisiana's article. As amended, the rule now extends substantive effect to prior consistent statements that rebut **other attacks on a witness's credibility**—such as charges of faulty memory or that the witness's testimony is inconsistent with his prior statement.[303]

300. *See* State v. Domino, 708 So. 2d 1143 (La. Ct. App. 1st Cir. 1998) (holding that the charge may come by way of opposing counsel's voir dire and opening statement suggesting that the witness may be biased); *See also* Force & Rault, Handbook, Art. 801(D)(1)(b)Author's Comment (3).

301. State v. Milto, 751 So. 2d 271 (La. Ct. App. 1st Cir. 1999).

302. Fed. R. Evid. 801(d)(1)(B)(ii) as amended effective December 1, 2014.

303. *See* Fed. R. Evid. 801(d)(1)(B) advisory committee's notes.

The amendment does not change the fact that the prior consistent statement may only be offered after the witness's credibility has been attacked, and is admissible subject to a Rule 403 balancing. Further, "[t]he amendment does not make any consistent statement admissible that was not admissible previously—the only difference is that prior consistent statements otherwise admissible for rehabilitation are now admissible substantively as well."[304]

Case on Prior Consistent Statements

State v. Milto
Court of Appeal of Louisiana, First Circuit
751 So. 2d 271
Nov. 5, 1999

PARRO, Judge.

On August 13, 1997, the defendant and Gregory Mitchell, his friend of approximately ten years, went out together for the evening. The defendant drove his own car, and Mitchell rode in the passenger seat. At approximately 2:00 a.m., they were stopped by Slidell police officer Kevin O'Neill, because the temporary license plate on the defendant's vehicle was not clearly visible. Mitchell testified that, at the time of the stop, the defendant told him to take his (defendant's) gun out of the glove compartment while he got out of the car to talk to the police officer. Mitchell complied and put the gun under the seat. Officer O'Neill testified he saw Mitchell's movements in the car and called for back-up. He ordered Mitchell out of the car and saw the gun sticking out from under the seat. At that point, he did a pat-down search for weapons and found a small amount of marijuana and a pipe in Mitchell's pocket. The officer also found a box of bullets for the gun in the glove compartment. At the scene, both men denied any knowledge of the gun. Mitchell was taken into custody. The defendant was cited with a summons for the license plate, given a field sobriety test, and released.

Officer O'Neill testified that when they got to the police station, Mitchell indicated that the gun belonged to him. Mitchell was charged only with possession of marijuana. He testified he told the police officer that the gun was his because he was concerned about getting the defendant into trouble. Mitchell was aware that his friend had a prior felony conviction. He testified that after talking to the lawyer he obtained to represent him on the marijuana charge, he went to the police to tell the truth about the ownership of the gun. He contacted Officer O'Neill, who advised him to come to the station to make a written statement.

On August 24, 1997, he went to the police station. Oscar Patrick, who worked with Mitchell at Kmart, accompanied him. Patrick also gave a written statement to police that evening. He stated he was familiar with the defendant, because the defendant had come to the store on a number of occasions to visit Mitchell. Patrick indicated that the defendant came to the store to visit Mitchell one night and discovered that he was on vacation. On that occasion, the defendant told Patrick that he had a gun and showed the gun to Patrick. Patrick said the defendant purchased bullets for the gun at Kmart that night. He said he

304. Fed. R. Evid. 801(d)(1)(B) advisory committee's notes.

knew the defendant purchased the bullets because it was his job to check the bags of customers when they exited the store through the garden center where he worked.

ASSIGNMENT OF ERROR NUMBER THREE

In his third assignment of error, the defendant contends the trial court erred in admitting, over defense objection, a prior statement by one of the state's witnesses. Patrick testified at trial that the defendant had shown him the gun in question on an occasion before the stop of the defendant and Mitchell. Defense counsel, during cross-examination, attempted to impeach Patrick by pointing out an alleged inconsistency in his original statement to the police, as well as by attacking his credibility on the basis that he had some bias or motive to lie. Counsel implied the witness would lie for Mitchell, due to the fact that he worked with Mitchell at Kmart and allegedly knew that Mitchell might have problems with his job if he got into trouble involving the weapon. Defense counsel also insinuated that, because Mitchell was an assistant manager at the store, Patrick might feel pressure to protect him in order to keep his (Patrick's) job.

Louisiana Code of Evidence article 801(D)(1) states that a prior statement of a witness is not hearsay if:

> [t]he declarant testifies at the trial or hearing and is subject to cross-examination concerning the statement, and the statement is: ... (b) [c]onsistent with his testimony and is offered to rebut an express or implied charge against him of recent fabrication or improper ... motive.

Former Louisiana Revised Statutes 15:497 contained additional language that "it is proper to show that the witness made a similar statement at a time when the supposed motive did not exist and the effect of such statement could not be foreseen." The Louisiana Code of Evidence, effective in 1989, is silent as to that requirement. The official comments to that article, while not authority, are helpful in determining whether the omission of that language effects a change in the admissibility of the type of statement complained of here. The comments indicate this section of the code is based on Federal Rule of Evidence 801(d)(1)(B) and "the requirement that the statement [be] made at an unsuspicious time has been eliminated. But see Article 403."

In a leading treatise on Louisiana evidence law, the authors' notes indicate that the analysis as to the admissibility of a statement under Article 801(D)(1)(b) of the Louisiana Code of Evidence would necessitate a determination of whether the statement was made at a time when the alleged bias or motive to lie did not exist, in order for it to satisfy the relevancy requirements of Articles 401 through 403.1 *See* George W. Pugh, Robert Force, Gerald A. Rault, Jr., and Kerry Triche, Handbook on Louisiana Evidence Law 464 (1999). The notes indicate that Article 801(D)(1)(b) "does not deal with relevancy.... Statements consistent with testimony made subsequent to the ... circumstances suggesting a motive to fabricate generally have insufficient relevancy to be admissible." *Id.* Again, the authors' notes are not authority; however, because this issue of Louisiana evidence law has not been addressed by this circuit or by the Louisiana Supreme Court since the adoption of the Code of Evidence, the authors' notes are persuasive as to the proper analysis to be used when examining the admissibility of a statement introduced under Article 801(D)(1)(b).[305]

The defendant contends that Patrick's out-of-court statement was inadmissible because defense counsel merely attempted to impeach the witness with an inconsistency in a

---

305. In *Tome v. U.S.*, 513 U.S. 150, 115 S.Ct. 696, 130 L.Ed.2d 574 (1995), the United States Supreme Court interpreted Federal Rule of Evidence 801(d)(1)(B) to include the pre-motive requirement in the determination of admissibility of the statement as non-hearsay.

portion of that statement. On the contrary, defense counsel asked numerous questions on cross-examination designed to show that the witness had a motive to lie for Mitchell and thus attacked Patrick's credibility, both on the basis of inconsistency and improper motive. The defendant further argues that, because of the inconsistencies pointed out by defense counsel, the statement did not qualify as a consistent statement in the first place.

Defense counsel attempted to impeach Patrick on the basis that he testified in court that, although he did see the defendant with the gun, he did not think he saw the defendant load the gun. Patrick's out-of-court statement indicated that while he was outside Kmart with the defendant at his car, the defendant loaded the gun. In fact, the testimony at trial was not inconsistent with Patrick's original statement. At trial the witness indicated that he recognized he had originally told the police that he had seen the defendant load the gun and he did not deny that it might be true, but he just did not remember it at the time of trial. Over a year elapsed between the making of the original statement and the day of trial. Patrick's testimony was substantially the same as his statement to the police; it therefore satisfies the requirement that it be a prior **consistent** statement. Because Patrick's credibility was attacked on the basis of the motive to lie, the prior consistent statement was potentially admissible under Article 801(D)(1)(b).

Although the statement met the technical requirements of Article 801(D)(1)(b), this court must still examine the circumstances to determine whether this prior consistent statement had sufficient relevance in the light of its only purpose, which was to rehabilitate a witness whose credibility in court had been challenged. In August 1997, Patrick had been an employee of Kmart for eight months. Mitchell had worked at the same store for seven years. Although the defense attorney attempted to characterize Patrick as a subordinate of Mitchell, Patrick's testimony as to his understanding of Mitchell's position indicated that he did not view Mitchell as having the authority to make decisions regarding his (Patrick's) employment. At the time of trial, Patrick had not worked at Kmart for a year. There was no evidence that he had maintained any social contact with Mitchell during that time. Under those circumstances, any motive he may have had to lie on behalf of Mitchell had surely dissipated. On the other hand, at the time of his out-of-court statement, all of the factors alluded to by defense counsel were in existence [Patrick worked with Mitchell at Kmart, allegedly knew that Mitchell might have problems with his job if he got into trouble involving the weapon, and because Mitchell was an assistant manager at the store, Patrick might feel pressure to protect him in order to keep his (Patrick's) job]. Therefore, the prior consistent statement, which was made when Patrick may have had a motive to lie about seeing the gun to protect Mitchell, was not relevant to determine whether his in-court statement was true. That in-court statement, made when the supposed motive no longer existed, could not be enhanced by a prior consistent statement made when there may have been such a motive. We conclude that although Patrick's prior consistent statement met the requirements of Article 801(D)(1)(b), and therefore was not hearsay, it did not meet the requirements of Articles 401–403, because it was not relevant for the purpose of substantiating his in-court testimony. For these reasons, the statement should not have been admitted.

Having found that the statement was inadmissible, we must review the record to determine whether the defendant suffered substantial prejudice as a result of its introduction, or whether this was harmless error....

... The admission of the improper evidence is harmless only if its effect is comparatively minimal so that it can be said it did not contribute to the verdict rendered. *State v. Spikes*, 96–0334 (La.App. 1st Cir.11/8/96), 683 So.2d 1363, *writ denied*, 97–0183 (La.9/19/97), 701 So.2d 164. In this case, Patrick's out-of-court statement was cumulative at best, and its effect was comparatively minimal. If anything, the introduction of that statement may have subtly undermined Patrick's credibility, since it was made under circumstances suggesting he may have had a motive to lie to protect Mitchell—circumstances which were no longer extant when he testified at trial. In light of the facts of the entire case, the evidence complained of cannot be said to have contributed to the jury's verdict, and therefore its admission constituted harmless error. *See State v. Hawkins,* 96–0766 (La.1/14/97), 688 So.2d 473.

...

CONVICTION AND SENTENCE AFFIRMED.

Discussion Questions

1. The *Milto* court addresses whether a prior consistent statement should predate any motive to lie. *Milto* analyzes the pre-motive requirement as a relevancy issue. If the prior consistent statement does not predate the motive to lie, is the prior statement relevant, i.e., does it truly rebut the charge of improper influence or motive for the purpose of substantiating the witness's in-court testimony? Such a situation might arguably have no more value than stating that the witness is telling the truth because he also stated the same thing this morning before the trial began. Thus, the court reasons that it fails Article 403 balancing. Do you agree? How would you argue the Article 403 balancing when the prior statement did not predate the motive to lie?
2. Prior to the 2014 amendment, Louisiana's article was identical to the corresponding Federal Rule of Evidence 801(d)(1)(B)(i). Given this, the *Milto* Court refers to *Tome v. U.S.,* 513 U.S. 150, 115 S.Ct. 696 (1995), in which the United States Supreme Court interpreted Federal Rule of Evidence 801(d)(1)(B) to include the pre-motive requirement in the determining the admissibility of the statement as non-hearsay. In *Tome* the U.S. Supreme Court also argues that the plain language of the rule makes it clear that the statement must pre-date the motive to lie, noting that:

   > The Rule speaks of a party rebutting an alleged motive, ... This limitation is instructive, not only to establish the preconditions of admissibility but also to reinforce the significance of the requirement that the consistent statements must have been made before the alleged influence, or motive to fabricate, arose. That is to say, the forms of impeachment within the Rule's coverage are the ones in which the temporal requirement makes the most sense. Impeachment by charging that the testimony is a recent fabrication or results from an improper influence or motive is, as a general matter, capable of direct and forceful refutation through introduction of out-of-court consistent statements that predate the alleged fabrication, influence, or motive. A consistent statement that predates the motive is a square rebuttal of the charge that the testimony was contrived as a consequence of that motive.[306]

   What do you think of the Court's argument here that evidence of pre-motive statement must directly rebut the impeachment method included in the rule?
3. A preliminary issue addressed in *Milto* was whether the prior statement was actually *consistent* with the current testimony in light of the fact that the witness stated that he "did not remember" whether or not he saw something, rather than that "he had not" seen it. The court found that the prior statement "was substantially the same" as

306. Tome v. U.S., 513 U.S. 150, 157–158, 115 S.Ct. 696 (1995).

the in-court testimony. Do you have a problem finding the prior statement to be consistent with the witness's current testimony?

4. *Milto* presents an interesting scenario in that the witness's prior statement was given when the alleged motive to lie existed, but no longer existed by the time his in-court testimony was given. The court reasons that under these circumstances the prior statement may have done more to hurt Patrick's testimony than to enhance it. What effect do you think the prior statement had in this situation? Did it enhance it? Hurt it? Have no impact at all?
5. Can you think of situations in which a prior consistent statement might rehabilitate a witness on grounds other than charges of recent fabrication or improper influence or motive? What if on cross-examination a witness was asked, "You don't really remember what happened, do you?" or "This is the first time you've ever mentioned this fact," or "So why didn't you report this earlier?" Would a prior consistent statement be relevant in these instances? Can you think of others?
6. Do you think Louisiana's rule should be amended, as the Federal Rule was amended, to allow substantive admissibility of prior consistent statements offered to rebut attacks on a witness on grounds other than merely charges of recent fabrication or improper influence or motive? What are justifications for and against such a change?

Key Points

The key points to keep in mind regarding the prior consistent statements.

1. Exempts from the hearsay rule a prior statement of a witness that is consistent with the witness's testimony at the present trial offered to rebut an express or implied charge against him of recent fabrication or improper influence or motive.
2. **The requirements for admissibility of a prior consistent statement are:**
   1. The declarant testifies at the trial or hearing;
   2. the declarant is subject to cross-examination concerning the prior statement;
   3. the statement is consistent with his current testimony;
   4. the statement is offered to rebut an express or implied charge against him of recent fabrication or improper influence or motive; and
   5. the statement was made prior to the motive or influence to lie.
3. Statement may be offered for rehabilitative as well as for substantive value.
4. The charge of recent fabrication or improper influence or motive may be express or implied from the questioning, opening statements, voir dire, case strategy, etc.
5. A witness's credibility cannot be supported until after it has been attacked (See Chapter 6 § 6.11, *infra*).

Problems on Prior Consistent Statements

PROBLEM 5-165. Blunt and Obliv were both arrested for possession of drugs with intent to distribute while transporting 50 kilos of cocaine on I-10E in the trunk of their vehicle. Blunt, who was driving, immediately took responsibility for all of the drugs. Blunt pled guilty, and again admitted that all of the drugs were his, citing his guilty plea, and was sentenced to 15 years in prison. At Obliv's trial, sometime later, Blunt testified for the defense and again stated that the drugs were his and that Obliv knew nothing about the drugs. On cross-examination, the prosecution accused Blunt of taking the rap only because he had already been convicted and sentenced and had nothing to lose from taking all responsibility for the charge. In response, the defense attempted to offer evidence that Blunt had said the same thing when they were originally arrested, and when he pleaded guilty at sentencing. The prosecution objected that the statements were hearsay. How should the court rule and why?

PROBLEM 5-166. Bill Billings is accused of firing a shot at Lefty Simpson from a secret passageway at the top of the Louisiana Grand Stadium. At the trial, Bill testifies during direct examination that he has never been to the Grand Stadium. His attorney then asks him to tell the jury what he told police when he was arrested for the crime, and Bill testifies that he told them that he had never been to the Grand Stadium. The prosecution objects that the statement is hearsay. How should the court rule and why?

PROBLEM 5-167. At George's trial for extortion, Mayor Mackey testifies that George demanded $200,000 from him or else he (George) would create a rumor that the Mayor was having an illicit affair with his secretary. At trial, George is claiming that the affair is real and that the Mayor is simply trying to cover up the affair by claiming that George created the rumor in retaliation for his not giving George $200,000. In response to George's accusation, the prosecution would like to call Secretary to the stand to testify that Mayor Mackey told her that someone was threatening to say that they were having an affair long before the rumor ever surfaced. In fact, at that time, the Mayor even offered to allow her to be transferred to another department to avoid her reputation being ruined. George objects that Secretary's testimony about what the Mayor said to her is hearsay. How will the court likely rule on the objection and why?

PROBLEM 5-168. Chloe's mom and dad always got along very well and enjoyed joint custody of Chloe for many years with no problems. One day, Chloe told her mother (Mom) and stepdad (Stepdad) that she didn't like going to her dad's (Dad) house because his friend touched her inappropriately. Chloe's mom began avoiding Dad on his custody weekends. Upset with dealing with this for over six months, Dad filed for sole custody of Chloe. Chloe hasn't mentioned the accusations again since she initially told Mom and Stepdad about it, and refuses to say anything about it at the trial. During cross-examination of Mom, Dad's lawyer asked her if she had told Chloe to make up the story about being molested at Dad's house to keep Dad from winning custody of Chloe. Mom adamantly denied the accusation and offered Chloe's statement through her husband that Chloe made about Dad's friend six months before the custody proceedings began. Dad objected that the statement is inadmissible hearsay. Should Chloe's prior statement be admissible? Why or why not?

Would your answer change if instead defense counsel had asked Chloe on cross-examination whether her mother told her to say such a thing? Why or why not?

§ 5.22.2 References and Additional Authority for Prior Consistent Statements [La. C.E. art. 801(D)(1)(b)]

1. La. C.E. art. 801(D)(1)(b) and Official Comments
2. Force & Rault, Handbook on Louisiana Evidence Law Art. 801(D)(1)(b) Author's Comments (West Publishing 2014)

3. Harges & Jones, LOUISIANA EVIDENCE Art. 801(D)(1)(b) Author's Comments (West Publishing 2014)
4. 19 La. Civ. L. Treatise, Evidence And Proof § 10.2 (2nd ed.)
5. **Prior Consistent Statement [La. C.E. art. 801(D)(1)(b)]**: *State v. Fisher*, 649 So. 2d 604 (La. Ct. App. 3d Cir. 1994) (The defendant argued that the lower court erred in not allowing the defense to offer prior consistent statements of the witness to rebut the charge against him of recent fabrication after being impeached by the state. The court ruled that the error was harmless.); *State v. Turner*, 82 So. 3d 1245 (La. Ct. App. 4th Cir. 2012) (The defendant argued that prior recorded statements of the witness were improperly admitted because the defense never implied or accused the witness of fabricating her story. The court ruled that the statements were properly admitted because the defense had attacked the witness's testimony.).
6. **Adult testifying to minor child's prior consistent statement**: *State v. Thomas*, 711 So. 2d 808, 815 (La. Ct. App. 2d Cir. 1998) (The defendant argued that the lower court erred in overruling his objection to testimony of the minor child's foster mother. The child's foster mother testified to prior consistent statements of the child after the defense implied that the child fabricated his story.); *State v. Holley*, 799 So. 2d 578 (La. Ct. App. 3d Cir. 2001) (holding that the trial court did not err in allowing minor child's social worker to testify about what the minor child said to rebut the implied claim that the minor fabricated her testimony).
7. **Inadmissible as Prior Consistent Statement**: *State v. Joyner*, 107 So. 3d 675 (La. Ct. App. 4th Cir. 2012) (holding that the trial court did not err in barring defense counsel from questioning Officer Mitchell on his prior statements after the State questioned Lieutenant Italiano about Officer Mitchell's statements to him because Officer Mitchell was never accused of fabricating his story).

§ 5.22.3 Identification [La. C.E. art. 801(D)(1)(c)]

> **Applicable Code Articles**
>
> * * *
>
> **D. Statements which are not hearsay.** A statement is not hearsay if:
>
> **(1) Prior statement by witness.** The declarant testifies at the trial or hearing and is subject to cross-examination concerning the statement, and the statement is:
>
> * * *
>
> (c) One of identification of a person made after perceiving the person; or
>
> * * *

Article 801(D)(1)(c) exempts prior identifications that a witness might have made from the hearsay rule. In a trial, particularly a criminal trial, the identity of a perpetrator is an important issue. A witness, usually a victim or eyewitness, will typically be called to testify in court and will be asked to identify the defendant as the person who committed the crime. Additionally, the prosecution will also seek to offer evidence that the witness was able to identify the suspect at a time closer to the incident in question, either in a

Requirements for an Identification

1. the declarant testifies at trial;
2. the declarant is subject to cross-examination concerning the statement; and
3. the statement is one of identification of a person made after perceiving the person.

photo lineup or show-up identification. A show-up identification is where the police bring a suspect back to the scene and ask the witness whether that person is the suspect in question, and after perceiving the person, the witness states, "*Yes, that's him. That's the guy who robbed me.*"

Provided the person who made the prior identification is present in court and capable of being cross-examined on the prior identification, evidence of the prior identification made after perceiving the person may be offered into evidence to prove the truth of the matter asserted.

The person testifying to the prior identification may be the person himself, or might be a police officer who coordinated the identification procedure or any other witness who has first-hand knowledge of the prior out-of-court identification. While the prior identification is technically hearsay under the definition, in that it is being offered to prove what is being asserted, this provision exempts such statements from the hearsay rule if the requirements are met.[307]

The requirements are:

1. the declarant testifies at the trial;
2. is subject to cross-examination concerning the statement; and
3. the statement is one of identification of a person made after perceiving the person.

As with all statements under Article 801(D)(1), for the prior statement of identification to be admissible, the declarant must testify at the trial or hearing and be subject to cross-examination concerning the statement. If the declarant is unavailable, the police officer or other witness who has first-hand knowledge of the identification would not be allowed to testify to the prior identification.

Further, the witness need not testify consistently with the prior identification for the exemption to apply. The witness might recant, deny making the statement, or be unable to remember whom he identified.[308] Provided the witness is present and capable of being cross-examined about the identification, the exemption applies.

---

307. *See* State ex rel. D.W., 47 So. 3d 1048 (La. Ct. App. 5th Cir. 2010) (finding that statement of identification of defendant was admissible at trial for substantive value after witness recanted at trial).

308. *Id.*

Key Points

The key points to keep in mind regarding identification.

1. Exempts a statement of identification of a person from the hearsay rule that was made outside of the present trial by a witness after perceiving the person.
2. **The requirements for admissibility of a prior consistent statement are:**
    1. the declarant testifies at the trial;
    2. is subject to cross-examination concerning the statement; and
    3. the statement is one of identification of a person made after perceiving the person.
3. Statement admissible for substantive value.
4. Declarant need not testify consistently with identification to be admissible. May recant, not remember, or etc., provided he is present and testifies.
5. Identifications include show-up, lineup, photographic identification.
6. Anyone with first-hand knowledge of statement may testify to it.

Problems on Identification

PROBLEM 5-169. In defendant's trial, the witness is unable to identify him when asked to do so in court. Furthermore, he has no recollection of many of the events of the assault, but he does recall that he made a prior identification, although when shown the lineup at trial he is unable to identify anyone. The officer takes the stand who showed him the lineup and proceeds to testify to which person the witness picked out of the lineup on the day of the robbery. The defense attorney objected that the officer's testimony regarding the identification is hearsay. How should the court rule?

PROBLEM 5-170. Before arresting the defendant for armed robbery, three of the bank tellers present during the robbery positively identified the defendant in a photographic lineup. At trial, one of the witnesses cannot be located, but the other two witnesses will testify. The prosecution intends to call the police officer to testify regarding who each of the witnesses identified in the photo lineup during his investigation. The defense objects that none of the identifications can be admitted through the police officer, and that only the witnesses themselves can testify to their out-of-court identifications and that, therefore, no evidence can be admitted regarding the witness's identification that cannot be located. How should the court rule on the objection and why?

§ 5.22.3 References and Additional Authority on Identification [La. C.E. art. 801(D)(1)(c)]

1. La. C.E. art. 801(D)(1)(c) and Official Comments
2. Force & Rault, HANDBOOK ON LOUISIANA EVIDENCE LAW Art. 801(D)(1)(c) Author's Comments (West Publishing 2014)
3. Harges & Jones, LOUISIANA EVIDENCE Art. 801(D)(1)(c) Author's Comments (West Publishing 2014)

4. 19 La. Civ. L. Treatise, Evidence And Proof § 10.2 (2nd ed.)
5. **Identification [La. C.E. art. 801(D)(1)(c)]:** *State v. Joyner*, 107 So. 3d 675 (La. Ct. App. 4th Cir. 2012) (The defendant argued that the trial court improperly admitted hearsay testimony without requiring the state to lay the proper foundation. The court ruled that the statement was non-hearsay because it was a statement of identification and foundation need not be laid for it.).

§ 5.22.4 Initial Complaint of Sexual Assault [La. C.E. art. 801(D)(1)(d)]

Applicable Code Articles

* * *

D. Statements which are not hearsay. A statement is not hearsay if:

(1) Prior statement by witness. The declarant testifies at the trial or hearing and is subject to cross-examination concerning the statement, and the statement is:

* * *

(d) Consistent with the declarant's testimony and is one of initial complaint of sexually assaultive behavior.

* * *

Article 801(D)(1)(d) exempts a statement from the hearsay rule that is an initial complaint of sexually assaultive behavior that is consistent with the declarant's testimony at trial. Under this article, evidence of the prior statement of sexually assaultive behavior is non-hearsay and is admissible to prove the truth of the matter asserted in the prior complaint.

The requirements for the exception to apply are:

1. the declarant testifies at the trial or hearing;
2. the declarant is subject to cross-examination concerning the statement;
3. the statement is consistent with the declarant's testimony;[309] and
4. the statement is one of *initial* complaint of sexually assaultive behavior.

Initial complaint only. To minimize confrontation problems in potentially having multiple people testify against a defendant to complaints of sexual assault, the exemption only applies to the *initial* complaint of sexually assaultive behavior.[310] In some instances, a question arises as to whether the statement at issue was the *initial* complaint. The initial complaint has been held to apply only to the first "friendly adult"[311] to which a complaint is made. Thus, a young child's statement to a friend would not apply. The exemption usually applies to the initial statement made to a parent, teacher, pastor, or similar adult.

309. *See, e.g.*, State v. Johnson, 726 So. 2d 1126 (La. Ct. App. 4th Cir. 1999).
310. *See* La. Code Evid. art. 801(D)(1)(d) Official Comment (e).
311. State v. Ste. Marie, 801 So. 2d 424 (La. Ct. App. 3d Cir. 2001).

Requirements for an Initial Complaint of Sexually Assaultive Behavior

1. the declarant testifies at the trial or hearing;
2. the declarant is subject to cross-examination concerning the statement;
3. the statement is consistent with the declarant's testimony;
4. the statement is one of *initial* complaint of sexually assaultive behavior.

After the initial complaint is made, the declarant may be asked to repeat the complaint to others, such as a social worker or a police officer. Such *subsequent* complaints would not be included in the exemption. It would also not apply to a statement that the person who received the initial statement made to someone else. For example, if the child makes the complaint to the teacher who calls the police and tells the police officer what the child said, then the statement to the police officer would constitute double hearsay. In order for the police officer to testify to what the teacher told him that the child said, the teacher's statement would have to conform to a separate exception or exemption to the hearsay rule to be admissible.

Witness testifies consistently at trial. This exemption also requires that the declarant testify at the trial or hearing and be subject to cross-examination on the prior statement. Additionally, the witness must testify consistently with the prior statement. If the witness recants, the prior statement is not admissible under this exemption.

Sexually assaultive behavior. The sexually assaultive behavior included in the exemption is broadly defined to include initial complaints of rape, aggravated rape, simple rape, sexual battery, aggravated sexual battery, carnal knowledge of a juvenile, molestation, crime against nature, and others.[312]

Federal Rules of Evidence Distinction. There is no corresponding provision in the federal rules.

Distinction from Complaint of Sexual Assault in Article 804(B)(5). As we covered in § 5.20, another exception that pertains to complaints of sexual assault is contained in Article 804(B)(5), which applies when the declarant is unavailable. The requirements for that exception are:

1. the declarant must be unavailable; and
2. the statement must be either: a) one of initial complaint of sexually assaultive behavior, ***or*** b) a trustworthy complaint of sexually assaultive behavior; and
3. the declarant must be a person under the age of twelve.

As outlined in the chart below, the requirements for the two exceptions are quite different. Under the Article 801(D)(1)(d) exemption, there is no age requirement, it only applies to the *initial* complaint of sexually assaultive behavior, not "other trustworthy complaints," and contrary to the Article 804(B)(5) exception that requires that the declarant be unavailable, the Article 801(D)(1)(d) exemption specifically requires that the witness be present at trial, has testified consistently with the prior statement of sexually assaultive behavior, and is capable of being cross-examined on the prior statement.

312. *See* La. Code Evid. art. 801(D)(1)(d) Official Comment (d).

Comparison of Sexual Assault Complaint Provisions

	Initial Complaint Sexual Assault Article 801(D)(1)(d)	Complaint of Sexual Assault Article 804(B)(5)
Availability	Declarant must be available. Declarant must testify at trial, and be subject to cross-examination on prior statement.	Declarant must be unavailable.
Substance of Statement	Must be *initial* complaint only of sexual assault to first friendly adult.	May be initial complaint of sexual assault ***or*** other trustworthy complaint of sexually assaultive behavior.
Age of Complainant	There is no age requirement.	The declarant must be under the age of 12 when complaint made.
Other Requirement	Prior statement must be consistent with declarant's testimony at trial.	

Key Points

The key points to keep in mind regarding initial complaint of sexually assaultive behavior.

1. Exempts a statement from the hearsay rule that is an initial complaint of sexually assaultive behavior that is consistent with the declarant's testimony at trial.
2. **The requirements for exemption of Initial Complaint of Sexually Assaultive Behavior:**
    1. the declarant testifies at the trial or hearing;
    2. the declarant is subject to cross-examination concerning the statement;
    3. the statement is consistent with the declarant's testimony; and
    4. the statement is one of *initial* complaint of sexually assaultive behavior.
3. The similar rule contained in **Article 804(B)(5) for an unavailable declarant** requires the following:
    1. the declarant must be unavailable;
    2. the statement must be either: a) one of initial complaint of sexually assaultive behavior; ***or*** b) be a trustworthy complaint of sexually assaultive behavior; and
    3. the declarant must be a person under the age of twelve.

Problems on Sexual Assault Complaint

PROBLEM 5-171. Mary is in the first grade. After acting out several times at school, her teacher Ms. Johnson pulled her aside and asked her if everything was okay at home. She told her that at night her grandfather comes into her bedroom and "plays" with her in ways that makes her uncomfortable. Ms. Johnson called CPS, who further investigated the case. Eventually, Mary's grandfather was arrested for molestation of Mary. At trial, Mary is traumatized by the ordeal, and suppressed the experience and refuses to talk about anything related to the events. The prosecutor would like to admit Mary's statement to her teacher to prove the case. Will the statement be admissible under Article 804(B)(5) or alternatively 801(D)(1)(d)? Explain.

PROBLEM 5-172. Mother walked in on her boyfriend sexually assaulting her daughter and asks her daughter what was going on. Her daughter says, he always does this when you're at work. Mother then asks her how long it's been going on, and she says for about a year. After asking her boyfriend to leave, Mother calls the police and tells her daughter to tell the police about what he's been doing. The daughter details the year of sexual abuse. Boyfriend is eventually arrested. At the trial, the police officer begins to testify about what daughter told him that led to the investigation, and the defense objects that the statements are hearsay. Do the statements fall with the "sexual assault complaint" exception? What requirements must be met for the exception to apply?

§ 5.22.4 References and Additional Authority on Sexual Assault Complaint [La. C.E. art. 801(D)(1)(d)]

1. La. C.E. art. 801(D)(1)(d) and Official Comments
2. Force & Rault, HANDBOOK ON LOUISIANA EVIDENCE LAW Art. 801(D)(1)(d) Author's Comments (West Publishing 2014)
3. Harges & Jones, LOUISIANA EVIDENCE Art. 801(D)(1)(d) Author's Comments (West Publishing 2014)
4. 19 La. Civ. L. Treatise, Evidence And Proof § 10.2 (2nd ed.)
5. **Must be consistent**: *State v. Greene*, 951 So. 2d 1226 (La. Ct. App. 5th Cir. 2007) (The court ruled that the minor victim's statement to the deputy that the defendant had intercourse with her was a prior consistent statement. The statement was admissible because it was offered after the victim was accused of fabricating her testimony.).
6. **Must be initial complaint to a "friendly adult"**: *State v. Noble*, 342 So. 2d 170 (La. 1977) (The minor child attempted to tell several adults in the nursery of the sexual assault, but no one took the time to listen. The court ruled that although the social worker was not the first person the minor child attempted to complain of sexual assault to, the social worker was the first person that took the time to discern what the minor child was saying; therefore, the statement was admissible because it was the initial complaint of sexual assault.).
7. **Courts have sometimes extended "initial" complaint beyond first friendly adult:** *State v. Reed*, 712 So. 2d 572 (La. Ct. App. 1st Cir. 1998) (The court ruled that there is no specific order that witnesses must testify. The victim need not be the first to testify. The victim spoke with two officers at the scene of the crime, but told the third officer her complete complaint. The court ruled that the complaint to the third officer was the initial complaint.); *State v. Free*, 643 So. 2d 767 (La. Ct. App. 2d Cir. 1994) (The defendant argued that the lower court erred in allowing the deputy to testify as to what the minor victim told her. Deputy was the fourth person that the minor told of the sexual assault. The defendant argued that the first complaint was to the child's mother. The court ruled that the complaint to her mother was not an initial complaint within the meanings of the article because the minor was crying while telling her mother and her mother could not understand everything that she was saying. The child spoke with a counselor and physician afterward, but the record does not state

what the child discussed with them. Therefore, the court ruled that the initial complaint was to the deputy.).

9. **Complaint over period of time:** *State v. Burks*, 905 So. 2d 394 (La. Ct. App. 5th Cir. 2005) (The defendant argued that because the minor child told the witness of the sexual assault over a couple of weeks, only the first statement minor child made to witness was admissible, but all other statements were inadmissible. The victim was available in court. The court cited *State v. Hillman*, 613 So. 2d 1053 (La. Ct. App. 3d Cir. 1993) and ruled that the victim giving details of the assault over a period of time does not exclude the statements from the provisions of this article.).

§ 5.23 Admissions [La. C.E. arts. 801(D)(2), (3)]

Applicable Code Articles

* * *

D. Statements which are not hearsay. A statement is not hearsay if:

* * *

(2) Personal, adoptive, and authorized admissions. The statement is offered against a party and is:

(a) His own statement, in either his individual or a representative capacity;

(b) A statement of which he has manifested his adoption or belief in its truth; or

(c) A statement by a person authorized by him to make a statement concerning the subject.

(3) Relational and privity admissions. The statement is offered against a party, and the statement is:

(a) A statement by an agent or employee of the party against whom it is offered, concerning a matter within the scope of his agency or employment, made during the existence of the relationship;

(b) A statement by a declarant while participating in a conspiracy to commit a crime or civil wrong and in furtherance of the objective of the conspiracy, provided that a prima facie case of conspiracy is established;

(c) In a civil case, a statement by a declarant when the liability, obligation, or duty of the party against whom it is offered is derivatively based in whole or in part upon a liability, obligation, or duty of the declarant, or when the claim or right asserted by that party is barred or diminished by a breach of duty by the declarant, and when the statement would be admissible if offered against the declarant as a party in an action involving that liability, obligation, or breach of duty;

(d) In a civil case, a statement by a declarant when a right, title, or interest in any property or claim asserted by the party against whom it is offered requires a determination that a right, title, or interest exists or existed in the declarant during the time that that party now claims the declarant was the holder of the right, title, or in-

> terest, and when the statement would be admissible if offered against the declarant as a party in an action involving that right, title, or interest;
>
> (e) A statement by a declarant offered against the party in an action for damages arising from the death of that declarant; or
>
> (f) A statement by a minor child offered against a party in an action to recover for injury to that child, or against the person responsible for the child in an action to recover damages for losses caused by the child.
>
> * * *

In this section we turn to **admissions**. Articles 801(D)(2) and (3) exempt admissions from the hearsay rule allowing them to be offered for the truth of the matter asserted within them. Admissions are statements made by a party to the action being offered against that party by his opponent. There are several different types of statements listed in Articles 801(D)(2) and (3) that are deemed to be a party's own statement in either his personal or representative capacity, or a statement attributable to him because he either adopted it, authorized it, or by virtue of his relationship to the person making the statement. In either case, for the exemption to apply, the party's opponent must offer his statement against him.

Thus, there are two very important **requirements that apply to all admissions**:

1. it is a statement **by a party** to the action or is attributed to him; and
2. the statement is being **offered *against* the party** by his opponent.

Because a party's own statement is being offered against him, the exemption is often referred to as a "party admission" or an "admission by a party opponent."[313] The theory in classing a party's own statements as non-hearsay lies in the fact that a person should not be able to complain that he cannot cross-examine himself or that he is not worthy of belief without being under oath.[314] These statements are not admissible because they are deemed to be any more reliable than other out-of-court statements; instead, as a matter of fairness, the exemption holds a party responsible for his own statements. Thus, a party's own statement, when offered against them, is not hearsay and may be offered by his opponent to prove the truth of the matter asserted within the statement.

With this is mind, for purposes of this exemption a statement will always overcome the *hearsay* rule if, in response to a hearsay objection, the proponent can say, **"Your Honor, it is *his* (☞) own statement"** *(pointing to the opponent)*. Whenever a party can point to his opponent, and respond, **"Your Honor, it is *his* (☞) own statement,"** you have overcome the hearsay bar.

It is important to bear in mind, however, that like all statements, an admission could be excluded for other reasons, such as for relevancy, or statements that were unconstitutionally obtained in violation of an accused's Fifth Amendment privilege against self-incrimination.[315] Additionally, if the statement is in writing or recorded, it would have to be properly authenticated as being that of the party against whom it is being offered.

---

313. *See, e.g.*, Harges & Jones, LOUISIANA EVIDENCE, Arts. 801(D)(2) and (3) Author's Comments (West Publishing 2014).

314. *See* Article 801(D)(2) Official Comment (b)(1988).

315. *See* U.S. Const. amends V, VI; La. Const. Art. I Secs. 13, 16 (1974); See also Art. 801(D)(2) Official Comments (a) (1988).

A court might even exclude portions of a statement for being unfairly prejudicial, particularly when offered against a defendant in a criminal trial. However, such a statement is ***not*** hearsay.

Offered Against a Party

The first key requirement under this exemption is that it is only applicable when the statement of a party is offered *against* him, i.e., the plaintiff is offering a statement made by the defendant, or vice versa. For example, the defendant runs into the back of another vehicle and jumps out and says, "*I'm sorry, I was dozing off and didn't see you.*" The plaintiff sues the defendant for negligence. At the trial for the accident, the plaintiff could offer evidence of the defendant's statement against him. While the statement would be hearsay under the definition, in that it is being offered to prove the truth of the matter asserted, that the defendant was dozing off and didn't see plaintiff, this article exempts such statements from the hearsay rule when offered against the party who made the statement. In such a case, the defendant's statement is not hearsay, and may be considered for its assertive value.

Similarly, the prosecution can offer a defendant's statement into evidence in a criminal trial, since he is a party to the action and his statement is being offered against him. However, this provision ***does not*** apply when a party attempts to offer his own statement into evidence at trial.[316] For example, if in the scenario above the defendant had instead told the police officer (or bystander) that the plaintiff hit *him*, he would not be able to offer the statement at trial under this provision. This article does not allow a party to offer his own statement into evidence. In such a case, the statement is inadmissible hearsay. The exemption only applies when a party's opponent offers his statement against him, hence the response, "**Your honor, it is *his* (☞) own statement.**" The response is ***not*** "Your honor, it is ***my*** own statement."

A Party's Own Statement (Or One Attributed to Him)

The second requirement that must be met for a statement to be offered against a party as an admission is that the statement must be the party's own statement, or one attributed to him. Articles 801(D)(2) and (3) include a broad range of statements that may be offered against a party as an admission and include not only those statements that are made by the party in his personal or representative capacity but also includes statements that are attributed to him because he either adopted it, authorized it, or by virtue of his relationship to the person making the statement such as an employer-employee, agent-principle, co-conspirators, as well as others.

There are five main types of statements that may be offered against a party as an admission that we will cover in more detail in this section and briefly address the others. For purposes of this article, a party's own statements and those attributed to him include:

1. His own personal statement (in his individual or representative capacity) [Art. 801(D)(2)(a)]
2. A statement in which he *adopted* [Art. 801(D)(2)(b)]

---

316. *See* State v. Freeman, 521 So. 2d 783 (La. App. 2d Cir. 1988); *See also* Force & Rault, HANDBOOK, Arts. 801(D)(2) and (3) Author's Comment (6).

3. A statement *authorized* by him [Art. 801(D)(2)(c)]
4. A statement of an agent/employee in course/scope of employment/agency [Art. 801(D)(3)(a)]
5. Statements of co-conspirators in furtherance of conspiracy [Art. 801(D)(3)(b)]

1. Personal Statement. Article 801(D)(2)(a) allows a statement to be offered against a party if it is a ***personal statement*** made by the party himself in his individual capacity or by his representative. The statement may be expressed orally, in writing, or may be tacit. A tacit admission, however, one that is by silence or action, must comply with the definition of a statement under Article 801(A), in that the declarant must have intended to assert a message by his silence or action to raise a hearsay issue. Such statements will be subject to the balancing of Article 403.[317]

A good example of a tacit admission by silence occurred in *State v. Romero*,[318] where after the defendant was arrested for first-degree murder, his father went to see him in jail. Evidence was offered against the son that in response to his father asking him, "Son, did you do this?" he gave an affirmative nod. The statement was assertive conduct under Article 801(A), conduct intended to assert the message that he'd committed the crime. It was a personal statement by the defendant offered against him as a tacit admission by action.

2. Adopted Admission. Article 801(D)(2)(b) allows a statement to be offered against a party if he "adopts" it or "manifests a belief in its truth." A person may ***expressly adopt*** a statement, or ***implicitly adopt*** it. A statement may be expressly adopted orally or in writing. For example, following an accident, a person who may be listening to another person telling a police officer what happened, might state, "*Yes, that's exactly how it happened*," expressly adopting the statement orally. The police officer might then write down what he has learned, then after reading it, the person might sign the statement, expressly adopting the statement in writing.

Additionally, a person could implicitly adopt a statement by either:

1. the party's **reliance** upon the contents of a ***statement in a related conversation or writing***; or
2. ***by silence*** under circumstances in which it would be natural to respond.

   Factors: Louisiana courts have considered a number of factors in determining whether a person in fact **adopted** a statement by silence:[319]

   - statement was made in defendant's **presence**
   - the defendant **heard** the statement
   - the defendant **understood** the statement
   - of such a nature and under circumstances where a **denial, explanation, or reply** would be **expected**
   - and where the defendant is **not in legal custody** and is at full liberty to speak
   - defendant **failed to deny or explain**

---

317. La. Code Evid. art. 801(D)(2) Official Comments.

318. State v. Romero, 552 So. 2d 45 (La. Ct. App. 3d Cir. 1989).

319. *See* State v. McClain, 254 La. 56, 222 So. 2d 855, 856, 857 (1969); *See also* Harges & Jones, Louisiana Evidence, Art. 801(D)(2) Author's Comments.

> If a person adopts a statement by silence, evidence of the statement and of the defendant's silence and failure to deny the statement may be offered to the jury against him as an admission.[320]

For example, following an accident, a person jumps out of a car, then tells the other driver, "*You ran the light! You were dialing a number on your phone!*" If that person doesn't respond to such an accusation, that person might be said to have adopted the statement by silence because the statement was of such a nature that a reasonable person would have denied it if it hadn't been true. For example, if the accusation were not true, a reasonable person might respond, "*I was not dialing a number. My phone was in my purse.*"

When a person fails to deny an accusation that a reasonable person would have likely denied or explained had the accusation not been true, he will likely be considered to have adopted the statement by silence provided the facts suggest that the person actually heard the statement, understood it, and there were no physical or emotional impediments that might have prevented him from responding.

Similarly, a party might implicitly adopt a statement by his reliance upon the contents of a statement in a related conversation or writing. For example, a student who sends his transcript to a potential employer has implicitly adopted the contents of the transcript. A person might attach a copy of his health physical prepared by a doctor to an application, expressing a belief in its truth.

Thus, a person may **adopt a statement expressly, orally or in writing; or may adopt it implicitly, by silence or reliance on a writing or words.** In either case, the adopted statement may be offered against the party as an admission to prove the truth of the matter asserted within the adopted statement.

Criminal cases—Fifth Amendment Privilege against self-incrimination. Keep in mind that in a criminal case, a suspect in *custody* of law enforcement has a right to remain silent and to not make any statements that may be used against him.[321] Under these circumstances a person's silence cannot be used against him as an admission of guilt.

3. Authorized Admission. Article 801(D)(2)(c) allows a statement to be offered against a party if it was made by a person authorized by the party to make a statement concerning the subject. The admissibility is based on basic agency principles and is often called representative or vicarious admissions. These agents are also referred to as "speaking agents,"[322] who are authorized to speak on that person or entity's behalf, and therefore the statements from that person can be attributed to the principle, and under this exemption, offered against him.

For example, the White House's press secretary is authorized to speak for the White House and President on certain topics, and therefore those statements can be attributed to the White House. A person's attorney is authorized to speak for him in court. A sports agent is authorized to speak for his client in negotiating a contract. The statements of the person authorized to speak on a person's behalf may be attributed to him and offered against him as an admission.

4. Agent/Employee in course/scope of agency/employment. Article 801(D)(3)(a) allows a statement to be offered against a party if it was made by an agent or employee of the

320. *See* State v. McClain, 254 La. 56, 222 So. 2d 855, 856, 857 (1969).

321. U.S. Const. Amend. V; *See also* Miranda v. Arizona, 384 U.S. 436 (1966).

322. La. Code Evid. art. 801(D)(3) Official Comment (b).

person against whom it is offered if it concerns a matter "within the scope" of the agency or employment, made "during the existence" of the relationship. This type of admission is a relational admission that is labeled such when it is not personal, adoptive, or truly authorized, but the statement is admissible based on considerations of fairness and completeness.[323]

This provision attributes a statement to a party and may be offered against him if the **following requirements are met**:

1. The statement must be made by an employee or agent of the party;
2. concerning a matter within the scope of his agency or employment;
3. during the existence of the relationship; and
4. offered against the principal/employee who is a party to the action.

The general rule is that the statement must have been within the scope of the agent's/employee's authority, although the agent need not have been specifically authorized to speak on the principal's behalf, which is commonly known as a "speaking agent," as discussed above. An agent/employee specifically authorized to speak on behalf of his principal/employer is covered in Article 801(D)(2) above, covering authorized admissions. Under this provision, a statement may be attributed to the principal "whenever the statement concerns a matter within the scope of the agency or employment"[324] and made during the existence of the relationship. Traditional agency principles are used to determine whether the relationship exists and the scope of the agency/employment relationship.

Example: Cane slipped and fell in a grocery store. Immediately after he fell, the store employee who sweeps, stocks, and mops floors ran over to him and stated, "I knew we put too much wax on the floors last night." Will the employee's statement be admissible against the grocery store?

5. Co-conspirators. Article 801(D)(3)(b) allows a statement to be offered against a party if it is made by a co-conspirator/declarant "while participating in" a conspiracy to commit a crime or civil wrong and "in furtherance of" the objective of the conspiracy. In order for the provision to apply the proponent must first establish a **prima facie case of conspiracy** between the declarant/co-conspirator and the party against whom the statement is offered. Once the conspiracy is established, a statement made by one of the co-conspirators during the conspiracy and in furtherance of the conspiracy may be offered against any of the other co-conspirators. This article treats such statements as admissions and exempts them from the hearsay ban. For this exemption to apply, **the following requirements must be met**:

1. Prima face case of conspiracy between declarant and party-litigant;
2. Statement made during the conspiracy;
3. Statement in furtherance of the conspiracy; and
4. Offered against a co-conspirator who is a party to the action.

The requirement that the statement be made during the conspiracy excludes statements made after the venture has ended, unless such statement might be deemed to be a part of a continuous transaction forming the criminal act. Further, the statement must be made in furtherance of the conspiracy. Additionally, the co-conspirator's state-

323. La. Code Evid. art. 801(D)(3) Official Comment (a).
324. La. Code Evid. art. 801(D)(3) Official Comment (b).

ments sought to be admitted may serve as evidence of the foundation requirement to establish the existence of the conspiracy.[325]

6. Other privity admissions. Article 801(D)(3)(c)–(f) contains statements referred to as privity admissions. Privity admissions are based on the principle that one who under substantive law stands in another's shoes for the purposes of a lawsuit should generally be made to take the bad with the good.[326] Thus, the statements of those in whose shoes the party stands for purpose of the lawsuit may be offered against them as a privity admission. Privity admissions under this article are supported by concepts of fairness and completeness.[327] These provisions apply only in civil cases and are not found in the Federal Rules of Evidence.[328]

Examples of privity admissions falling within Article 801(D)(3)(c) include statements of a principle debtor offered against his surety, statements of an assignor offered against the assignee, and statements by an insured offered against the beneficiary.[329] Examples of statements falling into Article 801(D)(3)(d) includes statements by a predecessor in title offered against his successor.

Additionally, Article 801(D)(3)(e) includes statement by a declarant offered against the party in an action for damages arising from the death of that declarant. This provision includes both actions for wrongful death as well as survival actions under Louisiana substantive law.[330] See *Bordelon v. Henderson*,[331] where a deceased patient's denial of medical treatment was treated as a privity admission under this provision against her heirs who brought the medical malpractice lawsuit arising out of the death of the declarant.[332]

Article 801(D)(3)(f) includes statement by a minor child offered against a party in an action to recover for injury to that child, or against the person responsible for the child in an action to recover damages for losses caused by the child.

Content of Statement

A common point of confusion when dealing with "admissions" is the idea that the statement in question must somehow be incriminating or otherwise be against the party's interest who made it. After all, why else would his opponent seek to offer it into evidence? However, Articles 801(D)(2) and (3) have no such requirement, as in the case of a statement against interest covered in Article 804(B)(3). This article applies to *any* relevant statement by the opponent, even if it is exculpatory or neutral.

---

325. *See* State v. Lobato, 603 So. 2d 739 (La. 1992); *See also* Bourjaily v. U.S., 483 U.S. 171, 107 S. Ct. 2775 (1987); 19 La. Civ. L. Treatise, Evidence and Proof § 10.3; *See* State v. Cox, 876 So. 2d 932 (La. Ct. App. 3d Cir. 2004) for discussion of *Crawford* in the context of a purported co-conspirator statement.

326. La. Code Evid. art. 801(D)(3) Official Comment (a).

327. La. Code Evid. art. 801(D)(3) Official Comment (d).

328. La. Code Evid. art. 801(D)(3) Official Comment (3).

329. La. Code Evid. art. 801(D)(3) Official Comment (e); *See also* Iberia Building Systems, Inc. v. Bank One, 768 So. 2d 106 (La. Ct. App. 3d Cir. 2000) (Bank secretary stole money from depositor by forging checks and cashing at bank. Secretary's admissions are admissible against the bank because bank's liability was derivatively based on Secretary's liability).

330. La. Code Evid. art. 801(D)(3) Official Comment (e).

331. Bordelon v. Henderson, 604 So. 2d 950 (La. 1992).

332. *See* Force & Rault, Handbook, Arts. 801(D)(2) and(3) Author's Comment (6); Ghetti, Louisiana Evidence (Unpublished 2008).

Additionally, unlike most other exceptions and exemptions to the hearsay rule, admissions may also include opinions and conclusions. Further, there is no requirement of personal knowledge for this exemption to apply.

Example: An employee of a business is shot and killed at work by a robber who entered the business just after they closed. The robbery occurred while the business owner was away. Several employees were present and didn't see how the robber entered but believed he entered through a back door that can be shimmied open even when locked. After the robbery occurred, the owner was called to the scene and spoke to the employees. When the police arrived, he told the police, "*A robber came into the business through the broken back door and shot and killed one of my employees.*" A lawsuit is later brought against the employer for the employee's death. The plaintiffs would like to offer the defendant/employer's statement into evidence to prove the truth of the matter asserted. The employer would like the evidence excluded. He is now claiming that he did not know how the robber got into the business because he was not present. Can his statement be offered against him? Why or why not?

Distinguishing Admissions and Statements Against Interest

As discussed in § 5.17, the "statements against interest" exception found in Article 804(B)(3) for unavailable declarants is often confused with "admissions," which, as we just covered, are non-hearsay. You should keep in mind that they are not the same and the requirements for each are different. There are four distinct differences in the two types of statements: 1) statements against interest do not require that the declarant be a party in the action, as in the case of admissions; 2) a statement against interest need not be offered *against* the declarant, as in the case of admissions; 3) an admission need not be a statement against the declarant's interest, but instead can be "any" statement made by a party that is being offered against him; and 4) a statement against interest requires that the declarant be unavailable for admissibility, whereas availability is immaterial with respect to an admission.

While the requirements for each are different, in some instances they do in fact overlap, such as in the case of the prosecution offering a defendant's statement against him. All of the requirements for both a statement against interest and for an admission are met. However, in most instances, a statement will fit into one category but not the other. The chart below lays out the differences.

Comparison of Statements Against Interest and Admissions

	Statement Against Interest	Admission
Party to action	Need not be a party to the action.	Must be a party to the action.
Substance of statement	Must be against the declarant's interest when made.	May be anything. Need not be against interest. May also include opinions, conclusions and no first-hand knowledge requirement.
Availability	Must be unavailable at trial.	Need not be unavailable. Here the declarant is a party.
Who may offer	May be offered by either party.	Must be offered by the opponent of the party making the statement.

Which of the following is an admission and which is a statement against interest or both?

1. In a civil case, the plaintiff offers a statement against the defendant that when he was informed by his neighbor that a tree in his backyard had fallen on his neighbor's fence he stated, "*I knew I should have cut that tree down when my wife mentioned it to me.*"
2. In a criminal trial for rape, the prosecution wishes to offer into evidence a statement made by the defendant to the police that while he was present in the vicinity of where the victim was raped, he did not rape the victim.

   Assume instead that the defendant wishes to offer a statement that the victim gave to the police several days after he was arrested for the rape where she stated that she had lied about the whole thing.
3. In a medical malpractice suit against her doctor, the plaintiff would like to offer a statement made to her by the doctor's nurse when the doctor stepped out of the room that, "*he should probably give you a couple more tests before he sends you home in this condition or at least hold you for observations.*"
4. The defendant, a store owner in a slip and fall case, would like to offer evidence that a few months after the plaintiff fell down in his store, he saw the plaintiff at an amusement park, and the plaintiff said to him, "*Hey Jim, doing great! Not hurt at all by the fall!*"

Cases on Admissions

Personal Admissions [Article 801(D)(2)(a)]

State v. Strickland
Supreme Court of Louisiana
683 So. 2d 218
Nov. 1, 1996

WATSON, Justice.

A Vernon Parish grand jury indicted Lawson Eugene Strickland and Christian Boyd for first-degree murder, armed robbery and conspiracy to commit the armed robbery of Jesse B. Pinsonneault. The indictment was amended prior to trial to charge only Strickland. A jury found Strickland guilty as charged on all counts. After a penalty hearing, the jury unanimously recommended a death sentence for the first degree murder, finding as an aggravating factor that the murder was committed during the commission of an armed robbery. The trial judge sentenced Strickland to death in accordance with the jury's recommendation....

FACTS

At 1:35 a.m. on November 3, 1992, the Vernon Parish Sheriff's Office responded to a report of robbery and shooting at the Merchants and Farmers Bank on Fort Polk Entrance Road southeast of Leesville, Louisiana. Officers dispatched to the scene saw Jesse Pinsonneault, the 23-year-old assistant manager of a nearby Sambino's pizza restaurant, lying in a pool of blood. Pinsonneault had been shot once in the upper right chest; a spent .380 cartridge casing lay nearby. The victim told officers he had come to put the day's receipts into the bank's night deposit when a man approached him from behind and said something to him. Pinsonneault turned toward the man, saying "What?" and was shot in the chest. The man then grabbed one of the two bank bags the victim carried, which contained $106.91 in cash and checks, and ran away.

Pinsonneault described his assailant as a white male, five feet eight inches to five feet nine inches tall, wearing dark clothing. Pinsonneault was rushed to a nearby hospital for treatment and then transferred to Rapides General Hospital in Alexandria, Louisiana. He died later that morning of his injuries.

Officers interviewed Donald Baker and Rogena Cravens. Baker, Pinsonneault's friend, had waited at Sambino's while Pinsonneault made out the night deposit. Cravens, a Sambino's employee, had cleaned up for the night. Baker and Cravens waited in front of Sambino's while Pinsonneault drove approximately 300 yards to make the night bank deposit.

Baker heard voices coming from the direction of the bank, then he and Cravens heard a gunshot and someone yelling for help. Baker told Cravens to get into his car, then ran toward the bank. Baker saw a man on a nearby hill run back toward the woods. Cravens saw another man dressed in black running across a parking lot 100 feet away toward the woods and heard heavy footsteps. Baker did not see the second man but heard his heavy running footsteps.

...

The police brought in tracking dogs that followed a trail through the woods. The scent was lost in a nearby military housing area beyond the woods. Officers canvassed the area without success.

On November 6, 1992 at 3:55 p.m., Dispatcher Lonnie Barrington of the Vernon Parish Sheriff's Office received a call from an anonymous male, stating that two escapees from the parish jail, Lawson Strickland and Christian Boyd, were staying with two girls named Amy and Jennifer in a trailer on Jeane Chapel Road. The caller gave directions to the trailer and warned that both men were armed and dangerous. Strickland and Boyd, facing burglary and theft charges, had escaped from the parish jail on October 28, 1992.

Police went to the described area. A young woman exited the trailer and was followed to her parents' residence in Leesville. The woman was Kimberly Atkins, known to the police as Lawson Strickland's girlfriend. When stopped, Atkins told police that Strickland and Boyd were not in the trailer she had just left and that she did not know where they might be. Police transported her back to the trailer, where she continued to insist that the men were not inside.

Police officers knocked on the trailer's front door; Amanda "Amy" Dempsey opened it. When officers asked if there were other people in the trailer, she stated that there were and called to the persons inside. Dempsey, Strickland and Boyd walked outside to the waiting officers, were placed on the ground and handcuffed. Jennifer McCormic, the trailer's lessee, was picked up from her job and escorted back to the trailer where she signed a consent to search form....

[After investigation] Strickland and Boyd were arrested for first degree murder, armed robbery and conspiracy to commit armed robbery. Dempsey and McCormic were arrested as material witnesses; charges were later dismissed against them.

Kimberly Atkins was also arrested and later pleaded guilty to accessory after the fact of first degree murder....

LAW AND DISCUSSION

...

At trial, defense counsel objected to the letters *[the letters follow this case]* on the basis of hearsay, relevancy, lack of proper foundation, and because they were "fruit of the poisonous tree". The trial judge overruled the objections. The trial judge had portions of the letters, either too inflammatory or inadmissible as relating to other crimes evidence, deleted from the letters shown to the jury. The letters, as Strickland's own statements, were not hearsay. La.C.E. art. 801(D)(2). The relevancy of the letters, in which Strickland urged Atkins to "stick to the story" and generally wrote about the crimes, is self-evident. Atkins testified about receiving the letters and also receiving telephone calls from Strickland discussing the fact that the letters were written; a proper foundation was laid for the letters' introduction.... The trial judge did not err in allowing the letters to be introduced in evidence.

GH,

Hey Baby. I was so happy to get your letter. I am happy to hear that you still Love me. Losing your love is the worst thing that could happen to me. At least no matter what happens to me I know that I will always have you in my heart. They cant take that away from me. you must understand how important that is to me. As the years go by this will all become a bad memorie for you and the Love we have and the times we spent together will slowly fade away, but for me these memories and that feeling of love will be All that I have. For the Rest of my life. My dreams will always be of being with you and sharing that love again. Do you realize that you are the last woman I will ever have sex with? Pretty wild huh. you are the last woman I will ever fall in love with, kiss, hold in my Arms. That is not the same for you. Now you under stand how these feelings will always live forever in me and slowly fade and die in you. But that is to be expected. I hope the best for you. I hope you have every thing you want. I will write you of course. I will always keep in touch. Im probably going to Angola but no matter what it will be in LA. If you wanted to you could visit me. Inmates Are Allowed to have <u>Contact</u> visits. Meaning we could touch and Everything. Whoa Now. Boyd will probably send me a little money Every month. you have to send money. Nothing else but letters gets in They have a store for the inmates. Thats the only way you can get your Cigarettes and soap and shit. Im sorry to break this to you but it's going to be more than a few years. Its going to be atleast 60 yrs if not the death penalty. I dont want you to wait for me or anything. Put this behind you and get on with your life. Just dont forget me. Dont forget what we had. I love you. I always will.

Now lets get down to the business at hand. If you told them anything then tell me. I need to know. Dont be afraid to tell me. It will help me more. Im not mad at anyone. Even if they told. If you didn't say shit then good. Now, if you didn't say anything here's what me and Chris need. we need you to say that Chris was not with me. He stayed at home with you. Amy and Jennifer were at work in Alex. so they dont know. You have to say that Boyd was not there. you and him had nothing to do with it. If you already told them you dropped me off then say it was just me and you didn't know what I was going to do. I said that I just wanted to look around. Then you went home. Boyd didn't even know. Im trying to get you and Boyd off. Im taking this hit. you and Chris will do me a lot more good on the outside than in Jail. you have to tell them you didn't know for sure. I never told you you have to stick to it. Its you and Chris's only chance. IF they are going to get you they are going to

Kim 1 of 2

get you anyways. So you might as well try. I know that they
have probably tried to get you to turn states Evidence against me.
They tried to get Boyd to. Thats O.K. That will help you. But if you
do then you have to stick to the story. Its the only way. we are
all in this together we have to try to help each other. Not fuck
Each other. Dont worry about what Amy and Jennifer say. They
weren't there. I want to try to make it look like it was an accid
that I shot him, get my charges dropped to 2nd degree murder
That doesn't carry the death Sentence. If the pressure you and
tell you that they now. I told you what happened then atleast
if you have to tell them I didn't mean to shoot the guy. That it
was an accident. The gun just went off during the struggle.
Chris is going to do the same. He is going to say that he was.
at the trailor. He didn't know. He is going to turn states evidence
against me. Its all part of the plan. Dont worry. I want to
help you two. I will take All the blame. They've Already got m
theres no need for all of us to get in trouble. You can get the
Acessary to Armed Robbery off you. Thats the big one. Aiding a
Escape aint shit. The most you could get is a $3,000 fine and
5 years in Jail. But you wont get that. you are a 1st offende
Plus you really didn't Aid the Escape. you just hid us. you
will probably get probation. Especially if you turn states. But
if you already told them every thing you need to tell me cause
then we will have to change plans. I'm trying to help you and Boyd
me and chris haven't said 1 word. After you get out you can

KIM

get with Amy and Jeniffer and tell them to suddenly get dumb. To say look. We were scared. We told you what we thought. We weren't there, we were in Alex working. We dont know for sure. That will help. Just try to cover you and chriss ASS. Dont worry about me. Tell one of those girls over there to write me a letter to let me know when you are gone so I will know when you get out. I will continue to write you at Chris's P.O. Box. Do you still have the key? I wont be able to write anything to you because they will probably read my mail. And you dont write anything to me about this cause they will probably read it. Dont use your name when I write you. I wont use your name either. When you get out Please mail me some cigarettes. Please. There are some at the trailer unless People already smoked them. And tell Amy and Jenn. to be quet about this. Dont tell everyone. After you bond out you cant come here to visit me. If you give me Brooks address I will write you there. Try to get Brooks T.V. tell him I will Rent it $10 every 2 weeks. If youve already told every thing then tell me its vecy important so that I will now what to do. Help me. I love you. Stay tough. I hope you feel better...

P.S.
Remember, I always have a Plan. Its not over yet.
I dont give up so easy.
Trust ME. Save some money. Do good in school!

I love you
Forever,

ME

Discussion Questions

1. *Strickland* demonstrates the classic situation in which admissions are commonly used—against defendants in a criminal case. Here, the statement is a written statement. The defendant is a party to the action, and his statement is offered against him. Is this provision a free-for-all to offer anything a defendant says against him? Strickland also reminds us that even though an out-of-court statement may not be excluded under the hearsay rule because it fits into an exception or exemption, it may still be excluded on other grounds, particularly in a criminal case. What are some limitations? Consider these issues:
    - *What if the defendant describes several other unrelated crimes in the statement and talked about a long criminal history?*
    - *What if the defendant described the gruesome details of how he committed a violent crime?*
    - *What if the defendant insists that he did not write the letter (statement) and there was no one around who could say that he did in fact write it?*
    - *What if the statement had been made to a police officer after the defendant asked for a lawyer?*

    Considering these issues and others, upon what grounds might a defendant's statement be excluded?
2. Upon what grounds did the defense object to the statement in *Strickland* being offered? How did the court address those issues?

Adoptive Admissions [Article 803(D)(2)(b)]

In *Hamilton v. Walker*, the court examines the adoptive admission in the context of a civil case.

Hamilton v. Walker
Court of Appeal of Louisiana, Third Circuit
893 So. 2d 1002
Feb. 9, 2005

SAUNDERS, Judge.

This suit revolves around an automobile accident. The trial court found Mr. Walker 100% at fault and awarded Ms. Hamilton damages. We affirm in part and reverse in part.

FACTS

On October 22, 1999, around 2:54 p.m., an automobile accident occurred involving Mr. Walker and Ms. Hamilton. At the time of the accident, Mr. Walker was traveling north on the service road that runs parallel to MacArthur Drive or U.S. Hwy. 71. Ms. Hamilton had crossed the four lanes of traffic on U.S. Hwy. 71 and was making a left turn onto that same service road when the two vehicles collided. Mr. Walker's lane was controlled by a yield sign, and the lane crossing U.S. Hwy. 71 was controlled by a red light signal, which Ms. Hamilton says was green.

Immediately following the accident, the police were notified and Officer Craig R. Mikel arrived to investigate the accident. Officer Mikel completed an accident report but did not issue any traffic citations.

Ms. Hamilton filed suit against Charles Walker and Allstate Insurance Company. Later, she amended her petition to name as a defendant her own insurance company, New Hampshire Insurance Company. Trial was held on August 6, 2004, with Ms. Hamilton being the only witness presented at trial. Ms. Hamilton's treating physician, Dr. Gregory Brian, provided a deposition on November 13, 2003, and this deposition was admitted at trial and evaluated by the trial judge. The defendant, Mr. Walker, did not testify at trial, but his deposition taken on June 20, 2003 was introduced at trial and also evaluated by the judge. Officer Mikel failed to appear at either of his two scheduled depositions, and, therefore his accident report was introduced into evidence. However, any information in the report representing the officer's opinion about how the accident occurred or who was at fault was excluded.

After hearing the testimony and evaluating the evidence, the trial judge determined that Mr. Walker was 100% at fault and awarded Ms. Hamilton damages. Mr. Walker and Allstate Insurance Company filed an appeal.

...

LAW AND ANALYSIS

... The appellant's second argument in support of this assignment of error is based on an adoptive admission they allege Ms. Hamilton made at the scene of the accident.

> Q. Okay. What happened after the accident?
>
> A. Well, I got out of the car and I was a little angry **and I told her, I said you run the red light and it was nothing said** and we started changing insurance information. (Emphasis added.)

Mr. Walker accused Ms. Hamilton of running the red light and appellants argue that Ms. Hamilton's failure to deny the allegation amounts to an adoptive admission. Appellants contend that this admission coupled with the officer's report should have established Ms. Hamilton's liability for the accident. According to *State v. McClain,* 254 La. 56, 222 So. 2d 855, 856–57 (1969) (citations omitted), *cert. denied,* 399 U.S. 911, 90 S. Ct. 2205, 26 L. Ed. 2d 566 (1970), an adoptive admission is defined as the following:

If a statement incriminating a defendant is made by another in the defendant's presence and hearing, under circumstances where a denial, explanation, or reply would be expected and where the defendant is not in legal custody and is at full liberty to speak, evidence of that statement, and of the defendant's silence and failure to deny or explain it, may be submitted to the jury for consideration as an admission by the defendant of that statement. State v. McClain, 254 La. 56, 222 So. 2d 855, 856, 857 (1969).

However, the adoptive admission in the case referred to by the appellants occurred in a criminal context and that case is not directly on point with the facts before us. In addition, a thorough study of the record failed to reveal any references to this alleged adoptive admission at trial. During the examination of Ms. Hamilton, neither party questioned her about this admission or even made reference to it. Also, during closing arguments, neither party discussed this admission. The only evidence presented of this was in Mr. Walker's deposition where he states that he told her she ran a red light, but there is no evidence to indicate that Ms. Hamilton even heard the accusation. In addition, he accuses her of running a red light, but specifically states that traffic attempting to cross over U.S. Hwy. 71 had a green light, which coincides with Ms. Hamilton's testimony. This statement to Ms. Hamilton, without more, is insufficient to establish Ms. Hamilton's liability for this accident. Therefore, we find this alleged "adoptive admission" argument lacking as even the defendant's statements are contradictory.

Therefore, as the appellants have provided no persuasive arguments, we find that the trial court did not commit manifest error in finding Mr. Walker 100% at fault.

Discussion Questions

1. Upon what basis did the court in *Hamilton* find the statement at issue was not an adoptive admission? What standard did the court use? What was missing?
2. Are adoptive admissions reliable? Don't people sometimes fail to respond to accusations for various reasons? Is it fair to then use the person's silence against him? Why or why not?
3. How much weight should adoptive admissions be given? Had the court found that the statement was an adoptive admission, should liability have been assessed to the plaintiff? How much?
4. The court makes an important distinction between considering such a statement in a civil context versus considering them in a criminal context when a defendant is in police custody due to a person's Fifth Amendment privilege against self-incrimination. The privilege prevents a person's silence from being used against him as an admission in a criminal case. What reasoning or rationale do you believe underlies this distinction in a civil context versus a criminal context?

State v. Carey
Ct. of Appeal of Louisiana, Second Circuit
628 So. 2d 27
Aug. 18, 1993

VICTORY, Judge.

Defendants, Demond Carey and Bobby Wallace, aka Bobby Young, Jr., were found guilty as charged by a jury of the second degree murder of Johnny Lee Atkins. Defendants appeal, urging among other complaints that the evidence was insufficient to sustain a conviction. We reverse the convictions, vacate the sentences and order the defendants discharged.

FACTS

According to the prosecution's theory of the case, on November 20, 1990 at approximately 9:00 p.m., defendants Carey and Wallace, accompanied by Wallace's cousin, Tronde Young, were riding around in the Martin Luther King Drive area of Shreveport in a brown or green Ford four-door. While driving down Willis Street, Carey forced three pedestrians, one of whom was the victim, Johnny Lee Atkins, off the road. Carey turned the car around and drove back to where Atkins was standing. The young men exchanged words and Wallace pulled out a firearm. As Atkins began to run away, Wallace fired one shot into his back, causing his demise.

Carey and Wallace were indicted for second degree murder. One of the state's eyewitnesses to the crime could not be located by the state. Tronde Young testified at trial, but denied being in the car or having any personal knowledge of the crime. Following extensive impeachment of Young's testimony by his prior inconsistent statements, the jury convicted defendants of second degree murder.

On appeal, defendants claim that the state failed to produce sufficient evidence that they committed the crime, specifically arguing that the jury was encouraged to and used the substance of inconsistent statements as proof of guilt. We agree.

LAW & DISCUSSION

... Eric Clinton's testimony was also used at trial to impeach Young's denials at trial. Clinton testified that, at about 9:30 p.m. on the night of the homicide, he encountered the defendants and Young by the washateria and Young told him that he, Carey and Wallace had been riding down Willis Street when "something happened." Defense counsel objected to Clinton's testimony as hearsay within hearsay since Young had denied being present at the scene of the crime.... Clinton also admitted that a week after the homicide he informed the police that Young told him that Wallace told Young, "I didn't fire four times, I just fired once"; that Carey said they did it, "for the money and the weed"; and, that Carey said Wallace hung out the window and fired the shot." ...

A jury is allowed by law to consider prior inconsistent statements as evidence that a witness is not telling the truth at trial. However, it may not accept the substance of the prior statements as the truth and use it to convict a defendant. *State v. Taylor, supra.*

CONCLUSION

Viewing the testimony in a light most favorable to the state, but not considering the substance of any prior inconsistent statements given by Young or Clinton, the state clearly failed to prove beyond a reasonable doubt that the defendants murdered Atkins....

Although the trial court charged the jury that contradictory statements "are admitted only to attempt to discredit the witness, not to show that the contradictory statements are true," it is clear that in convicting the defendants, the jury erroneously accepted the substance of some of the prior inconsistent statements as the truth.... Under these circumstances, we are required by law to reverse the convictions, vacate the sentences imposed and discharge the defendants on these charges....

ON REHEARING

In its application for rehearing in this case, the State argues for the first time that Tronde Young's statements to Eric Clinton, in the presence of defendants Carey and Wallace, together with their failure to respond, were an adoptive admission under *State v. McClain,* 254 La. 56, 222 So.2d 855 (1969), cert. den. 399 U.S. 911, 90 S.Ct. 2205, 26 L.Ed.2d 566 (1970). See Louisiana Code of Evidence Article 801(D)(2)(b). The State argues, that when these circumstances are viewed as an admission, along with the other evidence presented, the *Jackson v. Virginia* standard has been met.

In *State v. McClain,* the Louisiana Supreme Court stated:

> If a statement incriminating a defendant, is made by another in the defendant's presence and hearing, under circumstances where a denial, explanation, or reply would be expected and where the defendant is not in legal custody and is at full liberty to speak, evidence of that statement, and of the defendant's silence and failure to deny or explain it, may be submitted to the jury for consideration as an *admission* by the defendant of that statement.... ... Neither the witness to a verbalized admission nor the witness to an admission through silence is obliged to vouch for the truth of the content of the admission. Hinton's testimony is admitted not as truth of what McBroom said, but only to show the defendant's acquiescence in that statement through failure to deny or explain. Hence to admit this testimony is not a denial of the defendant's right of confrontation and cross-examination.

The statements in question were offered by the State only to impeach Tronde Young, who denied at trial that he had had a discussion with Clinton shortly after the shooting. Thereafter, as a witness for the State, Eric Clinton testified (after admitting he had first told the police that the incriminating statements were made to him *by the defendants*) Tronde Young told him at about 9:30 p.m. on the night of the shooting in the presence of the defendants that he, Carey and Wallace were riding down Willis Street, had just done something, that one shot, not four, was fired, that Wallace had leaned out the car window and said to the victim Atkins, "Where's the money, give me the money," and that Carey and Wallace had done it for the money and the weed. Undoubtedly, the defendants were close enough to Tronde Young to have heard these statements.

Viewing this evidence and the other circumstantial evidence in a light most favorable to the State, we now reverse our earlier ruling and conclude that the evidence was sufficient for a rational trier of fact to conclude beyond a reasonable doubt that the defendants were guilty.

Nonetheless, as pointed out in our original opinion, in its closing argument, the State repeatedly encouraged the jury to accept the substance of prior inconsistent statements as proof of the defendants' guilt. Although the defendants objected to these remarks, the trial judge did not stop the State from such arguments, but simply read the jury instruction on prior inconsistent statements. We are thoroughly convinced that the State's improper closing arguments influenced the jury and contributed to the verdict in this case, depriving the defendants of a fair trial....

For these reasons, our original judgment in this case is modified. The defendants' convictions are reversed, the sentences vacated, and the case is remanded for a new trial.

Discussion Questions

1. *Carey* deals with an adoptive admission in a criminal context. The court uses factors set out in *State v. McClain,* 222 So. 2d 855 (La. 1969), to determine whether the statement may be offered as an admission against the defendant. Do you agree that the defendant adopted the statement in *Carey*?
2. While the standard in *McClain* was established with the criminal context in mind, the court nonetheless used similar factors in deciding this case. Do you think there should be different considerations in a criminal versus a civil context considering the different consequences at stake?
3. Keep in mind that a statement may also be expressly adopted, and may be implicitly adopted by reliance on a statement in a writing or conversation. Can you think of examples in which a criminal defendant might expressly adopt a statement? How might a person implicitly adopt a statement by reliance upon a statement in a writing or conversation?

Relational Admissions—Agent/Principal, Employer/Employee [Article 801(D)(3)(a)]

Holloway v. Gulf Motors, Inc.
Court of Appeal of Louisiana, Second Circuit
588 So. 2d 1322
Oct. 30, 1991

NORRIS, Judge.

Rita Jo Holloway sued Gulf Motors, Inc., the seller, and General Motors Corp., the manufacturer, to rescind the sale of a 1989 Buick Century and restore the purchase price, and for damages, attorney fees and costs....

Evidence at the confirmation hearing

Mrs. Holloway testified that she bought the new Buick Century on October 18, 1988. Her invoice from Gulf verifies that she paid $18,116.00 for the car; she also testified that she paid $326.10 for insurance and $919.88 for tax, title and license.

About three days after she got the car, Mrs. Holloway's husband, who is a certified mechanic, noticed a ticking sound in the engine; she herself found the brakes had to be pushed almost to the floor. She called the salesman and told him these problems, and others: a high pitch noise in the front end, a clicking sound in the tires, the gas gauge did not work and the car was pulling badly to the right. She brought the car to Gulf on October 25; Gulf returned it later that day, saying nothing was wrong with it. Mrs. Holloway returned the car two days later and spoke to the Service manager, Mr. Carter, who felt the problem was a torque converter clutch in the transmission; this would have to be replaced and it would take two or three days. Mrs. Holloway brought them the car for this work on November 9. Gulf kept the car for 16 days, with Mr. Carter explaining that he had to send it to Shreveport for the work.

When she received the car in late November, Mrs. Holloway found all the problems still present, plus a popping sound whenever she would make a sharp turn. She went to Gulf's manager, Mr. Russell, on November 26 to complain. He told her they would put in a new transmission. She delivered the car for this work on December 8 and got it back on December 12, but all the problems were still present....

In late December Gulf hired a new manager, Mr. Veazey, who told Mrs. Holloway to bring in the car and they would try to fix it again. She brought the car on February 27, 1989, with all the old problems plus the trunk light was not working. She detailed all her complaints to Mr. Veazey. When they returned the car four days later, the problems were still there, though the popping was not as loud and the clicking occurred only in reverse; however, the cruise control no longer worked, the windows rolled down by themselves, the car vibrated at various speeds and the paint was chipping off.

Mrs. Holloway was convinced that she "just got a lemon" and twice asked Mr. Carter to take the car back, but he refused. She added that Mr. Russell had been "real ugly" with her.

...

Discussion

By its first assignment Gulf urges the trial court erred in rendering a default judgment without competent evidence. In particular, Gulf argues that Mrs. Holloway's testimony as to her husband's assessment of the mechanical problems was hearsay and not competent to prove the defects, and that there was no testimony to establish that Gulf was aware of the defects at the time of the sale....

...

Mrs. Holloway testified that her husband first noticed the ticking sound in the engine about three days after she bought the car, and that he would not drive it because he thought it was too dangerous. These statements are hearsay. La.C.Ev. art. 801 C. She also testified, however, that Mr. Carter [the service manager] told her on October 27 that the torque converter clutch in the transmission was defective and would have to be replaced; he also told her he sent the car to Shreveport for repairs. She testified that Mr. Russell [Gulf's manger] told her on November 26 that they would have to replace the transmission; and she testified that Mr. Veazey [Gulf's new manager] called her sometime after December 23, asking her to bring the car to "see if they could get it fixed." These are statements by employees of Gulf and offered against Gulf, concerning matters within the scope, and during the existence, of their employment. La.C.Ev. art. 801 D(3). They are *not* hearsay and were competent as part of Mrs. Holloway's prima facie case, together with her own testimony.

Redhibition is the avoidance of a sale on account of some vice or defect in the thing sold, which renders it either absolutely useless, or its use so inconvenient and imperfect that it must be supposed that the buyer would not have purchased it, had he known of the vice. La.C.C. art. 2520. The buyer must prove that the vice existed before the sale was made by him; however, if the vice appears within three days immediately following the sale, it is presumed to have existed before the sale. La.C.C. art. 2530.

Gulf's employees admitted the car needed a torque converter clutch and a whole new transmission. This is a major defect and sufficient to support a judgment of rescission. *Lee v. Shaw,* 402 So.2d 152 (La.App. 1st Cir.1981). Later they told her to return the car for work on her various other complaints. They worked on the car seven times and kept it 38 days, without avail; the car still exhibited the same problems. The car's condition had brought Mrs. Holloway to the brink of three accidents. This multiplicity of defects will also support a rescission. *Evangeline Medical & X–Ray Dist. Corp. v. Coleman Oldsmobile, Inc.,* 402 So.2d 208 (La.App. 1st Cir.1981). The finding that a defect warrants rescission or merely reduction is a factual matter in which the trial court has great discretion. *Davis v. Davis,* 353 So.2d 1060 (La.App. 2d Cir.1977).

Mrs. Holloway also testified that the major problems, in the transmission and brakes, became apparent within three days of the sale. In the absence of contrary evidence, these are presumed to have existed before the sale. La.C.C. art. 2530....

On this record, Mrs. Holloway made a prima facie case that the car suffered from defects which rendered its use so inconvenient that she would not have purchased it had she known of them, and that the defects were present at the time of the sale. Denial of new trial on the issue of redhibition is not plainly wrong.

...

Discussion Questions

1. In *Holloway*, another common type of admission is offered. Here an employee's statement is offered against his employer under Article 801(D)(3)(a). What are the requirements that must be met for this provision to apply? Analyze the facts in *Holloway.* How were each of the elements met here?
2. What policy reasons underlie this exemption allowing statements of agents and employees to be offered against their employers/principals?

Co-Conspirators [Article 801(D)(3)(b)]

In *Turner v. Ostrowe*, the court carefully lays out and applies the elements that must be met to offer a co-conspirator's statements against a party as an admission. This case is also a good example of the application of this rule in a civil case.

Turner v. Ostrowe
Court of Appeal of Louisiana, First Circuit
828 So. 2d 1212
Sept. 27, 2002

PARRO, Judge.

In this appeal of a judgment in her favor, Mary Ann Turner contends the trial court's $35,000 general damage award for her physical and psychological injuries is abusively low. Her ex-husband, Dr. Alan J. Ostrowe, against whom the judgment was rendered, also appealed, claiming the trial court's judgment in favor of Turner is legally and manifestly erroneous. We amend the judgment and affirm as amended.

FACTUAL AND PROCEDURAL BACKGROUND

This is a factually unusual, legally challenging, and emotionally charged case with a long history dating back to an event that occurred in 1972. Turner claims in this lawsuit that in 1972, her then-husband, Dr. Alan J. Ostrowe, an anesthesiologist, conspired with another Baton Rouge physician, Dr. Anthony B. Leggio, an obstetrician/gynecologist, to have a surgical procedure performed on her without her knowledge or consent. This procedure, sometimes called female circumcision, consists of the removal of the clitoral prepuce, which is the flap of skin that partially covers and protects the clitoris.[333] Dr. Leggio is deceased and unavailable to testify, but hospital records from Turner's 1972 surgery indicate that Dr. Leggio did, in fact, remove the prepuce of her clitoris.... Turner claims she endured severe pain for months following the surgery and was kept heavily sedated by Ostrowe during that time. Turner and Ostrowe eventually separated for other reasons and were divorced in 1983. Turner contends she believed the only surgery done during her 1972 hospitalization was the posterior repair, and she did not find out until late May or early June of 1988 that a female circumcision had been performed on her at Ostrowe's request. Ostrowe's response is that the couple discussed this procedure after reading about it, that Turner agreed to have a female circumcision in order to energize their sexual relationship, and that she knew and consented to the surgical procedure. Turner vehemently denies this and claims the discovery that she had been genitally mutilated and so intimately betrayed by her then-husband caused her serious emotional trauma in addition to the permanent residual physical effects of the surgery. These physical effects included both hypersensitivity and, conversely, numbness of her clitoral area, causing pain and a loss of sexual pleasure. This suit, seeking damages from Ostrowe for her physical and emotional injuries, was filed April 28, 1989.

... A jury trial commenced October 29, 1996, but ended in a mistrial on October 31, 1996. Ultimately, the parties agreed to a bench trial, which was held in March 2001.

In extensive written reasons, the trial court ruled in favor of Turner, finding that Ostrowe had been instrumental in having the female circumcision performed on her, that

---

333. This procedure was performed, ostensibly as a means of enhancing female sexual response, but according to documents and testimony in the record, it most often had the opposite result due to the exposure of the extremely sensitive nerve endings in the clitoris. Although for purposes of this opinion we will use the term female circumcision, physicians who testified in this case indicated the implied analogy to male circumcision is misleading; the more accurate analogy would be to the complete skinning of the penis, which, of course, is never done. The more recent medical literature includes female circumcision in a broad category called female genital mutilation.

she did not learn about this surgery until 1988, and that her failure to discover the condition was reasonable. A judgment was signed April 6, 2001, awarding her $35,000 in general damages.... Turner then appealed the quantum of the damage award, claiming the trial court applied a legally incorrect standard in making the award and that it was an abuse of discretion. Ostrowe also appealed, urging the trial court erred in making certain evidentiary rulings and claiming manifest error with respect to the court's factual findings....

ANALYSIS

Dr. Leggio's Statements to Dr. Pizzolatto

We address first Ostrowe's assignment of error claiming the trial court committed reversible error when it allowed into the record the "clear hearsay" testimony of Dr. Karl Pizzolatto, in which he recounted a comment allegedly made to him by Dr. Leggio.... Dr. Pizzolatto assisted Dr. Leggio in performing the 1972 surgery on Turner.[334] Dr. Pizzolatto testified that while he and Dr. Leggio were in the surgical suite and after the posterior repair was finished, Dr. Leggio whispered to him that there was an additional procedure to be done and described the female circumcision. When Dr. Pizzolatto asked why such an unusual procedure was being performed, Dr. Leggio purportedly responded that he was doing it as a favor to Ostrowe and that Turner did not know about it. Ostrowe objected to this entire line of testimony as hearsay and it was proffered.

However, on cross-examination of Dr. Pizzolatto, Ostrowe's attorney initiated the following colloquy:

> Q Do you have any evidence, by the way, do you yourself, Dr. Pizzolatto, have any knowledge at all that Dr. Leggio kept this a secret from Mary Ann Turner?
>
> A Yes, I do.
>
> Q That Dr. Leggio kept it a secret?
>
> A Yes.
>
> Q What is your testimony?
>
> A He said to me when we discussed this case that Dr. Ostrowe wanted this done because Mary Ann wasn't sensitive enough sexually, and Mary Ann didn't know it was being done.

...

The trial court based its ruling on Louisiana Code of Evidence article 801(D)(3)(b). Under that provision, a statement is not hearsay if it is offered against a party and is made by a declarant while participating in a conspiracy to commit a crime or civil wrong and in furtherance of the objective of the conspiracy, provided that a prima facie case of conspiracy is established. Ostrowe takes issue with the trial court's conclusion that a prima facie case of conspiracy had been established between him and Dr. Leggio to perform this surgery on Turner without her knowledge or consent, which is a civil battery. The trial court found there was sufficient evidence of such a conspiracy to admit Dr. Leggio's statements as a co-conspirator with Ostrowe.

A prima facie case of conspiracy is presented when evidence is introduced which, if unrebutted, would be sufficient to establish the facts of the conspiracy.... Statements made by co-conspirators, which are the object of the hearsay objection, may be considered

334. He is also the person who informed Turner in 1988 that, in addition to the posterior repair, a female circumcision had been done during that surgery.

by the trial court in making its determination as to whether a prima facie case of conspiracy has been established.... A trial court's determination as to the admissibility of such evidence will not be overturned absent clear error....

Our evaluation of the record reveals considerable evidence supporting the prima facie case of conspiracy between Ostrowe and Dr. Leggio. Ostrowe admitted that after he read an article about female circumcision as a means of enhancing a woman's sexual response, he became interested in having this procedure done on his wife for that purpose. He also admitted recommending to his wife that she go to Dr. Leggio for the posterior repair that Ostrowe thought she needed after the birth of their third child. Ostrowe further acknowledged that before his wife saw Dr. Leggio, he discussed with Dr. Leggio the possibility of performing a female circumcision on his wife. Of course, Ostrowe also said he and Turner jointly agreed that she would undergo the procedure; Turner denies ever discussing it with him or Dr. Leggio. Turner recalled that during her only office examination by Dr. Leggio before the surgery, he made a brief mention that she may have some excess tissue covering the clitoris, but did not suggest removing it and did not discuss it further, recommending only the posterior repair and D & C....

The consent for surgery that Turner signed did not describe any of the procedures to be performed. Ostrowe admitted giving her pre-operative sedatives. Although in a deposition Ostrowe denied six times that he was present in the operating room or even in the hospital during the surgery, Ostrowe admitted at trial, and Dr. Pizzolatto confirmed, that he was in the operating room next to the operating table while the surgery, including the female circumcision, was performed. The hospital charts from Turner's nine-day post-operative hospitalization show that Dr. Leggio left orders that Ostrowe could prescribe or administer medications to his wife. The medications given her during this period were described by other doctors who testified as heavy doses of sedatives and painkillers. Although Ostrowe denied administering any drugs to Turner in the hospital, Dr. Pizzolatto testified that he twice saw Ostrowe injecting his wife with valium. These injections do not appear on the hospital record. The removal of the clitoral prepuce also does not appear anywhere in the hospital records until three months following the surgery when the complete operative notes and progress notes were dictated for the record by Dr. Leggio. As Dr. Pizzolatto noted concerning this, "If you want to keep it a secret, you dictate it three months after it happened because nobody reads the records." Turner testified that after she got home from the hospital, she was in excruciating pain, and Ostrowe kept her heavily sedated for several months until the incisions healed....

The cumulative effect of this evidence suffices to establish a prima facie case that Ostrowe and Dr. Leggio conspired to perform a female circumcision on Turner without her knowledge or consent, which is a civil battery.[335] The statements made by Dr. Leggio to Dr. Pizzolatto during and after the surgical procedure were in furtherance of that conspiracy, in that Dr. Pizzolatto was assisting in the surgery. Also, by telling Dr. Pizzolatto that Turner did not know of the female circumcision, the clear implication was that Dr.

335. Ostrowe argues that none of this evidence proves that he knew that Turner did not know. Such proof of a mental state—what he did or did not know—can only be by circumstantial evidence. The trial court evaluated the credibility of the witnesses and concluded that Turner was more credible than Ostrowe and that there was more support for her version of events. Such evaluations of the evidence are the prerogative of the trial court and are entitled to great deference by this court. The circumstantial evidence in this case is sufficient to establish that it is more likely than not that Ostrowe deliberately concealed what had been done, and therefore knew that Turner did not know about the female circumcision.

Pizzolatto should join Dr. Leggio and Ostrowe in keeping the matter secret from her. Therefore, the trial court did not abuse its discretion in allowing Dr. Pizzolatto to testify about what Dr. Leggio told him concerning the female circumcision, Ostrowe's part in having it done, and Turner's lack of knowledge that this was being done to her....

CONCLUSION

The judgment of the trial court is amended and Ostrowe is ordered to pay Turner $125,000, plus legal interest from date of judicial demand and all court costs other than those associated with the first trial. In all other respects, the judgment of the trial court is affirmed. All costs of this appeal are assessed against Ostrowe.

Discussion Questions

1. A key issue in *Turner* is whether a prima face case of conspiracy to commit a civil wrong was established. What must be shown? Is this an issue for the judge or jury to determine?
2. Do you agree that a conspiracy between Dr. Leggio and Dr. Ostrowe was established? Why or why not?
3. The key statement that likely determined the outcome of this case was Dr. Leggio's statement to Dr. Pizzolatto that he was doing the female circumcision as a favor to Dr. Ostrowe and that Turner did not know about it. For a co-conspirator's statement to be offered against a party litigant, the statement must be: 1) made during the conspiracy; and 2) "in furtherance of" the conspiracy. Do you agree with the court that both of these requirements were met? Explain. When did the venture begin and end? How did the statement advance the conspiracy?
4. Do you think there should be any difference in the handling of the admissibility of co-conspirator statements in civil and criminal cases due to the additional rights that an accused has in a criminal case? Why or why not? What should be the difference?

Key Points

The key points to keep in mind regarding admissions.

1. A party's own statement offered against him is non-hearsay and may be considered for substantive value.
2. **Prerequisites that apply to all admissions:**
   a. they are statements **by a party** to the action or are attributed to him; and
   b. the statement is being **offered against the party.**
3. **Party's own statements:**
   a. His own personal statement (in his individual or representative capacity) [Article 801(D)(2)(a)].
   b. A statement in which he *adopted* [Article 801(D)(2)(b)].
   c. A statement *authorized* by him [Article 801(D)(2)(c)].
   d. A statement of an agent/employee in course/scope of employment/agency [Article 801(D)(3)(a)].

e. Statements of co-conspirators in furtherance of conspiracy [Article 801(D)(3)(b)].

4. His own ***personal*** statement (in his individual or representative capacity) — may be oral, written, or tacit. If tacit, should be similar to assertive conduct.
5. A statement in which he ***adopted*** — may be express or implied.
   a. Express Adoption:
      i. orally; or
      ii. in writing.
   b. Implicit Adoption:
      i. Reliance on contents of a statement related in a conversation or writing; or
      ii. Adoption by silence.

      Factors: statement was made in defendant's **presence;** the defendant **heard** the statement; the defendant **understood** the statement; of such a nature and under circumstances where a **denial, explanation, or reply** would be **expected;** and where the defendant is **not in legal custody** and is at full liberty to speak; defendant **failed to deny or explain**
6. A statement ***authorized*** by him — statements attributed to a person because they are authorized to speak on the person's behalf.
7. A statement of an ***agent/employee*** in course/scope of employment/agency: 1) made by an employee or agent of the party 2) concerning a matter within the scope of his agency or employment; 3) made during the existence of the relationship; and 4) offered against the principle/employer.
8. Statements of ***co-conspirators*** in furtherance of conspiracy. The proponent must show: 1) existence of conspiracy; 2) made during the conspiracy; 3) in furtherance of the conspiracy; and 4) offered against any of the co-conspirators.
9. **Content of statement.** May be any statement. Need not be incriminating. May include opinions, conclusions, and there is no requirement of first-hand knowledge.

Problems on Admissions

PROBLEM 5-173. Since Wayne Hospital treated the first diagnosed case of Ebola virus disease in the United States, Derrick Richards, patients have steered clear of the hospital. Patient rolls have plummeted, the hospital's revenue has fallen 25 percent in the 30 days following the patient's stay there, and emergency room visits have fallen 50 percent. Following criticism for initially failing to properly diagnose the patient on his first visit to the hospital, the hospital has hired crisis manager Octavia Prime to help put the hospital's image back on track. Live from the hospital in its first press conference, Prime states, "*We made many mistakes — there are too many to name. There are many things we should have done differently. But new measures have been put in place, and we are now prepared to properly treat cases of Ebola.*" In the family's lawsuit against Wayne Hospital, Derrick's family wishes to offer Prime's statement to help prove that the hospital did not properly treat Derrick. The defense objects that the statement is hearsay and inadmissible. How should the court rule and why?

PROBLEM 5-174. Ingrid, Bailey, and Neely were camping. When Bailey walked out of the room, Ingrid stated, "*Bailey is a cheater and a liar. He can't be trusted.*" Neely nodded and stated, "*Yes, that's true.*" In a lawsuit against Neely for slander, Bailey intends to offer Ingrid's statement against Neely. Neely objected that the statement is hearsay. How should the court rule and why?

PROBLEM 5-175. Twin brothers Tim and Tam, are partners in a restaurant called the TimTam Tavern. Under what circumstances will statements of either Tim or Tam be offered against the other twin, and/or the restaurant? Explain.

PROBLEM 5-176. Beverly walks into her house and hears her mother screaming from upstairs in the bathroom. She runs into the bathroom and her mother is lying face down in the tub and her father is standing over mother with wet hands. Beverly yells, "*You drowned her! You drowned her!*" Father says nothing. Can his silence be admitted against him in a criminal trial as an admission? Why or why not?

PROBLEM 5-177. Two weeks before Dion's pregnant wife is found dead, Dion says to his neighbor, "*I think my wife is cheating. I don't think that child is mine.*" Can Dion's statement be offered against him at his trial for killing his wife? Why or why not?

PROBLEM 5-178. Lefty Simpson's agent is negotiating another contract for him to continue on as quarterback with the Home Team for five more years. During negotiations with the team (Lefty is not present), his agent says, "*His arm is good for at least another four to five years.*" Two years after resigning Lefty to another five-year contract, Lefty's arm gives out and the team sues him for breach of contract. At the trial the team seeks to offer his agent's statement that the arm would be good for four to five years, an assertion they claim they relied upon in resigning Lefty for the lucrative five-year contract. Can the agent's statement be offered against Lefty in the trial? Why or why not?

PROBLEM 5-179. Sisters Zondra and Zanetta were headed home from a late night of partying when they were stopped by police. Zondra was driving. Both got out of the car and went to the rear of the car to speak to the officer. The officer asked Zondra for the vehicle's registration. When Zondra returned to the vehicle and was just out of earshot of Zanetta and the police officer, Zanetta said to the officer, "*Ya know we're really both wasted and were just trying to make it to our house just down the street.*" At Zondra's trial, the prosecution wishes to use Zanetta's statement to the police officer in its case-in-chief to help prove that Zondra was guilty of DWI. The defense objects that the statement is hearsay. The prosecution claims the statement is both an admission and a statement against interest. How should the court rule on the admissibility of Zanetta's statement against Zondra at her trial and why?

PROBLEM 5-180. Bob is a truck driver for Millikin Trucking, LLC. While texting behind the wheel, Bob negligently ran into the back of Kathy's car with Mildred as a passenger. After striking Kathy's car, Bob immediately jumped out of the truck and stated, "*My bad. I was texting and didn't realize you'd stopped.*" Under which of the following scenarios would Bob's statement be admissible as an admission? You may select more than one answer if applicable. Explain.

A. Kathy sues Millikin Trucking for damages arising from Bob's negligence.

B. Kathy learns that Millikin Trucking is insolvent and sues Bob personally for damages.

C. Assume both Bob and Millikin Trucking are insolvent, so Kathy sues her own insurance company under her uninsured motorist policy. In order to prove the accident was not her fault, she offers Bob's statement as an admission.

D. Mildred files a lawsuit against Kathy and Kathy's insurance company. Will Bob's statement come in as evidence of how the accident occurred?

E. None of the above.

PROBLEM 5-181. Morris is on trial for aggravated burglary. At his trial, his brother-in-law Ned will testify that the night of the burglary, his wife (Morris's sister) told him that Morris had called her and told her, "*I have a new television set, a computer, and several household items that I acquired earlier this evening. Y'all wanna buy anything?*" and she said no. At the trial, the defense objects to Ned's testimony. Should Ned be able to testify to what his wife told him? Why or why not?

PROBLEM 5-182. Sampson wants to be a pilot, which requires perfect vision. He gets an exam which shows less than perfect vision and attaches the exam to his application. He is denied admission to flight school and seeks to get social security for being disabled. At the hearing he offers the eye examination results as proof of his eye condition. The defense objects. How will the court rule?

Assume that Sampson was denied social security for disability, so he applied for another job requiring perfect vision and was denied. Sampson sued the company for discrimination and the company offered the exam results against Sampson. Sampson objects, claiming the exam results are hearsay. Would the result be different? Why?

PROBLEM 5-183. Professor Sampson teaches evidence. He learns that another professor has had an outstanding success rate in his class by having an "**A Guarantee**"—where he guarantees that a student will receive an "A" if they do everything on a list that he gives them, regardless to test performance. The list includes reading and briefing every case, writing out the answer to all problems, outlining the code articles, working old exams, outlining the course, allowing the professor to review sample model answers to old exams, among other things. The professor enthusiastically tells his class about how well it has worked and encourages his class to do those things as well to help them get a better grade in his class. He then adds the page that reads "**A Guarantee**" to the last page of his syllabus so they will know what to do. Several students completed all the requirements, but did not get A's. The professor says that he was not guaranteeing A's, but only attached the policy to let them know what they could do to improve their chances of getting a better grade. They sued the professor for their A's, and now the professor objects to the admissibility of the "**A Guarantee**" policy as inadmissible hearsay. What ruling and why?

PROBLEM 5-184. The clerk at the crime lab signs receipts for all evidence turned over to the lab. She is suspected of taking drugs that were turned in as evidence for her personal use. She is arrested. At the trial, the prosecution introduces several hundred receipts that she had signed for drug evidence that was later discovered to be missing. She objects that the evidence is hearsay. What ruling?

PROBLEM 5-185. A few days after Ben and Carter robbed the Kilgore Bank, Carter was stopped for an expired inspection sticker by police. Carter immediately jumped out of the car and stated that Ben had forced him to commit the robbery. At Ben's trial for robbery, the prosecution would like to use Carter's statement against Ben. The defense objects that the statement is hearsay. Should the statement be admitted into evidence?

Assume that following Carter's statement, police immediately went to Ben's residence and arrested him. After taking him to the stationhouse, police read him his *Miranda* rights and proceeded to question him about the incident, repeatedly stating, "You did it, didn't you? Carter told us everything. In fact, it was your idea, wasn't it? You coerced Carter into helping you, didn't you?" Ben never said anything. Eventually Ben was taken to his cell. At Ben's trial, the police would also like to use Ben's silence against him as an admission claiming he never denied their allegations and therefore, they must be true. Can Ben's silence be admitted against him at trial? Why or why not?

PROBLEM 5-186. Brothers Bates and Dow have a plan whereby they sell cheap products to schools as fundraising supplies for extremely high prices. They take pictures of nice items to put in the catalogs, and once customers place orders through the young kids and their parents, they ship very cheap merchandise to the customers after they receive payment. They are arrested and charged with conspiracy to defraud. The prosecutor seeks to offer against Bates the testimony of the superintendent of schools that Dow said to him, "We're making a killing off the kids. Do you think you could get us a couple contracts at other schools?" Will Dow's statement likely be admitted against Bates? Why or why not?

§ 5.23 References and Additional Authority on Admissions [La. C.E. arts. 801(D)(2), (3)]

1. La. C.E. arts. 801(D)(2), (3) and Official Comments
2. Force & Rault, Handbook on Louisiana Evidence Law Arts. 801(D)(2), (3) Author's Comments (West Publishing 2014)
3. Harges & Jones, Louisiana Evidence Arts. 801(D)(2), (3) Author's Comments (West Publishing 2014)
4. 19 La. Civ. L. Treatise, Evidence And Proof § 10.3 (2nd ed.)
5. **Admissions [La. C.E. art. 801(D)(2), (3)]:** *Doty v. USF Ins. Co.*, 84 So. 3d 666 (La. Ct. App. 3d Cir. 2012) (After carpenter told home builder that he did not have the proper equipment to secure a stairwell, home builder told carpenter to go to another job and that he (homebuilder) would secure the stairwell. The court ruled that the statements made by home builder were personal admissions that could be used against him.); *State v. Billiot*, 672 So. 2d 361 (La. Ct. App. 1st Cir. 1996) (holding that defendant's letter to his girlfriend wherein he stated, "how does it feel to be in love with a murderer ha ha," was admissible as an admission); *State v. Glynn*, 653 1288 (La. Ct. App. 1st Cir. 1995) (holding that defendant's statement to a fellow inmate was admissible as an admission and was not involuntarily made in response to promises by the prosecution); *State v. Romero*, 552 So. 2d 45 (La. Ct. App. 3d Cir. 1989) (holding that defendant's assertive head nod to his father while visiting him in jail after being asked, "Son did you do this?" was admissible as an admission).
6. **Statement not authorized**: *Turner v. Ostrowe*, 828 So. 2d 1212 (Trial court properly held that when plaintiff did not authorize any and statements by her psychologists when she allowed her former psychologist to release information to her current psychologist.).
7. **Co-conspirators**: *State v. Lang*, 128 So. 3d 330 (La. Ct. App. 5th Cir. 2013) (The trial court properly ruled that the statements within the text messages were not testimonial and because the state established a prima facie case of conspiracy, the text messages were admissible as non-hearsay statements of co-conspirators.).
8. **Privity** (Only applies in civil cases): *Hoerner v. ANCO Insulations, Inc.*, 812 So. 2d 45 (La. Ct. App. 4th Cir. 2002) (Maryland Casualty insurance company argued that the lower court erred in admitting the deposition of the wife of the founder of Marquette

Insulations, the company it insured. Maryland Casualty further argued that the deposition was inadmissible because it was not present at the time the deposition was taken. The court ruled that because the wife was a representative of Marquette Insulations and Maryland Casualty represented Marquette Insulations, the two were essentially the same party. Therefore, the court ruled that the deposition of the representative wife was admissible as a privity admission.).

9. **Not a privity admission**: *Clay v. International Harvester Co.*, 674 So. 2d 398 (La. Ct. App. 3d Cir. 1996) (The court ruled that the plaintiff's liability was not derivatively based on the liability of his co-employee and because employee/employer tort suits are barred by worker's compensation, the statement was inadmissible as a privity admission.).

§ 5.24 Things Said and Done [La. C.E. art. 801(D)(4)]

Applicable Code Articles

* * *

D. Statements which are not hearsay. A statement is not hearsay if:

* * *

(4) Things said or done. The statements are events speaking for themselves under the immediate pressure of the occurrence, through the instructive, impulsive and spontaneous words and acts of the participants, and not the words of the participants when narrating the events, and which are necessary incidents of the criminal act, or immediate concomitants of it, or form in conjunction with it one continuous transaction.

* * *

Article 801(D)(4) exempts "things said and done" during a criminal act from the hearsay rule. This exemption only applies to **criminal cases**[336] and includes statements made under the immediate pressure of the criminal act that are the instructive, impulsive and spontaneous words and acts of the participants, which are necessary incidents of the criminal act, the immediate concomitants of it, or form one continuous transaction. For example, this exception would exempt from the hearsay ban, the various instructive statements made by the perpetrators of the crime, such as "*Get on the floor*" or "*Put your hand up!*" as well as other spontaneous statements they may make, like "*Let's get out of here*" or "*Where's the cash?*" It would include the necessary concomitants of the criminal act, such as in a drug transaction statements like "*How much you want?*" or "*Give me $60 worth.*" It would also include statements by the victims and other participants as well, such as "*Please don't shoot me,*" "*I don't have any money,*" or "*Take all you want.*" Statements conforming to this rule are not hearsay.

336. *See* Goldsmith v. Green, 47 So. 3d 637 (La. Ct. App. 2d Cir. 2010) (In reversing the use of the exception in a civil case, the court stated, "res gestae has only been used by courts in criminal matters as a means of introducing evidence for convictions of defendants, not for determining the applicability of provisions in insurance policies."); *See also* Force & Rault, Handbook, Art. 801(D)(4) Author's Comments (8) (noting that if used at all in civil cases, should be given an extremely narrow interpretation).

Underlying policy. The idea here is that the various statements made during the pressure of a criminal act have indicia of reliability because the participants are unlikely to have an opportunity to reflect and fabricate their statements. "[I]t is believed that spontaneous and impulsive words which are spoken during the criminal transaction, or as part of it, are reliable statements,"[337] and are thus exempt from the hearsay ban. Thus it is important that the exception be limited to only those statements made during the criminal act by the participants of the act and not statements occurring after the incident has ended.

It is worth noting that similar policy underlies the "excited utterance" and "present sense impression" exceptions to the hearsay rule.[338] Thus, many of the statements conforming to this exemption might overlap with those exceptions and would nonetheless be admissible under either provision.

Requirements of the exemption:

1. applies in criminal cases;
2. made by participants of the crime and, in limited circumstances, some victims or witnesses;
3. made during the crime, both before and after the crime that forms a continuous transaction with it; and
4. statements are instructive, impulsive and spontaneous words and acts that are necessary incidents of the criminal act, or immediate concomitants of it.

Not narrating the events. Since the exemption only applies to statements that are a part of a continuous transaction of events that form the criminal act, someone who actually hears the statements as they are being made, must testify to what he heard. For example, the bank teller who was being robbed can testify to the things said by the participants of the crime during the criminal act, such as "*He said, 'Give me all of the money.'*" A rape victim can testify to what the perpetrator said during the rape, or during the kidnapping such as, "*Get in the car,*" or "*If you scream, I'll shoot you.*"

This exception does not include "words of the participants when narrating the events"[339] where a participant later tells someone about what was said during a crime after the incident is over. For example, if the bank teller later tells the police officer about what the perpetrator said during the crime, her statement to the police is not included in the exemption. Her statements are narrating the events. Thus, the police officer would not be able to testify under this exemption, "*The witness said that he told her to put her hands over her head.*" This exemption would only apply if the witness who actually heard the defendant say those words and who has first-hand knowledge of the statements testified to what was said and done.

Included statements. The types of statements included are those that are "the **instructive, impulsive** and **spontaneous words** and **acts** of the participants," statements that are "**necessary incidents** of the criminal act, or **immediate concomitants** of it." This would basically cover practically anything that the participants could say during the crime. Fur-

---

337. State v. Robinson, 634 So. 2d 1274 (La. Ct. App. 3d Cir. 1994).

338. *See* 19 La. Civ. L. Treatise, Evidence And Proof § 10.4 (2d ed.), noting that scholars and lawmakers originally opposing the provision noted that "declarations properly admissible under 'res gestae' would remain admissible under the codes, either as non-hearsay or under the hearsay exceptions for excited utterances, present sense impressions, statements of existing mental, emotional or physical condition, and statements for purposes of medical treatment."

339. La. Code Evid. art. 801(D)(4).

Requirements for Things Said and Done

1. applies in criminal cases;
2. made by participants of the crime (and sometimes victims, witnesses, or police officers);
3. made during the crime, both before and after the crime that forms a continuous transaction with it; and
4. statements are instructive, impulsive and spontaneous words and acts that are necessary incidents of the criminal act, or immediate concomitants of it.

thermore, the exemption "includes not only spontaneous utterances and declarations made before and after the commission of a crime, but also includes testimony of witnesses and police officers pertaining to what they heard or observed before, during, or after the commission of the crime if the continuous chain of events is evident under the circumstances."[340] For example, the exemption would include statements made before the crime, such as if a man were to say to the other man before shooting him, "*I told you I was going to do it,*"[341] and would also include statements made by the police officer or others after a crime while chasing or attempting to apprehend the suspect such as, "*He went that way,*" "*There he is,*" or "*Come out with your hands up!*"

Distinguish from "Res Gestae," or "Integral Part Evidence." Since this exemption refers to the things that are said and done during a criminal act, it is also referred to as the "res gestae" exception to the hearsay rule. However, it might be much easier to remember the scope of the exemption by accurately referring to it as, "things said and done," because it explains exactly what the exemption is intended to encompass—the things that are *said* and *done during* the criminal act, by the participants of the criminal act.

This exemption should not be confused with Article 404(B)(1) which allows certain "other crimes" to be admitted into evidence if they form an "integral part" of a charged crime. Under that rule, evidence of other crimes that form a part of the "res gestae" are generally not excluded from being offered against an accused at trial. To form a part of the res gestae, the other crimes must be integrally connected to the crime for which the defendant is on trial. The other crimes lend narrative completeness to the instant offense for which a defendant is on trial and are needed to tell a cohesive version of the events forming the instant offense.

For example, if an officer is attempting to stop a vehicle for driving while intoxicated that turns into a high speed chase and aggravated escape, evidence of the DWI would be admissible in the trial for the aggravated escape because it is an integral part of explaining how and why the officer came to be chasing the suspect. The prosecution would not be able to adequately explain the aggravated escape without reference to the DWI. Thus, it would be another crime that would be admissible because it forms a part of the "res gestae" of the crime for which the defendant is on trial.

While the res gestae exception in Article 404(B) refers to other criminal conduct that forms a part of the instant offense for which the defendant is on trial, this exception primarily refers to the statements made during a criminal act that form a part of criminal

340. State v. Crawford, 672 So. 2d 197 (La. Ct. App. 3d Cir. 1996).
341. *See* State v. Robinson, 634 So. 2d 1274 (La. Ct. App. 3d Cir. 1994) below.

transaction as well as the actions of the participants. Integral part evidence as it relates to other crimes is discussed in greater detail in Chapter 6, *infra*.

Federal Rules of Evidence Distinction. There is no corresponding provision in the Federal Rules of Evidence.

Case on Things Said and Done

State v. Robinson[342] presents a fairly straightforward application of the "things said and done" hearsay exemption. It also presents some of underlying policy and rationale supporting the exemption.

State v. Robinson
Court of Appeal of Louisiana, Third Circuit
634 So. 2d 1274
March 2, 1994

COOKS, Judge.

Noble Robinson, Jr., was indicted by a grand jury on the charge of second degree murder in violation of La.R.S. 14:30.1. The defendant was found guilty following a jury trial and was sentenced to life imprisonment at hard labor without benefit of parole, probation or suspension of sentence....

FACTS

On August 25, 1990, at approximately 3:45 p.m., the defendant rode his bicycle into the parking lot of Kelly's I.G. Grocery in Church Point, Louisiana and approached a parked vehicle. Inside the vehicle were the victim, Serita Thomas (the defendant's former girlfriend) and the couple's four year old son both seated in the back seat. Patricia Ann Pitre, Serita's girlfriend, was seated in the front passenger seat of the vehicle. A brief conversation ensued after which the defendant drew a .38 caliber revolver and proceeded to shoot Serita Thomas once in the thigh and once in the head.

The defendant then remounted his bicycle and rode to the Church Point Police Department where he informed the police dispatcher that he had shot Serita Thomas. He promptly unloaded the weapon placing both the bullets and the unloaded weapon on the dispatcher's desk. Immediately, he was arrested and informed of his *Miranda* rights....

ASSIGNMENT OF ERROR NUMBER 1

By this assignment, defendant contends the trial court erred in admitting the testimony of Patricia Ann Pitre. Specifically, he alleges the testimony introduced at trial constituted hearsay.

Patricia Pitre, a passenger in the vehicle, testified she heard the defendant say "I told you I was going to do it" seconds before he pulled the trigger. The defense objected. The state, however, noted that it was relying on ... distinct provisions of the evidence code which set forth exceptions to the hearsay rule: ... (2) things said or done.

---

342. State v. Robinson, 634 So. 2d 1274 (La. Ct. App. 3d Cir. 1994).

Hearsay statements are generally inadmissible because of their historic unreliability and because of the unfairness to the defendant who cannot test the truth of the statement....

... [T]he statement was also admissible under the "Things said or done" provision set forth in La.Code of Evidence art. 801(D)(4) which now codifies the concept of "*res gestae.*" This article provides:

> "D. Statements which are not hearsay. A statement is not hearsay if:
>
> (4) Things said or done. The statements are events speaking for themselves under the immediate pressure of the occurrence, through the instructive, impulsive and spontaneous words and acts of the participants, and not the words of the participants when narrating the events, and which are necessary incidents of the criminal act, or immediate concomitants of it, or form in conjunction with it one continuous transaction."

In *State v. Millet,* 356 So.2d 1380 (La.1978) the court recognized that utterances made before, during and immediately after a crime carry a special reliability. The court noted that:

> "[U]nlike statements made in the course of ordinary conversation when the speaker normally weighs his words as he talks, it is believed that spontaneous and impulsive words which are spoken during the criminal transaction, or as part of it, are reliable statements, admissible into evidence even without the usual safeguards of admitting only the testimony of those who are sworn to tell the truth and are available for cross examination. *Millet* at 1383."

The statements recalled by Patricia Ann Pitre took place as immediate concomitants of the defendant's criminal act. The words were spoken seconds before the fatal shooting as the defendant was leaning into the car on the passenger's side where Mrs. Pitre was seated and able to hear the conversation as it transpired. As such, the statement was admissible under ... the Evidence Code. This assignment of error lacks merit.

...

AFFIRMED

Discussion Questions

1. Do you agree that such statements made before, during, and immediately after a crime carry "special reliability" warranting exclusion from the hearsay ban? Compare such statements to "excited utterances" and "present sense impressions"—do they carry similar indicia of reliability? Explain.
2. Was the statement hearsay? Analyze the statement under the definition. What do you think?
3. Why do you suppose the statement was not simply offered as an admission? Do you think it would have been easier to fit into that exemption? Why or why not?
4. This exemption applies not only to statements made by perpetrators of an offense, but also to statements made by others involved in the crime including victims, witnesses and other participants who made statements that form a part of the criminal transaction.[343] Thus, the exception could apply to a victim of a crime begging for her life prior to being shot, "*Please don't shoot me.*" An area of concern, however, has been

343. *See* State v. Walters, 630 So. 2d 1371 (La. Ct. App. 2d Cir. 1994) (allowing statement by defendant's wife made four hours before crime); *See also* State v. Smith, 651 So. 2d 890 (La. Ct. App. 2 Cir. 1995).

that the exception seems to be becoming increasingly broader than originally intended.[344] Louisiana Courts have held that "[t]he res gestae doctrine is broad and includes not only spontaneous utterances and declarations made before and after the commission of a crime but also includes testimony of witnesses and police officers pertaining to what they heard or observed before, during, or after the commission of the crime if the continuous chain of events is evident under the circumstances."[345]

Do you believe the exception should apply to events transpiring before and after the crime, including statements made by police and other witnesses? Do such events carry the reliability of the statement made during the crime by the participants? The courts have held that the "amount of time that elapses between the statement and the occurrence of the crime is not the sole consideration in determining whether the statement is res gestae." What else should be considered?

5. A common area where the exception has been applied is to statements of co-conspirators[346] and to statements made during drug transactions.[347] A good example occurred in *State v. Thompson*,[348] where the undercover agents arrived on scene and called out to the defendant, *"Hey Mel!"* The defendant approached them and asked them what they wanted, to which they responded "*Sixty dollars' worth.*" The defendant then returned to the crowd and sent a deliveryman, "Rubin," back with three "rocks" who stated while handing them to the undercover agents, "*Here, Mel sent this.*" In finding that the statements were admissible under the "things said and done" exemption to the hearsay rule, the court stated:

   > We believe that Rubin's statement fits precisely within this definition. Rubin was a participant in the transaction. Deputy Pichon testified that she clearly saw the defendant give something (which later proved to be cocaine) to Rubin who immediately delivered it to the deputies and made the statement. The statement was an integral part of the continuous transaction, linking Rubin's action with the deputies' previous conversation with the defendant. As such, it forms part of the *res gestae* of the crime, and is admissible.

   Refer back to Article 801(D)(3)(b) that specifically exempts certain statements by co-conspirators from the hearsay rule. Is this provision broader or narrower for admitting such statements?

Key Points

The key points to keep in mind regarding things said and done.

1. Things said and done ("res gestae") exempts from the hearsay ban the things that are "said and done" during a criminal act.
2. **Requirements of the exemption**:

---

344. *See* Force & Rault, Handbook, Art. 801(D)(4) Author's Comments (8).

345. *See* State v. Crawford, 672 So. 2d 197 (La. Ct. App. 3d Cir. 1996) (allowing statements of rape victim immediately before rape and within 30 minutes after rape under the exception).

346. *See* State v. Howard, 888 So. 2d 375 (La. Ct. App. 3d Cir. 2004).

347. *See* State v. Caldwell, 616 So. 2d 713 (La. Ct. App. 3d Cir. 1993); *See also* State v. Kidd, 568 So. 2d 175, 180 (La. App. 2 Cir. 1990).

348. State v. Thompson, 665 So. 2d 686 (La. Ct. App. 2d Cir. 1995).

a. applies in criminal cases;

b. made by participants in the crime (and sometimes victims, witnesses, or police officers);

c. made before, during, and after the crime, and forms a continuous transaction with it; and

d. the statements are instructive, impulsive and spontaneous words and acts that are necessary incidents of the criminal act, or immediate concomitants of it.

3. May include statements of police officers or witnesses after the incident if they form a part of a continuous transaction of events.
4. Does not include a narration of the events after the incident has ended.
5. Applies in criminal cases only.
6. Not to be confused with "integral part evidence" found in Article 404(B).

Problems on Things Said and Done

PROBLEM 5-187. Ricky and his brother Ryan robbed a convenience store. They burst into the store, threw the customers out, locked the doors, then robbed the place. The clerk overheard Ryan saying, "*Remember the plan. Remember the plan. Clear the store. I'll cover the Clerk. Just get the stuff!*" After the store was cleared, Ryan tied up the clerk while Ricky proceeded to load up money, cigarettes, and liquor. Ricky then stated, "*I've got the money, the cigs, and the liquor, let's go!*" They then ran out of the store and were arrested just down the street. While Ricky and Ryan were taken downtown for booking, another police officer arrived at the store and spoke to the clerk about the details of what occurred. She told him about what the two robbers were saying and doing during the robbery. At the trial, the prosecution seeks to have the clerk testify to Ricky and Ryan's statements made during the robbery. The defense objects that the statements are hearsay. How should the court rule on the admissibility of the statements?

Assume instead that by the time the case goes to trial, the clerk cannot be located so the prosecution attempts to offer the statements through the responding police officer. The defense objects that the statements are double hearsay. What ruling?

PROBLEM 5-188. Cody and Trent robbed a drugstore. During the robbery, the cashier overheard Cody say to Trent, "*Trent, don't forget to get the video tape out of the VCR. Last time you almost messed us up with that!*" Trent grabbed the tape and the two of them left. Just as they were leaving, the police pulled up, and the clerk ran out behind Trent and Cody screaming, "*They went that way!*" The police saw two guys running and gave chase. While chasing the guys, the officer grabbed his radio and said to dispatch, "*On scene at 5100 block of Haney St. on foot chase of two suspects headed north into the Sable Run Apartment Complex. One is short, about 5'5", wearing a grey sweatshirt and the other one is average height, kinda heavy and is wearing a black hoodie.*" Other officers met the officer at the apartment complex, surrounded it, and about 2 hours later, Cody and Trent came out and surrendered. They were arrested for the robbery. At the trial, the prosecution seeks to offer the evidence of the statements made by the suspects, the cashier, and the police officer as he chased the suspects. The defense objects to the admissibility of all the statements claiming they are hearsay. How should the court rule on the admissibility of each statement? Explain.

§ 5.24 References and Additional Authority on Things Said and Done [La. C.E. art. 801(D)(4)]

1. La. C.E. art. 801(D)(4) and Official Comments
2. Force & Rault, Handbook on Louisiana Evidence Law Art. 801(D)(4) Author's Comments (West Publishing 2014)
3. Harges & Jones, Louisiana Evidence Art. 801(D)(4) Author's Comments (West Publishing 2014)
4. 19 La. Civ. L. Treatise, Evidence And Proof § 10.4 (2nd ed.)
5. **Things Said and Done [La. C.E. art. 801(D)(4)]:** *State v. Wilson*, 69 So. 3d 598 (La. Ct. App. 2d Cir. 2011) (holding that the statement by defendant to a police officer in which he stated he was "only going to smoke a little bit of marijuana," did not meet the requirements of "things said and done" because it did not relate to the event).

Part E
Hearsay vis à vis the Sixth Amendment Confrontation Clause

§ 5.25 Hearsay vis à vis the Sixth Amendment Confrontation Clause—*Crawford v. Washington*

Applicable Constitutional Provisions

Sixth Amendment of the United States Constitution

In all criminal prosecutions, the accused shall enjoy the right ... to be confronted with the witnesses against him; to have compulsory process for obtaining witnesses in his favor, and to have the Assistance of Counsel for his defense.

La. Const. Art. I Sec. 16 (1974): "Rights to a Fair Trial"

... An accused is entitled to confront and cross-examine the witnesses against him, to compel the attendance of witnesses, to present a defense, and to testify in his own behalf ...

The Sixth Amendment of the United States Constitution provides that, "[i]n all criminal prosecutions, the accused shall enjoy the right ... to be confronted with the witnesses against him."[349] Throughout this chapter you have often been reminded that while a statement may conform to a hearsay exception, the admissibility of such statement may not infringe upon the right of an accused person in a criminal trial to confront a witness against him as provided in the Sixth Amendment of the United States Constitution and Art. 1, § 16 of the Louisiana State Constitution. The two concepts are closely related in that hearsay statements are generally excluded *because* they are unconfronted[350] and are thus incapable of being tested by cross-examination. However, while a statement might overcome the hearsay bar because it is deemed reliable, the constitutional right of an accused to confront witnesses against him has been held to require more than mere reliability of a statement. In this section we will examine the rules for compliance with an accused's Sixth Amendment rights under the Confrontation Clause, despite the fact that the statement conforms to a hearsay exception.

Prior Standard for Admissibility: *Ohio v. Roberts*[351]

The right to confrontation applies in all criminal prosecutions in both state and federal court.[352] Despite this important right of an accused to confront witnesses against him at trial, for more than two decades prior to *Crawford v. Washington*,[353] once a court determined that a statement was not precluded by the hearsay rule (i.e., fit into a hearsay exception or exemption), the statement was deemed to have complied with any requirements of the

349. U.S. Const. amend. VI; La. Const. Art. 1, Sec. 16 (1974).
350. Giles v. California, 128 S. Ct. 2678 (2008).
351. Ohio v. Roberts, 448 U.S. 56 (1980).
352. Crawford v. Washington, 541 U.S. 36 (2004).
353. *Id.*

Confrontation Clause and was allowed into evidence.[354] In *Ohio v. Roberts*, the United States Supreme Court held:

> [W]hen a hearsay declarant is not present for cross-examination at trial, the Confrontation Clause normally requires a showing that he is unavailable. Even then, his statement is admissible only if it bears adequate "indicia of reliability." Reliability can be inferred without more in a case where evidence falls within a firmly rooted hearsay exception. In other cases, the evidence must be excluded, at least absent a showing of particularized guarantees of trustworthiness.[355]

Thus, the standard for admissibility under *Ohio v. Roberts* was: 1) unavailable declarant; and 2) reliability, which was "inferred without more" if the statement fell within a firmly rooted hearsay exception. Thus, under the bright-line rule of *Ohio v. Roberts*, once a statement conformed to a firmly rooted hearsay exception, no additional requirements were necessary to protect the rights of an accused to confront and cross-examine witnesses against him.

Current Standard for Admissibility: *Crawford v. Washington*[356]

In *Crawford v. Washington*,[357] the U.S. Supreme Court revisited the relationship between hearsay and the Confrontation Clause and rejected the standard set out in *Ohio v. Roberts*, that provided for a mere finding that the statement conformed with a firmly rooted hearsay exception. Instead, the Court held that a testimonial statement complied with confrontation requirements only if: 1) the declarant is currently unavailable; and 2) there was a prior opportunity for cross-examination.[358]

Crawford clarified that not all statements offered against an accused are subject to confrontation. The Sixth Amendment right to confrontation specifically applies to "**witnesses**" against an accused, i.e., "those who bear testimony."[359] Thus, only those statements that are "**testimonial**" in nature are subject to confrontation, not every "casual remark to an acquaintance"[360] that might be offered against him. It is the testimonial nature of a statement that causes a declarant to be a "witness" against the accused within the meaning of the Sixth Amendment.

Crawford concluded that the Confrontation Clause requires that when a testimonial statement is offered against an accused, if the witness is unavailable for confrontation at trial, the statement must be excluded unless the accused had a *prior* opportunity to cross-examine the declarant on the statement. Thus, a testimonial statement does not violate the Confrontation Clause if the accused has either a present or prior opportunity for cross-examination. Similarly, if the statement is not testimonial, then the accused has no right of confrontation, and the unconfronted statement may be offered against an accused without violating the Sixth Amendment right to confrontation.

Based on the requirements set out in *Crawford* for compliance with the Confrontation Clause, there are three scenarios in which a statement will not be excluded under the Sixth Amendment from being offered against a defendant in a criminal trial:

---

354. *See* Ohio v. Roberts, 448 U.S. 56 (1980).
355. *Id.* at 66.
356. Crawford v. Washington, 541 U.S. 36 (2004).
357. *Id.*
358. *Id.*
359. *Id.*
360. *Id.* at 51.

Statements that Comply with Sixth Amendment Confrontation Clause

1. The statement is non-testimonial, even if never crossed, and witness is currently unavailable.
2. The statement is a) testimonial, and b) witness is currently *available* for cross examination.
3. The statement is a) testimonial; b) witness is unavailable; and c) there was a prior opportunity to cross-examine the witness.

1. The statement is non-testimonial, even if never cross-examined, and the witness is currently unavailable;
2. The statement is: a) testimonial, and b) witness is currently *available* for cross-examination; or
3. The statement is: a) testimonial; b) witness is unavailable; and c) there was a prior opportunity to cross-examine the witness.

***Crawford* examples of "testimonial" statements.** Since the Confrontation Clause has been held to apply only to statements that are testimonial, the initial inquiry under *Crawford* is to determine whether or not the statement sought to be admitted is in fact "testimony." The *Crawford* Court declined to commit to a comprehensive definition of what constitutes "testimony," but noted several definitions that conform with what the framers of the United States Constitution apparently intended, including:

- "[P]rior testimony at a preliminary hearing, before a grand jury, or at a former trial; and to police interrogations,"
- "[*E*]*x parte* in-court testimony or its functional equivalent—that is, material such as affidavits, custodial examinations, prior testimony that the defendant was unable to cross-examine, or similar pretrial statements that declarants would reasonably expect to be used prosecutorially,"
- "[E]xtrajudicial statements ... contained in formalized testimonial materials, such as affidavits, depositions, prior testimony, or confessions," and
- "[S]tatements that were made under circumstances which would lead an objective witness reasonably to believe that the statement would be available for use at a later trial."[361]

Thus, when any of these types of statements are offered against an accused, the Sixth Amendment is implicated, and the requirements of *Crawford* must be met.

***Davis v. Washington* further defines "testimonial."** Just two years after *Crawford* was decided, the United States Supreme Court further clarified the definition of testimony for purposes of the Sixth Amendment Confrontation Clause in *Davis v. Washington*.[362] Evaluating a 911 call that a domestic violence victim made for help in the face of what the Court referred to as a "bona fide physical threat," as well as a distinguishable companion case[363] in which a domestic violence altercation had apparently subsided, the Court further distinguished testimonial and nontestimonial statements as follows:

---

361. Crawford v. Washington, 541 U.S. 36 (2004).
362. Davis v. Washington, 547 U.S. 813 (2006).
363. The Court also simultaneously considered Hammon v. Indiana in the *Davis* opinion.

- "Statements are **nontestimonial** when made in the course of police interrogation under circumstances objectively indicating that the primary purpose of the interrogation is to enable police assistance to meet an ongoing emergency."[364]
- "They are **testimonial** when the circumstances objectively indicate that there is no such ongoing emergency, and that the primary purpose of the interrogation is to establish or prove past events potentially relevant to later criminal prosecution"[365]

Confrontation Clause Analysis under *Crawford*

Following *Crawford*, when analyzing whether offering a statement against an accused would violate his Sixth Amendment right to confrontation, the first step is to determine whether the statement is ***testimonial*** under *Crawford* and *Davis*. Pursuant to definitions outlined above, a statement is testimonial, and subject to confrontation, if it is: prior testimony given at a hearing, grand jury, prior trial, affidavit, formal police interrogation, deposition, or other statement that would lead an objective witness reasonably to believe that the statement would be available for use at a later trial, as well as a statement made in the course of police interrogation when there is no ongoing emergency, and the primary purpose of which is to establish or prove past events potentially relevant to later criminal prosecution.

If a statement is ***nontestimonial***, then the accused has no right of confrontation and the statement may be offered against an accused without violating the Confrontation Clause. If the statement is ***testimonial***, the next inquiry is whether or not the declarant is ***currently available*** for cross-examination. If the declarant is available, the accused may exercise his confrontation rights at the trial.

If the declarant is ***unavailable***, then the next inquiry is whether there was a ***prior opportunity for cross-examination***. If so, then the accused's confrontation rights have been protected and the statement may be offered against him without violating the Confrontation Clause. If there was no prior opportunity to cross-examine the declarant on the statement, then offering the statement would violate the accused's confrontation rights. Thus, as outlined above, there are three scenarios in which a statement will not be excluded under the Sixth Amendment:

1. The statement is non-testimonial, even if never crossed and witness is currently unavailable
2. The statement is a) testimonial, and b) witness is currently *available* for cross-examination
3. The statement is a) testimonial; b) witness is unavailable; and c) prior opportunity to cross-examine the witness

Keep in mind that even though the statement may not be excluded under the Confrontation Clause, to be admitted, it must not be excluded by any other provision, including hearsay, relevancy and Article 403 balancing.

Forfeiture by Wrongdoing. As you recall from § 5.21, *supra*, an accused who procures the absence of a witness by his wrongdoing, with the intent and for the purpose of pre-

364. *Davis*, 547 U.S. at 822.
365. *Id.*

Figure 1. Analysis of Statement under *Crawford*

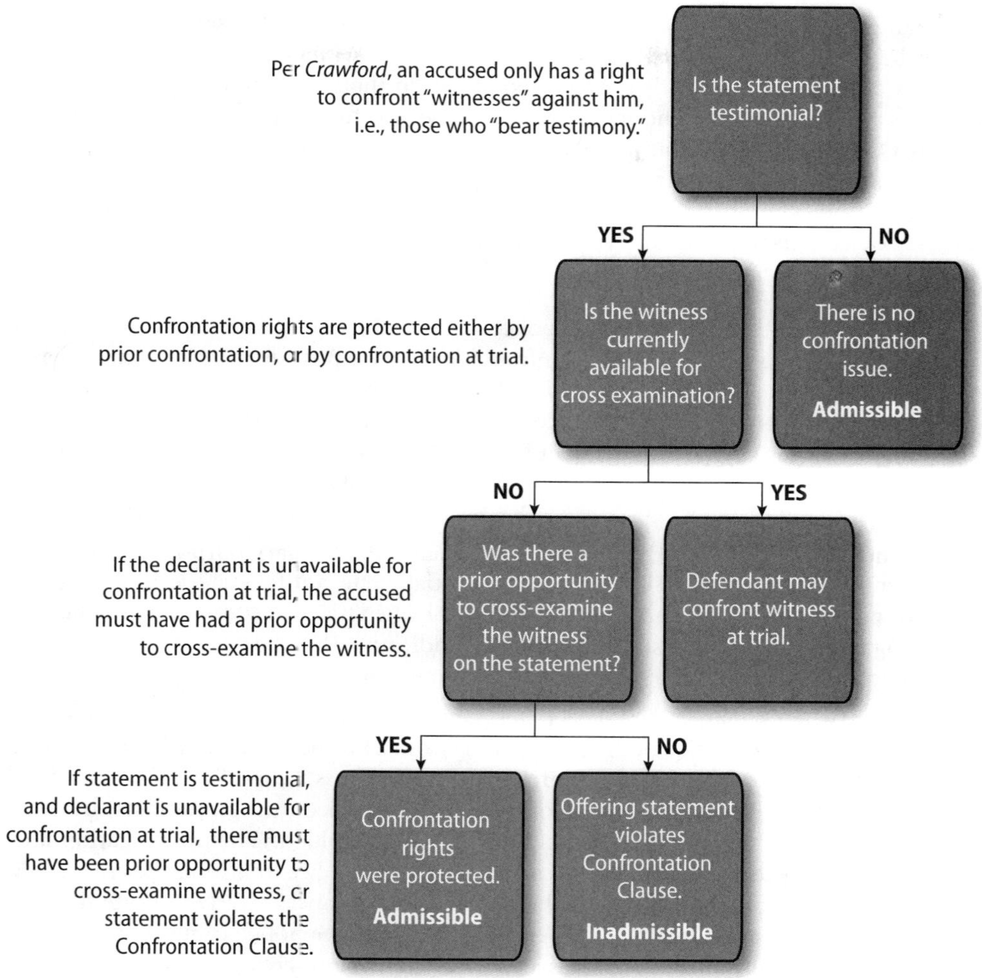

venting the witness from testifying against him at trial, forfeits his rights under the Confrontation Clause of the United States Constitution and Art. I § 16 of the Louisiana Constitution under the doctrine of "forfeiture by wrongdoing." However, pursuant to the United States Supreme Court in *Giles v. California*,[366] it must be shown that the accused procured the unavailability of the witness with the specific purpose of preventing the witness from testifying against him. If this standard is met, a testimonial statement may be offered against an accused without violating the Confrontation Clause.

Illustration of Confrontation Clause Analysis under *Crawford*

Randy is being tried for murdering his business partner Omar after Randy discovered that Omar had gambled away all of the money from their business. The week before the murder, Omar frantically called 911 one afternoon from inside of the closet in the business

---

366. *Giles*, 28 S. Ct. at 2684 (2008).

and reported that Randy had confronted him at knifepoint about the money and threatened to kill Omar if he got to him in the closet. Police came to the business to arrest Randy, but Randy left out of the back door of the business when he saw the police car drive up. After the police officers secured the scene, they sat down with Omar and took a more detailed statement about Randy's attempted attack so that they could get a warrant for Randy's arrest for assault. The very next day, Omar was found dead. In Randy's trial for killing Omar, the prosecution would like to admit Omar's 911 call as well as the detailed statement Omar made to the police after they arrived at the business. Randy objects to the admissibility of both statements on Sixth Amendment confrontation grounds. No hearsay objections were raised. Will either statement be admissible?

Discussion of 911 Call

The 911 call that Omar made to police will not likely be excluded on confrontation grounds. The Sixth Amendment Confrontation Clause provides that an accused has a right to confront witnesses against him at trial. Under *Crawford*, only those statements that are "testimonial" are subject to confrontation. If the statement is testimonial, then *Crawford* requires that the statement be excluded unless the witness is unavailable to testify and the defendant had a prior opportunity to cross-examine the declarant on the statement.

Under *Davis*, a statement may be testimonial if the primary purpose of the police interrogation is to establish past events potentially relevant to a later criminal prosecution. However, a statement is nontestimonial when made in the course of police interrogation under circumstances objectively indicating that the primary purpose is to enable police assistance to meet an ongoing emergency.

Here, when Omar made the 911 call, he was seeking assistance with an ongoing emergency. He was inside of the closet hiding from a business partner who was outside of the closet attempting to gain entry with a dangerous weapon to inflict harm on Omar while threatening to kill him. Omar was not recounting past facts, but was instead relating facts to the 911 operator as they unfolded. The interrogation and answers Omar provided were necessary to enable the police to resolve the emergency in the face of a bona fide physical threat. The circumstances clearly indicate that the primary purpose of Omar's statement was to enable the police to meet an ongoing emergency. Omar was not acting as a witness. He was not giving testimony.

Since Omar's statement to the 911 operator was not testimonial, it is not subject to the Confrontation Clause, and thus will not be excluded on confrontation grounds.

Detailed Statement to Police

The circumstances surrounding Omar giving the formal statement to the police are different. It is possible that a nontestimonial statement may evolve into a testimonial statement once the purpose has been achieved. While the police arrived at Omar's business in the face of an ongoing emergency, at the time Omar sat down to give the formal written statement to the police officer, the threat of the emergency he faced from Randy had subsided. Randy had left the scene and the police had secured the business. Omar then proceeded to give the police a detailed statement, at which time he began to recall past facts relevant to a criminal prosecution releative to Randy's threats and attempt to break into the closet to attack him. In fact, the police specifically told Omar that his statement would be used to obtain a warrant for Randy's arrest.

The circumstances surrounding the giving of Omar's second statement to the police clearly indicate that the primary purpose of the interrogation was to establish past facts for later use at trial. Thus, Omar's statement to the police was testimonial and as such, Randy has a right of confrontation. Under *Crawford*, since Omar is currently unavailable for cross-examination, the statement may only be used if Omar had a prior opportunity to cross-examine Omar on the statement. Based on the facts, there was no prior opportunity for Randy to cross-examine Omar, since Omar was killed the very next day after making the statement. Thus, the formal statement that Omar made to the police should be excluded on confrontation grounds.

Forfeiture by Wrongdoing

It is worth noting here that the doctrine of forfeiture by wrongdoing does not apply to this case. Under the doctrine, if an accused procures the unavailability of a witness due to his own wrongdoing, then he forfeits his rights to confront the witness and the statement may be offered against him. However, the doctrine only applies if the accused procures the unavailability of the witness for the specific purpose of preventing him from testifying at trial.

In this case, while Randy's wrongdoing is the reason Omar is unavailable for cross-examination, Randy did not kill him for the specific purpose of preventing him from testifying. Here, Randy killed Omar because Omar gambled away all of the money from their business, not to prevent Omar from testifying. Thus, Randy has not forfeited his right to confront Omar.

Cases on Confrontation Clause

Crawford v. Washington

Supreme Court of the United States
541 U.S. 36, 124 S. Ct. 1354
March 8, 2004

SCALIA, J., delivered the opinion of the Court, in which STEVENS, KENNEDY, SOUTER, THOMAS, GINSBURG, and BREYER, JJ., joined. REHNQUIST, C. J., filed an opinion concurring in the judgment, in which O'CONNOR, J., joined.

Petitioner Michael Crawford stabbed a man who allegedly tried to rape his wife, Sylvia. At his trial, the State played for the jury Sylvia's tape-recorded statement to the police describing the stabbing, even though [Crawford] had no opportunity for cross-examination. The Washington Supreme Court upheld petitioner's conviction after determining that Sylvia's statement was reliable. The question presented is whether this procedure complied with the Sixth Amendment's guarantee that, "[i]n all criminal prosecutions, the accused shall enjoy the right ... to be confronted with the witnesses against him."

I

On August 5, 1999, Kenneth Lee was stabbed at his apartment. Police arrested petitioner later that night. After giving petitioner and his wife *Miranda* warnings, detectives interrogated each of them twice. Petitioner eventually confessed that he and Sylvia had gone in search of Lee because he was upset over an earlier incident in which Lee had tried to rape her. The two had found Lee at his apartment, and a fight ensued in which Lee was stabbed in the torso and petitioner's hand was cut.

Petitioner gave the following account of the fight:

"Q. Okay. Did you ever see anything in [Lee's] hands?

"A. I think so, but I'm not positive.

"Q. Okay, when you think so, what do you mean by that?

"A. I coulda swore I seen him goin' for somethin' before, right before everything happened. He was like reachin', fiddlin' around down here and stuff ... and I just ... I don't know, I think, this is just a possibility, but I think, I think that he pulled somethin' out and I grabbed for it and that's how I got cut ... but I'm not positive. I, I, my mind goes blank when things like this happen. I mean, I just, I remember things wrong, I remember things that just doesn't, don't make sense to me later."

Sylvia generally corroborated petitioner's story about the events leading up to the fight, but her account of the fight itself was arguably different—particularly with respect to whether Lee had drawn a weapon before petitioner assaulted him:

"Q. Did Kenny do anything to fight back from this assault?

"A. (pausing) I know he reached into his pocket ... or somethin'... I don't know what.

"Q. After he was stabbed?

"A. He saw Michael coming up. He lifted his hand ... his chest open, he might [have] went to go strike his hand out or something and then (inaudible).

"Q. Okay, you, you gotta speak up.

"A. Okay, he lifted his hand over his head maybe to strike Michael's hand down or something and then he put his hands in his ... put his right hand in his right pocket ... took a step back ... Michael proceeded to stab him ... then his hands were like ... how do you explain this ... open arms ... with his hands open and he fell down ... and we ran (describing subject holding hands open, palms toward assailant).

"Q. Okay, when he's standing there with his open hands, you're talking about Kenny, correct?

"A. Yeah, after, after the fact, yes.

"Q. Did you see anything in his hands at that point?

"A. (pausing) um um (no)." *Id.,* at 137 (punctuation added).

The State charged petitioner with assault and attempted murder. At trial, he claimed self-defense. Sylvia did not testify because of the state marital privilege, which generally bars a spouse from testifying without the other spouse's consent. In Washington, this privilege does not extend to a spouse's out-of-court statements admissible under a hearsay exception, so the State sought to introduce Sylvia's tape-recorded statements to the police as evidence that the stabbing was not in self-defense. Noting that Sylvia had admitted she led petitioner to Lee's apartment and thus had facilitated the assault, the State invoked the hearsay exception for statements against penal interest, Rule Evid. 804(b)(3).

Petitioner countered that, state law notwithstanding, admitting the evidence would violate his federal constitutional right to be "confronted with the witnesses against him." Amdt. 6. [***Ohio v. Roberts***]. According to our description of that right in *Ohio v. Roberts,* 448 U.S. 56, 100 S.Ct. 2531, 65 L.Ed.2d 597 (1980), it does not bar admission of an unavailable witness's statement against a criminal defendant if the statement bears "adequate 'indicia of reliability.'" *Id.,* at 66, 100 S.Ct. 2531. To meet that test, evidence must either fall within a "firmly rooted hearsay exception" or bear "particularized guarantees of trustworthiness." *Ibid.* The trial court here admitted the statement on the latter ground, offering several reasons why it was trustworthy: Sylvia was not shifting blame but rather corroborating her husband's story that he acted in self-defense or "justified reprisal"; she had direct knowledge as an eyewitness; she was describing recent events; and she was being questioned by a "neutral" law enforcement officer. The prosecution played the tape for the jury and relied on it in closing, arguing that it was "damning evidence" that "completely refutes [petitioner's] claim of self-defense." The jury convicted petitioner of assault.

The Washington Court of Appeals reversed.... The Washington Supreme Court reinstated the conviction, unanimously concluding that, although Sylvia's statement did not fall under a firmly rooted hearsay exception, it bore guarantees of trustworthiness: "'[W]hen a codefendant's confession is virtually identical [to, *i.e.*, interlocks with,] that of a defendant, it may be deemed reliable.'"[367]

We granted certiorari to determine whether the State's use of Sylvia's statement violated the Confrontation Clause.

II

The Sixth Amendment's Confrontation Clause provides that, "[i]n all criminal prosecutions, the accused shall enjoy the right ... to be confronted with the witnesses against him." We have held that this bedrock procedural guarantee applies to both federal and state prosecutions. As noted above, *Roberts* says that an unavailable witness's out-of-court statement may be admitted so long as it has adequate indicia of reliability—*i.e.*, falls within a "firmly rooted hearsay exception" or bears "particularized guarantees of trustworthiness." Petitioner argues that this test strays from the original meaning of the Confrontation Clause and urges us to reconsider it.

A

The Constitution's text does not alone resolve this case. One could plausibly read "witnesses against" a defendant to mean those who actually testify at trial, those whose statements are offered at trial, or something in-between. We must therefore turn to the historical background of the Clause to understand its meaning.

The right to confront one's accusers is a concept that dates back to Roman times. The founding generation's immediate source of the concept, however, was the common law. English common law has long differed from continental civil law in regard to the manner in which witnesses give testimony in criminal trials. The common-law tradition is one of live testimony in court subject to adversarial testing, while the civil law condones examination in private by judicial officers.

Nonetheless, England at times adopted elements of the civil-law practice. Justices of the peace or other officials examined suspects and witnesses before trial. These examinations were sometimes read in court in lieu of live testimony, a practice that "occasioned frequent demands by the prisoner to have his 'accusers,' *i.e.* the witnesses against him, brought before him face to face." In some cases, these demands were refused.

Pretrial examinations became routine under two statutes passed during the reign of Queen Mary in the 16th century, 1 & 2 Phil. & M., c. 13 (1554), and 2 & 3 *id.*, c. 10

---

367. The court rejected the State's argument that guarantees of trustworthiness were unnecessary since petitioner waived his confrontation rights by invoking the marital privilege. It reasoned that "forcing the defendant to choose between the marital privilege and confronting his spouse presents an untenable Hobson's choice." The State has not challenged this holding here. The State also has not challenged the Court of Appeals' conclusion (not reached by the State Supreme Court) that the confrontation violation, if it occurred, was not harmless. We express no opinion on these matters.

(1555). These Marian bail and committal statutes required justices of the peace to examine suspects and witnesses in felony cases and to certify the results to the court. It is doubtful that the original purpose of the examinations was to produce evidence admissible at trial. Whatever the original purpose, however, they came to be used as evidence in some cases, resulting in an adoption of continental procedure.

The most notorious instances of civil-law examination occurred in the great political trials of the 16th and 17th centuries. One such was the 1603 trial of Sir Walter Raleigh for treason. Lord Cobham, Raleigh's alleged accomplice, had implicated him in an examination before the Privy Council and in a letter. At Raleigh's trial, these were read to the jury. Raleigh argued that Cobham had lied to save himself: "Cobham is absolutely in the King's mercy; to excuse me cannot avail him; by accusing me he may hope for favour." Suspecting that Cobham would recant, Raleigh demanded that the judges call him to appear, arguing that "[t]he Proof of the Common Law is by witness and jury: let Cobham be here, let him speak it. Call my accuser before my face...." The judges refused, and, despite Raleigh's protestations that he was being tried "by the Spanish Inquisition," the jury convicted, and Raleigh was sentenced to death.

One of Raleigh's trial judges later lamented that "'the justice of England has never been so degraded and injured as by the condemnation of Sir Walter Raleigh.'" Through a series of statutory and judicial reforms, English law developed a right of confrontation that limited these abuses. For example, treason statutes required witnesses to confront the accused "face to face" at his arraignment. Courts, meanwhile, developed relatively strict rules of unavailability, admitting examinations only if the witness was demonstrably unable to testify in person. Several authorities also stated that a suspect's confession could be admitted only against himself, and not against others he implicated.

One recurring question was whether the admissibility of an unavailable witness's pretrial examination depended on whether the defendant had had an opportunity to cross-examine him. In 1696, the Court of King's Bench answered this question in the affirmative, in the widely reported misdemeanor libel case of *King v. Paine*, 5 Mod. 163, 87 Eng. Rep. 584. The court ruled that, even though a witness was dead, his examination was not admissible where "the defendant not being present when [it was] taken before the mayor ... had lost the benefit of a cross-examination." The question was also debated at length during the infamous proceedings against Sir John Fenwick on a bill of attainder. Fenwick's counsel objected to admitting the examination of a witness who had been spirited away, on the ground that Fenwick had had no opportunity to cross-examine.... The examination was nonetheless admitted on a closely divided vote after several of those present opined that the common-law rules of procedure did not apply to parliamentary attainder proceedings—one speaker even admitting that the evidence would normally be inadmissible. Fenwick was condemned, but the proceedings "must have burned into the general consciousness the vital importance of the rule securing the right of cross-examination."

Paine had settled the rule requiring a prior opportunity for cross-examination as a matter of common law, but some doubts remained over whether the Marian statutes prescribed an exception to it in felony cases. The statutes did not identify the circumstances under which examinations were admissible, and some inferred that no prior opportunity for cross-examination was required. Many who expressed this view acknowledged that it meant the statutes were in derogation of the common law....

Nevertheless, by 1791 (the year the Sixth Amendment was ratified), courts were applying the cross-examination rule even to examinations by justices of the peace in felony cases.... Early 19th-century treatises confirm that requirement.... When Parliament amended the statutes in 1848 to make the requirement explicit, the change merely "introduced in terms" what was already afforded the defendant "by the equitable construction of the law." ... [368]

B

Controversial examination practices were also used in the Colonies. Early in the 18th century, for example, the Virginia Council protested against the Governor for having "privately issued several commissions to examine witnesses against particular men *ex parte,*" complaining that "the person accused is not admitted to be confronted with, or defend himself against his defamers." ... A decade before the Revolution, England gave jurisdiction over Stamp Act offenses to the admiralty courts, which followed civil-law rather than common-law procedures and thus routinely took testimony by deposition or private judicial examination.... Colonial representatives protested that the Act subverted their rights "by extending the jurisdiction of the courts of admiralty beyond its ancient limits." ... John Adams, defending a merchant in a high-profile admiralty case, argued: "Examinations of witnesses upon Interrogatories, are only by the Civil Law. Interrogatories are unknown at common Law, and Englishmen and common Lawyers have an aversion to them if not an Abhorrence of them." ...

Many declarations of rights adopted around the time of the Revolution guaranteed a right of confrontation. See Virginia; Pennsylvania; Delaware; Maryland; North Carolina; Vermont; Massachusetts; New Hampshire, all reprinted in 1 B. Schwartz, The Bill of Rights: A Documentary History (1971). The proposed Federal Constitution, however, did not. At the Massachusetts ratifying convention, Abraham Holmes objected to this omission precisely on the ground that it would lead to civil-law practices: "The mode of trial is altogether indetermined; ... whether [the defendant] is to be allowed to confront the witnesses, and have the advantage of cross-examination, we are not yet told.... [W]e shall find Congress possessed of powers enabling them to institute judicatories little less inauspicious than a certain tribunal in Spain, ... the *Inquisition.*" ... Similarly, a prominent Antifederalist writing under the pseudonym Federal Farmer criticized the use of "written evidence" while objecting to the omission of a vicinage [trial in your own community] right: "Nothing can be more essential than the cross examining [of] witnesses, and generally before the triers of the facts in question.... [W]ritten evidence ... [is] almost useless; it must be frequently taken ex parte, and but very seldom leads to the proper discovery of truth." ... The First Congress responded by including the Confrontation Clause in the proposal that became the Sixth Amendment.

Early state decisions shed light upon the original understanding of the common-law right. *State v. Webb,* 2 N.C. 103 (1794), decided a mere three years after the adoption of the Sixth Amendment, held that depositions could be read against an accused only if they were taken in his presence. Rejecting a broader reading of the English authorities, the court held: "[I]t is a rule of the common law, founded on natural justice, that no man shall be prejudiced by evidence which he had not the liberty to cross examine."

Similarly, in *State v. Campbell,* 1 Rich. 124, 1844 WL 2558 (S.C.1844), South Carolina's highest law court excluded a deposition taken by a coroner in the absence of the accused. It held: "[I]f we are to decide the question by the established rules of the common law, there could not be a dissenting voice. For, notwithstanding the death of the witness, and

368. There is some question whether the requirement of a prior opportunity for cross-examination applied as well to statements taken by a coroner, which were also authorized by the Marian statutes.... Whatever the English rule, several early American authorities flatly rejected any special status for coroner statements....

whatever the respectability of the court taking the depositions, the solemnity of the occasion and the weight of the testimony, such depositions are *ex parte*, and, therefore, utterly incompetent." The court said that one of the "indispensable conditions" implicitly guaranteed by the State Constitution was that "prosecutions be carried on to the conviction of the accused, by witnesses confronted by him, and subjected to his personal examination."

Many other decisions are to the same effect. Some early cases went so far as to hold that prior testimony was inadmissible in criminal cases *even if* the accused had a previous opportunity to cross-examine.... Most courts rejected that view, but only after reaffirming that admissibility depended on a prior opportunity for cross-examination.... Nineteenth-century treatises confirm the rule....

III

This history supports two inferences about the meaning of the Sixth Amendment.

A

First, the principal evil at which the Confrontation Clause was directed was the civil-law mode of criminal procedure, and particularly its use of *ex parte* examinations as evidence against the accused. It was these practices that the Crown deployed in notorious treason cases like Raleigh's; that the Marian statutes invited; that English law's assertion of a right to confrontation was meant to prohibit; and that the founding-era rhetoric decried. The Sixth Amendment must be interpreted with this focus in mind.

Accordingly, we once again reject the view that the Confrontation Clause applies of its own force only to in-court testimony, and that its application to out-of-court statements introduced at trial depends upon "the law of Evidence for the time being." ... Leaving the regulation of out-of-court statements to the law of evidence would render the Confrontation Clause powerless to prevent even the most flagrant inquisitorial practices. Raleigh was, after all, perfectly free to confront those who read Cobham's confession in court.

This focus also suggests that not all hearsay implicates the Sixth Amendment's core concerns. An off-hand, overheard remark might be unreliable evidence and thus a good candidate for exclusion under hearsay rules, but it bears little resemblance to the civil-law abuses the Confrontation Clause targeted. On the other hand, *ex parte* examinations might sometimes be admissible under modern hearsay rules, but the Framers certainly would not have condoned them.

The text of the Confrontation Clause reflects this focus. It applies to "witnesses" against the accused—in other words, those who "bear testimony." "Testimony," in turn, is typically "[a] solemn declaration or affirmation made for the purpose of establishing or proving some fact." An accuser who makes a formal statement to government officers bears testimony in a sense that a person who makes a casual remark to an acquaintance does not. The constitutional text, like the history underlying the common-law right of confrontation, thus reflects an especially acute concern with a specific type of out-of-court statement.

Various formulations of this core class of "testimonial" statements exist: "*ex parte* in-court testimony or its functional equivalent—that is, material such as affidavits, custodial examinations, prior testimony that the defendant was unable to cross-examine, or similar pretrial statements that declarants would reasonably expect to be used prosecutorially," "extrajudicial statements ... contained in formalized testimonial materials, such as affidavits, depositions, prior testimony, or confessions," "statements that were made under circumstances which would lead an objective witness reasonably to believe that the statement would be available for use at a later trial." These formulations all share a common nucleus and then define the Clause's coverage at various levels of abstraction around it.

Regardless of the precise articulation, some statements qualify under any definition—for example, *ex parte* testimony at a preliminary hearing.

Statements taken by police officers in the course of interrogations are also testimonial under even a narrow standard. Police interrogations bear a striking resemblance to examinations by justices of the peace in England. The statements are not *sworn* testimony, but the absence of oath was not dispositive. Cobham's examination was unsworn, yet Raleigh's trial has long been thought a paradigmatic confrontation violation. Under the Marian statutes, witnesses were typically put on oath, but suspects were not. Yet Hawkins and others went out of their way to caution that such unsworn confessions were not admissible against anyone but the confessor.[369]

That interrogators are police officers rather than magistrates does not change the picture either. Justices of the peace conducting examinations under the Marian statutes were not magistrates as we understand that office today, but had an essentially investigative and prosecutorial function.... England did not have a professional police force until the 19th century, so it is not surprising that other government officers performed the investigative functions now associated primarily with the police. The involvement of government officers in the production of testimonial evidence presents the same risk, whether the officers are police or justices of the peace.

In sum, even if the Sixth Amendment is not solely concerned with testimonial hearsay, that is its primary object, and interrogations by law enforcement officers fall squarely within that class.[370]

B

The historical record also supports a second proposition: that the Framers would not have allowed admission of testimonial statements of a witness who did not appear at trial unless he was unavailable to testify, and the defendant had had a prior opportunity for cross-examination. The text of the Sixth Amendment does not suggest any open-ended exceptions from the confrontation requirement to be developed by the courts. Rather, the "right ... to be confronted with the witnesses against him," Amdt. 6, is most naturally read as a reference to the right of confrontation at common law, admitting only those exceptions established at the time of the founding.... As the English authorities above reveal, the common law in 1791 conditioned admissibility of an absent witness's examination on unavailability and a prior opportunity to cross-examine. The Sixth Amendment there-

369. These sources—especially Raleigh's trial—refute THE CHIEF JUSTICE's assertion, *post,* at 1375 (opinion concurring in judgment), that the right of confrontation was not particularly concerned with unsworn testimonial statements. But even if, as he claims, a general bar on unsworn hearsay made application of the Confrontation Clause to unsworn testimonial statements a moot point, that would merely change our focus from direct evidence of original meaning of the Sixth Amendment to reasonable inference. We find it implausible that a provision which concededly condemned trial by sworn *ex parte* affidavit thought trial by *unsworn ex parte* affidavit perfectly OK. (The claim that unsworn testimony was self-regulating because jurors would disbelieve it, is belied by the very existence of a general bar on unsworn testimony.) Any attempt to determine the application of a constitutional provision to a phenomenon that did not exist at the time of its adoption (here, allegedly, admissible unsworn testimony) involves some degree of estimation—what THE CHIEF JUSTICE calls use of a "proxy,"—but that is hardly a reason not to make the estimation as accurate as possible. Even if, as THE CHIEF JUSTICE mistakenly asserts, there were no direct evidence of how the Sixth Amendment originally applied to unsworn testimony, there is no doubt what its application would have been.

370. We use the term "interrogation" in its colloquial, rather than any technical legal, sense. Just as various definitions of "testimonial" exist, one can imagine various definitions of "interrogation," and we need not select among them in this case. Sylvia's recorded statement, knowingly given in response to structured police questioning, qualifies under any conceivable definition.

fore incorporates those limitations. The numerous early state decisions applying the same test confirm that these principles were received as part of the common law in this country.[371]

We do not read the historical sources to say that a prior opportunity to cross-examine was merely a sufficient, rather than a necessary, condition for admissibility of testimonial statements. They suggest that this requirement was dispositive, and not merely one of several ways to establish reliability. This is not to deny, as THE CHIEF JUSTICE notes, that "[t]here were always exceptions to the general rule of exclusion" of hearsay evidence. Several had become well established by 1791. But there is scant evidence that exceptions were invoked to admit *testimonial* statements against the accused in a *criminal* case.[372] Most of the hearsay exceptions covered statements that by their nature were not testimonial—for example, business records or statements in furtherance of a conspiracy. We do not infer from these that the Framers thought exceptions would apply even to prior testimony.[373]

IV

Our case law has been largely consistent with these two principles. Our leading early decision, for example, involved a deceased witness's prior trial testimony. *Mattox v. United States,* 15 S.Ct. 337 (1895). In allowing the statement to be admitted, we relied on the fact that the defendant had had, at the first trial, an adequate opportunity to confront the witness: "The substance of the constitutional protection is preserved to the prisoner in the advantage he has once had of seeing the witness face to face, and of subjecting him to the ordeal of a cross-examination. This, the law says, he shall under no circumstances be deprived of...."

Our later cases conform to *Mattox's* holding that prior trial or preliminary hearing testimony is admissible only if the defendant had an adequate opportunity to cross-examine.... Even where the defendant had such an opportunity, we excluded the testimony where the government had not established unavailability of the witness.... We similarly excluded accomplice confessions where the defendant had no opportunity to cross-examine.... In contrast, we considered reliability factors beyond prior opportunity for cross-examination when the hearsay statement at issue was not testimonial....

---

371. THE CHIEF JUSTICE claims that English law's treatment of testimonial statements was inconsistent at the time of the framing, but the examples he cites relate to examinations under the Marian statutes. As we have explained, to the extent Marian examinations were admissible, it was only because the statutes *derogated* from the common law. Moreover, by 1791 even the statutory-derogation view had been rejected with respect to justice-of-the-peace examinations— ... and by implication in *King v. Radbourne.* None of THE CHIEF JUSTICE's citations proves otherwise.... In short, none of THE CHIEF JUSTICE's sources shows that the law in 1791 was unsettled *even as to examinations by justices of the peace under the Marian statutes.* More importantly, however, even if the statutory rule in 1791 were in doubt, the numerous early state-court decisions make abundantly clear that the Sixth Amendment incorporated the *common-law* right of confrontation and not any exceptions the Marian statutes supposedly carved out from it.... The common-law rule had been settled since *Paine* in 1696....

372. The one deviation we have found involves dying declarations. The existence of that exception as a general rule of criminal hearsay law cannot be disputed.... Although many dying declarations may not be testimonial, there is authority for admitting even those that clearly are.... We need not decide in this case whether the Sixth Amendment incorporates an exception for testimonial dying declarations. If this exception must be accepted on historical grounds, it is *sui generis.*

373. We cannot agree with THE CHIEF JUSTICE that the fact "[t]hat a statement might be testimonial does nothing to undermine the wisdom of one of these [hearsay] exceptions." Involvement of government officers in the production of testimony with an eye toward trial presents unique potential for prosecutorial abuse—a fact borne out time and again throughout a history with which the Framers were keenly familiar. This consideration does not evaporate when testimony happens to fall within some broad, modern hearsay exception, even if that exception might be justifiable in other circumstances.

Even our recent cases, in their outcomes, hew closely to the traditional line. *Ohio v. Roberts,* admitted testimony from a preliminary hearing at which the defendant had examined the witness. *Lilly v. Virginia,* excluded testimonial statements that the defendant had had no opportunity to test by cross-examination. And *Bourjaily v. United States,* 107 S.Ct. 2775 (1987), admitted statements made unwittingly to an FBI informant after applying a more general test that did *not* make prior cross-examination an indispensable requirement.[374]

Lee v. Illinois, 106 S.Ct. 2056 (1986), on which the State relies, is not to the contrary. There, we *rejected* the State's attempt to admit an accomplice confession. The State had argued that the confession was admissible because it "interlocked" with the defendant's. We dealt with the argument by rejecting its premise, holding that "when the discrepancies between the statements are not insignificant, the codefendant's confession may not be admitted." Respondent argues that "[t]he logical inference of this statement is that when the discrepancies between the statements *are* insignificant, then the codefendant's statement *may* be admitted." But this is merely a possible inference, not an inevitable one, and we do not draw it here. If *Lee* had meant authoritatively to announce an exception—previously unknown to this Court's jurisprudence—for interlocking confessions, it would not have done so in such an oblique manner. Our only precedent on interlocking confessions had addressed the entirely different question whether a limiting instruction cured prejudice to codefendants from admitting a defendant's *own* confession against him in a joint trial....

Our cases have thus remained faithful to the Framers' understanding: Testimonial statements of witnesses absent from trial have been admitted only where the declarant is unavailable, and only where the defendant has had a prior opportunity to cross-examine.[375]

Finally, we reiterate that, when the declarant appears for cross-examination at trial, the Confrontation Clause places no constraints at all on the use of his prior testimonial statements. See *California v. Green,* 90 S.Ct. 1930 (1970). It is therefore irrelevant that the reliability of some out-of-court statements "'cannot be replicated, even if the declarant testifies to the

---

374. One case arguably in tension with the rule requiring a prior opportunity for cross-examination when the proffered statement is testimonial is *White v. Illinois,* 112 S.Ct. 736 (1992), which involved, *inter alia,* statements of a child victim to an investigating police officer admitted as spontaneous declarations. It is questionable whether testimonial statements would ever have been admissible on that ground in 1791; to the extent the hearsay exception for spontaneous declarations existed at all, it required that the statements be made "immediat[ely] upon the hurt received, and before [the declarant] had time to devise or contrive anything for her own advantage." In any case, the only question presented in *White* was whether the Confrontation Clause imposed an unavailability requirement on the types of hearsay at issue. The holding did not address the question whether certain of the statements, because they were testimonial, had to be excluded *even if* the witness was unavailable. We "[took] as a given ... that the testimony properly falls within the relevant hearsay exceptions."

375. THE CHIEF JUSTICE complains that our prior decisions have "never drawn a distinction" like the one we now draw.... But nothing in these cases contradicts our holding in any way. *Mattox* and *Kirby* allowed or excluded evidence depending on whether the defendant had had an opportunity for cross-examination. That the two cases did not extrapolate a more general class of evidence to which that criterion applied does not prevent us from doing so now. As to *Burr,* we disagree with THE CHIEF JUSTICE's reading of the case. Although Chief Justice Marshall made one passing reference to the Confrontation Clause, the case was fundamentally about the hearsay rules governing statements in furtherance of a conspiracy. The "principle so truly important" on which "inroad[s]" had been introduced was the "rule of evidence which rejects mere hearsay testimony." Nothing in the opinion concedes exceptions to the Confrontation Clause's exclusion of testimonial statements as we use the term. THE CHIEF JUSTICE fails to identify a single case (aside from one minor, arguable exception), where we have admitted testimonial statements based on indicia of reliability other than a prior opportunity for cross-examination. If nothing else, the test we announce is an empirically accurate explanation of the results our cases have reached.

same matters in court.' " The Clause does not bar admission of a statement so long as the declarant is present at trial to defend or explain it. (The Clause also does not bar the use of testimonial statements for purposes other than establishing the truth of the matter asserted.)

V

Although the results of our decisions have generally been faithful to the original meaning of the Confrontation Clause, the same cannot be said of our rationales. *Roberts* conditions the admissibility of all hearsay evidence on whether it falls under a "firmly rooted hearsay exception" or bears "particularized guarantees of trustworthiness." This test departs from the historical principles identified above in two respects. First, it is too broad: It applies the same mode of analysis whether or not the hearsay consists of *ex parte* testimony. This often results in close constitutional scrutiny in cases that are far removed from the core concerns of the Clause. At the same time, however, the test is too narrow: It admits statements that *do* consist of *ex parte* testimony upon a mere finding of reliability. This malleable standard often fails to protect against paradigmatic confrontation violations.

Members of this Court and academics have suggested that we revise our doctrine to reflect more accurately the original understanding of the Clause.... They offer two proposals: First, that we apply the Confrontation Clause only to testimonial statements, leaving the remainder to regulation by hearsay law—thus eliminating the overbreadth referred to above. Second, that we impose an absolute bar to statements that are testimonial, absent a prior opportunity to cross-examine—thus eliminating the excessive narrowness referred to above.

In *White,* we considered the first proposal and rejected it.... Although our analysis in this case casts doubt on that holding, we need not definitively resolve whether it survives our decision today, because Sylvia Crawford's statement is testimonial under any definition. This case does, however, squarely implicate the second proposal.

A

Where testimonial statements are involved, we do not think the Framers meant to leave the Sixth Amendment's protection to the vagaries of the rules of evidence, much less to amorphous notions of "reliability." Certainly none of the authorities discussed above acknowledges any general reliability exception to the common-law rule. Admitting statements deemed reliable by a judge is fundamentally at odds with the right of confrontation. To be sure, the Clause's ultimate goal is to ensure reliability of evidence, but it is a procedural rather than a substantive guarantee. It commands, not that evidence be reliable, but that reliability be assessed in a particular manner: by testing in the crucible of cross-examination. The Clause thus reflects a judgment, not only about the desirability of reliable evidence (a point on which there could be little dissent), but about how reliability can best be determined.

The *Roberts* test allows a jury to hear evidence, untested by the adversary process, based on a mere judicial determination of reliability. It thus replaces the constitutionally prescribed method of assessing reliability with a wholly foreign one. In this respect, it is very different from exceptions to the Confrontation Clause that make no claim to be a surrogate means of assessing reliability. For example, the rule of forfeiture by wrongdoing (which we accept) extinguishes confrontation claims on essentially equitable grounds; it does not purport to be an alternative means of determining reliability.

The Raleigh trial itself involved the very sorts of reliability determinations that *Roberts* authorizes. In the face of Raleigh's repeated demands for confrontation, the prosecution responded with many of the arguments a court applying *Roberts* might invoke today: that Cobham's statements were self-inculpatory, that they were not made in the heat of passion, and that they were not "extracted from [him] upon any hopes or promise of Pardon". It is not plausible that the Framers' only objection to the trial was that Raleigh's judges did not properly weigh these factors before sentencing him to death. Rather, the problem was that the judges refused to allow Raleigh to confront Cobham in court, where he could cross-examine him and try to expose his accusation as a lie.

Dispensing with confrontation because testimony is obviously reliable is akin to dispensing with jury trial because a defendant is obviously guilty. This is not what the Sixth Amendment prescribes.

B

The legacy of *Roberts* in other courts vindicates the Framers' wisdom in rejecting a general reliability exception. The framework is so unpredictable that it fails to provide meaningful protection from even core confrontation violations.

Reliability is an amorphous, if not entirely subjective, concept. There are countless factors bearing on whether a statement is reliable; the nine-factor balancing test applied by the Court of Appeals below is representative. Whether a statement is deemed reliable depends heavily on which factors the judge considers and how much weight he accords each of them. Some courts wind up attaching the same significance to opposite facts. For example, the Colorado Supreme Court held a statement more reliable because its inculpation of the defendant was "detailed," while the Fourth Circuit found a statement more reliable because the portion implicating another was "fleeting." The Virginia Court of Appeals found a statement more reliable because the witness was in custody and charged with a crime (thus making the statement more obviously against her penal interest), while the Wisconsin Court of Appeals found a statement more reliable because the witness was *not* in custody and *not* a suspect. Finally, the Colorado Supreme Court in one case found a statement more reliable because it was given "immediately after" the events at issue, while that same court, in another case, found a statement more reliable because two years had elapsed.

The unpardonable vice of the *Roberts* test, however, is not its unpredictability, but its demonstrated capacity to admit core testimonial statements that the Confrontation Clause plainly meant to exclude. Despite the plurality's speculation in *Lilly,* that it was "highly unlikely" that accomplice confessions implicating the accused could survive *Roberts,* courts continue routinely to admit them.... One recent study found that, after *Lilly,* appellate courts admitted accomplice statements to the authorities in 25 out of 70 cases—more than one-third of the time ... Courts have invoked *Roberts* to admit other sorts of plainly testimonial statements despite the absence of any opportunity to cross-examine....

To add insult to injury, some of the courts that admit untested testimonial statements find reliability in the very factors that *make* the statements testimonial. As noted earlier, one court relied on the fact that the witness's statement was made to police while in custody on pending charges—the theory being that this made the statement more clearly against penal interest and thus more reliable. Other courts routinely rely on the fact that a prior statement is given under oath in judicial proceedings. That inculpating statements are given in a testimonial setting is not an antidote to the confrontation problem, but rather the trigger that makes the Clause's demands most urgent. It is not enough to point out that most of the usual safeguards of the adversary process attend the statement, when the single safeguard missing is the one the Confrontation Clause demands.

C

Roberts' failings were on full display in the proceedings below. Sylvia Crawford made her statement while in police custody, herself a potential suspect in the case. Indeed, she had been told that whether she would be released "depend[ed] on how the investigation continues." In response to often leading questions from police detectives, she implicated her husband in Lee's stabbing and at least arguably undermined his self-defense claim. Despite all this, the trial court admitted her statement, listing several reasons why it was reliable. In its opinion reversing, the Court of Appeals listed several *other* reasons why the statement was *not* reliable. Finally, the State Supreme Court relied exclusively on the interlocking character of the statement and disregarded every other factor the lower courts had considered. The case is thus a self-contained demonstration of *Roberts'* unpredictable and inconsistent application.

Each of the courts also made assumptions that cross-examination might well have undermined. The trial court, for example, stated that Sylvia Crawford's statement was reliable because she was an eyewitness with direct knowledge of the events. But Sylvia at one point told the police that she had "shut [her] eyes and ... didn't really watch" part of the fight, and that she was "in shock." The trial court also buttressed its reliability finding by claiming that Sylvia was "being questioned by law enforcement, and, thus, the [questioner] is ... neutral to her and not someone who would be inclined to advance her interests and shade her version of the truth unfavorably toward the defendant." The Framers would be astounded to learn that *ex parte* testimony could be admitted against a criminal defendant because it was elicited by "neutral" government officers. But even if the court's assessment of the officer's motives was accurate, it says nothing about Sylvia's perception of her situation. Only cross-examination could reveal that.

The State Supreme Court gave dispositive weight to the interlocking nature of the two statements—that they were both ambiguous as to when and whether Lee had a weapon. The court's claim that the two statements were *equally* ambiguous is hard to accept. Petitioner's statement is ambiguous only in the sense that he had lingering doubts about his recollection: "A. I coulda swore I seen him goin' for somethin' before, right before everything happened.... [B]ut I'm not positive." Sylvia's statement, on the other hand, is truly inscrutable, since the key timing detail was simply assumed in the leading question she was asked: "Q. Did Kenny do anything to fight back from this assault?" Moreover, Sylvia specifically said Lee had nothing in his hands after he was stabbed, while petitioner was not asked about that.

The prosecutor obviously did not share the court's view that Sylvia's statement was ambiguous—he called it "damning evidence" that "completely refutes [petitioner's] claim of self-defense." We have no way of knowing whether the jury agreed with the prosecutor or the court. Far from obviating the need for cross-examination, the "interlocking" ambiguity of the two statements made it all the more imperative that they be tested to tease out the truth.

We readily concede that we could resolve this case by simply reweighing the "reliability factors" under *Roberts* and finding that Sylvia Crawford's statement falls short. But we view this as one of those rare cases in which the result below is so improbable that it reveals a fundamental failure on our part to interpret the Constitution in a way that secures its intended constraint on judicial discretion. Moreover, to reverse the Washington Supreme Court's decision after conducting our own reliability analysis would perpetuate, not avoid, what the Sixth Amendment condemns. The Constitution prescribes a procedure for determining the reliability of testimony in criminal trials, and we, no less than the state courts, lack authority to replace it with one of our own devising.

We have no doubt that the courts below were acting in utmost good faith when they found reliability. The Framers, however, would not have been content to indulge this assumption. They knew that judges, like other government officers, could not always be trusted to safeguard the rights of the people; the likes of the dread Lord Jeffreys were not yet too distant a memory. They were loath to leave too much discretion in judicial hands. By replacing categorical constitutional guarantees with open-ended balancing tests, we do violence to their design. Vague standards are manipulable, and, while that might be a small concern in run-of-the-mill assault prosecutions like this one, the Framers had an eye toward politically charged cases like Raleigh's—great state trials where the impartiality of even those at the highest levels of the judiciary might not be so clear. It is difficult to imagine *Roberts'* providing any meaningful protection in those circumstances. * * *

Where nontestimonial hearsay is at issue, it is wholly consistent with the Framers' design to afford the States flexibility in their development of hearsay law—as does *Roberts,* and as would an approach that exempted such statements from Confrontation Clause scrutiny altogether. Where testimonial evidence is at issue, however, the Sixth Amendment demands what the common law required: unavailability and a prior opportunity for cross-examination. We leave for another day any effort to spell out a comprehensive definition of "testimonial."[376] Whatever else the term covers, it applies at a minimum to prior testimony at a preliminary hearing, before a grand jury, or at a former trial; and to police interrogations. These are the modern practices with closest kinship to the abuses at which the Confrontation Clause was directed.

In this case, the State admitted Sylvia's testimonial statement against petitioner, despite the fact that he had no opportunity to cross-examine her. That alone is sufficient to make out a violation of the Sixth Amendment. *Roberts* notwithstanding, we decline to mine the record in search of indicia of reliability. Where testimonial statements are at issue, the only indicium of reliability sufficient to satisfy constitutional demands is the one the Constitution actually prescribes: confrontation.

The judgment of the Washington Supreme Court is reversed, and the case is remanded for further proceedings not inconsistent with this opinion.

It is so ordered.

Discussion Questions

1. Explain the Court's primary basis for its criticism of the standard set out in *Ohio v. Roberts.* Explain the standard and its reasoning. Do you believe the *Roberts* rule sufficiently comported with the purpose and function of the Confrontation Clause?
2. While the Court does not give a final definition of "testimonial," what preliminary types of statements did the Court point out conformed to that requirement?
3. Do you agree that the Confrontation Clause should only apply to statements that are "testimonial" in nature? What reasoning or rationale underlies this distinction?
4. The court notes the following regarding the right of confrontation:

   "[c]lause's ultimate goal is to ensure reliability of evidence, but it is a procedural rather than a substantive guarantee. It commands, not that evidence be reliable, but that reliability be assessed in a particular manner: by testing in the crucible of cross-examination. The Clause thus reflects a judgment, not only about

376. We acknowledge THE CHIEF JUSTICE's objection that our refusal to articulate a comprehensive definition in this case will cause interim uncertainty. But it can hardly be any worse than the status quo. The difference is that the *Roberts* test is *inherently,* and therefore *permanently,* unpredictable.

the desirability of reliable evidence (a point on which there could be little dissent), but about how reliability can best be determined."[377]

What is your understanding of the value of confrontation and cross-examination for testing the reliability of a statement? Does it provide greater protection in ensuring an accused a fair trial, or is it merely form over substance? Explain.

5. The *Crawford* Court did not extend the ruling to dying declarations, statements by co-conspirators in furtherance of a conspiracy, and statements that may be offered for purposes other than the truth of the matter asserted. Do you agree that the requirement of confrontation and cross-examination have no place in those settings? Why or why not?

In *Davis v. Washington*,[378] the court provides additional guidance in defining what constitutes a "testimonial" statement. The Court further carves out what is commonly referred to as an "emergency exception" to the Confrontation Clause.

Davis v. Washington

Supreme Court of the United States
126 S. Ct. 2266
June 19, 2006.

SCALIA, J., delivered the opinion of the Court, in which ROBERTS, C. J., and STEVENS, KENNEDY, SOUTER, GINSBURG, BREYER, and ALITO, JJ., joined. THOMAS, J., filed an opinion concurring in the judgment in part and dissenting in part.

These cases require us to determine when statements made to law enforcement personnel during a 911 call or at a crime scene are "testimonial" and thus subject to the requirements of the Sixth Amendment's Confrontation Clause.

I

A

The relevant statements in *Davis v. Washington* were made to a 911 emergency operator on February 1, 2001. When the operator answered the initial call, the connection terminated before anyone spoke. She reversed the call, and Michelle McCottry answered. In the ensuing conversation, the operator ascertained that McCottry was involved in a domestic disturbance with her former boyfriend Adrian Davis, the petitioner in this case:

"911 Operator: Hello.

"Complainant: Hello.

"911 Operator: What's going on?

"Complainant: He's here jumpin' on me again.

"911 Operator: Okay. Listen to me carefully. Are you in a house or an apartment?

"Complainant: I'm in a house.

"911 Operator: Are there any weapons?

"Complainant: No. He's usin' his fists.

"911 Operator: Okay. Has he been drinking?

---

377. *Crawford*, 541 U.S. at 61.
378. Davis v. Washington, 547 U.S. 813 (2006).

"Complainant: No.

"911 Operator: Okay, sweetie. I've got help started. Stay on the line with me, okay?

"Complainant: I'm on the line.

"911 Operator: Listen to me carefully. Do you know his last name?

"Complainant: It's Davis.

"911 Operator: Davis? Okay, what's his first name?

"Complainant: Adrian

"911 Operator: What is it?

"Complainant: Adrian.

"911 Operator: Adrian?

"Complainant: Yeah.

"911 Operator: Okay. What's his middle initial?

"Complainant: Martell. He's runnin' now."

As the conversation continued, the operator learned that Davis had "just r[un] out the door" after hitting McCottry, and that he was leaving in a car with someone else. McCottry started talking, but the operator cut her off, saying, "Stop talking and answer my questions." She then gathered more information about Davis (including his birthday), and learned that Davis had told McCottry that his purpose in coming to the house was "to get his stuff," since McCottry was moving. McCottry described the context of the assault, after which the operator told her that the police were on their way. "They're gonna check the area for him first," the operator said, "and then they're gonna come talk to you."

The police arrived within four minutes of the 911 call and observed McCottry's shaken state, the "fresh injuries on her forearm and her face," and her "frantic efforts to gather her belongings and her children so that they could leave the residence."

The State charged Davis with felony violation of a domestic no-contact order. "The State's only witnesses were the two police officers who responded to the 911 call. Both officers testified that McCottry exhibited injuries that appeared to be recent, but neither officer could testify as to the cause of the injuries." McCottry presumably could have testified as to whether Davis was her assailant, but she did not appear. Over Davis's objection, based on the Confrontation Clause of the Sixth Amendment, the trial court admitted the recording of her exchange with the 911 operator, and the jury convicted him. The Washington Court of Appeals affirmed. The Supreme Court of Washington, with one dissenting justice, also affirmed, concluding that the portion of the 911 conversation in which McCottry identified Davis was not testimonial, and that if other portions of the conversation were testimonial, admitting them was harmless beyond a reasonable doubt.

B

In *Hammon v. Indiana* [the companion case] police responded late on the night of February 26, 2003, to a "reported domestic disturbance" at the home of Hershel and Amy Hammon. They found Amy alone on the front porch, appearing " 'somewhat frightened,' " but she told them that " 'nothing was the matter,' " She gave them permission to enter the house, where an officer saw "a gas heating unit in the corner of the living room" that had "flames coming out of the ... partial glass front. There were pieces of glass on the ground in front of it and there was flame emitting from the front of the heating unit."

Hershel, meanwhile, was in the kitchen. He told the police "that he and his wife had 'been in an argument' but 'everything was fine now' and the argument 'never became physical.'" By this point Amy had come back inside. One of the officers remained with Hershel; the other went to the living room to talk with Amy, and "again asked [her] what had occurred." Hershel made several attempts to participate in Amy's conversation with the police, but was rebuffed. The officer later testified that Hershel "became angry when I insisted that [he] stay separated from Mrs. Hammon so that we can investigate what had happened." After hearing Amy's account, the officer "had her fill out and sign a battery affidavit." Amy handwrote the following: "Broke our Furnace & shoved me down on the floor into the broken glass. Hit me in the chest and threw me down. Broke our lamps & phone. Tore up my van where I couldn't leave the house. Attacked my daughter."

The State charged Hershel with domestic battery and with violating his probation. Amy was subpoenaed, but she did not appear at his subsequent bench trial. The State called the officer who had questioned Amy, and asked him to recount what Amy told him and to authenticate the affidavit. Hershel's counsel repeatedly objected to the admission of this evidence. At one point, after hearing the prosecutor defend the affidavit because it was made "under oath," defense counsel said, "That doesn't give us the opportunity to cross examine [the] person who allegedly drafted it. Makes me mad." Nonetheless, the trial court admitted the affidavit as a "present sense impression," and Amy's statements as "excited utterances" that "are expressly permitted in these kinds of cases even if the declarant is not available to testify." The officer thus testified that Amy

> "informed me that she and Hershel had been in an argument. That he became irrate [sic] over the fact of their daughter going to a boyfriend's house. The argument became ... physical after being verbal and she informed me that Mr. Hammon, during the verbal part of the argument was breaking things in the living room and I believe she stated he broke the phone, broke the lamp, broke the front of the heater. When it became physical he threw her down into the glass of the heater.
>
> .....
>
> "She informed me Mr. Hammon had pushed her onto the ground, had shoved her head into the broken glass of the heater and that he had punched her in the chest twice I believe."

The trial judge found Hershel guilty on both charges, and the Indiana Court of Appeals affirmed in relevant part. The Indiana Supreme Court also affirmed, concluding that Amy's statement was admissible for state-law purposes as an excited utterance; that "a 'testimonial' statement is one given or taken in significant part for purposes of preserving it for potential future use in legal proceedings," where "the motivations of the questioner and declarant are the central concerns," and that Amy's oral statement was not "testimonial" under these standards. It also concluded that, although the affidavit was testimonial and thus wrongly admitted, it was harmless beyond a reasonable doubt, largely because the trial was to the bench.

II

The Confrontation Clause of the Sixth Amendment provides: "In all criminal prosecutions, the accused shall enjoy the right ... to be confronted with the witnesses against him." In *Crawford v. Washington,* 124 S.Ct. 1354 (2004), we held that this provision bars "admission of testimonial statements of a witness who did not appear at trial unless he was unavailable to testify, and the defendant had had a prior opportunity for cross-examination." A critical portion of this holding, and the portion central to resolution of the two cases now before us, is the phrase "testimonial statements." Only statements of this sort cause the declarant to be a "witness" within the meaning of the Confrontation

Clause. It is the testimonial character of the statement that separates it from other hearsay that, while subject to traditional limitations upon hearsay evidence, is not subject to the Confrontation Clause.

Our opinion in *Crawford* set forth "[v]arious formulations" of the core class of " 'testimonial' " statements, *ibid.*, but found it unnecessary to endorse any of them, because "some statements qualify under any definition." Among those, we said, were "[s]tatements taken by police officers in the course of interrogations." The questioning that generated the deponent's statement in *Crawford*—which was made and recorded while she was in police custody, after having been given *Miranda* warnings as a possible suspect herself—"qualifies under any conceivable definition" of an " 'interrogation.' " We therefore did not define that term, except to say that "[w]e use [it] ... in its colloquial, rather than any technical legal, sense," and that "one can imagine various definitions..., and we need not select among them in this case." The character of the statements in the present cases is not as clear, and these cases require us to determine more precisely which police interrogations produce testimony.

Without attempting to produce an exhaustive classification of all conceivable statements—or even all conceivable statements in response to police interrogation—as either testimonial or nontestimonial, it suffices to decide the present cases to hold as follows: Statements are nontestimonial when made in the course of police interrogation under circumstances objectively indicating that the primary purpose of the interrogation is to enable police assistance to meet an ongoing emergency. They are testimonial when the circumstances objectively indicate that there is no such ongoing emergency, and that the primary purpose of the interrogation is to establish or prove past events potentially relevant to later criminal prosecution.[379]

III

A

In *Crawford*, it sufficed for resolution of the case before us to determine that "even if the Sixth Amendment is not solely concerned with testimonial hearsay, that is its primary object, and interrogations by law enforcement officers fall squarely within that class." Moreover, as we have just described, the facts of that case spared us the need to define what we meant by "interrogations." The *Davis* case today does not permit us this luxury of indecision. The inquiries of a police operator in the course of a 911 call[380] are an interrogation in one sense, but not in a sense that "qualifies under any conceivable definition."

379. Our holding refers to interrogations because, as explained below, the statements in the cases presently before us are the products of interrogations—which in some circumstances tend to generate testimonial responses. This is not to imply, however, that statements made in the absence of any interrogation are necessarily nontestimonial. The Framers were no more willing to exempt from cross-examination volunteered testimony or answers to open-ended questions than they were to exempt answers to detailed interrogation. (Part of the evidence against Sir Walter Raleigh was a letter from Lord Cobham that was plainly *not* the result of sustained questioning.) And of course even when interrogation exists, it is in the final analysis the declarant's statements, not the interrogator's questions, that the Confrontation Clause requires us to evaluate.

380. If 911 operators are not themselves law enforcement officers, they may at least be agents of law enforcement when they conduct interrogations of 911 callers. For purposes of this opinion (and without deciding the point), we consider their acts to be acts of the police. As in *Crawford v. Washington*, therefore, our holding today makes it unnecessary to consider whether and when statements made to someone other than law enforcement personnel are "testimonial."

We must decide, therefore, whether the Confrontation Clause applies only to testimonial hearsay; and, if so, whether the recording of a 911 call qualifies.

...

The question before us in *Davis,* then, is whether, objectively considered, the interrogation that took place in the course of the 911 call produced testimonial statements. When we said in *Crawford, supra,* that "interrogations by law enforcement officers fall squarely within [the] class" of testimonial hearsay, we had immediately in mind (for that was the case before us) interrogations solely directed at establishing the facts of a past crime, in order to identify (or provide evidence to convict) the perpetrator. The product of such interrogation, whether reduced to a writing signed by the declarant or embedded in the memory (and perhaps notes) of the interrogating officer, is testimonial. It is, in the terms of the 1828 American dictionary quoted in *Crawford,* "'[a] solemn declaration or affirmation made for the purpose of establishing or proving some fact.'" (The solemnity of even an oral declaration of relevant past fact to an investigating officer is well enough established by the severe consequences that can attend a deliberate falsehood. A 911 call, on the other hand, and at least the initial interrogation conducted in connection with a 911 call, is ordinarily not designed primarily to "establis[h] or prov[e]" some past fact, but to describe current circumstances requiring police assistance.

The difference between the interrogation in *Davis* and the one in *Crawford* is apparent on the face of things. In *Davis,* McCottry was speaking about events *as they were actually happening,* rather than "describ[ing] past events." Sylvia Crawford's interrogation, on the other hand, took place hours after the events she described had occurred. Moreover, any reasonable listener would recognize that McCottry (unlike Sylvia Crawford) was facing an ongoing emergency. Although one *might* call 911 to provide a narrative report of a crime absent any imminent danger, McCottry's call was plainly a call for help against bona fide physical threat. Third, the nature of what was asked and answered in *Davis,* again viewed objectively, was such that the elicited statements were necessary to be able to *resolve* the present emergency, rather than simply to learn (as in *Crawford*) what had happened in the past. That is true even of the operator's effort to establish the identity of the assailant, so that the dispatched officers might know whether they would be encountering a violent felon. And finally, the difference in the level of formality between the two interviews is striking. Crawford was responding calmly, at the station house, to a series of questions, with the officer-interrogator taping and making notes of her answers; McCottry's frantic answers were provided over the phone, in an environment that was not tranquil, or even (as far as any reasonable 911 operator could make out) safe.

We conclude from all this that the circumstances of McCottry's interrogation objectively indicate its primary purpose was to enable police assistance to meet an ongoing emergency. She simply was not acting as a *witness;* she was not *testifying.* What she said was not "a weaker substitute for live testimony" at trial, like Lord Cobham's statements in *Raleigh's Case,* or Jane Dingler's *ex parte* statements against her husband in *King v. Dingler,* or Sylvia Crawford's statement in *Crawford.* In each of those cases, the *ex parte* actors and the evidentiary products of the *ex parte* communication aligned perfectly with their courtroom analogues. McCottry's emergency statement does not. No "witness" goes into court to proclaim an emergency and seek help.

Davis seeks to cast McCottry in the unlikely role of a witness by pointing to English cases. None of them involves statements made during an ongoing emergency. In *King v. Brasier,* 1 Leach 199, 168 Eng. Rep. 202 (1779), for example, a young rape victim, "immediately on her coming home, told all the circumstances of the injury" to her mother.

The case would be helpful to Davis if the relevant statement had been the girl's screams for aid as she was being chased by her assailant. But by the time the victim got home, her story was an account of past events.

This is not to say that a conversation which begins as an interrogation to determine the need for emergency assistance cannot, as the Indiana Supreme Court put it, "evolve into testimonial statements," once that purpose has been achieved. In this case, for example, after the operator gained the information needed to address the exigency of the moment, the emergency appears to have ended (when Davis drove away from the premises). The operator then told McCottry to be quiet, and proceeded to pose a battery of questions. It could readily be maintained that, from that point on, McCottry's statements were testimonial, not unlike the "structured police questioning" that occurred in *Crawford.* This presents no great problem. Just as, for Fifth Amendment purposes, "police officers can and will distinguish almost instinctively between questions necessary to secure their own safety or the safety of the public and questions designed solely to elicit testimonial evidence from a suspect," trial courts will recognize the point at which, for Sixth Amendment purposes, statements in response to interrogations become testimonial. Through *in limine* procedure, they should redact or exclude the portions of any statement that have become testimonial, as they do, for example, with unduly prejudicial portions of otherwise admissible evidence. Davis's jury did not hear the *complete* 911 call, although it may well have heard some testimonial portions. We were asked to classify only McCottry's early statements identifying Davis as her assailant, and we agree with the Washington Supreme Court that they were not testimonial. That court also concluded that, even if later parts of the call were testimonial, their admission was harmless beyond a reasonable doubt. Davis does not challenge that holding, and we therefore assume it to be correct.

B

Determining the testimonial or non-testimonial character of the statements that were the product of the interrogation in *Hammon* is a much easier task, since they were not much different from the statements we found to be testimonial in *Crawford.* It is entirely clear from the circumstances that the interrogation was part of an investigation into possibly criminal past conduct—as, indeed, the testifying officer expressly acknowledged. There was no emergency in progress; the interrogating officer testified that he had heard no arguments or crashing and saw no one throw or break anything. When the officers first arrived, Amy told them that things were fine, and there was no immediate threat to her person. When the officer questioned Amy for the second time, and elicited the challenged statements, he was not seeking to determine (as in *Davis*) "what is happening," but rather "what happened." Objectively viewed, the primary, if not indeed the sole, purpose of the interrogation was to investigate a possible crime—which is, of course, precisely what the officer *should* have done.

It is true that the *Crawford* interrogation was more formal. It followed a *Miranda* warning, was tape-recorded, and took place at the station house. While these features certainly strengthened the statements' testimonial aspect—made it more objectively apparent, that is, that the purpose of the exercise was to nail down the truth about past criminal events—none was essential to the point. It was formal enough that Amy's interrogation was conducted in a separate room, away from her husband (who tried to intervene), with the officer receiving her replies for use in his "investigat[ion]." What we called the "striking resemblance" of the *Crawford* statement to civil-law *ex parte* examinations is shared by Amy's statement here. Both declarants were actively separated from the defendant—officers forcibly prevented Hershel from participating in the interrogation. Both statements deliberately recounted, in response to police questioning, how potentially criminal past events began and progressed. And both took place some time after the events described were over. Such statements under official interrogation are an obvious substitute for live testimony, because they do precisely *what a witness does* on direct examination; they are inherently testimonial.[381]

...

Although we necessarily reject the Indiana Supreme Court's implication that virtually any "initial inquiries" at the crime scene will not be testimonial, we do not hold the opposite—that *no* questions at the scene will yield nontestimonial answers. We have already observed of domestic disputes that "[o]fficers called to investigate ... need to know whom they are dealing with in order to assess the situation, the threat to their own safety, and possible danger to the potential victim." Such exigencies may *often* mean that "initial inquiries" produce non-testimonial statements. But in cases like this one, where Amy's statements were neither a cry for help nor the provision of information enabling officers immediately to end a threatening situation, the fact that they were given at an alleged crime scene and were "initial inquiries" is immaterial....

IV

Respondents in both cases, joined by a number of their *amici,* contend that the nature of the offenses charged in these two cases—domestic violence—requires greater flexibility in the use of testimonial evidence. This particular type of crime is notoriously susceptible to intimidation or coercion of the victim to ensure that she does not testify at trial. When this occurs, the Confrontation Clause gives the criminal a windfall. We may not, however, vitiate constitutional guarantees when they have the effect of allowing the guilty to go free. But when defendants seek to undermine the judicial process by procuring or coercing silence from witnesses and victims, the Sixth Amendment does not require courts to acquiesce. While defendants have no duty to assist the State in proving their guilt, they *do* have the duty to refrain from acting in ways that destroy the integrity of the criminal-trial system. We reiterate what we said in *Crawford:* that "the rule of forfeiture by wrongdoing ... extinguishes confrontation claims on essentially equitable grounds." That is, one

---

381. The dissent criticizes our test for being "neither workable nor a targeted attempt to reach the abuses forbidden by the [Confrontation] Clause" (opinion of THOMAS, J.). As to the former: We have acknowledged that our holding is not an "exhaustive classification of all conceivable statements—or even all conceivable statements in response to police interrogation," but rather a resolution of the cases before us and those like them. For *those* cases, the test is objective and quite "workable." The dissent, in attempting to formulate an exhaustive classification of its own, has not provided anything that deserves the description "workable"—unless one thinks that the distinction between "formal" and "informal" statements qualifies. And the dissent even qualifies that vague distinction by acknowledging that the Confrontation Clause "also reaches the use of technically informal statements when used to evade the formalized process," and cautioning that the Clause would stop the State from "us [ing] out-of-court statements as a means of circumventing the literal right of confrontation." It is hard to see this as much more "predictable," than the rule we adopt for the narrow situations we address. (Indeed, under the dissent's approach it is eminently arguable that the dissent should agree, rather than disagree, with our disposition in *Hammon v. Indiana,* No. 05-5705.)

As for the charge that our holding is not a "targeted attempt to reach the abuses forbidden by the [Confrontation] Clause," which the dissent describes as the depositions taken by Marian magistrates, characterized by a high degree of formality: We do not dispute that formality is indeed essential to testimonial utterance. But we no longer have examining Marian magistrates; and we do have, as our 18th-century forebears did not, examining police officers, who perform investigative and testimonial functions once performed by examining Marian magistrates. It imports sufficient formality, in our view, that lies to such officers are criminal offenses. Restricting the Confrontation Clause to the precise forms against which it was originally directed is a recipe for its extinction.

who obtains the absence of a witness by wrongdoing forfeits the constitutional right to confrontation.

We affirm the judgment of the Supreme Court of Washington in No. 05-5224. We reverse the judgment of the Supreme Court of Indiana in No. 05-5705, and remand the case to that Court for proceedings not inconsistent with this opinion.

It is so ordered....

Discussion Questions

1. How does the Court distinguish between testimonial and nontestimonial statements? Do you foresee any potential difficulties in applying this rule? Upon what basis does the court draw the distinction? Why?
2. Do you think the Court should have provided further guidance for determining whether a statement is being made for the purpose of meeting an ongoing emergency versus making a testimonial statement? What additional clarification or factors would you suggest?
3. What about in cases in which a statement transitions from nontestimonial to testimonial? How should a court determine at what point the statement is testimonial? How does the Court suggest such statements should be handled?
4. Is it possible for a 911 call to be testimonial? Why or why not? The Court did not address the latter part of McCottry's call. Do you think it was testimonial? Why or why not?
5. Why was the outcome different in *Hammon* (the companion case)?
6. What truly constitutes an emergency? Must someone's life be in danger? Should time be a factor? Whether the suspect has left the scene? Is this a subjective or an objective standard? The U.S. Supreme Court revisited the issue in *Michigan v. Bryant*, 131 S. Ct. 1143 (2001), for further discussion (and possible expansion) of the emergency exception. Review *Bryant*. How does *Bryant* expand the definition of the "primary purpose" test?
7. Throughout this chapter we have often discussed statements made by young children to teachers, school officials, and other state workers regarding allegations of abuse and sexual assaults. Some of these statements might be the result of extensive questioning of the child by non-law enforcement officials. Does offering such a statement against an accused, when the child is unavailable to testify, violate his confrontation rights? In 2015, the United States Supreme Court decided this very issue in *Ohio v. Clark*, 576 U.S. ___ (2015). In reversing the Ohio Supreme Court in a 9–0 opinion, the Court applied the "primary purpose" test first set out in *Davis* above and expanded on *Bryant*, and held that, "L.P.'s statements clearly were not made with the primary purpose of creating evidence for Clark's prosecution."[382] The Court added that, "L.P.'s statements occurred in the context of an ongoing emergency involving suspected child abuse,"[383] and were, "informal and spontaneous,"[384] and nothing like the "formalized station-house questioning in *Crawford*."[385]
   a. Do you agree with the Court that such statement's made by a child to teachers are not testimonial? Why or why not?

---

382. Ohio v. Clark, 576 U.S. ___ (2015).
383. *Id.*
384. *Id.*
385. *Id.*

b. What facts or circumstances surrounding such questioning do you find most persuasive? The fact that there was a legitimate concern for L.P.'s safety? The fact that there was no law enforcement present? What other facts affected the Court's reasoning?

c. Can you think of situations where a statement made to non-law enforcement *could* be testimonial?

Affidavits of Crime Lab Reports

Let's turn now to the Confrontation Clause as it relates to affidavits reporting findings of forensic analysis, commonly referred to as "certificates of analysis" or "lab reports." Does the accused have the right to confront the forensic analyst who conducts tests such as DNA analysis, drug analysis, blood alcohol analysis, and the like? *Melendez-Diaz v. Massachusetts*[386] addresses this question in light of the confrontation requirements set out in *Crawford.*

Melendez-Diaz v. Massachusetts
Supreme Court of the United States
129 S. Ct. 2527
June 25, 2009

Justice SCALIA delivered the opinion of the Court.

The Massachusetts courts in this case admitted into evidence affidavits reporting the results of forensic analysis which showed that material seized by the police and connected to the defendant was cocaine. The question presented is whether those affidavits are "testimonial," rendering the affiants "witnesses" subject to the defendant's right of confrontation under the Sixth Amendment.

I

In 2001, Boston police officers received a tip that a Kmart employee, Thomas Wright, was engaging in suspicious activity. The informant reported that Wright repeatedly received phone calls at work, after each of which he would be picked up in front of the store by a blue sedan, and would return to the store a short time later. The police set up surveillance in the Kmart parking lot and witnessed this precise sequence of events. When Wright got out of the car upon his return, one of the officers detained and searched him, finding four clear white plastic bags containing a substance resembling cocaine. The officer then signaled other officers on the scene to arrest the two men in the car—one of whom was petitioner Luis Melendez-Diaz. The officers placed all three men in a police cruiser.

During the short drive to the police station, the officers observed their passengers fidgeting and making furtive movements in the back of the car. After depositing the men at the station, they searched the police cruiser and found a plastic bag containing 19 smaller plastic bags hidden in the partition between the front and back seats. They submitted the seized evidence to a state laboratory required by law to conduct chemical analysis upon police request.

Melendez-Diaz was charged with distributing cocaine and with trafficking in cocaine in an amount between 14 and 28 grams. Ch. 94C, §§ 32A, 32E(b)(1). At trial, the pros-

386. Melendez-Diaz v. Massachusetts, 129 S. Ct. 2527 (2009); *See also* Bullcoming v. New Mexico, 131 S. Ct. 2705 (2011) (reversible error to allow a lab official to testify to a blood alcohol analysis who did not sign the form nor perform or participate in analysis).

ecution placed into evidence the bags seized from Wright and from the police cruiser. It also submitted three "certificates of analysis" showing the results of the forensic analysis performed on the seized substances. The certificates reported the weight of the seized bags and stated that the bags "[h]a[ve] been examined with the following results: The substance was found to contain: Cocaine." The certificates were sworn to before a notary public by analysts at the State Laboratory Institute of the Massachusetts Department of Public Health, as required under Massachusetts law.

Petitioner objected to the admission of the certificates, asserting that our Confrontation Clause decision in *Crawford v. Washington,* required the analysts to testify in person. The objection was overruled, and the certificates were admitted pursuant to state law as "prima facie evidence of the composition, quality, and the net weight of the narcotic ... analyzed."

The jury found Melendez-Diaz guilty. He appealed, contending, among other things, that admission of the certificates violated his Sixth Amendment right to be confronted with the witnesses against him. The Appeals Court of Massachusetts rejected the claim, ... [and] the Supreme Judicial Court denied review. We granted certiorari.

II

The Sixth Amendment to the United States Constitution, made applicable to the States via the Fourteenth Amendment, provides that "[i]n all criminal prosecutions, the accused shall enjoy the right ... to be confronted with the witnesses against him." In *Crawford,* after reviewing the Clause's historical underpinnings, we held that it guarantees a defendant's right to confront those "who 'bear testimony'" against him. A witness's testimony against a defendant is thus inadmissible unless the witness appears at trial or, if the witness is unavailable, the defendant had a prior opportunity for cross-examination.

Our opinion described the class of testimonial statements covered by the Confrontation Clause as follows:

> "Various formulations of this core class of testimonial statements exist: *ex parte* in-court testimony or its functional equivalent—that is, material such as affidavits, custodial examinations, prior testimony that the defendant was unable to cross-examine, or similar pretrial statements that declarants would reasonably expect to be used prosecutorially; extrajudicial statements ... contained in formalized testimonial materials, such as affidavits, depositions, prior testimony, or confessions; statements that were made under circumstances which would lead an objective witness reasonably to believe that the statement would be available for use at a later trial."

There is little doubt that the documents at issue in this case fall within the "core class of testimonial statements" thus described. Our description of that category mentions affidavits twice. The documents at issue here, while denominated by Massachusetts law "certificates," are quite plainly affidavits: "declaration[s] of facts written down and sworn to by the declarant before an officer authorized to administer oaths." Black's Law Dictionary 62 (8th ed. 2004). They are incontrovertibly a "'solemn declaration or affirmation made for the purpose of establishing or proving some fact.'" The fact in question is that the substance found in the possession of Melendez-Diaz and his codefendants was, as the prosecution claimed, cocaine—the precise testimony the analysts would be expected to provide if called at trial. The "certificates" are functionally identical to live, in-court testimony, doing "precisely what a witness does on direct examination."

Here, moreover, not only were the affidavits "'made under circumstances which would lead an objective witness reasonably to believe that the statement would be available for use at a later trial,'" but under Massachusetts law the *sole purpose* of the affidavits was to provide "prima facie evidence of the composition, quality, and the net weight" of the analyzed substance. We can safely assume that the analysts were aware of the affidavits' evidentiary purpose, since that purpose—as stated in the relevant state-law provision—was reprinted on the affidavits themselves.

In short, under our decision in *Crawford* the analysts' affidavits were testimonial statements, and the analysts were "witnesses" for purposes of the Sixth Amendment. Absent a showing that the analysts were unavailable to testify at trial *and* that petitioner had a prior opportunity to cross-examine them, petitioner was entitled to "'be confronted with'" the analysts at trial.[387]

III

Respondent and the dissent advance a potpourri of analytic arguments in an effort to avoid this rather straightforward application of our holding in *Crawford*.... [Historical discussion at this point]. We turn now to the various legal arguments raised by respondent and the dissent.

A

Respondent first argues that the analysts are not subject to confrontation because they are not "accusatory" witnesses, in that they do not directly accuse petitioner of wrongdoing; rather, their testimony is inculpatory only when taken together with other evidence linking petitioner to the contraband. This finds no support in the text of the Sixth Amendment or in our case law.

The Sixth Amendment guarantees a defendant the right "to be confronted with the witnesses *against him*." To the extent the analysts were witnesses (a question resolved above), they certainly provided testimony *against* petitioner, proving one fact necessary for his conviction—that the substance he possessed was cocaine. The contrast between the text of the Confrontation Clause and the text of the adjacent Compulsory Process Clause confirms this analysis. While the Confrontation Clause guarantees a defendant the right to be confronted with the witnesses "against him," the Compulsory Process Clause guarantees a defendant the right to call witnesses "in his favor." U.S. Const., Amdt. 6. The text of the Amendment contemplates two classes of witnesses—those against the defendant and those in his favor. The prosecution *must* produce the former;[388] the defendant *may* call the latter. Contrary to respondent's assertion, there is not a third category of witnesses, helpful to the prosecution, but somehow immune from confrontation.

It is often, indeed perhaps usually, the case that an adverse witness's testimony, taken alone, will not suffice to convict. Yet respondent fails to cite a single case in which such

---

387. Contrary to the dissent's suggestion, we do not hold, and it is not the case, that anyone whose testimony may be relevant in establishing the chain of custody, authenticity of the sample, or accuracy of the testing device, must appear in person as part of the prosecution's case. While the dissent is correct that "[i]t is the obligation of the prosecution to establish the chain of custody," this does not mean that everyone who laid hands on the evidence must be called. As stated in the dissent's own quotation, "gaps in the chain [of custody] normally go to the weight of the evidence rather than its admissibility." It is up to the prosecution to decide what steps in the chain of custody are so crucial as to require evidence; but what testimony *is* introduced must (if the defendant objects) be introduced live. Additionally, documents prepared in the regular course of equipment maintenance may well qualify as nontestimonial records.

388. The right to confrontation may, of course, be waived, including by failure to object to the offending evidence; and States may adopt procedural rules governing the exercise of such objections.

testimony was admitted absent a defendant's opportunity to cross-examine. Unsurprisingly, since such a holding would be contrary to longstanding case law....

B

Respondent and the dissent argue that the analysts should not be subject to confrontation because they are not "conventional" (or "typical" or "ordinary") witnesses of the sort whose *ex parte* testimony was most notoriously used at the trial of Sir Walter Raleigh. It is true, as the Court recognized in *Crawford,* that *ex parte* examinations of the sort used at Raleigh's trial have "long been thought a paradigmatic confrontation violation." But the paradigmatic case identifies the core of the right to confrontation, not its limits. The right to confrontation was not invented in response to the use of the *ex parte* examinations in *Raleigh's Case,* 2 How. St. Tr. 1 (1603). That use provoked such an outcry precisely because it flouted the deeply rooted common-law tradition "of live testimony in court subject to adversarial testing."

In any case, the purported distinctions respondent and the dissent identify between this case and Sir Walter Raleigh's "conventional" accusers do not survive scrutiny. The dissent first contends that a "conventional witness recalls events observed in the past, while an analyst's report contains near—contemporaneous observations of the test." It is doubtful that the analyst's reports in this case could be characterized as reporting "near—contemporaneous observations"; the affidavits were completed almost a week after the tests were performed. But regardless, the dissent misunderstands the role that "near—contemporaneity" has played in our case law. The dissent notes that that factor was given "substantial weight" in *Davis,* but in fact that decision *disproves* the dissent's position. There the Court considered the admissibility of statements made to police officers responding to a report of a domestic disturbance. By the time officers arrived the assault had ended, but the victim's statements—written and oral—were sufficiently close in time to the alleged assault that the trial court admitted her affidavit as a "present sense impression." Though the witness's statements in *Davis* were "near—contemporaneous" to the events she reported, we nevertheless held that they could *not* be admitted absent an opportunity to confront the witness.

A second reason the dissent contends that the analysts are not "conventional witnesses" (and thus not subject to confrontation) is that they "observe[d] neither the crime nor any human action related to it." The dissent provides no authority for this particular limitation of the type of witnesses subject to confrontation. Nor is it conceivable that all witnesses who fit this description would be outside the scope of the Confrontation Clause. For example, is a police officer's investigative report describing the crime scene admissible absent an opportunity to examine the officer? The dissent's novel exception from coverage of the Confrontation Clause would exempt all expert witnesses—a hardly "unconventional" class of witnesses.

A third respect in which the dissent asserts that the analysts are not "conventional" witnesses and thus not subject to confrontation is that their statements were not provided in response to interrogation. As we have explained, "[t]he Framers were no more willing to exempt from cross-examination volunteered testimony or answers to open-ended questions than they were to exempt answers to detailed interrogation." Respondent and the dissent cite no authority, and we are aware of none, holding that a person who volunteers his testimony is any less a "'witness against' the defendant," than one who is responding to interrogation. In any event, the analysts' affidavits in this case *were* presented in response to a police request. If an affidavit submitted in response to a police officer's request to "write down what happened" suffices to trigger the Sixth Amendment's protection (as it apparently does), then the analysts' testimony should be subject to confrontation as well.

C

Respondent claims that there is a difference, for Confrontation Clause purposes, between testimony recounting historical events, which is "prone to distortion or manipulation," and the testimony at issue here, which is the "resul[t] of neutral, scientific testing." Relatedly, respondent and the dissent argue that confrontation of forensic analysts would be of little value because "one would not reasonably expect a laboratory professional ... to feel quite differently about the results of his scientific test by having to look at the defendant."

This argument is little more than an invitation to return to our overruled decision in *Roberts,* which held that evidence with "particularized guarantees of trustworthiness" was admissible notwithstanding the Confrontation Clause. What we said in *Crawford* in response to that argument remains true:

> "To be sure, the Clause's ultimate goal is to ensure reliability of evidence, but it is a procedural rather than a substantive guarantee. It commands, not that evidence be reliable, but that reliability be assessed in a particular manner: by testing in the crucible of cross-examination.... Dispensing with confrontation because testimony is obviously reliable is akin to dispensing with jury trial because a defendant is obviously guilty. This is not what the Sixth Amendment prescribes."

Respondent and the dissent may be right that there are other ways—and in some cases better ways—to challenge or verify the results of a forensic test.[389] But the Constitution guarantees one way: confrontation. We do not have license to suspend the Confrontation Clause when a preferable trial strategy is available.

Nor is it evident that what respondent calls "neutral scientific testing" is as neutral or as reliable as respondent suggests. Forensic evidence is not uniquely immune from the risk of manipulation. According to a recent study conducted under the auspices of the National Academy of Sciences, "[t]he majority of [laboratories producing forensic evidence] are administered by law enforcement agencies, such as police departments, where the laboratory administrator reports to the head of the agency." National Research Council of the National Academies, Strengthening Forensic Science in the United States: A Path Forward 6-1 (Prepublication Copy Feb. 2009) (hereinafter National Academy Report). And "[b]ecause forensic scientists often are driven in their work by a need to answer a particular question related to the issues of a particular case, they sometimes face pressure to sacrifice appropriate methodology for the sake of expediency." A forensic analyst responding to a request from a law enforcement official may feel pressure—or have an incentive—to alter the evidence in a manner favorable to the prosecution.

Confrontation is one means of assuring accurate forensic analysis. While it is true, as the dissent notes, that an honest analyst will not alter his testimony when forced to confront the defendant, the same cannot be said of the fraudulent analyst. See Brief for National Innocence Network as *Amicus Curiae* 15–17 (discussing cases of documented "drylabbing" where forensic analysts report results of tests that were never performed); National Academy Report 1-8 to 1-10 (discussing documented cases of fraud and error involving the use of forensic evidence). Like the eyewitness who has fabricated his account to the police, the analyst who provides false results may, under oath in open court, reconsider his false testimony. And, of course, the prospect of confrontation will deter fraudulent analysis in the first place.

389. Though surely not always. Some forensic analyses, such as autopsies and breathalyzer tests, cannot be repeated, and the specimens used for other analyses have often been lost or degraded.

Confrontation is designed to weed out not only the fraudulent analyst, but the incompetent one as well. Serious deficiencies have been found in the forensic evidence used in criminal trials. One commentator asserts that "[t]he legal community now concedes, with varying degrees of urgency, that our system produces erroneous convictions based on discredited forensics." Metzger, Cheating the Constitution, 59 Vand. L.Rev. 475, 491 (2006). One study of cases in which exonerating evidence resulted in the overturning of criminal convictions concluded that invalid forensic testimony contributed to the convictions in 60% of the cases. Garrett & Neufeld, Invalid Forensic Science Testimony and Wrongful Convictions, 95 Va. L.Rev. 1, 14 (2009). And the National Academy Report concluded:

> *"The forensic science system, encompassing both research and practice, has serious problems that can only be addressed by a national commitment to overhaul the current structure that supports the forensic science community in this country."* National Academy Report P-1 (emphasis in original).

Like expert witnesses generally, an analyst's lack of proper training or deficiency in judgment may be disclosed in cross-examination.

This case is illustrative. The affidavits submitted by the analysts contained only the bare-bones statement that "[t]he substance was found to contain: Cocaine." At the time of trial, petitioner did not know what tests the analysts performed, whether those tests were routine, and whether interpreting their results required the exercise of judgment or the use of skills that the analysts may not have possessed. While we still do not know the precise tests used by the analysts, we are told that the laboratories use "methodology recommended by the Scientific Working Group for the Analysis of Seized Drugs." At least some of that methodology requires the exercise of judgment and presents a risk of error that might be explored on cross-examination. See 2 P. Giannelli & E. Imwinkelried, Scientific Evidence § 23.03[c], pp. 532–533, ch. 23A, p. 607 (4th ed.2007) (identifying four "critical errors" that analysts may commit in interpreting the results of the commonly used gas chromatography/mass spectrometry analysis); Shellow, The Application of *Daubert* to the Identification of Drugs, 2 Shepard's Expert & Scientific Evidence Quarterly 593, 600 (1995) (noting that while spectrometers may be equipped with computerized matching systems, "forensic analysts in crime laboratories typically do not utilize this feature of the instrument, but rely exclusively on their subjective judgment").

The same is true of many of the other types of forensic evidence commonly used in criminal prosecutions. "[T]here is wide variability across forensic science disciplines with regard to techniques, methodologies, reliability, types and numbers of potential errors, research, general acceptability, and published material." National Academy Report S-5. See also *id.*, at 5-9, 5-12, 5-17, 5-21 (discussing problems of subjectivity, bias, and unreliability of common forensic tests such as latent fingerprint analysis, pattern/impression analysis, and toolmark and firearms analysis). Contrary to respondent's and the dissent's suggestion, there is little reason to believe that confrontation will be useless in testing analysts' honesty, proficiency, and methodology—the features that are commonly the focus in the cross-examination of experts.

D

Respondent argues that the analysts' affidavits are admissible without confrontation because they are "akin to the types of official and business records admissible at common law." But the affidavits do not qualify as traditional official or business records, and even if they did, their authors would be subject to confrontation nonetheless.

Documents kept in the regular course of business may ordinarily be admitted at trial despite their hearsay status. See Fed. Rule Evid. 803(6). But that is not the case if the regularly conducted business activity is the production of evidence for use at trial. Our decision in *Palmer v. Hoffman*, 318 U.S. 109, 63 S.Ct. 477, 87 L.Ed. 645 (1943), made that distinction clear. There we held that an accident report provided by an employee of a railroad company did not qualify as a business record because, although kept in the regular course of the railroad's operations, it was "calculated for use essentially in the court, not in the business." The analysts' certificates—like police reports generated by law enforcement officials—do not qualify as business or public records for precisely the same reason. See Rule 803(8) (defining public records as "excluding, however, in criminal cases matters observed by police officers and other law enforcement personnel").

Respondent seeks to rebut this limitation by noting that at common law the results of a coroner's inquest were admissible without an opportunity for confrontation. But as we have previously noted, whatever the status of coroner's reports at common law in England, they were not accorded any special status in American practice.

The dissent identifies a single class of evidence which, though prepared for use at trial, was traditionally admissible: a clerk's certificate authenticating an official record—or a copy thereof—for use as evidence. But a clerk's authority in that regard was narrowly circumscribed. He was permitted "to certify to the correctness of a copy of a record kept in his office," but had "no authority to furnish, as evidence for the trial of a lawsuit, his interpretation of what the record contains or shows, or to certify to its substance or effect." The dissent suggests that the fact that this exception was " 'narrowly circumscribed' " makes no difference. To the contrary, it makes all the difference in the world. It shows that even the line of cases establishing the one narrow exception the dissent has been able to identify simultaneously vindicates the general rule applicable to the present case. A clerk could by affidavit *authenticate* or provide a copy of an otherwise admissible record, but could not do what the analysts did here: *create* a record for the sole purpose of providing evidence against a defendant.

Far more probative here are those cases in which the prosecution sought to admit into evidence a clerk's certificate attesting to the fact that the clerk had searched for a particular relevant record and failed to find it. Like the testimony of the analysts in this case, the clerk's statement would serve as substantive evidence against the defendant whose guilt depended on the nonexistence of the record for which the clerk searched. Although the clerk's certificate would qualify as an official record under respondent's definition—it was prepared by a public officer in the regular course of his official duties—and although the clerk was certainly not a "conventional witness" under the dissent's approach, the clerk was nonetheless subject to confrontation.

Respondent also misunderstands the relationship between the business- and official-records hearsay exceptions and the Confrontation Clause. As we stated in *Crawford:* "Most of the hearsay exceptions covered statements that by their nature were not testimonial—for example, business records or statements in furtherance of a conspiracy." Business and public records are generally admissible absent confrontation not because they qualify under an exception to the hearsay rules, but because—having been created for the administration of an entity's affairs and not for the purpose of establishing or proving some fact at trial—they are not testimonial. Whether or not they qualify as business or official records, the analysts' statements here—prepared specifically for use at petitioner's trial—were testimony against petitioner, and the analysts were subject to confrontation under the Sixth Amendment.

E

Respondent asserts that we should find no Confrontation Clause violation in this case because petitioner had the ability to subpoena the analysts. But that power—whether pursuant to state law or the Compulsory Process Clause—is no substitute for the right of confrontation. Unlike the Confrontation Clause, those provisions are of no use to the defendant when the witness is unavailable or simply refuses to appear. Converting the prosecution's duty under the Confrontation Clause into the defendant's privilege under state law or the Compulsory Process Clause shifts the consequences of adverse-witness no-shows from the State to the accused. More fundamentally, the Confrontation Clause imposes a burden on the prosecution to present its witnesses, not on the defendant to bring those adverse witnesses into court. Its value to the defendant is not replaced by a system in which the prosecution presents its evidence via *ex parte* affidavits and waits for the defendant to subpoena the affiants if he chooses.

F

Finally, respondent asks us to relax the requirements of the Confrontation Clause to accommodate the "'necessities of trial and the adversary process.'" It is not clear whence we would derive the authority to do so. The Confrontation Clause may make the prosecution of criminals more burdensome, but that is equally true of the right to trial by jury and the privilege against self-incrimination. The Confrontation Clause—like those other constitutional provisions—is binding, and we may not disregard it at our convenience.

We also doubt the accuracy of respondent's and the dissent's dire predictions. The dissent, respondent, and its *amici* highlight the substantial total number of controlled-substance analyses performed by state and federal laboratories in recent years. But only some of those tests are implicated in prosecutions, and only a small fraction of those cases actually proceed to trial. See Brief for Law Professors as *Amici Curiae* 7–8 (nearly 95% of convictions in state and federal courts are obtained via guilty plea).[390]

Perhaps the best indication that the sky will not fall after today's decision is that it has not done so already. Many States have already adopted the constitutional rule we announce today, while many others permit the defendant to assert (or forfeit by silence) his Confrontation Clause right after receiving notice of the prosecution's intent to use a forensic analyst's report, *id.*, at 13–15 (cataloging such state laws). Despite these widespread practices, there is no evidence that the criminal justice system has ground to a halt in the States that, one way or another, empower a defendant to insist upon the analyst's appearance at trial. Indeed, in Massachusetts itself, a defendant may subpoena the analyst to appear at trial, and yet there is no indication that obstructionist defendants are abusing the privilege.

The dissent finds this evidence "far less reassuring than promised." But its doubts rest on two flawed premises. First, the dissent believes that those state statutes "requiring the defendant to give early notice of his intent to confront the analyst," are "burden-shifting statutes [that] may be invalidated by the Court's reasoning." That is not so. In their simplest form, notice-and-demand statutes require the prosecution to provide notice to the defendant of its intent to use an analyst's report as evidence at trial, after which the defendant is given a period of time in which he may object to the admission of the evidence absent

---

390. The dissent provides some back-of-the-envelope calculations regarding the number of court appearances that will result from today's ruling. Those numbers rely on various unfounded assumptions: that the prosecution will place into evidence a drug analysis certificate in every case; that the defendant will never stipulate to the nature of the controlled substance; that even where no such stipulation is made, every defendant will object to the evidence or otherwise demand the appearance of the analyst. These assumptions are wildly unrealistic, and, as discussed below, the figures they produce do not reflect what has in fact occurred in those jurisdictions that have already adopted the rule we announce today.

the analyst's appearance live at trial. See, *e.g.*,Ga.Code Ann. § 35-3-154.1 (2006); Tex.Code Crim. Proc. Ann., Art. 38.41, § 4 (Vernon 2005); Ohio Rev.Code Ann. § 2925.51(C) (West 2006). Contrary to the dissent's perception, these statutes shift no burden whatever. The defendant *always* has the burden of raising his Confrontation Clause objection; notice-and-demand statutes simply govern the *time* within which he must do so. States are free to adopt procedural rules governing objections. It is common to require a defendant to exercise his rights under the Compulsory Process Clause in advance of trial, announcing his intent to present certain witnesses. There is no conceivable reason why he cannot similarly be compelled to exercise his Confrontation Clause rights before trial. Today's decision will not disrupt criminal prosecutions in the many large States whose practice is already in accord with the Confrontation Clause.[391]

... Defense attorneys and their clients will often stipulate to the nature of the substance in the ordinary drug case. It is unlikely that defense counsel will insist on live testimony whose effect will be merely to highlight rather than cast doubt upon the forensic analysis. Nor will defense attorneys want to antagonize the judge or jury by wasting their time with the appearance of a witness whose testimony defense counsel does not intend to rebut in any fashion. The *amicus* brief filed by District Attorneys in Support of the Commonwealth in the Massachusetts Supreme Court case upon which the Appeals Court here relied said that "it is almost always the case that [analysts' certificates] are admitted without objection. Generally, defendants do not object to the admission of drug certificates most likely because there is no benefit to a defendant from such testimony." Given these strategic considerations, and in light of the experience in those States that already provide the same or similar protections to defendants, there is little reason to believe that our decision today will commence the parade of horribles respondent and the dissent predict.

* * *

This case involves little more than the application of our holding in *Crawford v. Washington*. The Sixth Amendment does not permit the prosecution to prove its case via *ex parte* out-of-court affidavits, and the admission of such evidence against Melendez-Diaz was error. We therefore reverse the judgment of the Appeals Court of Massachusetts and remand the case for further proceedings not inconsistent with this opinion.

It is so ordered.

Discussion Questions

1. As we noted above, a preliminary determination in any Sixth Amendment analysis under *Crawford* is to determine whether the statement in question is in fact "testimonial." The Court concludes that crime lab reports are affidavits and are thus, testimonial. What are affidavits? Why are they testimony within the meaning of the Confrontation Clause? Do you agree with the Court's reasoning?
2. Do you find a distinct difference between this type of sworn affidavit (forensic lab reports) and an affidavit by a domestic violence victim detailing domestic abuse by her

391. As the dissent notes, *some* state statutes, "requir[e] defense counsel to subpoena the analyst, to show good cause for demanding the analyst's presence, or even to affirm under oath an intent to cross-examine the analyst." We have no occasion today to pass on the constitutionality of every variety of statute commonly given the notice-and-demand label. It suffices to say that what we have referred to as the "simplest form [of] notice-and-demand statutes," is constitutional; that such provisions are in place in a number of States; and that in those States, and in other States that require confrontation without notice-and-demand, there is no indication that the dire consequences predicted by the dissent have materialized.

spouse? Do you view such an affidavit being offered against an accused, in lieu of live testimony, differently than lab results? Why or why not?

3. Among other arguments by the State as to why such affidavits should not be subject to confrontation is because the testimony does not recount historical events, which are "prone to distortion or manipulation," but instead, is the "result of neutral, scientific testing." The Court questions this point noting that, even in this setting, confrontation could expose fraud and incompetence, and other flaws in analysis. What are your thoughts? Is there value in confronting and cross-examining an analyst who conducted scientific testing? Explain.

4. The Respondents also argue that such reports are closely akin to business and public records, and thus share the same type of reliability that has led to those records overcoming the hearsay bar. Do you agree, and even if so, would that satisfy the Confrontation Clause? What did the court say about "reliability" of a statement and the Confrontation Clause?

5. Respondents also argue the potential burden on the judicial system if required to subpoena lab analysts. Should the burden on the system ever be a basis of depriving an accused a constitutional right intended to protect his rights to a fair trial?

6. The most important issue in this case, however, deals with whether an accused's constitutional right to confrontation is violated by a statute that effectively "shifts the burden" to the defendant to subpoena the analysts himself upon notice by the prosecution of its intent to offer the report. Prior to its 2010 amendment, Louisiana's statute for offering certificates of analysis also contained such a provision that had been upheld in 2005 by the Louisiana Supreme Court in *State v. Cunningham*[392] prior to the *Melendez-Diaz* decision. The provision was later held unconstitutional by the Louisiana Forth Circuit Court of Appeal in *State v. Simmons,*[393] in a post-*Melendez-Diaz* decision.

   In 2010, La. R.S. 15:501 was amended to what is commonly referred to as a "notice-and-demand" statute, of which the *Melendez-Diaz* Court expressed approval. Such "notice-and-demand" statutes provide that upon notice by the State of its intent to offer a certificate of analysis, the defense may demand that the State call the analyst to testify at the trial, rather than having to subpoena the witness himself as required under prior law. Sanctioning notice-and-demand statutes as compliance with Confrontation rights, the *Melendez-Diaz* Court notes:

   > Contrary to the dissent's perception, these statutes shift no burden whatever. The defendant *always* has the burden of raising his Confrontation Clause objection; notice-and-demand statutes simply govern the *time* within which he must do so ... It is common to require a defendant to exercise his rights under the Compulsory Process Clause in advance of trial, ... There is no conceivable reason why he cannot similarly be compelled to exercise his Confrontation Clause rights before trial.[394]

---

392. State v. Cunningham, 903 So. 2d 1110, 1121 (La. 2005) (holding that "[t]he statutes do not infringe upon defendant's constitutional right to confrontation").

393. State v. Simmons, 67 So. 3d 525, 535 (La. Ct. App. 4th Cir. 2011) (holding that "we find that the statutory scheme in effect at the time of Simmons' trial violated Simmons' rights under Melendez-Diaz. That is our reading of Melendez-Diaz is that the Confrontation Clause does not allow the burden to be shifted to the defendant to call as a witness the criminalist, a witness obviously against him ..." While the law had already changed at the time of the decision, the case was decided under the law in existence at the time of the trial court's decision on the issue.).

394. Melendez-Diaz v. Massachusetts, 129 S. Ct. 2527, 2541 (2007).

Reviewing Louisiana's statute below, compare the notice-and-demand statute with a statute that would require the defendant to subpoena the lab analysis himself upon receiving such notice. How do you distinguish the constitutionality of one from the other?

§ 501. Notice of opposing party and opportunity to cross-examine expert; certification of subpoena request[395]

A. The party seeking to introduce a certificate made in accordance with R. S. 15:499 shall, not less than forty-five days prior to the commencement of the trial, give written notice of intent to offer proof by certificate. Such notice shall include a copy of the certificate.

B. The attorney for the defendant, or the defendant acting in his own defense, if not represented by counsel, may demand that the person making the examination or analysis testify by filing a written demand and serving it upon the district attorney or attorney general seeking to introduce the certificate. If such a demand is made timely as set forth below, the certificate shall not constitute prima facie proof of the facts thereon as set forth in R.S. 15:500.

C. Demand for the testimony of the person making the examination or analysis shall be filed and served by counsel for the defendant, or by a defendant acting as his own counsel, within thirty days of the receipt of the notice provided for in Subsection A of this Section. The trial court may extend this thirty-day period for good cause shown if such request is made prior to the expiration of the thirty days.

D. If no request for additional time is made prior to the expiration of the thirty-day period, an extension of time in which to make such a demand may be made only upon a showing of exceptional circumstances. Any allegation that such circumstances exist shall constitute a preliminary plea on the defendant's behalf for the purposes of Louisiana Code of Criminal Procedure Article 580. The demand shall be made in writing and notice shall be served on the district attorney or the attorney general prosecuting the matter. The court shall conduct a contradictory hearing to determine if the extension is warranted.

E. The filing of a demand by the defendant does not prevent the admission of the certificate or its contents in any other manner otherwise appropriate pursuant to the Louisiana Code of Evidence or its ancillaries.

Illustration of Confrontation Clause and Certificates of Analysis

Dez is on trial for possession of cocaine. The prosecution intends to use the certificate of analysis prepared by the crime lab as evidence that the white powdery substance that was found inside of Dez's pocket was determined to be 100% cocaine. At trial, the prosecution offers the lab report into evidence without calling a witness. Dez objects that offering the lab report violates his Sixth Amendment confrontation rights. Is he correct? Using the analysis in *Melendez-Diaz*, explain whether lab reports are or are not subject to confrontation. How can the State comply with any confrontation requirements?

Discussion

Dez is correct that offering the crime lab report against him, without calling a witness that he may confront and cross-examine, violates his Sixth Amendment confrontation

395. Amended by Acts. Effective August 15, 2010; *See also* La. R.S. 15:499 As amended effective August 1, 2012 (dealing with the form of the lab reports); La. R.S. 15:500 (addressing the admissibility of lab reports).

rights because the analyst's statements contained in the report are "testimonial "under *Crawford/Davis* and therefore may only be admitted if the witness is unavailable and Dez had a prior opportunity to cross-examine the witness/analyst. Otherwise, the use of the evidence would violate his confrontation rights.

While numerous arguments have been made as to why lab reports should be exempt from the confrontation requirement, in *Melendez-Diaz*, the United States Supreme Court has held that lab reports are incontrovertibly a "solemn declaration or affirmation made for the purpose of establishing or proving some fact," "made under circumstances which would lead an objective witness reasonably to believe that the statement would be available for use at a later trial." As such, the reports are testimonial in nature and subject to the Confrontation Clause of the Sixth Amendment. Like experts in general, an analyst's lack of proper training or deficiency in judgment or fraud, as well as deficiencies in processes or procedures, may be disclosed in cross-examination. Thus, a defendant has a right to confront the analyst conducting such tests at a trial.

In *Melendez-Diaz*, the Court held that the prosecution can comply with a defendant's confrontation rights through the use of a notice-and-demand statute. Thus, pursuant to La. R.S. 15:501, the state can provide notice to Dez of its intent to use the lab results at least 45 days prior to trial, and require that within 30 days of receipt of the notice that Dez makes a written demand to have the person making the examination or analysis appear personally in court for confrontation and cross-examination. Additional time to demand the witness's presence may be available if timely requested or if exceptional circumstances exist. If Dez makes a timely demand to have the analyst testify, the certificate shall not be prima facie proof of the facts thereon, and the evidence may only be offered against Dez if the witness is present to testify. If Dez fails to make a timely demand for the witness's presence, the State may offer the report as evidence against Dez without violating his constitutional rights.

Key Points

The key points to keep in mind regarding hearsay and the Sixth Amendment Confrontation Clause

1. The Sixth Amendment requires that in all criminal cases an accused has a right to confront witnesses against him.

- The right includes the right to cross-examine witnesses.
- Applies in criminal cases.
- Applies in both state and federal courts.

2. ***Crawford*** provides that the Confrontation Clause only applies to **"testimonial"** statements. If a statement is testimonial, the Confrontation Clause requires that to be admissible: 1) the witness is currently unavailable; and 2) there was a *prior opportunity for cross-examination*.

- The Confrontation Clause also does not preclude a testimonial statement from being offered against an accused if the witness is currently *available* for cross-examination on the statement.

3. **The following statements are admissible under *Crawford*:**

A. The statement is non-testimonial, even if never cross-examined and witness is currently unavailable.

B. The statement is: a) testimonial; and b) witness is currently *available* for cross-examination.

C. The statement is: a) testimonial; b) witness is unavailable; and c) there was prior opportunity to cross-examine the witness.

4. **Testimony is defined as:**

- "it applies at a minimum to prior testimony at a preliminary hearing, before a grand jury, or at a former trial; and to police interrogations,"
- "*ex parte* in-court testimony or its functional equivalent—that is, material such as affidavits, custodial examinations, prior testimony that the defendant was unable to cross-examine, or similar pretrial statements that declarants would reasonably expect to be used prosecutorially,"
- "extrajudicial statements ... contained in formalized testimonial materials, such as affidavits, depositions, prior testimony, or confessions,"
- "statements that were made under circumstances which would lead an objective witness reasonably to believe that the statement would be available for use at a later trial."

Davis v. Washington **further defined testimony as:**

- "Statements are nontestimonial when made in the course of police interrogation under circumstances objectively indicating that the primary purpose of the interrogation is to enable police assistance to meet an ongoing emergency."
- "They are testimonial when the circumstances objectively indicate that there is no such ongoing emergency, and that the primary purpose of the interrogation is to establish or prove past events potentially relevant to later criminal prosecution."

5. **Forfeiture by Wrongdoing** (*Giles*)—An accused who procures the absence of a witness for the purpose of preventing the witness from testifying against him at trial forfeits his rights under the Confrontation Clause of the United States Constitution and Article I § 16 of the Louisiana Constitution.

6. ***Crawford*** **and Certificates of Analysis**—*Melendez-Diaz* provided that, under *Crawford,* affidavits of forensic analysis are "testimonial," and as such an accused has a right to confront the forensic analyst who conducted the test. Notice-and-demand statutes comply with the confrontation requirements.

Problems on Hearsay and the Sixth Amendment Confrontation Clause

PROBLEM 5-189. Part I: Marjorie was involved in an altercation with her husband. She ran into the bathroom and called 911. When the police arrived, Marjorie's husband had left the house. She went outside to talk to the police about what had happened. She pointed down the street and said he ran that way. The officer walked down the street and didn't see her husband. He returned to Marjorie's house and asked her to write a sworn statement detailing what happened. They went inside into the kitchen and prepared the statement.

Marjorie signed it and gave it to the officer. Just as Marjorie was finishing up the statement, she heard someone fiddling with the door knob at the back door. She began crying and screaming to the officer, "Please don't let him get in here. Please don't leave me with that monster. Please! I'm scare to death!" The officer then went outside and arrested Marjorie's husband. The next day another officer from the Domestic Violence Unit called Marjorie into the station for a detailed statement. Marjorie went to the station and gave an hour-long recorded interview.

Marjorie asserts her spousal testimonial privilege at her husband's trial and refuses to testify. The prosecution would like to offer all five of Marjorie's statements against her husband. Husband objects on Sixth Amendment confrontation grounds. The use of which, if any, of the statements would violate the Sixth Amendment? Why or why not?

1. The 911 call
2. Statement made in front yard to police
3. Affidavit of the incident at kitchen table
4. Marjorie's statement in kitchen when husband returned
5. The statement made to the DV Unit Officer

Part II: Would your answer change if Marjorie agreed to come to court and testify truthfully at the trial about all of the events of the day? How? Why or why not?

Part III: Marjorie informed her husband that she would be in court for the trial. He begged her not to testify against him. She insisted that she would. Husband told her that if she testified in court an old cellmate of his would kill her for him. Husband then had the cellmate drive to her house, get out of the car with an 18-inch machete, and show it to her. Marjorie immediately packed a bag, left town, and refused to answer any calls from the prosecution. Marjorie did not show up for trial and they don't know where she is. The prosecution would like to use all of Marjorie's statements. Defense objects on confrontation grounds. What ruling? Why?

PROBLEM 5-190. Part I: Bowen is on trial for the murder of a man he killed in a car accident. Kip testified at the grand jury proceedings for the prosecution that he saw Bowen speeding down the interstate driving east in the westbound lane when he struck the victim's vehicle in a head-on collision, immediately causing the victim to be ejected from his vehicle. He died immediately upon striking the ground headfirst. Prior to the trial, Kip is diagnosed with lung cancer and dies just four months later. At Bowen's trial, the prosecution seeks to admit Kip's testimony given before the grand jury. Bowen objects on Sixth Amendment confrontation grounds.

A) Will Kip's grand jury testimony be admissible against Bowen in his trial? Why or why not?

B) Would your answer change if Kip had lived, but was unable to speak (i.e., testify) as a result of the chemotherapy for his cancer? Why or why not?

C) Would your answer change (regarding Sixth Amendment Confrontation Clause only) if Kip had miraculously recovered from the cancer, and was willing to show up and take the stand to testify? Why or why not?

Part II: Assume instead that rather than a grand jury proceeding, Kip had testified at Bowen's preliminary examination, where Bowen's attorney cross-examined him. Kip actually does die from the cancer prior to trial. The prosecution would like to offer Kip's preliminary examination testimony at the trial. Bowen objected on both Sixth Amendment

Confrontation grounds as well as hearsay grounds. How would you respond to the hearsay objection as well as the Sixth Amendment Confrontation objection?

PROBLEM 5-191. Part I: Kaine is being tried for murdering his lawn guy, Omar. The week before the murder, Omar called 911 one afternoon after completing Kaine's lawn and reported that Kaine had confronted him at knifepoint earlier that day about possibly sleeping with Kaine's wife and had threatened to kill Omar if he ever came back around their home again. The next day, Omar was found dead. Kaine is charged with his murder. The prosecution would like to admit Omar's 911 call to the police. Kaine objects to the admissibility of the statement on Sixth Amendment confrontation grounds. (No hearsay objections were raised.) The prosecution claims Kaine "forfeited" his right to confront Omar when he killed him. Can the statement be offered against Kaine without violating the Confrontation Clause? Why or why not?

Part II: Assume that Omar's helper Ray was with him when Kaine made the threat, and had also made a statement to the police within a day or two before Omar was killed. Upon hearing of it, Kaine went over and threatened to do to him what he did to Omar, if he didn't stay out of his business. Ray left town. The prosecution would like to use Ray's statement he made to the police in the interrogation. Kaine objects on Sixth Amendment Confrontation and hearsay grounds. Should the statement be admitted over Kaine's objection? Why or why not?

Part III: Would your answer change if instead of threatening Ray, Kaine had called him up and asked him not to testify and explained to him that he and Omar had just had a misunderstanding between men? Still afraid, Ray ran away. Does use of Ray's statement against Kaine violate his Sixth Amendment confrontation rights? Why or why not?

§ 5.25 References and Additional Authority on Hearsay vis à vis the Sixth Amendment of the U.S. Constitution and Article I Section 16 of the Louisiana Constitution

1. La. C.E. Introductory Note to Chapter 8
2. Force & Rault, HANDBOOK ON LOUISIANA EVIDENCE LAW, Introduction to Chapter 8 Author's Comments (West Publishing 2014)
3. Harges & Jones, LOUISIANA EVIDENCE, Introduction to Chapter 8 Author's Comments (West Publishing 2014)
4. 19 La. Civ. L. Treatise, Evidence And Proof § 10.1 (2nd ed.)
5. **Commentary**: Aslett, *Crawford's Curious Dictum: Why Testimonial "Nonhearsay" Implicates the Confrontation Clause,* 82 Tul. L. Rev. 297 (2007); Gremillion, Amber, *"I'll Be Seeing You in Court: Melendez-Diaz v. Massachusetts' Flawed Decision and Its Impact on Louisiana*, 37 S.U.L. Rev. 255 (2010).
6. **Cases following *Crawford* excluded statement as violating Confrontation Clause:** *Johnson v. State*, 929 So. 2d 4 (Fl. Ct. App. 2d Dis. 2005) (The defendant argued that the admission of a lab report violated his confrontation rights. The court ruled that although *Crawford* stated that business records are non-testimonial, here, the lab report was prepared for the purposes of establishing an element of a crime and was

therefore testimonial. The court went on to determine whether the two-prong test from *Crawford* of unavailability and prior opportunity to cross-examine were met. The court concluded that the declarant was not unavailable and remanded the case.).

7. **Following *Crawford* found no violation of *Crawford***: *State v. Harris*, 781 So. 2d 73 (La. Ct. App. 4th Cir. 2001) (holding that the defendant's right to confront the witness against him was not violated because the defendant had no right to confront in a pretrial hearing; this case overruled *State v. Connerly*, 989 So. 2d 84 (La. 2008)).

8. **Emergency Exception**: *State v. Hugle*, 104 So. 3d 598 (La. Ct. App. 4th Cir. 2012) (holding that when a statement is made in the course of police interrogation for the purpose of aiding in the investigation, the statement is nontestimonial in regard to the confrontation clause).

§ 5.26 Practical Application Exercises

PAE 1: The parents of Minnie Williams are suing the defendant, Trish Simpson, and her insurance company for damages their daughter sustained in a car accident. They claim Trish intentionally rammed her vehicle into their daughter's car, inflicting a severe head injury that causes her to have periodic seizures. In support of their case, the Williamses would like to offer into evidence the medical record (below) from the first incident in which Minnie suffered a seizure, just five days after the accident occurred. The defense has objected that the medical record is hearsay. They further assert that, even if the medical record is admitted into evidence, portions of the record should be excluded as inadmissible multiple hearsay. Will any portion of the medical record be admitted? If so, under what exception will it be admissible? Are there multiple exceptions in which the medical record might be admissible? Explain each. If portions of the record are multiple hearsay, what exceptions would apply to those statements? Will portions have to be excised out of the record completely? Fully explain your answer.

STATE HOSPITAL MEDICAL RECORD

Emergency Department

PRESENTING COMPLAINT: apparent seizure, unconsciousness

ARRIVED BY: ambulance TIME: 8:48 p.m.

CONDITION ON ADMISSION: FAIR__ GOOD__ POOR: X

ALLERGIES: YES__ NO X SPECIFY:

Patient:
Minnie Lee Williams
117 Blackburn Street
Lake Providence, La. 71254

AGE: 16 DOB: 3/30/1999
PATIENT #: 0002 147 5486 2574

TEMP: 103 PULSE: 65 RESP. 25 B.P. 145/100 TIME: 9:10 p.m.

NOTES: On arrival patient mother reports that patient was doing homework at table when she began shaking and trembling uncontrollably. Episode lasted 3-5 minutes when patient suddenly lost consciousness. Called 911 NURSE SIGNATURE: Carrie N. Wallace

HISTORY: No prior episodes. Mother states that patient was involved in car accident 5 dys prior when jealous teen hit daughter's car. States that at time, patient reported no pain or injuries but had dull headache. Didn't see doctor. Mother states patient had small bump on head.

DOCTOR SUMMARY: 16year-old girl admitted after parents reported patient "went blank," then fell off chair, jerking, trembling, lost consciousness for 30-40 minutes. Upon regaining consciousness in ER, patient was slow in verbal response. Reported dizziness, confusion, Lab data abnormal. Chemistry profile abnormal. Brain MRI unremarkable. (see supplement for details)

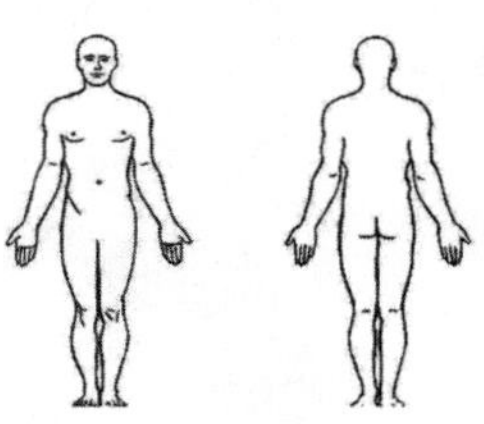

DISCHARGE CONDITION: fair TIME: 10:15 p.m.

DISCHARGE INSTRUCTIONS: Return in a.m. for CBC to check for Electrolyte levels, lumbar puncture, and toxicology screen Instructed to return to ER immediately if condition returns Severe headache, confusion, inability to walk/stand, or fever

PHYSICIAN: L.G. Perry, Jr. PATIENT: Minnie L. Williams

PAE 2: Billy is suing his cell phone insurance provider to reimburse him for charges he incurred while attempting to have his defective cell phone repaired. The insurance company has failed to pay, claiming that the bill surpasses the value of the phone and only wants to pay the amount of the defective phone. Billy is suing for the entire bill under his insurance agreement. In support of his claim, Billy offers the invoice (reproduced below) from the certified cell phone repair company who replaced the phone after they attempted to repair it. Assuming the evidence has been properly authenticated, ATV objects that the invoice is hearsay and/or multiple hearsay. What response(s) would you make to attempt to overcome the hearsay objections?

ATV Cellphone Repair Co.
111 Window World Ln
Little City, La. 70817

Customer:
Billy Caston
55943 Country Winding Rd.
Grey City, La. 61973

September 17, 2013

ITEM	QUANTITY/HR	HR RATE	Line Price
Customer complaint: Says phone will not charge. Customer plugs in power cord and points out that charge light not on and phone not charging even though plugged in.			
Tech notes: Tested battery, tested powercord, tested power input. Replaced defective phone.	4	$75	$300.00
		Tax	$ 27.00
		Total	$327.00

Billy Caston
CUSTOMER SIGNATURE

Mark Ryan
TECHNICIAN SIGNATURE

PAE 3: Peter is on trial for killing his wife. He claims she ran away from home. In Peter's defense he offers the note below that he claims his wife left on the kitchen table on the day that she disappeared. Peter plans to take the stand and authenticate the letter as being his wife's handwriting. The prosecution objects that the letter is hearsay. How should Peter's attorney respond to attempt to get the letter into evidence? What ruling?

> Dear Peter,
>
> Things have not been good for a while now. I don't think that staying together is in the best interest of the kids. It might be best that we finally part ways. So I'm leaving. I talked to the kids and they said they'd rather live with you. I'm sure this doesn't come as a surprise. Last week when I said I had plans in the works, you just smiled. I knew that you knew. We both have been so miserable over the last 5 years. We've argued and fought constantly. Remember that time I told you I wanted you dead? Well, I'm tired now. I'm sad. I want a brighter future for all of us. Don't look for me. Don't try to contact me. I do not want to be found. I appreciate all that you've done for me. I think you're a great father and husband. You're just not for me. I will always love you and the kids. Don't let them forget me. Goodbye!
>
> Lynette

Chapter 6

Character, Other Crimes & Credibility

§6.1 Character Generally [La. C.E. art. 404(A)]

Applicable Code Articles

Art. 404. Character evidence generally not admissible in civil or criminal trial to prove conduct; exceptions; other criminal acts

A. Character evidence generally. Evidence of a person's character or a trait of his character, such as a moral quality, is not admissible for the purpose of proving that he acted in conformity therewith on a particular occasion, except:

* * *

As discussed in Chapter 3 §3.2, although relevant, some evidence may be excluded because it may have an "**undue tendency to suggest decision on an improper basis,**"[1] namely, because it may adversely affect "the jury's attitude toward the defendant wholly apart from its judgment as to his guilt or innocence of the crime charged."[2] In other words, some evidence must be excluded because it may cause the jury to convict the defendant, not because of evidence that actually proves his guilt, but because of their feelings about the *kind* of person they believe he is, such as a *violent* person, a *mean* person, or a *dishonest* person. When you refer to **the *kind* of person someone is**, you speak of his "**character.**" "'Character' has been defined as a person's disposition or disposition in respect to a general trait."[3] Character evidence is deemed to be highly persuasive with a jury, so much so that it is feared to have the tendency to lead the jury to convict based solely on the character evidence itself, dismissing all other relevant evidence. Because of this, it has the potential to be **unfairly prejudicial**. Thus, several rules have been developed to limit the scope and circumstances under which such evidence may be offered against a person.

Character evidence generally inadmissible—The "Conformity Rule." Pursuant to Article 404(A), evidence of a person's character or a trait of his character is generally **not admissible** for the purpose of proving that the person **acted in conformity** with the par-

1. See Fed. Rules of Evid. art. 403 advisory committee notes.

2. U.S. v. Bailleaux, 685 F.2d 1105 (9th Cir. 1982); *See also* State v. Rose, 949 So. 2d 1236 (2007) (explaining the term "prejudicial effect" of other crimes as it pertains to a criminal case, as a "substantial risk of grave prejudice to the defendant").

3. *See* Bell v. Whitten, 722 So. 2d 1057 (La. Ct. App. 1st Cir. 1998) *citing* McCormick on Evidence §195 (5th ed., 1992).

ticular character trait on a particular occasion. For example, evidence that a person is dishonest would not be admissible to prove that the person committed a forgery. Evidence that a person is violent, mean, or quick-tempered cannot be offered to prove the person committed a murder. Similarly, evidence that a man is jealous and egotistical may not be offered to prove that he battered his wife, nor can evidence that a person is lustful be offered to prove that he committed a rape. This exclusion of character evidence applies in both civil and criminal cases and is referred to as the "conformity rule," because it precludes evidence of a person's character to prove that he acted in conformity with the character trait on the occasion in question. "Stated differently, the prosecution is not allowed to suggest to the jury that because the defendant has a 'propensity' to do certain things, the defendant is guilty in the case before"[4] them. Thus, this rule is also referred to as the "**propensity bar**."[5]

Examples of character traits. To help you better understand the kind of evidence excluded under Article 404(A), the following are examples of character traits. They are generalized descriptions of a person's disposition and may not be offered to prove that a person with the character trait in question acted in conformity with the particular trait on the occasion in question.

Negative character traits: greedy, dishonest, disrespectful, angry, flamboyant, arrogant, evil, bossy, unfair, unfaithful, fearless, foolish, reckless, foul, careless, childish/immature, ungrateful, inconsiderate, uncooperative, grouchy, grumpy, cowardly, cruel, harsh, curious, hateful, dangerous, daring, ignorant, rough, rowdy, impatient, rude, impolite, selfish, jealous, lazy, sly, sneaky, mean, messy, stingy, mysterious, naughty, stubborn, noisy, disobedient, obnoxious, thoughtless, picky, unfriendly, wicked, irrational, unreliable, irresponsible, lustful.

Good character traits: dependable, honest, ambitious, respectful, easygoing, attentive, efficient, fair, faithful, brilliant, calm, careful, cautious, friendly, charming, mature, gentle, concerned, good, confident, considerate, cooperative, courageous, helpful, patient, polite, considerate, independent, industrious, kind, sharp, skillful, loving, loyal, smart, sweet, nice, talented, obedient, thankful, thoughtful, peaceful, tolerant, pleasant, polite, trusting, trustworthy, friendly, positive, modest, warm, quick, quiet, wise, reliable, worried, religious, responsible.

Exceptions. While character evidence is generally inadmissible, there are exceptions to the rule in which evidence of a person's character may be offered at a trial. Article 404(A), specifically lists three exceptions in which character evidence is admissible that will be discussed throughout this chapter:

1. Character of the **defendant** when he puts his own, usually good, character at issue (discussed *infra* § 6.3);
2. Character of the **victim** (discussed *infra* § 6.8); and
3. Character of a **witness** for his truthfulness or untruthfulness (discussed *infra* § 6.9).

Additionally, under Article 405, character evidence is admissible when character is an essential element of a claim, charge, or defense (discussed *infra* § 6.4). When character is an essential element of a claim, charge, or defense, it may also be proven by specific instances of conduct.

---

4. Harges & Jones, Louisiana Evidence Art. 404 Author's Comments.
5. *Id.*

§ 6.2 Proving Character [La. C.E. arts. 405(A), (C)]

Applicable Code Articles

Art. 405. Methods of proving character

A. Reputation. Except as provided in Article 412, in all cases in which evidence of character or a trait of character of a person is admissible, proof may be made by testimony as to general reputation only. On cross-examination of the character witness, inquiry is allowable into relevant specific instances of conduct.

* * *

C. Foundation. Before a person may be permitted to testify to the reputation of another person, a foundation must be established that the witness is familiar with that reputation.

General reputation only. Pursuant to Article 405, except as provided in Article 412 and Article 405(B),[6] **in all cases** in which evidence of a person's character is admissible, it must be proven by testimony as to **general reputation** only. This includes the exceptions listed in §6.1. Additionally, before a person may be permitted to testify to the reputation of another person, a **foundation** must be established that the witness is familiar with that reputation. Under Louisiana law, a person's character may not be proven by specific instances of conduct or by a person's opinion of another person's character. Character may only be proven by testimony as to general reputation in the community, with proper foundation that establishes that the witness is competent to testify as to that person's character.

For example, if a defendant is on trial for forgery, he can offer a character witness to testify that his general reputation in the community is for being an honest, trustworthy person. However, that witness may neither testify that in his *opinion* the defendant is honest, nor can he testify to *specific instances* to prove the defendant's honesty, such as the fact that he saw the defendant find and return a lost wallet to its owner. While returning a lost wallet to its owner is an example of honesty, it is a "specific instance of conduct," which is generally not a permissible method of proving a person's character under Louisiana law.

Foundation. It is important to keep in mind that before testifying to a person's general reputation in the community for the particular character trait, the proponent must ask questions to establish that the witness is in fact familiar with that person's reputation.[7] Furthermore, the *community* in which the witness learned of the person's character could be that person's work, church, school, organization, or any other community in which the witness would have had an opportunity to learn of the person's reputation for the character trait.[8] To establish the foundation for character evidence, the attorney offering the evidence might question the witness as follows:

---

6. La. Code Evid. art. 412 relative to sexual assault victims is discussed *infra* § 6.9, and La. Code Evid. art. 405(B) relative to cases in which character is an essential element discussed *infra* § 6.4.

7. La. Code Evid. art. 405(C).

8. *See* La. Code Evid. art. 405 Official Comment (b); *See also* State v. Clark, 402 So. 2d 684, 687 (La. 1981) ("[A]ny substantial community of people among whom he is well known, such as the group with whom he works, does business or goes to school.").

Q: How long have you known Mr. Williams?

A: About 7 years.

Q: In what capacity have you known him?

A: We are both members of the same lodge.

Q: As members of the same lodge, what is the nature and extent of your interaction with Mr. Williams and others who know him?

A: Well, the organization meets twice a week and we also have various committee meetings throughout the month. Additionally, the members perform community projects together on the weekends and overall spend quite a bit of time together running the organization.

Q: In the course of knowing Mr. Williams and others who know him, have you had an occasion to discuss his reputation for honesty?

A: Yes, I have.

Q: And through your discussions about his reputation for honesty, have you become familiar with his reputation for honesty and integrity?

A: Yes, I have.

Q: What is his reputation?

A: Mr. Williams has **a reputation for being a very honest man and for being a man of great integrity.**

Through this line of questioning, the proponent of the character evidence has established that, through the witness's interactions with the person and with others who know him, he is familiar with the person's character in the community (the lodge).

Pertinent character trait. When character evidence is admissible, the trait offered must be pertinent, or relevant, to the case. For example, in a forgery case, honesty is pertinent; however, evidence that the person is punctual is not a pertinent character trait and would not be admissible in that trial. Similarly, if the character witness will testify to the witness's character for truthfulness/untruthfulness pursuant to Article 404(A)(3), the pertinent character trait is whether the witness is in fact truthful or honest. Evidence that the witness is dependable, wise, or patient would not be a pertinent character trait and should not be permitted.

Cross-examination of a character witness. Once a witness has testified about a particular character trait of a person, that witness may then be cross-examined about relevant specific instances of conduct that go to the heart of the character trait in question. For example, if a witness is called to testify that someone is honest, he may be cross-examined about whether *he has heard* that the person had stolen money from his last employer—a specific instance of conduct that pertains to the character trait in question, honesty. This allows the jury to determine the weight and credibility they will give the witness's testimony regarding the person's character about which the witness has testified.[9]

A jury would be interested to know that a witness was aware that a person was fired for stealing, yet testified that the person was honest. Similarly, the jury would be interested

9. *See* La. Code Evid. art. 405 Official Comment (c).

to know that a person testified that someone was honest, who did not know that the person had been fired for stealing. In such a case, it would be shown that either the witness clearly does not know the person very well whose character he is attesting to, or that the witness is biased in his assessment of the witness's character, despite what he has heard. Thus, the jury would be better able to determine the weight and credibility they will attach to the witness's testimony regarding the person's character.

Further, the specific instances in question need not be convictions—they could include arrests that did not result in a conviction,[10] bad acts for which the person was not arrested, or even rumors and gossip that are currently being discussed in the community, even if the character witness has not heard about them.[11]

"Have you heard . . . ?" When cross-examining a character witness about specific instances of conduct, the questions must be in the form of asking the witness whether he or she "*has heard*" about each of the specific instances of conduct in question. For example, the witness should be asked, "*Have you heard* that Mary was fired from her job for stealing?" It would be inappropriate to ask the witness, "*Did you know* that Mary was fired for stealing?" or, "*Would you be surprised to learn* that Mary was fired from her job for stealing?" as well as, "*Were you aware* of the fact that Mary was fired from her job for stealing?"

Because character evidence may only be in the form of general reputation in the community, it is essentially a summary of what the witness has *heard* being discussed in the community about the person.[12] Thus, in testing the witness's credibility concerning the character testimony he has given, all that is relevant is what the witness might have *heard* about the person's reputation in question. Thus, the witness may only be cross-examined about whether he has heard about the specific instances of conduct rather than if he was aware of or knew about them.

Precautions before cross-examining character witnesses on specific instances. In order to minimize the prejudice to a defendant when a character witness is cross-examined about the defendant's prior bad acts, arrests, or convictions, the Louisiana Supreme Court has established safeguards that should be recognized regarding the specific instances about which the character witness may be cross-examined. Under *State v. Johnson*,[13] before allowing a witness to be questioned about specific instances that may prejudice the jury, the trial judge should conduct a preliminary inquiry out of the presence of the jury regarding the conduct in question and he should satisfy himself:[14]

1. that there is **no question as to the fact** of the subject matter of the rumor, that is, of the previous arrest, conviction, or other pertinent misconduct of the defendant;
2. that a reasonable likelihood exists that the previous arrest, conviction or other pertinent misconduct would have been **bruited about the neighborhood** or **community** prior to the alleged commission of the offense on trial;
3. that neither the event or conduct nor the rumor concerning it occurred **at a time too remote** from the present offense;
4. that the earlier event or misconduct and the rumor **concerned the specific trait involved** in the offense for which the accused is on trial;

10. *See* State v. Warner, 116 So. 3d 811 (La. Ct. App. 4th Cir. 2013) (allowing cross-examination of character witness about prior arrests).

11. Harges & Jones, Louisiana Evidence Art. 405 Author's Comments.

12. *Id.*

13. State v. Johnson, 389 So. 2d 372 (La. 1980).

14. *Id.*

5. that the examination will be conducted in the **proper form**, that is: '**Have you heard**,' etc., not 'Do you know,' etc. (citations omitted); and
6. if a conclusion is reached to allow the interrogation, the jury should be informed of its **exact purpose** either at the conclusion thereof or in the charge.[15]

This preliminary inquiry into the specific instances of conduct, commonly referred to as a "**Johnson hearing**,"[16] will help minimize prejudice because it can help to ensure that the specific instances referred to are in fact relevant to testing the credibility of the character witness, that the cross-examiner has credible grounds for asking the questions, and that they are not merely a bad faith attempt to present potentially highly prejudicial information before the jury. By requiring the trial court to ensure that the conduct in question in fact occurred, would likely have been discussed about the community, is not too remote in time to be relevant, and involves the character trait in question, the potential for abuse and unfair prejudice are significantly reduced.

Rebuttal by opponent. One final component of the procedures for proving character at trial is that once a party has called a character witness to testify to a pertinent character trait, the opponent may offer rebuttal evidence of the person's character through another character witness. For example, after a defendant offers character witnesses to testify as to his good character trait, and has opened the door to his character, the prosecution may call character witnesses to testify as to the defendant's character as well. When a character witness is called to testify in rebuttal to testimony given by another character witness, all of the procedures discussed above apply to the rebuttal character witness that applied to the original character witness. Specifically, the witnesses may only testify as to the person's general reputation and may be cross-examined on specific instances of conduct.

Federal Rules of Evidence Distinction. Louisiana's rules for offering character evidence differ widely from the Federal Rules of Evidence, which provide that character may also be proven by *opinion* testimony of the witness in addition to reputation testimony.[17] Thus, in federal court, either an expert witness or a lay witness can testify as to their opinion of the person's pertinent character trait.[18] As with reputation, a witness must have sufficient familiarity with the person to be qualified to express an opinion as to the person's character.[19] Additionally, as in Louisiana, the character witness may be cross-examined about relevant specific instances of conduct. However, under the Federal Rules, the witness may be questioned in the form of either "*have you heard*," "*do you know*," or even "*were you aware*" of the specific relevant conduct in question, regardless to whether he testified in the form of opinion or to reputation.[20]

These distinctions are quite significant in comparison to the Louisiana rules, where a witness may only give character evidence in the form of reputation in the community and may only be cross-examined in the form of "have you heard." One final distinction

15. *Id.*, *quoting* State v. Steensen, 35 N.J. Super. 103, 113 A.2d 203 (App. Div. 1955).

16. *See, e.g.,* State v. Henderson, 740 So. 2d 240 (La. Ct. App. 2d Cir. 1999); State v. Houghton, 619 So. 2d 765 (La. Ct. App. 4th Cir. 1993).

17. *See* Fed. R. Evid. 405(a).

18. Steven Goode & Olin Guy Wellborn III, Courtroom Evidence Handbook Rule 405 Author's Comments (5) (West Publishing 2010–2011).

19. *Id.*; *See also*, United States v. Koessel, 706 F.2d 271, 275 (8th Cir. 1983) (excluding a witness's opinion testimony finding that the witness who had only met the person once was not qualified to give opinion of person's character).

20. United States v. Scholl, 166 F.3d 964, 974 (9th Cir. 1999), cert. Denied, 528 U.S. 873, 120 S. Ct. 176 (1999).

that is quite significant is that under the Federal Rules, there are no specific procedures or factors like those Louisiana has developed in *Johnson* to help minimize the prejudicial effect of the prior offenses about which a character witness may be cross-examined. Under the Federal Rules, the state need only have a "good faith basis" for believing the prior offenses occurred. However, in Louisiana there must be "no question as to the fact of the subject matter of the rumor" that forms the basis of the conduct about which the witness may be cross-examined. This is yet another instance in which the state court provides greater protection for a defendant than the Federal Rules do.

Key Points

The key points to keep in mind regarding proving character.

1. Instances where character evidence is admissible: 1) defendant puts his own character at issue; 2) character of a witness for truthfulness; and 3) character of a victim.
2. **Proving character**: In all instances in which character is admissible, it must comply with the following procedures:
    1. proven by general reputation in the community;
    2. it must be a pertinent character trait;
    3. a foundation must be laid to establish that the witness is familiar with the person's reputation in the community;
    4. the "community" in which the knowledge was obtained can be school, work, neighborhood, or any other setting in which the witness interacted with the person and other associates enough to have learned of the person's reputation for that particular character trait;
    5. the character witness may be cross-examined on specific instances of conduct that must: a) go to the pertinent character trait in issue; and b) be in the form of "have you heard";
    6. prior conduct subject to a preliminary hearing on the *Johnson* safeguards; and
    7. the opponent may also call character witnesses to rebut the character witnesses called by the defendant. Prosecution's witnesses must also comply with all requirements for offering character evidence: a) proven by general reputation in the community; b) pertinent character trait only; c) foundation to establish that they are familiar with reputation in a community; d) may be any substantial community of people; and e) they may also be cross-examined in the form of "have you heards" on specific instances of conduct that must go to the pertinent character trait at issue.
3. ***Johnson* Safeguards:** For testing the prior specific instances of conduct about which character witnesses will be cross-examined.
    1. that there is no question as to the fact of the subject matter of the rumor, that is, of the previous arrest, conviction, or other pertinent misconduct of the defendant;
    2. that a reasonable likelihood exists that the previous arrest, conviction or other pertinent misconduct would have been bruited about the neighborhood or community prior to the alleged commission of the offense on trial;

3. that neither the event or conduct nor the rumor concerning it occurred at a time too remote from the present offense;
4. that the earlier event or misconduct and the rumor concerned the specific trait involved in the offense for which the accused is on trial;
5. that the examination will be conducted in the proper form, that is: 'Have you heard,' etc., not 'Do you know,' etc. (citations omitted); and
6. if a conclusion is reached to allow the interrogation, the jury should be informed of its exact purpose either at the conclusion thereof or in the charge.

Problem on Proving Character

PROBLEM 6-1

Part I: Mary, an accountant, is a defendant in a forgery case and plans to call one or more character witnesses to testify on her behalf. Which of the following witnesses will be able to testify as proposed?

a. William takes the stand, and testifies that he has known Mary all of her life and that in his opinion Mary doesn't appear to be the kind of person who would forge something.

b. Milton will take the stand and will testify that he has worked with Mary at an accounting firm for 12 years and that around the office she is known to be thorough, accurate, and fair.

c. Bill testifies that Mary gives $5000 to the office Christmas charity foundation each year, and clearly could not be stealing if she can give so much.

d. Bo takes the stand and says that although he doesn't know Mary personally, he lives in her subdivision and she's the treasurer for the HOA, so if they trust her, she must be a good person.

e. Crystal is Mary's best friend and will testify that Mary is known in their circle for being very strong, dependable, and a great confidant. She also testifies that Mary is an outstanding mother to her children.

f. The mayor also knows Mary, and she will testify that she is familiar with Mary's reputation in the community, and Mary is known for being very outgoing, energetic and fun.

g. Reverend Simmons will testify that he is Mary's pastor and that in the church she is known for being extremely honest.

Part II: Can any of the character witnesses (whose testimony is admissible) be cross-examined by the prosecution regarding the following:

a. Whether they had heard that Mary had been convicted of income tax fraud.

b. Whether they had heard that Mary had suffered from depression and was a recluse.

c. Whether they knew that Mary had tried to bribe a police officer.

d. Would they be surprised to learn that Mary had had an affair.

e. Would it change their opinion of Mary to learn that Mary had been charged for impersonating a police officer.

Part III: The prosecution wishes to call a character witness to rebut the evidence to which Mary's witness(es) have testified. Which character witness can the prosecution call in rebuttal?

a. One of Mary's former coworkers who will testify that Mary was fired from a former job.

b. One of Mary's former employers who will testify that around the office Mary had a reputation for being deceptive and untrustworthy.

c. A member from the local State Accountant Association who will testify that Mary has a reputation in the organization for being a loud, boisterous woman.

d. A former college roommate who will testify that when Mary was in college, about 15 years ago, Mary was known for being unreliable because she was elected president of an organization, but never showed up for a meeting.

§ 6.3 Character of Accused (Defendant Puts Own Character at Issue) [La. C.E. art. 404(A)(1)]

Applicable Code Articles

Art. 404. Character evidence generally not admissible in civil or criminal trial to prove conduct; exceptions; other criminal acts

A. Character evidence generally. Evidence of a person's character or a trait of his character, such as a moral quality, is not admissible for the purpose of proving that he acted in conformity therewith on a particular occasion, except:

(1) **Character of accused.** Evidence of a pertinent trait of his character, such as a moral quality, offered by an accused, or by the prosecution to rebut the character evidence; provided that such evidence shall be restricted to showing those moral qualities pertinent to the crime with which he is charged, and that character evidence cannot destroy conclusive evidence of guilt.

* * *

As discussed above, the conformity rule precludes evidence of a person's character from being offered against him to prove that he acted in conformity with that character trait on a particular occasion. Thus, the prosecution cannot offer evidence of a defendant's character in its case-in-chief in a trial to help prove a defendant's guilt. However, Article 404(A)(1) sets forth an exception to this general rule that applies in criminal cases. It provides that an accused may offer evidence of a pertinent trait of his character, such as a moral quality, provided that such evidence shall be restricted to showing those moral qualities pertinent to the crime with which he is charged. Thus, while the prosecution cannot put the defendant's character at issue, if a defendant chooses to, he may offer evidence of his own (usually good) character relative to a pertinent character trait in a trial. By doing this, the defendant puts his character at issue, and opens the door to evidence of his character being offered by the prosecution in rebuttal as well. The procedures for offering evidence of the character of the accused must be in accordance with Article 405 (as outlined above in § 6.2), which are:

1. proven by general reputation in the community;
2. it must be a pertinent character trait;
3. a foundation must be laid to establish that the witness is familiar with the person's reputation in the community;
4. the "community" in which the knowledge was obtained can be school, work, neighborhood, or any other setting in which the witness interacted with the person and other associates enough to have learned of the person's reputation for that particular character trait;
5. the character witness may be cross-examined on specific instances of conduct that must: a) go to the pertinent character trait in issue; and b) be in the form of "have you heard";
6. prior conduct subject to a preliminary hearing on *Johnson* safeguards; and
7. the opponent may also call character witnesses to rebut the character witnesses called by the defendant. Prosecution's witnesses must also comply with all requirements for offering character evidence: a) proven by general reputation in the community; b) pertinent character trait only; c) foundation to establish that they are familiar with reputation in a community; d) may be any substantial community of people; and e) they may also be cross-examined in the form of "have you heards" on specific instances of conduct that must go to the pertinent character trait at issue.

How defendant puts character at issue. The law is clear that only a defendant may put his character at issue, not only opening the door to his witnesses being cross-examined about any bad acts, convictions, or arrests he may have, but also to character witnesses being called by the prosecution in rebuttal to testify to his character. A defendant does not open the door to his general character by merely taking the stand, as discussed below in *State v. James*. While a defendant, like all witnesses, puts his *credibility* at issue when he takes the stand, he does not generally put his character at issue simply by testifying.[21]

A defendant may only put his character at issue by offering evidence of his character—evidence that describes the kind of person he is—either through another witness or by his own testimony. While such evidence is usually intentionally offered, a defendant (or his witness) may inadvertently open the door to the defendant's character. For example, if during the defendant's testimony, he is asked whether he was at the location where the crime occurred, a known crack house, and he responds, "*No, I would never go to a place like that. I'm an upstanding law-abiding citizen who doesn't do such things*," then he may have inadvertently put his character at issue by testifying to his character as an upstanding person. By doing this, he has opened the door to additional character evidence being offered by the prosecution to rebut the character trait to which he has testified.

Federal Rules of Evidence Distinction. Like Louisiana's Article 404(A), the Federal Rule of Evidence 404(a) similarly precludes the use of character evidence to prove action in conformity therewith. Both provisions also contain this exception to the general rule that applies in criminal cases. However, unlike the Federal Rule of Evidence 404(a)(1), Louisiana's Article 404(A)(1) specifically provides that "character evidence cannot destroy conclusive evidence of guilt." This distinction is significant because some federal courts allow the trial court to instruct the jury that evidence of the defendant's good character,

21. Only a witness's character for truthfulness or untruthfulness as it relates to credibility is placed at issue simply by testifying as provided in Articles 608 and 404(A); *See also* La. Code Evid. art. 404(A) Official Comments to Paragraph A (d)(1998).

standing alone, may be sufficient evidence to create reasonable doubt, even though the courts have held that the accused is not entitled to such an instruction.[22]

In accordance with Louisiana's provision limiting the use of such evidence, the prosecution is entitled to a limiting instruction to the jury that they are not to assume the defendant's innocence because of the character evidence he offers. Thus, in federal court, evidence of the accused's character has the potential to have a much greater impact on the case than in a Louisiana court.

Cases on Defendant Putting His Own Character at Issue

State v. Johnson

Supreme Court of Louisiana
389 So. 2d 372
Oct. 6, 1980

DENNIS, Justice.

Defendant, Nicholas L. Johnson, was charged by bill of information with the crime of armed robbery, a violation of La.R.S. 14:64. After trial by jury, he was found guilty and sentenced to serve eight years at hard labor. On appeal, defendant relies on two assignments of error, both involving impermissible cross-examination of the defendant and his character witness about defendant's prior criminal record. Although we find that the prosecution's questioning was objectionable, we must affirm defendant's conviction and sentence because he did not properly present the errors for our review. The abuses revealed in the record, however, move us to adopt safeguards for future cases.

The state's case against the defendant consisted entirely of testimony given by one eyewitness, Edna Burke, an employee of a grocery store that was robbed on the morning of February 12, 1979. Ms. Burke testified that a man she identified as the defendant entered the store around nine o'clock a. m. while she was alone at the cashier's counter, brandished a revolver partially protruding out of a paper sack, and indicated by motioning with the weapon that he wanted the money in the register. She emptied the register and the robber then fled the store on foot. According to Ms. Burke, the entire incident took less than two minutes, during which time she had the opportunity to get a good look at the man, whom she described as between 5'7 and 5'9 in height, with black hair, a heavy beard, and a smooth dark complexion.

Ms. Burke testified that about a month after the incident, the defendant entered the store to buy beer and cigarettes. At this time she immediately identified him as the man who had robbed the store and tried unsuccessfully to alert the store manager, John Lewis, to his presence. On several occasions thereafter the defendant, who admitted living in the neighborhood, would come and go from the store and the manager would be unsuccessful in stopping his employee's suspect before defendant's departure. Finally, on April 23, 1979, on a pre-arranged signal from Ms. Burke, Lewis caught sight of the defendant as he left the store and followed him to a carwash. Lewis then summoned police, who took the defendant into custody. Ms. Burke was brought to the scene and she identified the

---

22. *See* United v. Pujana-Mena, 949 F.2d 24, 28 n. 2 (2d Cir. 1991); *See also* United States v. Foley, 598 F.2d 1323, 1336–37 (4th Cir. 1979), cert. denied, 444 U.S. 1043 (1980); United States v. Lewis, 482 F.2d 632, 637 (D.C. Cir. 1973).

defendant as the same man who had robbed the store on February 12. Defendant was then arrested for armed robbery.

At trial, defendant placed himself at work pouring concrete forms during the day of February 12, 1979. Two defense witnesses corroborated this story. Robert Williams, who along with the other witness, Anthony Roberts, operated an independent contracting business, testified that the defendant was employed by him at the time of the offense. On cross-examination, he conceded that it was possible for the defendant to have missed work on that particular day. Anthony Roberts testified that defendant was employed by his business on the day of the offense and would have been at work that day because he "never skipped a day" of work.

Defendant then called Roy Lee Jarrell, who had lived next door to the defendant for a year, and worked with him for two years in Baton Rouge, to testify as a character witness. Mr. Jarrell testified that he never had heard the defendant being accused of stealing, and otherwise knew him to be an honest person.

On cross-examination of Mr. Jarrell, the prosecution asked the witness three separate questions concerning the defendant's prior criminal record: "Would it change your opinion of Mr. Johnson if I told you that in November of 1968, he was arrested for selling a narcotic drug?" "Mr. Jarrell, would it change your opinion about Mr. Johnson if I told you that in March of 1974 that he was arrested for possession of weapons and danger (sic) instruments?" "Would it change your opinion about Mr. Johnson if I told you that in July '74 he pled guilty to criminal possession of a controlled dangerous substance?" Following the second question, defense counsel objected to any reference to arrests on cross-examination of the witness. After the third question, defense counsel objected on grounds that the question should include the specific possessory offense charged. All three defense objections were overruled.

Defendant Johnson followed Jarrell to the stand. On direct examination, defendant was asked whether the prior conviction was of a violent nature, or involved the traits of honesty or veracity, and whether he had ever been convicted of carrying a gun or any type of offense related to the possession of a gun. Defendant replied to all of these questions in the negative. On cross-examination, the prosecution elicited from the defendant that the conviction involved possession of marijuana, for which defendant had served time in jail. The prosecution then proceeded to go into an extended inquiry into the defendant's prior arrests, including the details of the arrest for possession of a dangerous weapon. Defendant explained that this involved a blunt club found in the car he was driving at the time of the arrest for the narcotics violation. The club was not his but rather belonged to the owner of the car, and the charge was subsequently dropped. Defense counsel offered no objection to these questions.

On appeal, defendant assigns as error the trial court's ruling on his objections to the interrogation of the character witness, Mr. Jarrell. He also assigns error to the denial of his motion for a new trial, which was based partially on the prosecution's interrogation of Jarrell and also on the prosecution's interrogation of the defendant regarding his previous arrests. In his brief, defendant argues that the questions put to the witness Jarrell were in improper form, and involved charges that were too remote and irrelevant to the offense charged. Defendant further maintains that the cross-examination of both Mr. Jarrell and the defendant about the defendant's prior criminal record was an improper and highly prejudicial use of other crimes evidence that could have warranted a mistrial.

We agree that the potential for abuse of such evidence indicates that some regulation of character witness cross-examination is needed and adopt safeguards to be applied in future cases. However, these safeguards may not be applied in the present case to reverse defendant's conviction because he did not preserve the error for our review by a properly grounded contemporaneous objection at trial.

In interpreting our statutory rules concerning character evidence, see La.R.S. 15:479-481, this Court has held that "it is not reversible error for the prosecution to question a defense witness about his knowledge of prior arrests of the defendant." State v. Harvey, 329 So.2d 731 (La.1976); State v. Banks, 307 So.2d 594 (La.1975).

This type of rule has been criticized for a number of reasons both within and without our state. It trenches close to the widely condemned practice of proving other crimes extrinsically in order to show bad reputation as a logical result, presenting the danger that the jury, finding the prior crime, will shortcut the reputation process and use it more directly to convict in the case on trial. McCormick on Evidence, s 191, p. 457 (Cleary ed. 1972). See, Michelson v. United States, 335 U.S. 469, 477–87, 69 S.Ct. 213, 219–224, 93 L.Ed. 168, 174–179 (1948); 3 A. Wigmore, Evidence, s 988, pp. 920–21 (Chadbourn rev.1970). In order to alleviate some of the danger, the witness should not be asked "if he knows" that the accused has committed such other crimes, but only whether he "has heard" that defendant has committed particular acts inconsistent with the reputation vouched for on direct. McCormick, supra, at pp. 456–57. See also, G. Pugh and J. McClelland, The Work of the Louisiana Appellate Courts for the 1972–1973 Term—Evidence, 34 La. L. Rev. 443, 447 (1974). Even so, a rule permitting the cross-examiner to ask the character witness whether he "has heard" of other particular crimes of accused involving the same trait is pregnant with possibilities of destructive prejudice. McCormick, supra, at p. 457. Although the courts agree that propounding such a question in bad faith may be ground for reversal, establishing bad faith may be a hopeless task for an accused in the absence of judicial intervention. McCormick, supra, at p. 458; 3 A. Wigmore, supra, s 988.

Wigmore and McCormick recommend that the trial judge, before permitting the prosecuting attorney to cross-examine the character witness on rumors of misconduct of the accused, should question the prosecutor in the absence of the jury, as to whether he has credible grounds for asking the question. McCormick, supra, s 191; 3 A. Wigmore, supra, s 988. Several jurisdictions have approved, recommended, or required this or a similar practice.

The Superior Court of New Jersey has formulated perhaps the most thoughtful guidelines to assist trial judges in determining whether the prosecutor has reasonable grounds for cross-examining the character witness about convictions, arrests or other misconduct of the accused. In determining whether to allow the cross-examination, the trial court should conduct a preliminary inquiry out of the presence of the jury and he should satisfy himself:

> "(1) that there is no question as to the fact of the subject matter of the rumor, that is, of the previous arrest, conviction, or other pertinent misconduct of the defendant;
>
> "(2) that a reasonable likelihood exists that the previous arrest, conviction or other pertinent misconduct would have been bruited about the neighborhood or community prior to the alleged commission of the offense on trial;
>
> "(3) that neither the event or conduct nor the rumor concerning it occurred at a time too remote from the present offense;
>
> "(4) that the earlier event or misconduct and the rumor concerned the specific trait involved in the offense for which the accused is on trial; and

"(5) that the examination will be conducted in the proper form, that is: 'Have you heard,' etc., not 'Do you know,' etc. (citations omitted)

"And if the conclusion is reached to allow the interrogation, the jury should be informed of its exact purpose either at the conclusion thereof or in the charge."

In reviewing the questions propounded by the state in the instant case, we are convinced that the asserted dangers of our present practice are real and that some regulation of character witness examination is necessary. The legitimate function of the prosecution in subjecting the character witness's testimony to the crucible of cross-examination to enable the jury to assess his familiarity with defendant's reputation and the quality of his report thereof can be performed without the suggestion or assertion of facts in such a way as to arouse undue prejudice within the jury. In order to promote this legitimate function of the prosecution and to insure that a defendant is protected from possible abusive cross-examination, we conclude that the safeguards which have been advocated by the scholars, Wigmore and McCormick, approved by the United States Supreme Court in *Michelson v. United States* and articulated by the New Jersey Superior Court should be adopted as fully set forth earlier in this opinion.

Defendant may not avail himself of these safeguards, however, because he failed to make a contemporaneous objection on these grounds at trial....

Because we find no reversible error in those matters properly before us on appeal, we affirm defendant's conviction and sentence. However, in future cases prejudicial error resulting from a trial court's failure to enforce the safeguards adopted herein during the cross-examination of character witnesses will require reversal, if properly objected to an assigned.

Discussion Questions

1. According to the court, the *Johnson* safeguards are designed to protect defendants from "abusive cross-examinations." What does the court mean by this? What are some of the dangers, mentioned in *Johnson*, of not having these safeguards in place?
   a. Can you think of any additional dangers of not having these safeguards in place *not* mentioned by the court?
   b. Why do these examinations have the potential for such unfair prejudice?
2. One of the requirements to allow the prosecution to cross-examine the character witness about convictions, arrests, or other misconduct of the accused, is that neither the event or conduct nor the rumor concerning it must be at a time "too remote" from the present offense. Can you think of an example or circumstances of when an event or conduct or the rumor concerning the event or conduct might be too remote?
   a. What factors should the court consider in making the determination?
   b. Why is this such an important inquiry?
3. What is the importance and rationale behind the court specifically requiring the cross-examination in the form of "Have you heard ..." rather than some of the other variations discussed: "Did you know ... ?" "Were you aware of ... ?" "Would you be surprised to learn ... ?" How is "have you heard" less prejudicial than the other forms of questioning?
   a. How or why does this form of questioning go to the heart of the type of character evidence given, i.e., "reputation in the community"?

4. The court says there must be "no question as to the fact of the subject matter of the rumor," which might include a conviction, arrest not resulting in a conviction, a bad act for which there was no arrest, or even random gossip. As it pertains to gossip, should the prosecution be required to determine whether gossip or a rumor is actually true, or is the interest furthered either way? In other words, if a rumor is being bruited about the community, even if not true, doesn't questioning a character witness about it test the credibility of the character witness either way? What are arguments for and against it?
5. *Johnson* decided the defendant had not properly preserved the issue for appeal by generally objecting to "any reference to arrests on cross-examination of the witness" rather than specifically objecting to the form in which the questions were asked, i.e., "have you heard." How should the defense counsel have objected to questions about the defendant's prior criminal record to preserve these objections on appeal?
6. What are your thoughts on the Federal Rules allowing opinion testimony as to character as well as cross-examination in the form of "did you know" and "were you aware of the fact that"? Which is more reliable, opinion or reputation? Which is more prejudicial? Why do you believe Louisiana excludes opinion testimony regarding character?
7. Finally, the *Johnson* court requires that "if the conclusion is reached to allow the interrogation, the jury should be informed of its exact purpose either at the conclusion thereof or in the charge." What is the reason for so advising the jury? Does it accomplish its goals, or bring more attention to the other bad act(s)?

State v. Galliano

Court of Appeal of Louisiana, First Circuit
639 So. 2d 440
June 24, 1994

CRAIN, Judge.

Defendant, Lynn Paul Galliano, was charged by grand jury indictment with aggravated rape, a violation of LSA-R.S. 14:42. Defendant pled not guilty and, after trial by jury, was found guilty as charged....

The record reflects that the instant offense occurred in Houma, Louisiana, on or about June 10, 1992, during the early morning hours. The victim of the offense was a female, approximately thirty-nine years of age.

On the day prior to the offense, defendant and the victim were assisting Tammy Baudoin in moving into an apartment next door to the victim's residence. Later that day after the move apparently had been completed, the victim accompanied defendant to a lounge.

According to the victim she and defendant stayed at the lounge for about forty-five minutes. They left the lounge when the victim asked defendant to take her home. However, defendant indicated to the victim that he wanted to stop at his home to show her something. When they arrived at defendant's home, they exited defendant's vehicle; and the victim followed defendant inside his home. Defendant started locking the house from the inside. At that point, the victim "thought [she] was in trouble." She asked defendant why he was locking the doors. Defendant did not answer her. He started turning off the lights. The victim asked him what he was doing. Again, defendant did not answer her.

Defendant walked to his bedroom. The victim followed him and told him she wanted to go home. Defendant walked to the side of his bed, leaned underneath it, and pulled out a .38 revolver. He put the gun to the victim's head and told her that if she did not do what he wanted he would "blow [her] f [____] brains out." Defendant then pushed her down on the bed, removed his and the victim's clothes and raped her. [He then raped her two more times.] ...

At that point, the victim asked defendant if he would call a taxicab for her. Defendant complied with this request. He unlocked the door and told her to walk down the street to meet the taxicab so as not to cause his dogs to start barking.

The victim walked down the street. Tammy Baudoin drove up. The victim related to Baudoin what had happened to her. Shortly thereafter at about 2:00 a.m., the taxicab driver arrived. The driver testified that the victim told him that she had been raped. He radioed his company's dispatcher and had the dispatcher contact the police....

At the scene, after being advised of his constitutional rights, defendant made a statement to Perkins. Defendant admitted to having had sex with the victim, but he maintained that it had been consensual. The officers asked defendant for and received from him a signed consent to search his residence. During the search, the officers seized various items, including the revolver, the shotgun, bedclothes, and hosiery and underpants belonging to the victim....

Dr. Randall Kenneth Lillich, a medical doctor, physically examined the victim at Terrebonne General Hospital at 4:10 a.m. on June 10, 1992. His examination revealed that the victim had sustained trauma....

At trial, defendant took the stand in his own defense and related a different version of the facts from that given by the victim. Consistent with his earlier statements to the police, he testified that he and the victim had engaged in consensual sexual intercourse....

ASSIGNMENT OF ERROR NUMBER THREE:

By means of this assignment, defendant contends that the trial court erred "in refusing to permit defendant to call Laurie Clement [as a character witness on his behalf] in fear of having Tammy Baudoin testify in 'rebuttal'." Defendant submits that the trial court's action denied him his constitutional right to call witnesses in his behalf.

...

At trial, during defendant's presentation of his case, the jury was removed from the courtroom at defense counsel's request. At that point, defense counsel indicated that he had intended to call Laurie Clement as his next witness to establish that a previous relationship between defendant and Clement was not "anything out of line that would indicate an attempt to rape or an attempt to have unconsented to (sic) sexual intercourse with her." Relying on LSA-C.E. art. 404A(1) and Official Comment (d) to that article, the trial court implicitly ruled that such testimony by Clement was admissible, stating that if Clement testified that any sexual relations she had with defendant were consensual and not by force, this testimony would open the door for the state to present Baudoin's testimony in rebuttal. Defense counsel objected to the ruling and stated that he would not call Clement as a witness....

LSA-C.E. art. 404 A generally disallows admission of evidence of a person's character or a trait of his character for the purpose of proving he acted in conformity therewith on a particular occasion. However, as a limited exception to the general rule, Article 404A(1) allows admission of evidence of a pertinent trait of an accused's character, such as a moral quality, offered by him or by the prosecution to rebut the character evidence; provided that such evidence shall be restricted to showing those moral qualities pertinent to the charged crime and cannot destroy conclusive evidence of guilt. For this exception to apply, the requirements of LSA-C.E. article 405 also must be met. Generally article 405 allows a party to prove a person's character with testimony as to "general reputation" only, and a particular foundation is required. LSA-C.E. art. 405 A & C. In this case, defendant never attempted, nor expressed a desire, to meet these requirements. To the contrary, the record reflects that the character evidence defendant sought to introduce was by specific instances of alleged good conduct and not a pertinent trait of his character provable by testimony as to general reputation only. Thus, the testimony sought to be introduced was inadmissible under LSA-C.E. art. 404A(1).

On the other hand, proof of character by specific instances of conduct is admissible but only "[i]n cases in which character or a trait of character of a person is an essential element of a charge, claim, or defense such as in a prosecution for defamation or when there is a defense of entrapment." ... Proof that defendant did not attempt to rape or engage in non-consensual sexual intercourse with someone other than the victim was clearly not an essential element of the charged offense or a defense to the charge and, therefore, was not admissible under article 405 B.

Hence, we find that the trial court erred to the extent that it implicitly ruled that the testimony anticipated from Clement was admissible. Nevertheless, under these circumstances in which the trial court's ruling would apparently have allowed defendant to elicit the inadmissible testimony, but defendant chose not to elicit the testimony, defendant was clearly not prejudiced. Moreover, we believe that, if defendant had chosen to elicit the testimony at issue, defendant would have opened the door to similar contradictory testimony in rebuttal, i.e., the testimony of Tammy Baudoin concerning her alleged rape by defendant.

This assignment lacks merit.

Discussion Questions

The defendant may put his own character at issue. This is an exception to the general rule in which character evidence is admissible. The law is clear that in situations in which character evidence is admissible, it must be in the form of "general reputation in the community," and must go toward the pertinent character trait at issue. It cannot be specific instances of conduct, as the defendant here sought to introduce.

1. What would have been the appropriate way for the defendant to put his character at issue in *Galliano*? Who may testify to it? What foundational requirements must be met? Specifically, to what type of evidence can a character witness testify?
2. What is the pertinent character trait that is at issue in a rape case? That the defendant is respectful toward women? A nice guy? Does not have a lustful disposition? What type of pertinent character trait would you expect to hear about in an aggravated rape case?
3. If Galliano had properly offered his character evidence, putting his character at issue, what rights would the State have had with respect to cross-examining the character witness? Might the evidence of the alleged rape of Tammy Baudoin have come out anyway? What precautions are put in place to potentially reduce the prejudicial effect of such evidence?
4. Additionally, if Galliano had properly offered his character evidence, to what type of evidence would he have opened the door for the State to offer in rebuttal? Specifically, to what would the State's witnesses have been permitted to testify? What foundation must they have laid? What would have been the scope of their testimony?
5. What are your thoughts in general regarding the impact of "opening the door" to otherwise inadmissible testimony? Does this prevent the defendant from presenting a de-

fense, or is it a fair exchange for what the defendant stands to gain for the positive testimony he will receive on direct examination?

State v. James

Court of Appeal of Louisiana, First Circuit
569 So. 2d 135
Oct. 16, 1990

ALFORD, Judge.

Paul C. James was charged by bill of information with possession of cocaine, a violation of La.R.S. 40:967C. Defendant pled not guilty, and, after a trial by jury, was found guilty as charged. Defendant was subsequently sentenced to serve eighteen months at hard labor. Defendant appeals, alleging that the trial court erred in allowing the state to cross-examine him as to prior bad acts, namely previous cocaine usage....

Defendant was arrested in Covington, Louisiana, on May 8, 1988, when a deputy from the St. Tammany Parish Sheriff's Office observed him drop a small piece of white paper upon the deputy's approach. Upon further investigation, the paper was found to contain cocaine.

Defendant took the stand at trial and claimed that he was not in possession of cocaine on the night in question....

While being cross-examined by the prosecutor, defendant was asked: "Do you use cocaine or have you ever used cocaine?" Defense counsel objected to this line of questioning, and his objection was initially sustained. The prosecutor argued, however, that when a defendant takes the stand he subjects the entirety of his character to cross-examination by the state. The prosecutor further argued that, if a defendant is on trial for drug charges, the question of whether or not he is a drug user goes to his credibility as a witness and has nothing to do with whether or not he has committed prior crimes. At this point, the trial court called a bench conference and then stated:

> I think that the Court believes that the context in which the question is offered is going to be allowed. I am going to overrule the objection and I'm going to instruct the jury that this question only goes to the truth and veracity and credibility of this witness and is not to be considered in any other context. He's only on trial for one, for one alleged crime here and it cannot be considered in connection with anything else, except his truth and veracity in this case, and so admonish the jury to only so consider the question and whatever the answer may be.

After this ruling, defense counsel reurged his prior objection. Defendant was asked again whether or not he had used cocaine before; and he answered: "I might have tried cocaine before." Defense counsel objected again and also moved for a mistrial, both of which were denied by the trial court.

In his brief to this Court, defendant contends that the prosecutor overstated his case when he asserted that a defendant who puts himself on the stand subjects the entirety of his character to cross-examination by the state. He further asserts that a defendant's character may be raised only by the accused (which he claims was not done herein) and only then may the state use evidence of a defendant's character solely to rebut the issues raised by defendant. Defendant grants the proposition that an accused, as any other witness, is subject to impeachment on cross-examination; however, defendant contends that he was not subject to cross-examination based on any prior convictions, because he had no prior convictions. Moreover, defendant submits that particular acts, vices, or courses of conduct of a witness may not be inquired into for the purpose of attacking his character for truthfulness, other than a conviction for a crime.

The state, on the other hand, argues to this Court that, since defendant claimed at trial that he was not in possession of cocaine at the time he was arrested, the prosecution's attempt to impeach his credibility with the question of whether or not he was a drug user was permissible. The state further argues that the trial court limited the above line of questioning and sufficiently admonished the jury that such questioning was for the limited purpose of determining the defendant's credibility as a witness. Therefore, it submits that the limited purpose for which the question was allowed should not constitute the basis upon which defendant's conviction is overturned.

For the following reasons, we disagree. First, as defendant submits in his brief to this Court, he did not raise the issue of his character; therefore, it was not properly before the jury while he was being cross-examined by the state.... [23] Next, the credibility of a witness may be attacked by any party; and, in doing so, such party may examine the witness concerning any matter having a reasonable tendency to disprove the truthfulness or accuracy of his testimony. Nevertheless, particular acts, vices or courses of conduct of the witness may not be inquired into or proved by extrinsic evidence for the purpose of attacking his character for truthfulness, other than ... as provided by La.C.E. art. 609.1. *See* La.C.E. arts. 607 A. and C. and 608 B.

...

Moreover, we do not feel that the prosecutor's questioning of defendant as to his possible prior usage of cocaine was harmless error, pursuant to La.C.Cr.P. art. 921....

Thus, we find that the trial court erred by allowing the state to cross-examine defendant concerning prior bad acts which he may have committed. Accordingly, defendant's conviction is reversed and the case is remanded to the trial court for further proceedings consistent with our opinion herein.

Discussion Questions

1. Distinguish a defendant putting his character at issue from putting his credibility at issue. Why is the defendant's character not at issue upon taking the stand in his own defense, but his credibility is?
2. What types of prejudicial effects, constitutional issues or otherwise, do you foresee coming into play if the full breadth of a defendant's character could be inquired into each time he took the stand?
3. Sometimes a defendant inadvertently puts his character at issue even when he does not intend to do so by something that he says while testifying. What type of question and answer might the defendant have responded to on direct examination that might have inadvertently opened the door to his character?

---

23. La.R.S. 15:479 et seq. were repealed by Acts 1988, No. 515, § 8. Comment (d) to La.C.E. art. 404 states that § A. (1) of art. 404 preserves the traditional rule that an accused has the option to introduce evidence of his character with respect to the pertinent trait involved in the crime charged. If the accused affirmatively exercises this option, the prosecution may then offer evidence to rebut the character evidence thus offered by the accused as to the pertinent character trait involved in the crime. By taking the stand as a witness, an accused does not thereby put his general character at issue, nor his character as to the pertinent trait involved in the crime, but only his credibility as a witness, as provided in La.C.E. art. 608.

4. Why do you think convictions may be used to attack credibility, but not arrests?

Key Points

The key points to keep in mind regarding proving character.

1. Character is generally inadmissible to prove that a person acted in conformity with it on a particular occasion.
2. Instances in which character evidence is admissible: 1) defendant puts his own character at issue; 2) character of a witness for truthfulness; and 3) character of a victim.
3. In all instances in which character evidence is admissible, it must comply with the following procedures:
   1. proven by general reputation in the community;
   2. it must be a pertinent character trait;
   3. a foundation must be laid to establish that the witness is familiar with the person's reputation in the community;
   4. the "community" in which the knowledge was obtained can be school, work, neighborhood, or any other setting in which the witness interacted with the person and other associates enough to have learned of the person's reputation for that particular character trait;
   5. the character witness may be cross-examined on specific instances of conduct that must: a) go to the pertinent character trait in issue; and b) be in the form of "have you heard";
   6. prior conduct subject to a preliminary hearing on *Johnson* safeguards; and
   7. the opponent may also call character witnesses to rebut the character witnesses called by the defendant. Prosecution's witnesses must also comply with all requirements for offering character evidence: a) proven by general reputation in the community; b) pertinent character trait only; c) foundation to establish that they are familiar with reputation in a community; d) may be any substantial community of people; and e) they may also be cross-examined in the form of "have you heards" on specific instances of conduct that must go to the pertinent character trait at issue.
4. When character is an essential element of a claim or charge, it may be proven by general reputation as well as specific instances of conduct (discussed in §6.4 *infra*).
5. **Character of the accused**. A defendant may put his own character at issue. He does not put his character at issue by taking the stand. He puts his credibility at issue by taking the stand, but not his character. When defendant puts character at issue, he must fully comply with requirements above for proving character.

Problems on Proving Character of the Accused

PROBLEM 6-2. Lionel is a small business owner. He is charged with fraud in federal court for filing a false IRS tax return. At trial, his attorney calls Lionel's neighbor Derek to testify. The attorney then laid a foundation regarding the close relationship between the accused and the witness, as well as his knowledge of Lionel's reputation around town. The witness testifies that in his opinion Lionel is a great father, a quiet neighbor, and a generous person. The prosecution objects to the evidence. Upon what grounds should he object? How should the court rule and why?

PROBLEM 6-3. The defendant is on trial for armed robbery. Explain why each of the following is an example of the defendant *properly* putting his own character at issue at his trial for armed robbery:

A. Defendant takes the stand and testifies in his own defense that he was out of town on the day of the offense, and has no knowledge of the charged offense.

B. The defense calls his pastor to the stand to testify that he regularly attends church every Sunday and teaches Sunday school.

C. The defense calls his daughter to testify that he is an outstanding father, who has been there for his children in tough times, sacrificing his own wellbeing for their benefit.

D. The defense calls his employer to testify that he is a dependable employee who has been with the company for 17 years and that he'd trust him with anything that he has.

PROBLEM 6-4. Sam is a doctor and has a small family practice. Gretchen takes care of his billing. One day, Gretchen stole one of Sam's company checks and purchased food for her family. At the time of the purchase, Gretchen forged Sam's name on the check as she had become very familiar with his signature over the years. When Sam found out about the theft and forged check, he immediately called the police and Gretchen was arrested. Gretchen claims she neither stole the check nor forged Sam's signature. At Gretchen's forgery trial, her attorney attempts to introduce evidence that Gretchen had an excellent reputation for honesty in their small town. The prosecution objects to the evidence. How should the judge rule and why?

PROBLEM 6-5. Ned is on trial for extortion. At his trial the defense offers evidence of all the work he has done in the community, working for various organizations building houses and feeding the needy. The prosecution objects to the evidence. What ruling?

PROBLEM 6-6. John-Paul is accused of murdering a 13-year-old girl in the community by choking her to death, then tossing her body in the creek. As part of the State's case, the prosecution would like to call a witness in its case-in-chief to testify that for the past ten years she has lived in the same small town as John-Paul and she knows him to have a reputation for violence and for being a bully. John-Paul objects. How will the court rule and why?

PROBLEM 6-7. Beau is on trial for murder. At his trial, he takes the stand in his own defense to testify to his version of the murder. Beau basically testifies that he was not responsible for the murder and was not present when it occurred. On cross-examination, the prosecution begins to attempt to cross-examine Beau about his prior involvement with a street gang responsible for murdering more than a dozen people. The defense objects claiming that the evidence is inadmissible bad character evidence. The prosecution responds that Beau put his character at issue when he took the stand. How should the court rule and why?

PROBLEM 6-8. Sally is being charged with theft. She is the first lady of a large mega church. In Sally's defense her attorney calls a church member to testify that she is a good religious woman to prove that she would never steal anything. Should the judge allow the testimony? Why or why not?

PROBLEM 6-9. Jada is on trial for attempted robbery. She seeks to admit testimony from her employer for her volunteer work with underprivileged children and the elderly to show that she is a compassionate woman who could never rob anyone. Should the judge allow the employer's testimony? Why or why not?

PROBLEM 6-10. Benny is a member of the city council who is on trial for malfeasance in office. At his trial, the defense offers testimony from a former president of Homes for Homeless (HFH), an organization that builds houses for homeless families, to testify that Benny has contributed thousands of hours of community service to the organization building houses, and has also contributed money towards supplies and other HFH community initiatives. The prosecution objects to the evidence. How should the court rule and why?

PROBLEM 6-11. Sam is on trial for beating up the coach of his son's baseball team. He takes the stand in his defense and testifies that he is not a violent man and that he is actually very peaceful and considerate of others. The judge allows the testimony. On cross-examination, the prosecution seeks to question Sam about an altercation with his wife in a bar that occurred about a year prior to the instant offense that led to Sam's arrest. The charges in that case were dismissed after Sam completed court-ordered anger management classes. The prosecution would also like to question Sam about the anger management classes and on the fact that he skipped some of the classes in defiance. The defense objects. Did Sam open the door to cross-examination on the named incidents? Why or why not?

PROBLEM 6-12. Wade is on trial for sexually assaulting a colleague at work. In an effort to prove his innocence, he wishes to call his minister Bishop Perry to testify that he is familiar with Wade's reputation in their church, and it is one for being an upstanding, law-abiding citizen, and for being respectful and considerate of women. On cross-examination, the prosecution asks Bishop Perry if he would be surprised to learn that Wade had also been accused of sexually assaulting another woman at his job? On what grounds should the defense object? How should the judge rule and why?

PROBLEM 6-13. James is on trial for the first-degree murder of Bill. In its case-in-chief, the defense seeks to offer testimony of James' older sister who will testify that she has known James all of his life and that she knows his reputation in the family and in the community, and it is one for being a peaceful man and for being jovial, happy, and an easygoing person. Is her testimony proper? Why or why not?

Assume the judge allows her testimony. The prosecution wishes to cross-examine her regarding whether she had heard that her brother James was a member of a gang and was known for fighting and carrying a knife. The defendant objects. Are the questions appropriate for cross-examination of the character witness? Explain.

Assume that after the defense rests, the State requests that it be allowed to reopen its case in rebuttal to call a witness, a former long-time fellow gang member, to testify that James: 1) has a reputation in the community for violence; and 2) that James is a member of the gang and has killed in the past. Will the State be allowed to call the witness to rebut the sister's testimony? Why or why not?

PROBLEM 6-14. Harry is charged with stealing Barry's expensive gold watch. At Harry's trial, the State calls Larry to testify in its case-in-chief that Harry's reputation in the community is for being dishonest and for not being a law-abiding citizen. Harry's lawyer timely objects. How should the court rule? Explain.

PROBLEM 6-15. Wanda is on trial for battery of her ex-husband's new wife, Kirsten. At the trial, the State calls Kirsten's sister Melissa to testify as a character witness in its case-in-chief. Melissa testifies, "Wanda has a reputation around town for being crazy, and it is commonly known that last year she went to her ex-husband's job and slashed his tires and broke the windows out of his car." Defense counsel objects to Melissa's testimony. How will the court likely rule and why?

PROBLEM 6-16. Moose is on trial for battering a security guard while being held in the Parish jail on other charges. At the jail, Moose is known for being a bully, for being bossy, and for taking whatever he wants from the little guys. One day Moose tried to force a cook to give him a second serving of his favorite jailhouse meal. Once the guard stepped in and instructed Moose to move on down the line, Moose pushed the guard and the instant charges were brought against him for battery of a security guard. At the trial, the prosecution would like to call several inmates as witnesses from the jail to testify to Moose's reputation to prove that he likely committed the battery against the security guard. The defense objects? How should the court rule?

§§ 6.1–6.3 References and Additional Authority on Proving Character and Defendant Putting His Own Character at Issue [La. C.E. art. 404(A)(1)]

1. La. C.E. arts. 404, 404(A)(1) and Official Comments
2. Force & Rault, Handbook on Louisiana Evidence Law Art. 404(A)(1) Author's Comments (West Publishing 2014)
3. Harges & Jones, Louisiana Evidence Art. 404(A)(1) Author's Comments (West Publishing 2014)
4. 19 La. Civ. L. Treatise, Evidence And Proof § 5.2 (2nd ed.)
5. **Knowledge of reputation in the community insufficient**: *State v. Jenkins*, 456 So. 2d 174 (La. Ct. App. 2d Cir. 1984) (holding a community insufficient even though witness testified that he frequented the same bars as the victim, had seen the victim a few times in those bars, and heard people talk about the victim's reputation, but did not know the victim himself); *State v. Deaton*, 412 So. 2d 586 (La. 1982) (holding that witness was unable to give testimony pertaining to the defendant's bad character because the witness did not know the defendant from any community that the defendant was associated with); *State v. Ciaccio*, 112 So. 486 (La. 1927) (upholding the lower court's decision that the testimony offered by the defendant pertaining to his character should be excluded because the witness had never heard the defendant's character being discussed in the community).
6. **Character witness improperly cross-examined**: *State v. Marquer*, 446 So. 2d 1258 (La. Ct. App. 4th Cir. 1984) (holding that the State improperly questioned defendant's character witness in the form of, "would it surprise you to learn," instead of "have you heard"; however, only when improper questioning of the character witness prejudices the defendant will the defendant's conviction be overturned); *State v. Anderson*, 784 So. 2d 666 (La. Ct. App. 1st Cir. 2001) (holding that the testimony of the State's witness was not admissible when the witness stated on direct examination that he saw the defendant intoxicated on a prior occasion).
7. **Defining character and how proven**: *Michelson v. U.S.*, 345 U.S. 469 (1948) (for an excellent discussion of the definition of character and how proven).

8. **Character witness properly cross-examined**: *State v. Dauzat*, 590 So. 2d 768 (La. Ct. App. 3d Cir. 1991) (holding that the question asked to the witnesses whether they had heard anybody in the community talking about the defendant taking money from an insurance company on cross-examination by the prosecution was properly asked); *State v. Warner*, 116 So. 3d 811 (La. Ct. App. 4th Cir. 2013) (holding that the court properly allowed defendant's good character witness to be cross-examined about knowledge of defendant's prior arrests).
9. **Defendant improperly put character at issue (specific instances):** *State v. Murray*, 827 So. 2d 488 (La. Ct. App. 2d Cir. 2002) (not allowing the defendant to show an exhibit with pictures of him participating in extracurricular activities with his children because they are considered specific acts); *State v. Harmon,* 448 So. 2d 264 (La. Ct. App. 3d Cir. 1984) (not allowing the victim's brother to answer whether or not his brother had been convicted of a crime because it referred to a specific act and not general reputation); *State v. Hughes*, 841 So. 2d 718 (La. 2003) (not allowing defendant to offer testimony of a psychologist to testify that defendant did not have psychology of sexual predator; holding that defendant must prove character by general reputation in the community).
10. **Defendant inadvertently put character at issue, opening the door**: *State. v. Warner*, 116 So. 3d 811 (La. Ct. App. 4th Cir. 2013) (holding that in prosecution for second-degree murder, defendant put his character at issue by opening the door when a character witness testified that defendant was a "good quality person"); *State v. Robinson*, 33 So. 3d 1019 (La. App. 4th Cir. 2010) (holding that statement of character witness for defendant saying that she knew the defendant to do odd jobs around the community for neighbors and run errands for them allowed State to ask questions pertaining to the defendant's prior criminal convictions because the defense opened the door on examination of the character witness); *State v. Hurst*, 828 So. 2d 1165 (La. App. Ct. 4th Cir. 2002) (holding that defense opened the door by asking the defendant's mother whether she knew her son to be a violent person; the State was then able to ask questions pertaining to the defendant's prior arrests for armed robbery); *State v. Singletary*, 461 So. 2d 481 (La. Ct. App. 3d Cir. 1984) (holding that the prosecution's rebuttal was proper because the accused put his own character at issue when his counsel cross-examined his girlfriend and roommate about his temper); *State v. Norfleet*, 721 So. 2d 506 (La. Ct. App. 4th Cir. 1998) (holding that the accused put his own character at issue when his character witnesses testified on direct examination by the defense counsel that the defendant was obedient, willing to learn, truthful, and very respectful, and therefore the prosecution could bring up specific instances of conduct on cross-examination); *State v. Francis*, 2011-1082 La. App. 4 Cir. 11/7/12, 2012 WL 6619022 (La. Ct. App. 4th Cir. 2012) (holding that defendant's good character witness put defendant's character at issue by testifying that defendant "didn't get into trouble" as a child).
11. **Sufficient foundation to testify to reputation in community:** *State v. Clark*, 402 So. 2d 684 (La. 1981) (upholding the trial court's verdict that stated that the parish, other than the one the defendant lived in, was a substantial community of people to whom the victim was well known).
12. **Federal Rules of Evidence on use of "Did you know":** Fed. R. Evid. 405 Advisory Committee Notes stating that "the opinion witness would be asked 'whether he knew,'" as well as 'whether he had heard'"; *U.S. v. Scholl*, C.A.9 (Ariz.) 1999, 166 F.3d 964, amended on denial of rehearing, certiorari denied 120 S. Ct. 176, 528 U.S. 873, 145 L.Ed.2d 149 (Use of "Did you know ... ?" form of question instead of "Have you heard ... ?" in cross-examination of character witnesses was proper).

§ 6.4 Character Essential Element [La. C.E. arts. 405(A) and (B)]

Applicable Code Article

Art. 405. Methods of proving character

A. Reputation. Except as provided in Article 412, in all cases in which evidence of character or a trait of character of a person is admissible, proof may be made by testimony as to general reputation only. On cross-examination of the character witness, inquiry is allowable into relevant specific instances of conduct.

B. Specific instances of conduct. In cases in which character or a trait of character of a person is an essential element of a charge, claim, or defense, such as in a prosecution for defamation or when there is a defense of entrapment, proof may also be made of specific instances of his conduct.

* * *

Article 405(B) provides that in cases in which character or a trait of character of a person is an **essential element of a charge, claim, or defense**, proof of character may be made, not only by evidence of the person's reputation in the community, but may also be proven by **specific instances of conduct**. Character is an essential element of a claim, charge, or defense when the existence or nonexistence of the character trait determines the **rights and liabilities of the parties**.[24] Common claims and defenses in which character is an essential element include prosecution for defamation, defense of entrapment, negligent entrustment cases, and child custody cases. For example, in a child custody case each parent's character is at issue because the judge must determine the *kind* of person each parent is as she decides who is better suited to have custody of the child. In such a case, the existence or nonexistence of the character trait itself, determines the rights of the parties. Thus, the judge would not only be able to consider the fact that a parent has a reputation for being irresponsible, he could also consider evidence that the parent has abused the child on several occasions—specific instances of conduct that directly bear on the parent's fitness to be the custodial parent.

Character is an essential element of only a few rare charges, claims, or defenses as listed above. The cases below demonstrate how character is presented as an essential element of a claim or defense.

Defamation. A claim in which character is an essential element is in a libel case where truth of the statement is an absolute defense. For example, if a newspaper published a story stating that a company CEO was a womanizer, and maintains as their defense that the statement is true, they may prove their defense by offering evidence of specific instances of conduct showing that the plaintiff is in fact a womanizer. In such a case, the plaintiff's character, whether he is a womanizer, is an element of the defense in that it will determine the liability of the parties, and thus may be proven by specific instances of contact. So, in the newspaper's defense, it would be able to offer evidence, for example, that the com-

24. *See* Schafer v. Time, 142 F.3d 1361 (U.S. Ct. App. 11th Cir. 1998).

pany CEO had been sued for sexual harassment, and had been publicly accused of an affair, specific instances of conduct, to prove that the CEO was, in fact, a womanizer.

Additionally, in a defamation case, the plaintiff typically seeks to recover for damage to his reputation. In such a case, specific instances of conduct could be offered by the defendant to show the plaintiff's reputation was bad, for example, before the statement was made—thus placing the plaintiff's character at the center of the issue. The court in *Shaffer* below, explains how specific instances of conduct may be used in such a way to overcome a claim for damages to a person's reputation.

Case on Character as an Essential Element

Schafer v. Time, Inc.
U.S. Court of Appeals, Eleventh Circuit
142 F.3d 1361
June 8, 1998

BIRCH, Circuit Judge.

On December 21, 1988, Pan Am Flight 103 exploded in mid-flight over Lockerbie, Scotland, causing the death of everyone on board. A terrorist's bomb was then, and is now, widely suspected to be the source of that explosion. On April 20, 1992, defendant-appellee, Time, Inc. ("Time"), published a cover story entitled "The Untold Story of Pan Am 103." The article purported to debunk the then-prevailing theory that the government of Libya had sponsored the attack on Pan Am 103. Instead, the article posited that a Palestinian group, with connections to Syrian drug traffickers, had targeted Pan Am 103 to eliminate several of the passengers who were members of a United States counter terrorism team attempting to rescue United States hostages in Lebanon. The article claims that these passengers had discovered an unsavory, covert relationship between the Syrian drug traffickers and a unit of the United States Central Intelligence Agency and intended to expose it upon their return to the United States.

The article further stated that an American agent, David Lovejoy, had become a double agent and had leaked information regarding the team's travel plans to forces hostile to the United States. The article included a photograph of a man identified by the following caption:

> David Lovejoy, a reported double agent for the U.S. and Iran, is alleged to have told Iranian officials that McKee [one of the U.S. agents] was booked on Flight 103.

The article went on to imply that the information Lovejoy disclosed to hostile forces led to the attack on Pan Am 103.

The photograph in question apparently became associated with the Pam Am 103 bombing in connection with a civil case filed by the families of the Pan Am 103 victims. The families' law suit claimed that Pan Am had failed to take adequate security precautions to prevent the bombing. One of Pan Am's lawyers in that case, James Shaughnessy, filed a sworn affidavit that contained a variety of assertions about the attack that he hoped to explore through discovery in the Pan Am litigation. Shaughnessy's affidavit alleged that unnamed sources had identified Lovejoy, the double agent whose treachery facilitated the attack on Pan Am 103, as the man in an attached photograph. The man in the photograph, however, is Michael Schafer, the plaintiff-appellant in this case. Time's article, therefore, erroneously identified Schafer, then working in his family's janitorial business in Austell, Georgia, both as a traitor to the United States government and a player in the bombing of Pan Am 103.[25]

Upon discovering his picture in the magazine, Schafer demanded and eventually received a retraction from Time. Schafer filed suit against Time, making claims under Georgia's libel laws. A jury returned a verdict in Time's favor, finding no liability for the error. After filing a motion for a new trial, which the district court denied, Schafer filed this timely appeal....

DISCUSSION

...

II. Evidentiary Issues

Schafer also argues that the district court committed reversible error by permitting Time's counsel to question Schafer regarding a number of "specific acts of misconduct" during cross-examination and by excluding from evidence a memorandum discussing the credibility of Time's sources for the Pan Am 103 article....

A. *Specific Acts of Misconduct*

Evidence of a person's character is viewed with some suspicion under the law and generally is disfavored in the Federal Rules of Evidence. *See* Fed.R.Evid. 404 (character evidence generally inadmissible to prove conforming conduct). In an action for defamation or libel, however, the issue of the plaintiff's reputation and character scarcely can be avoided because the plaintiff typically seeks to recover compensation for damage to his or her reputation. Even in such cases, however, the rules of evidence prescribe particular methods for broaching the issue of character. *See* Fed.R.Evid. 405 ("Methods of Proving Character").

Before trial, the district court instructed the parties that Time would not be permitted to introduce and explore a number of specific acts and events in Schafer's life as they were irrelevant to the issues before the jury. At that time, however, the district court warned both parties that the court would revisit the character issue to the extent that particular acts and events were shown to be relevant to the question of damages or how Schafer's picture might have become associated with the Pan Am case. During the course of the trial, the district court made a preliminary ruling permitting Time to explore selective incidents and acts in Schafer's background but excluding evidence of others. Specifically, the district court ruled that Time would be permitted to question Schafer about a felony conviction, a possible violation of his subsequent parole, convictions for driving under the influence, an arrest for writing a bad check, failure to file tax returns, failure to pay alimony and child support, and evidence concerning Schafer's efforts to change his name and social security number.[26] Schafer attacks the district court's ruling and argues that these specific acts were inadmissible.

The Federal Rules of Evidence detail the circumstances under which character evidence is admissible and the methods available for presenting such evidence. In all cases in which

25. The record in this case provides no definitive explanation of how Shaughnessy obtained Schafer's picture or how Schafer became identified as David Lovejoy. At trial, Schafer speculated that Lester Coleman, named as a source in the Time article, provided the picture to Pan Am's team of investigators and lawyers. Schafer worked with Coleman in Beirut, Lebanon in 1985, when they were both employed by the Christian Broadcast Network, and testified that he provided Coleman with a number of pictures of himself in the course of his employment there.

26. Schafer changed his name from Michael Franks at the age of 32 when he discovered that he had never legally been adopted. *See* R21 at 4–5. The issue was relevant at trial because "Michael Franks" was one of Lovejoy's purported aliases.

character evidence is admissible, a party may offer reputation or opinion testimony on the issue of a person's character. *See* Fed. R. Evid. 405(a). Only in cases in which a person's character is "an essential element of a charge, claim or defense," however, may a party offer evidence of specific instances of conduct. *See* Fed.R.Evid. 405(b).[27]

Character evidence does not constitute an "essential element" of a claim or charge unless it alters the rights and liabilities of the parties under the substantive law.... Our determination of whether character constitutes an essential element requires us to examine the "authoritative statutory or common law statement of the elements of the prima facie case and defenses." *Keiser,* 57 F.3d at 856 n. 20.[28] The advisory committee's notes to the Federal Rules of Evidence provide two examples in which character evidence constitutes such an essential element: "[1] the chastity of a victim under a statute specifying her chastity as an element of the crime of seduction, or [2] the competency of the driver in an action for negligently entrusting a motor vehicle to an incompetent driver." ... In addition to these examples, a charge of defamation or libel commonly makes damage to the victim's reputation or character an essential element of the case.... Georgia law confirms that an assertion of damage to reputation in a libel case makes the plaintiff's character an issue under the substantive law.... Since the plaintiff's character is substantively at issue in a libel case under Georgia law, Rule 405(b) permits the admission of evidence regarding specific instances of the plaintiff's conduct on that issue.[29] ... Given the plain language of Rule 405(b), Schafer's arguments that specific acts remain inadmissible to prove character in an action for libel are unpersuasive.

For the sake of completing the analysis, however, we note that even though evidence of specific acts is admissible to prove character in a libel case under Rule 405(b), a district court must still determine whether such acts pass muster under Federal Rule of Evidence 401 (relevance) and Federal Rule of Evidence 403 (prejudice).... The district court's decision to admit the evidence at issue here cannot be said to constitute an abuse of discretion under these rules.

Accordingly, we find no error in Time's exploration of these and other issues of character during its cross-examination of Schafer. To the extent that Time strayed from the specific issues of character enumerated in the district court's preliminary ruling, including Time's questions regarding Schafer's work for *Soldier of Fortune* magazine,[30] Time's questions fell

---

27. The advisory committee notes to Rule 405 provide some insight as to the rule's limitations on the use of specific acts to prove character:

> Of the three methods of proving character provided by the rule, evidence of specific instances of conduct is the most convincing. At the same time it possesses the greatest capacity to arouse prejudice, to confuse, to surprise, and to consume time. Consequently the rule confines the use of evidence of this kind to cases in which character is, in the strict sense, in issue and hence deserving of a searching inquiry.

28. As the *Keiser* court noted, this inquiry is a legal rather than factual one, *see Keiser,* 57 F.3d at 856 n. 20, and as a result, our review of the district court's decision on this matter is *de novo. Id.* at 852 n. 6.

29. Schafer's argument that this analysis puts "the horse before the cart" because Rule 404 governs the question of whether character evidence is admissible is unavailing. Rule 404 forbids the use of character evidence to prove "action in conformity therewith on a particular occasion," or as the advisory committee's notes describe it, the "circumstantial" use of character evidence. *See* Fed.R.Evid. 404(a) adv. comm. notes. Rule 404 does not bar the admission of character evidence when character or a particular character trait is actually at issue. *Id.* Rule 404 permits the character evidence in dispute here, and Rule 405 governs the acceptable methods for introducing it.

30. It strikes us that the district court could have permitted Time to challenge Schafer's direct testimony about his travels and work history without reference to the name of this particular publication,

within the scope of Federal Rules of Evidence 405(a) and 608(b).[31] We cannot say that the district court's decisions on these matters rose to the level of an abuse of discretion, nor can we say that Schafer suffered a "substantial prejudicial effect." ...

...

CONCLUSION

... We find no error in the district court's decision to admit specific instances of conduct to prove character under Federal Rule of Evidence 405(b) and its decision to exclude the Pondisco memorandum under Federal Rule of Evidence Rule 403....

Discussion Questions

1. Explain how using character evidence to prove "action in conformity therewith on a particular occasion" is regarded as "circumstantial" use of character evidence. What does that mean, and how does it differ from the way the evidence is used in *Shaffer*?
2. Specific instances of conduct offered should go the pertinent character trait. Do the specific instances of Lovejoy's background that *Time* delved into go to the heart of the character trait at issue? In other words, do they actually show that the plaintiff's reputation was not damaged or less damaged by the publication in the way that Lovejoy claims his reputation was damaged?
3. Should a proponent of bad acts evidence offered to rebut a claim of damage to reputation have to show that the general public actually *knew* of those bad acts? In other words, does the fact that Lovejoy had prior misconduct (a DWI and felony conviction, a parole violation, an arrest for writing a bad check, failure to file tax returns and to pay alimony and child support), mean his reputation had not been damaged by the *Time* publication? What if no one knew of the prior misconduct? Should *Time* be required to show that the prior bad acts were generally known in order to make them relevant to the issue of Lovejoy's reputation prior to the publication?
4. The court points out that specific instances of conduct are indeed more convincing in proving a person's character than evidence of general reputation. For example, evidence that a person has a reputation for being honest is not nearly as persuasive as evidence that the person once found $5,000 in a wallet in the park and returned it to the owner. In situations in which character evidence may be offered, why do you think such evidence may not be proven by specific instances of conduct, and thus, be more convincing?

Defense of Entrapment

Article 405(B) specifically refers to the defense of entrapment as another instance in which the defendant's character is an essential element of the defense,[32] and as such, proof of the defendant's character may be proven by both general reputation in the community as well as by specific instances of conduct. As discussed below in *State v. Taylor*,[33] when a

---

the variable to which Schafer apparently attaches prejudice. Given the parties' failure to suggest such an option, however, we cannot find that the district court abused its discretion in this matter.

31. Rule 405(a) permits cross examination regarding specific instances of conduct when character evidence is admissible. Rule 608(b) permits cross-examination regarding specific instances of conduct to attack the credibility of a witness.

32. La. Code Evid. art. 405(B).

33. State v. Taylor, 888 So. 2d 272 (La. Ct. App. 5th Cir. 2004).

defendant raises an entrapment defense, he claims that he would not have committed the crime charged had it not been for the inducement of the state agent. Thus, he's stating that he was not predisposed to commit the crime, i.e., that he did not have the *propensity* to commit it.

In rebuttal, the prosecution must prove that the defendant was, in fact, predisposed to or had the propensity to commit the criminal act, even without the government involvement. Thus, the defendant's character, his criminal propensity, is an element of the defense. The defendant's rights are dependent upon the existence or nonexistence of the of the character trait. As such, it may be proven by specific instances of conduct, namely through the defendant's past criminal history of committing similar criminal acts.[34] A defendant's past criminal acts can show that the defendant was, in fact, predisposed to commit the crime, even without the government involvement.

State v. Taylor

Court of Appeal of Louisiana, Fifth Circuit
888 So. 2d 272
Oct. 26, 2004

THOMAS F. DALEY, Judge.

On July 16, 2001, at approximately 2:00 p.m., Agent Robin Jones was working undercover in the area of the Acre Road Housing Project in Marrero attempting to purchase narcotics from "anyone that was willing to sell it." Agent Jones stopped at a store on Acre Road and met a man later identified as the defendant. Agent Jones asked the defendant for "two 20s," street slang for two rocks of crack cocaine. The defendant stated he wanted the money up front and requested a ride from Agent Jones. Agent Jones refused both requests. The defendant then instructed Agent Jones to meet him at a different location approximately two blocks away. When Agent Jones met the defendant at the location, the defendant directed her to Betty Street. Once on Betty Street, Agent Jones handed the defendant the money and the defendant gave her two off-white rock-like objects. A field test performed on the objects immediately after the transaction was negative for cocaine.

The entire transaction was captured on videotape. The videotape was reviewed by Sergeant Joe Williams who recognized the defendant as the perpetrator of the offense. A photographic lineup was prepared and shown to Agent Jones who positively identified the defendant as the person who sold her the alleged cocaine.

DISCUSSION

In his sole Assignment of Error, the defendant argues that the trial court erred in denying his Motion in Limine to exclude the defendant's prior criminal history.

A trial court's ruling on the admissibility of evidence of other crimes will not be disturbed absent an abuse of discretion. LSA–C.E. art. 404(B)(1) states in pertinent part that:

> Except as provided in Article 412, evidence of other crimes, wrongs, or acts is not admissible to prove the character of a person in order to show that he acted in conformity therewith. It may, however, be admissible for other purposes, such as proof of motive, opportunity, intent, preparation, plan, knowledge, identity, absence of mistake or accident ...

---

34. *See* State v. Taylor, 888 So. 2d 272 (La. Ct. App. 5th Cir. 2004).

The admissibility of such evidence is determined by:

First, whether the evidence at issue has some independent relevance or is an element of the crime charged. *State v. Dickerson,* 772 So.2d at 851.

Second, whether the State has met the requirement to prove the defendant committed these other acts by clear and convincing evidence. *Id.*

Third, whether even though independently relevant the evidence's probative value is substantially outweighed by the dangers of unfair prejudice, confusion of the issues, misleading of the jury, or by considerations of undue delay, or waste of time. *Id.*

Finally, the *Prieur* requirements must be met under which the State must provide written notice of its intent to use other acts or crimes evidence, describe these acts in sufficient detail within a reasonable time before trial, and specify the exception to the general exclusionary rule for the admissibility of the evidence....

In the present case, on the day of trial, the defendant filed a Motion in Limine in which he sought to exclude any evidence of his prior criminal history in case he pursued an entrapment defense. A hearing on the motion was held prior to trial. Specifically, the defendant sought to exclude a 1989 conviction for possession of heroin and a 1995 conviction for distribution of cocaine3. During the hearing, the defense counsel admitted that the State would be required to show the defendant had a predisposition to commit the crime should the defendant present an entrapment defense. However, the defense counsel argued that the prior convictions were too remote to be of any probative value regarding his predisposition to commit the presently alleged crime occurring on July 16, 2001, and should be inadmissible because they lacked similar character to the charged offense of knowingly and intentionally distributing a substance falsely represented to be counterfeit Cocaine.

During the hearing, the State argued that if the defendant presented an entrapment defense showing by a preponderance of the evidence that there was State inducement to commit the charged offense, then the State should be allowed to present any relevant arrests and convictions showing the defendant's predisposition to commit this type of crime. The State argued that both of the defendant's prior convictions were similar in character to the present crime, because they all involved distribution of drugs. The State noted that while the defendant pled guilty in 1989 to possession of heroin, he was initially arrested and charged with distribution of heroin....

... Nevertheless, the State contends that the trial court properly denied the Motion in Limine, because the evidence of defendant's criminal history would have been admissible to show the defendant's predisposition to commit the charged crime, if the defendant raised an entrapment defense.

The Sixth Amendment of United States Constitution and the Louisiana Constitution, Article I § 16 (1974) guarantees a criminal defendant the right to present a defense. *State v. Lewis.* The focal point of inquiry with an entrapment defense is the predisposition of the defendant to commit the crime, as well as the conduct of the police. *Id.* The entrapment occurs when a law enforcement official or a person cooperating with the official solicits, encourages, or otherwise induces another person to commit an offense when he is not then otherwise predisposed in order to obtain evidence of the commission of an offense. *Id.* That is, a defendant must be induced in some way to commit a criminal act, which he otherwise would not otherwise commit. *Id.* It is not entrapment, if the officers or its agents have merely furnished a defendant predisposed to commit the crime with the opportunity. *Id.* In order to prevail in an entrapment defense, the defendant must prove an inducement by a State agent to commit an offense, and the lack of predisposition to commit the offense on the part of the defendant. *Id.* Upon raising an entrapment defense, the burden of proof is on the defendant to show by a preponderance of evidence that a State agent induced him to commit a crime. *Id.* The burden then shifts to the State to prove beyond a reasonable doubt that the defendant was predisposed to commit the crime prior to the State's involvement. *Id.* The Louisiana Supreme Court recognized that, if a defendant chooses to pursue an entrapment defense, evidence of his other criminal activity may be relevant in determining whether he had a predisposition to commit the present crime. *State v. Batiste*, 363 So. 2d 639, 642 (La. 1978). Before such evidence of other criminal activity may be admissible, it must first be clear that the defendant will invoke the entrapment defense. Id., at 643. If the defendant raises an entrapment defense, the State can utilize evidence of prior crimes of similar character to prove predisposition. *Id.* Even if the evidence is relevant to the defendant's predisposition to commit a crime, it should be excluded, if its prejudicial effect outweighs its probative value. *Id.*

...

In the instant case, the defendant never raised an entrapment defense, but rather sought to exclude convictions that occurred twelve and almost six years prior to the current offense, just in case he chose to raise the defense.

... The trial court found that after removing the periods of time in which he was incarcerated, the defendant's prior convictions in 1989 and 1995 were not too remote.

... Since, the defendant has raised his objection to the alleged periods of incarceration presented by the State for the first time on appeal, there is no ruling for this court to review. Therefore, based on the record, the trial court did not abuse its discretion in denying the Motion in Limine prior to trial.

... The defendant was not prevented from presenting an entrapment defense, but rather chose not to for apparently tactical reasons. ... The trial court's ruling simply allowed the State the ability upon the defendant's presentation of an entrapment defense to rebut the defendant's claim of entrapment by showing his predisposition to commit the crime through his past criminal history. We find no legal error in the trial court's ruling.

...

SENTENCE AFFIRMED; MATTER REMANDED.

Discussion Questions

1. Why is a defendant's character directly at issue when pursuing an entrapment defense? Explain.
2. How does a defendant's prior criminal history refute the entrapment defense?
3. Obviously, not all prior criminal acts will be relevant or probative of whether a defendant has the propensity to commit a particular crime at hand. How should a court determine which prior offenses are relevant to determining a defendant's predisposition to commit a particular crime?
4. Louisiana courts have recognized that even in this context, evidence of past criminal acts has the potential for unfair prejudice. As a result, the court has developed safeguards governing the admissibility of other crimes in this context. What are those safeguards?
5. What factors should be considered in determining the prejudicial effect of prior criminal acts when considered for an entrapment defense? What factors should be considered in determining the probative value of the prior criminal acts?

Key Points

The key points to keep in mind regarding character as an essential element.

1. When character is an essential element of the charge, claim, or defense, proof may be made by both: 1) reputation in the community; and 2) specific instances of conduct.
2. The existence or nonexistence of the character trait affects the rights and liabilities of the parties.
3. Examples of claims, charges, or offenses where character is at issue include: prosecution for defamation, defense of entrapment, child custody cases, negligent hiring.

Problems on Character as an Essential Element

PROBLEM 6-17. Sister Watson accused her mega-church pastor, Bishop T.P. Mills, of sexually assaulting her during a spiritual counseling session, which she claims led to an ongoing nonconsensual affair between the two of them as she claims she feared retaliation if she refused his advances. The church's Board of Directors conducted a thorough investigation with plans of possible removal of Bishop Mills if the allegations were confirmed. Numerous witnesses in the church were interviewed by investigators and the incident received national media coverage. At the conclusion of the investigation, no charges were filed against Bishop Mills. After the investigation concluded, Bishop Mills brought an action for slander against Sister Watson seeking to recover for damages to his reputation in the church and nationally. In the trial, Sister Watson would like to offer evidence that Bishop Mills, who is married, is known in the church for being a promiscuous womanizer, and for having fathered four illegitimate children by three different women in the church. How should the court rule on the admissibility of the evidence?

PROBLEM 6-18. Mike was killed in a car accident when the vehicle he was driving was negligently struck by an 18-wheeler. Mike was killed on impact. Mike's wife, Mary Ann, has filed a wrongful death lawsuit against the driver and his employer. Mary Ann seeks damages for loss of consortium, including loss of love and affection, society, and companionship. In response, the company would like to introduce evidence that Mike was a very despondent and dismissive husband, who was actually quite aloof, to address the damages that Mary Ann claims to have suffered by Mike's death. Mary Ann objects. How should the court rule and why?

PROBLEM 6-19. Kenny and Amanda Stalling are in litigation for the custody of their five-year-old daughter Miranda. Kenny is a teacher, and a couple of years before Miranda was born, Kenny was fired from his job teaching at a local high school after he was arrested and convicted of battery against one of his students. During the custody litigation for Miranda, Amanda would like to offer evidence of the prior battery charge as well as evidence that Kenny was fired from his job around young kids because of the charge and subsequent conviction. Should the court allow Amanda's lawyer to introduce the evidence during the proceedings to show Kenny's fitness to have custody of their daughter?

PROBLEM 6-20. Bob hires Danielle to work at his house cleaning company. Bob had been notified by one of Danielle's previous employers that Danielle had four prior convictions of theft and embezzlement of company funds that occurred within the last two years. Bob hired Danielle anyway because she was cheap labor. Shortly after Danielle was hired, several pieces of expensive jewelry were reported missing from one of Bob's client's houses that Danielle had cleaned. It was later discovered that Danielle had pawned the missing jewelry the same day that she cleaned the client's house. In an action against Bob by the client for negligent hiring, will his knowledge of Danielle's prior convictions be admissible? Why or why not?

PROBLEM 6-21. Ron and Harold both had sons on the peewee baseball team. Ron sued Harold for slander after Ron volunteered to be the head coach, and Harold told all the parents at a team meeting that Ron was abusive to children and often used foul language. Harold maintains as his defense that the statements he made about Ron are true. To prove his defense, Harold would like to offer evidence that Ron was arrested for child abuse last year. He would also like to call a coach from last season to testify to language Ron used around the kids. Ron objects that the specific instances of conduct are not admissible. What ruling?

§ 6.4 References and Additional Authority on Character as an Essential Element [La. C.E. arts. 405(A) and (B)]

1. La. C.E. arts. 405(A), 405(B) and Official Comments
2. Force & Rault, Handbook on Louisiana Evidence Law Arts. 405(A), (B) Author's Comments (West Publishing 2014)
3. Harges & Jones, Louisiana Evidence Arts. 405(A), (B) Author's Comments (West Publishing 2014)
4. 19 La. Civ. L. Treatise, Evidence And Proof § 5.2 (2nd ed.)
5. **Standard of proof for entrapment defense:** *State v. Batiste*, 363 So. 2d 639 (La. 1978) (providing that evidence is not admissible unless it has been demonstrated clearly that the entrapment defense will be invoked; also requiring that it be of similar character, not too remote in time, and admitted subject to a 403 balancing test); *State v. Taylor*, 888 So. 2d 272 (La. Ct. App. 5th Cir. 2004) (requiring proof by clear and convincing evidence of the prior offense, and subject to safeguards of *State v. Prieur*, 277 So. 126 (La. 1973), and 403 balancing).
6. **Character essential element in child custody case:** *Fernandez v. Pizzalato*, 902 So. 2d 1112 (La. Ct. App. 4th Cir. 2005) (holding that in a child custody case in which the mother sought a change of custody, evidence of the defendant's arrest record that contained a DWI should have been admitted into evidence because it showed that living with the defendant was not in the best interest of the child); *L.E.P.S. v. R.G.P.*, 11 So. 3d 633 (La. Ct. App. 3d Cir. 2009) (holding that evidence of father's arrest for drug use and carnal knowledge of juvenile relevant in child custody case).
7. **Good moral character essential to admission to the bar:** *Ex Parte Minor*, 280 So. 2d 217 (La. 1973) (Two applicants were denied admission to the Bar for failure to sign a waiver of their confidentiality. Applicants must produce satisfactory evidence of good moral character. The applicants stated that the admissions committee lacked the statutory authority to look through their records, at any given time. The court stated that the Committee has an obligation to inquire into the moral character of the applicants and affirmed the denial of the applications.); *See also* Supreme Court Rule

XVII, § 5(B) ("The term 'good moral character' includes, but is not limited to, the qualities of honesty, fairness, candor, trustworthiness, observances of fiduciary responsibility and of the laws of the State of Louisiana and of the United States of America, and a respect for the rights of other persons." "In satisfying the requirements of good moral character and fitness, applicants should be persons whose record of conduct justifies the trust of clients, adversaries, courts and others with respect to the professional duties owed to them. A record manifesting a significant deficiency in the honesty, trustworthiness, diligence or reliability of an applicant may constitute a basis for denial of admission.").

8. **Character as essential element in negligent hiring cases:** *Corkern v. Smith*, 960 So. 2d 1152 (La. Ct. App. 3d Cir. 2007) (holding that state trooper's personnel file and other evidence of specific instances of conduct admissible in excessive force case where plaintiff claimed that State of Louisiana negligently hired state trooper).
9. **Character as essential element in defense of entrapment case:** *State v. Tate*, 593 So. 2d 864 (La. Ct. App. 2d Cir. 1992) (holding that the trial court, in a case where the defendant used the defense of entrapment, properly admitted the question to the witness of whether he had previously known the defendant to distribute narcotics); *State v. Konylis*, 12/27/13 (Not published) (holding that when the defendant claims the defense of entrapment, and on direct examination testifies that prior to the event in which he is now being accused he never wanted to sell drugs, the trial court properly allowed but limited the opposing attorney's argument to specific instances of conduct that negate that part of the defendant's conduct).
10. **Felon in possession of firearm:** *State v. Morvan*, 725 So. 2d 515 (La. Ct. App. 2 Cir. 1998) (holding that "evidence of defendant's previous conviction is admissible as proof of an essential element of the crime of illegal possession of firearm").

§ 6.5 Habit/Routine Practice [La. C.E. art. 406]

Applicable Code Article

Art. 406. Habit; routine practice; methods of proof

Evidence of the habit of a person or of the routine practice of an organization, whether corroborated or not and regardless of the presence of eyewitnesses, is relevant to prove that the conduct of the person or organization on a particular occasion was in conformity with the habit or routine practice. The evidence may consist of testimony in the form of an opinion or evidence of specific instances of conduct sufficient in number to warrant a finding that the habit existed or that the practice was routine.

Article 406 provides that evidence of a person's **habit** or of the **routine practice** of an organization may be offered to prove that the person or organization acted in conformity with the habit or routine practice on a particular occasion. The article applies to both the *habits* of a person as well as to the *routine practices* of businesses, and allows evidence of the habit or routine practice to be offered into evidence to prove what the person or business did on a particular occasion in which their conduct is in question. Such evidence is allowed, even though there were no witnesses to it or corroborating circumstances to support it. For example, if it is established that a person's habit is to always lock the door behind him when he enters his home, evidence of that habit may be offered to prove that he locked the door behind himself on the occasion in question. Similarly, if it is established that the business's routine practice is to always mail out orders on the same day the order is received, evidence of the routine practice may be offered to prove that on the particular occasion in question, the business acted in conformity with that routine practice, and mailed out the order on the same day it was received.

What is habit/routine practice? Habit has been defined as "a course of behavior of a person regularly repeated under like circumstances."[35] A person's habit is the way that the person invariably responds whenever he is confronted with the specific situation. For example, a person's habit might be that every time he gets into the car, he puts on his seatbelt, or every night before he goes to bed, he brushes his teeth. In each case, the conduct is practically a semi-automatic reflexive response whenever the person is confronted with the situation.

Thus, defining a person's habit would include words like "always," "invariably," "every time," "habitually," or "instinctively." A person's habit is *not* something that is done "often," "occasionally," "usually," "sometimes," or "frequently." The probative value of evidence of habit lies in the fact that the person's response invariably *always* occurs when the situation is presented.

The routine practice of an organization is the same. It is "a course of behavior of an organization or group of persons regularly repeated under like circumstances."[36] Like the habit of a person, the routine practice of a business is what the business does each and every time the situation is presented—mails out letters before 8 a.m., shreds sensitive documents, or gives each customer a receipt.

Habit v. Character. Habit is different from character. While character is a generalized description of a person's disposition, e.g., that the person is *scary,* a person's habit would be screaming whenever the lights go out. Screaming would be a person's automatic reflexive response to the situation of the lights going out. The Louisiana Second Circuit Court of Appeal explains the difference between the two by quoting evidence scholar Charles McCormick:

> Character and habit are close akin. Character is a generalized description of one's disposition, or of one's disposition in respect to a general trait, such as honesty, temperance, or peacefulness. "Habit," in modern usage, both lay and psychological, is more specific. It describes one's regular response to a repeated specific situation. If we speak of character for care, we think of the person's tendency to act prudently in all the varying situations of life, in business, family life, in handling automobiles and in walking across the street. A habit, on the other hand, is the person's regular practice of meeting a particular kind of situation with a specific type of conduct, such as the habit of going down a particular stairway two stairs at a time, or of giving the hand signal for a left turn, or of alighting from railway cars while they are moving. The doing of the habitual acts may become semi-automatic.[37]

In comparing the two, character is general and broad, e.g., that the person is a "careful or cautious driver," while evidence of habit is specific and invariable, e.g., that the person

---

35. Force & Rault, Handbook, art. 406, Author's note (1) (West Publishing 2013).

36. *Id.*

37. Stapleton v. Great Lakes Corporation, 616 So. 2d 1311, 1317–1318 (La. Ct. App. 2d Cir. 1993) *quoting* McCormick's Handbook of the Law of Evidence (2d ed. 1972) § 195, at 462–3.

"always drives the speed limit, stops at stop signs, or looks both ways before crossing the street."[38] While evidence of a person's character may not be used to infer the person's conduct on a particular occasion based on the kind of person he is, a person's habit may be used to infer the person's behavior on a particular occasion based on what he habitually does.

Offered to prove action in conformity on a particular occasion. Once it is established that a person has a particular habit, he is deemed to habitually and invariably act in accordance with that habit. Thus, evidence of a person's habit is relevant in inferring the person's behavior on a particular occasion when eyewitnesses or corroborating circumstances may not exist. So, a person may offer evidence of his habit of stopping at stop signs as evidence that on the particular occasion in question, he stopped at the stop sign, even though no one observed him doing it. Evidence of habit need not be corroborated by any additional facts or eyewitnesses to be admissible. If the habit is established, it may be offered as proof that it occurred on the occasion in question.

Similarly, if an issue arose as to whether a hospital did something on a particular occasion, such as sterilized equipment before using it on a patient, evidence that it is the hospital's routine practice to always sterilize equipment before it is used on a patient may be offered to prove that the business sterilized the equipment on the occasion in question. While evidence of habit or routine practice is admissible, it is not conclusive, and may be weighed with or counterbalanced by other available evidence.[39]

How habit/routine practice proven. Evidence to establish a habit or routine practice may consist of either: 1) testimony in the form of an opinion; or 2) evidence of specific instances of conduct sufficient in number to warrant a finding that the habit existed or that the practice was routine. Thus, one or more witnesses may testify that they have observed the person on several occasions doing the particular thing, and the court must determine whether the number of instances is sufficient to prove that the conduct is the person's habit or that the practice of the business is routine.

For example, if a person rode to work with someone every morning for two years, the driver would be able to testify to what the driver does every morning driving to work, such as stopping at all stop signs, taking a particular route, or putting on his seat belt. One or more witnesses testifying that the person or business always, or invariably responds to the situation in the particular way could prove that the habit or routine practice existed. However, evidence that the person or business "often" or "occasionally" did something would not be sufficient. For example, three DWI convictions would not prove a habit. A habit would be if *every* time the person left a particular bar he drove home intoxicated, not that on three occasions he drove home intoxicated.

Proof of habit/routine practice by opinion. The article also provides that a habit may be proven by a witness's *opinion* that the person had the relevant habit. The article does not authorize opinion testimony as to what the person *did* on the occasion in question, only his opinion as to whether the habit existed. When a person offers an opinion of a person's habit, a foundation must be laid to establish that the witness is competent to testify as to the habit or routine practice under the same foundational requirements for

---

38. *See* Stapleton v. Great Lakes Corporation, 627 So. 2d 1358 (La. 1993) (finding that evidence of driver's "two million miles of safe driving and awards from the National Safety Council" was character evidence rather than habit evidence).

39. *See* Force & Rault, HANDBOOK ON LOUISIANA EVIDENCE LAW, art. 406, Author's note (1) (West Publishing 2013); *See also* Brown v. Permanent General Ins. Co., 783 So. 2d 467 (La. Ct. App. 5th Cir. 2001).

all lay witness opinions under Article 701. The witness must be able to point to specific perceptions or observations of which he has first-hand knowledge upon which he based his opinion. For example, a person may testify that she has observed the woman always properly strapping her baby into the car seat before driving off, and as a result, it is her opinion that it is the woman's habit to always properly strap her baby into the car seat before driving away.

Corbello v. Southern Pacific Transportation Co.

Court of Appeal of Louisiana, Third Circuit
586 So. 2d 1383
Aug. 7, 1991

STOKER, Judge.

Paul and Dorothy Corbello seek damages for wrongful death in this suit. A train owned and operated by Southern Pacific Transportation Co. (defendant) struck the automobile driven by their daughter, Sabrina. Sabrina Corbello died as a result of the collision. The jury apportioned fault among the parties and held defendant had been 75% negligent and that the deceased girl had been 25% negligent. The jury awarded wrongful death damages to each parent in the amount of $250,000 and $75,000 for funeral and related expenses.

III.

Finally, we turn to the train engineer's alleged failure to blow the train's whistle to warn Sabrina of the train's approach. Under LSA-R.S. 32:168, a train must, on approaching at grade any street or highway crossing, sound a bell, whistle or horn for a distance of at least three hundred yards from the crossing. The purpose of this statute is to protect motorists who are traversing train crossings. Failure to comply with this statutory duty constitutes negligence....

At the trial, the members of the Southern Pacific train crew testified positively that the train whistle was sounded timely before the train reached the crossing. Two independent witnesses who were in close proximity to the crossing testified as witnesses for the defendant. Their testimony was positive and supported the testimony of the railroad crew. For the plaintiffs, numerous residents of the area of the crossing testified that the crews operating defendant's trains did not customarily sound the whistle when it approached the crossing.

Defendant's counsel objected to admission of the purely negative testimony of plaintiffs' witnesses to oppose the positive testimony of its own witnesses....

In support of the admissibility of the negative testimony, plaintiffs urge the applicability of Article 406 of the Louisiana Code of Evidence, relating to evidence of habit and routine practice. The article provides:

> "Evidence of the habit of a person or of the routine practice of an organization, whether corroborated or not and regardless of the presence of eyewitnesses, is relevant to prove that the conduct of the person or organization on a particular occasion was in conformity with the habit or routine practice. The evidence may consist of testimony in the form of an opinion or evidence of specific instances of conduct sufficient in number to warrant a finding that the habit existed or that the practice was routine."

We deem this article authorized the admission of the negative testimony of plaintiffs' witness on the issue of the sounding of the horn. As a legislative expression, it must be given effect over the jurisprudence cited on behalf of the defendant. This is particularly true when the text of Article 406 is viewed in light of the Author's Notes pertaining to the article, particularly paragraphs three, four and five of the notes. Inasmuch as we feel the negative testimony could properly be heard by the jury, the jury was entitled to accord to it whatever value it felt proper, even to the extent of rejecting the positive testimony to the contrary. In view of the fact that the jury answered the jury interrogatories to the effect that Southern Pacific was guilty of fault that was a cause in fact of the accident in the proportion of 75%, we must conclude that the jury found that the whistle was in fact not sounded. We may not disturb the finding.

...

AFFIRMED.

Discussion Questions

1. What does the court mean by "negative testimony"? Can you think of other examples of negative testimony of habit?
2. Do you believe the testimony here was sufficient to establish the negative habit? How many witnesses, or number of occasions, would you require to find that the habit existed?

Routine Practice of an Organization

Brandt v. Engle
Supreme Court of Louisiana
791 So. 2d 614
June 29, 2001

VICTORY, Judge.

Plaintiff, Shirley Brandt, was referred to defendant, Dr. Alan Engle, in August of 1993 for the treatment of corns on the second and fourth toes of her right foot.... Although Dr. Engle told her that surgery could alleviate her corns, she chose instead to continue conservative treatment at that time.

However, in August of 1994, Ms. Brandt returned to Dr. Engle and told him that she was about to lose her insurance coverage and wanted to have the surgery to relieve her corns. Dr. Engle performed arthroplasty surgery on Ms. Brandt's second and fourth toes of her right foot on August 26, 1994, and as a result of the surgery, Ms. Brandt developed "floppy toe," a condition in which she has no control over the toes on which Dr. Engle operated, and which prevents her from wearing high heels, causes pain, and prevents her from walking long distances. Ms. Brandt brought suit against Dr. Engle and Boston Old Colony Insurance Company alleging that had she been informed of the risk of developing "floppy toe" as a result of the surgery, she would not have consented to the surgery. She also alleged that she never consented to the surgery that was performed and only consented to having her bone shaved.

At trial, testimony conflicted as to whether Dr. Engle told Ms. Brandt that the surgery involved shaving of the bone or the removal of part of the bone of her toes. Ms. Brandt testified that Dr. Engle told her that he was going to make a little incision and shave the bones of her two toes in order to relieve the corns. Dr. Engle testified that he could not remember exactly what he told Ms. Brandt but that he followed his usual routine when discussing arthroplasty with her and that he had performed this procedure approximately 30 times per year since 1982. The trial court allowed Dr. Engle to testify that his usual routine was to show the patient a diagram with a chart of the foot, and describe the procedure, including informing the patient that he would make an incision over the toe and cut the tendon, then go down to the bone and take out a portion of the bone from the joint. He testified that he would also show the patient the amount of bone he would remove.

...

The jury found in favor of the defendants, finding specifically that Ms. Brandt consented to arthroplasty, rather than shaving of the bones, and that "floppy toe" was not a material risk of this procedure. The court of appeal reversed, finding that the trial court erred (1) in allowing Dr. Engle to testify as to his habit and routine in advising his patients about arthroplasty.... We granted defendants' writ application. *Brandt v. Engle,* 00–3416, 784 So.2d 652 (La.2/9/01).

DISCUSSION

... Plaintiff claims that although she signed an informed consent form which described the procedure as arthroplasty and removal of a bone, Dr. Engle verbally told her that he was going to shave the bone, a different procedure altogether. Thus, one of the main issues in the case was whether Dr. Engle misrepresented to Ms. Brandt that her surgery involved shaving the bone, and that her consent was induced by this misrepresentation. The trial court allowed Dr. Engle to explain to the jury his routine habit and practice in describing the arthroplasty surgery to his patients prior to surgery, which included testimony that he tells his patients that he will be removing a portion of the bone and shows them on a diagram how much bone he will be removing. Dr. Engle further testified that he never tells his arthroplasty patients that he will be merely shaving the bone.

Article 406 of the Louisiana Code of Evidence provides as follows:

> Evidence of the habit of a person or of the routine practice of an organization, whether corroborated or not and regardless of the presence of eyewitnesses, is relevant to prove that the conduct of the person or organization on a particular occasion was in conformity with the habit or routine practice. The evidence may consist of testimony in the form of an opinion or evidence of specific instances of conduct sufficient in number to warrant a finding that the habit existed or that the practice was routine.

Thus, under Art. 406, Dr. Engle's testimony was highly relevant to show that he routinely advises his arthroplasty patients that the surgery involves removing a bone in the toe and that his conduct with regard to Ms. Brandt was in conformity with this routine.

...

Discussion Questions

1. Do you find the evidence of the doctor's routine practice to be persuasive? How much weight do you believe the jury gives to such evidence?
2. Evidence of habit or routine practice is not conclusive, and may be weighed with or counterbalanced by other available evidence. Since there are typically no eyewitnesses or corroborating evidence that the person acted in conformity with the habit or routine practice on the occasion in question, what type of evidence could be offered in cases such as this to counterbalance the evidence offered?

Key Points

The key points to keep in mind regarding habit or routine practice.

1. Evidence of a person's habit or the routine practice of an organization may be offered to prove that the person acted in conformity with the habit, or the business acted in conformity with the routine practice on a particular occasion in question.
2. Habit relates to a person; routine practices relate to organizations.
3. **Habit is defined as:** a semi-automatic reflexive response every time the person is confronted with the situation, e.g., always fastens seatbelts, stops at railroad tracks, etc.

   Compared to character. Character is broad and general, i.e., a careful, cautious person. Habit is specific, i.e., a ways follows speed limit, stops at stop signs.
4. **Routine practice is defined as:** a course of behavior of an organization or group of persons regularly repeated uncer like circumstances, e.g., always gives customers receipts, always checks identification before selling alcoholic beverages, always mails notices, etc.
5. **Proof of a habit/routine practice** may be made by: 1) a sufficient number of instances to prove the habit or routine practice existed; or 2) opinion that the habit or routine practice existed, with proper foundation.
6. Once the habit or routine practice is established, evidence of it may be offered to prove that the person acted in conformity with the habit or routine practice on a particular occasion.
7. Need not have corroborating circumstances nor eyewitnesses to the habit or routine practice on the occasion in question.
8. Evidence of the habit or routine practice is not conclusive, and may be weighed with or counterbalanced by other available evidence.

Problems on Habit/Routine Practice

PROBLEM 6-22. Perrin was beaten by police officers following an encounter while police were investigating a hit and run. Perrin brought an action against the police force and city for damages. Defendants claim the plaintiff was the first aggressor and that they reasonably believed their life was in danger. At the trial, the defense seeks to introduce the testimony of four police officers to testify that they had been involved previously in violent encounters with Perrin. These officers plan to testify to Perrin's apparent hatred or fear of uniformed officers and his consistently violent response to any contact with them.

For example, defendants will present evidence that on one occasion he rammed his head into the bars and walls of his cell requiring administration of a tranquilizer. Another time while barefoot, Perrin kicked loose a porcelain toilet bowl that was bolted to the floor. One officer will testify that he encountered Perrin while responding to a public drunk call. He will testify that Perrin attacked him, and during the following struggle, Perrin tried to reach for his weapon. The officer and his back-up had to carry Perrin handcuffed, kicking and screaming, to the squad car, where Perrin then kicked the windshield out of the car. Another officer will testify that Perrin attacked him after Perrin was stopped at a vehicle checkpoint. During the ensuing struggle, three policemen were needed to subdue Perrin, including one 6' 2½" officer weighing 250 pounds, and one 6' 6½" officer weighing 350 pounds. Defendants seek to introduce this evidence to prove that Perrin was the first aggressor in the fight. The plaintiffs will offer no evidence of any peaceful encounter between Perrin and the police. Should the evidence be admissible to prove Perrin's habit? [See *Perrin v. Anderson*, 784 F. 2d 1040 (10th Cir. 1986).]

PROBLEM 6-23. Silvia has brought an action against Sunbelt Medical Health Clinic (SMHC) for breach of confidentiality of her medical records for improperly disposing of her medical records by throwing them away in the public dumpsters. The company would like to offer evidence that over the last five years since the clinic opened, it has routinely shredded its medical records as well as accounting and billing documents within 30 days of service, and only maintains electronic copies. Can SMHC offer evidence of this practice as proof that Silvia's medical records were shredded within 30 days of service in accordance with their practice? Explain.

PROBLEM 6-24. Donna has always taken her lunch break from 11:00 a.m.–12:00 noon at a café across the street from the courthouse for the two years that she has worked as a secretary there. One day, just before noon, a safe inside of the conference room was broken into and $5,000 was taken. Donna is accused of the crime because she knows the combination to the safe, needed the money, and bought a car right after the incident. Will Donna be able to offer evidence of her daily lunch routine as evidence that she was likely at lunch during the incident? Explain.

PROBLEM 6-25. Thomas is suing his fraternity for injuries he suffered during the initiation ritual that involved a great deal of strenuous physical activity and physical abuse. Thomas claims he was not made aware of the ritual when he decided to join the fraternity and would not have joined had he known about it. The fraternity offers evidence that it is the routine practice of the organization to discuss all of the initiation policies and procedures on permitted use of physical activity with new prospective members at the first interest meeting. They maintain that the evidence will help prove that Thomas was made aware of the policy and consented to taking part in the initiation procedures when he signed up. Should the evidence be admissible as the routine practice of the organization to prove that the organization covered the policies on use of physical force with Thomas at the first interest meeting? Explain.

PROBLEM 6-26. Monty is on trial for vehicular homicide after hitting a caravan that killed a baby properly fastened into his baby seat in the back of the vehicle. Monty was leaving a local bar when the accident occurred. The defendant offers testimony of Ralph, a witness from the bar to testify that Monty has given him a ride home on several occasions after a night of partying, and Monty usually does not drive drunk and is a very cautious driver. Will Ralph's testimony likely be admissible as evidence of habit? What about character? Explain.

PROBLEM 6-27. Nate is on trial for first-degree murder. He claims an intoxication defense. To bolster his defense, he seeks to have his girlfriend testify that it is very common that on the Saturday nights that Nate goes out, he usually gets drunk and high on cocaine. Should the court accept her testimony as sufficient to prove that it was Nate's habit to be drunk and high on the weekends to prove that he was likely drunk and high on the night of the incident in question? Why or why not? [See *State v. Davis*, 637 So. 2d 1012 (La. 1994).]

PROBLEM 6-28. Bubba is on trial for negligent homicide. Bubba has owned a local tire shop for forty years and has been accused of failing to tighten the lug nuts on Ms. Daisy's Cadillac, causing her tire to come off the car while speeding down the highway. After leaving the tire shop, Ms. Daisy hit a tree and died on impact. Chip, Bubba's assistant manager, is called to testify that with every balance and rotation they perform, he checks and then Bubba rechecks the tightness of all lug nuts. They don't remember Ms. Daisy's car, but they are sure they did this with her car. Will Chip's testimony be admissible to prove that they checked and rechecked the lug nuts on Ms. Daisy's Cadillac? Explain.

PROBLEM 6-29. From the list below, identify which evidence would be permissible character evidence, which would be evidence of habit, and which evidence would be neither character nor habit:

A. John is generally a good guy and an all-around helpful friend.
B. Willie gives $50.00 in tithes and offerings to his church every Sunday.
C. Kimberly is a nice and positive person.
D. Sandra is known in the community as an upstanding, law-abiding citizen.
E. Daniel is a loving, caring father to his three children.
F. Gia used to steal a pack of gum every now and then.
G. Jerry is very sneaky and sly.
H. Gibson pulls over to the side of the road every time he sees a police officer to allow the officer to pass him.
I. Gertrude is very spoiled.
J. People say that George is a crook.
K. Bob is very clumsy.
L. When Allen comes home in the evening, he always stops at the mailbox, gets the mail, pulls into the driveway and reads all of his mail before going into the house.
M. Roland tries to cook for his wife whenever he can.

PROBLEM 6-30. Robert owns a new construction company. He was only in business for two months when a family sued him for injuries sustained by their son when he used Robert's company ladder that was left at the residence to climb on top of the house, where he fell and broke his leg. Robert maintains that he is sure the ladder was removed from the house and placed on the ground because his company always removes upright ladders from houses before they leave the jobsite for the day and they walk around the house to double check before they leave. They've done this on every job they've had over the last couple months, a couple times per week. Can Robert offer evidence of this practice as proof that they removed the ladder from the house on the day in question and also walked around the house to double check before they left the premises that day? Why or why not?

PROBLEM 6-31. Terry is charged with armed robbery. Terry's lawyer calls a witness to the stand to testify that Terry is very rich and donates large amounts of money to the Salvation Army and other worthy causes to show that Terry does not need to steal. The prosecution objects to the line of questioning. Terry's lawyer claims the evidence is habit evidence. Is he correct? What ruling and why?

PROBLEM 6-32. Ivan, who's been driving buses for ten years, is charged with negligent homicide for the death of several passengers who were on his bus when it was hit by a train while Ivan was attempting to cross the tracks. At the trial, Ivan plans to call five witnesses to the stand who have ridden the bus on numerous occasions to testify that whenever they have been on the bus, Ivan always stopped at all railroad crossings and looked both ways before traveling over them as evidence that Ivan stopped at the railroad crossing and looked both ways before crossing on the day of the accident in question. The State objects to the witnesses' testimony. How will the court rule on the objection?

PROBLEM 6-33. Beth was seriously injured in a car accident when she was thrown from the car after her vehicle was struck by another car. Beth sued the driver of the car that hit her. In his defense, he would like to offer evidence that Beth had received four tickets for failure to wear a seatbelt in the last year to prove that Beth was likely not wearing her seatbelt when she was hit, to offset the amount of Beth's damages, for which he should be held liable. Will the tickets be admissible as evidence that it is Beth's habit not to wear her seatbelt? Why or why not?

PROBLEM 6-34. Jonathan, owner of Carat Jewelers, is being charged with selling counterfeit diamonds. Usually, he purchases and receives a large shipment of loose diamonds from Liberia. However, it was discovered that several customers had purchased counterfeit diamonds from Carat that were "Made in China." Jonathan says he was not aware that he was in possession of the counterfeit diamonds because he has only ever purchased diamonds from Liberia. At his trial, he plans to call his store manager, who purchases all diamonds for his store, to testify that in over five years since Carat Jewelers opened, they have only purchased diamonds from Liberia. Can Jonathan offer this evidence of his company's procedure for how they purchase diamonds to prove that they have only purchased diamonds from Liberia and not diamonds made in China? Explain.

PROBLEM 6-35. Marcus was arrested and charged with a burglary that occurred the previous Sunday at around at 2:00 p.m. Marcus would like to offer evidence that every Sunday for the last eight years when the home team has a home game, he attends the game. On the date of the burglary, the team played at home at noon, and Marcus claims he was at the game. Can Marcus introduce evidence that he always attends home games of his favorite team to show that he was at the game during the burglary? Why or why not?

PROBLEM 6-36. Maple purchased a used car from Bayou Self Car Sales. Maple had driven only 150 miles when the motor blew up. Maple brought an action against Bill Bayou to recover the cost of the vehicle under the vehicle's warranty. Bill Bayou, owner of Bayou Self, maintains that the vehicle was sold "as is." He plans to testify that he always routinely covers a list of items with each customer before leaving the premises that includes explaining that the vehicles are sold "as is" and that there are no warranties. He explains that he does this with each and every car sold, without exception, and even points out his company motto, "Once you leave the car lot, you are Bayou Self." Can Bill offer evidence that he routinely tells his customers that there are no warranties to prove that he told this to Maple when her car was purchased? Explain.

§ 6.5 References and Additional Authority on Habit and Routine Practice [La. C.E. art. 406]

1. La. C.E. arts. 404, 406 and Official Comments
2. Force & Rault, Handbook on Louisiana Evidence Law Arts. 404, 406 Author's Comments (West Publishing 2014)
3. Harges & Jones, Louisiana Evidence Arts. 404, 406 Author's Comments (West Publishing 2014)
4. 19 La. Civ. L. Treatise, Evidence And Proof § 5.2 (2nd ed.)
5. **Admitting evidence of routine practice:** *Spurrell v. Ivey*, 630 So. 2d 1378 (La. Ct. App. 2d Cir. 1994) (holding that it was the routine practice to always forward written notices to the insurer once information was received from the insured); *Brown v. Permanent Gen. Ins. Co.*, 783 So. 2d 467 (La. Ct. App. 5th Cir. 2001) (holding that the evidence presented by ABC was insufficient to prove that it was the routine practice of the business to immediately forward endorsements).

6. **Admitting evidence of habit:** *State v. Brown*, 395 So. 2d 1301 (La. 1981) (allowing the victim to testify that she had known for the defendant to carry a gun on his person wherever he went because this testimony constituted a habit of the defendant); *Boutte v. Kelly*, 863 So. 2d 530 (La. Ct. App. 4th Cir. 2003) (allowing habit testimony that the plaintiff's fiancée was wearing a seatbelt on the day of the accident; it was her habit to always wear a seatbelt).
7. **Insufficient number of instances to prove the habit or routine practice existed:** *State v. Martin*, 582 So. 2d 306 (La. Ct. App. 1 Cir. 1991) (holding that the two or three instances in which complaints were made against an agent were insufficient to prove that it was the agent's habit to be vulgar); *Chunn v. Brookshire Grocery Co.*, 18 So. 3d 179 (La. Ct. App. 2d Cir. 2009) (holding that photographs of store traffic on busy holiday weekend were insufficient to prove the routine traffic of the business); *Munar v. State Farm Ins. Co.*, 972 So. 2d 1273 (La. Ct. App. 3d Cir. 2007) (holding that evidence that truck driver had had several other accidents was insufficient to establish pattern of habit, so prior accident could not be offered to show inattention on occasion in question); *State v. Davis*, 637 So. 2d 1012 (La. 5/23/94) (holding that in first-degree murder prosecution evidence that defendant used cocaine and drank on weekends was insufficient to establish habit to bolster his intoxication defense); *State v. Adams*, 119 So. 3d 46 (La. Ct. App. 5th Cir. 2013) writ denied, 129 So. 3d 531 (La. 2013) (holding that one single incident of a detective obtaining a false confession by coercion was insufficient to establish that detective had a habit of obtaining false confessions by coercion).
8. **Distinguishing character from habit**: *State v. Stringer*, 949 So. 2d 464 (La. Ct. App. 3d Cir. 2006) (distinguishing character from habit evidence, the court held that "evidence of a father's domineering nature demonstrates a character trait of the father, and not necessarily a habit or specified, routine practice between the men"); *Stapleton v. Great Lakes Chemical Corp.*, 616 So. 2d 1311 (La. Ct. App. 2d Cir. 1993) (distinguishing character and habit, court found evidence of safe driving record was evidence of character rather than habit).

§6.6 Non-Conformity [La. C.E. art. 404(B)]

Applicable Code Article

Art. 404. Character evidence generally not admissible in civil or criminal trial to prove conduct; exceptions; other criminal acts

* * *

B. Other crimes, wrongs, or acts. (1) Except as provided in Article 412, evidence of other crimes, wrongs, or acts is not admissible to prove the character of a person in order to show that he acted in conformity therewith. It may, however, be admissible for other purposes, such as proof of motive, opportunity, intent, preparation, plan, knowledge, identity, absence of mistake or accident, provided that upon request by the accused, the prosecution in a criminal case shall provide reasonable notice in advance of trial, of the nature of any such evidence it intends to introduce at trial for such purposes, or when it relates to conduct that constitutes an integral part of the act or transaction that is the subject of the present proceeding.

(2) In the absence of evidence of a hostile demonstration or an overt act on the part of the victim at the time of the offense charged, evidence of the victim's prior threats against the accused or the accused's state of mind as to the victim's dangerous character is not admissible; provided that when the accused pleads self-defense and there is a history of assaultive behavior between the victim and the accused and the accused lived in a familial or intimate relationship such as, but not limited to, the husband-wife, parent-child, or concubinage relationship, it shall not be necessary to first show a hostile demonstration or overt act on the part of the victim in order to introduce evidence of the dangerous character of the victim, including specific instances of conduct and domestic violence; and further provided that an expert's opinion as to the effects of the prior assaultive acts on the accused's state of mind is admissible.

In § 6.1 we studied the non-conformity rule found in Article 404(A). The non-conformity rule generally precludes evidence of a person's character from being offered to prove that the person acted in conformity with a particular character trait on a particular occasion. Article 404(B) generally extends the non-conformity rule to also exclude evidence of **specific instances of conduct** from being offered against a person to prove he acted in conformity therewith. Article 404(B) specifically refers to **other crimes, wrongs, and bad acts**, and precludes their use in both civil and criminal cases from being offered against a person to prove that because of the prior bad act, the person likely acted in conformity with such behavior in the instant case. This rule is particularly important in criminal cases, where evidence of a defendant's past criminal conduct or bad acts could have the potential for unfair prejudice, because of its tendency to lead the jury to convict the defendant based on their perception of the kind of person they believe the defendant is because of his prior conduct, rather than on the evidence before them. Thus, the admissibility of other crimes, wrongs, or bad acts is significantly limited under this article and prevailing case law.

Permissible purposes. While Article 404(B) generally excludes prior crimes, wrongs, or bad acts from being offered for conformity purposes, it provides that the evidence may be offered to prove **other relevant purposes** in the case. The article gives an illustrative list of relevant reasons in which such evidence may be offered—to prove ***motive, opportunity, intent, preparation, plan, knowledge, identity, and absence of mistake or accident.*** To be admissible, evidence of other crimes must have independent relevance apart from its propensity purposes. For example, if a person is on trial for murdering a man (Ted), evidence may be offered to show that Ted witnessed the defendant committing another crime, to prove the defendant's *motive* for killing Ted, the victim in the current murder trial. Another example would be if a person is on trial for robbing a bank, evidence might be offered to show that two weeks before the robbery the defendant stole the getaway car used in the robbery in *preparation* for the bank robbery. In both instances, the evidence of the prior criminal conduct has independent relevance towards proving issues and elements in the instant case, rather than being offered only to show that the defendant was a bad person acting in conformity with his past bad behavior.

The list of non-conformity purposes contained in Article 404(B) is only illustrative, and the evidence may be offered for other relevant purposes that the circumstances may present.

Admissibility requirements. Because of the potential for unfair prejudice whenever evidence of other crimes is offered against an accused, the prosecution must comply with specific admissibility requirements as set forth in Article 404(B), and by the courts in *State v. Prieur*[40] and *State v. Davis*.[41] Article 404(B) specifically provides that upon *request* by the accused, the prosecution in a criminal case shall provide reasonable *notice* in advance of trial, of the nature of any such evidence it intends to introduce at trial, and for what purposes. The prosecution's notice must *specify the evidence* they intend to use, and must specify the specific *purpose* for which it will be offered to prove. After providing the required "notice of intent" to offer other crimes evidence, a *hearing* is set in which the admissibility of the other crimes is determined by the court applying safeguards established in *State v. Prieur*.

While Article 404(B) specifically provides that the defendant must request notice of the prosecution's intent to offer evidence of other crimes, wrongs, or acts, the Louisiana Supreme Court, in *State v. Blank*,[42] has held that the prosecution must provide such notice whether it is specifically requested by the accused or not, in order to use such evidence.[43]

The *Prieur* Hearing. In *State v. Prieur*,[44] the Louisiana Supreme Court established the safeguards that must be used in determining the admissibility of other crimes evidence when offered to prove a non-conformity purpose such as motive, knowledge, plan, or intent under Article 404(B). In what is commonly referred to as the "*Prieur* hearing," the court ensures compliance with the safeguards which were designed to protect the defendant's constitutional rights to confrontation and cross-examination[45] and to protect him from unfairly prejudicial evidence. The safeguards are as follows:

1. **Notice**. Within a reasonable time prior to trial, the prosecution gives the defense a detailed written notice: a) of the nature and circumstances of the other crime, wrong, or bad act; and b) specifying the purpose for which the evidence is being offered;
2. **Prerequisite Determination**. Prior to introducing the evidence, the prosecution satisfies the court that the evidence, otherwise admissible, serves the purpose for which it is being offered, and is not repetitive or cumulative; that its admission is not a subterfuge for depicting the accused as a person of bad character; and that the prosecution will introduce clear and convincing evidence that the accused in fact committed the other criminal act;
3. **Preliminary Instruction**. At the time the evidence is admitted, the court, if requested, instructs the jury as to the limited purpose for which the evidence was received and may be considered; and
4. **Final Instruction**. In its final charge to the jury, the court instructs the jury as to the limited purpose for which the evidence was received and may be considered, and further instructs the jury it may not convict the accused of any crime other than the one charged or a crime responsive to the once charged.[46]

---

40. State v. Prieur, 277 So. 2d 126 (La. 1973).
41. State v. Davis, 993 So. 2d 295 (La. Ct. App. 5th Cir. 2008).
42. State v. Blank, 955 So. 2d 90 (La. 2007).
43. The requirement that notice be "upon request by accused ..." was added by Act 51 of the 1994 Third Extraordinary Legislative Session. Although the statute appeared to conflict with the requirements of State v. Prieur, the Louisiana Supreme Court has since clarified the issue in State v. Blank, 955 So. 2d 90 (La. 2007), providing that the requirement of *Prieur* remains viable.
44. State v. Prieur, 277 So. 2d 126 (La. 1973).
45. Harges & Jones, Louisiana Evidence art. 404 Author's Comments.
46. *See* State v. Prieur, 277 So. 2d 126 (La. 1973); *See also* Force & Rault, Handbook, Art. 404(B) Author's note (4).

Stated purpose must actually be at issue.[47] The purpose for which the prosecution seeks to offer the evidence must actually be at issue in the case, and the other crime or bad act must also be probative of the named purpose. For instance, evidence being offered to prove that the accused had the requisite intent to commit a crime may not be allowed if intent is not required for the crime, is not at issue in the case, or if the evidence does not actually help to prove intent. Another commonly stated purpose for offering evidence of other crimes is to prove identity. For example, in a case in which the defendant is charged with burglary, the prosecution might attempt to offer evidence of one or more of defendant's prior burglary convictions with a stated purpose of showing identity, i.e., that the person who committed the prior burglaries, committed the present one. In such cases, the prior crime must be "distinctively similar to the one charged, especially in terms of time, place and manner of commission," to say that the prior crime and the instant offense were committed by the same person.[48] Otherwise, the evidence is not probative of the issue of identity.

If the stated purpose is motive, it must be shown that the prior bad act somehow compelled the defendant to commit the present crime, such as a drug addiction that might compel a person to commit a robbery, or evidence that a murder was committed in revenge against someone who might have turned the defendant in for a prior crime. The overall point is that the prior bad act must actually serve the purpose for which it is being offered and not be a subterfuge for depicting the accused as a person of bad character.[49] The prior bad act must actually be *relevant* in the case, and even then, it may only be admitted if it passes an Article 403 balancing test.

Standard of proof of other crime. There is no requirement in Article 404(B) that the accused have been convicted of the prior crime, wrong, or bad act to be admissible. In addition to convictions, the prior bad act could be a full range of bad acts, or vices, including arrests, accusations for crimes that might not have resulted in an arrest, alcohol or drug use, gambling, being fired from a job, particularly for doing something inappropriate such as watching pornography at work or for sexual harassment, and numerous other types of conduct. The prosecution need only demonstrate by "clear and convincing evidence" that the other crime, wrong, or act was in fact committed.[50] Thus, while a conviction is not nec-

---

47. *See* State v. Leday, 97 So. 3d 501, 506 (La. Ct. App. 5th Cir. 2012) (finding that the stated purposes, of knowledge, intent, motive, were not at issue in the case and the prior bad act was improperly admitted).

48. State v. Leday, 97 So. 3d 501 (La. Ct. App. 5th Cir. 2012); *See* State v. Prieur, 277 So. 2d 126 (La. 1973); *See also* State v. Carr, 620 So. 2d 288, 291 (La. Ct. App. 1st Cir. 1993) (allowing hearsay evidence to establish clear and convincing evidence that other prior bad act occurred); *See also* State v. Blank, 955 So. 2d 90, 95 (La. 2007) (upholding the clear and convincing standard that state must meet in proving the other bad act occurred).

49. State v. Prieur, 277 So. 2d 126 (La. 1973).

50. Act 51 of the 1994 Third Extraordinary Legislative Session Section 2 (now La. Code Evid. art. 1104) specifically provided that "[t]he burden of proof in a pretrial hearing held in accordance with State v. Prieur shall be identical to the burden of proof required by Federal Rules of Evidence 404, which appeared to have provided for a preponderance of the evidence standard, as applied under the Federal Rules. *See* Huddleson v. U.S., 485 U.S. 681, 108 S. Ct. 1496 (1988). However, in a series of cases, the Louisiana Supreme Court has clarified that the requirement of *Prieur* remain viable providing for a "clear and convincing evidence" standard. *See* State v. Blank, 955 So. 2d 90, 95 (La. 2007) (upholding the clear and convincing standard that the State must meet in proving the other bad act occurred); *See also* State v. Prieur, 277 So. 2d 126 (La. 1973); State v. Carr, 620 So. 2d 288, 291 (La. Ct. App. 1st Cir. 1993) (allowing hearsay evidence to establish clear and convincing evidence that other prior bad act occurred).

essary, there must be enough evidence to establish that the prior bad act in fact was committed.

Admitted subject to the Article 403 balancing test. Prior to admissibility, the evidence must also pass an Article 403 balancing test in which the probative value of the prior bad act toward proving the relevant non-conformity purpose is weighed against its potential for unfair prejudice. The evidence is admissible unless the prejudicial effect substantially outweighs the probative value. In situations in which the evidence only tentatively proves the non-conformity purpose, or the connection between the two is only speculative, such as in the burglary example above, the probative value of the evidence is minimal. When such evidence is balanced against what has the potential to be highly prejudicial evidence of other crimes, the evidence should properly be excluded. All evidence of other crimes offered against a defendant in a criminal trial under 404(B) is subject to the Article 403 balancing test.

Integral part evidence. Integral part evidence, formerly "res gestae" evidence, is evidence of another crime that forms a part of the sequence of events leading to the charged offense. It is evidence so "related [to] and intertwined with the charged offense to such an extent that the State could not ... accurately present[] its case without reference to it."[51] For example, if a police officer attempts to stop a suspected drunk driver who refuses to stop, leading to a high speed chase, the person may only be charged with aggravated escape, but evidence of the DWI may be offered because it forms a part of the sequence of events leading to the charged offense for which the defendant is being tried. Although evidence of the DWI is evidence for *another* crime for which the defendant is not on trial, it is admitted because the prosecution's case would lack narrative completeness without it.

In determining whether evidence forms an integral part of the instant offense, the court considers its proximity to the instant offense in time and place[52] and whether the evidence "forms a continuous chain of events leading to the defendant's arrest."[53] For the evidence to be admitted as an integral part of the instant offense, it must be "so important the prosecution could not prove the crime without the evidence."[54] Under *State v. Prieur*, the prosecution need not give notice of its intent to use integral part evidence. Because of its close connection to the instant offense in time and place, the defendant is deemed to reasonably anticipate its admissibility in connection with the instant offense, and be prepared to meet it.

Federal Rules of Evidence Distinction. Federal Rule of Evidence 404(b) does not contain language providing for the admissibility of other crimes that form an integral part of the crime charged.

Subject to harmless error rule. Erroneously admitted other crimes evidence is admitted subject to the harmless error rule.

51. State v. Brewington, 601 So. 2d 656, 657 (La. 1992), *citing* State v. Boyd, 359 So. 2d 931, 942 (La. 1978); *See also* State v. Clift, 339 So. 2d 755, 760 (La. 1976).

52. State v. Taylor, 838 So. 2d 729 (La. 2003).

53. State v. Wallace, WL 1551736 (La. Ct. App. 1st Cir. 2012).

54. Harges & Jones, Louisiana Evidence art. 404 Author's Comments.

Cases on Non-Conformity

Anderson v. Warden, Louisiana State Penitentiary

United States District Court, W.D. Louisiana, Shreveport Division
2013 WL 1405423
March 19, 2013

MARK L. HORNSBY, United States Magistrate Judge.

The body of Richard "Hot Dog" Holloway was discovered in a wooded area near Benton in Bossier Parish. He had been shot multiple times, including twice to the head. Carlos and Alice Stewart testified at trial that Petitioner was at their home several weeks later for dinner when he told them that he had killed a man named Hot Dog because the man stole three rocks of crack cocaine from him. There was ample evidence that Petitioner was involved in dealing crack, and most of the witnesses had multiple drug-related arrests and convictions.

The Stewarts testified that Petitioner stayed late that night after dinner. Alice eventually went to take a bath. Carlos testified that Petitioner kept saying he was trying to get a ride from his girlfriend, and he often stepped outside to make calls. Petitioner said at one point that he was going outside to investigate some gunshots they heard in the distance. He then returned with his hoodie pulled over his head and shot Carlos with a .45 caliber pistol, but Carlos survived.

A comparison of .45 caliber casings found near Hot Dog's body and casings found at the Stewart home show they were fired by the same weapon. Police arrested Petitioner and charged him with second degree murder. Latarsha Smith, Petitioner's girlfriend at the time of the murder, testified at trial that Petitioner came to her home the evening of the murder accompanied by Holloway and Daniel Lewis. Petitioner told Smith that he wanted her to drive the men to a location near Benton where they were going to break in a house.

... She drove the men home, and Lewis departed. Smith asked Petitioner what he did it for, and Petitioner told her she did not have to worry because he would never hurt her. Smith admitted that she heard Hot Dog had stolen dope from Petitioner, but Petitioner never told her about his business or why he killed Hot Dog.

...

Lewis testified that he saw Petitioner shoot Holloway in the head.... Lewis testified that Petitioner told him that he killed Holloway because the man had stolen crack cocaine from him.

...

Other Crimes Evidence

Louisiana law provides that evidence of other acts of misconduct are generally not admissible because of the risk the defendant will be convicted of the present offense because the unrelated evidence establishes him as a bad person. Evidence of other crimes may be admissible, however, if the State establishes an independent and relevant reason such as proof of identity, and the probative value outweighs its prejudicial effect. The prosecution typically must give pretrial notice of intent to use such evidence and make a proper showing before it is admitted.

Petitioner argued on direct appeal that the trial court erred when it allowed the Stewarts to testify about his alleged shooting at their home, without first conducting a hearing pursuant to *State v. Prieur*, 277 So.2d 126 (La.1973). The state appellate court found that the State did give pretrial notice of intent to use other crimes evidence in two separate pleadings and, early in the trial, the court heard arguments on the issue and ruled the evidence admissible. Identity of the person who fired the murder weapon was a key issue, and the Stewart testimony linked Petitioner directly to the weapon. The state court thus found no error in admitting the evidence. *State v. Anderson*, 942 So.2d at 629–30.

...

Prosecutorial Misconduct
A. Introduction

Petitioner argued in his post-conviction application that the prosecutor engaged in misconduct when she (1) solicited from witnesses hearsay and other crimes evidence for which the State did not give pretrial notice, ...

B. Other Crimes; Drug Dealing

The prosecutor asked Latarsha Smith, Mr. and Mrs. Stewart, and Daniel Lewis if Petitioner had told them why he killed Hot Dog. Each testified that Petitioner sold crack cocaine, Hot Dog was a customer, and Petitioner said he killed Hot Dog because he had stolen his crack. Petitioner argued in his post-conviction application that these questions introduced evidence of other crimes (drug dealing) for which there had not been proper pretrial notice. The State trial court noted that, to warrant relief, the reference must be to another crime as to which evidence is not admissible and substantial prejudice results. The court ultimately did not address the merits because it found the claim was procedurally barred because it had been raised on direct appeal. A review of Petitioner's appellate brief and the appellate decision, however, show that the other crimes argument on direct appeal was focused on admission of the shooting at the Stewart home rather than the drug dealing. In any event, the State has not attempted to assert a procedural bar defense to this claim.

Relief is not warranted on the merits of the claim because there is no doubt the court would have ruled the evidence admissible had the prosecutor given pretrial notice as argued for by Petitioner. Other crimes evidence is generally not admissible, but a well-known exception is when the evidence has independent relevance to motive. La. C.E. art. 404(B)(1). The drug-dealer evidence was directly relevant to motive and almost certainly would have been ruled admissible by any reasonable judge. The prosecutor may have fallen short of Louisiana procedural requirements for giving pretrial notice of such evidence, but when the issue is viewed in light of the entire record there is no basis to find a due process violation that would warrant vacating the conviction.

...

Discussion Questions

1. Strictly construing Article 404(B)(1), was the prosecution required to give the defendant notice of its intent to introduce the defendant's drug dealing into evidence to prove motive? Considering the Louisiana Supreme Court's decision in *Blank* regarding the prosecution's obligation to give notice, discussed above, how do you think such a case would turn out on appeal?
2. In *Anderson*, what if the defendant admitted that he had the intent to kill, but did so for example, in self-defense. Would evidence of defendant's motive still have been relevant? Would the court have likely admitted the evidence for that purpose? In other words, while we know that the "purpose" for which evidence is offered must be relevant, must it also be controverted?

3. Why do you think it is sufficient that the prosecution need only prove that a prior crime was committed by "clear and convincing" evidence, a much lower standard than proof beyond a reasonable doubt? Are a defendant's rights well protected by use of such a standard?

State v. Griffin

Court of Appeal of Louisiana, Second Circuit
618 So. 2d 680
May 5, 1993

STEWART, Judge.

On August 25, 1991, Pamela Griffin met Gary Braggs at the house of a friend. After socializing together for a while, Griffin and Braggs drove in his pick-up out into the woods where they parked, intending to engage in sexual activities and smoke "crack" cocaine. They undressed and began to smoke the "crack." After about two hours, Griffin got out of the truck, telling Braggs that she needed to use the restroom. When she got to the back of the truck, she asked Braggs to join her and told him she thought she heard something. As he leaned over, looking through the bushes, she shot him in the back of the head with a gun that she had taken from underneath the truck seat. After Braggs fell to the ground, she shot him once more in the head. He then played dead until she jumped in the truck. As she drove off, he got up and ran, wearing only tennis shoes, through the woods to a nearby house in search of help. Upon seeing the naked and bleeding man outside, the occupants of the house summoned the police.

Meanwhile, Griffin, also naked, continued her escape. After driving the truck into a tree, she managed to reach the parish road where she lost control of the vehicle again and ran it into a ditch. She apparently dressed, got out of the truck which she left with its engine and lights on, took Braggs clothes and started walking down the road. Approximately 1/4 to 1/2 mile later, she threw the clothes down in the road. At this point, Craig Harris came by in his company truck. He had seen the wreck and stopped to ask Griffin if she needed help. Pointing the pistol at him, she forced him out of the truck, and fired two shots at him, one of which struck Harris in the head. A short time later, passing motorists found him lying in the road and took him to a hospital where he died.

When the police investigated the disturbance at the house, the information obtained from Braggs led to the issuance of an A.P.B. for the arrest of Griffin. The next day she was found hiding in the bathtub of a friend's house in El Dorado, Arkansas, arrested and returned to Louisiana.

Griffin was indicted by the Union Parish grand jury on charges of first-degree murder for which the state sought the death penalty. After a trial, held on April 20–25, 1992, the defendant was convicted as charged and sentenced to life imprisonment.

DISCUSSION

...

ASSIGNMENTS OF ERROR 3 & 26

The trial court erred in finding that the *Prieur* notice was sufficient and in allowing the admission of "other crimes" evidence.

At the hearing on various pretrial motions, the defendant argued that the *Prieur* notice failed to specify which exception to the general exclusionary rule was the basis for introducing evidence of other crimes.

The "other crimes" evidence intended to be used was listed as: (1) possession of cocaine; (2) attempted first degree murder of Gary Braggs; (3) failure to maintain control of Gary Braggs' vehicle; (4) reckless operation of Gary Braggs' vehicle; (5) illegal carrying of a weapon; (6) extortion; (7) prostitution; and (8) illegal possession of stolen goods; and (9) possession of drug paraphernalia.

The notice stated that the purpose of using the evidence was to establish

> the defendant's motive, and/or opportunity, and/or intent, and/or preparation, and/or plan, and/or knowledge, and/or identity, and/or absence of mistake or accident, and/or the conduct relates to conduct that constitutes an integral part of the act or transactions [sic] that is the subject of the present proceeding.

The trial court found that the state intended to rely upon all of the exceptions listed and that, because the evidence constituted an integral part of the subject act, *Prieur* notice was not even required. We agree.

Article 404 of the Louisiana Code of Evidence states in pertinent part:

> B. (1) Except as provided in Article 412, evidence of other crimes, wrongs, or acts is not admissible to prove the character of a person in order to show that he acted in conformity therewith. It may, however, be admissible for other purposes, such as proof of motive, opportunity, intent, preparation, plan, knowledge, identity, absence of mistake or accident, or when it relates to conduct that constitutes an integral part of the act or transaction that is the subject of the present proceeding.

This article neither codifies nor affects the law of other crimes evidence, as set forth in *State v. Prieur,* 277 So.2d 126 (La.1973); *State v. Davis,* 449 So.2d 466 (La.1984); *State v. Moore,* 278 So.2d 781 (La.1973) and their progeny. LSA–C.E. Art. 1103. However, the notice requirements of *Prieur* and its progeny are not applicable to evidence of offenses which constitute part of the res gestae. *State v. Goza,* 408 So.2d 1349 (La.1982). The Code of Evidence article 404 B(1) phrase, "or when it relates to conduct that constitutes an integral part of the act or transaction that is the subject of the present proceeding", refers to that which was formerly called "res gestae". *Comment* (m), LSA–C.E. Art. 404. Accordingly, *Prieur* notice is not required for evidence of offenses which are an integral part of the act or transaction that is the subject at bar.

In *State v. Brewington,* 587 So.2d 189 (La.App. 3d Cir.1991), the court of appeal found that, during trial for second degree murder, testimony about defendant's claim of cocaine possession was inadmissible "other crimes" evidence. The appellate court reversed the defendant's conviction for second degree murder and remanded for a new trial. In its per curiam reversal of the appellate judgment, *State v. Brewington,* 601 So.2d 656 (La.1992), the Louisiana Supreme Court stated the following (citations omitted):

> This court has approved the admission of other crimes evidence when it is related and intertwined with the charged offense to such an extent that the state could not have accurately presented its case without reference to it. In such cases, the purpose served by admission of other crimes evidence is not to depict the defendant as a bad man, but rather to complete the story of the crime on trial by proving its immediate context of happenings near in time and place. The concomitant other crimes do not affect the accused's character, because they were done, if at all, as parts of a whole; therefore, the trier of fact will attribute all of the criminal conduct to the defendant or none of it. And, because of the close connection in time and location, the defendant is unlikely to be unfairly surprised.

The other crimes, referred to in the instant *Prieur* notice and described during trial, constituted one continuous transaction. The connected string of offenses began with the drug use and sexual activity, the shooting of Braggs and theft of his truck, gun and clothes. Griffin continued the crime spree by wrecking Braggs' truck, threatening Harris with the stolen gun to get him out of his truck, shooting Harris, and fleeing down backroads to Arkansas in another stolen truck. Each crime occurred as a result of, or in close time and proximity with, a previous crime. All of these offenses took place within a short time period, and there existed a very close connexity between the charged offense and the other crimes. *[Citations omitted]*.

Moreover, the evidence of "other crimes" was of probative value on the issues of Griffin's intent, opportunity, preparation, plan, knowledge, identity, and absence of mistake or accident. Griffin's defense was that her "crack" intoxication prevented her from forming the requisite specific intent. Therefore, the question of her intent was both an element of the offense and a controverted issue.

For the foregoing reasons, we find no error in the trial court's rulings regarding this evidence of other crimes. These assignments of error lack merit.

. . .

AFFIRMED.

Discussion Questions

1. Louisiana courts have stated that "integral act" (*res gestae*) evidence in Louisiana incorporates a rule of narrative completeness without which the State's case would lose its narrative cohesiveness, "with power not only to support conclusions but to sustain the willingness of jurors to draw the inferences, whatever they may be, necessary to reach an honest verdict."[55] What does the court mean by this statement?
   a. Why is "narrative completeness" important to the admissibility of "integral part" evidence?
   b. Do you recall discussing narrative completeness in *Old Chief*, which we studied in Chapter 3 in the context of the admissibility of other crimes? How is the role of other crimes in this context similar to the role of "other crimes evidence" in the context of *Old Chief*?
2. Why was no notice required in *Griffin*? Why is notice not required "in general" when the prosecution plans to present integral part evidence?
3. Would it have been possible for the prosecution to have told this story without reference to the other events that transpired leading up to the murder? Explain.
4. Do you think there could be a situation in which integral part evidence might be so unfairly prejudicial that it should nonetheless be excluded? Can you think of an example?
5. The court in *Griffin* also found that the evidence was of "probative value on the issues of Griffin's intent, opportunity, preparation, plan, knowledge, identity, and absence of mistake or accident" because of Griffin's defense that her "crack" intoxication prevented her from forming the requisite specific intent. Do you find the other crimes to be probative of those issues? Even so, if admitted solely for those purposes, would they pass the Article 403 balancing test?

---

55. State v. Napoleon, 119 So. 3d 238, 243 (La. Ct. App. 5th Cir. 2013) (quoting State v. Colomb, 747 So. 2d 1074, 1076 (La. 1999)).

Key Points

The key points to keep in mind regarding admissibility of other crimes, wrongs, and acts for non-conformity purposes.

1. Other crimes, wrongs, and bad acts are generally inadmissible to prove action in conformity therewith.
2. Applies to both civil and criminal cases.
3. **Admissible for other relevant purposes**: such as proof of motive, opportunity, intent, preparation, plan, knowledge, identity, and absence of mistake or accident.
4. **Admissibility requirements.** Because of the potential for prejudice, under Article 404(B) and *State v. Prieur*, the following safeguards must be met to offer evidence of other crimes in a criminal case:
   a. **Request** by accused of prosecution's intent to use other crimes, although notice should be given even without request;
   b. **Notice** to accused from prosecution of intent to use other crimes evidence. Notice must include: 1) the specific evidence to be offered; and 2) the specific purpose it will be offered to prove;
   c. ***Prieur* hearing.** Prosecution must satisfy the court that the evidence serves the purpose for which it is being offered, and is not repetitious or cumulative; that its admission is not a subterfuge for depicting the accused as a person of bad character; and that the prosecution will introduce clear and convincing evidence that the accused in fact committed the other criminal act;
   d. **Preliminary instruction.** If requested, when the evidence is presented, the jury may be instructed of the limited purpose for which evidence is to be used; and
   e. **Final instruction.** In final instruction, court instructs jury of limited purpose for which evidence may be considered, and that defendant may only be convicted of charged crime.
5. **Stated purpose must actually be at issue.** The stated purposed for which the prosecution intends to offer the evidence must actually be at issue in the case and other bad acts must be probative of the stated purpose.
6. **Standard of proof of other crime.** The prosecution must be able to prove that the other crime was committed by the "*clear and convincing evidence*" standard.
7. **Admitted subject to Article 403 balancing.** Evidence is subject to Article 403 balancing test, weighing its probative value towards proving the stated purpose (motive, intent, etc.) against its potential for unfair prejudice.
8. **Integral part evidence.** Formerly known as "res gestae" evidence, evidence is generally admissible if it forms an integral part of the transaction of evidence giving rise to the instant offense, such as the escape of the suspect from the scene. Notice need not be given of intent to introduce integral part evidence.
9. Erroneously admitted other crimes evidence is subject to the harmless error rule.

Problems on Non-Conformity

PROBLEM 6-37. Moses is a new Assistant District Attorney. As he is reviewing his files, he comes across a number of cases in which he notices that a number of criminal defendants have prior convictions and other bad acts. As Moses prepares the "Notice of Intent to Use Other Crimes, Wrongs, or Acts" in his cases, he must determine the relevant non-conformity purpose for which the evidence may be admitted under Article 404(B). For each of the following cases, for what purpose is evidence of the listed prior bad act most relevant? Please indicate if you do not believe the evidence will be admitted under Article 404(B) because it is not probative of the non-conformity purpose, or because it would be unfairly prejudicial to admit it.

A. DJ is charged with snatching purses. He has two prior convictions for purse snatching. In both of the prior cases, the defendant pretended to help an elderly lady across the street, then gave her several compliments and hugs before snatching her purse. He then ran into the subway station where he jumped on a train and got away. The current offense for which the defendant is on trial was committed in the same manner. For what purposes might Moses offer evidence of the prior purse snatching convictions?

B. Deen is on trial for killing Victor. At the trial, the prosecution would like to offer evidence that two years prior to the murder, Deen robbed Victor and was later convicted and served 18 months for simple robbery. In that case, Victor identified Deen in a photo lineup and testified against him at the trial. Deen has always maintained his innocence in that case and claims Victor falsely identified him. For what purpose might Moses offer evidence of Deen's prior robbery of Victor?

C. Bobby is on trial for burglary of a vehicle. He is accused of breaking into a vehicle in a downtown parking garage and stealing a very expensive ladies handbag and cell phone from the vehicle. On six prior occasions, Bobby has been accused of stealing various expensive items (purses, GPS systems, cell phones, sunglasses, etc.) from the inside of vehicles that were parked in various locations downtown. In each instance, Bobby was quickly apprehended and was released or charges were dropped after the items were returned to the owners. He has no prior convictions for any of the prior incidents, but police reports were filed. For what purpose might Moses offer evidence of the prior offenses?

D. Dale is on trial for second-degree battery for breaking his girlfriend's arm during an altercation. The defendant claims that the victim's arm was mistakenly broken during a minor struggle when she forcefully pulled away from him and fell backwards down the stairs. About thirteen years prior to the incident, Dale was convicted for the brutal rape and murder of his first wife, which was a highly publicized case because of the brutality used to commit the crime. Dale served twelve years for the crime. For what purpose might Moses offer evidence of the prior rape and murder?

E. Donald is on trial for armed robbery and attempted murder. The prosecution would like to offer evidence that Donald stole a box of 9mm bullets the day before the murder. The forensic testing has established that the bullet pulled from the victim's arm was fired from a 9mm handgun. For what purpose might Moses offer evidence of the theft of the bullets?

F. Henry is charged with murder. The prosecution has evidence that the murdered victim witnessed Henry steal a Ford Mustang. For what purpose might the prior theft be relevant?

G. Jonathan is on trial for passing counterfeit bills. Jonathan claims that he received the bills during a transaction at a store and had no idea they were counterfeit. Jonathan has a prior conviction for the same offense 2 ½ years prior to the instant offense. For what purpose might Moses offer evidence of the prior conviction?

H. Jim is married and is accused of raping his neighbor in his apartment complex. Evidence shows that the night of the rape, a lady he'd been having an affair with broke it off with him. Jim was distraught and angry. The rape occurred just two hours later. Jim claims the affair would be offered only to put him in a negative light. For what purpose might Moses offer evidence of the affair?

I. On Monday, Marlon and Jamie were arrested and charged with burglary. About eight months earlier, Marlon and Jamie had stolen a car. Marlon didn't have a car, so he used the stolen car as his own for the eight months prior to the burglary. During that time, several people had seen him in the car around town. When Marlon and Jamie went to commit the burglary, they used the stolen car as the getaway vehicle, which the witness described. For what purpose might the State offer evidence in the burglary trial that Marlon and/or Jamie had stolen the car?

PROBLEM 6-38. Cantrell is on trial for first-degree murder for killing a member of a rival gang. In Cantrell's trial, the prosecution would like to offer evidence that Cantrell is a member of a violent gang known as the Kingheads, and that the week before the murder, Cantrell and the Kingheads had been involved in a violent altercation with another violent gang known as the Scorpions. The altercation resulted in several arrests, numerous injuries, and one death. The prosecution plans to offer evidence that the Kingheads member that was killed was Cantrell's mentor and "jumpman" (*the gang member who initiated Cantrell into the Kingheads*), who was violently murdered by who was believed to be the Scorpion member Cantrell is accused of killing. Cantrell's defense is that he did not commit the murder, and he objects to any evidence being offered at trial regarding gang membership and the prior altercation, claiming it is inadmissible character evidence and other bad acts offered only to put him in a bad light before the jury. What procedural safeguards should be followed? What must be shown? What standard of proof? How should the court rule on the admissibility of the evidence following the *Prieur* hearing and why?

PROBLEM 6-39. Abe, Bob, and Ced are good friends and decided to rob a bank. Abe stole masks in preparation for the bank heist. Bob stole a Chevrolet Suburban to use as the getaway car a couple of weeks before the robbery. The day before the robbery, Abe, Bob, and Ced stole guns from Abe's parents' house. Following the robbery, Abe and Bob got away from the scene, but Ced ran the wrong way and was apprehended. Prior to Ced's trial for armed robbery, the prosecution provided reasonable notice of its intent to introduce the other crimes of Abe, Bob, and Ced. Ced objects to the crimes of all three of them. Are there any grounds upon which Ced can have Abe and Bob's crimes excluded? What about the theft of the guns in which he participated? How should the court rule?

PROBLEM 6-40. David is on trial for the armed robbery of a young female college student in her apartment just around the corner from the college campus. David denies being in the small college town where the robbery occurred during the time the robbery was committed. David lives about 75 miles away. He also claimed he doesn't know the female and never met her in an initial statement made to the police. Which of the following evidence will likely be admissible against David and for what purpose?

A) Evidence that David received a speeding ticket in the town where the robbery occurred the day before the robbery;

B) Evidence of the receipt from David's purchase of a gun a couple of days before the robbery;

C) Evidence that David had cocaine in his pocket when he was arrested for the robbery;

D) Evidence of a police report that the victim filed with the campus police that she was being stalked by David about six months before the offense;

E) Evidence that a couple months before the robbery, David had been asked by the management to stay away from the apartment complex that the victim lived in because he was always hanging around there but didn't live there.

PROBLEM 6-41. Tango is on trial for forgery and felony theft. Tango managed to steal $150,000 by printing up checks in his capacity as CFO of Marx Co. and then signing the CEO's signature to pass the checks. Tango's defense is that he wasn't trying to "steal" the money, but that he believed he deserved the money because of all the overtime that he'd put in on the job, but hadn't been paid for. The prosecution has learned that Tango was fired from his last job as a bank teller a couple years prior to the incident because on several occasions his bank drawer came up short. Tango was arrested for embezzlement for the acts at the bank, but was found not guilty at the trial because the CEO did not show up to testify. The prosecution would like to offer evidence of the embezzlement charge from the bank against Tango in its case-in-chief in the upcoming trial on the forgery and felony theft at Marx Co. For what purpose should they attempt to offer it? How will the court likely rule and why? Will the acquittal affect the admissibility of the evidence?

PROBLEM 6-42. Elmo is on trial for the armed robbery of a bank that is directly across the street from a pawnshop. The prosecution would like to offer evidence that, just before the robbery, Elmo stole a pistol from the pawnshop and ran across the street and robbed the bank with it. Should the theft from the pawnshop be admissible against Elmo in the armed robbery trial?

PROBLEM 6-43. Assume an officer noticed several guys gathered around a car parked in an area known for drug trafficking. As a result of this observation, the officer approached the car, and with permission of the owner, searched it and found a gun. Subsequently, the officer asked the car owner if he had any drugs on him. After a short chat, the car owner showed the officer a bag of marijuana that he'd placed under his shirt during the search. He was thereafter arrested for illegal possession of a firearm by a convicted felon. At the trial, the prosecution would like to introduce evidence of the marijuana. The State claims marijuana possession is an integral part of the charge of illegal possession of a firearm by a felon in this instance. Do you think the court should allow this evidence under the theory of "res gestae"? Why or why not? [See generally, *State v. Colomb*, 747 So. 2d 1074 (La. 1999).]

§ 6.6 References and Additional Authority on Admissibility of Other Crimes, Wrongs, or Acts for Non-Conformity Purposes [La. C.E. art. 404(B)]

1. La. C.E. arts. 404, 404(B) and Official Comments
2. Force & Rault, HANDBOOK ON LOUISIANA EVIDENCE LAW Art. 404(B) Author's Comments (West Publishing 2014)
3. Harges & Jones, LOUISIANA EVIDENCE Art. 404(B) Author's Comments (West Publishing 2014)

4. 19 La. Civ. L. Treatise, Evidence And Proof § 5.2 (2nd ed.)

5. **Commentary**: Jones, Russell, *Other Crimes Evidence: How Should it Work? The Louisiana Approach*, 29 S.U. L. Rev. 129 (Spring 2002).

6. **Court finds evidence of integral part evidence:** *State v. Joseph*, 854 So. 2d 914 (La. Ct. App. 3d Cir. 2003) (holding that other crimes the defendant committed were an integral part of the charge of possession of a firearm by a convicted felon); *State v. Colomb*, 747 So. 2d 1074 (La. 1999) (holding that finding the defendant in possession of marijuana after finding a semi-automatic weapon in the vehicle that the defendant was driving was an integral part of the crime charged and therefore was admissible); *State v. Alsup*, 968 So. 2d 1152 (La. Ct. App. 2d Cir. 2007) (allowing evidence of the victim's use of stolen checks the defendant obtained from a burglary in order to show an integral part of the burglary).

7. **Admissible "other crimes" to show motive:** *State v. Colbert*, 990 So. 2d 76 (La. Ct. App. 4th Cir. 2008) (allowing prior bad acts of the defendant that showed a pattern of obsession toward a woman to be used by the prosecution to show the defendant's intent to keep the woman from seeing other men and his motive for killing a man that the woman was seeing); *State v. Grady*, 47-622 La. App. 2 Cir. 1/16/13, 2013 WL 163767 (La. Ct. App. 2d Cir. 2013) (holding that a fight between the defendant and victim several months before house fire relevant to prove defendant's motive for arson).

8. **Admissible "other crimes" to prove intent:** *State v. Winn*, 978 So. 2d 1239 (La. Ct. App. 2d Cir. 2008) (allowing a witness to testify about prior threats made to her by the defendant in order to show the defendant's intent, motive, or plan to use insanity defense to evade prosecution); *State v. Blank*, 955 So. 2d 90 (La. 2007) (holding that five other capital murders and two attempted murders in a capital murder trial admissible to show intent); *State v. Bruce*, 93 So. 3d 717 (La. Ct. App. 2d Cir. 2012) (holding evidence of repeated pattern of contracting to do work, receiving payment, and leaving admissible to show intent to defraud).

9. **Admissible "other crimes" to show preparation:** *State v. Cooley*, 92 So. 3d 1095 (La. Ct. App. 2d Cir. 2012) (holding evidence of defendant's robbery where he took car to drive to pawnshop to commit robbery admissible to show preparation for crime); *State v. Chambers*, 2011-1499 La. App. 3 Cir. 6/20/12, 2012 WL 2327701 (La. Ct. App. 3d Cir. 2012) (unpublished) (holding evidence that defendant provided alcohol, cocaine to rape victims admissible to prove preparation and plan to commit rapes).

10. **Admissible "other crimes" to show identity:** *State v. Mathieu*, 980 So. 2d 17 (La. Ct. App 4th Cir. 2008) (allowing into evidence recorded phone calls from the defendant to his mother and brother in which the defendant stated that he was still in jail because he had not killed a witness; recordings were offered to prove the defendant's identity as the murderer).

11. **Admissible "other crimes" to show identity and motive**: *State v. Rose*, 925 So. 2d 34 (La. Ct. App. 4th Cir. 2006) (holding that evidence of the defendant's conviction of manslaughter of his first wife was admissible to prove the defendant's identity and motive in killing his second wife); *State v. Martin*, 645 So. 2d 190 (La. 1994) (holding that evidence that defendant wore a mask during each robbery was admissible to prove identity; defendant's statement that his past unsuccessful attempt to complete robbery that resulted in his incarceration showed his motive to rob the gas station).

§ 6.7 Criminal Convictions (for Credibility) [La. C.E. arts. 609 and 609.1]

Articles 609 and 609.1 provide for the admissibility of **prior criminal convictions** on the issue of the *credibility* of a witness. Throughout this chapter we have generally discussed character evidence and the admissibility of various types of specific instances of conduct, including criminal convictions, for various purposes. While on the subject of criminal convictions, it is important to understand the full scope of when such convictions may be admitted for comparison purposes.Under this provision, criminal convictions are not being offered to prove the character of a person or any issues or elements directly related to the substantive law. Under Articles 609 and 609.1, evidence of a criminal conviction may be offered only on the issue of the witness's credibility, i.e., his truthfulness or veracity.

Credibility of a witness. As we have pointed out thus far, whenever a witness takes the stand, his credibility is *always* at issue. By testifying at trial, a witness in essence asks the trier of fact to believe his testimony is true. Thus, any evidence that bears upon the witness's truthfulness, veracity, or credibility is relevant and generally admissible. One such issue that is deemed to bear upon a witness's credibility is whether he has been convicted of a crime. You may be familiar with the old saying, "If you'll lie, you'll steal." Well, this provision is premised upon the presumption that "If you'll steal, you might lie." In other words, the law presumes that a trier of fact, usually a jury, is justified in knowing whether a witness in a trial has been convicted of a crime in assessing whether the witness is telling the truth.

This provision applies to *convictions* only, and does not apply to an arrest, the issuance of an arrest warrant, an indictment, a prosecution, or an acquittal, nor to a conviction that has been the subject of a pardon or an annulment. The details surrounding admissibility of such evidence depends upon whether the evidence is being offered in a civil or criminal trial.

Civil Cases (La. C.E. art. 609)

Applicable Code Article

Art. 609. Attacking credibility by evidence of conviction of crime in civil cases

A. General civil rule. For the purpose of attacking the credibility of a witness in civil cases, no evidence of the details of the crime of which he was convicted is admissible. However, evidence of the name of the crime of which he was convicted and the date of conviction is admissible if the crime:

(1) Was punishable by death or imprisonment in excess of six months under the law under which he was convicted, and the court determines that the probative value of admitting this evidence outweighs its prejudicial effect to a party; or

(2) Involved dishonesty or false statement, regardless of the punishment.

B. Time limit. Evidence of a conviction under this Article is not admissible if a period of more than ten years has elapsed since the date of the conviction.

C. Effect of pardon or annulment. Evidence of a conviction is not admissible under this Article if the conviction has been the subject of a pardon, annulment, or other equivalent procedure explicitly based on a finding of innocence.

D. Juvenile adjudications. Evidence of juvenile adjudications of delinquency is generally not admissible under this Article.

E. Pendency of appeal. The pendency of an appeal there from does not render evidence of a conviction inadmissible. When evidence of a conviction is admissible, evidence of the pendency of an appeal is also admissible.

F. Arrest, indictment, or prosecution. Evidence of the arrest, indictment, or prosecution of a witness is not admissible for the purpose of attacking his credibility.

Article 609 provides that for the purpose of attacking the credibility of a witness in **civil cases**, evidence of the **name** of the crime of which the witness was convicted and the **date** of conviction is admissible if the crime:

(1) Was punishable by death or imprisonment in excess of six months under the law under which he was convicted, and the court determines that the probative value of admitting the evidence outweighs its prejudicial effect to a party; or

(2) Involved dishonesty or false statement, regardless of the punishment.

Further, no more than ten years must have elapsed since the date of the conviction. Thus, in civil cases, only the **name** and **date** of convictions **punishable in excess of six months** may be admitted subject to a balancing of interests, as well as the **name** and **date** of any conviction involving **dishonesty** or **false statement**. Both must have occurred **within 10 years**.

Convictions punishable in excess of six months. Under this article, two categories of convictions are admissible to attack a witness's credibility. The first category of convictions involves those crimes that are **punishable** by **death** or **imprisonment in excess of six months**. This category of convictions includes all felony convictions under Louisiana law as well as a small group of misdemeanors, such as stalking, tattooing a minor, and battery of a schoolteacher (by a student).

Such convictions may only be admitted if the court finds that the probative value of admitting the evidence outweighs its prejudicial effect. Contrary to the language of Article 403, which excludes evidence if the probative value is substantially outweighed by the prejudicial effect, here the evidence is admitted only if the probative value outweighs the prejudicial effect. Thus, while Article 403 favors admissibility, here the evidence is excluded unless the proponent of the prior criminal conviction can convince the judge that the evidence should be admitted.

When a conviction is admissible under this provision in a civil case to attack a witness's credibility, only the: 1) **name**; and 2) **date** of the prior conviction are admissible.

Convictions involving dishonesty or false statement. A second category of convictions that are admissible under Article 609 to attack a witness's credibility in a civil case includes those crimes (including misdemeanors) involving dishonesty or false statement. This category includes crimes such as fraud, perjury, or embezzlement. These crimes are admissible without the need for balancing the probative value against the prejudicial effect because they are deemed to have a direct bearing on a witness's credibility. When such crimes are admissible under this article, only the: 1) **name**; and 2) **date** of the conviction, is admissible.

Exclusions. This article only applies to convictions for crimes and does not include crimes for which there has only been an arrest, indictment, or prosecution of a witness, or a conviction that has been subject to a pardon or an annulment based upon a finding of innocence. Further, juvenile adjudications are not ordinarily inquired into under this article. Additionally, convictions are not admissible under this article if more than ten years has elapsed since the date of conviction. The fact that a conviction is on appeal does not preclude its use for impeachment purposes.

Scope of cross-examination. On cross-examination of a witness, counsel may question a witness under this provision as follows regarding the name and date of the conviction. The witness may not be questioned regarding any of the facts or details surrounding the crime, nor the sentence imposed. Further, a witness may be questioned about her prior convictions without any foundation as follows:

Q: *Ms. Witness, you have been convicted of two crimes?*

A: *Yes, I have.*

Q: *You have been convicted of illegal possession of stolen things?*

A: *Yes.*

Q: *And that conviction occurred on January 10, 2007?*

A: *Yes.*

Q: *You were also convicted of impersonating a police officer?*

A: *That's correct.*

Q: *That conviction occurred on April 21, 2011?*

A: *Yes, that's right.*

This is the extent of a cross-examination relative to prior criminal convictions in a civil case. Counsel must move on to the next topic on which he wishes to cross-examine the witness.

Extrinsic evidence admissible. When a witness is cross-examined about his prior conviction(s) under this article, if he fails to admit it, extrinsic evidence may be offered to prove that he was in fact so convicted. Extrinsic evidence is any evidence outside of the witness himself that may prove something—a document, recording, or another witness. Extrinsic evidence of the conviction may only be offered after the proponent has first fairly directed the witness's attention to his prior conviction, and the witness has been given the opportunity to admit the fact and has failed distinctly to do so. Thus, if a witness refuses to admit the conviction when asked about it, counsel may then offer outside proof of it, such as certified court minutes showing the conviction.

The admissibility of extrinsic evidence to prove the prior conviction is governed under Article 613, and is more thoroughly covered in §6.11, *infra*.

Criminal Cases (La. C.E. art. 609.1)

Applicable Code Article

Art. 609.1. Attacking credibility by evidence of conviction of crime in criminal cases

A. General criminal rule. n a criminal case, every witness by testifying subjects himself to examination relative to his criminal convictions, subject to limitations set forth below.

B. Convictions. Generally, only offenses for which the witness has been convicted are admissible upon the issue of his credibility, and no inquiry is permitted into matters for which there has only been an arrest, the issuance of an arrest warrant, an indictment, a prosecution, or an acquittal.

C. Details of convictions. Ordinarily, only the fact of a conviction, the name of the offense, the date thereof, and the sentence imposed is admissible. However, details of the offense may become admissible to show the true nature of the offense:

(1) When the witness has denied the conviction or denied recollection thereof;

(2) When the witness has testified to exculpatory facts or circumstances surrounding the conviction; or

(3) When the probative value thereof outweighs the danger of unfair prejudice, confusion of the issues, or misleading the jury.

D. Effect of pending post-conviction relief procedures. The pendency of an appeal or other post-conviction relief procedures does not render the conviction inadmissible, but may be introduced as bearing upon the weight to be given the evidence of the conviction.

E. Effect of pardon or annulment. When a pardon or annulment, based upon a finding of innocence, has been granted, evidence of that conviction is not admissible to attack the credibility of the witness.

F. Juvenile adjudications. Evidence of juvenile adjudications of delinquency is generally not admissible under this Article, except for use in proceedings brought pursuant to the habitual offender law, R.S. 15:529.1.

Article 609.1 provides for the admissibility of a witness's criminal convictions in a **criminal case**. There are several distinctions between the admissibility of criminal convictions in a criminal case and a civil case. In a criminal case, a witness may be cross-examined relative to any type of criminal conviction, whether felony or misdemeanor, regardless of whether the crime involves dishonesty or false statement. Additionally, in a criminal case, not only can the **name** and **date** of the conviction be admitted, but also the **sentence imposed** for such conviction. Further, there is no time limitation within which the conviction must have occurred. Under this article, no matter how much time has passed since the conviction occurred, it may be offered on the issue of the witness's credibility.

Details of the crime. Ordinarily, only the **fact** of a conviction, the **name** of the offense, the **date** thereof, and the **sentence imposed** is admissible. However, there are three instances in Article 609.1 in which the details of the offense may become admissible to show the true nature of the offense:

1. When the witness has denied the conviction or denied recollection thereof;
2. When the witness has testified to exculpatory facts or circumstances surrounding the conviction; or

3. When the probative value thereof outweighs the danger of unfair prejudice, confusion of the issues, or misleading the jury.

Thus, if the witness **denies he was convicted** of the crime, **denies recollection** of it, or **testifies to exculpatory facts**, then details of the crime may be inquired into. For example, if the witness is asked on cross-examination, "Weren't you convicted of possession of a firearm by a convicted felon?" and the witness responds, "Yes, but it wasn't my car. I didn't even know that gun was in the car," then he has opened the door to the details of the crime to show the true nature of the offense. Thus, the cross-examination may continue as follows: "But isn't it true that you'd been in possession of the vehicle for the six months leading up to the offense?" or "Didn't you attempt to hide the gun when the officer initiated the stop?" These questions, inquiring into the details of the crimes of which the witness was convicted, are only permissible when any of the three circumstances listed in Article 609.1(C) exists, such as if the witness testifies to exculpatory facts as above.

Exclusions. Article 609.1 only authorizes the admissibility of convictions to impeach the witness, and does not permit inquiry into matters for which there has only been an arrest, the issuance of an arrest warrant, an indictment, a prosecution, or an acquittal. Additionally it does not apply when a pardon or annulment has been granted based upon a finding of innocence, nor to juvenile adjudications of delinquency.

Scope of cross-examination. When cross-examining a witness relative to prior convictions under Article 609.1, counsel may only question the witness regarding the fact of a conviction, the name of the offense, the date thereof, and the sentence imposed as follows:

Q: Mr. Witness, you have been convicted of two crimes?

A: Yes.

Q: You have been convicted of illegal possession of stolen things?

A: Yes.

Q: And that conviction occurred on January 10, 1997?

A: That's correct.

Q: As a result of that conviction, you received a sentence of 6 months in the parish jail, which time was suspended, and you were placed on supervised probation for 6 months, right?

A: Yes, that's correct.

Q: You have also been convicted of soliciting a prostitute?

A: Well . . .

Q: Well, weren't you convicted of soliciting a prostitute?[56]

A: Well, she wasn't a prostitute. She was an undercover police officer.

Q: Mr. Witness, isn't it true that on July 4, 2004 you walked up to a woman standing on the corner of Bourbon St. in New Orleans and asked her what you could get for $20?

A: Yes.

56. See discussion of State v. Tolbert, 849 So. 2d 32 (La. 2003) below, regarding the admissibility of misdemeanor convictions for impeachment purposes.

Q: And when you made her that offer, you had no idea that she was an undercover police officer, did you?

A: No, not at that time.

Q: Then the two of you subsequently agreed upon a price?

A: Yes.

Q: And you agreed upon a place?

A: Yes.

Q: At that point you handed over the money to her, right?

A: Yes.

Q: That's when you were arrested for soliciting a prostitute, weren't you?

A: Yes, I was arrested for that.

Q: You were later convicted of soliciting a prostitute for your conduct that night, weren't you?

A: Yes, that's right.

Q: And you were sentenced to 90 days in the parish jail as a result of it?

A: Yes, I was.

In the examination above, the prosecution was permitted to inquire into the details of the conviction only after the witness testified to exculpatory facts. The prosecutor must now move on to the next topic.

Extrinsic evidence admissible to prove prior conviction. As with civil cases, if the witness fails to admit the prior criminal conviction in a criminal case, extrinsic evidence of the conviction may be offered to prove it—evidence outside of the witness's own testimony, such as another witness or document. Pursuant to Article 613, the proponent may only offer extrinsic evidence of the conviction after he has first fairly directed the witness's attention to his prior conviction, and the witness has been given the opportunity to admit the fact and has failed distinctly to do so. Thus, only after the witness has been asked whether he has the prior conviction, and denies it, may the proponent offer other evidence to prove that he was in fact convicted of the crime, such as by offering a copy of certified court minutes showing the conviction.

It is not permissible to offer extrinsic evidence of the conviction when a witness has admitted to the conviction, or before asking a witness if he has been convicted of the crime.

Cases on Convictions for Credibility in Criminal Cases

State v. Ash
Court of Appeal of Louisiana, Fourth Circuit
729 So. 2d 664
Feb. 10, 1999

BYRNES, Judge.

On April 23, 1996, New Orleans Police officers Bryan Lampard and Jake Schnapp were on proactive patrol around the intersection of Josephine and LaSalle Streets. As the officers proceeded in an uptown direction on LaSalle towards Jackson Avenue, they observed Ash and an unknown female engaged in a conversation. When the officers approached the middle of the block, they noticed that Ash had his right hand extended. The female was looking down at his hand. Ash looked up, saw the approaching police vehicle, quickly closed his hand, and started walking in a lake bound direction on Josephine Street. The officers followed Ash and turned onto Josephine Street. The officers observed Ash sitting in front of 2415 Josephine Street next to a man later identified as Kenneth Williams. When the officers stopped the police vehicle, Ash started running in a river bound direction on Josephine Street. Ash turned in a downtown direction when he got to the intersection of Josephine Street and LaSalle Street. The officers broadcast the defendant's description and location.

Officer Lampard pursued Ash on foot as he ran down LaSalle Street towards St. Andrew Street. As he reached St. Andrew Street, Ash entered a vacant lot. When Ash reached a tree stump in the lot, he took two objects from his waistband and discarded them. Ash lost his footing and fell face down in the lot. Officer Lampard apprehended Ash, handcuffed him, and patted him for weapons. The officer found no weapons on Ash. After Officer Schnapp arrived, Lampard turned Ash over to Schnapp. Lampard then walked back to the two objects that the officer had seen Ash discard. The officer found two plastic Ziploc-type bags on top of a piece of plywood. One of the bags contained eight pieces of crack cocaine. The other bag contained thirteen pieces of crack cocaine and eighteen smaller bags of cocaine powder. Ash subsequently was arrested and advised of his rights. Thirty-six dollars were found on Ash during a search incident to the arrest. It was stipulated at trial that the substances found in the plastic bags tested positive for cocaine.

... Ash denied having any drugs on him. He further stated he did not throw anything down. He had been working at Avondale Shipyards and at an uniform store since he was released from jail. Ash admitted that he had three prior convictions for possession of cocaine.

...

Assignment of Error No. 3

Ash also contends that he received ineffective assistance of counsel when his trial counsel failed to object to the state's improper cross-examination of the defendant concerning the defendant's prior convictions.

Generally, the issue of ineffective assistance of counsel is a matter more properly addressed in an application for post conviction relief, filed in the trial court where a full evidentiary hearing can be conducted. *State v. Johnson,* 557 So.2d 1030 (La.App. 4 Cir. 1990). Only if the record discloses sufficient evidence to rule on the merits of the claim do the interests of judicial economy justify consideration of the issues on appeal. *State v. Seiss,* 428 So.2d 444 (La. 1983); *State v. Landry,* 499 So.2d 1320 (La.App. 4 Cir. 1986).

...

Ash contends his trial counsel erroneously failed to object to the state's cross-examination concerning Ash's three prior convictions for possession of cocaine. During direct examination, defense counsel asked Ash about his prior convictions. Ash stated that he had two or three prior convictions. Upon cross-examination, the state sought to clarify the number of Ash's prior convictions. The state elicited from Ash that he had been convicted three times for possession of cocaine. Each conviction was based upon an arrest in the vicinity of LaSalle and Josephine Streets.

La.Code of Evidence article 609.1 sets forth the limitations on the use of a witness' convictions in order to impeach the witness' credibility. La.C.E. art. 609.1 provides in pertinent part:

A. General criminal rule. In a criminal case, every witness by testifying subjects himself to examination relative to his criminal convictions, subject to limitations set forth below.

B. Convictions. Generally, only offenses for which the witness has been convicted are admissible upon the issue of his credibility, and no inquiry is permitted into the matters for which there has only been an arrest, the issuance of an arrest warrant, an indictment, a prosecution, or an acquittal.

C. Details of convictions. Ordinarily, only the fact of a conviction, the name of the offense, the date thereof, and the sentence imposed is admissible. However, the details of the offense may become admissible to show the true nature of the offense:

(1) When the witness has denied the conviction or denied recollection thereof;

(2) When the witness has testified to exculpatory facts or circumstances surrounding the conviction; or

(3) When the probative value thereof outweighs the danger of unfair prejudice, confusion of the issues, or misleading the jury.

In the present case, Ash originally denied recollection of all three prior convictions. Ash acknowledged two prior convictions during cross-examination by the state. Ash testified that he served sentences on two prior convictions. When asked about a third conviction, Ash stated that he did not know if he had two or three convictions. The state then questioned Ash about his arrests for the three convictions. The state went through each conviction and ascertained that all three convictions arose from arrests in the area of LaSalle and Josephine Streets. As Ash denied his third prior conviction for possession of cocaine, the state was allowed to use details of the arrest and conviction to prompt Ash's memory. The evidence of the locations of Ash's prior arrests was used to refresh Ash's memory of his prior convictions. As such questioning was permissible under La.C.E. article 609.1, Ash's trial counsel had no basis to object to the state's examination of the defendant, and counsel was not ineffective for failing to object.

...

AFFIRMED.

Discussion Questions

1. Did Ash open the door to the prosecutor delving into the details of all of his prior convictions or only to the one in which he denied recollection?
2. In this case, the prior convictions were of the same type for which the defendant was on trial. Do you believe that fact had the potential for more prejudice in leading a jury to improperly use the priors toward finding Ash guilty? Should additional care and precautions be taken when the witness is the defendant himself? What would be your suggestions?
3. Apply the Article 403 balancing test to the facts in *Ash*. What outcome?
4. You have studied Article 404(B) where prior bad acts may be offered for non-conformity purposes. Do you think there was any purpose for which the priors might have been relevant in this case that would have allowed the prosecution to offer them in their case-in-chief? [See *State v. Lockett*, 754 So. 2d 1128 (La.Ct. App. 1st Cir. 2000).]
5. Attorneys have an important role in assisting their clients in deciding whether to take the stand when they have prior convictions that may be inquired into on cross-

examination under Article 609.1. While the defendant must make the final decision, an attorney has an obligation to properly inform his client of the pros and cons of such a decision. How would you handle such a situation? What should be considered in making such a decision?

Revisit *State v. James*, 569 So. 2d 135 (La. Ct. App. 1st Cir. 1990) (discussed *supra* § 6.3)

If you recall, over the defendant's objection, the prosecution was allowed to ask the defendant on cross-examination, "Do you use cocaine or have you ever used cocaine?" The court allowed the question after the prosecution argued, "when a defendant takes the stand he subjects the entirety of his character to cross-examination by the state." The prosecutor further argued that, "if a defendant is on trial for drug charges, the question of whether or not he is a drug user goes to his credibility as a witness and has nothing to do with whether or not he has committed prior crimes."[57]

In reversing the trial court conviction and sentence, the First Circuit Court of Appeal held:

> First, as defendant submits in his brief to this Court, he did not raise the issue of his character; therefore, it was not properly before the jury while he was being cross-examined by the state. *See* La.C.E. art. 404 A. (1). Next, the credibility of a witness may be attacked by any party; and, in doing so, such party may examine the witness concerning any matter having a reasonable tendency to disprove the truthfulness or accuracy of his testimony. Nevertheless, particular acts, vices or courses of conduct of the witness may not be inquired into or proved by extrinsic evidence for the purpose of attacking his character for truthfulness, other than conviction of a crime as provided by La.C.E. art. 609.1. *See* La.C.E. arts. 607 A. and C. and 608 B.
>
> La.C.E. art. 609.1 states, in pertinent part, as follows:
>
> In a criminal case, every witness by testifying subjects himself to examination relative to his criminal convictions....
>
> Generally, only offenses for which the witness has been convicted are admissible upon the issue of his credibility, and no inquiry is permitted into matters for which there has only been an arrest, the issuance of an arrest warrant, an indictment, a prosecution, or an acquittal.[58]

Discussion Questions

The *James* court reiterated that when a defendant takes the stand that only his credibility is at issue, not his character.[59] As such, only convictions may be offered to impeach his credibility, not arrests, nor any other particular acts, vices, or course of conduct pursuant to Article 608(B) (discussed *infra* § 6.11).

1. As discussed above in *Ash*, do you think that drug addiction might be relevant for some non-conformity purpose under Article 404(B), similar to what the prosecution argued? Even so, do you think it should properly be excluded under Article 403? Why or why not?

57. State v. James, 569 So. 2d 135 (La. Ct. App. 1st Cir. 1990).

58. *Id.*

59. However, in § 6.10 *infra*, we will study the admissibility of a witness's character for truthfulness or untruthfulness on the issue of his credibility under Article 608.

2. Compare the potential for prejudice in *James* in cross-examining the defendant regarding "prior cocaine use" with the potential prejudice in *Ash*, in cross-examining the defendant regarding "prior possession of cocaine convictions." Of course, the cross-examination in *Ash* was permissible under Article 609.1, but not in *James*. Do you see a valid reason for the distinction under the law? Do you agree or disagree with the distinction and limitation regarding only allowing *convictions* on the issue of credibility with respect to specific instances of conduct?

Federal Rules of Evidence Distinction. Under Federal Rule of Evidence 609, there is no distinction between civil and criminal cases regarding the types of prior convictions that may be offered against a witness to attack his credibility. In either civil or criminal cases in federal court, the only convictions that may be used to impeach a witness are for convictions for crimes: 1) punishable by death or imprisonment of more than one year (which are generally felony convictions); and 2) crimes involving honesty or false statement. The Federal Rule does not provide that in a criminal case, *any* criminal conviction may be offered regardless of whether it involves dishonesty or false statement, as in the Louisiana Code. Additionally, the Federal Rule provides for a 403 balancing test for any crime that does not involve dishonesty or false statement. Louisiana only provides for a balancing similar to Article 403 in civil cases and only for convictions that do not involve dishonesty or false statement.

This distinction shows the intent under the Federal Rules to only allow impeachment of a witness with convictions for serious crimes or for minor crimes only if they directly bear on the witness's credibility. This is a significant distinction from Louisiana law where *any* criminal conviction may be used to impeach a witness in a criminal case regardless of the seriousness of the crime, or how long ago it occurred, including municipal ordinances, as discussed below.

Municipal ordinances. In *State v. Tolbert*, 849 So. 2d 32 (La. 2003), the Louisiana Supreme Court held that a conviction for a municipal ordinance could be used for impeachment purposes, overruling prior law that had held that it could not. See *State v. Ramos*, 390 So. 2d 1262, 1264 (La. 1980). In *Tolbert*, the defendant, a New Orleans police officer charged with aggravated crime against nature, sought to impeach the victim with several municipal violations, including prostitution and lewd conduct. In overruling *Ramos*, the court held:

> We repudiate the decision and, to the extent it remains valid after the repeal of La. R.S. 15:495, overrule it.
>
> With the repeal of former La. R.S. 15:495 in 1989, impeachment of witnesses by prior convictions in criminal cases now falls exclusively under the provisions of La. C.E. art. 609.1 and varies significantly from the rules prevailing under the Federal Rules of Evidence, the source for many of the provisions in our Code of Evidence. At the federal level, in both civil and criminal cases,
>
>> evidence that a witness other than an accused has been convicted of a crime shall be admitted, subject to Rule 403, if the crime was punishable by death or imprisonment in excess of one year under the law under which the witness was convicted, and evidence that an accused has been convicted of such a crime shall be admitted if the court determines that the probative value of admitting this evidence outweighs its prejudicial effect to the accused....
>
> Fed.R.Evid. 609(a)(1). These restrictions, which clearly preclude impeachment by relatively minor convictions, *see, e.g., U.S. v. Cox*, 536 F.2d 65 (5th Cir.1976) (prostitution), do not apply if the prior conviction "involved dishonesty or false

statement, regardless of the punishment." Fed.R.Evid. 609(a)(2). Federal law in this area clearly influenced the provisions of La. C.E. art. 609 regarding impeachment of witnesses in civil cases by convictions for crimes "punishable by death or imprisonment in excess of six months under the law under which [the witness] was convicted" when the court "determines that the probative value of admitting this evidence outweighs its prejudicial effect to a party...." La. C.E. art. 609(A)(1). As does its federal counterpart, the statute excepts from these restrictions crimes involving "dishonesty or false statement, regardless of the punishment." La. C.E. art. 609(A)(2).

On the other hand, La. C.E. art. 609.1(A) provides broadly that in criminal cases, "every witness by testifying subjects himself to examination relative to his criminal convictions, subject to" certain limitations. The limitations that follow this broad rule of impeachment in no way limit the class of convictions available for impeachment purposes. Section (B) states that only "*offenses* for which the witness has been convicted are admissible upon the issue of his credibility, and no inquiry is permitted into matters for which there has only been an arrest, the issuance of an arrest warrant, an indictment, a prosecution, or an acquittal." La. C.E. art. 909.1(B) (emphasis added).

Unlike former article 15:495, which spoke in terms of conviction of a "crime," art. 609.1 speaks in terms of "offenses" for which the witness has been convicted. The term "offenses" is not defined in the Code of Evidence. It is, however, defined in the Code of Criminal Procedure as including "both a felony and a misdemeanor." La.C.Cr.P. art. 933(1). "Misdemeanor," in turn, is defined as "any offense other than a felony, and includes the violation of an ordinance providing a penal sanction." La.C.Cr.P. art. 933(4). Thus, a municipal conviction that carries the possibility of a penal sanction is properly termed an offense. It therefore appears clear that municipal convictions subject to punishment are included within the scope of art. 609.1.

In light of the broad language employed in La. C.E. art. 609.1 in obvious distinction to that used in Article 609, its civil counterpart, the lack of limitations imposed by the legislature on the class of convictions available for impeachment purposes, and the use in art. 609.1 of the term "offenses," we conclude that municipal convictions subject to a penal sanction may be used for impeachment purposes in criminal cases pursuant to the provisions of and subject to the limitations provided in La. C.E. art. 609.1.[60]

Discussion Questions

1. What crimes truly have a bearing on a witness's credibility? Should the seriousness of the crime matter? Should the nature of the crime matter, i.e., the exact charge? Do convictions for minor crimes such as littering, door-to-door peddling, or loud music have any true bearing on a person's credibility?
2. Why do you suppose Louisiana allows a witness to be impeached with any criminal conviction, whether or not it actually bears on the witness's credibility? What reasoning or rationale do you believe underlies such a distinction?

60. State v. Tolbert, 849 So. 2d 32, 37–38 (La. 2003).

Key Points

The key points to keep in mind regarding convictions for credibility.

CIVIL CASES (Article 609)

1. **Type of convictions:** 1) convictions punishable by more than 6 months, subject to Article 403 balancing; or 2) convictions involving dishonesty or false statement.
2. **What may be admitted**: Evidence of the <u>name</u> of the crime of which the witness was convicted and the <u>date</u> of conviction is admissible.
3. **Does not include:** Arrest, indictment, prosecution, pardon, annulment based upon a finding of innocence, or juvenile adjudications.
4. **Appeal.** An appeal of a conviction does not preclude its use.
5. **Time limitation.** Not more than **10 years** must have elapsed since the conviction.
6. **Extrinsic evidence admissible.** If the witness denies the conviction, evidence outside of the witness may be offered to prove the conviction occurred.

CRIMINAL CASES (Article 609.1)

1. **Type of convictions.** Any type of conviction, whether felony or misdemeanor regardless of nature of the crime.
2. **What may be admitted:** 1) **fact** of a conviction; 2) the **name** of the offense; 3) the **date** thereof; and 4) the **sentence** imposed.
3. **Details of crime.** Details of the offense may become admissible to show the true nature of the offense under the following circumstances:
   (1) **When the witness has denied the conviction or denied recollection thereof;**
   (2) **When the witness has testified to exculpatory facts or circumstances surrounding the conviction; or**
   (3) **When the probative value thereof outweighs the danger of unfair prejudice, confusion of the issues, or misleading the jury.**
4. **Does not include.** Mere arrest, arrest warrant, an indictment, a prosecution, an acquittal, a pardon or annulment granted based upon a finding of innocence, or to juvenile adjudications of delinquency.
5. **Time limitation.** There are no time limitations as to when the conviction occurred.
6. **Extrinsic evidence admissible.** If the witness denies the conviction, evidence outside of the witness may be offered to prove the conviction occurred.

Problems on Convictions for Credibility

PROBLEM 6-44. Witness is testifying for the defense in a criminal case and has a prior conviction eight years ago for fraudulent misconduct (a misdemeanor). Plaintiff wants to introduce this conviction to prove that the witness cannot be believed. Can plaintiff cross-examine the witness regarding the conviction? Why or why not?

PROBLEM 6-45. Douglas sues his insurance company to force them to pay under an insurance policy Douglas had on his home at the time his home burned down in a fire. The insurance company has refused to pay because it is believed that Douglas set fire to the house to collect the insurance proceeds. Douglas has been charged with arson and the charges are still pending against him. At the trial against the insurance company, Douglas called Shannon to testify that at the time of the fire, she and Douglas were together at a football game 100 miles away from Douglas' home. On cross-examination, the defense plans to cross-examine Shannon regarding a perjury conviction that she received 12 years prior to the trial, for which she served a four-year sentence. Douglas' attorney objects that the cross-examination is improper. 1) Should the judge allow the defense to cross-examine Shannon regarding the prior conviction? 2) If Douglas takes the stand, should the defense (the insurance company), be allowed to cross-examine him regarding the pending criminal charge to attack his credibility? Why or why not?

PROBLEM 6-46. Shaun is on trial for misdemeanor theft and takes the stand in his own defense. At trial, Shaun testifies that he is an honest, hardworking man. The prosecution seeks to introduce evidence of Shaun's adjudication of delinquency when he was 16 years old, for possession of stolen property. The defense objects to the admissibility of the evidence. How should the court rule and why?

PROBLEM 6-47. Sarah is on trial for forgery and plans to call her co-worker Kimberly as a fact witness to testify in her defense. The prosecution has learned the information below about Kimberly. Which of the following will they be able to cross-examine Kimberly on to attack her credibility? Explain.

E1: That Kimberly's boyfriend is a drug dealer.

E2: That Kimberly was also charged with a similar offense (another forgery) five years ago for which she was acquitted.

E3: That Kimberly was convicted of tax fraud 17 years ago.

E4: That Kimberly was convicted of loitering 6 months ago.

PROBLEM 6-48. Amere is on trial for theft. Leon was present at the time it allegedly occurred. Amere plans to call Leon to testify to what he saw. At trial, the defense attempts to attack Leon's credibility by cross-examining him regarding a conviction for possession of child pornography six months prior to the trial, that Leon has appealed. The defense objects and states that Leon cannot be cross-examined on the conviction because it is currently on appeal. What ruling?

PROBLEM 6-49. Rodney is suing Billy for damages he suffered after Billy negligently ran into his vehicle causing serious bodily injury to Rodney. Rodney's father, who was riding with Rodney at the time of the offense, testifies on Rodney's behalf. During cross-examination of Rodney's father, Billy's attorney asks him if he has been convicted of disturbing the peace three times within the last 5 years. Rodney's attorney objects that the question is impermissible. 1) What ruling? Explain. 2) Would your answer change if it was a criminal case? Why or why not?

PROBLEM 6-50. Mayor Pimberly currently has criminal charges pending for taking kickbacks in exchange for awarding city contracts. At trial, the State wants to impeach a defense witness with evidence that the witness was convicted three months prior to the trial of a misdemeanor for disorderly conduct. Is evidence of the conviction admissible?

PROBLEM 6-51. Ian is a witness in a civil case for the defense. On cross-examination, the plaintiff attempts to impeach him by asking: "Weren't you kicked out of law school for cheating on an examination?" Can Ian be impeached with this evidence? Why or why not?

PROBLEM 6-52. Wally is on trial for attempted murder. During a fight with his best friend Greg, Wally shot him three times. At his trial, Wally testifies in his own defense.

On cross-examination the prosecution would like to offer evidence that Wally has a prior conviction for aggravated battery and served five years in prison before recently being released on parole, during which time the instant offense occurred. Further, the prosecution would like to offer evidence that during Wally's time in prison on the charge, he beat up a fellow prisoner and was often placed in solitary confinement because of his poor attitude. The defense objects to the extent of the testimony. What evidence can the prosecution present against Wally? Explain.

PROBLEM 6-53. Devin has been sued for breach of contact. On cross-examination of a plaintiff's witness, Devin's attorney asks him if he was convicted in 2012 of impersonating a police officer (a misdemeanor). The witness admits that he was. Devin's attorney continues, "The uniform you were wearing at the time belonged to your father, who is a retired police officer, correct?" The plaintiff objects to the question. How should the court rule and why?

PROBLEM 6-54. Jordan is on trial for murder. At trial, his girlfriend, Cindy, is called as a witness to provide an alibi for Jordan's whereabouts on the night of the murder. The prosecution wants to introduce evidence that Cindy was charged with aiding and abetting a former boyfriend, but the charges were dismissed after she completed a pre-trial diversion program. Admissible?

PROBLEM 6-55. The University has been sued by several former members of the football team because they claim that the school's football coach, Coach Pentrony, molested them when they were on the team. The University called Sam Dusty as a character witness for Coach Pentrony. Coach Dusty was an assistant coach during several of the years in question. Coach Dusty was allowed to testify that Coach Pentrony had a reputation of being very caring, supportive and respectful of other people among the players, coaches, and the university. The prosecution would like to discredit Coach Dusty. They learn the following about Coach Dusty: 1) that Coach Dusty has a conviction for presenting a fake identification card (misdemeanor) about seven years ago; and 2) Coach Dusty was in charge of raising money to buy new uniforms for his son's high school football team, but in almost two years, the kids haven't received the uniforms. They think he stole their money. Which of the two prior wrongs or acts will most likely be admissible against Coach Dusty in the trial?

PROBLEM 6-56. Jerry was on trial for second-degree battery and took the stand in his own defense. On cross-examination by the prosecution, he was asked whether he'd been convicted of robbery on 9/15/2005, to which he responded that he had. He was then asked if he'd also been convicted of possession of a firearm by a convicted felon just two months later on 11/18/2005, with the 9/15 robbery being the underlying felony. Jerry admitted this conviction as well, but added that after he pleaded guilty to the robbery on 9/15, knowing he was not to be in possession of a firearm, he called his probation officer the very next day and asked him for a suggestion as to how he should get rid of his shotgun that he'd owned for many years. He testifies that he was told that it was okay for him to pawn it. He stated that he was on the way to the pawnshop that same day when he was stopped for speeding and subsequently arrested for possessing the shotgun. The prosecution then asked him whether he'd also gone to work that day and had driven around for hours before heading to the pawnshop. The defense objects that the prosecution cannot ask Jerry about the specifics of the prior conviction. What ruling and why?

§ 6.7 References and Additional Authority on Convictions on the Issue of Credibility [La. C.E. arts. 609, 609.1]

1. La. C.E. arts. 609, 609.1 and Official Comments
2. Force & Rault, HANDBOOK ON LOUISIANA EVIDENCE LAW Arts. 609, 609.1 Author's Comments (West Publishing 2014)
3. Harges & Jones, LOUISIANA EVIDENCE Arts. 609, 609.1 Author's Comments (West Publishing 2014)
4. 19 La. Civ. L. Treatise, Evidence And Proof § 9.3 (2nd ed.)
5. **Commentary**: Menon, *Impeaching Witnesses in Criminal Cases with Evidence of Convictions: Putting Louisiana's Rule in Context*, 79 Tul. L. Rev. 701 (2005).
6. **Allowing misdemeanors for impeachment**: *State v. Odom*, 273 So. 2d 261 (La. 1973) (after defense counsel's objection to the DA's questioning pertaining to the defendant's prior conviction of a misdemeanor, the court stated that it never heard any rule stating that a misdemeanor conviction could not be used for impeachment purposes and ruled that the objection had no validity); *State v. Bradford*, 298 So. 2d 781 (La. 1974) (Defense counsel objected to the State asking the defendant on cross-examination whether the defendant had been convicted of any offense while serving in the Armed Services because it was a misdemeanor; the court overruled the objection that only felony convictions could be used to impeach a witness).
7. **Counsel "improperly" inquired into details of prior conviction:** *State v. Williams*, 575 So. 2d 452 (La. Ct. App. 4th Cir. 1991) (After defendant mistakenly stated that her bond for her previous conviction was $100,000, the State proceeded to ask questions concerning how defendant was able to bond out at that amount when State knew bond was actually $10,000 and that defendant stated the wrong amount); *State v. Leonard*, 932 So. 2d 660 (La. 2006) (finding harmless error when state attempted to go into detail of the defendant's prior conviction of simple battery after the defendant admitted the prior conviction); *State v. Singleton*, 589 So. 2d 1166 (La. Ct. App. 4th Cir. 1991) (holding that the State's attempt at questioning the defendant regarding the details of guilty pleas made by the defendant was improper cross-examination).
8. **Proper inquiry into details of conviction:** *State v. Williams*, 862 So. 2d 108(La. Ct. App. 5th Cir. 2003) (allowing the State to ask questions concerning the details of the defendant's prior conviction because the defendant attempted to explain why he did not admit his prior sexual offense. By doing this, the defendant was testifying to exculpatory facts, which made the details of his prior conviction admissible.); *State v. Ash*, 729 So. 2d 664 (La. Ct. App. 4th Cir. 1999) (allowing inquiry into details of defendant's prior conviction when defendant claimed lack of memory); *State v. Tolliver*, 714 So. 2d 1273 (La. Ct. App. 5th Cir. 1998) (allowing inquiry into details of defendant's conviction for robbery permissible after defendant denied conviction).
9. **Criminal conviction for credibility in civil cases:** *Williams v. United Fire Cas. Co.*, 594 So. 2d 455 (La. Ct. App. 1st Cir. 1991) (allowing evidence of the plaintiff's conviction of attempted possession of cocaine and two misdemeanor convictions because the plaintiff lied in his deposition when he stated that he did not have any criminal convictions).
10. **Counsel improperly inquired into acquittal or pardon or arrests or nolle prosequi:** *State v. Johnson*, 664 So. 2d 94 (La. 11/27/95) (finding harmless error in trial court improperly permitting five nolle prosequi burglaries).

11. **Prior conviction excluded under 403 balancing:** *Gage v. Potts*, 653 So. 2d 1183 (La. Ct. App. 1st Cir. 1995) (holding that evidence of plaintiff's prior conviction for aggravated sexual assault in civil personal injury action was improperly admitted when the prior conviction was more than ten years old and had very little probative value).
12. **Conviction excluded in civil case where more than 10 years since conviction:** *Perniciaro v. Liberty Mutual Ins. Co.*, 834 So. 2d 1161 (La. Ct. App. 4th Cir. 2002) (burglary conviction excluded because more than 10 years old).

§ 6.8 Character of Victims [La. C.E. art. 404(A)(2) and La. C.E. art. 404(B)(2)]

Applicable Code Article

Art. 404. Character evidence generally not admissible in civil or criminal trial to prove conduct; exceptions; other criminal acts

A. Character evidence generally. Evidence of a person's character or a trait of his character, such as a moral quality, is not admissible for the purpose of proving that he acted in conformity therewith on a particular occasion, except:

* * *

(2) Character of victim. (a) Except as provided in Article 412, evidence of a pertinent trait of character, such as a moral quality, of the victim of the crime offered by an accused, or by the prosecution to rebut the character evidence; provided that in the absence of evidence of a hostile demonstration or an overt act on the part of the victim at the time of the offense charged, evidence of his dangerous character is not admissible; provided further that when the accused pleads self-defense and there is a history of assaultive behavior between the victim and the accused and the accused lived in a familial or intimate relationship such as, but not limited to, the husband-wife, parent-child, or concubinage relationship, it shall not be necessary to first show a hostile demonstration or overt act on the part of the victim in order to introduce evidence of the dangerous character of the victim, including specific instances of conduct and domestic violence; and further provided that an expert's opinion as to the effects of the prior assaultive acts on the accused's state of mind is admissible; or

(b) Evidence of a character trait of peacefulness of the victim offered by the prosecution in a homicide case to rebut evidence that the victim was the first aggressor;

* * *

Art. 404. Character evidence generally not admissible in civil or criminal trial to prove conduct; exceptions; other criminal acts

* * *

B. Other crimes, wrongs, or acts

* * *

(2) In the absence of evidence of a hostile demonstration or an overt act on the part of the victim at the time of the offense charged, evidence of the victim's prior threats

> against the accused or the accused's state of mind as to the victim's dangerous character is not admissible; provided that when the accused pleads self-defense and there is a history of assaultive behavior between the victim and the accused and the accused lived in a familial or intimate relationship such as, but not limited to, the husband-wife, parent-child, or concubinage relationship, it shall not be necessary to first show a hostile demonstration or overt act on the part of the victim in order to introduce evidence of the dangerous character of the victim, including specific instances of conduct and domestic violence; and further provided that an expert's opinion as to the effects of the prior assaultive acts on the accused's state of mind is admissible.

A second exception to the general rule excluding character evidence from being offered to prove action in conformity with the character trait is in situations in which evidence of a *victim's* character is admissible in criminal cases. Pursuant to Article 404(A)(2), an accused may offer evidence of any pertinent trait of character of the victim of the crime, except the character trait of being "dangerous," to prove that the victim acted in conformity with the character trait at the time of the incident in question. An accused may only offer evidence of the ***dangerous*** character of the victim if he can first show appreciable evidence of a ***hostile demonstration*** or an ***overt act*** on the part of the victim at the time of the offense charged. Once the accused has offered such evidence, Article 404(B)(2) additionally provides that he may also introduce evidence of the victim's prior threats against him, as well as evidence showing his state of mind as to the victim's dangerous character.

Article 404(A)(2) provides an exception to the rule for offering evidence of the dangerous character of a victim in domestic violence situations. The article provides that the accused need not first show evidence of a hostile demonstration or overt act on the part of the victim in order to introduce evidence of the dangerous character of the victim if: 1) the accused pleads self-defense; 2) there is a history of assaultive behavior between the victim and the accused; and 3) the accused lived in a familial or intimate relationship such as the husband-wife or parent-child relationship.

This exception, which is commonly referred to as the "domestic violence exception" or "battered spouse exception," also allows the accused to introduce specific instances of conduct and domestic violence in addition to general reputation. Article 404(B)(2) also contains a domestic violence exception that applies when the requirements above have been met that further allows the battered spouse to introduce evidence of the victim's prior threats against the accused as well as evidence of the accused's state of mind as to the victim's dangerous character. The accused may also offer an expert's opinion as to the effects of the prior assaultive acts on the accused's state of mind.

Additionally, as with all character evidence, if the defendant introduces evidence of a victim's character, whether for dangerousness or otherwise, the prosecution may offer character evidence to rebut whatever character evidence the accused offers. If the accused offers evidence that the victim was the first aggressor in a homicide case, the prosecution may also offer evidence of the character trait of *peacefulness* of the victim to rebut such evidence.

As you can see, the admissibility of character evidence under Article 404(A)(2) and Article 404(B)(2) differs slightly from the general rules governing the admissibility of character evidence as provided in Article 405. Under these articles, in addition to evidence of general reputation, in some situations evidence of specific instances of conduct may also be introduced to prove character. The types of character evidence that may be introduced and the purposes for which it may be offered depend upon whether the character evidence is: 1) offered by an accused when there has been no evidence of a hostile demonstration or overt act; 2) offered by an accused when there is evidence of a hostile demonstration or overt act (non-domestic violence); 3) offered by an accused in certain domestic violence situations; or 4) offered by the prosecution to rebut character evidence offered by an accused. It is important to distinguish the situations in which evidence may be proven by general reputation only from those in which evidence of specific instances of conduct may be introduced. Additionally, you must distinguish the different purposes for which each type of evidence may be offered.

Types of Admissible Evidence of Victim's Character

Pursuant to Article 404(A)(2) and 404(B)(2) and the applicable case law discussed below (see *Edwards* and *Lee*), there are several different scenarios under which character of the victim may be introduced in the form of either: 1) general reputation; or 2) specific instances of conduct of the victim. Five circumstances involve general character evidence of the victim, and two involve specific instances of conduct.

In the following five instances, evidence of the victim's character may be offered into evidence in the form of general reputation in the community:

1. Evidence of a ***pertinent trait of character*** of the victim of a crime (*not dangerousness*) offered by an accused (Article 404(A)(2)(a)).
2. Evidence of a ***pertinent character trait*** of the victim (*not dangerousness*) offered by prosecution to rebut character evidence offered by the accused (Article 404(A)(2)(a)).
3. Evidence of ***dangerous character*** of the victim offered by the accused after offering appreciable evidence of a *hostile demonstration or overt act* by the victim at the time of the charged offense (non-domestic violence cases) (Article 404(A)(2)(a)).
4. Evidence of ***dangerous character*** of the victim (*including specific instances and domestic violence*) offered by the accused without the need for an overt act at time of offense when: 1) defendant claims self-defense; 2) history of assaultive behavior; and 3) familial or intimate relationship (Article 404(A)(2)(a)).
5. Evidence of ***peacefulness*** of the victim offered by the prosecution in homicide to rebut defendant's claim that the victim was the first aggressor (Article 404(A)(2)(b)).

In the following two instances evidence of specific instances of conduct may be offered.

1. **Overt Act/Hostile Demonstration**. When accused has offered evidence of an overt act or hostile demonstration (*non-domestic violence*), in addition to character for dangerousness, he may also introduce evidence of the following specific instances:
   a. Evidence of the victim's ***prior threats*** against the accused (Article 404(B)(2)).
   b. Evidence of the accused's ***state of mind*** regarding the dangerousness of the victim, which would include ***threats, reputation, and other specific acts against the accused or others*** upon which the state of mind is based (Article 404(B)(2)).
2. **Domestic Violence Exception**. When: 1) the accused claims self-defense; 2) history of assaultive behavior; and 3) familial or intimate relationship, in addition to dangerous character, the accused may introduce evidence of the following specific instances:
   a. Evidence of ***specific instances of conduct*** (Article 404(A)(2)(a)).

b. ***Domestic violence*** may be offered (Article 404(A)(2)(a)).

c. Evidence of victim's ***prior threats*** against the accused (Article 404(B)(2)).

d. Evidence of the accused's ***state of mind*** regarding the dangerousness of victim, which would include ***threats, reputation, and other specific acts against the accused or others*** upon which the state of mind is based (Article 404(B)(2)).

The cases that follow will explain the two purposes for which evidence of specific instances of conduct listed above may be offered, and which types of specific instances may be offered for each purpose.

Federal Rules of Evidence Distinction. Federal Rule of Evidence 404(a)(2) is not quite as complex as the comparable Louisiana article. It merely provides that the accused may offer evidence of a pertinent trait of character of the victim in a criminal case, that the prosecution may rebut such evidence offered by the accused, and that the prosecution may also offer evidence of the character trait of peacefulness of the victim to rebut evidence that the victim was the first aggressor. The Federal Rule does not provide for specific requirements that must be met to offer evidence of the dangerous character of the victim, threats, specific instances of conduct, and state of mind as is provided in Articles 404(A)(2) and 404(B)(2), nor does it contain a domestic violence exception. Further, unlike Louisiana Article 404(B)(2) which contains a provision relative to the admissibility of specific instances of conduct of the victim (including threats and state of mind), Federal Rule of Evidence 404(b) makes no mention whatsoever of the admissibility of specific instances of conduct of the victim.

Another significant distinction is that Federal Rule of Evidence 404(a)(1) provides that if the accused offers evidence of a trait of character of the victim, the prosecution may offer evidence of the same trait of character of the accused. The Louisiana Code does not contain such a provision.

§ 6.8.1 Character of the Victim/Self-Defense (Non-Domestic Violence Cases)

Overt Act/Hostile Demonstration at time of offense. In order to introduce evidence of the **dangerous character**, **threats**, and **specific instances of conduct** of the victim, as well as evidence of the accused's **state of mind**, as outlined above, the accused must first offer "**appreciable evidence**"[61] **of an overt act or hostile demonstration** by the victim at the time of the commission of the offense. An overt act, as it relates to self-defense, means "any act of the victim that manifests to the mind of a reasonable person a present intention on his part to kill or do great bodily harm."[62] For example, if the defendant is on trial for killing the victim and claims self-defense, if he wishes to introduce evidence of the victim's dangerous character, prior threats, and specific dangerous acts, he must first offer appreciable evidence that at the time of the incident, the victim did something that would "create in the mind of a reasonable person the belief that he was in imminent danger of losing his life or suffering great bodily harm."[63] Such an act might include evidence that the victim reached for a gun, knife, or other object to be used to strike the accused, or actually pulled a weapon on him.

---

61. *See* State v. Lee, 331 So. 2d 455 (La. 1975); *See also* La.C.Cr.P. Art. 802(2); and La.R.S. 15:482.

62. *See* State v. Edwards, 420 So. 2d 663 (La. 1982) *quoting* State v. Brown, 172 La. 121, 133 So. 383 (1931).

63. State v. Lee, 331 So.2d 455 (La. 1975) *quoting* State v. Brown 172 La. 121, 133 So. 383 (1931).

In meeting this standard, the accused is not required to *prove* the hostile demonstration or overt act; rather, he need only offer evidence into the record "relevantly tending to establish the overt act"[64] or hostile demonstration. While this is a relatively low standard of proof, it will typically require more than the self-serving word of the accused alone that the victim did the alleged act.[65] Typically, the court will require corroborating circumstances or witnesses supporting the accused's assertion. Once this standard is met, the trial court cannot infringe upon the fact-determination function of the jury and exclude the evidence by making credibility determinations as to the sufficiency of the evidence in proving the overt act.[66] The court must permit the accused to present a defense and allow the jury to make credibility determinations and findings of fact as to what events may have actually transpired.[67]

Purposes for which evidence may be offered. Once the accused establishes that the victim made an overt act or hostile demonstration at the time of the instant offense, only then may he offer evidence of the victim's ***dangerous*** **character**. Additionally, the accused may introduce evidence of the victim's **prior threats** against him as well as evidence that shows the **accused's state of mind** as to the victim's dangerous character. He may show his state of mind through evidence of the victim's **threats**, **dangerous reputation**, and **violent acts**, whether against the accused or others, **that the accused knew about** at the time of the offense, upon which his state of mind is based. The evidence of dangerous character of the victim, threats, and violent acts are relevant to a plea of self-defense for **two purposes**:

1. to help determine who was the **first aggressor**; and
2. to show the accused **state of mind**, i.e., whether the accused acted reasonably.[68]

With respect to the two relevant purposes for which the character evidence and specific acts may be offered, it may be introduced as follows:

1. **To help determine who was first aggressor.** On the issue of who was the first aggressor, the accused may offer evidence of the ***dangerous character of the victim*** in the form of general reputation as provided in Article 405, as well as evidence of the ***victim's threats*** to the accused. Evidence of the victim's threats and dangerous character are relevant to the issue of who was the first aggressor whether or not the accused knew about the threats or dangerous character. As demonstrated in *Edwards* below, if the victim tells someone that he is going to kill the accused, and the accused later claims that the victim did, in fact, attempt to kill him, the victim's statement is relevant to whether the victim did what he said he was going to do, even if the accused didn't know that the victim had made the statement. The statement is relevant in determining whether the victim was the first aggressor as the accused alleges.
2. **State of mind of the accused**. Evidence of the victim's state of mind is also relevant in a self-defense claim because an issue is whether the accused was reasonable in his belief that the force used was necessary to protect himself from the victim or to show the accused's reasonable apprehension of danger justifying his conduct. On this issue, the accused may introduce evidence regarding ***prior threats against***

64. *See* State v. Lee, 331 So. 2d 455 (La. 1975).

65. *See* State v. Felder, 809 So. 2d 360 (La. Ct. App. 1st Cir. 2001).

66. *See* State v. Lee, 331 So. 2d 455 (La. 1975).

67. *See* State v. Lee, 331 So. 2d 455 (La. 1975); *See also*, Force & Rault, Handbook on Louisiana Evidence Law, Art. 404(A) Author's Comment (2) (West Publishing 2014).

68. *See* State v. Edwards, 420 So. 2d 663 (La. 1982).

the accused or others, ***reputation for dangerousness***, and other ***specific acts of violence against the accused or others*** if the accused ***knew*** about them. If the accused knew about the victim's violent acts, threats, and dangerous character, it helps to establish that he may have been justified in his belief that the victim posed a threat of danger to him, i.e., that he acted reasonably. For purposes of the accused's state of mind, he must have been **aware of** the prior acts, threats, and dangerous character, and the acts may be admissible whether directed towards the accused or someone else.

Illustration of dangerous character. The following diagram illustrates the relationship of the concepts contained in 404(A)(2) and 404(B)(2), discussed above, relative to the dangerous character of the victim. The diagram shows that once the overt act or hostile demonstration on the part of victim is established, evidence of threats and of the victim's dangerous character (center) may be offered for two issues: 1) on the issue of who was the first aggressor (left), threats against the accused are admissible whether he knew about them or not, as well as evidence of the dangerous character of the accused whether or not the accused knew of the dangerous character; and 2) on the issue of the accused state of mind (right), evidence of threats, specific acts of violence, and general reputation for dangerousness are admissible to show the accused's reasonable apprehension of dangerousness, i.e., whether he acted reasonably.

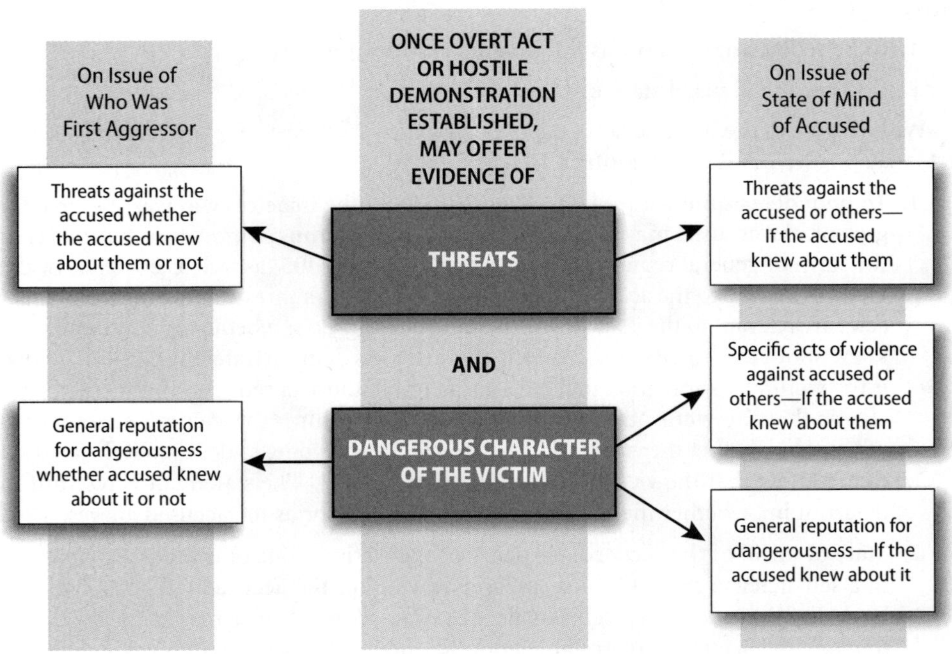

Example: Dale (D) is on trial for killing Victor (V). If Dale offers evidence that at the time of the shooting Victor lunged at him with a knife (overt act), which of the following may Dale offer into evidence, and for what purpose:

1. Victor has a general reputation for being a dangerous or violent person.

This evidence is relevant and admissible whether or not Dale knew about it at the time he killed Victor on the issue of who was the first aggressor.

2. Victor told his best friend that whenever he saw Dale he was going to stab Dale, but Dale did not know Victor said this.

This evidence is relevant and admissible on the issue of who was the first aggressor whether or not Dale knew about the threat to help prove that Victor was the first aggressor, and did, in fact, attempt to stab Dale when he saw him as Dale alleges.

3. Dale knew that Victor had once stabbed a man in the neck during a fight at a nightclub.

Because Dale knew about this incident, it is relevant and admissible because it will help to establish that Dale was reasonable in believing that his conduct was justified. It goes to his state of mind.

4. Dale killed someone several years ago, but Victor was not aware of it when he killed Victor.

This evidence is inadmissible, because Dale didn't know about it. Thus, it does not help prove his state of mind.

Cases on Character of the Victim/Non-Domestic Violence

State v. Edwards
Supreme Court of Louisiana
420 So. 2d 663
Sept. 7, 1982

WILLIAM NORRIS, III, Judge Ad Hoc.

Defendant Nancy L. Edwards was indicted for second degree murder in violation of La.R.S. 14:30.1 in connection with the death of her husband, Don Edwards. After trial by jury, defendant was found guilty of manslaughter by a verdict of 11 to 1 and sentenced to serve 10 years imprisonment at hard labor. It is from this conviction and the resulting sentence that defendant appeals.

FACTS

On November 11, 1980, at approximately 6:00 a.m., defendant while carrying a loaded .38 caliber pistol, forcibly entered the rear entrance of the residence of Mrs. Audlee Outz, located in Minden, Louisiana, where she found her husband completely nude and Mrs. Outz clad only in black panties in the bedroom. Thereafter, she fired her pistol five times striking Mr. Edwards four times inflicting wounds which resulted in his death after which she called the police. When the officers arrived they found Mr. Edwards' body on the bedroom floor close to the doorway leading into the kitchen, Mrs. Outz intoxicated in her state of undress and Mrs. Edwards.

Prior to the shooting, defendant and her husband had a violent confrontation at their family home in Dubberly shortly after midnight. According to Mrs. Edwards' testimony, her intoxicated husband had physically abused her and threatened to beat their eight year old daughter to death. Mrs. Edwards testified that after her husband threatened the child, he "jumped up and started toward her." Mrs. Edwards then grabbed a crowbar, struck him on the head as hard as she could, and fled with her child to a neighbor's home where she called the police to inform them of the incident. Thereafter, Mr. Edwards went to the hospital for treatment and several hours later to the Webster Parish Courthouse where

Mr. and Mrs. Edwards confronted each other in the parking lot. It was there that Mrs. Edwards retrieved her car, returned home to unlock the door so Mr. Edwards would not break it down, and left. Mr. Edwards later returned home with a deputy sheriff, got his truck and left.

Mrs. Edwards was afraid to return home so she went to the home of her paramour, Melvin Reeves, where she engaged in sexual relations with him before she left to go to work at approximately 5:30 a.m. On her way to work she attempted to determine her husband's whereabouts. Failing to see his truck at a truck stop he frequented, she drove by Mrs. Outz's residence, a place he had gone on a prior occasion, where she saw his truck parked. She then pulled into the driveway, picked up the gun which she always carried with her, and proceeded to knock on the front door. Receiving no answer and finding the door locked, she walked around the side of the house and passed a bedroom window where she heard her husband and Mrs. Outz "making love." She then proceeded to the rear door, knocked, found it locked, pushed a hole in the screen to open its latch, and leaned against the main door forcing it open.

After entering the house, she went through the back bedroom and the kitchen into the bedroom where she found her husband and Mrs. Outz. Mrs. Edwards turned on the bedroom light with the hand in which she held the gun.

According to the testimony of Mrs. Edwards, Mrs. Outz came toward her, turned to the right and went into the hallway toward the bathroom. Mrs. Edwards saw her husband sitting on the side of one of the two beds in the room and told him, without pointing the gun at him, that she knew he would be there. At that point, Mr. Edwards sprang from the bed saying "you G-d son-of-a-bitch, I told you I'd kill you if you come (sic) here again," coming toward her with his hands up in a threatening manner. She then started to run, hit a door or doorframe, and was unable to retreat. When she saw her husband almost upon her, she shot to keep Mr. Edwards from killing her.

After the shooting, Mrs. Edwards laid her gun on the bed and called the police from the bedroom phone to report the shooting.

The only other witness to the shooting was Mrs. Outz, who had been drinking heavily for a prolonged period prior to the shooting with Mrs. Maggie Townsend. While admittedly she was "pretty high" at the time of the shooting, she recalls Mr. Edwards' calling to tell her he was coming over but she could not recall what time he called, when he arrived or which bed she was on at the time of the shooting. She testified that she did not see Mrs. Edwards until the first shot was fired. At one point, she indicated she was sitting on the bed but later testified that she was awakened by the first shot. She further stated that she heard no talk prior to the shooting and that Mrs. Edwards had fired five shots from the kitchen while Mr. Edwards was standing. She also testified that the deceased only fell forward with "his brains blowed out" after the five shots were fired and that he was never within two feet of Mrs. Edwards during the shooting. She further testified that Mrs. Edwards never entered the bedroom but used the phone in the front room to call the police. Nothing was moved in the bedroom before the arrival of the police.

Three law enforcement personnel who arrived at the scene minutes after the shooting testified that defendant met them at the door of the Outz residence and informed them she had shot her husband. She further related essentially the same sequence of events which she testified to at trial.

...

Mrs. Edwards has never denied shooting her husband. She contends and always has contended that she never had any intention of killing her husband until he came at her in a threatening manner that made her believe he was going to kill her. It is her contention that she was justified in killing him in self-defense.

ASSIGNMENTS OF ERROR NOS. 20, 8, 14 AND 36

These assignments of error deal with the trial court's refusal to allow evidence of prior specific threats and acts of violence by the victim toward the defendant and evidence of the victim's bad character and reputation for violence.

Evidence of the victim's dangerous character or threats against the accused supports a plea of self-defense because it is relevant to show that the victim was the aggressor and to show that defendant's apprehension of danger was reasonable.

The foundation for the admissibility of such evidence is found in La.R.S. 15:482:

> In the absence of evidence of hostile demonstration or of overt act on the part of the person slain or injured, evidence of his dangerous character or of his threats against accused is not admissible.

The term "overt act" as used in connection with prosecutions where the plea of self-defense is involved, means any act of the victim that manifests to the mind of a reasonable person a present intention on his part to kill or do great bodily harm. See *State v. Brown,* 172 La. 121, 133 So. 383 (1931).

Prior to 1952, La.R.S. 15:482 required "proof" of an overt act or hostile demonstration before evidence of the victim's threats or dangerous character was admissible. Thus, we held that the overt act or hostile demonstration must be established to the satisfaction of the trial court. *State v. Terry,* 221 La. 1109, 61 So.2d 888 (1952); *State v. Tobias,* 218 La. 226, 48 So.2d 905 (1950).

However, the legislature amended La.R.S. 15:482 in 1952 to require "evidence" rather than "proof" of an overt act. In *State v. Lee, supra,* we held this amendment meant that:

> "... when appreciable evidence is in the record relevantly tending to establish the overt act, the trial court cannot exercise its discretion to infringe upon the fact-determination function of the jury by disbelieving this defense testimony and thus, deny the accused a defense permitted him by law." (331 So.2d at 459.)

See also La.C.Cr.P. Art. 802(2).

In the instant case, this is precisely what the trial court repeatedly did. It exercised a "credibility evaluation" to refuse the defendant the right to have the jury determine the merits of her plea of self-defense.

Defendant claimed initially she was looking for her husband on her way to work because of her concern for his condition that was caused by the blow she inflicted with the crowbar. Failing to locate him at several places, she drove to Mrs. Outz's residence. She testified that after finding his truck there, she intended to go inside to let him know she knew he was there, to embarrass him and to inform him she intended to get a divorce. She stated that she carried the gun because she could talk to him without incident when it was in her possession or within her reach. Admittedly, she forced her way through the back door of the residence and turned on the light with the hand holding the gun. However, she stated that she never pointed the gun at him and only told him at the outset that she knew he would "be here again." Her version of the incident was that at that point the victim sprang from the bed, cursed her, and told her "... I told you I'd kill you if you come (sic) here again." She then testified that he came at her with his hands raised as he had done many times before, she started to retreat and she was prevented from successfully doing so because she ran or backed into the door or doorframe. She then looked at her husband again, saw he was almost upon her, and began shooting because "he had that same look as he had the time he tried to cut my throat ..." She further stated that she kept shooting because he kept coming toward her. She believed that he was "right on her" and actually made contact with her arm before he fell. After the shooting, she stepped around her husband, who was still trying to grab her with his hands, placed the gun on the small bed, picked up the telephone on the night table between the beds and called the police.

Mrs. Outz's version of the incident was contrary to that of the defendant. However, she was clearly intoxicated, and there are inconsistencies in her testimony. Dr. McCormick's testimony contradicts her testimony insofar as his investigation revealed facts not inconsistent with defendant's statements that the defendant was charging her at the time he was shot. Mrs. Outz's testimony that Mrs. Edwards never entered the bedroom could be contradicted by the finding of the gun in the bedroom on the bed when the officers arrived a short time after the shooting.

Mrs. Edwards' version of the incident as told to the officers upon their arrival at the scene was consistent with her testimony at trial. The pictures of the bruises on her arm, buttocks, and back introduced at trial tend to corroborate her version that her husband made contact with her and that she backed into something while attempting to retreat. Additionally, Raymond Potter's testimony together with the exhibits showing string tracings from where the various bullets were fired also tends to corroborate Mrs. Edwards' version of the shooting.

We conclude that all of the aforediscussed evidence is sufficient to satisfy the "appreciable evidence of an overt act or hostile demonstration" test set forth in *State v. Lee, supra.* Defendant should not have been denied the right to have the jury determine the merits of her plea of self-defense based on all admissible evidence. The evidence of the victim's dangerous character and of prior threats against the defendant was erroneously excluded by the trial court.

Once evidence of an overt act is established on the part of the victim evidence of threats and of the victim's dangerous character is admissible for two distinct purposes: (1) to show the defendant's reasonable apprehension of danger which would justify her conduct; and (2) to help determine who was the aggressor in the conflict.

As pointed out in *Lee,* when the evidence is sought to be introduced to show the accused's state of mind, it must be shown that the defendant knew of the victim's prior threats or reputation. Once it is shown that the defendant had such knowledge, the scope of evidence allowed to indicate the victim's character is not limited to evidence of general reputation, but includes evidence of specific threats or acts of violence by the victim against the accused. *State v. Boss,* 353 So.2d 241 (La.1977). Conversely, when evidence of the victim's dangerous character [character evidence] is sought to be introduced by a defendant for the second purpose [to prove that the victim was the aggressor], there is no requirement that the defendant have knowledge of the victim's prior acts or reputation. However, consistent with the evidentiary rule, which is not premised on defendant's knowledge of the victim's character, there still remains the general rule that character, whether good or bad, "depends upon the general reputation that a man has among his neighbors." La.R.S. 15:479. Under this rule, proof of a victim's character tending to prove who is the aggressor in a conflict must be established by the general reputation of the victim, not by specific acts. Only evidence of general reputation, not evidence of specific acts or personal opinion, is admissible to establish who was the aggressor in the conflict. *State v. Boss, supra.*

Thus, under the jurisprudence set forth above, only evidence of general reputation, not evidence of specific acts or personal opinion, is admissible to establish who was the aggressor in the conflict. Conversely, evidence of prior threats and violent acts [whether against the accused or against others] while inadmissible as character evidence, is admissible if defendant knew of them at the time of the offense for the purpose of showing defendant's reasonable apprehension of danger which would justify her conduct.

The trial court refused to allow defendant to offer the testimony of Deputy Steve Shaw to the effect that during the early morning hours of November 11, 1980 around 1:30 a.m. he saw the victim at the Minden Medical Center where he threatened to kill the defendant if she ever confronted him again. The defense does not argue that Mrs. Edwards was aware of or heard this threat, for if she did the evidence would have been admissible. The contention is that this threat is admissible to show the state of mind of the victim at the time of the fatal confrontation, relevant to who was the aggressor.

We hold that under the circumstances of the instant case the threat, even if uncommunicated to the defendant, is admissible. It is undisputed that the victim's state of mind is highly relevant in the instant case because defendant contended that she did not threaten him nor point the gun at him before he charged her, cursed her and told her he was going to kill her. The threat in question was not remote in time but uttered only some four and one-half hours prior to the fatal confrontation. Under these unique circumstances, the trial court erred in refusing to allow Deputy Shaw to testify regarding this threat....

Professor Wigmore would not disagree with this conclusion:

> Where on a charge of homicide the excuse is self-defense, and the controversy is whether the deceased was the aggressor, the deceased's threats against the accused are relevant. The deceased's design to do violence upon the defendant is of some value to show that on the occasion in question he did carry out, or attempt to carry out his design. Moreover, it is the fact of his design, irrespective of its communication to the defendant, that is evidential ... Wigmore on Evidence 3d Ed. § 110 at page 546.

...

Finding merit in these assignments of error, we must therefore reverse the conviction and sentence of the defendant in this case because she was erroneously denied the right to introduce admissible evidence in support of her claim of self-defense.

Discussion Questions

1. What does "appreciable evidence ... relevantly tending to establish the overt act" mean? Do you consider it to be a high standard, or a relatively easy standard for a defendant to meet in proving the "overt act" or "hostile demonstration"? Where is this standard on the continuum of standards of proof? How would you define it in your own words?
2. How does one prove that an overt act or hostile demonstration occurred? In *Edwards*, the court found corroborating circumstances of the defendant's contentions, that the victim charged at her prior to shooting him, by her wounds and testimony from the coroner and the police officer about the possible distance from which the gun was shot. Many of these types of incidents do not have witnesses. What type of evidence might assist a judge in finding appreciable evidence of a hostile demonstration or overt act?
3. Did the victim's conduct in *Edwards* constitute an overt act or hostile demonstration? Would a reasonable person have believed his life was in danger or that he would suffer serious bodily harm from what the victim did? Why or why not?
4. Does the fact that the defendant went searching for the victim and broke into someone else's home while armed with a gun give you hesitation about her claim of self-defense? Where, if anywhere, should *her* conduct fit into the analysis, i.e., her state of mind, who was first aggressor, etc.?

5. The court defines an overt act in this context as an "act of the victim that manifests to the mind of a reasonable person a present intention on his part to kill or do great bodily harm." In *Edwards* the overt act occurred when the victim came at the defendant with his hands raised. Other than someone coming towards someone with a knife or gun, what other type of conduct would you think might be sufficient? What are your thoughts on the following:
    1. A heated argument. [See *State v. Taylor*, 850 So. 2d 5 (La. Ct. App. 4th Cir. 2003)]
    2. After an argument, victim goes to car and puts his gun in his lap. [See *State v. Claiborne*, 2012 WL 996880 (La. Ct. App. 1 Cir. 2012)]
    3. Trespassing on another's property. [See *State v. McGuffie*, 42-536 La. App. 2 Cir. 9/26/07, 2007 WL 2783383]
    4. Cursing and reaching in pocket. [See *State v. Schexnayder*, 708 So. 2d 851 (La. Ct. App. 1st Cir. 1998)]
    5. A person goes to another's house to "settle a beef." [See *State v. Loston*, 874 So. 2d 197 (La. Ct. App. 1st Cir. 2004)]

State v. Lee

Supreme Court of Louisiana
331 So. 2d 455
Nov. 3, 1975

TATE, Justice.

The defendant Lee was convicted of second degree murder, La.R.S. 14:30.1 (1973), and sentenced to life imprisonment at hard labor. We must reverse. We find that the trial court erred in refusing to receive testimony as to the decedent's dangerous character in support of the accused's plea of self-defense, after the defendant had laid the requisite foundation by producing appreciable evidence that the decedent had made a hostile overt act against the accused.

Context Facts

The defendant Lee and the victim Etchieson were part of a group of transient blacktop roof repairers, who with their families had moved from Mississippi to a mobile trailer park near Monroe, Louisiana, about a week before the offense charged. For the most part, they were related to one another by blood or marriage and moved from job-site to job-site over several southern states.

On the Sunday morning of the incident, Etchieson's daughter and Lee's son, both five years of age, had gotten into a fight while they waited near the road for the Sunday school bus. Etchieson came out of his trailer in anger and headed toward the children.

Lee's son ran towards his father, who was nearby standing with three other men preparing to go squirrel hunting. Lee had with him a 12-gauge shotgun.

Lee testified that Etchieson sprang at him and cut him with a knife and shouted, 'I'm going to cut off your head.' (The three state witnesses, the decedent's wife chiefly, testified Etchieson had no knife.[69]) Lee shot Etchieson, causing his almost immediate death. He

69. However, on the motion for new trial, two witnesses were produced, allegedly not discoverable by the exercise of due diligence prior to the trial. (They were in Texas and Florida then, neither of them being in Louisiana from immediately after the shooting.) They testified respectively that (a) one saw the knife in Etchieson's hand and saw Etchieson's wife pick it up and throw it in the back of a

immediately turned himself in to the police, who found a small reddened slashmark (scratch) on his left chest beneath a ripped shirt.

The decedent was a big man, over six feet in height, weighing about 210 pounds. The accused was a much smaller man.

The defense upon which the accused relied was that he shot the decedent in self-defense, in the reasonable belief that his own life was in danger. The defendant Lee was permitted to describe his own difficulties with the decedent Etchieson and to testify to a violent act he had seen him commit; but state objections were sustained to questions asked of him and of another defense witness that prevented him from attempting to establish the decedent's dangerous and violent character. For reasons to be set forth, these objections erroneously hampered to a substantial degree the evidence he tendered for his plea of self-defense.

Evidence as to the Decedent's Dangerous Character in Support of Plea of Self-Defense

In direct contradiction to the state's three eyewitnesses, the first defense witness testified that she had seen the victim make two or three jumps toward defendant and swing at him with 'something'. After he was shot, the victim staggered back and dropped a knife.

The second defense witness testified that immediately after the shooting, she saw a knife laying on the ground beside the victim.

The defense counsel then attempted to elicit testimony from this witness as to the victim's dangerous character and reputation.[70] The trial court sustained the state's objection to the introduction of this testimony. Similarly, when the defendant took the stand and attempted to respond to questions concerning his own knowledge of the victim's dangerous history,[71] the trial judge refused to admit such testimony.

The evidence was sought in support of a plea of self-defense, authorized by La.R.S. 14:20: 'A homicide is justifiable: (1) When committed in self-defense by one who reasonably believes that he is in imminent danger of losing his life or receiving great bodily harm and that the killing is necessary to save himself from that danger * * *.'

Evidence of the decedent's dangerous character or of his threats against the accused may be admissible in support of this plea of self-defense, provided that the accused first produces evidence that the decedent had made a hostile demonstration or overt act against the accused at the time of the incident. See La.R.S. 15:482 (quoted below).

---

pickup after the shooting, and (b) one heard Etchieson's wife admit (contrary to her trial testimony) that her husband had cut Lee prior to the shooting.

70. Q. No. 1: 'Did you ever ... ever hear or ever know of any ... dangerous characteristics of Lane's?'

Q. No. 2: 'Had you ever seen Lane ... do anything violent?'

Q. No. 3: 'Did you ever see him do anything physical to anyone?'

These questions form the basis of Assignments 1–3. The second and third questions may have been subject to objection as vague, but the thrust of the state's objection was that the witness could not be asked whether she had seen the decedent do any particular violent act in proof of his dangerous character.

71. The questions asked of the defendant himself, to which objections were sustained (Assignments 4 and 5), were:

> Q. No. 4: At the time of the incident, 'had you ever heard of any violent acts he had committed on anyone?'
>
> Q. No. 5: 'Do you know of any overt act that Lane Etchieson had ever committed towards anyone?'

As explained in State v. Brown, 172 La. 121, 133 So. 383, 386 (1931), summarizing the well-settled principle: 'An overt act is a hostile demonstration of such character as to create in the mind of a reasonable person the belief that he is in immediate danger of losing his life or of suffering great bodily harm. The term 'overt act,' as used in connection with prosecutions for murder where the plea of self-defense is involved, means any act of the deceased which manifests to the mind of a reasonable person a present intention on his part to kill defendant or do him great bodily harm.'

As amended by Act 239 of 1952, La.R.S. 15:482 provides: 'In the absence of evidence of hostile demonstration or of overt act on the part of the person slain or injured, evidence of his dangerous character or of his threats against accused is not admissible.' The 1952 amendment specifically permitted dangerous character evidence, if 'evidence' instead of 'proof' (the pre-1952 wording) was made of the overt act or hostile demonstration.

Prior to the 1952 amendment, this court had held that by the pre-1952 wording the 'proof' of the overt act must be established to the satisfaction of the trial judge before evidence of the decedent's dangerous character or of his threats against the accused could be received.... Chief Justice O'Niell repeatedly dissented from these rulings, strongly urging that by them the trial judge, by rejecting the credibility of defense witnesses on a merit-issue, was permitted to invade the trial jury's function of evaluating the evidence.

The legislative intent reflected by the 1952 amendment was to overrule legislatively our decisions that permitted the trial judge's discretion to determine incredible the defendant's evidence of an overt act and thus, without jury evaluation of it to withhold from the jury evidence tendered by the defendant in support of his position that he was acting reasonably in self-defense. This is the explicit purport of the amendment, and the prior academic and judicial criticism of the former interpretation (unique to Louisiana) reenforces our view that such was the legislative intent.

Despite the specific evidence by the first and second defense witnesses that the decedent had attacked the accused with a knife, the trial court did not permit the dangerous-character evidence to go to the jury, apparently upon its own credibility evaluation that the evidence was untruthful. As our trial brother stated, 'In view of the uniformity of positive evidence from state's witnesses as to what had occurred and the absence of any weapon connected with the deceased, the Court was extremely doubtful that at this point in the trial there had been Sufficient evidence to show an overt act or hostile demonstration by the deceased toward defendant at the time of the shooting.' (Italics ours.)

The trial court thus committed error in its ruling, for it ignored the effect of the 1952 amendment. By it, when appreciable evidence is in the record relevantly tending to establish the overt act, the trial court cannot exercise its discretion to infringe on the fact-determination function of the jury by disbelieving this defense testimony and thus, deny the accused a defense permitted him by law.... ...

The statute and jurisprudence require that an overt act be established before the dangerous-character and threat evidence concerning the decedent may be introduced....

But, once the overt act is established, this type of evidence is admissible in support of a plea of self-defense in a murder prosecution for two distinct purposes: (1) to show defendant's reasonable apprehension of danger which would justify his conduct; and (2) to help determine who was the aggressor in the conflict.

When the evidence is introduced for the first purpose, it is admissible to show the accused's state of mind, based on what he himself knew of the decedent's reputation or threats. As explained in State v. McMillian, 223 La. 96, 64 So.2d 856, 857, reversing for refusal to permit introduction of evidence concerning specific prior acts between the parties, such evidence 'was admissible and relevant to show the reasonableness of the defendant's fear of an impending attack or of suffering great bodily harm at the time of the homicide. It would have tended to negative intent and was thus relevant and admissible under (La.R.S.15:)Article 441 of the Code of Criminal Procedure, which provides: 'Relevant evidence is that tending * * * to negative the commission of the offense and the intent.''...

The reason for the overt-act foundation required to let in such evidence to prove aggression is explained by Wigmore, Section 63 at pp. 489–490: 'There ought, of course, to be some other appreciable evidence of the deceased's aggression, for the character-evidence can hardly be of value unless there is otherwise a fair possibility of doubt on the point; moreover, otherwise the deceased's bad character is likely to be put forward to serve improperly as a mere excuse for the killing....

Based on these authorities, the trial court committed error in failing to permit the accused to elicit from a witness evidence as to the dangerous character of the accused and in failing to permit the accused to testify as to his own knowledge of prior acts by the decedent which manifested the decedent's dangerous character.

In the context of the facts, the series of questions to the first defense witness (Footnote 2) were to develop incidents of violence known to all members of the closely-knit family group with which both the decedent and the accused had lived in various places over the preceding year or so; while questions 2 and 3 (Footnote 2), as asked, were subject to objection as not tied in more specifically to this aim, the effect of sustaining the state's objection was to terminate examination of this witness to this end. Question 1, however, sought to elicit evidence as to the decedent's known dangerous character, relevant both on the aggressor issue and on the accused's state of mind.

It is true that questions two through five (see Footnotes 2 and 3) sought to elicit testimony of specific acts by the victim. The traditional rule is that character evidence is established by general reputation, not by specific acts....

Nevertheless, the evidence of specific acts is relevant not to show the victim's character, but to show the defendant's state of mind.... The accused's state of mind (his reasonable belief of his own danger) is a material issue in this case.

Therefore, though prior threats and violent acts, (whether against the accused or against others) might be inadmissible as character evidence, they are admissible if defendant knew of them at the time of the offense.[72] As the objections of the state and the rulings of the trial court show (with regard to Question 1 also), the defendant was denied the right to produce evidence of prior dangerous acts of the decedent unless directed against the accused himself or else witnessed by the latter.

The erroneous rulings had the effect of depriving him of substantial evidence in support of proving his own state of mind, that is, his reasonable belief that he himself, from what he knew or had heard of the decedent's violent propensities, was in danger of serious bodily harm when the decedent came up to him as a result of the fight between their two children....

---

72. However, as noted above, such evidence is inadmissible until the issue of self-defense has been raised by the introduction of evidence of the victim's overt acts or hostile demonstration at the time of the offense.

Discussion Questions

1. The court explains why there must first be a showing of an "overt act" or "hostile demonstration" on the part of the victim prior to offering evidence of the dangerous character of the victim and other evidence in a self-defense claim. Explain the necessity for this requirement.

2. In *Lee*, the Louisiana Supreme Court emphasized that judges are not to make credibility evaluations while deciding whether the accused has presented appreciable evidence of a hostile demonstration or overt act. The *Lee* court criticized the trial judge for making certain findings of fact that should have been reserved for the jury. Specifically, the *Lee* court took issue with the trial judge stating:

   > In view of the uniformity of positive evidence from state's witnesses as to what had occurred and the absence of any weapon connected with the deceased, the court was extremely doubtful that at this point in the trial there had been [s]ufficient evidence to show an overt act or hostile demonstration by the deceased toward defendant at the time of the shooting.

   How should the determination of whether there is "appreciable evidence" of an overt act or hostile demonstration be handled by the court? Is this an issue for the judge or jury? What is the reasoning behind your answer? If not exercised properly, what are the potential implications? What rights might be affected?

3. In *Lee*, two witnesses testified that they saw the victim attack the defendant with a knife before the shooting. What if no witnesses were present when the victim went after the defendant with a knife before the shooting? Would there have been "appreciable evidence" of an overt act shown here? Would the defendant have likely been able to present a defense? In the absence of witnesses, what evidence might an accused present to meet this standard to be able to offer his defense?

4. Consider the two purposes for which evidence of dangerous character, threats, and specific instances of conduct may be offered under Article 404(A)(2) and 404(B)(2). For each purpose, explain what evidence is admissible and how the evidence actually helps to prove these relevant issues in the case.

   Think back to your study of relevance in Chapter 3, and the inferential steps between the proffered evidence and the ultimate issues and elements that must be proven at trial. Explain the inferential steps between the admissible types of evidence, i.e., dangerous character, threats, etc., and the purposes for which the evidence may be offered, and the issues that must be proven in a murder trial.

5. What, if any, limits should be imposed for admitting character evidence of the victim once the overt act or hostile demonstration has been shown? Should the door be open to all specific instances of conduct, no matter how many or when they occurred?

Key Points

The key points to keep in mind regarding evidence of the character of the victim.

Instances where victim's character may be proven by general reputation only:

1. Evidence of a ***pertinent trait of character*** of the victim of a crime (*not dangerousness*) offered by an accused (Article 404(A)(2)(a)).

2. Evidence of a ***pertinent character trait*** of victim (*not dangerousness*) offered by prosecution to rebut character evidence offered by accused (Article 404(A)(2)(a)).
3. Evidence of ***dangerous character*** of victim offered by the accused after he offers appreciable evidence of a *hostile demonstration or overt act* by victim at time of charged offense (non-domestic violence cases) (Article 404(A)(2)(a)).
4. Evidence of ***dangerous character*** of victim (*including specific instances and domestic violence*) offered by the accused without the need for overt act at time of offense when 1) D claims self-defense; 2) history of assaultive behavior; and 3) familial or intimate relationship (Article 404(A)(2)(a)).
5. Evidence of ***peacefulness*** of victim offered by prosecution in homicide to rebut D claim that victim was first aggressor (Article 404(A)(2)(b)).

Specific instances of conduct admissible

6. **Overt Act/Hostile Demonstration** (*non-domestic violence*). May also offer evidence of: ***prior threats*** against accused; and evidence of the accused's ***state of mind*** regarding the dangerousness of victim, for two purposes:
   a. **First aggressor** — may offer threats against the accused and dangerous character whether he knew about them or not; and
   b. **State of mind of accused** — evidence of *threats*, specific acts of violence, and general reputation for dangerousness show the accused reasonable apprehension of dangerousness, i.e., whether he acted reasonably.
7. **Domestic Violence Exception. Requirements**: 1) the accused claims self-defense; 2) history of assaultive behavior between the accused and the victim; and 3) familial or intimate relationship between the accused and the victim.
   a. Once the requirements are met, the accused may introduce the following types of evidence: 1) dangerous or violent character; 2) specific violent acts against the accused or others; 3) domestic violence; 4) prior threats against accused; and 5) state of mind evidence.
   b. Evidence may be admitted for two purposes:
      1. **Who was first aggressor.** May offer evidence of dangerous character, domestic violence, threats against the accused, whether or not the accused knew about it.
      2. **The accused's reasonable apprehension of danger, or state of mind.** May offer evidence of dangerous character, prior violent acts and threats against the accused or others if the accused knew about it, as well as domestic violence.

Problems on Character of the Victim (Non-Domestic Violence)

PROBLEM 6-57. When Bo looked outside and saw his son Bobby arguing with Lucas, his neighbor's son, he grabbed his gun and went outside to stop the feud. Lucas' father, Luke, saw Bo outside with a gun, grabbed his knife and ran outside as well. An argument between Bo and Luke ensued. Luke then reached for the knife in his waistband, that Bo saw protruding from underneath Luke's shirt, and Bo immediately shot and killed Luke before Luke could retrieve it. Bo is charged with murder and claims self-defense. He would like to offer the following evidence in the trial. Which if any would be admissible, and why?

1. Luke has a reputation in the neighborhood for being a very dangerous person.
2. Only weeks before the shooting, Bo had found out that Luke stabbed his own brother in the chest about 5 years ago.
3. Sometime within the past year, Bo had overheard Luke threatening another father in the neighborhood to kill him if he said anything to his son Lucas.
4. Shortly after the shooting, Bo also learned that Luke had choked a guy at a nightclub a few years back.

Discussion

Generally, only a pertinent character trait of a victim, other than dangerousness, may be offered by an accused, unless he can offer appreciable evidence of an overt act or hostile demonstration on the part of the victim at the time of the commission of the offense. Once the overt act or hostile demonstration on the part of the victim is offered, the accused may offer evidence of threats against the accused or character of the victim for dangerousness for two purposes: 1) to show who was the first aggressor; and 2) to show the state of mind of the accused, i.e., that he acted reasonably in his conduct. As it pertains to who was first aggressor, the accused may offer threats against the accused and reputation in the community for dangerousness, whether or not the accused knew about them. On the issue of state of mind of the accused, he may offer evidence of threats, reputation for violence/dangerousness, and specific acts of violence against himself or others, if he knew about them.

In this case, Bo will be able to show appreciable evidence of an overt act or hostile demonstration on the part of Luke at the time of the commission of the offense because prior to killing Luke, Luke reached for a large knife he was carrying in his waistband. That was an act of the victim that would manifest to the mind of a reasonable person a present intention on his part to kill or do great bodily harm. With the evidence of Luke's overt act and hostile demonstration, Bo will be able to offer the following:

1. Evidence of Luke's reputation in the neighborhood for being a dangerous person is admissible whether or not Bo knew about it on the issue of who was the first aggressor in the incident.
2. Evidence that Luke stabbed his own brother in the chest about 5 years ago is also admissible because it is a specific instance of violence against another person that Bo knew about. The evidence is admissible on the issue of Bo's state of mind, i.e., whether he acted reasonably in believing his conduct was justified.
3. Evidence that Bo had overheard Luke threaten to kill another father in the neighborhood if he said anything to his son Lucas will also be admissible, because this is a threat against another person that Luke knew about. This evidence is admissible on the issue of Bo's state of mind to help determine if Bo was justified in his conduct in believing the force used was reasonable and necessary.
4. Evidence that Luke had choked a guy at a nightclub after the shooting would not be admissible, because specific acts of violence are admissible only if the accused knew about them at the time of the commission of the offense, to go to his state of mind as to whether he acted reasonably in apprehending danger, justifying his conduct. Since this incident had not occurred at the time Bo shot Luke, he could not have relied on that information in believing Luke would pose a threat of danger to his life at the time he shot Luke.

PROBLEM 6-58. Prior to killing the victim, the defendant alleged that as he was talking with the victim, who was seated in her car, she told him that she was going to kill him, then turned and picked up a gun and pointed it at him. The sole evidence to support this version is defendant's own testimony. There were no eyewitnesses who could corroborate the defendant's testimony, and the physical evidence conflicts with his testimony as well. Do you think the court will likely find the defendant's testimony sufficient to find that he presented appreciable evidence of an overt act or hostile demonstration on the part of the victim? Why or why not? [See *State v. Sylvester*, 438 So. 2d 1277, 1280 (La. Ct. App. 3d Cir. 1983).]

PROBLEM 6-59. Baron confronted Roger over rumors that Roger was having an affair with Baron's wife at a local bar. Several people saw the guys arguing, but didn't really pay much attention, when out of nowhere, Roger was seen laid out on the floor unconscious. Baron claims that while he was nicely speaking to Roger, Roger swung at him, at which time he swung back and Roger fell backwards and hit his head on the concrete floor. Roger was seriously injured as a result of the altercation. Baron was charged with second-degree battery. At the trial, Baron would like to offer evidence of Roger's reputation for dangerous character. Several witnesses in the bar will testify that Roger swung at Baron before Baron hit him, and several witnesses claim that Roger did not do anything prior to Baron striking him. Should Baron be able to offer the evidence of the overt act and subsequent testimony regarding Roger's dangerous character? How should the court handle the issue? Explain.

PROBLEM 6-60. Mason is on trial for the murder of Steve. Mason claims that he had borrowed money from Steve about six months prior to the incident and that Steve had come over to his house and demanded the money back. When Mason was unable to pay, Mason claims that he thought Steve was leaving his house, but instead, Steve retrieved a tire iron from the trunk of his car and returned to Mason's front door and began banging on it. As Steve continued banging and pushing on the door, Mason fired a shot through the door, immediately killing Steve. When the police arrived, Steve was lying just outside of Mason's front door with a tire iron lying near him. A hole was in the center of the front door at just about the height of where the bullet entered Steve's stomach. At Mason's trial, he claims self-defense and would like to offer evidence of Steve's reputation for being dangerous and aggressive and that Steve had beat a man with a lead pipe on a prior occasion. The prosecution argues that Mason cannot show appreciable evidence of an overt act or hostile demonstration at the time of the incident, both because Steve was outside of Mason's house and because there are no witnesses to the incident. How should the court rule and why?

PROBLEM 6-61. Danika was charged with aggravated battery of Vicky. Vicky and Danika had an ongoing dispute between them because of a man both had dated. One day Vicky went to Danika's job at Burger Yard to harass and annoy her. The two of them became involved in a dispute over the counter and began grabbing each other's hair. They were separated by the staff. As Vicky turned to leave the restaurant, Danika went into the cooking area of the restaurant, dipped some hot grease out from where French fries were cooking, ran after Vicky and threw it on Vicky just before Vicky exited the restaurant. Vicky's skin sizzled as the grease hit her, and her hair shriveled up and melted. Her skin immediately began to blister, and her eyes were swollen shut for weeks. Vicky was immediately taken to the hospital for treatment. At Danika's trial, she wishes to offer evidence that for months leading up to the incident, Vicky has harassed her since she began dating Vicky's ex-boyfriend with whom Vicky has a child. Vicky has cut her tires, has thrown a brick through the front window of her house, often calls and hangs up the phone and comes to her job often and calls her names across the counter as she is waiting on her.

Will any of Vicky's prior conduct be admissible in Danika's trial? Why or why not? [See *State v. Littleton*, 996 So. 2d 421 (La. Ct. App. 2d Cir. 2008).]

§ 6.8.2 Character of the Victim—Domestic Violence Exception

As stated above, Article 404(A)(2) and Article 404(B)(2) both contain a domestic violence exception to the rule governing the admissibility of the dangerous character of the victim of an offense. The exception relaxes the requirement that an accused first show a hostile demonstration or overt act prior to offering such evidence when the incident in question arose out of a domestic violence situation. The rule takes into account the effects that the prior abuse had on the battered spouse, and presumes that while there may not have been an overt act *at the time* of the instant offense, since the prior abuse likely led to the incident, evidence of it is a sufficient prerequisite to offering evidence of the victim's dangerous character, and other violent acts in the accused's defense that were in response to it.

The articles provide that if the accused: 1) pleads self-defense; 2) there is a history of assaultive behavior between the victim and the accused; and 3) the accused lived in a familial or intimate relationship with the victim, an accused may introduce evidence of the dangerous character of the victim, specific instances of violent conduct, domestic violence, the victim's prior threats against the accused, as well as evidence of the accused's state of mind as to the victim's dangerous character. The exception also permits expert testimony as to the effects of the prior assaultive acts on the accused's state of mind. Because of the extensive amount of evidence of character and prior violent acts admitted under this exception, it is imperative that all requirements for the exception are met to prevent abuse and unfair prejudice to the victim of a crime.

Requirements for the domestic violence exception.

If the following three requirements are met, a battered spouse need not first show appreciable evidence of an overt act or hostile demonstration at the time of the instant offense to offer evidence of the dangerous character of the victim, domestic violence and other violent acts:

1. the accused claims self-defense;
2. history of assaultive behavior between the accused and the victim; and
3. familial or intimate relationship between the accused and the victim.

Familial or intimate relationship. An important requirement of the domestic violence exception is that the accused and the victim have lived in an intimate or familial relationship. A familial or intimate relationship includes, but is not limited to, the husband-wife, parent-child, or concubinage relationship. To satisfy this requirement, the accused must show "the critical issues of the **seriousness** and **duration** of the relationship. An intermittent or short-term relationship with the deceased does not qualify as a familial relationship" under this Article.[73] The exception envisions that only a close emotional connection arising out of living in a domestic situation can give rise to the type of intense psychological impact on the abused precipitating the need for such an exception.

73. Harges & Jones, LOUISIANA EVIDENCE, Art. 404 Author's Comments.

For purposes of the article, the relationship may continue to exist for some time even after the individuals have separated and are no longer living in the same household.[74] The courts have recognized that because of the emotional connection involved, the relationships, and the resulting turmoil, often continue beyond a couple physically living together for a period of time after the couple has separated. In *Rodrigue* below, the Louisiana Supreme Court notes that "[t]he domestic violence exception, ... certainly did not contemplate that the battered party would not have the benefit of the provision when the batterer, as frequently happens, confronts and assaults the former mate shortly after the break-up of the intimate relationship." "[T]he length of time intervening between the alleged offense and the violent act is material only to the credibility and weight to be given to such evidence."[75]

History of assaultive behavior. A second requirement for this exception is that the accused must offer evidence of a history of assaultive behavior between the victim and the accused that generally consists of prior instances of physical abuse by the victim. The prior instances may be proven by the defendant, the victim (if alive) or by friends, relatives, or neighbors of the accused who are familiar with the relationship between the victim and the defendant.[76] Additionally, there will often be documented cases of prior assaultive behavior from prior police visits, arrests, or convictions for domestic battery related incidents.

Self-Defense. The final requirement for the exception is that the accused must "plead" self-defense.[77] While Louisiana does not formerly recognize a "plea"[78] of self-defense, it is clear that "the legislative intent of the requirement was that the accused must rely in the particular case on self-defense as a defense to the prosecution,"[79] basically claiming that her conduct was justified under the circumstances because the victim posed a threat to her life or of serious bodily injury as provided in La.R.S. 14:19 and 14:20 of the Louisiana Criminal Code.[80] Thus, while the exception does not require evidence of an overt act at the time of the offense, the accused must be able to show evidence sufficient to justify a claim of self-defense.[81]

Expert opinion regarding effects of prior abuse. In situations in which the domestic violence exception applies, expert witnesses may testify as to the effects of the prior assaultive acts on the accused's state of mind.[82] "The expert may testify that the "battered wife" type defendant was in fear of losing her life or of suffering great bodily harm"[83] due to the history of assaultive behavior. Here, the expert is not testifying that the battered spouse was incapable of distinguishing between right or wrong[84] or that he or she was in-

---

74. *See* State v. Coleman, 121 So. 3d 703 (La. Ct. App. 2d Cir. 2013).
75. State v. McMillian, 223 La. 96, 64 So. 2d 856 (1953).
76. Harges & Jones, Louisiana Evidence, Art. 404 Author's Comments.
77. La. Code Evid. art. 404(A)(2) and La. Code Evid. art. 404(B)(2).
78. *See* La. C.Cr.P. Art. 552 authorizing only the following pleas at arraignment: (1) guilty; (2) not guilty; (3) not guilty and not guilty by reason of insanity; and (4) nolo contendere.
79. *See* State v. Rodrigue, 734 So. 2d 608 (La. 1999).
80. La.R.S. 14:19 sets forth the requirements that justify the use of force in self-defense that does not result in death and 14:20 sets forth the requirements that justify the use of force in self-defense that results in death.
81. Professor Michelle Ghetti, Louisiana Evidence, Cases and Materials (Unpublished 2008).
82. La. Code Evid. art. 404(A)(2)(a) and La. Code Evid. art. 404(B)(2).
83. Harges & Jones, Louisiana Evidence Art. 404 Author's Comment (c).
84. In Louisiana, the definition of insanity is defined in La.R.S. 14:14 as follows: If the circumstances indicate that because of a mental disease or mental defect the offender was incapable of distinguishing between right and wrong with reference to the conduct in question, the offender shall be exempt from criminal responsibility.

Requirements for Domestic Violence Exception

1. the accused claims self-defense;
2. history of assaultive behavior between the accused and the victim; and
3. familial or intimate relationship between the accused and the victim.

capable of forming whatever mental element was required for the offense, such as specific intent. Here, the expert is only testifying that due to the history of assaultive behavior, the battered spouse likely believed her life was in danger at the time of the offense.

Specific Instances and Domestic Violence Admissible. Once the accused has established the requirements for the domestic violence exception, he may then introduce various types of evidence in support of his claim of self-defense. Bear in mind that the provision of both Article 404(A)(2)(a) and Article 404(B)(2) should be read together in applying the full extent of the exception and understanding the purposes for which such evidence may be offered. Article 404(A)(2)(a) generally addresses the admissibility of character evidence and provides for the admissibility of "*evidence of dangerous character of the victim, including specific instances of conduct and domestic violence of the accused.*" Article 404(B)(2) relates to specific instances of conduct and specifically provides for the admissibility of "*evidence of the victim's dangerous character, the victim's prior threats against the accused or the accused's state of mind as to the victim's dangerous character, including specific instances of conduct and domestic violence.*"

Under these articles and the case law interpreting it[85] discussed below, once the requirements for the exception are met, the accused may introduce the following types of evidence: 1) dangerous or violent character; 2) specific violent acts against the accused or others; 3) domestic violence; 4) prior threats against accused; and 5) state of mind evidence (including specific instances of conduct, threats, character that accused knew about).[86] *State v. Terry* provides that such evidence is admissible for two purposes:

1. to show defendant's reasonable apprehension of danger which would justify his conduct, i.e., his state of mind; and
2. to help determine whether or not the victim was the aggressor in the instant conflict.[87]

In order for evidence to be admissible to show the defendant's reasonable apprehension of danger, or his **state of mind**, it must be shown that the defendant ***knew*** of the victim's prior acts of violence or reputation for violence.[88] As it pertains to state of mind, a full range of prior conduct may be admitted provided the defendant was aware of it and claims that, because of it, she feared for her life. On the issue of who was the **first aggressor in the conflict**, there is no requirement that the defendant have knowledge of the victim's prior acts or reputation.[89] The evidence is admissible solely because it is being offered to prove that the victim acted in conformity with his violent reputation and threats in bringing on the physical altercation with the accused.

---

85. *See* State v. Terry below.
86. *Terry*; *Cf.* State v. Lee, 331 So. 2d 455, 461 (La. 1975).
87. State v. Terry, 654 So. 2d 455 (La. Ct. App. 1st Cir. 1995).
88. *Id.*
89. *Id.*

Cases on Domestic Violence Exception

State v. Rodrigue
Supreme Court of Louisiana
734 So. 2d 608
April 13, 1999

LEMMON, Justice.

In this prosecution for second degree murder, we granted defendant's application for certiorari to determine whether her constitutional right to present a defense under La. Const. art. I, § 16 was violated when the prosecution objected, and the trial court sustained the objections, to evidence of the dangerous character of the homicide victim.

FACTS

An investigating police officer, responding to an anonymous call, found the homicide victim's nude and decomposing body on the bedroom floor of his small house. The victim had been stabbed once in the chest near the neck.

The detective discovered through police records that defendant had made a 911 call some weeks earlier, complaining of a family dispute at the residence where the body had been discovered. The detective also learned from the victim's family that defendant had been the victim's girlfriend.

When the detective sought to question defendant about the homicide, she voluntarily accompanied him to the station and gave a statement. She stated that she and the victim had lived together for about six months and had separated about two weeks before the homicide. On the day of the stabbing, according to defendant, she and the victim argued near the home where they previously had lived together, and the victim forcibly dragged her to his house. Defendant said that the victim held her in the house for several hours against her will, beat her, took off her clothes and raped her, and eventually tried to have anal sex with her, at which point she grabbed a knife that was on top of the dresser, stabbed the victim once, got dressed and fled. Defendant later directed police to a place away from the scene of the homicide where defendant had hidden the knife.

At trial, defendant relied on a defense of justification. During the state's case-in-chief, the prosecutor called the victim's sister, who testified that she saw defendant and the victim walking arm-in-arm near the victim's house on the afternoon of the homicide. She further testified that defendant greeted her as "sister-in-law," and there was no indication that the victim and defendant had been fighting. On cross-examination, defense counsel asked the victim's sister whether the victim had a drinking problem. The prosecutor objected, and the trial judge entertained arguments out of the jury's hearing. Defense counsel explained that he intended to present evidence of the victim's violent character under the domestic violence exception in La.Code Evid. art. 404A(2). The trial court disallowed the evidence, explaining that defendant could not present evidence of the victim's dangerous character because the intimate relationship between the victim and defendant, according to her own statement to the police, did not exist *at the time of the crime.*

During the defense's case-in-chief, defense counsel called defendant's sister, who testified that the victim and defendant were "boyfriend and girlfriend." When defense counsel attempted to elicit further testimony in an effort to establish the intimate nature of the relationship between the victim and defendant, the prosecution again objected. After an untranscribed side-bar, no further evidence concerning the relationship was admitted.

The trial court also denied defense counsel's proffer of evidence, but allowed defense counsel to explain that he had intended to present defendant's sister and mother to testify further about the relationship between the victim and defendant and about the victim's allegedly abusive treatment of defendant. Thus defense counsel was not allowed to establish whether the victim and defendant had an intimate relationship shortly before the homicide, and whether that relationship included a history of the victim's assaultive behavior against defendant. The jury found defendant guilty of second degree murder as charged.

Affirming, the court of appeal concluded that defendant failed to establish either of the two exceptions to the general rule excluding evidence of the victim's dangerous character. 97-1517 (La.App. 1st Cir.5/15/98), 714 So.2d 203. The court noted that defendant had not laid a foundation of an "overt act" by the victim against her, and that defendant's statement and other references in the record to the relationship between defendant and the victim "provided insufficient information concerning the critical issues of the seriousness and duration of the relationship." 714 So.2d at 209....

Applicability of Domestic Violence Exception

La.Code Evid. art. 404 A, governing the admissibility of character evidence, provides in part:

> A. Character evidence generally. Evidence of a person's character or a trait of his character, such as a moral quality, is not admissible for the purpose of proving that he acted in conformity therewith on a particular occasion, except:
>
> ...
>
> (2) Character of victim. (a) Except as provided in Article 412, evidence of a pertinent trait of character, such as a moral quality, of the victim of the crime offered by an accused, or by the prosecution to rebut the character evidence; provided that in the absence of evidence of a hostile demonstration or an overt act on the part of the victim at the time of the offense charged, evidence of his dangerous character is not admissible; *provided further that when the accused pleads self-defense and there is a history of assaultive behavior between the victim and the accused and the accused lived in a familial or intimate relationship such as, but not limited to, the husband-wife, parent-child, or concubinage relationship, it shall not be necessary to first show a hostile demonstration or overt act on the part of the victim in order to introduce evidence of the dangerous character of the victim, including specific instances of conduct and domestic violence;* ... (emphasis added).

Thus evidence of a person's character generally is inadmissible to prove that the person acted in conformity with his or her character on a particular occasion. However, there are several specific exceptions to this general rule. With respect to evidence of the dangerous character of the victim of a crime, such evidence is admissible (1) when the accused offers appreciable evidence of a hostile demonstration or an overt act on the part of the victim at the time of the offense charged, or (2) when the accused, relying on the defense of self-defense, establishes (a) a history of assaultive behavior between the victim and the accused and (b) a familial or intimate relationship between the victim and the accused. When the latter exception has been established, the accused may offer evidence of specific instances of dangerous conduct and domestic violence without establishing a hostile demonstration or overt act by the victim.

Inasmuch as we decide the present case on the basis of the domestic violence exception, it is not necessary to address whether the accused presented appreciable evidence of a hostile demonstration or an overt act by the victim.

The trial court rejected defendant's use of the domestic violence exception because the accused and the victim were not living in an intimate relationship at the time of the commission of this crime. Further noting there is no such plea as self-defense, the trial judge also mentioned, but did not expressly rule upon, the requirement of a history of assaultive behavior between the victim and the accused. We will address separately each of the three requirements for application of the domestic violence exception.

First, Article 404 A(2)(a) states that the exception is applicable "when the accused pleads self-defense." The only pleas authorized by the Code of Criminal Procedure are guilty; not guilty; not guilty and not guilty by reason of insanity; and nolo contendere. La.Code Crim. Proc. art. 552. Self-defense is not a plea authorized by the Code, but the Legislature, obviously knowing this, nevertheless included in Article 404 A(2)(a) the requirement that an accused plead self-defense in order to avail himself or herself of the domestic violence exception.

The statutory language must have some meaning, and it is the function of the court to give a genuine construction to the language. La.Rev.Stat. 14:3; *State v. Jones,* 481 So.2d 598 (La.1986). We conclude that the legislative intent of the requirement was that the accused must rely in the particular case on self-defense as a defense to the prosecution.

In the present case, defendant clearly relied on the defense of self-defense. From the time of her initial statement to the police, she admitted all of the essential elements of the crime of murder. However, she justified her conduct in stabbing the victim on the basis that he had dragged her into the home, forcefully detained and assaulted her, and attempted to force her to have anal sex against her will. Thus defendant "pleaded" self-defense, in the only possible way to do so, and relied on that defense as a justification for her conduct.

As to the second requirement for use of the domestic violence exception, police records showed defendant had made at least one 911 emergency call for police assistance during a domestic dispute about the time of their break-up. Defense counsel attempted to introduce further evidence of alleged prior threats and assaults, but was denied the opportunity because of objections from the prosecutor that were sustained by the trial court.

While defendant did not testify at trial, her statement to the police (introduced by the prosecutor) and the testimony of a police officer as to the 911 call tended to prove the required history of assaultive behavior between the accused and the victim. The defense offered further evidence of the alleged assaultive behavior, which the judge excluded because defendant and the victim were not living together in an intimate relationship at the time of the homicide.

As to the third requirement of a familial or intimate relationship, defendant asserted in her statement to the police that they had lived together in an intimate relationship for about six months and had separated only about two weeks before the incident. Defendant's sister testified that the two were "boyfriend and girlfriend," and the victim's sister referred to the victim's house as "their house." Defense counsel also attempted to call defendant's mother to testify further about the victim's relationship with the accused and his allegedly assaultive behavior, but the prosecutor's objection prevented the introduction of additional evidence of the intimate relationship.

As noted above, the trial court rejected the applicability of the domestic violence exception, not because of insufficiency of evidence (the issue on which the court of appeal's decision appears to turn), but because the accused and the victim were not living in an intimate relationship *at the time of the incident.* Because of this reasoning, the defense was precluded from introducing additional evidence of the intimate relationship. The court of appeal also suggested the requirement of a *current* intimate relationship. 714 So.2d at 209. The statute, however, contains no such requirement. Indeed, such a requirement would be contrary to the purpose of the statute, which "was designed to provide a certain measure of relief for defendants in the so-called battered wife cases," as well as for a broader category of accused persons....

The domestic violence exception, as observed by the dissenting judge in the court of appeal, certainly did not contemplate that the battered party would not have the benefit of the provision when the batterer, as frequently happens, confronts and assaults the former mate shortly after the break-up of the intimate relationship. *See State v. Thibeaux,* 366 So.2d 1314, 1317 (La.1978) (pre-Code of Evidence case discussing the effect of time between past violent acts and the crime charged); *State v. McMillian,* 223 La. 96, 64 So.2d 856 (1953) (the length of time intervening between the alleged offense and the violent act is material only to the credibility and weight to be given to such evidence).

We conclude that the trial court erred in rejecting the applicability of the domestic violence exception in La.Code Evid. art. 404A(2)(a) and in preventing defense counsel from introducing further support for use of the domestic violence exception that would permit evidence of the allegedly dangerous character of the victim. Furthermore, we cannot say that the guilty verdict "was surely unattributable to the error" of disallowing this opportunity to present evidence of the victim's allegedly dangerous character. *Sullivan v. Louisiana,* 508 U.S. 275, 279, 113 S.Ct. 2078, 124 L.Ed.2d 182 (1993). Since defendant was erroneously deprived of her constitutional right to present a defense, she is entitled to a new trial before a jury that, in weighing the defense of self-defense, will have the benefit of the excluded evidence of the dangerous character of the victim (if the foundation is properly laid.)

Accordingly, the judgment of the court of appeal is set aside, the conviction is reversed, and the case is remanded to the district court for further proceedings.

Discussion Questions

In his article entitled *"A License to Kill Your Spouse: A Critical Look at the Admissibility of Prior Acts Evidence as it Relates to the Louisiana Domestic Violence Exception,"*[90] Southern University Law Center Professor Donald North[91] raises a number of questions regarding the requirements that trigger the domestic violence exception of Article 404(A)(2), as well as the breadth of evidence the exception allows. Consider these points for discussion purposes.

1. "The Court in *Rodrigue,* stated that the defendant's claim of self-defense from the moment of her initial contact with the police justified her conduct on the basis that the victim 'dragged her into the home, forcefully detained and assaulted her, and attempted to force her to have anal sex against her will.' She pleaded self-defense and relied on the defense of justification. Why, then, was it necessary to allow evidence of prior assaultive behavior?"[92] In other words, based on the facts at hand, were the circumstances sufficient to support a claim of self-defense even without the prior assaultive behavior?

90. Donald North, *"A License to Kill Your Spouse: A Critical Look at the Admissibility of Prior Acts Evidence as it Relates to the Louisiana Domestic Violence Exception,"* 27 S.U. L. Rev. 181 (2000) [hereinafter North, *A License to Kill Your Spouse*] (this article is based on actual events related in Louisiana courtroom proceedings in which Professor North was intimately involved).

91. Professor North is the Johnnie Cochran, Jr. Endowed Professor of Law at the Southern University Law Center, where he previously served as the director of the Clinical Education Program/Criminal Law Clinic. He is a former Assistant Attorney General with the Louisiana Department of Justice and retired Lt. Colonel of the United States Army's Judge Advocate General Corps.

92. North, *A License to Kill Your Spouse,* 27 S.U. L. Rev. 181, 187.

2. Why do you believe this exception was created? What factors and underlying policy concerns come into play in domestic violence cases that may justify the exception?

3. Among the requirements to trigger the domestic violence exception is that there be a "history of prior assaultive behavior" between the victim and the accused. Professor North posits that for purposes of this provision, "what constitutes prior assaultive behavior?" "Does it matter who started the argument or the intensity of the argument?"[93] Whether the police were called? Does it only include physical abuse or should assaultive abuse be considered? What facts or circumstances surrounding the prior incidents would you require in order to satisfy this prerequisite?

4. In the same vein, specifically which instances of prior assaultive behavior should be deemed relevant to an instant offense? Article 404(A)(2) sets no specific limitations in terms of what instances should be admissible, and which should not. Should all prior incidents between a couple be deemed relevant, no matter how minor or when it occurred? Consider an incident that occurred 25 years prior to the incident in question—Professor North writes that such incidents are "unreliable because they cannot be related to the defendant's present reasonable apprehension of danger."[94] "How does this historical event show the defendant's reasonable apprehension of danger?"[95]

5. Professor North continues that, "[o]nce the door is opened concerning prior abuse, other testimony regarding the victim's good character can [also] be entered, thereby creating an avalanche of character testimony involving the victim and the defendant, creating confusion for the fact-finders." Do you believe there are instances in which the extent of admissible prior assaultive behavior and domestic abuse could have the effect of confusing the issues regarding the incident in question? What about waste of time? What relevant factors should be considered in applying an Article 403 balancing test?

6. Further, he writes, "[w]hat constitutes an intimate relationship?"[96] While marriage would certainly qualify, what elements must be proven to trigger the exception? Further, how long after the relationship "ends" should a spouse be able to claim that the "familial or intimate relationship" still exists? As the court reasons, the end of relationships can be some of the most volatile moments for a couple leading to abuse. What factors or considerations should the court consider in determining whether this requirement of the domestic violence exception has been satisfied?

7. Does the fact that "any marital or intimate relationship is inherently, by its nature, private"[97] frustrate the judicial process? "When the accused is allowed to introduce specific acts of violence by a deceased spouse, the State is thereby forced to produce evidence to rebut the same, which is most likely impossible given that the only rebuttal witness is dead."[98] Does the State have a fair opportunity to meet such evidence offered by an accused?

8. Prof. North further posits that under Article 404(A)(2) "certain unconstitutionally protected classes of people (i.e., battered spouses) are given preferential treatment when compared to others accused of similar crimes. In *State v. Flowers*,[99] the defendant argued that he should be allowed to introduce evidence of specific acts to show the

93. *Id.*
94. *Id.*
95. *Id.*
96. *Id.*
97. North, *A License to Kill Your Spouse,* 27 S.U. L. Rev. 181, 192.
98. *Id.*
99. State v. Flowers, 574 So. 2d 448 (La. Ct. App. 2d Cir. 1991).

victim's homosexual tendencies and habits.[100] *Flowers* maintained that evidence of specific acts would show that the victim was in the habit of offering rides to young men and thereafter taking them to his apartment where he would make sexual advances. The court stated that even though this evidence was relevant, the evidence did not satisfy the codal requirements for the admissibility of character evidence"[101] through specific instances of conduct under Article 405. Do you think that "battered spouses" receive preferential treatment in presenting a defense? Even so, do you believe it is warranted considering the nature of the psychological and physical abuse precipitating the incident?

State v. Terry (I)[102]
Court of Appeal of Louisiana, First Circuit
654 So. 2d 455
April 7, 1995

WHIPPLE, Judge.

Defendant, William Jerome Terry, III, was charged by grand jury indictment with aggravated rape (count one) and attempted second degree murder (count two), violations of LSA–R.S. 14:42, LSA–R.S. 14:27 and LSA–R.S. 14:30.1, respectively. Defendant was tried by a jury, which acquitted him of the aggravated rape charge and found him guilty as charged of attempted second degree murder. The trial court sentenced defendant to imprisonment at hard labor for fifty years. Defendant has appealed, ...

During the night of August 26, 1992, a black male came to a nursing home in East Baton Rouge Parish where Henry Aucoin, a charge nurse, was at work. The black male told him there was a female who had been attacked at an apartment building behind the nursing home and that she needed help. Aucoin called the 911 emergency service line.

In response, Baton Rouge City Police Officer J. Foley and Reserve Officer Gary Marino went to the 4700 block of Annette Street. Defendant, an individual with whom the victim previously had a romantic relationship, was standing on the corner across the street from the apartment building, which was vacant and abandoned. Defendant advised the officers that he was the individual who was responsible for the emergency call. At defendant's direction, the officers entered the apartment building. They found the thirty-four-year old female victim lying on the floor in one of the apartments. She was bleeding, had sustained numerous injuries and was unable to tell the officers anything. The victim, accompanied by defendant, was transported to the hospital. Later, Officer Ben Odom interviewed the victim at the hospital; and during the interview she identified defendant as her assailant. Defendant's arrest followed.

The victim's testimony reveals the following version of the facts. She spoke with defendant on the telephone shortly before the instant incident, to let defendant know that she would be a witness for him in his endeavor to obtain unemployment compensation. At about 11:45 p.m. on August 25, approximately twenty minutes after the call, defendant drove up to the house where the victim was staying. She answered defendant's knock at the door. Defendant declined her offer to come inside the house, indicating he wanted

100. *Id.*
101. North, *A License to Kill Your Spouse,* 27 S.U. L. Rev. 181, 194.
102. State v. Terry is revisited in § 6.10.

to remain in the car. She got into the car with defendant but was not planning to leave the residence. Once inside the car, their conversation was initially friendly. Defendant attempted to kiss her. She "jerked away" from him. Defendant grabbed her by her neck, locked the car door, started the car, and drove off, taking her to the apartment building. Defendant told the victim that he was going to kill her. He parked the car, exited it and pulled the victim out of the car. Outside the apartment building, defendant slapped her. Her head hit a brick area, and one of her earrings fell out. Defendant pulled her into the apartment building.

When defendant got the victim into the apartment building, he picked up a piece of pipe and used it to hit her at least three times on her head. She fell to her knees, and defendant used the pipe to hit her across her back. After she had fallen, defendant hit her across her face and on her legs with the pipe. Defendant rolled her over and pulled off her tights and underpants. Defendant performed oral sex on her, and had vaginal sexual intercourse with her. At the time, she could not move and did not consent to having intercourse. She was telling defendant to stop and to get off of her.

Defendant then picked up the victim and carried her into another part of the apartment. At some point, defendant said he was going to get beer for them and left. Her intention was to get out of the building, but she could not see where she was and could not walk. She did crawl but was unable to exit the building. When defendant returned to the building, he gave her a soft drink and helped her to drink it. He also made her smoke a cigarette. When she finished the soft drink, defendant told the victim that it was time for her to die.

When defendant returned to the building, he also had a pack of razor blades with him, which he used to cut the victim's wrists. Defendant threatened to cut her throat. He took a gold chain that she was wearing around her neck, telling her that "where you're going you won't need it." Defendant shaved or cut off the victim's hair and had nonconsensual anal sexual intercourse with her. Defendant was constantly telling her that he was going to kill her and that she had to die, was going to die and was "not leaving the place." Defendant wrapped her in a "carpet or whatever it was." Defendant told her he was glad she was going to die. The victim stated that she thinks that at some point defendant left the building again. She indicated that at times she would lose consciousness and then regain it and lose it.

At some point, the victim told defendant how much she wanted to live, that she loved him, forgave him and wanted to go to the hospital. She also told defendant that she had some money and would give it to him. She indicated to defendant that all he had to do was get her medical attention and that she would not tell the police what he had done to her. Instead, she would say that "some guys" had attacked her. According to the victim, defendant believed her and went for help. Defendant later returned to the building, told her help was on the way and threatened her if she later told the police what he had done. When the ambulance transported her to the hospital, defendant accompanied her.

Several physicians attended to the victim at Earl K. Long Charity Hospital where she was taken. The victim suffered numerous injuries, including a pneumothorax (collapsed lung) and trauma (both blunt and penetrating) to her head, neck and chest. There were lacerations to her scalp and lacerations of both wrists, which included severed tendons, nerves and arteries. She suffered a fractured rib and fractures of her right hand. The victim also had fractures to her face, a right zygomatic complex fracture, a small fracture of the right maxillary buttress and an isolated zygomatic arch fracture on her left side. Several surgeries were required as part of the victim's treatment. According to the victim, she suffered permanent loss of all use of her left hand and loss of movement in two fingers on her right hand.

Several of her attending physicians gave testimony indicating that if she had not received medical treatment she could have bled to death. Due to the severe blood loss she had sustained, the victim's treatment included transfusions of four units of blood, representing replacement of the victim's loss of sixty percent of her blood volume.

Defendant took the stand at trial in his own defense and presented an entirely different version of the facts pertaining to the instant incident than that related through the victim's testimony....

Defendant denied that he hit the victim with a piece of pipe or that he shaved her head. According to defendant, only when he kicked the victim in the side did she become helpless. They had consensual sexual relations at the apartment building; and, when he left the apartment building, he perceived her as being "all right," not knowing the extent of her injuries. Additionally, he had no intention of killing the victim.

ASSIGNMENTS OF ERROR NUMBERS TWO, FIVE AND SIX

In assignment of error number two, defendant contends that the trial court erred in sustaining the state's objection to defense counsel's cross-examination of the victim concerning her alleged history of domestic violence. In assignment of error number five, defendant claims that the trial court erred in sustaining the state's objection to defense counsel's questioning of defendant on redirect examination concerning his knowledge of alleged fights between the victim and her family. In assignment of error number six, defendant contends that the trial court erred in sustaining the state's objection to the presentation of testimony of defense witness Acqueline Burnette concerning whether or not the victim had injured Burnette in 1987.

During the victim's direct examination, she gave the following testimony. In January of 1992, she and defendant began a romantic relationship. They began living together during the following month. They lived together until the victim left defendant and began living with her "auntee" in August, 1992, approximately three weeks before the instant offense. The victim stated that the reason she left defendant was because they were constantly fighting, with him abusing her.

Thereafter, on cross-examination, the victim testified as follows. In February or March of 1992, she and defendant "got into it;" and she cut defendant with a razor blade. In approximately May of 1992, while she and defendant were living at the Universal Motel, they "got into it," she cut him and he gave her a black eye. During this incident, the victim had to be taken to a hospital on a stretcher. She indicated that on this occasion she was only protecting herself. Later, during the time the victim and defendant were living with his aunt, she and defendant again "got into it." On this occasion, the victim threw something at defendant and she assumed that it hit him.

The victim further testified that she had lived with her mother in the past. At that point in cross-examination of the victim, defense counsel posed the question which prompted the court's ruling forming the basis for assignment of error number two. The question was whether the victim had ever "attack[ed]" her mother at any time while she was living with her mother. The state objected to the question. Outside the presence of the jury, the state essentially contended that under LSA–C.E. art. 404, evidence of the victim's character was limited to incidents between the victim and defendant and that any incident between the victim and her mother accordingly was irrelevant and inadmissible. Defense counsel argued a contrary view. In sustaining the state's objection, the court indicated that, while defense counsel's questioning concerning the alleged incidents between defendant and the victim was permissible, his questioning in regard to the alleged incident between the victim and her mother was impermissible under LSA–C.E. art. 404 and would not be allowed.

During his testimony on direct examination, defendant stated that he and the victim began a sexual relationship in December of 1991 and that she moved in with him in January or February of the following year. He stated that the victim had a drug habit and indicated that when she is under the influence of drugs, she becomes violent. He stated they had engaged in "fights." On one occasion, the victim cut him on his chest with a razor blade. On another occasion, she stabbed him in the shoulder with a knife. In July of 1992, while he and the victim were living with defendant's aunt, Elizabeth Odom Chapman, the victim hit him in the head with a vase. According to defendant, he stayed with the victim because she is a very loving and understanding person when she is not taking drugs and he thought he could help her with her drug problem. Consistent with his version of the facts, defendant emphatically stated that the victim attacked him and that all he did was defend himself.

After the state's cross-examination of defendant, defense counsel asked defendant during redirect examination if the victim had ever told him about any "altercations she had had with family members." The prosecutor objected to the question on two grounds, one of which was that the question sought to elicit testimony that exceeded the proper scope of redirect examination.1 The trial court sustained the state's objection on the basis that the question was beyond the scope of matters covered on cross-examination, which ruling formed the basis of assignment of error number five.

Later, defendant called Acqueline Burnette, the victim's sister, as a defense witness. During her direct examination, defense counsel asked Burnette whether or not she had been "injured by" the victim in 1987. The state objected to the question on the ground that defendant had not presented any evidence of his personal knowledge of any instance of violence between the victim and her sister and that, accordingly, the testimony sought to be elicited by the question was irrelevant. The trial court sustained the objection, indicating that had defendant presented some evidence during his direct examination that he knew of some alleged violence by the victim against someone other than defendant, the court's ruling might be different. This ruling served as the basis for assignment of error number six.

Subject to specified exceptions, Louisiana Code of Evidence article 404 A. generally disallows admission of evidence of a person's character or a trait of his character for the purpose of proving he acted in conformity therewith on a particular occasion. One of these exceptions is set forth in LSA–C.E. art. 404 A. (2), which provides:

> (2) Character of victim. (a) Except as provided in Article 412, evidence of a pertinent trait of character, such as a moral quality, of the victim of the crime offered by an accused, or by the prosecution to rebut the character evidence; provided that in the absence of evidence of a hostile demonstration or an overt act on the part of the victim at the time of the offense charged, evidence of his dangerous character is not admissible; provided further that when the accused pleads self-defense and there is a history of assaultive behavior between the victim and the accused and the accused lived in a familial or intimate relationship such as, but not limited to, the husband-wife, parent-child, or concubinage relationship, it shall not be necessary to first show a hostile demonstration or overt act on the part of the victim in order to introduce evidence of the dangerous character of the victim, including specific instances of conduct and domestic violence; and

> further provided that an expert's opinion as to the effects of the prior assaultive acts on the accused's state of mind is admissible; or
>
> (b) Evidence of a character trait of peacefulness of the victim offered by the prosecution in a homicide case to rebut evidence that the victim was the first aggressor;

Additionally, LSA–C.E. art. 404 B. (2), entitled **"Other crimes, wrongs, or acts[,]"** provides as follows:

> (2) In the absence of evidence of a hostile demonstration or an overt act on the part of the victim at the time of the offense charged, evidence of the victim's prior threats against the accused or the accused's state of mind as to the victim's dangerous character is not admissible; provided that when the accused pleads self-defense and there is a history of assaultive behavior between the victim and the accused and the accused lived in a familial or intimate relationship such as, but not limited to, the husband-wife, parent-child, or concubinage relationship, it shall not be necessary to first show a hostile demonstration or overt act on the part of the victim in order to introduce evidence of the dangerous character of the victim, including specific instances of conduct and domestic violence; and further provided that an expert's opinion as to the effects of the prior assaultive acts on the accused's state of mind is admissible.

On appeal, defendant asserts that, because he pled self-defense and there was evidence of a familial relationship and a history of assaultive behavior between the defendant and the victim, the trial court erred by construing LSA–C.E. art. 404 as limited to specific instances of conduct and domestic violence between the victim and the accused and, thus, in precluding him from introducing evidence of specific instances of conduct and domestic violence between the victim and her mother and between the victim and her sister. Defendant argues that the trial court unfairly restricted his redirect examination by not allowing him to testify as to whether or not the victim had ever told him that she had had any fights with members of her family. Defendant submits that, because he claimed self-defense, his state of mind was relevant and that he should have been allowed to show that he feared the victim because of his knowledge of her prior acts of violence against other individuals. Defendant claims that the ruling precluding the introduction of such evidence denied defendant his constitutional rights to present a defense and to a fair trial.

In this case, defendant claimed self-defense. Both he and the victim gave testimony reflecting that they had lived in a familial relationship shortly before the instant incident and that there was a history of assaultive behavior between the victim and defendant, as revealed by the testimony of the victim and defendant summarized above. We find that, once this foundation was established, evidence of the victim's dangerous character would have been admissible for two purposes: (1) to show defendant's reasonable apprehension of danger which would justify his conduct; and (2) to help determine whether or not the victim was the aggressor in the instant conflict. *See State v. Ducre,* 596 So.2d 1372, 1379 (La.App. 1st Cir.), *writ denied,* 600 So.2d 637 (La.1992). The pertinent provisions of LSA–C.E. art. 404 quoted above, under appropriate circumstances, authorize the admission of evidence of the victim's dangerous character which includes specific instances of conduct and domestic violence by the victim whether against the accused or others. *Cf. State v. Lee,* 331 So.2d 455, 461 (La.1975). However, in order for evidence to be admissible to show the defendant's reasonable apprehension of danger, it must be shown that the defendant knew of the victim's prior acts of violence or reputation for violence. On the other hand, if the evidence is to be introduced to help determine who was the aggressor in the conflict, there is no requirement that the defendant have knowledge of the victim's prior acts or reputation. However, only evidence of general reputation, not evidence of specific acts or personal opinion, is admissible to establish who was the aggressor. *State v. Edwards,* 420 So.2d 663, 671 (La.1982); *State v. Johnson,* 553 So.2d 865, 871 (La.App. 1st Cir.1989), *writ denied,* 558 So.2d 600 (La.1990).

Consequently, the trial court erred by construing the pertinent provisions of LSA–C.E. art. 404 as being limited to evidence of specific instances of conduct and domestic violence by the victim against defendant. However, because defense counsel's question to defendant on redirect examination as to whether or not "[the victim] had ever told [him] about any altercations she had had with family members" was beyond the subject matter covered on cross-examination, it was within the court's discretion to refuse to allow defendant to bring out such new matter on redirect. *See* LSA–C.E. art. 611 D.

...

CONVICTION AFFIRMED; SENTENCE VACATED; REMANDED FOR RESENTENCING.

Discussion Questions

1. Why was it necessary for the defense attorney to first ask the defendant about whether he knew about prior violent acts of the victim against her family members prior to eliciting the information from others?
2. Explain why the evidence the defense sought to introduce should have been allowed.
3. In this case, the entire issue of the admissibility of the violent acts against others was pretermitted by the fact that the defendant did not attempt to address it until redirect examination. Had the defense attempted to elicit the information during direct examination, and it had been improperly excluded by the court, what outcome do you think would have resulted? In other words, do you think the case would have been reversed with the court finding that a substantial right of the defendant was affected or do you think any error would have been harmless?
4. As a refresher, what is the scope of cross-examination, redirect examination, and recross-examination?

Key Points

The key points to keep in mind regarding the domestic violence exception to victim's character.

1. **Requirements for the domestic violence exception**:
   1. the accused claims self-defense;
   2. history of assaultive behavior between the accused and the victim; and
   3. familial or intimate relationship between the accused and the victim.
2. Once the requirements are met, the accused may introduce the following types of evidence: 1) dangerous or violent character of the victim; 2) specific violent acts against the accused or others; 3) domestic violence; 4) prior threats against accused; and 5) state of mind evidence (including specific instances of conduct, threats, character that accused knew about).
3. Evidence may be admitted for **two purposes**:

1. **Who was first aggressor.** May offer evidence of dangerous character, domestic violence, threats against the accused, whether or not the accused knew about it.
2. **The accused's reasonable apprehension of danger, or state of mind.** May offer evidence of dangerous character, prior violent acts and threats against the accused or others if the accused knew about it, as well as domestic violence.

4. Expert opinion may be offered on the effects that the prior abusive acts had on the accused.

Problems on Character of the Victim—Domestic Violence Exception

PROBLEM 6-62. Wendy and John were married for several years. Over time the flame burned out and John left Wendy. John moved on quickly and began seeing another lady named Candy. Just days after breaking off the relationship with Wendy, Wendy visited John's new apartment where she found John and Candy in bed. Wendy went berserk and brandished the pistol she always carried for protection. John lunged from the bed screaming, "Didn't I tell you don't be coming around here? I'll kill you! This is my house." Wendy pulled the trigger, shooting John once in the chest, killing him. John had never in the past attacked Wendy prior to the confrontation and subsequent shooting, although she had known him to be violent toward others on a couple occasions and a few threats. He'd hit a man over the head with a bottle once at a nightclub and beat up a coworker at the plant where he worked. Wendy wishes to offer the evidence as part of her self-defense plea. She maintains that when she shot John, she believed that when he lunged at her, he was going to kill her in a fit of rage. Will Wendy be able to offer evidence of John's character for dangerousness, threats to others, and two prior specific violent acts in order to prove her state of mind after the threat and lung?

Discussion:

While generally, only a pertinent character trait of the victim, other than dangerousness, may be offered by the accused: 1) when the accused pleads self-defense; 2) there is a history of assaultive behavior between the victim and the accused; and 3) the accused lived in a familial or intimate relationship with the victim, the accused may offer evidence of the dangerous character of the victim, specific instances of conduct and domestic violence by the victim. It is not necessary to first show an overt act or hostile demonstration at the time of the commission of the offense to offer evidence of the dangerous character, specific acts, and domestic violence when these requirements are met. Here, Wendy and John live in a familial/intimate relationship because they were married for several years, and have only been separated for a few days. It is irrelevant that John has gotten another apartment of his own and has a new girlfriend; under this fact pattern, the relationship still satisfies the requirement for the provision because it is so soon after the relationship ended, and the couple is most likely still married. Further, the courts have recognized that some of the most volatile times in a relationship are when the couple is breaking up, so this period of time was indeed intended to be covered under the exception. The victim also claims self-defense in this case. However, since the couple does not have a history of assaultive behavior, the domestic violence exception does not apply.

Since the domestic violence exception does not apply, Wendy would have to show appreciable evidence of an overt act or hostile demonstration on John's part at the time of the commission of the offense to offer evidence of his dangerous character, threats, and specific instances of violence, to go toward the issues of: 1) who was the first aggressor, and 2) to show the state of mind of the accused, i.e., the reasonableness of her conduct.

Here, prior to Wendy opening fire on John, he lunged from the bed at her screaming, "Didn't I tell you don't be coming around here? I'll kill you! This is my house." This act and words would have manifested to the mind of a reasonable person a present intention on his part to kill or do great bodily harm to them. She will likely be able to show appreciable evidence of the overt act since a witness was there to testify to John's conduct, if she so testifies. As a result of John's overt act, Wendy can now offer evidence of John's character for dangerousness and evidence of threats he made to others, whether or not she knew about them, to show that he was the first aggressor. The character evidence, threats, and specific instances of violence that she is aware of may also be offered on the issue of her state of mind since she knew about them and thus likely affected whether she reasonably believed she was in danger of death or of receiving serious bodily injury at the time she shot John.

PROBLEM 6-63. Freddie was suspicious that his wife was having an affair with her boss ("Boss"). One evening after his wife was very late getting home from work, Freddie traveled to her job and found only her car and Boss' cars in the parking lot. Freddie began banging on the back door, and when Boss opened the door, Freddie immediately jumped on top of him and began punching him in the face. While continuously being punched, Boss managed to scoot across the floor over to his briefcase where he retrieved his gun and shot Freddie once in the stomach during the scuffle, immediately killing Freddie. Boss is charged with murder and claims self-defense. In his defense, he would like to offer evidence of the following. Which of the following will be admissible?

E-1: That he was aware that Freddie had, in fact, killed a man in the past.

E-2: That another employee had told him that Freddie was telling folks that he'd kill Boss if he found out that Boss was having an affair with his wife.

E-3: That since the murder, he has learned that Freddie also threatened to kill another guy with whom he thought his wife was having an affair.

E-4: That he knew that Freddie had a reputation for being very violent and dangerous in their small town.

PROBLEM 6-64. Kelly is on trial for shooting her live-in boyfriend Mark in the stomach one Friday night following a long evening of fussing and fighting, which is common after Mark gets paid on Friday and gets drunk. The two have lived together about eight months. On the Friday night in question, while arguing in the kitchen, Mark threatened Kelly, saying, "*I will bust yo (expletive) mouth open if you say another (expletive) word!!!!*" Kelly stood speechless as Mark got up, grabbed her by the neck and pointed in her face repeatedly asking, "*Do you (expletive) hear me? Do you hear me, (expletive)?*" Afraid to say anything, Kelly grabbed a knife from the drawer and stabbed Mark in the stomach with it. Kelly is charged with second-degree battery and claims self-defense. Which of the following will be admissible at Kelly's trial?

E1: All of the past incidents of domestic violence between Kelly and Mark.

E2: Evidence that Mark used to beat his ex-wife and often bragged about it to Kelly.

E3: Evidence of Mark's dangerous character.

E4: Evidence that Kelly knew that Mark physically assaulted a woman at his job just a few weeks prior to the incident and sent her to the hospital, after she and Mark had a minor disagreement at work.

E5: Evidence from one of Mark's co-workers that Mark had told him that same day before leaving work that he was going home to whip Kelly—but Kelly didn't know he'd told him that at the time.

PROBLEM 6-65. Benita is on trial for killing her husband, Benny. Benita testified that Benny often beat her if she did not cook for him every night of the week, and had threatened to "finish her off" if she did it again. Benita shot Benny when he entered the house one evening when she had not cooked for him, and claimed self-defense. Benita would like to offer evidence of Benny's dangerous and violent character, and of his prior threats against her and the beatings. Will the evidence be admissible?

PROBLEM 6-66. Kacy and Kenneth began dating while Kenneth was in the Air Force. A couple of months after they began dating, Kacy became pregnant. Kenneth then informed her that he was being deployed to Afghanistan for nine months. Right after Kenneth left, Kacy suffered a miscarriage. Kacy and Kenneth continued their relationship via social media, email, and video phone calls during the 9 months that Kenneth was deployed. After Kenneth returned home from Afghanistan, he got an apartment across town from Kacy. About a month after Kenneth had returned home, Kacy unexpectedly showed up at Kenneth's apartment after a night out partying with her girlfriends. Following an altercation, Kacy stabbed Kenneth 64 times, including a stab in the neck that killed him. At Kacy's trial for second-degree murder, Kacy sought to introduce evidence from her neighbor who lived underneath her, that a couple weeks before the stabbing, he had overheard an argument between Kacy and Kenneth and had gone up to Kacy's apartment to ask Kenneth to leave. He will testify that as Kenneth left he stated, "I'll take care of her later." The prosecution objected to the neighbor's testimony. He claimed the testimony was evidence of a specific instance of conduct of the victim and that the defense had not established the requirements of the domestic violence exception because there was no 1) history of assaultive behavior; and 2) no intimate or familial relationship between the two of them. How should the court rule on the objection? [See *State v. Coleman*, 121 So. 3d 703 (La. Ct. App. 2d Cir. 2013).]

PROBLEM 6-67. Defendant and victim were both serving life sentences in prison. They had been sharing a 10' x 10' cell for about six weeks. During that time, the defendant had made several requests to be moved to another cell, and continued complaining that the victim was a bully. One night deputies overheard both the defendant and victim screaming. They ran to the cell and when they arrived the defendant was on top of the victim and had stabbed him over twenty times in the chest, killing him. The deputies recovered a makeshift knife from the defendant. The victim had no weapon. At the defendant's trial, he sought to introduce evidence of the victim's character for being a bully around the prison. He sought to have witnesses testify to several arguments they had heard between the gentlemen. The defendant claimed that while their relationship was not sexual, it was familial because they lived together in a small cell. [See *State v. Kelly*, 935 So. 2d 205 (La. Ct. App. 1st Cir. 2006).]

PROBLEM 6-68. Jasmine's estranged husband is on trial for aggravated battery because he burst a bottle across Jasmine's head. The bottle fractured and left a large laceration on Jasmine's head. At the defendant's trial, the prosecution calls Jasmine's best friend from her childhood and current neighbor to testify as a witness in its case-in-chief. After the proper foundation is laid, Jasmine's friend testifies that Jasmine has a reputation in the community for being a very peaceful and non-violent woman. The defense counsel objects to the admissibility of the friend's testimony. How should the court respond?

PROBLEM 6-69. Bruce and Angela had been married for 15 years. Over that time Bruce had beat Angela often—at least five to six times per year. The police had been called to the residence on several occasions, and Bruce had been arrested three times. One night Bruce beat Angela badly because of an outfit that one of Bruce's friends told him he saw Angela wearing. That night as Angela looked into the mirror and tried to figure out how she would explain the bruising the next day at work, she decided she was done. She retrieved Bruce's gun from the safe, and went into their bedroom and shot Bruce in the back of the head, immediately killing him. Angela claimed self-defense and wishes to offer evidence of the beatings, evidence of Bruce's dangerous character and evidence of several violent acts Bruce has committed against others as well. What, if any, of the evidence is admissible? What would have to be established prior to admitting any of the evidence?

§ 6.8 References and Additional Authority on Offering Character of the Victim [La. C.E. arts. 404(A)(2), 404(B)(2)]

1. La. C.E. arts. 404(A)(2), 404(B)(2) and Official Comments
2. Force & Rault, Handbook on Louisiana Evidence Law Arts. 404(A)(2), 404(B)(2) Author's Comments (West Publishing 2014)
3. Harges & Jones, Louisiana Evidence Art. 404(A)(2), 404(B)(2) Author's Comments (West Publishing 2014)
4. 19 La. Civ. L. Treatise, Evidence And Proof § 5.2 (2nd ed.)
5. **Commentary**: North, *A License to Kill Your Spouse: A Critical Look at the Admissibility of Prior Acts Evidence as it Relates to the Louisiana Domestic Violence Exception*, 27 S.U. L. Rev. 181 (2000).
6. **Court found no "overt act":** *State v. Taylor*, 850 So. 2d 5 (La. Ct. App. 4th Cir. 2003) (argument between defendant and victim insufficient overt act); *State v. Lathan*, 953 So. 2d 890 (La. Ct. App. 2d Cir. 2007) (holding that evidence that victim had HIV was insufficient to show an overt act or hostile demonstration); *State v. Loston,* 874 So. 2d 197 (La. Ct. App. 1st Cir. 2004) (not allowing the defense to bring in specific acts of the victim to show the victim's bad character after defendant claimed that the unarmed victim made an overt act simply because he had "beef" with the defendant*); State v. Bell,* 647 So. 2d 498 (La. Ct. App. 3d Cir. 1994) (holding that a 2' long and 1" in diameter stick was a dangerous weapon used against the victim and defendant could not prove that there was any evidence of an overt act on the part of the victim; therefore, character evidence of the victim was inadmissible); *State v. Scott*, 720 So. 2d 415, 31,379 (La.App. 2 Cir. 10/28/98) (holding that evidence that victim pushed defendant was insufficient evidence of "overt act" to support admission of evidence of victim's dangerous character in murder prosecution); *State v. Ducre*, 596 So. 2d 1372 (La. Ct. App. 1st Cir. 1992) (holding that victim's approach toward defendant while making certain hand gestures toward him during an argument was not an "overt act" so as to allow defendant to introduce evidence of victim's dangerous character, even if victim had gun in his back pocket).
7. **Court finds sufficient overt act (knife, gun, bat, etc.):** *State. v. Brice*, 808 So. 2d 615 (La. Ct. App. 1st Cir. 2001) (holding that although the defendant had established an overt act on the part of the victim by testifying that the victim had choked, slapped, and threatened to rape her, prior acts of the defendant were inadmissible because the

defendant did not have knowledge of the victim's prior conviction for rape at the time of the current offense and the prior conviction was a specific instance); *State v. Brooks*, 734 So. 2d 1232 (La.App. 1 Cir. 4/15/99) (holding that victim's active pursuit with three friends of defendant and his female friend, victim's threat of "war" directed at defendant, and victim's lunging at defendant after warning shots had been fired constituted overt hostile acts, for purposes of determining admissibility of evidence of victim's allegedly violent character in manslaughter prosecution); *State v. Carter*, 550 So. 2d 805 (La. Ct. App. 2d Cir 1989) (holding that in a prosecution for second-degree murder in which the defendant was claiming self-defense, defendant offered appreciable evidence of hostile overt acts by the victim towards the defendant, allowing him to introduce evidence of the victim's dangerous character, where there was evidence that the victim grabbed the defendant and spun him around, and that victim reached into his pocket as if to draw a knife, and advanced on defendant after being warned).

8. **Cases where excluded evidence of overt act because not "appreciable evidence":** *State v. Felder*, 809 So. 2d 360 (La. Ct. App. 1st Cir. 1991) (not allowing the defense to introduce evidence of the victim's character after the defendant claimed that he shot the victim because he saw the victim pull "something black" out of his pocket; finding that the victim's sudden hand movement from his pocket while allegedly engaged in an argument was not appreciable evidence of overt act by the victim); *State v. Jones*, La. App. 5 Cir. 5/23/13 WL 2249168 (La. Ct. App. 5th Cir. 2013) (unpublished) (holding that defendant's own testimony that he saw victim reach into pocket for what appeared to be a rag with something black in it that looked like a gun or knife was not "appreciable evidence" of overt act or hostile demonstration).
9. **Familial/Intimate relationship found, but inapplicable:** *State v. Coleman*, 121 So. 3d 703 (La. Ct. App. 2d Cir. 2013) (holding that although a familial/intimate relationship existed between the victim and the defendant, the domestic violence exception did not apply because the defendant was unable to establish prior assaultive behavior by the victim).
10. **Character for peacefulness:** *State v. Ducksworth*, 469 So. 2d 624 (La. Ct. App. 1st Cir 1986) (holding that court properly permitted witness to testify to victim's reputation for peacefulness in rebuttal to vast amount of evidence offered of victim's dangerous, aggressive character).

§ 6.9 Sexual Assault Victim Character [La. C.E. arts. 412, 412.1, 412.2, and 412.3]

The Louisiana Code of Evidence contains several articles that govern the admissibility of prior sexual conduct in sexual assault cases. In § 6.9 we will address these articles. Article 412 governs the admissibility of the past sexual behavior of the victim of a sexual assault, including victims of sexual trafficking; Article 412.1 governs the admissibility of the victim's attire in sexual assault cases; Article 412.2 governs the admissibility of prior sexual conduct and other prior acts of the accused in sexual assault cases; and Article 412.3 governs the admissibility of certain statements made by victims of sexual trafficking in sex trafficking cases.

Some of these rules will virtually turn everything you've learned about the admissibility of character and other crimes on its head. However, many of the rules and procedures for admitting evidence under these articles overlap with the rules you've studied thus far, so it is important to learn and study these concepts in the context of studying the admissibility of character and other crimes in general. It is also important to understand and keep in mind the policy considerations underlying the articles relative to sexual assault. The reasoning should help to guide you in your understanding and application of these rules.

§ 6.9.1 Rape Shield Statute [La. C.E. art. 412]

Applicable Code Articles

Art. 412. Victim's past sexual behavior in sexual assault cases; trafficking offenses

A. (1) Opinion and reputation evidence; sexual assault cases. When an accused is charged with a crime involving sexually assaultive behavior, reputation or opinion evidence of the past sexual behavior of the victim is not admissible.

(2) Other evidence; exceptions. When an accused is charged with a crime involving sexually assaultive behavior, evidence of specific instances of the victim's past sexual behavior is also not admissible except for:

(a) Evidence of past sexual behavior with persons other than the accused, upon the issue of whether or not the accused was the source of semen or injury; provided that such evidence is limited to a period not to exceed seventy-two hours prior to the time of the offense, and further provided that the jury be instructed at the time and in its final charge regarding the limited purpose for which the evidence is admitted; or

(b) Evidence of past sexual behavior with the accused offered by the accused upon the issue of whether or not the victim consented to the sexually assaultive behavior.

* * *

Article 412 is Louisiana's Rape Shield Statute and generally excludes evidence of the prior sexual behavior of the victim of a sexual assault from being introduced and inquired into at trial. Historically, victims of sexual assaults, usually women, were discouraged from reporting sexual assaults because of the experiences they incurred at trial. Victims of sexual assaults were often embarrassed and harassed as their prior sexual history and sexual predisposition were fair game to be exploited by the defense before the jury. The experiences at trial ultimately led to significant underreporting of sexual assaults.[103] In response, most states across the country and the federal government have enacted rape shield statutes. Rape shield statutes are designed to abate the victim's ordeal at trial.[104] By excluding evidence of unrelated prior sexual conduct that has little to no probative value toward proving the instant offense, they lessen the possibility of unjust influence by inflammatory evidence, avoid confusion of issues and waste of time, and encourage reports of rape.[105]

Louisiana's Rape Shield Statute provides that when an accused is charged with a crime involving sexually assaultive behavior, the following evidence is inadmissible: **1) opinion evidence, 2) reputation evidence, and 3) specific instances of conduct regarding the**

103. According to a recent study by the U.S. Department of Justice: Bureau of Justice Statistics titled, "Rape and Sexual Assault: Reporting to Police and Medical Attention, 1992–2000" published in 2002, 63% of completed rapes, 65% of attempted rapes, and 74% of completed and attempted sexual assaults against females were not reported to the police during the relevant time period.

104. State v. Vaughn, 448 So. 2d 1260 (La. 1984).

105. *See* State v. Vaughn, 448 So. 2d 1260 (La. 1984).

past sexual behavior of the victim of the sexual assault. Thus, in a rape trial, the defendant cannot offer evidence that the victim had a *reputation* for being easy, or promiscuous; evidence of anyone's *opinion* that the victim slept around or was loose; nor evidence regarding other people with whom the victim might have had sexual relations.

For purposes of Article 412, all sexual behavior, other than the sexual behavior with respect to which the offense of sexually assaultive behavior is alleged, is generally excluded. The exclusion is broad, and even includes past instances of sexual conduct between the victim and the accused, except as provided below. Further, the article **only applies to criminal cases**. In civil cases, the general rule of inadmissibility of character evidence and specific instances of conduct are governed by Article 404 and 405.[106]

Exceptions. Louisiana's Rape Shield Statute contains two narrow exceptions in which the defendant may offer evidence of specific instances of past sexual behavior of the victim:

1. Evidence of past sexual behavior with persons **other than the accused** that took place **within 72 hours** prior to the time of the incident, on the issue of whether or not the accused was the source of semen or injury; and
2. Evidence of past sexual behavior **with the accused** offered by the accused upon the issue of whether or not the **victim consented** to the sexually assaultive behavior.

The two exceptions found in Article 412(A)(2) do not confer an absolute right to admissibility. The evidence may only be admitted following a pretrial hearing in which the court determines that the evidence which the accused seeks to offer is: 1) **relevant**; and 2) that the **probative value of such evidence outweighs the danger of unfair prejudice**.

When considering the prejudicial effect of offering past sexual behavior of the victim, the court should consider not only factors such as the possibility that the evidence may confuse the issues or mislead the jury, but also the possibility that it may unduly invade the privacy of the victim.[107] The procedures for admitting evidence under these exceptions are more fully discussed below.

Constitutional Implications of the Rape Shield Statute. The Louisiana Supreme Court has recognized that whenever an accused is restricted in his ability to offer evidence in his defense at trial, as provided in Article 412, an accused's constitutional rights to confrontation, cross-examination, and the right to present a defense may be implicated.[108] While the article does not expressly contain a provision specifically stating that the exclusion might not be applied if it would violate an accused's constitutional rights, it is well recognized that all evidentiary rules in the Code are subject to the provisions of the Constitution. Specifically, the Official Comments to Article 102(b) state that, "[i]n criminal matters especially, the Articles of this code must be interpreted and applied in light of and within the confines mandated by the Louisiana and federal constitutions."[109] The comments go on to state that under certain factual circumstances the provisions of the code must "bow to these notions of fundamental fairness."[110] Thus, in some instances, a defendant will be permitted to introduce evidence of a sexual assault victim's prior sexual conduct that might otherwise be excluded under this provision, if necessary to protect his constitutional right to present a defense.

---

106. *See* La. Code Evid. art. 412 Official Comment (h).

107. *See* La. Code Evid. art. 412 Official Comment (d).

108. State v. Vaughn, 448 So. 2d 1260 (La.1984); *See also*, La. Code Evid. art. 412 Official Comment (b).

109. La. Code Evid. art. 102 Official Comment (b).

110. La. Code Evid. art. 102 Official Comment (b).

Sexually assaultive behavior. Louisiana's Rape Shield Statute is applicable in all cases in which the accused is charged with crimes involving sexually assaultive behavior. "Sexually assaultive behavior" as used in the article applies to a broad range of conduct related to sexual offenses, including: rape, aggravated rape, forcible rape, simple rape, sexual battery, aggravated sexual battery, carnal knowledge of a juvenile, indecent behavior with a juvenile, pornography involving juveniles, molestation of a juvenile, crime against nature, aggravated crime against nature, and attempt of any of the foregoing offenses. This enumeration is intended to be illustrative and not exclusive.[111]

Prior sexual assault to attack credibility. While the Rape Shield Statute generally excludes evidence of prior sexual behavior of the victim, it does not exclude such evidence that tends to show *bias, interest, or corruption.*[112] For instance, evidence that the victim accused her father of molesting her after her father learned of her sexual relationship with another man and, as a result, prevented her from seeing him, would be admissible to show the victim's motive to lie. Similarly, evidence that a witness is currently in a relationship with the victim (other sexual conduct), would be relevant to show the witness's bias. Prior sexual behavior that shows bias, interest, or corruption is governed under the provisions relative to impeachment of witnesses rather than Article 412.

Further, the article does not preclude evidence regarding *prior false allegations*[113] concerning sexual behavior offered for impeachment purposes. Prior false allegations are also governed under the provisions relative to impeachment of witnesses. In situations in which the accused intends to offer evidence of prior false allegations to attack the witness's credibility, while a 412 hearing is not necessary, the accused must present sufficient evidence such that "reasonable jurors could find, based upon the evidence presented by the defendant, that the victim had made prior false accusations."[114] It is not sufficient that the accused merely *claim* the prior allegations are false. If the accused meets the standard, the issue should go to the jury. This issue is further addressed in *State v. Handy* below.

Federal Rules of Evidence Distinction. The Federal Rule of Evidence Rape Shield Statute is found in Rule 412. It similarly excludes evidence of prior sexual behavior of the victims of sexual assault. However, the Federal Rule contains three exceptions in which evidence of the victim's prior sexual conduct may be admissible. Two of them are the same as in Louisiana relative to: 1) prior sexual conduct with the accused on the issue of consent; and 2) prior sexual conduct with someone other than the accused occurring within 72 hours of the offense on the issue of the source of semen or injury. The third exception under the Federal Rule specifically provides for the admissibility of evidence of a victim's past sexual behavior when "the exclusion of the evidence would violate the constitutional rights of the defendant."[115] While Louisiana's rule may be interpreted to have such a construction, as stated above, the Federal Rule specifically provides that an accused's constitutional right to present a defense and to a fair trial may require the admissibility of such evidence.

Further, the Federal Rule specifically provides that the rule also applies in civil cases, while Louisiana's statute only applies to criminal cases. Federal Rule of Evidence 412(b)(2) provides that, "in a civil case, evidence offered to prove the sexual behavior or sexual pre-

111. La. Code Evid. art. 412 Official Comment (e).

112. *See* La. Code Evid. art. 412 Official Comments (1988); *See also* Force & Rault, Handbook, Art. 412 Author's Note (5).

113. *See* Force & Rault, Handbook, Art. 412 Author's Note (5).

114. State v. Smith, 743 So. 2d 199 (La. 1999).

115. *See* Fed. R. Evid. 412(B)(1)(C).

disposition of any alleged victim is admissible if it is otherwise admissible under these rules and its probative value substantially outweighs the danger of harm to any victim and of unfair prejudice to any party."[116] Thus, in a civil case, such evidence is admissible provided it is not unfairly prejudicial to any party.

Procedures for Offering Evidence under Exceptions

Applicable Code Articles

Art. 412. Victim's past sexual behavior in sexual assault cases; trafficking offenses

* * *

C. Motion. (1) Before the person, accused of committing a crime that involves sexually assaultive behavior, human trafficking, or trafficking of children for sexual purposes, may offer under Subparagraph (A)(2) or (B)(2) of this Article evidence of specific instances of the victim's past sexual behavior, the accused shall make a written motion in camera to offer such evidence. The motion shall be accompanied by a written statement of evidence setting forth the names and addresses of persons to be called as witnesses.

(2) The motion and statement of evidence shall be served on the state which shall make a reasonable effort to notify the victim prior to the hearing.

D. Time for a motion. The motion shall be made within the time for filing pre-trial motions specified in Code of Criminal Procedure Article 521, except that the court shall allow the motion to be made at a later date, if the court determines that:

(1) The evidence is of past sexual behavior with the accused, and the accused establishes that the motion was not timely made because of an impossibility arising through no fault of his own; or

(2) The evidence is of past sexual behavior with someone other than the accused, and the accused establishes that the evidence or the issue to which it relates is newly discovered and could not have been obtained earlier through the exercise of due diligence.

E. Hearing. (1) If the court determines that the statement of evidence contains evidence described in Subparagraph (A)(2) or (B)(2), the court shall order a hearing which shall be closed to determine if such evidence is admissible. At such hearing the parties may call witnesses.

(2) The victim, if present, has the right to attend the hearing and may be accompanied by counsel.

(3) If the court determines on the basis of the hearing described in Subparagraph (E)(1) that the evidence which the accused seeks to offer is relevant and that the probative value of such evidence outweighs the danger of unfair prejudice, such evidence may be admissible in the trial to the extent an order made by the court specifies evidence which may be offered and areas with respect to which the victim may be examined or cross-examined. Introduction of such evidence shall be limited to that specified in the order.

(4) Any motion made under Subparagraph C and any statement of evidence, brief, record of a hearing, or like material made or used in connection with the motion shall be

116. *See* Fed. R. Evid. 412(b)(2).

kept in a separate, sealed package as part of the record in the case. Nothing in this Article shall preclude the use of the testimony at such hearing in a subsequent prosecution for perjury or false swearing.

F. Past sexual behavior defined. For purposes of this Article, the term "past sexual behavior" means sexual behavior other than the sexual behavior with respect to which the offense of sexually assaultive behavior is alleged.

Notice/Hearing. The admissibility of the evidence contained in the exceptions to Article 412(A)(2) must be in strict compliance with the notice and hearing requirements of Article 412(C)–(E). Prior to admitting the evidence, the accused must make a written motion on camera to offer the evidence. The motion must contain a statement of the evidence that he intends to offer along with the names and addresses of the witnesses he intends to call. The motion must be served on the State, who must make a reasonable effort to notify the victim. After examining the motion, if the court is satisfied that the motion sets forth evidence contained in an exception to the article, the matter is set for a hearing.

At the hearing, which is closed, the court will determine the admissibility of the evidence. The parties may call witnesses. The victim has the right to attend and may be accompanied by counsel. In determining the admissibility of the evidence, the court will weigh the probative value of the evidence towards proving the stated purpose, against the danger of unfair prejudice. When considering the prejudicial effect of offering past sexual behavior of the victim, among other factors, the court will also consider the possibility that it may unduly invade the victim's privacy.

If the court determines that the evidence which the accused seeks to offer is: 1) **relevant**; and 2) that the **probative value** of such evidence **outweighs** the danger of **unfair prejudice**, such evidence may be admissible in the trial to the extent specified by the court in an order. The court's order shall specify the evidence which may be offered and the areas with respect to which the victim may be examined or cross-examined. Introduction of such evidence shall be limited to that specified in the order.

The time for filing a motion to offer evidence under this provision is typically made in accordance with La. C.Cr.P. art. 521; however, the court may allow additional time under extraordinary circumstances, such as if the evidence is newly discovered and could not have been obtained earlier through due diligence of the defendant.

Evidence of prior false allegations are not subject to the notice and hearing requirement of Article 412.

Cases on Rape Shield Statute

State v. Smith
Supreme Court of Louisiana
743 So. 2d 199
Sept. 8, 1999

TRAYLOR, Justice.

FACTS AND PROCEDURAL HISTORY

During the summer of 1996, the alleged victim, who was twelve years old at the time, told her mother's friend that the defendant, her grandmother's husband, had touched her in inappropriate places, on and off, for several years. The victim claimed that when she was four or five years old, defendant rubbed her "butt" while she lay on a sofa. The victim further testified that when she was about nine years old, defendant would touch her inappropriately when she slept at her grandmother's house. She stated that defendant had touched her bare breasts, kissed her bare back, and touched her vaginal area over her pants and underwear. She also stated she would wake up with her "pants undone." When the victim threatened to tell her father about the incidents, defendant stated, "I know secrets about you, and you know secrets about me; and we're not going to tell anybody." Because the victim did not claim the defendant attempted penetration in any manner, there was no physical evidence of abuse, and the outcome of trial rested entirely on her credibility.

During trial, defense counsel cross-examined the victim's mother's friend, Julie, regarding similar accusations the victim had made against her cousin and allegedly subsequently recanted. The State thereafter moved to prevent any further such questioning in accordance with La. C.E. art. 412, the so-called "rape shield statute." In response, defense counsel argued the evidence was not barred by Article 412 because the allegation was false and not of prior sexual behavior, but rather evidence of the victim's state of mind.

Relying on this court's decision in *State v. Allen*, 97-1058 (La.4/30/97), 693 So.2d 728, the trial judge held a hearing outside the presence of the jury "under Code of Evidence Article 412" to determine whether the victim actually made the allegations and, if so, whether such allegations were false. The defense first called the victim's mother who testified that the victim made allegations of molestation against her cousin, T.S. When asked whether the victim later retracted those allegations, the witness stated, "Not to me, no." Furthermore, she stated she had no reason to believe those allegations were false. The defense then called the victim, who claimed the accusations were true and denied retracting them. Finally, the defense called the younger brother of T.S., who was also the victim's cousin. The younger brother, M.S., testified that he, T.S., and the victim played together on a regular basis. M.S. testified that when they were rollerblading, the victim said that T.S. had "touched her and all" when she spent the night with her cousins. M.S. stated T.S. denied touching the victim and the victim skated away, but returned and told T.S. she was just joking. After hearing the testimony presented, the trial judge ruled as follows:

> All right. Based on the testimony that we just heard in this hearing under Code of Evidence Article 412, I find that there were no prior false allegations of sexual molestation by the victim. And pursuant to Article 412, if there were, in fact, incidents of sexual molestation, I find that specific instances of the victim's past sexual behavior are not admissible and that the exceptions of their inadmissibility

> under Paragraph B-1 and 2 do not apply in this case. Therefore, I will not permit any evidence of prior sexual misconduct, nor will I allow the cross-examination of the victim or evidence of prior false allegations at the trial.

The trial resumed, and defendant was subsequently convicted of attempted indecent behavior with a juvenile.

The court of appeal affirmed defendant's conviction, finding there was no abuse of discretion in the trial court's refusal to permit the presentation of evidence concerning the allegedly false prior allegations of molestation....

We granted certiorari to address defendant's argument that defense counsel should have been allowed to present to the jury testimony and cross-examination of witnesses regarding the allegations of prior molestation, which were subsequently allegedly recanted, to impeach the victim's credibility at trial.

DISCUSSION

As a general rule, a party may attack the credibility of a witness by examining him or her concerning any matter having a reasonable tendency to disprove the truthfulness of his or her testimony. La. C.E. art. 607(C). In cases involving sexually assaultive behavior, however, La. C.E. art. 412 bars the introduction of evidence of the victim's past sexual behavior, except that evidence of the victim's past sexual behavior with persons other than the accused within seventy-two hours prior to the time of the offense is admissible to challenge the source of semen or injury, and evidence of past sexual behavior with the defendant is admissible to show the victim consented to the behavior. In sexual assault cases involving an issue of prior false allegations of sexual assault, La. C.E. art. 412 may be viewed as being at odds with the long-established principle that "[a] witness' corruption may be evidenced by conduct indicating a general scheme to make false charges or claims." *State v. Cappo,* 345 So.2d 443, 445 (La.1977). This is especially true in those cases, such as the one at issue, where there is no physical evidence of sexual assault and the outcome of trial hinges on the trier of fact's credibility determinations.

...

Thus, in the instant case, when accusations of prior false allegations surfaced, the trial judge, mindful of this court's earlier decision in *Allen,* held a hearing "under Code of Evidence Article 412" to determine whether prior false allegations of sexual molestation had, in fact, been made by the victim. Defendant argues that La. C.E. art. 412 is inapplicable to the instant situation as evidence that the victim had previously accused another male of molesting her and then quickly retracted those accusations is not evidence of past sexual behavior of the victim, but rather impeachment evidence used to attack the victim's credibility. We agree.

As previously discussed, Article 412 prevents the introduction of evidence of the victim's past sexual behavior, with certain limited exceptions. The statute defines "past sexual behavior" as "sexual behavior other than the sexual behavior with respect to which the offense of sexually assaultive behavior is alleged." La. C.E. art. 412(F). It has also been described as "sexual history," although not limited to sexual intercourse. *State v. Everidge,* 96-2647 (La.12/2/97), 702 So.2d 680. Here, by attempting to introduce evidence that the victim had accused her cousin of molestation and then retracted the accusation, defendant was not seeking to prove that the victim had engaged in prior sexual behavior or that she had an unchaste character. Rather, defendant sought to prove for impeachment purposes that the victim had, in the past, made false allegations regarding sexual activity. Because the evidence defendant attempted to introduce did not concern the victim's prior sexual behavior, history or reputation for chastity, we conclude that prior false allegations of sexual assault by the victim do not constitute "past sexual behavior" for purposes of our rape shield statute.2 We hold, therefore, that Article 412 is inapplicable in sexual assault cases where defendant seeks to question witnesses regarding the victim's prior false allegations concerning sexual behavior for impeachment purposes. Consequently, no Article 412 hearing is required when defendant seeks to introduce such evidence. To the extent *State v. Allen* suggests otherwise, it is hereby overruled.

In this case, because the rape shield statute was inapplicable, an Article 412 hearing to determine whether the evidence of prior false allegations of molestation made by the victim was admissible should not have been held. Instead, when considering the admissibility of such evidence, the question for the trial court is not whether it believed the prior allegations were false, but whether reasonable jurors could find, based on the evidence presented by defendant, that the victim had made prior false accusations. *See Huddleston v. United States,* 485 U.S. 681, 108 S.Ct. 1496 (1988) (in ruling on the admissibility of other crimes evidence, the district court "neither weighs credibility nor makes a finding that the Government has proved the conditional fact by a preponderance, [but] simply examines all the evidence in the case and decides whether the jury could reasonably find the conditional fact ... by a preponderance of the evidence"). In *Ellison v. State,* 198 Ga.App. 75, 400 S.E.2d 360, 361 (1990), the court reviewed a trial court's ruling that the defendant failed to carry his burden of proving that previous allegations were false. The court stated,

> In our view, the trial court abused its discretion in determining that there was no reasonable probability that the prosecutrix had made prior false allegations. The prosecutrix admitted the prior accusation (albeit she did not concede that the accusation was false) and defendant presented the testimony of an independent third party that the prior accusation was false. Defendant could hardly have made a clearer showing. The trial court erred in excluding the defendant's evidence of prior false accusations.

Likewise, in the instant case, the victim admitted, and other witnesses agreed, that she had accused her cousin of improper sexual behavior. Defendant presented the testimony of M.S. who stated that shortly after making accusations which T.S. denied, the victim recanted those accusations. We conclude the evidence presented by defendant is sufficient to allow reasonable jurors to find that the victim has made false allegations of molestation in the past. As such, this evidence directly concerning the victim's credibility could have been admitted provided the trial court determined it met all other standards for admissibility.

CONCLUSION

We find that La. C.E. art. 412 is inapplicable to cases involving prior false allegations of sexual behavior. When a defendant seeks to introduce evidence that the victim has made such prior false accusations, the trial judge must evaluate that evidence by determining whether reasonable jurors could find, based on the evidence presented by defendant, that the victim had made prior false accusations and whether all other requirements of the Code of Evidence have been satisfied. Because the outcome of this case rested entirely upon the jury's perception of the victim's veracity, the trial court's ruling regarding the victim's prior false allegations of sexual molestation cannot be said to be harmless. Therefore, because defendant has been prejudiced by the confused and erroneous state of the law applied in his case and because his right to a fair trial has been impeded, we must reverse the conviction and remand the case to the trial court for a new trial to be held.

REVERSED AND REMANDED.

Discussion Questions

1. What is the standard the court should apply when determining whether to permit evidence of prior false accusations? Why is it that when this standard is met, it is inappropriate for a judge to exclude such evidence?
2. Why is Article 412 inapplicable to prior false allegations?
3. Upon what basis did the court find that the error here was not harmless?

State v. Handy

Court of Appeal of Louisiana, Fourth Circuit
732 So. 2d 134
April 7, 1999

JONES, Judge.

Relator avers that he is accused of raping his eighteen-year-old former girlfriend on November 9, 1997, at approximately 4:00 a.m. The rape allegedly occurred at the victim's home and was reported at approximately 12:15 p.m. on November 9th. The victim was examined at Charity Hospital on the same date at approximately 3:00 p.m. The emergency room report and physical examination for sexual assault form reflect that the victim suffered a one-half centimeter abrasion/laceration anterior to the cervix on the vaginal mucosa. No external trauma to the genital-rectal area was noted. The victim did have facial abrasions and a bite mark on the neck. The internal and external swabs were negative for seminal fluid and spermatozoa. Relator asserts that he did not rape the victim.

In his motion to present evidence of the victim's prior sexual activity, relator argues that the victim had also engaged in sexual relations with Theo McGriff on the night of the alleged rape; Mr. McGriff's testimony was presented to the trial court at the December 14, 1998 hearing. Mr. McGriff testified that he was at the victim's home from approximately 8:00 p.m. until 1:00 a.m. on November 8–9, 1997. He also testified that he engaged in sexual intercourse with the victim, without a condom, but did not ejaculate inside of her. Mr. McGriff also testified that he was not rough with the victim and he testified that he did not hear the victim complain that he was being rough or that the intercourse was hurting her. Mr. McGriff further testified that the defendant came to the victim's house while he was present, and that the victim and the relator argued until relator later left. However, the victim did not tell Mr. McGriff of the alleged rape until recently.

DISCUSSION

Relator argues to this Court that the trial court erred when it denied his motion to present the evidence of the victim's prior sexual activity with Mr. McGriff. The relator further argues that the evidence is relevant and fits within the exception provided by Article 412 of the Louisiana Code of Evidence, also known as the "rape shield law." Additionally, he argues that exclusion of the evidence would violate his constitutional right to confrontation of his accusers and violate his Due Process rights.

...

Pursuant to art. 412, the relator's motion was timely filed and presented testimony which apparently fits within the exception of paragraph (B) of Article 412. The prior sexual activity referred to in relator's motion allegedly occurred within seventy-two hours of the incident. Relator seeks to present evidence to show that the victim's sexual intercourse with Mr. McGriff was the source of the abrasion/laceration—the only physical evidence of the alleged rape.

At the hearing, the State's primary argument against the granting of relator's motion was that McGriff's testimony did not fit the exception of LSA–C.E. art 412 because he only testified that the victim did not complain of painful physical intercourse with him. However, article 412(B) provides that the evidence is admissible "upon the issue of whether or not the accused was the source of the semen or injury." Nothing in LSA–C.E. article 412 implies that the evidence should be excluded simply because the other sexual activity may not be the source of the injury—an issue which presumably is for the jury to decide.

Furthermore, relator argues that his constitutional right to confront his accusers must also be considered. The Second Circuit addressed this issue in State v. Womack, 592 So.2d 872 (La.App. 2 Cir.1991), writ denied, 600 So.2d 675 (La.1992), where the defense sought to introduce evidence of the victim's alleged sexual intercourse with another man that occurred approximately one year prior to the alleged rape by the defendant. The court acknowledged that this evidence would not fall within the exceptions of art. 412(B), but it then noted:

> The Louisiana Supreme Court has indicated that a restriction of a defendant's offer to introduce testimony as to the victim's prior sexual history may violate defendant's right to confrontation and fair trial. State v. Vaughn, 448 So.2d 1260 (La.1983); LSA–C.E. Art. 412 comment (b). The Federal Rules of Evidence have addressed this problem by explicitly providing for the admissibility of some evidence of a victim's past sexual behavior when such evidence is constitutionally required to be admitted. In criminal matters, the articles of the Louisiana Code of Evidence must be interpreted and applied in light of and within the confines mandated by the Louisiana and Federal Constitutions. LSA–C.E. Art. 102 comment (b). The constitutional "exception" to LSA–C.E. Art. 412 is "intended to cover those infrequent instances where, because of an unusual chain of circumstances, the general rule of inadmissibility, if followed, would result in denying the defendant a constitutional right." House of Representatives, 120 Cong. Rec. 34, 912 (1978). In Vaughn, the Louisiana State Supreme Court concluded "that evidence of a single instance of sexual intercourse between the victim and another individual five days prior to the rape is not relevant to a determination of whether the act with defendant was consensual." Further, the Supreme Court held that where the evidence sought to be admitted is not relevant, the right to confrontation is not affected. Vaughn, supra.*Womack*, 592 So.2d at 879.

...

In the instant case, the evidence presented in relator's motion appears to fit within the exception of Article 412. Although Article 412(E)(3) provides that the court could still exclude the evidence if it finds that the probative value outweighs the danger of unfair prejudice, the trial court here denied the motion without explanation. Moreover, the State never argued that the evidence was probative or unduly prejudicial; instead it argued that the exception was not shown. The court apparently accepted this argument after both parties confirmed that no semen was present. Considering that the exception in Article 412(B) states semen or injury, the lack of semen is not dispositive of the issue. In *State v. Ragas*, 607 So.2d 967, 970 (La.App. 4 Cir.1992), writ denied 612 So.2d 97 (La.1993), this Court recognized that injury in Article 412(B) as "injury suffered in the crime involving the sexually assaultive behavior."

The State did not indicate that the abrasion/laceration was not going to be used to corroborate that a rape occurred. Nevertheless, because this is a pretrial writ, the evidence to be presented is not fully developed.

. . .

WRIT APPLICATION GRANTED.

Discussion Questions

1. How does this case fit within the exception of Article 412? In other words, what are the requirements of Article 412, and how are those requirements met in *Handy*? Explain.
2. The courts have recognized that the limitations of Article 412 have the potential in some instances to deprive the defendant of his constitutional rights to confrontation and cross-examination and to present a defense. How does the construction of Article 412, with respect to the exceptions, tend to strike a balance between the defendant's constitutional rights and the policy implications behind Article 412 of attempting to protect victims of sexual assault from embarrassment and revictimization?
3. Are there other exceptions not listed in Article 412 that you believe should be listed in the Rape Shield Statute, i.e., instances or circumstances where you believe prior sexual conduct of the victim should be allowed?

§ 6.9.2 Victim's Attire in Sexual Assault Cases [La. C.E. art. 412.1]

Applicable Code Articles

Art. 412.1. Victim's attire in sexual assault cases

When an accused is charged with the crime of aggravated rape, forcible rape, simple rape, sexual battery, or second degree sexual battery, the manner and style of the victim's attire shall not be admissible as evidence that the victim encouraged or consented to the offense; however, items of clothing or parts thereof may be introduced in order to establish the presence or absence of the elements of the offense and the proof of its occurrence.

When an accused is charged with certain sexual assault offenses, evidence of the manner and style of the victim's attire shall not be admissible as evidence to prove the victim encouraged or consented to the offense. For instance, the defendant cannot argue that victim *wanted* the sex because the victim wore tight clothing, a short skirt, no panties, or any other reference to the victim's attire. Similarly, the accused cannot argue that the victim *enticed* or *encouraged* the sex because of the victim's clothing. This provision specifically applies to an accused charged with aggravated rape, forcible rape, simple rape, sexual battery, or second-degree sexual battery. It is not as broad as the Rape Shield Statute found in Article 412 that applies generally to "sexually assaultive behavior." This article is specifically limited to the enumerated offenses.

Federal Rules of Evidence Distinction. There is no counterpart to this article in the Federal Rules of Evidence.

Exception to the rule. The exclusion of victim's attire in certain sexual assault cases does not apply if the evidence is offered to show the presence or absence of an element of the offense or the proof of its occurrence. For instance, the defendant might offer evidence of the victim's clothing to demonstrate that the offense could not have occurred as the victim claims, such as if the victim claims "he tore my pants off," yet the pants are clearly not torn. Additionally, some authorities have posited that in other extraordinary circumstances the accused may have a constitutional right to present evidence of the victim's attire tending to corroborate his version of the incident.[117]

Court's interpretation in *State v. Anders*.[118] While there is not much case law interpreting Article 412.1, *State v. Anders* demonstrates the exact type of evidence the statute is designed to exclude. In attempting to offer evidence of the victim's attire in *Anders*, the following evidence was elicited by the defense at the hearing on the motion in limine:

> ... [D]efense counsel informed the trial court that D.H. and the Defendant acknowledged, in their statements to police, that the Defendant was admitted into D.H.'s home between 1:00 and 2:00 a.m. and D.H. had gotten out of bed, was in her underwear, and had wrapped a blanket around herself. Additionally, D.H. remained that way for approximately an hour, at which time the alleged offense occurred. Defense counsel argued that the information regarding D.H.'s attire should be available to the jury "to judge consent, simply because it's the hour and the location. This is not at a bar. This is her home under two o'clock in the morning, and that's the way she allows somebody to come into the—to her home, and stays that way for at least an hour."

The Defendant further argued:

> D.H.'s lack of attire would have supported his assertion that she consented to sexual intercourse and, as he was not allowed to present testimony regarding her attire, he was deprived of his constitutional right to due process and the right to confront his accuser. The Defendant also asserts that, had the jury heard evidence of how D.H. was clothed, it would have been in a better position to weigh the credibility of D.H. and himself. The Defendant contends that, once D.H. realized there was no emergency, she had ample opportunity to either end the conversation with him or excuse herself to dress in more appropriate clothing, as the blanket D.H. used to cover herself cannot be considered attire for purposes of Article 412.1.

In upholding the trial court's decision to exclude evidence of the victim's attire, the *Anders* court noted, "it appears the Defendant is taking the exact position La. Code Evid. art. 412.1 prohibits—that women wearing certain clothing are '"asking for it" and consent to sex via a wardrobe.' Article 412.1 clearly prohibits testimony regarding D.H.'s attire at the time of the offense in order to prove consent. On that basis, the trial court properly excluded any testimony regarding D.H.'s attire."

Finally, the *Anders* court noted that in some limited circumstances such evidence might be admissible for other purposes such as, "if it were being used to prove the presence or absence of an element of the offense ... [such as] to show the condition of the clothing after the offense." However, the defendant made no such argument in *Anders*.[119]

Discussion Questions

1. Can you think of a situation in which the victim's attire in a sexual assault case might be relevant for a purpose other than showing that the victim encouraged or consented to the sexual assault?

---

117. *See* Force & Rault, HANDBOOK, 412.1 Author's Note (1).
118. *See* State v. Anders, 941 So. 2d 93 (La. Ct. App. 3d Cir. 2006).
119. *Id.*

2. Why do you think Article 412.1 is only limited to certain sex offenses, while the Rape Shield Statute is much broader in applying generally to "sexually assaultive behavior"?

§ 6.9.3 Prior Sex Offenses in Sex Offense Cases [La. C.E. art. 412.2]

> **Applicable Code Articles**
>
> **Art. 412.2. Evidence of similar crimes, wrongs, or acts in sex offense cases**
>
> A. When an accused is charged with a crime involving sexually assaultive behavior, or with acts that constitute a sex offense involving a victim who was under the age of seventeen at the time of the offense, evidence of the accused's commission of another crime, wrong, or act involving sexually assaultive behavior or acts which indicate a lustful disposition toward children may be admissible and may be considered for its bearing on any matter to which it is relevant subject to the balancing test provided in Article 403.
>
> B. In a case in which the state intends to offer evidence under the provisions of this Article, the prosecution shall, upon request of the accused, provide reasonable notice in advance of trial of the nature of any such evidence it intends to introduce at trial for such purposes.
>
> C. This Article shall not be construed to limit the admission or consideration of evidence under any other rule.

Article 412.2 provides that when an accused is charged with a crime involving sexually assaultive behavior, or with acts that constitute a sex offense involving a victim who was under the age of seventeen at the time of the offense, evidence of the accused's commission of another crime, wrong, or act involving sexually assaultive behavior or acts which indicate a lustful disposition toward children may be admissible. Such crimes may be considered for their bearing on any matter to which they are relevant subject to Article 403 balancing.

The article applies in two situations:

1) when the accused is charged with a crime involving sexually assaultive behavior; ***or***

2) when the accused is charged with a sex offense involving a victim under seventeen years old at the time of the offense.[120]

In the first instance, in which the accused is charged with a crime involving sexually assaultive behavior, the article provides that other crimes, wrongs, or acts of sexually assaultive behavior may be admissible. Similarly, when the accused is charged with a sex offense where the victim is under the age of seventeen, other sex offenses or acts which indicate a lustful disposition toward children may be admissible.

In either case, the article specifically provides that the other crimes, wrongs, or acts ***may*** be admissible and **may** be considered for their bearing **on any relevant issue**, subject to an **Article 403 balancing**. In other words, if the court determines that the probative value toward the relevant reasons for which the evidence is proffered is not substantially

120. *See* State v. Wright, 79 So. 2d 309 (La. 2011); *See also* Force & Rault, Handbook on Louisiana Evidence Law, Art. 412.2 Author's Note (1) (West Publishing 2013).

outweighed by its prejudicial effect, then the court *may* admit the evidence, but is not required to do so, even though it passes the Article 403 balancing test. This article is written to leave great discretion to the court in determining the admissibility of the evidence, due to the potential of such evidence for unfair prejudice.

Admissible prior offenses. Under this provision, a wide range of other crimes, wrongs, or acts may be admissible, including offenses or bad acts for which the accused may never have been arrested or even charged, as well as an offense for which the defendant was acquitted, since the burden of proof is lower for admission under 412.2 than for finding guilt at trial.[121] Additionally, the article makes clear that the other acts need not be a "sex" crime, per se, to be considered toward proving lustful disposition toward a child. For instance, the other act might be evidence that the accused trespassed on school property to gain access to children, evidence that the accused wrote several letters to the child expressing his desires, or that he maintained photos of the child.

Additionally, the other act might have occurred either before or after the offense for which the accused is on trial[122] and may even involve a victim of a different sex than in the instant offense.[123] The article also does not provide for a specific time limitation as to when the prior crime must have been committed. Some courts have upheld prior offenses occurring ten[124] and even thirty years[125] prior to the instant offense. The amount of time that has passed since the prior act would only be a relevant factor the court would consider in applying the Article 403 balancing test.[126] The court in *State v. Henry*,[127] below, further elaborates on this issue.

The prior offense must be proven by "clear and convincing" evidence as in the case of other crimes offered under Article 404(B). Like Article 404(B), the evidence must be relevant to proving some issue or element in the case, subject to Article 403.

Notice. Upon request of the accused, the prosecution is required to give reasonable notice in advance of trial of the nature of any such evidence it intends to use at the trial under this provision. While notice is required prior to the use of such evidence against an accused, in *State v. Williams*,[128] the La. Supreme Court held that the procedural requirements of *State v. Prieur* do not apply to Article 412.2 cases. If requested, however, counsel is entitled to a limiting instruction to the jury on the appropriate use of the prior offenses.[129]

Federal Rules of Evidence Distinction. The federal counterparts to this article are found in Federal Rules of Evidence 413, 414, and 415. Rule 413 applies to the admissibility of another offense *or* offense of sexual assault when the accused is charged with **sexual assault**, and Rule 414 applies to the admissibility of another offense or other offense of child molestation when the accused is charged with **child molestation**. Louisiana

---

121. State v. Harris, 83 So. 3d 269 (La. Ct. App. 5th Cir. 2011); *See also* State v. Cotton, 778 So. 2d 569 (La. 2001).

122. *See* State v. Friday, 73 So. 3d 913 (La. Ct. App. 1st Cir. 2011).

123. *See* State v. Wright, 79 So. 2d 309 (La. 2011).

124. *See* State v. Scoggins, 70 So. 3d 145 (La. Ct. App. 4th Cir. 2011) (permitted an incident that occurred 10 years prior to the instant offense).

125. *See* State v. Buckenberger, 984 So. 2d 751 (La. Ct. App. 1st Cir. 2008) (permitted 25-year-old offenses).

126. *See* State v. Scoggins, 70 So. 3d 145 (La. Ct. App. 4th Cir. 2011).

127. State v. Henry, 102 So. 2d 1016 (La. Ct. App. 4th Cir. 2011).

128. State v. Williams, 830 So. 2d 984 (La. 2002).

129. *See* State v. Brown, 874 So. 2d 318 (La. Ct. App. 3d Cir. 2004) (court found it reversible error for trial court to refuse to comply with defense counsel's request of limiting instruction).

contains provisions similar to both Rules in the same article rather than breaking them up into two separate articles.

Additionally, in contrast to the Louisiana article, which provides that the other crimes evidence *may* be admissible subject to Article 403, the Federal Rules of Evidence provide that such evidence *is* admissible. In fact, Congress' legislative judgment has been that such evidence "'normally' should be admitted."[130] Thus in Louisiana, the courts have more discretion than federal courts on whether to admit the prior offenses under this article.[131]

Additionally, Federal Rule of Evidence 413 and Rule 414 specifically state that the rules apply **only in criminal cases**. Federal Rule of Evidence 415 provides for the admissibility of such evidence in **civil cases** and specifically provides that the evidence should be admissible in civil cases as provided in Rule 413 and Rule 414. Louisiana's article only applies to criminal cases and has no such provision making the articles applicable in civil cases.

Case on Prior Sex Offenses in Sex Offense Cases

State v. Henry
Court of Appeal of Louisiana, Fourth Circuit
102 So. 3d 1016
Oct. 24, 2012

ROSEMARY LEDET, Judge.

This is a criminal appeal. The defendant, David Henry, appeals his conviction and sentence for aggravated and forcible rape. The principal issue raised on appeal is whether the trial court erred in allowing the State to introduce evidence of a prior sex crime—a 1978 conviction for attempted aggravated rape—under La. C.E. art. 412.2. Finding no error, we affirm.

...

STATEMENT OF THE FACTS

Mr. Henry was tried and convicted for the aggravated rape of R.C. between March 1, 2007 and May 4, 2008, and the forcible rape of R.C. between May 5, 2008 and June 15, 2009. At the time of trial (April 2011), the victim, R.C., was fifteen years old and in the eighth grade. According to R.C., in 2008, she lived in Algiers with her mother, her two brothers, and Mr. Henry, who she referred to as "Mr. David." R.C. identified Mr. Henry in court. She testified that he was her mother's boyfriend. She further testified that he forced her to have sex with him on multiple occasions.

R.C. testified that the first rape occurred in 2008 when she was twelve years old; ... He threatened that if she told anyone he would kill her, her mother, and her brothers.

R.C. testified that the last rape occurred when she was fourteen years old; however, she did not recall the details of that occurrence. She further testified that Mr. Henry raped her every time her mother or her brothers were gone....

In July 2009, R.C. went to Atlanta, Georgia to visit her older sister, I.F., for about a month. R.C. testified that she made the trip to Atlanta because she wanted to get away

---

130. *See also* Force & Rault, Handbook, Art. 412.2 Author's Note (3).
131. *Id.*

from Mr. Henry and "[t]he raping." While she was in Atlanta, R.C. noticed that her stomach was getting big and that she was throwing up every morning....

In mid-August 2009 when I.F. brought R.C. back to New Orleans for school, I.F. and her cousin tricked R.C. into giving a urine sample; they told R.C. that the cousin needed it to submit for an employment drug screening. After they obtained the urine sample, they performed two home pregnancy tests that both came back positive. When confronted with the test results, R.C. began crying. R.C. stated that she did not want to be pregnant, that it was not her fault, and that her mother's boyfriend had been raping her....

After disclosing to S.C. that she had been raped, R.C. talked to both the police and physicians....

In November 2009, R.C. gave birth to a baby girl. A few days after the baby was born, Detective Ross came to the hospital and obtained buccal swabs from the inner jaw of R.C. and her baby....

Kathryn Moyse, a DNA analyst from Scales Biolab in Camden, Mississippi, was qualified by joint stipulation as an expert in forensic DNA analysis.... In February 2010, a new set of samples were submitted and the testing was done again from scratch. Ms. Moyse testified that the testing of the second set of DNA samples established that the DNA of Mr. Henry matched that of R.C.'s baby such that it was 99.99% certain that Mr. Henry was her baby's father.

...

N.O.P.D. Officer Joseph Pollard, who was qualified by joint stipulation as a fingerprint expert, identified the fingerprints belonging to Mr. Henry that he took in court that day. He then identified a certified copy of an arrest register and the matching certified pack from case No. 260–856. These documents showed that Mr. Henry had pled guilty in 1978 to attempted aggravated rape....

DISCUSSION

...

ASSIGNMENT OF ERROR NO. 1

Mr. Henry's first assignment of error is that the trial court erred in admitting evidence of Mr. Henry's prior conviction for attempted aggravated rape. Before trial the State filed a notice of its intent to use evidence of similar crimes pursuant to La. C.E. art. 412.2. In that notice, the State expressed its intent to introduce evidence of Mr. Henry's previous sex crime with a juvenile victim; to wit:

> Defendant, David Henry, committed the Aggravated Rape of then 10 year old, N.M. (female, dob: 8/16/66) on July 13, 1977. Defendant subsequently plead guilty to one count of Attempted Aggravated Rape in Orleans Parish Criminal District Court, Case No. 260–856.

On October 12, 2010, the trial court granted the State's request to introduce La. C.E. art. 412.2 evidence at trial. At trial, the State, over the defense's objection, introduced evidence of Mr. Henry's 1978 conviction for the July 1977 rape. On appeal, Mr. Henry contends that it was an abuse of discretion to admit the "other crimes" evidence under the guise of proving his purported "lustful disposition."

A trial court's ruling on the admissibility of evidence will not be overturned absent an abuse of discretion. *State v. Wright,* 79 So.3d 309, 316. This same standard is applied to rulings on the admission of other crimes evidence under La. C.E. art. 404(B)(1) and evidence under La. C.E. art. 412.2. *Wright, supra.*

The governing statutory provision on this issue is La. C.E. art. 412.2, which provides, in pertinent part:

> A. When an accused is charged with a crime involving sexually assaultive behavior, or with acts that constitute a sex offense involving a victim who was under the age of seventeen at the time of the offense, evidence of the accused's commission of another crime, wrong, or act involving sexually assaultive behavior or acts which indicate a lustful disposition toward children may be admissible and may be considered for its bearing on any matter to which it is relevant subject to the balancing test provided in Article 403.

In order for any evidence deemed to fall within La. C.E. art. 412.2 to be admissible, it must pass the balancing test of La. C.E. art. 403, which provides: "[a]lthough relevant, evidence may be excluded if its probative value is substantially outweighed by the dangers of unfair prejudice, confusion of the issues, or misleading the jury, or by considerations of undue delay, or waste of time."

Addressing the meaning of the "unfair prejudice" component of the balancing test, the Louisiana Supreme Court in *State v. Rose,* 949 So.2d 1236, 1244, noted that "[a]ny inculpatory evidence is 'prejudicial' to a defendant, especially when it is 'probative' to a high degree." *Id.* The Supreme Court further noted that "[a]s used in the balancing test, 'prejudicial' limits the introduction of probative evidence of prior misconduct only when it is unduly and unfairly prejudicial." *Id.*...

In this case, Mr. Henry argues that the other crime evidence was "so stale as to have greatly diminished any probative value it may have originally provided." He emphasizes that he was only sixteen years old—a child himself—at the time of the prior crime. He thus submits that the prior crime was a criminal sexual act committed by one child against another, and did not, thirty years thereafter, serve to indicate his lustful disposition toward children. The State counters that Mr. Henry erred in focusing his argument solely on the "lustful disposition toward children" aspect of La. C.E. art. 412.2. The State points out that La. C.E. art. 412.2 also provides that "evidence of the accused's commission of another crime, wrong, or act involving sexually assaultive behavior ... may be considered for its bearing on any matter to which it is relevant subject to the balancing test provided in Article 403." The State argues that Mr. Henry failed to establish prejudice based on either the remoteness in time or his youth at the time of the prior offense.

Summarizing the jurisprudence addressing the lack of a temporal limit on sex crimes admissible under Article 412.2, a commentator states:

> The legislature did not address a temporal limitation for sex crimes in Article 412.2. Under current Louisiana jurisprudence, the acts that are admissible under Article 412.2 could occur prior to or subsequent to the charged crime. Moreover, the courts have not set a limit on the number of years a sex crime could have occurred before or after the charged crime. The age of the prior sex crime is a consideration for the trial judge when he does the 403 balancing test to determine whether the prior crime should be admitted. However, it is only one factor to be considered and prior sex crimes that occurred several years earlier have not been excluded because of the length of time.

Bobby Harges & Russell Jones, La. Prac. Evidence, Art. 412.2, n. 28 (2012 ed.) (citing *State v. Buckenberger,* 07–1422 (La.App. 1 Cir. 2/8/08), 984 So.2d 751; and *State v. Willis,* 05–218 (La.App. 3 Cir. 11/2/05), 915 So.2d 365). Accordingly, "the fact that the prior sex offenses occurred many years before trial is not significant as the legislature did not set forth a time limitation in Article 412.2." *Willis,* 915 So.2d at 388.

Likewise, this court in *State v. Scoggins,* 70 So.3d 145, rejected the argument that the remoteness in time of a prior sex offense rendered it inadmissible....

On appeal, the defendant in *Scoggins* argued that the single instance of his assaultive behavior on the female family friend that occurred ten years before the crime for which he was being tried was so remote in time as to have had no probative value. Rejecting that argument, this court reasoned that "[r]emoteness in time, in most cases, is only one factor to be considered when determining whether the probative value of the evidence outweighs its prejudicial effect." *Scoggins,* at 154 (citing *State v. Jackson,* 625 So.2d 146 (La.1993)). We also noted the general rule that "a lapse in time will go to the weight of the evidence, rather than to its admissibility." *Id.*

...

The instant case presents unusual circumstances given the difference between Mr. Henry's age at the time of the prior offense, sixteen years old, and at the time of the instant offenses, approximately forty-six to forty eight years old. Mr. Henry was six years older than the victim of the prior offense, but forty-one to forty-three years older than the victim of the instant offenses. Another difference is that the prior victim was ten years old at the time of the offense; the victim in the instant case was fourteen and fifteen years old at the time of the instant offenses. The first offense was a single incident; the instant offenses occurred on an unknown number of times. (As noted earlier, R.C. testified that Mr. Henry raped her whenever her mother or her brothers were out of the house, and she said he mother left for work at 4:00 a.m. on Monday through Friday.) The victim in the prior offense was someone who resided near the then sixteen-year-old Mr. Henry, but she had never talked to him. Here, the victim of the instant offenses resided with Mr. Henry; Mr. Henry was the victim's mother's boyfriend.

Despite the age differences between the parties to the prior offense and the instant offenses, and the significant lapse of time between the two offenses, it cannot be said, considering all of the facts and circumstances of this case, that the trial court abused its discretion in concluding that the probative value of the prior offense was not substantially outweighed by its prejudicial effect.

...

AFFIRMED

Discussion Questions

1. Do you agree with the court in *Henry*? Why or why not?
2. What procedural requirements must the State comply with to offer evidence of prior offenses in sexual assault cases? What steps did the State take in *Henry* to comply with the requirements to admit prior sexual offenses?
3. The State in *Henry* points out that under the statute, evidence may be offered that shows "lustful disposition toward children" or the State may offer evidence of any "crime, wrong, or act involving sexually assaultive behavior" for its bearing on "any matter to which it is relevant subject to the balancing test provided in Article 403." While the State effectively concedes that the evidence did not show a lustful disposition toward children, it never specifically stated an alternative purpose for which the evidence was relevant. If not to show lustful disposition toward children, for what purpose do you find the 1978 conviction to be relevant in *Henry*?

4. In general, what are some reasons you believe prior sexual crimes might be relevant to show in a sexual assault case under Article 412.2, other than to show lustful disposition toward children, if anything?
5. Expound upon the Article 403 balancing test conducted in *Henry*. Discuss the probative value toward proving the relevant purpose in the case. Discuss the prejudicial effect of the evidence. Other than the passage of time, what other factors are useful in determining whether the probative value of the evidence outweighs its prejudicial effect?
6. Since this issue is subject to a harmless error standard, do you think the fact that there was overwhelming evidence in the case, e.g., the impregnation of the victim, played a role in the court's decision?

§ 6.9.4 Prior Sexual Behavior in Sexual Trafficking Cases [La. C.E. art. 412(B), La. C.E. art. 412.3]

Applicable Code Articles

Art. 412. Victim's past sexual behavior in sexual assault cases; trafficking offenses

* * *

B. (1) Opinion and reputation evidence; trafficking. When an accused is charged with a crime involving human trafficking or trafficking of children for sexual purposes, reputation or opinion evidence of the past sexual behavior of the victim is not admissible.

(2) Evidence of specific instances of the victim's past sexual behavior is not admissible unless the evidence is offered by the prosecution in a criminal case to prove a pattern of trafficking activity by the defendant.

* * *

Art. 412.3. Statements made by victims of trafficking during investigations

If a victim of human trafficking or trafficking of children for sexual purposes is also a defendant in any case arising from unlawful acts committed as part of the same trafficking activity, any inculpatory statement made by the victim as a result of questioning by any person then known by the victim to be a law enforcement officer is inadmissible against the victim, except pursuant to Article 801 of this Code or in any prosecution of the victim for perjury, at a trial of the victim for the unlawful acts committed by the victim as part of the same trafficking activity if all of the following conditions exist:

(1) The victim cooperates with the investigation and prosecution, including the giving of a use-immunity statement as directed by the prosecuting attorney.

(2) The victim testifies truthfully at any hearing or trial related to the trafficking activity, or agrees, either in writing or on the record, to testify truthfully at any hearing or trial related to the trafficking activity in any prosecution of any other person charged with an offense arising from the same trafficking activity, regardless of whether the testimony is unnecessary due to entry of a plea by the other person.

(3) The victim has agreed in writing to receive services or participate in a program that provides services to victims of human trafficking or trafficking of children for sexual purposes, if such services are available.

In the 2014 Regular Legislative Session, Louisiana amended its Rape Shield Statute to include laws relative to human trafficking and sexual trafficking. Article 412(B) provides that when an accused is charged with a crime involving "human trafficking" or "trafficking of children for sexual purposes," reputation or opinion evidence of the past sexual behavior of the victim is not admissible. Thus, evidence by the defendant such as, "He/She was doing this long before I came along," or "He/She has been doing this all of his/her life," is inadmissible. The article **excludes reputation**, **opinion**, and specific **past sexual behavior of the victim** in such cases.

Exception. An exception to this rule is found in Article 412(B)(2) and provides that the evidence may be admissible if offered by the prosecution in a criminal case to prove a **pattern of trafficking activity by the defendant**. In such instances, the evidence must be admitted in accordance with the same procedures outlined above in 6.9.1, for introducing other evidence of past sexual conduct under the Rape Shield Statute.

Procedures for offering evidence. The proponent must make a written motion on camera to offer the evidence. The motion must contain a statement of the evidence that the proponent intends to offer along with the names and addresses of the witnesses he intends to call. The motion must be served on the opposing party. After examining the motion, if the court is satisfied that the motion sets forth evidence contained in an exception to the article, the matter is set for a hearing. At the hearing, which is closed, the court will determine the admissibility of the evidence. The parties may call witnesses. In determining the admissibility of the evidence, the court will weigh the probative value of the evidence toward proving the stated purpose against the danger of unfair prejudice. When considering the prejudicial effect of offering past sexual behavior of the victim, among other factors, the court will also consider the possibility that it may unduly invade the victim's privacy.

If the court determines that the evidence which the accused seeks to offer is: 1) relevant; and 2) that the probative value of such evidence outweighs the danger of unfair prejudice, such evidence may be admissible in the trial to the extent specified by the court in an order which sets forth the areas with respect to which the victim may be examined or cross-examined. Introduction of such evidence shall be limited to that specified in the order.

The time for filing such motions is typically made in accordance with La. C.Cr.P. art. 521; however, the court may allow additional time under extraordinary circumstances, such as if the evidence is newly discovered and could not have been obtained earlier through due diligence of the defendant.

Statements made by victims of trafficking during investigations inadmissible in victim's trial. If a victim of human trafficking or trafficking of children for sexual purposes is also a defendant in any case arising from unlawful acts committed as part of the same trafficking activity, any inculpatory statement made by the victim as a result of questioning by any person then known by the victim to be a law enforcement officer is inadmissible against the victim at a trial of the victim for the unlawful acts committed by the victim as part of the same trafficking activity if all of the following conditions exist:

1. The victim cooperates with the investigation and prosecution, including the giving of a use-immunity statement as directed by the prosecuting attorney.
2. The victim testifies truthfully at any hearing or trial related to the trafficking activity, or agrees, either in writing or on the record, to testify truthfully at any hearing or trial related to the trafficking activity in any prosecution of any other person charged with an offense arising from the same trafficking activity, regardless of whether the testimony is unnecessary due to entry of a plea by the other person.

3. The victim has agreed in writing to receive services or participate in a program that provides services to victims of human trafficking or trafficking of children for sexual purposes, if such services are available.

This provision does not apply to Article 801 of this Code or in any prosecution of the victim for perjury.

Key Points

The key points to keep in mind regarding prior sexual conduct in sexual assault cases.

1. **Louisiana's Rape Shield Statute (Article 412) excludes:** 1) opinion evidence, 2) reputation evidence, and 3) specific instances of conduct regarding the past sexual behavior of the victim of the sexual assault in a sexual assault case. **Two exceptions**:

   i) if it is with the accused on the issue of consent; or ii) if it was with another person occurring within 72 hours of incident on issue of source of semen or injury.

2. **Sex Trafficking Cases**: Rape Shield Statute also excludes evidence of reputation, opinion and past sexual behavior of the victim of sexual trafficking in sexual/human trafficking cases.

   Exception: if offered by the prosecution in a criminal case to prove a pattern of trafficking activity by the defendant.

3. **Credibility exceptions.** The exclusion of prior sexual conduct of the victim in sexual assault cases does not apply to conduct tending to show bias, interest, or corruption, or to prior false allegations.

4. **Procedures for admitting prior sexual behavior under Rape Shield Statute (including sex trafficking cases)**:

   a. Accused makes written motion in camera to offer the evidence.

   b. Motion must contain evidence to be offered and names/addresses of witnesses.

   c. Motion served on State, who gives notice to victim.

   d. Judge examines motion, and if it sets forth sufficient evidence, it is set for hearing.

   e. At the closed hearing, court may admit the evidence if: 1) relevant; and 2) probative value outweigh danger of unfair prejudice.

   f. If admitted, court specifies evidence which may be offered and areas in which victim may be examined or cross-examined.

   g. Introduction of evidence limited to the scope of the order.

   h. Notice is given to victim that such evidence will be offered.

5. **Victim's Attire.** (Article 412.1) Evidence of victim's attire is also excluded to show victim encouraged or consented to assault. **Exceptions**: May be admitted to show presence or absence of elements of offense.

6. **Admissible prior sexual offenses of the accused**. (Article 412.2) When the accused is charged with:

   a. a crime involving sexually assaultive behavior — other crimes of sexually assaultive behavior *may* be admissible, if probative value outweighs prejudice; and

b. a sex offense involving a victim under seventeen years old at the time of the offense—other crimes that show lustful disposition toward children *may* be admissible if probative value outweighs prejudice.

Upon request by accused, prosecution must give notice of intent to use crimes under 412.2, but no *Prieur* hearing is required. Reversible error for court to deny a limiting jury instruction.

7. **Statements of victims of sexual trafficking** to law enforcement are inadmissible in victim's trial arising out of same trafficking activity if: 1) victim cooperates; 2) agrees to testify truthfully at trial to the trafficking activity; and 3) the victim agrees to receive services for victims of sexual trafficking. (Article 412.3)

Problems on Prior Sexual Conduct in Sexual Assault Cases

PROBLEM 6-70. Derrick is accused of raping Katrina. The two of them had been having a casual sexual relationship for the six months leading up to the time that the alleged rape occurred. Derrick would like to offer evidence that during the same time, Katrina was also involved in an on-again, off-again sexual relationship with Cole, a man who Katrina had hopes of marrying. Derrick would like to show that Katrina is only claiming he raped her because Cole found a used condom wrapper next to her bed and she did not want to admit to having sex with Derrick while she was also seeing Cole. As a result, Derrick claims she made up the rape story. The prosecution objects to the admissibility of any evidence that Katrina was having sex with Cole as inadmissible past sexual behavior of the victim in a sexual assault case. What procedures must be followed to offer the evidence? How should the court rule on the admissibility of the evidence of Katrina's intimate relationship with Cole? Explain.

PROBLEM 6-71. James is charged with raping Tiffany in her hotel room while both were attending the National Basketball Conference Championship. James would like to offer evidence that Tiffany gave him her room number and when he arrived at Tiffany's hotel room around 2 a.m., Tiffany answered the door in her panties and a sheet, and laid across the bed as he visited with her. He claims she never tried to get dressed or cover herself. Should the judge allow James to offer evidence that Tiffany answered the door and remained in panties the entire time he was in her hotel room? Why or why not?

PROBLEM 6-72. Devin has been accused of raping Victoria. Victoria's boyfriend, Peter, testifies at trial because he saw Victoria immediately after the rape in the parking lot of Devin's apartment complex. He then called the police and took her to the hospital. At the trial, Devin would like to elicit testimony that Peter is having intimate relations with Victoria, and that on the night of the alleged rape, Peter was in his (Devin's) apartment complex only because he suspected Victoria of cheating on him. Devin claims Peter is only testifying because he is sleeping with Victoria and wants to get rid of Devin because he doesn't want Victoria to see Devin again. The prosecution objects that Devin cannot drag Victoria's sex life through the mud and that the whole line of questioning is inadmissible. Will the evidence of Victoria's sexual relationship with Peter be admissible?

PROBLEM 6-73. Moe was on trial for raping Katrina. Moe and Katrina had dated briefly for about 6 months. During that time, Moe and Katrina often met for lunch to have sex. Katrina has even had sex in her office at work with Moe on her lunch break. The rape allegedly occurred in Moe's car at the pier by the lake where he took Katrina after picking her up from her office to treat her to lunch. Katrina claims she agreed to go but told him that she couldn't stay long because she had to return to work. She claims that once they arrived at the pier and were alone, Moe raped her after she refused to do it again for "old times' sake." Can Moe offer evidence of all the prior occasions in which he and Katrina had sex during their lunch break to show that Katrina agreed to have sex with him on the day in question? Why or why not?

PROBLEM 6-74. In defendant's trial for aggravated rape, he sought to introduce a videotape of himself and the victim having consensual sexual intercourse about a year before the incident. The video was an explicit depiction of the two of them in various sexual positions for over two hours. The prosecution objects to the videotape and claims that it is offensive and lacks probative value. Further, the prosecution has offered to stipulate that the victim and defendant once had a relationship, the time and length of the relationship, and that a videotape was made of the two of them having sex during the course of the relationship with a general summary of the contents. How should the court rule on the admissibility of the videotape? What should the court consider in coming to its conclusion? See *State v. Myers*, 981 So. 2d 214 (La. Ct App. 5th Cir. 2008).

PROBLEM 6-75. Jimmy was on trial for raping his neighbor Amber. The day after the alleged rape, Amber tested positive for an STD. Jimmy would like to offer evidence that Amber had an STD at trial, and that he did not have one at the time of the alleged rape, to explain why she is claiming that she was raped. Jimmy claims that Amber made up the rape story to explain an STD that she apparently got from cheating on her boyfriend. Should the judge allow evidence of Amber's STD, possible cheating, and that she has a boyfriend? Explain.

PROBLEM 6-76. Phillip is charged with raping his neighbor Monique. Phillip would like to offer evidence that on the night of the alleged rape, he knows that Monique had an overnight guest because he saw him enter her apartment and he did not leave until the next morning. He asserts that Monique may have been raped by that man and is now blaming it on him. Should the judge allow Phillip to testify that a man spent the night at Monique's house the night of the alleged rape? Why or why not?

PROBLEM 6-77. Part I: Melody is 15 years old, and her stepfather is on trial for molesting her. During cross-examination of Melody in the trial, the defense asks her if it was true that her stepfather had walked into her bedroom one night and found a boy in there that she had sneaked into the house, who her stepfather subsequently banned from ever coming there again? The prosecution objects that the question goes into specific instances of bad conduct and that it is also banned by the Rape Shield Statute. How should the court rule and why?

Part II: Assume that after the court resolves that issue, the defense then attempts to question Melody about prior allegations of molestations that she had made against two of her mother's former boyfriends shortly after her mother divorced Melody's father where charges were never filed. The defense claims the allegations against the prior boyfriends were false. Melody claims the allegations she made were true. How should the court handle the issue to determine whether to allow the questioning? Should the questioning be allowed?

PROBLEM 6-78. Monty is charged with the forcible rape of his 12-year-old stepdaughter. According to the victim, it had occurred five or six times. His wife walked in and caught the defendant raping her daughter one evening when she returned from work early. Monty has a prior molestation conviction of a 14-year-old girl that occurred 7 years prior to the instant offense as well as a prior carnal knowledge of a juvenile that occurred 14 years prior to the instant offense of which he was acquitted at trial. The prosecution would like to used both offenses in the trial of the forcible rape. What steps should they take to be able to use the evidence? For what purpose might it be relevant? Does it pass the Article 403 balancing test? Will the evidence likely be admitted?

PROBLEM 6-79. Vicky is 15 years old. Her uncle is charged with raping her. He would like to offer evidence that Vicky is a very promiscuous girl and had sex with several boys on her prom night. Should the evidence by admissible?

PROBLEM 6-80. Martin is charged with raping Agnes. He claims Agnes has slept with several of his business partners in exchange for gifts and money. He claims the evidence that Agnes had consensual sex with his business partners is relevant to show that Agnes consented to have sex with him hoping to get the same benefits. He claims she only claimed rape when he refused to give her money. Should the evidence of Agnes' sexual behavior with Martin's business partners be permissible at trial? Explain.

§ 6.9 References and Additional Authority on the Admissibility of Prior Sexual Conduct in Sexual Assault Cases [La. C.E. arts. 412, 412.1, 412.2, 412.3]

1. La. C.E. arts. 412, 412.1, 412.2, 412.3 and Official Comments
2. Force & Rault, Handbook on Louisiana Evidence Law Arts. 412, 412.1, 412.2, 412.3; Author's Comments (West Publishing 2014)
3. Harges & Jones, Louisiana Evidence Arts. 412, 412.1, 412.2, 412.3; Author's Comments (West Publishing 2014)
4. 19 La. Civ. L. Treatise, Evidence And Proof § 9.3 (2nd ed.)
5. **Commentary**: Collier, *State v. Jackson: Evidence of Allegations of Prior Sexual Abuse by Accused in an Intra-Family Context*, 55 La. L. Rev. 1191 (1995); Jones, Russell, *Louisiana Code of Evidence Article 412.2: Has It Destroyed a Well-Established Evidentiary Rule*? 50 La. B.J. 90 (August/September, 2002).
6. **Prior sex with defendant to show consent:** *State v. Everidge*, 702 So. 2d 680 (La. 1997) (holding that court improperly excluded evidence that prior to the sexual encounter, the defendant and victim were hugging and kissing several hours beforehand because the evidence showed prior sexual conduct with the defendant); *State v. Myers*, 981 So. 2d 214 (La. Ct. App. 5th Cir. 2008) (The defendant appealed the judgment of the trial court which excluded evidence of a videotape offered to show that the defendant and the victim had a consensual sexual relationship. The court ruled that the probative value of the videotape was outweighed by the unfair prejudice to the victim and was inadmissible.).
7. **Source of injury/semen within 72 hours:** *State v. Breaux*, 2011-15 (La. Ct. App. 1st Cir. 2011) (not allowing the defendant to offer evidence that his five-year-old daughter, the victim in the case, was raped by her uncle because it occurred more than 72 hours prior to the current sexual abuse).
8. **Prior false allegation:** *State v. Dixon*, 982 So. 2d 146 (La. Ct. App. 5th Cir. 2008) (In holding evidence of prior false allegations inadmissible, the court distinguished *State v. Smith, supra*, by stating that the defendant in the instant case did not present any evidence to support prior false allegations made on the part of the victim; the defendant is the only person who stated that the victim made prior false allegations.).

9. **Bias, interest, motive:** *State v. Pitts*, 87 So. 3d 306 (La. Ct. App. 3d Cir. 2012) (holding evidence inadmissible because the defendant failed to show that by presenting evidence that the victim, who was thirteen at the time of the offense, having sex with someone his own age showed bias toward the defendant); *State v. Blackwell*, 953 So. 2d 207 (La. Ct. App. 1st Cir. 2007) (The defendant attempted to offer evidence of the victim's prior sexual acts with other men in order to show the victim's motive for making an allegation against him. The court ruled that evidence of the victim's sexual acts with other men was inadmissible, but evidence of disagreements between the defendant and victim was admissible.).
10. **Procedures/hearing/no notice:** *State v. Frith*, 747 So. 2d 1269 (La. Ct. App. 2d Cir. 1999) (holding that in order for a defendant to offer the victim's past sexual behavior under one of the exceptions in article 412, he must first file a notice of intent; the court then holds a closed hearing to determine the admissibility of the evidence); *State v. Willis*, 915 So. 2d 365 (La. Ct. App. 3d Cir. 2005) (holding State's notice of offenses committed in LaSalle Parish sufficient under Article 412; notice included the defendant's previous victims' names and the years that the offenses occurred).
11. **Attire:** *State v. Anders*, 941 So. 93 (La. Ct. App. 3d Cir. 2006) (holding inadmissible the defendant's attempt to offer testimony regarding the victim's attire in order to show the victim's consent).
12. **412.2 prior acts showing lustful disposition and very old prior sexual acts:** *State v. Fisher*, 40 So. 3d 1020 (La. Ct. App. 4th Cir. 2010) (The defendant argued that evidence given by the defendant's daughter was more prejudicial than it was probative. The court ruled that the evidence showed the defendant's propensity to sexually abuse young girls; therefore, the evidence was admissible.); *State v. Driggers*, 554 So. 2d 720 (La. Ct. App. 2d Cir. 1989) (allowing prior acts that occurred between seven and twenty-six years prior to the current offense and showed a lustful disposition for children as evidence against the defendant because it showed what motivated the defendant to act in the manner that he did); *State v. Hotard*, 975 So. 2d 16 (La. Ct. App. 5th Cir. 2007) (allowing evidence of a letter written by the defendant in which the defendant expressed a sexual interest for young girls to show the defendant's lustful disposition for children); *State v. Caston*, 996 So. 2d 480 (La. Ct. App. 2d Cir. 2008) (allowing evidence of the defendant's prior convictions of aggravated sexual battery and incest because the other crimes showed the defendant's lustful disposition for children).

§ 6.10 Character of Witness for Truthfulness/Credibility [La. C.E. arts. 404(A)(3), 608]

Applicable Code Articles

Art. 404. Character evidence generally not admissible in civil or criminal trial to prove conduct; exceptions; other criminal acts

A. Character evidence generally. Evidence of a person's character or a trait of his character, such as a moral quality, is not admissible for the purpose of proving that he acted in conformity therewith on a particular occasion, except:

* * *

(3) Character of witness. Evidence of the character of a witness, as provided in Articles 607, 608, and 609.

Art. 608. Attacking or supporting credibility by character evidence

A. Reputation evidence of character. The credibility of a witness may be attacked or supported by evidence in the form of general reputation only, but subject to these limitations:

(1) The evidence may refer only to character for truthfulness or untruthfulness.

(2) A foundation must first be established that the character witness is familiar with the reputation of the witness whose credibility is in issue. The character witness shall not express his personal opinion as to the character of the witness whose credibility is in issue.

(3) Inquiry into specific acts on direct examination while qualifying the character witness or otherwise is prohibited.

B. Particular acts, vices, or courses of conduct. Particular acts, vices, or courses of conduct of a witness may not be inquired into or proved by extrinsic evidence for the purpose of attacking his character for truthfulness, other than conviction of crime as provided in Articles 609 and 609.1 or as constitutionally required.

C. Cross-examination of character witnesses. A witness who has testified to the character for truthfulness or untruthfulness of another witness may be cross-examined as to whether he has heard about particular acts of that witness bearing upon his credibility.

As we have studied thus far, while character evidence may not be offered to prove that a person acted in conformity with his character on a particular occasion, it may be offered for other purposes. Article 404(A)(1)–(3) specifically lists three situations in which character evidence is admissible, and we have covered two of them. In § 6.3 we covered an accused putting his own character at issue as provided in Article 404(A)(1), and in § 6.8 we covered the character of a victim as provided in Article 404(A)(2). Additionally, in § 6.4 we have studied the admissibility of character evidence when it is an essential element of the charge, claim, or defense. In this section we will discuss the admissibility of character evidence of a witness for truthfulness or untruthfulness as provided in Article 404(A)(3). Unlike situations in which a witness is testifying to the character of the accused or of a victim, **this section deals with a witness who is called to testify to the character of another witness on the issue of that witness's credibility, i.e., his truthfulness or veracity**.

For clarification purposes, throughout this section we will refer to the initial witness who testified in a case (usually a fact witness) as the "**principal witness**," and the witness testifying to that witness's character for truthfulness will be referred to as the "**character witness**."

Character of witness for truthfulness admissible. As we have covered throughout the book, whenever a witness takes the stand, his credibility is *always* at issue. The jury, who is usually the trier of fact, must make credibility determinations as they listen to a witness's testimony to decide what evidence to accept or reject in making factual determinations. Since a witness's credibility is always at issue, any evidence bearing on the witness's truthfulness or veracity is relevant. So far, we have only discussed one way in which a witness's credibility may be attacked—by impeachment with prior convictions under Article 609 and Article 609.1, covered in §6.7. In this section we address another useful method of offering evidence that bears on a witness's credibility—by offering evidence of the witness's character for truthfulness or untruthfulness.

Up until this point, we have primarily discussed character and credibility separately, noting that when a witness takes the stand, he does not generally put his character at issue, only his credibility. However, there is one pertinent character trait that *is* at issue when a witness takes the stand—**his character relative to his truthfulness**. Thus, as you study Article 404(A)(3), there are two important points to keep in mind: 1) when a witness takes the stand, evidence of his character for truthfulness (the pertinent character trait) is admissible and relevant; and 2) character in this situation must be proven by the same procedures discussed in §6.2. The text of Article 404(A)(3) specifically points to Article 608 for the procedures for proving character of a witness for truthfulness, and they are as follows:

1. proven by general reputation in the community;
2. it must be a pertinent character trait (*truthfulness or untruthfulness is the only pertinent character trait permissible*);
3. a foundation must be laid to establish that the witness is familiar with the person's reputation in the community for truthfulness (but no specific instances in foundation);
4. the "community" in which the knowledge was obtained can be school, work, neighborhood, or any other setting in which the witness interacted with the person and other associates enough to have learned of the person's reputation for that particular character trait;
5. the character witness may be cross-examined on specific instances of conduct that must: a) go to the pertinent character trait in issue (*truthfulness/untruthfulness*); and b) cross-examination must be in the form of "have you heard";
6. prior conduct subject to a preliminary hearing on *Johnson* safeguards; and
7. the opponent may also call character witnesses to rebut the testimony of the character witness who testifies to the character of the principle witness. For example, if a party calls a character witness to testify that a fact witness is not truthful, the opponent may call a character witness in rebuttal to testify that the fact witness is, in fact, truthful. The same procedures apply for offering the rebuttal character evidence.

General reputation for truthfulness. Pursuant to Article 608(A), as in all cases of proving character, except when it is an essential element and under Article 412, it must be in the form of the witness's general reputation in the community for the pertinent character trait (*here, truthfulness or untruthfulness*). Such testimony requires the proper foundation to establish how the witness has become familiar with the witness's reputation for truthfulness. A witness's testimony addressing the character of the principle witness cannot be in the form of opinion evidence. Further, in laying the foundation on direct examination to establish how the witness is familiar with the principle witness's character for truthfulness, counsel may not inquire into specific instances of conduct. In other words, the witness may not give specific examples of incidents or events that may explain how the principle witness got his reputation. For example, the witness would not be able to testify, "*Well, Jim has a reputation for being honest because everyone knows that he broke off an affair and told his wife he'd cheated and she didn't even know about the affair.*" Such specific instances are not permissible. The witness may only testify to the principle witness's reputation in the community for truthfulness, as follows: "*Witness X has a reputation in our church for being a very truthful, honest person of high integrity.*"

Specific instances cannot be inquired into. Article 608(B) specifically precludes the use of specific instances of conduct for the purpose of attacking a witness's character for truthfulness, with the exception of Articles 609 and 609.1 relative to criminal convictions. This article reaffirms the fact that character, even on the issue of a witness's credibility, may only be proven by **general reputation** in the community with the limited exceptions we have discussed. For example, when a witness takes the stand and testifies, he cannot be cross-examined regarding the fact that he was fired from his job for stealing as a way of attacking his credibility. However, he may be questioned regarding a *conviction* for stealing as discussed above relative to Articles 609 and 609.1. We saw this issue play out in *James* and *Ash*, *supra*, § 6.7. While Ash could be questioned about his prior *conviction* for possession of cocaine under Article 609.1, James could not be questioned about whether he had ever *used* cocaine because it was not a conviction. This exclusion applies to a full range of particular acts, vices or courses of conduct including arrests, drug addiction, cheating in school, or even getting kicked out of school. They are all examples of specific instances of conduct and may not be inquired into to prove truthfulness or untruthfulness of a witness.

Keep in mind that while this article precludes the particular acts from being offered for the sole purpose of attacking or proving a witness's character for truthfulness, they may be relevant for other purposes, discussed in § 6.11, *infra*, relative to credibility.

Specific instances cannot be proven by extrinsic evidence. Not only can specific instances of conduct not be **inquired into** under this article, but they also cannot be **proven** by extrinsic evidence, other than as it relates to convictions under Articles 609 and 609.1. As we briefly discussed relative to convictions offered on the issue of credibility, extrinsic evidence is evidence other than what the witness himself has testified to—it may be another witness, physical evidence, or even a document offered to prove what the witness has refused to testify to. For instance, if a witness is questioned about whether he has been convicted of a crime and denies it, counsel may offer evidence outside of his testimony to prove that he has, in fact, been convicted of the crime, such as by offering a certified copy of the clerk of court minutes. The minutes are extrinsic evidence to prove what the witness failed to admit to. Extrinsic evidence is not admissible to prove specific acts or vices of a witness on the issue of his credibility. Thus, if a witness is questioned as to whether he was expelled from law school for cheating and denies it (an impermissible question in itself), counsel may not then call the Dean of the school to testify that he was so expelled.

Credibility cannot be supported until it has been attacked. It is important to keep in mind that, pursuant to Article 607(B), the credibility of a witness may not be attacked until after the witness has been sworn, and **may not be supported unless it has been attacked**. For example, if the prosecution calls a child witness in a sexual assault case who testifies that her grandfather molested her, the prosecution cannot then call a neighbor of the family to testify that the victim/girl has a reputation in the community for being credible and truthful in an effort to bolster her credibility. Since the child's credibility has not been attacked, it cannot be supported by the neighbor's testimony. It is not until *after* the defense has attacked the credibility of the witness that the prosecution can call a witness to support the witness's credibility. However, if on cross-examination of the child witness, the defense suggests that the witness was lying or was being coached, then the prosecution could properly call the neighbor to testify that the witness has a reputation for being truthful.

While counsel could call a witness to testify that a principle witness has a reputation for being *untruthful* anytime after a witness has been sworn, attacking the credibility of a witness, a witness may not be called to testify that a principle witness has a reputation for being *truthful*, supporting his credibility, until after the witness's credibility has been attacked. Thereafter the full list of procedures outlined above for offering character evidence for truthfulness should be followed.

Same procedures as for all character witnesses. The procedures outlined above for proving character as laid out in Article 404(A)(3), Article 607 and Article 608 are the same as for all character witnesses, with the exception that the witness's credibility must first be attacked prior to offering a character witness for truthfulness (not untruthfulness). Thereafter, the procedures above apply. Additionally, the specific instances in which the character witness may be cross-examined in the form of "have you heard" must bear on the character trait of truthfulness as well. For example, the character witness may be asked, "Have you heard the principal witness lied on his income taxes?" Additionally, rebuttal witnesses may be called to rebut the character witness's testimony as to the same trait. Keep in mind that the requirements of *Johnson* apply to the specific bad acts about which the witness may be cross-examined to reduce the risk of unfair prejudice.

Federal Rules of Evidence Distinction. As in all instances under the Federal Rules of Evidence where character evidence is admissible, the character of a witness for truthfulness may also be proven by both reputation in the community and opinion evidence of a witness to the principle witness's character for truthfulness. Sufficient foundation must be laid to establish how the witness became familiar with the reputation for truthfulness or untruthfulness. Similarly, foundation must be laid to establish that the witness is acquainted with the witness. Whether the witness testifies to reputation or to opinion, he may be cross-examined on specific instances of conduct of the principle witness—preferably in the form of "have you heard," if the testimony was in reputation, or "did you know" if the testimony was in the form of opinion. However, either form of questioning is sufficient in either case. Counsel need only have a "good faith basis" for asking the "have you heard" or "did you know" question.[132]

Case on Character of the Witness for Truthfulness

State v. Terry (II)
Court of Appeal of Louisiana, First Circuit
654 So. 2d 455
April 7, 1995

WHIPPLE, Judge.

[The facts of the case are set forth in *Terry (I)* in § 6.8, *supra.*]

ASSIGNMENT OF ERROR NUMBER FOUR

By means of this assignment, defendant contends that the trial court erred in sustaining the state's objection to defense counsel's cross-examination of Mathis Holiday, by which counsel sought to elicit testimony concerning the victim's reputation for untruthfulness. He asserts that this ruling unfairly restricted his right to attack the credibility of the victim and to present a defense. He submits that the trial court erred by concluding that the requisite foundation under LSA–C.E. art. 608 had not been met.

LSA–C.E. art. 608 provides as follows:

> **A. Reputation evidence of character.** The credibility of a witness may be attacked or supported by evidence in the form of general reputation only, but subject to these limitations:

132. United States v. Monteleone, 77 F.3d 1086, 1090–91, (6th Cir. 1996).

(1) The evidence may refer only to character for truthfulness or untruthfulness.

(2) A foundation must first be established that the character witness is familiar with the reputation of the witness whose credibility is in issue. The character witness shall not express his personal opinion as to the character of the witness whose credibility is in issue.

(3) Inquiry into specific acts on direct examination while qualifying the character witness or otherwise is prohibited.

B. Particular acts, vices, or courses of conduct. Particular acts, vices, or courses of conduct of a witness may not be inquired into or proved by extrinsic evidence for the purpose of attacking his character for truthfulness, other than conviction of crime as provided in Articles 609 or 609.1 or as constitutionally required.

C. Cross-examination of character witnesses. A witness who has testified to the character for truthfulness or untruthfulness of another witness may be cross-examined as to whether he has heard about particular acts of that witness bearing upon his credibility.

On cross-examination, state witness Mathis Holiday testified that he had lived in Baton Rouge for almost sixteen years, knew the victim well and had heard people in the community talk about her. When defense counsel asked Holiday what kind of reputation the victim had based on the conversations he had heard, the prosecutor objected to the question. Outside the presence of the jury, the prosecutor stated that the defense had not established the foundation required by LSA-C.E. art. 608 to attack the victim's credibility. At that point, defense counsel was allowed to question Holiday (out of the jury's presence) during which the following exchange occurred:

By Mr. Mitchell:

Q. Mr. Holiday, how long have you lived in the community where you live now?

A. About four years and some months.

Q. Have you lived in the same community with [the victim]?

A. I was staying [sic] when she was staying with [defendant's] aunt, and I stayed around Zion City and Rosenwald.

Q. Have you spoken with people in either of those communities who talked about [the victim's] reputation for truth?

A. A few.

Q. What do you call a few?

A. About maybe three or four.

Q. And the people that you've talked to who talked about her reputation did they express their knowledge of her, that they know her?

A. Yeah.

Q. Did they express opinions as to her truthfulness?

A. Yes.

Q. Are these people related to you or to the defendant?

A. They're not related to him, and not related to me.

Q. And what is that reputation in the community?

A. Okay. When they first saw her come into Brookstown and saw him and her be [sic] walking the streets sometimes—

Q. Mr. Holiday, my question is, what is the community's opinion of [the victim's] truthfulness or untruthfulness?

A. Well, they said she wasn't so.

By the court:

Q. Wasn't what?

A. Wasn't what you—explain what you're saying.

By Mr. Mitchell:

Q. Is she truthful or is she not? Does she have a reputation for being truthful or does she have a reputation for being untruthful?

A. Well, they said she had a bad reputation, okay? I'll put it like that.

Q. Does she have a reputation for lying or telling the truth?

A. Well, they say for lying. And they say for fooling with other things. Like I said, you know.

Mr. Mitchell:

Your honor, I intend to limit it to her truthfulness.

The court:

Well, you can limit it to that. He's talked to three or four people. If you talk to the right three or four people they might call me a lying S.O.B., or whatever. I don't know. I don't think that represents a community. It depends on which three or four you get.

Mr. Mitchell:

Your honor, I believe the jurisprudence is that the witness is credible, the persons that he's talked to is credible. There is no set number of persons that he has to talk to.

The court:

That isn't what the code says.

Mr. Mitchell:

The code also doesn't give a number.

The court:

No, it doesn't give a number, but I know that a community—I think I can almost take judicial notice of the fact that Brookstown is a community that is significantly greater than three or four people. If he told me three or four dozen or three or four hundred even, maybe you might have something, but not three or four people. Like I said, if you get the right three or four people you can hear anything you want to hear. Objection of the state is sustained....

Character testimony is the opinion by a member of the community exposed over an extended period of time to hearing the discussion by other members of the community shared by himself and the person whose reputation is at issue. Before being permitted to testify, the reputation witness must be shown to be qualified to testify on the subject as a member of the community in a position to speak with authority on the subject. *State v. Deaton,* 412 So.2d 586, 589 (La.1982). Proof of general reputation attacking or supporting credibility may be made not only of the reputation of the person where he lives, but also of his repute, as long as it is general and established, in any substantial community of people among whom he is well known, such as the group with whom he works, does business or goes to school. *State v. Clark,* 402 So.2d 684, 687 (La.1981).

Citing *State v. Taylor,* 621 So.2d 141, 153 (La.App. 2nd Cir.1993), *writ denied,* 93–2054 (La. 2/11/94), 634 So.2d 371, defendant asserts that the trial court erred by ruling that he failed to establish the required foundation for Holiday's testimony as to the victim's reputation for untruthfulness. We disagree.

In *Taylor,* the reputation witness had learned of the defendant's reputation through discussions with his family members, their pastor, students at school and Haynesville Mayor Tom Crocker. In finding the foundation adequate for the witness' reputation evidence, the *Taylor* court indicated that without this identification of the persons with whom the reputation witness had held discussions, the foundation issue might have given the court cause for concern. We find the instant situation distinguishable from that in *Taylor* but analogous to the situation presented in another case decided by the Second Circuit Court of Appeal, *State v. Jenkins,* 456 So.2d 174, 177–178 (La.App. 2nd Cir.), *writ denied,* 460 So.2d 1043 (La.1984). The court in *Jenkins* upheld the trial court's ruling sustaining the state's objection to the adequacy of the foundation for reputation evidence. In reaching its decision, the court noted:

> At best, the testimony of this witness was to the effect that he had known the victim, had frequented bars himself, had seen the victim at bars, and had heard "some" or a "few" unidentified people talk about her reputation without specificity as to whom he had heard talking, how many times he had heard them discussing the victim, over what length of time he had heard these conversations, and how well the people who had discussed her were known to either the victim or this witness. Clearly, this was an insufficient foundation to determine that this evidence of repute was based on reputation of the victim among those who knew her well. *Jenkins,* 456 So.2d at 178.

In the instant case, Holiday testified that he lived in the community, knew the victim and had spoken with a few (three or four) unidentified people in the community about the victim's reputation for truthfulness. Although Holiday stated that the persons to whom he had spoken were not related to him or the defendant, there was no specificity setting forth with whom Holiday had spoken, how many times or when the discussions had occurred, or how well these people were known to either the victim or Holiday. Clearly, the trial court did not err in ruling that an insufficient foundation had been laid to admit the testimony of this character witness.

This assignment lacks merit.

...

Discussion Questions

1. Do you agree with the court's decision in *Terry* above? Based on reading the transcript of what transpired in the hearing while laying foundation, do you think sufficient foundation had been established that the witness was familiar enough with the victim's reputation to testify to her reputation in the community? What more would you have asked the witness?
2. To how many people must a character witness have spoken to be familiar with a person's reputation? In *Terry*, the trial judge stated the following: "*If he told me three or four dozen or three or four hundred even, maybe you might have something, but not three or four people. Like I said, if you get the right three or four people you can hear anything*

you want to hear." Does one need to speak to three or four hundred people to learn of a person's reputation? Does it depend upon the size of the community? For example, how many people would you think you'd need to speak with in the law school to become familiar with a person's reputation—five to six, fifty to sixty, or two to three hundred? What's the standard? What should be considered?

3. What weight do you believe such evidence has with the jury? Do you believe it is very persuasive or not in discrediting a witness?
4. What are your thoughts on not allowing foundation on specific instances of conduct? Do you think, even if outside of the presence of the jury, that it would assist a judge in determining whether the witness was qualified to testify on a person's truthfulness? Why do you think such evidence is not allowed?

Key Points

The key points to keep in mind regarding the character of a witness.

1. Character evidence is admissible to prove the character of a witness on the issue of the witness's credibility, by offering evidence of the witness's character for truthfulness
2. Before character may be offered to bolster a witness's credibility (truthfulness), it must first be attacked.
3. The procedures for proving the character of a witness are as follows:
    1. proven by general reputation in the community;
    2. it must be a pertinent character trait (*truthfulness or untruthfulness is the pertinent character trait*);
    3. a foundation must be laid to establish that the witness is familiar with the person's reputation in the community for truthfulness (but no specific instances in foundation);
    4. the "community" in which the knowledge was obtained can be school, work, neighborhood, or any other setting in which the witness interacted with the person and other associates enough to have learned of the person's reputation for that particular character trait;
    5. the character witness may be cross-examined on specific instances of conduct that must: a) go to the pertinent character trait in issue (*truthfulness/untruthfulness*); and b) be in the form of "have you heard";
    6. prior conduct subject to a preliminary hearing on *Johnson* safeguards; and
    7. the opponent may also call character witnesses to rebut the testimony of the first character witness. For example, if a party calls a character witness to testify that a fact witness is not truthful, the opponent may call a character witness in rebuttal to testify that the fact witness is, in fact, truthful. Same procedures apply for offering the rebuttal character evidence.
4. Specific instances of conduct may not be inquired into in laying foundation for a character witness.
5. Specific instances (acts, vices, or courses of conduct) may not be asked of a witness to attack his character, except under 609/609.1; and extrinsic evidence may not be offered to prove specific instances.

Problems on Character of a Witness

PROBLEM 6-81. Ted was robbed and identified Pete, the defendant, as the robber. Ted testifies for the prosecution. During the defense's case, they call Kimble to testify to Ted's character for truthfulness. Kimble works at the courthouse, and testifies that word around the courthouse is that Ted has testified in three or four cases for the prosecution where the defendant was subsequently found not guilty. The prosecution objects that the testimony is an improper impeachment of Ted. How should the court rule and why?

PROBLEM 6-82. Paul is a plaintiff in a personal injury action arising out of a car accident. At the time of the accident, Webster was a passenger in Paul's car. Paul calls Webster at the trial to testify to how the accident occurred. After Webster testifies, Paul then calls Webster's twin brother Wesley to testify about Webster's good reputation for truthfulness. Can Paul do this? Why or why not?

PROBLEM 6-83. Samantha is a plaintiff in a civil case against Big Town Department Store, where she slipped and fell, injuring her back. In Samantha's case she called Wilma, who was shopping with her on the day she fell, to testify to how the incident occurred. After the plaintiff rested, Big Town called a witness to testify that Wilma is not credible because she too has filed a frivolous lawsuit. The plaintiff objects. How should the court rule?

PROBLEM 6-84. After all foundational requirements were met, Diane testified that Kaleb, the plaintiff's star witness, has a reputation in the community for being honest and highly trustworthy. On cross-examination by the defense, the attorney asks Diane whether she had heard about the fact that Kaleb had a child abuse case pending for beating his son. Is the question proper? Why or why not?

PROBLEM 6-85. The defendant testified in his own defense at trial. After his credibility was attacked by the prosecution, the defense called a witness to testify that the defendant had a reputation for being truthful in the community. The defense complied with all the procedures for properly offering the character evidence. After the defense rested, the prosecution called a witness in rebuttal to testify to the defendant's character for truthfulness/untruthfulness. After foundation was laid that the witness was familiar with the defendant's reputation for truthfulness, he testified that the defendant has a reputation for being untruthful because everybody knows that the defendant lied about receiving a large settlement in a lawsuit, when it was actually money that he received when his father died. Admissible? Why or why not?

PROBLEM 6-86. Carney is called by the plaintiffs to testify to another witness's character for untruthfulness in a civil case. In laying foundation for Carney's testimony, Carney testifies that she and the principal witness both grew up in the same part of town and that over the years the witness's name has come up a couple of times and they have discussed her reputation for truthfulness/untruthfulness. Counsel then asked Carney what is that reputation? Upon what basis should the defense object? How should the court likely rule and why?

PROBLEM 6-87. The defendant is charged with indecent behavior with a juvenile. He testified in his own defense. During his testimony, he was cross-examined regarding a prior felony conviction. The defense then calls Nick to testify to the defendant's character for truthfulness. While laying foundation to establish how Nick became familiar with the defendant's reputation, he testifies that they have worked together as high school teachers for the last 17 years, and that during that time the defendant has repeatedly encouraged students to come clean to their parents or school officials about many incidents in which they were involved. He also states that the defendant has been the teacher who has come clean on events involving the faculty. As a result, Nick states that he is now familiar with the defendant's character for truthfulness. Is there anything objectionable about this questioning? Should it be allowed? Explain.

PROBLEM 6-88. Taylor is called by the plaintiff to testify to the plaintiff's character for truthfulness after the plaintiff's character was attacked by the defense on cross-examination. After laying foundation that Taylor is familiar with the plaintiff's reputation for truthfulness because of their interactions in a non-profit organization, Taylor testifies that the plaintiff is the most honest and trustworthy person she knows because the plaintiff is the treasurer on the Board of Directors of their organization, which takes in over $7 million per year. Upon what basis should the defense object? How should the court likely rule and why?

PROBLEM 6-89. Lt. Frazier is a police officer who investigated an aggravated arson, and was called to testify for the prosecution about his investigation that led to the defendant's arrest. During cross-examination, the defense suggested that Lt. Frazier was corrupt. They claim that he and the entire police force often planted evidence and would do anything to get a conviction. He also cross-examined the officer about a prior conviction for a minor offense of violation of open container law, to which the officer openly admitted. Following Lt. Frazier's testimony, the prosecution then called another witness from the police force who has known Lt. Frazier for 17 years to testify to Lt. Frazier's character for truthfulness. After the foundation was laid, the witness testified that Lt. Frazier had an excellent reputation for truth and veracity among the officers on the police force. The defense then sought to cross-examine the witness on the following. Which of the following will they be able to ask about Lt. Frazier on cross-examination?

1. Have you heard that Lt. Frazier was arrested for domestic battery?
2. Have you heard that Lt. Frazier was convicted of violating the open container law?
3. Have you heard that Lt. Frazier was suspended without pay for 2 weeks, about 11 years ago, while they investigated a complaint that he propositioned a prostitute he'd arrested? The allegations were not substantiated.
4. Have you heard that Lt. Frazier falsely represented himself as a federal agent once to gain access to a federal prison?

PROBLEM 6-90. Phyllis is a witness in a trial for the prosecution. Ricky is called to testify to Phyllis' reputation for truth and veracity. Ricky says, "Phyllis does not have a good reputation for truthfulness. In fact, she was fired from her job for stealing money, then lying that she was robbed." Admissible? Why or why not?

§ 6.10 References and Additional Authority on Character of a Witness for Truthfulness/Untruthfulness [La. C.E. art. 404(A)(3), 608]

1. La. C.E. arts. 404(A)(3), 608 and Official Comments
2. Force & Rault, HANDBOOK ON LOUISIANA EVIDENCE LAW Arts. 404(A)(3), 608; Author's Comments (West Publishing 2014)
3. Harges & Jones, LOUISIANA EVIDENCE Arts. 404(A)(3), 608; Author's Comments (West Publishing 2014)
4. 19 La. Civ. L. Treatise, Evidence And Proof § 5.2,9.2 (2nd ed.)
5. **Foundation not laid for witness to testify (no knowledge of reputation):** *State v. Lambert*, 749 So. 2d 739 (La. Ct. App. 4th Cir. 1999) (holding that foundation had not

been laid for the witness to testify to the victim's reputation because the witness was not familiar with the victim's reputation for truthfulness or untruthfulness); *State v. Burrell*, 561 So. 2d 692 (La. 1990) (The defense counsel made no attempt to lay the proper foundation for the witness to testify to the reputation of the victim. Instead, the defense counsel immediately asked the witness if she knew the victim's reputation in the community and if it was bad or good. The court ruled that this evidence was inadmissible because no foundation had been laid.); *State v. Hotoph*, App. 5 Cir. 1999, 750 So. 2d 1036, 99-243 (La.App. 5 Cir. 11/10/99), writ denied 765 So. 2d 1062, writ denied 765 So. 2d 1066 (holding that insufficient foundation laid to establish that witness could testify to victim's reputation in trial for oral sexual battery and aggravated incest when witness testified that he had met victim a couple of times but that he did not know her).

6. **Proper foundation laid for witness to testify**: *State v. Taylor*, 621 So. 2d 141 (La. Ct. App. 2d Cir. 1993) (holding that the foundation had been laid for witness to testify about defendant's reputation; character witness had lived next door to defendant for several years and she had knowledge of the defendant's reputation for truth through his family and pastor).
7. **Counsel attempts to have witness testify to specific instances of conduct (or specific acts or vices) instead of character for truthfulness in form of reputation in the community:** *State v. Adams*, App. 5 Cir. 2013, 119 So. 3d 46, 11-1052 (La. App. 5 Cir. 5/16/13), writ denied 129 So. 3d 531, 2013-1413 (La. 12/6/13) (Improper attempt to use evidence of specific acts, vices, or course of conduct to impeach police office concerning the alleged false confession that police officer obtained in an unrelated criminal case); *State v. Joyner*, App. 4 Cir. 2012, 107 So. 3d 675, 2011-1397 (La.App. 4 Cir. 10/24/12), writ denied 118 So. 3d 388, 2012-2494 (La. 5/31/13) (Improper attempt to use specific acts to impeach credibility of police officer in murder trial with police officer's personnel file, which contained specific acts including a provoked attack on a fellow officer, a neglect of duty charge, an insubordination violation of departmental rules, a lack of truthfulness charge, and a mishandling evidence and mishandling an injured subject charge).
8. **Specific instances of conduct permissible on cross-examination of character witness:** *State v. Simpson*, 175 So. 2d 255 (La. 1965) (holding that a character witness may be asked about specific conduct of the defendant once the victim has testified to the good character of the defendant); *State v. Guss*, 775 So. 2d 622 (La. Ct. App. 4th Cir 2000) (holding that after character witness for the defendant testified that she had never known defendant to be violent and that the defendant was respectful, the state was then able to question the character witness on whether she was aware of the defendant's pending charge for armed robbery).
9. **Reputation for truthfulness/untruthfulness only, not "general reputation"**: *State v. Burrell*, Sup.1990, 561 So. 2d 692, rehearing denied, certiorari denied 111 S. Ct. 799, 498 U.S. 1074, 112 L.Ed.2d 861 (holding that character witness who testified that she was familiar with witness's reputation in the community was improperly questioned as to whether reputation of witness was "good or bad" rather than witness's reputation for truthfulness/untruthfulness).
10. **Denial of constitutional right to prevent a defense—reversible error:** *State v. Bairnsfather*, 591 So. 2d 686 (La. 1991) (finding reversible error when trial court refused to allow the defense to impeach the credibility of victim's testimony, which was sole substantive evidence against defendant; denial of defendant's right to impeach the credibility of sole witness prevents the defendant from presenting a defense).

11. **Federal Rules of Evidence:** Unlike Louisiana Evidence, the Federal Rules of Evidence allow reputation and opinion testimony to attack or support the credibility of a witness. Fed. R. Evid. 608(a).

§ 6.11 Other Attacks on Credibility of Witnesses — Impeachment [La. C.E. arts. 607, 613]

Applicable Code Articles

Art. 607. Attacking and supporting credibility generally

A. Who may attack credibility. The credibility of a witness may be attacked by any party, including the party calling him.

B. Time for attacking and supporting credibility. The credibility of a witness may not be attacked until the witness has been sworn, and the credibility of a witness may not be supported unless it has been attacked. However, a party may question any witness as to his relationship to the parties, interest in the lawsuit, or capacity to perceive or to recollect.

C. Attacking credibility intrinsically. Except as otherwise provided by legislation, a party, to attack the credibility of a witness, may examine him concerning any matter having a reasonable tendency to disprove the truthfulness or accuracy of his testimony.

D. Attacking credibility extrinsically. Except as otherwise provided by legislation:

(1) Extrinsic evidence to show a witness' bias, interest, corruption, or defect of capacity is admissible to attack the credibility of the witness.

(2) Other extrinsic evidence, including prior inconsistent statements and evidence contradicting the witness' testimony, is admissible when offered solely to attack the credibility of a witness unless the court determines that the probative value of the evidence on the issue of credibility is substantially outweighed by the risks of undue consumption of time, confusion of the issues, or unfair prejudice.

Art. 613. Foundation for extrinsic attack on credibility

Except as the interests of justice otherwise require, extrinsic evidence of bias, interest, or corruption, prior inconsistent statements, conviction of crime, or defects of capacity is admissible after the proponent has first fairly directed the witness' attention to the statement, act, or matter alleged, and the witness has been given the opportunity to admit the fact and has failed distinctly to do so.

An attack on a witness's credibility is referred to as "impeachment" — the introduction of evidence designed to call into question the truthfulness or accuracy of a witness's testimony. So far we have studied two primary ways in which a witness may be impeached: 1) through criminal convictions pursuant to Article 609 and 609.1; and 2) through evidence regarding a witness's character for truthfulness/untruthfulness pursuant to Article 608.

Article 607 and Article 613 govern several additional ways in which a witness may be impeached. Generally, a witness's credibility may be attacked through the introduction of various forms of evidence having **a reasonable tendency to disprove the truthfulness or accuracy of the witness's testimony**. In addition to the two forms of impeachment previously discussed, other common forms of impeachment include evidence that shows bias, interest, corruption, prior inconsistent statements, defects of capacity, and witness's relationship to the parties.

Certain specific acts *are* admissible. While specific instances of conduct (bad acts, vices, courses of conduct) may not be inquired into to prove a witness's character for truthfulness as outlined above in § 6.10, specific instances may be inquired into to show other things, such as: **bias, interest, corruption, prior inconsistent statements, defects of capacity, or witness's relationship to the parties.**

For example, it would be permissible to inquire of a witness who is testifying against the school principal whether the principal kicked him out of school for cheating. In such a case, while the act is a specific instance of conduct and a bad act because the witness is accused of cheating, it may be inquired into because it tends to show the witness's bias in testifying against the principal of the school. Additionally, a witness might be asked if he suffers from a mental disease or defect, or was under the influence of drugs or alcohol at the time he observed the incident about which he is testifying, solely to attack the witness's capacity to perceive or recollect.

Throughout this chapter we have studied the limited admissibility of specific instances of conduct to only those situations in which the conduct is relevant and probative of a purpose other than merely placing a person in a negative light before the jury, such as in Article 404(B). Here, evidence of specific bad acts, vices, or courses of conduct may be offered if it bears on the witness's credibility, i.e., if it would show bias, interest, corruption, or have any reasonable tendency to disprove the truthfulness or accuracy of the witness's testimony.

Common methods of impeachment. A witness may be examined regarding a wide range of issues that directly bear on the witness's credibility. The following are some of the most common:

Bias. A witness may be impeached by evidence that shows that the witness might have a reason to slant or favor one side or the other in his testimony, such as because of a relationship to the parties, interest, or otherwise. For example, a witness may be questioned regarding whether he received a plea agreement from the prosecution in exchange for his testimony to show that he has an incentive to testify against the defendant due to what he stands to gain. A witness's bias will usually always be exposed because it may tend to affect a witness's truthfulness, whether intentional or not.

Interest in Lawsuit. A witness may also be impeached by showing that he has an interest in the outcome of the case. For example, a person could be asked, "If the D is found liable, that would affect you as well, because you have ownership in the company, don't you?"

Defect of capacity. A witness may be shown to have some defect in capacity that might affect his ability to perceive or recollect. As stated above, a witness might be questioned concerning whether he was under the influence of alcohol or drugs, or whether he might have been suffering from a mental disease or defect at the time of the event about which he is testifying that might have affected his ability to perceive or recollect. Additionally, a witness could be questioned about something as simple as whether he was wearing his glasses at the time of the event he claims to have witnessed. In some instances it may be shown that the witness's testimony is not truthful, not because he intends to be dishonest, but simply because his capacity to perceive was impaired.

Impeachment with prior inconsistent statements. A witness may also be shown to have made a statement that is inconsistent with his testimony at trial. For instance, a witness may testify differently than he did in a deposition or statement made to the police or in an affidavit. This is different than under Article 801(D)(1)(A) where a person's statement may be offered in a criminal case for substantive value if certain foundational requirements are met.[133] Here, the prior inconsistent statement is being offered only to cast doubt on the truthfulness of the witness's testimony.

Who may attack credibility. Article 607(A) provides that the credibility of a witness may be attacked by any party, including the party calling him.

Cannot support credibility until after attacked. Article 607(B) provides that the credibility of a witness may not be attacked until the witness has been sworn, and the credibility of a witness may not be supported unless it has been attacked.

Intrinsic and Extrinsic Attack on Credibility

There is a distinct difference between inquiring into matters that can impeach a witness by examining the witness himself (intrinsic attack), versus offering evidence that impeaches a witness outside of his own testimony if the witness denies the matter (extrinsic attack). Clearly, impeaching a witness's credibility would have little effect if a witness could simply deny every matter about which he is questioned that might bear on his truthfulness. For example, if a witness could simply testify that he has never been convicted of a crime, or has not made a prior inconsistent statement, and so on, then questioning the witness regarding the issues would be futile. The matters would not fairly assist the jury in assessing the witness's credibility if the witness could not be forced to tell the truth about the issues, or if counsel could not prove the matter by other methods. Thus, Article 607 provides that certain impeachment evidence may be proven only by examining the witness himself, an intrinsic attack on credibility, while other impeachment evidence may also be proven by other evidence outside of the witness if the witness denies the matter, an extrinsic attack on credibility.

Intrinsic Attack on Credibility. Article 607(C) governs intrinsic attacks on credibility and provides that to attack the credibility of a witness, a party may examine him concerning any matter having a reasonable tendency to disprove the truthfulness or accuracy of his testimony, including: his relationship to the parties, interest in the lawsuit, capacity to perceive or to recollect. Additionally, a witness may be questioned regarding any matter that may show bias, interest, defects in capacity, prior inconsistent statement, or on any other matter bearing on his credibility. Attacking a witness's credibility is very broad in terms of the matters that may be inquired into from the witness *himself*, if it could have a tendency to bear on his credibility.

Extrinsic Attack on Credibility. Extrinsic attacks on a witness's credibility have more limitations. Article 607(D)(1) provides that extrinsic evidence may be offered to show a witness's bias, interest, corruption, or defect of capacity to attack the credibility of the witness. Article 607(D)(2) provides that other extrinsic evidence, including prior inconsistent statements and evidence contradicting the witness's testimony, is admissible when offered solely to attack the credibility of a witness unless the court determines that the probative

133. Pursuant to La. Code Evid. art. 801(D)(1)(a), a prior inconsistent statement is not hearsay and may be considered for substantive value if the declarant is present and capable of being cross-examined on the prior statement, provided that the proponent has first fairly directed the witness's attention to the prior statement and the witness has been given an opportunity to admit the fact and there exists evidence to corroborate the matter asserted in the prior inconsistent statement.

Intrinsic Attack
(May ask the witness himself about)

- Bias
- Interest
- Defects in capacity
- Prior inconsistent statement
- Relationship to parties
- Interest in lawsuit
- Capacity to perceive or recollect
- Any matter having a reasonable tendency to disprove the truthfulness or accuracy of his testimony

value of the evidence on the issue of credibility is substantially outweighed by the risks of undue consumption of time, confusion of the issues, or unfair prejudice. While extrinsic proof of *certain* impeachment evidence *may always be admitted*, evidence of *other types* of impeachment evidence may only be admitted *subject to Article 403 balancing.*

For example, if a person testifies at trial differently than he did in a prior statement, such as a deposition, the prior statement may be offered into evidence to prove that the witness in fact made a statement that is different than his current testimony. The out-of-court statement is not hearsay because it is not being offered to prove the truth of the matter asserted in the prior statement, but is offered only to show that the prior statement is different than the witness's current testimony. It is being offered only on the issue of the witness's credibility. Pursuant to Article 607(D)(2), however, the prior statement will only be admissible if the court determines that the probative value of the evidence on the issue of credibility is substantially outweighed by the risks of undue consumption of time, confusion of the issues, or unfair prejudice. However, extrinsic evidence that shows bias is admissible under Article 607(D)(1) without being subject to an Article 403 balancing test. The text boxes list the types of evidence that may be used for intrinsic attack on credibility, that which may also be proven by extrinsic evidence, and that which is only admissible subject to an Article 403 balancing test.

Foundation for extrinsic attack on credibility. Article 613 sets forth the foundation that must be laid prior to admitting extrinsic evidence attacking a witness's credibility in situations in which extrinsic evidence is permissible. The article provides that evidence of bias, interest, corruption, prior inconsistent statement, conviction of crime, or defects of capacity is admissible after the proponent has first fairly directed the witness's attention to the statement, act, or matter alleged, and the witness has been given the opportunity to admit the fact and has failed distinctly to do so.

Thus, a witness should always be questioned first about matters that attack his credibility. It is **only after the witness denies that fact or matter alleged** that extrinsic evidence should be offered on the point. If the witness admits the matter, such as a prior conviction, then counsel may not properly offer extrinsic evidence to prove the matter.

Extrinsic Attack
*(May ask the witness about, but if witness **denies**, may prove through other witness, document, or otherwise)*

- Bias
- Interest
- Corruption
- Defect of capacity
- Conviction of crime (subject to Article 403 balancing)
- Other extrinsic evidence (subject to Article 403 balancing)
- Prior inconsistent statements (subject to Article 403 balancing)
- Evidence contradicting testimony (subject to Article 403 balancing)

Impeachment with Prior Inconsistent Statements

As stated above, one of the most effective and common methods of impeaching a witness is with a prior inconsistent statement. A prior inconsistent statement is a statement that is inconsistent with a witness's testimony at trial. The prior statement may be oral or written, sworn or unsworn. It is important to remember, however, that when a witness is impeached with a prior inconsistent statement, the prior statement is not being offered to prove the truth of the matter asserted, but is only being offered to show that the witness is testifying differently than in the original statement and therefore should not be believed. Thus, it would be improper to argue the substance of the statement to the jury.

For example, the witness testifies at trial that the light was *red* when he went through it, but stated to the police officer at the scene of the accident that the light was *green* when he went through it. The attorney would not be able to argue that the light was actually red when witness went through it by claiming that the witness said so in his deposition. Such an argument would be using the out-of-court statement to prove *the truth of the matter asserted*, which is excluded by the hearsay rule. Instead it would only be appropriate for the attorney to argue that the witness cannot be believed because the witness has testified differently today than in his previous statement. Thus, under Article 607 the prior inconsistent statement may not be used for its "substantive value."

If you recall in Chapter 5, Part D, in our discussion of Statutory Non-Hearsay, under Article 801(D)(1)(A) a person's statement may be offered in a criminal case for substantive value if certain foundational requirements are met.[134] If those foundational requirements are not met in a criminal case, and in civil cases, the prior statement may only be used for its impeachment value.

Procedures for offering extrinsic evidence of prior inconsistent statement. In all instances, whether criminal for impeachment or substantive value, or in a civil case, in order to introduce extrinsic evidence of a prior inconsistent statement, the witness's attention

134. Pursuant to La. Code Evid. art. 801(D)(1)(a), a prior inconsistent statement is not hearsay and may be considered for substantive value if: 1) in a criminal trial; 2) the witness testifies differently than in a prior statement; 3) the declarant is present and capable of being cross-examined on the prior statement; 4) the proponent has first fairly directed the witness's attention to the prior statement and the witness has been given an opportunity to admit the fact and denies it; and 5) there exists evidence to corroborate the matter asserted in the prior inconsistent statement.

must first be directed toward the prior statement and given an opportunity to admit it. If he fails to do so, then extrinsic evidence of the prior statement may be offered. The following demonstrates how to impeach a witness with a prior inconsistent statement. Keep in mind that the impeachment will usually occur on cross-examination where leading questions are permissible.

Impeachment of Witness with Prior Inconsistent Statement

Q: And when you went through the light, it was red wasn't it, Mr. Witness? *(Pg. 6/Ln. 15)*

A: No, the light was actually green when I went through it.

Q: Mr. Witness, wasn't the light actually red when you went through it?

A: No, Sir. I am sure that the light was green when I went through it.

Q: Mr. Witness, didn't you previously make a statement where you indicated that the light was red when you went through it?

A: No, I did not. I've always said the light was green.

(*Counsel would then ask the witness the following litany of questions as foundation for impeachment.*)

Q: You gave a deposition/statement to police/affidavit?

Q: Before you gave the deposition, you took an oath to tell the truth?

Q: That's the same oath you took today?

Q: After you gave the deposition, you had a chance to look it over?

Q: To make sure there were no mistakes or missing facts?

Q: And after you were certain that there were no mistakes or missing facts, you signed it, correct?

Your honor, may I approach the witness? (*Tell opposing counsel page and line number.*)

Q: Mr. Witness, this is your deposition correct? *(Handing deposition to witness.)*

Q: Is this your signature?

Q: Look at page 6, line 15.

Option I: You may read aloud yourself

Q: Isn't it true that you were asked "what color was the light when you went through it?"

A: Yes.

Q: And you answered "the light was red," correct?

A: Yes, I did.

Option II: You may have the witness read

Q: Could you read page 6, line 15 **aloud,** please?

A: The question was, "Mr. Witness, what color was the light when you went through it?" My answer was "The light was red."

(Take deposition back from the witness, and restate original question.)

Q: So let me ask you again, Mr. Witness. The light was red when you went through it, wasn't it?

A: Yes, it was red when I went through it.

There are a few important points to keep in mind when impeaching a witness with a prior inconsistent statement. First, when you ask a witness whether he has made a prior statement as to a fact, the witness may very well admit that he made the prior statement and that he was lying or mistaken at that time and is currently telling the truth. If this happens, then there are no grounds for offering the prior statement in that the witness has not "failed to admit" the matter. The witness admits the statement, but claims it is not correct or accurate. Introducing the prior statement would do nothing more than what the witness has already stated.

Secondly, the witness's testimony must in fact be **inconsistent** with the prior statement to impeach the witness with it. For example, if the witness testifies that the light was green when her husband went through it, but her deposition states that she was sleeping when the accident occurred, the deposition would not be a prior inconsistent statement even though the inference is that the witness could not have known what color the light was if she was asleep. Instead the witness should be asked, "weren't you asleep when the accident occurred?" If the witness testifies that she was not asleep, then it would be appropriate to impeach her with her prior statement where she indicated that she was asleep when the accident occurred.

Additionally, counsel must get a **commitment** from the witness as to his current testimony to ensure that his current testimony is inconsistent with the prior statement. For example, if the witness testifies that he is not sure what color the light was, that he does not remember what color the light was, or that the light *might* have been the color counsel claims, then an impeachment may not be proper, since the witness has not affirmatively testified inconsistently with his prior statement. Counsel should attempt to refresh the witness's memory if the witness claims he does not remember. However, in order to impeach the witness, counsel should have the witness commit to his current testimony, and it should be inconsistent with his prior statement.

Finally, as noted in the questions above, the witness is **reasked the question** after the impeachment. This is very important because if the witness now testifies that the light was red, as he did in his deposition, then the answer is his current testimony and may be argued to the jury for its substantive value. If the witness never testifies to the fact, then his prior statement may not be argued to the jury for its substantive value because it is hearsay. Thus, if counsel wishes to argue the substance of the prior statement, he should reask the question. However, the witness could still maintain his new position and claim the prior statement was incorrect.

Federal Rules of Evidence Distinction. The Federal Rules of Evidence specifically provide for impeachment of a witness by testimony regarding the witness's character for truthfulness or untruthfulness pursuant to Rule 608 and through impeachment by prior inconsistent statements under Rule 613. However, contrary to the Louisiana Code, the Federal Rules do not specifically address many of the other commonly used forms of impeachment specifically listed in the Louisiana Code of Evidence, such as: bias, interest, corruption, defects of capacity, witness's relationship to the parties, interest in the lawsuit, or capacity to perceive or to recollect. Those methods, however, are well recognized methods of impeachment through federal case law.[135]

135. *See* United States v. Abel, 469 U.S. 45, 52 (1984) (citations omitted) ("[I]t is permissible to impeach a witness by showing his bias under the Federal Rules of Evidence just as it was permissible, to do so before their adoption.").

Key Points

The key points to keep in mind regarding impeachment of witnesses.

1. An attack on a witness's credibility is impeachment.
2. **Specific acts.** While bad acts may not be used generally to attack credibility, bad acts, vices, courses of conduct (other than convictions) may be inquired into if it specifically shows bias, interest, corruption, prior inconsistent statements, defects of capacity, or witness's relationship to the parties.
3. **Common methods of impeachment** include bias, interest in lawsuit, defect of capacity, prior inconsistent statements.
4. **Who may attack credibility.** Any party may attack credibility, including the party calling him.
5. **When may credibility be attacked.** Cannot attack a witness's credibility until after a witness has been sworn, and may not support credibility until after it has been attacked.
6. **Intrinsic attack on credibility**: May ask the witness himself about virtually any matter having a reasonable tendency to disprove the truthfulness or accuracy of his testimony.

   Examples: bias, interest, defects in capacity, prior inconsistent statement, relationship to parties, interest in lawsuit, capacity to perceive or recollect
7. **Extrinsic attack on credibility:** If a witness is asked about a matter and fails to admit it, may ask another witness, or introduce document or other evidence to prove it. Some matters may only be proven by extrinsic evidence if it passes the Article 403 balancing test:

   Example: bias, interest, corruption, defect of capacity, conviction of crime (403), prior inconsistent statements (403), evidence contradicting testimony (403)
8. **Foundation for extrinsic attack.** Proponent must first fairly direct the witness's attention to the statement, act, or matter alleged, and the witness has been given the opportunity to admit the fact and failed distinctly to do so.
9. **Impeaching with prior inconsistent statement.**
   a. Prior statement offered for impeachment purposes only, not substantive value.
   b. Counsel must first direct the witness's attention to the prior statement and the witness must fail to admit the fact. If witness admits prior statement and that it was different, then there is no impeachment.
   c. The witness's current statement must be inconsistent with the prior statement. If witness claims he doesn't remember, he should be refreshed, not impeached.
   d. Counsel may read the prior statement aloud or may have witness read the prior statement aloud.
   e. Counsel should re-ask the question, and if witness now changes testimony, counsel may argue the substance of the witness's testimony.

Problems on Impeaching Witnesses

PROBLEM 6-91. Coach Kincaid is the head football coach at University USA. One of his star athletes, Jake Stride, is on trial for beating up his girlfriend and has been suspended from the team pending the outcome of the charges. At the trial, Coach Kincaid testifies as a character witness for the defense with proper foundation that Jake is known for being a very gentle man, who is very peaceful and non-violent. The prosecution does not know of any specific instances about which to ask Coach Kincaid. Instead, the prosecution asks Coach whether he had posted the bond for Jake to get out of jail on the charges, whether Jake could help his team win, and whether he received raises and promotions for winning games. The defense adamantly objected to the line of questions as improper attacks on the coach's credibility. How should the court rule and why?

PROBLEM 6-92. Maria has brought an action against her employer for wrongful termination. She calls her sister as a witness in the trial. On cross-examination the defense asks the witness whether she is the plaintiff's sister. Maria's attorney stands up and objects, claiming that the issue is irrelevant, and that even if she is, it doesn't mean that she is not telling the truth. How should the court rule on the objection and why?

PROBLEM 6-93. During the defense's cross-examination of one of the prosecution's eyewitnesses, she is asked whether she saw the defendant's face during the robbery. She states that she did, in fact, see his face during the robbery. The defense asks her whether she is sure, and she states that she is sure. The defense asks her whether she previously testified that she did not see the robber's face. She states that she has always maintained that she could clearly see the robber's face and that it was the defendant who robbed the bank. The defense has a handwritten statement by this witness where she states, "Things were moving so quickly, all I could see were shapes and shadows. I really couldn't see any faces." Is there anything he can do to have the statement offered into evidence? Can he read it? Can he have her read it? What should he do next? What questions should he ask?

PROBLEM 6-94. Zachery and Law School Dean William Zaine Carmichael are involved in a collision. At trial, Joe, a witness for Zachery, testifies that he saw Chancellor Carmichael run a red light and hit Zachery's car. On cross-examination, Joe is asked: *"Weren't you thrown out of Law School for stealing money from the SBA while you were SBA President?"* Joe denies it, and opposing counsel seeks to offer proof that it's true. Is the evidence admissible, even though Joe was never charged with any offense?

PROBLEM 6-95. Hunter is a witness for the plaintiffs in a civil action. During cross-examination of Hunter, the defense asks him if he has ever been convicted of a crime. Hunter responds that he's never been convicted of a crime. The defense then asks Hunter if he has been convicted of possession of a controlled dangerous substance with the intent to distribute, which is a felony? Hunter maintains that he has not. The defense knows that Hunter has in fact been convicted of the crime. What, if anything, can they do to impeach Hunter? What steps should they take? What questions should be asked?

PROBLEM 6-96. Beau has testified for the prosecution in an aggravated rape trial. He testifies that he was headed to work and heard screams in the neighbor's apartment and went up there. He broke into the apartment and the defendant got up and ran past him and escaped before police arrived. During cross-examination of the witness, the defense asks him whether he told the police that he was headed to the store when he heard the screams coming from his neighbor's apartment. Beau testified that he is pretty sure he was headed to work. The defense would like to call Beau's employer to the stand to testify that Beau was not scheduled to work that day and in fact did not go to work that day to impeach Beau. Upon what basis should the prosecution object? How should the court likely rule and why?

PROBLEM 6-97. Nina is testifying for the defense in a criminal case. She was a customer in a bank when it was robbed. After she finishes testifying to the description of the suspect (which didn't match the defendant), the defense then asks her whether that was the same version she told the police on the night in question. Upon what basis (other than hearsay) should the prosecution object? How should the court likely rule and why?

PROBLEM 6-98. Tiffany is testifying as a witness for the plaintiff in a civil case. The plaintiffs are suing the City for the wrongful death of their son who was killed by the police during a high-speed chase that ended when the son drove into a tree. The collision occurred in a high crime area commonly known to be frequented by drug dealers, drug users, and prostitutes. Tiffany was in the vicinity of the collision when it occurred. She saw the collision and the subsequent conduct of the police, which is also at issue for being improper. During the defense's cross-examination of Tiffany, they would like to ask her questions about whether she is a drug user, whether she was high on drugs on the night of the incident, and/or whether she is a prostitute. The plaintiffs have objected to the line of questioning. The defense concedes that they have no evidence one way or the other but they would like to inquire into the line of questioning because they know that the area has several drug users and prostitutes there, and they believe the issues are relevant to her capacity to perceive or recollect. Should the court allow the questions? Why or why not?

§ 6.11 References and Additional Authority on Attacking Credibility of a Witness [La. C.E. art. 607, 613]

1. La. C.E. arts. 607, 613 and Official Comments
2. Force & Rault, HANDBOOK ON LOUISIANA EVIDENCE LAW Arts. 607, 613; Author's Comments (West Publishing 2014)
3. Harges & Jones, LOUISIANA EVIDENCE Arts. 607, 613; Author's Comments (West Publishing 2014)
4. 19 La. Civ. L. Treatise, Evidence And Proof § 9.1-§ 9.10(2nd ed.)
5. **Specific instances permitted on issue of bias**: *State v. Berry*, 645 So. 2d 757 (La. Ct. App. 5th Cir. 1994) (court properly allowed victim in second-degree battery prosecution to be cross-examined about retaining attorney in civil suit to show possible bias); *State v. Jefferson*, 922 So. 2d 577 (La. Ct. App. 4th Cir. 2005) (finding no error in the trial court's decision to exclude references made to the witness's misdemeanor charge because it does not show the witness bias or interest that may arise from arrests, or pending criminal charge, or the prospect of prosecution).
6. **Prior inconsistent statement**: *State v. Givens*, 41 So. 3d 589 (La. Ct. App. 2d Cir. 2010) (court properly allowed defendant's girlfriend to be cross-examined on prior inconsistent statement of domestic battery complaints in defendant' trial for second-degree murder, after she testified that defendant provided a nonviolent home for his family).
7. **Specific instances permitted to show interest**: *State v. Quinn*, 123 So. 3d 320 (La. App. 4th Cir. 2013) (holding that the trial court's decision to limit the cross-exami-

nation of the witness's other prior felony convictions was harmless error because the opponent was able to cross-examine the witness on his numerous convictions to show bias or interest); *State v Bowie*, 813 So. 2d 377 (La. 4/3/02) (holding that plea bargains or other inducement permissible to show interests).

8. **Question on capacity of witness**: *State v. Robinson*, 817 So. 2d 1131 (La. 5/17/02) (finding reversible error for court to refuse to allow defendant to cross-examine State's key witness on history of mental problems on issue of capacity as a violation of his Sixth Amendment confrontation rights).
9. **Extrinsic evidence used for impeachment**: *State v. Burbank*, 872 So. 2d 1049 (La. 4/23/04) (trial court erred in refusing to allow extrinsic evidence of witness's prior inconsistent statement); *Kampen v. Conway Southwest Exp.*, 655 So. 2d 380 (La. Ct. App. 5th Cir. 1995) (finding that extrinsic evidence was allowed after witness denied ever having epilepsy, having seizures, or having received psychiatric treatment prior to accident).
10. **Improper foundation for extrinsic evidence:** *State v. Robledo v. Orr Motors of Louisiana, Inc.*, 582 So. 2d 892 (La. Ct. App. 2d Cir. 1991) (holding that extrinsic evidence not permissible when witness admits the fact); *State v. Davis*, 818 So. 2d 76 (La. Ct. App. 1st Cir. 2001) (reversing the ruling of the trial court because the trial court prevented the defendant from offering extrinsic evidence with respect to the interest or corruption of the witness by refusing to allow him to lay the foundation for cross-examination); *Thongsavanh v. Schexnayder*, 40 So. 3d 989 (La. Ct. App. 1st Cir. 2010) (holding that foundation for introduction of prior written statement was improper when counsel failed to allow witness opportunity to admit or deny the statement and testimony was not inconsistent with prior written statement); *State v. Johnson*, 595 So. 2d 789 (La. Ct. App. 2d Cir. 1992) (citing *State v. Taylor*, 593 So. 2d 431 (La. Ct. App. 2d Cir.) (holding that evidence of prior statement inadmissible when witness admits to making the prior statement)).

§ 6.12 Chapter Overview — How the Concepts Relate to Each Other

Now that you have studied the admissibility of character and other crimes evidence, it is important that you consider these concepts in terms of how they relate to one another. When you think of other crimes, wrongs, bad acts, convictions, and character, in many instances the conduct might all look the same. A conviction for armed robbery is a crime, it's a bad act, it's a conviction, and it has bearing on a person's character and credibility under the law. However, as we've just studied, the rules are strict regarding the circumstances in which such evidence may be offered, whether by the prosecution or only by the defense, in the case-in-chief, on rebuttal, or only during cross-examination. Further, there are limitations on the purpose for which the evidence may be offered — whether only toward the credibility of a witness, to attack the credibility of a character witness, to prove some relevant issue in the case such as motive or opportunity to commit a crime, or offered to prove a person's character when his character is at issue.

From the **prosecution's perspective**, upon receiving a file it will likely contain a rap sheet that lists various arrests — some will have resulted in convictions, some might have been dismissed, some might be juvenile convictions and others might still be pending. Additionally, he might become aware of other bad acts through witness statements and the police officer reports that could reveal what might be integral part evidence. Looking at all of this, he must decide how this evidence might be used, what is relevant and what is not, and what procedural steps must be taken to ensure that he can properly advance his case without unfairly prejudicing the defendant.

From the **defense's perspective**, he will also be aware of similar information regarding his client. He should understand the limits for which it may be offered, what may be offered in the prosecution's case-in-chief, or what may only be offered if the defendant opens the door to it. Additionally, it will be his job to ensure that the prosecution complies with all procedural requirements, and to ensure that evidence is only used, i.e., argued to the jury, for the purpose for which it was admitted.

This section is designed to assist you in thinking about and learning these concepts together and from a practical perspective.

Overview of Character, Other Crimes, Bad Acts, Credibility

First let's review the types of evidence that we've studied in this chapter. All of the evidence in this chapter can be broken down into two main categories:

1. evidence in the form of general reputation in the community; and
2. evidence in the form of specific instances of conduct.

You have learned that in all situations in which character evidence is admissible, it must be in the form of "general reputation in the community." Although there are a few exceptions, you should follow this general rule, and when offering evidence of a person's character in the situations authorized by law, present it in the form of "general reputation in the community" in accordance with the procedures we covered in § 6.2.

There are also several instances in which evidence of specific instances of conduct are admissible — criminal convictions, arrests, bad acts, etc. In some situations, the law provides that the evidence may be offered in the form of both general reputation in the community as well as by specific instances of conduct, such as character of victims for dangerousness, and when character is an essential element of claim, charge, or defense.

In order to help you remember the situations in which character is admissible in the form of general reputation, and those in which evidence of specific instances is admissible, the charts below describe the provision, the purpose for which it may be offered, how its proven, and whether extrinsic evidence may be offered.

Evidence of General Reputation in the Community

Table 6.12.1 below lists nine different scenarios in which evidence of character may be offered in a trial in the form of **general reputation only**. Article 404(A) specifically lists 3 scenarios in which evidence of character may be offered: 1) character of the defendant; 2) character of the victim; and 3) character of a witness. This chart also breaks down the admissibility of character that may be offered to rebut character that may be offered. This is listed separately because it will be a different party who can offer the character evidence in rebuttal, so the provision creates a wholly separate opportunity for a different party to present character through a different character witness. The situations in which character is permissible in rebuttal are in bold italics as a reminder that it is only offered in response to other character evidence offered.

For example, in 404(A)(1), the defendant may offer evidence of his character for a pertinent character trait, in the form of general reputation in the community. If he does this, the prosecution may offer character evidence of the defendant in rebuttal to rebut

Table 6.12.1 Admissibility of Character Evidence — General Reputation

Article	Admissible Character Evidence	Who May Offer	Proven by	May Be Offered to Prove	Extrinsic Evidence
404(A)(1)	Defendant puts his own character at issue	Defendant	General reputation in community	Any pertinent character trait	Yes
	Character evidence of defendant offered to ***rebut*** character offered by defendant	Prosecution	General reputation in community	Character trait that rebuts character offered by defendant	Yes
404(A)(2)	Character of the victim offered by defendant (other than dangerousness)	Defendant	General reputation in community	Pertinent character trait other than dangerousness	Yes
	Character of victim (other than dangerousness) offered to ***rebut*** character offered by defendant	Prosecution	General reputation in community	Character trait that rebuts character offered by defendant	Yes
	Character of victim for dangerousness (overt act/hostile demonstration)*	Defendant	General reputation in community	Character for dangerousness	Yes
	Character of victim (domestic violence exception)*	Defendant	General reputation in community	Character for dangerousness	Yes
	Character of victim for peacefulness (homicide case, to ***rebut*** evidence that victim was first aggressor)	Prosecution	General reputation in community	Character for peacefulness	Yes
404(A)(3)	Character of a witness	Either party	General reputation in community	Character for truthfulness	Yes
405(B)	Character is an essential element of a crime*	Either party	General reputation in community	Pertinent character trait	Yes

* May also offer evidence of specific instances of conduct as discussed below.

the character evidence offered by the defendant. Thus, in a forgery trial, if the defendant offers evidence of his character for having a general reputation in the community for honesty, the prosecution may offer a character witness in rebuttal that the defendant is not an honest, trustworthy person. In both situations the evidence is being offered by extrinsic evidence because it is evidence about the defendant being proven by evidence outside of the defendant himself—through a character witness.

Note also that asterisks are placed next to situations in which character may also be proven by specific instances of conduct, which are outlined in Table 6.12.2 below.

Specific Instances of Conduct

Table 6.12.2 illustrates situations/evidentiary provisions in which evidence of ***specific instances of conduct*** (specific crimes, wrongs, or acts) may be offered in a trial by a party. The conduct listed ranges from criminal convictions to conduct that is not convictions, and in some articles require specific types of prior conduct, such as past sexual conduct showing lustful disposition toward victims.

Table 6.12.2 Admissibility of Specific Instances of Conduct

Article	Admissible Types of Specific Acts Evidence	Who May Offer	Proven by	For What Purpose Admissible	Extrinsic Evidence
404(B)	Other crimes, wrongs, or acts	Prosecution	Evidence of other crimes, wrongs, or acts	Motive, opportunity, plan, preparation, knowledge, etc.	Yes
	Integral part evidence ("res gestae")	Prosecution	Specific acts forming Res gestae	Forms an integral part of the crime charged	Yes
404(A)(1)	Cross-examination of character witness with specific acts	Opponent of party calling W	"Have you heard" about specific acts pertinent trait of character that contradicts character witness's testimony	To attack credibility and competency of character witness	No
404(A)(2)/ 404(B)(2)	Character of victim (overt act/hostile demonstration)*	Defendant	Threats, specific instance of conduct that go to State of mind	Dangerous character of victim/who was 1st aggressor and state of mind of accused	Yes
	Character of victim (domestic violence exception)*	Defendant	Threats, domestic violence, specific instances of conduct that go to state of mind	Dangerous character of victim, who was first aggressor, and state of mind of accused	Yes
405(B)	Character essential element of crime, charge or defense*	Party with burden of proof	Specific instances of conduct	To prove essential element of crime, charge or defense	Yes
609 & 609.1	Criminal convictions on issue of credibility/civil cases	Party calling witness or opponent	Felony convictions and crimes involving dishonesty/ false statement (10 yrs)	Credibility of witness	Yes
	Criminal convictions on issue of credibility/ criminal cases	Party calling witness or opponent	Any conviction	Credibility of witness	Yes
412	Victim past conduct with D to show consent	Defendant	Past sexual conduct of victim	Victim consent in sexual assault case	Yes
	Victim past sexual conduct within 72 hrs to show source of semen/ injury	Defendant	Past sexual conduct of V within 72 hrs of offense	To show source of semen/injury in sexual assault case	Yes
	Past sexual trafficking of sex trafficking V to prove pattern of trafficking by defendant	Prosecution	Specific instance of past sexual trafficking	To prove pattern of sexual trafficking in sex trafficking case	Yes
412.2	Other crimes of sexually assaultive behavior in sex assault case	Prosecution	Specific instances of sexually assaultive behavior	Any relevant purpose	Yes
	Crimes showing lustful disposition towards children in sex assault case involving victim under 17	Prosecution	Specific instances of sexually assaultive behavior	To show lustful disposition toward children	Yes
608	Specific acts that show bias, interest, to attack credibility	Party calling W or opponent	Specific acts showing bias, interest, motive, etc.	For its bearing on credibility	No

* May also offer evidence of specific instances of conduct as discussed below.

The chart is a basic overview of all of the provisions covered in Chapter 6 with the exception of evidence of habit/routine practice covered in § 6.5, addressed below. As we studied earlier in the chapter, habit is distinctly different from character in that habit is the way a person invariably responds when he is confronted with a given situation (i.e., he always puts on seatbelt), whereas character is a generalized description of a person's disposition (safe driver). Habit is also not a specific instance of conduct, but instead, conduct *always* exercised by a person when he is confronted with a specific situation offered to prove that he likely acted in conformity with the habit or routine practice on an occasion in question.

Table 6.12.3 Evidence of Habit/Routine Practice

Article	Admissible Types of Evidence	Who May Offer	Proven by	For What Purpose Admissible	Extrinsic Evidence
406	Habit or routine practice	Either party	Opinion or Specific instances that are sufficient in number to prove the habit or routine practice	Action in conformity with habit or routine practice on particular occasion	Yes

Order of Trial

Now that we have briefly reviewed the different types of and purposes for which character and evidence of specific instances of conduct may be offered in a trial that we covered in Chapter 6, let's talk about how to effectively use this evidence at trial. But first, we also need to briefly review the order of trial.

As you may recall from Chapter 1, the prosecution in a criminal trial (plaintiff in civil trial) has the burden of proving each and every element of the crime charged (cause of action in civil case). The prosecution's case-in-chief is the time in which the prosecution presents its case to prove the elements of the crime. To do this, the prosecution calls witnesses and presents physical evidence, documents, photographs, or whatever other evidence they have to prove its case.

During the prosecution's case-in-chief, the defense cross-examines the prosecution's witnesses, but does not call witnesses of its own. When the prosecution has called all of the witnesses that they have and have presented all of the evidence, they will "rest" their case. When the prosecution rests, they must have presented sufficient evidence to support a jury finding in their favor for every proposition for which they bear the burden of proving—this is referred to as a "prima facie" case. This basically means that the plaintiff has offered enough evidence in its case-in-chief to prove each and every element of the crime or cause of action brought, and if uncontroverted and uncontradicted, the jury could find in his favor.

After the prosecution rests, the defense will have an opportunity to present its case-in-chief. At that time, the defense may call witnesses and present evidence that contradicts what the State has offered and to prove any affirmative defenses they may raise.

It is important to have this frame of reference in mind, because as you have learned throughout this chapter and reviewed above, there is certain evidence that may be introduced in the prosecution's case-in-chief, while other evidence may only be brought out after the defendant has raised the issue or on rebuttal. For example, in § 6.3 you learned that only a defendant may put his character at issue. Thus, this is something that will usually occur in the defendant's case-in-chief. The prosecution does not call witnesses to testify to the defendant's character in its case-in-chief because they must wait until the defendant presents his case and puts his character at issue before they may offer character witnesses to rebut the evidence introduced by the defendant. As a result, any character witnesses the prosecution would call would have to occur in rebuttal, after the defendant has rested its case.

As a brief side note here, it is possible for the defendant to put his character at issue during the prosecution's case-in-chief. For example, say the defendant is on trial for murdering his wife to obtain insurance proceeds, and the prosecution calls as a witness, the victim's sister to testify about how the husband constantly insisted that his wife (victim) take out a large insurance policy. If on cross-examination of the witness, the defense asks her questions such as, *"Have you ever known defendant to be anything other than a loving, caring husband to your sister?" "Did your sister ever once mention that he was anything other than a loyal, faithful husband?"* or *"He has never been violent with your sister has he?"* Such questions would certainly open up the door to the defendant's character in the prosecution's case-in-chief, and the witness would certainly be able to respond that she knows of husband's conduct that is not wonderful, loving, or loyal, such as if her sister (victim) had found out he was having an affair with his secretary the previous year.

While this is not the common scenario, since defense attorneys are usually careful about asking such questions, it is *possible* that the defendant may sometimes open up the door to his character during the prosecution's case-in-chief. But either way, it must be the defendant, and not the prosecution who puts the defendant's character at issue, and it is usually (and properly) done by the defendant calling a character witness in his case-in-chief to testify to his general reputation in the community to a pertinent character trait in the trial.

Prosecution's Case-In-Chief

Now that we've reviewed the types of evidence at issue here and how the trial works, let's examine how to use this evidence at trial. We'll first take a look at it from the perspective of the prosecution's case-in-chief and will address the defense's case-in-chief below.

General reputation in the community. Based on what we've studied about character evidence generally, the prosecution is most often limited to offering character evidence in *rebuttal* or in response to character evidence offered by the defendant. In this chapter, and as outlined in the chart below, there are four basic types of evidence that may be offered in the form of general reputation in the community that we're looking at:

1. character of the accused
2. character of the victim
3. character of witness (truthfulness/untruthfulness)
4. character as an essential element (that may also include specific instances)

Clearly, we know that the prosecution cannot offer evidence of the defendant's character in its case-in-chief, nor can the prosecution first offer character evidence of the victim of a crime. The prosecution may only offer evidence to *rebut* character evidence of the victim after presented from the defense; thus, such evidence will not be offered in the prosecution's case-in-chief either.

As it pertains to character evidence of a witness, you should recall form § 6.11 that while a party calling a witness may attack his own witness's credibility, he cannot support the credibility until after the credibility has been attacked. Thus, in the prosecution's case-in-chief, they can attack their own witness's credibility, but they cannot support it until after it has been attacked by the defense. Since the defense would not be able to call a witness to testify to the character of the prosecution's witness for untruthfulness until their case-in-chief (Article 608), the prosecution will not be able to call a witness to rebut such evidence until after the defense witness is called, which would have to occur in their rebuttal.

Let's take an example: In the defendant's trial for simple rape, the prosecution calls three witnesses as noted in the diagram below—Ann (victim), Bob, and Ced. After the prosecution rests, in the defense's case-in-chief they call two witnesses, Abe and Bill. Abe is a fact witness, who testifies to the events he observed at the scene. Bill is a character witness. He will testify as to Ann's character (that she is untruthful) pursuant to Article 608. After the appropriate foundation is laid, Bill testifies that Ann's general reputation in the community is for being a very dishonest, untruthful person. The prosecution is allowed to cross-examine the character witness (Bill) about specific instances of Ann's conduct that contradict the character evidence he gave about Ann.

After the defense rests, the prosecution may reopen its case in rebuttal. To rebut the defense's character witness, the prosecution may now call a character witness to rehabilitate Ann's character for truthfulness. The prosecution calls Dell to testify in rebuttal that Ann actually has a reputation in the community for being a very truthful and honest person. The defense can cross-examine Dell about specific instances of conduct in the form of "have you heards," just as the prosecution cross-examined Bill about specific instances of Ann's conduct.

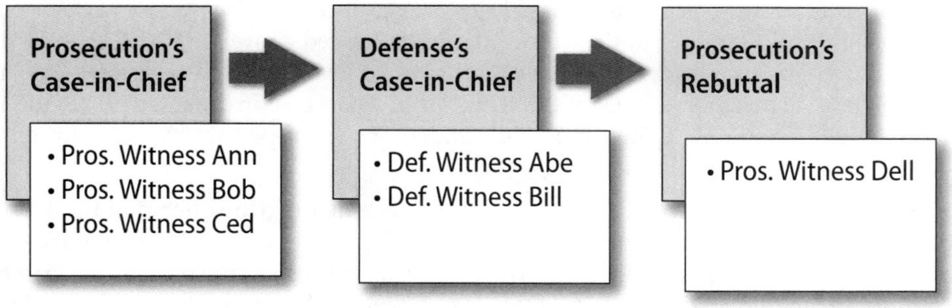

Thus, as you can see, the prosecution will not usually present character evidence in its case-in-chief for two reasons. **First**, a party cannot support a witness's character until after it has been attacked. Thus, the prosecution had to wait until Ann's character was attacked in the defense's case-in-chief by Bill before they could offer evidence of her truthful character in rebuttal by Dell. They could not call Dell in their case-in-chief because Ann's credibility had not been attacked yet. **Second**, when a party calls a character witness, the other party may call a witness to rebut the character evidence presented by the witness. Since the defense cannot call a witness until their case-in-chief, the prosecution could not rebut it until they reopened its case in rebuttal. It could not have been done in its case-in-chief.

The same would be true if the defendant calls a character witness to testify to his good character or calls a character witness to testify to a character trait of the victim. In either case, the prosecution could cross-examine the witness on specific instances of conduct that pertain to (and contradict) the character trait to which the witness has testified, but the prosecution would have to wait until its rebuttal to call a character witness to rebut the character evidence offered by the defense.

Therefore, as far as character in the form of general reputation is concerned, the prosecution will generally only be able to present one type in its case-in-chief without waiting for any prerequisite conduct from the defense, and that is in situations in which ***character is an essential element of the crime, charge, or defense.*** When character is an essential element, it may be proven by character in general reputation as well as specific instances of conduct. One example is a felon in possession of a firearm. In such a case, since a specific instance of conduct is an element of the crime (the underlying felony), the prosecution must present the evidence in its case-in-chief, along with all of the other elements of the crime. With respect to the other types of general character, the prosecution must wait to rebut evidence offered by the defense.

Specific instances of conduct. With respect to specific instances of conduct the prosecution has much more leeway. Let's talk about these seven types of evidence:

1. Nonconformity evidence
2. Character essential element
3. Integral part evidence
4. Past sexual trafficking of V to prove pattern of trafficking of D
5. Other crimes of sexually assaultive behavior in sex assault case
6. Crimes showing lustful disposition towards children in cases with victim under 17
7. Credibility (609.1 and 608)

Character essential element. As you know, the prosecution must prove all elements of a crime in its case-in-chief. Thus, if a specific instance of conduct is an essential element, the prosecution *must* offer it in their case-in-chief. As stated above, one such crime is a felon in possession of a firearm. The prosecution must prove that the defendant was in fact a convicted felon as an element of the crime. Thus, in its case-in-chief the prosecution may offer evidence to prove the defendant's underlying felony without waiting for any action on the part of the defense first.

Non-conformity evidence. Another type of evidence that may be offered in the prosecution's case-in-chief is non-conformity evidence. If you recall from § 6.6, the prosecution may offer evidence of specific instances of conduct for a relevant purpose in the crime such as to prove motive, opportunity, plan, intent, knowledge, and absence of mistake. For example, the prosecution may offer evidence that the defendant stole a truck a month before the bank robbery in preparation for the robbery to acquire the getaway car that he used in the robbery. The prior bad act is not being offered to prove that he is a bad person, but only to show that he prepared for and planned the crime, and it also connects him to the crime by showing how he came into possession of the getaway car.

Article 404(B) contains an illustrative list of relevant purposes for which evidence of other crimes may be offered. However, due to the potential prejudice of such evidence, keep in mind the strict guidelines that must be followed to admit such as evidence as we studied in § 6.6: 1) the notice of intent to use the evidence stating the evidence to be offered and the purpose for which it will be offered; 2) the *Prieur* hearing, where it is shown that the evidence will actually further the stated purpose and the bad act is proven by clear and convincing evidence; and 3) the limiting instructions to the jury as to the purpose for which the evidence may be considered.

Integral part evidence. Under Article 404(B), the prosecution may offer evidence of another crime that forms an integral part of the offense for which the defendant is on trial. This is evidence so related to the charged offense that the State could not present its case without reference to it. If evidence is an integral part of the charged offense, the prosecution may offer such evidence without any notice requirement as provided for offering non-conformity evidence.

Past sexual trafficking of victim to prove pattern of trafficking of defendant. Article 412 allows the prosecution in a sexual or human trafficking case to offer evidence in its case-in-chief of past sexual behavior of the victim of sexual trafficking to prove a pattern of trafficking of the defendant as discussed in § 6.9.

Other crimes of sexually assaultive behavior in sex assault case. Further, under Article 412.2 the prosecution may offer evidence of prior sexual offenses in cases where the accused is charged with a sexual assault offense. This provision also allows the prosecution to offer evidence of prior crimes showing lustful disposition towards children in a sexual assault case with a victim under the age of 17. Such evidence is admissible if the probative value outweighs the prejudicial effect. The prosecution must give notice of intent to use such evidence, but no *Prieur* hearing is required.

Credibility (Article 609.1). Additionally, if the prosecution calls a witness to testify who has been convicted of a crime, they may question their own witness about the fact that the witness has a criminal conviction as a preemptive move. Keep in mind that when a witness takes the stand his credibility is always at issue. Evidence that goes to his credibility may be offered. Under Article 609.1 evidence that a witness has been convicted of a crime may be offered on the issue of his credibility. Since the person who calls a witness may attack the credibility of his own witness, the prosecution can ask the witness whether he has been convicted of a crime to take the wind out of the issue that it would have had if brought out on cross-examination for the first time. The witness may be asked the question again on cross-examination, but provided the witness admits the prior conviction, there will be no additional action that may be taken by the defense on the issue.

Credibility (Article 608). Finally, the prosecution may offer evidence of specific instances of conduct that may show bias, interest, or motive on the issue of their witness's credibility. Keep in mind here that since the prosecution does not necessarily know which witnesses may be called by the defense, they would be limited to introducing such evidence as it relates to their own witness. The prosecution may do this, as we stated, because a party may attack the credibility of their own witness. Of course the only benefit the prosecution would truly seek to gain in attacking the credibility of their own witness would be to avoid the evidence coming out from the defense for the first time. Thus, the prosecution might ask their own key witness, "You also have a criminal case pending with the District Attorney's Office don't you?" (Yes). "Are you testifying here today to curry favor for the disposition of your case?" (No, I'm not.) "Have you been promised anything in exchange for your testimony today?" (No.).

Also keep in mind here, that as you know, a party cannot support or bolster a witness's credibility before it has been attacked. So you may get that objection for such a line of questioning. But even without a witness's credibility being attacked a party may ask basic questions regarding whether a witness has been offered anything in exchange for their testimony, has a relationship to the parties, etc. This is general information that may be asked upon calling any witness, so the above questioning should be allowed on such grounds.

Defendant's Case-In-Chief

As outlined above, the defense need not prove elements of the crime, but may offer evidence to refute such evidence offered by the prosecution in its case-in-chief. To do so, the defense also calls witnesses on his behalf and presents evidence. As it pertains to general reputation in the community, as we discussed above, in the defendant's case-in-chief they may offer evidence of:

1. the character of accused;
2. character of the victim; or
3. character of a witness.

The defense can offer evidence of his good character that is inconsistent with the crime charged. He does it pursuant to the procedures we covered in § 6.2, which includes opening himself up to character witnesses being offered in rebuttal by the prosecution. Additionally, the defense can offer character evidence of the victim as we discussed at length in § 6.8. He may offer any pertinent character trait of the victim, except character for dangerousness, with no prerequisite showing. To offer evidence for dangerous character the accused must either show a hostile demonstration or overt act, or in the alternative, the evidence may be admissible under the domestic violence exception if the requirements are met—familial relationship, history of assaultive behavior, and claim of self-defense. Additionally, the defense may offer evidence of the character of any of the prosecution's witnesses for untruthfulness in their case-in-chief. All of these measures assist the defendant in presenting a defense by refuting the evidence offered by the prosecution.

Specific instances of conduct. There are also limited situations in which the defense may offer evidence of specific instances of conduct in his case-in-chief.

Character of the victim. Under 404(A)(1) and (2), if the defendant is able to show an overt act or hostile demonstration at the time of the offense charged or under the domestic violence exception, the defendant may be able to offer specific instances of conduct of the victim in addition to character for dangerousness as we covered in § 6.8. If he establishes the preliminary requirements for admissibility he may offer evidence of threats against him and specific instances of conduct to prove that the victim was the first aggressor and his state of mind, i.e., whether he acted reasonably. In a domestic violence case, he may also offer evidence of the prior domestic violence for the same reasons.

While the defense may offer such evidence in its case-in-chief without any prior conduct from the prosecution, offering such evidence opens the door to the prosecution offering evidence of the victim's character for peacefulness in rebuttal.

Victim's past sexual conduct. As we discussed in § 6.9.1, under the Rape Shield Statute (Article 412) a defendant may offer evidence of a victim's past sexual conduct in only two situations: 1) if with the accused on the issue of consent; or 2) if with a third party to explain the source of semen or injury. Keep in mind the specific procedural requirements with which the defendant must comply to offer such evidence as outlined in the statute.

Criminal convictions for credibility. Like the prosecution, the defense may also question their witness, including the defendant himself if he takes the stand, about prior convictions. If the defendant takes the stand, of course, he does not generally put his character at issue, only his credibility, so specific acts for which he was not convicted cannot be inquired into.

Specific acts that show bias, interest, motive. The defense may also question its own witness on direct examination regarding specific instances of conduct that may go to the witness's credibility before he is cross-examined on the issue by the prosecution. For example, if the witness was also arrested for the same charge, has already pled guilty, and is now taking the stand to accept all of the blame for the crime, the defense might question him about this fact so that the witness will have an opportunity to explain that the perceived interest, bias, or motive has no bearing on the substance of his testimony.

Rebuttal by Prosecution

As we stated above, depending on what is offered in the defense's case, the prosecution may be allowed to reopen its case to rebut evidence offered by the defense. The prosecution may call character witnesses to rebut character witnesses offered by the defense that testified to the character of the defendant, a witness, or the victim of the crime. Any character witnesses called will be subject to cross-examination by the defense.

Cross-Examination

Also keep in mind, that during cross-examination (whether the defense cross-examining the prosecution's witnesses or the prosecution cross-examining the defendant's witness), the credibility of all witnesses is at issue. So the witness will be subject to cross-examination regarding prior convictions under 609.1 (criminal trials), and regarding any specific instances of conduct that would have bearing on his credibility, such as evidence that would show bias, interest, or motive. As in the example above, the witness could be questioned regarding any pending charges with the DA's office that might affect whether he has a motive to curry favor with the DA's office to get a better deal in his case.

Additionally, character witnesses are always subject to cross-examination regarding specific instances of conduct that could contradict the character evidence to which they have testified.

Argue Stated Purpose Only

One final point here to always keep in mind is that evidence should only ever be argued for the purpose for which it is admissible. For instance, if criminal convictions of a witness were introduced into evidence under Article 609/609.1 (including those of the defendant if he testifies), it should only be argued to the jury for that purpose—for its bearing on the witness's credibility. It would be entirely impermissible and inappropriate to argue the evidence to the jury for any other reason, such as by stating that he's got the other conviction so he likely did this as well. If a defendant's other crime has been offered into evidence to prove his motive, it should only be argued to the jury for that purpose. Counsel should never use one provision as a ruse to introduce evidence into the record to inappropriately use for another impermissible purpose.

Example and Application

PROBLEM 6-99. Kent is arrested for armed robbery of a small convenience store. The prosecution learns the information listed below about Kent. Which, if any, of the following would be admissible? Please explain upon what basis and under what circumstances the evidence would be admissible against Kent by the prosecution. Also explain for what purposes the evidence may be offered against Kent. What procedural requirements would have to be met?

1. Kent is addicted to cocaine and has stolen goods in the past to obtain money to purchase cocaine.
2. Kent has a prior conviction for armed robbery of a small convenience store that occurred five years ago.
3. Kent has been arrested six times within the last ten years for various grades of theft, but no convictions.
4. When Kent was arrested for the instant offense, he had a small amount of crack cocaine in his possession, for which he was not charged.

5. Kent has two convictions for simple battery (misdemeanors), which occurred five and seven years ago.
6. Police suspected Kent of being involved in burglarizing a house in his neighborhood and burning it down to cover it up, but have no evidence.
7. A lady says that Kent tried to snatch her purse one afternoon, but she beat him with it until he went away.

Discussion of #1 above.

1. The prosecution will likely be able to offer evidence of Kent's cocaine addiction in its case-in-chief to show his motive for the armed robbery, particularly in light of the fact that he has been shown to have stolen to further his addiction in the past. While evidence of other crimes, wrongs, or acts is generally inadmissible to prove the character of a person in order to show that the person acted in conformity with the particular character trait on a particular occasion, Article 404(B) provides that such evidence may be offered for other purposes such as to prove motive, opportunity, plan, or for other relevant purposes. In this case, evidence of Kent's addiction to cocaine may be relevant to show his *motive* to commit the robbery. It is likely he committed the robbery to obtain money to use to buy drugs.

   To offer evidence under this provision the prosecution must provide notice to Kent of its intent to offer evidence of his addiction to prove his motive for committing the crime. Then the parties should set a *Prieur* hearing in which the prosecution will have to establish by "clear and convincing" evidence that the bad act (Kent's addiction) actually exists. The prosecution will also have to show that the addiction actually will help to prove his motive for committing the crime and is not a subterfuge for portraying Kent as a bad person. If admitted, upon request, Kent would also be entitled to a preliminary instruction and also a final instruction to the jury on the limited purpose for which it may be used whether he requests it or not. The court will also apply an Article 403 balancing to ensure the evidence is not unfairly prejudicial.

   In this case, provided the prosecution can actually prove that Kent has the cocaine addiction, it will likely be admitted since it could show what might have *compelled* Kent to commit the crime. The court is likely familiar with the strength of the addiction compelling a person to want to acquire the drugs and resorting to conduct such as robbery to obtain them. Thus, the evidence would be highly probative of the purpose for which it is offered. It will not likely be unfairly prejudicial, because although it is a bad act the evidence is not so compelling or deviant that it might compel the jury to want to convict Kent based solely on their belief that he is a bad person.

   Thus, following a *Prieur* hearing, and an Article 403 balancing test, the evidence of Kent's addiction will likely be admissible in the prosecution's case-in-chief to prove Kent's motive for committing the armed robbery.

Practical Application Exercise

PAE-1. Please use the fact pattern and the rap sheet below to complete the exercise.

Jeremy P.J. Templeton was arrested on November 29, 2014 on the charges listed below after police suspected he was driving while intoxicated. Realizing there was a warrant out for his arrest, Jeremy tried to evade capture and accelerated, ran red lights and barely escaped hitting a pedestrian before stopping. After Jeremy failed the field sobriety tests, Jeremy was arrested and searched. The search yielded cocaine in Jeremy's pocket and officers found a gun in the console of the vehicle which is registered to Jeremy. Jeremy emphatically denies ownership of the gun. You are the prosecutor and you have just received the file which includes the rap sheet below. You are prosecuting him on the Aggravated Escape and Felon in Possession of Firearm only. Jeremy emphatically objects to any other character or bad acts evidence being admitted against him at trial. As you prepare your case, what if any of the bad acts listed on Jeremy's rap sheet (prior or current arrests, convictions, etc.) might be able to come into evidence against Jeremy, by whom, and for what purpose(s) (*i.e., by prosecution in case-in-chief to prove ... ; only on cross-examination, etc.*)? What procedures, if any, must be followed?

★ CITY POLICE DEPARTMENT ★

UNIFORM ARREST AND DISPOSITION RECORD

Name: Jeremy P.J. Templeton
Known Alias: "Temp"
Date of Birth: 06/19/1985
Place of Birth: Franklinville, La.
SSN: 441-22-0000

ARREST CHARGES: Possession of firearm by convicted felon, aggravated escape, Driving While Intoxicated, Possession of Schedule II CDS (Cocaine)

SUMMARY OF ARREST: On 11/29/2014 suspect was weaving across dividing line on Hwy. 195. I got behind subject. He accelerated to high rate of speed and drove through two red lights. Narrowly avoided hitting pedestrian. Suspect apprehended after short chase. Failed SFST's. Arrested for DWI, etc. (as listed). Search revealed cocaine, weapon (suspect not to possess weapons due to felon status). Found active warrant from 10.10.2014 for Armed Robbery.

ARREST DATE	OFFENSE	DISPOSITION
1. 02/24/2000	Joyriding	Adjudicated delinquent - Probation 2 years
2. 05/28/2004	Open container	PG - 30 days PJ
3. 09/22/2005	Carrying a concealed weapon	PG - Probation 1 year
4. 11/14/2008	Simple Burglary	FG - 2 years HL. State Penitentiary
5. 04/17/2010	Aggravated Burglary (with dangerous weapon)	PG - 2 yrs. State Penitentiary Paroled 5/16/09
6. 05/09/2013	Armed Robbery	PG - simple robbery, 1 yr. HL
7. 09/07/2014	Illegal Discharge of Weapon	Dismissed
8. 10/10/2014	Armed Robbery	BW - Failure to appear (charges pending)

Chapter 7

Expert Witnesses and Scientific Evidence

§ 7.1 Expert Witnesses Generally [Arts. 702–705]

Applicable Code Articles

Art. 702. Testimony by experts

A witness who is qualified as an expert by knowledge, skill, experience, training, or education may testify in the form of an opinion or otherwise if:

(1) The expert's scientific, technical, or other specialized knowledge will help the trier of fact to understand the evidence or to determine a fact in issue;

(2) The testimony is based on sufficient facts or data;

(3) The testimony is the product of reliable principles and methods; and

(4) The expert has reliably applied the principles and methods to the facts of the case.

As noted in Chapter 4 relative to our discussion of lay witness opinions, all witnesses testify as either an expert witness or a lay witness. If a witness is not qualified as an expert to testify in a particular field, he is testifying as a lay witness, even if he could have been qualified as an expert in a particular field.[1] While a lay witness may only testify to opinions or inferences that are rationally based on his personal perceptions, a person qualified as an expert witness in a particular field may be allowed to express more in-depth opinions and provide other information that can help the jury understand and resolve complex issues that require scientific, technical, or other specialized knowledge.

Expert witnesses are given wide latitude when testifying. In addition to expressing opinions in his area of expertise and giving other helpful background information on the subject matter, an expert witness may also answer hypothetical questions posed to him by either counsel.[2] Additionally, an expert may be asked leading questions on direct examination,[3] and oftentimes, may be exempt from the rule of sequestration pursuant to Article 615 if his presence is needed in the courtroom to assist counsel in the presentation of his case.

1. These individuals are commonly referred to as "quasi-experts," and although they might easily be qualified as an expert in the field, the witness has not been so qualified. Courts are reluctant to accept such testimony. This issue is more thoroughly addressed in Chapter 4 § 4.4 relative to lay witness opinions.

2. La. Code Evid. art. 703 Official Comment (d).

3. La. Code Evid. art. 611(C); *See also* La. Code Evid. art. 702 Official Comment (2); The Federal Rules of Evidence do not specifically authorize this.

Further, an expert's opinion testimony need not be based on first-hand knowledge of the underlying facts, as is the case for lay witnesses. In addition to basing his opinions on facts or data personally perceived by him, an expert witness may also base his opinions or inferences on facts or data made known to him at or before the hearing, and in some instances, may even base his opinions on inadmissible facts and data. Thus, expert witnesses can be an invaluable asset to a party's case in helping the jury understand complex issues that are beyond the realm of common knowledge.

Since expert testimony has the potential to weigh heavily with the jury, there are several rules as well as important caselaw that govern its admissibility that are discussed in this chapter. The rules governing the admissibility of expert witness testimony are contained in Articles 702–706.

Requirements for expressing expert opinions. The general rule governing the admissibility of expert testimony is contained in Article 702. Under the article, a witness who is qualified as an expert may express opinions and other information in areas of scientific, technical, or other specialized knowledge, if the following five requirements are met:

1. the witness is qualified by knowledge, skill, experience, training, or education, or any combination thereof;
2. the expert's scientific, technical, or other specialized knowledge will help the trier of fact to understand the evidence or to determine a fact in issue;
3. the expert's testimony is based on sufficient facts or data;
4. the testimony is the product of reliable principles and methods; and
5. the expert has reliably applied the principles and methods to the facts of the case.

Based on these requirements, this chapter will examine four primary issues related to expert witnesses: 1) qualifications (§ 7.2); 2) scope of opinion (including opinions on ultimate issue and helpfulness) (§ 7.3); 3) basis of opinion (§ 7.4); and 4) reliable methodology (§ 7.5).

§ 7.2 Qualifications of Experts [Art. 702]

Witness qualifications/Basis of expertise. A witness may be qualified as an expert in a particular field based on education, training, practical application, experience, or any combination thereof, that forms the basis of his expertise. Formal education or a college degree is not necessary, provided the witness has sufficient experience in the field. For example, a person who has worked his entire life changing tires would have specialized knowledge that would enable him to give opinions in that field. The trial court has broad discretion in determining "who should or should not be permitted to testify as an expert."[4] His findings as to whether a witness should be qualified as an expert will generally not be overturned on appeal absent an abuse of that discretion.

When qualifying a witness as an expert, counsel should question the witness about his education, training, experience, skills, and any other information upon which the witness bases his expertise. Since there are such a vast number of areas in which a person could claim expertise, there will be a broad range of qualifications upon which a person's expertise could be based. A witness will typically be questioned about his educational background,

4. La. Code Evid. art. 702 Official Comment (d).

including any advanced degrees he may have earned, any additional training he may have in the field, as well as any special certifications or specializations he may have.

Additionally, the witness's work experience would be highly relevant along with any opportunities he may have had to apply the information or knowledge. A person may have also acquired additional knowledge through teaching in the area and from conducting research and publishing in the field. The test of the competency of an expert witness is his knowledge of the subject about which he is called upon to express an opinion[5]—however it may have been acquired. All relevant information should be presented to the court to demonstrate this point.

Qualifying a witness as expert/Procedures. Prior to testifying as an expert, the attorney must "qualify" the witness as an expert in the field in which he will express expert opinions. In other words, the witness must be *shown* to possess the necessary qualifications to express expert opinions in that field. While the procedures outlined below are usually used to qualify an expert witness, the law does not specifically require any formal procedure for qualifying an expert witness, nor is there a requirement that a judge formally declare that a witness has been accepted as an expert witness. A witness is implicitly accepted as an expert witness when the judge allows the witness to testify as an expert after the attorney elicits testimony regarding the witness's qualifications. Most often, however, a judge expressly states that a witness has or has not been accepted as an expert in the field in which he has been tendered.

Qualifying a witness usually takes place *during* the trial immediately prior to the witness beginning to testify to the substantive issues in the case. The questioning is also usually done in the presence of the jury. Keep in mind that this procedure is different than a *Daubert*[6] hearing, discussed, *infra*, § 7.4, where the court determines the reliability of the methodology and principles used by the witness in coming to the opinions to which he seeks to testify. A *Daubert* hearing is typically held pre-trial in a separate hearing outside of the presence of a jury. During *this* procedure, qualifying a witness as an expert, the judge is evaluating this particular witness's qualifications to determine whether he is competent to testify as an expert in the field in which he is tendered.

The usual procedures followed when qualifying a witness as an expert are:

1. **Question witness on qualifications**. The proponent of the witness must ask questions concerning the witness's qualifications to testify as an expert, i.e., questions concerning his experience, training, education, certifications, publications, teaching, memberships in professional organizations, ongoing training to stay up-to-date on advancements in his field, and about any other matters upon which the witness bases his expertise. Additionally witnesses are asked if they have ever testified as an expert witness before, the number of times, and in which courts. Note, however, that there are no special or additional requirements that must be met for a witness being qualified as an expert for the first time.[7] Counsel should seek to elicit all relevant information regarding the witness's qualifications as an expert in the field.
2. **Tender witness as expert**. After questioning the witness on his qualifications, the witness is tendered to the court as an expert in a particular area of expertise based

---

5. Harges & Jones, LOUISIANA EVIDENCE, art. 702 Author's Comments.
6. Daubert v. Merrill Dow Pharmaceuticals, Inc., 509 U.S. 579 (U.S. Cal., 1993) (the U.S. Supreme Court established the standard for determining whether the scientific methodology and principles used by an expert witness is reliable).
7. See Force & Rault, HANDBOOK, Art. 702 Author's Comments (5); *See also* State v. Allen, 942 So. 2d 1244 (La. Ct. App. 2d Cir. 2006).

on the qualifications elicited, e.g., as a forensic psychiatrist, a forensic pathologist, an accident reconstructionist, a fingerprint analyst, etc.

3. **Cross-examination on qualifications.** After the witness is tendered as an expert in a particular field, the opposing party is given an opportunity to question the witness about his qualifications. This examination is also known as a "voir dire" of the expert witness. This cross-examination is limited to the witness's qualifications to testify as an expert. The substantive issues in the case at hand are not relevant here. While oftentimes opposing counsel will question the witness about any biases he may possess during the voir dire, i.e., whether he's being paid, or whether he always testifies for a particular side in cases, etc., those are credibility issues that go to the weight to be given to the expert's testimony, and do not go to the issue of whether the witness should be allowed to give expert testimony.
4. **Objection/Argument.** After both parties have questioned the witness on his qualifications to testify as an expert in the field in which he is tendered, the opposing party may or may not object to the witness being accepted as an expert in the field. Both parties would be allowed to make arguments to support their position. In some instances, if there is no dispute as to the witness's qualifications, with which the judge is also familiar, an opponent may offer to stipulate that the witness is an expert in the field in which he is being offered. In such a case, the proponent of the witness may accept the stipulation or reject it. Strategically speaking, a party offering an expert may want to fully lay out his expert's qualifications in the presence of the jury and reject the offer to stipulate.
5. **Judge accepts as expert.** Following any arguments on the witness's qualifications, the judge then determines if the witness is competent to testify as an expert as tendered. The Court usually formally declares that the witness has been accepted as a witness in a particular field, however, there is no requirement in the law that a judge formally accept or declare that a witness is an expert. The judge may implicitly accept the witness as an expert by simply allowing the witness to testify as tendered.

   If the judge does not allow the witness to give expert testimony as tendered, the proponent of the witness should object to the court's ruling and proffer the substance of the proposed expert's testimony to preserve the issue for appeal.

Qualifying an Expert Witness — Sample

- Please state your name and spell it for the record.
- What is your current occupation?
- What exactly is a biomedical engineer?
- Where are you employed?
- How long have you been so employed?
- What do your duties entail?
- What other jobs have you had in this field prior to joining University Hospital?
- Could you tell us the education you received to become a biomedical engineer?
- What other training have you received in this field?
- Have you *published* in the field of biomedical engineering?
  - Could you list your publications in the field?

- Are you a member of any professional *organizations*?
  - Which organizations are they?
- Do you hold any *certifications*?
  - Which certifications do you hold?
- Have you recently attended any *seminars* in the field of biomedical engineering?
  - Could you name them?
- Have you *lectured* in the field of biomedical engineering?
- Do you stay abreast of updates or changes in the field of biomedical engineering?
  - How do you do so? Seminars, research, publications, membership in professional organizations all contribute to staying abreast of the latest advances in biomedical engineering.
- Have you testified as an *expert* in a court proceeding?
- In what fields did you testify as an expert?
- How many times have you qualified and subsequently testified as an expert in the field of biomedical engineering?
- In which courts have you testified as an expert in the field?
- Have there been any occasions when you were not accepted as an expert as tendered?

At this time your honor, I will tender the witness as an expert in the field of biomedical engineering, qualified by his experience and training to testify in the field of biomedical engineering. And I will tender the witness to opposing counsel for voir dire on his qualifications to testify as an expert in the field of biomedical engineering.

Once the witness is tendered for voir dire by opposing counsel for questioning on his qualifications as an expert in the field in which he has been tendered, the voir dire would likely proceed as follows:

Sample Voir Dire of Expert Witness on Qualifications by Opposing Counsel

- You testified that you have no publications in the field of biomedical engineering, correct?
- You have never lectured or taught in this field either, have you?
- There are a number of various specializations in the field of biomedical engineering, aren't there?
- However, you have no particular specialization, do you?
- Specifically, you do not specialize in the particular field in which the issues in this case are based, do you?
- You also do no have any particular certifications in this field, do you?
- And so on ...

These and other questions of this nature would be the basis upon which counsel would object to the witness being allowed to give expert testimony.

Case on Qualifications of Experts

Pyles v. Weaver

Court of Appeal of Louisiana, Fourth Circuit
958 So. 2d 753
May 16, 2007

PATRICIA RIVET MURRAY, Judge.

On September 19, 2001, Kimberly Pyles filed the instant petition against Anthony Weaver and Rick's Cabaret alleging that she was injured on February 8, 2001, while working as an independent contractor dancer at a gentlemen's club operated by Rick's Cabaret on Bourbon Street in New Orleans. Ms. Pyles alleged her injuries were caused by defendant Anthony Weaver, a patron of the club, who deliberately threw a heavy rock glass at her, striking her in the face; and by the negligence of Rick's Cabaret in failing to provide adequate security to protect her. The case was tried March 21–29, 2006, and the jury found in favor of the plaintiff and determined that she suffered damages in the amount of $450,000 (including $300,000 for pain and suffering; $100,000 for mental anguish; and $50,000 for past medical costs)....

ISSUES ON APPEAL

Regarding the merits, appellant Rick's Cabaret asserts a single issue: the trial court erred by assigning any liability to Rick's Cabaret because the plaintiff failed to prove adequate security would have prevented the incident that caused her injuries. Specifically, Rick's Cabaret argues that the trial court committed legal error by admitting the testimony of plaintiff's sole security expert, Larry Preston Williams, despite his lack of qualifications; alternatively, defendant contends that Mr. William's testimony was insufficient to prove that additional security would have deterred Anthony Weaver from throwing the glass.

...

EVIDENCE PRESENTED AT TRIAL

... The plaintiff also presented five experts on damages, including her treating physicians (a chiropractor, a neurosurgeon, a neuropsychologist, and a maxillofacial prosthodontist); and one security expert, Larry Preston Williams. The defense offered its own security expert, Dr. Wade Schindler, and its own expert in neurosurgery, Dr. Robert Applebaum....

Ms. Pyles testified she was an independent contractor who paid a fee to dance at Rick's Cabaret; therefore, she had no employee benefits. At the time of the incident, she was dancing on stage number two, also known as the piano stage, on the first floor....

On the evening in question, after performing a two-song routine on the main stage, Ms. Pyles moved to the piano stage. As she approached the stage, the dancer who had preceded her, Holly Malave, warned Ms. Pyles that there was a table near the stage that was "rowdy." Ms. Pyles performed her routine, dancing topless as usual. Near the end of her second song, a man from the rowdy table, whom she later learned was Anthony Weaver, approached the stage with a dollar in his hand, offering it to her if she would expose more of her body. Ms. Pyles testified that she immediately knew there was a problem, because Mr. Weaver had an angry look, his pupils were dilated, and he was obviously intoxicated. She then cut off her routine before her relief arrived, left the stage, grabbed her clothes and put them on as she walked toward the place where the VIP host was stationed, intending to tell him what had happened.... Then, as Ms. Pyles was walking past the men's room, she was knocked unconscious by something that struck her in the face.

Ms. Pyles stated she did not know how long she remained unconscious, but when she awoke she was lying on the ground with blood, glass and teeth in her mouth....

Plaintiff's final witness on liability was security expert Larry Preston Williams, who opined that the failure of Rick's Cabaret to provide adequate security contributed to Ms. Pyles' injury.

...

ASSIGNMENT OF FAULT TO RICK'S CABARET

... The only possible basis for the jury to find fault on the part of Rick's Cabaret is the failure of Rick's Cabaret to provide adequate security for its dancers. In order to show there was a lack of security at the club, plaintiff presented the testimony of Larry Preston Williams, who was accepted as an expert in security. Rick's Cabaret first contends that Mr. Williams should not have been qualified as an expert under *Daubert. v. Merrell Dow Pharmaceuticals,* 509 U.S. 579, 113 S.Ct. 2786, 125 L.Ed.2d 469 (1993). Alternatively, defendant argues that plaintiff failed to prove the lack of adequate security noted by Mr. Williams caused Ms. Pyles' injury because the evidence did not show that additional reasonable security measures would have prevented Mr. Weaver from throwing the glass.

The requirements of expert testimony are set forth in La. C.E. art. 702, which provides:

> If scientific, technical or other specialized knowledge will assist the trier of fact to understand the evidence or to determine a fact in issue, a witness qualified as an expert by knowledge, skill, experience, training or education may testify thereto in the form of an opinion or otherwise.

Formal education or training in a particular field is not always necessary to qualify as an expert in a particular field; experience alone is sufficient. *Id.* (citations omitted). It is well-established that the trial judge has wide discretion in determining whether to allow a witness to testify as a expert, and his judgment will not be disturbed by an appellate court unless clearly erroneous....

In the instant case, Mr. Williams testified that he had been self-employed as a security consultant since 1993 and as an investigative consultant since 1986. He received a Bachelor's Degree in Criminology from Loyola University in 1971. From 1968 until 1974, Mr. Williams worked in the Intelligence Division of the New Orleans Police Department, and from 1974 until 1977 he worked as a Special Investigator for the District Attorney's office. Having received a Juris Doctorate from Loyola in 1976, Mr. Williams practiced law from 1977 until 1985. He admitted he stopped practicing law when the Louisiana Supreme Court first suspended, then revoked, his license for multiple instances of misconduct, including converting client funds to his own personal use. Mr. Williams testified that he had published an article on protecting tourists and another on protecting rural churches from fire-bombs; that he had been appointed in 1998 to a Louisiana Department of Education task force on school violence; and that he had lectured on preventing violence in schools. He also testified that he had been accepted as an expert in a Plaquemines Parish court and in a Florida court, but admitted that he had never testified as an expert on security as it applies to a gentlemen's club, night club, or other establishment that serves alcohol. He also admitted he had never designed or analyzed security for such an establishment. He testified he was not a certified protection professional, nor did he belong to any organization of security professionals. The trial judge accepted Mr. Williams as an expert in security based upon his "extensive experience in law enforcement and security-related issues."

Although Mr. Williams lacked the level of expertise possessed by the defendants' expert, Dr. Schindler, we cannot say the trial court abused its discretion by allowing him to testify as an expert on security. The fact that he was disbarred for misconduct as a lawyer, while it may relate to his credibility, has no bearing upon Mr. William's expertise in security-related issues. His degree in Criminology and experience as a police officer and special investigator provide at least the minimum credentials necessary to qualify him as an expert capable of giving an opinion as to the effectiveness of the security at Rick's Cabaret. It is well settled that the trier of fact is charged with the determination of what credibility it assigns to expert witnesses and the decision as to which expert among those testifying is more credible. In the instant case it was not error for the trial judge to afford the jury the opportunity to hear both experts, to assess their credibility, and to determine what weight it should place on the opinion of each.

...

Accordingly, we conclude that the trial court did not commit reversible legal error in this case.

CONCLUSION

For the reasons stated, we affirm the judgment of the trial court.

AFFIRMED.

Discussion Questions

1. Do you agree that the witness possessed the qualifications to testify as an expert in the field of nightclub security? What more, if anything, could be required? Is the standard sometimes too high to qualify as an expert?
2. What steps should an attorney take at the trial level to preserve his right to challenge an expert's qualifications on appeal? *See State v. Williams,* 2012-0252 (La. App. 4 Cir. 4/17/13), 115 So. 3d 600, 613–14 (La. Ct. App.) *writ denied,* 2013-1141 (La. 11/22/13), 126 So. 3d 477.
3. Opposing parties may stipulate to an expert's qualifications. This means that the opposing parties voluntarily agree that the expert is qualified to testify as an expert in the field. If the parties do indeed stipulate to the expert's qualifications, there is no need to qualify the expert before he testifies. In other words, the party presenting the expert witness will not ask questions like, "What degrees do you hold? How many years have you specialized in your field? What articles have you published?"

   Can you think of any advantages and disadvantages to stipulating to an expert witness's qualification? Note that qualifying an expert is typically done in the presence of the jury.
4. In *Pyles,* the Fourth Circuit Court of Appeal distinguishes between the security expert being "qualified" to testify as an expert in the particular field, and the security expert being "credible." As the court said while referencing the security expert, "The fact that he was disbarred for misconduct as a lawyer, while it may relate to his credibility, has no bearing upon Mr. Williams' expertise in security-related issues." Define what it means for an expert to be "qualified" and what it means for an expert to be "credible." How are the two different? Does an expert's qualifications ever bear on his credibility or are they mutually exclusive? How so? *See* 1 La. Prac. Pers. Inj. § 3:119.
5. Any expert may be subject to scrupulous cross-examination by opposing counsel. As a practicing attorney, how would you verify the qualifications of your expert? Is examining his curriculum vitae combined with his word sufficient? Are there any other approaches you would take to verify his qualifications? *See* 1 La. Prac. Pers. Inj. § 3:119.

§ 7.3 Scope of Expert Testimony [Arts. 702, 704]

Once a witness is qualified as an expert, he may testify in the form of his opinions (or otherwise) in his area of expertise. He may not give expert opinions in areas outside of or beyond the scope of the area in which he has been qualified as an expert. For instance, if the witness is qualified as an expert in the area of neurology, and has testified that the cause of death was a neurological disorder, he cannot testify to the amount of money the decedent would likely have made had he lived ten additional years. That testimony would be outside of the witness's area of expertise. In any area outside of the witness's area of expertise, his testimony is limited to that of a lay witness.

In addition to testimony directly related to the witness's area of expertise, an expert witness may give relevant background information that may be helpful to the jury in understanding the issues, his testimony, and ultimately his opinions. Further, when expressing opinions, an expert witness may be asked hypothetical questions. For example, if an economist has testified in a wrongful death action that had the decedent lived to the average lifespan (an additional 25 years) he would have earned a certain amount of money in his lifetime, he may be asked to give an opinion as to the amount of money the decedent would have likely earned if he had only lived an additional 10 years. The idea is that the underlying facts may be disputed amongst the parties, and must be proven by other evidence; but the expert is merely testifying that given this set of facts, this is what his opinion would be.

Applicable Code Articles

Art. 704. Opinion on ultimate issue

Testimony in the form of an opinion or inference otherwise admissible is not to be excluded solely because it embraces an ultimate issue to be decided by the trier of fact. However, in a criminal case, an expert witness shall not express an opinion as to the guilt or innocence of the accused.

Excluded testimony/Ultimate issues. Some early opinions suggested that expert opinions that embraced ultimate issues were inadmissible. However, Article 704 specifically provides that expert testimony shall not be excluded solely because it embraces an ultimate issue to be decided by the trier of fact, provided the testimony will nonetheless be *helpful* to them. For example, if a witness qualified as an expert in forensic psychology testifies that the defendant was insane at the time of the offense, the opinion goes to the ultimate issue to be decided in the case.

The law continues to prefer the more concrete testimony rather than the less concrete, and as the subject matter of the opinion approaches an ultimate issue, the presentation of the more concrete becomes more helpful, and conclusory testimony generally less so.[8] For example, it is more concrete to testify that a defendant was not capable of understanding the difference between right and wrong, than to testify that he was "insane," which is more abstract. Specific words or actions of the defendant that demonstrate his inability to distinguish between right and wrong are even more concrete. The more concrete

8. La. Code Evid. art. 702 Official Comment (c).

the testimony, the more helpful it will be to the jury in coming to its *own* conclusions in deciding the issues, rather than simply allowing the expert to tell them how to decide.

While such testimony is not automatically excluded because it embraces the ultimate issue to be decided in the case, this fact "should be taken into account in determining whether it is, on balance, helpful or unduly prejudicial."[9] The evidence may be excluded if its probative value in assisting the trier of fact in deciding a fact in issue is outweighed by its prejudicial effect in suggesting the result to be reached.

While expert witnesses are given great latitude in the issues to which they may testify, in a criminal case, an expert witness shall not express an opinion as to the guilt or innocence of the accused.[10] For example, testimony that the defendant possessed the specific intent to kill in a first-degree murder trial would be excluded. Such testimony is the equivalent of stating that the defendant is guilty. However, the Louisiana Code of Criminal Procedure expressly authorizes the appointment of a sanity commission to inquire into the mental condition of the accused (pleading insanity or mental incompetency to proceed) and to testify as to their findings at the trial.[11] Other expert evidence on the accused's mental condition is also admissible.[12]

Federal Rules of Evidence Distinction. The Federal Rules of Evidence specifically preclude expert testimony as to *any* "mental state or condition of a defendant in a criminal case." Such testimony is deemed to be a matter for the trier of fact to decide.[13] Louisiana has not adopted this provision, and concerns exist as to whether the provision violates a defendant's constitutional rights to present a defense.[14]

Credibility of witnesses. Additionally, an expert witness cannot give expert opinion regarding the **credibility of another witness**, i.e., whether in his expert opinion the witness is telling the truth. This is an issue that often arises in child sexual abuse cases. Louisiana courts have repeatedly held that expert opinions on credibility are inadmissible.[15]

Helpfulness requirement. As outlined above, the opinion or other testimony to which an expert will testify must help the trier of fact to understand the evidence or determine a fact in issue. The official comments to Article 702 specifically state that the criterion for allowing expert testimony is "not whether the question in issue involves knowledge obtained only by means of special training or experience," but rather, "whether the particular specialized knowledge would 'assist the trier of fact to understand the evidence or to determine a fact in issue.' "[16] Expert testimony that is not helpful to the trier of fact is not admissible.

Among the factors to consider in determining the helpfulness of the evidence is whether it embraces an ultimate issue, which, rather than assisting the jury, has been said to "invade the province of the jury." In other words, rather than assisting the jury in its determination

---

9. La. Code Evid. art. 702 Official Comment (f); *See also* La. Code Evid. art. 704 and State v. Wheller, 416 So. 2d 78 (La. 1982).

10. La. Code Evid. art. 704.

11. La. Code Evid. art. 704 Official Comment (b); *See also* La.C.Cr.P. art. 643 et seq.

12. La. Code Evid. art. 704 Official Comment (b); *See also* State v. Claibon, 395 So. 2d 770 (La. 1981).

13. As amended by Pub.L. 98-473, Title III, § 406, October 12, 1984, 98 State. 2067; *See also* La. Code Evid. art. 704 Official Comment (b).

14. La. Code Evid. art. 704 Official Comment (b).

15. *See* La. Code Evid. art. 702 Comment (e); *See also* La. Code Evid. art. 608 and discussion in Chapter 4 relative to credibility.

16. La. Code Evid. art. 702 Official Comment (a).

of guilt or innocence, it makes the determination for them. Keep in mind though that evidence is not excluded based *solely* on the fact that it embraces an ultimate issue, provided it is in fact helpful.

Evidence has also been held to be unhelpful when the fact finder could reasonably draw the same inferences based on his own knowledge and experience[17] without aid of an expert. For example, any reasonable finder of fact could likely conclude based on his own knowledge and experience that a driver's intoxication likely played a role in causing the driver to crash. In such a case, testimony from an expert witness qualified in accident reconstruction is not needed or helpful.[18]

Keep in mind, however, that expert testimony is not inadmissible simply "because the matter in issue is within the knowledge of ordinary citizens as was [the case] under prior law."[19] Like matters embracing ultimate issues, opinions within the knowledge of ordinary people, may be admissible if the opinions are nonetheless helpful to the jury.

Case on Scope of Expert Testimony

State v. Johnson
Court of Appeal of Louisiana, Fourth Circuit
780 So. 2d 403
November 29, 2000

WALTZER, Judge.

... On 7 September 1999, the court sentenced Johnson, on the conviction for possession with intent to distribute ... and on the conviction for attempted possession with intent to distribute ...

STATEMENT OF FACTS

Detective Michael Lohman, NOPD officers and DEA Agents participated in obtaining a search warrant for, and conducting surveillance of, C & G Liquor store, located in the 5500 block of North Galvez Street. At approximately 1:30 p.m. on 9 October 1998, Detective Lohman observed Terrance Johnson, one of the targets of the investigation, loitering in front of the liquor store. Detective Lohman noted several instances where a subject would approach Johnson, engage in brief conversation, and then enter the store followed by Johnson. Moments later the individual would exit the store, not carrying any items, and then leave the area. Johnson would then resume loitering in front of the store, counting money in his hands, until the next subject approached him. Based on these observations, Detective Lohman suspected narcotics activity. Shortly before 2:00 p.m., Russell Harris arrived in a black Mitsubishi Diamonte accompanied by Mario Breedlove. Both men entered the store followed by Johnson. Shortly thereafter, Johnson exited the store and resumed his suspect behavior. Satisfied there was drug activity at the location, Detective Lohman signaled back up officers to execute the warrant.

---

17. *See* Theriot v. Lasseigne, 640 So. 2d 1305, 1308 n5 (La. 7/5/1994).

18. Theriot v. Lasseigne, 640 So. 2d 1305, 1308 n5 (La. 7/5/94) ("[e]xpert testimony is not necessary when a factfinder can reasonably draw inferences based on his own knowledge and experience"; court could have reasonably found that alcohol consumption may have played a role in combined negligence of parties even though no expert testimony was introduced on effect of consumption of alcohol on a person's driving ability).

19. La. Code Evid. art. 702 Official Comment (c).

Johnson walked across the street to another store where he was intercepted by officers and returned to the target location. As officers entered C & G they encountered four individuals behind the counter, who were secured, and advised of the search warrant. Detective Lohman advised the detainees of their Miranda rights, placed them under arrest, and began searching the store. Officers found a "slab" of rock cocaine and $191 in the cash register. A search of the beverage cooler yielded 23 grams of crack cocaine. Russell Harris, Terrance Johnson, Greg Morris and Mario Breedlove were arrested for possession of cocaine.

Searching the store further, the officers discovered a razor blade containing a white residue; two cigar boxes containing glass tubes, wire mesh and small plastic bags, items common to narcotics consumption and packaging; one digital and twelve handheld metal scales....

... Officer Harry O'Neal, drug chemist with the NOPD crime lab and expert in the analysis of controlled dangerous substances, was ... qualified as an expert in the identification of drug paraphernalia and the use, packaging and distribution of controlled dangerous substances, particularly cocaine. Officer O'Neal explained his testing methods on the contraband seized from the C & G liquor store and the Alabo Street residence. The evidence tested positive for cocaine. He further testified that in his twelve and a half years of police experience with controlled substances, the type of scales confiscated at the liquor store are frequently used to weigh contraband before packaging. Upon examination of the glass tubes, copper mesh wire and plastic bags seized in the search of the liquor store and residence, Officer O'Neal said that the objects were the type associated with drug paraphernalia. Further explaining "drug paraphernalia", the officer testified that wire mesh and glass tubes are used in making crack pipes and the scales and plastic bags are employed in packaging drugs, particularly cocaine and marijuana, for street sale. For "demonstrative purposes" Officer O'Neal displayed crack pipes from other cases to show how the pipe is constructed from glass tubes and wire mesh....

JOHNSON — ASSIGNMENT OF ERROR

... In a sole assignment, Johnson contends the trial court erred in allowing the State's expert to render an opinion as to an ultimate issue of fact. The defense objected to the State's qualifying Officer Harry O'Neal as an expert in the identification of drug paraphernalia and the use, packaging and distribution of cocaine on the basis that this type of testimony should not be labeled as expert "value".

During his testimony, Officer O'Neal reviewed the evidence retrieved, including the quantity of cocaine found on the defendants, and the scales, baggies and glass tubes. The officer testified that the items were consistent with distribution. The defendant argues that this testimony constituted giving an opinion on an ultimate issue of guilt, the intent to distribute, in violation of the holdings in *State v. Montana*, 421 So.2d 895 (La.1982); *State v. Wheeler*, 416 So.2d 78 (La.1982); *State v. White*, 450 So.2d 648 (La.1984), *State v. Evans*, 593 So.2d 900 (La.App. 4 Cir.1992), writ denied 598 So.2d 371 (La.1992), and *State v. Dabney*, 452 So.2d 775 (La.App. 4 Cir.1984).

LSA–C.E. art. 702 provides that "[I]f scientific, technical, or other specialized knowledge will assist the trier of fact to understand the evidence or to determine a fact in issue, a witness qualified as an expert by knowledge, skill, experience, training, or education, may testify thereto in the form of an opinion or otherwise."

In *Wheeler*, the defendant was charged with possession of marijuana with the intent to distribute. The prosecutor asked the police officer-expert a hypothetical question in which the details exactly mirrored the facts of the case. The expert was then asked, in his expert opinion "... what is the likelihood of this [hypothetical] individual being involved in the distribution of marijuana" to which he replied "[i]n my opinion the person would be involved in the distribution of marijuana ..." *Wheeler*, supra at 79. On appeal, the Louisiana Supreme Court found that the trial court had erred when it overruled the defendant's objection to the hypothetical question because the testimony "was tantamount to an opinion that the defendant was guilty of the crime charged, an indirect abstract inference as to the ultimate issue in the case." *Wheeler*, supra at 81.

In *State v. Montana*, the court held that where an expert gives his opinion as to the ultimate issue of the defendant's guilt, i.e. whether the defendant intended to distribute drugs, he has improperly usurped the function of the jury. The court in *Montana* found reversible error where a police officer, qualified as an expert in the packaging and distribution of illegal drugs, was given a factual situation similar to the circumstances surrounding the defendant's arrest, and the officer gave his opinion that "they [the defendants] had it for sale." *Montana*, supra at 900.

Likewise in *State v. White*, the State posed a hypothetical factual situation virtually identical to the actual evidence produced at defendant's trial. The officer testified that in his opinion, "a person standing on the street corner with a matchbox containing say twenty-seven tin foils containing heroin, would be there for the purpose of selling or distributing." Once again, the court found reversible error concluding that the officer was usurping the jury's function as finder of fact.

In *State v. Evans*, this court reversed the defendant's conviction because the State failed to establish a proper foundation qualifying the officer to testify as an expert in the field of narcotics, where the basis of the officer's expertise, such as amount of time he had been with the police force or with the narcotics division, was not disclosed. Moreover, this court indicated that the officer's testimony that "the quantity is possession with intent to distribute", was in effect an opinion as to the defendant's guilt.

In *State v. Dabney*, the defendant's conviction was reversed because the expert gave an opinion as to whether a person in possession of an exact number of "sets of Ts and Blues" (i.e. the same number of sets as was taken from the defendant) was possessing them for personal use. This Court found that the expert, who had already testified to the packaging and marketing of "Ts and blues" on a wholesale level, had given the equivalent of a direct statement that the defendant possessed the drugs with the intent to distribute.

In this case, during examination by the State, Officer O'Neal testified that he had been on the police force for twenty-four years. For half of those years, he was a narcotics detective and participated in excess of several thousand narcotics arrests. He has interviewed numerous drug users and dealers, and is very familiar with and knowledgeable of the street methodology of packaging and distribution of narcotics, as well as items used in preparation of narcotics for retail sale. Based upon Officer O'Neal's background, the trial court qualified him as an expert in the packaging of narcotics for retail distribution. The State proceeded to question the officer as an expert. Officer O'Neal explained that his testing and quantifying the evidence indicated that the officers seized in excess of seventy-five grams of cocaine from the defendants. He further testified that the scales, baggies, and glass tubes confiscated in the investigation are commonly used in the retail sale and packaging of street level narcotics, particularly crack cocaine.

Officer O'Neal's testimony assisted the jury in understanding how cocaine is packaged for retail sale. Such testimony was helpful to the jury because of their lack of exposure to narcotics trafficking. The officer's testimony merely assisted the jury in its determination. Unlike the testifying experts in *Montana*, *Wheeler*, *White*, *Evans* and *Dabney*, Officer O'Neal did not give the jury an opinion as to the defendant's guilt or innocence, only that the paraphernalia confiscated in the case was consistent with paraphernalia used in narcotics distribution. The officer's testimony assisted the jury in determining whether defendant's denial of guilt was credible. As such, it does not appear that the trial court erred in qualifying the officer as an expert and allowing him to testify as the packaging of narcotics for retail sales. This assignment is without merit.

...

Discussion Questions

1. Do you take issue with the police officer's testimony in this case? Did it embrace the ultimate issue of guilt/innocence? Was his testimony helpful to the jury? Why or why not?
2. While hypothetical scenarios are permissible with experts, the courts are sometimes skeptical of hypothetical scenarios that closely relate to the facts at issue. The expert witnesses are often asked to give an opinion as to an ultimate issue in the "hypothetical" situation, which clearly answers the issue in the instant case. In *Johnson*, the defendant was charged with possession with intent to distribute. After testifying to what he found in defendant's possession, would it have been appropriate for the prosecution to then ask the officer the following: "*Hypothetically speaking, Officer O'Neal, would a person in possession of more than seventy-five grams of cocaine, scales, baggies, and glass tubes, have the intent to distribute the cocaine?*" Why or why not?

   How is that question different from what the officer actually testified to—that the items confiscated, "are commonly used in the retail sale and packaging of street level narcotics, particularly crack cocaine"?
3. A primary concern with allowing opinions on ultimate issues is that it is said to "invade the province of the jury." What does this mean in this context? Why is this issue of such concern?
4. In *Johnson*, the Louisiana Fourth Circuit Court of Appeal listed several case examples where experts gave impermissible opinions embracing ultimate issues of the case. Ultimately, the Fourth Circuit decided *Johnson* was different than the listed cases. What is different between the expert's testimony in *Johnson* and the experts' testimonies in the listed cases that were excluded?

Opinions on Defendant's Sanity

Revisit *State v. Butler*. Another issue in which expert opinions often approach opinions on guilt or innocence is in the context of a defendant's sanity at the time of an offense, or his competency to stand trial. Let's revisit *State v. Butler*,[20] which we covered in Chapter 4 § 4.4, relative to lay witness opinions.

If you recall, the defendant was indicted for second-degree murder after he shot and killed his former girlfriend, Michelle Y. Poche, after confronting her and her escort in front of her apartment complex. The defendant pled not guilty and not guilty by reason of insanity.

In support of his insanity defense, the defense unsuccessfully sought to elicit testimony from a co-worker whom he spoke to immediately after the shooting, that the defendant

20. State v. Butler, 563 So. 2d 976 (La. Ct. App. First Cir. 1990).

appeared to be "in a trance" when he saw him. The court of appeal upheld the trial court's[21] ruling, finding that even if the witness had been allowed to testify as proposed, the testimony would not have been helpful to the jury in understanding the defendant's sanity—a requirement for admitting lay witness opinion. Further the court held that the testimony was nonetheless presented to the jury through other questioning.

At the trial, both the defense and the prosecution presented expert witnesses to testify to the defendant's mental condition at the time of the offense.

Defendant's expert. The defense presented the testimony of psychologist, Dr. Marc Zimmerman, who "testified that he had examined defendant and had determined that, at the time of the incident, 'he moved across the line from sanity into insanity.'" Dr. Zimmerman further testified that defendant had "decompensated into a state where he lost contact with reality, a psychotic state, and I had never put a diagnosis on it, but some form of schizophrenia from what he described."[22]

When Dr. Zimmerman was asked about whether the defendant was aware of "social structures, morals, or values,"[23] Dr. Zimmerman testified at the time of the incident, the defendant "was not aware of them,"[24] and because of his "rage he had 'literally lost contact with reality' so that 'he was not able to say wait a second, this is wrong according to what I was taught in Sunday school or what the law says or whatever.'"[25] Defense counsel then asked Dr. Zimmerman:

> Q. And at that point he was unable really to premeditate or to understand really the effects of what he's doing in a legal sense at least, is that—[26]

The state objected to this question arguing that it embraced an ultimate issue of guilt or innocence. The court sustained the objection, and the witness was not allowed to testify any further on the issue.

Prosecution's expert. In the same trial, the state also called an expert witness, Dr. Hypolite Landry. On the issue of defendant's sanity, the state questioned him as follows:

> Q. Particularly as to the third thing you listed that the judge was interested in your examination of Mr. Butler as to his sanity at the time of the commission of the offense on May 11, 1988, as to the legal definition of sanity of his ability at that time to determine right from wrong—
>
> A. Yes, sir.
>
> Q. What was your conclusion?[27]

Over defendant's objection, the state's expert witness was allowed to testify as follows: "I have no reason—I have no reason to believe that he did not know right from wrong on that day. As I stated, I didn't elicit a history of a psychosis on that day which would render him incapable of doing that or on any other day."[28]

---

21. The trial judge in the 19th Judicial District Court at the time was Judge Freddie Pitcher, Jr., who later went on to become a judge for the Louisiana First Circuit Court of Appeal, and from 2003–2015, Chancellor of the Southern University Law Center.

22. State v. Butler, 563 So. 2d 976, 982 (La. Ct. App. First Cir. 1990).

23. *Id.*

24. *Id.*

25. *Id.*

26. *Id.*

27. *Id.*

28. *Butler*, 563 So. 2d 976, 982.

Jury instruction on insanity. The trial court instructed the jury on the insanity as follows: "Insanity at the time of the commission of the crime exempts the offender from criminal responsibility. If the circumstances indicate that because of a mental disease or a mental defect that the defendant was incapable of distinguishing between right and wrong with reference to the conduct in question, the defendant must be found not guilty by reason of insanity."[29]

Discussion Questions

1. Under the definition of insanity above, do you believe either expert's opinion crossed the line into expressing an opinion of guilt or innocence? Why or why not?
2. Should Dr. Zimmerman have been allowed to answer the last question posed by the defense?
3. Did the prosecution go too far with its last question to Dr. Landry? Why or why not?
4. Dr. Landry seems to have answered a slightly different question than was asked of him in the final question. Does this make a difference to you in terms of whether his testimony was an opinion on guilt or innocence? Why or why not?
5. How do you think the Louisiana First Circuit Court of Appeal decided these issues and why? See *State v. Butler,* 563 So. 2d 976 (La. Ct. App. First Cir. 1990).

Specific Intent to Kill

In a first-degree murder trial, should a prosecutor be able to ask an expert witness whether, based on the facts and circumstances, the defendant had the "specific intent to kill"? Does the question go to guilt or innocence?

In *State v. Deal,*[30] the defendant was indicted with first-degree murder after he killed his two-month-old son by stuffing a paper towel down his throat. In a recorded statement to the police, the defendant stated:

> ... I go back there in the room, picked the baby up out his bed, feed him his bottle. Okay. He spits up and he starts whining and I took this rag and stuffed it into his mouth and spun it, turned it, like to wash his mouth out, and that was before—let me back myself up—I was trying to make him go to the bathroom, squeezing on his tummy and pushing on his legs, and that's when he spit up—take that back. That's when he spit up and then that kind of made me angry, did that. Took the baby, which the baby bed is to my left, took him and just more or less slung him and flung him into the bed and he bounced and hit his head into the side of the railing of the baby bed. And then I noticed that he wasn't breathing. Took him out and put him on the—back onto the bed and I get concerned because I can't get him the breath. I was giving him CPR. Go and get my wife up, said "Jerry, he's not breathing. He's not breathing." She panics, so I went and called 911 and the man tried to tell me what to do, to hold his head back and everything ...
>
> DET. EATMAN: Why did you throw him in the baby bed?
>
> MR. DEAL: Because he kept bawling and stuff like that and I was trying to get him to go to sleep and it was late and I was wanting to go to bed myself and I was drinking, and when I been drinking I sometimes lose—I got a temper.

---

29. *Id.* at 987.
30. State v. Deal, 802 So. 2d 1254 (La. 2001).

DET. EATMAN: So you got mad at the baby.

MR. DEAL: Yeah, and I—did like that and it bounced, bam, hit that side of that rail, bounced up on the bed. Sir, I didn't kill that boy just to be killing him. I didn't. That's my son.

...

DET. EATMAN: Didn't you think it was going to cause a problem for the baby, you leaving a paper towel in his mouth?

MR. DEAL: Well, that's the thing about it, I didn't know it was in his mouth. I didn't know.

DET. EATMAN: You stuck it in there.

MR. DEAL: I know I stuck it in there though, but I had a paper towel, two of them together, stuck in there and turned it like this and pulled it back out, chunked it in the garbage like that—[31]

...

The Louisiana Supreme Court found reversible error in the court allowing two expert witnesses to testify that at the time of the offense, the defendant had the specific intent to kill. At the trial, the prosecution called the coroner, a forensic pathologist, who testified that "in his expert opinion, the fatal injuries suffered by the victim, a skull fracture and a blocked airway, illustrated a specific intent to kill or inflict great bodily harm."[32] Dr. McCormick was also presented with a hypothetical scenario that mimicked the facts of the case and further testified that in "his opinion that specific intent to kill or inflict great bodily harm was present."[33]

Adding to this testimony "in the guilt phase, the prosecutor questioned the defense's expert witness Dr. Mark Vigan, as the defense psychologist, about the defendant's intent when he asked, 'And Mr. Deal did specifically intend to kill and inflict great bodily harm on his son Joshua when he killed him, did he not?' The doctor replied, 'I think so. His behavior is, you know, we can't read intention, we can only infer intention from behavior. But I certainly agree with you.' Shortly thereafter, the prosecutor repeated Dr. Vigan's testimony during his cross-examination of the doctor, stating, '[Y]ou're convinced he has specific intent to kill or inflict great bodily harm.'"[34]

Discussion Questions

1. Should the trial court have allowed the expert witnesses to testify that the defendant had the specific intent to kill? Why or why not? Was the testimony equivalent to an opinion on guilt or innocence?
2. Did the testimony invade the province of the jury—deciding issues usually preserved for the trier of fact?
3. Do you think this testimony was helpful to the jury?
4. The court typically prefers expert testimony that is "concrete" rather than "abstract." For example, testimony that the defendant "could not distinguish between right and wrong" rather than "he was insane." In this case, can you think of ways in which the

31. *Id.*
32. *Id.*
33. *Id.*
34. *Id.*

testimony might have been presented to be more concrete from which the jury would have been able to determine for themselves whether the defendant had the specific intent to kill?

5. Dr. McCormick, the coroner who testified for the prosecution, is a forensic pathologist, a medical doctor. They usually testify to the cause, manner, and fact of death. Do you think that it is within the realm of expertise of a forensic pathologist to testify to *any* mental states of the defendant? Is this within his area of expertise? Why or why not?

§ 7.4 Basis of Expert Opinion [Arts. 703, 705]

Applicable Code Articles

Art. 703. Bases of opinion testimony by experts

The facts or data in the particular case upon which an expert bases an opinion or inference may be those perceived by or made known to him at or before the hearing. If of a type reasonably relied upon by experts in the particular field in forming opinions or inferences upon the subject, the facts or data need not be admissible in evidence.

Art. 705. Disclosure of facts or data underlying expert opinion; foundation

A. Civil cases. In a civil case, the expert may testify in terms of opinion or inference and give his reasons therefor without prior disclosure of the underlying facts or data, unless the court requires otherwise. The expert may in any event be required to disclose the underlying facts or data on cross-examination.

B. Criminal cases. In a criminal case, every expert witness must state the facts upon which his opinion is based, provided, however, that with respect to evidence which would otherwise be inadmissible such basis shall only be elicited on cross-examination.

An important distinction between an expert witness and a lay witness giving opinions is that an expert may base his opinion on information **perceived by** *or* **made known to him at or before the hearing**, whereas a lay witness must have first-hand knowledge of the underlying facts upon which he bases his opinions or inferences.[35] In most instances an expert will not likely have first-hand knowledge of the matters to which he will render an expert opinion at trial. Usually, an expert will be provided with information that the attorney calling him obtains through discovery upon which he will base his opinion. Specifically, experts are usually provided with factual accounts about the case, witness statements, depositions, forensic tests, photographs, police reports, medical reports, and a full range of other information that might assist him in developing his opinions. Oftentimes an expert will visit the scene where an incident occurred, and even take measurements and photos.

Additionally, an expert may base his opinions on information made known to him at the hearing itself.[36] If needed, an expert can be exempted from the rule of sequestration to remain in the courtroom during the testimony of other witnesses so that he can be later

35. La. Code Evid. art. 703 Official Comment (c).

36. La. Code Evid. art. 703 Official Comment (d).

questioned about the testimony, usually in the form of hypothetical questions.[37] For instance, an expert might be asked, if given this set of facts as true, what would your opinion be?

Further, in some instances an expert may even base his opinion on inadmissible facts or data if it's the type of information **reasonably relied upon by experts in the field**. Ultimately, expert witnesses are given a great deal of leeway in basing their opinions on a wide variety of information made known to them and even hypothetical scenarios. The idea is that while the expert will not be able to testify that the underlying facts and other information unequivocally exist in the case at hand, he is only testifying that given those facts, his opinion would be as such. It is up to the parties to prove, by other evidence, whether or not those facts actually exist.

Inadmissible facts and data. As stated above, Article 703 also provides that in some instances an expert witness may base his opinion on inadmissible facts or data, if of a type reasonably relied upon by experts in the particular field in forming opinions or inferences upon the subject.[38] In such a case, however, the expert cannot necessarily testify to the inadmissible information upon which he based his opinion.[39] For example, an accident reconstructionist might give an expert opinion about how an accident occurred. In doing so, he will usually rely, among other things, on eyewitness accounts of an accident. Witnesses might give information about the location, speed, or other circumstances surrounding an accident. Because this is the type of information upon which an accident reconstructionist would usually rely in forming an opinion about how an accident occurred, he may rely on inadmissible information in coming to his opinion. Thus, if one or more of the witness's statements was inadmissible hearsay that will not be brought out at trial, the expert would not be precluded from relying on the inadmissible statement in coming to his conclusion.

Keep in mind though, that while the expert may use the inadmissible information to form an opinion, and may testify to the opinion to which he arrived, this rule does not automatically permit the expert to testify to the inadmissible information upon which he based his opinion. The rule does not permit a proponent of the expert opinion to "backdoor" inadmissible facts into evidence. It merely allows the expert to consider the information in coming to his opinions or inferences.

As we stated above, the expert is merely testifying that given those facts, this is what his opinion would be. He has no first-hand knowledge in such a situation, as to whether the facts exist and thus, any testimony he gives regarding the factual basis of his opinions should not be given any substantive weight.[40] The proponents must prove the underlying facts to support the expert's opinion by other reliable evidence.

An opponent of an expert's opinion may always attack the basis of an expert's opinion, claiming the facts are not as the ones upon which the expert relied. However, attacks on the basis of an expert's opinion goes only to the credibility of the expert witness's testimony, an issue for the trier of fact to decide—it does not go to its admissibility. An opposing party may attack the factual basis of an expert witness's opinion through cross-examination and by offering contradicting information into evidence. It is only when the expert opinion is so fundamentally unsupported by the proven facts that it can offer no assistance to the jury, that the testimony should not be admitted.

---

37. La. Code Evid. art. 703 Official Comment (d).

38. La. Code Evid. art. 703; La. Code Evid. art. 703 Official Comment (d).

39. La. Code Evid. art. 703 Official comment (f); *See also* La. Code Evid. art. 705 governing disclosure of underlying facts.

40. Force & Rault, Handbook on Louisiana Evidence Law, Art. 705 Author's Comment (1) (West Publishing 2014).

Disclosure of underlying facts. Article 705 outlines the circumstances under which an expert must disclose the underlying facts upon which he bases his opinions. In a ***civil case***, an expert may testify as to his opinions or inferences without first disclosing the facts upon which his opinion is based, unless the court requires otherwise. He may be required, however, to disclose the facts or data underlying his opinion on cross-examination. Thus, in a civil case, an expert would not be required to disclose the factual basis of his testimony at all if the opposing party does not inquire into it on cross-examination.

The requirements are different in a ***criminal case***. In a criminal case, an expert is *required* to state the facts upon which his opinion is based. The proponent of the expert testimony does not have the option, as in a civil case, of only having to disclose the information on cross-examination. However, this is not the case with any *inadmissible* facts or data upon which the witness may rely. If the expert witness relies on inadmissible evidence in forming his opinions, such as inadmissible hearsay, the proponent of the expert's opinion *cannot* disclose the inadmissible facts or data. In such a case, only the opposing party may elicit the information on cross-examination.

So for example, if an expert witness testifies in a criminal case for the prosecution, and some of the information upon which he relied is inadmissible hearsay, he must disclose the facts and data upon which he based his opinion with the exception of the inadmissible information. The inadmissible facts and data may only be elicited by the defense on cross-examination if they choose to do so.

Federal Rules of Evidence Distinction—Disclosure of Underlying Facts. The Federal Rules of Evidence differ with respect to disclosure of underlying facts. Under Federal Rule of Evidence 705, no distinction is made between experts testifying in civil cases and criminal cases. In either instance, the expert may testify to his opinions or inferences without first testifying to the underlying facts upon which his opinion is based, unless the court requires otherwise. The expert *may* be required to disclose the facts and data underlying his opinions and inferences on cross-examination. This is different than under Louisiana law, where in a *criminal case* the underlying facts or data *must* be disclosed, even if not inquired into on cross-examination, with the exception of inadmissible evidence.

As it pertains to inadmissible evidence under the Federal Rules of Evidence, the inadmissible underlying facts shall not be disclosed by the proponent of the expert opinion *unless* the court finds that its probative value in assisting the jury outweighs its prejudicial effect. So effectively, inadmissible evidence could possibly be disclosed by the proponent of the expert testimony if it passes Federal Rule of Evidence 403 balancing. Louisiana has a blanket exclusion against admitting the inadmissible underlying bases of expert testimony by the proponent of the expert testimony that relies upon it. Such testimony may only be inquired into on cross-examination by the opposing party.

Article 403 Balancing. Expert testimony is subject to the balancing test of Article 403.[41] When balancing the admissibility of expert testimony, the court considers its probative value toward its helpfulness in assisting the jury to understand the evidence or determine a fact in issue, and weighs it against the prejudicial effect of such testimony. In addition to the prejudicial effect outlined above relative to embracing ultimate issues, expert testimony could also risk confusing the issues due to the complexity of some technical evidence, or of misleading the jury by having them assign undue weight to the expert testimony.

41. La. Code Evid. art. 702 Official Comment (f).

Case on Basis of Expert Testimony

Turner v. Lyons
Court of Appeal of Louisiana, Fourth Circuit
867 So. 2d 13
Jan. 28, 2004

TERRI F. LOVE, Judge.

... On August 1, 1995, between 9:30 to 10:00 p.m., sixty-year-old Emma Turner ("Mrs. Turner") was crossing from the lake to the riverside of Canal Street in the block between North Galvez and North Miro, when she was injured by a New Orleans Police Department ("N.O.P.D.") vehicle, being driven by Officer Michael Lyons. Mrs. Turner was transported to Charity Hospital where she underwent immediate surgery to repair her two broken legs and a broken arm caused by the accident. That same night, while in the process of recovery, she suffered a heart attack.... Mrs. Turner died on May 31, 1996.

...

LAW AND DISCUSSION

On appeal, Michael Lyons and the City of New Orleans allege ...

> (1) The trial court erred by relying upon the testimony of an accident reconstruction expert to impose liability, where that expert's opinions were based on undefined and unproven facts;

...

First Assignment of Error

... In the first assignment of error, defendants assert that plaintiff's expert testimony was based upon inadmissible evidence and accordingly, the trial court's reliance upon the expert testimony was erroneous. Defendants conclude that the trial court's imposition of liability upon Officer Lyons based on this testimony is reversible error.

The appellants, Officer Michael Lyons and the City of New Orleans contend that the testimony of plaintiff's expert, Dr. Frank Griffith, a physicist and plaintiff's accident reconstruction expert, was inadmissible because his opinion was based upon inadmissible evidence. Appellants contend that the inadmissible evidence Dr. Griffith relied upon in forming his opinion was the N.O.P.D. Police Report and the N.O.P.D. Internal Report. Appellants assert that the trial court based its finding of liability against Officer Lyons upon Dr. Griffith's testimony and should therefore be reversed. We find no merit in this argument. Louisiana Code of Evidence Article 703 provides:

> [t]he facts or data in the particular case upon which an expert bases an opinion or inference may be those perceived by or made known to him at or before the hearing. If of a type reasonably relied upon by experts in the particular field in forming opinions or inferences upon the subject, the facts or data need not be admissible in evidence.

In *Wiley v. City of New Orleans,* 2000-1544 (La.App. 4 Cir. 5/16/01), 809 So.2d 151, the testimony of an expert in the field of land surveying and design, construction, maintenance and safety of public roads and streets was challenged by the appellants as being inadmissible because it was based upon an inadmissible (hearsay) police accident report. According to Article 703 of the Louisiana Code of Evidence, this court found the expert's testimony admissible even though it was a based upon inadmissible hearsay *per se.* In

Wiley this court referenced the 1988 official comments (d) to the Louisiana Code of Evidence Article 703 states:

> Under this Article the facts or data underlying the expert witness' opinion may properly be: ... (3) under designated circumstances, facts or data not admissible in evidence (because, for example, their source is inadmissible hearsay), if they are of a kind reasonably relied upon by experts in the particular field in arriving at their opinions or inferences ... Whether the facts or data may be reasonably relied upon" in this Fashion is a question for the court under Article 104(A).

During direct examination, Dr. Griffith testified:

> Q: Right. Okay. Now, Doctor, would you tell the Court what information you reviewed in connection with the matter of Emma Turner?
>
> A: I reviewed the accident report, the deposition of Officer Lyons, a report Sergeant Glasser, which was the internal report, and the deposition of Dr. Liuzza. Those were the documents that I reviewed. In addition to that, I did a sight visit where measurements were made and photographs were taken on the 19th of April, this year.

Dr. Griffith also testified that he based his opinions upon the trial testimony of defendant Officer Lyons, reviewed the specifications of the type of police vehicle Officer Lyons was driving at the time of the accident, and made calculations regarding its stopping time. Additionally, Dr. Griffith reviewed the Motor Vehicle Traffic Regulations, a textbook pertaining to pedestrian accident reconstruction as well as videos with pedestrian accident reconstructions. The evidence indicates that Dr. Griffith based his opinions on various sources including, but not limited to the N.O.P.D. Police Report and Internal Report, such that the admissibility of the two documents are irrelevant to the overall admissibility of his testimony. Moreover, as in *Wiley*, Dr. Griffith's reliance upon the N.O.P.D. Police Report and Internal Report does not render his testimony inadmissible as they are of the kind of facts and/or data reasonably relied upon by experts in his particular field.

...

After a complete review of the record and the trial court's reasons for ruling, we cannot find that the trial court's ruling assigning liability to Officer Lyons was manifestly erroneous. We find no error in the trial court's ruling that the evidence was inadmissible hearsay *per se*, but could be used as a basis of expert testimony.

...

Discussion Questions

1. Why was the witness in *Lyons* permitted to rely on the inadmissible information in forming his opinions?
2. While reliance on inadmissible facts/data of the kind reasonably relied upon by experts in that field does not render opinions based on such facts/data inadmissible, what, if any, effect does it or should it have on an expert's opinion?
3. Are there any circumstances in which the inadmissible information in *Lyons* could have been disclosed to the jury? Would your answer change if this were a criminal case for negligent homicide against Officer Lyons rather than a civil case?
4. Should an expert relying on inadmissible facts and data be limited on how heavily he relies on the inadmissible information? Should it matter? Here, the court noted that the witness's reliance on the two documents was basically irrelevant in light of the

other information he relied on. Do you think the outcome of the case would have been different had the witness not had the other information on which to also rely? What effect, if any, should the availability of other corroborating information have on the witness's ability to rely on inadmissible information?

5. When an expert is required to disclose underlying data under the Rules, he need only disclose facts or data upon which he actually *relies*, not information that he may have seen or come across but did not rely. Just as an expert's opinion may be attacked on what he chooses to base his opinion on, it may also be attacked based on which information he chooses to disregard.[42] For example, say the police reports the expert reviewed had conflicting witness information—some stating that the vehicle that caused the accident was traveling at around 45 mph, and another stating that the same vehicle was traveling around 60 mph. Suppose the expert bases his opinion only on the witness's testimony that stated that the vehicle was traveling at 60 mph.

   How would you suggest an attorney use discrepancies in facts to his advantage in terms of proving his case, arguing the case, and in questioning the expert? Should an expert be allowed to testify when conflicting facts or data exist?

§ 7.5 Reliability of Principles and Methodology (*Excluding "Junk Science"*) [Art. 702]

Suppose that a plaintiff offers an expert witness who holds a Ph.D. in chemistry and who has conducted extensive research and teaching in his field over the last 35 years (highly qualified) to testify that he utilizes a process by which he can conduct a rain dance using a person's urine to determine whether that person is the biological parent of a child. There is no doubt that this "junk science" would be rejected by the court as not being a reliable scientific methodology for determining paternity, irrespective of the witness's qualifications or specialized knowledge in the field. In some instances, however, it would not be so easy to determine whether the scientific methodology used by an expert in arriving at his opinions are reliable, particularly since scientific testimony can be quite complicated and technical. Because of the weight juries tend to place on expert testimony, the courts have gone to great measures to ensure that sufficient procedures are put in place to evaluate the reliability of scientific principles and methodology in determining the admissibility of scientific evidence.

Old Law/The *Frye* Standard. For more than 70 years, most states and the federal courts relied upon a standard first set out in the case of *Frye v. U.S.*, 293 F. 1013 (D.C.Cir. 1923), in which the court held that only scientific evidence that was **"generally accepted in the scientific community"** could be relied on by an expert at trial. If a scientific methodology was not generally accepted in the scientific community, as was the case for the relatively new polygraph testing that was rejected by the *Frye* court, the methodology and any expert opinions relying on those principles were not admissible in court. This test was known as the "general acceptance test" and remained the prevailing standard for several decades

42. A practice tip is to serve a subpoena duces tecum on an opposing counsel's expert to produce his files in advance of his deposition and "examine him on all facts and data considered, and not necessarily relied on in forming his opinion. It may affect the credibility of an expert if he considered and then disregarded evidence favorable to your case in arriving at an opinion favorable to your opponent." La. Prac. Civ. Trial § 7:92.

until the U.S. Supreme Court revisited the issue in *Daubert v. Merrell Dow Pharmaceuticals*, 113 S. Ct. 2786 (1993).

Current Standard/*Daubert v. Merrell Dow Pharmaceuticals*. In *Daubert* (below), the United States Supreme Court rejected the *Frye* standard, finding that Federal Rule of Evidence 702 (practically identical to Louisiana's Article 702) contained no requirement of a "general acceptance" test[43] and that there was nothing to indicate Congress' intent to adopt that standard. The *Daubert* Court noted that "[t]he drafting history makes no mention of *Frye*, and a rigid 'general acceptance' requirement would be at odds with the 'liberal thrust' of the Federal Rules and their general approach of relaxing the traditional barriers to 'opinion' testimony."[44]

Thus, as an alternative to the *Frye* standard, the *Daubert* Court imposed a requirement on **trial courts** to determine the admissibility of scientific evidence by acting in **a "gatekeeping" role** to ensure that scientific evidence is both relevant and reliable.[45] It held that in doing so, the court should make a preliminary determination as to whether the evidence "relates to 'scientific knowledge,'" and will "assist the trier of fact to understand the evidence or to determine a fact in issue."[46] In other words, the *Daubert* Court reasoned that rather than looking to the scientific community to determine the reliability of scientific methodology, Rule 702 assigns the trial judge the task of ensuring that an expert's testimony rests on reliable foundation and is relevant to the task at hand.

Under the *Daubert* standard, in order to be admissible, scientific evidence must meet two basic requirements:

1. It must be ***"relevant"*** to the task at hand; and
2. It must be shown to be ***"reliable,"*** or more specifically, ***"scientifically valid."***

The Relevancy Requirement. In this prong of the analysis, the court must ensure that the evidence is "sufficiently tied to the facts of the case that it will aid the jury in resolving a factual dispute."[47] "Expert testimony which does not relate to any issue in the case is not relevant and, ergo, non-helpful."[48] The court noted an illustration that if an issue in a case is whether it was dark on a certain night, then an expert on the phases of the moon could testify to whether there was moonlight on that particular night. Such testimony would "fit" the facts of the case. However, the expert would not be able to testify that a person behaved irrationally based on the phase the moon was in on that night.[49] This expert testimony would not *fit* the facts of the case, i.e., it would not be relevant to the task at hand, or otherwise "aid the jury in resolving a factual dispute." "Rule 702's 'helpfulness' standard requires a valid scientific connection to the pertinent inquiry as a precondition to admissibility."[50]

The Reliability Requirement. Additionally, the Court held, to be admissible the reasoning and methodology used must be reliable. In order to be reliable, the scientific reasoning

---

43. *See* Daubert v. Merrell Dow Pharmaceuticals, 509 U.S. 579, 588 (1993).

44. *Id.*; Beech Aircraft Corp. v. Rainey, 488 U.S. 153, at 169 (citing Rules 701 to 705).

45. *See* Daubert v. Merrell Dow Pharmaceuticals, 509 U.S. 579 (1993); *See also* Force & Rault, Handbook, Art. 702 Author's Comments (5).

46. *See* Daubert v. Merrell Dow Pharmaceuticals, 509 U.S. 579 (1993).

47. *See* Force & Rault, Handbook, Art. 702 Author's Comments (6).

48. *Daubert*, 509 U.S. at 591 (1993).

49. *Daubert*, 509 U.S. at 591 (1993).

50. *Daubert*, 509 U.S. at 592 (1993).

and methodology used must be **"scientifically valid"** and must constitute "scientific knowledge." The court developed the following factors to be used in determining the scientific validity of the reasoning and methodology underlying expert testimony.[51]

1. Can and has the method been reliably **tested**?
2. Has the theory or technique been subject to **peer review** and **publication**?
3. The known or potential **rate of error**.
4. The existence and maintenance of **standards** controlling the techniques operation.
5. Identification of a relevant scientific community and an express determination of whether the technique has become **generally accepted** within that scientific community.

Expounding on these factors, the Court noted that if a method has been tested, it is certainly more likely to be reliable. Similarly, if the methodology has been subject to the scrutiny of peers in the scientific community, then any substantive flaws in the methodology would likely have been detected. A low rate of error would also contribute to the reliability of the techniques. Additionally, courts can consider whether there are any standards controlling the techniques, such as any that might be imposed by a professional organization or otherwise. Finally, the Court maintained the general acceptance standard of *Frye* as only a relevant factor rather than the sole issue for determining admissibility. "The fact that a theory or technique is widely accepted can be an important factor in favor of admissibility,"[52] whereas "a known technique which has been able to attract only minimal support within the community"[53] may properly be viewed with skepticism.[54]

The Court reasoned that the factors above were **not exclusive** and that courts should also apply any other factors that could aid in assessing the scientific validity of the scientific methodology used by experts.[55] Congress subsequently amended Federal Rule of Evidence 702 to incorporate the *Daubert* standard.[56]

Louisiana adopts *Daubert* Standard. In *State v. Foret*, 628 So. 2d 1116 (La. 1993) (below), Louisiana adopted the requirements of *Daubert* to be used in assessing the reliability of methodology used by experts. Recognizing the fact that Louisiana's Code of Evidence art. 702 is virtually identical to the Federal Rule of Evidence 702, the court noted:

> "similarity between the federal and Louisiana rules on the admission of expert testimony, coupled with similar guidelines for the admissibility of expert scientific testimony pronounced by this court in *Catanese,* persuade this court to adopt *Daubert*'s requirement that expert scientific testimony must rise to a threshold level of reliability in order to be admissible under La.C.E. art. 702. As we find the *Daubert* court's 'observations' on what will help to determine this threshold

---

51. *See Daubert*, 509 U.S. at 592–595 (1993).

52. Force & Rault, Handbook, Art. 702 Author's Comments (6).

53. *Daubert*, 509 U.S. at 595 (1993) (citing *Downing*, 753 F.2d at 1238).

54. *Id.*

55. *See, e.g.*, Daubert v. Merrell Dow Pharmaceuticals, 43 F.3d 1311 (9th Cir.1995), on remand from the U.S. Supreme Court also considered whether the technique "grows naturally out of work that the testifying expert was conducting independently, or was developed specifically for the litigation" as another factor in determining the reliability of the scientific evidence offered in *Daubert.*

56. *See* Fed. R. Evid. 702 (amended 2000).

level of reliability to be an effective guide, we shall adopt these 'observations,' as well."[57]

Thus in Louisiana the threshold requirement for the admissibility of scientific evidence is that the methodology must be **reliable** under the *Daubert* standard. In the 2014 regular legislative session, Article 702 was amended to its current version[58] to specifically incorporate the reliability requirements into the statute. As noted above, Article 702 now reads as follows:

> A witness who is qualified as an expert by knowledge, skill, experience, training, or education may testify in the form of an opinion or otherwise if:
>
> (1) The expert's scientific, technical, or other specialized knowledge will help the trier of fact to understand the evidence or to determine a fact in issue;
>
> (2) The testimony is based on sufficient facts or data;
>
> (3) The testimony is the product of reliable principles and methods; and
>
> (4) The expert has reliably applied the principles and methods to the facts of the case.

In addition to the helpfulness requirement in Article 702(1), providing that the expert's scientific, technical, or other specialized knowledge must "**help the trier of fact** to understand the evidence or to determine a fact in issue;" Article 702(2)–(4) address requirements affecting the reliability of the testimony consistent with *Daubert*. Article 702(2) requires that the testimony be based on "**sufficient facts or data**." Article 702(3) sets forth the reliability requirement, providing that the testimony be the product of **reliable principles and methods**. Finally, Article 702(4) sets forth the requirement that the expert has **reliably applied** the principles and methods to the facts of the case.

While the statute does not specifically list the *Daubert* factors, the factors remain relevant law in determining the reliability of scientific evidence under Louisiana law.[59] The Louisiana courts have held that "the factors to be applied by the trial court in performing its role as gate keeper" should not be applied mechanically and that even if one of the factors is not satisfied, the evidence should not be automatically excluded."[60] With the 2014 amendment, Louisiana's law is now identical to the Federal Rule again.

Application of *Daubert* in Louisiana. Since the adoption of the *Daubert* standard in Louisiana, a number of courts have been called upon to determine the admissibility of scientific evidence. Louisiana courts "have used the *Daubert/Foret* analysis to allow expert testimony about the causes of silicosis,[61] whether an automobile restraint system caused

---

57. State v. Foret, 628 So. 2d 1116, 1123 (La. 1993).

58. Prior to the 2014 amendment, La. Code Evid. art. 702 read as follows:

Art. 702. Testimony by experts

If scientific, technical, or other specialized knowledge will assist the trier of fact to understand the evidence or to determine a fact in issue, a witness qualified as an expert by knowledge, skill, experience, training, or education, may testify thereto in the form of an opinion or otherwise.

59. Cases using *Daubert* factors: *See* Clement v. Griffin, 634 So. 2d 412, 432 (La. Ct. App. 4th Cir. 1994).

60. Force & Rault, Handbook, Art. 702 Author's Comments (6); *See also* Young v. Logue, 660 So. 2d 32, 50 (La. Ct. App. 4th Cir. 1995).

61. Young v. Logue, 660 So. 2d 32 (La. Ct. App. 4th Cir. 1995).

an occupant's injuries,[62] the causes of an automobile battery explosion,[63] about the reliability of DNA evidence,[64] and about firearms identification and examination,[65] [and] the pattern of injuries sustained by the victim during a car accident."[66]

Similarly, in a number of decisions, Louisiana courts have excluded expert testimony under the *Daubert/Foret* analysis. For example, courts have excluded "testimony of an expert who desired to testify about a methodology used to determine the cause of a tread separating from a tire,[67] about the cause of a blowout of a tire,[68] that the biodynamic forces resulting from an accident could not have caused particular injuries,[69] as an accident reconstructionist,[70] and about false confessions and the influence of high-control organizations."[71]

***Daubert* standard extended to all expert testimony**. In another important U.S. Supreme Court case, *Kumho Tire Co., Ltd. v. Carmichael*, 119 S. Ct. 1167 (1999), the Court extended *Daubert*'s standard for testing the reliability of scientific evidence to all types of expert testimony, including testimony based on "technical" or "other specialized knowledge." For instance, if a witness will be proffered as an expert in roofing or plumbing, based on his experience, the U.S. Supreme Court has held that the factors should also be applied in these contexts. However, "the factors will not be a definitive checklist." Some of the factors may not be readily applied in a particular situation, and others may need to be added.[72]

Challenging the expert testimony. An attorney who wishes to challenge the scientific validity of the methodology used by an expert, should file a motion to exclude expert testimony or a motion for a *Daubert* hearing, which must be held pre-trial in civil cases.[73] At that time the court can consider the scientific validity of the methodology used by the

62. Harges, *citing* Fussell v. Roadrunner Towing and Recovery, Inc., 765 So. 2d 373 (La. Ct. App. 1st Cir. 2000) (finding that trial court committed reversible error when it refused to allow expert to determine speed and acceleration rate of wrecker and whether injury was consistent with those forces); Perret v. Nelson, 722 So. 2d 1118 (La. Ct. App. 5th Cir. 1998) (allowing expert in accident reconstruction to testify about tests used to calculate G forces on a car during a collision); Dufrene v. Willingham, 721 So. 2d 1026, 1031 (La. Ct. App. 5th Cir. 1998) (*Daubert* nor *Foret* prevents experts in accident reconstruction from testifying although they are "hired guns"); Boutte v. Nissan Motor Corp., 663 So. 2d 154 (La. Ct. App. 3d Cir. 1995).

63. Citing Hickman v. Exide, Inc., 679 So. 2d 527 (La. Ct. App. 2d Cir. 1996).

64. Citing State v. Ledet, 792 So. 2d 160 (La. Ct. App. 5th Cir. 2001); Hays v. State, 856 So. 2d 64 (La. Ct. App. 2d Cir. 2003) (toxicity characteristic leaching procedure was properly admitted by trial judge).

65. Citing State v. Williams, 974 So. 2d 157 (La. Ct. App. 2d Cir. 2008).

66. Harges & Jones, Louisiana Evidence Art. 702; Author's Comments *citing*, State v. Knight, 36 So. 3d 1163 (La. Ct. App. 2d Cir. 2010).

67. Citing Mitchell v. Uniroyal Goodrich Tire Co., Inc., 666 So. 2d 727 (La. Ct. App. 4th Cir. 1995).

68. Citing Clement v. Griffin, 634 So. 2d 412, 426–428, (La. Ct. App. 4th Cir. 1994).

69. Citing, Davis v. Martel, 790 So. 2d 767 (La. Ct. App. 3d Cir. 2001).

70. Citing Garcia v. Louisiana Dept. of Transp. and Development, 787 So. 2d 1142 (La. Ct. App. 4th Cir. 2001); Locke v. Young, 973 So. 2d 831 (La. Ct. App. 2d Cir. 2007).

71. Harges & Jones, Louisiana Evidence Art. 702; Author's Comments *citing*, State v. Lamonica, 44 So. 3d 895 (La. Ct. App. 1st Cir. 2010) (finding lower court properly excluded expert testimony regarding false confessions and the influence of high-control organizations when such testimony failed to satisfy the Daubert standards and would have added nothing to enhance the jury's understanding of the facts but instead would have only confused the issues).

72. Force & Rault, Handbook, Art. 702 Author's Comments (6); *See also* Isla Resources, LLC v. Frey, 931 So. 2d 1233 (La. Ct. App. 3d Cir. 2006).

73. *See* La. C.C. Pr. art. 1425 (F) (as amended 2008). There is no such requirement for criminal cases.

expert and make a ruling on the reliability and therefore admissibility of the expert testimony. A *Daubert* hearing is conducted outside of the presence of a jury.

While challenges to the reliability of the expert testimony go the admissibility of the expert testimony, other challenges to the expert's findings go to the weight that the trier of fact will give to the expert testimony. For example, if a party calls an expert and it is determined that the expert was mistaken or misinterpreted an underlying fact upon which he based a conclusion, that issue does not make the expert's testimony inadmissible. The information will only go to the weight in which the trier of fact will give to the expert's testimony.

The same is true for other issues bearing on the expert's credibility, as in *Pyles* above, where the expert who testified to security measures had been previously disbarred from the practice of law. Such issues go to the weight to give to the expert's opinion, not to the admissibility of his testimony. The expert witness's testimony is excluded only if his testimony is not reliable, determined by whether or not their methodology is scientifically valid.

Additionally, keep in mind that a *Daubert* hearing is not the same as qualifying a witness as an expert. A *Daubert* hearing is a challenge to the expert's methodologies, not his qualifications.

Louisiana Supreme Court summarized requirements for expert testimony. *Cheairs v. La. Dept. of Transportation & Development*, 861 So. 2d 536 (La. 2003). In order to clarify and simplify full compliance with all issues and requirements related to the admissibility of expert witness testimony, the Louisiana Supreme Court set forth a three-part inquiry, all of which must be met to admit an expert's testimony:

(1) the expert is qualified to testify competently regarding the matters he intends to address;

(2) the methodology by which the expert reaches his conclusions is sufficiently reliable as determined by the sort of inquiry mandated in *Daubert*; and

(3) the testimony assists the trier of fact, through the application of scientific, technical, or specialized expertise, to understand the evidence or to determine a fact in issue.[74]

Cases on Reliability of Scientific Principles

Daubert v. Merrell Dow Pharmaceuticals, Inc.

Supreme Court of the United States
509 U.S. 579, 113 S. Ct. 2786
June 28, 1993

Justice BLACKMUN delivered the opinion of the Court.

In this case we are called upon to determine the standard for admitting expert scientific testimony in a federal trial.

I

Petitioners Jason Daubert and Eric Schuller are minor children born with serious birth defects. They and their parents sued respondent in California state court, alleging that the birth defects had been caused by the mothers' ingestion of Bendectin, a prescription

74. Cheairs v. La. Dept. of Transportation & Development, 861 So. 2d 536, 542 (La. 2003).

antinausea drug marketed by respondent. Respondent removed the suits to federal court on diversity grounds.

After extensive discovery, respondent moved for summary judgment, contending that Bendectin does not cause birth defects in humans and that petitioners would be unable to come forward with any admissible evidence that it does. In support of its motion, respondent submitted an affidavit of Steven H. Lamm, physician and epidemiologist, who is a well-credentialed expert on the risks from exposure to various chemical substances. Doctor Lamm stated that he had reviewed all the literature on Bendectin and human birth defects—more than 30 published studies involving over 130,000 patients. No study had found Bendectin to be a human teratogen (*i.e.*, a substance capable of causing malformations in fetuses). On the basis of this review, Doctor Lamm concluded that maternal use of Bendectin during the first trimester of pregnancy has not been shown to be a risk factor for human birth defects.

Petitioners did not (and do not) contest this characterization of the published record regarding Bendectin. Instead, they responded to respondent's motion with the testimony of eight experts of their own, each of whom also possessed impressive credentials. These experts had concluded that Bendectin can cause birth defects. Their conclusions were based upon "in vitro" (test tube) and "in vivo" (live) animal studies that found a link between Bendectin and malformations; pharmacological studies of the chemical structure of Bendectin that purported to show similarities between the structure of the drug and that of other substances known to cause birth defects; and the "reanalysis" of previously published epidemiological (human statistical) studies.

The District Court granted respondent's motion for summary judgment. The court stated that scientific evidence is admissible only if the principle upon which it is based is " 'sufficiently established to have general acceptance in the field to which it belongs.' " The court concluded that petitioners' evidence did not meet this standard. Given the vast body of epidemiological data concerning Bendectin, the court held, expert opinion which is not based on epidemiological evidence is not admissible to establish causation. Thus, the animal-cell studies, live-animal studies, and chemical-structure analyses on which petitioners had relied could not raise by themselves a reasonably disputable jury issue regarding causation. Petitioners' epidemiological analyses, based as they were on recalculations of data in previously published studies that had found no causal link between the drug and birth defects, were ruled to be inadmissible because they had not been published or subjected to peer review.

The United States Court of Appeals for the Ninth Circuit affirmed. Citing *Frye v. United States*, 54 App.D.C. 46, 47, 293 F. 1013, 1014 (1923), the court stated that expert opinion based on a scientific technique is inadmissible unless the technique is "generally accepted" as reliable in the relevant scientific community. The court declared that expert opinion based on a methodology that diverges "significantly from the procedures accepted by recognized authorities in the field ... cannot be shown to be 'generally accepted as a reliable technique.' "

The court emphasized that other Courts of Appeals considering the risks of Bendectin had refused to admit reanalyses of epidemiological studies that had been neither published nor subjected to peer review. Those courts had found unpublished reanalyses "particularly problematic in light of the massive weight of the original published studies supporting [respondent's] position, all of which had undergone full scrutiny from the scientific community." Contending that reanalysis is generally accepted by the scientific community only when it is subjected to verification and scrutiny by others in the field, the Court of

Appeals rejected petitioners' reanalyses as "unpublished, not subjected to the normal peer review process and generated solely for use in litigation." The court concluded that petitioners' evidence provided an insufficient foundation to allow admission of expert testimony that Bendectin caused their injuries and, accordingly, that petitioners could not satisfy their burden of proving causation at trial.

We granted certiorari, in light of sharp divisions among the courts regarding the proper standard for the admission of expert testimony.

II

A

In the 70 years since its formulation in the *Frye* case, the "general acceptance" test has been the dominant standard for determining the admissibility of novel scientific evidence at trial. Although under increasing attack of late, the rule continues to be followed by a majority of courts, including the Ninth Circuit. The *Frye* test has its origin in a short and citation-free 1923 decision concerning the admissibility of evidence derived from a systolic blood pressure deception test, a crude precursor to the polygraph machine. In what has become a famous (perhaps infamous) passage, the then Court of Appeals for the District of Columbia described the device and its operation and declared:

> "Just when a scientific principle or discovery crosses the line between the experimental and demonstrable stages is difficult to define. Somewhere in this twilight zone the evidential force of the principle must be recognized, and while courts will go a long way in admitting expert testimony deduced from a well-recognized scientific principle or discovery, the thing from which the deduction is made must be sufficiently established to have gained general acceptance in the particular field in which it belongs."

Because the deception test had "not yet gained such standing and scientific recognition among physiological and psychological authorities as would justify the courts in admitting expert testimony deduced from the discovery, development, and experiments thus far made," evidence of its results was ruled inadmissible.

The merits of the *Frye* test have been much debated, and scholarship on its proper scope and application is legion. [Court cites article in footnote]

Petitioners' primary attack, however, is not on the content but on the continuing authority of the rule. They contend that the *Frye* test was superseded by the adoption of the Federal Rules of Evidence. We agree.

We interpret the legislatively enacted Federal Rules of Evidence as we would any statute. *Beech Aircraft Corp. v. Rainey*, 488 U.S. 153 (1988). Rule 402 provides the baseline:

> "All relevant evidence is admissible, except as otherwise provided by the Constitution of the United States, by Act of Congress, by these rules, or by other rules prescribed by the Supreme Court pursuant to statutory authority. Evidence which is not relevant is not admissible."

"Relevant evidence" is defined as that which has "any tendency to make the existence of any fact that is of consequence to the determination of the action more probable or less probable than it would be without the evidence." Rule 401. The Rule's basic standard of relevance thus is a liberal one.

Frye, of course, predated the Rules by half a century. In *United States v. Abel,* 469 U.S. 45 (1984), we considered the pertinence of background common law in interpreting the Rules of Evidence. We noted that the Rules occupy the field, but, quoting Professor Cleary, the Reporter, explained that the common law nevertheless could serve as an aid to their application:

> "'In principle, under the Federal Rules no common law of evidence remains. "All relevant evidence is admissible, except as otherwise provided...." In reality, of course, the body of common law knowledge continues to exist, though in the somewhat altered form of a source of guidance in the exercise of delegated powers.'"

We found the common-law precept at issue in the *Abel* case entirely consistent with Rule 402's general requirement of admissibility, and considered it unlikely that the drafters had intended to change the rule. In *Bourjaily v. United States*, 483 U.S. 171 (1987), on the other hand, the Court was unable to find a particular common-law doctrine in the Rules, and so held it superseded.

Here there is a specific Rule that speaks to the contested issue. Rule 702, governing expert testimony, provides:

> "If scientific, technical, or other specialized knowledge will assist the trier of fact to understand the evidence or to determine a fact in issue, a witness qualified as an expert by knowledge, skill, experience, training, or education, may testify thereto in the form of an opinion or otherwise."

Nothing in the text of this Rule establishes "general acceptance" as an absolute prerequisite to admissibility. Nor does respondent present any clear indication that Rule 702 or the Rules as a whole were intended to incorporate a "general acceptance" standard. The drafting history makes no mention of *Frye*, and a rigid "general acceptance" requirement would be at odds with the "liberal thrust" of the Federal Rules and their "general approach of relaxing the traditional barriers to 'opinion' testimony." *Beech Aircraft Corp. v. Rainey* (citing Rules 701 to 705). See also Weinstein, Rule 702 of the Federal Rules of Evidence is Sound; It Should Not Be Amended, 138 F.R.D. 631 (1991) ("The Rules were designed to depend primarily upon lawyer-adversaries and sensible triers of fact to evaluate conflicts"). Given the Rules' permissive backdrop and their inclusion of a specific rule on expert testimony that does not mention "'general acceptance,'" the assertion that the Rules somehow assimilated *Frye* is unconvincing. *Frye* made "general acceptance" the exclusive test for admitting expert scientific testimony. That austere standard, absent from, and incompatible with, the Federal Rules of Evidence, should not be applied in federal trials.

B

That the *Frye* test was displaced by the Rules of Evidence does not mean, however, that the Rules themselves place no limits on the admissibility of purportedly scientific evidence.[75] Nor is the trial judge disabled from screening such evidence. To the contrary, under the Rules the trial judge must ensure that any and all scientific testimony or evidence admitted is not only relevant, but reliable.

The primary locus of this obligation is Rule 702, which clearly contemplates some degree of regulation of the subjects and theories about which an expert may testify. "*If scientific,* technical, or other specialized *knowledge will assist the trier of fact* to understand the evidence or to determine a fact in issue" an expert "may testify *thereto.*" The subject of an expert's testimony must be "scientific ... knowledge." The adjective "scientific"

75. THE CHIEF JUSTICE "do[es] not doubt that Rule 702 confides to the judge some gatekeeping responsibility," *post*, at 2800, but would neither say how it does so nor explain what that role entails. We believe the better course is to note the nature and source of the duty.

implies a grounding in the methods and procedures of science. Similarly, the word "knowledge" connotes more than subjective belief or unsupported speculation. The term "applies to any body of known facts or to any body of ideas inferred from such facts or accepted as truths on good grounds." Webster's Third New International Dictionary 1252 (1986). Of course, it would be unreasonable to conclude that the subject of scientific testimony must be "known" to a certainty; arguably, there are no certainties in science. See, *e.g.*, Brief for Nicolaas Bloembergen et al. as *Amici Curiae* 9 ("Indeed, scientists do not assert that they know what is immutably 'true'—they are committed to searching for new, temporary, theories to explain, as best they can, phenomena"); Brief for American Association for the Advancement of Science et al. as *Amici Curiae* 7–8 ("Science is not an encyclopedic body of knowledge about the universe. Instead, it represents a *process* for proposing and refining theoretical explanations about the world that are subject to further testing and refinement" (emphasis in original)). But, in order to qualify as "scientific knowledge," an inference or assertion must be derived by the scientific method. Proposed testimony must be supported by appropriate validation—*i.e.*, "good grounds," based on what is known. In short, the requirement that an expert's testimony pertain to " scientific knowledge" establishes a standard of evidentiary reliability.

Rule 702 further requires that the evidence or testimony "assist the trier of fact to understand the evidence or to determine a fact in issue." This condition goes primarily to relevance. " Expert testimony which does not relate to any issue in the case is not relevant and, ergo, non-helpful." 3 Weinstein & Berger ¶ 702[02], p. 702-18. See also *United States v. Downing*, 753 F.2d 1224, 1242 (CA3 1985) ("An additional consideration under Rule 702—and another aspect of relevancy—is whether expert testimony proffered in the case is sufficiently tied to the facts of the case that it will aid the jury in resolving a factual dispute"). The consideration has been aptly described by Judge Becker as one of "fit." *Ibid.* "Fit" is not always obvious, and scientific validity for one purpose is not necessarily scientific validity for other, unrelated purposes. See Starrs, *Frye v. United States* Restructured and Revitalized: A Proposal to Amend Federal Evidence Rule 702, 26 Jurimetrics J. 249, 258 (1986). The study of the phases of the moon, for example, may provide valid scientific "knowledge" about whether a certain night was dark, and if darkness is a fact in issue, the knowledge will assist the trier of fact. However (absent creditable grounds supporting such a link), evidence that the moon was full on a certain night will not assist the trier of fact in determining whether an individual was unusually likely to have behaved irrationally on that night. Rule 702's "helpfulness" standard requires a valid scientific connection to the pertinent inquiry as a precondition to admissibility.

That these requirements are embodied in Rule 702 is not surprising. Unlike an ordinary witness, see Rule 701, an expert is permitted wide latitude to offer opinions, including those that are not based on firsthand knowledge or observation. See Rules 702 and 703. Presumably, this relaxation of the usual requirement of firsthand knowledge—a rule which represents "a 'most pervasive manifestation' of the common law insistence upon 'the most reliable sources of information,'" Advisory Committee's Notes on Fed.Rule Evid. 602, 28 U.S.C.App., p. 755 (citation omitted)—is premised on an assumption that the expert's opinion will have a reliable basis in the knowledge and experience of his discipline.

C

Faced with a proffer of expert scientific testimony, then, the trial judge must determine at the outset, pursuant to Rule 104(a), whether the expert is proposing to testify to (1) scientific knowledge that (2) will assist the trier of fact to understand or determine a fact in issue. This entails a preliminary assessment of whether the reasoning or methodology underlying the testimony is scientifically valid and of whether that reasoning or methodology properly can be applied to the facts in issue. We are confident that federal judges possess the capacity to undertake this review. Many factors will bear on the inquiry, and we do not presume to set out a definitive checklist or test. But some general observations are appropriate.

Ordinarily, a key question to be answered in determining whether a theory or technique is scientific knowledge that will assist the trier of fact will be whether it can be (and has been) tested. "Scientific methodology today is based on generating hypotheses and testing them to see if they can be falsified; indeed, this methodology is what distinguishes science from other fields of human inquiry." Green 645. See also C. Hempel, Philosophy of Natural Science 49 (1966) ("[T]he statements constituting a scientific explanation must be capable of empirical test"); K. Popper, Conjectures and Refutations: The Growth of Scientific Knowledge 37 (5th ed. 1989) ("[T]he criterion of the scientific status of a theory is its falsifiability, or refutability, or testability").

Another pertinent consideration is whether the theory or technique has been subjected to peer review and publication. Publication (which is but one element of peer review) is not a *sine qua non* of admissibility; it does not necessarily correlate with reliability, see S. Jasanoff, The Fifth Branch: Science Advisors as Policymakers 61–76 (1990), and in some instances well-grounded but innovative theories will not have been published, see Horrobin, The Philosophical Basis of Peer Review and the Suppression of Innovation, 263 JAMA 1438 (1990). Some propositions, moreover, are too particular, too new, or of too limited interest to be published. But submission to the scrutiny of the scientific community is a component of "good science," in part because it increases the likelihood that substantive flaws in methodology will be detected. See J. Ziman, Reliable Knowledge: An Exploration of the Grounds for Belief in Science 130–133 (1978); Relman & Angell, How Good Is Peer Review?, 321 New Eng.J.Med. 827 (1989). The fact of publication (or lack thereof) in a peer reviewed journal thus will be a relevant, though not dispositive, consideration in assessing the scientific validity of a particular technique or methodology on which an opinion is premised.

Additionally, in the case of a particular scientific technique, the court ordinarily should consider the known or potential rate of error, see, *e.g., United States v. Smith*, 869 F.2d 348, 353–354 (CA7 1989) (surveying studies of the error rate of spectrographic voice identification technique), and the existence and maintenance of standards controlling the technique's operation, see *United States v. Williams*, 583 F.2d 1194, 1198 (CA2 1978) (noting professional organization's standard governing spectrographic analysis), cert. denied, 439 U.S. 1117, 99 S.Ct. 1025, 59 L.Ed.2d 77 (1979).

Finally, "general acceptance" can yet have a bearing on the inquiry. A "reliability assessment does not require, although it does permit, explicit identification of a relevant scientific community and an express determination of a particular degree of acceptance within that community." *Downing*. Widespread acceptance can be an important factor in ruling particular evidence admissible, and "a known technique which has been able to attract only minimal support within the community," *Downing*, may properly be viewed with skepticism.

The inquiry envisioned by Rule 702 is, we emphasize, a flexible one. Its overarching subject is the scientific validity and thus the evidentiary relevance and reliability of the principles that underlie a proposed submission. The focus, of course, must be solely on principles and methodology, not on the conclusions that they generate.

Throughout, a judge assessing a proffer of expert scientific testimony under Rule 702 should also be mindful of other applicable rules. Rule 703 provides that expert opinions based on otherwise inadmissible hearsay are to be admitted only if the facts or data are "of a type reasonably relied upon by experts in the particular field in forming opinions or inferences upon the subject." Rule 706 allows the court at its discretion to procure the assistance of an expert of its own choosing. Finally, Rule 403 permits the exclusion of relevant evidence "if its probative value is substantially outweighed by the danger of unfair prejudice, confusion of the issues, or misleading the jury...." Judge Weinstein has explained: "Expert evidence can be both powerful and quite misleading because of the difficulty in evaluating it. Because of this risk, the judge in weighing possible prejudice against probative force under Rule 403 of the present rules exercises more control over experts than over lay witnesses." Weinstein, 138 F.R.D., at 632.

III

We conclude by briefly addressing what appear to be two underlying concerns of the parties and *amici* in this case. Respondent expresses apprehension that abandonment of "general acceptance" as the exclusive requirement for admission will result in a "free-for-all" in which befuddled juries are confounded by absurd and irrational pseudoscientific assertions. In this regard respondent seems to us to be overly pessimistic about the capabilities of the jury and of the adversary system generally. Vigorous cross-examination, presentation of contrary evidence, and careful instruction on the burden of proof are the traditional and appropriate means of attacking shaky but admissible evidence. See *Rock v. Arkansas*, 483 U.S. 44, 61 (1987). Additionally, in the event the trial court concludes that the scintilla of evidence presented supporting a position is insufficient to allow a reasonable juror to conclude that the position more likely than not is true, the court remains free to direct a judgment, Fed.Rule Civ.Proc. 50(a), and likewise to grant summary judgment, Fed.Rule Civ.Proc. 56.... These conventional devices, rather than wholesale exclusion under an uncompromising "general acceptance" test, are the appropriate safeguards where the basis of scientific testimony meets the standards of Rule 702.

Petitioners and, to a greater extent, their *amici* exhibit a different concern. They suggest that recognition of a screening role for the judge that allows for the exclusion of "invalid" evidence will sanction a stifling and repressive scientific orthodoxy and will be inimical to the search for truth. See, *e.g.*, Brief for Ronald Bayer et al. as *Amici Curiae*. It is true that open debate is an essential part of both legal and scientific analyses. Yet there are important differences between the quest for truth in the courtroom and the quest for truth in the laboratory. Scientific conclusions are subject to perpetual revision. Law, on the other hand, must resolve disputes finally and quickly. The scientific project is advanced by broad and wide-ranging consideration of a multitude of hypotheses, for those that are incorrect will eventually be shown to be so, and that in itself is an advance. Conjectures that are probably wrong are of little use, however, in the project of reaching a quick, final, and binding legal judgment—often of great consequence—about a particular set of events in the past. We recognize that, in practice, a gatekeeping role for the judge, no matter how flexible, inevitably on occasion will prevent the jury from learning of authentic insights and innovations. That, nevertheless, is the balance that is struck by Rules of Evidence designed not for the exhaustive search for cosmic understanding but for the particularized resolution of legal disputes.

IV

To summarize: "General acceptance" is not a necessary precondition to the admissibility of scientific evidence under the Federal Rules of Evidence, but the Rules of Evidence—especially Rule 702—do assign to the trial judge the task of ensuring that an expert's testimony both rests on a reliable foundation and is relevant to the task at hand. Pertinent evidence based on scientifically valid principles will satisfy those demands.

The inquiries of the District Court and the Court of Appeals focused almost exclusively on "general acceptance," as gauged by publication and the decisions of other courts. Accordingly, the judgment of the Court of Appeals is vacated, and the case is remanded for further proceedings consistent with this opinion.

It is so ordered.

Chief Justice REHNQUIST, with whom Justice STEVENS joins, concurring in part and dissenting in part.

The petition for certiorari in this case presents two questions: first, whether the rule of *Frye v. United States*, 54 App.D.C. 46, 293 F. 1013 (1923), remains good law after the enactment of the Federal Rules of Evidence; and second, if *Frye* remains valid, whether it requires expert scientific testimony to have been subjected to a peer review process in order to be admissible. The Court concludes, correctly in my view, that the *Frye* rule did not survive the enactment of the Federal Rules of Evidence, and I therefore join Parts I and II-A of its opinion. The second question presented in the petition for certiorari necessarily is mooted by this holding, but the Court nonetheless proceeds to construe Rules 702 and 703 very much in the abstract, and then offers some "general observations."

"General observations" by this Court customarily carry great weight with lower federal courts, but the ones offered here suffer from the flaw common to most such observations—they are not applied to deciding whether particular testimony was or was not admissible, and therefore they tend to be not only general, but vague and abstract. This is particularly unfortunate in a case such as this, where the ultimate legal question depends on an appreciation of one or more bodies of knowledge not judicially noticeable, and subject to different interpretations in the briefs of the parties and their *amici*. Twenty-two *amicus* briefs have been filed in the case, and indeed the Court's opinion contains no fewer than 37 citations to *amicus* briefs and other secondary sources....

I do not doubt that Rule 702 confides to the judge some gatekeeping responsibility in deciding questions of the admissibility of proffered expert testimony. But I do not think it imposes on them either the obligation or the authority to become amateur scientists in order to perform that role. I think the Court would be far better advised in this case to decide only the questions presented, and to leave the further development of this important area of the law to future cases.

Discussion Questions

1. Why do you suppose the *Frye* "general acceptance" test remained the prominent standard for determining the admissibility of novel scientific evidence at trial for more than 70 years before the significant change in the law in *Daubert*? Do you think there could be prominent social changes, such as the evolution of science or other factors that could have called for a change in the standard? Explain.
2. Do you think that the *Frye* standard effectively gives the scientific community the task of determining the admissibility of scientific evidence, rather than the court? If so, do you think that was appropriate? Who is in the best position to determine the reliability of scientific evidence, the relevant scientific community or the courts? Explain.
3. *Daubert* places a "gatekeeping" function on the trial court, requiring *courts* to determine the admissibility of scientific evidence. The courts must ensure that the evidence is both relevant and reliable. What factors does the court state must be considered in resolving each of these requirements? How is relevancy determined? How is reliability determined?

4. What does the court mean by "fit"—that the methodology must "fit" the facts at hand? Does the Court's analogy to the phases of the moon provide insight to the fit requirement, i.e., the relevancy prong of the analysis?
5. Explain how each of the factors the court considers for assessing the reliability of the methodology help the trial courts in their assessment of the reliability of the scientific methodology.
    a. Can and has the method been reliably **tested**;
    b. Has the theory or technique been subject to **peer review** and **publication**;
    c. The known or potential **rate of error**;
    d. The existence and maintenance of **standards** controlling the techniques operation; and
    e. Identification of a relevant scientific community and an express determination of whether the technique has become **generally accepted** within that scientific community.
6. In addition to the factors specifically set out in *Daubert*, the court points out that other factors may also be used for determining the scientific reliability of expert testimony. Can you think of any additional factors? In *In re Vioxx Products Liability Litigation*, 414 F. Supp. 2d 574 (E.D. La. 2006), additional factors considered by the court included: (1) whether the expert's opinion is based on incomplete or inaccurate dosage or duration data; (2) whether the expert has identified the specific mechanism by which the drug supposedly causes the alleged disease; (3) whether the expert has unjustifiably extrapolated from an accepted premise to an unfounded conclusion; (4) whether the expert has adequately accounted for alternative explanations; and (5) whether the expert proposes to testify about matters growing directly out of research he or she has conducted independent of the litigation. What do you think of these factors? Can you think of others?[76]

State v. Foret
Supreme Court of Louisiana
628 So. 2d 1116 (La. 1993)

HALL, Justice.

I.

The defendant, Hypolite Foret, was convicted of attempting to molest his step-daughter over a one-and-a-half to two-year period, when the victim was twelve to fourteen years old. The victim testified that the repeated incidences of abuse took place at the family residence when her mother was asleep or not at home. The alleged initial acts of molestation involved hugging, kissing, and rubbing the victim's breasts, culminating with the defendant rubbing under the victim's clothes and inserting his finger into her vagina.

These alleged acts of abuse were discovered upon the return of the victim after she ran away from the family home. The victim had been having problems with both the defendant

76. *See* 1 La. Prac. Pers. Inj. § 3:127.

and her mother, namely that they were strict and steadfastly refused to allow her to date an older (by approximately eight years) boyfriend. Upon her return home, she was interviewed by a child protection worker, Cindy Ordoyne, and, during that interview, she detailed molestations allegedly made by her stepfather. The interview set forth a series of events that resulted in the court-ordered removal of the victim from the family home and the defendant being charged with molestation of a juvenile.

At trial, the defendant denied that he had abused the victim, but believed that she might have been abused by someone else. He admitted that he may have touched the victim's private parts, but maintained that the touching occurred accidentally during horseplay or tickling....

The state offered two expert witnesses to support its case-in-chief. The first was a physician qualified as an expert in the field of family medicine, who testified that, although an examination of the victim after the abuse was reported yielded no positive physical evidence of abuse, the lack of positive physical evidence of abuse was not unusual in this type of case. The second witness was a child psychologist, Dr. William Janzen, Ph.D., who was qualified as an expert in the field of psychology with expertise in child sexual abuse. Defendant objected to Dr. Janzen being allowed to testify, claiming that his not being given Dr. Janzen's report until the morning of trial when the state had possessed it for a week prior to trial was a prejudicial discovery violation, as there was insufficient time to prepare an effective cross-examination of the expert. This objection was overruled.

Dr. Janzen testified that he interviewed the victim on three separate occasions and concluded that, in his expert opinion, she was telling the truth about being the victim of sexual abuse. He based his conclusions on the following: the victim gave detailed accounts of the acts of abuse and conversations she had with the defendant; the victim described common feelings of disgust and sadness; the victim claimed that the defendant was possessive of her and did not want her to be with other boys; the victim felt that she had done something wrong; and, finally, the defendant told her to keep the molestations a secret.

Dr. Janzen explained his methods for evaluation of sexual abuse allegations, focusing on questioning the victim:

> And then on the basis of what I get from the child, the type of detail that I get from the child to make some conclusions about whether or not what she is telling me suggests that she has been sexually abused, or another way of putting it, on the basis of what I get from the child I make some conclusions about whether or not what she is telling me is consistent with what we know about the dynamics of sexual abuse....

The State then posed the following question:

> Doctor, after the interviews you had with [the victim], the testing and the conversations and so on that you had with her, is it your opinion that she was sexually abused?

The defendant objected, claiming that the State was asking the expert to comment upon "the fact and [sic] issue here", but the trial court allowed the question to be answered, simply cautioning the doctor not to "identi[fy] ... any person who may be responsible." Dr. Janzen then answered:

> The details that she gave me are consistent with the dynamics of sexual abuse and so my conclusion would, therefore, be that she has been sexually abused and should be in counseling to help her cope with that.

Later summing up his direct examination, Dr. Janzen noted that, given the details related to him by the victim and considering the various dynamics of sexual abuse, his "only conclusion" was that the victim had "been sexually abused."

Based largely on the testimony of the victim, as bolstered by Dr. Janzen, the jury returned a verdict of guilty of attempted molestation.

II.

Prior to trial, defendant moved for discovery of all reports of examinations and tests that were made by the State, pursuant to La.C.Cr.P. art. 719:

> Upon motion of the defendant, the court shall order the district attorney to permit or authorize the defendant to inspect and copy ... any results or reports ... of physical or mental examination, and of scientific tests or experiments, made in connection with or material to the particular case, that are in the possession, custody, control, or knowledge of the district attorney and intended for use at trial.
>
> ...

The report in question was dated September 29, 1991, and was mailed to the State on October 2, 1991. The appellate court determined that at the earliest, the state would have received the report the day after it was mailed, and, thus, had the report for seven days before giving it to defendant on the morning of trial. Although the report was not promptly given to the defendant, the appellate court was unwilling to find reversible error for the violation in the absence of a showing of actual prejudice to the defendant.

The court of appeal focused on prejudice arising from the defendant's inability to proffer his own expert to rebut Dr. Janzen. It held that the failure of the defendant to make a specific showing as to how another expert would have been able to attack the findings of the psychologist was fatal. The court of appeal failed, however, to focus on the inherent prejudice of the last minute disclosure in precluding adequate time to prepare to rebut the expert's testimony either by effective cross-examination or by offering the testimony of a defense expert. Perhaps more importantly, the court of appeal failed to consider whether this type of expert testimony was itself properly admitted into evidence, considering the significant problems that this type of testimony has created in other jurisdictions as recognized by reservations expressed by the concurring Justices in *State v. Brossette*, 599 So.2d 1092 (La.1992) (Dennis and Hall, JJ., concurring):

> ... the introduction of expert opinion testimony as to the psychological characteristics of the victim or her testimony is fraught with serious res nova constitutional and evidentiary problems. While this type of evidence is absolutely not admissible for some purposes ... but might be admissible for others, it should be allowed only after careful study and under strict control by the trial court....

The reluctance to embrace this kind of testimony was brought on by a fear of prejudice resulting from potential inaccuracy and the undue persuasive value of the very evidence itself, as opposed to whether or not it was properly rebutted. This prejudicial effect might have been avoided if the trial court carefully weighed and controlled this testimony. In this case, however, the tardy disclosure of the report deprived not only the defendant, but also the trial court of the opportunity for "careful study" of the matter so as to limit the expert testimony to the areas in which courts have generally agreed that the probative value of a child sexual abuse profile outweighs its potential for prejudice. In an effort to guide trial courts in the future, we shall explore what commentators and other jurisdictions consider to be the proper, non-prejudicial use of such expert testimony. This necessarily requires us to set out the general guidelines for the admissibility of expert testimony, as well as setting forth guidelines for admission of this particular kind of expert testimony.

III.

La.C.E. art. 702 sets forth the general rule for the admissibility of expert testimony in Louisiana:

> If scientific, technical, or other specialized knowledge will assist the trier of fact to understand the evidence or to determine a fact in issue, a witness qualified as an expert by knowledge, skill, experience, training, or education, may testify thereto in the form of an opinion or otherwise.

As this provision is virtually identical to its source provision in the Federal Rules of Evidence, F.R.E. 702 and in several states' evidentiary rules, we will examine and consider federal jurisprudence and other states' jurisprudence interpreting the proper application of this rule.

"Subsumed in the requirements of Rule 702 is the premise that expert testimony must be reliable to be admissible." A recent United States Supreme Court case, *Daubert v. Merrell Dow Pharmaceuticals, Inc.*, 509 U.S. 579 (1993), set forth a means for determining reliability of expert scientific testimony and answered many questions as to proper standards for admissibility of expert testimony.

In *Daubert,* the court was concerned with determining the admissibility of new techniques as basis for expert scientific testimony. Formerly, the test for admissibility of expert scientific testimony was based on a "short, citation-free 1928 decision" of the District of Columbia Court of Appeals, *Frye v. United States*, 54 App.D.C. 46, 293 F. 1013 (1923). In *Frye,* the rule for admissibility of expert testimony was delineated as requiring "general acceptance" of a technique in its respective scientific field before the technique is considered admissible. Finding that "a rigid 'general acceptance' requirement would be at odds with 'the liberal thrust of the Federal Rules'," the Court concluded that *Frye*'s "austere standard, absent from and incompatible with [this liberal thrust] should not be applied in federal trials."

The court replaced *Frye* with a new standard that requires the trial court to act in a "gatekeeping" function to "ensure that any and all scientific testimony or evidence admitted is not only relevant, but reliable." This requirement stems from a belief that the rules on expert testimony serve to relax "the usual requirement of first-hand knowledge" to ensure reliability on the part of a witness. This relaxation is justified so long as "the expert's opinion (has) a reliable basis in the knowledge and experience of his discipline."

The reliability of expert testimony is to be ensured by a requirement that there be "a valid scientific connection to the pertinent inquiry as a precondition to admissibility." This connection is to be examined in light of "a preliminary assessment" by the trial court "of whether the reasoning or methodology underlying the testimony is scientifically valid and of whether the reasoning or methodology properly can be applied to the facts in issue." The court went on to make some suggestions as to how a court could fulfill its gatekeeping role. These involve whether or not the technique had been subjected to peer review and/or publication, the "known or potential rate of error", the existence of "standards controlling the technique's operation", the technique's "refutability" or, more simply put, testability, and, finally, an incorporation of the *Frye* general acceptance in the scientific community as only a factor in the analysis.

The court also stated that other rules of evidence govern this testimony, mainly F.R.E. 403's balancing test that will exclude probative evidence if outweighed by its potential for unfair prejudice. The Court noted the possibility that the expert's testimony can be quite misleading and prejudicial if this gatekeeping role is not properly satisfied, requiring a flexible approach and a careful evaluation of the methodology surrounding the testimony and its conclusions:

La.C.E. art. 403 is almost identical:

> Although relevant, evidence may be excluded if its probative value is substantially outweighed by the danger of unfair prejudice, confusion of the issues, or misleading the jury, or by considerations of undue delay, or waste of time.

Conjectures that are probably wrong are of little use, however, in the project of reaching a quick, final, and binding legal judgment—often of great consequence—about a particular set of events in the past. We recognize that in practice, a gatekeeping role for the judge, no matter how flexible, inevitably on occasion will prevent the jury from learning of authentic insights and innovations. That, nevertheless, is the balance struck by Rules of Evidence designed not for the exhaustive search for cosmic understanding but for the particularized resolution of legal disputes.

Since much of the Louisiana Code of Evidence is patterned after the Federal Rules of Evidence in an attempt to facilitate a "movement towards a uniform national law of evidence", it seems appropriate for Louisiana courts to, "especially where the language of the Louisiana Code is identical or virtually identical with that used ... in the federal rules" utilize this "body of persuasive authority which may be instructive in interpreting the Louisiana Code." As the Louisiana Code of Evidence provision on expert testimony is identical to the federal Rule, it follows that this court should carefully consider the *Daubert* decision that soundly interprets an identical provision in the federal law of evidence.

Past decisions of this court have espoused similar sentiments regarding the admission of expert scientific testimony. In *State v. Catanese*, 368 So.2d 975 (La.1979), this court rejected *Frye*'s "general acceptance" in the scientific community as the only test for the admissibility of polygraph results in criminal trials. This court held that, although the validity of polygraph evidence was not "universally accepted" in the scientific community, the evidence should be admissible in a limited fashion in post-trial proceedings. This court noted that such scientific evidence should be admitted in those proceedings whenever the trial court, after balancing the probative value of the evidence against its prejudicial effect, determines that "the evidence is reliable and will aid in a decision." The admission of the evidence was subject to the "discretion of the trial judge."

Like *Catanese, Daubert* refuses to precondition admissibility of expert scientific testimony solely upon its "general acceptance" in the scientific community, and is also similar to *Catanese* in its reliance upon the evidence's admissibility provided that the trial court properly exercise its gatekeeping function in balancing the probative value of the evidence against its prejudicial effect. *Daubert* goes further than *Catanese* in that it sets forth clearer guidelines as to how a trial court can determine the reliability of expert testimony in its consideration of the probative value aspect of the *Catanese* balancing test. The above-noted similarity between the federal and Louisiana rules on the admission of expert testimony, coupled with similar guidelines for the admissibility of expert scientific testimony pronounced by this court in *Catanese,* persuade this court to adopt *Daubert*'s requirement that expert scientific testimony must rise to a threshold level of reliability in order to be admissible under La.C.E. art. 702. As we find the *Daubert* court's "observations" on what will help to determine this threshold level of reliability to be an effective guide, we shall adopt these "observations", as well.

It is not lost upon us that this new standard serves to remove some of the barriers in the admission of expert testimony in many fields, including child sexual abuse cases.

Nevertheless, Dr. Janzen's testimony still fails to satisfy the requirements for admissibility, even under the new *Daubert* standard. The reasons for this failure are several, and will now be discussed.

IV.

[Since no pre-trial hearing on admissibility was conducted, the record is limited for purposes of examining it for the use of CSAAS to diagnose sexual abuse because] ...

Child Sexual Abuse Accommodation Syndrome ("CSAAS") is a psychological phenomenon prevalent amongst victims of child sexual abuse.... The principal factors (or "dynamics") include secrecy, helplessness, entrapment and accommodation, delayed/conflicted/ and/or unconvincing disclosure, and retraction. The stated purpose in the dissemination of information relating to this "syndrome" was to create a "common language" for treaters of abused children.

Despite this stated purpose, the "syndrome" came to be used as a tool for determining whether or not abuse has occurred, as opposed to the intended use of the "syndrome" as a treatment device:

> ...
>
> Summit did not intend the accommodation syndrome as a diagnostic device. Rather, it assumes the presence of abuse, and explains the child's reactions to it.... Thus, the accommodation syndrome is not probative of abuse....

Myers, Bays, Becker, Berliner, Corwin, and Saywitz, "Expert Testimony in Child Sexual Abuse Litigation", 68 Neb.L.R. 1, 68–69 (1989). Commentators seized upon this as an "abuse" of the "syndrome":

...

The "syndrome's" "discoverer" has stated that ... [t]he CSAAS is used appropriately in court testimony not to prove a child was molested but to rebut the myths which prejudice endorsement of delayed or inconsistent disclosure." [Summit, "Abuse of the Child Sexual Abuse Accommodation Syndrome", 1 Journal of Child Sexual Abuse 160 (1992)] In this opinion he is joined by commentators who take issue with the use of CSAAS as a diagnostic tool to show to a court that sexual abuse has indeed occurred:

> The accommodation syndrome has a place in the courtroom. The syndrome helps explain why many sexually abused children delay reporting their abuse, and why many children recant allegations of abuse and deny that anything occurred. If the use of the syndrome is confined to these rehabilitative functions, the confusion clears, and the accommodation syndrome serves a useful function.

Myers, at 68.

In the instant case, Dr. Janzen used the "dynamics" of the syndrome not as a "common language" to facilitate treatment of the disorder as Dr. Summit and other therapists in the field intended, but as a tool for diagnosing whether or not abuse had occurred. This use of CSAAS is seen as having highly dubious value by many members of the psychological treatment community, since "(g)enerally speaking, the psychological evaluation of a child suspected of being sexually abused is, at best, an inexact science." Even experts utilizing CSAAS for determinations of the existence of abuse have been compelled to admit that "the evaluation of such a (sexually abused) child is partly a science and partly an art form." *Id.* Thus, the use of this technique for determinations of the victim's truthfulness in his or her allegations of abuse is not one that, even after peer review, has been embraced by the scientific community. Due to this failure, use of CSAAS-like techniques for determinations of the existence of abuse fails to satisfy the *Frye* element ("general acceptance" in the community) of the *Daubert* test.

This type of testimony also suffers from a number of difficulties inherent with all types of psychodynamic psychology. It is essentially "irrefutable", as the only way to test it is by proposing theoretical explanations for behavior and then testing the theories upon patients. Regardless of opinions on the accuracy of psychodynamic theories such as the one at bar, we must agree with Professor Morse's conclusion that psychodynamic theories on the explanation of human behavior is, at best, a science that is difficult to impossible to test for accuracy. This untestability comes from its very nature as an **opinion** as to the causes of human behavior, and the fact that the methods for testing the results of psychoanalysis are rife with the potential for inaccuracy. Thus, the "key question" of testability in determining whether a technique is valid enough for admissibility cannot be conclusively answered.

Finally, we must examine the "known or potential rate of error.". One of the few sources for validation of expert determinations of the existence of child sexual abuse is found in a study conducted that examined over 100 cases of child sexual abuse where the perpetrators confessed or acknowledged the abuse. Faller, "Criteria for Judging the Credibility of Children's Statements About Their Sexual Abuse", 67 Child Welfare 389 (1988), cited in Myers, *supra,* at 75–76. Faller described three factors that were crucial in determinations of abuse. They were "information about the context of the sexual abuse, the description or demonstration of the sexual victimization, and the victim's emotional state." Faller, at 391. The factors relied upon by clinicians in their determinations were prevalent in 68% of the cases, leading Faller to the conclusion that "clinical criteria employed by evaluators of sexually abused children are indeed valid predictors of whether children have been sexually abused...."

While Dr. Faller might have been content with a 32% margin of error, we are not so comfortable, especially remembering that "[t]he integrity of the criminal trial process is too important to permit it to be compromised by the admission of dynamic speculations." This type of testimony has been labeled as "so inherently unreliable that they cannot aid decisionmaking in the criminal justice system." ...

In short, it is unclear at best whether CSAAS can be relied upon in any fashion. Given these questions about the reliability of this sort of testimony at all it is only logical that this court should be reluctant to allow it to be broadly used for a purpose which it was not intended — a credibility evaluation tool.

Therefore, this court finds that this type of evidence is of highly questionable scientific validity, and fails to unequivocally pass the *Daubert* threshold test of scientific reliability. In any capacity, it is highly unlikely that it will be useful to a jury on the issue of a witness's credibility, especially as a tool for determining whether or not abuse actually occurred. Even if it were, the trial court made no such finding, and, by failing to exercise its "gatekeeping" role per *Daubert,* failed to satisfy what this court believes is a prudent and necessary standard for evaluation of expert testimony in criminal cases. Even assuming, *arguendo,* that CSAAS-based testimony itself does indeed pass the *Daubert* test for scientific validity, we now explore whether or not its use to bolster the victim's credibility was improper so as to unfairly prejudice the defendant.

V.

La.C.E. art. 702 sets up a scheme wherein the expert testifies only as to matters that are calculated to be helpful to the jury. Of course, this helpfulness to the jury is to be balanced by a due consideration of the probative value/prejudicial effect balancing test mandated by La.C.E. art. 403. As this provision generally follows the federal rule and is similar to other state evidentiary rules on testimony as to credibility, we look once again to federal and other state jurisprudence on this matter.

The question of whether or not such testimony on CSAAS is "helpful" to the jury in its determination of a victim's credibility has been one that, although it has generated much litigation in other jurisdictions, is *res nova* in this state. These other jurisdictions have repeatedly wrestled with the problem of admissibility of CSAAS-based testimony for the purpose of bolstering a victim's credibility, and they almost uniformly hold that the testimony is inadmissible:

> [u]nlike some aspects of expert testimony on child sexual abuse, courts approach unanimity when it comes to expert testimony on credibility. The great majority of courts reject expert testimony which comments directly on the credibility of individual children or on the credibility of sexually abused children as a class.

The rationales for excluding the evidence all seem to focus on the factfinding role of juries and that part of this role involves a determination as to the credibility of each witness. Testimony by an expert is not particularly helpful to a jury that must rely upon its own common sense as a barometer for the evaluation of truthfulness. The cases all seem to focus on, in the face of such expert testimony, fears of the jury surrender[ing] its own common sense in weighing [victim] testimony and deferr[ing] to [a] diagnosis [of sexual abuse] without knowing that the diagnosis was nothing more than a subjective opinion favoring [the victim]....

This bolstering of credibility has the effect of unfairly prejudicing a criminal defendant, and, as such, the use of CSAAS-based testimony for the purpose of bolstering a witness' credibility creates a risk of prejudice that outweighs its questionable probative value. Given the near unanimity of other jurisdictions' disapproval of CSAAS-based testimony as a determinant of abuse, coupled with our observations of the risk of prejudice inherent in CSAAS, this court now concludes that such opinion testimony as a determinant of a victim/witness' credibility is not admissible.

VI.

... The proper presentation of this sort of expert testimony must focus on explaining to a jury why "superficially bizarre" reactions such as delayed reporting, etc. take place in such cases. The opinion testimony must "seek to demonstrate or explain in general terms the behavioral characteristics of child abuse victims in disclosing alleged incidents," without giving "testimony directly concerning the particular victim's credibility." If the testimony is limited in this fashion, then it is of assistance to the jury in evaluating the psychological dynamics and resulting behavior patterns of alleged victims of child abuse, where the child's behavior is not within the common experience of the average juror....

The expert testimony on why victims might recant or delay reporting is being offered to rebut attacks on the victim's credibility. So long as the expert limits the testimony to general characteristics that would explain delays in reporting, recantations, and omission of details, the testimony will not substitute [the expert's] estimation of credibility for that of the jury. Rather, it is to provide a scientific perspective for the jury according to which it can evaluate the complainant's testimony for itself....

In the instant case, the expert testified as to his expert opinion on the victim's credibility, and did not limit his testimony to general information about possible psychiatric explanations for the delay in reporting. In fact, the expert based most of his opinion upon the "level of detail" of the child's description of the sexual abuse. He concluded with an objected-to summation that, in his expert opinion, the witness was telling the truth on that occasion as to whether abuse had occurred. This expert assessment of the witness' credibility was improper, making the trial court's overruling of the objection erroneous....

REVERSED AND REMANDED....

Discussion Questions

1. How does the Louisiana Supreme Court ultimately determine that the *Daubert* standard for the admissibility of evidence should be adopted in Louisiana? How does the court's reasoning in *Cantonese* and the Article 403 balancing test help to support the court's reasoning for adopting *Daubert* under Louisiana law?
2. After adopting the *Daubert* standard for admissibility of scientific evidence, the court applies the standard to the instant case and determines that the use of Child Sexual Abuse Accommodation Syndrome ("CSAAS") is not a reliable scientific methodology. Explain the court's analysis of the *Daubert* factors. Why does CSAAS fail to meet the standard of being a reliable methodology?
3. The courts have also repeatedly held that expert testimony is not appropriate for evaluating witness truthfulness. Why do you suppose this is the case? Is such testimony not reliable? Is this determination one that should properly be left to the jury? Explain your answer.
4. How would a party go about placing the *Daubert* issue before the court? Is a court required to hold a *Daubert* hearing? What issues must be decided at the hearing? Does the court inquire into the qualification of the expert? How does a party preserve a ruling either accepting or rejecting an expert's methodology?

Kumho Tire Co., Ltd. v. Carmichael

Supreme Court of the United States
526 U.S. 137, 119 S. Ct. 1167
March 23, 1999

Justice BREYER delivered the opinion of the Court.

In *Daubert v. Merrell Dow Pharmaceuticals, Inc.*, 509 U.S. 579 (1993), this Court focused upon the admissibility of scientific expert testimony. It pointed out that such testimony is admissible only if it is both relevant and reliable. And it held that the Federal Rules of Evidence "assign to the trial judge the task of ensuring that an expert's testimony both rests on a reliable foundation and is relevant to the task at hand." The Court also discussed certain more specific factors, such as testing, peer review, error rates, and "acceptability" in the relevant scientific community, some or all of which might prove helpful in determining the reliability of a particular scientific "theory or technique."

This case requires us to decide how *Daubert* applies to the testimony of engineers and other experts who are not scientists. We conclude that *Daubert's* general holding—setting forth the trial judge's general "gatekeeping" obligation—applies not only to testimony based on "scientific" knowledge, but also to testimony based on "technical" and "other specialized" knowledge. See Fed. Rule Evid. 702. We also conclude that a trial court *may* consider one or more of the more specific factors that *Daubert* mentioned when doing so will help determine that testimony's reliability. But, as the Court stated in *Daubert*, the test of reliability is "flexible," and *Daubert's* list of specific factors neither necessarily nor exclusively applies to all experts or in every case. Rather, the law grants a district court the same broad latitude when it decides *how* to determine reliability as it enjoys in respect to its ultimate reliability determination. See *General Electric Co. v. Joiner*, 522 U.S. 136, (1997) (courts of appeals are to apply "abuse of discretion" standard when reviewing district court's reliability determination). Applying these standards, we determine that the District Court's decision in this case—not to admit certain expert testimony—was within its discretion and therefore lawful.

I

On July 6, 1993, the right rear tire of a minivan driven by Patrick Carmichael blew out. In the accident that followed, one of the passengers died, and others were severely injured. In October 1993, the Carmichaels brought this diversity suit against the tire's maker and its distributor, whom we refer to collectively as Kumho Tire, claiming that the tire was defective. The plaintiffs rested their case in significant part upon deposition testimony provided by an expert in tire failure analysis, Dennis Carlson, Jr., who intended to testify in support of their conclusion.

Carlson's depositions relied upon certain features of tire technology that are not in dispute. A steel-belted radial tire like the Carmichaels' is made up of a "carcass" containing many layers of flexible cords, called "plies," along which (between the cords and the outer tread) are laid steel strips called "belts." Steel wire loops, called "beads," hold the cords together at the plies' bottom edges. An outer layer, called the "tread," encases the carcass, and the entire tire is bound together in rubber, through the application of heat and various chemicals. The bead of the tire sits upon a "bead seat," which is part of the wheel assembly. That assembly contains a "rim flange," which extends over the bead and rests against the side of the tire....

Carlson's testimony also accepted certain background facts about the tire in question. He assumed that before the blowout the tire had traveled far. (The tire was made in 1988 and had been installed some time before the Carmichaels bought the used minivan in March 1993; the Carmichaels had driven the van approximately 7,000 additional miles in the two months they had owned it.) Carlson noted that the tire's tread depth, which was 11/32 of an inch when new, App. 242, had been worn down to depths that ranged from 3/32 of an inch along some parts of the tire, to nothing at all along others. He conceded that the tire tread had at least two punctures which had been inadequately repaired.

Despite the tire's age and history, Carlson concluded that a defect in its manufacture or design caused the blowout. He rested this conclusion in part upon three premises which, for present purposes, we must assume are not in dispute: First, a tire's carcass should stay bound to the inner side of the tread for a significant period of time after its tread depth has worn away. Second, the tread of the tire at issue had separated from its inner steel-belted carcass prior to the accident. Third, this "separation" caused the blowout.

Carlson's conclusion that a defect caused the separation, however, rested upon certain other propositions, several of which the defendants strongly dispute. First, Carlson said that if a separation is *not* caused by a certain kind of tire misuse called "overdeflection" (which consists of underinflating the tire or causing it to carry too much weight, thereby generating heat that can undo the chemical tread/carcass bond), then, ordinarily, its cause is a tire defect. Second, he said that if a tire has been subject to sufficient overdeflection to cause a separation, it should reveal certain physical symptoms. These symptoms include (a) tread wear on the tire's shoulder that is greater than the tread wear along the tire's center, *id.*, at 211; (b) signs of a "bead groove," where the beads have been pushed too hard against the bead seat on the inside of the tire's rim; (c) sidewalls of the tire with physical signs of deterioration, such as discoloration; and/or (d) marks on the tire's rim flange, *id.*, at 219–220. Third, Carlson said that where he does not find *at least two* of the four physical signs just mentioned (and presumably where there is no reason to suspect a less common cause of separation), he concludes that a manufacturing or design defect caused the separation.

Carlson added that he had inspected the tire in question. He conceded that the tire to a limited degree showed greater wear on the shoulder than in the center, some signs of "bead groove," some discoloration, a few marks on the rim flange, and inadequately filled puncture holes (which can also cause heat that might lead to separation). But, in each instance, he testified that the symptoms were not significant, and he explained why he believed that they did not reveal overdeflection. For example, the extra shoulder wear, he said, appeared primarily on one shoulder, whereas an overdeflected tire would reveal equally abnormal wear on both shoulders. Carlson concluded that the tire did not bear at least two of the four overdeflection symptoms, nor was there any less obvious cause of separation; and since neither overdeflection nor the punctures caused the blowout, a defect must have done so.

Kumho Tire moved the District Court to exclude Carlson's testimony on the ground that his methodology failed Rule 702's reliability requirement. The court agreed with Kumho that it should act as a *Daubert*-type reliability "gatekeeper," even though one might consider Carlson's testimony as "technical," rather than "scientific." The court then examined Carlson's methodology in light of the reliability-related factors that *Daubert* mentioned, such as a theory's testability, whether it "has been a subject of peer review or publication," the "known or potential rate of error," and the "degree of acceptance ... within the relevant scientific community." The District Court found that all those factors argued against the reliability of Carlson's methods, and it granted the motion to exclude the testimony (as well as the defendants' accompanying motion for summary judgment).

The plaintiffs, arguing that the court's application of the *Daubert* factors was too "inflexible," asked for reconsideration. And the court granted that motion. After reconsidering the matter, the court agreed with the plaintiffs that *Daubert* should be applied flexibly, that its four factors were simply illustrative, and that other factors could argue in favor of admissibility. It conceded that there may be widespread acceptance of a "visual-inspection method" for some relevant purposes. But the court found insufficient indications of the reliability of "the component of Carlson's tire failure analysis which most concerned the Court, namely, the methodology employed by the expert in analyzing the data obtained in the visual inspection, and the scientific basis, if any, for such an analysis."

It consequently affirmed its earlier order declaring Carlson's testimony inadmissible and granting the defendants' motion for summary judgment.

The Eleventh Circuit reversed. See *Carmichael v. Samyang Tire, Inc.*, 131 F.3d 1433 (1997). It "review[ed] ... *de novo*" the "district court's legal decision to apply *Daubert*." Id., at 1435. It noted that "the Supreme Court in *Daubert* explicitly limited its holding to cover only the 'scientific context,'" adding that "a *Daubert* analysis" applies only where an expert relies "on the application of scientific principles," rather than "on skill- or experience-based observation." Id., at 1435–1436. It concluded that Carlson's testimony, which it viewed as relying on experience, "falls outside the scope of *Daubert*," that "the district court erred as a matter of law by applying *Daubert* in this case," and that the case must be remanded for further (non–*Daubert*-type) consideration under Rule 702. 131 F.3d, at 1436.

Kumho Tire petitioned for certiorari, asking us to determine whether a trial court "may" consider *Daubert's* specific "factors" when determining the "admissibility of an engineering expert's testimony." Pet. for Cert. i. We granted certiorari in light of uncertainty among the lower courts about whether, or how, *Daubert* applies to expert testimony that might be characterized as based not upon "scientific" knowledge, but rather upon "technical" or "other specialized" knowledge. Fed. Rule Evid. 702. [Citations omitted.]

II

A

In *Daubert*, this Court held that Federal Rule of Evidence 702 imposes a special obligation upon a trial judge to "ensure that any and all scientific testimony ... is not only relevant, but reliable." The initial question before us is whether this basic gatekeeping obligation applies only to "scientific" testimony or to all expert testimony. We, like the parties, believe that it applies to all expert testimony. See Brief for Petitioners 19; Brief for Respondents 17.

For one thing, Rule 702 itself says:

> "If scientific, technical, or other specialized knowledge will assist the trier of fact to understand the evidence or to determine a fact in issue, a witness qualified as an expert by knowledge, skill, experience, training, or education, may testify thereto in the form of an opinion or otherwise."

This language makes no relevant distinction between "scientific" knowledge and "technical" or "other specialized" knowledge. It makes clear that any such knowledge might become the subject of expert testimony. In *Daubert*, the Court specified that it is the Rule's word "knowledge," not the words (like "scientific") that modify that word, that "establishes a standard of evidentiary reliability." 509 U.S., at 589–590, 113 S.Ct. 2786. Hence, as a matter of language, the Rule applies its reliability standard to all "scientific," "technical," or "other specialized" matters within its scope. We concede that the Court in *Daubert* referred only to "scientific" knowledge. But as the Court there said, it referred to "scientific" testimony "because that [wa]s the nature of the expertise" at issue.

Neither is the evidentiary rationale that underlay the Court's basic *Daubert* "gatekeeping" determination limited to "scientific" knowledge. *Daubert* pointed out that Federal Rules 702 and 703 grant expert witnesses testimonial latitude unavailable to other witnesses on the "assumption that the expert's opinion will have a reliable basis in the knowledge and experience of his discipline" (pointing out that experts may testify to opinions, including those that are not based on firsthand knowledge or observation). The Rules grant that latitude to all experts, not just to "scientific" ones.

Finally, it would prove difficult, if not impossible, for judges to administer evidentiary rules under which a gatekeeping obligation depended upon a distinction between "scientific" knowledge and "technical" or "other specialized" knowledge. There is no clear line that divides the one from the others. Disciplines such as engineering rest upon scientific knowledge. Pure scientific theory itself may depend for its development upon observation and properly engineered machinery. And conceptual efforts to distinguish the two are unlikely to produce clear legal lines capable of application in particular cases. [Citations omitted].

Neither is there a convincing need to make such distinctions. Experts of all kinds tie observations to conclusions through the use of what Judge Learned Hand called "general truths derived from ... specialized experience." ... The trial judge's effort to assure that the specialized testimony is reliable and relevant can help the jury evaluate that foreign experience, whether the testimony reflects scientific, technical, or other specialized knowledge.

We conclude that *Daubert's* general principles apply to the expert matters described in Rule 702. The Rule, in respect to all such matters, "establishes a standard of evidentiary reliability." 509 U.S., at 590, 113 S.Ct. 2786. It "requires a valid ... connection to the pertinent inquiry as a precondition to admissibility." Id., at 592, 113 S.Ct. 2786. And where such testimony's factual basis, data, principles, methods, or their application are called sufficiently into question, see Part III, *infra*, the trial judge must determine whether the testimony has "a reliable basis in the knowledge and experience of [the relevant] discipline."

B

Petitioners ask more specifically whether a trial judge determining the "admissibility of an engineering expert's testimony" *may* consider several more specific factors that *Daubert* said might "bear on" a judge's gatekeeping determination. Brief for Petitioners i. These factors include:

—Whether a "theory or technique ... can be (and has been) tested";

—Whether it "has been subjected to peer review and publication";

—Whether, in respect to a particular technique, there is a high "known or potential rate of error" and whether there are "standards controlling the technique's operation"; and

—Whether the theory or technique enjoys " 'general acceptance' " within a " 'relevant scientific community.' "

Emphasizing the word "may" in the question, we answer that question yes.

Engineering testimony rests upon scientific foundations, the reliability of which will be at issue in some cases. In other cases, the relevant reliability concerns may focus upon personal knowledge or experience. As the Solicitor General points out, there are many different kinds of experts, and many different kinds of expertise.... *Daubert* makes clear that the factors it mentions do *not* constitute a "definitive checklist or test." And *Daubert* adds that the gatekeeping inquiry must be " 'tied to the facts' " of a particular "case." (quoting *United States v. Downing*, 753 F.2d 1224, 1242 (C.A.3 1985)....

Daubert itself is not to the contrary. It made clear that its list of factors was meant to be helpful, not definitive. Indeed, those factors do not all necessarily apply even in every instance in which the reliability of scientific testimony is challenged....

At the same time, and contrary to the Court of Appeals' view, some of *Daubert's* questions can help to evaluate the reliability even of experience-based testimony. In certain cases, it will be appropriate for the trial judge to ask, for example, how often an engineering expert's experience-based methodology has produced erroneous results, or whether such a method is generally accepted in the relevant engineering community. Likewise, it will at times be useful to ask even of a witness whose expertise is based purely on experience, say, a perfume tester able to distinguish among 140 odors at a sniff, whether his preparation is of a kind that others in the field would recognize as acceptable.

We must therefore disagree with the Eleventh Circuit's holding that a trial judge may ask questions of the sort *Daubert* mentioned only where an expert "relies on the application of scientific principles," but not where an expert relies "on skill- or experience-based observation." 131 F.3d, at 1435....

To say this is not to deny the importance of *Daubert's* gatekeeping requirement. The objective of that requirement is to ensure the reliability and relevancy of expert testimony. It is to make certain that an expert, whether basing testimony upon professional studies or personal experience, employs in the courtroom the same level of intellectual rigor that characterizes the practice of an expert in the relevant field. Nor do we deny that, as stated in *Daubert*, the particular questions that it mentioned will often be appropriate for use in determining the reliability of challenged expert testimony. Rather, we conclude that the trial judge must have considerable leeway in deciding in a particular case how to go about determining whether particular expert testimony is reliable. That is to say, a trial court should consider the specific factors identified in *Daubert* where they are reasonable measures of the reliability of expert testimony.

The trial court must have the same kind of latitude in deciding *how* to test an expert's reliability, and to decide whether or when special briefing or other proceedings are needed to investigate reliability, as it enjoys when it decides *whether or not* that expert's relevant testimony is reliable. Our opinion in *General Electric v. Joiner*, 522 U.S. 166 (1997), makes clear that a court of appeals is to apply an abuse-of-discretion standard when it "review[s] a trial court's decision to admit or exclude expert testimony." That standard applies as much to the trial court's decisions about how to determine reliability as to its ultimate conclusion.... Thus, whether *Daubert's* specific factors are, or are not, reasonable measures of reliability in a particular case is a matter that the law grants the trial judge broad latitude to determine.

III

We further explain the way in which a trial judge "may" consider *Daubert's* factors by applying these considerations to the case at hand, a matter that has been briefed exhaustively by the parties and their 19 *amici*. The District Court did not doubt Carlson's qualifications, which included a masters degree in mechanical engineering, 10 years' work at Michelin America, Inc., and testimony as a tire failure consultant in other tort cases. Rather, it excluded the testimony because, despite those qualifications, it initially doubted, and then found unreliable, "the methodology employed by the expert in analyzing the data obtained in the visual inspection, and the scientific basis, if any, for such an analysis." ... After examining the transcript in "some detail," 923 F.Supp., at 1518–1519, n. 4, and after considering respondents' defense of Carlson's methodology, the District Court determined that Carlson's testimony was not reliable. It fell outside the range where experts might reasonably differ, and where the jury must decide among the conflicting views of different experts, even though the evidence is "shaky." *Daubert*, 509 U.S., at 596, 113 S.Ct. 2786. In our view, the doubts that triggered the District Court's initial inquiry here were reasonable, as was the court's ultimate conclusion.

For one thing, and contrary to respondents' suggestion, the specific issue before the court was not the reasonableness *in general* of a tire expert's use of a visual and tactile inspection to determine whether overdeflection had caused the tire's tread to separate from its steel-belted carcass. Rather, it was the reasonableness of using such an approach, along with Carlson's particular method of analyzing the data thereby obtained, to draw a conclusion regarding *the particular matter to which the expert testimony was directly relevant.* That matter concerned the likelihood that a defect in the tire at issue caused its tread to separate from its carcass. The tire in question, the expert conceded, had traveled far enough so that some of the tread had been worn bald; it should have been taken out of service; it had been repaired (inadequately) for punctures; and it bore some of the very marks that the expert said indicated, not a defect, but abuse through overdeflection. The relevant issue was whether the expert could reliably determine the cause of *this* tire's separation.

Nor was the basis for Carlson's conclusion simply the general theory that, in the absence of evidence of abuse, a defect will normally have caused a tire's separation. Rather, the expert employed a more specific theory to establish the existence (or absence) of such abuse. Carlson testified precisely that in the absence of *at least two* of four signs of abuse (proportionately greater tread wear on the shoulder; signs of grooves caused by the beads; discolored sidewalls; marks on the rim flange), he concludes that a defect caused the separation. And his analysis depended upon acceptance of a further implicit proposition, namely, that his visual and tactile inspection could determine that the tire before him had not been abused despite some evidence of the presence of the very signs for which he looked (and two punctures).

For another thing, the transcripts of Carlson's depositions support both the trial court's initial uncertainty and its final conclusion. Those transcripts cast considerable doubt upon the reliability of both the explicit theory (about the need for two signs of abuse) and the implicit proposition (about the significance of visual inspection in this case). Among other things, the expert could not say whether the tire had traveled more than 10, or 20, or 30, or 40, or 50 thousand miles, adding that 6,000 miles was "about how far" he could "say with any certainty." The court could reasonably have wondered about the reliability of a method of visual and tactile inspection sufficiently precise to ascertain with some certainty the abuse-related significance of minute shoulder/center relative tread wear differences, but insufficiently precise to tell "with any certainty" from the tread wear whether a tire had traveled less than 10,000 or more than 50,000 miles. And these concerns might have been augmented by Carlson's repeated reliance on the "subjective[ness]" of his mode of analysis in response to questions seeking specific information regarding how he could differentiate between a tire that actually had been overdeflected and a tire that merely looked as though it had been. They would have been further augmented by the fact that Carlson said he had inspected the tire itself for the first time the morning of his first deposition, and then only for a few hours. (His initial conclusions were based on photographs.)

Moreover, prior to his first deposition, Carlson had issued a signed report in which he concluded that the tire had "not been ... overloaded or underinflated," not because of the absence of "two of four" signs of abuse, but simply because "the rim flange impressions ... were normal." ...

Finally, the court, after looking for a defense of Carlson's methodology as applied in these circumstances, found no convincing defense. Rather, it found (1) that "none" of the *Daubert* factors, including that of "general acceptance" in the relevant expert community, indicated that Carlson's testimony was reliable; (2) that its own analysis "revealed no countervailing factors operating in favor of admissibility which could outweigh those identified in *Daubert*," App. to Pet. for Cert. 4c; and (3) that the "parties identified no such factors in their briefs," *ibid.* For these three reasons *taken together,* it concluded that Carlson's testimony was unreliable.

Respondents now argue to us, as they did to the District Court, that a method of tire failure analysis that employs a visual/tactile inspection is a reliable method, and they point both to its use by other experts and to Carlson's long experience working for Michelin as sufficient indication that that is so. But no one denies that an expert might draw a conclusion from a set of observations based on extensive and specialized experience. Nor does anyone deny that, as a general matter, tire abuse may often be identified by qualified experts through visual or tactile inspection of the tire.... As we said before, *supra,* at 1977, the question before the trial court was specific, not general. The trial court had to decide whether this particular expert had sufficient specialized knowledge to assist the jurors "in deciding the particular issues in the case."

The particular issue in this case concerned the use of Carlson's two-factor test and his related use of visual/tactile inspection to draw conclusions on the basis of what seemed small observational differences. We have found no indication in the record that other experts in the industry use Carlson's two-factor test or that tire experts such as Carlson normally make the very fine distinctions about, say, the symmetry of comparatively greater shoulder tread wear that were necessary, on Carlson's own theory, to support his conclusions. Nor, despite the prevalence of tire testing, does anyone refer to any articles or papers that validate Carlson's approach....

Respondents additionally argue that the District Court too rigidly applied *Daubert's* criteria. They read its opinion to hold that a failure to satisfy any one of those criteria automatically renders expert testimony inadmissible. The District Court's initial opinion might have been vulnerable to a form of this argument. There, the court, after rejecting respondents' claim that Carlson's testimony was "exempted from *Daubert*-style scrutiny" because it was "technical analysis" rather than "scientific evidence," simply added that "none of the four admissibility criteria outlined by the *Daubert* court are satisfied." 923 F.Supp., at 1521. Subsequently, however, the court granted respondents' motion for reconsideration. It then explicitly recognized that the relevant reliability inquiry "should be 'flexible,'" that its "'overarching subject [should be] ... validity' and reliability," and that "*Daubert* was intended neither to be exhaustive nor to apply in every case." App. to Pet. for Cert. 4c (quoting *Daubert*, 509 U.S., at 594–595, 113 S.Ct. 2786). And the court ultimately based its decision upon Carlson's failure to satisfy either *Daubert's* factors *or any other* set of reasonable reliability criteria. In light of the record as developed by the parties, that conclusion was within the District Court's lawful discretion.

In sum, Rule 702 grants the district judge the discretionary authority, reviewable for its abuse, to determine reliability in light of the particular facts and circumstances of the particular case. The District Court did not abuse its discretionary authority in this case. Hence, the judgment of the Court of Appeals is *Reversed.*

Justice SCALIA, with whom Justice O'CONNOR and Justice THOMAS join, concurring.

I join the opinion of the Court, which makes clear that the discretion it endorses—trial-court discretion in choosing the manner of testing expert reliability—is not discretion to abandon the gatekeeping function. I think it worth adding that it is not discretion to perform the function inadequately. Rather, it is discretion to choose among *reasonable* means of excluding expertise that is *fausse* and science that is junky. Though, as the Court makes clear today, the *Daubert* factors are not holy writ, in a particular case the failure to apply one or another of them may be unreasonable, and hence an abuse of discretion.

Justice STEVENS, concurring in part and dissenting in part.

The only question that we granted certiorari to decide is whether a trial judge "[m]ay ... consider the four factors set out by this Court in *Daubert* in a Rule 702 analysis of admissibility of an engineering expert's testimony." Pet. for Cert. i. That question is fully and correctly answered in Parts I and II of the Court's opinion, which I join.

Part III answers the quite different question whether the trial judge abused his discretion when he excluded the testimony of Dennis Carlson. Because a proper answer to that question requires a study of the record that can be performed more efficiently by the Court of Appeals than by the nine Members of this Court, I would remand the case to the Eleventh Circuit to perform that task....

Discussion Questions

1. Overall, how does the court conclude that the *Daubert* factors should be used in determining the reliability of "technical, or other specialized knowledge"? Can the factors be properly applied to technical and other areas of specialized knowledge? Why or why not?
2. In determining whether there should be a different rule when evaluating "scientific" versus "technical" knowledge, is there a clear line that divides one from the other?

Would it be easy or practical to have a different standard for evaluating scientific versus technical knowledge?

Key Points

The key points to keep in mind regarding expert witnesses and scientific testimony.

1. **Helpfulness.** Expert testimony may be offered if scientific, technical, or other specialized knowledge will assist the trier of fact in understanding the evidence or determining a fact in issue.
2. **Qualifications.** The witness must be qualified as an expert by knowledge, skill, experience, training, or education, or any combination thereof—a college degree is not required.
3. **Qualifying a witness at trial**: Proponent questions witness on qualifications; proponent tenders witness as expert in field; opposing party cross-examines witness on qualifications; opposing party may object or stipulate; parties argue issue; judge accepts or rejects as expert.
4. **No formalities necessary:** There are no formal procedures required for qualifying an expert. An expert witness need not be formally tendered, and judge need not formally accept witness as expert. The judge may implicitly accept a witness as an expert.
5. **Scope of testimony.** The expert witness may express opinions and provide other information in areas of expertise. He may answer hypothetical questions.
6. **Opinion on ultimate issue**. Expert testimony is not excluded solely for embracing an ultimate issue, if it is still helpful. However, an expert witness cannot testify to guilt/innocence of accused in a criminal trial. Experts may testify to mental state of defendant on issue of insanity or competency to proceed.
7. **Basis of opinion.** An expert witness may base his opinion on information/facts perceived by him or made known to him at or before the proceeding, including other witnesses testifying at the trial. He may even base opinions on inadmissible information if of the type commonly relied upon by experts rendering such opinions.
8. **Disclosure of underlying facts**. In a civil case, an expert need not disclose underlying facts on direct examination, but may be required to disclose on cross-examination. In criminal cases, expert *must* disclose underlying facts on direct examination. As to inadmissible facts, the proponent of the expert cannot disclose inadmissible facts/data, but the opponent can elicit the inadmissible underlying facts and data on cross-examination.
9. ***Daubert* sets standard for admissibility of scientific evidence.** Must be: 1) **relevant** to task at hand; and 2) **reliable**.
   a. Methodology is **reliable** if **scientifically valid**, which is determined by five *Daubert* factors: 1) Has method been reliably **tested**; 2) Has the theory or technique been subject to **peer review** and **publication**; 3) The known or potential **rate of error**; 4) The existence and maintenance of **standards** controlling the techniques operation; and 5) Is method **generally accepted** within that scientific community.
   b. *Daubert* overruled *Frye's* general acceptance standard.
   c. Louisiana adopted the *Daubert* standard in *State v. Foret.*

d. *Kumho Tire* extended the *Daubert* standards to all expert testimony.

10. **Article 403 Balancing**. Expert testimony admitted subject to Article 403 balancing of helpfulness against risk of prejudice.

11. **2014 Amendment of Article 702.** Louisiana's expert witness statute was amended in 2014 to encompass the reliability standard of *Daubert*. The statute does not change the law. *Daubert* factors are still the law under *Foret*.

12. **Summarization for requirements for experts**. In *Cheairs* the Louisiana Supreme Court summarized the requirements for expert witnesses to avoid confusion: "(1) the expert must be competently qualified in area in which he will testify; (2) the expert's methodology is reliable under *Daubert*; and (3) the expert testimony must assist the trier of fact to understand the evidence or to determine a fact in issue."

Problems on Expert Witnesses and Scientific Testimony

PROBLEM 7-1. PART I: Brandon is a licensed civil engineer practicing for over 17 years. He has been qualified as an expert at trial in civil engineering with a specialization in structural engineering which includes the construction and maintenance of bridges. In a lawsuit against the City after a bridge gave way during a storm, killing hundreds of commuters traversing the bridge and injuring thousands more, Brandon testifies for the plaintiffs that the bridge was not properly constructed to handle the estimated capacity the bridge would have to support on the major thoroughfare it covered. He will also testify that the bridge was not properly maintained and inspected to prevent, detect, and repair signs that the bridge was routinely being used over capacity and would likely give way. Brandon was asked the following questions on the stand during direct examination. *[Note: Civil engineering is a professional engineering discipline that deals with the design, construction, and maintenance of the physical and naturally built environments, including works like roads, bridges, canals, dams and buildings. Structural engineering is concerned with the structural design and structural analysis of buildings, bridges, towers, overpasses, tunnels, and other structures.]*

i. "Could you explain ways in which the bridge could have been made safer?"

ii. "How often and what types of inspections should be conducted on a bridge of this nature to detect damage in need of repair?"

iii. "Do the injuries sustained by the plaintiffs appear to be consistent with the type of injury that would be expected from this type of accident?"

iv. "After examining the bridge, what indicators did you detect, that led you to conclude that the bridge had been showing signs of disrepair for more than five years?"

v. "How would you distinguish your findings that the bridge gave way due to insufficient construction, inspections, and maintenance, from the defense expert's findings that the bridge gave way due to unforeseeable circumstances caused by the storm?"

vi. "Hypothetically speaking, let's say the bridge was operating at the capacity in which it was designed to carry. How much longer would this bridge have likely lasted?"

Which questions will most likely be **objectionable**, that Brandon will **not** likely be allowed to answer? Explain.

PART II: During cross-examination of Brandon, the defense attorney asks him if he is familiar with the *Treatise on Structural Engineering Technology*. He states that every engineer worth a grain of salt is familiar with the publication because it is the most noted authority in the field. The attorney then cross-examines him from the publication, asking him to explain various statements made in the publication for the jury. He reads what the publication states, then asks Brandon if it is a true statement, and to reconcile his testimony with the treatise. Opposing counsel objects that the statements in the book are hearsay.

1. Can Brandon be cross-examined regarding the contents of the treatise? Is it hearsay? Why or why not?
2. For what purpose did the defense attorney ask Brandon whether he was familiar with the treatise? Is it or some other question of similar nature relevant and/or required? Why or why not?

PROBLEM 7-2. Professor Heather Lane sued University for wrongful termination after she was denied tenure and terminated from employment after a year of excessive class cancellations and failure to complete her research projects. Her theory is that a medical condition caused her poor performance, and that she should not have been punished for it, but instead should have been offered treatment. To support her case at the trial, Professor Lane would like to call her therapist Dr. Stillman, a licensed clinical psychologist, who has not been qualified as an expert in any field, to testify that Professor Lane had been clinically depressed over the last two years, and that it was her depression that caused her poor performance at work. Dr. Stillman will further testify that with proper treatment, Professor Lane could have performed her duties. The defense objects to Dr. Stillman's testimony. How should the court rule?

PROBLEM 7-3. Wilson had four children, three of which were left out of his will when he passed away. The will was executed about a year before he died. The excluded children bring an action to challenge the will claiming Wilson lacked testamentary capacity to execute the will. They plan to call a psychiatrist to testify that although he never met or personally examined Wilson, he had an opportunity to review psychiatric evaluations for the two years prior to executing the will, he interviewed several of Wilson's associates, friends, family, and doctors, and based on his expert opinion, Wilson lacked testamentary capacity at the time the will was executed. The defense objects on the following grounds:

1. The psychiatrist cannot testify to Wilson's capacity because he never met him.
2. The psychiatrist's opinion embraces the ultimate issue.

Should the psychiatrist be allowed to testify as proposed? Why or why not?

PROBLEM 7-4. Dr. Philson is qualified as an expert in the field of clinical psychology. Which of the following is within the scope of the field of clinical psychology that he may be able to testify to? Which would be beyond the scope of the field in which he is qualified to testify as an expert?

1. That the person he examined was suffering from a mental disease.
2. That the person he examined could likely benefit from treatment for the mental disorder.
3. That certain things could exacerbate his condition.
4. That it was not likely that a particular thing could have caused the mental disorder.

PROBLEM 7-5. Dr. Milton Pera is a licensed medical doctor with a specialization in the field of neurology. Must he be qualified as an expert to testify as to the cause of the neurological disorder that a particular person has, or is he presumed to be an expert in the field because of his experience and training?

PROBLEM 7-6. Edward Finley has been qualified as expert in accident reconstruction. He will testify as to how an accident occurred. Is he required to go the scene of where the accident occurred? Why or why not?

PROBLEM 7-7. Bo has been working at the chemical plant for 25 years. He started right after high school and never went to college. His job entails draining a particular toxic chemical in a certain way so as to avoid leakage that can kill if it comes in contact with the body. Over the years he has seen several accidents that resulted in permanent damage to other employees, has been retrained each year to safety measures that should be taken, and has been involved in testing of new measures. In a lawsuit filed by one of Bo's coworkers against their employer, the plant would like to call Bo to testify to how the chemical should have been handled in order for the employee to have avoided his injury. Can he be qualified as an expert in how to handle toxic chemicals?

PROBLEM 7-8. An economist has been qualified as an expert in economics in a wrongful death case in the damages phase of the trial (liability has already been found) and has been qualified as an expert in economics with a specialization in salary/income projection. The plaintiffs had already called another expert to testify to life expectancy of the decedent based on his age, health, lifestyle, family history, etc. They seek to elicit testimony from the expert regarding the amount of income the decedent would have likely made had he lived to the projected age of 78–82 years old (40–44 additional years) had it not been for the conduct of the defendant in negligently causing decedent's death. The plaintiff then asked the witness the following questions:

1. What if the plaintiff had only lived another 10 more years, to the age of 45 years old? What would have been the projected lifetime income?
2. What if the plaintiff had only lived to the age of 55 years old? What would have been the projected lifetime income?
3. What if the plaintiff had only lived to the age of 65 years old? What would have been the projected lifetime income?

Can the witness be asked the hypothetical questions? Can the witness give the testimony? Why or why not?

PROBLEM 7-9. In each of the following, would a lay witness, an expert witness or neither be able to give the following testimony:

1. Results of DNA analysis
2. Testimony that radiation-induced cataracts can be identified through mere observation
3. Evidence matching a shoeprint to a particular shoe
4. Testimony regarding the accuracy of eyewitness identification
5. Fingerprint matches
6. Testimony as to whether the release of fumes was caused by fire or chemicals
7. Testimony about the meaning of certain slang terms
8. Testimony about surveillance and counter-surveillance techniques

9. An opinion that driver of vehicle was in "total control" prior to accident
10. That a substance thrown was urine
11. That the person had the smell of alcohol on them
12. The value of the services a person has provided in his field (ex. If a lawyer completes a succession, another lawyer testifies as to how much the service is worth)
13. Whether a bridge is constructed properly
14. Whether it was the amount of weight on a staircase or its construction that led to it collapsing
15. Whether the victim in an alleged rape was being "deceitful"
16. Whether a driver's intoxication caused the death of the decedent

PROBLEM 7-10. Wayne is charged with second-degree murder of his adult son. He has pled not guilty and not guilty by reason of insanity. The State alleges that the defendant had the specific intent to kill or inflict great bodily harm when he choked his son to death during an argument. The defense claims that the defendant "snapped" and in that moment, in a state of psychosis, he was incapable of distinguishing between right and wrong. The State's witness who was qualified as an expert in forensic psychology testified that he examined the defendant on several occasions, reviewed all reports, witness statements, and psychological evaluations of the defendant over the last 3 years and concluded that the defendant was not insane at the time of the offense, and that he knew the difference between right and wrong, and was capable of understanding his actions. Among the information upon which the expert relied in coming to this conclusion was that in one of his interviews with the defendant, the defendant disclosed that he had had several violent fights with his son in the past and that he had prepared for his son on this occasion. He stated how he had planned to attack his son the next time they had a fight and that he had been in jail in the past and did not mind going back to show his son a lesson. Following a motion in limine to exclude the statement by the defendant because it disclosed "other crimes, wrongs, or bad acts," the judge ruled any evidence regarding the defendant's statement of the other fights and planning inadmissible.

1. May the expert witness still consider the information in coming to his conclusions on the defendant's sanity? Why or why not?
2. Are there any circumstances under which the inadmissible facts or data may be admissible? Explain.
3. If the expert is allowed to consider the information in coming to his conclusion, are there any circumstances under which the information may be disclosed?

PROBLEM 7-11. John represents the defendant in a personal injury action. The State has called a witness to testify as an expert in the field. John objects to the witness being able to testify as an expert because he knows that the witness never went to college. John has had his paralegal quickly draft and bring over a motion for a *Daubert* hearing. How should the judge rule on the motion and why?

PROBLEM 7-12. Procedural basics:

A. Describe the procedure at trial for a witness to testify as an expert witness, from qualifying the expert to cross-examination and redirect examination of the expert, including the roles of each attorney and the judge.

B. What are some common objections that may arise dealing with qualifying experts?

C. What might a trial judge likely consider and examine in determining whether to allow a witness to testify as an expert?

D. What evidence and questions might be used to cross-examine and impeach experts?

E. Explain the difference between a lay witness and an expert witness. What questions may be asked of each, what knowledge is required for each to testify, and what is the difference between the matter and manner of the testimony that is allowed by each?

PROBLEM 7-13. Using the facts below in each scenario, please determine whether the court would likely find the witness qualified to give the listed expert opinion. Provide an explanation for why you believe the witness will or will not be allowed to testify as proposed.

i. A man was accused of rape. Traces of phencyclidine, a drug that causes hallucinations, were found in the man's bloodstream the night of the rape. At trial, a physician specializing in toxicology and pathology, who mainly had expertise in the toxic effects of phencyclidine, testified that ingesting the drug could have rendered the defendant incapable of distinguishing between right and wrong. The prosecution objects that the physician was not qualified to give the opinion. How should the court rule and why? [*See State v. Rives*, 407 So. 2d 1195 (La. 1981)].

ii. An internal medicine physician provided emergency medical care to an 82-year-old woman. He released the woman knowing she had an extremely high heart rate. Shortly after her release, the woman died. At trial, a registered nurse was asked whether an internal medicine physician releasing a patient from emergency care was a breach of the applicable standard of care. The nurse testified that there was a breach. The defense objects that the nurse was not qualified to give such an opinion. How should the court rule and why? [*See Taplin v. Lupin*, 700 So. 2d 1160 (La. Ct. App. 4th Cir. 1997)].

iii. A man trespassed on his neighbor's land and removed several trees. To calculate the market value of the removed trees, a skilled forester, with many years of experience in planting, managing, and caring for trees, testified to the commercial value of the removed timber so the court could multiply the commercial value by three to determine treble damages to award the plaintiff. The defendant objects that the forester was not qualified to give the opinion. How should the court rule and why? [*See Gewin v. Willamette Industries, Inc.*, 406 So. 2d 730 (La. Ct. App. 3d Cir. 1981)].

iv. Plaintiff seeks to introduce the expert testimony of a person in the carpet-cleaning and repair business for 20 years to testify as a safety expert in a case where a customer tripped on a floor mat in a store. Should the witness be allowed to testify as proposed? Why or why not?

PROBLEM 7-14. An inmate in solitary confinement was in a small room by himself with no windows 23 hours/day. The inmate's sole interactions with other people were when the guardsmen brought food to him and the doctor visited him. On the forty-seventh day of confinement, the inmate choked a guardsman to death while the guardsman was delivering his food. The inmate is now on trial for first-degree murder. At trial, the inmate's defense is that the killing was a result of a psychotic episode the inmate was having from being in solitary confinement for forty-seven days straight that prevented him from controlling his actions and from forming the requisite intent for the crime. The prosecution calls a psychiatrist and qualifies him as an expert witness in the field of forensic psychiatry. The psychiatrist will testify that in his professional opinion an inmate will not become psychotic from confinement for forty-seven days, and so it is very likely that at the time the inmate committed the offense the inmate was capable of controlling his actions and forming the requisite intent to commit the crime. The defense objects that the opinion is not helpful and is the equivalent of an opinion on guilt or innocence. How should the court rule on the objection and why? Is the opinion permissible?

PROBLEM 7-15. Tiffany was injured at a college football game when the railing gave way as several students were cheering and leaning against it when the team scored a touchdown. Tiffany and several other students fell headfirst onto the football field, and several other students fell on top of her. Tiffany is paralyzed from the neck down as a result of the accident. Tiffany's parents sue the school claiming the school failed to adequately maintain the railing, and the manufacturer for the construction and installation of it. At the trial, Tiffany calls as an expert witness an engineer who has designed such railings for major facilities such as stadiums and the like for over 20 years. He will testify that the railing was not properly designed, installed, or maintained. In coming to his conclusions, he relies on the following:

1) testimony given at the trial by longtime stadium workers that the railings were never inspected or maintained;
2) an email to the coordinator of facilities at the university from a university official telling him not to "waste time" on railings—a statement that will be excluded from trial because it cannot be authenticated;
3) information given in depositions by engineers for the manufacturer;
4) designs for sturdier railings installed at other university stadiums;
5) statements made by a lead design engineer, who is now deceased, to the installers to "just get it done," to which they responded in haste in installing the railings; and
6) handwritten statements made by students who were eyewitnesses to the incident, who have since graduated and cannot be located and will not testify at the trial. Some of the statements were not signed and their origins are unknown.

What, if any, of the information should the expert be allowed to rely upon in forming the opinions to which he will testify? What information will he be allowed to disclose during his testimony in giving his opinions? If any of the information is inadmissible, are there any circumstances under which it might be disclosed at trial? Explain.

PRACTICAL APPLICATION EXERCISE PAE 7-1. Select a partner in class. One of you will represent the prosecution and the other the defense. The defendant has pled not guilty and not guilty by reason of insanity in a murder trial. You should prepare an examination to qualify your designated expert witness (see chart below) as an expert in the field of forensic psychology. You must also prepare a voir dire of the expert offered by your opposing counsel. Voir dire is where you cross-examine the opposing expert on his qualifications to testify as an expert witness in the field tendered. Be prepared to present in class if called on.

Prosecution's Expert Witness
Chris C.W. Franciscus, Ph.D.
3287 Willow Dr.
Grey City, La. 61973

Education
- State University, May 1997 (*honors*)
  Ph.D. in Clinical Phycology
  Dissertation Topic: *"The Prevalence of Abusive Backgrounds on Death Row"*
- State University, May 1993
  M.A. Psychology
  Thesis: *"The Murderer's Mind"*
- State University at SW Campus 5/91
  B.A. Psychology

Employment
- Franciscus & Associates
  Forensic Clinical Psychologist
  Sept. 2013 — Present
- Staff Psychologist
  State Prison
  May 1997 — Sept. 2013

Published Articles
- *"The Chronic Murderer"*
  Forensic Psychology 3/14
- *"Why Men Murder"*
  Forensic Psychology
- *"I Can't Help Myself"*
  American Psychology Journal 1/09

Professional Organizations
- American Psychology Association
- National Psychology Association
- Mental Health National Society

Licenses
- Licensed Clinical Psychologist in Louisiana, Texas, and Georgia

Defense's Expert Witness
Louis G. Fitzgerald, Sr. Ph.D.
48567 Ocean Lane, Ste. 213
Grey City, La. 61973

Education
- Langford University, May 1981
  Ph.D. in Clinical Psychology
  Dissertation Topic: *"Chronic Effects of Post-Traumatic Stress Disorder"*
- State University, May 1970
  B.A. Psychology

Employment
- Staff Psychologist
  State Mental Health Hospital
  Oct. 1985–Present
- Adjunct Professor of Psychology
  State University, 1995–Present
- Staff Psychologist
  City Mental Health Clinic
  May 1981–October 1985

Published Articles
- Weekly article in *"Mental Health Weekly"* (371 consecutive weeks) (see attachment for topics)

Professional Organizations
- American Psychology Association

Licenses
- Licensed Clinical Psychologist in State of Louisiana

Specialization
- Forensic Psychology

Chapter References and Additional Authority on Expert Witnesses and Scientific Evidence [La. C.E. arts. 702–706]

1. La. C.E. arts. 702–706 and Official Comments
2. Force & Rault, Handbook on Louisiana Evidence Law Arts. 702–706 Author's Comments (West Publishing 2014)
3. Harges & Jones, Louisiana Evidence Arts. 702–706; Author's Comments (West Publishing 2014)
4. 19 La. Civ. L. Treatise, Evidence And Proof § 11.3–§ 11.7 (2nd ed.)
5. **Commentary**: Davis, Comment, "*Admissibility of Expert Testimony After Daubert and Foret; A Wider Gate, A More Vigilant Gatekeeper*," 54 La. L. Rev. 1307 (1994).
6. **Experts accepted on experience and training alone**: *State v. Gipson*, 850 So. 2d 973 (La. Ct. App. 2d Cir. 2003) (holding that "A combination of specialized training, work experience, and practical application of the expert's knowledge can combine to demonstrate that a person is an expert"); *Manchack v. Willamette Industries, Inc.*, 621 So. 2d 649, 653 (La. Ct. App. 2d Cir. 1993) (holding that "experience alone is sufficient to qualify a witness as an expert; a college degree is not required"); *Dixon v. Tucker*, 92 So. 3d 1100 (La. Ct. App. 2d Cir. 2012) (finding a police officer with nine years of experience investigating accidents was sufficient to qualify him as an expert witness).
7. **Expert opinion not helpful**: *Hattori v. Peairs*, 662 So. 2d 509 (La. Ct. App. 1st Cir. 1995) (holding that "we cannot say that such testimony would be helpful to the trier of fact in reaching an objective determination of whether Mr. Peairs' actions that evening were reasonable.... [T]estimony on this point was not needed."); *Theriot v. Lasseigne*, 640 So. 2d 1305 (La. 1994) (holding that expert testimony was not helpful to determine that alcohol consumption could affect a person's driving ability, and thus could have played a role in negligence of parties; "[e]xpert testimony is not necessary when a factfinder can reasonably draw inferences based on his own knowledge and experience").
8. **Witness not permitted to give expert opinion in particular field**: *Robertson v. Hessler*, 13 So. 3d 1214 (La. Ct. App. 4th Cir. 2009) (finding that court errs in qualifying witness as expert in crime scene reconstruction and investigation where his training and experience, although extensive, did not include training in crime scene investigation); *Washauer v. J.C. Penney Co., Inc.*, 879 So. 2d 195, 198–99 (La. Ct. App. 1st Cir. 2004) (not allowing witness to testify as a safety expert since witness had no superior knowledge or experience that would help the finder of fact); *Lafayette City-Parish Consol. Government v. Entergy Gulf States, Inc.*, 975 So. 2d 177 (La. Ct. App. 3d Cir. 2008) (not allowing witness to give an electric utility economic valuation because witness was not a certified appraiser); *State v. Qutoum*, 839 So. 2d 323, 327 (La. Ct. App. 5th Cir. 2003) (not permitting witness to testify as an arson expert).
9. **Expert's methodology rejected**: *Davis v. Martel*, 790 So. 2d 767 (La. Ct. App. 3d Cir. 2001) (not permitting witness to give expert testimony as to the lateral speed of the vehicles, that the forward speed had no bearing on the impact of the vehicles, and that the plaintiff could not have suffered injury as a result of the accident in a "sideswipe" accident when the expert had not been to the accident scene and no evidence was submitted that the method the expert used to reach his opinion was generally accepted within the scientific community).

10. **Inadmissible opinion on ultimate issue**: *State v. Wilson*, App. 3 Cir. 1996, 677 So. 2d 471, 1996-46 (La.App. 3 Cir. 5/8/96), writ denied 699 So. 2d 49, 1996-1893 (La. 8/27/97) (holding that physician's expert testimony inadmissible as to effects of various drugs on hypothetical individual's ability to perceive, recall and remember regarding aggravated rape victim's credibility, when hypothetical individual exactly matched victim's profile and circumstances, and physician's opinion would have been used to decide ultimate issue); *State v. Mitchell*, 572 So. 2d 800 (La. Ct. App. 4th Cir. 1990), writ denied 576 So. 2d 47 (holding that in second-degree murder trial where defendant's specific intent was disputed, expert testimony concerning amount of alcohol needed to impair an alcoholic's volition was not admissible where expert's opinion was based on factual situation directly paralleling actual situation presented in court, and expert opinion concerned ultimate issue of whether defendant had specific intent to kill); *State v. Johnson*, 52 So. 3d 110 (La. Ct. App. 5th Cir. 2010), writ denied 60 So. 3d 1248, 2010-2546 (La. 4/1/11) (holding that police lieutenant's responses to prosecutor's "hypothetical" questions in prosecution for possession with intent to distribute cocaine came too close to commenting on the ultimate issue of guilt when the prosecutor's "hypothetical" tracked the specific facts of the case at trial down to the number of pieces of crack recovered from defendant and the weight of the large piece of crack recovered from defendant's apartment).
11. **Distinguishing reliability of methodology and the conclusions drawn from use of the methodology:** *Dirett v. Lakeside Hosp.*, 811 So. 2d 116 (La. Ct. App. 4th Cir. 2002) (holding that court erred in excluding expert testimony under *Daubert* that blood transfusion can cause Hepatitis C, due to conflicting evidence that it was scientifically impossible to determine source of infection; methodology was not questioned, only conclusions reached by applying the methodology to the facts).
12. **Beyond scope of lay witness—expert witness needed:** *Robin v. Hebert*, 2012-1417 La. App. 3 Cir. 5/1/13, 2013 WL 1809821, So. 3d (La. Ct. App. 3d Cir. 2013) (holding that claims by a medical malpractice victim that a certain medication was both inappropriately prescribed to the patient and prescribed in an inappropriate dosage are complex medical issues that could require expert evidence).
13. **Inadmissible evidence as basis:** *Dixon v. Tucker*, 92 So. 3d 1100 (La. Ct. App. 2d Cir. 2012) (allowing witness to rely on hearsay police reports and investigation reports in accident reconstruction).

Chapter 8

Privileges

§ 8.1 Introduction to Privileges

In this chapter we now turn to the study of **privileges**. The law governing privileges is contained in Chapter 5 of the Louisiana Code of Evidence.[1] A privilege is the legal right to preclude the disclosure of relevant and, in some cases, highly probative evidence from trial. You might have heard of a person asserting a spousal witness privilege, an attorney-client privilege, or a doctor-patient privilege. In all cases, the privilege allows the person asserting it to refuse to disclose potentially relevant evidence. As such, privileges are said to actually "inhibit[] the truth seeking function of [the] adversary trial."[2] Thus, the question becomes, why are they allowed?

Privileges are justified based on public policy interests that are furthered by the existence of the privilege. For example, if a spouse asserts the spousal testimonial privilege and refuses to testify against her husband, she might likely have highly relevant and probative evidence that will be withheld from the trial. However, the spousal witness privilege is designed to show respect for and support the sanctity of marriage by promoting marital harmony. Needless to say, things will not go over very well at home in a marriage after a spouse has just given harmful testimony against the other spouse. Thus, we deem the importance of the marital union to justify and outweigh the harm of allowing the spouse to refuse to disclose the relevant evidence.

All privileges are based on personal or public policy interests sought to be furthered by the existence of the privilege and are allowed only when such interests are deemed to be of such importance to outweigh the potential harm of excluding the relevant evidence from trial. Other privileges contained in the Code, including the spousal communications privilege, the attorney-client privilege, and the doctor-patient privilege, protect confidential communications within those relationships where such open communication is essential to furthering the nature and purpose of the relationships. Privileges also exist for the support and maintenance of certain relationships themselves, to prevent a person from perjuring himself if he were compelled to disclose such information, and several other interests that we will discuss later in this chapter.

While the Louisiana Code of Evidence does not purport to contain all privileges that may exist under various state and federal statutes, or the state and federal constitutions, Chapter 5 of the Code contains the most significant, including: the spousal communications privilege, lawyer-client privilege, healthcare provider-patient privilege, clergyman-penitent privilege, accountant-client privilege, and others.

Holder of the privilege/Waiver. The holder of a privilege is the person or party for whose benefit the privilege operates—protecting *his* information, relationship, or other

1. Added by Acts 1992, No. 376, § 1, eff. Jan. 1, 1993.
2. State v. Taylor, 642 So. 2d 160 (La. 1994).

enumerated interest. Privileges are personal to the holder (or holders) who has the sole right to waive it, allowing for the disclosure of the protected information. While others may assert a privilege on behalf of the holder, such as an attorney who may assert the attorney-client privilege on behalf of his client and refuse to disclose the content of their communications, only the holder of a privilege may waive the privilege. Waiver of a privilege may be express or implied, and generally occurs when the holder "voluntarily discloses or consents to disclosure of any significant part of the privileged matter."[3] Disclosure by a non-holder does not constitute a waiver of the privilege.[4]

Proceedings in which privileges are applicable. As outlined in Article 1101 (A)(2), "except as otherwise provided by legislation, the provisions pertaining to privileges in Chapter 5 of the Code apply to all stages of all actions, cases, and proceedings where there is power to subpoena witnesses, including administrative, juvenile, legislative, military courts-martial, grand jury, arbitration, medical review panel, and judicial proceedings,"[5] worker's compensation cases, child custody cases, revocation of probation hearings, preliminary examinations in criminal cases, proceedings in mayor's courts and justice of the peace courts, peace bond hearings, extradition hearings, and several other types of hearings and proceedings.[6]

The provisions make clear that the rules governing privileges have much broader scope than the other rules of evidence, and are generally applicable to all types of hearings where a person may be required to give testimony in a government-authorized trial, hearing, or other proceeding.[7] The idea is that if information is confidential, disclosure at any point would destroy that confidentiality. Thus, privileged information is protected in a broad range of proceedings.

Federal Rules of Evidence Distinction. The Federal Rules do not contain a chapter on privileges. Federal Rule of Evidence 501 provides "The common law—as interpreted by United States courts in the light of reason and experience—governs a claim of privilege unless any of the following provides otherwise: the United States Constitution; a federal statute; or rules prescribed by the Supreme Court. But in a civil case, state law governs privilege regarding a claim or defense for which state law supplies the rule of decision."[8] "The rationale underlying the proviso is that federal law should not supersede that of the States in substantive areas such as privilege absent a compelling reason. The Committee believes that in civil cases in the federal courts where an element of a claim or defense is not grounded upon a federal question, there is no federal interest strong enough to justify departure from State policy."[9] Thus, in federal court, privileges are governed under the common law, except in civil cases when the matter to be proved is regarding a "claim or defense" as to which state law supplies the "rule of decision," such as in diversity cases. In such cases, state law would govern the privilege in federal court.

Throughout this chapter, we will study the most common of the privileges, those that have been the subject of the most litigation and debate. They include: the spousal communications privilege, lawyer-client privilege, healthcare provider-patient privilege, and clergyman-penitent privilege. Other privileges will be briefly summarized.

---

3. La. Code Evid. art. 502(A).
4. *See* La. Code Evid. art. 502 Official Comment (c).
5. La. Code Evid. art. 1101(A)(2).
6. *See* La. Code Evid. art. 1101(B) and (C).
7. La. Code Evid. art. 1101 Official Comment (e).
8. *See* Fed. R. Evid. 501.
9. Fed. R. Evid. 501, Notes of Committee on the Judiciary, House Report No. 93–650.

§8.2 Spousal Communications Privilege [La. C.E. art. 504]

Applicable Code Articles

Art. 504. Spousal confidential communications privilege

A. Definition. A communication is "confidential" if it is made privately and is not intended for further disclosure unless such disclosure is itself privileged.

B. Confidential communications privilege. Each spouse has a privilege during and after the marriage to refuse to disclose, and to prevent the other spouse from disclosing, confidential communications with the other spouse while they were husband and wife.

C. Confidential communications; exceptions. This privilege does not apply:

(1) In a criminal case in which one spouse is charged with a crime against the person or property of the other spouse or of a child of either.

(2) In a civil case brought by or on behalf of one spouse against the other spouse.

(3) In commitment or interdiction proceedings as to either spouse.

(4) When the communication is offered to protect or vindicate the rights of a minor child of either spouse.

(5) In cases otherwise provided by legislation.

There are two privileges that relate to spouses in the Louisiana Code of Evidence—one is the spousal **confidential communications privilege** that protects certain confidential communications between spouses, and the other privilege is the **spousal testimonial privilege** that prevents spouses from being compelled to testify against each other at trial. The spousal confidential communications privilege is discussed in this section. The spousal testimonial privilege will be discussed in §8.3.

The spousal confidential communications privilege is contained in Article 504 and provides that each spouse has a privilege during and after the marriage to refuse to disclose, and to prevent the other spouse from disclosing confidential communications with the other spouse made during the existence of the marriage. As briefly discussed above, this privilege encourages open communications between spouses because a spouse can be confident in knowing that he or she can preclude the other spouse from disclosing such communications in judicial proceedings. We deem open communication within a marriage to be essential to the maintenance and support of the relationship, and thus justify not having the relevant information disclosed in a judicial proceeding.

The key components of the spousal confidential communications privilege are:

1. applies to "communications" only;
2. the communications must be "confidential"; and
3. must be made "during" the existence of a lawful marriage.

Applies to *communications* only. The confidential communications privilege only applies to *communications* between the spouses made during the marriage. For purposes of the provision, communications include "information intentionally imparted to the other spouse" whether written or oral. The privilege does not apply to actions or observations,

> **Key components of spousal communications privilege:**
> 1. applies to "communications" only;
> 2. the communications must be "confidential";
> 3. must be made during the existence of lawful marriage; and
> 4. applies both during and after marriage.

unless the spouse intends to assert a message by his actions, as we studied in Chapter 5 relative to hearsay. For example, if Wife observes Husband sitting on the bed counting money stolen during an armed robbery, Husband cannot claim that his conduct done in the presence of Wife was a confidential communication. He did not intend to communicate with her. Conduct, in some cases, could be a communication if it is indeed intended as an assertion. For example, if Wife believes Husband has killed someone and asks him if he did it, and he then takes a gun out and points at it, he might intend to communicate that he did, in fact, kill the person, in which case the communication would be protected under the rule.

Similarly, the privilege does not apply to situations in which the spouse may have been talking in his sleep, to himself, or if a spouse inadvertently reads information that the other spouse has written, say in a text message or diary entry. In such situations, the information was not "intentionally imparted to the other spouse." This situation is discussed further in *State v. Gaudet*,[10] below. If the information was not a "communication" within the meaning of the article, it is not protected under this provision.

Applies to *confidential* communications only. Further, the privilege does not apply to all communications between spouses, but only those that are intended to be *confidential.* A communication is "confidential" if it is made privately and is not intended for further disclosure unless such disclosure is itself privileged. Usually, communications made privately between the spouses are deemed to be confidential, while those made in the presence of third parties or when the spouses should have reason to know that a third party might overhear the conversation, are not confidential. For example, if a spouse shares information with the other spouse at a restaurant that is overheard by the waiter or people at the next table, the information is not likely to be deemed confidential because the spouse had reason to know that others could have overheard their conversation.

However, if the statement is not made under circumstances in which the spouse should have known that it would be overheard, the presence of an eavesdropper will not destroy the confidentiality of the statement, as between the spouses. The eavesdropper to the confidential husband-wife communications may testify to the communications, at least where the eavesdropper overhears the conversation without the cooperation or connivance of one of the spouses.[11] If a spouse takes part in facilitating the presence of another party, the communication is not confidential and the privilege does not apply, even as to the spouses.

Whether a communication is "confidential" is a preliminary determination to be made by the trial court that will consider the "totality of the circumstances surrounding the making of the communication and the probable intent of the parties at the time of the

10. State v. Gaudet, 638 So. 2d 1216 (La. Ct. App. 1st Cir. 1994).
11. Force & Rault, HANDBOOK, Art. 504 Author's Note (1).

communication."[12] In making the determination of whether the communication is confidential the court is prohibited from looking to the content of the communication itself to determine whether it was made in confidence.[13]

Communications made *during* the marriage. Further, the privilege only applies to communications made *during the existence of a lawful marriage*. It does not apply to statements made before a couple was married or after the marriage has ended. It only applies to those communications that occurred *during* the existence of a lawful marriage under the laws of the state. Thus, since Louisiana does not recognize a Louisiana common-law marriage, the privilege would not apply to statements made during the existence of such relationships, regardless of whether or how long the couple may have lived in a domestic or familial relationship.

Keep in mind though that while Louisiana does not recognize a Louisiana common-law marriage, under the Full Faith and Credit Clause of the United States Constitution, Louisiana will likely recognize the existence of the privilege for statements made during the existence of a lawful common-law marriage recognized by another state. Thus, if a couple who has a common-law marriage, say in the state of Texas, moves to Louisiana and makes confidential communications to his or her spouse during the existence of the Texas common-law marriage, the statements will likely be protected. However, common-law marriages purporting to have been established in Louisiana do not exist and are not recognized under the privilege.

Applies during and after the marriage. While the communications must be made during the marriage, the privilege to prevent disclosure of such communications continues after the marriage ends. Thus, a person may refuse to disclose or prevent the former spouse from disclosing confidential communications made while the couple was married, even after the couple divorces. For example, suppose Wife privately tells Husband during their marriage that she is stealing money from her employer. The couple later divorces and charges are subsequently brought against the Wife for the embezzlement. Wife can prevent ex-husband from testifying to what she told him during the marriage, even though they are no longer married.

Keep in mind though that in this situation, this privilege (protecting confidential communications) does not entitle ex-husband to refuse to testify against his ex-wife altogether. That is the spousal testimonial privilege. Under *this* privilege, if the couple divorces, the ex-husband can be compelled to testify against his ex-wife. However, the wife can prevent the husband from testifying to the confidential communications she made to him while they were married. The husband may, however, testify to other things—actions, communications that are not confidential, etc. Under this privilege, while the protected communications must be made *during* the marriage, the privilege to prevent disclosure of such statements continues even after the marriage ends.

Below in § 8.3, we will discuss the spousal testimonial privilege that gives a testifying spouse the right to refuse to testify against a person to whom she is currently married that ceases to exist after the marriage ends. Under that privilege, while a spouse may be compelled to testify after the marriage ends, the confidential communications made under this privilege continue to be protected. We will further compare the two privileges below after we have studied the spousal testimonial privilege.

Either spouse may prevent other from disclosing. The spousal communications privilege belongs to **both spouses**, and as such, either spouse may assert the privilege to prevent the

12. *Id.*
13. *Id.*

other spouse from disclosing the confidential communications made during the marriage. Thus, as we pointed out in the example above, the defendant spouse (the Wife) can assert the privilege and prevent the husband from testifying against her in a trial.

As we will study below, under the spousal *witness* privilege, only the witness spouse is the single holder of the privilege and as such, only he may assert and waive it and voluntarily testify against the defendant spouse if he chooses to.

Exceptions to the privilege. There are several exceptions to this privilege in which the privilege does not apply and include:

1. domestic violence cases (spouse or child);
2. civil case against other spouse;
3. commitment or interdiction as to either spouse; and
4. offered to protect or vindicate the rights of a minor child of either spouse.

In these situations, relevant communications made by a spouse are not privileged and thus their disclosure cannot be precluded. For example, in a trial in which the communicating spouse battered the other spouse or child, the communicating spouse would not be able to assert the privilege and preclude the witness from testifying to confidential communications made by him. The same applies to the other exceptions.

Applies in civil and criminal cases. The privilege applies in both civil and criminal cases in a full range of proceedings as discussed above in § 8.1.

Case on Spousal Communications Privilege

State v. Gaudet
Court of Appeal of Louisiana, First Circuit
638 So. 2d 1216
June 24, 1994

LOTTINGER, Chief Judge.

On February 18, 1984, Connie Guidry Gaudet ("the victim") mysteriously disappeared. The victim, who had been married to defendant since September 1978, had two young daughters, ages four and one. On the day of her disappearance, the victim worked until 6:30 p.m., picked up her two daughters from their grandmother's care, and returned to the house she shared with defendant in Lockport, Louisiana. The youngest daughter's second birthday was approximately one week away. The victim was twenty-three years of age at the time of her disappearance....

Following her disappearance, defendant filed for a divorce from the victim. Defendant obtained the divorce. Subsequently, in June 1985, defendant married Donna Foret. Defendant and Foret were married until November 1988. During her marriage to defendant, Foret lived in the same house that defendant shared with the victim....

In February 1991, defendant sold the residence he had shared with the victim to Joyce Toups.... In November 1991, after inheriting another residence from a relative, Toups sold the house she had bought from defendant to Jerry and Monica Knight.... The Knights contacted defendant and asked him for information on the drain fields. Defendant met with the Knights and the sewer contractor to determine the best location to place the system.

... Defendant suggested that the excavation be as close to the fence as possible. Furthermore, defendant advised the Knights to avoid the area around the slab because of tree stumps. Defendant left the Knights believing that they would follow his advice. Ultimately, the Knights and the contractor decided to place the system in a location different from the one suggested by defendant.... During the installation process, the slab was broken up by heavy machinery.

On Sunday, November 10, 1991, Jerry Knight decided to clean the yard following the installation project. While cleaning, he discovered what appeared to be part of a human jawbone lying on the soil surface. The Knights brought the bone to a family physician. The physician concluded the bone was of human origin, but deferred to a pathologist for a final confirmation. After further examination established the sample was from a human skeleton, the police excavated the yard. A substantial portion of a skeleton, wrapped in a mattress cover, was exhumed. Moreover, dental records established that the remains removed from the yard were those of the victim. Thereafter, defendant was arrested and charged with her murder.

Defendant was indicted by the Lafourche Parish grand jury for the second degree murder of his wife. He was tried by a jury, which convicted him as charged....

ISSUES

The presentation of defendant's briefed assignments of error raises the following ... questions ... in light of the spousal privilege, did the trial court err by allowing defendant's second wife to testify about statements that he made concerning the victim? ...

SPOUSAL PRIVILEGE

... [D]efendant submits that the trial court erred by permitting his second wife, Donna Foret, to testify about the statements he made concerning the victim. Defendant argues this evidence was introduced in violation of the spousal privilege.

La.Code of Evid. art. 504(B), establishing the spousal privilege to confidential communications, provides as follows:

> Each spouse has a privilege during and after the marriage to refuse to disclose, and to prevent the other spouse from disclosing, confidential communications *with* the other spouse while they were husband and wife. (Emphasis added.)

Whether a particular communication is protected as a confidential communication is a question of fact to be determined by the trial court. Accordingly, the trial court must assess the totality of the circumstances surrounding the alleged confidential communication and the probable intent of the divulging spouse at the time it was made.

Defendant and Foret were married from June 1985, to November 1988. At trial Foret testified about three separate incidents wherein she overheard defendant apparently "speaking" to the victim when he was unaware that she could hear him. The first occasion was before their marriage. Foret testified that she was in defendant's bedroom, seated at his desk, when defendant emerged from the shower. As he looked in the mirror, wiping his face with a towel, defendant stated, "Connie, I'm so sorry I did what I did. I miss you. The kids miss you." Defendant then noticed that Foret was in the room. She and defendant argued over the remarks. Further, Foret wanted to leave. However, defendant ordered her to stay and not to let anyone know she was upset by what she had heard. Foret did as he instructed.

After the couple was married, Foret overheard defendant apparently speaking to the victim one morning as he was getting ready for work. She heard him call the victim's name. Then, she heard him compliment the victim on the meal she had prepared the preceding evening and how well she had done with the children because they were learning to behave better and "they have just become a whole loving family." Apparently, defendant was attributing Forte's actions to the victim. Foret became upset and questioned him about the comments. However, defendant denied making the statements, telling her that she was "hearing things."

The third statement overheard by Foret occurred after she sustained an illness precluding sexual intercourse for several weeks. On the night that she and defendant resumed sexual relations, Foret overheard defendant in the bathroom, addressing the victim and telling her how well the children were doing and how pleased he was with their conduct. Then, defendant stated, "Connie, you were the best lover tonight that you ever have been." Foret testified that she confronted defendant about the statements when he came out of the bathroom. However, defendant denied making the statements, telling her that she was dreaming.

The legislature enacted La.Code of Evid. art. 504(B) to instill and preserve confidence within the marital relationship. However, not every word uttered by one spouse that happens to be heard by the other spouse is entitled to this shield of secrecy. Hence, as emphasized above, the spousal privilege applies only to confidential communications "with" the other spouse. Although "confidential communications" embody both words and acts, the privilege only extends where the information was intentionally imparted to the other spouse. In other words, there must be an intentional sharing of the confidential information.

The first instance about which Foret testified occurred prior to their marriage. Hence, the spousal privilege does not even arguably extend to this instance. The other two statements were remarks made by defendant which he apparently did not intend for Foret to hear.

In determining that the statements were admissible, the trial court ruled as follows:

> The words of a statute, of course, are supposed to be given their ordinary meaning. And as I read 504(B) what is protected here is not the generalized interest in privacy, but specifically communications with the spouse, communications between one spouse and another spouse.
>
> Accordingly, I interpret Article 504 as excluding from the privilege statements that were made in the presence of the spouse that were not in fact, and not intended to be, communications or expressions by one spouse with the other. I think that had the legislature intended to give a broader protection to protect a broader interest, it easily could have done so.

The trial court's reasoning is correct. As evidenced from the context in which they were made, these statements were not intended to be communications between defendant and Foret. Although defendant claims that he obviously intended for Foret to hear the statements because he was on notice of her distress after hearing the first incident, the circumstances under which the comments were made, especially the fact that on both occasions defendant apparently believed Foret was asleep in an adjacent room, simply do not support his claim that the communication was intentional.

Accordingly, defendant's assignment of error is without merit....

AFFIRMED.

Discussion Questions

1. You have studied the policy interests in protecting confidential communications between spouses. What are those interests? Are these interests furthered by protecting communications that were *not* intentionally imparted to the other spouse, as in *Gaudet,*

or if a spouse inadvertently reads a text message on the other spouse's phone, etc.? Why or why not?

2. Do you find the defendant's argument persuasive that he intended that the statements be heard, "because he was on notice of her distress after hearing the first incident"? Examining the facts, do you find any validity in this argument?

§ 8.3 Spousal Testimonial Privilege [La. C.E. art. 505]

Applicable Code Articles

Art. 505. Spousal witness privilege

In a criminal case or in commitment or interdiction proceedings, a witness spouse has a privilege not to testify against the other spouse. This privilege terminates upon the annulment of the marriage, legal separation, or divorce of the spouses. This privilege does not apply in a criminal case in which one spouse is charged with a crime against the person of the other spouse or a crime against the person of a child including but not limited to the violation of a preliminary or permanent injunction or protective order and violations of R.S. 14:79.

The other privilege that applies to spouses is the **spousal *witness* privilege**. This privilege is contained in Article 505 and provides that a witness has a privilege not to be compelled to testify against her current spouse in a criminal case or in commitment or interdiction proceedings. As we explained above, this privilege promotes and supports the sanctity of marriage by furthering marital harmony in not compelling a person to give harmful testimony against her current spouse in a criminal, commitment, or interdiction proceeding. Thus, the privilege exists even though it results in the exclusion of relevant evidence at trial. The key components of the privilege include:

1. Applies to "testimony" at trial;
2. Only applies "during" the existence of lawful marriage;
3. Only "testifying" spouse is holder, and may assert or waive; and
4. Applies during criminal trial, commitment, or interdictions proceedings.

Witness spouse sole holder of privilege. The witness spouse is the sole holder of this privilege, and therefore may assert it and refuse to testify against the other spouse, or she may waive it and freely testify if she chooses to do so. Thus, in a criminal trial, if Wife were called to testify against Husband (the defendant), she could assert the spousal witness privilege and refuse to testify against her husband. However, because the witness is the sole holder of the privilege and may waive it if she chooses to, Wife could testify against Husband and he could not prevent her from doing so.

Only applies *during* a lawful marriage. Unlike the spousal communications privilege, the spousal witness privilege is only applicable *during* the marriage. A witness only has a privilege to refuse to testify against a person to whom she is currently married at the time she is called to testify. The privilege terminates upon annulment, legal separation or divorce. Thus, even if the testifying spouse is testifying as to events that occurred during the marriage, if she is no longer married when the witness is called to testify, she may not assert the testimonial privilege. As we discussed in the last section, however, while the witness does not

Key components of spousal witness privilege:

1. Must be "testifying";
2. Only applies "during" the existence of lawful marriage;
3. Witness spouse is sole holder, and may assert or waive; and
4. Applies during criminal trial or interdictions proceedings.

have a privilege to refuse to testify once the marriage has ended, the witness may not testify to confidential communications made during the existence of the marriage unless the other spouse (the communicating spouse) waives the privilege. As you learned in the last section, the communications privilege continues even after the marriage has ended.

Further, the privilege does not apply to common-law marriages purporting to have originated in the State of Louisiana, as Louisiana does not recognize a Louisiana common-law marriage. However, the privilege likely applies to common-law marriages recognized by another state.

Applies to *testifying* only. Further, the privilege does not apply to statements made by a spouse against the other spouse in contexts outside of testifying in court. In other words, the privilege only applies to the spouse's in-court testimony; it does not preclude other statements the spouse might have made at other times or to other individuals. For example, the privilege would not preclude the prosecution from offering a wife's statement against her defendant/husband that she might have previously made to law enforcement, to a friend or to a family member. Thus, if Wife tells her best friend that her husband committed a crime, Wife could not prevent Friend from testifying about what Wife told her under this privilege. Similarly, if Wife made a statement to law enforcement, she could not preclude the statement from being offered against her husband under this privilege. While the statement might be excluded under other provisions of the Code, such as hearsay, they are not privileged under the spousal witness privilege in that they are not "testimony."[14]

Domestic violence exception. Prior to 2006, the spousal witness privilege did not contain an exception for domestic violence situations as the spousal communications privilege contains. Thus, a person could refuse to testify against her spouse even in a situation where her refusal was a result of intimidation or fear of the person accused of the forcible offense against her. In 2006, the spousal testimonial privilege was amended to include an exception in criminal cases in which one spouse is charged with a crime against the person of the other spouse or of a child. The exception also applies in cases involving violations of a preliminary or permanent injunction or protective order.

The Louisiana Supreme Court addressed the issue in *State v. Taylor*[15] below, holding that "in a case where the testifying spouse is the victim of the offense charged, and where the evidence supports a finding that the victim spouse asserting the spousal privilege is more probable than not acting under fear, threats or coercion, or that the marriage itself is a sham confected for the purpose of making the privilege available, the purpose of the privilege is not served and may, in the court's discretion, be considered as not applicable." Thus, while the article did not contain a domestic violence exception prior to 2006, a

14. *See* State v. Walters, 630 So. 2d 1371 (La. Ct. App. 2d Cir. 1994).
15. State v. Taylor, 642 So. 2d 160 (La. 1994).

spouse who was a victim of violence from the accused spouse could have been compelled to testify against her spouse under the authority of *Taylor*. The *Taylor* court reasoned that the privilege did not apply to domestic violence situations because the public policy interests sought to be furthered (furthering marital harmony) are not furthered by allowing a witness to refuse to testify in such situations. Following the 2006 amendment, Article 505 now specifically excepts such situations from the privilege.

It is worth noting that as we studied in the last section, the spousal communications privilege in Article 504 has contained a domestic violence exception since the statute was enacted in 1992. The reasoning there was that since the accused spouse could assert the communications privilege and prevent the witness spouse from disclosing confidential communications, the exception was *needed* to enable a witness spouse who was the victim of violence to be allowed to testify to the relevant communications. Otherwise, the defendant spouse could prevent the witness from testifying to the communications. It was believed that such an exception was not necessary for the *witness* privilege since the witness, being the holder of the privilege, could waive the privilege and testify if she chose to. However, *Taylor* recognized that even with the power to waive the testimonial privilege, in many instances the victim of a crime might not feel free to do so due to fear, threats, or coercion from the defendant spouse. Thus, such an exception is also needed under this privilege—hence, the 2006 amendment.

The statute does not specifically extend to excepting the "sham marriage" from the privilege, where a couple marries solely for the purpose of asserting the spousal testimonial privilege. However, such situations might still be excepted from the privilege under the authority of *Taylor*.

Applies when called to testify *against* spouse. Some authorities[16] are of the opinion that since the provision specifically grants the privilege to a witness being called to testify *against* her spouse, it would not apply if the witness is called to testify *for* her spouse, i.e., she would not be able to refuse to testify for her spouse under this provision. Extending the privilege to such a situation could potentially implicate the defendant's Sixth Amendment right to present a defense.

Distinctions in spousal witness privilege and spousal communications privilege. As you study the two spousal privileges, you should keep in mind these major distinctions between the two of them, and that they each act independently of the other.

Types of cases:

- Spousal testimonial privilege—applies in criminal, interdiction, commitment proceedings
- Spousal communications privilege—applies in criminal or civil cases

What/who it applies to:

- Spousal testimonial privilege—applies only to current spouse
- Spousal communications privilege—applies to communications made during the marriage, even after marriage ends

Holder of privilege:

- Spousal testimonial privilege—only the witness spouse holds testimonial privilege and may assert or waive it

---

16. *See* Force & Rault, Handbook, Art. 505 Author's Note (3); *Cf.* State v. Chatman, 683 So. 2d 1236 (La. Ct. App. 3d Cir. 1996).

- Spousal communications privilege—both spouses hold the privilege and may assert the communications privilege to prevent the other from disclosing the confidential communications made during marriage

Duration of privilege:

- Spousal testimonial privilege applies only during the marriage
- Spousal communications privilege applies both during and after the marriage

Case on Spousal Testimonial Privilege

State v. Taylor
Supreme Court of Louisiana
642 So. 2d 160
Sept. 6, 1994

HALL, Justice.

The state contends that beginning at about 7:00 p.m. on May 16, 1993, and continuing until approximately 2:00 a.m. the following morning, Kenneth Taylor, then a New Orleans police officer, assaulted, threatened to kill and brutally beat his then girlfriend, Glenda Richard. He used his fists as well as his police-issue flashlight and 9mm Beretta semi-automatic service weapon to pummel the victim into a state of semiconsciousness. It is alleged that several times in these hours Taylor placed his Beretta inside the victim's mouth and threatened to pull the trigger. After the beating, Taylor put Richard and the couple's five-month-old daughter into his car and drove them to the Richard home in Violet, Louisiana. The victim's sister called an ambulance, and Glenda Richard spent several days at Chalmette Medical Center and Charity Hospital recovering from her injuries. The Internal Affairs division of the New Orleans Police Department investigated the matter and Richard cooperated. She gave a typed statement describing the beating, executed an affidavit setting forth her desire to prosecute, and appeared on video-tape. Richard was unable to read her statement because her eyes were swollen shut and because the injuries to her mouth rendered coherent speech difficult, but the video recorded her acknowledgment that the typed statement describing the attack was her own.

Pursuant to a warrant executed at defendant's home, investigators seized his broken police flashlight and bloodied 9mm Beretta. Photographs taken inside depicted blood-stained carpets, towels, walls, bed and a police uniform. Taylor was arrested May 17, 1993, and charged with aggravated battery, a violation of LSA-R.S. 14:34. He entered a plea of not guilty and trial was set for December 14, 1993.

On the morning of trial, the victim appeared with her own attorney to advise that she no longer wished to prosecute and, further, that she would not testify against the defendant. When the state's motion for a continuance was denied, it entered a nolle prosequi.

The state later reinstituted prosecution and, following Taylor's arraignment in January of 1994, a status hearing was scheduled for February 24. At the hearing, the prosecution learned that the victim and the defendant were married February 14, 1994. The hearing was continued. The state then filed a motion in limine which sought (1) to bar the victim's assertion of a claim of spousal privilege, and (2) to have her written, oral and video-taped statements declared admissible. The state made an oral motion that the victim be compelled to testify.

When the hearing resumed March 15, the victim appeared, took the stand and was questioned by the court. Mrs. Taylor acknowledged that she had initiated the call to police, that she filed a complaint and that she had identified defendant as the person responsible for her injuries. She remembered having pictures taken of her face and that she had assured the district attorney's office of her willingness to prosecute, but now, she stated, she had changed her mind. The trial judge denied the state's motion with the following remarks:

> ... I think if this woman's crazy enough to want to get beat up by her husband to within an inch of her life, and she wants to go back and marry him, that's her business. And I couldn't stop her if she wanted to get up on a ledge and jump off the building, if I wasn't close to her. It's her life. I've seen the pictures. I think she's crazy. But what am I going to do? I'll deny your Motion in Limine.

No evidence, other than the brief testimony of the victim described above, was presented at the hearing nor was there any discussion or argument on the state's request for a ruling on the admissibility of the victim's statements.

The state applied to the court of appeal for writs seeking a reversal of the trial court's denial of its motion in limine and its request for an order compelling the testimony of Glenda Richard Taylor against her husband. The state's application included a copy of the couple's marriage certificate, as well as an affidavit from Aubrey Richard, the victim's mother, executed March 17, 1994, subsequent to the trial court hearing. In the affidavit, Aubrey Richard stated that three days after her daughter and the defendant were married, her daughter moved back home. She also believed that her daughter was afraid of the defendant and afraid to testify against him.

The court of appeal denied the state's writ application without assigning reasons.

We issued a stay order and granted the state's writ application, *State v. Taylor,* 635 So.2d 1141 (La.1994).

II.

The spousal witness privilege in Louisiana has a long history and can be traced to the common law. In 1805, the legislature adopted the Crimes Act which implemented the common law as Louisiana's criminal law. See Sydney B. Galloway, *Evidence-The Husband-Wife Testimony Privilege,* 19 La.L.Rev. 427 (1954). The common law provided that the husband and wife were incompetent and disqualified from testifying against one another. By Act 29 of 1886 this principle was codified in Louisiana. The act provided "[t]hat the competent witness in all criminal matters, shall be a person of proper understanding; provided, that the husband cannot be a witness for or against his wife, nor the wife for or against her husband, except in such cases as is now provided by law." This same language was carried over in Act 185 of 1902. Since these statutes were based on the common law, the exceptions that were recognized in the common law were also applicable in Louisiana. One of the exceptions from the disqualification of the spouses to testify for or against one another was where the wife had sustained a personal injury from her husband. *State v. McDavid,* 15 La.Ann. 403 (1860); *State v. Pain,* 48 La.Ann. 311, 19 So. 138 (La.1896). The rationale for this policy was set forth in *State v. Parker,* 42 La.Ann. 972, 8 So. 473 (La.1890), where the husband was charged with the attempted murder of his wife. In rejecting the defendant-husband's claims that the trial court erred in admitting the testimony of the wife, this court held:

> The injured person is the wife of the accused. The common law authorities admit the testimony of the wife against the husband for the purpose of proving the crime committed by him on her person. The law's purpose in excluding the testimony is to respect and protect relations of faith, reliance, and confidence be-

> tween the spouses. When one attempts to destroy the other, the great necessity and importance of the exclusion no longer exists. The rules of evidence in the prosecution of crimes shall be according to the common law, unless otherwise provided. Acts 1805, p. 440. Where a crime has been committed on the person of the wife, she is a competent witness.

By Act 41 of 1904, the legislature added the exception that the privilege did not apply in bigamy cases, but retained the same language as was included in the previous acts. However, a major change occurred when Act 157 of 1916 adopted both the confidential communication privilege and the spousal witness privilege.6 With regard to the witness privilege, the act stated: "Neither husband nor wife shall be compelled to be a witness on any trial upon an indictment, complaint or other criminal proceeding, against the other." This same provision was reaffirmed by Act 2 of 1928 and later moved to the Code of Evidence by Act 376 of 1992. Currently, the spousal witness privilege is codified in Louisiana in LSA-C.E. art. 505. The privilege provides:

> In a criminal case or in commitment or interdiction proceedings, a witness spouse has a privilege not to testify against the other spouse. This privilege terminates upon the annulment of the marriage, legal separation, or divorce of the spouses.
>
> This privilege is held by the witness spouse and can be waived by her. The statute provides that neither spouse may be compelled to be a witness against the other in a criminal trial. However, the statute does not prohibit a spouse from voluntarily taking the stand against the defendant spouse. *State v. Triplett,* 313 So.2d 227, 229 (La.1975).

On the other hand, the confidential communication privilege is found in LSA-C.E. art. 504. That article provides in part:

> B. Confidential communications privilege. Each spouse has a privilege during and after the marriage to refuse to disclose, and to prevent the other spouse from disclosing, confidential communications with the other spouse while they were husband and wife.
>
> C. Confidential communications; exceptions. This privilege does not apply:
>
> (1) In a criminal case in which one spouse is charged with a crime against the person or property of the other spouse or of a child of either.

This court explained the difference between the two privileges when it discussed LSA-R.S. 15:461,[17] where both privileges were contained before being moved to the Code of Evidence:

> This statute, in effect, creates two distinct privileges. The first of these is the privilege which attaches to private conversations between husband and wife and which may be asserted by the defendant-spouse. Secondly, the statute establishes a privilege in favor of a spouse called to testify against the other spouse by providing that neither spouse shall be compelled to be a witness against the other

---

17. LSA-R.S. 15:461 provided:

The competent witness in any criminal proceeding, in a court or before a person having authority to receive evidence, shall be a person of proper understanding, but;

(1) Private conversations between husband and wife shall be privileged.

(2) Neither husband nor wife shall be compelled to be a witness on any trial upon an indictment, complaint or other criminal proceeding, against the other.

(3) In the trial of all indictments, complaints and other proceedings against persons charged with the commission of crimes or offenses, a person so charged shall, at his own request, but not otherwise, be deemed a competent witness.

> in a criminal proceeding. The exercise of this privilege rests with the testifying spouse alone and may not be invoked by the defendant-spouse.

State v. Bennett, 357 So.2d 1136, 1139–40 (La.1978). The fact that the defendant spouse can invoke the confidential communications privilege led the legislature to create a statutory exception in cases where "one spouse is charged with a crime against the person or property of the other spouse or a child of either." LSA-C.E. art. 504(C)(1).

By the passage of Act 157 of 1916, and the subsequent acts thereafter, the legislature abrogated the common law rule and the common law exceptions in Louisiana. *State v. Dejean,* 159 La. 900, 106 So. 374 (La.1925). The common law rule that one spouse was incompetent or disqualified from testifying against the other spouse was replaced by a privilege that provided that the spouse could not be compelled to testify, but could voluntarily do so. If a witness spouse voluntarily agreed to testify against a defendant spouse, the defendant spouse could not object unless the testimony included confidential communications and the defendant spouse invoked the confidential communications privilege. The fact that the privilege is vested solely in the witness spouse rendered unnecessary the common law exception in cases where the defendant spouse had caused personal injury to the testifying spouse, because there was no absolute bar to the spouse's testimony, the defendant spouse could not prevent its admissibility, and the victim spouse could voluntarily testify.

Statutory privileges should be given a genuine construction. Although privileges serve to foster a relationship (in this instance the husband-wife relationship), they disserve the truth-seeking function of the adversary trial. Therefore, in determining the applicability of a privilege, a court should determine whether the testimony that is claimed to be privileged is in the class whose exclusion will advance the policy sought to be furthered by the privilege. *State v. Fuller,* 454 So.2d 119, 122 (La.1984); *State v. Aucoin,* 362 So.2d 503, 506 (La.1978). The policies for adopting the witness spouse privilege were an interest in preserving the family unit and "society's desire to preserve the harmony of the existing marriage by preventing ill feeling between the spouses that might result if one were required to give unfavorable testimony against the other." Galloway, supra at 428–9.

III.

The state contends that the court should establish an exception to the spousal witness privilege in cases where one spouse is the victim of abuse by the other spouse, as is the case with the confidential communication privilege, LSA-C.E. art. 504. The state believes that the refusal of this court to apply the exception in LSA-C.E. art. 504 to LSA-C.E. art. 505 would render the exception ineffective, since the testifying spouse could circumvent the exception and hinder justice by simply invoking the spousal witness privilege. It is argued that this would contravene the purpose of the evidence statutes "to secure fairness and efficiency in administration of the law of evidence to the end that truth may be ascertained and proceedings justly determined." LSA-C.E. art. 102.

Additionally, the state argues that the spousal witness privilege should not apply in this case and all cases where the crime occurs before marriage and the marriage between the victim and the defendant is used as a means to foreclose the victim from testifying at the criminal trial.

The state also provides cases and codal provisions from other jurisdictions in support of its proposed interpretation of Louisiana's testimonial privileges. However, no clear or hard and fast rule is discernible, given the differences in other jurisdictions' statutory language, intricacies of evidentiary and procedural rules, and judicial interpretations. Therefore, the bulk of what the state offers from other states provides neither support for its position nor is particularly persuasive.

IV.

LSA-C.E. art. 504 makes an exception where the spouse is the victim for the confidential communication privilege. LSA-C.E. art. 504 makes no such exception for the spousal witness privilege. The reason for the distinction is clear: the confidential communication privilege can be exercised by the defendant, barring the victim spouse from testifying even though the victim spouse wishes to testify; the spousal witness privilege cannot be exercised by the defendant, leaving the victim spouse perfectly free to testify if the victim spouse wishes to do so.

The spousal witness privilege, as explained above, has been a part of Louisiana law for a long time, and it was recently affirmed by the legislature when it was considered and included in the Evidence Code adopted in 1992 without any exception as to victim spouses. As a longstanding and recently affirmed legislative enactment, the court would not be justified in reading into the statute an exception purposely omitted by the legislature, regardless of the court's view as to whether or not such an exception represents better policy.

Similarly, the code article makes no exception for acts occurring prior to marriage. It is generally held that the competency of one spouse as a witness depends on the existence of the relationship at the time he or she is offered as a witness, and not upon whether the relationship existed at the time of the occurrence of the events about which he or she is expected to testify. *See State v. Dejean,* 159 La. 900, 106 So. 374 (La.1925); 81 Am.Jur.2d, *Witnesses,* § 245, p. 249 (1992); Annotation, *Marriage for Purpose of Barring Testimony,* 13 A.L.R. 4th 1305. There is no exception in the governing Louisiana code article making the spousal witness privilege inapplicable to testimony about acts occurring prior to marriage.

However, the dynamics of spousal abuse and domestic violence cannot be ignored. Fear, self-blame, and other emotional factors often leave a battered spouse unable to make a sound judgment as to whether to testify against an abusive spouse. Exercise of the spousal witness privilege may be the result of coercion, fear, subjugation, or undue influence, perhaps not even consciously recognized by the abused spouse in some circumstances.

Recognizing these dynamics, and the barrier the spousal witness privilege erects to the prosecution of criminal offenses which are, after all, offenses against society as a whole, the privilege has been legislatively abolished in many states, and judicially limited in decisions of other state and federal courts.

While we do not feel justified or empowered to impose by judicial fiat a victim spouse exception to the legislatively established spousal witness privilege, we nevertheless feel justified and even compelled to limit exercise of the privilege where facts and circumstances established by proper evidence indicate the privilege is being exercised because of fear, threats, or coercion, especially where the marriage giving rise to the privilege is itself the result of fear, threats, or coercion or a mere sham confected to make the privilege available. We do not believe it was the legislative intent to make the privilege available under circumstances such as these, where sanctity of the marriage and marital harmony are hardly served. Also, a defendant should not be able to prevent the introduction of damaging evidence through threats, fear or coercion of a spouse witness anymore than any other witness.

Thus, in a case where the testifying spouse is the victim of the offense charged, and where the evidence supports a finding that the victim spouse asserting the spousal witness privilege is more probably than not acting under fear, threats or coercion, or that the marriage itself is a sham confected for the purpose of making the privilege available, the purpose of the privilege is not served and may, in the court's discretion, be considered as not applicable.

Applying these precepts to the instant case, we note that the evidence was not fully developed at the hearing held in the district court. Nevertheless, the facts established raise a strong inference of both fear and coercion and a sham marriage. The alleged brutal beating, the initial willingness of the victim spouse to cooperate with the law enforcement authorities, the change of heart on the day of trial, the subsequent marriage after charges were reinstated, and (although the affidavit of the victim's mother is not considered) the lack of evidence that the victim and defendant have actually established a genuine marital relationship, create an inference that circumstances exist that would support the non-applicability of the privilege in this case.

Considering that we pronounce new rules in this opinion that were not available to the parties or the court at the time the hearing was held, we deem it in the interest of justice and the development of the true facts upon which a determination of the applicability of the privilege can be made to remand this case to the trial court for reconsideration and the taking of further evidence on the issue of whether the privilege is to be applied in this case and whether the victim spouse can be compelled to testify.

The ruling of the district court is set aside and the case is remanded to the district court for further proceedings consistent with this opinion.

REVERSED AND REMANDED.

Discussion Questions

1. Do you agree that the policy interests sought to be furthered by the spousal witness privilege are not furthered in domestic violence situations? Why or why not?
2. Explore the policy reason(s) behind why the domestic violence exception was not originally thought to be needed for the spousal testimonial privilege, but was included in the spousal communications privilege. Why do you think the article was amended to include the exception in 2006?
3. What are your thoughts on the "sham marriage"? Is the court in a position to determine whether a marriage is a sham and done only for the purpose for invoking the exception? Does this inquiry give courts an overreaching authority to delve into the privacy of married couples—assessing their love and affection for one another?
4. Why do you think the Louisiana Legislature did not include the "sham marriage" provision in the 2006 amendment?

Key Points

The key points to keep in mind regarding spousal privileges.

Spousal Testimonial Privilege

1. Testifying spouse is sole holder—can invoke and refuse to testify, or can waive the privilege and testify against the other spouse.
2. Only applies during marriage. If divorced, legally separated, or annulled, the exception doesn't exist. Must be a lawfully recognized marriage in Louisiana.
3. Doesn't apply in domestic violence cases in which the spouse or child is the victim in the case in which the spouse is called to testify.

Spousal Communications Privilege

1. Both spouses hold privilege, and can refuse to disclose and prevent the other from disclosing confidential communications. Thus, a spouse can prevent the other spouse from disclosing confidential communications made to them in a trial.
2. Includes communications only — not observations, or conduct, unless intended to assert a fact. Also doesn't include statements not intended to impart information to other spouse (e.g., talking in sleep, etc.).
3. While the communicating spouse cannot prevent the other spouse from testifying, in general, since the testifying spouse holds *that* privilege alone, he can prevent them from testifying to the confidential communications made to him.
4. Only applies to communications made *during* the marriage.
5. Privilege continues after marriage ends.
6. If statements made in presence of others, not considered confidential.
7. Exceptions: 1) domestic violence cases (spouse or child; 2) civil case against other spouse; 3) commitment or interdiction as to either spouse; 4) offered to protect or vindicate the rights of a minor child of either spouse.
8. Applies in civil or criminal cases.

Distinction between Two Privileges

Types of cases:

- Spousal testimonial privilege — applies in criminal, interdiction, commitment proceedings
- Spousal communications privilege — applies in criminal or civil cases

What/who it applies to:

- Spousal testimonial privilege — applies only to current spouse
- Spousal communications privilege — applies to communications made during the marriage, even after marriage ends

Holder of privilege:

- Spousal testimonial privilege — only the witness spouse holds testimonial privilege and may assert or waive it
- Spousal communications privilege — both spouses hold the privilege and may assert the communications privilege to prevent the other from disclosing the confidential communications made during marriage

Duration of privilege:

- Spousal testimonial privilege applies only during the marriage
- Spousal communications privilege applies both during and after the marriage

Problems on Spousal Privileges

PROBLEM 8-1. The defendant is charged with robbing a local convenience store. One night after the robbery, his wife said to him, *"I'm tired of being broke. You never have any money. When are you gonna get a job?"* Husband then gets up and silently goes over to the closet, pulls a laundry bag out from underneath a pile of clothes and pours the contents out onto the bed, which were thousands of balled up large bills of money. Wife became extremely upset, called the police, and her husband was arrested. She now wants to testify for the prosecution, but her husband insists that she cannot tell anyone what he showed her. Can the defendant prevent his wife from testifying regarding what she saw? If she chooses not to testify at all, can she be compelled to do so?

PROBLEM 8-2. One of your classmates has been severely beaten by her boyfriend. You encourage her to contact the police, which she did, and her boyfriend is arrested and charged with battering her. By the time the case goes to trial, six months later, the classmate has married her boyfriend and is pregnant. She refuses to testify. Can she be compelled to testify in the trial against her now-husband for the battery against her? Why or why not?

PROBLEM 8-3. Cam and his wife Jill have carefully planned to rob the Hillbrook Bank. On the day of the robbery, Cam leaves the following note on the whiteboard in their kitchen on the refrigerator: "*Jill: 5:00pm—Hillbrook Branch on Hillbrook Dr. Don't forget the bag! —Kids this is for your mother. Do not erase!*" The kids and housekeeper saw the note and did not erase it. The prosecution would like to offer the note on the whiteboard against husband at trial for the robbery. He has objected that it was a communication to his wife. Is the note protected by the spousal communications privilege? Why or why not?

PROBLEM 8-4. Lora and her husband Jim are on vacation and were taking a tour of the city on a tour bus. After one of their stops, Lora opened her purse and whispered to Jim, "Look at this expensive watch I snatched from that vendor on the corner." Unbeknownst to Lora, the couple sitting behind her and Jim on the bus overheard what she told Jim and reported the incident to the police. Lora was arrested. At the trial, can Lora prevent the couple from testifying to what they overheard her saying to her husband? If Jim wants to testify, can Lora prevent Jim from testifying to what she said?

PROBLEM 8-5. Sam and Delilah have been married for 15 years. During that time, Sam confided in Delilah that one day he was going to start committing burglaries and robberies and taking what he wants. Shortly after telling her that, they had three children. Feeling the financial strains, Sam decided to put his plan into action. Sam robbed several of their neighbors' houses and some local convenience stores and a bank. One night after Sam got home from robbing a store, he threw the money on the bed and began jumping around in it. He then took off his clothes and put the clothes, the mask, and the gun in the trash, as Delilah stood in the door in amazement at what she was seeing. Please answer the following questions:

A. Can Sam prevent Delilah from testifying against him in his robbery trial?

B. Can Delilah testify to Sam's statement that he was going to start committing robberies one day if she chooses to?

C. Can Sam prevent Delilah from testifying about him coming home with the money, jumping in it, and throwing the clothes, gun and mask away after his last robbery?

D. Can Delilah refuse to testify against Sam altogether?

PROBLEM 8-6. Biff and Sandra have been married for 10 years. Biff has owned his own business for 7 of those years. Biff is on trial for tax evasion and the State wants Sandra to testify about various statements and conversations between her and her husband as well as various business practices of the company that she may know about. She doesn't plan to testify against her husband. However, she has discussed the case extensively with her mother, who now knows everything. At the trial, Sandra refuses to testify against Biff. Sandra's mother tells the prosecution that she knows the whole story and will testify. The prosecution calls Sandra's mother to the stand. Biff objects that the information she will testify to is protected by both the spousal testimonial privilege and the spousal witness privilege. How should the judge rule and why? Assume that no hearsay objections were raised.

PROBLEM 8-7. Diane and Cantrell lived together for two years before getting married. During that time, Cantrell witnessed quite a bit of Diane's unlawful activity. Diane explained to him how she used computers to make bad checks and to process fake IDs to open accounts in other people's names to rip them off. Diane and Cantrell later get married. Can Cantrell be forced to testify against Diane in a criminal trial as to how Diane explained to him how she processed the bad checks? Why or why not?

§ 8.2 and § 8.3 References and Additional Authority on Spousal Witness and Spousal Communications Privileges [La. C.E. arts. 504, 505]

1. La. C.E. arts. 504, 505 and Official Comments
2. Force & Rault, HANDBOOK ON LOUISIANA EVIDENCE LAW Arts. 504, 505 Author's Comments (West Publishing 2014)
3. Harges & Jones, LOUISIANA EVIDENCE Arts. 504, 505 Author's Comments (West Publishing 2014)
4. 19 La. Civ. L. Treatise, Evidence And Proof § 8.11 (2nd ed.)
5. MCCORMICK ON EVIDENCE §§ 78–86 (5th ed., 1999)
6. **Commentary**: Deshazo, Michael, "*Louisiana Code of Evidence Article 504 and the Spousal Confidential Communications Privilege*," 57 La. B. J. 84 (2009).
7. **Spousal Communications Privilege could be asserted**: *State v. Smith*, 489 So. 2d. 255 (La. Ct. App. 5h Cir. 1986) (holding that although the wife was able to waive her testimonial privilege, only the defendant can waive the spousal communications privilege; lower court erred in ruling that the communications were not privileged).
8. **Communications privilege did not apply:** *State v. Hughes*, 587 So. 2d 31 (La. Ct. App. 2d Cir. 1991) (Spouse attempted to assert privilege, but failed because she testified that her husband had never been involved in drug activity. By testifying to exculpatory statements, the witness spouse opened the door and was cross-examined on prior acts committed by her husband.); *State v. Bennett*, 357 So. 2d 1136 (La. 1978) (Defendant attempted to assert his spousal communications privilege in order to prevent his wife from testifying against him. After his wife waived her testimonial privilege, she was allowed to testify about communications that were not privileged between her and her husband.).
9. **Authority on observations being outside the privilege**: *State v. Nash*, 821 So. 2d 678 (La. Ct. App. 2d Cir. 2002) (Defendant argued that the trial court should have barred his wife from testifying to confidential communications shared between the two of them. The defendant's wife waived her right not to testify against her husband under Article 505. The court ruled that the defendant's wife was able to testify to matters that she observed and that were not confidential.).
10. **Unavailability to Louisiana common law marriage:** *State v. Williams*, 688 So. 2d 1277 (La. Ct. App 3d Cir. 1997) (In a pre-code case, the defendant argued that his girlfriend

should not have been allowed to testify against him under La. R. S. 15:461. The defendant and his girlfriend had been together off and on for three years and also had three children together. Although Louisiana courts give full, faith, and credit to common-law marriage outside of the state, it does not recognize common-law marriages within the state. The court held that because the defendant and his girlfriend were not married, the spousal privilege did not exist.).

11. **No expectation of confidentiality:** *State v. Lilly*, 111 So. 3d 45 (La. Ct. App. 1st Cir. 2012) (holding that privilege could not be asserted because the husband and wife made statements to each other while on a monitored prison phone call while the husband was incarcerated; both parties were aware that the phone call was being recorded).

12. **Attempted to invoke testimonial privilege, but privilege did not exist**: *State v. Parent*, 836 So. 2d 494 (La. Ct. App. 5th Cir. 2002) (Defendant argued that the court erred in allowing his ex-wife to testify against him regarding prior threats the defendant made against her. The court ruled that the spousal testimonial privilege ended when they divorced. The court also ruled that by testifying to threats the defendant made toward her, which were not privileged, the ex-wife did not violate the spousal communications privilege.).

§8.4 Attorney-Client Privilege [La. C.E. arts. 506–509]

Applicable Code Articles

Art. 506. Lawyer-client privilege

* * *

B. General rule of privilege. A client has a privilege to refuse to disclose, and to prevent another person from disclosing, a confidential communication, whether oral, written, or otherwise, made for the purpose of facilitating the rendition of professional legal services to the client, as well as the perceptions, observations, and the like, of the mental, emotional, or physical condition of the client in connection with such a communication, when the communication is:

(1) Between the client or a representative of the client and the client's lawyer or a representative of the lawyer.

(2) Between the lawyer and a representative of the lawyer.

(3) By the client or his lawyer, or a representative of either, to a lawyer, or representative of a lawyer, who represents another party concerning a matter of common interest.

(4) Between representatives of the client or between the client and a representative of the client.

(5) Among lawyers and their representatives representing the same client.

(6) Between representatives of the client's lawyer.

* * *

The attorney-client privilege confers a right to a client not to disclose and to prevent his lawyer from disclosing any confidential communications between the two of them relating to the professional relationship. This privilege exists to encourage open communication between the lawyer and client in furtherance of the professional relationship.

The privilege belongs to the client. As such, only the client can waive the privilege, as discussed below. However, while the attorney may invoke or assert the privilege on behalf of his client, and refuse to disclose privileged information, he cannot waive it. The client is the exclusive holder of the privilege in an attorney-client relationship.

Who is a lawyer? For purposes of this provision, a **lawyer** is a person authorized to practice law in any state or nation, or is reasonably believed by the client to be authorized to practice law. Thus, by these terms, the privilege could apply between a person and someone who is not actually licensed to practice law, if the circumstances were such that the person reasonably believed that person was authorized to practice law. This might include a person who, unbeknownst to the client, might have been recently disbarred, or a person believed to have recently passed the bar exam. The privilege also extends to communications made to the lawyer's representatives or a person hired by the lawyer to assist him in the rendition of professional legal services, such as the attorney's paralegal.

The privilege does not, however, extend to a jailhouse lawyer who does not hold himself out to be a lawyer, and in most cases is known not to actually be a lawyer.

Who is a "client?" A **client** is a person or entity (business, corporation, etc.) to whom professional legal services are rendered by a lawyer, or a person who consults a lawyer for the purpose of obtaining professional legal services from him. The privilege does not only include communications made by the client to the lawyer, but also includes communications made by the client's representative to the lawyer or the lawyer's representatives. A representative of the client includes persons authorized to act on the client's behalf in obtaining legal services, or to act on the advice of the lawyers.

Further, since a "client" for purposes of the privilege includes a person who "consults a lawyer for the purpose of obtaining professional legal services from him," it would include statements made to a lawyer who might not end up actually representing the person for the consulted matter.

Must relate to the rendition of legal services. The privilege does not include any and all communications with a lawyer about any topic, even if intended to be confidential. To be within the privilege, the communications with the attorney (or his representative, or a person reasonably believed to be an attorney) must relate to the **rendition of legal services.** Communications about other things are not included within the privilege, such as plans to participate in future criminal conduct, taxes, political advice, or any other random topics.

Privileged information. The privilege not only extends to **confidential communications**, whether oral, written, or otherwise, made for the purpose of facilitating the rendition of professional legal services to the client, but also to **perceptions and observations relating to the mental, emotional, or physical condition** of the client in connection with such a communication. For instance, if a person called the lawyer after committing a crime, and upon meeting, the person appeared to be bloody or sweaty, not only would the person's statement to the lawyer be privileged, but also the fact that he was bloody, sweaty, and appeared to be out of breath at the time the lawyer came in contact with him.

The privilege would not, however, include observations that third parties could have also made, such as a cut on D's hand that he tells the lawyer he got during the crime. While his statement to the lawyer that he got the cut during the crime would certainly be covered, the fact that it exists is not confidential since anyone viewing the defendant would see it.

The privilege also does not include the concealment of evidence that the lawyer might obtain from the client, i.e., a weapon used to kill the victim. In this case, any statements the client might have made to the lawyer in connection with the delivery of the evidence would be privileged, and the lawyer would not have to disclose it unless it were shown that the statements were made in furtherance of a plan or conspiracy to commit a *future* crime, including a conspiracy to conceal the evidence in question.

Applies to confidential communications only. The privilege applies only to *confidential* communications made by the client to the lawyer for the purpose of obtaining legal services. The client must intend for the communications to be confidential. Thus, in most instances, the presence of third parties would destroy the confidentiality. However, there are exceptions where the presence of third parties would not destroy the confidentiality of attorney-client communications. The confidentiality of a communication is not destroyed if made in the presence of third parties **reasonably necessary for the transmission of the communication** or, when special circumstances warrant, those who are present at the **behest of the client** who are **reasonably necessary to facilitate the communication.**[18] The provision specifically limits third parties to only those who are reasonably necessary to facilitate the communications for the purpose of furthering the legal services. It does not extend to third parties the client may seek to bring into the conference for moral support, such as a mother or friend. The presence of individuals who are not reasonably necessary to facilitate rendition of the legal services could destroy the confidentiality of the communications and any such communications made in their presence would therefore not be privileged.

Applicable Code Articles

Art. 506. Lawyer-client privilege

* * *

D. Who may claim privilege. The privilege may be claimed by the client, the client's agent or legal representative, or the successor, trustee, or similar representative of a client that is a corporation, partnership, unincorporated association, or other organization, whether or not in existence. The person who was the lawyer or the lawyer's representative at the time of the communication is presumed to have authority to claim the privilege on behalf of the client, former client, or deceased client.

Who may claim. As stated above, while the client is the sole holder of the privilege and as such, only he can waive it, the privilege may be claimed by his attorney, legal representative, or agent. The attorney-client privilege continues after the relationship ends, into death. Thus, even after the client dies, if the attorney is called upon to disclose confidential communications related to him by his client, he may assert the privilege on behalf of his deceased client and refuse to disclose the privileged information.

18. La. Code Evid. art. 506(A)(5)(a)–(c).

Applicable Code Articles

Art. 506. Lawyer-client privilege

* * *

C. Exceptions. There is no privilege under this Article as to a communication:

(1)(a) If the services of the lawyer were sought or obtained to enable or aid anyone to commit or plan to commit what the client or his representative knew or reasonably should have known to be a crime or fraud.

(b) Made in furtherance of a crime or fraud.

(2) Which was with a client now deceased relevant to an issue between parties who claim through that client, regardless of whether the claims are by testate or intestate succession or by transaction inter vivos.

(3) Which is relevant to an issue of breach of duty by a lawyer to the client or by a client to the client's lawyer.

(4)(a) Which is relevant to an issue of authenticity or capacity concerning a document which the lawyer signed as a witness or notary.

(b) Concerning the testimony of a representative of a lawyer regarding a communication relevant to an issue of authenticity or capacity concerning a document to which the representative is a witness or notary.

(5) Which is relevant to a matter of common interest between or among two or more clients if the communication was made by any of them or their representative to a lawyer or his representative retained or consulted in common, when subsequently offered by one client against the other in a civil action.

(6) Concerning the identity of the lawyer's client or his representative, unless disclosure of the identity by the lawyer or his representative would reveal either the reason for which legal services were sought or a communication which is otherwise privileged under this Article.

* * *

Exceptions to the privilege. Article 506(C) specifically sets out exceptions to the attorney-client privilege in which communications between a lawyer and client are not privileged. The most common exception is when communications are made in furtherance of a crime or fraud, or the lawyer's services are sought or obtained to aid in the commission of what the client knew or reasonably should have known to be a crime or fraud. This exception does not pertain to situations in which a crime has already been committed and the client speaks to the lawyer with a view towards obtaining the lawyer's representation, even if no representation occurs. The exception only pertains to plans to commit *future* crimes or fraud, in which such communications do not further the interests sought to be protected by the privilege and as such, are not protected by the privilege.

Other exceptions to the attorney-client privilege include:

1. *Breach of duty.* Communications relevant to a breach of duty of either lawyer or client;
2. *Claim through deceased clients.* Communication which was with a client now deceased relevant to an issue between parties who claim through that client, regardless of whether the claims are by testate or intestate succession or by transaction inter vivos;

3. *Joint clients.* Communications relevant to a matter of common interest between or among two or more clients if the communication was made by any of them or their representative to a lawyer or his representative retained or consulted in common, when subsequently offered by one client against the other in a civil action;
4. *Documents attested to.* Communications concerning an issue of authenticity or capacity concerning a document which the lawyer signed as a witness or notary;
5. *Identity.* Communications concerning the identity of the lawyer's client or his representative, unless disclosure of the identity by the lawyer or his representative would reveal either the reason for which legal services were sought or a communication which is otherwise privilege.

Procedures for obtaining testimony from lawyer regarding client. While a lawyer may not reveal privileged communications between him and his client, in some instances a lawyer may have information that is **not privileged** that may be disclosed. Articles 507 and 508 list the procedures that must be followed prior to issuing a subpoena to a lawyer requiring him to reveal such information about a client or former client obtained in the course of representing him. "This Article is intended to strike a balance between the attorney-client privilege and the need of the prosecution to obtain otherwise unprivileged information about a client from his attorney or former attorney."[19] It is designed to provide breathing room for the privilege by setting forth appropriate procedural steps that must be followed in order to subpoena a lawyer for the purpose of obtaining information about a client or former client.[20] Article 507 pertains to criminal cases, and Article 508 pertains to civil cases.

Criminal Cases (Article 507)

In order to obtain unprivileged information from a lawyer about his client in a criminal case, a **contradictory hearing** is required wherein a judge determines that:

1. the information requested is **not protected** by the attorney-client privilege or work product rule;
2. the information sought is **essential** to the successful completion of an **ongoing investigation, prosecution, or defense**;
3. the purpose of seeking the information is **not to harass** the attorney or his client;
4. with respect to a subpoena, the **subpoena lists the information sought** with particularity, is reasonably limited as to subject matter and period of time, and gives timely notice; and
5. there is **no practicable alternative means** of obtaining the information.

Civil Cases (Article 508)

In order to obtain unprivileged information from a lawyer about his client in civil cases, a **contradictory hearing** is also required wherein a judge must determine the following:

1. that the information is **not protected** by the attorney-client privilege or work product rule;

---

19. La. Code Evid. art. 507 Official Comment.
20. La. Code Evid. art. 507 Official Comment.

2. the information sought is **essential** to the successful completion of an ongoing investigation, is essential to the case of the party seeking the information, and is not merely peripheral, cumulative, or speculative;
3. the purpose of seeking the information is **not to harass** the attorney or his client;
4. with respect to a subpoena, the **subpoena lists the information sought** with particularity, is reasonably limited as to subject matter and period of time, and gives timely notice; and
5. there is **no practicable alternative means** of obtaining the information.

In order for the determination that the privilege is not applicable to certain information about the client to be binding on the client, **the client must have been given notice of the time, place, and substance of the hearing** and must have been given an **opportunity to fully participate in the hearing.** Failure to timely object to non-compliance with the procedural requirements of the article constitutes a waiver of such protections but does not constitute a waiver of the privilege.[21]

In 2007 both provisions were amended to make clear that the provisions also apply to lawyers who serve as prosecutors at any level.[22]

Effect on Work Product Rule. Article 509 makes clear that the provisions concerning the attorney-client privilege do not in any way affect the protections of information the attorney may have gotten by reason of his representation under the work product rule. The attorney work product rule is much broader than the attorney-client privilege, also protecting from discovery "**reports, memoranda, or other internal documents made by the other side or statements obtained from witnesses in anticipation of litigation or in preparation for trial.**"[23]

The work product rule for criminal proceedings is contained in the C.Cr.P. Arts. 723 and 728; the provisions for civil cases are contained in C.Civ.Pr. art. 1424.

Key Points

The key points to keep in mind regarding attorney-client privilege.

1. **Holder.** Client is sole holder of privilege and may assert it or waive it.
2. **Who may assert.** Attorney can assert privilege on behalf of client, but cannot waive it.
3. **Communications between.** Client and his representative and the attorney and his representative.
4. **Who is an attorney?** The attorney includes the lawyer, his representative hired to assist in rendition of legal services (not other tasks, such as answering telephones), and those who a person would reasonably believe is an attorney.
5. **Must relate to.** Must relate to the rendition of legal services—not other things, such as taxes, political advice, etc.

---

21. La. Code Evid. art. 507(B) and La. Code Evid. art. 508(B).
22. *See* 2007 Acts., No. 23; *See also* La. Code Evid. art. 507 (E) and La. Code Evid. art. 508(E).
23. Harges & Jones, Louisiana Evidence, Art. 509 Author's notes (West Publishing 2014).

6. **Privileged information.** Oral or written communications, as well as perceptions and observations relating to the mental, emotional, or physical condition of the client in connection with such a communication.
7. **Doesn't apply to** concealment of evidence, but does apply to any statements that may have been made in connection with delivery of such evidence, as well as any perceptions or observations relating to the mental, emotional, or physical condition of the client at that time.
8. **Confidentiality/Presence of third parties.** May only be made in presence of parties "reasonably necessary" to facilitate the rendition of legal services, not other persons, such as those that may be present for moral support.
9. **Exceptions to privilege.** Does not include any communications relating to commission of future crime or fraud. Another common exception includes a claim arising out of breach of duty of either lawyer or client.
10. **Procedures for obtaining information from attorney**. The procedures to compel an attorney to reveal information about a current or former client are found in arts. 507 and 508 and generally require that, in addition to finding that the information sought is not privileged, the court also find that: 1) the information sought is essential to the successful completion of an ongoing investigation, prosecution, or defense; 2) the purpose of seeking the information is not to harass the attorney or his client; 3) with respect to a subpoena, the subpoena lists the information sought with particularity, is reasonably limited as to subject matter and period of time, and gives timely notice; and (4) there is no practicable alternative means of obtaining the information.

Problems on Attorney-Client Privilege

PROBLEM 8-8. Jerry is having dinner with his best friend Fred, who is a lawyer, and confides in him that he has had an extramarital affair. In a later divorce proceeding, Jerry's wife would like to call Fred to the stand to testify that Jerry was having an affair. Jerry objects that the statements are protected by the attorney-client privilege. Are they? Why or why not?

A. Would your answer change if right before Jerry begins telling Fred about his affair he hands him a dollar and says, "Here you go man. Okay now you're my lawyer. Look, I'm having an affair. Give me some advice. How do I juggle the two women?"

B. What if Jerry states, "Look, I'm having an affair and need to get rid of my wife to be with my mistress. Can you help me get rid of her?" Would the statements be protected by the attorney-client privilege?

C. Would your answer change if instead Jerry had stated, "Look, I've been having an affair for the last two years. Last week I decided to get rid of my wife. I'm thinking of turning myself in to the police. What should I do? If I'm arrested and charged will you represent me?" Fred responds, "Well I wouldn't be able to represent you if you're arrested because you know your wife is a good friend of mine too. You'll have to find another attorney." Would Jerry's statements to Fred be protected by the attorney-client privilege in a murder trial for Jerry's wife's murder? Why or why not?

PROBLEM 8-9. Roman graduates from law school in May and takes the bar exam in July. His best childhood friend Pete supports him all the way and even helps Roman paint and set up his new office. When the bar results come out in October, Roman doesn't tell Pete that he failed the bar exam. A couple of months later, Pete is involved in a car accident and asks Roman to represent him. Roman agrees. Pete tells Roman about the case and admits fault in the accident. Are Pete's statements to Roman privileged? Explain.

PROBLEM 8-10. Larry has just killed his wife. He goes straight to his lawyer Rob's house with blood all over him. Upon arrival at Rob's house, Larry tells him, "I did something very bad," and gives his lawyer the gun. He is sweating profusely and is extremely upset and nervous. Larry is arrested for the murder. Rob cannot represent him because he is swamped with other cases, so Larry hires another lawyer. Please answer the following:

A. Since Rob no longer represents Larry, are Larry's statements to Rob protected by the attorney-client privilege? Why or why not?

B. Can Rob be compelled to testify as to Larry's appearance, demeanor, or emotional state when he saw him on the night of the murder? Why or why not?

C. Can Rob be compelled to hand over the weapon to law enforcement that Larry gave to him? Why or why not?

PROBLEM 8-11. Chris hired Attorney Ram Harper to represent him in a criminal case. During Chris' meetings with Ram, Ram's paralegal comes in to take notes to conduct research on the case. Are Chris' statements to Ram privileged? Why or why not?

PROBLEM 8-12. Chaz (22) commits a crime, then goes home and tells his parents what he has done. They convince him to turn himself in, and they immediately bond him out of jail and help him hire a lawyer. Chaz, his parents, and his girlfriend go to Attorney Wright's office, and Chaz recounts exactly what he did the night he committed the crime in the presence of his parents and girlfriend. When he is done, Attorney Wright agrees to represent him and Chaz's parents pay him and they leave. Are Chaz's statements to the lawyer privileged? Explain.

PROBLEM 8-13. Bubba is deceased and his children are in a dispute over his estate. They wish to call the attorney that represented Bubba on a number of affairs before he died to testify on several issues involving the various cases in which he represented Bubba. Does the attorney-client privilege still exist even though Bubba is now deceased? If so, can Bubba's lawyer assert it on Bubba's behalf? If Bubba's lawyer chooses to, can he waive the privilege and testify to the communications he had with Bubba while representing him before he died? Explain.

PROBLEM 8-14. Mildred is in law school and attends the Bar Association Annual Christmas party to network with local attorneys. As she chats with Attorney Augustine about which classes she enjoys and those she does not enjoy, she learns he is quite knowledgeable about successions. Learning this, she tells him about a dispute arising out of property left by her father who recently passed. She tells him that they hadn't opened the succession because she had heard that there might be another sibling out there, so they were waiting to see if that sibling might come forward, but she doesn't know how to find out if it was true. She asked him how should they go about handling the situation? He advised her. Sometime after that, Mildred and her family hired the Long Law Firm to handle the succession. Young Casey, the long-lost illegitimate daughter surfaces, and would like Attorney Augustine to testify about what Mildred told him about the succession (that she knew or should have known about another sibling). Can Mildred prevent Augustine from testifying about her conversation with him? Why or why not?

PROBLEM 8-15. Charles visits his attorney (Attorney 1) and asks for his help in setting up a real investment company. He plans to focus on getting the elderly to invest in the real estate because he believes they are more "influential" and have more disposable income. The attorney agrees. As Attorney 1 is setting up the company, he requests several documents from Charlie regarding the properties which Charlie is unable to provide. Suspicious, he asks Charlie if he even has any property, to which Charlie responds that he doesn't actually have the real estate, but "they don't have to know that." He then offers Attorney 1 a share of it if he completes the deal. Attorney 1 declines to do so, and discontinues his services to Charlie. Charlie gets the company set up by another Attorney 2, but his scheme is quickly discovered. He's being prosecuted for fraud. He consults with Attorney 3 about the incident and tells him exactly what he did. Disgusted, Attorney 3 refuses to represent him. He then contacts Attorney 4 about the fraud charges. Attorney 4 agrees to represent Charlie on the fraud charges in the criminal case. At the trial, the prosecution calls both Attorney 1, Attorney 2 and Attorney 3 to testify against Charlie. Charlie objects claiming the information shared with all Attorneys is protected by the attorney/client privilege. How will the judge rule on Charlie's objection? Are Charlie's communications to each attorney protected by the attorney-client privilege? Explain.

PROBLEM 8-16. Ben steals lumber from a local lumber dealership. He hears that the police are on his trail and want to interview him. He goes to his longtime lawyer (Tony) and tells him all about what he did and also tells him that the police want to speak with him. He then tells Tony where he hid the lumber. He and Tony go to the location where the lumber is hidden on Ben's grandfather's farm. Tony suggests that they remove the lumber from that location in case the police get a search warrant. They take the lumber to an abandoned shed near a local lake. Tony suggests that Ben remove any remnants of lumber from the property and from his truck. Days later Tony contacts the police and informs them that he has gotten a tip from around town as to where the lumber is located. He says that his client is innocent and he will not let them speak to his client, but will tell them where the property is located. Tony tells them where the lumber is and meets them there where the lumber is confiscated by the police. Charges are subsequently brought against Ben for stealing the lumber. The prosecution wants to call Tony as a witness to testify in the case as to how he came to learn of the location of the property. They claim that no attorney-client privilege exists because Tony was involved in a cover-up of a crime. Tony claims that his responsibility was to turn over the evidence, but not to implicate his client. Are Ben's statements and actions covered under the attorney-client privilege? (At the time of the trial Tony does not represent Ben because his license is suspended due to an unrelated matter.)

PROBLEM 8-17. Colin meets with a lawyer to discuss representing him in a civil matter. After the meeting Colin hires the lawyer. He is instructed to fax over some paperwork regarding the case that afternoon. Later that afternoon, Colin faxes over 40 pages of documents related to the case. The papers lay on the fax machine all afternoon and several folks in the office see the documents including the receptionists, law clerks, and even the cleaning crew. Is the information on the documents privileged? Explain.

§ 8.4 References and Additional Authority on Attorney-Client Privilege

1. La. C.E. arts. 506–509 and Official Comments
2. Force & Rault, Handbook on Louisiana Evidence Law Arts. 506–509 Author's Comments (West Publishing 2014)
3. Harges & Jones, Louisiana Evidence Arts. 506–509 Author's Comments (West Publishing 2014)
4. 19 La. Civ. L. Treatise, Evidence And Proof § 8.6 (2nd ed.)
5. McCormick on Evidence §§ 88–97 (5th ed., 1999)
6. **Commentary**: Smith, Gregory, "*Confidentiality and the Attorney-Client Privilege: A Few Fundamentals*," 47 La. B. J. 326 (1999).
7. **Finding privilege existed:** *State v. Bright*, 676 So. 2d 189 (La. Ct. App. 4th Cir. 1996) (holding that the lower court was correct in ordering the defendant's attorney to produce the defendant's diary or tell of its whereabouts since not made in anticipation of litigation; however, if the attorney did not have it and only knew of its whereabouts through confidential communications with the defendant, such information is subject to the attorney-client privilege).
8. **Information not subject to privilege:** *State v. Brown,* 115 So. 3d 564 (La. Ct. App. 4th Cir. 2013) (holding that attorney-client privilege not violated when attorney's office provided law enforcement with defendant's name, the time of day he visited his attorney, which was on the day of the incident, and his phone number, when circumstances do not indicated information was intended to be confidential); *State v. A.D.L.*, 92 So. 3d 989 (La. Ct. App. 3d Cir. 2012) (holding that by testifying to whether the defendant knowingly and intelligently waived his right to trial by jury, his attorney did not violate the attorney-client privilege).
9. **Waiver**: *State v. Williams*, 786 So. 2d 203 (La Ct. App. 2d Cir. 2001) (Asserting an alibi defense, witness was asked by prosecution whether he'd discussed the case with his attorney to which he responded he had. The court held that the defendant waived the attorney-client privilege when he then asked whether he'd told the attorney about the alibi witnesses, and he responded he had. Court then allowed attorney to testify about information given to him by witness.).
10. **Obtaining information from attorney in criminal case (Article 507):** *State v. Gates*, 17 So. 3d 41 (La. Ct. App. 1st Cir. 2009) (holding that defendant's request for subpoenas met the requirements of Article 507 when the defendant sought to subpoena the assistant district attorneys in order for them to testify as to what they told defense counsel and sheriff's counsel, and not for them to testify to what was said in conversations to the district attorney).
11. **Obtaining information from attorney in civil case (Article 508):** *McClanahan v. McClanahan*, 27 So. 3d 862 (La. Ct. App. 5th Cir. 2009) (holding that the subpoena did not meet the requirements of Article 508 because the purpose of the subpoena was to acquire information about a client or former client; therefore, the privilege could be invoked).
12. **Was not attorney (jailhouse):** *State v. Fleury*, 545 So. 2d 1208 (La. Ct. App. 4th Cir. 1989) (holding that attorney-client privilege did not exist between two inmates to pre-

vent the admissibility of communications defendant made to a fellow inmate who was acting as his attorney who defendant claimed held himself out to be an attorney); *State v. Myers*, 839 So. 2d 1183 (La. Ct. App. 3d Cir. 2003) (holding that attorney-client privilege did not apply to communications defendant made to a fellow inmate where defendant did not present any evidence to show that he reasonably believed that his fellow inmate was an attorney).

13. **Exception (criminal conduct):** *State v. Menard*, 844 So. 2d 1117 (La. Ct. App. 3d Cir. 2003) (communications made in furtherance of conspiracy to commit crime not protected); *State v. Johns*, 24 So. 2d 462 (La. 1945) (The appellant (attorney) argues that the indictment against him alleging that he committed perjury by counseling his client to lie is not valid because the communication is privileged. The court ruled that the privilege does not apply as to future criminal conduct of the attorney or client.).

§ 8.5 Physician-Patient Privilege [La. C.E. art. 510]

The Code also contains a privilege for communications between a physician and patient. The privilege is contained in Article 510 and varies slightly depending upon whether the statements are sought to be admitted in a civil proceeding or a criminal proceeding as discussed below.

Civil Proceedings

In a non-criminal proceeding, a patient has a privilege to refuse to disclose and to prevent another person from disclosing a confidential communication made for the purpose of advice, diagnosis or treatment of his health condition between or among himself or his representative, and his healthcare provider, or their representatives.

Who is a "healthcare provider"? For the privilege to apply, the confidential communication in question must be made to a person's healthcare provider, or their representative. For purposes of this privilege, a healthcare provider is broadly defined, and includes: a physician licensed to practice medicine in any state,[24] a psychotherapist,[25] which is a physician engaged in the diagnosis or treatment of a mental or emotional condition, a licensed or certified psychologist, a licensed professional counselor or social worker.[26] For purposes of this privilege, a healthcare provider also includes a person who is engaged in any office, center, or institution referred to as a rape crisis center who has undergone at least forty hours of sexual assault training and who is engaged in rendering advice, counseling, or assistance to victims of sexual assault.[27]

Additionally, for purposes of this privilege, the communication in question may be made to any of the "representatives" of any of the above, which would include any persons acting under their supervision, direction, control, or at the request of the healthcare provider as outlined above, as well as any personnel of a hospital whose duties relate to the healthcare

24. La. Code Evid. art. 510(A)(3)–(5).
25. La. Code Evid. art. 510(A)(2)–(6).
26. *Id.*
27. La. Code Evid. art. 510(A)(2).

of patients or to maintenance of records.[28] For purposes of this privilege, a healthcare provider would also include anyone that the patient reasonably believed to be any of the above.[29]

Must relate to health condition. The privilege applies only when the confidential communication is made for the purposes of obtaining **advice**, **diagnosis**, or **treatment** of any **physical**, **mental**, or **emotional condition**, including a condition induced by alcohol, drugs, or other substance.[30]

Confidential Communications/Presence of Third Parties. A confidential communication is the transmittal or acquisition of information not intended to be disclosed to persons other than 1) a healthcare provider and a representative of a healthcare provider; 2) those **reasonably necessary** for the transmission of the communication; 3) persons who are **participating in the diagnosis** and **treatment** under the direction of the physician or psychotherapist; 4) a patient's **healthcare insurer**, including any entity that provides indemnification to a patient; or 5) when special circumstances warrant, those who are present at the behest of the patient, physician, or psychotherapist and are **reasonably necessary** to facilitate the communication.[31]

Confidential communication includes any **information**, **substance**, or **tangible object** obtained incidental to the communication process and any opinion formed as a result of the consultation, examination, or interview, and also includes medical and hospital records made by healthcare providers and their representatives.[32]

Exceptions to the privilege.[33] There is no privilege under this Article in a noncriminal proceeding as to a communication:

(a) that relates to the health condition of a patient who brings or asserts a **personal injury claim** in a **judicial or worker's compensation** proceeding.[34]

(b) When the communication relates to the health condition of a **deceased patient in a wrongful death, survivorship, or worker's compensation** proceeding brought as a result of the death or injury of the deceased patient.[35]

(c) When the communication is relevant to an issue of the health condition of the patient in any proceeding in which the patient is a party and relies upon the condition as an **element of his claim or defense** or, after the patient's death, in any proceeding in which a party deriving his right from the patient relies on the patient's health condition as an element of his claim or defense.[36]

(d) When the communication relates to the health condition of a patient when the patient is a party to a proceeding for **custody or visitation of a child** and the condition has a substantial bearing on the fitness of the person claiming custody or visitation, or when the patient is a child who is the subject of a custody or visitation proceeding.[37]

---

28. La. Code Evid. art. 510(7).
29. La. Code Evid. art. 510(A).
30. La. Code Evid. art. 510(3).
31. La. Code Evid. art. 510(A)(1)(a).
32. La. Code Evid. art. 510(A)(1)(b).
33. La. Code Evid. art. 510(B)(2).
34. La. Code Evid. art. 510(B)(2)(a).
35. La. Code Evid. art. 510(B)(2)(b).
36. La. Code Evid. art. 510(B)(2)(c).
37. La. Code Evid. art. 510(B)(2)(d).

(e) When the communication made to the health care provider was intended to assist the patient or another person to **commit or plan to commit** what the patient knew or reasonably should have known to be a **crime or fraud.**[38]

(f) When the communication is made in the course of an **examination ordered by the court with respect to the health condition of a patient,** the fact that the examination was so ordered was made known to the patient prior to the communication, and the communication concerns the particular purpose for which the examination was made, unless the court in its order directing the examination has stated otherwise.[39]

(g)(i) When the communication is made by a patient who is the subject of an **interdiction or commitment proceeding** to his current healthcare provider when such patient has failed or refused to submit to an examination by a healthcare provider appointed by the court regarding issues relating to the interdiction or commitment proceeding, provided that the patient has been advised of such appointment and the consequences of not submitting to the examination.

(ii) Notwithstanding the provisions of Subitem (i) of this Item, in any commitment proceeding, the court-appointed physician may review the medical records of the patient or respondent and testify as to communications therein, but only those **which are essential to determine whether the patient is dangerous to himself, dangerous to others, or unable to survive safely in freedom or protect himself from serious harm.** However, such communications shall not be disclosed unless the patient was informed prior to the communication that such communications are not privileged in any subsequent commitment proceedings. The court-appointed examination shall be governed by Item B(2)(f).[40]

(h) When the communication is relevant in proceedings held **by peer review committees** and other disciplinary bodies to determine whether a particular healthcare provider has deviated from applicable **professional standards.**[41]

(i) When the communication is one regarding the **blood alcohol level** or other test for the presence of drugs of a patient and an action for damages for injury, death, or loss has been brought against the patient.[42]

(j) When disclosure of the communication is necessary for the **defense of the healthcare provider in a malpractice action** brought by the patient.[43]

(k) When the communication is relevant to proceedings **concerning issues of abuse** (child, elder, disabled, or incompetent).[44]

(l) When the communication is relevant after the death of a patient, concerning the **capacity of the patient to enter into the contract** which is the subject matter of the litigation.[45]

(m) When the communication is relevant in an **action contesting any testament** executed or claimed to have been executed by the patient now deceased.[46]

---

38. La. Code Evid. art. 510(B)(2)(e).
39. La. Code Evid. art. 510(B)(2)(f).
40. La. Code Evid. art. 510(B)(2)(g).
41. La. Code Evid. art. 510(B)(2)(h).
42. La. Code Evid. art. 510(B)(2)(i).
43. La. Code Evid. art. 510(B)(2)(j).
44. La. Code Evid. art. 510(B)(2)(k).
45. La. Code Evid. art. 510(B)(2)(l).
46. La. Code Evid. art. 510(B)(2)(m).

Criminal Proceedings

In a criminal proceeding, a patient has a privilege to refuse to disclose and to prevent another person from disclosing a confidential communication made for the purpose of advice, diagnosis or treatment of his health condition between or among himself, his representative, and his physician or psychotherapist, and their representatives.[47]

Statements made to. For the privilege to apply, the statements must be made to his healthcare provider, or their representative. For purposes of this privilege, a healthcare provider is broadly defined as outlined above as it relates to civil proceedings, and includes a physician, psychotherapist, any of their representatives, and anyone who the patient reasonably believes to be any of the above.

Statements relating to. As in the case of civil proceedings, the communications covered in criminal proceedings must be made for the purpose of **advice, diagnosis, or treatment** of any **physical**, **mental**, or **emotional condition**, including a condition induced by alcohol, drugs, or other substance.

The confidentiality of statements/presence of third parties. Just as in the case of civil proceedings, a confidential communication is the transmittal or acquisition of information not intended to be disclosed to persons other than 1) a healthcare provider and a representative of a healthcare provider; 2) those **reasonably necessary** for the transmission of the communication; 3) persons who are **participating in the diagnosis and treatment** under the direction of the physician or psychotherapist; 4) a patient's **healthcare insurer**, including any entity that provides indemnification to a patient; or 5) when special circumstances warrant, those who are present at the behest of the patient, physician, or psychotherapist and are **reasonably necessary to facilitate the communication.**[48]

Confidential communication includes any **information**, **substance**, or **tangible object**, obtained incidental to the communication process and any opinion formed as a result of the consultation, examination, or interview and also includes medical and hospital records made by healthcare providers and their representatives.[49]

Exceptions. There are generally six exceptions to this rule where the healthcare provider privilege would not apply in criminal proceedings. The privilege does not exist in a criminal case as to a communication:

(a) that is relevant to an issue of the health condition of the accused in any proceeding in which the accused relies upon the condition as an **element of his defense.**[50]

(b) that was intended to assist the patient or another person to **commit or plan to commit** what the patient knew or reasonably should have known to be a **crime or fraud.**[51]

(c) that was made in the course of an **examination ordered by the court** in a criminal case to determine the health condition of a patient, provided that a copy of the order was served on the patient prior to the communication.[52]

---

47. La. Code Evid. art. 510(C)(1).
48. La. Code Evid. art. 510(A)(1)(a).
49. La. Code Evid. art. 510(A)(1)(b).
50. La. Code Evid. art. 510(C)(2)(a).
51. La. Code Evid. art. 510(C)(2)(b).
52. La. Code Evid. art. 510(C)(2)(c).

(d) that is a record of the **results of a test for blood alcohol level or drugs** taken from a patient **who is under arrest**, or who was subsequently arrested for an offense related to the test.[53]

(e) that is **in the form of a tangible object**, including a bullet, that is removed from the body of a patient and which was in the body as a result of the crime charged.[54]

(f) that is relevant to an **investigation of or prosecution for abuse** (of child, the elderly, disabled, or incompetent persons).[55]

Who may claim the privilege. In both civil and criminal proceedings, the privilege may be claimed by the patient or by his legal representative. The physician may also claim the privilege on behalf of the patient or deceased patient.[56]

Waiver. The exceptions to the privilege set forth in Paragraph B(2) shall constitute a waiver of the privilege only as to testimony at trial or to discovery of the privileged communication by one of the discovery methods authorized by Code of Civil Procedure Article 1421 et seq., or pursuant to R.S. 40:1299.96 or R.S. 13:3715.1.[57]

Medical malpractice. The healthcare provider-patient privilege also does not apply in medical malpractice claims related to the patient's current treatment or physical condition.[58]

Problems on Physician-Patient Privilege

PROBLEM 8-18. Beth was suffering from severe depression. Her symptoms had become significantly worse after finding out her husband was having an affair. During several of her counseling sessions with her therapist, she stated that she wanted her husband or his mistress dead. In her most recent session she told her therapist that she had purchased a gun. Beth's counselor is wondering if he may disclose this information to authorities or to the victim or someone to prevent any possible harm that Beth may cause. Is Beth's statement to the therapist privileged under the psychotherapist-patient privilege? Why or why not?

PROBLEM 8-19. Johnny Ray is charged with murder and has pled not guilty and not guilty by reason of insanity. He has been examined by court-appointed therapists who will testify at the trial. Johnny Ray has not objected to any of those records being given to the prosecution, which are all evaluations that took place since he was arrested and accused of killing an unarmed man in a nightclub brawl. Additionally, the prosecution would like to obtain records from where Johnny Ray was examined by a psychiatrist about five years before the murder for which he was charged. Johnny Ray has objected to those records and claims that they are privileged. Are they? Why or why not?

PROBLEM 8-20. Bo and Mary were involved in an altercation while their three children were present and crying very loudly. Mary shot her husband in the knee, and he was taken to the hospital. Mary was arrested. The police called Child Protective Services, and a social worker arrived on scene and took custody of the children. The social worker subsequently interviewed the children, Mary, and Bo—all separately. Mary subsequently pled guilty to

---

53. La. Code Evid. art. 510(C)(2)(d).
54. La. Code Evid. art. 510(C)(2)(e).
55. La. Code Evid. art. 510(C)(2)(f).
56. La. Code Evid. art. 510(D).
57. La. Code Evid. art. 510(E).
58. La. Code Evid. art. 510(F).

the charge and was placed on probation. She and Bo resumed the relationship and continued with custody of their children. About two years after the incident, Bo and Mary divorced. Bo sought to obtain sole custody of the children and subpoenaed the records from the social worker regarding her interviews of the children and Mary following the incident when he was shot. The social worker claims the records from the interview with the children and Mary are privileged and that she cannot disclose them. Are the records privileged in the custody action?

PROBLEM 8-21. Kendyl seeks to obtain worker's compensation for an injury he sustained at work. The defense has requested Kendyl's medical records from his primary healthcare provider. Are the records privileged? Why or why not?

PROBLEM 8-22. During Bertha's throat surgery it was discovered that she was HIV positive. Does the physician-patient privilege prevent the doctor from reporting the HIV status in accordance with La. R.S. 40:1065(A)?

PROBLEM 8-23. Isis is an eyewitness to an accident and is expected to be called as a witness by the plaintiff to testify that the defendant ran into the back of the plaintiff's vehicle while sending a text message. The defense learns that Isis has received psychiatric treatment some time in her past and plans to cross-examine her about it to attack her capacity at the trial. The defense seeks her psychiatric records from her past therapists. The plaintiffs assert the records are privileged. Does the privilege apply? Why or why not?

§ 8.5 References and Additional Authority on Physician-Patient Privilege

1. La. C.E. art. 510 and Official Comments
2. Force & Rault, HANDBOOK ON LOUISIANA EVIDENCE LAW Art. 510 Author's Comments (West Publishing 2014)
3. Harges & Jones, LOUISIANA EVIDENCE Art. 510 Author's Comments (West Publishing 2014)
4. 19 La. Civ. L. Treatise, Evidence And Proof § 8.5, § 8.8 (2nd ed.)
5. **Privilege existed:** *State v. Baker*, 582 So. 2d 1320 (La. Ct. App. 4th Cir. 1991) (holding that psychiatric and psychological records were privileged and inadmissible to impeach a witness).
6. **Records not privilege:** *Chenevert v. Hilton*, 978 So. 2d 1078 (La. Ct. App. 3d Cir. 2008) (holding that medical records related to plaintiff's alcohol treatment not privileged in civil suit against sheriff's deputy because plaintiff put his physical condition at issue in suit on issue of plaintiff's recollection or reporting of the events); *Hortman v. Louisiana Steel Works*, 696 So. 2d 625 (La. Ct. App. 1st Cir. 1996) (After client-plaintiff failed to disclose all information to physician, defense counsel provided the undisclosed information to the physician. The court ruled that where an attorney disclosed information about a client to a physician, the physician-patient privilege is not violated.); *Hebert v. Conner-Monceaux General Contractors*, 922 So. 2d 1236 (La. Ct. App. 3d Cir. 2006) (holding that records to patient's insurer (here provider of worker's compensation benefits) not subject to the privilege).
7. **Waiver:** *Merhige v. Gubbles*, 657 So. 2d 1098 (La. Ct. App. 4th Cir. 1995) (holding that partial disclosure of medical records in divorce/custody proceeding constituted waiver in subsequent unrelated proceeding).

8. **Insanity defense:** *State v. Prince*, 688 So. 2d 643 (La. Ct. App. 2d Cir. 1997) (holding that a defendant who has pled not guilty and not guilty by reason of insanity may not invoke the privilege as to medical records to exclude statements made to a court-appointed physician); *State v. Carter*, 84 So. 3d 499 (La. 2012) (holding that when defendant pleads not guilty and not guilty by reason of insanity, the privilege does not apply to information or opinions relevant to defendant's mental health).
9. **Other exceptions:** *State v. Rupp*, 614 So. 2d 1323 (La. Ct. App. 3d Cir. 1993) (child abuse exception).

§ 8.6 Communications to Clergymen [La. C.E. art. 511]

Applicable Code Articles

Art. 511. Communications to clergymen

A. Definitions. As used in this Article:

(1) A "clergyman" is a minister, priest, rabbi, Christian Science practitioner, or other similar functionary of a religious organization, or an individual reasonably believed so to be by the person consulting him.

(2) A communication is "confidential" if it is made privately and not intended for further disclosure except to other persons present in furtherance of the purpose of the communication.

B. General rule of privilege. A person has a privilege to refuse to disclose and to prevent another person from disclosing a confidential communication by the person to a clergyman in his professional character as spiritual adviser.

C. Who may claim the privilege. The privilege may be claimed by the person or by his legal representative. The clergyman is presumed to have authority to claim the privilege on behalf of the person or deceased person.

The communications to clergymen privilege provides that a person who makes confidential communications to a clergyman in his professional capacity as a spiritual advisor has a privilege to refuse to disclose and to prevent another person from disclosing such communications. This privilege is designed to show further respect for and to encourage open communications between a communicant and a clergyman from whom the person seeks spiritual advice. Whether the privilege applies is determined by a totality of the circumstances test:

> (1) it must be determined that the person to whom the communication was received is a "clergyman;" (2) it must be determined that the purpose of the communication was to seek spiritual advice or consolation; (3) it must be determined that the communication was made privately and was not intended for further disclosure except to other persons present in furtherance of the purpose of the communication; and (4) even if those explicit requirements of the article are met, it must also be determined whether or not the communicant waived the application of the privilege.[59]

59. State v. Mudd, 69 So. 3d 574 (La. Ct. App. 2d Cir. 2011).

Who are clergymen? For purposes of this privilege, a "clergyman" would include "a minister, priest, rabbi, Christian Science practitioner, or other similar functionary of a religious organization, or an individual reasonably believed so to be by the person consulting him."[60] This provision makes it clear that the privilege extends to communications made to anyone that the communicant may reasonably believe is a member of the clergy, who he consulted in such a capacity, even if that person may not have been officially ordained as such. The circumstances must truly suggest that the person was reasonable in his belief in order for the privilege to apply.

In *State v. Mudd*, the La. Second Circuit Court of Appeal held that the privilege did not apply to a statement that the defendant (Mudd) made to a lady (Herman) who periodically volunteered at the halfway house where she and Mudd had met. Herman periodically volunteered to "encourage" the young people. After Mudd stabbed and killed another resident of the halfway house, Herman went to the jail to talk to her to find out what happened. Mudd confessed before praying with Herman. In finding that the communications to clergy privilege did not apply, the court noted:

> According to Herman, she did not hold herself out to be a minister to Mudd, or anyone else. She did not hold herself out to be a counselor, nor did she go to minister to Mudd. She simply "wanted to find out what happened at the halfway house." It took Mudd a few minutes to recognize her from the house. When Mudd asked why she was there, Herman said "Vertrice [the house manager] and Stephanie wanted to know how she was doing." Herman did not lead Mudd to believe the conversation would be private. After Herman spoke with Mudd, she asked Mudd if she wanted to pray. The women prayed before Herman left.[61]

Confidentiality/Presence of Third Parties. A communication is "confidential" if it is made privately and not intended for further disclosure except to other persons present in furtherance of the purpose of the communication. This provision makes clear that the presence of certain third persons will not automatically destroy the confidentiality of such communication if the persons are present **in furtherance of the purpose of the communication**, such as in the case of a husband and wife seeking marital counseling.[62] Additionally, the article makes clear that testimony by an eavesdropper to a communication that is otherwise subject to a valid claim of privilege is also subject to a valid claim of privilege.[63]

However, in some instances the presence of third parties can destroy the privilege. An excellent example of this is in *State v. Gray*[64] below, where the Louisiana Supreme Court held the privilege inapplicable when the defendant confessed to a minister in the presence of his aunt and his codefendant cousin, and did not object when the minister contacted his superior to determine how to proceed in light of the information received. The determining factor in most instances will be whether the third party's presence is, in fact, "in furtherance" of the communication. In *Gray*, the aunt's presence did not destroy the confidentiality since she was the person who actually contacted the minister and facilitated the communication. However, the presence of the cousin and contact with a second minister were not deemed to be "in furtherance" of the communications and therefore destroyed the privilege.

---

60. La. Code Evid. art. 511(A)(1).

61. State v. Mudd, 69 So. 3d 574, 579 (La. Ct. App. 2d Cir. 2011).

62. *See* La. Code Evid. art. 511 Official Comment (h).

63. La. Code Evid. art. 511 Official Comment (f); *Cf.* State v. Morgan, 147 La. 205, 84 So. 589 (192).

64. State v. Gray, 891 So. 2d 1260 (La. 2005).

Termination of privilege. The article also makes clear that the privilege survives a person's death, by the language contained in 511(C) that the privilege may be claimed by the person or their "legal representative" as well as by the clergyman on behalf of the person "or deceased person."[65] Thus, if a person seeks to have a clergyman disclose statements made to him covered after the communicant has died, the clergyman may invoke the privilege on the deceased communicant's behalf.

Holder/Waiver. The communicant is the sole holder of this privilege, and while the clergyman may claim the privilege on behalf of the communicant and refuse to disclose the content of the privileged communication, only the communicant can waive the privilege.

Case on Communications to Clergyman Privilege

State v. Gray
Supreme Court of Louisiana
891 So. 2d 1260
January 19, 2005

VICTORY, Judge.

We granted this writ application to determine whether the trial court erred in denying defendant's motion to suppress a statement made to a clergyman under Louisiana's clergyman privilege. After reviewing the record and the applicable law, we reverse the judgement of the court of appeal and hold that the trial court correctly ruled that the statement was not privileged under the clergyman privilege.

FACTS AND PROCEDURAL HISTORY

Deonta and Jonta Gray are cousins charged by Bill of Information with the attempted second-degree murder of Kayon Brumfield, a taxi cab driver, in violation of La. R.S. 14:27, 14:30.1. Before they were arrested and charged, Keyanta Gray, who is Deonta's aunt and Jonta's mother, arranged for them to meet with her minister, Reverend Jeffrey Woolridge, at a motel room at the Colonial Inn in Amite, Louisiana. Reverend Woolridge was the director of the Men's Discipleship Program at the All Nations Ministry in Amite. Keyanta asked Woolridge to meet with Deonta and Jonta "to talk to her boys about a matter and lead them to Christ." At the meeting, in which both Keyanta and Jonta were present, Keyanta told the cousins to tell "Brother Jeff" what happened and Deonta related to him that "they were getting high, called a cab driver to rob him, he came, he reached for a gun, and he shot him." Woolridge requested no details and none were provided. Instead, he spoke to them "about the life that they were living and the game and the lifestyle that they were living, what it had finally brought them to and to get them to recognize that this way of life, this is what the outcome was."

After being told of the shooting, Woolridge, in the presence of Deonta and Jonta, and Keyanta, called his superior at the church, Pastor Eldolinus Sniff, for advice on what to do in response to hearing this information. Pastor Sniff then spoke to Keyanta, who became very emotional upon hearing what he had to say, and then instructed Woolridge to notify the authorities after leaving the Grays.... Before leaving, Woolridge prayed with

65. *See* La. Code Evid. art. 511 Official Comment (g).

the Grays and he later testified that Deonta seemed to be seriously interested in changing his life. Several days after calling the police as instructed, Woolridge was contacted by a New Orleans Police Department detective to whom he voluntarily gave a statement, relating what Deonta had told him.

Deonta filed a motion to suppress the statement, arguing that his statements to Woolridge were privileged under La.Code Evid. art. 511....

After the hearing, the trial judge granted the defendant's motion to suppress Woolridge's statement to police, finding that, although there were two other persons present when Deonta confessed to Woolridge, the court was "not convinced that the presence of either the mother or the brother in any way diminished the sanctity or the applicability of the privilege within the facts of this particular case." The court of appeal reversed the trial court and remanded the case. *State v. Gray,* 03–0779 (La.App. 4 Cir. 6/5/03)....

After considering Deonta's testimony, the trial court denied the motion to suppress, ruling as follows:

> The Court heard the testimony that there were two other people present in the room during the time these activities were taking place; that at least one phone call was made to an unidentified person dealing with an unspecified matter. The witness testified that he was not aware of the nature of the conversation that was going on. The Court did not hear any testimony as to the defendant's familiarity with this particular minister. His testimony was he didn't attend church; there was no previous contact with clergy on matters of confidence. And the Court heard no testimony that would re-enforce the notion that the defendant had any expectations of privacy or, if you will, privilege, when he approached this particular minister.

The defendants then sought supervisory writs. The court of appeal denied the application finding that the trial court did not abuse its vast discretion. *State v. Gray,* 03–1240 (La.App. 4 Cir. 8/14/03), unpub. On review, this Court remanded the matter to the court of appeal for briefing, argument, and opinion. *State v. Gray,* 03–2604 (La.1/9/04), 864 So.2d 128. On remand, the Fourth Circuit reversed the trial court's judgment, finding that the trial court's original suppression of the statement was not manifestly erroneous, and that, in the absence of a finding by the trial court after the second hearing that it did not find Deonta credible in his testimony that he intended the statement to be confidential, or that he did not make the statement for spiritual or penitential considerations, the court of appeal found that it was required to uphold the plain, precise language contained in art. 511 and suppressed the statement. *State v. Gray,* 03–1240 (La.App. 4 Cir. 4/28/04), 874 So.2d 893. We granted the State's writ application. *State v. Gray,* 04–1197 (La.10/1/04), 883 So.2d 1003.

DISCUSSION

For only the third time in 80 years,[2] this Court has the opportunity to discuss Louisiana's clergyman privilege, presently incorporated in La. C.E. art. 511 but dating back in the criminal law to 1928 La. Acts 2, § 1, art. 477.[3] La. C.E. art. 511 provides as follows:

> **Art. 511. Communications to clergymen**
>
> **A. Definitions.** As used in this Article:
>
> (1) A "clergyman" is a minister, priest, rabbi, Christian Science practitioner or other similar functionary of a religious organization, or an individual reasonably believed so to be by the person consulting him.

(2) A communication is "confidential" if it is made privately and not intended for further disclosure except to other persons present in furtherance of the purpose of the communication.

B. General rule of privilege. A person has a privilege to refuse to disclose and to prevent another person from disclosing a confidential communication by the person to a clergyman in his professional character as spiritual adviser.

C. Who may claim the privilege. The privilege may be claimed by the person or by his legal representative. The clergyman is presumed to have authority to claim the privilege on behalf of the person or deceased person.

Thus, there are three legal prerequisites to finding that the clergyman privilege applies. First, it must be determined that the person to whom the communication was received is a "clergyman." Second, it must be determined that the purpose of the communication was to seek spiritual advice or consolation. *See State v. Berry, supra; State v. Tart, supra.* Third, it must be determined that the communication was made privately and was not intended for further disclosure except to other persons present in furtherance of the purpose of the communication. However, even if those explicit requirements of the article are met, it must also be determined whether or not the communicant waived the application of the privilege. *See* La. C.E. art. 502(A) ("A person upon whom the law confers a privilege against disclosure waives the privilege if he or his predecessor while holder of the privilege voluntarily discloses or consents to disclosure of any significant part of the privileged matter.").

Whether the prerequisites to the recognition of the privilege are present is a determination to be made by the trial judge under La. C.E. art. 104(A).4 In making this determination, the trial court considers whether the totality of the circumstances presented indicate that the statements made by the defendant are within the communications protected by the privilege. *See State v. Tart,* 93–0772 (La.2/9/96), 672 So.2d 116; A trial court's ruling on a motion to suppress is subject to an abuse of discretion standard. *See State v. Hobley,* 98–2460 (La.12/15/99), 752 So.2d 771, 790.

The testimony was uncontroverted that Reverend Woolridge was a full-time minister, licensed by his church, and working at the church of All Nations Ministry in Amite. Based on the evidence in the record, undoubtedly Reverend Woolridge was a "clergyman" within the meaning of the statute.

The second issue is whether the purpose of Deonta's visit to Reverend Woolridge was to seek spiritual advice or consolation. Unlike the factual situations presented in *Berry* and *Tart,* in this case the testimony was uncontroverted that Deonta visited Reverend Woolridge at his aunt's suggestion or insistence and that the purpose of his visit was "[t]o speak with a priest and for spiritual guidance." Further, once there, Reverend Woolridge prayed with him and Woolridge testified that Deonta appeared genuinely interested in changing his life. Woolridge further testified that he was there as a spiritual advisor and to "lead them to Christ." While Deonta testified that he did not know Woolridge prior to this visit, that he did not attend church, and that he was unaware of any sort of proceeding like confession in the Catholic Church, these factors do not necessarily preclude the privilege from attaching, but are only factors in considering the totality of the circumstances. As the court of appeal found, "the communicant may be a first time communicant if he or she reasonably believes, based upon the communicant's knowledge, that the communication will be held confidential and is motivated by penitential considerations." 874 So.2d at 904. While the trial court noted in denying the motion to suppress that the defendant was unfamiliar with the minister, and that he did not attend church and that he was a first time penitent, these factual considerations do not appear to have been directed at a finding that defendant did not speak to the minister for spiritual purposes, but rather toward a general finding that the privilege did not apply based upon the totality of the circumstances. Thus, the evidence supports Deonta's claim that the purpose of his visit was spiritual.

The next issue is whether the communication was made privately and not intended for further disclosure except to other persons present in furtherance of the purpose of the communication. There is no doubt that this communication was not made privately as two other persons were present, Jonta and Keyanta. However, as Deonta's aunt and a person with a spiritual connection to the minister, we find that Keyanta's presence was "in furtherance of the purpose of the communication." On the other hand, it is unclear why Jonta was there. He did not say a word and did not seek spiritual guidance. Furthermore, the fact that he was an alleged participant in the act confessed by Deonta does not cause this communication to be considered private. Jonta's presence was not in furtherance of the purpose of Deonta's communication.

The last issues, which are somewhat interrelated, are whether Deonta intended the communication to be confidential and/or whether he waived the privilege. "One indicia of the absence of intent to make a confidential communication is ... where the contents of the communication are shown to have been intended to be transmitted to a third party." Wright and Miller, *Federal Practice and Procedure,* § 561 (1992); La. C.E. art. 502(A) (the privilege is waived if the penitent voluntarily discloses or consents to disclosure of any significant part of the privileged matter); *see also Perry v. State,* 280 Ark. 36, 655, 655 S.W.2d 380 So. W.2d 380, 381 (1983) ("We agree with the trial court that Perry told about everyone he could about killing his wife and, therefore, waived any privilege he might claim [with respect to statements made to his minister]."); *State v. Andrews,* 187 Kan. 458, 357 P.2d 739, 744 (1960) ("Where the one making the privileged conversation tells the facts to other third parties, the privilege is waived and the minister, physician or lawyer may be allowed to testify as to the communication made to him."). In this case, there are at least two instances which indicate that either Deonta waived the privilege or did not have any expectation of privacy in his statement to Woolridge.

First, when Reverend Woolridge got on his cellular telephone to Pastor Sniff for advice on what he should do about the information imparted by Deonta, Deonta effectively waived any expectation in the confidentiality of Deonta's disclosure by remaining silent during the call and thereby consenting to disclosure of the information. Although Deonta testified at the reopened hearing that he did not know who was on the other end of the phone and did not know what was discussed because he "wasn't listening to them on the phone," Woolridge clearly told Pastor Sniff on the phone in Deonta's presence that Deonta had told him that he and Jonta had committed this crime. In addition, after Keyanta got on the phone with the pastor for a brief conversation of her own, she became emotional in front of all of them, because, according to Woolridge, she had received advice from Pastor Sniff to surrender the defendants to the police. Finally, after ending the call to the Pastor, Woolridge testified that he "instructed [Keyanta] on what [Sniff] had told me to do that she was to do, to turn them in, you know, tell her she should turn them in." That Deonta remained oblivious to the content of all these conversations and all these events is incredible. That fact that all this occurred in his presence clearly establishes that he either waived the privilege or had no expectation of privacy in the first place.

Secondly, the State argues that the privilege was waived because either Deonta or Jonta told Keyanta that they had shot the cab driver, thereby leading Keyanta to take them to see Reverend Woolridge. We agree that it is reasonable to conclude from Reverend Woolridge's testimony at the hearing that the cousins had previously informed Jonta's mother about the incidents, as she instructed the boys to "tell Brother Jeff what happened" once Woolridge arrived at the motel room.

Accordingly, the State argues that by disclosing information about the attempted robbery/murder to third parties, and then by implicitly consenting to disclosure of the same information by Woolridge to his superior at his church, Deonta waived any privilege that he may otherwise have enjoyed. Thus, whatever the technical distinctions between the existence or applicability of the privilege and waiver of that privilege, the state contends that the end result remains the same; the cousins do not have the benefit of the privilege and may not invoke it at trial to preclude admission of Deonta's statements to Woolridge.

Although the trial court on original hearing granted the motion to suppress, finding that the presence of Jonta and Keyanta did not "diminish[ ] the sanctity or the applicability of the privilege within the facts of this particular case," the trial court found otherwise after the second hearing at which Deonta testified as to his intent in speaking with Woolridge. In that ruling, which is the ruling now under review, the trial court denied the motion to suppress, apparently relying in part on the fact that two other people were present in the room, at least one phone call was made to an unidentified person revealing the contents of the confession, and Deonta testified he was unaware of the nature of the phone conversation. However, while the trial court did not expressly say so, it clearly found Deonta's testimony as to his intent to be incredible, by concluding that it had "heard no testimony that would re-enforce the notion that the defendant had any expectations of privacy or, if you will, privilege, when he approached this particular minister."

CONCLUSION

Whether the clergyman privilege of La. C.E. art. 511 applies is determined under a totality of the circumstances test, in which all of the following requirements must be shown to exist: (1) it must be determined that the person to whom the communication was received is a "clergyman;" (2) it must be determined that the purpose of the communication was to seek spiritual advice or consolation; (3) it must be determined that the communication was made privately and was not intended for further disclosure except to other persons present in furtherance of the purpose of the communication; and (4) even if those explicit requirements of the article are met, it must also be determined whether or not the communicant waived the application of the privilege. In this case, although it is clear from the record that Reverend Woolridge was a clergyman under the article, and that Deonta consulted him and confessed to him for spiritual purposes, the requirements of confidentiality and lack of waiver were not shown. The trial judge was in the best position to judge the credibility of the witnesses and explicitly found that the testimony did not show that Deonta "had any expectations of privacy when he approached that particular minister." We agree, and find that, after a review of the record in its entirety, and considering the totality of the circumstances as described above, the clergyman privilege does not apply in this case and the trial court did not abuse its discretion in denying the motion to suppress.

DECREE

For the reasons stated herein, the judgment of the court of appeal is reversed and the trial court judgment denying the defendant's motion to suppress is reinstated. The matter is remanded to the trial court for further proceedings.

REVERSED AND REMANDED.

CALOGERO, C.J., concurs and assigns reasons.

KIMBALL, J., concurs in the result and assigns reasons.

JOHNSON, J., dissents.

CALOGERO, Chief Justice, concurring.

I agree with the court of appeal that this case is a close one. However, I disagree with the appellate court's conclusion that the district court on remand did not make a finding with regard to the defendant's credibility. While the appellate court was correct that the district court did not make an explicit statement as to the defendant's credibility, the district court unquestionably discounted the defendant's testimony when it stated that it had "heard no testimony that would re-enforce the notion that the defendant had any expectations of privacy or, if you will, privilege, when he approached this particular minister." Given that the defendant testified he had expected his statement to remain confidential, implicit within the district court's factual finding is the determination that the defendant's testimony on this issue was not credible.

Accordingly, I concur in the majority's conclusion that the district court did not abuse its discretion in denying the motion to suppress the evidence. On the record before this court, I find no error in the district court's factual appreciation that the defendant, who is invoking the clergy-communicant privilege, failed to establish that his communication to Reverend Woolridge was "not intended for further disclosure...," and thus was "confidential" as defined in La.Code Evid. art. 511(A)(2).

KIMBALL, Justice, concurring in result.

I agree with the result reached by the majority in this case; however, in my view, Deonta Gray did not waive the privilege or indicate that he did not have any expectation of privacy in his statement to Reverend Woolridge when he remained silent during Reverend Woolridge's telephone call to Pastor Sniff, his superior at the church. In my opinion, a clergyman's disclosure of confidential information to his superior solely for advice on what he should do in regards to this imparted information should not be considered a disclosure to a third-party which would defeat the privilege for confidential communications to a clergyman. This situation is analogous to that when an associate attorney seeks the advice of his supervising partner or attorney regarding a client communication, and would never be considered a waiver of the attorney-client privilege. *See* La. C.E. art. 506. Likewise, Reverend Woolridge's disclosure of Denota's statement to his superior, Pastor Sniff, for the purpose of determining his next course of action in this sensitive matter should not be considered a waiver of the clergyman's privilege.

Discussion Questions

1. Ultimately the court found that the third element had not been met—that the statement was not intended to be private due to Jonta's presence, and that even if the privilege existed, Deonta subsequently waived it when he allowed the minister to contact the head pastor. Do you agree with the Court that Jonta's (co-defendant) presence destroyed the confidentiality, particularly in light of the fact that Deonta knew that Jonta was already aware of the information to be divulged? What effect do you believe Jonta's presence had on the privacy of the communication? Explain.
2. Do you agree that Deonta waived the privilege when he did not object to the minister calling Pastor Sniff? Why or why not?
3. What are your thoughts on Justice Kimball's concurring opinion where she analogizes speaking with a senior pastor to speaking with a senior attorney in a law firm, which she states would "never be considered a waiver of the attorney-client privilege." Do you agree with this point?

Key Points

The key points to keep in mind regarding communication to clergy privilege.

1. The communicant is the sole holder of the privilege. Only he may waive it.
2. The clergyman can claim the privilege on his behalf.
3. Must be made to a member of clergy—minister, priest, rabbi, or an individual reasonably believed a member of the clergy.
4. Purpose must be to seek spiritual advice.
5. Must be confidential—with only those around whose presence in furtherance of the purpose of the communication.
6. The privilege survives a person's death.

Problem on Confidential Communications to Clergy Privilege

PROBLEM 8-24. Fourteen-year-old Olivia and her family were longtime active members of a Catholic Church. During that time a well-known, long-time parishioner and active member of the church, 64-year-old priest Father Marnier befriended Olivia. Over a period of time, the two began to communicate quite regularly and became very close. The parents were concerned about the number of calls and emails between the two of them. At some point Olivia became confused and scared, and during confession before mass on three occasions she confessed to another Priest, Father Tinsley, that she and Father Marnier had engaged in inappropriate sexual acts. She stated that it began as emails, then the emails became more racy and then escalated to kissing and fondling. Father Tinsley told her that she "needed to handle the situation herself because otherwise, too many people would be hurt." In another confession she was told to "sweep it under the floor and get rid of it." No further action was taken.

Olivia's parents began to suspect that something was not quite right about the relationship that Olivia had with Father Marnier so they met with church officials and then later confronted Olivia about the relationship at which time Olivia told them the true nature of her relationship with Father Marnier. Subsequently, Olivia's parents brought an action against several parties including Father Marnier, the Church, and Father Tinsley claiming that he was a mandatory reporter (La. Ch.C. art. 603(15), 609, 610) who failed to report the abuse allegations. Father Tinsley sought to preclude disclosure of the confessions claiming they were privileged, that he was not required to disclose the matters learned during confession, and that compulsion to disclose would violate the First Amendment Religion Clause as it pertains to protecting the rights of clergy and priests not to disclose information obtained during a confession.

How do you think these issues should be resolved? Should Father Tinsley be compelled to disclose the subject of the confession if the communicant waives the privilege? Can he invoke it on her behalf nonetheless? Does the duty to disclose violate the First Amendment Religion Clause?

A similar scenario was recently presented in *Parents of Minor Child v. Charlet,* et al., 135 So. 3d 1177 (La. 2014). Review the case and see how the Louisiana Supreme Court resolved these issues and be prepared to discuss.

§ 8.6 References and Additional Authority on Communications to Clergymen [La. C.E. art. 511]

1. La. C.E. art. 511 and Official Comments
2. Force & Rault, HANDBOOK ON LOUISIANA EVIDENCE LAW Art. 511 Author's Comments (West Publishing 2014)
3. Harges & Jones, LOUISIANA EVIDENCE Art. 511 Author's Comments (West Publishing 2014)
4. 19 La. Civ. L. Treatise, Evidence And Proof § 8.12 (2nd ed.)
5. **Privilege applies:** *State v. Marrero*, 92 So. 3d 21 (La. Ct. App. 1st Cir. 2012) (holding that victim's communications to clergyman was privileged because the clergyman was counseling the victim at the time of the communication, thus clergy could not be examined on communications to impeach the victim's testimony).
6. **Communications not privileged:** *State v. Mudd*, 69 So. 3d 574 (La. Ct. App. 2d Cir. 2011) (Defendant argued that the trial court erred in denying her motion in limine and allowing the State's witness to testify about communications with the defendant. Defendant claimed that the communications she had with the State's witness were protected under this privilege because the witness ministered to her. The court ruled that the State's witness never held herself out to be a minister; therefore, the privilege did not apply.).

§ 8.7 Other Privileges

Other privileges contained in the Louisiana Code of Evidence include: a privilege protecting the tenor of a person's vote lawfully cast in a political election (Article 512); that protects a trade secret owned by a person that does not conceal fraud or otherwise work injustice (Article 513); that protects the identity of a person who has furnished information in order to assist in an investigation of a possible violation of a criminal law (Article 514); and that protects communications made for the purpose of obtaining professional accounting services, as well as the perceptions, observations, and the like, of the mental, emotional, or physical condition of the client in connection with such a communications (Articles 515–517). Like the other exceptions discussed above, they are all policy-based, and all of them include exceptions as to when the privilege does not apply when the public policy interests would not be furthered by the exercise and recognition of such privilege.

§ 8.7 References and Additional Authority on Other Privileges [La. C.E. art. 514]

1. La. C.E. art. 514 and Official Comments
2. Force & Rault, HANDBOOK ON LOUISIANA EVIDENCE LAW Art. 514 Author's Comments (West Publishing 2014)
3. Harges & Jones, LOUISIANA EVIDENCE Art. 514 Author's Comments (West Publishing 2014)

4. 19 La. Civ. L. Treatise, Evidence And Proof § 8.7, § 8.10, § 8.13–§ 8.15 (2nd ed.)

5. **Privilege of state to withhold identity of informer:** *State v. Regis*, 25 So. 3d 183 (La. Ct. App. 4th Cir. 2009) (The defendant argued that his Sixth Amendment Confrontation rights were violated when the lower court denied his motion to disclose the confidential informant's identity. The court ruled that because the informant was not a participant in the crime the defendant is being charged for, the defense has no right to compel the identity of the informant.); *State v. Griffin*, 984 So. 2d 97 (La. Ct. App. 1st Cir. 2008) (Defendant argued that the lower court erred in denying his motion to reveal the identity of the informer. The court stated that this privilege is not applicable only under exceptional circumstances such as if the informer participated in the crime that the defendant is currently charged with. The court ruled that because the informer only set up the meeting between the defendant and the detective, the privilege was not waived.).

Chapter 9

Social Policy Issues

In this chapter we will cover a number of rules that were developed to further public policy interests similar to the public policy interests we addressed in the last chapter relative to privileges. In this chapter we will study, for example, rules designed to encourage owners of property on which an injury occurred to repair the dangerous condition by not allowing the fact of the repair to be offered against the owner as evidence of his negligence. We will also cover rules that encourage litigants to attempt to freely settle claims by not allowing things said in their plea or compromise negotiations to be used against them at trial. This chapter covers these and other rules that encourage socially responsible behavior. We deem the value of promoting the social policy issue to outweigh the minimal probative value of the conduct in proving negligence. Thus, the evidence may not be offered for such purposes. However, in all of these situations you will learn that the evidence might be used for other relevant purposes, such as to show ownership, control, or authority, as discussed below.

§ 9.1 Subsequent Remedial Measures [La. C.E. art. 407]

Applicable Code Articles

Art. 407. Subsequent remedial measures

In a civil case, when, after an event, measures are taken which, if taken previously, would have made the event less likely to occur, evidence of the subsequent measures is not admissible to prove negligence or culpable conduct in connection with the event. This Article does not require the exclusion of evidence of subsequent measures when offered for another purpose, such as proving ownership, authority, knowledge, control, or feasibility of precautionary measures, or for attacking credibility.

One of the most common types of social policy rules that arises in civil litigation relates to **subsequent remedial measures**. Subsequent remedial measures are measures taken *after* an event occurs (usually an accident) that if taken *before* the incident, would have made the incident less likely to occur. For example, if a business installs a handrail on a staircase after a customer falls down the stairs, the subsequent installation of the handrail is a subsequent remedial measure. It is a measure taken after the accident that if the business had taken before the incident, would have made the incident (the customer falling down the stairs) less likely to have occurred. This article provides that evidence of such measures may not be offered in a civil trial to prove that the party was negligent or culpable in connection with the event. Thus, this article would preclude the plaintiff from offering evidence that the business installed the handrail after the customer fell down the stairs, to prove that the business was negligent in not having the handrail.

Evidence of subsequent remedial measures is excluded to **encourage the owner of property to take such remedial measures** by not allowing such action to be used against them. The rule is policy-based and is **designed to encourage social responsibility.**[1] It is recognized that it is in the best interest of the public for a party to take such remedial measures that clearly would not be taken if the party's conduct could be used against him to prove his negligence in a trial. Thus, the rule seeks to protect the public from the potential harm caused by the continued potentially harmful condition. A second reason for the rule is that evidence of post-accident improvements to a product is not relevant as it "has no probative value on the issue of whether the product was defective at the time"[2] of the incident.

The following must be met for the exclusion to apply:

1. **civil action only**;
2. measure must be taken **"subsequent"** to an incident;
3. the measure must be **"remedial,"** i.e., if taken before the accident it would have made the event less likely to have occurred;
4. measure must be **taken by party** accused of the negligent conduct, not a third party; and
5. **not offered for a permissible purpose** such as ownership, authority, knowledge, control, or feasibility.

What constitutes a "remedial measure." As defined by the statute, remedial measures are those which, if taken previously, would have made the event less likely to have occurred. This could include a full range of different types of measures, including: "post-accident repairs, installation of safety devices, changes in design, the removal of dangerous conditions, changes in procedure, the dismissal of an employee charged with causing an accident, changes in regulations, and changes in labels or instructions,"[3] implementation of new policies, posting of warning signs, among other measures.

Civil cases only. The rule only applies in civil cases. It does not apply in products liability or strict liability cases. In such cases, the applicability of the rule is determined by applying the Article 403 balancing test.

Permissible uses. As stated above, while evidence of subsequent remedial measures may not be used to prove negligence or culpable conduct, the evidence **may be offered** for **other purposes**, such as to prove **ownership**, **authority, knowledge, control, feasibility** of **precautionary measures**, or for **attacking credibility**. For example, if the person denied he owned the property in question where an accident occurred, evidence that he, rather than some other person or entity, made the repairs to the property would show that he in fact owned the property in question. If the party claimed that the thing could not be made safer, evidence of his subsequent remedial measure making the product safer could be offered to prove feasibility of precautionary measures.

The following examples illustrate the exceptions to admissibility:

---

1. *See* Advisory Committee Notes to Federal Rule 407; *See also* Force & Rault, HANDBOOK, Art. 407, Author's Comment (1).

2. Lovell v. Earl Grissmer Co., Inc., 422 So. 2d 1344 (La. App. 1st Cir. 1982), writ den., 427 So. 2d 871 (La. 1983).

3. Northern Assurance Co v. Louisiana Power & Light Co., 580 So. 2d 351, 357 (La. 1991).

Ownership. Janet fell in a hole on Timothy's property. Timothy denied it was his property. The day after Janet fell, Timothy fixed the hole. Janet would like to offer evidence of Timothy fixing the hole to help refute his claim that it was not his property.

Feasibility of precautionary measures. Janet fell in a hole on Timothy's property. The city had informed Timothy of the massive sinkhole on his property, but Timothy maintained that the hole could not be fixed. The day after Janet fell, Timothy fixed the hole. Janet would like to offer evidence that Timothy fixed the hole to refute his position that the hole could not be fixed.

Authority. Janet fell into a hole on one of the properties that Timothy's company manages. Timothy claimed that his company was not responsible for making those types of repairs. Following the fall, Timothy had the hole repaired. Janet would like to offer evidence that Timothy fixed the hole to refute his claim that he was not responsible for making the repairs.

Credibility/Cover-up. Janet fell into a hole on Timothy's property. Timothy claimed there was no hole on his property. Janet would like to offer evidence that Timothy fixed the hole on his property the day after she fell in an effort to cover up the fact that he had a hole on the property.

Each of the examples above demonstrates a purpose other than negligence for which evidence of a subsequent remedial measure may be offered. While each purpose will ultimately assist the trier of fact in finding that the party acted negligently, for example in showing that there were measures that could have been reasonably taken, the evidence is not offered merely to show his consciousness of fault or negligence in not taking the action.

Federal Rules of Evidence Distinction. It is important to note that Federal Rule of Evidence 407 specifically states that the rule does not require the exclusion of such evidence if offered to prove "ownership, control, or feasibility of precautionary measures, *if controverted*, or impeachment."[4] Inclusion of the language "if controverted" ensures that the measure may only be offered for these "other" purposes, if the other purpose is actually at issue in the case. In other words, the defendant should be disputing the issue of ownership, control, etc. in order for the evidence to be admitted. This is important language to ensure that a plaintiff is not merely claiming that the evidence is being offered for such a reason when that purpose is not a disputed issue. As illustrated in the examples above, the defendant should be disputing, in his answer or otherwise, the issue that the evidence is being offered to address.

While the "if controverted" language is not specifically included in Louisiana's Article 407,[5] a proper application of the provision should require the matter to be at issue, otherwise the provision would have no effect in that in all cases the plaintiff could merely articulate the exception and the rule would not be applied.

Only limits the admissibility of party's own remedial measures, not those of others. Take the following example: Janet's son fell into a hole on Timothy's property after Timothy allowed the grass to grow up covering up a dangerous hole. Janet wishes to offer evidence that after her son fell into the hole, the city cleaned off Timothy's property. Janet would like to offer the evidence to help prove Timothy's negligence in failing to maintain his property. Would this article preclude evidence of the city's actions in cleaning off Timothy's property?

4. Fed. R. Evid. 407.

5. *See* Force & Rault, Handbook, Art. 407, Author's Comment (1) ("1988 Senate Bill No. 155 as originally introduced likewise included that qualification. It was deleted from the Article by Senate Committee amendment").

The article does not limit the admissibility of measures **taken by third persons or entities**, only the party's **own subsequent remedial measures**. The theory here is that a party (here the City) is not likely to be discouraged from taking remedial action just because their conduct is offered in a case in which they are not a party. Excluding such evidence would not further the policy underlying the rule. Similarly, the rule would not exclude evidence that other landowners in the surrounding area also cleaned off *their* property following the accident, if relevant for some reason. The rule only excludes the subsequent remedial measures of the party himself.

Excluded measures must be *subsequent*, not *before* the incident. This article, excluding evidence of subsequent remedial measures, only **applies to measures taken *after* the incident** in question. It does not exclude remedial measures taken before the incident in question. For example, evidence that prior to the time that plaintiff was injured by her airbag when it prematurely deployed, Motors, Inc. had two other designs that they'd tested before settling on using the one in question, would not be excluded under the provision. The designs were not *after* an incident. However, in some instances it is not so clear-cut as to whether the measure was actually taken before or after the incident in question. In some instances, a company may have contemplated a new policy or procedure that had not yet been implemented, and in some instances, the policy was in place, but was not in use or being followed at the time. How should these instances be resolved?

This rule does not exclude evidence of a policy that was already in place and was not being followed at the time in question. In fact, that would be the very basis of liability—that the defendants were not doing what they should have done at the time in question based on their own policy.[6] However, a policy that may have been contemplated, but had not been implemented until after the incident would be excluded under this rule. A similar issue is addressed in *Thornton v. National Railroad Passenger Corp.*[7] below.

Case on Subsequent Remedial Measures

Thornton, Sr. v. National Railroad Passenger Corporation
Court of Appeal of Louisiana, Fourth Circuit
802 So. 2d 816
Nov. 14, 2001

PLOTKIN, Judge.

Mr. Thornton was employed as a Carman by Amtrak on May 21, 1997, the date of the injury at issue. At the time of the injury, Mr. Thornton was working to replace bolster springs on an Amtrak Superliner Coach. While performing this task, the wood blocking used to support the Superliner gave way, pinning Mr. Thornton's hands between "pinch points" for a period of approximately five minutes. The resulting injuries included lacerations on the left and right hands, as well as fractures of the right small finger, and to both the left ring and small finger. The injuries on his left hand required amputation of his small finger and a pin fixation of his ring finger.

To replace bolster springs on the railcars, the cars must be supported in such a way as to make it possible to compress the springs and expose the bolts securing the springs in

6. *See* Northern Assurance Co. v. Louisiana Power & Light Co., 580 So. 2d 351 (La. 1991).
7. Thornton v. National Railroad Passenger Corp., 802 So. 2d 816 (La. Ct. App. 4th Cir. 2001).

place. It was common practice at the Amtrak facility in New Orleans for a car to be supported by wood blocking to compress these springs and expose the bolts, allowing them to be removed by the carmen. In the instant case, Mr. Thornton unscrewed the nuts and bolts by hand, placing his hands between "pinch points," a position in which they could be pinned by the machinery.

...

Mr. Thornton filed suit against Amtrak under FELA. Following the trial in the matter, the jury returned a verdict finding Amtrak 90 percent at fault, Mr. Thornton one percent at fault, and "any other person" nine percent at fault....

Amtrak appeals the trial court decision, assigning three errors: (1) that the trial court erred in admitting into evidence documents which indicate subsequent remedial measures; ...

ADMISSION OF AMTRAK DOCUMENTS

First, Amtrak claims that the trial court improperly admitted documents generated after Mr. Thornton's accident and injury, which it claims contain evidence of subsequent remedial measures to be taken by Amtrak as a result of the accident. First, Amtrak complains of the trial court's decision to admit Exhibit P-2, an Amtrak Investigation Committee Report dated May 21, 1997, the date of Mr. Thornton's accident. This report included a section labeled "Committee Recommendations," recommending that Amtrak "construct a piece of equipment that will be used in place of blocking to support spring plank and procure or manufacture socket to remove swing hanger nuts." Second, Amtrak complains of the trial court's decision to admit Exhibit P-9, an Amtrak "Accident Prevention" Safety Alert also dated May 21, 1997. Exhibit P-9 contained a section labeled "Preventive Measures" recommending that Amtrak "design a jig to be used in place of blocking and a tool to remove the hanger bolts."

Amtrak claims that Mr. Thornton's sole purpose for introducing the two exhibits was to prove that his accident and injury were caused by Amtrak's negligence. Amtrak claims that the two Amtrak documents are inadmissible for that purpose under the provisions of La. C.E. art. 407, which states as follows:

> In a civil case, when, after an event, measures are taken which, if taken previously, would have made the event less likely to occur, evidence of the subsequent measures is not admissible to prove negligence or culpable conduct in connection with the event. This Article does not require the exclusion of evidence of subsequent measures when offered for another purpose, such as proving ownership, authority, knowledge, control, or feasibility of precautionary measures, or for attacking credibility.

... Amtrak contends that this evidence was directed at proving one of Mr. Thornton's two main contentions—i.e., that Amtrak failed to provide adequate tools for the job of changing bolster springs at its New Orleans facility.

...

Mr. Thornton contends that the two exhibits at issue were properly admitted under the provisions of La. C.E. art. 407 for two reasons. First, he claims that the information contained in the documents does not qualify as subsequent remedial measures. Alternatively, Mr. Thornton claims that the documents were offered for attacking credibility, an "other purpose" specifically sanctioned by La. C.E. art. 407.

First, Mr. Thornton claims that the information in the Amtrak documents recommending the use of an alternative to wooden blocking does not qualify as evidence of subsequent remedial measures both because metal blocking was being used at the Chicago Amtrak facility prior to his accident and because New Orleans Amtrak officials were aware of this alternative, safer method for performing the task he was performing at the time he was injured. In support of this argument, Mr. Thornton points to the testimony of Constantine Falaris, a New Orleans Amtrak foreman. Mr. Thornton claims the documents do not contain evidence of measures taken after the event in question, his injury, as metal blocking was used prior to the accident and information of this type was shared throughout the Amtrak system.

In support of this argument, Mr. Thornton cites *Fontenot v. Hollier & Sons,* 478 So.2d 1379 (La.App. 3 Cir.1985) and *Northern Assurance Company v. Louisiana Power & Light Co.,* 580 So.2d 351 (La.1991). In *Fontenot,* the appellate court found that the trial judge properly admitted a Service Information Memorandum and Operator's Manual containing revised procedures for operating defendant's machinery. The appellate court affirmed the trial judge's decision to admit the documents, finding that the exhibits actually reflected a decision to change procedures made prior to the plaintiff's accident. In *Northern Assurance Co.,* the Louisiana Supreme Court affirmed a trial court decision to admit pictures of house fires that occurred after the fire which formed the basis of the case at hand because they showed an alternative procedure for cutting off electricity during a house fire. The court found that the pictures were not evidence of subsequent remedial measures because the alternative procedure had been used prior to the fire in question.

Amtrak seeks to distinguish the *Fontenot* and *Northern Assurance* cases, claiming that the exhibits offered in this case contain no indication that the recommended changes were adopted prior to the accident or that they were in general practice. Amtrak also claims that the mere fact that an alternative method of performing a particular job was already in use at the Chicago facility did not indicate a previous decision to change the procedure and equipment used at the New Orleans facility. Finally, Amtrak claims that the recommendation to change procedures at the local office constitutes subsequent remedial measures specifically for the New Orleans facility and that practices and equipment used at other facilities does not affect the status of these documents.

We find no abuse of discretion in the trial court's decision to admit the documents at issue in the instant case. First, we agree with Mr. Thornton's argument that the recommendations in the exhibits simply refer to alternative methods for performing the same task in use within the Amtrak system prior to Mr. Thornton's accident. As such, they do not qualify as subsequent remedial measures under the rules set forth in *Fontenot* and *Northern Assurance Co.* Moreover, we note that the recommendation relative to the use of metal blocking in place of the wooden blocking traditionally used in the New Orleans facility is a common sense recommendation that would obviously make a dangerous task less hazardous.

We also agree with Mr. Thornton's alternative claim that the documents fall within an exception to La. C.E. art. 407 because they were offered for an "other purpose" than proving negligence or culpable conduct. Under the express provisions of La. C.E. art. 407, admission of evidence of subsequent remedial measures is allowed when they are offered for any "other purpose" besides proving negligence or culpable conduct. The article contains the following examples of "other purposes" for which subsequent remedial measures are admissible: "knowledge, control, or feasibility of precautionary measures, or for attacking credibility." Mr. Thornton argues that, even if the documents did contain evidence of subsequent remedial measures, they were properly admitted to attack credibility.

At trial, two Amtrak foremen testified that the wood blocking and pipewrench provided by Amtrak to its New Orleans employees were adequate to safely perform the job of changing bolster springs. Mr. Thornton argues that the documents were properly admitted to show that the foremen knew prior to his accident that the equipment provided was inadequate for performing the task safely. Additionally, Mr. Thornton argues that the documents in question were properly admitted to rebut Amtrak's claims that Mr. Thornton was contributorily negligent. Mr. Thornton claims that the documents show that the same persons who testified that the accident was caused by Mr. Thornton's improper use of the equipment provided knew that the equipment provided was itself inadequate for the task. For this reason also, we find no abuse of the trial judge's discretion in his decision to admit the documents challenged by Amtrak.

...

AFFIRMED

Discussion Questions

1. Exactly what "measure" is in dispute in *Thornton*? If the measure was merely, "recommending" the changes, was it in fact "remedial," in that if Amtrak had actually taken that measure prior to the accident (made the recommendation), would it have reduced the likelihood that the accident would have occurred? If not that measure, what measure was in dispute?
2. Would the issue surrounding the subsequent remedial measure be altogether different had Amtrak actually implemented the policy at the New Orleans Station after the accident? How, if at all, would the analysis change?
3. The case turned on whether the measures were deemed to be *subsequent to* or *prior to* the accident. What are the two arguments raised by the plaintiff as to why the measures were not actually subsequent to the accident? What were Amtrak's arguments as to why they were, in fact, subsequent remedial measures? Were the measures subsequent, or were they actually already in place?
4. Even if the measures were taken subsequent to the accident, do you think the plaintiffs sufficiently articulated an "other purpose" for why the evidence should be admitted? Explain how the evidence attacked the credibility of the Amtrak executives. Compare to *Young v. Armadores de Cabotaje, S.A.* 617 So. 2d 517 (La. Ct. App. 4th Cir. 1993).
5. Could there also be a "feasibility of precautionary measures" argument to make for the admissibility of this evidence? Explain.
6. An overarching consideration, that must always be considered when deciding these cases, is the overriding policy interests. Would excluding the evidence under this particular fact situation further the underlying policy considerations of this rule, or would it go against the policy sought to be furthered by excluding such evidence?
7. Can a jury really be expected to put aside the implications of negligence in these types of cases? How do you think such evidence is used by juries?

Key Points

The key points to keep in mind regarding subsequent remedial measures.

1. Applies in civil cases only.
2. Subsequent remedial measures are inadmissible to prove negligence or culpable conduct.
3. **Remedial measures may include**: post-accident repairs, installations of safety devices, changes in design, changes in procedures, dismissal of employee charged with causing

accident, changes in regulations, changes in labels or instructions, implementation of new policies, posting of warning signs, etc.

4. **Exceptions to rule**: Subsequent remedial measures may be offered to show ownership, control, feasibility of precautionary measures, authority, credibility/cover-up. Issue should most likely be "controverted."
5. Excluded measures must be **subsequent to** accident, not before. If policy already in place, or already in use (even if not used in the instance in question), it is admissible.
6. This exclusion does not limit admissibility of measures that may have been taken by a third party, only the party's own subsequent measures.
7. Does not apply in strict liability or products liability cases. Admissible subject to Article 403 balancing.

Problems on Subsequent Remedial Measures

PROBLEM 9-1. Following an accident, caution lights were installed at the on-ramp to a new bridge that was under construction by a private construction company. The city claims the accident site was under the authority of the construction company at the time of the accident; however, the construction company claims the city had authority over the intersection. In an action against the construction company, the plaintiff would like to offer evidence that following the accident the construction company installed the caution lights to show authority over the construction site. The construction company claims that the evidence is a "subsequent remedial measure" and is precluded under Article 407. How should the court rule?

PROBLEM 9-2. After several children opened bottles of dangerous drugs and ingested them, the manufacturer of the pill bottles changed the design so that the lid would have to be simultaneously pressed and turned in order to open them. Can the plaintiffs offer the evidence at trial to show that the defendants were negligent in their original lid design?

What if the company had argued that there were no alternative designs that could have been used to create a safer lid to the medicine bottles? Can the plaintiff offer the evidence that the lids were subsequently made safer after the injuries occurred?

PROBLEM 9-3. Several children were injured at a construction site. Following the injuries, new barriers were placed along the perimeter of the site along with signs stating, ***"Warning: Do not cross the red line. Construction in progress! Enter at own risk!"*** The plaintiffs wish to offer evidence at trial that the barriers and warning signs were placed at the construction site after the accident. Should the evidence be allowed to show the measures that the construction company should have followed to begin with?

PROBLEM 9-4. Donna owned a restaurant. Several of the steps entering the restaurant were rotting and one finally gave way one night as a customer exited the restaurant, causing the customer to fall and break her leg. The next day, Donna installed new steps. Can the customer offer evidence that Donna fixed the steps the day after the accident occurred? Why or why not? Can you think of scenarios where the evidence would certainly be admissible?

PROBLEM 9-5. Tom was injured when his car was struck by Driver, who was operating a tow truck owned by D company. After the accident, the D company fired the driver. Tom sued the D company and wishes to offer evidence that Driver had worked for the company and had been fired to show that at the time of the accident Driver was under the authority of the D company and was their employee. The D company claims that Driver was not their employee at the time of the accident and objects to any evidence being offered regarding him supposedly being fired as a subsequent remedial measure. Should the evidence be admissible? Why or why not?

PROBLEM 9-6. Marissa is injured after she rents a car with faulty brakes from a local rental car company affiliated with a major rental car company franchise. Marissa sues the local company. The rental car company claims that the parent company is responsible for maintenance and repair of vehicles. Marissa would like to offer evidence that following the accident the local rental company fixed the brakes to show that they were responsible for inspecting and repairing the vehicles. Should the evidence be admissible? Why or why not?

PROBLEM 9-7. In a lawsuit against Children's Drug Co., plaintiff seeks to offer evidence that after numerous reported cases that children were taking Children's Drug Co.'s pills thinking that the bright colored pills were candy, Children's Pills, Inc. (another company) changed the color of *their* pills, which were also brightly colored, to a less attractive color. The defendant (Children's Drug Co.) objects that the evidence is a subsequent remedial measure and is barred from admissibility. How should the court rule and why?

PROBLEM 9-8. In a lawsuit against Childco, the manufacturer of a popular baby crib, the plaintiff would like to offer evidence that, following several reported cases of babies being hung in their Childco cribs, Mega Dept. Store, Co. stopped carrying the brand and model. The defendant objects that the evidence is excluded as a subsequent remedial measure. What ruling?

PROBLEM 9-9. Burger Barn, a 24-hour burger joint, had a store policy to always have a security guard in the parking lot at night, but they rarely kept anyone in the lot. After Mary was kidnapped in the Burger Barn parking lot one night, Burger Barn began routinely following their policy, ensuring that a security guard was in the parking lot 24 hours per day. Mary would like to offer evidence that Burger Barn routinely puts a security guard in the parking lot after dark only since her accident to help show their negligence. Burger Barn objects that the evidence is a subsequent remedial measure and should be excluded. Mary argues that the policy was already in place and is not a subsequent measure. Should the evidence be excluded or allowed? For a similar issue, see generally *Northern Assurance Co. v. Louisiana Power & Light Co.*, 580 So. 2d 351 (La. 1991).

PROBLEM 9-10. Desmond and three of his friends were severely injured when they fell out of an amusement park ride at a state fairground. In their lawsuit against the amusement park and the ride manufacturer, they would like to offer evidence that the manufacturer of the ride considered several alternative designs for the ride before they finally settled on the design used. The defendants object that the evidence is inadmissible. What ruling?

PROBLEM 9-11. Bo rented furniture from a furniture company, and the morning after the first night sleeping in the bed, he woke up scratching all over his body. He went to the doctor and discovered he'd likely been bitten by bed bugs. He went home and called the company, and they immediately sent over a new bed to his apartment and took the old one. After thinking about the situation a little bit, he called the furniture company and requested to take photos of the bed. He was told that it had been destroyed. Bo learned that after his incident the furniture company implemented a new policy on getting rid of furniture with bed bugs to prevent the spread of the bed bugs to other furniture, by having the beds immediately destroyed and never even returned to the warehouse. Bo subsequently filed suit against the company for his injuries and sought to introduce evidence that the company implemented the new policy and destroyed the bed to prevent him from having the evidence. The furniture company claims the evidence is inadmissible because it is a subsequent remedial measure. How should the court rule and why?

§ 9.1 References and Additional Authority on Subsequent Remedial Measures [La. C.E. art. 407]

1. La. C.E. art. 407 and Official Comments
2. Force & Rault, Handbook on Louisiana Evidence Law Art. 407 Author's Comments (West Publishing 2014)
3. Harges & Jones, Louisiana Evidence Art. 407 Author's Comments (West Publishing 2014)
4. 19 La. Civ. L. Treatise, Evidence And Proof § 5.3 (2d ed.)
5. McCormick on Evidence § 263 (6th ed. 2006)
6. **Commentary:** Bienvenu, Jr., David, "*Subsequent Remedial Measures and the Louisiana Code of Evidence: Some Thoughts on Interpretation*," 51 La. L. Rev. 1069 (May 1991); Lutkewitte, Erin, "*A Problem in Need of Repair: Louisiana's Subsequent Remedial Measures Rule*," 67 La. L. Rev. 195 (2006).
7. **Cases excluding evidence as subsequent remedial measure:** *Tilden v. Blanca, L.L.C.*, 119 So. 3d 962 (La. Ct App. 4th Cir. 2013) (Patron filed a suit against restaurant after slipping and injuring her shoulder, back and neck. The trial court excluded the evidence of the defendant placing additional rugs out after the accident. Plaintiffs offered the evidence to prove the credibility of the defendant. Since there were no issues regarding the deposition and live testimony, the court excluded the evidence as subsequent remedial measures.); *Allums v. Parish of Lincoln*, 15 So. 3d 1117 (La. Ct. App. 2d Cir. 2009), *rehearing denied, writ denied*, 09-1938 (La. 2009) (holding that in a wrongful death and survival action brought by the decedent's wife against the Parish after decedent was killed in a rollover truck accident on a rural parish road, the trial court properly excluded evidence regarding the placement of an advisory speed plate, advising the speed to be 35 mph, on the curve after the accident).
8. **Admissible to show knowledge:** *Conques v. Wal-Mart Stores, Inc.*, 779 So. 2d 1094 (La. Ct App. 3d Cir. 2001), *writ denied*, 01-0715 (La. 2001), 790 So. 2d 643 (Store patron sued the store, manufacturer of the door and the door service company when she was injured by the automatic doors while entering the store. Court held that the trial court erred in excluding evidence that the store added a safety beam for the said door following the plaintiff's incident as a subsequent remedial measure as the evidence showed knowledge of the store but not as to the door service company or the manufacturer of the door.).
9. **Admissible to show authority/ownership/control:** *Patterson v. City of New Orleans*, 686 So. 2d 87 (La. Ct. App. 4th Cir. 1996), *writ denied*, 97-0140 (La. 1997), 689 So. 2d 1384 (A claim against a sewage and water board regarding the accident caused by algae growth on railroad underpass from water seepage. Testimony was offered showing that the city designed a remedy for the clogged perforated pipes prior to the accident but due to costs, the city did not implement the remedy. The testimony indicated that the remedy was implemented after the accident. The court held that the evidence

could be used for the limited purpose of showing that the city had control over the filter bed and that the filter beds were the responsibility of the city rather than the other defendants in the case.).

10. **Not remedial measure for incident in question:** *Thomas v. A.P. Green Industries, Inc.*, 933 So. 2d 843 (La. Ct. App. 4th Cir. 2006) (Decedent's surviving spouse and children filed suit against the owner of a power plant when he was exposed to asbestos. Plaintiff sought to introduce into evidence the subsequent root cause analysis report regarding the grinding of the asbestos gasket on the unit in the power plant. The trial court ruled that the subsequent remedial measure rule did not bar admission of the report because the report did not involve the measures taken in response to the said event but for a subsequent event.).

§ 9.2.1 Compromise and Offers to Compromise [La. C.E. art. 408] and Settlement or Tender [La. C.E. art. 413]

Applicable Code Articles

Art. 408. Compromise and offers to compromise

A. Civil cases. In a civil case, evidence of (1) furnishing or offering or promising to furnish, or (2) accepting or offering or promising to accept, anything of value in compromising or attempting to compromise a claim which was disputed as to either validity or amount, is not admissible to prove liability for or invalidity of the claim or its amount. Evidence of conduct or statements made in compromise negotiations is likewise not admissible. This Article does not require the exclusion of any evidence otherwise admissible merely because it is presented in the course of compromise negotiations. This Article also does not require exclusion when the evidence is offered for another purpose, such as proving bias or prejudice of a witness, negativing a contention of undue delay, or proving an effort to obstruct a criminal investigation or prosecution.

B. Criminal cases. This Article does not require the exclusion in a criminal case of evidence of the actions or statements described in Paragraph A, above, or of a giving or offer to give anything of value by the accused in direct or indirect restitution to a victim.

Art. 413. Settlement or tender

Any amount paid in settlement or by tender shall not be admitted into evidence unless the failure to make a settlement or tender is an issue in the case.

In this section we will cover compromise and offers to compromise claims which are contained in Article 408. We will also cover the related article that governs the use of amounts paid in settlements or tender which is covered in Article 413. Generally Article 408 limits the use of statements made during settlement negotiation in a trial in an attempt to encourage resolution of lawsuits. Recognizing the importance of settling cases out of court, and the need for open communications between the parties if such compromises are to be reached, this provision precludes such statements from being offered in a subsequent trial.

Specifically, Article 408 excludes evidence at trial of any offers or promises to pay or to accept anything of value to settle or compromise any claim where there is dispute as to validity or amount, to prove either liability for the claim, the validity of the claim, or the amount of the claim. For example, if a person who has been sued offers to settle the case for $100,000, a plaintiff who rejected the offer would not be able to offer evidence at trial that the defendant knows the plaintiff has a valid claim because he offered to settle the case for $100,000. Similarly the plaintiff would be precluded from offering evidence at trial that the case is worth at least $100,000 because the defendant offered to settle it for such an amount.

Only by excluding such evidence from being offered at trial are parties encouraged to openly and freely discuss the merits of the claims and make legitimate offers to settle them. The exclusion applies when all the following are met:

1. a civil case;
2. evidence of offers/promises to **pay** or offers/promises to **accept** anything of value;
3. to settle or compromise any claim;
4. where there is **dispute** as to **validity** or **amount** of claim;
5. to prove either **liability** for the claim, the **validity** of the claim, or the **amount** of the claim; and
6. also excludes **conduct** and **other statements** made in compromise negotiations.

Amount or validity in dispute. The exclusion only applies if the claim is in dispute as to its validity or amount. Thus, if a party concedes liability and the amount the other party demands to settle the claim, then the exclusion does not apply.

Collateral statements/conduct also inadmissible. Additionally, evidence of **conduct** or **collateral statements** made in compromise or settlement negotiations is likewise not admissible. For instance, if the defendant said to the plaintiff during settlement negotiations, "Look I was drunk, I admit it, so what can we do to make this go away? Will you take $10,000?" In this situation, the admission of driving drunk would also be inadmissible. The statement is considered to be *collateral* to the actual offer to compromise the case, "Will you take $10,000?" But such statements are also inadmissible under this article because the law presumes that parties must feel free to openly discuss the merits of the case in order to come to agreements and settle cases. Thus, collateral statements made in the course of such negotiations are also excluded.

Additionally conduct is also excluded under the article. Thus, a party who perhaps cries or otherwise shows remorse, or perhaps even a heated altercation would also be excluded under this rule.

Statements otherwise admissible. This article does not require the exclusion of any evidence when it is otherwise admissible, such as evidence already known or discoverable, just because it happened to be discussed in the course of compromise negotiations. This portion of the article precludes a party from discussing an issue during settlement negotiations for the sole purpose of attempting to make it inadmissible at trial under this rule. Thus, if information is already known or would be known through the ordinary discovery process, the mere fact that it was mentioned during settlement negotiations does not make it inadmissible.

Exceptions to the rule. While such evidence may not be offered for the purpose of proving either **liability** for the claim, the **validity** of the claim, or the **amount** of the claim, the evidence may be offered for other reasons. Namely, such evidence may be offered to prove: 1) bias or prejudice of a witness; 2) negativing a contention of undue delay; or 3) an effort to obstruct a criminal investigation or prosecution.

For example, if there are two plaintiffs and one settles with the defendant and subsequently testifies in favor of the defense, evidence of his settlement is admissible to show that the witness may be biased due to his settlement agreement or promise to settle with the defense. Thus on cross-examination of the defense witness, the following would be proper: "Isn't it true, Mr. Witness, that the defense has promised (or has paid) you $100,000 to settle your claim?"

Amounts paid in settlement. Article 413 also precludes the admissibility of any ***amount paid*** in settlement or by **tender** unless the failure to make a settlement or tender is an issue in the case. This provision focuses on the actual amount of any settlement, and limits admissibility of such evidence with a perceived goal of not allowing the plaintiff to be prejudiced by having the trier of fact limit recovery based on any amounts received. Authorities have questioned whether the intent of this article was to allow evidence of settlement amounts in cases in which such evidence may be relevant for other purposes, such as to show bias, prejudice, or for some other purpose as provided in article 408.[8] The La. Third Circuit Court of Appeal tackled this issue in *Alexander v. Tate*, 30 So. 2d 1122 (La. Ct. App. 3d Cir. 2010) below, and concludes the provision likely implicitly contains such an exception.

Federal Rules of Evidence Distinction. There is no comparable provision under the Federal Rules of Evidence.

§ 9.2.2 Payment of Medical and Similar Expenses [La. C.E. art. 409]

Applicable Code Articles

Art. 409. Payment of medical and similar expenses

In a civil case, evidence of furnishing or offering or promising to pay expenses or losses occasioned by an injury to person or damage to property is not admissible to prove liability for the injury or damage nor is it admissible to mitigate, reduce, or avoid liability therefor. This Article does not require the exclusion of such evidence when it is offered solely for another purpose, such as to enforce a contract for payment.

Article 409 also excludes statements offering to pay **medical** or **other expenses** or **losses** from being admitted at trial when offered to prove **liability** for **injury** or **damage**, or to **mitigate**, **reduce**, or **avoid liability**. This provision applies to statements such as, "I'll pay your medical bills," or "I'll pay for the damage to your car," or "Look I'll pay your medical bills and for the days you missed work." Like settlement negotiations, this provisions encourages such offers and recognizes that these types of offers would not be made if the statement could be offered into evidence to prove liability of the party or to avoid liability. Thus, such statements are excluded.

This exclusion is covered here alongside offers to compromise because such statements are often made in connection with attempts to settle a claim, and may thus be deemed settlement negotiations. For example, a person might state, "Look, how about I pay all

8. *See, e.g.*, Harges & Jones, Louisiana Evidence Art. 413 Author's Comments; *See also*, Force & Rault, Handbook, Art. 413 Author's Notes (1).

your expenses and make this whole thing go away?" It is important to understand the distinction between the two exclusions because of the different manner in which collateral statements are treated in settlement negotiations versus how they are treated in mere offers to pay expenses. As we discussed in § 9.2.1, collateral statements made in connection with settlement negotiations are also *excluded* to encourage open discussions to settle claims. However, with offers to pay expenses, **collateral statements are not excluded** simply because they are made in connection with the offer.

For example, if a person were to say: "*Look, I admit I was drunk, so how about I pay your medical bills and fix the car,*" while the offer to pay medical expenses would be inadmissible under this article, the statement "Look, I admit I was drunk" would be admissible as a collateral statement to the offer. The courts and legislature reason that while there is an interest in encouraging free settlement negotiations, and thus excluding collateral statements made during such negotiations, no such interest exists when offering to pay medical bills, so collateral statements and conduct need not be excluded.

Thus, in statement #1 below, the entire statement is excluded because it is in furtherance of settling the claim and is thus an offer to compromise a claim under Article 408. Here, the collateral statements are also excluded. However, in statement #2 only the portion offering to pay the medical bills is excluded. In such statements, collateral statements are not excluded.

~~1. "Look, I admit I was drunk, so how about I pay your medical bills and fix the car so that we can make this thing go away.~~

~~2.~~ "Look, I admit I was drunk, ~~so how about I pay your medical bills and fix the car."~~

Exception. This Article does not require the exclusion of such evidence when it is offered solely for another purpose, such as to enforce a contract for payment.

Cases on Compromise, Settlement or Tender, and Payment of Medical Expenses

Calcagno v. Gonzales[9] is a good example of how evidence of amounts tendered or paid can affect a jury's award of damages.

Calcagno, et al. v. Gonzales, et al.

Court of Appeal of Louisiana, Fifth Circuit
802 So. 2d 643
Oct. 13, 1999

CANNELLA, J.

Plaintiffs, Joseph and Lynne Calcagno, appeal a judgment for damages in an automobile accident case filed against their uninsured/underinsured motorist (UM) carrier, Progressive Insurance Company (Progressive.) We reverse the denial of the motion in limine, affirm liability and amend the damages.

9. Calcagno v. Gonzales, 802 So. 2d 643 (La. Ct. App. 5th Cir. 1999).

Plaintiffs were involved in an automobile accident on March 24, 1996. While traveling on Power Boulevard in Metairie, Louisiana, their vehicle was struck in the rear by an automobile owned and driven by Donald Gonzales.

Plaintiffs filed suit on June 4, 1996 against Progressive, plaintiffs' UM insurer. Suit was amended to add Gonzales and his alleged insurer. However, it was subsequently discovered that Gonzales was uninsured.

Prior to trial, Progressive unconditionally tendered $27,000 and $2,500 in medical payments to Lynne Calcagno and unconditionally tendered $29,500 and $2,500 in medical payments to Joseph Calcagno. On March 17, 1998, plaintiffs filed a Motion in Limine to exclude any evidence of the medical payments and the unconditional tenders. The trial judge denied the motion and on March 20, 1998, this Court denied relief, finding no error in the admissibility of the evidence.

A jury trial was held on March 18, 19 and 20, 1998, during which, the evidence of the medical payments and tenders were admitted. The jury awarded each plaintiff the amount of $500 for general damages and medical expenses to Lynne Calcagno of $1,038 and to Joseph Calcagno of $925.

On appeal, plaintiffs assert that the trial judge erred in allowing the evidence of the medical payments and tenders to be admitted. Further, they contend that this Court should perform a de novo review of the damages because of that legal error and the damages should be increased.

EVIDENCE OF TENDERS

The admissibility of evidence of compromise, settlement and tender are regulated by La.C.E. arts. 408, 409, 411 and 413. Under C.E. art. 408 A, evidence of an offer and/or acceptance of compromise of a claim which was disputed as to either validity or amount, is not admissible to prove liability for or invalidity of the claim or its amount, unless it is offered for another purpose, such as proving bias or prejudice of a witness, negativing a contention of undue delay or proving an effort to obstruct a criminal investigation or prosecution. C.E. Art. 409 provides that evidence of furnishing or offering or promising to pay expenses or losses is not admissible to prove liability, nor is it admissible to mitigate, reduce, or avoid liability, unless the evidence is offered solely for another purpose, *such as to enforce a contract.* C.E. art. 411 prohibits communicating the amount of an insurance policy to a jury, unless the amount of the policy is in dispute. Finally, C.E. art. 413 states that, "Any amount paid in settlement or by tender shall not be admitted into evidence unless the failure to make a settlement or tender is an issue in the case."

We find no cases directly on point to our issue. However, we conclude that even if evidence of the tenders were admissible under C.E. art. 409, as alleged by defendant, the evidence of the amounts is not admissible under C.E. art. 413. Further, this lawsuit is not to enforce a contract, which would make evidence of the tenders admissible under C.E. art. 409. This is a suit for damages. Defendant does not dispute that it owes anything under the contract. In fact, it has paid certain sums under the contract. Defendant here only disputes the amount to which the plaintiffs are entitled. The jury in this case was called upon to determine the whole of plaintiffs' damages, not whether the contract should be enforced. Further, considering the award by the jury, it is apparent that they considered the tendered amounts in reaching the verdict. Since this was legal, prejudicial error, we agree with plaintiffs that this Court must conduct a de novo review of the damages. *Ferrell v. Fireman's Fund Ins. Co.,* 94–1252 (La.2/20/95), 650 So.2d 742, 745–746 and cases cited therein.

DAMAGES

[Thorough review of evidence of damages sustained by plaintiffs]

... Accordingly, the judgment of the trial court is affirmed in part and affirmed as amended to award Lynne Calcagno general damages in the amount of $55,000 and medical expenses in the amount of $11,567. Joseph Calcagno is awarded general damages in the amount of $30,000, plus medical expenses of $13,648. These awards are subject to the insurance policy provisions. Furthermore, Progressive is entitled to credit for prior payments made ...

Discussion Question

Do you agree with the public policy consideration underlying this rule? Is it needed? Explain.

Alexander v. Tate

Court of Appeal of Louisiana, Third Circuit
30 So. 3d 1122
Feb. 3, 2010

DAVID E. CHATELAIN, Judge Pro Tempore.

... On August 3, 2005, Donald Alexander's vehicle was hit broadside by a vehicle driven by Ira Tate when Mr. Tate failed to see Mr. Alexander's vehicle as he approached the intersection of Louisiana Highway 85 and Hubertville Road in Iberia Parish. Mr. Alexander testified that he saw Mr. Tate's vehicle stopping at the stop sign as he approached it and thought Mr. Tate was stopped. According to Mr. Alexander, Mr. Tate's vehicle kept creeping forward, so he moved to the other lane of travel to avoid a collision and hit his brakes, but the vehicles collided anyway. Mr. Alexander sued Mr. Tate; Mr. Tate's employer, the owner of the vehicle driven by him; and the insurer of Mr. Tate's employer to recover damages he suffered as a result of the collision.

Mr. Alexander was forty-six years of age at the time of the accident. The Social Security Administration had declared him disabled due to a heart condition. After the accident, an ambulance transported him to the New Iberia Medical Center emergency room. He complained of abrasions to his right forehead and right elbow and pain on the left side of his neck and in his low back. The emergency room doctor prescribed Flexeril for muscle spasm and Voltaren for pain. X rays taken that day revealed degenerative changes in Mr. Alexander's middle and low cervical spine. Thereafter, Mr. Alexander sought medical treatment for his injuries from Dr. Keith Mack, a general practitioner; Dr. Allen J. Johnston, an orthopedist; and Dr. Sandra Weitz, an anesthesiologist and pain management specialist.

[Discussion of Mr. Alexander's medical complaints and treatment over next two years]

On March 3, 2008, Mr. Alexander was in another automobile accident, and he returned to Dr. Johnston on April 25, 2008. Upon his return to Dr. Johnston, he rated his pain as eight on a scale of one to ten; his pain had been four on scale of one to ten in December 2007.

Mr. Alexander pursued a claim for damages he suffered as a result of the March 2008 accident, which he settled for $8,000. Issues regarding causation arose herein with regard to injuries Mr. Alexander suffered in that accident, i.e., what, if any, injuries did the second accident cause; what pain and/or limitations were attributable to his pre-existing degenerative spine conditions; and what, if any, impact did the March 2008 accident have on the injuries caused by the August 2005 accident. At trial, Mr. Alexander sought to inform the jury that he settled his claim regarding the March 2008 accident for $8,000. The defendants objected, but the trial court ruled that the evidence was admissible.

The jury returned a verdict in favor of Mr. Alexander, assessing him with 10% fault and awarding him the following damages: Past Medical Expenses: $20,082; Bodily Injury, Past and Future Physical and Mental Pain and Suffering, Mental Anguish, and Disability: $192, 000; and Loss of Enjoyment of Life: $50,000.

The defendants appeal and assign four errors: ... (2) the trial court erred in allowing Mr. Alexander to introduce evidence of the settlement amount of the claim he made regarding his March 3, 2008 automobile accident; ...

DISCUSSION

...

Admission of Settlement Information

After his March 2008 accident, Mr. Alexander sought damages for injuries he sustained in the accident. He settled his claim for $8,000 and sought to introduce evidence of this settlement amount at trial [in the instant case] to establish that he was not seriously injured in that accident. The defendants objected to introduction of the settlement amount, claiming it was irrelevant and prohibited by La.Code Evid. art. 413 which provides: "Any amount paid in settlement or by tender shall not be admitted into evidence unless the failure to make a settlement or tender is an issue in the case." After arguments in an unrecorded sidebar conference, the trial court denied the defendants' objection and allowed Mr. Alexander to state that he settled the claim for $8,000.

The defendants argue that Article 413 prohibited the admission of the settlement amount. This evidentiary ruling is subject to the manifest error standard of review. *Lam v. State Farm Mut. Auto. Ins. Co.,* 05–1139 (La.11/29/06), 946 So.2d 133.

In support of their argument, the defendants cite *Calcagno v. Gonzales,* 99–287 (La.App. 5 Cir. 10/13/99), 802 So.2d 643.... The appellate court ... held that the trial court erred in allowing the amount of the tenders to be made known to the jury.

Mr. Alexander argues that the amount of the settlement was relevant and admissible because the defendants made the March 2008 accident and the extent of the injuries he suffered therein an issue at trial. He claims that the settlement amount was relevant to establish that the March 2008 accident merely aggravated injuries he sustained in the August 2005 accident, that the aggravation resolved shortly after the accident, and that he thereafter returned to his pre-March 2008 accident condition.

Mr. Alexander urges that Article 413 should be read in conjunction with La.Code Evid. art. 408(A), which prohibits the admission of evidence concerning compromise or offers to compromise a disputed claim "to prove liability for or invalidity of the claim or its amount" but does not prohibit evidence that is otherwise admissible "merely because it is presented in the course of compromise negotiations" or when "the evidence is offered for another purpose, such as proving bias or prejudice of a witness, negativing a contention of undue delay, or proving an effort to obstruct a criminal investigation or prosecution." La.Code Evid. art. 408(A). As support for his claim, Mr. Alexander relies on comments the authors of the "Handbook on Louisiana Evidence Law" made regarding Article 413. Those opinions state in part:

> This Article was particularly designed to protect a plaintiff in a personal injury suit from the introduction of evidence that would inform the jury of the amount

> plaintiff received in settlement from other alleged tortfeasors, or the amount received by other claimants in settlement of their claims against the defendant, when the purpose of such evidence is to minimize the value of plaintiff's claim, or suggests that he has already received adequate compensation.

George W. Pugh, Robert Force, Gerald A. Rault, Jr., and Kerry Triche, Handbook on Louisiana Evidence Law, 410 (2008 ed.). The authors then correlate Article 413 to Article 408, explaining that while Article 408 excludes evidence of settlements for the limited purpose of "proving or disproving liability or amount thereof," Article 413 is written in broader terms than Article 408 and that it "seemingly mak[es] evidence of settlements ... inadmissible for any purpose." *Id.* The authors continue, however, noting: "It is believed that [Article 413] should not be given such broad scope, and where the amount paid in settlement or tender has a relevance independent of its tacitly forbidden use, it should be held admissible, subject, of course, to the balancing test of Article 403." *Id.*...

We find the Handbook on Louisiana Evidence Law's observations regarding Article 413 and the federal jurisprudence persuasive and conclude that the trial court did not commit manifest error when it allowed Mr. Alexander to state the amount for which he settled his claim arising out of the March 2008 accident. Clearly, the settlement of this second accident did not involve the parties to this litigation, and it was relevant as to the severity of the injuries Mr. Alexander sustained in that accident....

AFFIRMED.

Discussion Questions

1. Do you agree that Article 413 is likely intended to be interpreted as not precluding evidence of settlement amount if it will show some other relevant purpose, such as bias, knowledge, etc. as is written in Article 408 and other social-policy-based exclusions? Why or why not?
2. It seems that if the legislature had intended the exception to apply, it would have been included in the article as it was in the other social policy-based exclusions where it applies. Why do you suppose such language was not included? Do you think the article was intended to be read "in conjunction" with Article 408 as noted by the court and the plaintiff?
3. Assuming Article 413 may be admissible for "other" reasons, does it pass the Article 403 balancing test in *Tate*? Discuss its probative value toward proving the extent of the plaintiff's injuries in that accident. What prejudicial effect could it have?

Key Points

The key points to keep in mind regarding the rule of compromise, offers to compromise, settlement or tender, and offers to pay medical and other expenses.

COMPROMISE, OFFER TO COMPROMISE

1. Excludes offers to pay or to accept anything of value to settle or compromise a case where there is a dispute over validity of claim or amount of claim to prove liability for claim, validity of claim, or amount of claim.
2. The claim must be in dispute as to validity or amount.

3. The exclusion only applies if the compromise is offered to prove: liability for claim, validity of claim, or amount of claim.
4. Collateral statements made during settlement negotiations are also excluded, such as admissions of guilt or liability like, "I know I was in the wrong."
5. Statements otherwise admissible and discoverable are not excluded just because they are made in course of settlement negotiations.
6. Exceptions to rule: to prove bias, prejudice of a witness, negativing a contention of undue delay, or proving an effort to obstruct a criminal investigation or prosecution.

SETTLEMENT OR TENDER

7. The amount actually paid in settlement or tender is likewise not admissible (Article 413). Most likely intended to be read as allowing evidence of settlement to show other reason, such as bias, prejudice, or for some other reason.

OFFER TO PAY MEDICAL OR OTHER EXPENSES

8. Offers to pay medical or other expenses (e.g., fix car, pay wages missed from work, etc.) excluded to prove liability, or to mitigate, reduce, or avoid liability.
9. Collateral statements are not excluded with offers to pay expenses; so if a person admitted fault or admitted to being drunk while offering to pay expenses, it could be offered against them.
10. The exclusion doesn't apply if offered for another reason such as to enforce a contract.

Problems on Compromise and Offers to Compromise, Settlement or Tender, and Payment of Medical and Similar Expenses

PROBLEM 9-12. The defendant negligently hits the plaintiff's car and immediately jumps out of the car and makes the following statements. Analyze each statement to determine which of the statements, or portions of statements, would likely be admissible against the defendant to prove liability. Explain why any statement or portion of the statement would be inadmissible.

A. "Oh my goodness, I'm so sorry. I must have dozed off. It was my fault."

B. "Oh my goodness, I'm so sorry. I was reading a stupid text message. It was my fault. I'll pay you $5,000 to settle."

C. "Oh my goodness, I'm so sorry. I was taking a selfie. It was my fault. I'll pay your medical bills and any other expenses you may have."

D. "Wow, I can't believe this. I look down for one second, and boom!!!! This is all my fault. I'll pay your medical bills to get rid of this case."

E. "Listen, I know it was my fault. I'll even concede that what you're asking is reasonable. But you know how long this thing can drag out in the courts, and you may get nothing. How about I give you half that amount today and call it a deal?"

F. "Hey, I'm sorry. It's all my fault. My son had just called, and I was trying to answer the phone. That's not more than $1,000 in damage. How about I give you $2,500 today and we forget about this?"

PROBLEM 9-13. Casey and Kim were both injured when they were struck in the crosswalk by Kendall when he failed to stop at a traffic light. Both of them sue Kendall. Casey promptly settles with Kendall for $8,500 and agrees to testify for Kendall at the trial. Kim and Kendall are unable to come to an agreement, so the case goes to trial. Casey testifies on Kendall's behalf at trial. On cross-examination of Casey, Kim's attorney asks Casey, "*Didn't you settle with Kendall for $8,500?*" Kendall objects, claiming settlements are inadmissible. What ruling?

PROBLEM 9-14. During settlement negotiations, the D company acknowledged several things that they did wrong to explain why they were willing to make such a generous offer. The attorney agreed and stated, "We know you did those things and plan to prove them at trial, so you may as well settle." Since there was no settlement, plaintiffs want to offer evidence at trial of all of the "things" that D did wrong that they argued about in the negotiations. The defendant objects that the information is inadmissible because it was discussed during settlement negotiations. What ruling?

PROBLEM 9-15. Jimmy is the defendant in a criminal case for domestic abuse battery of his estranged wife Tiffany. He offers Tiffany $5,000 not to testify against him. She refuses. Can the prosecution offer evidence of the offer in the obstruction of justice case against Jimmy? Why or why not?

PROBLEM 9-16. Morris negligently installed brakes on Maria's car, and as a result Maria caused a severe accident injuring herself and another driver, and totaled out both cars. She demanded $150,000 from Morris for all of her damages. During settlement negotiations Morris admits that the accident was all his fault and is very apologetic. Then after reviewing the records submitted by Maria's lawyer, he also agrees that the damages are about right. Would the statements made during the settlement negotiations be admissible at trial? Why or why not?

PROBLEM 9-17. Jay sues his home insurer for payment he claims he's entitled to for storm damage to his roof. The insurer disputes the amount of the claim, asserting that Jay failed to mitigate damages by allowing the roof to remain uncovered, damaging the floor and walls inside. Jay claims that the repairs were not made because the insurance company refused to pay and he was unable to make the repairs. The insurance company would like to offer evidence of several timely offers they made to settle the case, all of which Jay rejected. Jay objects, claiming that offers to settle are inadmissible. What ruling?

PROBLEM 9-18. Kaitlyn sued her doctor and hospital for medical malpractice. In the trial, the doctor sought to introduce evidence of the amount Kaitlyn received from the hospital settlement to show that she had been fully compensated for the injuries she suffered. Admissible?

§ 9.2 References and Additional Authority on Compromises, Offers [La. C.E. art. 408, 413] and Payment of Medical and Similar Expenses [La. C.E. art. 409]

1. La. C.E. arts. 408, 409, 413 and Official Comments
2. Force & Rault, Handbook on Louisiana Evidence Law Arts. 408, 409, 413 Author's Comments (West Publishing 2014)

3. Harges & Jones, LOUISIANA EVIDENCE Art. 408, 409, 413 Author's Comments (West Publishing 2014)
4. 19 La. Civ. L. Treatise, Evidence And Proof § 5.6, § 5.7, § 5.9 (2d ed.)
5. MCCORMICK ON EVIDENCE §§ 266–267 (6th ed. 2006)
6. **Excluded as compromise**: *Red Ball Oxygen, Inc. v. Swilley*, 82 So. 3d 360 (La. Ct. App. 3d Cir. 2011) (Former employee sought unpaid fees from former employer; however, the trial court dismissed the employee's claims. Defendant attempted to introduce into evidence an offer to compromise and argued that she was entitled to introduce the offer as evidence because the plaintiff introduced interrogatories and answers which contained the offer. The court held that the offer to compromise was not admissible and it was irrelevant that the answers refer to an offer. They reasoned that the reference to an offer by the introduction of the interrogatories does not waive the provision of Article 408.).
7. **Excluded as settlement or tender**: *Hoerner v. ANCO Insulations, Inc.*, 812 So. 2d 45 (La. Ct. App. 4th Cir. 2002), *writ denied*, 02-0938 (La. 2002), 819 So. 2d 1023 (Asbestos worker and his wife brought suit against employers and others from his contraction of asbestosis. Defendants wanted to introduce the evidence of settlement agreements to prove the amount of liability shared among one another. The court held that the amounts the plaintiff received from some defendants were irrelevant because liability is reduced by each defendant that was proved to be liable for the injuries to the plaintiff.).
8. **Exception to compromise:** *Reeves v. Grove*, 72 So. 3d 1010 (La. Ct. App. 4th Cir. 2011) (In a suit for personal injuries, the plaintiff testified that she had not undergone tooth implant surgery due to her inability to afford it. The trial court then properly allowed the introduction of funds received by plaintiff during her treatment on issue of plaintiff's credibility and veracity.).
9. **Exception to payment of medical expenses**: *Drago v. Winn Dixie Louisiana, Inc.*, 643 So. 2d 212 (La. Ct. App. 4th Cir. 1994) (Plaintiff brought suit against the store when she suffered injuries from a slip and fall. Plaintiff was allowed to introduce into evidence the store manager's promise to pay for her medical bills to enforce a contract for payment.).

§ 9.3 Inadmissibility of Plea Discussions [La. C.E. art. 410]

Applicable Code Articles

Art. 410. Inadmissibility of pleas, plea discussions, and related statements

A. General rule. Except as otherwise provided in this Article, evidence of the following is not, in any civil or criminal proceeding, admissible against the party who made the plea or was a participant in the plea discussions:

(1) A plea of guilty or of nolo contendere which was later withdrawn or set aside;

(2) In a civil case, a plea of nolo contendere;

(3) Any statement made in the course of any court proceeding concerning either of the foregoing pleas, or any plea discussions with an attorney for or other representative of the prosecuting authority regarding either of the foregoing pleas; or

(4) Any statement made in the course of plea discussions with an attorney for or other representative of the prosecuting authority which do not result in a plea of guilty or which result in a plea of guilty later withdrawn or set aside.

B. Exceptions. However, such a statement is admissible:

(1) In any proceeding wherein another statement made in the course of the same plea or plea discussions has been introduced and the statement ought in fairness be considered contemporaneously with it; or

(2) In a criminal proceeding for perjury or false statement if the statement was made by the defendant under oath, on the record and in the presence of counsel.

Article 410 is the criminal counterpart to Article 408. This article limits the admissibility of statements made in the course of plea discussions or negotiations in an effort to come to an agreement to resolve a criminal charge, as well as any actual pleas that may be entered as a result of a criminal charge from being admitted against a person at a subsequent civil or criminal trial. Like statements made during settlement negotiations, statements made during plea negotiations are excluded to encourage attempts to come to agreements in criminal cases. Specifically, the article provides that:

1. in a criminal or civil case,
2. evidence of the following statements:
    a. a plea of **guilty** or of **nolo contendere** which was later **withdrawn** or **set aside**;
    b. in a **civil case**, a plea of **nolo contendere**;
    c. any **(collateral) statements** made in the course of any court proceeding concerning either of the foregoing pleas; or
    d. any **plea discussions** with an attorney (or other representative) of the prosecuting authority regarding either of the foregoing pleas; or
    e. any statement made in the course of **plea discussions** with an attorney (or other representative) of the prosecuting authority which **does not result** in a **plea of guilty**; or
    f. any statement made in the course of plea discussions with an attorney (or other representative) of the prosecuting authority, which results in a plea of **guilty later withdrawn** or **set aside.**[10]
3. are not admissible against the party who made the plea nor against any other participant in the plea discussions.

Generally this article **excludes pleas and plea negotiations** (with the prosecuting attorney or their representative) that either **do not result in a plea**, or if they do, the **plea is later withdrawn or set aside**. Additionally, it includes statements made in court proceedings relative to a plea that is later withdrawn or set aside.

10. La. Code Evid. art. 410.

Policy interests. As with other provisions in this section, the rule is policy-based. This rule is designed to encourage "unrestrained condor between the prosecutor and the defense counsel that leads to effective plea bargaining"[11] "by giving the defendant protection from involuntary self-incrimination at two ends of the plea-bargaining spectrum: while he is negotiating over the disposition of case and while he is offering or entering a plea that is rejected or later withdrawn."[12] The State has a genuine interest in encouraging plea negotiations in that all or even most cases could not be tried to a jury. Such negotiations would be significantly hampered if those statements could then be used against a defendant in a trial.

Excludes statements offered *against party* or *participant* in negotiations. This provision specifically excludes the statements outlined above from being offered against the party who made them or against a party who was a participant in the plea negotiations. Thus, the prosecution would be precluded from offering such statements against a defendant, and similarly, the defense would be precluded from offering statements against the prosecution (a party) who was also a "participant in the plea negotiations." However, the article should not be construed to preclude the admissibility of pleas or plea negotiations of a nonparty witness that may be offered for impeachment purposes.

What constitutes plea negotiations? The determination of whether the statements in question were made in the course of plea negotiations[13] is a preliminary question for the trial court to determine under Article 104(A). The standard for determining whether plea negotiations were actually taking place is set out in *U.S. v. Robertson*[14] in a two-tiered analysis, stating that the trial court must determine, "first, whether the accused exhibited an actual subjective expectation to negotiate a plea at the time of the discussion, and second whether the accused's expectation was reasonable given the totality of the objective circumstances."[15] If both a **subjective** and an **objective intent to enter into plea-bargaining** are not met, then the statements will not be excluded under this rule.

Exceptions: The article contains two exceptions in which such statements may be admitted:

(1) In any proceeding wherein **another statement** made in the course of the same plea or plea discussions has been **introduced** and the statement ought in fairness be **considered contemporaneously** with it; or

(2) In a criminal **proceeding for perjury** or **false statement** if the statement was made by the **defendant under oath**, on the record and in the presence of counsel.[16]

Federal Rules of Evidence Distinction. This article is different from Federal Rule of Evidence 410, which only excludes a "statement made in the course of

11. State v. Lewis, 539 So. 2d 1199 (1989).
12. State v. Lewis, 539 So. 2d 1199, 1202 (1989).
13. In State v. Crockett, 886 So. 2d 1139 (La. Ct. App. 5th Cir. 2004), court found statements not made in course of plea negotiations when defendant offered to make statements on the record despite prosecution's statement on the record that no deal was on the table and that statements made would be used against defendant in trial set to begin the next day.
14. U.S. v. Robertson, 582 F.2d 1356 (5th Cir. 1978).
15. U.S. v. Robertson, 582 F.2d 1356, 1366 (5th Cir. 1978); *See also*, Harges & Jones, Louisiana Evidence, art. 410 Author's Notes.
16. La. Code Evid. art. 410(B).

plea discussions with an **attorney for the prosecuting authority**."[17] It does not include statements made to "**other representative**[s] of the prosecuting attorney" as under the Louisiana article. Thus, Louisiana gives greater protection because it would also preclude statements made during plea negotiations from being offered against an accused made to other *representatives* of the prosecuting authority including investigators, victim/witness advocates, or others. Statements made to such individuals in federal proceedings are not covered under the federal rule, and would thus be admissible against a criminal defendant in federal court.

Case on Plea Negotiations

State v. Crockett
Court of Appeal of Louisiana, Fifth Circuit
886 So. 2d 1139
Oct. 12, 2004

JAMES L. CANNELLA, Judge.

Harmon Wright (Wright), the victim, testified that, on November 10, 2002, he got off work at 4:00 p.m. and went to the apartment of a friend, Donald Johnson (Johnson), where he had been residing. Wright had a paycheck for $550 in his pocket and $75 in cash from a catering event that he had worked the previous night. Johnson accompanied Wright as he cashed his check. Wright and Johnson then went shopping for groceries. They went back to Johnson's apartment and Wright cooked dinner for a group including himself, Johnson, the Defendant, and another "guy." They then watched a movie. When the movie ended, Johnson left the apartment with the "guy," leaving the Defendant and Wright alone in the apartment. While the Defendant and Wright were watching television, a young lady came to the apartment, sat on the sofa next to the Defendant, and said to him, "Black, let's go get something off the corner." The Defendant and the lady then left.

A minute or two later, at approximately 11:00 or 11:30 p.m., the Defendant came back inside the house with a red shirt wrapped around his head. He produced a rust-colored .9 mm gun and told Wright to "give it up." Wright gave the Defendant the cash that he had in his pocket, which was approximately $600. The Defendant told Wright to go into the kitchen and the Defendant then left the apartment. Wright put his belongings into his vehicle and went to the police station around the corner to report the robbery....

Once Wright got to the police station, he told an officer that he had just been robbed by an individual named "Anthony." Wright was eventually shown a photographic lineup and positively identified the Defendant as the robber, immediately and without hesitation. Wright also positively identified the Defendant in court....

... Lt. Schultz issued a warrant for the Defendant's arrest and the Defendant was arrested a day or two later. Lt. Schultz read the Defendant his rights and the Defendant waived them. Lt. Schultz then took a statement from the Defendant.

In his first statement dated November 13, 2002, the Defendant said ... [Defendant details first statement]

Jefferson Parish Sheriff's Office Detective Kevin Decker testified that, on July 17, 2003, the State requested that he come to court because the Defendant had advised his attorney

17. Fed. R. Evid. 410.

that he had additional information in reference to the investigation. He read the Defendant his rights, which the Defendant waived, and the Defendant gave a statement in the presence of his attorney.

[Defendant details a second factual account of the sequence of events that transpired on the night in question]

...

ASSIGNMENT OF ERROR NUMBER ONE

The Defendant argues that the trial court erred in failing to suppress the second statement he made which he contends was made during the course of plea negotiations....

The State argues that the Defendant's second statement was not part of a plea discussion and, therefore, it was properly admitted....

On the morning originally scheduled for trial, defense counsel said that he was ready to pick a jury, but that the Defendant had informed him that he had information he would like to share with the district attorney's office and the sheriff's office which could possibly lead to bringing the proper parties before the court. The prosecutor stated that she wanted to put a couple of things on the record:

> Number one, there are no deals on the table, nor will there — there ever be for the foreseeable future, so I don't want this to be construed as a deal in progress. There are no deals, he is charged with armed robbery, he will be tried for armed robbery, as we stand right now.

She said that it was her understanding that the Defendant was waiving his rights and willing to give a statement and that Detective Decker was on his way to court to take a statement from him. She stated that she would like the court to question the Defendant regarding waiving his rights and giving a statement.

The trial judge continued the trial from July 17, 2003 to July 22, 2003. He advised the Defendant that on July 22, 2003 his trial was going forward absent the defense or the State saying they did not want to go forward that day. The trial judge stated:

> Okay, that's all I wanted — to understand, and the very last thing I want to understand is, from this moment on, there are no deals on the table, that, as far as I'm concerned, we do go to trial Tuesday morning. Understand that?

The Defendant indicated that he understood. Defense counsel said that the Defendant was previously offered eleven years but refused that, maintaining his innocence. Defense counsel further stated:

> Any deals, obviously, all deals are off the table. I think he understands that. But he also refused any deals that were offered to him before that.

...

On July 22, 2003, the State called this case for trial. Defense counsel stated that he had filed a motion to suppress the second statement and that he was ready to go forward with it. The State said it would get the officer there.

On July 23, 2003, in support of his motion, defense counsel argued that the State not be allowed to introduce into evidence the Defendant's second statement because it violated the hearsay rules and because it was made as part of plea negotiations. The prosecutor noted that she had made it very clear on the record that whatever statement was given she intended to use at trial, that the Defendant had waived his rights, and that there was no deal under consideration....

After hearing arguments of counsel, the trial judge ruled that the two statements could be used by the State. He found that the statement was not hearsay and that there had been no deal made with the prosecutor prior to the Defendant giving his second statement.

The law regarding the admissibility of statements made during plea discussions is found in La. C.E. art. 410, which provides in pertinent part:

> Except as otherwise provided in this Article, evidence of the following is not, in any civil or criminal proceeding, admissible against the party who made the plea or was a participant in the plea discussions:
>
> ....
>
> (4) Any statement made in the course of plea discussions with an attorney for or other representative of the prosecuting authority which do not result in a plea of guilty or which result in a plea of guilty later withdrawn or set aside.

In *State v. Lewis,* 539 So.2d 1199 (La.1989), cited by both the Defendant and the State in their briefs, the Louisiana Supreme Court discussed the law regarding statements made during plea discussions:

> The rules serve to promote negotiated disposition of criminal cases by giving the defendant protection from involuntary self-incrimination at two ends of the plea-bargaining spectrum: while he is negotiating over the disposition of his case and while he is offering or entering a plea that is rejected or later withdrawn....
> *Id.* at 1202 (citations omitted).

...

In the instant case, the record indicates that the Defendant's second statement was not made in the course of plea discussions and, therefore, that the trial judge did not err in admitting it into evidence.

Defense counsel advised the prosecutor that the Defendant wanted to provide information that the sheriff's office could use to bring the party or parties who committed the crime to court. The prosecutor agreed to consider the information and to continue the trial for investigation of the claims that the Defendant made in his second statement. The prosecutor clearly stated on the record that no deals were on the table nor would there ever be for the foreseeable future, and that she did not want this to be construed as a deal in progress. Additionally, the trial judge stated that he understood that there were no deals on the table.

... Thus, we find that the trial court did not err in denying the motion to suppress the second statement.

...

AFFIRMED AND REMANDED.

Discussion Questions

1. A preliminary question in determining the applicability of Article 410 is whether the statement in question is actually made in the course of plea negotiations. Could a reasonable argument be made in *Crockett* that the statements were actually in furtherance of a plea agreement?
   a. How could the facts have been changed so that the outcome of the case might have been different?
   b. While the defendant's statement is not included in the case above because it was only a lengthy alternative factual account of events, what if during the defendant's

statement he'd actually offered to plead guilty, or asked for an offer? Would that have been appropriate to present to the jury?

2. Is there a requirement that both parties agree or consent to "plea negotiations" taking place? What about in the common scenario in which defendants often send letters from jail to the prosecutor handling their cases offering to plead guilty to a particular charge? Are those letters subject to the Article 410 exclusion? In answering this question, consider whether the public policy interests are furthered by excluding such statements.
3. All of the public policy exclusions in Chapter 4 typically have exceptions in which the information may be offered for other reasons. While none of the exceptions in Article 410(B) apply to the situation in *Crockett*, should such a statement also be offered to attack a defendant's credibility in the instance in which the defendant contradicts other statements made by him?
   a. Should this question be answered by balancing the state's interest in fostering open plea negotiations, against a state's interest in presenting evidence of the defendant's credibility at trial, even in the event the defendant does not take the stand? How would you resolve this issue?

Key Points

The key points to keep in mind regarding pleas, plea discussions, and negotiations.

1. The purpose is to encourage open plea negotiations without fear that statements will later be used against the defendant.
2. Pleas, plea discussions or plea negotiations relate to efforts to resolve a criminal case.
3. The exclusion refers to the following pleas, negotiations and plea discussions, including plea discussions that do not result in a plea, or a plea of guilty or nolo contendere that is later withdrawn or set aside (Art. 894 or 893).
4. The exclusion also includes statements made by a defendant to other representatives of the prosecuting attorney (e.g., police, investigators, etc.).
5. Excludes statements from being offered against a party making the statement or against a party who was a participant in the negotiations.
6. Whether a plea was actually taking place is determined by: 1) whether defendant has an actual subjective expectation to negotiate a plea at the time of the discussion (subjective standard); and 2) whether the accused expectation was reasonable given the totality of the objective circumstances (objective standard).
7. Two exceptions: 1) if another statement was made during the plea negotiations is offered, and it should also be offered in fairness; and 2) in a criminal proceeding for perjury or false statement if the statement was made by the defendant under oath, on the record and in the presence of counsel.

Problems on Pleas, Plea Discussions, and Related Statements

PROBLEM 9-19. At Courtney's armed robbery trial, the prosecution would like to offer evidence that Courtney offered to plead guilty as charged with a sentence of ten years (an offer rejected by the prosecution) to help prove he committed the crime. Admissible?

PROBLEM 9-20 Eddie was charged with second-degree battery. Without his attorney's knowledge, Eddie wrote a letter to the prosecutor offering to plead guilty to simple battery with credit for time served. Eddie apologized for his actions and said that he sympathized for the victim who lost vision in one eye. He stated he wishes he could take it back, and that he'd learned his lesson. At the trial, the prosecution sought to admit the letter into evidence with the intention of reading the portion of the letter to the jury where the defendant admitted to the offense, apologized, and wished he could take it back. Is any portion of the letter admissible? How should the court rule and why? [See, *State v. Robertson*, 924 So. 2d 1201 (La. Ct. App. 3d Cir. 2006)].

PROBLEM 9-21. Mildred was testifying in the defendant Dan's trial. Dan, Mildred, and several others had been arrested in connection with a rash of burglaries in their neighborhood. They were all charged with five counts of simple burglary. At the trial, Mildred testified on behalf of the State. During the cross-examination of Mildred, she was asked if she'd gotten a deal from the prosecution. The prosecution objected that the statement related to plea negotiations and was inadmissible. What ruling?

PROBLEM 9-22. Defendant was charged with aggravated rape. In the defendant's case-in-chief, the defendant took the stand in his own defense. During the examination, the defendant's attorney asked the defendant why he had gone to trial on the charge. He stated that he went to trial because he was innocent. The defendant was asked whether he'd received an offer from the prosecution to plead guilty to a lesser charge that he'd rejected. The defense then sought to admit a letter from the Assistant District Attorney where an offer was made to the defendant for a lesser charge, in support of their position that the defendant had rejected an opportunity to plead guilty to a lesser charge because he was innocent. The prosecution objected to further testimony regarding the plea negotiations. How should the court rule and why?

PROBLEM 9-23. Derrick (D) was incarcerated on the charge of simple arson. He wrote a letter to the prosecutor offering to plead guilty as charged with credit for time served, in that he had been incarcerated for some time. Derrick confided in his cellmate that he'd written the letter to the prosecutor. He further explained that the prosecutor should take the offer because he was aware that he had no evidence against him. He stated that he made sure that he burned up all of the evidence, fingerprints, and anything else tying him to the crime when he committed the offense. Derrick's cellmate contacted the DA's office and told them what Derrick said. The prosecutor called the cellmate to the stand to testify as to what Derrick said, including the offer to plead guilty, and why he stated the prosecutor should accept the offer. The defense objected, claiming that the statements were plea negotiations. How should the court rule on the cellmate's testimony and why? [See, *State v. Divers*, 889 So. 2d 335 (La. Ct. App. 2d Cir. 2004)].

Would your answer change if the statements had been made to a sheriff's deputy working at the prison? What about a sheriff's deputy that the prosecutor had requested to talk to Derrick about the plea? Explain.

PROBLEM 9-24. The defendant was charged with aggravated battery of his wife. In the defendant's final court appearance before his case was scheduled to proceed to trial the next week, the defendant became upset with his attorney because he wanted his attorney to tell the judge that his wife was not going to show up and testify. He believed the State would drop the charges and would not prosecute. As his attorney tried to hush him and tell him it was not the time or place, the defendant yelled out in court, "Y'all might as well drop the charges. She ain't coming. She won't dare come down here Monday." At the trial the next week, the prosecution sought to admit the defendant's statement against him made in court the previous week to show his dangerous nature against his wife. The defense objected that the statement was made in the course of plea negotiations as the defense sought to resolve the case. How should the court rule and why? Would your answer change if similar statements were made regarding the witness's willingness to testify in more formal plea negotiations? Why or why not?

§ 9.3 References and Additional Authority on Inadmissibility of Plea Discussions [La. C.E. art. 410]

1. La. C.E. art. 410 and Official Comments
2. Force & Rault, Handbook on Louisiana Evidence Law Art. 410 Author's Comments (West Publishing 2014)
3. Harges & Jones, Louisiana Evidence Art. 410 Author's Comments (West Publishing 2014)
4. 19 La. Civ. L. Treatise, Evidence And Proof § 5.6
5. **Excluded as plea discussion**: *Brasseaux v. Town of Mamou*, 713 So 2d. 742 (La. Ct. App. 3d Cir. 1998) (holding that the introduction of the district attorney's entire file was inadmissible because portions of the file would contain pleas, plea discussions, and other related statements).
6. **Statements not a part of plea discussions:** *State v. Lewis*, 539 So. 2d 1199 (La. 1989) (Defendant provided statements to the district attorney more than a week after an agreement was signed. The statements were found to be outside the course of plea discussion and were not barred for introduction of evidence.).

§ 9.4 Liability Insurance [La. C.E. art. 411]

Applicable Code Articles

Art. 411. Liability insurance

Although a policy of insurance may be admissible, the amount of coverage under the policy shall not be communicated to the jury unless the amount of coverage is a disputed issue which the jury will decide.

Federal Rules of Evidence Distinction. Although the fact that a party is covered by insurance is admissible in Louisiana, evidence of the ***amount*** of coverage under the policy is not admissible at trial. This statute is different than the federal rule, which also precludes evidence of the fact that a party is covered by insurance on the issue of proving negligence. The Federal Rules do, however, allow such evidence to prove other issues such as agency, ownership, control, bias, or prejudice. Under Louisiana law, the fact of insurance is admissible, but the amount of coverage under the policy shall not be communicated to the jury unless the amount of coverage is a disputed issue which the jury will decide.

Problem on Liability Insurance

PROBLEM 9-25. Donovan is injured in a serious accident negligently caused by the driver of a large 18-wheeler owned by a major retail chain. Donovan wants to offer the following evidence at trial. Which would be permissible and why?

A. Evidence that the company is covered by $500 million in insurance to prove that the company can pay the cost of any damages awarded to the plaintiff.

B. Evidence that the company is covered by insurance to prove that the company can pay the cost of any damages awarded to the plaintiff.

C. Evidence that the company pays insurance for the driver to prove that the driver is an employee of the company and not an independent contractor.

§ 9.5 Workers' Compensation Payments [La. C.E. art. 414]

Applicable Code Articles

Art. 414. Workers' compensation payments

Evidence of the nature and extent of a workers' compensation claim or of payment of past or future workers' compensation benefits shall not be admissible to a jury, directly or indirectly, in any civil proceeding with respect to a claim for damages relative to the same injury for which the workers' compensation benefits are claimed or paid. Such evidence shall be admissible and presented to the judge only.

In a civil case, the fact and amount of any past or future workers' compensation payments the plaintiff may have received in connection with the injury that is also the subject of the current lawsuit shall not be made known to the jury. Further, evidence of the nature and extent of such a claim is also inadmissible. Such information may only be presented to the judge alone. The purpose of the provision is to prevent the jury from considering any worker's compensation in minimizing any award amount to which the plaintiff may be entitled. As in the case of Article 408, this article might be construed to allow for the admissibility of such evidence if relevant for another purpose, such as to attack the credibility of a witness.

Federal Rules of Evidence Distinction. There is no comparable provision in the Federal Rules of Evidence.

Problem on Workers' Compensation Payments

PROBLEM 9-26. Erin, the defendant in a case, would like to offer evidence in the jury trial that Christina, the plaintiff in the case, received workers' compensation to compensate her for her injuries to show that Christina should not recover because she has already been compensated for her injuries. Should the judge allow the evidence?

A. Assume instead that Christina was denied her workers' compensation claim because it was determined that she was not engaged in the course and scope of employment at the time of her injury. Should the judge allow this evidence to be presented to the jury?

B. May the judge receive either of the evidence referenced above? Why or why not?

§ 9.6 Act of Contacting an Attorney [La. C.E. art. 415]

> **Applicable Code Articles**
>
> **Art. 415. Act of contacting or retaining an attorney**
>
> In any criminal proceeding, the act of contacting or retaining an attorney shall not be admissible against any individual or entity, unless such act falls within an established exception for crime or fraud.

The fact that a party or entity contacted an attorney is inadmissible against the party or entity in any criminal proceeding, unless such act falls within an established exception for crime or fraud. For example, the State would not be able to ask the witness, "So if you were innocent, then why did you hire a lawyer?" The rule is designed to limit such questions that would imply that a witness contacted an attorney because of consciousness of guilt.

Federal Rules of Evidence Distinction. The Federal Rules of Evidence do not contain a corresponding provision.

Problem on the Act of Contacting or Retaining an Attorney

PROBLEM 9-27. Mayor Linstrom was suspected of malfeasance in office. During the investigation, it was discovered that the governor was having an extramarital affair with his accountant during an examination of his telephone records. Immediately after the accountant testified in the grand jury proceedings about the affair, she hired a lawyer. It was later discovered that she perjured herself in the proceedings. In her perjury trial, the prosecution would like to offer evidence that the accountant hired a lawyer immediately after the proceedings as proof of her guilty conscious after her testimony. Should the prosecution be able to offer the fact that the accountant hired a lawyer in her perjury trial for such purposes?

§ 9.3–§ 9.6 References and Additional Authority on Liability Insurance [La. C.E. art. 411], Act of Contacting Attorney [La. C.E. art. 415], and Workers' Compensation [La. C.E. art. 414]

1. La. C.E. arts. 411, 414, 415 and Official Comments
2. Force & Rault, Handbook on Louisiana Evidence Law Arts. 411, 414, 415 Author's Comments (West Publishing 2014)

3. Harges & Jones, Louisiana Evidence Art. 411, 414, 415 Author's Comments (West Publishing 2014)
4. 19 La. Civ. L. Treatise, Evidence And Proof § 5.8, § 5.10 (2d ed.)
5. **Liability insurance cases (Article 411)**: *Mack v. Transport Ins. Co.*, 577 So. 2d 112 (La. Ct. App. 1st Cir. 1991) (holding that the introduction into evidence of insurance limits is not admissible to prove the ability of a party to pay for damages).
6. **Act of contacting attorney (Article 415)**: *State v. Berry*, 645 So. 2d 757 (La. Ct. App. 5th Cir. 1994) (Victim of a battery filed a civil suit against the accused. In the criminal proceeding, the accused sought to question the victim about the hiring of an attorney to sue the defendant for damages. The trial court denied defendant the opportunity to question the victim regarding the civil matter. The appellate court held that the scope of Article 415 was not to prohibit matters of bias when someone files a lawsuit against the accused for damages arising out of a criminal matter.).
7. **Workers' compensation (Article 414)**: *Tolbird v. Wyble*, 892 So. 2d 103 (La. Ct. App. 2d Cir. 2004) (Employee filed a personal injury action against a tortfeasor and its insurer. The employee received worker's compensation benefits from an accident during the course and scope of his employment. During the trial, the parties attempted to introduce the worker's compensation payments received by the employee. The trial court found that the evidence was inadmissible because the evidence was being used to confuse the jury as to the proper calculation of damages to be awarded.).

Chapter 10

Authentication and Identification and the Requirement of the Original

§ 10.1 Authentication and Identification [La. C.E. arts. 901–905]

Applicable Code Articles

Art. 901. Requirement of authentication or identification

A. General provision. The requirement of authentication or identification as a condition precedent to admissibility is satisfied by evidence sufficient to support a finding that the matter in question is what its proponent claims.

* * *

Other than testimony, the primary way in which a party establishes the facts to prove his case at trial is through the introduction of items such as physical evidence, documents, diagrams, and photographs into evidence. Prior to admitting a matter into evidence at trial, the proponent must first establish that the matter in question is what he claims it is. This process is referred to as "authenticating" the evidence. Authentication is a condition precedent to the admissibility of all evidence. For example, if the proponent of a letter claims that the letter was written by the victim of the crime to the defendant prior to the alleged crime and was found at the crime scene, he must first establish that the letter he seeks to offer into evidence is in fact *that* letter, and not for example, one that someone else may have written or that the attorney offering it may have even written himself. In other words, the letter must be "authenticated" before it may be admitted into evidence and received by the trier of fact.

Authentication of evidence is an important part of the truth-finding process at trial. By requiring the proponent of evidence to first show that the item is what he claims it is, it helps to ensure that accurate and trustworthy evidence is being received by the jury. Additionally, it shows the relevance of the item to the case at hand, and it also adds to the weight and credibility the trier of fact can give to the evidence because it has been shown to be what the proponent claims it is in their presence.

In the example above, the person who wrote the letter or a person who may be familiar with the victim's handwriting would be able to authenticate the letter—providing sufficient evidence that the letter was in fact written by the victim. A person who saw the victim write the letter, and who perhaps delivered it to the defendant, would be able to testify to its authenticity as well as the defendant himself who could testify that he received the letter from the victim in which she responds to questions or conversations they've had.

In most cases there are many ways and through several people this process may be done. Chapter 9 of the Code of Evidence governs the requirement of authentication, sets the standard that must be met for authenticating evidence, and sets forth an illustrative list of ways of conforming with the authentication requirement.

The standard for admissibility. The standard for authenticating evidence is set forth in Article 901 which provides that the requirement of authentication or identification as a condition precedent to admissibility is satisfied by **"evidence sufficient to support a finding"** that the matter in question is what its proponent claims. This is an evidentiary determination made by the trial judge under the authority granted to judges under Article 104(B).

If you recall in Chapter 2 we studied conditional relevancy under Article 104(B) where you learned that in some instances the relevancy of evidence depends upon the determination of a preliminary question. With respect to the admissibility of evidence, its authenticity determines its relevance. For instance, as with the letter above, it is only relevant if it can be shown that the victim did in fact write it.[1] Clearly, if the letter was written by someone other than the victim (a fake or forgery), it would not be relevant to the case at hand. Under the standard of Article 104(B), the judge may admit the evidence upon a showing of evidence "sufficient to support a finding" that the letter (or other item) is what the proponent claims. Evidence is deemed to be sufficient to support a finding that it is what the proponent claims it is if **"a reasonable juror could find the existence of the fact."** So provided the proponent can offer evidence wherein a reasonable juror could find that the victim wrote the letter (or whatever the proponent may claim the evidence may be in another instance), the standard is met, and the evidence should be admitted.

This is a different and lower standard than the "preponderance of the evidence" standard that a judge typically uses in determining other preliminary questions. Here, the proponent of the evidence need only offer evidence in which "a rational juror could conclude"[2] that the evidence is what the proponent claims it is. Once this precondition is met, the judge should allow the evidence to be admitted at trial. Thereafter it will be left to the jury to make the final determination as to whether the evidence actually is what the proponent claims it is, and they will also decide the weight and credibility to give to the evidence.[3]

It is important to remember, however, as we pointed out in other portions of the casebook, the fact that evidence has been sufficiently authenticated does not automatically make it admissible. The other evidentiary rules still apply. The evidence must also overcome other objections such as hearsay, relevance, Article 403 balancing, requirement of the original (discussed in the next section), as well as not be excluded under any other provisions.

Procedure for admitting evidence: The following is a summary of the general procedure to keep in mind when preparing to offer a matter into evidence.

1. **Appropriate witness**. An appropriate witness must be called who is competent to testify that the evidence is what the proponent claims, by one of the ways listed below or by another manner in which they can establish that the evidence is what the proponent claims it is.
2. **Foundation laid.** Foundation must be laid to establish how the witness will be able to authenticate the evidence, e.g., how the witness is familiar with the signature,

---

1. *See also* FED. R. EVID. 104(b) advisory committee notes.
2. LA. CODE EVID. art. 104 Official Comment (f).
3. *See* Force & Rault, HANDBOOK, Art. 104, Author's Note (2).

how he is familiar with the voice, how he knows the distinguishing characteristics, or how he acquired other relevant knowledge to authenticate the evidence.

3. **Identification/authentication.** The witness identifies the evidence on the stand, and testifies as to how he knows the evidence is what it purports to be. (The litany is below for authenticating the evidence.)
4. **Evidence offered into evidence/subject to objections.** After the evidence is authenticated, the matter is offered into evidence and must overcome any other objections to admissibility, e.g., relevancy, hearsay, requirement of the original, etc.
5. **Published to jury.** If no objections to admissibility are sustained, or if there are no objections, and the exhibit is admitted into evidence, it may be viewed by the jury. The jury may only see or hear evidence that has been admitted into evidence.

If evidence is self-authenticating (discussed below § 10.2), no extrinsic evidence, i.e., a witness and foundation, is necessary prior to admitting it into evidence. The evidence is simply offered into evidence without the need for extrinsic evidence of authenticity.

Applicable Code Articles

Art. 901. Requirement of authentication or identification

* * *

B. Illustrations. By way of illustration only, and not by way of limitation, the following are examples of authentication or identification conforming with the requirements of this Article:

(1) Testimony of witness with knowledge. Testimony that a matter is what it is claimed to be.

(2) Nonexpert opinion on handwriting. Nonexpert opinion as to the genuineness of handwriting, based upon familiarity not acquired for purposes of the litigation.

(3) Comparison by trier or expert witness. Comparison by the trier of fact or by expert witnesses with specimens which have been authenticated.

(4) Distinctive characteristics and the like. Appearance, contents, substance, internal patterns, or other distinctive characteristics, taken in conjunction with circumstances.

(5) Voice identification. Identification of a voice, whether heard firsthand or through mechanical or electronic transmission or recording, by opinion based upon hearing the voice at any time under circumstances connecting it with the alleged speaker.

(6) Telephone conversations. Telephone conversations, by evidence that a call was made to the number assigned at the time by the telephone company to a particular person or business, if:

(a) In the case of a person, circumstances, including self-identification, show the person answering to be the one called; or

(b) In the case of a business, the call was made to a place of business and the conversation related to business reasonably transacted over the telephone.

(7) Public records or reports. Evidence that a writing authorized by law to be recorded or filed and in fact recorded or filed in a public office, or a purported public record, report, statement, or data compilation, in any form, is from the public office where items of this nature are kept.

(8) Ancient documents or data compilation. Evidence that a document or data compilation, in any form:

(a) Is in such condition as to create no suspicion concerning its authenticity;

(b) Was in a place where it, if authentic, would likely be; and

(c) Has been in existence thirty years or more at the time it is offered.

(9) Process or system. Evidence describing a process or system used to produce a result and showing that the process or system produces an accurate result.

(10) Methods provided by legislation. Any method of authentication or identification provided by Act of Congress or by Act of the Louisiana Legislature.

Methods of Authenticating Evidence

So how do we meet the standard for authenticating evidence? How does the proponent show that the evidence is what he claims it is? Since most evidence is admitted through witnesses, when a proponent of evidence seeks to admit evidence at trial, he must consider ***who*** can authenticate the evidence, and ***by what means*** the witness will be able to identify it or authenticate it. For example, if the prosecution seeks to admit a knife into evidence that he claims the defendant used to kill the victim, he must first consider who can authenticate it, i.e., who can testify that the knife in question is in fact the one used in the crime. He must also consider by what means the witness will be able to authenticate it, i.e., by some identifying mark on it or some unique characteristic, etc.

Clearly the defendant would be able to authenticate the knife that he used to commit a crime. But that witness would be unavailable to the prosecution. So they must consider other witnesses through whom the evidence can be admitted. The victim, if alive, might be able to testify to the knife used in a crime if she had an opportunity to view it or had some other way of being able to determine that it was in fact the knife used. Additionally, the crime scene investigator might be able to authenticate the knife. He'd be able to testify that he collected it from the scene, and put identifying marks on the packaging or label such as the case number or his signature.

There are many different types of evidence that a party may wish to introduce into evidence to prove his case. A party may wish to introduce physical evidence such as a knife, gun, shoe, jacket, book, pen, glove, pants, or some other tangible evidence. He may wish to offer a letter, a business record, a receipt, invoice, photograph, diagram, email, social media post, recording, video, or a full range of other items that may help to prove facts to support his case. Whatever the evidence, the proponent must authenticate it. Article 901(B) contains an illustrative list of ways to authenticate evidence. The list is merely examples of ways to authenticate evidence that satisfy the requirement of the article. Other ways of authenticating evidence may be used provided it meets the standard discussed above.

Some of the common methods of authenticating evidence contained in Article 901(B) include: witness with knowledge, nonexpert opinion on handwriting, comparison by trier or expert, distinctive characteristics and the like, process or system, voice identification, and others. Some of the more common methods are discussed below.

1. *Witness with knowledge or distinctive characteristics.* Two of the most common methods of authenticating evidence are by testimony of a witness with knowledge that the matter is what it is claimed to be or by distinctive characteristics such as the "appearance, contents, substance, internal patterns, or other distinctive characteristics, taken in conjunction with circumstances."[4] A witness who is familiar with the distinctive characteristics, shown by proper foundation, examines the evidence on the stand, testifies to what the evidence is, then testifies to the distinctive characteristics of the evidence which enables him to testify that the evidence is what the proponent claims. The litany that is used to authenticate evidence is below.

2. *Nonexpert opinion on handwriting.* Another commonly used way of authenticating handwritten documents is by "nonexpert opinion as to the genuineness of handwriting, based upon familiarity not acquired for purposes of the litigation."[5] A person familiar with another's handwriting can take the stand and after establishing the foundation of how the person is familiar with the handwriting of the writer, would then have an opportunity to review the writing in question and testify to whether it was written by the person in question. The provision stipulates that the knowledge of the person's handwriting must not have been acquired for purposes of litigation, but must have existed prior to the litigation in question. Typically, a person's spouse, child, or even a co-worker or employee who is familiar with the handwriting could testify as to whether the handwriting in question is that of the person it's claimed to be.

3. *Comparison by expert or trier of fact.* Additionally, an expert witness or trier of fact could authenticate evidence by comparing the object in question with a known specimen that has been authenticated. For example, an expert witness could compare a known sample of the person's handwriting with the handwriting in a letter in question to determine if both were made by the same person. Authentication by comparison of the objects may also be done by the trier of fact, the jury or the judge in a bench trial, but the article does not provide for comparison of objects by a lay witness.

An example of authentication by comparison might occur in a situation in which a person accused of murder might claim that the victim committed suicide and left a suicide note. The prosecution might claim the note wasn't written by the victim. The defense could authenticate the letter, and have it admitted into evidence by calling an expert witness to compare a known sample of the victim's handwriting with the suicide note. If the witness determines that the letter was in fact written by the victim, his testimony is sufficient to establish that the letter is what the proponent claims, i.e., a suicide note written by the victim.

4. *Opinion on voice.* A voice, such as in a recording, may be authenticated by opinion testimony based upon hearing the voice and evidence establishing that the person identifying the voice is familiar with the person's voice in question. For instance, the person who made a 911 call could authenticate the 911 call by testifying that the voice on the tape was her voice, and that the conversation on the tape accurately depicted the conversation that she had with the 911 operator.[6] It would not be necessary to call the custodian of records at the 911 dispatch center, although that person could also authenticate the 911 call based on the manner in which the calls are logged and stored in connection with the incident with which they are associated.

5. *Ancient documents.* An ancient document may be authenticated by evidence to establish that it has been in existence for 30 or more years and is in such condition as to create no suspicion concerning its authenticity and was in a place where it, if authentic,

4. La. Code Evid. art. 901(B)(4).
5. La. Code Evid. art. 901(B)(2).
6. State v. Taylor, 875 So. 2d 962 (La. Ct. App. 5th Cir. 2004).

would likely be. A will, for example, that has been sitting in a person's home safe for 40 years could possibly be authenticated this way, provided there is no evidence to create suspicion about its authenticity.

Article 901 lists common ways in which evidence may be authenticated, and most evidence can be authenticated by one of these methods, however, other ways may be used provided the standard is met as outlined below.

Chain of custody to authenticate evidence. In some instances, chain of custody may be used to authenticate evidence, and establish that the matter in question is what it purports to be. For example, in a possession of marijuana case the State must prove that the substance being offered into evidence in the defendant's trial was the substance that was actually possessed by the defendant on the date in question and that it tested positive for marijuana. Since the witness would not be able to identify the marijuana from any identifying characteristics, the prosecution usually seeks to authenticate the marijuana through establishing the chain of custody from its collection to its presence at trial.

To accomplish this, the prosecution would call the police officer to testify that he recovered the substance from the suspect, put identifying marks on the packaging and took it to the crime lab, where he checked it in with the clerk at the crime lab. The clerk at the crime lab would be called to testify that she in fact checked the substance in and would identify her signature logging it into the crime lab. The crime lab technician would then be called to testify that she checked it out for testing, and put her signature on the log showing the date and time she checked it out, and would show the date and time in which she logged the evidence back in after it was tested. The clerk could testify that she logged the evidence back in after it was tested; and finally, the police officer could testify that he logged the evidence out from the crime lab after it was tested and brought it to court for trial.

All of the witnesses' testimony taken together would establish that the evidence in question was the matter that was recovered from the suspect, that tested positive for marijuana, and that is being offered into evidence at the trial. By showing the chain of custody, it is sufficiently established that the evidence in question is what it purports to be. The chain of custody has authenticated the evidence.

The courts have consistently held that a break in the chain of custody "goes to the weight of the evidence rather than its admissibility."[7] Thus, if the clerk at the crime lab is unable to testify, a break in the chain of custody, the marijuana would not be inadmissible. The break would only be an issue that the defense could argue should be considered in the weight the jury should give to the evidence. However, a break in the chain of custody would not prevent the evidence from being admitted into evidence at trial.

Circumstantial evidence of authenticity. Another method of authenticating evidence is through circumstantial evidence. One recognized method of authenticating evidence by circumstantial evidence is by what is known as the "reply letter doctrine." Under this doctrine, it may be established that a letter signed by a particular person was actually written by that person through circumstantial evidence. "One circumstance recognized as sufficient is the fact that the letter discloses knowledge that only the purported signer would be likely to have. *Moreover, a convenient practice recognizes that if a letter has been written to X, and the letter now offered in evidence purports to be written by X and purports to be a reply to the first letter (that is either refers to it, or is responsive to its terms) and has*

---

7. State v. Bonhomme, 544 So. 2d 640 (La. Ct. App. 3d Cir. 1989); *See also, e.g.,* State v. Hansbro, 796 So. 2d 185 (La. Ct. App. 2d Cir. 2001); Duzon v. Stallworth, 866 So. 2d 837 (La. Ct. App. 1st Cir. 2002).

been received without unusual delay, these facts authenticate it as a reply letter."[8] Thus, this concept is referred to as the "reply letter doctrine."

This same principle could also be applied to other situations, including "a written reply to an oral inquiry, to a telephonic response to an oral or written inquiry, and so forth."[9] Today, this same principle could be used to authenticate an email, a text message or even a posting on a social media website. "The essentials are to establish by evidence independent of the reply that the original inquiry was put, and to find in the reply itself (or for that matter in surrounding circumstances) some indication that the author was indeed responding to the inquiry."[10]

Social media accounts are commonly being authenticated by the use of circumstantial evidence. The nature of the posts, being information only within the purported owner's knowledge, photographs, and other information surrounding the page, can be circumstantial evidence sufficient to establish that the page belongs to the person in question.

Foundation for authentication. Prior to allowing a witness to authenticate evidence, the proponent should lay the proper foundation to establish the grounds upon which the witness will be able to authenticate it. If you recall from Chapter 4, you learned that before a witness testifies to any information, Art. 602 requires that evidence be introduced sufficient to support a finding that the witness has personal knowledge of the matter about which he will testify. This rule also applies to a witness who will authenticate or identify a matter being offered into evidence. Prior to authenticating a matter, sufficient foundation must be established to support a finding that the witness has first-hand knowledge of the information to which he will testify regarding the matter being offered into evidence—e.g., that he is personally familiar with the identifying marks on the object, that he is personally familiar with a voice on the tape, or that his is personally familiar with the person's handwriting that he will identify.

When the proponent asks questions to show that the witness has such first-hand knowledge, he is said to be "laying foundation." By laying foundation the proponent establishes how the witness knows what he is about to testify to. Thus, if the witness will testify as to what a person was wearing, it must first be established how the witness knows—that he saw him, at this particular time, and at this particular place. Thereafter the witness can testify as to what the person was wearing.

Similarly, if the witness will testify that the gun in question is in fact the gun that is owned by the defendant, sufficient foundation must be laid to establish how the witness knows that the gun in question belongs to the defendant. The witness may testify that on several occasions he has seen the defendant in possession of the gun, that he has borrowed the gun, or has used the gun, and as a result, is familiar with what the gun looks like. After having laid the foundation as to how the witness acquired the information to which he will testify, the witness can be asked to identify the gun in question in court.

"Real" evidence v. "Demonstrative" evidence. Real evidence is evidence including physical or tangible objects that actually play a role in the matter in question, such as the actual knife used in the crime at hand, the actual drugs recovered from the defendant, or the actual gloves worn by the suspect at the time of the incident. These items are typically

8. Malloy v. VanWinkle, 662 So. 2d 96, 100 (La. Ct. App. 4th Cir. 1995).

9. Malloy v. VanWinkle, 662 So. 2d 96, 100 (La. Ct. App. 4th Cir. 1995) (citing 5 C.B. Mueller, Federal Evidence § 518 at 50–51 (2nd ed., 1994).

10. *Id.*

authenticated by a witness who can testify that the object in question is what the proponent claims it is, as outlined above.

Demonstrative evidence, on the other hand, did not play an actual role in the incident in question, but it illustrates some fact or evidence that may be helpful to the trier of fact in deciding the case. Demonstrative evidence may include maps, charts, models, photographs, videotapes, sound recordings, or other evidence that did not play a tangible role in the incident in question.

The authentication requirements are quite similar for both real evidence and demonstrative evidence with only a slight difference. In either case a competent witness must be able to testify that the matter is what it purports to be, whether it's a knife (real evidence) or a 911 call (demonstrative evidence), after sufficient foundation has been laid to establish how the witness can testify to such. However, in authenticating real evidence, the witness must be able to testify that the evidence is in the ***"same or substantially same condition"*** that it was at the time in question. Keep in mind that in the case of objects that are not readily identifiable, such as narcotics, additional foundation and/or authentication of the object may be needed since the witness would not be able to identify it from its physical characteristics. Establishing the chain of custody and having the officer testify as to identifying marks placed on the packaging, such as his signature, labeling, case number, etc., would be sufficient to authenticate real evidence not readily identifiable.

For demonstrative evidence a witness must be able to testify that the evidence ***"fairly and accurately depicts"***[11] what it purports to depict. For example, if a picture is of a bloody crime scene, anyone who can testify that the photograph fairly and accurately depicts the crime scene, as it was at the time in question, can authenticate the photo. This might include anyone who actually saw the crime scene—the police officers on the scene, the crime scene investigator, the detective, the person who took the photos, or even the victim if she was aware of her surroundings. However, a person who may have seen the scene before the incident (neighbor, or even a resident who was not present at the time), would not be able to testify that the photo represents the scene *as it was when the crime was committed.*

Litany for admitting "real" evidence. Any witness who can testify that the evidence is in ***"the same or substantially same condition"*** that it was at the time in question, with sufficient foundation as to how he can testify to such, can authenticate physical evidence.

Litany for Admitting Physical Evidence

- *Allow me to direct your attention to what has been previously marked for purposes of identification as plaintiff's exhibit P-1.*
- *Let the record reflect that I am showing defense counsel what has been previously marked for identification as plaintiff's exhibit P-1.*
- *Your honor, may I approach the witness?*
- *I am handing you what has been marked for identification purposes as plaintiff's exhibit P-1.*
- *Take a moment to examine this please.*
- *Have you had an opportunity to examine it?*

11. State v. Hall, 549 So. 2d 373 (La. Ct. App. 2d Cir. 1989); *See also* State v. Lanieux, 39 So. 3d 606 (La. Ct. App. 5th Cir. 2010).

- *Do you know what it is?*
- *What is it?*
- *How do you know?*
- *Is it in the "**same or substantially the same condition**" as when you first came into contact with it on (date)?*
- *Have there been any "**changes in its condition or appearance**"?*
- *Your honor, I offer plaintiff's exhibit P-1 for admission as evidence. (judge admits evidence)*
- *May I publish exhibit P-1 to the jury.*

Admitting demonstrative evidence. Demonstrative evidence includes photographs, videotapes, recordings, maps, diagrams, etc. Any witness who can testify that the evidence ***"fairly and accurately depicts the subject matter therein,"*** with sufficient foundation as to how he can testify to such, can authenticate it.

Litany for Admitting Photographs (or other demonstrative evidence)

- *Allow me to direct your attention to what has been previously marked for purposes of identification as plaintiff's exhibit P-1.*
- *Let the record reflect that I am showing defense counsel what has been previously marked for identification as plaintiff's exhibit P-1.*
- *Your honor, may I approach the witness?*
- *I am handing you what has been marked for identification purposes as plaintiff's exhibit P-1.*
- *Take a moment to examine this please.*
- *Have you had an opportunity to examine it?*
- *Do you know what it is?*
- *What is it?*
- *How do you know?*
- *Does it "**fairly and accurately depict the subject matter therein**" as it was on (date/time, place in question)?*
- *Has it been altered in any way?*
- *Your honor, I offer plaintiff's exhibit P-1 for admission as evidence. (judge admits)*
- *May I publish exhibit P-1 to the jury.*

Authentication Case

It is important to keep in mind that while a document may be sufficiently authenticated, it must not be excluded under any other exception to be admissible. Quite often a document must also overcome hearsay objections because it is an out-of-court statement being offered to prove what is asserted within it. Many documents will conform with the business records exception, but it is important to lay the proper foundation for that exception with a competent witness as discussed *supra* in § 5.11. Below, in *Malloy v. Vanwinkle,* after being authenticated under the reply doctrine, the letter is admitted as a statement against interest to overcome any hearsay objections.

Malloy v. Vanwinkle

Court of Appeal of Louisiana, Fourth Circuit
662 So. 2d 96
Sept. 28, 1995

ARMSTRONG, Judge.

The plaintiff, Mark Malloy, went to Gulfport, Mississippi to visit the beach. While there, he met Steven Vanwinkle. They spent some time on the beach there and Mr. Malloy drank some beer and he saw Mr. Vanwinkle drink one beer. That evening, while at the home of Mr. Vanwinkle or someone else in Gulfport, Mr. Malloy drank peppermint schnapps and observed Mr. Vanwinkle drink one shot of peppermint schnapps. Also that evening, Mr. Vanwinkle started to drive Mr. Malloy back to where Mr. Malloy had left his car. On the way, Mr. Vanwinkle's car hit a tree and Mr. Malloy was injured.

Mr. Malloy sued Mr. Vanwinkle as tortfeasor. However, Mr. Vanwinkle never made any appearance in this action and had no involvement in the trial below. In fact, Mr. Vanwinkle did not even testify either in person or by deposition.

Mr. Malloy sued State Farm Mutual Automobile Insurance Company ("State Farm") as his alleged uninsured motorist ("UM") insurer. Mr. Malloy lived with his parents. He alleges that his parents had a State Farm insurance policy which included UM coverage and that, as a member of their household, he was covered. He also alleged that Mr. Vanwinkle had no liability insurance.

...

State Farm's second argument on appeal is that Mr. Malloy did not prove, with proper evidence, that Mr. Vanwinkle was uninsured. State Farm points out that Mr. Malloy did not use the methods provided by La.R.S. 22:1406(D)(6) to prove that Mr. Vanwinkle was uninsured. However, the methods of proving uninsured status provided by that statute are not exclusive and uninsured status can be proven by other evidence.

The evidence that Mr. Vanwinkle was uninsured was an exchange of letters between him and Mr. Malloy's counsel. Specifically, Mr. Malloy's counsel wrote to Mr. Vanwinkle on August 15, 1990, stating that she represented Mr. Malloy in connection with the accident of July 31, 1990, and requesting that he have his liability insurer contact her. On September 12, 1990, Mr. Malloy's counsel received a reply letter, bearing the signature "Steven Vanwinkle" referencing Mr. Mallory and the July 31, 1990 accident date, and stating in relevant part: "Unfortunately, I have no insurance of any kind, also I am a student with limited funds. My only asset [his car] was lost in the accident."

State Farm argues that the Vanwinkle letter was not authenticated and, thus, not admissible. Authentication is the process whereby something is shown to be what it purports to be. La.Code Evid. art. 901 *See* G.W. Pugh, et al., *Handbook On Louisiana Evidence Law* at 504 (1995). In a situation like the present, a letter may be authenticated under the "reply letter doctrine."

> When a letter, signed with the purported signature of X, is received "out of the blue," with no previous correspondence, the traditional "show me" skepticism of the common law trial practice prevails, and the purported signature is not accepted as authentication, unless authenticity is confirmed by additional facts.

> One circumstance recognized as sufficient is the fact that the letter discloses knowledge that only the purported signer would be likely to have. *Moreover, a convenient practice recognizes that if a letter has been written to X, and the letter now offered in evidence purports to be written by X and purports to be a reply to the first letter (that is either refers to it, or is responsive to its terms) and has been received without unusual delay, these facts authenticate it as a reply letter.* This result may be rested upon the knowledge-principle, mentioned above. In view of the regularity of the mails the first letter would almost invariably come exclusively into the hands of X, or those authorized to act for him, who would alone know of the terms of the letter. It is supported also by the fact that in common experience we know that reply letters do come from the person addressed in the first letter.

2. J.W. Strong, ed., *McCormick On Evidence* § 225 at 49–50 (4th ed. 1992) (emphasis added).

> *Reply letter doctrine.* The reply letter doctrine, long recognized at common law, represents but a particular application of the more general method of authentication here discussed. If it can be shown that an inquiry was directed to a particular person, and that in due course an apparent reply was received, which expressly refers to or seems implicitly to acknowledge the earlier inquiry, these facts suffice as the basis for concluding that the reply was sent by the person to whom the inquiry was directed. Only he was likely to have received the inquiry; hence only he was likely to know of it, and to respond. In the typical case, both inquiry and reply are by means of letters sent through the mail, whence comes the name "reply letter doctrine." But there is nothing magic in form, and the principle applies equally to a written reply to an oral inquiry, to a telephonic response to an oral or written inquiry, and so forth, regardless of whether the mails are involved. The essentials are to establish by evidence independent of the reply that the original inquiry was put, and to find in the reply itself (or for that matter in surrounding circumstances) some indication that the author was indeed responding to the inquiry, for these points are the necessary predicate underlying the inference that the author of the reply is the person to whom the inquiry was put.

5 C.B. Mueller, *Federal Evidence* § 518 at 50–51 (2nd ed. 1994).

In fact, the reply letter doctrine has been applied in the exact same context as the present case (proof of uninsured status) by the Supreme Court in *Campbell v. American Home Assur Co.,* 260 La. 1047, 258 So.2d 81, 85 (1972). *See also* G.W. Pugh, *Louisiana Evidence Law* at 445 (1974) (discussing *Campbell*). Thus, we are confident that Mr. Vanwinkle's letter was properly authenticated.

State Farm has not raised the issue of whether Mr. Vanwinkle's letter is hearsay. In any event, the letter would be admissible under the "statement against interest" exception to the hearsay rule, La.Code Evid. art. 804.B(3), because, by admitting lack of insurance, Mr. Vanwinkle was admitting to a violation of Mississippi's Motor Vehicle Financial Responsibility Law. Miss.Stat. 303.010 et seq. *See Campbell,* 258 So.2d at 85–86. This hearsay exception applies only when the declarant is unavailable to testify in court, La.Code Evid. art. 804. However, as Mr. Vanwinkle lives in Mississippi, beyond the subpoena power of the trial court, and as Mr. Malloy testified as to being unable to locate Mr. Vanwinkle, it is apparent that Mr. Vanwinkle was unavailable. La.Code Evid. art. 804.A(5).

Mr. Vanwinkle's letter was admitted properly. Mr. Malloy proved that Mr. Vanwinkle was uninsured.

...

AFFIRMED.

Discussion Questions

1. For another excellent discussion by the Louisiana Supreme Court of the rules relevant to authenticating writings, see *State v. Magee*, 103 So. 3d 285 (La. 2012). In *Magee*, the court admitted a letter over the defendant's objection that the letter was hearsay and that it could not be authenticated because it was unsigned, undated, and had not been sent. In finding that the letter had been properly authenticated, the court held, "Tracy testified that she stood over and watched as Adrienne typed portions of the letter and read over it when Adrienne finished. From her personal knowledge, she identified the letter (although unsigned and undated) as an original document and denied that any alterations had been made to it. The defendant's protestations notwithstanding, Tracy's testimony provided a sufficient foundation to admit the letter as authentic." *Id.* at 316. The court continued to address whether the letter should nonetheless be excluded as inadmissible hearsay holding that, "the fact that evidence is found to satisfy the authenticity requirement does not mean it is necessarily admissible. It may be excluded by other rules, such as those relating to hearsay." *Id.* The court concluded that the letter in question was erroneously admitted because it did not satisfy the requirements of the "then existing mental condition" exception to the hearsay rule under Article 803(3) because the statements were of the declarant's memory or belief recalling past events rather than her then existing mental condition. Further, the statements were offered to prove the actions of a third person, her husband, rather than her own. For what purposes might such issues be considered?
2. Other than objections to hearsay, what other common objections would you expect to get when offering either real or demonstrative evidence? What would be the nature of your responses?

§ 10.2 Self-Authenticating Evidence [La. C.E. art. 902]

Applicable Code Articles

Art. 902. Self-authentication

Extrinsic evidence of authenticity as a condition precedent to admissibility is not required with respect to the following

(1) Domestic public documents under seal. A document bearing a seal purporting to be that of the United States, or of any state, district, commonwealth, territory, or insular possession thereof, or the Panama Canal Zone, or the Trust Territory of the Pacific Islands, or of a political subdivision, department, officer, or agency thereof, and a signature purporting to be an attestation or execution.

(2) Domestic public documents not under seal. (a) Domestic public documents generally. A document purporting to bear the signature in his official capacity of an officer or employee of any entity included in Paragraph (1) hereof, having no seal, if a public officer having a seal and having official duties in the district or political subdivision of the officer or employee certifies under seal that the signer has the official capacity and that the signature is genuine.

(b) Certified Louisiana public documents. A purported record, book, paper, or other document of the State of Louisiana, or of a department, board, or agency thereof or of a political subdivision of the state or a department, board, or agency of such a subdivision when certified as being the original by an officer or employee who identifies his official position and who either has custody of the document or who is otherwise authorized to make such a certification.

(3) Foreign public documents. A document purporting to be executed or attested in his official capacity by a person authorized by the laws of a foreign country to make the execution or attestation, and accompanied by a final certification as to the genuineness of the signature and official position (a) of the executing or attesting person, or (b) of any foreign official whose certificate of genuineness of signature and official position relates to the execution or attestation or is in a chain of certificates of genuineness of signature and official position relating to the execution or attestation. A final certification may be made by a secretary of embassy or legation, consul general, consul, vice consul, or consular agent of the United States, or a diplomatic or consular official of the foreign country assigned or accredited to the United States. If reasonable opportunity has been given to all parties to investigate the authenticity and accuracy of official documents, the court may, for good cause shown, order that they be treated as presumptively authentic without final certification or permit them to be evidenced by an attested summary with or without final certification.

(4) Presumptions under Acts of Congress and the Louisiana Legislature. Any signature, document, or other matter declared by Act of Congress or by Act of the Louisiana Legislature to be presumptively or prima facie genuine or authentic.

(5) Official publications. Books, pamphlets, or other publications purporting to be issued by public authority.

(6) Newspapers and periodicals. Printed materials purporting to be newspapers or periodicals.

(7) Trade inscriptions and the like. Inscriptions, signs, tags, or labels purporting to have been affixed in the course of business and indicating ownership, control, or origin.

(8) Authentic acts, acknowledged acts, and other instruments attested by witnesses. (a) Authentic acts, acts under private signature duly acknowledged, and instruments attested by witnesses and accompanied by affidavits, as provided by Louisiana law, whether executed in Louisiana or elsewhere. (b) Documents executed in a jurisdiction other than Louisiana accompanied by a certificate of acknowledgment executed in the manner provided by the laws of that jurisdiction by a notary public or other officer authorized by law to take acknowledgments.

(9) Commercial paper and related documents. Commercial paper, signatures thereon, and documents relating thereto to the extent provided by general commercial law.

(10) Labor reports. A copy of a report from the Department of Labor, or from any state or federal reporting agency, which is in the possession of a field officer of the support enforcement services program, office of family support, Department of Social Services, introduced as evidence in any child or spousal support proceeding. "Field officer" means any person designated or authorized as a field officer pursuant to the provisions of R.S. 46:236.1(K).

Articles 902, 904, and 905 refer to self-authenticating evidence. This means that no extrinsic evidence of authenticity is needed prior to admitting the evidence. The proponent simply offers the evidence into the record, and it may be received by the jury. Some common documents that are self-authenticating include public documents under seal, certified state documents, certified copies of state documents,[12] official publications (state books, pamphlets), newspapers, periodicals, trade inscriptions, including signs, tags, or labels purporting to have been affixed in the course of business and indicating ownership, control, or origin; authentic acts, acknowledged acts, and other instruments attested by witnesses; authentic acts, acts under private signature duly acknowledged, and instruments attested by witnesses and accompanied by affidavits, as provided by Louisiana law, and others.

The proponent may simply offer these documents into evidence without the need to call any particular witness to testify that the document is what it purports to be. The evidence intrinsically establishes its authenticity by evidence sufficient to satisfy the standard required in the statute.

Key Points

The key points to keep in mind regarding authentication and identification.

Authentication/Identification

1. **Appropriate witness.** An appropriate witness must be called who is competent to testify that the evidence is what the proponent claims, by one of the ways listed above or other ways sufficient to establish the standard for admissibility.
2. **Foundation.** Sufficient evidence must be established to show how the witness knows (has first-hand knowledge of) the information to which he will testify, e.g., how the witness is familiar with signature, etc.
3. **Identification/authentication.** Using the trial litanies, the witness is given opportunity to identify the evidence, authenticate it using a method contained in art. 901 or by other means.
   a. Identify voice, or other identifying marks, chain of custody, comparison by it.
   b. If real evidence, witness must testify that matter is in "same or substantially the same condition."
   c. If demonstrative evidence, witness must testify that matter "fairly and accurately depicts the subject matter therein."
   d. If matter is "self-authenticating" then no foundation or authentication is needed.
4. **Evidence offered into evidence/subject to objections.** After the evidence is authenticated, the matter is offered into evidence and must overcome any other objections to admissibility, e.g., insufficient foundation or authentication (has not met standard), relevancy, hearsay (must articulate an exception), requirement of the original, etc.
5. **Published to jury.** If no objections to admissibility are sustained, and the exhibit is admitted into evidence, it may be viewed by the jury. The jury may only see or hear evidence that has been admitted into evidence.

12. La. Code Evid. art. 904.

Problems on Authenticating Evidence

PROBLEM 10-1. Officer Kilborne is a witness in a murder trial he investigated. He collected the gun from the crime scene. At trial he is asked if he recognized the gun, and the officer responds: "Yes, this is the gun I collected from the scene. That is my signature on the evidence tag. That is also the correct date, case number, and location." Has the gun been properly authenticated for trial? Explain.

PROBLEM 10-2. Bo is on trial for killing his wife, Mary Anne. Bo claims she killed herself and gave the police a note claiming it was a suicide note left by his wife, Mary Anne. Which of the following are valid ways in which the letter may be authenticated?

A. Mary Anne's 15-year-old daughter can testify that it is her mother's handwriting.

B. The jury can take the note and compare it to a known sample of Mary Anne's handwriting.

C. Any witness can take the stand and compare the letter to a known sample of Mary Anne's handwriting.

D. Mary Anne's girlfriend testifies that she bought the stationery for Mary Anne that the letter is written on and explains how Mary Anne always talked about how she liked putting little lines under key words when she writes as indicated on the note.

E. An expert witness in handwriting analysis takes the stand and compares the writing to a known sample of Mary Anne's handwriting.

PROBLEM 10-3. Eric is arrested for vehicular homicide after he slams into the side of another vehicle in the intersection when he failed to stop for the red light. The victim was pronounced dead at the scene. Eric was given field sobriety tests on scene by Officer Demery and arrested after failing the tests. The officer also recovered several empty beer cans from Eric's car. Eric was taken to the hospital for a small bump on his head where a blood draw was taken for chemical analysis by a nurse and sent to the lab for testing by a lab technician that showed he had a BAC of .263 and other drugs in his system. At the trial, the prosecution wishes to offer the following into evidence. What witness should she call through whom to introduce the evidence? How can the following be authenticated? Explain.

A. the beer can

B. the video of Eric performing the field sobriety tests

C. the blood test results

D. the picture of the crime scene

E. photos of victim from autopsy taken by coroner

F. a diagram of the intersection

PROBLEM 10-4. Paula is a plaintiff in a civil action and claims her vehicle was damaged when the defendant ran into the rear of her vehicle. At trial, Paula's attorney shows her a picture of a vehicle and asks her what it is. Paula responds that it is a picture of a vehicle. What additional questions must Paula's attorney ask her to properly authenticate the photograph?

PROBLEM 10-5. A woman was brutally raped and left for dead in her home. She miraculously survived and was found in her home still lying in the pool of blood days later when her husband returned from a business trip. The kids were away at grandma's house. The chief detective arrived on scene and contacted the crime scene investigator who collected the evidence, took photographs, measurements, and collected fingerprints. The house was cleaned before the kids and husband were allowed back inside. Which of the following individuals can authenticate the photographs of the crime scene: a) the CSI; b) the victim; c) the husband; d) the detective; E) the kids? Explain why each may or may not be able to authenticate the photos.

PROBLEM 10-6. The children of the decedent and the decedent's wife are in a contest over the decedent's will. The children testify that the will is in their father's handwriting. The wife testifies that the will is not in the handwriting of the decedent because she has seen his handwriting for years since they've been married. Should the will be allowed into evidence? How should the court rule?

If the judge allows the will into evidence will the jury be required to accept the will as having been written by the decedent? Why or why not?

PROBLEM 10-7. Can Tiffany authenticate the 911 call she made at the time of the alleged incident after it is played? How or why can she do this?

PROBLEM 10-8. An attorney would like to offer a newspaper to show the headline and lead story for the day (which is relevant in the particular case). The prosecution objects that the paper must be authenticated by a person from the paper, such as an editor, writer, etc., to prove that the paper at hand is in fact their publication for that particular day. Is this needed? Why or why not?

PROBLEM 10-9. The prosecution must prove the defendant's underlying felony conviction and offers a certified copy of the Clerk of Court minutes showing the conviction as well as a certified copy of the bill of information showing the crime with which he was charged. The defense objects that someone from the clerk's office is needed to authenticate the documents. What ruling?

PROBLEM 10-10. Meredith was fired for violating her office social media policy. The policy stated that they could not make any posts about anyone with whom they worked, or about any events that transpired at work. They also couldn't post anything about their feelings about work, nor about how they felt about anyone with whom they worked. Meredith sued the company for wrongful termination claiming she didn't violate the policy. At the trial, the defense sought to offer into evidence a screenshot of a post they claim was posted on Meredith's social media page. Meredith claims it is not her account and that they can't prove it. The name on the account is listed as Meredith Crane, which is the name under which Meredith is employed and known. The photo is also a picture of Meredith. Several employees have communicated with Meredith about various issues via her social media page and have continued the discussions at work. They have inboxed Meredith as well. And there are over ten photo albums attached to the account with photos of Meredith on various trips and at various events. If you were representing the company in this case, how would you seek to authenticate the social medial account/post in order to use it against Meredith at trial? Will the post likely be admissible? Why or why not?

PROBLEM 10-11. Dale was involved in an accident while operating his boat on the lake on Memorial Day. He hit a jet ski after the kid jumped off to avoid being hit by Dale. Dale did not stop and render aid to help the kid. Dale was subsequently located and charged. Dale claims that he followed all recommended and required boating safety tips. At trial Dale offers a pamphlet published by the Dept. of Wildlife and Fisheries Boating Safety and Waterway titled, "Boating Safety," which lays out the rules and tips for safe boating. Who or what is needed to authenticate the pamphlet?

PROBLEM 10-12. The plaintiffs in a personal injury action allege that a bridge was improperly constructed and gave way killing 73 people and injuring several others when they fell into a lake during rush hour while traversing the bridge. At the trial, they wish to offer into evidence an animation that shows how the bridge's hinges broke apart causing the bridge to collapse. The animation coincides with the plaintiff's expert engineer's opinion as to how the collapse occurred. A separate animation company developed the animation working with the expert. To handle the issue of authenticity, the plaintiff's have filed a motion in limine on the admissibility of the animation and the matter has been set for pre-trial ruling on its admissibility. At the hearing the plaintiffs must authenticate the video. What witness(s) should they call? What must be shown? Should the video animation be admitted? Why or why not?

PROBLEM 10-13. Carl is charged with fraud for opening a bank account in his mother's name. He claims that he has a power of attorney that includes the authority to handle all of her financial affairs. At Carl's trial in his defense, he offers the original notarized copy of the Power of Attorney signed by him and his mother. The prosecution objects that the mother must be there to authenticate the POA. Is this true? How should the judge rule on the objection?

PROBLEM 10-14. Ricky and his brother Ryan robbed a gas station. The entire incident was caught on black and white surveillance video. The video showed them bursting into the store, throwing the customers out, locking the doors, and then robbing the place. After the robbery, they then ran out of the store and were arrested just down the street. The clerk had activated the silent alarm and police were on the way. The police went back to the store, collected the video and took Ricky and Ryan downtown for booking. At the trial, the prosecution called the store manager to testify about the robbery. He explained who was working that night and what inventory was missing. The prosecution then offered the video into evidence through the manager and prepared to play it. The defense objects that the manager cannot authenticate the video. Can he? Why or why not? If so, how does he? If not, who can authenticate it?

PROBLEM 10-15. While executing a search warrant at Dillon's home the police located his check stub, which had his name and social security number on it. The prosecution would like to offer the check stub into evidence through the officer who located it for reasons that are relevant in the case. Is the fact that Dillon's name and social security number are on the check sufficient to support a finding that the check stub belongs to Dillon, or will someone from his job, such as someone from Human Resources or his boss, be needed to authenticate the evidence?

§ 10.1 and § 10.2 References and Additional Authority on Authentication of Evidence [La. C.E. art. 901] and Self-Authentication [La. C.E. art. 902]

1. La. C.E. arts. 901, 902 and Official Comments
2. Force & Rault, Handbook on Louisiana Evidence Law Arts. 901, 902 Author's Comments (West Publishing 2014)
3. Harges & Jones, Louisiana Evidence Arts. 901, 902 Author's Comments (West Publishing 2014)
4. 19 La. Civ. L. Treatise, Evidence And Proof § 12.1 (2nd ed.)
5. **Authenticating by custodian**: *State v. Norah*, 131 So. 3d 172 (La. Ct. App. 4th Cir. 2013) (holding that jailhouse calls that implicated defendant in shooting were properly authenticated by testimony of telecommunications supervisor for the Orleans Parish

Sheriff's Office who testified that he maintained the archives of recorded prisoners' calls and he was also the custodian of records, even though he was unable to identify voice as that of defendant).

6. **Authenticating voice by recognition**: *State v. Martin,* 131 So. 3d 121 (La. Ct. App. 4th Cir. 2013) (Defendant argued that the State did not properly authenticate recordings of a conversation between him and the State's witness. The witness verified his voice and the defendant's voice on the recordings, and the court ruled that the recordings were sufficiently authenticated.).

7. **Failure of authentication**: *Calcasieu Marine Nat. Bank of Lake Charles v. Miller*, 590 So. 2d 1365 (La. Ct. App. 3d Cir. 1991) (Plaintiffs filed a petition for Deficiency Judgment against defendant on a promissory note. The defendant argued that he did not sign the promissory note and that his signature was forged. The defendant presented his driver's license that had his signature on it and he also signed his name on a piece of paper in court. The court ruled that because the plaintiff did not prove beyond the preponderance of evidence that it was the defendant's signature on the promissory note, the plaintiff's claim was denied.); *Artificial Lift, Inc. v. Production Specialties, Inc.*, 626 So. 2d 859 (La. Ct. App. 3d Cir. 1993), *writ denied* 634 So. 2d 394, 1994-0112 (La. 3/11/94) (holding that customers' cancelled checks written to equipment manufacturer were inadmissible for lack of foundation in an action by a sales representative against manufacturer to recover unpaid sales commissions when no person representing customer was present to attest to circumstances surrounding payment).

8. **Self-authentication:** *Price v. Roy O. Martin Lumber Co.*, 915 So. 2d 816 (La. Ct App. 1st. Cir. 2005) (Defendant argued that the trial court erred in admitting a letter from the Louisiana Department of Health because it was not properly authenticated. Plaintiffs presented a copy of a letter containing an official certification that was a true and correct copy of official records of the Louisiana Department of Environmental Quality. The court ruled that the letter was admissible because it was self-authenticating.).

9. **Not self-authenticating:** *Shexnayder v. Gish*, 948 So. 2d 1259 (La. Ct. App. 2d Cir. 2007) (Plaintiffs argue that the trial court erred in admitting a letter from the Louisiana Real Estate Commission because the letter was hearsay and was not properly authenticated. The court stated that although the letter was hearsay, it must first be properly authenticated. The court ruled that although the letter was from a Louisiana State agency, because it was not properly certified it was not self-authenticating.).

10. **Judge's role and trier of fact's role in determining authenticity of evidence:** *Cross v. Cutter Biological, Div. of Miles Inc.*, 676 So. 2d 131 (La. Ct. App. 4th Cir. 1996) (Initial authentication decision as to admissibility of evidence is made by trial judge by determining whether there is evidence sufficient to support finding that matter in question is what its proponent claims, and if trial judge determines that item is sufficiently genuine and its admission could assist trier of fact, factfinder ultimately determines whether evidence is genuine.).

11. **Authentication by chain of custody for drugs:** *State v. Henton*, 682 So. 2d 777 (La. Ct. App. 2d Cir. 1996) (holding that cocaine prosecution claims was sold to undercover officer by defendant was authenticated by chain of custody by testimony of officers that purchasing officer transferred cocaine to case officer, who immediately placed cocaine in envelope and wrote transaction number on envelope that corresponded with particular purchase recorded on surveillance video, then placed evidence in locked desk drawer until transported to crime lab and released to criminalist, and criminalist testified that substance contained cocaine).

12. **Demonstrative evidence:** *State v. Duncan*, 761 So. 2d 586 (La. Ct. App. 4th Cir. 2000) (allowing State to use a baseball bat as demonstrative aid during closing argument to illustrate the type of weapon used on murder victim, even though it was not the actual bat used, since the actual bat was probably burned in fire and defendant admitted that he hit victim with baseball bat, and there was no assertion by State that the bat was the actual bat used to attack the victim).

13. **Photographs:** *State v. Gates*, 630 So. 2d 1345 (La. Ct. App. 2d Cir. 1994) (holding that photographs were properly authenticated by coroner, even though there was no evidence as to who took photographs, through his testimony that photos accurately depicted what they purported to portray); *State v. LeBlanc*, 76 So. 3d 572 (La. Ct. App. 4th Cir. 2011), *writ denied* 75 So. 3d 446, 2011-2300 (La. 11/18/11) (holding that photographs of truck containing cable wire in back were properly authenticated in theft prosecution by testimony of owner of truck and employee for telephone company through testimony that the photographs depicted exactly what they depicted, including the symbols on it, size and volume); *State v. Bates*, 397 So. 2d 1331, Sup.1981 (holding that photograph need not be identified by person who took it to be admissible); *State v. Gordon*, 582 So. 2d 285 (La. Ct App. 1st Cir. 1991) (holding that photographs depicting defendant's face and scars on the back of his right hand and identified by sheriff's detective as true and correct representations of what he observed were properly admitted in evidence, even though detective could not recall being present when photographs were taken and was not certain who took them).

14. **Authentication by process or system:** *McLaughlin v. Fireman's Fund Ins. Co.*, 582 So. 2d 203 (La. Ct. App. 1st Cir. 1991), on rehearing, *writ denied* 586 So. 2d 536. (holding that blood alcohol test results of decedent were properly admitted in wrongful death action brought by decedent's parents by testimony that coroner drew blood sample, placed it in appropriate forensic blood collection kit vial, that laboratory dispatched courier to pick up specimen, that laboratory's records demonstrate that it received blood sample within 24 hours after it was taken, and that test was performed with all necessary precautions in order to render valid analysis).

§ 10.3 Requirement of the Original [La. C.E. arts. 1001–1008]

Applicable Code Articles

Art. 1002. Requirement of original

To prove the content of a writing, recording, or photograph, the original writing, recording, or photograph is required, except as otherwise provided by this Code or other legislation.

Art. 1003. Admissibility of duplicates

A duplicate is admissible to the same extent as an original unless:

(1) A genuine question is raised as to the authenticity of the original;

(2) In the circumstances it would be unfair to admit the duplicate in lieu of the original; or

(3) The original is a testament offered for probate, a contract on which the claim or defense is based, or is otherwise closely related to a controlling issue.

Article 1002 sets forth the requirement of the original. The **"requirement of the original"** is commonly and formerly referred to as the **"best evidence rule."** The rule requires that to prove the *content* of a writing, recording, or photograph, the original writing, recording, or photograph is required rather than secondary evidence of the matter. Basically this means that in order to prove what a photograph depicts, the photograph itself should be offered into evidence rather than testimony of what was depicted in the photograph. Similarly, in order to prove what was contained in a writing, the writing itself is needed rather than testimony of what was contained in the writing. For example, in order to prove the terms of contract, rather than have a witness testify that clause one contained this fact, and clause two contained that fact, the contract itself should be offered into evidence instead of having a witness testify to the various clauses of the contract. The witness's memory is clearly not the best evidence of the terms (or contents) or the contract (the writing).

This rule can be a bit confusing at times because a witness who has first-hand knowledge of information that just happens to also be contained in a writing, recording, or photograph can testify to that information without violating the rule.[13] However if a witness is only testifying to what was actually depicted in the photo, or what was said in the recording, then the photo or recording itself is needed, rather than his testimony on the issue.

For example, a man who is being stalked can testify that a woman has threatened to kill him, and left such messages on his answering machine. However, if he calls the police and allows the police officer to hear the recordings of the threats, the officer would not be able to testify that he listened to the tape and that on the tape he heard the witness say, "I'm going to make you regret you were ever born." While the witness/victim has first-hand knowledge of the threats that the witness made, and can testify to the threats, the officer is specifically testifying to the "content" of the recording, and under this rule, the actual recording would be needed rather than relying on his memory of what the recording says. The officer's testimony is not the "best evidence" of the content of the recording. This article requires the "original" rather than the testimony of what the recording contained.

Similarly, if a witness testifies that he saw the photos of the missing artwork, and proceeds to explain how valuable the artwork in the photos appeared to be, e.g., "the piece depicted in one of the photos was very large, and appeared to have been etched in oil," his testimony would violate the rule. He would clearly be testifying to the content of the photograph, and consequently the photograph would be needed. However, a witness who knows what the artwork looks like can certainly testify to what it looked like, in which case he is not testifying to what is depicted in the photo, he is testifying to something of which he has first-hand knowledge.

This article does not apply to all physical evidence, it **only applies to writings, recordings, and photographs**. Like the other rules, the content of the writing, recording or photograph must also be relevant to the case, and must also be authenticated in accordance with Article 901.

Admissibility of duplicates. Article 1003 provides that duplicates of writings, recordings, or photos are generally admissible to the same extent as an original unless a genuine question is raised as to the authenticity of the original; under the circumstances it would be unfair to admit the duplicate in lieu of the original; or the original is a testament offered for probate, a contract on which the claim or defense is based, or is otherwise closely

---

13. *See* La. Code Evid. art. 1002 Official Comment (b).

related to a controlling issue.[14] For the most part, duplicates may be admissible provided it doesn't appear that there are questions regarding its trustworthiness, such as if it appears as though there were changes or alterations made to it. Additionally, duplicates may be excluded if it is central to the controlling issue in the case, such as in the case of a will.

Applicable Code Articles

Art. 1004. Admissibility of other evidence of contents

The original is not required, and other evidence of the contents of a writing, recording, or photograph is admissible if:

(1) Originals lost or destroyed. All originals are lost or have been destroyed, unless the proponent lost or destroyed them in bad faith;

(2) Original not obtainable. No original can be obtained by any available judicial process or procedure;

(3) Original in possession of opponent. At a time when an original was under the control of the party against whom offered, he was put on notice, by the pleadings or otherwise, that the contents would be a subject of proof at the hearing, and he does not produce the original at the hearing;

(4) Collateral matters. The writing, recording, or photograph is not closely related to a controlling issue; or

(5) Impracticality of producing original. The original, because of its location, permanent fixture, or otherwise, cannot as a practical matter be produced in court; or the cost or other consideration to be incurred in securing the original is prohibitive and it appears that a copy will serve the evidentiary purpose.

Exceptions to the rule. A number of exceptions to the rule are contained in Article 1004, in which case other evidence of the content of the writing, recording, or photograph may be offered. The exceptions apply in situations in which **the original is lost or destroyed, not obtainable, in the possession of the opponent, impractical to produce, or the writing is collateral.** When the exceptions apply other evidence such as testimony from a witness or other evidence regarding the content of the writing, recording, or object may be offered.

Key Points

The key points to keep in mind regarding requirement of the original.

1. Requires that when the content of a writing, recording, or photograph is being proven, the actual writing, recording, or photograph must be offered.
2. A duplicate (photocopy) is admissible to the same extent as the original unless there are genuine questions raised as to their authenticity; it would be unfair under the circumstances; or the original is a testament offered for probate or a contract on which the claim is based.

---

14. La. Code Evid. art. 1003.

3. Does not exclude witness testimony of information of which he has first-hand knowledge that just happens to also be included in a writing, recording, or photocopy. Only applies when witness is testifying to "what the photo depicts," "what the writing says," or "what was in the recording."
4. Exceptions when secondary evidence is admissible: the original is lost or stolen; original is in possession of the opponent; the writing, recording, or photograph relates only a collateral matter not central to the case; or impracticality of producing the original (location, permanent fixture, cost, and other considerations).

Problems on Requirement of the Original

PROBLEM 10-16. On the brink of filing for bankruptcy, Muffins Co. has finally entered into an agreement with Hot Ovens, Inc. who will buy out several of the company's brands, including pastries, to continue production and sales for the hefty sum of $2 billion. After extensive negotiations, their lawyers finalize the agreement and everyone signs off making it official. The City Times Newspaper breaks the news of the agreement on the front page of the paper, detailing the amount of the buyout along with how and when the payments will be made. In a lawsuit filed by the labor union against Muffins Co. for unpaid benefits under *their* agreement, they offer a copy of the newspaper article explaining and detailing the agreement between Muffins Co. and Hot Ovens, Inc. and how much money Muffins Co. will make off the deal to support the amount to which they claim entitlement. The article is offered into evidence following the testimony of the labor union president, before he steps down from the stand. Muffins makes the following objections to the admissibility of the newspaper:

Objection, the newspaper article violates the "original writing requirement."

Objection, the newspaper article has not been properly authenticated.

How will the court likely rule on each of the objections and why?

PROBLEM 10-17. Which, if any, of the following pieces of evidence will likely be excluded under the requirement of the original (*formerly "best evidence rule"*)?

A. Kerry, the claims adjuster for the insurance company, testifies that he saw the photos of the stolen artwork and proceeds to explain what the artwork depicted in the photos that he used in satisfying the claim.

B. Kiera took photos of the damage to her vehicle. She left the photos at home, but proceeds to explain the damage to her vehicle.

C. The undercover officer recorded the drug transaction with a hidden recorder in the vehicle as he listened to the transaction. He can't find the recordings, but at trial he proceeds to testify as to the conversation between the defendant and accomplice that was recorded on the tapes.

D. Fred testifies that he can't find the letter his landlord wrote to him evicting him, but he remembers what it said, and proceeds to testify as to what was written.

PROBLEM 10-18. Dr. A was terminated from employment at the clinic after a series of medical malpractice lawsuits. When he was terminated he took, and likely destroyed, several of the files with him from the cases he was accused of misdiagnosing. One of the plaintiffs brought a suit against Dr. A claiming that he failed to diagnose her lung cancer.

To support her claim she called another doctor from the clinic who had seen the x-rays of her lungs several months after the misdiagnosis to testify to what was shown in the x-ray. The doctor testified, "It was actually pretty clear. In the upper right corner of the x-ray in the chest area there was a large cloudy looking white mass. That was the early stages of the cancer." Must the x-ray be presented or is the testimony allowable?

PROBLEM 10-19. Bank, Inc. is suing Matt for breach of contract. The bank president takes the stand to testify to the terms of the contract. He testifies that Matt was supposed to pay $250/month for 39 months, on the first of the month, at an interest rate of 5%. Matt's attorney objects that the president's testimony is not the best evidence of the terms of the contract. How should the court rule on the objection?

Assume the court sustains the objection. President sends an associate back to the bank and he comes back with a photocopy of the contract with Matt. Matt objects again to the photocopy under the best evidence rule. How should the court rule on the objection?

PROBLEM 10-20. Handsome is charged with bigamy. The prosecution claims he is still legally married to another woman in another state. Handsome testifies at trial that he divorced that woman years ago, and gives the date the divorce was final. The prosecution objects that Handsome cannot testify to the divorce and that the judgment is needed to prove he is divorced. How should the judge rule on the objection?

Would it affect your answer if Handsome testifies that he does not remember the date the judgment was finalized nor the judgment number, but refers to the judgment and testifies that the judgment indicates that the divorce was finalized on January 16, 2010, and has "Judgment #2010 4498621" written on it?

PROBLEM 10-21. The children of the decedent and the decedent's wife are in a contest over the decedent's will, which cannot be located. Can the lawyer who drafted the will testify that in the will the decedent left everything to his children?

Assume instead that although the lawyer does not have the actual will that was signed and notarized by the decedent, he has a copy of the document that was saved in a word file that he knows is exactly what the decedent signed. Can they use that document in the proceeding to prove the content of the will?

PROBLEM 10-22. In a defamation action, the plaintiff claims the defendant sent an email around the workplace with untruthful disparaging comments about her that ruined her reputation. She seeks to testify to what the email said about her. Does she need a copy of the email or is her testimony sufficient to prove what was written?

PROBLEM 10-23. Kelly is accused of possessing a stolen television. In her defense at trial she claims she paid for the television in cash and it belongs to her. The prosecution claims that she must have the receipt to prove the television was paid off. Does Kelly need the receipt or can she testify that she paid for the television?

PROBLEM 10-24. Sissy sued her landlord for breach of contract because she rented a house based on a photograph that the landlord emailed to her. She says that when she arrived it was a different house. At the trial, Sissy testifies that she deleted the email with the photograph in it, but begins to describe how large and nice the house was that was in the photograph that she received from the landlord in the mail. The defendant objects that the evidence is not the best evidence of the content of the photo. How should the court rule?

§ 10.3 References and Additional Authority on Requirement of Original [La. C.E. art. 1001–1008]

1. La. C.E. arts. 1002–1008 and Official Comments
2. Force & Rault, Handbook on Louisiana Evidence Law Arts. 1002–1008 Author's Comments (West Publishing 2014)
3. Harges & Jones, Louisiana Evidence Arts. 1002–1004 Author's Comments (West Publishing 2014)
4. 19 La. Civ. L. Treatise, Evidence And Proof § 13.2 (2nd ed.)
5. **Testimony in lieu of writing:** *State v. Hawkins*, 667 So. 2d 1070 (La. Ct. App. 4th Cir. 1995) (Defendant argued that the trial court erred in not allowing the jury to view documents from the crime lab report. After the crime lab technician testified extensively on the evidence found at the crime scene, the court ruled that the report was properly excluded because the testimony of the crime lab technician was the best evidence.).
6. **Original lost or destroyed:** *State v. Jackson*, 714 So. 2d 87 (La. Ct. App. 2d Cir. 1998) (Defendant argued that the trial court erred in allowing the State to read the transcript of the defendant's statement after the State lost the audio tape. Defendant argued that the audiotape itself was the best evidence. After testimony proved that the tape had only been misplaced and the State made a diligent effort to find it. Because the court found that no wrongdoing was done, the transcript was properly admitted.); *State v. Shumaker*, 945 So. 2d 277 (La. Ct. App. 2d Cir. 2006) (After the original warrant was lost, the State offered a duplicate copy of the warrant at trial. The defendant presented a copy of the search warrant that did not contain everything that the State's duplicate original contained. After discovering that the copy the defendant presented had been tampered with, the court ruled that the State's duplicate original was admissible because it contained the carbon copy signature and date.).

Chapter 11

Other Ways of Proving Facts

Judicial Notice, Presumptions, Burdens of Proof

Another way of proving facts at trial is to have the court take judicial notice of the fact. There are certain facts of which there is no reasonable dispute as to their existence. As a result, it is in the interest of judicial economy that the court and parties recognize their existence without the need for any formal proof of the fact at trial. For example, a party may ask the court to take judicial notice of the fact that a certain date fell on a certain day of the week, for reasons relevant in the trial. Since this would not be an issue subject to reasonable dispute, a party could request that the court take judicial notice of the fact. As a result, the parties could argue the fact to the jury without having to offer formal proof of the fact in the trial, such as offering a calendar into evidence. Rather, by taking judicial notice of the fact, the court merely instructs the jury as to its existence. A court may take judicial notice of certain adjudicative facts, governed by Article 201, as well as certain legal matters, governed by Article 202.

§ 11.1 Judicial Notice of Adjudicative Facts [La. C.E. art. 201]

Applicable Code Articles

Art. 201. Judicial notice of adjudicative facts generally

A. Scope of Article. This Article governs only judicial notice of adjudicative facts. An "adjudicative fact" is a fact normally determined by the trier of fact.

B. Kinds of facts. A judicially noticed fact must be one not subject to reasonable dispute in that it is either:

(1) Generally known within the territorial jurisdiction of the trial court; or

(2) Capable of accurate and ready determination by resort to sources whose accuracy cannot reasonably be questioned.

C. When discretionary. A court may take judicial notice, whether requested or not.

D. When mandatory. A court shall take judicial notice upon request if supplied with the information necessary for the court to determine that there is no reasonable dispute as to the fact.

E. Opportunity to be heard. A party is entitled upon timely request to an opportunity to be heard as to the propriety of taking judicial notice and the tenor of the matter noticed.

> In the absence of prior opportunity to be heard, the request may be made after judicial notice has been taken.
>
> **F. Time of taking notice.** A party may request judicial notice at any stage of the proceeding but shall not do so in the hearing of a jury. Before taking judicial notice of a matter in its instructions to the jury, the court shall inform the parties before closing arguments begin.
>
> **G. Instructing jury.** In a civil case, the court shall instruct the jury to accept as conclusive any fact judicially noticed. In a criminal case, the court shall instruct the jury that it may, but is not required to, accept as conclusive any fact judicially noticed.

One type of fact that a court may take judicial notice of is an **adjudicative fact.** Adjudicative facts are facts normally determined by the trier of fact.[1] In order for a fact to be appropriate for a court to take judicial notice, it must be one that is "not subject to reasonable dispute" in that it is either "generally known within the territorial jurisdiction of the trial court,"[2] or "capable of accurate and ready determination by resort to sources whose accuracy cannot reasonably be questioned."[3] If a party requests the court to take judicial notice of an adjudicative fact, he must present to the court sufficient evidence to establish that there is no reasonable dispute as to its existence or accuracy.[4] There is no set standard as to what information must be provided to the court to satisfy the requirement. The evidence offered could be as simple as showing the judge a calendar that shows a particular day/date, to providing a computer printout from a map website that shows the distance and directions from one place to another.

If reasonable dispute exists as to the existence of the fact, then the judge should not take judicial notice of it. Instead, the parties should have the opportunity to offer evidence of the fact at trial. For example, the court should reject a request that it take judicial notice that alcohol takes approximately two hours to dissipate from a person's system, because there will be reasonable dispute as to the amount of time it takes based on various factors such as a person's size, weight, the food he has eaten, etc. In such a case, both parties should have an opportunity to offer such evidence to the trier of fact for determination.

Undisputable facts. What types of facts can be said to have no reasonable dispute as to their existence? Facts appropriate for taking judicial notice have also been described as facts **"forming part of the common knowledge of every person of ordinary understanding and intelligence."**[5] For example, there would be no reasonable dispute as to the distance between two locations, whether a city is located within a particular parish, or who was mayor, governor, or President during a particular time. Perhaps a party would want the court to take judicial notice of the number of people making up a particular board at a particular time, i.e., six people on the school board, or twelve people on the city council. The court could take judicial notice that it's dark outside in Louisiana at 10:00 p.m., or of the day/date a particular natural disaster took place, i.e., Hurricane Katrina made

1. La. Code Evid. art. 201(A).
2. La. Code Evid. art. 201(B)(1).
3. La. Code Evid. art. 201(B)(2).
4. Force & Rault, Handbook, Art. 201 Author's note (4).
5. Neal v. Players Lake Charles, LLC, 787 So. 2d 1213 (La. Ct. App. 3d Cir. 2001).

landfall on a Monday morning. Additionally, a court could take judicial notice that a certain number of schools are located within a parish, that a particular business is located on a particular street, or that a parish or city has a certain number of people who live within it. Louisiana courts have also taken judicial notice of "geographical facts,[6] laws of nature,[7] time measurement,[8] facts of the calendar,"[9] and of various other matters. In all such situations, if the appropriate documentation is provided, there would be no reasonable dispute as to its existence, and the matter would be appropriate for a court to take judicial notice.

In the alternative, if the opposing party can show that a reasonable dispute exists as to the fact, the party should be given an opportunity to offer evidence of the fact at trial. For example, in *Walker v. Halliburton Services, Inc.*, 654 So. 2d 365 (La. Ct. App. 3d Cir. 1995), the court held that it was not appropriate for the trial court to have taken judicial notice of the fact that it takes six weeks for soft tissue injuries to heal. Clearly, in such a situation, various factors could affect the amount of time it would take a certain type of injury to heal, and each party should have an opportunity to present evidence to support their theory at trial.

When mandatory.[10] A court has the discretion of taking judicial notice of any fact whether requested or not, but is required to take judicial notice of adjudicative facts when requested by a party who has provided sufficient evidence that there is no reasonable dispute as to the fact.

Opportunity to be heard.[11] Prior to taking judicial notice of a fact, a party is entitled to have a fair opportunity to be heard as to whether a matter is one that is appropriate for the court to take judicial notice, i.e., that there is no reasonable dispute as to its existence. If a party is able to show that "there is a reasonable dispute either as to the existence of the fact or as to its incontestability,"[12] then the court should not take judicial notice of the fact.

The article does not expressly provide that parties be specifically given notice of the court's intention to take judicial notice of a matter prior to its doing so, but notice is somewhat implied in the article's requirement that parties be given an opportunity to be heard on the issue. Additionally, Article 201(F) specifically provides that the court shall

---

6. Harges & Jones, Louisiana Evidence, Art. 201 Author's Comments (citing State v. Scramuzza, 408 So. 2d 1316 (La. 1982) (location of named street); State v. Rittiner, 341 So. 2d 307 (La. 1976) (Lake Charles is located in Calcasieu Parish); State v. Gatch, 669 So. 2d 676 (La. Ct. App. 2d Cir. 1996)).

7. Harges & Jones, Louisiana Evidence, Art. 201 Author's Comments (citing S.J. Lemoine, Inc. v. St. Landry Parish School Bd., 527 So. 2d 1150 (La. Ct. App. 3d Cir. 1988) (it rains in Louisiana); Humble Pipe Line Co. v. Wm. T. Burton Industries, Inc., 221 So. 2d 526 (La. Ct. App. 1st Cir. 1969) (cane harvesting season); Josey v. Granite State Fire Ins. Co., 122 So. 2d 303 (La. Ct. App. 2d Cir. 1960) (time of rising and setting of moon and sun on a particular day)).

8. Harges & Jones, Louisiana Evidence, Art. 201 Author's Comments (citing State v. Fonseca, 378 So. 2d 389, 392 (La. 1979) (taking judicial notice that 10:45 p.m. was later than one-half hour after sunset and 11:45 p.m. was earlier than one-half hour before sunrise)).

9. Harges & Jones, Louisiana Evidence, Art. 201 Author's Comments (citing Castille v. Castille, 221 So. 2d 834 (La. Ct. App. 1st Cir. 1969) (there were 29 days in February in 1968); Diaz v. Nicosia, Licciardi & Nunez, LLC, 94 So. 3d 793 (La. Ct. App. 4th Cir. 2012) (the court took judicial notice that October 31, 2009, fell on a Saturday, a legal holiday)).

10. La. Code Evid. art. 201(D).

11. La. Code Evid. art. 201(E).

12. Force & Rault, Handbook, Art. 201 Author's note (1).

inform the parties of its intention to take judicial notice of a matter prior to closing arguments beginning.

Time of taking judicial notice.[13] A party may request that the court take judicial notice of an adjudicative fact at any stage of the proceedings, but shall not do so in the presence of the jury.

Jury instruction.[14] If a court takes judicial notice of an adjudicative fact in a **civil case** he shall instruct the jury to accept it as conclusive evidence. In a **criminal case**, the court shall instruct the jury that it may, but is not required to accept as conclusive evidence, the fact judicially noticed.

§ 11.2 Judicial Notice of Legal Matters [La. C.E. art. 202]

Applicable Code Articles

Art. 202. Judicial notice of legal matters

A. Mandatory. A court, whether requested to do so or not, shall take judicial notice of the laws of the United States, of every state, territory, and other jurisdiction of the United States, and of the ordinances enacted by any political subdivision within the court's territorial jurisdiction whenever certified copies of the ordinances have been filed with the clerk of that court.

B. Other legal matters. (1) A court shall take judicial notice of the following if a party requests it and provides the court with the information needed by it to comply with the request, and may take judicial notice without request of a party of:

(a) Proclamations of the President of the United States and the governor of this state.

(b) Rules of boards, commissions, and agencies of this state that have been duly published and promulgated in the Louisiana Register.

(c) Ordinances enacted by any political subdivision of the State of Louisiana.

(d) Rules which govern the practice and procedure in a court of the United States or of any state, territory, or other jurisdiction of the United States, and which have been published in a form which makes them readily accessible.

(e) Rules and decisions of boards, commissions, and agencies of the United States or of any state, territory, or other jurisdiction of the United States which have been duly published and promulgated and which have the effect of law within their respective jurisdictions.

(f) Law of foreign countries, international law, and maritime law.

(2) A party who requests that judicial notice be taken and the court, if notice is taken without request shall give reasonable notice during trial to all other parties.

---

13. La. Code Evid. art. 201(F).
14. La. Code Evid. art. 201(G).

> **C. Information by court.** The court may inform itself of any of the foregoing legal matters in such manner as it may deem proper, and the court may call upon counsel to aid it in obtaining such information.
>
> **D. Time of taking notice.** Judicial notice of the foregoing legal matters may be taken at any stage of the proceeding, provided that before taking judicial notice of a matter in its instructions to the jury, the court shall inform the parties before closing arguments begin.
>
> **E. Question for court.** The determination of the foregoing legal matters shall be made by the court.

In addition to adjudicative facts, a court may also take **judicial notice of legal matters.** This provision does not only include certain state and federal laws, but also includes rules and decisions of state and federal boards, commissions, and agencies, as well as laws of foreign countries, and other legal matters as outlined below.

Federal Rules of Evidence Distinction. There is no comparable provision in federal law. Under the Federal Rules of Evidence, the court may take judicial notice of adjudicative facts as outlined in Article 201 above, but there is no authority for taking judicial notice of legal matters as outlined Article 202.

Mandatory Legal Matters. A court is required to take judicial notice of the following, whether requested by a party or not: laws of the United States, of every state, territory, and other jurisdiction of the United States, and of the ordinances enacted by any political subdivision within the court's territorial jurisdiction whenever certified copies of the ordinances have been filed with the clerk of that court.[15]

The court is required to take judicial notice of the following only if requested by a party who provided the court with the information needed by it to comply with the request: (a) proclamations of the President of the United States and the governor of this state; (b) rules of boards, commissions, and agencies of this state that have been duly published and promulgated in the Louisiana Register; (c) ordinances enacted by any political subdivision of the State of Louisiana; (d) rules which govern the practice and procedure in a court of the United States or of any state, territory, or other jurisdiction of the United States, and which have been published in a form which makes them readily accessible; (e) rules and decisions of boards, commissions, and agencies of the United States or of any state, territory, or other jurisdiction of the United States which have been duly published and promulgated and which have the effect of law within their respective jurisdictions; and (f) law of foreign countries, international law, and maritime law.[16]

Discretionary legal matters. If neither party requests that the court take judicial notice of the items listed above in (a)–(f), the court may, but is not required to take judicial notice.[17]

Notice to parties. Unlike Article 201, this article specifically provides that a party who requests that judicial notice be taken, and the court, if notice is taken without request, shall give reasonable notice during trial to all other parties that judicial notice of a legal matter has been taken.[18]

---

15. La. Code Evid. art. 202(A).
16. La. Code Evid. art. 202(B)(a)–(f).
17. La. Code Evid. art. 202(B).
18. La. Code Evid. art. 202(B)(2).

Time of taking. As with adjudicative facts, the courts may take judicial notice of legal matters at any stage in the proceeding.[19]

Case on Judicial Notice

Neal v. Players Lake Charles, LLC, et al.
Court of Appeal of Louisiana, Third Circuit
787 So. 2d 1213
June 6, 2001

GREMILLION, Judge.

FACTUAL AND PROCEDURAL BACKGROUND

On August 20, 1997, Victoria, then eighty-four years old, fell and fractured her left wrist as she was walking through the casino owned by Players. She, thereafter, sued Players alleging that the floor was an unreasonably dangerous walking surface. The trial court concluded the floor surface was unreasonably dangerous after taking judicial notice of several facts and awarded the Neals $22,987.49. Players then filed this appeal, assigning as error:

1. The trial court's judicial notice of facts that were not properly subject to judicial notice, and

2. The trial court's failure to require the Neals to carry the burden of proving the liability of Players by a preponderance of the evidence.

JUDICIAL NOTICE

Players urges that it was an error of law for the trial court to take judicial notice of technical, disputed facts concerning the effects of a sealant applied by Players to its casino floor. The Neals argue that the trial court did not take improper judicial notice of any facts but, instead, made inferences based upon the testimony given at trial. The question before us is whether the trial court's findings concerning the alleged sealant build-up resulted from the improper use of judicial notice of facts not susceptible to the doctrine. We agree with Players and find that the trial court's factual conclusions were an improper use of judicial notice and constituted an error of law.

La.Code Evid. art. 201(B) states:

> **Kinds of facts.** A judicially noticed fact must be one not subject to reasonable dispute in that it is either:
>
> (1) Generally known within the territorial jurisdiction of the trial court; or
>
> (2) Capable of accurate and ready determination by resort to sources whose accuracy cannot reasonably be questioned.

The trial court determined that the Armorkote sealant used by the casino every two weeks must have necessarily built up over time. We can find no evidence to support that conclusion in our review of the record. The trial court opined that the floor should probably be stripped every so often and sealed again to prevent this "build-up" of sealant

19. La. Code Evid. art. 202(D).

product. Again, this determination was based purely on conjecture as there is no witness testimony or documentary evidence to support this supposition. In the same vein, without any evidence before us, we could determine that no such build-up occurred because of the heavy traffic experienced by a casino open for business twenty-four hours a day. Thus, the bi-weekly application simply replenished the worn away sealer. However, without any evidence to this effect, neither we nor the trial court are qualified to make such findings regarding the chemical properties of floor sealant products. This simple example clearly displays that the qualities pertaining to the floor sealant are not facts "forming part of the common knowledge of every person of ordinary understanding and intelligence." *Walker v. Halliburton Servs., Inc.*, 93–722, p. 3 (La.App. 3 Cir. 3/1/95); 654 So.2d 365, 368, *writ denied*, 95–1507 (La.9/22/95); 660 So.2d 481. Whether the floor sealant "built-up" so as to cause the floor to become slick and cause Victoria's fall is a disputed fact, and not one subject to judicial notice. Accordingly, we conduct a de novo review of the entire record and render a judgment on the merits. *Rosell v. ESCO*, 549 So.2d 840 (La.1989).

BURDEN OF PROOF

In a slip and fall case, the plaintiff must prove, among other things, that the condition of the floor presented an unreasonable risk of harm. La.R.S. 9:2800.6 B(1). Based on the evidence in the record, we find that Victoria failed to meet that burden. The evidence presented for our review can be summed up as follows: It was undisputed that there was no foreign substance on the floor, and that the sealant produced a highly glossy, polished, and shiny *appearance*. There was no evidence to suggest that the floor was actually slick, only testimony that it looked slick and shiny....

Based on this evidence, we are unable to find that the Neals met their burden of proving an unreasonable danger of harm to Victoria. The Neals proved nothing, other than that the floor at the casino had a shiny, glossy appearance, which is exactly what the Armorkote applied to it was intended to do.

CONCLUSION

The trial court committed an error of law in taking judicial notice of facts that were not of the type commonly known among ordinary persons, and the Neals failed to meet their burden of proving that Players Lake Charles, LLC and Zurich–American Insurance Group presented an unreasonable risk of danger to Victoria. Therefore, the finding of the trial court is reversed, and all costs are assessed against the plaintiffs-appellants, John and Victoria Neal.

REVERSED.

Discussion Questions

1. In *Neal*, the court notes that when varying factors could affect whether the fact in issue actually exists, here the heavy amount of traffic in a business open 24 hours/day, the fact is not appropriate for judicial notice. The parties should be allowed to present evidence to determine the exact factual circumstances presented in the case. Is there other evidence that the casino might have been able to present that might have disputed the existence of the fact?

2. What are your thoughts as to whether it would be appropriate for a court to take judicial notice of the following facts? Is there no reasonable dispute, or is it possible for the parties to present evidence to dispute the fact? a) The amount of time it would take for a broken leg to mend to support a plaintiff's damages claim as to the amount

of time he was out of work. b) The fact that it "rains a lot" in Louisiana in a builder's defense that he was unable to timely complete construction of a school due to inclement weather. [See *S.J. Lemoine, Inc. v. St. Landry Parish School Bd.*, 527 So. 2d 1150 (La. Ct. App. 3d Cir. 1988)].

Key Points

The key points to keep in mind regarding judicial notice.

Adjudicative Facts

1. Adjudicative facts are facts usually decided by the jury.
2. A court may take judicial notice of an adjudicative fact if it is "not subject to reasonable dispute" because it is: a) generally known within the jurisdiction; or 2) capable of accurate and ready determination from undisputable source.
3. The requesting party must present sufficient evidence to the court that there is no reasonable dispute as to its existence or accuracy.
4. There is no set standard for what evidence is sufficient.
5. Mandatory: when requested by a party who has provided sufficient evidence that there is no reasonable dispute as to the fact.
6. Discretionary: if not requested by a party, the court has discretion to take judicial notice of a fact of which there is no reasonable dispute.
7. Opportunity to be heard: A party requesting judicial notice should have an opportunity to be heard as to whether his request should be granted. The opposing party can argue as to whether the fact is subject to reasonable dispute and should not be granted.
8. A party may request that a court take notice at any stage of the proceeding, but not in presence of jury.
9. In a civil case, the jury is instructed to accept the fact as conclusive evidence. In a criminal case, jury is instructed that they may or may not accept fact as conclusive evidence.

Legal Matters

1. A court may also take judicial notice of legal matter: laws, rules, regulations, etc.
2. Judicial notice is mandatory *whether requested or not* regarding: federal laws, state law of any state, local ordinances in its own jurisdiction.
3. Judicial notice is mandatory *if requested with supporting information*: presidential proclamations, rules of any state or federal board, commissions, agencies, local ordinances outside of its own jurisdiction, and several other legal matters.
4. Judicial notice is discretionary regarding: any listed in "3" above that was not requested by a party.
5. The court may take judicial notice of such facts at any time during the proceedings.

Problems on Judicial Notice

PROBLEM 11-1. Penelope Smithers represents the plaintiff in a vehicular homicide that took place on University Campus on November 27, 2009. She has arrived in court on the last motions/hearings date before the trial with a list of items of which she would like the court to take judicial notice. The notice, which is in proper form, requests that the court take judicial notice of the following items. *(Assume, for purposes of the problem, that all the items are relevant, and she is prepared to offer proof.)* How should the court rule on the motion to take judicial notice on these items:

JN1: The area of the University campus is 4.2 square miles.

JN2: The president of the University in 2009 was Ralph Simpson.

JN3: November 27, 2009 was a Friday.

JN4: That during the fall 2009 school term, the university did not hold classes on Fridays.

JN5: That under the campus policy, the curfew for all on-campus residents was 10:00 p.m.

JN6: That at 6:30 p.m. on November 27, 2009, it was dark outside.

JN7: In November 2009, there was a city ordinance in place that prohibited open beverage containers in vehicles.

JN8: It takes approximately 2.5 hours for alcohol to dissipate from a person's system.

PROBLEM 11-2. John is the plaintiff in a lawsuit against Billy arising out of an accident that occurred while Billy was commuting from school at NSU to his home in Lafayette. During the trial, Billy realizes that the time it takes him to get home from school is becoming a heated issue at trial. He would like to ask the court to take judicial notice of the fact that NSU is exactly 91 miles from Lafayette. What type of information must he present to the court with his request?

PROBLEM 11-3. Ram Harper represents the plaintiff in a slip and fall action that took place at the local Country Market grocery store. Before the trial begins, Harper requests that the court take judicial notice of the following three facts during the trial, and is prepared to offer "some" proof:

JN1: That over time polishing and waxing floors builds up a residue causing a slippery surface.

JN2: That it takes approximately 1.5 hours for a floor to dry after a waxing.

JN3: That soft tissue injuries heal within 6 weeks.

How should the court rule on Ram's request to take judicial notice on the preceding items?

PROBLEM 11-4. In the damages phase of trial, the plaintiff's attorney has asked the court to take judicial notice of the average salary earned by individuals in her profession nationwide as listed on the U.S. Department of Labor website. Assuming the plaintiffs are prepared to print out the page from the U.S. Department of Labor website containing the listing of "Common American Jobs and Salaries," should the court take judicial notice of the fact listed? Why or why not?

PROBLEM 11-5 Maria would like for the court to take judicial notice that traffic accidents took place on Interstate 10 on three particular days in question. Maria has offered accident reports generated by the Louisiana State Police with details of the accidents and their locations on Interstate 10. The defense objects. Should the court take judicial notice of the requested facts—that there was an accident that took place on I-10 on the particular days in question, during the particular time listed? Why or why not?

§ 11.1 and § 11.2 References and Additional Authority on Judicial Notice [La. C.E. arts. 201, 202]

1. La. C.E. arts. 201, 202 and Official Comments
2. Force & Rault, Handbook on Louisiana Evidence Law Arts. 201, 202 Author's Comments (West Publishing 2014)
3. Harges & Jones, Louisiana Evidence Arts. 201, 202 Author's Comments (West Publishing 2014)
4. 19 La. Civ. L. Treatise, Evidence And Proof § 4.4, § 4.1 (2nd ed.)
5. McCormick on Evidence § 328(6th ed. 2006)
6. **Courts have taken judicial of the following adjudicative facts:** *State v. Mason*, 59 So. 3d 419 (La. Ct. App. 5th Cir. 2011) (distances); *State v. Temple*, 789 So. 2d 639 (La. Ct. App. 4th Cir. 2001) (Population, supported by information from U.S. Census); *Fidelity Nat. Bank of Baton Rouge v. Calhoun*, 11 So. 3d 1119 (La. Ct. App. 1st Cir. 2009) (court took judicial notice of change in bank's name supported by certificate of the United States Comptroller of the Currency that verified name change); *State in Interest of C.M.*, 128 So. 3d 1118 (La. Ct. App. 5th Cir. 2013), *writ denied*, 13-2796 (La. 2014), 140 So. 3d 1172 (A trial judge was able to take judicial notice of a juvenile's age for illegal possession of a firearm during the trial to determine his age at the time of the incident when the defendant was asked his age during a hearing.); *State v. Sterling*, 479 So. 2d 641 (La. Ct. App. 1st Cir. 1985) (The court was able to take judicial notice of notorious drug trafficking which was referred to as "the shooting gallery."); *State v. Coutee*, 545 So. 2d 571 (La. Ct. App. 2d Cir. 1989) (Judicial notice was taken that "coke" was used as slang for "cocaine".).
7. **Courts have taken judicial notice of the following legal matters:** *State v. Francis*, 977 So. 2d 187 (La. Ct. App. 4th Cir. 2008) (court took judicial notice of the Governor's executive order interrupting the prescriptive period for criminal proceedings in the wake of Hurricane Katrina); *State v. Price*, 952 So. 2d 112 (La. Ct. App. 1st Cir. 2006) (court took judicial notice of a regulation of the Department of Public Safety regarding the procedures for obtaining samples for chemical tests for people arrested for drunk driving); *Wood v. Louisiana Department of Employment Security*, 632 So. 2d 899 (La. Ct. Appeal 2d Cir. 1994) (A security guard was disqualified from receiving all unemployment compensation benefits because he was discharged. The Department of Labor's regulations would disqualify the guard from all benefits if one separation is found to disqualify the individual. Here, the court of appeal found that the regulations were not included in the record nor presented to the trial court thus, not allowing the court to take notice. Therefore, it was found that the guard was not disqualified from all of his benefits because the record could not indicate what regulations applied and the guard's actions which would violate the regulations.); *Johnson v. Nationwide Life Ins. Co.*, 388 So. 2d 464 (La. Ct. App. 2d Cir. 1980) (when proof of the law of another state, the court will take judicial notice of said law).

§ 11.3 Burdens and Presumptions [La. C.E. arts. 301–308]

Applicable Code Articles

Art. 301. Scope of Chapter

This Chapter applies only to civil cases. It defines and clarifies the foundation, weight, and other effects of presumptions and prima facie evidence or proof as used in legislation but does not apply where more specific legislation provides otherwise. It does not create new presumptions, nor does it apply to or directly affect mixed questions of law and fact, such as the inference of negligence arising from the doctrine of res ipsa loquitur.

Art. 302. Definitions

The following definitions apply under this Chapter:

(1) The "burden of persuasion" is the burden of a party to establish a requisite degree of belief in the mind of the trier of fact as to the existence or nonexistence of a fact. Depending on the circumstances, the degree of belief may be by a preponderance of the evidence, by clear and convincing evidence, or as otherwise required by law.

(2) A "predicate fact" is a fact or group of facts which must be established for a party to be entitled to the benefits of a presumption.

(3) A "presumption" is an inference created by legislation that the trier of fact must draw if it finds the existence of the predicate fact unless the trier of fact is persuaded by evidence of the nonexistence of the fact to be inferred. As used herein, it does not include a particular usage of the term "presumption" where the content, context, or history of the statute indicates an intention merely to authorize but not to require the trier of fact to draw an inference.

(4) An "inference" is a conclusion that an evidentiary fact exists based on the establishment of a predicate fact.

Art. 303. Conclusive presumptions

A "conclusive presumption" is a rule of substantive law and is not regulated by this Chapter.

Art. 304. Rebuttable presumptions

Presumptions regulated by this Chapter are rebuttable presumptions and therefore may be controverted or overcome by appropriate evidence.

Art. 305. Effect of presumptions if there is no controverting evidence

If the trier of fact finds the existence of the predicate fact, and there is no evidence controverting the fact to be inferred, the trier of fact is required to find the existence of the fact to be inferred.

Art. 306. Effect of presumptions if there is controverting evidence

If the trier of fact finds the existence of the predicate fact, and if there is evidence controverting the fact to be inferred, it shall find the existence of the inferred fact unless it is persuaded by the controverting evidence of the nonexistence of the inferred fact.

Art. 307. Jury instructions

In jury cases, upon request, the jury shall be instructed of the existence of a presumption and instructed as to its effect in accordance with Articles 305 and 306.

Art. 308. Effect of the term "prima facie" in legislation

A. Legislation providing that a document or other evidence is prima facie evidence or proof of all or part of its contents or of another fact establishes a presumption under this Chapter. When, however, the content, context, or history of the legislation indicates an intention not to shift the burden of persuasion, such legislation establishes only an inference and in a jury case, the court on request shall instruct the jury that if it finds the existence of the predicate fact it may but need not find the inferred fact.

B. Other uses of the term "prima facie", such as those that merely provide for the admissibility of specified evidence, do not create presumptions or inferences and are not regulated by this Chapter.

Civil cases only. This chapter applies only to **civil cases**. It defines and clarifies the foundation, weight, and other effects of presumptions and prima facie evidence or proof as used in legislation but does not apply where more specific legislation provides otherwise. It does not create new presumptions, nor does it apply to or directly affect mixed questions of law and fact, such as the inference of negligence arising from the doctrine of res ipsa loquitur.[20]

Rebuttable presumptions only. This chapter regulates rebuttable presumptions only.[21] A "presumption" is an inference created by legislation that the trier of fact must draw if it finds the existence of the predicate fact unless the trier of fact is persuaded by evidence of the nonexistence of the fact to be inferred.[22] A "rebuttable presumption" is one that **may be controverted or overcome by appropriate evidence.**[23] True evidentiary presumptions address evidentiary facts, not legal conclusions, and are classically styled in the form: "If A, then B," or more explicitly "If [evidentiary fact] A [is established], then [evidentiary fact] B [shall be considered established]," unless the opponent meets a certain specified burden[24] that rebuts the inference. Thus, the effect of establishing the predicate fact is to shift the burden of persuasion to the party against whom the presumption operates to show that the inference is not true.[25]

For example, Louisiana Civil Code Article 2340 creates a presumption that things in possession of a spouse during the existence of a marriage are community property. Once the predicate facts are established, the existence of marriage and possession of property, then the presumption exists. Thereafter, the party against whom the presumption operates, here, the party claiming that the property is separate property, has the burden of proving that the property is not community property.

The articles do not specifically state the specific standard the opponent must meet to overcome the presumption, but provides that "depending on the circumstances, the degree of belief may be by a preponderance of the evidence, by clear and convincing evidence, or as otherwise required by law."[26] As it pertains to the community property presumption

20. La. Code Evid. art. 301.
21. La. Code Evid. art. 304.
22. La. Code Evid. art. 302(3).
23. La. Code Evid. art. 304.
24. La. Code Evid. art. 301 Official Comment (a).
25. Force & Rault, Handbook, art. 303 Author's Note (1).
26. La. Code Evid. art. 302(1).

mentioned above, the Louisiana Supreme Court has held that the presumption is rebuttable by a preponderance of the evidence.[27] Evidence attacking the presumption of a person's capacity to contract must meet the "clear and convincing" standard.[28]

Thus, "if the trier of fact finds the existence of the predicate facts necessary to be entitled to the benefits of the rebuttable presumption, and there is *no* evidence controverting the fact to be inferred, the trier of fact is *required* to find the existence of the fact to be inferred."[29] However, even if there *is* evidence controverting the fact to be inferred, the trier of fact must nevertheless find the existence of the inferred fact *unless* it is persuaded by the controverting evidence of the nonexistence of the inferred fact.[30]

Not covered by this chapter. This chapter does not regulate "conclusive presumptions," which are rules of substantive law.[31] Conclusive presumptions may not be controverted or overcome by evidence to the contrary. Additionally, as stated above, this chapter only covers legislatively created presumptions; it does not cover judicially created presumptions.

Jury instructions. "In jury cases, upon request, the jury shall be instructed of the existence of a presumption and instructed as to its effect in accordance with Articles 305 and 306."[32]

Effect of the term "prima facie" in legislation. Legislation providing that a document or other evidence is prima facie evidence or proof of all or part of its contents or of another fact establishes a presumption under this Chapter. When, however, the content, context, or history of the legislation indicates an intention not to shift the burden of persuasion, such legislation establishes only an inference and in a jury case, the court on request shall instruct the jury that if it finds the existence of the predicate fact it *may* but need not find the inferred fact.

Other uses of the term "prima facie," such as those that merely provide for the admissibility of specified evidence, do not create presumptions or inferences and are not regulated by this Chapter.[33]

Application of law in Louisiana Courts. In ***Hall v. Folger Coffee Co.,*** 874 So 2d 90 (La. 2004), the Louisiana Supreme Court gives an excellent explanation of the analysis to be used in determining the effect of presumptions under this Chapter. In *Hall*, a default judgment was rendered against the defendants Folger Coffee Co. They brought an action for nullity claiming their agent had not been properly served with process of the petition. The plaintiff presented a completed sheriff's return, which under Louisiana law, C.C.Pr. Art. 1292, creates a presumption of proper service, thus shifting the burden to the defendant Folger to present evidence controverting the inference to prove that their agent had not, in fact, been properly served. In reversing the Court of Appeal, reinstating the judgment of the district court which annulled the default judge against the defendants, the court held:

> Under the provisions of La.Code of Civ. Proc. art. 1292, a sheriff's return of service of process "shall be considered prima facie correct." The impact of that statement is explained by reference to the provisions of La. Code of Evidence,

---

27. *See* Talbot v. Talbot, 864 So. 2d 590 (La. 2003); *See also* Force & Rault, Handbook, Art. 302, Author's Note (4).

28. Force & Rault, Handbook, Art. 302, Author's Note (4); *See also* La.C.C. art. 1482.

29. La. Code Evid. art. 305.

30. La. Code Evid. art. 306.

31. *See* La. Code Evid. art. 303.

32. La. Code Evid. art. 307.

33. La. Code Evid. art. 308.

Chapter 3, "Effect in Civil Cases of Presumptions and Prima Facie Evidence." According to that chapter, "[l]egislation providing that a document or other evidence is prima facie evidence ... establishes a presumption under this Chapter." "Presumption" is defined as "an inference created by legislation that the trier of fact must draw if it finds the existence of the predicate fact unless the trier of fact is persuaded by evidence of the nonexistence of the fact to be inferred." The only presumptions regulated by Chapter 3 of the La. Code of Evidence "are rebuttable presumptions [that] therefore may be controverted or overcome by appropriate evidence." "If the trier of fact finds the existence of the predicate fact, and if there is evidence controverting the fact to be inferred, it shall find the existence of the inferred fact unless it is persuaded by the controverting evidence of the nonexistence of the inferred fact."

The rule that may be extracted from reference to all of the above provisions is stated in Official Comment (b) to La. Code of Evid. 308, which states that "[w]hen the predicate fact is established it shifts the burden of persuasion of the non-existence of the inferred fact to the opponent." The phrase "burden of persuasion" is defined as "the burden of a party to establish a requisite degree of belief in the mind of the trier of fact as to the existence or nonexistence of a fact." The "degree of belief" required "may be by a preponderance of the evidence, by clear and convincing evidence, or as otherwise required by law." According to this court's most recent pronouncement on the subject, the burden of persuasion that applies to a party seeking to overcome the rebuttable presumption afforded a completed sheriff's return of service by La. Code of Civ. Proc. art. 1292 is preponderance of the evidence. *Roper v. Dailey,* 393 So.2d 85 (La.1981). Accordingly, the party attacking service must prove that, more probably than not, proper service was not made. *Id.,* 393 So.2d at 88.

Consideration of all of the above principles reveals the following method for determining a Nullity Action based on insufficient service of process:

1. The trier of fact must determine the existence of the "predicate fact"—i.e., whether the record contains a completed sheriff's return of service.

2. If the predicate fact exists, the trier of fact must draw the inference created by the legislature—i.e., that the sheriff's return of service is valid.

3. The party attacking the validity of the sheriff's return of service must be allowed to present "appropriate evidence" to controvert or overcome the presumption created by the first two steps.

4. The trier of fact must determine whether it is persuaded by the controverting evidence of the nonexistence of the inferred fact.

5. If the trier of fact is not persuaded by the controverting evidence of the nonexistence of the inferred fact, it must find the existence of the inferred fact.

6. If, based on a preponderance of the evidence, the trier of fact is persuaded by the controverting evidence of the nonexistence of the inferred fact, it may find that the inferred fact does not exist.

The record in the instant case indicates that the district court properly applied the rebuttable presumption of validity afforded the completed sheriff's return. Following a trial on the merits, the district court found that the evidence presented by Folger was sufficient to overcome the presumption. In effect, the district court's judgment is based on her being persuaded by the controverting evidence presented by Folger of the non-existence of the inferred fact—the latter being that service had been properly made on CT Corporation. Accordingly, the district court annulled the default judgment against Folger.[34]

§ 11.3 References and Additional Authority on Burdens and Presumptions [La. C.E. arts. 301–308]

1. La. C.E. arts. 301–308 and Official Comments
2. Force & Rault, HANDBOOK ON LOUISIANA EVIDENCE LAW Arts. 301–308 Author's Comments (West Publishing 2014)
3. Harges & Jones, LOUISIANA EVIDENCE Arts. 301–308 Author's Comments (West Publishing 2014)
4. 19 La. Civ. L. Treatise, Evidence And Proof § 4.3 (2nd ed.)
5. MCCORMICK ON EVIDENCE § 335(6th ed. 2006)
6. **Presumptions in criminal cases as shaped by the constitutional considerations**: See e.g., *County Court of Ulster Cty. v. Allen*, 99 S. Ct. 2213 (1979), and *State v. Lindsey*, 491 So. 2d 371 (La. 1986).
7. **Examples of rebuttable presumptions:** La. C.C. Art. 1918 (that all persons are presumed to have the capacity to contract); La. C.C. Art. 1470 (that all persons are capable of donating property *inter vivo* and *mortis causa*); La. R.S. 33:2581 (creates a presumption that when heart disease or infirmity manifests after the first five years of their employment, it is presumed to be caused by their work; La. R.S. 23:1081 (when an employee is injured on the job, refusal to consent to drug and alcohol tests creates a presumption of intoxication, and once the intoxication is proven, the accident is presumed to have been caused by the intoxication); La. R.S. 22:905 (written notice required before lapse of life policy is presumed to have been given when duly addressed and mailed by the insurer issuing such policy).
8. **Cases on the effect of rebuttable presumptions**: *Carsice v. Empire*, 2 So. 3d 553 (La. Ct. App. 4th Cir. 2008) (stating that "La. R.S. 23:1081 creates two separate and distinct presumptions. First, if an injured employee refuses to submit to drug and alcohol tests, then the employee is presumed to be intoxicated. Second, if the employer meets its burden of proof and proves the injured employee was intoxicated at the time of the accident, or if the presumption of intoxication is not rebutted, then it is presumed that the accident was caused by the intoxication" citing *Franks v. Air Conditioning Appliance Corp.*, 670 So. 2d 322, 325–26 (La. Ct. App. 3d Cir. 1996)); *Kessler v. Great Western Life & Annuity Ins. Co.*, 997 So. 2d 590 (La. Ct. App. 4th Cir. 2008) (summary judgment upheld when no evidence was introduced to rebut presumption of receipt of letter that had been properly addressed and mailed under La. R.S. 22:177); *Davies v. Johnson Controls, Inc.*, 830 So. 2d 462 (La. Ct. App. 2d Cir. 2002) (Claimant of a worker's compensation claim failed to establish that her carpal tunnel syndrome occurred through or during her employment.); See also *Succession of Hollis*, 897 So. 2d 387 (La. App. 2d Cir. 2008) (presumption of capacity to contract); *Cupples v. Pruitt*, 754 So. 2d 328 (La. Ct App. 2d Cir. 2000) (presumption in favor of testamentary

---

34. Hall v. Folger Coffee Co., 874 So. 2d 90, 96–97 (La. 2004).

capacity); *McMillan v. City of Monroe*, 108 So. 3d 869 (La. Ct. App. 2d Cir. 2013) (Firefighter's Heart and Lung Statute creates a presumption that a firefighter's work caused, contributed to, accelerated or aggravated his heart disease or infirmity if it manifests after the first five years of employment).

Louisiana Code of Evidence

Effective January 1, 1989
Including Amendments Effective through August 2014

CHAPTER 1. GENERAL PROVISIONS

Art. 101. Scope

This Code governs proceedings in the courts of Louisiana to the extent and with the exceptions stated in Article 1101.

Art. 102. Purpose and construction

These articles shall be construed to secure fairness and efficiency in administration of the law of evidence to the end that the truth may be ascertained and proceedings justly determined.

Art. 103. Rulings on evidence

A. **Effect of erroneous ruling.** Error may not be predicated upon a ruling which admits or excludes evidence unless a substantial right of the party is affected, and

(1) **Ruling admitting evidence.** When the ruling is one admitting evidence, a timely objection or motion to admonish the jury to limit or disregard appears of record, stating the specific ground of objection; or

(2) **Ruling excluding evidence.** When the ruling is one excluding evidence, the substance of the evidence was made known to the court by counsel.

B. **Record of ruling.** The court may add any other or further statement which shows the character of the evidence, the form in which it was offered, the objection made, and the ruling thereon.

C. **Hearing of jury.** In jury cases, proceedings shall be conducted, to the extent practicable, so as to prevent inadmissible evidence from being suggested to the jury by any means, such as making statements or asking questions in the hearing of the jury.

Art. 104. Preliminary questions

A. **Questions of admissibility generally.** Preliminary questions concerning the competency or qualification of a person to be a witness, the existence of a privilege, or the admissibility of evidence shall be determined by the court, subject to the provisions of Paragraph B. In making its determination it is not bound by the rules of evidence except those with respect to privileges.

B. **Relevancy conditioned on fact.** Subject to other provisions of this Code, when the relevancy of evidence depends upon the fulfillment of a condition of fact, the court shall admit it upon, or subject to, the introduction of evidence sufficient to support a finding of the fulfillment of the condition.

C. **Hearing of jury.** Hearings on matters to be decided by the judge alone shall be conducted out of the hearing of the jury when the interests of justice require. Hearings on the admissibility of confessions or admissions by the accused or evidence allegedly unlawfully obtained shall in all cases be conducted out of the hearing of the jury, but when there has been a ruling prior to trial, it shall not be necessary to conduct another hearing as to admissibility before presentation of the evidence to a jury.

D. **Weight and credibility.** The preliminary determination by the court that evidence is admissible does not limit the right of a party to introduce evidence relevant to weight or credibility at the trial.

Art. 105. Limited admissibility

When evidence which is admissible as to one party or for one purpose but not admissible as to another party or for another purpose is admitted, the court, upon request, shall restrict the evidence to its proper scope and instruct the jury accordingly. Failure to restrict the evidence and instruct the jury shall not constitute error absent a request to do so.

CHAPTER 2. JUDICIAL NOTICE

Art. 201. Judicial notice of adjudicative facts generally

A. **Scope of Article.** This Article governs only judicial notice of adjudicative facts. An "adjudicative fact" is a fact normally determined by the trier of fact.

B. **Kinds of facts.** A judicially noticed fact must be one not subject to reasonable dispute in that it is either:

(1) Generally known within the territorial jurisdiction of the trial court; or

(2) Capable of accurate and ready determination by resort to sources whose accuracy cannot reasonably be questioned.

C. **When discretionary.** A court may take judicial notice, whether requested or not.

D. **When mandatory.** A court shall take judicial notice upon request if supplied with the information necessary for the court to determine that there is no reasonable dispute as to the fact.

E. **Opportunity to be heard.** A party is entitled upon timely request to an opportunity to be heard as to the propriety of taking judicial notice and the tenor of the matter noticed. In the absence of prior opportunity to be heard, the request may be made after judicial notice has been taken.

F. **Time of taking notice.** A party may request judicial notice at any stage of the proceeding but shall not do so in the hearing of a jury. Before taking judicial notice of a matter in its instructions to the jury, the court shall inform the parties before closing arguments begin.

G. **Instructing jury.** In a civil case, the court shall instruct the jury to accept as conclusive any fact judicially noticed. In a criminal case, the court shall instruct the jury that it may, but is not required to, accept as conclusive any fact judicially noticed.

Art. 202. Judicial notice of legal matters

A. **Mandatory.** A court, whether requested to do so or not, shall take judicial notice of the laws of the United States, of every state, territory, and other jurisdiction of the United States, and of the ordinances enacted by any political subdivision within the court's territorial jurisdiction whenever certified copies of the ordinances have been filed with the clerk of that court.

B. **Other legal matters.**

(1) A court shall take judicial notice of the following if a party requests it and provides the court with the information needed by it to comply with the request, and may take judicial notice without request of a party of:

(a) Proclamations of the President of the United States and the governor of this state.

(b) Rules of boards, commissions, and agencies of this state that have been duly published and promulgated in the Louisiana Register.

(c) Ordinances enacted by any political subdivision of the State of Louisiana.

(d) Rules which govern the practice and procedure in a court of the United States or of any state, territory, or other jurisdiction of the United States, and which have been published in a form which makes them readily accessible.

(e) Rules and decisions of boards, commissions, and agencies of the United States or of any state, territory, or other jurisdiction of the United States which have been duly published and promulgated and which have the effect of law within their respective jurisdictions.

(f) Law of foreign countries, international law, and maritime law.

(2) A party who requests that judicial notice be taken and the court, if notice is taken without request shall give reasonable notice during trial to all other parties.

C. **Information by court.** The court may inform itself of any of the foregoing legal matters in such manner as it may deem proper, and the court may call upon counsel to aid it in obtaining such information.

D. **Time of taking notice.** Judicial notice of the foregoing legal matters may be taken at any stage of the proceeding, provided that before taking judicial notice of a matter in its instructions to the jury, the court shall inform the parties before closing arguments begin.

E. **Question for court.** The determination of the foregoing legal matters shall be made by the court.

CHAPTER 3. EFFECT IN CIVIL CASES OF PRESUMPTIONS AND PRIMA FACIE EVIDENCE

Art. 301. Scope of Chapter

This Chapter applies only to civil cases. It defines and clarifies the foundation, weight, and other effects of presumptions and prima facie evidence or proof as used in legislation but does not apply where more specific legislation provides otherwise. It does not create new presumptions, nor does it apply to or directly affect mixed questions of law and fact, such as the inference of negligence arising from the doctrine of res ipsa loquitur.

Art. 302. Definitions

The following definitions apply under this Chapter:

(1) The "burden of persuasion" is the burden of a party to establish a requisite degree of belief in the mind of the trier of fact as to the existence or nonexistence of a fact. Depending on the circumstances, the degree of belief may be by a prepon-

derance of the evidence, by clear and convincing evidence, or as otherwise required by law.

(2) A "predicate fact" is a fact or group of facts which must be established for a party to be entitled to the benefits of a presumption.

(3) A "presumption" is an inference created by legislation that the trier of fact must draw if it finds the existence of the predicate fact unless the trier of fact is persuaded by evidence of the nonexistence of the fact to be inferred. As used herein, it does not include a particular usage of the term "presumption" where the content, context, or history of the statute indicates an intention merely to authorize but not to require the trier of fact to draw an inference.

(4) An "inference" is a conclusion that an evidentiary fact exists based on the establishment of a predicate fact.

Art. 303. Conclusive presumptions

A "conclusive presumption" is a rule of substantive law and is not regulated by this Chapter.

Art. 304. Rebuttable presumptions

Presumptions regulated by this Chapter are rebuttable presumptions and therefore may be controverted or overcome by appropriate evidence.

Art. 305. Effect of presumptions if there is no controverting evidence

If the trier of fact finds the existence of the predicate fact, and there is no evidence controverting the fact to be inferred, the trier of fact is required to find the existence of the fact to be inferred.

Art. 306. Effect of presumptions if there is controverting evidence

If the trier of fact finds the existence of the predicate fact, and if there is evidence controverting the fact to be inferred, it shall find the existence of the inferred fact unless it is persuaded by the controverting evidence of the nonexistence of the inferred fact.

Art. 307. Jury instructions

In jury cases, upon request, the jury shall be instructed of the existence of a presumption and instructed as to its effect in accordance with Articles 305 and 306.

Art. 308. Effect of the term "prima facie" in legislation

A. Legislation providing that a document or other evidence is prima facie evidence or proof of all or part of its contents or of another fact establishes a presumption under this Chapter. When, however, the content, context, or history of the legislation indicates an intention not to shift the burden of persuasion, such legislation establishes only an inference and in a jury case, the court on request shall instruct the jury that if it finds the existence of the predicate fact it may but need not find the inferred fact.

B. Other uses of the term "prima facie", such as those that merely provide for the admissibility of specified evidence, do not create presumptions or inferences and are not regulated by this Chapter.

CHAPTER 4. RELEVANCY AND ITS LIMITS

Art. 401. Definition of "relevant evidence"

"Relevant evidence" means evidence having any tendency to make the existence of any fact that is of consequence to the determination of the action more probable or less probable than it would be without the evidence.

Art. 402. Relevant evidence generally admissible; irrelevant evidence inadmissible

All relevant evidence is admissible, except as otherwise provided by the Constitution of the United States, the Constitution of Louisiana, this Code of Evidence, or other legislation. Evidence which is not relevant is not admissible.

Art. 403. Exclusion of relevant evidence on grounds of prejudice, confusion, or waste of time

Although relevant, evidence may be excluded if its probative value is substantially outweighed by the danger of unfair prejudice, confusion of the issues, or misleading the jury, or by considerations of undue delay, or waste of time.

Art. 404. Character evidence generally not admissible in civil or criminal trial to prove conduct; exceptions; other criminal acts

A. **Character evidence generally.** Evidence of a person's character or a trait of his character, such as a moral quality, is not admissible for the purpose of proving that he acted in conformity therewith on a particular occasion, except:

(1) **Character of accused.** Evidence of a pertinent trait of his character, such as a moral quality, offered by an accused, or by the prosecution to rebut the character evidence; provided that such evidence shall be restricted to showing those moral qualities pertinent to the crime with which he is charged, and that character evidence cannot destroy conclusive evidence of guilt.

(2) **Character of victim.**

(a) Except as provided in Article 412, evidence of a pertinent trait of character, such as a moral quality, of the victim of the crime offered by an accused, or by the prosecution to rebut the character evidence; provided that in the absence of evidence of a hostile demonstration or an overt act on the part of the victim at the time of the offense charged, evidence of his dangerous character is not admissible; provided further that when the accused pleads self-defense and there is a history of assaultive behavior between the victim and the accused and the accused lived in a familial or intimate relationship such as, but not limited to, the husband-wife, parent-child, or concubinage relationship, it shall not be necessary to first show a hostile demonstration or overt act on the part of the victim in order to introduce evidence of the dangerous character of the victim, including specific instances of conduct and domestic violence; and further provided that an expert's opinion as to the effects of the prior assaultive acts on the accused's state of mind is admissible; or

(b) Evidence of a character trait of peacefulness of the victim offered by the prosecution in a homicide case to rebut evidence that the victim was the first aggressor;

(3) **Character of witness.** Evidence of the character of a witness, as provided in Articles 607, 608, and 609.

B. Other crimes, wrongs, or acts. (1)Except as provided in Article 412, evidence of other crimes, wrongs, or acts is not admissible to prove the character of a person in order to show that he acted in conformity therewith. It may, however, be admissible for other purposes, such as proof of motive, opportunity, intent, preparation, plan, knowledge, identity, absence of mistake or accident, provided that upon request by the accused, the prosecution in a criminal case shall provide reasonable notice in advance of trial, of the nature of any such evidence it intends to introduce at trial for such purposes, or when it relates to conduct that constitutes an integral part of the act or transaction that is the subject of the present proceeding.

(2) In the absence of evidence of a hostile demonstration or an overt act on the part of the victim at the time of the offense charged, evidence of the victim's prior threats against the accused or the accused's state of mind as to the victim's dangerous character is not admissible; provided that when the accused pleads self-defense and there is a history of assaultive behavior between the victim and the accused and the accused lived in a familial or intimate relationship such as, but not limited to, the husband-wife, parent-child, or concubinage relationship, it shall not be necessary to first show a hostile demonstration or overt act on the part of the victim in order to introduce evidence of the dangerous character of the victim, including specific instances of conduct and domestic violence; and further provided that an expert's opinion as to the effects of the prior assaultive acts on the accused's state of mind is admissible.

Art. 405. Methods of proving character

A. **Reputation.** Except as provided in Article 412, in all cases in which evidence of character or a trait of character of a person is admissible, proof may be made by testimony as to general reputation only. On cross-examination of the character witness, inquiry is allowable into relevant specific instances of conduct.

B. **Specific instances of conduct.** In cases in which character or a trait of character of a person is an essential element of a charge, claim, or defense, such as in a prosecution for defamation or when there is a defense of entrapment, proof may also be made of specific instances of his conduct.

C. **Foundation.** Before a person may be permitted to testify to the reputation of another person, a foundation must be established that the witness is familiar with that reputation.

Art. 406. Habit; routine practice; methods of proof

Evidence of the habit of a person or of the routine practice of an organization, whether corroborated or not and regardless of the presence of eyewitnesses, is relevant to prove that the conduct of the person or organization on a particular occasion was in conformity with the habit or routine practice. The evidence may consist of testimony in the form of an opinion or evidence of specific instances of conduct sufficient in number to warrant a finding that the habit existed or that the practice was routine.

Art. 407. Subsequent remedial measures

In a civil case, when, after an event, measures are taken which, if taken previously, would have made the event less likely to occur, evidence of the subsequent measures is not admissible to prove negligence or culpable conduct in connection with the event. This Article does not require the exclusion of evidence of subsequent measures when offered for another purpose, such as proving ownership, authority, knowledge, control, or feasibility of precautionary measures, or for attacking credibility.

Art. 408. Compromise and offers to compromise

A. **Civil cases.** In a civil case, evidence of (1) furnishing or offering or promising to furnish, or (2) accepting or offering or promising to accept, anything of value in compromising or attempting to compromise a claim which was disputed as to either validity or amount, is not admissible to prove liability for or invalidity of the claim or its amount. Evidence of conduct or statements made in compromise negotiations is likewise not admissible. This Article does not require the exclusion of any evidence otherwise admissible merely because it is presented in the course of compromise negotiations. This Article also does not require exclusion when the evidence is offered for another purpose, such as proving bias or prejudice of a witness, negativing a contention of undue delay, or proving an effort to obstruct a criminal investigation or prosecution.

B. **Criminal cases.** This Article does not require the exclusion in a criminal case of evidence of the actions or statements described in Paragraph A, above, or of a giving or offer to give anything of value by the accused in direct or indirect restitution to a victim.

Art. 409. Payment of medical and similar expenses

In a civil case, evidence of furnishing or offering or promising to pay expenses or losses occasioned by an injury to person or damage to property is not admissible to prove liability for the injury or damage nor is it admissible to mitigate, reduce, or avoid liability therefor. This Article does not require the exclusion of such evidence when it is offered solely for another purpose, such as to enforce a contract for payment.

Art. 410. Inadmissibility of pleas, plea discussions, and related statements

A. **General rule.** Except as otherwise provided in this Article, evidence of the following is not, in any civil or criminal proceeding, admissible against the party who made the plea or was a participant in the plea discussions:

(1) A plea of guilty or of nolo contendere which was later withdrawn or set aside;

(2) In a civil case, a plea of nolo contendere;

(3) Any statement made in the course of any court proceeding concerning either of the foregoing pleas, or any plea discussions with an attorney for or other representative of the prosecuting authority regarding either of the foregoing pleas; or

(4) Any statement made in the course of plea discussions with an attorney for or other representative of the prosecuting authority which do not result in a plea of guilty or which result in a plea of guilty later withdrawn or set aside.

B. **Exceptions.** However, such a statement is admissible:

(1) In any proceeding wherein another statement made in the course of the same plea or plea discussions has been introduced and the statement ought in fairness be considered contemporaneously with it; or

(2) In a criminal proceeding for perjury or false statement if the statement was made by the defendant under oath, on the record and in the presence of counsel.

Art. 411. Liability insurance

Although a policy of insurance may be admissible, the amount of coverage under the policy shall not be communicated to the jury unless the amount of coverage is a disputed issue which the jury will decide.

Art. 412. Victim's past sexual behavior in sexual assault cases; trafficking offenses

A. (1) **Opinion and reputation evidence; sexual assault cases.** When an accused is charged with a crime involving sexually assaultive behavior, reputation or opinion evidence of the past sexual behavior of the victim is not admissible.

(2) **Other evidence; exceptions.** When an accused is charged with a crime involving sexually assaultive behavior, evidence of specific instances of the victim's past sexual behavior is also not admissible except for:

(a) Evidence of past sexual behavior with persons other than the accused, upon the issue of whether or not the accused was the source of semen or injury; provided that such evidence is limited to a period not to exceed seventy-two hours prior to the time of the offense, and further provided that the jury be instructed at the time and in its final charge regarding the limited purpose for which the evidence is admitted; or

(b) Evidence of past sexual behavior with the accused offered by the accused upon the issue of whether or not the victim consented to the sexually assaultive behavior.

B. (1) **Opinion and reputation evidence; trafficking.** When an accused is charged with a crime involving human trafficking or trafficking of children for sexual purposes, reputation or opinion evidence of the past sexual behavior of the victim is not admissible.

(2) Evidence of specific instances of the victim's past sexual behavior is not admissible unless the evidence is offered by the prosecution in a criminal case to prove a pattern of trafficking activity by the defendant.

C. **Motion.** (1) Before the person, accused of committing a crime that involves sexually assaultive behavior, human trafficking, or trafficking of children for sexual purposes, may offer under Subparagraph (A)(2) or (B)(2) of this Article evidence of specific instances of the victim's past sexual behavior, the accused shall make a written motion in camera to offer such evidence. The motion shall be accompanied by a written statement of evidence setting forth the names and addresses of persons to be called as witnesses.

(2) The motion and statement of evidence shall be served on the state which shall make a reasonable effort to notify the victim prior to the hearing.

D. **Time for a motion.** The motion shall be made within the time for filing pre-trial motions specified in Code of Criminal Procedure Article 521, except that the court shall allow the motion to be made at a later date, if the court determines that:

(1) The evidence is of past sexual behavior with the accused, and the accused establishes that the motion was not timely made because of an impossibility arising through no fault of his own; or

(2) The evidence is of past sexual behavior with someone other than the accused, and the accused establishes that the evidence or the issue to which it relates is newly discovered and could not have been obtained earlier through the exercise of due diligence.

E. **Hearing.** (1) If the court determines that the statement of evidence contains evidence described in Subparagraph (A)(2) or (B)(2), the court shall order a hearing which shall be closed to determine if such evidence is admissible. At such hearing the parties may call witnesses.

(2) The victim, if present, has the right to attend the hearing and may be accompanied by counsel.

(3) If the court determines on the basis of the hearing described in Subparagraph (E)(1) that the evidence which the accused seeks to offer is relevant and that the probative value of such evidence outweighs the danger of unfair prejudice, such evidence may be admissible in the trial to the extent an order made by the court specifies evidence which may be offered and areas with respect to which the victim may be examined or cross-examined. Introduction of such evidence shall be limited to that specified in the order.

(4) Any motion made under Subparagraph C and any statement of evidence, brief, record of a hearing, or like material made or used in connection with the motion shall be kept in a separate, sealed package as part of the record in the case. Nothing in this Article shall preclude the use of the testimony at such hearing in a subsequent prosecution for perjury or false swearing.

F. **Past sexual behavior defined.** For purposes of this Article, the term "past sexual behavior" means sexual behavior other than the sexual behavior with respect to which the offense of sexually assaultive behavior is alleged.

Art. 412.1. Victim's attire in sexual assault cases

When an accused is charged with the crime of aggravated rape, forcible rape, simple rape, sexual battery, or second degree sexual battery, the manner and style of the victim's attire shall not be admissible as evidence that the victim encouraged or consented to the offense; however, items of clothing or parts thereof may be introduced in order to establish the presence or absence of the elements of the offense and the proof of its occurrence.

Art. 412.2. Evidence of similar crimes, wrongs, or acts in sex offense cases

A. When an accused is charged with a crime involving sexually assaultive behavior, or with acts that constitute a sex offense involving a victim who was under the age of seventeen at the time of the offense, evidence of the accused's commission of another crime, wrong, or act involving sexually assaultive behavior or acts which indicate a lustful disposition toward children may be admissible and may be considered for its bearing on any matter to which it is relevant subject to the balancing test provided in Article 403.

B. In a case in which the state intends to offer evidence under the provisions of this Article, the prosecution shall, upon request of the accused, provide reasonable notice in advance of trial of the nature of any such evidence it intends to introduce at trial for such purposes.

C. This Article shall not be construed to limit the admission or consideration of evidence under any other rule.

Art. 412.3. Statements made by victims of trafficking during investigations

If a victim of human trafficking or trafficking of children for sexual purposes is also a defendant in any case arising from unlawful acts committed as part of the same trafficking activity, any inculpatory statement made by the victim as a result of questioning by any person then known by the victim to be a law enforcement officer is inadmissible against the victim, except pursuant to Article 801 of this Code or in any prosecution of the victim for perjury, at a trial of the victim for the unlawful acts committed by the victim as part of the same trafficking activity if all of the following conditions exist:

(1) The victim cooperates with the investigation and prosecution, including the giving of a use-immunity statement as directed by the prosecuting attorney.

(2) The victim testifies truthfully at any hearing or trial related to the trafficking activity, or agrees, either in writing or on the record, to testify truthfully at any hearing or trial related to the trafficking activity in any prosecution of any other person charged with an offense arising from the same trafficking activity, regardless of whether the testimony is unnecessary due to entry of a plea by the other person.

(3) The victim has agreed in writing to receive services or participate in a program that provides services to victims of human trafficking or trafficking of children for sexual purposes, if such services are available.

Art. 413. Settlement or tender

Any amount paid in settlement or by tender shall not be admitted into evidence unless the failure to make a settlement or tender is an issue in the case.

Art. 414. Workers' compensation payments

Evidence of the nature and extent of a workers' compensation claim or of payment of past or future workers' compensation benefits shall not be admissible to a jury, directly or indirectly, in any civil proceeding with respect to a claim for damages relative to the same injury for which the workers' compensation benefits are claimed or paid. Such evidence shall be admissible and presented to the judge only.

Art. 415. Act of contacting or retaining an attorney

In any criminal proceeding, the act of contacting or retaining an attorney shall not be admissible against any individual or entity, unless such act falls within an established exception for crime or fraud.

CHAPTER 5. TESTIMONIAL PRIVILEGES

Art. 501. Scope of privileges

Privileges as recognized in this Chapter are evidentiary in nature, do not of themselves create causes of action or other substantive rights, and are applicable to proceedings enumerated in Article 1101. Nothing in this Chapter is intended to regulate the content or waiver of constitutional rights, nor inferences to be drawn from their invocation.

Art. 502. Waiver of privilege

A. Waiver. A person upon whom the law confers a privilege against disclosure waives the privilege if he or his predecessor while holder of the privilege voluntarily discloses or consents to disclosure of any significant part of the privileged matter. This rule does not apply if the disclosure itself is privileged.

B. Disclosure under compulsion or without opportunity to claim. A claim of privilege is not defeated by a disclosure which was compelled or made without opportunity to claim the privilege.

C. Joint holders. Where two or more persons are joint holders of a privilege, a waiver of the right of one joint holder to claim the privilege does not affect the right of another joint holder to claim the privilege.

Art. 503. Comment on or inference from claim of privilege; instructions; exception

A. Comment, inference, and instructions.

(1) The claim of privilege, whether in the present proceeding or upon a prior occasion, is not a proper subject of comment by judge or counsel. No inferences may be drawn therefrom.

(2) In jury cases, proceedings shall be conducted, to the extent practicable, so as to facilitate the making of claims of privilege without the knowledge of the jury.

(3) Upon request, any party against whom the jury might draw an adverse inference from a claim of privilege is entitled to an instruction that no inference may be drawn therefrom.

B. **Exception in non-criminal proceedings.** In non-criminal proceedings, under exceptional circumstances in the interest of justice, if a claim of privilege is sustained counsel may comment thereon, and, upon request, the court shall instruct the trier of fact that it may draw all reasonable inferences therefrom.

Art. 504. Spousal confidential communications privilege

A. **Definition.** A communication is "confidential" if it is made privately and is not intended for further disclosure unless such disclosure is itself privileged.

B. **Confidential communications privilege.** Each spouse has a privilege during and after the marriage to refuse to disclose, and to prevent the other spouse from disclosing, confidential communications with the other spouse while they were husband and wife.

C. **Confidential communications; exceptions.** This privilege does not apply:

(1) In a criminal case in which one spouse is charged with a crime against the person or property of the other spouse or of a child of either.

(2) In a civil case brought by or on behalf of one spouse against the other spouse.

(3) In commitment or interdiction proceedings as to either spouse.

(4) When the communication is offered to protect or vindicate the rights of a minor child of either spouse.

(5) In cases otherwise provided by legislation.

Art. 505. Spousal witness privilege

In a criminal case or in commitment or interdiction proceedings, a witness spouse has a privilege not to testify against the other spouse. This privilege terminates upon the annulment of the marriage, legal separation, or divorce of the spouses. This privilege does not apply in a criminal case in which one spouse is charged with a crime against the person of the other spouse or a crime against the person of a child including but not limited to the violation of a preliminary or permanent injunction or protective order and violations of R.S. 14:79.

Art. 506. Lawyer-client privilege

A. **Definitions.** As used in this Article:

(1) "Client" is a person, including a public officer, corporation, partnership, unincorporated association, or other organization or entity, public or private, to whom professional legal services are rendered by a lawyer, or who consults a lawyer with a view to obtaining professional legal services from the lawyer.

(2) "Representative of the client" is:

(a) A person having authority to obtain professional legal services, or to act on advice so obtained, on behalf of the client.

(b) Any other person who makes or receives a confidential communication for the purpose of effectuating legal representation for the client, while acting in the scope of employment for the client.

(3) "Lawyer" is a person authorized, or reasonably believed by the client to be authorized, to practice law in any state or nation.

(4) "Representative of the lawyer" is a person engaged by the lawyer to assist the lawyer in the lawyer's rendition of professional legal services.

(5) A communication is "confidential" if it is not intended to be disclosed to persons other than:

(a) Those to whom disclosure is made in furtherance of obtaining or rendering professional legal services for the client.

(b) Those reasonably necessary for the transmission of the communication.

(c) When special circumstances warrant, those who are present at the behest of the client and are reasonably necessary to facilitate the communication.

B. General rule of privilege. A client has a privilege to refuse to disclose, and to prevent another person from disclosing, a confidential communication, whether oral, written, or otherwise, made for the purpose of facilitating the rendition of professional legal services to the client, as well as the perceptions, observations, and the like, of the mental, emotional, or physical condition of the client in connection with such a communication, when the communication is:

(1) Between the client or a representative of the client and the client's lawyer or a representative of the lawyer.

(2) Between the lawyer and a representative of the lawyer.

(3) By the client or his lawyer, or a representative of either, to a lawyer, or representative of a lawyer, who represents another party concerning a matter of common interest.

(4) Between representatives of the client or between the client and a representative of the client.

(5) Among lawyers and their representatives representing the same client.

(6) Between representatives of the client's lawyer.

C. Exceptions. There is no privilege under this Article as to a communication:

(1)(a) If the services of the lawyer were sought or obtained to enable or aid anyone to commit or plan to commit what the client or his representative knew or reasonably should have known to be a crime or fraud.

(b) Made in furtherance of a crime or fraud.

(2) Which was with a client now deceased relevant to an issue between parties who claim through that client, regardless of whether the claims are by testate or intestate succession or by transaction inter vivos.

(3) Which is relevant to an issue of breach of duty by a lawyer to the client or by a client to the client's lawyer.

(4)(a) Which is relevant to an issue of authenticity or capacity concerning a document which the lawyer signed as a witness or notary.

(b) Concerning the testimony of a representative of a lawyer regarding a communication relevant to an issue of authenticity or capacity concerning a document to which the representative is a witness or notary.

(5) Which is relevant to a matter of common interest between or among two or more clients if the communication was made by any of them or their representative to a lawyer or his representative retained or consulted in common, when subsequently offered by one client against the other in a civil action.

(6) Concerning the identity of the lawyer's client or his representative, unless disclosure of the identity by the lawyer or his representative would reveal either the reason for which legal services were sought or a communication which is otherwise privileged under this Article.

D. **Who may claim privilege.** The privilege may be claimed by the client, the client's agent or legal representative, or the successor, trustee, or similar representative of a client that is a corporation, partnership, unincorporated association, or other organization, whether or not in existence. The person who was the lawyer or the lawyer's representative at the time of the communication is presumed to have authority to claim the privilege on behalf of the client, former client, or deceased client.

Art. 507. Subpoena of lawyer or his representative in criminal cases

A. **General rule.** Neither a subpoena nor a court order shall be issued to a lawyer or his representative to appear or testify in any criminal investigation or proceeding where the purpose of the subpoena or order is to ask the lawyer or his representative to reveal information about a client or former client obtained in the course of representing the client unless the court after a contradictory hearing has determined that the information sought is not protected from disclosure by any applicable privilege or work product rule; and all of the following:

(1) The information sought is essential to the successful completion of an ongoing investigation, prosecution, or defense.

(2) The purpose of seeking the information is not to harass the attorney or his client.

(3) With respect to a subpoena, the subpoena lists the information sought with particularity, is reasonably limited as to subject matter and period of time, and gives timely notice.

(4) There is no practicable alternative means of obtaining the information

B. **Waiver.** Failure to object timely to non-compliance with the terms of this Article constitutes a waiver of the procedural protections of this Article, but does not constitute a waiver of any privilege.

C. **Binding effect of determination; notice to client.** The determination that a lawyer-client privilege is not applicable to the testimony shall not bind the client or former client unless the client or former client was given notice of the time, place, and substance of the hearing and had an opportunity fully to participate in that hearing.

D. **Exceptions.** This Article shall not apply in habitual offender proceedings when a lawyer is called as a witness for purposes of identification of his client or former client, or in post-conviction proceedings when a lawyer is called as a witness on the issue of ineffective assistance of the lawyer.

E. The procedural provisions and protections afforded by Paragraph A of this Article shall extend to lawyers serving as prosecutors in state, parish, or municipal courts, whether those functions are exercised in the name of the state of Louisiana or any parish or municipality, and whether the lawyer is the attorney general or assistant attorney general, a district attorney or assistant district attorney, or a parish or municipal prosecutor, and shall extend to lawyers employed by either house of the Louisiana Legislature.

Art. 508. Subpoena of lawyer or his representative in civil cases

A. **General rule.** Neither a subpoena nor a court order shall be issued to a lawyer or his representative to appear or testify in any civil or juvenile proceeding, including pretrial discovery, or in an administrative investigation or hearing, where the purpose of the subpoena or order is to ask the lawyer or his representative to reveal information about a client or former client obtained in the course of representing the client unless, after a contradictory hearing, it has been determined that the information sought is not protected from disclosure by any applicable privilege or work product rule; and all of the following:

(1) The information sought is essential to the successful completion of an ongoing investigation, is essential to the case of the party seeking the information, and is not merely peripheral, cumulative, or speculative.

(2) The purpose of seeking the information is not to harass the attorney or his client.

(3) With respect to a subpoena, the subpoena lists the information sought with particularity, is reasonably limited as to subject matter and period of time, and gives timely notice.

(4) There is no practicable alternative means of obtaining the information.

B. Waiver. Failure to object timely to non-compliance with the terms of this Article constitutes a waiver of the procedural protections of this Article, but does not constitute a waiver of any privilege.

C. Binding effect of determination; notice to client. The determination that a lawyer-client privilege is not applicable to the testimony shall not bind the client or former client unless the client or former client was given notice of the time, place, and substance of the hearing and had an opportunity fully to participate in that hearing.

D. Scope. Nothing in this Article is intended to affect the provisions of Code of Civil Procedure Articles 863 and 1452(B).

E. The procedural provisions and protections afforded by Paragraph A of this Article shall extend to lawyers representing the state or any political subdivision, whether the lawyer is the attorney general or assistant attorney general, a district attorney or assistant district attorney, a parish attorney or assistant parish attorney; or a municipal or city attorney or assistant municipal or assistant city attorney; and shall extend to lawyers employed by either house of the Louisiana Legislature.

Art. 509. Work product rule not affected

Nothing in this Chapter shall be construed as derogating from the protection afforded by the rules relating to work product.

Art. 510. Health care provider-patient privilege

A. Definitions. The definitions of health care provider, physician, psychotherapist, and their representatives as provided in this Article include persons reasonably believed to be such by the patient or his representative. As used in this Article:

(1) (a) "Confidential communication" is the transmittal or acquisition of information not intended to be disclosed to persons other than:

(i) A health care provider and a representative of a health care provider.

(ii) Those reasonably necessary for the transmission of the communication.

(iii) Persons who are participating in the diagnosis and treatment under the direction of the physician or psychotherapist.

(iv) A patient's health care insurer, including any entity that provides indemnification to a patient.

(v) When special circumstances warrant, those who are present at the behest of the patient, physician, or psychotherapist and are reasonably necessary to facilitate the communication.

(b) "Confidential communication" includes any information, substance, or tangible object, obtained incidental to the communication process and any opinion formed as a result of the consultation, examination, or interview and also includes medical and hospital records made by health care providers and their representatives.

(2) "Health care provider" is a person or entity defined as such in R.S. 13:3734(A)(1), and includes a physician and psychotherapist as defined below, and also includes a person who is engaged in any office, center, or institution referred to as a rape crisis center, who has undergone at least forty hours of sexual assault training and who is engaged in rendering advice, counseling, or assistance to victims of sexual assault.

(3) "Health condition" is a physical, mental, or emotional condition, including a condition induced by alcohol, drugs, or other substance.

(4) "Patient" is a person who consults or is examined or interviewed by another for the purpose of receiving advice, diagnosis, or treatment in regard to that person's health.

(5) "Physician" is a person licensed to practice medicine in any state or nation.

(6) "Psychotherapist" is:

(a) A physician engaged in the diagnosis or treatment of a mental or emotional condition, including a condition induced by alcohol, drugs, or other substance.

(b) A person licensed or certified as a psychologist under the laws of any state or nation.

(c) A person licensed as a licensed professional counselor or social worker under the laws of any state or nation.

(7) "Representative" of a physician, psychotherapist, or other health care provider is:

(a) A person acting under the supervision, direction, control, or request of a physician, psychotherapist, or health care provider engaged in the diagnosis or treatment of the patient.

(b) Personnel of a "hospital," as defined in R.S. 13:3734(A)(3), whose duties relate to the health care of patients or to maintenance of patient records.

(8) "Representative of a patient" is any person who makes or receives a confidential communication for the purpose of effectuating diagnosis or treatment of a patient.

B. (1) **General rule of privilege in civil proceedings.** In a non-criminal proceeding, a patient has a privilege to refuse to disclose and to prevent another person from disclosing a confidential communication made for the purpose of advice, diagnosis or treatment of his health condition between or among himself or his representative, his health care provider, or their representatives.

(2) **Exceptions.** There is no privilege under this Article in a noncriminal proceeding as to a communication:

(a) When the communication relates to the health condition of a patient who brings or asserts a personal injury claim in a judicial or worker's compensation proceeding.

(b) When the communication relates to the health condition of a deceased patient in a wrongful death, survivorship, or worker's compensation proceeding brought or asserted as a consequence of the death or injury of the deceased patient.

(c) When the communication is relevant to an issue of the health condition of the patient in any proceeding in which the patient is a party and relies upon the condition as an element of his claim or defense or, after the patient's death, in any proceeding in which a party deriving his right from the patient relies on the patient's health condition as an element of his claim or defense.

(d) When the communication relates to the health condition of a patient when the patient is a party to a proceeding for custody or visitation of a child and the condition has a substantial bearing on the fitness of the person claiming custody or visitation, or when the patient is a child who is the subject of a custody or visitation proceeding.

(e) When the communication made to the health care provider was intended to assist the patient or another person to commit or plan to commit what the patient knew or reasonably should have known to be a crime or fraud.

(f) When the communication is made in the course of an examination ordered by the court with respect to the health condition of a patient, the fact that the examination was so ordered was made known to the patient prior to the communication, and the communication concerns the particular purpose for which the examination was made, unless the court in its order directing the examination has stated otherwise.

(g)(i) When the communication is made by a patient who is the subject of an interdiction or commitment proceeding to his current health care provider when such patient has failed or refused to submit to an examination by a health care provider appointed by the court regarding issues relating to the interdiction or commitment proceeding, provided that the patient has been advised of such appointment and the consequences of not submitting to the examination.

(ii) Notwithstanding the provisions of Subitem (i) of this Item, in any commitment proceeding, the court-appointed physician may review the medical records of the patient or respondent and testify as to communications therein, but only those which are essential to determine whether the patient is dangerous to himself, dangerous to others, or unable to survive safely in freedom or protect himself from serious harm. However, such communications shall not be disclosed unless the patient was informed prior to the communication that such communications are not privileged in any subsequent commitment proceedings. The court-appointed examination shall be governed by Item B(2)(f).

(h) When the communication is relevant in proceedings held by peer review committees and other disciplinary bodies to determine whether a particular health care provider has deviated from applicable professional standards.

(i) When the communication is one regarding the blood alcohol level or other test for the presence of drugs of a patient and an action for damages for injury, death, or loss has been brought against the patient.

(j) When disclosure of the communication is necessary for the defense of the health care provider in a malpractice action brought by the patient.

(k) When the communication is relevant to proceedings concerning issues of child abuse, elder abuse, or the abuse of persons with disabilities or persons who are incompetent.

(l) When the communication is relevant after the death of a patient, concerning the capacity of the patient to enter into the contract which is the subject matter of the litigation.

(m) When the communication is relevant in an action contesting any testament executed or claimed to have been executed by the patient now deceased.

C. (1) **General rule of privilege in criminal proceedings.** In a criminal proceeding, a patient has a privilege to refuse to disclose and to prevent another person from disclosing a confidential communication made for the purpose of advice, diagnosis or treatment of his health condition between or among himself, his representative, and his physician or psychotherapist, and their representatives.

(2) **Exceptions.** There is no privilege under this Article in a criminal case as to a communication:

(a) When the communication is relevant to an issue of the health condition of the accused in any proceeding in which the accused relies upon the condition as an element of his defense.

(b) When the communication was intended to assist the patient or another person to commit or plan to commit what the patient knew or reasonably should have known to be a crime or fraud.

(c) When the communication was made in the course of an examination ordered by the court in a criminal case to determine the health condition of a patient, provided that a copy of the order was served on the patient prior to the communication.

(d) When the communication is a record of the results of a test for blood alcohol level or drugs taken from a patient who is under arrest, or who was subsequently arrested for an offense related to the test.

(e) When the communication is in the form of a tangible object, including a bullet, that is removed from the body of a patient and which was in the body as a result of the crime charged.

(f) When the communication is relevant to an investigation of or prosecution for child abuse, elder abuse, or the abuse of persons with disabilities or persons who are incompetent.

D. **Who may claim the privilege.** In both civil and criminal proceedings, the privilege may be claimed by the patient or by his legal representative. The person who was the physician, psychotherapist, or health care provider or their representatives, at the time of the communication is presumed to have authority to claim the privilege on behalf of the patient or deceased patient.

E. **Waiver.** The exceptions to the privilege set forth in Paragraph B(2) shall constitute a waiver of the privilege only as to testimony at trial or to discovery of the privileged communication by one of the discovery methods authorized by Code of Civil Procedure Article 1421 et seq., or pursuant to R.S. 40:1299.96 or R.S. 13:3715.1

F. **Medical malpractice.** (1) There shall be no health care provider-patient privilege in medical malpractice claims as defined in R.S. 40:1299.41 et seq. as to information directly and specifically related to the factual issues pertaining to the liability of a health care provider who is a named party in a pending lawsuit or medical review panel proceeding.

(2) In medical malpractice claims information about a patient's current treatment or physical condition may only be disclosed pursuant to testimony at trial, pursuant to one of the discovery methods authorized by Code of Civil Procedure Article 1421 et seq., pursuant to R.S. 40:1299.96 or R.S. 13:3715.1.

G. **Sanctions.** Any attorney who violates a provision of this Article shall be subject to sanctions by the court.

Art. 511. Communications to clergymen

A. **Definitions.** As used in this Article:

(1) A "clergyman" is a minister, priest, rabbi, Christian Science practitioner, or other similar functionary of a religious organization, or an individual reasonably believed so to be by the person consulting him.

(2) A communication is "confidential" if it is made privately and not intended for further disclosure except to other persons present in furtherance of the purpose of the communication.

B. **General rule of privilege.** A person has a privilege to refuse to disclose and to prevent another person from disclosing a confidential communication by the person to a clergyman in his professional character as spiritual adviser.

C. **Who may claim the privilege.** The privilege may be claimed by the person or by his legal representative. The clergyman is presumed to have authority to claim the privilege on behalf of the person or deceased person.

Art. 512. Political vote

Every person has a privilege to refuse to disclose the tenor of his vote at a political election conducted by secret ballot unless the vote was cast illegally.

Art. 513. Trade secrets

A person has a privilege, which may be claimed by him or his agent or employee, to refuse to disclose, and to prevent another person from disclosing, a trade secret owned by him, if the allowance of the privilege will not tend to conceal fraud or otherwise work injustice. When disclosure is directed, the judge shall take such protective measure as the interests of the holder of the privilege and of the parties and the furtherance of justice may require.

Art. 514. Identity of informer

A. **General rule of privilege.** The United States, a state, or subdivision thereof has a privilege to refuse to disclose, and to protect another from required disclosure of, the identity of a person who has furnished information in order to assist in an investigation of a possible violation of a criminal law.

B. **Who may claim the privilege.** The privilege may be claimed by the prosecuting authority or an appropriate representative of the public entity to which the information was furnished.

C. **Inapplicability of privilege.** No privilege shall be recognized if:

(1) The informer appears as a witness for the government and testifies with respect to matters previously disclosed in confidence.

(2) The identity of the informer has been disclosed to those who have cause to resent the communication by either the informer or the prosecution, or in a civil case, a person with authority to claim the privilege.

(3) The party seeking to overcome the privilege clearly demonstrates that the interest of the government in preventing disclosure is substantially outweighed by exceptional circumstances such that the informer's testimony is essential to the preparation of the defense or to a fair determination on the issue of guilt or innocence.

(4) In a criminal case, the prosecution objects.

D. **Order to disclose identity.** If the court orders disclosure of the identity of an informer and the prosecution opposes the disclosure, the court:

(1) In a criminal case, shall enter one of the following orders exclusively:

(a) An order suppressing the evidence concerning which the identity of the informer has been ordered.

(b) An order declaring a mistrial.

(2) In a civil case, may make any order justice requires.

Art. 515. Accountant-client privilege

A. **Definitions.** As used in this Article:

(1) "Client" is a person, including a public officer, corporation, partnership, unincorporated association, or other organization or entity, public or private, to whom professional services are rendered by an accountant, or who consults an accountant with a view to obtaining professional services from the accountant.

(2) "Representative of the client" is either of the following:

(a) A person having authority to obtain professional services from an accountant, or to act on advice so obtained, on behalf of the client.

(b) Any other person who makes or receives a confidential communication for the purpose of effectuating representation by an accountant for the client, while acting in the scope of employment for the client.

(3) "Accountant" is the holder of a license issued pursuant to the Louisiana Accountancy Act and shall include all persons and entities within the definition of licensee in R.S. 37:73(8).

(4) "Representative of the accountant" means a person engaged by the accountant to assist the accountant in the accountant's rendition of professional services.

(5) "Confidential communication" is any communication not intended to be disclosed to persons other than:

(a) Those to whom disclosure is made in furtherance of obtaining or rendering professional accounting services for the client.

(b) Those reasonably necessary for the transmission of the communication.

(c) When special circumstances warrant, those who are present at the behest of the client and are reasonably necessary to facilitate the communication.

B. **General rule of privilege.** A client has a privilege to refuse to disclose, and to prevent another person from disclosing, a confidential communication, whether oral, written, or otherwise, made for the purpose of facilitating the rendition of professional accounting services to the client, as well as the perceptions, observations, and the like, of the mental, emotional, or physical condition of the client in connection with such a communication. This privilege includes the protection of other confidential information or material obtained by the accountant from the client for the purpose of rendering professional services. This privilege exists when the communication is:

(1) Between the client or a representative of the client and the client's accountant or a representative of the accountant.

(2) Between the accountant and a representative of the accountant.

(3) By the client or his accountant or a representative of either, to an accountant or lawyer, or representative of an accountant or lawyer, who represents another party concerning a matter of common interest.

(4) Between representatives of the client or between the client and a representative of the client.

(5) Among accountants and their representatives representing the same client.

(6) Between representatives of the client's accountant.

C. **Exceptions.** There is no privilege under this Article as to a communication:

(1)(a) If the services of the accountant were sought or obtained to enable or aid anyone to commit or plan to commit what the client or his representative knew or reasonably should have known to be a crime or fraud.

(b) Made in furtherance of a crime or fraud.

(2) Which was with a client now deceased relevant to an issue between parties who claim through that decedent, regardless of whether the claims are by testate or intestate succession or by transaction inter vivos.

(3) Which is relevant to an issue of breach of duty by an accountant to the client or by a client to the client's accountant.

(4) (a) Which is relevant to an issue of authenticity or capacity concerning a document which the accountant signed as a witness or notary.

(b) Concerning the testimony of a representative of an accountant regarding a communication relevant to an issue of authenticity or capacity concerning a document to which the representative is a witness or notary.

(5) Which is relevant to a matter of common interest between or among two or more clients if the communication was made by any of them or their representative to an accountant or his representative retained or consulted in common, when subsequently offered by one client against the other in a civil action.

(6) Concerning the identity of the accountant's client or his representative, unless disclosure of the identity by the accountant or his representative would reveal either the reason for which accounting services were sought or a communication which is otherwise privileged under this Article.

(7) Concerning information required to be disclosed by the standards of the public accounting profession in reporting on the examination of financial statements whose proceedings are protected from discovery pursuant to R.S. 37:86.

(8) Concerning disclosures in investigations or proceedings of the State Board of Certified Public Accountants of Louisiana pursuant to the provisions of Part I of the Louisiana Accountancy Act whose proceedings are protected from discovery pursuant to R.S. 37:86.

(9) Concerning disclosures in ethical investigations of an accountant conducted by private professional organizations whose proceedings are protected from discovery pursuant to R.S. 37:86 or in the course of quality or peer reviews.

(10) In any domestic proceeding including the partition of community property and the settlement of claims arising from matrimonial regimes, spousal support, and child support.

D. **Who may claim privilege.** The privilege may be claimed by the client, the client's agent or accountant, or the successor, trustee, or similar representative of a client that is a corporation, partnership, unincorporated association, or other organization, whether or not in existence. The person who was the accountant or the accountant's representative at the time of the communication is presumed to have authority to claim the privilege on behalf of the client, former client, or deceased client.

E. **Scope.** Nothing in this Article is intended to affect the absolute privileges against disclosure contained in R.S. 37:86(B) through (E).

Art. 516. Subpoena of accountant or his representative in criminal cases

A. **General rule.** Neither a subpoena nor a court order shall be issued to an accountant or his representative to appear or testify in any criminal investigation or proceeding when the purpose of the subpoena or order is to ask the accountant or his representative to reveal information about a client or former client obtained in the course of representing the client unless the party issuing the subpoena executes and attaches to the subpoena an affidavit that:

(1) The information sought is essential to the successful completion of an ongoing investigation, prosecution, or defense.

(2) The purpose of seeking the information is not to harass the accountant or the client.

(3) With respect to a subpoena, the subpoena lists the information sought with particularity, is reasonably limited as to subject matter and period of time, and gives timely notice.

(4) There is no practicable alternative means of obtaining the information.

B. **Waiver.** Failure to object timely to noncompliance with the terms of this Article constitutes a waiver of the procedural protections of this Article, but does not constitute a waiver of any privilege.

C. **Binding effect of determination; notice to client.** The determination that an accountant-client privilege is not applicable to the testimony shall not bind the client or former client unless the client or former client was given notice of the subpoena.

D. **Exceptions.** This Article shall not apply in habitual offender proceedings when an accountant is called as a witness for purposes of identification of his client or former client.

E. **Scope.** Nothing in this Article is intended to affect the absolute privileges against disclosure contained in R.S. 37:86(B) through (E).

Art. 517. Subpoena of accountant; civil, juvenile, administrative proceedings

A. **General rule.** Neither a subpoena nor a court order shall be issued to an accountant or his representative to appear or testify in any civil or juvenile proceeding, including pretrial discovery, or in an administrative investigation or hearing, except proceedings by the State Board of Accountancy as provided in the Louisiana Accountancy Act, where the purpose of the subpoena or order is to ask the accountant or his representative to reveal information about a client or former client obtained in the course of representing the client unless the court determines, after a contradictory hearing held after service of actual notice to the accountant and the client at least ten days prior to the contradictory hearing, that the information sought is not protected from disclosure by any applicable privilege or work product rule and all of the following apply:

(1) The information sought is essential to the successful completion of an ongoing investigation, is essential to the case of the party seeking the information, and is not merely peripheral, cumulative, or speculative.

(2) The purpose of seeking the information is not to harass the accountant or his client.

(3) With respect to a subpoena, the subpoena lists the information sought with particularity, is reasonably limited as to subject matter and period of time, and gives timely notice.

(4) There is no practicable alternative means of obtaining the information.

B. **Waiver.** Failure to object timely to noncompliance with the terms of this Article constitutes a waiver of the procedural protections of this Article, but does not constitute a waiver of any privilege

C. **Binding effect of determination; notice to client.** The determination that an accountant-client privilege is not applicable to the testimony shall not bind the client or former client unless the client or former client was given notice within the time period set forth in Subsection A of this Section, of the time, place, and substance of the hearing and had an opportunity fully to participate in that hearing.

D. **Scope.** Nothing in this Article is intended to affect the absolute privileges against disclosure in R.S. 37:86(B) through (E).

Art. 518. Trained peer support member privilege

A. (1) A trained peer support member shall not, without consent of the emergency responder making the communication, be compelled to testify about any communication made to the trained peer support member by the emergency responder while receiving peer support services. The trained peer support member shall be designated as such by the emergency service agency or entity, prior to the incident that results in receiving peer support services. The privilege only applies when the communication was made to the trained peer support member.

(2) The privilege does not apply to any of the following if:

(a) The trained peer support member was an initial responding emergency responder, a witness, or a party to the incident which prompted the delivery of peer support services to the emergency responder.

(b) A communication reveals the intended commission of a crime or harmful act and such disclosure is determined to be necessary by the trained peer support member to protect any person from a clear, imminent risk of serious mental or physical harm or injury, or to forestall a serious threat to the public safety.

B. For purposes of this Section, a "trained peer support member" is an emergency responder or civilian volunteer of an emergency service agency or entity, who has received training in Critical Incident Stress Management to provide emotional and moral support to an emergency responder who needs those services as a result of an incident in which the emergency responder was involved while acting in his official capacity.

A "trained peer support member" also includes a volunteer counselor or other mental health services provider who has been designated by the emergency service agency or entity to provide emotional and moral support and counseling to an emergency responder who needs those services as a result of an incident in which the emergency responder was involved while acting in his official capacity.

Art. 519. Subpoena of judge or his representative in civil and criminal cases

A. **General rule.** Neither a subpoena nor a court order shall be issued to a judge or his representative to appear or testify in any civil, criminal, or juvenile proceeding, including pretrial discovery or an administrative hearing, unless, after a contradictory hearing, it has been determined that the information sought is not protected from disclosure by the judicial deliberative process privilege, and all of the following:

(1) The information sought is essential to the case of the party seeking the information and is not merely peripheral, cumulative, or speculative.

(2) The purpose of seeking the information is not to harass the judge, nor for the mere purpose of seeking recusal of the judge.

(3) With respect to a subpoena, the subpoena lists the information sought with particularity, is reasonably limited as to subject matter and period of time, and gives timely notice.

(4) There is no practical alternative means of obtaining the information.

B. **Waiver.** Failure to object timely to a party's non-compliance with the provisions of this Article constitutes a waiver of the procedural protections of this Article, but does not constitute a waiver of any privilege.

C. The procedural provisions of and the protections afforded by Paragraph A of this Article shall extend to any judge of any court provided for by Article V of the Constitution of Louisiana and to any commissioner or special master of such court.

CHAPTER 6. WITNESSES

Art. 601. General rule of competency

Every person of proper understanding is competent to be a witness except as otherwise provided by legislation.

Art. 602. Lack of personal knowledge

A witness may not testify to a matter unless evidence is introduced sufficient to support a finding that he has personal knowledge of the matter. Evidence to prove personal knowledge may, but need not, consist of the testimony of the witness himself. This Article is subject to the provisions of Article 703, relating to opinion testimony by expert witnesses.

Art. 603. Oath or affirmation

Before testifying, every witness shall be required to declare that he will testify truthfully, by oath or affirmation administered in a form calculated to awaken his conscience and impress his mind with his duty to do so.

Art. 604. Interpreters

An interpreter is subject to the provisions of this Code relating to qualification as an expert and the administration of an oath or affirmation that he will make a true translation.

Art. 605. Disqualification of judge as witness

The judge presiding at the trial may not testify in that trial as a witness. No objection need be made in order to preserve the point.

Art. 606. Disqualification of juror as witness

A. **At the trial.** A member of the jury may not testify as a witness before that jury in the trial of the case in which he is sitting as a juror. If he is called so to testify, the opposing party shall be afforded an opportunity to object out of the presence of the jury.

B. **Inquiry into validity of verdict or indictment.** Upon an inquiry into the validity of a verdict or indictment, a juror may not testify as to any matter or statement occurring during the course of the jury's deliberations or to the effect of anything upon his or any other juror's mind or emotions as influencing him to assent to or dissent from the verdict or indictment or concerning his mental processes in connection therewith, except that a juror may testify on the question whether any outside influence was improperly brought to bear upon any juror, and, in criminal cases only, whether extraneous prejudicial information was improperly brought to the jury's attention. Nor may his affidavit or evidence of any statement by him concerning a matter about which he would be precluded from testifying be received for these purposes.

Art. 607. Attacking and supporting credibility generally

A. **Who may attack credibility.** The credibility of a witness may be attacked by any party, including the party calling him.

B. **Time for attacking and supporting credibility.** The credibility of a witness may not be attacked until the witness has been sworn, and the credibility of a witness may not be supported unless it has been attacked. However, a party may question any witness as to his relationship to the parties, interest in the lawsuit, or capacity to perceive or to recollect.

C. **Attacking credibility intrinsically.** Except as otherwise provided by legislation, a party, to attack the credibility of a witness, may examine him concerning any matter having a reasonable tendency to disprove the truthfulness or accuracy of his testimony.

D. **Attacking credibility extrinsically.** Except as otherwise provided by legislation:

(1) Extrinsic evidence to show a witness' bias, interest, corruption, or defect of capacity is admissible to attack the credibility of the witness.

(2) Other extrinsic evidence, including prior inconsistent statements and evidence contradicting the witness' testimony, is admissible when offered solely to attack the credibility of a witness unless the court determines that the probative value of the evidence on the issue of credibility is substantially outweighed by the risks of undue consumption of time, confusion of the issues, or unfair prejudice.

Art. 608. Attacking or supporting credibility by character evidence

A. **Reputation evidence of character.** The credibility of a witness may be attacked or supported by evidence in the form of general reputation only, but subject to these limitations:

(1) The evidence may refer only to character for truthfulness or untruthfulness.

(2) A foundation must first be established that the character witness is familiar with the reputation of the witness whose credibility is in issue. The character witness shall not express his personal opinion as to the character of the witness whose credibility is in issue.

(3) Inquiry into specific acts on direct examination while qualifying the character witness or otherwise is prohibited.

B. **Particular acts, vices, or courses of conduct.** Particular acts, vices, or courses of conduct of a witness may not be inquired into or proved by extrinsic evidence for the purpose of attacking his character for truthfulness, other than conviction of crime as provided in Articles 609 and 609.1 or as constitutionally required.

C. **Cross-examination of character witnesses.** A witness who has testified to the character for truthfulness or untruthfulness of another witness may be cross-examined as to whether he has heard about particular acts of that witness bearing upon his credibility.

Art. 609. Attacking credibility by evidence of conviction of crime in civil cases

A. **General civil rule.** For the purpose of attacking the credibility of a witness in civil cases, no evidence of the details of the crime of which he was convicted is admissible. However, evidence of the name of the crime of which he was convicted and the date of conviction is admissible if the crime:

(1) Was punishable by death or imprisonment in excess of six months under the law under which he was convicted, and the court determines that the probative value of admitting this evidence outweighs its prejudicial effect to a party; or

(2) Involved dishonesty or false statement, regardless of the punishment.

B. **Time limit.** Evidence of a conviction under this Article is not admissible if a period of more than ten years has elapsed since the date of the conviction.

C. **Effect of pardon or annulment.** Evidence of a conviction is not admissible under this Article if the conviction has been the subject of a pardon, annulment, or other equivalent procedure explicitly based on a finding of innocence.

D. **Juvenile adjudications.** Evidence of juvenile adjudications of delinquency is generally not admissible under this Article.

E. **Pendency of appeal.** The pendency of an appeal therefrom does not render evidence of a conviction inadmissible. When evidence of a conviction is admissible, evidence of the pendency of an appeal is also admissible.

F. **Arrest, indictment, or prosecution.** Evidence of the arrest, indictment, or prosecution of a witness is not admissible for the purpose of attacking his credibility.

Art. 609.1. Attacking credibility by evidence of conviction of crime in criminal cases

A. **General criminal rule.** In a criminal case, every witness by testifying subjects himself to examination relative to his criminal convictions, subject to limitations set forth below.

B. **Convictions.** Generally, only offenses for which the witness has been convicted are admissible upon the issue of his credibility, and no inquiry is permitted into matters for which there has only been an arrest, the issuance of an arrest warrant, an indictment, a prosecution, or an acquittal.

C. **Details of convictions.** Ordinarily, only the fact of a conviction, the name of the offense, the date thereof, and the sentence imposed is admissible. However, details of the offense may become admissible to show the true nature of the offense:

(1) When the witness has denied the conviction or denied recollection thereof;

(2) When the witness has testified to exculpatory facts or circumstances surrounding the conviction; or

(3) When the probative value thereof outweighs the danger of unfair prejudice, confusion of the issues, or misleading the jury.

D. **Effect of pending post-conviction relief procedures.** The pendency of an appeal or other post-conviction relief procedures does not render the conviction inadmissible, but may be introduced as bearing upon the weight to be given the evidence of the conviction.

E. **Effect of pardon or annulment.** When a pardon or annulment, based upon a finding of innocence, has been granted, evidence of that conviction is not admissible to attack the credibility of the witness.

F. **Juvenile adjudications.** Evidence of juvenile adjudications of delinquency is generally not admissible under this Article, except for use in proceedings brought pursuant to the habitual offender law, R.S. 15:529.1.

Art. 610. Religious beliefs or opinions

Except as provided in Article 613, evidence of the beliefs or opinions of a witness on matters of religion is not admissible for the sole purpose of showing that by reason of their nature his credibility is impaired or enhanced.

Art. 611. Mode and order of interrogation and presentation

A. **Control by court.** Except as provided by this Article and Code of Criminal Procedure Article 773, the parties to a proceeding have the primary responsibility of presenting the evidence and examining the witnesses. The court, however, shall exercise reasonable control over the mode and order of interrogating witnesses and presenting evidence so as to:

(1) Make the interrogation and presentation effective for the ascertainment of the truth;

(2) Avoid needless consumption of time; and

(3) Protect witnesses from harassment or undue embarrassment.

B. **Scope of cross-examination.** A witness may be cross-examined on any matter relevant to any issue in the case, including credibility. However, in a civil case, when a party or person identified with a party has been called as a witness by an adverse party to testify only as to particular aspects of the case, the court shall limit the scope of cross-examination to matters testified to on direct examination, unless the interests of justice otherwise require.

C. **Leading questions.** Generally, leading questions should not be used on the direct examination of a witness except as may be necessary to develop his testimony and in examining an expert witness on his opinions and inferences. However, when a party calls a hostile witness, a witness who is unable or unwilling to respond to proper questioning, an adverse party, or a witness identified with an adverse party, interrogation may be by leading questions. Generally, leading questions should be permitted on cross-examination. However, the court ordinarily shall prohibit counsel for a party from using leading questions when that party or a person identified with him is examined by his counsel, even when the party or a person identified with him has been called as a witness by another party and tendered for cross-examination.

D. **Scope of redirect examination; recross examination.** A witness who has been cross-examined is subject to redirect examination as to matters covered on cross-examination and, in the discretion of the court, as to other matters in the case. When the court has allowed a party to bring out new matter on redirect, the other parties shall be provided an opportunity to recross on such matters.

E. **Rebuttal evidence.** The plaintiff in a civil case and the state in a criminal prosecution shall have the right to rebut evidence adduced by their opponents.

Art. 612. Writing used to refresh memory

A. **Civil cases.** In a civil case, any writing, recording, or object may be used by a witness to refresh his memory while testifying. If a witness asserts that his memory is refreshed he must then testify from memory independent of the writing, recording, or object. If, before or during testimony, a witness has used or uses a writing, recording, or object to refresh his memory for the purpose of testifying in court, an adverse party is entitled, subject to Paragraph C, to have the writing, recording, or object produced, if practicable, at the hearing, to inspect it, to examine the witness thereon, and to introduce in evidence those portions which relate to the testimony of the witness. If production of the writing, recording, or object at the hearing is impracticable, the court may make any appropriate order, including one for inspection.

B. **Criminal cases.** In a criminal case, any writing, recording, or object may be used by a witness to refresh his memory while testifying. If a witness asserts that his memory is refreshed he must then testify from memory independent of the writing, recording, or object. If while testifying a witness uses a writing, recording, or object to refresh his memory an adverse party is entitled, subject to Paragraph C, to inspect it, to examine the witness thereon, and to introduce in evidence those portions which relate to the testimony of the witness.

C. **Claim of irrelevance.** If it is claimed that a writing or recording contains matters not related to the subject matter of the testimony the court shall examine it in camera, excise any portions not so related, and order delivery of the remainder to the party entitled thereto. Any portion withheld over objections shall be preserved and made available to the appellate court in the event of an appeal.

D. **Failure to produce.** If a writing, recording, or object is not produced or delivered pursuant to an order under this Article, the court shall make any order justice requires, except that in criminal cases when the prosecution elects not to comply, the order shall only be one excluding the testimony or, if the court in its discretion determines that the interests of justice so require, declaring a mistrial.

Art. 613. Foundation for extrinsic attack on credibility

Except as the interests of justice otherwise require, extrinsic evidence of bias, interest, or corruption, prior inconsistent statements, conviction of crime, or defects of capacity is admissible after the proponent has first fairly directed the witness' attention to the statement, act, or matter alleged, and the witness has been given the opportunity to admit the fact and has failed distinctly to do so.

Art. 614. Calling and questioning of witnesses by court

A. **Calling by court.** The court, at the request of a party or if otherwise authorized by legislation, may call witnesses, and all parties are entitled to examine witnesses thus called.

B. **Questioning by court.** The court may question witnesses, whether called by itself or by a party.

C. **Objections.** Objections to the calling of witnesses by the court or to questioning of witnesses by it may be made at the time or at the next available opportunity when the jury is not present.

D. **Exception.** In a jury trial, the court may not call or examine a witness, except upon the express consent of all parties, which consent shall not be requested within the hearing of the jury.

Art. 615. Exclusion of witnesses

A. **As a matter of right.** On its own motion the court may, and on request of a party the court shall, order that the witnesses be excluded from the courtroom or from a place where they can see or hear the proceedings, and refrain from discussing the facts of the case with anyone other than counsel in the case. In the interests of justice, the court may exempt any witness from its order of exclusion.

B. **Exceptions.** This Article does not authorize exclusion of any of the following:

(1) A party who is a natural person.

(2) A single officer or single employee of a party which is not a natural person designated as its representative or case agent by its attorney.

(3) A person whose presence is shown by a party to be essential to the presentation of his cause such as an expert.

(4) The victim of the offense or the family of the victim.

C. **Violation of exclusion order.** A court may impose appropriate sanctions for violations of its exclusion order including contempt, appropriate instructions to the jury, or when such sanctions are insufficient, disqualification of the witness.

CHAPTER 7. OPINIONS AND EXPERT TESTIMONY

Art. 701. Opinion testimony by lay witnesses

If the witness is not testifying as an expert, his testimony in the form of opinions or inferences is limited to those opinions or inferences which are:

(1) Rationally based on the perception of the witness; and

(2) Helpful to a clear understanding of his testimony or the determination of a fact in issue.

Art. 702. Testimony by experts

A witness who is qualified as an expert by knowledge, skill, experience, training, or education may testify in the form of an opinion or otherwise if:

(1) The expert's scientific, technical, or other specialized knowledge will help the trier of fact to understand the evidence or to determine a fact in issue;

(2) The testimony is based on sufficient facts or data;

(3) The testimony is the product of reliable principles and methods; and

(4) The expert has reliably applied the principles and methods to the facts of the case.

Art. 703. Bases of opinion testimony by experts

The facts or data in the particular case upon which an expert bases an opinion or inference may be those perceived by or made known to him at or before the hearing. If of a type reasonably relied upon by experts in the particular field in forming opinions or inferences upon the subject, the facts or data need not be admissible in evidence.

Art. 704. Opinion on ultimate issue

Testimony in the form of an opinion or inference otherwise admissible is not to be excluded solely because it embraces an ultimate issue to be decided by the trier of fact. However, in a criminal case, an expert witness shall not express an opinion as to the guilt or innocence of the accused.

Art. 705. Disclosure of facts or data underlying expert opinion; foundation

A. **Civil cases.** In a civil case, the expert may testify in terms of opinion or inference and give his reasons therefor without prior disclosure of the underlying facts or data, unless the court requires otherwise. The expert may in any event be required to disclose the underlying facts or data on cross-examination.

B. **Criminal cases.** In a criminal case, every expert witness must state the facts upon which his opinion is based, provided, however, that with respect to evidence which would otherwise be inadmissible such basis shall only be elicited on cross-examination.

Art. 706. Court appointed experts

A. **Civil cases.** In a civil case, the court may on its own motion or on the motion of any party enter an order to show cause why expert witnesses should not be appointed, and may request the parties to submit nominations. The court may appoint any expert witnesses agreed upon by the parties, and may appoint expert witnesses of its own selection. An expert witness shall not be appointed by the court unless he consents to act. A witness so appointed shall be informed of his duties by the court in writing, a copy of which shall be filed with the clerk, or at a conference in which the parties shall have opportunity to participate. A witness so appointed shall advise the parties of his findings, if any; his deposition may be taken by any party; and he may be called to testify by the court or any party.

B. **Disclosure of appointment.** In a civil case, in the exercise of its discretion, the court may authorize disclosure to the jury of the fact that the court appointed the expert witness.

C. **Parties' experts of own selection.** Nothing in this Article limits the parties in calling expert witnesses of their own selection.

D. **Criminal cases.** In a criminal case, the court may appoint an expert witness only when specifically authorized by statute, or as constitutionally required.

CHAPTER 8. HEARSAY

Art. 801. Definitions

The following definitions apply under this Chapter:

A. **Statement.** A "statement" is:

(1) An oral or written assertion; or

(2) Nonverbal conduct of a person, if it is intended by him as an assertion.

B. **Declarant.** A "declarant" is a person who makes a statement.

C. **Hearsay.** "Hearsay" is a statement, other than one made by the declarant while testifying at the present trial or hearing, offered in evidence to prove the truth of the matter asserted.

D. **Statements which are not hearsay.** A statement is not hearsay if:

(1) **Prior statement by witness.** The declarant testifies at the trial or hearing and is subject to cross-examination concerning the statement, and the statement is:

(a) In a criminal case, inconsistent with his testimony, provided that the proponent has first fairly directed the witness' attention to the statement and the witness has been given the opportunity to admit the fact and where there exists any additional evidence to corroborate the matter asserted by the prior inconsistent statement;

(b) Consistent with his testimony and is offered to rebut an express or implied charge against him of recent fabrication or improper influence or motive;

(c) One of identification of a person made after perceiving the person; or

(d) Consistent with the declarant's testimony and is one of initial complaint of sexually assaultive behavior.

(2) **Personal, adoptive, and authorized admissions.** The statement is offered against a party and is:

(a) His own statement, in either his individual or a representative capacity;

(b) A statement of which he has manifested his adoption or belief in its truth; or

(c) A statement by a person authorized by him to make a statement concerning the subject.

(3) **Relational and privity admissions.** The statement is offered against a party, and the statement is:

(a) A statement by an agent or employee of the party against whom it is offered, concerning a matter within the scope of his agency or employment, made during the existence of the relationship;

(b) A statement by a declarant while participating in a conspiracy to commit a crime or civil wrong and in furtherance of the objective of the conspiracy, provided that a prima facie case of conspiracy is established;

(c) In a civil case, a statement by a declarant when the liability, obligation, or duty of the party against whom it is offered is derivatively based in whole or in part upon a liability, obligation, or duty of the declarant, or when the claim or right asserted by that party is barred or diminished by a breach of duty by the declarant, and when the statement would be admissible if offered against the declarant as a party in an action involving that liability, obligation, or breach of duty;

(d) In a civil case, a statement by a declarant when a right, title, or interest in any property or claim asserted by the party against whom it is offered requires a determination that a right, title, or interest exists or existed in the declarant during the time that that party now claims the declarant was the holder of the right, title, or interest, and when the statement would be admissible if offered against the declarant as a party in an action involving that right, title, or interest;

(e) A statement by a declarant offered against the party in an action for damages arising from the death of that declarant; or

(f) A statement by a minor child offered against a party in an action to recover for injury to that child, or against the person responsible for the child in an action to recover damages for losses caused by the child.

(4) **Things said or done.** The statements are events speaking for themselves under the immediate pressure of the occurrence, through the instructive, impulsive and

spontaneous words and acts of the participants, and not the words of the participants when narrating the events, and which are necessary incidents of the criminal act, or immediate concomitants of it, or form in conjunction with it one continuous transaction.

E. **Optical Disk Imaging System.** "Optical disk imaging system" means a storage system that utilizes non-erasable Write Once Read Many (WORM) optical storage technology to record information on an optical disk with the use of laser technology, and that utilizes laser technology to retrieve and read previously stored information.

Art. 802. Hearsay rule

Hearsay is not admissible except as otherwise provided by this Code or other legislation.

Art. 803. Hearsay exceptions; availability of declarant immaterial

The following are not excluded by the hearsay rule, even though the declarant is available as a witness:

(1) **Present sense impression.** A statement describing or explaining an event or condition made while the declarant was perceiving the event or condition, or immediately thereafter.

(2) **Excited utterance.** A statement relating to a startling event or condition made while the declarant was under the stress of excitement caused by the event or condition.

(3) **Then existing mental, emotional, or physical condition.** A statement of the declarant's then existing state of mind, emotion, sensation, or physical condition (such as intent, plan, motive, design, mental feeling, pain, and bodily health), offered to prove the declarant's then existing condition or his future action. A statement of memory or belief, however, is not admissible to prove the fact remembered or believed unless it relates to the execution, revocation, identification, or terms of declarant's testament.

(4) **Statements for purposes of medical treatment and medical diagnosis in connection with treatment.** Statements made for purposes of medical treatment and medical diagnosis in connection with treatment and describing medical history, or past or present symptoms, pain, or sensations, or the inception or general character of the cause or external source thereof insofar as reasonably pertinent to treatment or diagnosis in connection with treatment.

(5) **Recorded recollection.** A memorandum or record concerning a matter about which a witness once had knowledge but now has insufficient recollection to enable him to testify fully and accurately, shown to have been made or adopted by the witness when the matter was fresh in his memory and to reflect that knowledge correctly. If admitted, the memorandum or record may be read into evidence and received as an exhibit but may not itself be taken into the jury room. This exception is subject to the provisions of Article 612.

(6) **Records of regularly conducted business activity.** A memorandum, report, record, or data compilation, in any form, including but not limited to that which is stored by the use of an optical disk imaging system, of acts, events, conditions, opinions, or diagnoses, made at or near the time by, or from information transmitted by, a person with knowledge, if made and kept in the course of a regularly conducted business activity, and if it was the regular practice of that business activity to make

and to keep the memorandum, report, record, or data compilation, all as shown by the testimony of the custodian or other qualified witness, unless the source of information or the method or circumstances of preparation indicate lack of trustworthiness. This exception is inapplicable unless the recorded information was furnished to the business either by a person who was routinely acting for the business in reporting the information or in circumstances under which the statement would not be excluded by the hearsay rule. The term "business" as used in this Paragraph includes business, institution, association, profession, occupation, and calling of every kind, whether or not conducted for profit. Public records and reports which are specifically excluded from the public records exception by Article 803(8)(b) shall not qualify as an exception to the hearsay rule under this Paragraph.

(7) **Absence of entry in records of regularly conducted business activity.** Evidence that a matter is not included in the memoranda, reports, records, or data compilations, in any form, kept in accordance with the provisions of Paragraph (6), to prove the nonoccurrence or nonexistence of the matter, if the matter was of a kind of which a memorandum, report, record, or data compilation was regularly made and preserved unless the sources of information or other circumstances indicate lack of trustworthiness.

(8) **Public records and reports.**

(a) Records, reports, statements, or data compilations, in any form, of a public office or agency setting forth:

(i) Its regularly conducted and regularly recorded activities;

(ii) Matters observed pursuant to duty imposed by law and as to which there was a duty to report; or

(iii) Factual findings resulting from an investigation made pursuant to authority granted by law. Factual findings are conclusions of fact reached by a governmental agency and may be based upon information furnished to it by persons other than agents and employees of that agency.

(b) Except as specifically provided otherwise by legislation, the following are excluded from this exception to the hearsay rule:

(i) Investigative reports by police and other law enforcement personnel.

(ii) Investigative reports prepared by or for any government, public office, or public agency when offered by that or any other government, public office, or public agency in a case in which it is a party.

(iii) Factual findings offered by the prosecution in a criminal case.

(iv) Factual findings resulting from investigation of a particular complaint, case, or incident, including an investigation into the facts and circumstances on which the present proceeding is based or an investigation into a similar occurrence or occurrences.

(9) **Records of vital statistics.** Records or data compilations, in any form, of birth, filiation, adoption, or death, including fetal death, still birth, and abortion, or of marital status, including divorce and annulment, if the report thereof was made to a public office pursuant to requirements of law, and any record included within the Louisiana Vital Statistics Laws.

(10) **Absence of public record or entry.** To prove the absence of a record, report, statement, or data compilation, in any form, or the nonoccurrence or nonexistence

of a matter of which a record, report, statement, or data compilation, in any form, was regularly made and preserved by a public office or agency, evidence in the form of a certification in accordance with Article 902, or testimony, that diligent search failed to disclose the record, report, statement, or data compilation, or entry.

(11) **Records of religious organizations.** Statements of births, marriages, divorces, deaths, filiation, ancestry, relationship by blood or marriage, or other similar facts of personal or family history, contained in a regularly kept record of a religious organization.

(12) **Marriage, baptismal, and similar certificates.** Statements of fact contained in a certificate that the maker performed a marriage or other ceremony or administered a sacrament, made by a clergyman, public official, or other person authorized by the rules or practices of a religious organization or by law to perform the act certified, and purporting to have been issued at the time of the act or within a reasonable time thereafter.

(13) **Family records.** Statements of fact concerning personal or family history contained in family Bibles, genealogies, charts, engravings on rings, inscriptions on family portraits, engravings on urns, crypts, or tombstones, or the like.

(14) **Records of documents affecting an interest in property.** Records of documents purporting to establish or affect an interest in property to the extent that their admission is authorized by other legislation.

(15) **Statements in documents affecting an interest in property.** A statement contained in a document purporting to establish or affect an interest in property if the matter stated was relevant to the purpose of the document, unless dealings with the property since the document was made have been inconsistent with the truth of the statement or the purport of the document.

(16) **Statements in ancient documents.** Statements in a document in existence thirty years or more the authenticity of which is established, or statements in a recorded document as provided by other legislation.

(17) **Market reports, commercial publications.** Market quotations, tabulations, lists, directories, or other published compilations, generally used and relied upon by the public or by persons in particular occupations.

(18) **Learned treatises.** To the extent called to the attention of an expert witness upon cross-examination or, in a civil case, relied upon by him in direct examination, statements contained in published treatises, periodicals, or pamphlets on a subject of history, medicine, or other science or art, established as a reliable authority by the testimony or admission of the witness or by other expert testimony or by judicial notice. If admitted, such a statement may be read into evidence and received as an exhibit but may not be taken into the jury room.

(19) **Reputation concerning personal or family history.** Reputation, arising before the controversy, among members of his family by blood, adoption, or marriage, or among his associates, or in the community, concerning a person's birth, adoption, marriage, divorce, death, filiation, relationship by blood, adoption, or marriage, ancestry, or other similar fact of his personal or family history.

(20) **Reputation concerning boundaries or general history.** Reputation in a community, arising before the controversy, as to boundaries of or customs affecting lands in

the community, and reputation as to events of general history important to the community or state or nation in which located.

(21) **Reputation as to character.** Reputation of a person's character among his associates or in the community.

(22) **Judgment of previous conviction.** Evidence of a final judgment, entered after a trial or upon a plea of guilty (but not upon a plea of nolo contendere), adjudging a person guilty of a crime punishable by death or imprisonment in excess of six months, to prove any fact essential to sustain the judgment. This exception does not permit the prosecutor in a criminal prosecution to offer as evidence the judgment of conviction of a person other than the accused, except for the purpose of attacking the credibility of a witness. The pendency of an appeal may be shown but does not affect admissibility.

(23) **Judgment as to personal, family, or general history, or boundaries.** Judgments as proof of matters of personal, family, or general history, or boundaries, essential to the judgment, if the same would be provable by evidence of reputation.

(24) **Testimony as to age.** A witness' testimony as to his own age.

Art. 803.1. Hearsay exceptions; foreign records of regularly conducted activity

A. (1) Except as otherwise provided by this Code, in a criminal proceeding, a foreign record of regularly conducted activity, or a copy of such record, shall not be excluded as evidence by the hearsay rule if a foreign certification attests to the following:

(a) Such record was made, at or near the time of the occurrence of the matters set forth, by or from information transmitted by, a person with knowledge of those matters; and

(b) Such record was kept in the course of a regularly conducted business activity; and

(c) The business activity made such a record as a regular practice; and

(d) If such record is not the original, such record is a duplicate of the original, unless the source of information or the method or circumstances of preparation indicate lack of trustworthiness.

(2) A party intending to offer in evidence pursuant to this Article a foreign record of regularly conducted activity shall provide written notice of that intention to each other party not less than ten days prior to trial. A motion opposing admission in evidence of such record shall be made by the opposing party and determined by the court before trial. Failure by a party to file such motion before trial shall constitute a waiver of objection to such record or duplicate, but the court for cause shown may grant relief from the waiver.

B. As used in this Article:

(1) "Foreign record of regularly conducted activity" means a memorandum, report, record, or data compilation, in any form, of acts, events, conditions, opinions, or diagnoses, maintained by a business domiciled in a jurisdiction outside the territorial limits of the state of Louisiana.

(2) "Foreign certification" means a written declaration made and signed in a jurisdiction outside the territorial limits of the state of Louisiana by the custodian of a business record of regularly conducted activity or another qualified person that, if falsely made, would subject the maker to criminal penalty under the laws of the state of Louisiana.

(3) "Business" includes a business, institution, association, profession, occupation, and calling of every kind, whether or not conducted for profit.

Art. 804. Hearsay exceptions; declarant unavailable

A. **Definition of unavailability.** Except as otherwise provided by this Code, a declarant is "unavailable as a witness" when the declarant cannot or will not appear in court and testify to the substance of his statement made outside of court. This includes situations in which the declarant:

(1) Is exempted by ruling of the court on the ground of privilege from testifying concerning the subject matter of his statement;

(2) Persists in refusing to testify concerning the subject matter of his statement despite an order of the court to do so;

(3) Testifies to a lack of memory of the subject matter of his statement;

(4) Is unable to be present or to testify at the hearing because of death or then existing physical or mental illness, infirmity, or other sufficient cause; o

(5) Is absent from the hearing and the proponent of his statement has been unable to procure his attendance by process or other reasonable means. A declarant is not unavailable as a witness if his exemption, refusal, claim of lack of memory, inability, or absence is due to the procurement or wrong-doing of the proponent of his statement for the purpose of preventing the witness from attending or testifying.

B. **Hearsay exceptions.** The following are not excluded by the hearsay rule if the declarant is unavailable as a witness:

(1) **Former testimony.** Testimony given as a witness at another hearing of the same or a different proceeding, if the party against whom the testimony is now offered, or, in a civil action or proceeding, a party with a similar interest, had an opportunity and similar motive to develop the testimony by direct, cross, or redirect examination. Testimony given in another proceeding by an expert witness in the form of opinions or inferences, however, is not admissible under this exception.

(2) **Statement under belief of impending death.** A statement made by a declarant while believing that his death was imminent, concerning the cause or circumstances of what he believed to be his impending death.

(3) **Statement against interest.** A statement which was at the time of its making so far contrary to the declarant's pecuniary or proprietary interest, or so far tended to subject him to civil or criminal liability, or to render invalid a claim by him against another, that a reasonable man in his position would not have made the statement unless he believed it to be true. A statement tending to expose the declarant to criminal liability and offered to exculpate the accused is not admissible unless corroborating circumstances clearly indicate the trustworthiness of the statement.

(4) **Statement of personal or family history.** (a) A statement, made before the controversy, concerning the declarant's own birth, adoption, marriage, divorce, filiation, relationship by blood, adoption, or marriage, ancestry, or other similar fact of personal or family history, even though declarant had no means of acquiring personal knowledge of the matter stated; or

(b) A statement, made before the controversy, concerning the foregoing matters, and death also, of another person, if the declarant was related to the other by blood, adoption, or marriage or was so intimately associated with the other's family as to be likely to have accurate information concerning the matter declared.

(5) **Complaint of sexually assaultive behavior.** A statement made by a person under the age of twelve years and the statement is one of initial or otherwise trustworthy complaint of sexually assaultive behavior.

(6) **Other exceptions.** In a civil case, a statement not specifically covered by any of the foregoing exceptions if the court determines that considering all pertinent circumstances in the particular case the statement is trustworthy, and the proponent of the evidence has adduced or made a reasonable effort to adduce all other admissible evidence to establish the fact to which the proffered statement relates and the proponent of the statement makes known in writing to the adverse party and to the court his intention to offer the statement and the particulars of it, including the name and address of the declarant, sufficiently in advance of the trial or hearing to provide the adverse party with a fair opportunity to prepare to meet it. If, under the circumstances of a particular case, giving of this notice was not practicable or failure to give notice is found by the court to have been excusable, the court may authorize a delayed notice to be given, and in that event the opposing party is entitled to a recess, continuance, or other appropriate relief sufficient to enable him to prepare to meet the evidence.

(7) (a) **Forfeiture by wrongdoing.** A statement offered against a party that has engaged or acquiesced in wrongdoing that was intended to, and did, procure the unavailability of the declarant as a witness.

(b) A party seeking to introduce statements under the forfeiture by wrongdoing hearsay exception shall establish, by a preponderance of the evidence, that the party against whom the statement is offered, engaged or acquiesced in the wrongdoing.

Art. 805. Hearsay within hearsay

Hearsay included within hearsay is not excluded under the hearsay rule if each part of the combined statements conforms with an exception to the hearsay rule provided by legislation.

Art. 806. Attacking and supporting credibility of declarant

When a hearsay statement, or a statement defined in Article 801(D)(2)(c) or (D)(3), has been admitted in evidence, the credibility of the declarant may be attacked, and if attacked may be supported, by any evidence which would be admissible for those purposes if declarant had testified as a witness. Evidence of a statement or conduct by the declarant at any time, offered to attack the declarant's credibility, is not subject to any requirement that he may have been afforded an opportunity to deny or explain. If the party against whom a hearsay statement has been admitted calls the declarant as a witness, the party is entitled to examine him on the statement as a witness identified with an adverse party.

CHAPTER 9. AUTHENTICATION AND IDENTIFICATION

Art. 901. Requirement of authentication or identification

A. **General provision.** The requirement of authentication or identification as a condition precedent to admissibility is satisfied by evidence sufficient to support a finding that the matter in question is what its proponent claims.

B. **Illustrations.** By way of illustration only, and not by way of limitation, the following are examples of authentication or identification conforming with the requirements of this Article:

(1) **Testimony of witness with knowledge.** Testimony that a matter is what it is claimed to be.

(2) **Nonexpert opinion on handwriting.** Nonexpert opinion as to the genuineness of handwriting, based upon familiarity not acquired for purposes of the litigation.

(3) **Comparison by trier or expert witness.** Comparison by the trier of fact or by expert witnesses with specimens which have been authenticated.

(4) **Distinctive characteristics and the like.** Appearance, contents, substance, internal patterns, or other distinctive characteristics, taken in conjunction with circumstances.

(5) **Voice identification.** Identification of a voice, whether heard firsthand or through mechanical or electronic transmission or recording, by opinion based upon hearing the voice at any time under circumstances connecting it with the alleged speaker.

(6) **Telephone conversations.** Telephone conversations, by evidence that a call was made to the number assigned at the time by the telephone company to a particular person or business, if:

(a) In the case of a person, circumstances, including self-identification, show the person answering to be the one called; or

(b) In the case of a business, the call was made to a place of business and the conversation related to business reasonably transacted over the telephone.

(7) **Public records or reports.** Evidence that a writing authorized by law to be recorded or filed and in fact recorded or filed in a public office, or a purported public record, report, statement, or data compilation, in any form, is from the public office where items of this nature are kept.

(8) **Ancient documents or data compilation.** Evidence that a document or data compilation, in any form:

(a) Is in such condition as to create no suspicion concerning its authenticity;

(b) Was in a place where it, if authentic, would likely be; and

(c) Has been in existence thirty years or more at the time it is offered.

(9) **Process or system.** Evidence describing a process or system used to produce a result and showing that the process or system produces an accurate result.

(10) **Methods provided by legislation.** Any method of authentication or identification provided by Act of Congress or by Act of the Louisiana Legislature.

Art. 902. Self-authentication

Extrinsic evidence of authenticity as a condition precedent to admissibility is not required with respect to the following

(1) **Domestic public documents under seal.** A document bearing a seal purporting to be that of the United States, or of any state, district, commonwealth, territory, or insular possession thereof, or the Panama Canal Zone, or the Trust Territory of the Pacific Islands, or of a political subdivision, department, officer, or agency thereof, and a signature purporting to be an attestation or execution.

(2) **Domestic public documents not under seal.**

(a) **Domestic public documents generally.** A document purporting to bear the signature in his official capacity of an officer or employee of any entity included in Paragraph (1) hereof, having no seal, if a public officer having a seal and having official duties in the district or political subdivision of the officer or employee certifies under seal that the signer has the official capacity and that the signature is genuine.

(b) **Certified Louisiana public documents.** A purported record, book, paper, or other document of the State of Louisiana, or of a department, board, or agency thereof or of a political subdivision of the state or a department, board, or agency of such a subdivision when certified as being the original by an officer or employee who identifies his official position and who either has custody of the document or who is otherwise authorized to make such a certification.

(3) **Foreign public documents.** A document purporting to be executed or attested in his official capacity by a person authorized by the laws of a foreign country to make the execution or attestation, and accompanied by a final certification as to the genuineness of the signature and official position (a) of the executing or attesting person, or (b) of any foreign official whose certificate of genuineness of signature and official position relates to the execution or attestation or is in a chain of certificates of genuineness of signature and official position relating to the execution or attestation. A final certification may be made by a secretary of embassy or legation, consul general, consul, vice consul, or consular agent of the United States, or a diplomatic or consular official of the foreign country assigned or accredited to the United States. If reasonable opportunity has been given to all parties to investigate the authenticity and accuracy of official documents, the court may, for good cause shown, order that they be treated as presumptively authentic without final certification or permit them to be evidenced by an attested summary with or without final certification.

(4) **Presumptions under Acts of Congress and the Louisiana Legislature.** Any signature, document, or other matter declared by Act of Congress or by Act of the Louisiana Legislature to be presumptively or prima facie genuine or authentic.

(5) **Official publications.** Books, pamphlets, or other publications purporting to be issued by public authority.

(6) **Newspapers and periodicals.** Printed materials purporting to be newspapers or periodicals.

(7) **Trade inscriptions and the like.** Inscriptions, signs, tags, or labels purporting to have been affixed in the course of business and indicating ownership, control, or origin.

(8) **Authentic acts, acknowledged acts, and other instruments attested by witnesses.** (a) Authentic acts, acts under private signature duly acknowledged, and instruments attested by witnesses and accompanied by affidavits, as provided by Louisiana law, whether executed in Louisiana or elsewhere. (b) Documents executed in a jurisdiction other than Louisiana accompanied by a certificate of acknowledgment executed in the manner provided by the laws of that jurisdiction by a notary public or other officer authorized by law to take acknowledgments.

(9) **Commercial paper and related documents.** Commercial paper, signatures thereon, and documents relating thereto to the extent provided by general commercial law.

(10) **Labor reports.** A copy of a report from the Department of Labor, or from any state or federal reporting agency, which is in the possession of a field officer of the

support enforcement services program, office of family support, Department of Social Services, introduced as evidence in any child or spousal support proceeding. "Field officer" means any person designated or authorized as a field officer pursuant to the provisions of R.S. 46:236.1(K).

Art. 903. Subscribing witness' testimony unnecessary

The testimony of a subscribing witness is not necessary to authenticate a writing unless required by the laws of the jurisdiction whose laws govern the validity of the writing.

Art. 904. Self-authentication of copies of public documents

When an original public document is deemed authentic without proof by extrinsic evidence as provided in Article 902(1), (2), or (3), a purported copy of the document also shall be deemed authentic when certified as true or correct by the custodian or other person authorized to make that certification, by certificate complying with Article 902(1), (2), or (3).

Art. 905. Self-authentication of other public records

A. **Self-authentication.** Extrinsic evidence of authenticity as a condition precedent to admissibility is not required with respect to a document purporting to be a document authorized by law to be recorded or filed and actually recorded or filed in a public office, including data compilations in any form, when it is certified as being true or correct by the custodian or other person authorized to make the certification, by certificate complying with Article 902(1), (2), or (3) and when, by statute, it is made to be presumptively or prima facie genuine or authentic.

B. **Copy of original document described in Paragraph A.** A document which purports to be a copy of an original document described in Paragraph A shall be deemed as authentic as the original when certified as true or correct by the custodian or other person authorized to make the certification, by certificate complying with Article 902(1), (2), or (3).

C. **Copy of other public records.** A document which purports to be a copy of an original document, other than a document described in Paragraph A, which is recorded or filed in a public office, including a data compilation in any form, shall be prima facie evidence that the copy accurately reflects the contents of the document which is filed or recorded when the copy is certified as true or correct by the custodian or other person authorized to make the certification, by certificate complying with Article 902(1), (2), or (3).

CHAPTER 10. CONTENTS OF WRITINGS, RECORDINGS, AND PHOTOGRAPHS

Art. 1001. Definitions

For purposes of this Chapter the following definitions are applicable:

(1) **Writings and recordings.** "Writings" and "recordings" consist of letters, words, numbers, sounds, or their equivalent, set down by handwriting, typewriting, printing, photostating, photographing, magnetic impulse, mechanical or electronic recording, or other form of data compilation.

(2) **Photographs.** "Photographs" include still photographs, X-ray films, video tapes, motion pictures, and their equivalents.

(3) **Original.** An "original" of a writing or recording is the writing or recording itself or any counterpart intended to have the same effect by a person executing or issuing it. An "original" of a photograph includes the negative or any print therefrom. If data are stored in or copied onto a computer or similar device, including any portable or hand-held computer or electronic storage device, any printout or other output readable by sight, shown to reflect the data accurately, is an "original".

(4) **Optical disk imaging system.** An "optical disk imaging system" is a storage system that utilizes non-erasable Write Once Read Many (WORM) optical storage technology to record information on an optical disk with the use of laser technology, and that utilizes laser technology to retrieve and read previously stored information.

(5) **Duplicate.** A "duplicate" is a counterpart produced by the same impression as the original, or from the same matrix, or by means of photography, including enlargements and miniatures, or by mechanical or electronic re-recording, or electronic imaging, or by chemical reproduction, or by an optical disk imaging system, or by other equivalent techniques, which accurately reproduces the original.

(6) **Electronic imaging.** "Electronic imaging" is the process of storing and retrieving any record, document, data, or other information through the use of electronic data processing, or computerized, digital, or optical scanning, or other electronic imaging system.

Art. 1002. Requirement of original

To prove the content of a writing, recording, or photograph, the original writing, recording, or photograph is required, except as otherwise provided by this Code or other legislation.

Art. 1003. Admissibility of duplicates

A duplicate is admissible to the same extent as an original unless:

(1) A genuine question is raised as to the authenticity of the original;

(2) In the circumstances it would be unfair to admit the duplicate in lieu of the original; or

(3) The original is a testament offered for probate, a contract on which the claim or defense is based, or is otherwise closely related to a controlling issue.

Art. 1003.1. Electronic duplicates

A duplicate may not be deemed inadmissible or excluded from evidence solely because it is in electronic form or is a reproduction of electronically imaged or stored records, documents, data, or other information.

Art. 1004. Admissibility of other evidence of contents

The original is not required, and other evidence of the contents of a writing, recording, or photograph is admissible if:

(1) **Originals lost or destroyed.** All originals are lost or have been destroyed, unless the proponent lost or destroyed them in bad faith;

(2) **Original not obtainable.** No original can be obtained by any available judicial process or procedure;

(3) **Original in possession of opponent.** At a time when an original was under the control of the party against whom offered, he was put on notice, by the pleadings or otherwise, that the contents would be a subject of proof at the hearing, and he does not produce the original at the hearing;

(4) **Collateral matters.** The writing, recording, or photograph is not closely related to a controlling issue; or

(5) **Impracticality of producing original.** The original, because of its location, permanent fixture, or otherwise, cannot as a practical matter be produced in court; or the cost or other consideration to be incurred in securing the original is prohibitive and it appears that a copy will serve the evidentiary purpose.

Art. 1005. Public records

The contents of an official record, or of a document authorized to be recorded or filed and actually recorded or filed, including data compilations in any form, if otherwise admissible, may be proved by copy, certified as correct in accordance with Article 902 or testified to be correct by a witness who has compared it with the original. If a copy which complies with the foregoing cannot be obtained by the exercise of reasonable diligence, then other evidence of the contents may be given.

Art. 1006. Summaries

The contents of otherwise admissible voluminous writings, recordings, or photographs which cannot conveniently be examined in court may be presented in the form of a chart, summary, or calculation. The originals, or duplicates, shall be made available for examination or copying, or both, by other parties at a reasonable time and place. The court may order that they be produced in court.

Art. 1007. Testimony or written admission of party

Contents of writings, recordings, or photographs may be proved by the testimony or, in a civil case, deposition of the party against whom offered or by his written admission, without accounting for the nonproduction of the original.

Art. 1008. Functions of court and jury

When the admissibility of other evidence of contents of writings, recordings, or photographs under these articles depends upon the fulfillment of a condition of fact, the question whether the condition has been fulfilled is ordinarily for the court to determine in accordance with the provisions of Article 104. However, when an issue is raised (1) whether the asserted writing ever existed, or (2) whether another writing, recording, or photograph produced at the trial is the original, or (3) whether other evidence of contents correctly reflects the contents, the issue is for the trier of fact to determine as in the case of other issues of fact.

CHAPTER 11. MISCELLANEOUS RULES

Art. 1101. Applicability

A. **Proceedings generally; rule of privilege.**

(1) Except as otherwise provided by legislation, the provisions of this Code shall be applicable to the determination of questions of fact in all contradictory judicial proceedings and in proceedings to confirm a default judgment. Juvenile adjudication hearings in non-delinquency proceedings shall be governed by the provisions of this Code applicable to civil cases. Juvenile adjudication hearings in delinquency proceedings shall be governed by the provisions of this Code applicable to criminal cases.

(2) Furthermore, except as otherwise provided by legislation, Chapter 5 of this Code with respect to testimonial privileges applies to all stages of all actions, cases, and

proceedings where there is power to subpoena witnesses, including administrative, juvenile, legislative, military courts-martial, grand jury, arbitration, medical review panel, and judicial proceedings, and the proceedings enumerated in Paragraphs B and C of this Article.

B. **Limited applicability.** Except as otherwise provided by Article 1101(A)(2) and other legislation, in the following proceedings, the principles underlying this Code shall serve as guides to the admissibility of evidence. The specific exclusionary rules and other provisions, however, shall be applied only to the extent that they tend to promote the purposes of the proceeding.

(1) Worker's compensation cases.

(2) Child custody cases.

(3) Revocation of probation hearings.

(4) Preliminary examinations in criminal cases, and the court may consider evidence that would otherwise be barred by the hearsay rule.

(5) All proceedings before mayors' courts and justice of the peace courts.

(6) Peace bond hearings.

(7) Extradition hearings.

(8) Hearings on motions and other summary proceedings involving questions of fact not dispositive of or central to the disposition of the case on the merits, or to the dismissal of the case, excluding in criminal cases hearings on motions to suppress evidence and hearings to determine mental capacity to proceed.

C. **Rules inapplicable.** Except as otherwise provided by Article 1101(A)(2) and other legislation, the provisions of this Code shall not apply to the following:

(1) The determination of questions of fact preliminary to admissibility of evidence when the issue is to be determined by the court under Article 104.

(2) Proceedings with respect to release on bail.

(3) Disposition hearings in juvenile cases.

(4) Sentencing hearings except as provided in Code of Criminal Procedure Article 905.2 in capital cases.

(5) Small claims court proceedings except as provided in R.S. 13:5203 and 13:5207.

(6) Proceedings before grand juries except as provided by Code of Criminal Procedure Article 442.

D. **Discretionary applicability.** Notwithstanding the limitations on the applicability of this Code stated in Paragraphs A, B, and C of this Article, in all judicial proceedings a court may rely upon the provisions of this Code with respect to judicial notice, authentication and identification, and proof of contents of writings, recordings, and photographs as a basis for admitting evidence or making a finding of fact.

Art. 1102. Title

This Code may be known and cited as the "Louisiana Code of Evidence."

Art. 1104. *State v. Prieur*; pretrial; burden of proof

The burden of proof in a pretrial hearing held in accordance with *State v. Prieur*, 277 So.2d 126 (La. 1973), shall be identical to the burden of proof required by Federal Rules of Evidence Article IV, Rule 404.

Index to Major Topics